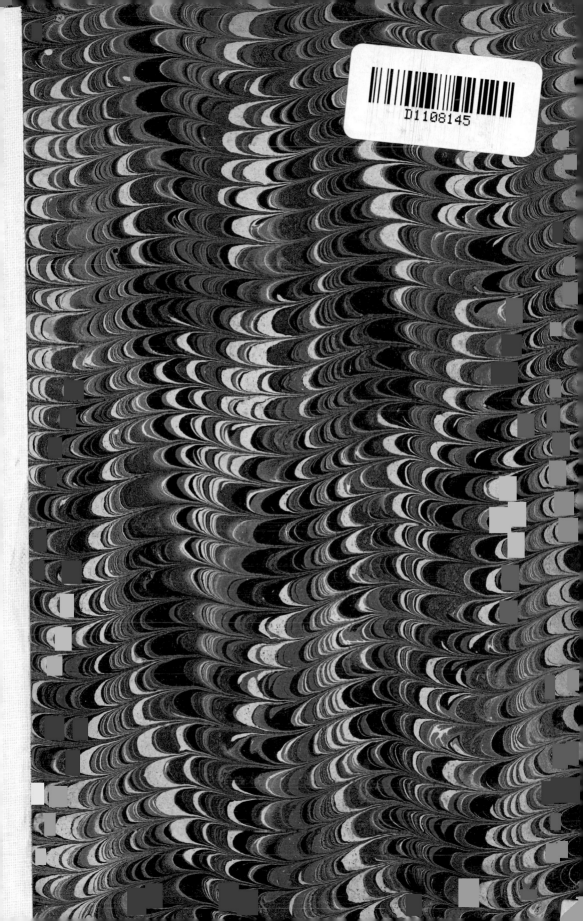

Geo. E. Cadwallader.

H.B. Hall.

From a recent Photograph by Brady.

Winfield Scott
Lieut Genl. &c. &c.

THE

REBELLION RECORD:

A Diary of American Events,

WITH

DOCUMENTS, NARRATIVES, ILLUSTRATIVE INCIDENTS, POETRY, ETC.

EDITED BY

FRANK MOORE,

AUTHOR OF "DIARY OF THE AMERICAN REVOLUTION."

WITH

AN INTRODUCTORY ADDRESS,

ON THE CAUSES OF THE STRUGGLE, AND THE GREAT ISSUES BEFORE THE COUNTRY

By EDWARD EVERETT.

FIRST VOLUME.

WITH ELEVEN PORTRAITS ON STEEL, A COLORED MAP, AND VARIOUS DIAGRAMS.

NEW YORK: G. P. PUTNAM.
C. T. EVANS, GENERAL AGENT.
1862.

JOHN F. TROW,
PRINTER, STEREOTYPER, AND ELECTROTYPER,
46, 48 & 50 Greene Street,
New York.

PREFACE.

In the initial number of the Rebellion Record, it was stated that the work proposed to furnish, "in a digested and systematic shape, a comprehensive history of this struggle; sifting fact from fiction and rumor; presenting the poetical and picturesque aspects, the notable and characteristic incidents, separated from the graver and more important documents."

It was observed that we did not aim either to "supersede or to keep pace with the newspapers, but to subject them, both North and South, to the crucible of *time;* following them at such distance as may be required to verify and classify all that is best worth preserving out of the immense mass of leaders, speeches, letters, and reports, which crowd the daily press;" "every important document and extended narrative being given in consecutive order, and numbered, with references from the Diary."

The editor, aiming at entire impartiality, has collected, from *every quarter*, whatever appeared to be of general interest, in any way connected with the great topics of the day, or likely to elucidate, in the slightest degree, the questions at issue, or the spirit and temper of the people, whether loyal or otherwise. Thus it will be found that a very considerable portion of the volume is occupied with "secession documents," or articles from the "secession" press, reprinted *verbatim*, without alteration, or comment. Every individual who has spoken or written with effect on either side, or "on the fence," has been placed "on record," and his utterances are here electrotyped for the benefit of future generations.

The volume is paged in three divisions, viz., I. Diary of Events; II. Documents and Narratives; III. Poetry, Rumors, Incidents, etc. A full Index and a Table of Contents are added; and the whole is preceded by the able and comprehensive address by Mr. Edward Everett, discussing with even more than his accustomed vigor, eloquence, and force, the principles and conclusions involved in this great contest.

The work will be continued during the rebellion, and will embrace its entire history. The concluding numbers will contain a comprehensive historical sketch, in which the whole story will be presented in a clear and connected narrative form. To do this properly at present, in the midst of the turmoil, and the conflicting reports and opinions of the day, is manifestly impossible. When the smoke of the battle shall be fairly cleared away; when the results shall be correctly ascertained; and when the nation is restored, as all *faith*ful citizens believe it will be speedily, to a peaceful and prosperous Union, it will be time enough to trace accurately and consecutively the outline of the most extraordinary and unjustifiable conspiracy and rebellion which the world has ever witnessed.

In closing this volume, the Editor acknowledges his obligations to the numerous individuals from whom he has received valuable assistance; and especially to the officers of the United States Army and Navy, and of the various State Governments, for the facility with which he has been enabled to make use of their valuable official collections.

New York, *October*, 1861.

The following omissions in the "Diary of Events" occurred during the progress of the work:

April 18.—Four hundred Pennsylvania volunteers, escorted by three hundred regular United States troops from Carlisle Barracks, (Pa.,) arrived at Washington this evening at ten o'clock, and bivouacked at the capitol.—*N. Y. Times, April* 19.

May 8.—An act to prevent the collection of debts owing by citizens of Tennessee, to citizens of non-slaveholding States during hostilities, passed the legislature of that State. —*N. Y. Herald, June* 7.

May 8.—Jefferson Davis submitted to the Confederate Congress the correspondence between Judge John A. Campbell and Secretary Seward, on the subject of the evacuation of Fort Sumter, and a "peaceful adjustment of the pending difficulties" between the North and South. (*Doc.* 267.)

REBELLION RECORD.

CONTENTS OF THE FIRST VOLUME.

III.—Poetry ....Page

INCIDENTS, RUMORS, ETC.

ILLUSTRATIONS.

MAPS.

DIARY OF EVENTS.

INTRODUCTION.

ADDRESS BY EDWARD EVERETT.

ADDRESS.*

BY EDWARD EVERETT.

WHEN the Congress of the United States, on the 4th of July, 1776, issued the ever memorable Declaration which we commemorate to-day, they deemed that a decent respect for the opinions of mankind required a formal statement of the causes which impelled them to the all-important measure. The eighty-fifth anniversary of the great Declaration finds the loyal people of the Union engaged in a tremendous conflict, to maintain and defend the grand nationality, which was asserted by our Fathers, and to prevent their fair Creation from crumbling into dishonorable Chaos. A great People, gallantly struggling to keep a noble framework of government from falling into wretched fragments, needs no justification at the tribunal of the public opinion of mankind. But while our patriotic fellow-citizens, who have rallied to the defence of the Union, marshalled by the ablest of living chieftains, are risking their lives in the field; while the blood of your youthful heroes and ours is poured out together in defence of this precious legacy of constitutional freedom, you will not think it a misappropriation of the hour, if I employ it in showing the justice of the cause in which we are engaged, and the fallacy of the arguments employed by the South, in vindication of the war, alike murderous and suicidal, which she is waging against the Constitution and the Union.

PROSPEROUS STATE OF THE COUNTRY LAST YEAR.

A twelvemonth ago, nay, six or seven months ago, our country was regarded and spoken of by the rest of the civilized world, as among the most prosperous in the family of nations. It was classed with England, France, and Russia, as one of the four leading powers of the age.† Remote as we were from the complications of foreign politics, the extent of our commerce and the efficiency of our navy won for us the respectful consideration of Europe. The United States were particularly referred to, on all occasions and in all countries, as an illustration of the mighty influence of free governments in promoting the prosperity of States. In England, notwithstanding some diplomatic collisions on boundary questions and occasional hostile reminiscences of the past, there has hardly been a debate for thirty years in parliament on any topic, in reference to which this country in the

---

* Delivered, by request, at the Academy of Music, New York, July 4, 1861. Large portions of this address were, on account of its length, necessarily omitted in the delivery.

† The Edinburgh Review for April, 1861, p. 555.

nature of things afforded matter of comparison, in which it was not referred to as furnishing instructive examples of prosperous enterprise and hopeful progress. At home, the country grew as by enchantment. Its vast geographical extent, augmented by magnificent accessions of conterminous territory peacefully made; its population far more rapidly increasing than that of any other country, and swelled by an emigration from Europe such as the world has never before seen; the mutually beneficial intercourse between its different sections and climates, each supplying what the other wants; the rapidity with which the arts of civilization have been extended over a before unsettled wilderness, and, together with this material prosperity, the advance of the country in education, literature, science, and refinement, formed a spectacle, of which the history of mankind furnished no other example. That such was the state of the country six months ago was matter of general recognition and acknowledgment at home and abroad.

THE PRESIDENTIAL ELECTION AND ITS RESULTS

There was, however, one sad deduction to be made, not from the truth of this description, not from the fidelity of this picture for that is incontestable, but from the content, happiness, and mutual good will which ought to have existed on the part of a People, favored by such an accumulation of Providential blessings. I allude, of course, to the great sectional controversies which have so long agitated the country, and arrayed the people in bitter geographical antagonism of political organization and action. Fierce party contentions had always existed in the United States, as they ever have and unquestionably ever will exist under all free elective governments; and these contentions had, from the first, tended somewhat to a sectional character. They had not, however, till quite lately, assumed that character so exclusively, that the minority in any one part of the country had not had a respectable electoral representation in every other. Till last November, there has never been a Southern Presidential Candidate, who did not receive electoral votes at the North, nor a Northern Candidate who did not receive electoral votes at the South.

At the late election and for the first time, this was not the case; and consequences the most extraordinary and deplorable have resulted. The country, as we have seen, being in profound peace at home and abroad, and in a state of unexampled prosperity—Agriculture, Commerce, Navigation, Manufactures, East, West, North, and South recovered or rapidly recovering from the crisis of 1857—powerful and respected abroad, and thriving beyond example at home, entered in the usual manner upon the electioneering campaign, for the choice of the nineteenth President of the United States. I say in the usual manner, though it is true that parties were more than usually broken up and subdivided. The normal division was into two great parties, but there had on several former occasions been three; in 1824 there were four, and there were four last November. The South equally with the West and the North entered into the canvass; conventions were held, nominations made, mass meetings assembled; the platform, the press enlisted with unwonted vigor; the election in all its stages, conducted in legal and constitutional form, without violence and without surprise, and the result obtained by a decided majority.

No sooner, however, was this result ascertained, than it appeared on the part of one of the Southern States, and her example was rapidly followed by others, that it had by no means been the intention of those States to abide by the result of the election, except on the one condition, of the choice of their candidate. The reference of the great sectional controversy to the peaceful arbitrament of the ballot box, the great safety valve of republican institutions, though made with every appearance of good faith, on the part of our brethren at the South, meant but this : if we succeed in this election, as we have in fifteen that have preceded it, well and good ; we will consent to govern the country for four years more, as we have already governed it for sixty years ; but we have no intention of acquiescing in any other result. We do not mean to abide by the election, although we participate in it, unless our candidate is chosen. If he fails we intend to prostrate the Government and break up the Union ; peaceably, if the States composing the majority are willing that it should be broken up peaceably ; otherwise, at the point of the sword.

SOUTH CAROLINA SECEDES FROM THE UNION.

The election took place on the 6th of November, and in pursuance of the extraordinary programme just described, the State of South Carolina, acting by a Convention chosen for the purpose, assembled on the 17th of December, and on the 20th, passed unanimously what was styled " an ordinance to dissolve the Union between the State of South Carolina and other States united with her, under the compact entitled the Constitution, of the United States of America." It is not my purpose on this occasion to make a documentary speech, but as this so-called " Ordinance " is very short, and affords matter for deep reflection, I beg leave to recite it in full :—

" We, the People of the State of South Carolina, in Convention assembled, do declare and ordain, and it is hereby declared and ordained, that the ordinance adopted by us in Convention on the 23d day of May, in the year of our Lord 1788, whereby the Constitution of the United States was ratified, and also all acts and parts of acts of the general assembly of this State, ratifying the amendments of the said Constitution, are hereby repealed, and that the Union now subsisting between South Carolina and other States, under the name of the United States of America, is dissolved."

This remarkable document is called an " Ordinance," and no doubt some special virtue is supposed to reside in the name. But names are nothing except as they truly represent things. An ordinance, if it is any thing clothed with binding force, is a Law, and nothing but a Law, and as such this ordinance, being in direct violation of the Constitution of the United States, is a mere nullity. The Constitution contains the following express provision : "This Constitution and the Laws of the United States made in pursuance thereof, and the treaties made or which shall be made under the authority of the United States, shall be the supreme law of the land, and the judges in every State shall be bound thereby, any thing in the Constitution or laws of any State to the contrary notwithstanding." Such being the express provision of the Constitution of the United States, which the people of South Carolina adopted in 1788, just as much as they ever adopted either of their State Constitutions, is it not trifling with serious things to claim that, by the simple expedient of passing a law under the name of an ordinance, this provision and

2

every other provision of it may be nullified, and every magistrate and officer in Carolina, whether of the State or Union, absolved from the oath which they have taken to support it?

But this is not all. This secession ordinance purports to "repeal" the ordinance of 23d May, 1788, by which the Constitution of the United States was ratified by the people of South Carolina. It was intended, of course, by calling the act of ratification an ordinance to infer a right of repealing it by another ordinance. It is important, therefore, to observe that the act of ratification is not, and was not at the time called, an ordinance, and contains nothing which by possibility can be repealed. It is in the following terms:—

"The Convention [of the people of South Carolina], having maturely considered the Constitution, or form of government, reported to Congress by the convention of delegates from the United States of America, and submitted to them, by a resolution of the Legislature of this State passed the 17th and 18th days of February last, in order to form a more perfect Union, establish justice, ensure domestic tranquillity, provide for the common defence, promote the general welfare, and secure the blessings of liberty to the people of the said United States and their posterity, do, in the name and in behalf of the people of this State, hereby assent to and ratify the same."

Here it is evident that there is nothing in the instrument which, in the nature of things, can be repealed; it is an authorized solemn assertion of the People of South Carolina, that they assent to, and ratify a form of government, which is declared in terms to be paramount to all State laws and constitutions. This is a great historical fact, the most important that can ever occur in the history of a people. The fact that the People of South Carolina, on the 23d of May, 1788, assented to and ratified the Constitution of the United States, in order, among other objects, to secure the blessings of liberty for themselves and "their posterity," can no more be repealed in 1861, than any other historical fact that occurred in Charleston in that year and on that day. It would be just as rational, at the present day, to attempt by ordinance to repeal any other event, as that the sun rose or that the tide ebbed and flowed on that day, as to repeal by ordinance the assent of Carolina to the Constitution.

Again: it is well known that various amendments to the Constitution were desired and proposed in different States. The first of the amendments proposed by South Carolina was as follows:—

"Whereas it is essential to the preservation of the rights reserved to the several States and the freedom of the People under the operation of the General Government, that the right of prescribing the manner, times, and places of holding the elections of the Federal Legislature should be *forever inseparably* annexed to the sovereignty of the States; this Convention doth declare that the same ought to remain to *all posterity*, a perpetual and fundamental right in the *local*, exclusive of the interference of the *general* Government, except in cases where the Legislature of the States shall refuse or neglect to perform or fulfil the same, according to the tenor of the said Constitution."

Here you perceive that South Carolina herself in 1788 desired a provision to be made and annexed inseparably to her sovereignty, that she should forever have the power of prescribing the time, place, and manner of holding the elections of members of Congress;—but even in making this express reservation, to operate for all posterity, she was willing to provide that, if the State Legislatures refuse or neglect to perform the duty, (which is precisely the case of the Seceding States at the present day,) then the General Government was, by this South Carolina amendment, expressly authorized to do it. South Carolina in 1788, by a sort of prophetic foresight, looked forward to the possibility that the States might "refuse or neglect" to coöperate in carrying on the Government, and admitted, in that case, that the General Government must go on, in spite of their delinquency.

I have dwelt on these points at some length, to show how futile is the attempt, by giving the name of "ordinance" to the act, by which South Carolina adopted the Constitution, and entered the Union, to gain a power to leave it by a subsequent ordinance of repeal.*

IS SECESSION A CONSTITUTIONAL RIGHT, OR IS IT REVOLUTION?

Whether the present unnatural civil war is waged by the South, in virtue of a supposed constitutional right to leave the Union at pleasure; or whether it is an exercise of the great and ultimate right of revolution, the existence of which no one denies, seems to be left in uncertainty by the leaders of the movement. Mr. Jefferson Davis, the President of the new confederacy, in his inaugural speech delivered on the 18th of February, declares that it is "an abuse of language" to call it "a revolution." Mr. Vice-President Stephens, on the contrary, in a speech at Savannah, on the 21st of March, pronounces it "one of the greatest revolutions in the annals of the world." The question is of great magnitude as one of constitutional and public law; as one of morality it is of very little consequence whether the country is drenched in blood, in the exercise of a right claimed under the Constitution, or the right inherent in every community to revolt against an oppressive government. Unless the oppression is so extreme as to justify revolution, it would not justify the evil of breaking up a government, under an abstract constitutional right to do so.

NEITHER A GRANTED NOR A RESERVED RIGHT.

This assumed right of Secession rests upon the doctrine that the Union is a compact between Independent States, from which any one of them may withdraw at pleasure in virtue of its sovereignty. This imaginary right has been the subject of discussion for more than thirty years, having been originally suggested, though not at first much dwelt upon, in connection with the kindred claim of a right, on the part of an individual State, to "nullify" an Act of Congress. It would, of course, be impossible within the limits of the hour to review these elaborate discussions. I will only remark, on this occasion, that none of the premises from which this remarkable conclusion is drawn, are recognized in the Constitution, and that the right of Secession, though claimed to be a "reserved" right, is not *expressly* reserved in it. That instrument does not purport to be a "compact," but a Constitution of Government. It appears, in its first sentence, not to have been entered into by the States, but to have been ordained and established by the People of the United States, for "themselves and their posterity." The States are not named in it; nearly all the characteristic powers of sovereignty are expressly granted to the

* See Appendix A.

General Government and expressly prohibited to the States, and so far from reserving a right of secession to the latter, on any ground or under any pretence, it ordains and establishes in terms the Constitution of the United States as the Supreme Law of the land, any thing in the Constitution or Laws of any State to the contrary notwithstanding.

It would seem that this is as clear and positive as language can make it. But it is argued, that, though the right of secession is not reserved in terms, it must be considered as implied in the general reservation to the States and to the People of all the powers not granted to Congress nor prohibited to the States. This extraordinary assumption, more distinctly stated, is that, in direct defiance of the express grant to Congress and the express prohibition to the States of nearly all the powers of an independent government, there is, *by implication,* a right reserved to the States to assume and exercise all these powers thus vested in the Union and prohibited to themselves, simply in virtue of going through the ceremony of passing a law called an Ordinance of Secession. A general reservation to the States of powers not prohibited to them, nor granted to Congress is an implied reservation to the States of a right to exercise these very powers thus expressly delegated to Congress and thus expressly prohibited to the States !

The Constitution directs that the Congress of the United States shall have power to declare war, grant letters of marque and reprisal, to raise and support armies, to provide and maintain a navy, and that the President of the United States, by and with the advice and consent of the Senate, shall make treaties with foreign powers.

These express grants of power to the Government of the United States are followed by prohibitions as express to the several States :—

"No State shall enter into any treaty, alliance, or confederation, grant letters of marque or reprisal: no State shall, without the consent of Congress, lay any duty of tonnage, keep troops or ships of war in time of peace, enter into any agreement or compact with another State, or with a foreign power, or engage in war, unless actually invaded, or in such imminent danger as will not admit of delay."

These and numerous other express grants of power to the General Government, and express prohibitions to the States, are further enforced by the comprehensive provision, already recited, that the Constitution and Laws of the United States are paramount to the laws and Constitution of the separate States.

And this Constitution, with these express grants and express prohibitions, and with this express subordination of the States to the General Government, has been adopted by the People of all the States ; and all their judges and other officers, and all their citizens holding office under the government of the United States or the individual States, are solemnly sworn to support it.

In the face of all this, in defiance of all this, in violation of all this, in contempt of all this, the seceding States claim the right to exercise every power expressly delegated to Congress and expressly prohibited to the States by that Constitution, which every one of their prominent men, civil and military, is under oath to support. They have entered into a confederation, raised an army, attempted to provide a navy, issued letters of marque and reprisal, waged war, and that war,— Merciful Heaven forgive them,—not with a foreign enemy, not with the wild tribes which still desolate the unprotected frontier ; (they, it is said, are swelling, armed with tomahawk and scalping-knife, the Confederate forces ;) but with their own countrymen, and the mildest and most beneficent government on the face of the earth!

BEFORE THE REVOLUTION THE COLONIES WERE A PEOPLE.

But we are told all this is done in virtue of the Sovereignty of the States; as if, because a State is Sovereign, its people were incompetent to establish a government for themselves and their posterity. Certainly the States are clothed with Sovereignty for local purposes; but it is doubtful whether they ever possessed it in any other sense; and if they had, it is certain that they ceded it to the General Government, in adopting the Constitution. Before their independence of England was asserted, they constituted a provincial people, (Burke calls it "a glorious Empire,") subject to the British crown, organized for certain purposes under separate colonial charters, but, on some great occasions of political interest and public safety, acting as one. Thus they acted when, on the approach of the great Seven Years' War, which exerted such an important influence on the fate of British America, they sent their delegates to Albany to concert a plan of union. In the discussions of that plan which was reported by Franklin, the citizens of the colonies were evidently considered as a People. When the passage of the Stamp Act in 1765 roused the spirit of resistance throughout America, the Unity of her People assumed a still more practical form. "Union," says one of our great American historians,* "was the hope of Otis. Union that 'should knit and work into the very blood and bones of the original system every region as fast as settled.'" In this hope he argued against writs of assistance, and in this hope he brought about the call of the Convention at New York in 1765. At that Convention, the noble South Carolinian Christopher Gadsden, with prophetic foreboding of the disintegrating heresies of the present day, cautioned his associates against too great dependence on their colonial charters. "I wish," said he, "that the charters may not ensnare us at last, by drawing different Colonies to act differently in this great cause. Whenever that is the case all is over with the whole. *There ought to be no New England man, no New Yorker, known on the Continent, but all of us Americans.*"†

While the patriots in America counselled, and wrote, and spoke as a people, they were recognized as such in England. "Believe me," cried Colonel Barré in the House of Commons, "I this day told you so, the same spirit of Freedom which actuated *that People* at first will accompany them still. The people, I believe, are as truly loyal as any subjects the king has, but a People jealous of their liberties, and who will vindicate them, should they be violated."

When ten years later the great struggle long foreboded came on, it was felt, on both sides of the Atlantic, to be an attempt to reduce a free People beyond the sea to unconditional dependence on a parliament in which they were not represented. "What foundation have we," was the language of Chatham on the 27th Jan. 1775, "for our claims over America? What is our right to persist in such cruel and vindictive measures against *that loyal, respectable People?* How have this respectable people behaved under all their grievances? Repeal, therefore, I say. But bare repeal will not satisfy *this enlightened and spirited People.*" Lord Camden, in the same debate, exclaimed, "You have no right to tax America; the natural rights of man, and the immutable laws of Nature, are with *that People.*" Burke,

---

* Bancroft's History of the United States, vol. v., p. 292.   † Ibid., p. 335.

two months later, made his great speech for conciliation with America. " I do not know," he exclaimed, " the method of drawing up an indictment against a WHOLE PEOPLE." In a letter written two years after the commencement of the war, he traces the growth of the colonies from their feeble beginnings to the magnitude which they had attained when the revolution broke out, and in which his glowing imagination saw future grandeur and power beyond the reality. " At the first designation of these colonial assemblies," says he, " they were probably not intended for any thing more (nor perhaps did they think themselves much higher) than the municipal corporations within this island, to which some at present love to compare them. But nothing in progression can rest on its original plan ; we may as well think of rocking a grown man in the cradle of an infant. Therefore, as the Colonies prospered and increased to A NUMEROUS AND MIGHTY PEOPLE, spreading over a very great tract of the globe, it was natural that they should attribute to assemblies so respectable in the formed Constitution, some part of the dignity of the great nations which they represented."

The meeting of the first Continental Congress of 1774 was the spontaneous impulse of the People. All their resolves and addresses proceed on the assumption that they represented a People. Their first appeal to the Royal authority was their letter to General Gage, remonstrating against the fortifications of Boston. " We entreat your Excellency to consider," they say, " what a tendency this conduct must have to irritate and force a *free People*, hitherto well disposed to peaceable measures, into hostilities." Their final act, at the close of the Session, their address to the King, one of the most eloquent and pathetic of State papers, appeals to him " in the name of all your Majesty's faithful People in America."

THE DECLARATION OF INDEPENDENCE RECOGNIZES A PEOPLE.

But this all-important principle in our political system is placed beyond doubt, by an authority which makes all further argument or illustration superfluous. That the citizens of the British Colonies, however divided for local purposes into different governments, when they ceased to be subject to the English crown, became *ipso facto* one People for all the high concerns of national existence, is a fact embodied in the Declaration of Independence itself. That august Manifesto, the *Magna Charta*, which introduced us into the family of nations, was issued to the world, so its first sentence sets forth—because " a decent respect for the opinions of mankind requires " such solemn announcement of motives and causes to be made, " when in the course of human events it becomes necessary for *one People* to dissolve the political bonds which have connected them with another." Mr. Jefferson Davis, in his message of the 29th of April, deems it important to remark, that, by the treaty of peace with Great Britain, " the several States were each by name recognized to be independent." It would be more accurate to say that the United States each by name were so recognized. Such enumeration was necessary, in order to fix beyond doubt, which of the Anglo-American colonies, twenty-five or six in number, were included in the recognition.* But it is surely a far more significant circumstance, that the separate States are not named in the Declaration

---

* Burke's account of " the English settlements in America," begins with Jamaica, and proceeds through the West India Islands. There were also English settlements on the Continent, Canada—and Nova Scotia,—which it was necessary to *exclude* from the Treaty, by an enumeration of the *included* Colonies.

of Independence, that they are called only by the collective designation of the United States of America; that the manifesto is issued "in the name and by the authority of the good people" of the Colonies, and that they are characterized in the first sentence as "One People."

Let it not be thought that these are the latitudinarian doctrines of modern times, or of a section of the country predisposed to a loose construction of laws and Constitutions. Listen, I pray you, to the noble words of a Southern revolutionary patriot and statesman:—

"The separate independence and individual sovereignty of the several States were never thought of by the enlightened band of patriots who framed the Declaration of Independence. The several States are not even mentioned by name in any part of it, as if it was intended to impress this maxim on America, that our Freedom and Independence arose from our Union, and that without it we could neither be free nor independent. Let us then consider all attempts to weaken this Union, by maintaining that each State is separately and individually independent, as a species of political heresy, which can never benefit us, and may bring on us the most serious distresses."* These are the solemn and prophetic words of Charles Cotesworth Pinckney; the patriot, the soldier, the statesman; the trusted friend of Washington, repeatedly called by him to the highest offices of the Government; the one name that stands highest and brightest, on the list of the great men of South Carolina.†

THE ARTICLES OF CONFEDERATION.

Not only was the Declaration of Independence made in the name of the one People of the United States, but the war by which it was sustained was carried on by their authority. A very grave historical error, in this respect, is often committed by the politicians of the Secession School. Mr. Davis, in his message of the 29th of April, having called the old Confederation "a close alliance," says: "under this contract of alliance the war of the revolution was successfully waged, and resulted in the treaty of peace with Great Britain of 1783, by the terms of which the several States were each by name recognized to be independent." I have already given the reason for this enumeration, but the main fact alleged in the passage is entirely without foundation. The Articles of Confederation were first signed by the delegates from eight of the States, on the 9th of July, 1778, more than three years after the commencement of the war, long after the capitulation of Burgoyne, the alliance with France, and the reception of a French Minister. The ratification of the other States was given at intervals the following years, the last not till 1781, seven months only before the virtual close of the war, by the surrender of Cornwallis. Then, and not till then, was "the Contract of Alliance" consummated. Most true it is, as Mr. Davis bids us remark, that, by these Articles of Confederation the States retained "each its sovereignty, freedom, and independence." It is not less true, that their selfish struggle to exercise and enforce their assumed rights as separate sovereignties was the source of the greatest difficulties and dangers of the Revolution, and risked its success; not less true, that most of the great powers of a sovereign State were nominally conferred even by these

---

* Elliott's Debates, vol. iv., p. 301.

† See an admirable sketch of his character in Trescot's Diplomatic History of the Administrations of Washington and Adams, pp. 169—171.

articles on the Congress, and that that body was regarded and spoken of by Washington himself as THE "SOVEREIGN OF THE UNION." *

But feeble as the old Confederation was, and distinctly as it recognized the sovereignty of the States, it recognized in them no right to withdraw at their pleasure from the Union. On the contrary, it was specially provided that "the Articles of Confederation should be inviolably preserved by every State," and that "the Union should be perpetual." It is true that in a few years, from the inherent weakness of the central power, and from the want of means to enforce its authority on the individual citizen, it fell to pieces. It sickened and died from the poison of what General Pinckney aptly called "the heresy of State Sovereignty," and in its place a Constitution was ordained and established "in order to form a more perfect Union;" a Union more binding on its members than this "contract of alliance," which yet was to be "inviolably observed by every State;" more durable than the old Union, which yet was declared to be "perpetual." This great and beneficent change was a Revolution—happily a peaceful revolution, the most important change probably ever brought about in a government, without bloodshed. The new government was unanimously adopted by all the members of the old Confederation, by some more promptly than by others, but by all within the space of four years.

THE STATES MIGHT BE COERCED UNDER THE CONFEDERATION.

Much has been said against *coercion*, that is, the employment of force to compel obedience to the laws of the United States, when they are resisted under the assumed authority of a State; but even the old Confederation, with all its weakness, in the opinion of the most eminent contemporary statesmen possessed this power. Great stress is laid by politicians of the Secession School on the fact, that in a project for amending the articles of Confederation brought forward by Judge Paterson in the Federal Convention, it was proposed to clothe the Government with this power and the proposal was not adopted. This is a very inaccurate statement of the facts of the case. The proposal formed part of a project which was rejected *in toto*. The reason why this power of State coercion was not granted *eo nomine*, in the new Constitution, is that it was wholly superfluous and inconsistent with the fundamental principle of the Government. Within the sphere of its delegated powers, the General Government deals with the individual citizen. If its power is resisted, the person or persons resisting it do so at their peril and are amenable to the law. They can derive no immunity from State Legislatures or State Conventions, because the Constitution and laws of the United States are the Supreme Law of the Land. If the resistance assumes an organized form, on the part of numbers too great to be restrained by the ordinary powers of the law, it is then an insurrection, which the General Government is expressly authorized to suppress. Did any one imagine in 1793, when General Washington called out 15,000 men to suppress the insurrection in the Western counties of Pennsylvania, that if the insurgents had happened to have the control of a majority of the Legislature, and had thus been able to clothe their rebellion with a pretended form of law, that he would have been obliged to disband his troops, and return himself baffled and discomfited to Mount Vernon? If John Brown's raid at Harper's Ferry, instead of being the

* Sparks' Washington, vol. ix., pp. 12, 23, 29.

project of one misguided individual and a dozen and a half deluded followers, had been the organized movement of the States of Ohio and Pennsylvania, do the Seceders hold that the United States would have had no right to protect Virginia, or punish the individuals concerned in her invasion? Do the seceding States really mean, after all, to deny, that if a State law is passed to prevent the rendition of a fugitive slave, the General Government has any right to employ force to effect his surrender?

But, as I have said, even the old Confederation, with all its weakness, was held by the ablest contemporary statesmen, and that of the State rights school, to possess the power of enforcing its requisitions against a delinquent State. Mr. Jefferson, in a letter to Mr. Adams of the 11th of July, 1786, on the subject of providing a naval force of 150 guns to chastise the Barbary Powers, urges, as an additional reason for such a step, that it would arm " the Federal head with the safest of all the instruments of coercion, over its delinquent members, and prevent it from using what would be less safe," viz. : a land force. Writing on the same subject to Mr. Monroe a month later, (11 Aug. 1786,) he answers the objection of expense thus : " It will be said, ' There is no money in the Treasury.' There never will be money in the Treasury till the Confederacy shows its teeth. *The States must see the rod, perhaps it must be felt by some of them.* Every rational citizen must wish to see an effective instrument of coercion, and should fear to see it on any other element than the water. A naval force can never endanger our liberties nor occasion bloodshed ; a land force would do both." In the following year, and when the Confederation was at its last gasp, Mr. Jefferson was still of the opinion that it possessed the power of coercing the States, and that it was expedient to exercise it. In a letter to Col. Carrington of the 4th of April, 1787, he says : " It has been so often said as to be generally believed, that Congress have no power by the Confederation to enforce any thing, for instance, contributions of money. It was not necessary to give them that power expressly, they have it by the law of nature. *When two parties make a compact, there results to each the power of compelling the other to execute it.* Compulsion was never so easy as in our case, when a single frigate would soon levy on the commerce of a single State the deficiency of its contributions."

Such was Mr. Jefferson's opinion of the powers of Congress, under the " old contract of alliance." Will any reasonable man maintain that under a constitution of government there can be less power to enforce the laws?

STATE SOVEREIGNTY DOES NOT AUTHORIZE SECESSION.

But the cause of secession gains nothing by magnifying the doctrine of the Sovereignty of the States or calling the Constitution a compact between them. Calling it a compact does not change a word of its text, and no theory of what is implied in the word " Sovereignty " is of any weight, in opposition to the actual provisions of the instrument itself. *Sovereignty* is a word of very various signification. It is one thing in China, another in Turkey, another in Russia, another in France, another in England, another in Switzerland, another in San Marino, another in the individual American States, and it is something different from all in the United States. To maintain that, because the State of Virginia, for instance, was in some sense or other a sovereign State, when her people adopted the Federal Constitution, (which in terms was ordained and established not only for the people of that day, but for their posterity,) she may therefore at pleasure secede from the Union existing under that Constitution, is simply to beg the question. That question is not what was the theory or form of government existing in Virginia, before the Constitution, but what are the provisions of the Constitution which her people adopted and made their own? Does the Constitution of the United States permit or forbid the States to enter into a confederation? Is it a mere loose partnership, which any of the parties can break up at pleasure, or is it a Constitution of government, delegating to Congress and prohibiting to the States most of the primal functions of a sovereign power;—Peace, War, Commerce, Finance, Navy, Army, Mail, Mint; Executive, Legislative, and Judicial functions? The States are not named in it; the word Sovereignty does not occur in it; the right of secession is as much ignored in it as the precession of the Equinoxes, and all the great prerogatives which characterize an independent member of the family of nations are by distinct grant conferred on Congress by the People of the United States and prohibited to the individual States of the Union. Is it not the height of absurdity to maintain that all these express grants and distinct prohibitions, and constitutional arrangements, may be set at nought by an individual State under the pretence that she was a sovereign State before she assented to or ratified them; in other words, that an act is of no binding force because it was performed by an authorized and competent agent?

In fact, to deduce from the sovereignty of the States the right of seceding from the Union is the most stupendous *non sequitur* that was ever advanced in grave affairs. The only legitimate inference to be drawn from that sovereignty is precisely the reverse. If any one right can be predicated of a sovereign State, it is that of forming or adopting a frame of government. She may do it alone, or she may do it as a member of a Union. She may enter into a loose pact for ten years or till a partisan majority of a convention, goaded on by ambitious aspirants to power, shall vote in secret session to dissolve it; or she may, after grave deliberation and mature counsel, led by the wisest and most virtuous of the land, ratify and adopt a constitution of government, ordained and established not only for that generation, but their posterity, subject only to the inalienable right of revolution possessed by every political community.

What would be thought in private affairs of a man who should seriously claim the right to revoke a grant, in consequence of having an unqualified right to make it? A right to break a contract, because he had a right to enter into it? To what extent is it more rational on the part of a State to found the right to dissolve the Union on the competence of the parties to form it; the right to prostrate a government on the fact that it was constitutionally framed?

PARALLEL CASES: IRELAND, SCOTLAND.

But let us look at parallel cases, and they are by no means wanting. In the year 1800, a union was formed between England and Ireland. Ireland, before she entered into the union, was subject, indeed, to the English crown, but she had her own parliament, consisting of her own Lords and Commons, and enacting her own laws. In 1800 she entered into a constitutional union with England on the basis of articles of agreement, jointly accepted by the two parliaments.* The union was

* Annual Register, xlii., p. 190

opposed at the time by a powerful minority in Ireland, and Mr. O'Connell succeeded, thirty years later, by ardent appeals to the sensibilities of the people, in producing an almost unanimous desire for its dissolution. He professed, however, although he had wrought his countrymen to the verge of rebellion, to aim at nothing but a constitutional repeal of the articles of union by the parliament of Great Britain. It never occurred even to his fervid imagination, that, because Ireland was an independent government when she entered into the union, it was competent for her at her discretion to secede from it. What would our English friends, who have learned from our Secessionists the "inherent right" of a disaffected State to secede from our Union, have thought, had Mr. O'Connell, in the paroxysms of his agitation, claimed the right on the part of Ireland, by her own act, to sever her union with England?

Again, in 1706, Scotland and England formed a Constitutional Union. They also, though subject to the same monarch, were in other respects Sovereign and independent Kingdoms. They had each its separate parliament, courts of justice, laws, and established national church. Articles of union were established between them; but all the laws and statutes of either kingdom not contrary to these articles, remained in force.* A powerful minority in Scotland disapproved of the Union at the time. Nine years afterward an insurrection broke out in Scotland under a prince, who claimed to be the lawful, as he certainly was the lineal, heir to the throne. The rebellion was crushed, but the disaffection in which it had its origin was not wholly appeased. In thirty years more a second Scottish insurrection took place, and, as before, under the lead of the lineal heir to the crown. On neither occasion that I ever heard of, did it enter into the imagination of rebel or loyalist, that Scotland was acting under a reserved right as a sovereign kingdom, to secede from the Union, or that the movement was any thing less than an insurrection; revolution if it succeeded; treason and rebellion if it failed. Neither do I recollect that, in less than a month after either insurrection broke out, any one of the friendly and neutral powers made haste, in anticipation even of the arrival of the ministers of the reigning sovereign, to announce that the rebels "would be recognized as belligerents."

VIRGINIA VAINLY ATTEMPTS TO ESTABLISH A RESERVED RIGHT.

In fact, it is so plain, in the nature of things, that there can be no constitutional right to break up a government unless it is expressly provided for, that the politicians of the secession school are driven back, at every turn, to a *reserved* right. I have already shown that there is no such *express* reservation, and I have dwelt on the absurdity of getting by *implication* a reserved right to violate every *express* provision of a constitution. In this strait, Virginia, proverbially skilled in logical subtilties, has attempted to find an express reservation, not, of course, in the Constitution itself, where it does not exist, but in her original act of adhesion, or rather in the declaration of the "impressions" under which that act was adopted. The ratification itself of Virginia, was positive and unconditional. "We, the said delegates, in the name and behalf of *the People of Virginia*, do, by these presents, assent and ratify the Constitution recommended on the 17th day of September, 1787, by the Federal Convention, *for the government of the United States,* hereby announcing

* Rapin's History of England, vol. iv., p. 741-6.

to all those whom it may concern, that the said Constitution is binding upon the said *People*, according to an authentic copy hereunto annexed. Done in Convention this 26th day of June, 1788."

This, as you perceive, is an absolute and unconditional ratification of the Constitution by the People of Virginia. An attempt, however, is made, by the late Convention in Virginia, in their ordinance of secession, to extract a reservation of a right to secede, out of the declaration contained in the preamble to the act of ratification. That preamble declares it to be an "impression" of the people of Virginia, that the powers granted under the Constitution, being derived from the people of the United States, may be resumed BY THEM, whenever the same shall be perverted to their injury or oppression. The ordinance of secession passed by the recent convention, purporting to cite this declaration, omits the words *by them*, that is, by the People of the United States, not by the people of any single State, thus arrogating to the people of Virginia alone what the Convention of 1788 claimed only, and that by way of "impression," for the People of the United States.

By this most grave omission of the vital words of the sentence, the Convention, I fear, intended to lead the incautious or the ignorant to the conclusion, that the Convention of 1788 asserted the right of an individual State to resume the powers granted in the Constitution to the General Government; a claim for which there is not the slightest foundation in Constitutional history. On the contrary, when the ill-omened doctrine of State nullification was sought to be sustained by the same argument in 1830, and the famous Virginia resolutions of 1798 were appealed to by Mr. Calhoun and his friends, as affording countenance to that doctrine, it was repeatedly and emphatically declared by Mr. Madison, the author of the resolutions, that they were intended to claim, not for an individual State, but for the United States, by whom the Constitution was ordained and established, the right of remedying its abuses by constitutional ways, such as united protest, repeal, or an amendment of the Constitution.* Incidentally to the discussion of nullification, he denied over and over again the right of peaceable secession; and this fact was well known to some of the members of the late Convention at Richmond. When the secrets of their assembly are laid open, no doubt it will appear that there were some faithful Abdiels to proclaim the fact. Oh, that the venerable sage, second to none of his patriot compeers in framing the Constitution, the equal associate of Hamilton in recommending it to the People; its great champion in the Virginia Convention of 1788, and its faithful vindicator in 1830, against the deleterious heresy of nullification, could have been spared to protect it, at the present day, from the still deadlier venom of Secession! But he is gone; the principles, the traditions, and the illustrious memories which gave to Virginia her name and her praise in the land, are no longer cherished; the work of Washington, and Madison, and Randolph, and Pendleton, and Marshall is repudiated, and nullifiers, precipitators, and seceders gather in secret conclave to destroy the Constitution, in the very building that holds the monumental statue of the Father of his Country!

THE VIRGINIA RESOLUTIONS OF 1798.

Having had occasion to allude to the Virginia resolutions of 1798, I may observe that of these famous resolves, the subject of so much political romance, it is

---

* Maguire's Collection, p. 213.

time that a little plain truth should be promulgated. The country, in 1798, was vehemently agitated by the struggles of the domestic parties, which about equally divided it, and these struggles were urged to unwonted and extreme bitterness, by the preparations made and making for a war with France. By an act of Congress, passed in the summer of that year, the President of the United States was clothed with power to send from the country any alien whom he might judge dangerous to the public peace and safety, or who should be concerned in any treasonable or secret machinations against the Government of the United States. This act was passed as a war measure; it was to be in force two years, and it expired by its own limitation on the 25th of June, 1800. War, it is true, had not been formally declared; but hostilities on the ocean had taken place on both sides, and the army of the United States had been placed upon a war footing. The measure was certainly within the war power, and one which no prudent commander, even without the authority of a statute, would hesitate to execute in an urgent case within his own district. Congress thought fit to provide for and regulate its exercise by law.

Two or three weeks later (14th July, 1798) another law was enacted, making it penal to combine or conspire with intent to oppose any lawful measure of the Government of the United States, or to write, print, or publish any false and scandalous writing against the Government, either House of Congress, or the President of the United States. In prosecutions under this law, it was provided that the Truth might be pleaded in justification, and that the Jury should be judges of the law as well as of the fact. This law was by its own limitation to expire at the close of the then current Presidential term.

Such are the famous alien and sedition laws, passed under the Administration of that noble and true-hearted revolutionary patriot, John Adams, though not recommended by him officially or privately; adjudged to be constitutional by the Supreme Court of the United States; distinctly approved by Washington, Patrick Henry, and Marshall; and, whatever else may be said of them, certainly preferable to the laws which, throughout the Seceding States, Judge Lynch would not fail to enforce at the lamp-post and tar-bucket against any person guilty of the offences against which these statutes were aimed.

It suited, however, the purposes of party at that time, to raise a formidable clamor against these laws. It was in vain that their Constitutionality was affirmed by the Judiciary of the United States. "Nothing," said Washington, alluding to these laws, "will produce the least change in the conduct of the leaders of the opposition to the measures of the General Government. They have points to carry from which no reasoning, no inconsistency of conduct, no absurdity can divert them." Such, in the opinion of Washington, was the object for which the Legislatures of Virginia and Kentucky passed their famous resolutions of 1798, the former drafted by Mr. Madison, and the latter by Mr. Jefferson, and sent to a friend in Kentucky to be brought forward. These resolutions were transmitted to the other States for their concurrence. The replies from the States which made any response were referred the following year to committees in Virginia and Kentucky. In the Legislature of Virginia, an elaborate report was made by Mr. Madison, explaining and defending the resolutions; in Kentucky another resolve reaffirming those of the preceding year was drafted by Mr. Wilson Cary Nicholas, not by Mr. Jefferson, as stated by General McDuffie. Our respect for the distinguished men who took the lead on this occasion, then ardently engaged in the warfare of politics, must not make us fear to tell the truth, that the simple object of the entire movement was to make " political capital " for the approaching election, by holding up to the excited imaginations of the masses the Alien and Sedition laws, as an infraction of the Constitution, which threatened the overthrow of the liberties of the People. The resolutions maintained that, the States being parties to the Constitutional compact, in a case of deliberate, palpable, and dangerous exercise of powers not granted by the compact, the States have a right and are in duty bound to *interpose* for preventing the progress of the evil.

Such, in brief, was the main purport of the Virginia and Kentucky resolutions. The sort of interposition intended was left in studied obscurity. Not a word was dropped of secession from the Union. Mr. Nicholas's resolution in 1799 hinted at "nullification" as the appropriate remedy for an unconstitutional law, but what was meant by the ill-sounding word was not explained. The words " null, void, and of no effect," contained in the original draft of the Virginia resolutions, were, on motion of John Taylor of Caroline, stricken from them, on their passage through the assembly ; and Mr. Madison, in his report of 1799, carefully explains that no extra constitutional measures were intended. One of the Kentucky resolutions ends with an invitation to the States to unite in a petition to Congress to repeal the laws.

These resolutions were communicated, as I have said, to the other States for concurrence. From most of them no response was received ; some adopted dissenting reports and resolutions ; NOT ONE CONCURRED. But the resolutions did their work—all that they were intended or expected to do—by shaking the Administration. At the ensuing election, Mr. Jefferson, at whose instance the entire movement was made, was chosen President by a very small majority ; Mr. Madison was placed at the head of his administration as Secretary of State ; the obnoxious laws expired by their own limitation ; not repealed by the dominant party, as Mr. Calhoun with strange inadvertence asserts ; * and Mr. Jefferson proceeded to administer the Government upon constitutional principles quite as lax, to say the least, as those of his predecessors. If there was any marked departure in his general policy from the course hitherto pursued, it was that, having some theoretical prejudices against a navy, he allowed that branch of the service to languish. By no Administration have the powers of the General Government been more liberally construed—not to say further strained—sometimes beneficially, as in the acquisition of Louisiana, sometimes perniciously as in the embargo. The resolutions of 1798, and the metaphysics they inculcated, were surrendered to the cobwebs which habitually await the plausible exaggerations of the canvass after an election is decided. These resolutions of 1798 have been sometimes in Virginia waked from their slumbers at closely contested elections as a party cry ; the report of the Hartford Convention, without citing them by name, borrows their language ; but as representing in their modern interpretation any system on which the Government ever was or could be administered, they were buried in the same grave as the Laws which called them forth.

Unhappily during their transient vitality, like the butterfly which deposits its egg in the apple blossoms that have so lately filled our orchards with beauty and

---

* Mr. Calhoun's Discourse on the Constitution, p. 359.

perfume—a gilded harmless moth, whose food is a dew drop, whose life is a mid-summer's day—these resolutions, misconceived and perverted, proved, in the minds of ambitious and reckless politicians, the germ of a fatal heresy. The butterfly's egg is a microscopic speck, but as the fruit grows, the little speck gives life to a greedy and nauseous worm, that gnaws and bores to the heart of the apple, and renders it, though smooth and fair without, foul and bitter and rotten within. In like manner, the theoretical generalities of these resolutions, intending nothing in the minds of their authors but constitutional efforts to procure the repeal of obnoxious laws, matured in the minds of a later generation into the deadly paradoxes of 1830 and 1860—kindred products of the same soil, *venenorum ferax ;*—the one asserting the monstrous absurdity that a State, though remaining in the Union, could by her single act nullify a law of Congress; the other teaching the still more preposterous doctrine, that a single State may nullify the Constitution. The first of these heresies failed to spread far beyond the latitude where it was engendered. In the Senate of the United States, the great acuteness of its inventor, (Mr. Calhoun,) then the Vice-President, and the accomplished rhetoric of its champion, (Mr. Hayne,) failed to raise it above the level of a plausible sophism. It sunk forever discredited beneath the sturdy common sense and indomitable will of Jackson, the mature wisdom of Livingston, the keen analysis of Clay, and the crushing logic of Webster.

Nor was this all : the venerable author of the Resolutions of 1798 and of the report of 1799 was still living in a green old age. His connection with those State papers and still more his large participation in the formation and adoption of the Constitution, entitled him, beyond all men living, to be consulted on the subject. No effort was spared by the Leaders of the Nullification school to draw from him even a qualified assent to their theories. But in vain. He not only refused to admit their soundness, but he devoted his time and energies for three laborious years to the preparation of essays and letters, of which the object was to demonstrate that his resolutions and report did not, and could not bear the Carolina interpretation. He earnestly maintained that the separate action of an individual State was not contemplated by them, and that they had in view nothing but the concerted action of the States to procure the repeal of unconstitutional laws or an amendment of the Constitution.*

With one such letter written with this intent, I was myself honored. It filled ten pages of the journal in which with his permission it was published. It unfolded the true theory of the Constitution and the meaning and design of the resolutions, and exposed the false gloss attempted to be placed upon them by the Nullifiers, with a clearness and force of reasoning which defied refutation. None, to my knowledge, was ever attempted. The politicians of the Nullification and Secession school, as far as I am aware, have from that day to this made no attempt to grapple with Mr. Madison's letter of August, 1830.† Mr. Calhoun certainly made no such attempt in the elaborate treatise composed by him, mainly for the purpose of expounding the doctrine of nullification. He claims the support of these resolutions, without adverting to the fact that his interpretation of them had been repudiated

---

* A very considerable portion of the important volume containing a selection from the Madison papers, and printed "exclusively for private distribution " by J. C. McGuire, Esq., in 1853, is taken up with these letters and essays.

† North American Review, vol. xxxi., p. 567.

by their illustrious author. He repeats his exploded parodoxes as confidently, as if Mr. Madison himself had expired with the Alien and Sedition laws, and left no testimony to the meaning of his resolutions; while, at the present day, with equal confidence, the same resolutions are appealed to by the disciples of Mr. Calhoun as sustaining the doctrine of secession, in the face of the positive declaration of their author, when that doctrine first began to be broached, that they will bear no such interpretation.

MR. CALHOUN DID NOT CLAIM A CONSTITUTIONAL RIGHT OF SECESSION.

In this respect the disciples have gone beyond the master. There is a single sentence in Mr. Calhoun's elaborate volume in which he maintains the right of a State to secede from the Union. (Page 301.) There is reason to suppose, however, that he intended to claim only the inalienable right of revolution. In 1828, a declaration of political principles was drawn up by him for the State of South Carolina, in which it was expressly taught, that the people of that State by adopting the Federal Constitution had "modified *its original right of sovereignty*, whereby its individual consent was necessary to any change in its political condition, and by becoming a member of the Union, had placed that power in the hands of three-fourths of the States, [the number necessary for a Constitutional amendment,] in whom the highest power known to the Constitution actually resides." In a recent patriotic speech of Mr. Reverdy Johnson, at Frederick, Md., on the 7th of May, the distinct authority of Mr. Calhoun is quoted as late as 1844 against the right of separate action on the part of an individual State, and I am assured by the same respected gentleman, that it is within his personal knowledge, that Mr. Calhoun did not maintain the peaceful right of secession.*

SECESSION AS A REVOLUTION.

But it may be thought a waste of time to argue against a Constitutional right of peaceful Secession, since no one denies the right of Revolution; and no pains are spared by the disaffected leaders, while they claim indeed the Constitutional right, to represent their movement as the uprising of an indignant People against an oppressive and tyrannical Government.

IS THE GOVERNMENT OF THE UNITED STATES OPPRESSIVE AND TYRANNICAL?

An oppressive and tyrannical government! Let us examine this pretence for a few moments, first in the general, and then in the detail of its alleged tyrannies and abuses.

This oppressive and tyrannical Government is the successful solution of a problem, which had tasked the sagacity of mankind from the dawn of civilization; viz.: to find a form of polity, by which institutions purely popular could be extended over a vast empire, free alike from despotic centralization and undue preponderance of the local powers. It was necessarily a complex system; a Union at once federal and national. It leaves to the separate States the control of all matters of purely local administration, and confides to the central power the management of Foreign affairs and of all other concerns in which the United family have a joint interest. All the organized and delegated powers depend directly or very nearly

* See Appendix B.

so on popular choice. This Government was not imposed upon the People by a foreign conqueror ; it is not an inheritance descending from barbarous ages, laden with traditionary abuses, which create a painful ever-recurring necessity of reform ; it is not the conceit of heated enthusiasts in the spasms of a revolution. It is the recent and voluntary frame-work of an enlightened age, compacted by wise and good men, with deliberation and care, working upon materials prepared by long Colonial discipline. In framing it, they sought to combine the merits and to avoid the defects of former systems of government. The greatest possible liberty of the citizen is the basis ; just representation the ruling principle, reconciling with rare ingenuity the federal equality of the States, with the proportionate influence of numbers. Its legislative and executive magistrates are freely chosen at short periods ; its judiciary alone holding office by a more permanent, but still sufficiently responsible, tenure. No money flows into or out of the Treasury but under the direct sanction of the representatives of the People, on whom also all the great functions of Government for peace and war, within the limits already indicated, are devolved. No hereditary titles or privileges, no distinction of ranks, no established church, no courts of high commission, no censorship of the press, are known to the system ; not a drop of blood has ever flowed under its authority for a political offence ; but this tyrannical and oppressive Government has certainly exhibited a more perfect development of equal republican principles, than has ever before existed on any considerable scale. Under its benign influence, the country, every part of the country, has prospered beyond all former example. Its population has increased ; its commerce, agriculture, and manufactures have flourished ; manners, arts, education, letters, all that dignifies and ennobles man, have in a shorter period attained a higher point of cultivation than has ever before been witnessed in a newly settled region. The consequence has been consideration and influence abroad and marvellous well-being at home. The world has looked with admiration upon the Country's progress ; we have ourselves contemplated it, perhaps, with undue self-complacency. Armies without conscription ; navies without impressment, and neither army nor navy swelled to an oppressive size ; an overflowing treasury without direct taxation or oppressive taxation of any kind ; churches without number and with no denominational preferences on the part of the State ; schools and colleges accessible to all the people ; a free and a cheap press ; —all the great institutions of social life extending their benefits to the mass of the community. Such, no one can deny, is the general character of this oppressive and tyrannical government.

But perhaps this Government, however wisely planned, however beneficial even in its operation, may have been rendered distasteful, or may have become oppressive in one part of the country and to one portion of the people, in consequence of the control of affairs having been monopolized or unequally shared by another portion. In a Confederacy, the people of one section are not well pleased to be even mildly governed by an exclusive domination of the other. In point of fact this is the allegation, the persistent allegation of the South, that from the foundation of the Government it has been wielded by the people of the North for their special, often exclusive, benefit, and to the injury and oppression of the South. Let us see. Out of seventy-two years since the organization of the Government, the Executive chair has, for sixty-four years, been filled nearly all the time by Southern

3

Presidents; and when that was not the case, by Presidents possessing the confidence of the South. For a still longer period, the controlling influences of the Legislative and Judicial departments of the Government have centred in the same quarter. Of all the offices in the gift of the central power in every department, far more than her proportionate share has always been enjoyed by the South. She is at this moment revolting against a Government, not only admitted to be the mildest and most beneficent ever organized this side Utopia, but one of which she has herself from the first, almost monopolized the administration.

CAUSE OF THE REVOLUTION ALLEGED BY SOUTH CAROLINA.

But are there no wrongs, abuses, and oppressions, alleged to have been suffered by the South, which have rendered her longer submission to the Federal Government intolerable, and which are pleaded as the motive and justification of the revolt ? Of course there are, but with such variation and uncertainty of statement as to render their examination difficult. The manifesto of South Carolina of the 20th of Dec. last, which led the way in this inauspicious movement, sets forth nothing but the passage of State laws to obstruct the surrender of fugitive slaves. The document does not state that South Carolina herself ever lost a slave in consequence of these laws, it is not probable she ever did, and yet she makes the existence of these laws, which are wholly inoperative as far as she is concerned, and which probably never caused to the entire South the loss of a dozen fugitives, the ground for breaking up the Union and plunging the country into a civil war. But I shall presently revert to this topic.

Other statements in other quarters enlarge the list of grievances. In the month of November last, after the result of the presidential election was ascertained, a very interesting discussion of the subject of secession took place at Milledgeville, before the members of the Legislature of Georgia and the citizens generally, between two gentlemen of great ability and eminence, since elected, the one Secretary of State, the other Vice-President of the new Confederacy; the former urging the necessity and duty of immediate secession;—the latter opposing it. I take the grievances and abuses of the Federal Government, which the South has suffered at the hands of the North, and which were urged by the former speaker as the grounds of secession, as I find them stated and to some extent answered by his friend and fellow-citizen (then opposed to secession) according to the report in the Milledgeville papers.

CAUSES ALLEGED BY GEORGIA: THE FISHING BOUNTIES.

And what, think you, was the grievance in the front rank of those oppressions on the part of the North, which have driven the long-suffering and patient South to open rebellion against "the best Government that the history of the world gives any account of" ? It was not that upon which the Convention of South Carolina relied. You will hardly believe it; posterity will surely not believe it. "We listened," said Mr. Vice-President Stephens, in his reply, "to my honorable friend last night, (Mr. Toombs,) as he recounted the evils of this Government. *The first was the fishing bounties paid mostly to the sailors of New England.*" The bounty paid by the Federal Government to encourage the deep-sea fisheries of the United States !

You are aware that this laborious branch of industry has, by all maritime States, been ever regarded with special favor as the nursery of naval power. The fisheries of the American colonies before the American Revolution drew from Burke one of the most gorgeous bursts of eloquence in our language,—in any language. They were all but annihilated by the Revolution, but they furnished the men who followed Manly, and Tucker, and Biddle, and Paul Jones to the jaws of death. Reviving after the war, they attracted the notice of the First Congress, and were recommended to their favor by Mr. Jefferson, then Secretary of State. This favor was at first extended to them in the shape of a draw-back of the duty on the various imported articles employed in the building and outfit of the vessels and on the foreign salt used in preserving the fish. The complexity of this arrangement led to the substitution at first of a certain bounty on the quantity of the fish exported ; afterwards on the tonnage of the vessels employed in the fisheries. All administrations have concurred in the measure ; Presidents of all parties,—though there has not been much variety of party in that office,—have approved the appropriations. If the North had a local interest in these bounties, the South got the principal food of her laboring population so much the cheaper ; and she had her common share in the protection which the navy afforded her coasts, and in the glory which it shed on the flag of the country. But since, unfortunately, the deep-sea fisheries do not exist in the Gulf of Mexico, nor, as in the " age of Pyrrha," on the top of the Blue Ridge, it has been discovered of late years that these bounties are a violation of the Constitution ; a largess bestowed by the common treasury on one section of the country, and not shared by the other ; one of the hundred ways, in a word, in which the rapacious North is fattening upon the oppressed and pillaged South. You will naturally wish to know the amount of this tyrannical and oppressive bounty. It is stated by a senator from Alabama (Mr. Clay) who has warred against it with perseverance and zeal, and succeeded in the last Congress in carrying a bill through the Senate for its repeal, to have amounted, on the average, to an annual sum of 200,005 dollars ! Such is the portentous grievance which in Georgia stands at the head of the acts of oppression, for which, although repealed in one branch of Congress, the Union is to be broken up, and the country desolated by war. Switzerland revolted because an Austrian tyrant invaded the sanctity of her firesides, crushed out the eyes of aged patriots, and compelled her fathers to shoot apples from the heads of her sons ; the Low Countries revolted against the fires of the Inquisition, and the infernal cruelties of Alva ; our fathers revolted because they were taxed by a parliament in which they were not represented ; the Cotton States revolt because a paltry subvention is paid to the hardy fishermen who form the nerve and muscle of the American Navy.

But it is not, we shall be told, the amount of the bounty, but the principle, as our fathers revolted against a three-penny tax on tea. But that was because it was laid by a parliament in which the Colonies were not represented, and which yet claimed the right to bind them in all cases. The Fishing Bounty is bestowed by a Government which has been from the first controlled by the South. Then how unreasonable to expect or to wish, that, in a country so vast as ours, no public expenditure should be made for the immediate benefit of one part or one interest that cannot be identically repeated in every other. A liberal policy, or rather the necessity of the case, demands, that what the public good, upon the whole, requires, should under constitutional limitations be done where it is required, offsetting the local benefit which may accrue from the expenditure made in one place and for one object, with the local benefit from the same source, in some other place for some other object. More money was expended by the United States in removing the Indians from Georgia, eight or ten times as much was expended for the same object in Florida, as has been paid for Fishing Bounties in seventy years. For the last year, to pay for the expense of the post-office in the seceding States, and enable our fellow-citizens there to enjoy the comforts of a newspaper and letter mail to the same extent as they are enjoyed in the other States, three millions of dollars were paid from the common Treasury. The post-office bounty paid to the seceding States exceeded seventeen fold the annual average amount of the Fishing Bounty paid to the North. In four years that excess would equal the sum total of the amount paid since 1792 in bounties to the deep-sea fishery! This circumstance probably explains the fact, that the pride of the Southern Confederacy was not alarmed at having the mails still conveyed by the United States, three or four months after the forts had been seized, the arsenals emptied, and the mints plundered.

NAVIGATION LAWS.

The second of the grievances under which the South is laboring, and which, according to Mr. Stephens, was on the occasion alluded to pleaded by the Secretary of State of the new Confederacy as a ground for dissolving the Union, is the Navigation Laws, which give to American vessels the exclusive enjoyment of our own coasting trade. This also is a policy coeval with the Government of the United States, and universally adopted by maritime powers, though relaxed by England within the last few years. Like the fishing bounty, it is a policy adopted for the purpose of fostering the commercial and with that the naval marine of the United States. All administrations of all parties have favored it; under its influence our commercial tonnage has grown up to be second to no other in the world, and our navy has proved itself adequate to all the exigencies of peace and war. And are these no objects in a national point of view? Are the seceding politicians really insensible to interests of such paramount national importance? Can they, for the sake of an imaginary infinitesimal reduction of coastwise freights, be willing to run even the risk of impairing our naval prosperity? Are they insensible to the fact that nothing but the growth of the American commercial marine protects the entire freighting interest of the country, in which the South is more deeply interested than the North, from European monopoly? The South did not always take so narrow a view of the subject. When the Constitution was framed, and the American Merchant Marine was inconsiderable, the discrimination in favor of United States vessels, which then extended to the foreign trade, was an object of some apprehension on the part of the planting States. But there were statesmen in the South at that day, who did not regard the shipping interest as a local concern. "So far," said Mr. Edward Rutledge, in the South Carolina Convention of 1788, "from not preferring the Northern States by a navigation act, it would be politic to increase their strength by every means in our power; for we had no other resource in our day of danger than in the naval force of our Northern friends, nor could we ever expect to become a great nation till we were powerful on the waters."* But "powerful

Elliott's Debates, vol. iv., p. 299.

on the waters" the South can never be. She has live oak, naval stores, and gallant officers; but her climate and its diseases, the bars at the mouth of nearly all her harbors, the *Teredo*, the want of a merchant marine and of fisheries, and the character of her laboring population, will forever prevent her becoming a great naval power. Without the protection of the Navy of the United States, of which the strength centres at the North, she would hold the ingress and egress of every port on her coast at the mercy, I will not say of the great maritime States of Europe, but of Holland, and Denmark, and Austria, and Spain—of any second or third-rate power, which can keep a few steam frigates at sea.

It must be confessed, however, that there is a sad congruity between the conduct of our seceding fellow-citizens and the motives which they assign for it. They attempt a suicidal separation of themselves from a great naval power, of which they are now an integral part, and they put forward, as the reason for this self-destructive course, the legislative measures which have contributed to the growth of the navy. A judicious policy designed to promote that end has built up the commercial and military marine of the Union to its present commanding stature and power; the South, though unable to contribute any thing to its prosperity but the service of her naval officers, enjoys her full share of the honor which it reflects on the country, and the protection which it extends to our flag, our coasts, and our commerce, but under the influence of a narrow-minded sectional jealousy, she is willing to abdicate the noble position which she now fills among the nations of the earth; to depend for her very existence on the exigencies of the cotton market, to live upon the tolerance of the navies of Europe, and she assigns as leading causes for this amazing fatuity, that the Northern fisheries have been encouraged by a trifling bounty, and that the Northern commercial marine has the monopoly of the coastwise trade. And the politicians, who, for reasons like these, almost too frivolous to merit the time we have devoted to their examination, are sapping a noble framework of government, and drenching a fair and but for them prosperous country in blood, appeal to the public opinion of mankind for the justice of their cause, and the purity of their motives, and lift their eyes to Heaven for a blessing on their arms!

THE TARIFF.

But the tariff is, with one exception, the alleged monster wrong—for which South Carolina in 1832 drove the Union to the verge of a civil war, and which, next to the slavery question, the South has been taught to regard as the most grievous of the oppressions which she suffers at the hands of the North, and that by which she seeks to win the sympathy of the manufacturing States of Europe. It was so treated in the debate referred to. I am certainly not going so far to abuse your patience, as to enter into a discussion of the constitutionality or expediency of the protective policy, on which I am aware that opinions at the North differ, nor do I deem it necessary to expose the utter fallacy of the monstrous paradox, that duties, enhancing the price of imported articles, are paid, not by the consumer of the merchandise imported, but by the producer of the last article of export given in exchange. It is sufficient to say that for this maxim, (the forty-bale theory so called,) which has grown into an article of faith at the South, not the slightest authority ever has been, to my knowledge, adduced from any political economist of any school. Indeed, it can be shown to be a shallow sophism, inasmuch as the *consumer* must be, directly or indirectly, the *producer* of the equivalents given in exchange for the article he consumes. But without entering into this discussion, I shall make a few remarks to show the great injustice of representing the protective system as being in its origin an oppression, of which the South has to complain on the part of the North.

Every such suggestion is a complete inversion of the truth of history. Some attempts at manufactures by machinery were made at the North before the Revolution, but to an inconsiderable extent. The manufacturing system as a great Northern interest is the child of the restrictive policy of 1807—1812, and of the war. That policy was pursued against the earnest opposition of the North, and to the temporary prostration of their commerce, navigation, and fisheries. Their capital was driven in this way into manufactures, and on the return of peace, the foundations of the protective system were laid in the square yard duty on cotton fabrics, in the support of which Mr. Calhoun, advised that the growth of the manufacture would open a new market for the staple of the South, took the lead. As late as 1821 the Legislature of South Carolina unanimously affirmed the constitutionality of protective duties, though denying their expediency,—and of all the States of the Union Louisiana has derived the greatest benefit from this policy ; in fact, she owes the sugar culture to it, and has for that reason given it her steady support. In all the tariff battles while I was a member of Congress, few votes were surer for the policy than that of Louisiana. If the duty on an article imported is considered as added to its price in our market, (which, however, is far from being invariably the case,) the sugar duty, of late, has amounted to a tax of five millions of dollars annually paid by the consumer, for the benefit of the Louisiana planter.

As to its being an unconstitutional policy, it is perfectly well known that the protection of manufactures was a leading and avowed object for the formation of the Constitution. The second law, passed by Congress after its formation, was a revenue law. Its preamble is as follows : " Whereas it is necessary for the support of Government, for the discharge of the debts of the United States, and the encouragement and protection of manufactures, that duties be laid on goods, wares, and merchandise imported." That act was reported to the House of Representatives by Mr. Madison, who is entitled as much as any one to be called the father of the Constitution. While it was pending before the House, and in the first week of the first session of the first Congress, two memorials were presented praying for protective duties ; and it is a matter of some curiosity to inquire, from what part of the country this first call came for that policy, now put forward as one of the acts of Northern oppression, which justify the South in flying to arms. The first of these petitions was from Baltimore. It implored the new Government to lay a protecting duty on all articles imported from abroad, which can be manufactured at home. The second was from the shipwrights, not of New York, not of Boston, not of Portland, but of Charleston, South Carolina, praying for " such a general regulation of trade and the establishment of such a NAVIGATION ACT, as will relieve the particular distresses of the petitioners, in common with those of their fellow-shipwrights throughout the Union " ! and if South Carolina had always been willing to make common cause with their fellow-citizens throughout the Union, it would not now be rent by civil war.

THE COTTON CULTURE INTRODUCED UNDER PROTECTION.

But the history of the great Southern staple is most curious and instructive. His Majesty "King Cotton," on his throne, does not seem to be aware of the influences which surrounded his cradle. The culture of cotton, on any considerable scale, is well known to be of recent date in America. The household manufacture of cotton was coeval with the settlement of the country. A century before the piano-forte or the harp was seen on this continent, the music of the spinning-wheel was heard at every fire-side in town and country. The raw materials were wool, flax, and cotton, the last imported from the West Indies. The colonial system of Great Britain before the Revolution forbade the establishment of any other than household manufactures. Soon after the Revolution, cotton mills were erected in Rhode Island and Massachusetts, and the infant manufacture was encouraged by State duties on the imported fabric. The raw material was still derived exclusively from the West Indies. Its culture in this country was so extremely limited and so little known, that a small parcel sent from the United States to Liverpool in 1784 was seized at the custom-house there, as an illicit importation of British colonial produce. Even as late as 1794, and by persons so intelligent as the negotiators of Jay's treaty, it was not known that cotton was an article of growth and export from the United States. In the twelfth article of that treaty, as laid before the Senate, Cotton was included with Molasses, Sugar, Coffee, and Cocoa, as articles which American vessels should not be permitted to carry from the islands *or from the United States* to any foreign country.

In the Revenue law of 1789, as it passed through the House of Representatives, cotton, with other raw materials, was placed on the free list. When the bill reached the Senate a duty of 3 cents per pound was laid upon cotton, not to encourage, not to protect, but to *create* the domestic culture. On the discussion of this amendment in the House, a member from South Carolina declared that "Cotton was in contemplation" in South Carolina and Georgia, "and *if good seed could be procured he hoped it might succeed.*" On this hope the amendment of the Senate was concurred in, and the duty of three cents per pound was laid on cotton. In 1791, Hamilton, in his report on the manufactures, recommended the repeal of this duty, on the ground that it was "a very serious impediment to the manufacture of cotton," but his recommendation was disregarded.

Thus, in the infancy of the cotton manufacture of the North, at the moment when they were deprived of the protection extended to them before the Constitution by State laws, and while they were struggling against English competition under the rapidly improving machinery of Arkwright, which it was highly penal to export to foreign countries, a heavy burden was laid upon them by this protecting duty, to enable the planters of South Carolina and Georgia to explore the tropics for a variety of cotton seed adapted to their climate. For seven years at least, and probably more, this duty was in every sense of the word a protecting duty. There was not a pound of cotton spun, no not for candle-wicks to light the humble industry of the cottages of the North, which did not pay this tribute to the Southern planter. The growth of the native article, as we have seen, had not in 1794 reached a point to be known to Chief Justice Jay as one of actual or probable export. As late as 1796, the manufacturers of Brandywine in Delaware petitioned

Congress for the repeal of this duty on imported cotton, and the petition was rejected on the Report of a Committee, consisting of a majority from the Southern
States, on the ground, that " to repeal the duty on raw cotton imported would be
to damp the growth of cotton in our own country."   Radicle and plumule, root and
stalk, blossom and boll, the culture of the cotton plant in the United States was
in its infancy the foster-child of the Protective System.

When therefore the pedigree of King Cotton is traced, he is found to be the
lineal child of the tariff; called into being by a specific duty ; reared by a tax laid
upon the manufacturing industry of the North, to create the culture of the raw
material in the South.   The Northern manufacturers of America were slightly protected in 1789 because they were too feeble to stand alone.   Reared into magnitude under the restrictive system and the war of 1812, they were upheld in 1816
because they were too important to be sacrificed, and because the great staple of
the South had a joint interest in their prosperity.   King Cotton alone, not in his
manhood, not in his adolescence, not in his infancy, but in his very embryo state,
was pensioned upon the Treasury,—before the seed from which he sprung was
cast " in the lowest parts of the earth."   In the book of the tariff " his members were
written, which in continuance were fashioned, when as yet there were none of
them."

But it was not enough to create the culture of cotton at the South, by taxing the
manufactures of the North with a duty on the raw material ; the extension of that
culture and the prosperity which it has conferred upon the South are due to the
mechanical genius of the North.   What says Mr. Justice Johnson of the Supreme
Court of the United States, and a citizen of South Carolina ?   " With regard to the
utility of this discovery " (the cotton gin of Whitney) " the court would deem it a
waste of time to dwell long upon this topic.   Is there a man who hears us that has
not experienced its utility ?   The whole interior of the Southern States was lan-
guishing, and its inhabitants emigrating, for want of some object to engage their
attention and employ their industry, when the invention of this machine at once
opened views to them which set the whole country in active motion.   From child
hood to age it has presented us a lucrative employment.   Individuals who were
depressed in poverty and sunk in idleness, have suddenly risen to wealth and
respectability.   Our debts have been paid off, our capitals increased, and our lands
trebled in value.   We cannot express the weight of obligation which the country
owes to this invention ; the extent of it cannot now be seen."—Yes, and when happier days shall return, and the South, awakening from her suicidal delusion, shall
remember who it was that sowed her sunny fields with the seeds of those golden
crops with which she thinks to rule the world, she will cast a veil of oblivion over
the memory of the ambitious men who have goaded her to her present madness,
and will rear a monument of her gratitude in the beautiful City of Elms, over the
ashes of her greatest benefactor—ELI WHITNEY.

INTERFERENCE WITH SLAVERY THE GREAT ALLEGED GRIEVANCE.

But the great complaint of the South, and that which is admitted to be the immediate occasion of the present revolt, is the alleged interference of the North in
the Southern institution of slavery ; a subject on which the sensibilities of the two
sections have been so deeply and fearfully stirred, that it is nearly impossible to

speak words of impartial truth. As I have already stated, the declaration of South Carolina, of the causes which prompted her to secede from the Union, alleged no other reason for this movement than the enactment of laws to obstruct the surrender of fugitive slaves. The declaration does not state that South Carolina ever lost a slave by the operation of these laws, and it is doubtful whether a dozen from all the States have been lost from this cause. A gross error on this subject pervades the popular mind at the South. Some hundred of slaves in the aggregate escape annually ; some to the recesses of the Dismal Swamp ; some to the everglades of Florida ; some to the trackless mountain region, which traverses the South ; some to the Mexican States and the Indian tribes ; some across the free States to Canada. The popular feeling of the South ascribes the entire loss to the laws of the free States, while it is doubtful whether these laws cause any portion of it. The public sentiment of the North is not such, of course, as to dispose the community to obstruct the escape or aid in the surrender of slaves. Neither is it at the South. No one, I am told, at the South, not called upon by official duty, joins in the hue and cry after a fugitive ; and whenever he escapes from any States south of the border tier, it is evident that his flight must have been aided in a community of slave-holders. If the North Carolina fugitive escapes through Virginia, or the Tennessee fugitive escapes through Kentucky, why are Pennsylvania and Ohio alone blamed ? On this whole subject the grossest injustice is done to the North. She is expected to be more tolerant of slavery than the South herself ; for while the South demands of the North entire acquiescence in the extremest doctrines of slave property, it is a well-known fact, and as such alluded to by Mr. Clay in his speech on the compromises of 1850, that any man who habitually traffics in this property is held in the same infamy at Richmond and New Orleans that he would be at Philadelphia or Cincinnati.*

While South Carolina, assigning the cause of secession, confines herself to the State laws for obstructing the surrender of fugitives, in other quarters, by the press, in the manifestoes and debates on the subject of secession, and in the official papers of the new Confederacy, the general conduct of the North, with respect to Slavery, is put forward as the justifying, nay, the compelling cause of the revolution. This subject, still more than that of the tariff, is too trite for discussion, with the hope of saying any thing new on the general question. I will but submit a few considerations to show the great injustice which is done to the North, by representing her as the aggressor in this sectional warfare.

The Southern theory assumes that, at the time of the adoption of the Constitution, the same antagonism prevailed as now between the North and South, on the general subject of Slavery ; that, although it existed to some extent in all the States but one of the Union, it was a feeble and declining interest at the North, and mainly seated at the South ; that the soil and climate of the North were soon found to be unpropitious to slave labor, while the reverse was the case at the South ; that the Northern States, in consequence, having, from interested motives, abolished Slavery, sold their slaves to the South, and that then, although the existence of Slavery was recognized, and its protection guaranteed by the Constitution, as soon as the Northern States had acquired a controlling voice in Congress, a persistent and organized system of hostile measures, against the rights of the owners

* See Appendix, C.

of slaves in the Southern States, was inaugurated and gradually extended, in violation of the compromises of the Constitution, as well as of the honor and good faith tacitly pledged to the South, by the manner in which the North disposed of her slaves.

Such, in substance, is the statement of Mr. Davis in his late message ; and he then proceeds, seemingly as if rehearsing the acts of this Northern majority in Congress, to refer to the anti-slavery measures of the State Legislatures, to the resolutions of abolition societies, to the passionate appeals of the party press, and to the acts of lawless individuals, during the progress of this unhappy agitation.

THE SOUTH FORMERLY OPPOSED TO SLAVERY.

Now, this entire view of the subject, with whatever boldness it is affirmed, and with whatever persistency it is repeated, is destitute of foundation. It is demonstrably at war with the truth of history, and is contradicted by facts known to those now on the stage, or which are matters of recent record. At the time of the adoption of the Constitution, and long afterwards, there was, generally speaking, no sectional difference of opinion between North and South, on the subject of Slavery. It was in both parts of the country regarded, in the established formula of the day, as "a social, political, and moral evil." The general feeling in favor of universal liberty and the rights of man, wrought into fervor in the progress of the Revolution, naturally strengthened the anti-slavery sentiment throughout the Union. *It is the South which has since changed, not the North.* The theory of a change in the Northern mind, growing out of a discovery made *soon after* 1789, that our soil and climate were unpropitious to Slavery, (as if the soil and climate then were different from what they had always been,) and a consequent sale to the South of the slaves of the North, is purely mythical—as groundless in fact as it is absurd in statement. I have often asked for the evidence of this last allegation, and I have never found an individual who attempted even to prove it. But however this may be, the South at that time regarded Slavery as an evil, though a necessary one, and habitually spoke of it in that light. Its continued existence was supposed to depend on keeping up the African slave trade ; and South as well as North, Virginia as well as Massachusetts, passed laws to prohibit that traffic ; they were, however, before the revolution, vetoed by the Royal Governors. One of the first acts of the Continental Congress, unanimously subscribed by its members, was an agreement neither to import, nor purchase any slave imported, after the first of December, 1774. In the Declaration of Independence, as originally drafted by Mr. Jefferson, both Slavery and the slave trade were denounced in the most uncompromising language. In 1777 the traffic was forbidden in Virginia, by State law, no longer subject to the veto of Royal Governors. In 1784, an ordinance was reported by Mr. Jefferson to the old Congress, providing that after 1800 there should be no Slavery in any Territory, ceded or to be ceded to the United States. The ordinance failed at that time to be enacted, but the same prohibition formed a part by general consent of the ordinance of 1787, for the organization of the northwestern Territory. In his Notes on Virginia, published in that year, Mr. Jefferson depicted the evils of Slavery in terms of fearful import. In the same year the Constitution was framed. It recognized the existence of Slavery, but the word was carefully excluded from the instrument, and Congress was authorized to abolish the traffic in twenty years. In 1796, Mr. St. George Tucker, law professor in William and Mary College in Virginia, published a treatise entitled, "a Dissertation on Slavery, with a proposal for the gradual abolition of it in the State of Virginia." In the preface to the essay, he speaks of the "abolition of Slavery in this State as an object of the first importance, not only to our moral character and domestic peace, but even to our political salvation." In 1797 Mr. Pinkney, in the Legislature of Maryland, maintained that "by the eternal principles of justice, no man in the State has the right to hold his slave a single hour." In 1803, Mr. John Randolph, from a committee on the subject, reported that the prohibition of Slavery by the ordinance of 1787, was "a measure wisely calculated to promote the happiness and prosperity of the North-western States, and to give strength and security to that extensive frontier." Under Mr. Jefferson, the importation of slaves into the Territories of Mississippi and Louisiana was prohibited in advance of the time limited by the Constitution for the interdiction of the slave trade. When the Missouri restriction was enacted, all the members of Mr. Monroe's Cabinet—Mr. Crawford of Georgia, Mr. Calhoun of South Carolina, and Mr. Wirt of Virginia—concurred with Mr. Monroe in affirming its constitutionality. In 1832, after the Southampton massacre, the evils of Slavery were exposed in the Legislature of Virginia, and the expediency of its gradual abolition maintained, in terms as decided as were ever employed by the most uncompromising agitator. A bill for that object was introduced into the Assembly by the grandson of Mr. Jefferson, and warmly supported by distinguished politicians now on the stage. Nay, we have the recent admission of the Vice-President of the seceding Confederacy, that what he calls "the errors of the past generation," meaning the anti-slavery sentiments entertained by Southern statesmen, "still clung to many as late as *twenty years* ago."

To this hasty review of Southern opinions and measures, showing their accordance till a late date with Northern sentiment on the subject of Slavery, I might add the testimony of Washington, of Patrick Henry, of George Mason, of Wythe, of Pendleton, of Marshall, of Lowndes, of Poinsett, of Clay, and of nearly every first-class name in the Southern States. Nay, as late as 1849, and after the Union had been shaken by the agitations incident to the acquisition of Mexican territory, the Convention of California, although nearly one-half of its members were from the slaveholding States, *unanimously* adopted a Constitution, by which slavery was prohibited in that State. In fact, it is now triumphantly proclaimed by the chiefs of the revolt, that the ideas prevailing on this subject when the Constitution was adopted were fundamentally wrong; that the new Government of the Confederate States "rests upon exactly the opposite ideas; that its foundations are laid and its corner-stone reposes upon the great truth, that the negro is not equal to the white man; that Slavery—subordination to the superior race—is his natural and normal condition. This our new Government is the first in the history of the world based upon this physical, philosophical, and moral truth." So little foundation is there for the statement, that the North, from the first, has been engaged in a struggle with the South on the subject of Slavery, or has departed in any degree from the spirit with which the Union was entered into, by both parties. The fact is precisely the reverse.

NO ANTI-SLAVERY MEASURES ENACTED BY CONGRESS.

Mr. Davis, in his message to the Confederate States, goes over a long list of measures, which he declares to have been inaugurated, and gradually extended, as soon as the Northern States had reached a sufficient number to give their representatives a controlling voice in Congress.   But of all these measures, not one is a matter of Congressional legislation, nor has Congress, with this alleged controlling voice on the part of the North, ever either passed a law hostile to the interests of the South, on the subject of Slavery, nor failed to pass one which the South has claimed as belonging to her rights or needed for her safety.   In truth, the North, meaning thereby the anti-slavery North, never has had the control of both Houses of Congress, never of the judiciary, rarely of the Executive, and never exerted there to the prejudice of Southern rights.   Every judicial or legislative issue on this question, with the single exception of the final admission of Kansas, that has ever been raised before Congress, has been decided in favor of the South ; and yet she allows herself to allege " a persistent and organized system of hostile measures against the rights of the owners of slaves," as the justification of her rebellion.

The hostile measures alluded to are, as I have said, none of them matters of Congressional legislation.   Some of them are purely imaginary as to any injurious effect, others much exaggerated, others unavoidably incident to freedom of speech and the press.   You are aware, my friends, that I have always disapproved the agitation of the subject of Slavery for party purposes, or with a view to infringe upon the Constitutional rights of the South.   But if the North has given cause of complaint, in this respect, the fault has been equally committed by the South.   The subject has been fully as much abused there as here for party purposes ; and if the North has ever made it the means of gaining a sectional triumph, she has but done what the South, for the last twenty-five years, has never missed an occasion of doing.   With respect to every thing substantial in the complaints of the South against the North, Congress and the States have afforded or tendered all reasonable, all possible satisfaction.   She asked for a more stringent fugitive slave law in 1850, and it was enacted.   She complained of the Missouri Compromise, although adopted in conformity with all the traditions of the Government, and approved by the most judicious Southern statesmen ; and after thirty-four years' acquiescence on the part of the people, Congress repealed it.   She wished for a judicial decision of the territorial question in her favor, and the Supreme Court of the United States, in contravention of the whole current of our legislation, so decided it.   She insisted on carrying this decision into effect, and three new Territories, at the very last session of Congress, were organized in conformity to it, as Utah and New Mexico had been before it was rendered.   She demanded a guarantee against amendments of the Constitution adverse to her interests, and it was given by the requisite majority of the two Houses.   She required the repeal of the State laws obstructing the surrender of fugitive slaves, and although she had taken the extreme remedy of revolt into her hands, they were repealed or modified.   Nothing satisfied her, because there was an active party in the cotton-growing States, led by ambitious men determined on disunion, who were resolved not to be satisfied.   In one instance alone the South has suffered defeat.   The North, for the first time since the foundation of the Government, has chosen a President by her unaided electoral vote; and that is the occasion of the present unnatural war. I cannot appropriate to myself any portion of those cheers, for, as you know, I did not contribute, by my vote, to that result; but I did enlist under the Banner of "the Union, the Constitution, and the enforcement of the laws." Under that Banner I mean to stand, and with it, if it is struck down, I am willing to fall. Even for this result the South has no one to blame but herself. Her disunionists would give their votes for no candidate but the one selected by leaders who avowed the purpose of effecting a revolution of the cotton States, and who brought about a schism in the Democratic party directly caclulated, probably designed, to produce the event which actually took place, with all its dread consequences.

REPRESENTATION OF THREE-FIFTHS OF THE SLAVES.

I trust I have shown the flagrant injustice of this whole attempt to fasten upon the North the charge of wielding the powers of the Federal Government to the prejudice of the South. But there is one great fact connected with this subject, seldom prominently brought forward, which ought forever to close the lips of the South, in this warfare of sectional reproach. Under the old Confederation, the Congress consisted of but one House, and each State, large and small, had but a single vote, and consequently an equal share in the Government, if Government it could be called, of the Union. This manifest injustice was barely tolerable in a state of war, when the imminence of the public danger tended to produce unanimity of feeling and action. When the country was relieved from the pressure of the war, and discordant interests more and more disclosed themselves, the equality of the States became a positive element of discontent, and contributed its full share to the downfall of that short-lived and ill-compacted frame of Government.

Accordingly, when the Constitution of the United States was formed, the great object and the main difficulty was to reconcile the equality of the States, (which gave to Rhode Island and Delaware equal weight with Virginia and Massachusetts,) with a proportionate representation of the people. Each of these principles was of vital importance; the first being demanded by the small States, as due to their equal independence, and the last being demanded by the large States, in virtue of the fact that the Constitution was the work and the Government of the people, and in conformity with the great law in which the Revolution had its origin, that representation and taxation should go hand in hand.

The problem was solved, in the Federal Convention, by a system of extremely refined arrangements, of which the chief was that there should be two Houses of Congress, that each State should have an equal representation in the Senate, (voting, however, not by States, but *per capita*,) and a number of representatives in the House in proportion to its population. But here a formidable difficulty presented itself, growing out of the anomalous character of the population of the slave-holding States, consisting as it did of a dominant and a subject class, the latter excluded by local law from the enjoyment of all political rights, and regarded simply as property. In this state of things, was it just or equitable that the slaveholding States, in addition to the number of representatives to which their free population entitled them, should have a further share in the government of the country, on account of the slaves held as property by a small portion of the ruling class? While property of every kind in the non-slaveholding States was unrepresented, was it just that this species of property, forming a large proportion of the entire property of the South, should be allowed to swell the representation of the slave-holding States ?

This serious difficulty was finally disposed of, in a manner mutually satisfactory, by providing that Representatives and direct Taxes should be apportioned among the States on the same basis of population, ascertained by adding to the whole number of free persons three-fifths of the slaves. It was expected at this time that the Federal Treasury would be mainly supplied by direct taxation. While, therefore, the rule adopted gave to the South a number of representatives out of proportion to the number of her citizens, she would be restrained from exercising this power to the prejudice of the North, by the fact that any increase of the public burdens would fall in the same increased proportion on herself. For the additional weight which the South gained in the presidential election, by this adjustment, the North received no compensation.

But now mark the practical operation of the compromise. Direct taxation, instead of being the chief resource of the Treasury, has been resorted to but four times since the foundation of the Government, and then for small amounts; in 1798 two millions of dollars, in 1813 three millions, in 1815 six millions, in 1816 three millions again, in all fourteen millions, the sum total raised by direct taxation in seventy-two years, less than an average of 200,000 dollars a year. What number of representatives, beyond the proportion of their free population, the South has elected in former Congresses I have not computed. In the last Congress she was represented by twenty members, in behalf of her slaves, being nearly one-eleventh part of the entire House. As the increasing ratio of the two classes of population has not greatly varied, it is probable that the South, in virtue of her slaves, has always enjoyed about the same proportionate representation in the House, in excess of that accruing from her free population. As it has rarely happened in our political divisions that important measures have been carried by large majorities, this excess has been quite sufficient to assure the South a majority on all sectional questions. It enabled her to elect her candidate for the Presidency in 1800, and thus effect the great political revolution of that year, and is sufficient of itself to account for that approach to a monopoly of the Government which she has ever enjoyed.

Now, though the consideration for which the North agreed to this arrangement, may be said to have wholly failed, it has nevertheless been quietly acquiesced in. I do not mean that in times of high party excitement it has never been alluded to as a hardship. The Hartford Convention spoke of it as a grievance which ought to be remedied ; but even since our political controversies have turned almost wholly on the subject of slavery, I am not aware that this entire failure of the equivalent, for which the North gave up to the South what has secured to her, in fact, the almost exclusive control of the Government of the country, has been a frequent or a prominent subject of complaint.

So much for the pursuit by the North of measures hostile to the interests of the South ;—so much for the grievances urged by the South as her justification for bringing upon the country the crimes and sufferings of civil war, and aiming at the prostration of a Government admitted by herself to be the most perfect the world has seen, and under which all her own interests have been eminently protected and favored ; for to complete the demonstration of the unreasonableness of her com-plaints, it is necessary only to add, that, by the admission of her leading public men, there never was a time when her " peculiar institution " was so stable and prosperous as at the present moment.*

WHY SHOULD WE NOT RECOGNIZE THE SECEDING STATES?

And now let us rise from these disregarded appeals to the truth of history and the wretched subtilties of the Secession School of Argument, and contemplate the great issue before us, in its solemn practical reality. " Why should we not," it is asked, " admit the claims of the seceding States, acknowledge their independence, and put an end at once to the war ? " " Why should we not ? "　I answer the question by asking another : " Why should we ? "　What have we to gain, what to hope from the pursuit of that course ?　Peace ?　But we were at peace before. Why are we not at peace now ?　The North has not waged the war, it has been forced upon us in self-defence ; and if, while they had the Constitution and the Laws, the Executive, Congress, and the Courts, all controlled by themselves, the South, dissatisfied with legal protections and Constitutional remedies, has grasped the sword, can North and South hope to live in peace, when the bonds of Union are broken, and amicable means of adjustment are repudiated ?　Peace is the very last thing which Secession, if recognized, will give us ; it will give us nothing but a hollow truce,—time to prepare the means of new outrages.　It is in its very nature a perpetual cause of hostility ; an eternal never-cancelled letter of marque and reprisal, an everlasting proclamation of border-war.　How can peace exist, when all the causes of dissension shall be indefinitely multiplied ; when unequal revenue laws shall have led to a gigantic system of smuggling ; when a general *stampede* of slaves shall take place along the border, with no thought of rendition, and all the thousand causes of mutual irritation shall be called into action, on a frontier of 1,500 miles not marked by natural boundaries and not subject to a common jurisdiction or a mediating power ?　We did believe in peace, fondly, credulously, believed that, cemented by the mild umpirage of the Federal Union, it might dwell forever beneath the folds of the Star-Spangled Banner, and the sacred shield of a common Nationality.　That was the great *arcanum* of policy ; that was the State mystery into which men and angels desired to look ; hidden from ages, but revealed to us :—

> Which Kings and Prophets waited for,
> And sought, but never found :

a family of States independent of each other for local concerns, united under one Government for the management of common interests and the prevention of internal feuds.　There was no limit to the possible extension of such a system.　It had already comprehended half of North America, and it might, in the course of time, have folded the continent in its peaceful, beneficent embrace.　We fondly dreamed that, in the lapse of ages, it would have been extended till half the Western hemi-sphere had realized the vision of universal, perpetual peace.　From that dream we have been rudely startled by the array of ten thousand armed men in Charleston Harbor, and the glare of eleven batteries bursting on the torn sky of the Union, like the comet which, at this very moment, burns " In the Arctic sky, and from his

---

* See Appendix, D.

horrid hair shakes pestilence and war." These batteries rained their storm of iron hail on one poor siege-worn company, because, in obedience to lawful authority, in the performance of sworn duty, the gallant Anderson resolved to keep *his* oath. That brave and faithful band, by remaining at their post, did not hurt a hair of the head of a Carolinian, bond or free. The United States proposed not to reënforce, but to feed them. But the Confederate leaders would not allow them even the poor boon of being starved into surrender; and because *some* laws had been passed *somewhere*, by which it was alleged that the return of *some* slaves (not one from Carolina) had been or might be obstructed, South Carolina, disclaiming the protection of courts and of Congress, which had never been withheld from her, has inaugurated a ruthless civil war. If, for the frivolous reasons assigned, the seceding States have chosen to plunge into this gulf, while all the peaceful temperaments and constitutional remedies of the Union were within their reach, and offers of further compromise and additional guarantees were daily tendered them, what hope, what possibility of peace can there be, when the Union is broken up, when, in addition to all other sources of deadly quarrel, a general *exodus* of the slave population begins, (as, beyond all question, it will,) and nothing but war remains for the settlement of controversies? The Vice-President of the new Confederacy states that it rests on slavery; but from its very nature it must rest equally on war; eternal war, first between North and South, and then between the smaller fragments into which some of the disintegrated parts may crumble. The work of demons has already begun. Besides the hosts mustered for the capture or destruction of Washington, Eastern Virginia has let loose the dogs of war on the loyal citizens of Western Virginia; they are straining at the leash in Maryland and Kentucky; Tennessee threatens to set a price on the head of her noble Johnson and his friends; a civil war rages in Missouri. Why, in the name of Heaven, has not Western Virginia, separated from Eastern Virginia by mountain ridges, by climate, by the course of her rivers, by the character of her population, and the nature of her industry, why has she not as good a right to stay in the Union which she inherited from her Washington, as Eastern Virginia has to abandon it for the mushroom Confederacy forced upon her from Montgomery? Are no rights sacred but those of rebellion; no oaths binding but those taken by men already foresworn; are liberty of thought, and speech, and action nowhere to be tolerated except on the part of those by whom laws are trampled under foot, arsenals and mints plundered, governments warred against, and where their patriotic defenders are assailed by ferocious and murderous mobs?

SECESSION ESTABLISHES A FOREIGN POWER ON THE CONTINENT.

Then consider the monstrous nature and reach of the pretensions in which we are expected to acquiesce; which are nothing less than that the United States should allow a Foreign Power, by surprise, treachery, and violence, to possess itself of one-half of their territory and all the public property and public establishments contained in it; for if the Southern Confederacy is recognized, it becomes a Foreign Power, established along a curiously dove-tailed frontier of 1,500 miles, commanding some of the most important commercial and military positions and lines of communication for travel and trade; half the sea-coast of the Union; the navigation of our Mediterranean Sea, (the Gulf of Mexico, one-third as large as the Mediterranean of Europe,) and, above all, the great arterial inlet into the heart of the Continent, through which its very life-blood pours its imperial tides. I say we are coolly summoned to surrender all this to a Foreign Power. Would we surrender it to England, to France, to Spain? Not an inch of it; why, then, to the Southern Confederacy? Would any other Government on earth, unless compelled by the direst necessity, make such a surrender? Does not France keep an army of 100,000 men in Algeria to prevent a few wandering tribes of Arabs, a recent conquest, from asserting their independence? Did not England strain her resources to the utmost tension, to prevent the native Kingdoms of Central India (civilized States two thousand years ago, and while painted chieftains ruled the savage clans of ancient Britain) from reëstablishing their sovereignty; and shall we be expected, without a struggle, to abandon a great integral part of the United States to a Foreign Power?

Let it be remembered, too, that in granting to the seceding States, jointly and severally, the right to leave the Union, we concede to them the right of resuming, if they please, their former allegiance to England, France, and Spain. It rests with them, with any one of them, if the right of secession is admitted, again to plant a European Government side by side with that of the United States on the soil of America; and it is by no means the most improbable upshot of this ill-starred rebellion, if allowed to prosper. Is this the Monroe doctrine for which the United States have been contending? The disunion press in Virginia last year openly encouraged the idea of a French Protectorate, and her Legislature has, I believe, sold out the James River canal, the darling enterprise of Washington, to a company in France supposed to enjoy the countenance of the emperor. The seceding patriots of South Carolina were understood by the correspondent of the London "Times," to admit that they would rather be subject to a British prince, than to the Government of the United States. Whether they desire it or not, the moment the seceders lose the protection of the United States, they hold their independence at the mercy of the powerful governments of Europe. If the navy of the North should withdraw its protection, there is not a Southern State on the Atlantic or the Gulf, which might not be recolonized by Europe, in six months after the outbreak of a foreign war.

IMMENSE COST OF THE TERRITORIES CLAIMED BY SECESSION.

Then look at the case for a moment, in reference to the cost of the acquisitions of territory made on this side of the continent within the present century,—Florida, Louisiana, Texas, and the entire coast of Alabama and Mississippi; vast regions acquired from France, Spain, and Mexico, within sixty years. Louisiana cost 15,000,000 dollars, when our population was 5,000,000, representing, of course, a burden of 90,000,000 of dollars at the present day. Florida cost 5,000,000 dollars in 1820, when our population was less than 10,000,000, equal to 15,000,000 dollars at the present day, besides the expenses of General Jackson's war in 1818, and the Florida war of 1840, in which some 80,000,000 of dollars were thrown away, for the purpose of driving out a handful of starving Seminoles from the Everglades. Texas cost $200,000,000 expended in the Mexican war, in addition to the lives of thousands of brave men; besides $10,000,000 paid to her in 1850, for ceding a tract of land which was not hers to New Mexico. A great part of the expense of

4

the military establishment of the United States has been incurred in defending the South-Western frontier. The troops, meanly surprised and betrayed in Texas, were sent there to protect her defenceless border settlements from the tomahawk and scalping-knife. If to all this expenditure we add that of the forts, the navy yards, the court-houses, the custom-houses, and the other public buildings in these regions, 500,000,000 dollars of the public funds, of which at least five-sixths have been levied by indirect taxation from the North and North-West, have been expended in and for the Gulf States in this century. Would England, would France, would any government on the face of the earth surrender, without a death-struggle, such a dear-bought territory?

THE UNITED STATES CANNOT GIVE UP THE CONTROL OF THE OUTLET OF THE MISSISSIPPI.

But of this I make no account; the dollars are spent; let *them* go. But look at the subject for a moment in its relations to the safety, to the prosperity, and the growth of the country. The Missouri and the Mississippi Rivers, with their hundred tributaries, give to the great central basin of our continent its character and destiny. The outlet of this mighty system lies between the States of Tennessee and Missouri, of Mississippi and Arkansas, and through the State of Louisiana. The ancient province so-called, the proudest monument of the mighty monarch whose name it bears, passed from the jurisdiction of France to that of Spain in 1763. Spain coveted it, not that she might fill it with prosperous colonies and rising States, but that it might stretch as a broad waste barrier, infested with warlike tribes, between the Anglo-American power and the silver mines of Mexico. With the independence of the United States, the fear of a still more dangerous neighbor grew upon Spain, and in the insane expectation of checking the progress of the Union westward, she threatened, and at times attempted, to close the mouth of the Mississippi, on the rapidly increasing trade of the West. The bare suggestion of such a policy roused the population upon the banks of the Ohio, then inconsiderable, as one man. Their confidence in Washington scarcely restrained them from rushing to the seizure of New Orleans, when the treaty of San Lorenzo El Real in 1795 stipulated for them a precarious right of navigating the noble river to the sea, with a right of deposit at New Orleans. This subject was for years the turning point of the politics of the West, and it was perfectly well understood, that, sooner or later, she would be content with nothing less than the sovereign control of the mighty stream from its head spring to its outlet in the Gulf; *and that is as true now as it was then.*

So stood affairs at the close of the last century, when the colossal power of the first Napoleon burst upon the world. In the vast recesses of his Titanic ambition, he cherished as a leading object of his policy, to acquire for France a colonial empire which should balance that of England. In pursuit of this policy, he fixed his eye on the ancient regal colony which Louis XIV. had founded in the heart of North America, and he tempted Spain by the paltry bribe of creating a kingdom of Etruria for a Bourbon prince, to give back to France the then boundless waste of the territory of Louisiana. The cession was made by the secret treaty of San Ildefonso of the 1st of October, 1800, (of which one sentence only has ever been published, but that sentence gave away half a continent,) and the youthful conqueror concentrated all the resources of his mighty genius on the accomplishment of the vast project. If successful, it would have established the French power on the mouth and on the right bank of the Mississippi, and would have opposed the most formidable barrier to the expansion of the United States. The peace of Amiens, at this juncture, relieved Napoleon from the pressure of the war with England, and every thing seemed propitious to the success of the great enterprise. The fate of America trembled for a moment in a doubtful balance, and five hundred thousand citizens in that region felt the danger, and sounded the alarm.*

But in another moment the aspect of affairs was changed, by a stroke of policy, grand, unexpected, and fruitful of consequences, perhaps without a parallel in history. The short-lived truce of Amiens was about to end, the renewal of war was inevitable. Napoleon saw that before he could take possession of Louisiana it would be wrested from him by England, who commanded the seas, and he determined at once, not merely to deprive her of this magnificent conquest, but to contribute as far as in him lay, to build up a great rival maritime power in the West. The Government of the United States, not less sagacious, seized the golden moment—a moment such as does not happen twice in a thousand years. Mr. Jefferson perceived that, unless acquired by the United States, Louisiana would in a short time belong to France or to England, and with equal wisdom and courage he determined that it should belong to neither. True he held the acquisition to be unconstitutional, but he threw to the winds the resolutions of 1798, which had just brought him into power; he broke the Constitution and he gained an Empire. Mr. Monroe was sent to France to conduct the negotiation, in conjunction with Chancellor Livingston, the resident Minister, contemplating, however, at that time only the acquisition of New Orleans and the adjacent territory.

But they were dealing with a man that did nothing by halves. Napoleon knew, *and we know*—that to give up the mouth of the river was to give up its course. On Easter-Sunday of 1803, he amazed his Council with the announcement, that he had determined to cede the whole of Louisiana to the United States. Not less to the astonishment of the American envoys, they were told by the French negotiators, at the first interview, that their master was prepared to treat with them not merely for the Isle of New Orleans, but for the whole vast province which bore the name of Louisiana; whose boundaries, then unsettled, have since been carried on the North to the British line, on the West to the Pacific Ocean; a territory half as big as Europe, transferred by a stroke of the pen. Fifty-eight years have elapsed since the acquisition was made. The States of Louisiana, Arkansas, Missouri, Iowa, Minnesota, and Kansas, the territories of Nebraska, Dacotah, Jefferson, and part of Colorado, have been established within its limits, on this side of the Rocky Mountains; the State of Oregon and the territory of Washington on their western slope; while a tide of population is steadily pouring into the region, destined in addition to the natural increase, before the close of the century, to double the number of the States and Territories. For the entire region west of the Alleghanies and east of the Rocky Mountains, the Missouri and the Mississippi form the natural outlet to the sea. Without counting the population of the seceding States, there are ten millions of the free citizens of the country, between Pittsburg and Fort Union, who claim the course and the mouth of the Mississippi, as belonging to the United States. It is theirs by a transfer of truly imperial origin and

---

* Speech of Mr. Ross, in the Senate of the United States, 14th February, 1803.

magnitude; theirs by a sixty years' undisputed title; theirs by occupation and settlement; theirs by the Law of Nature and of God.   Louisiana, a fragment of this Colonial empire, detached from its main portion and first organized as a State, undertakes to secede from the Union, and thinks by so doing that she will be allowed by the Government and People of the United States to revoke this imperial transfer, to disregard this possession and occupation of sixty years, to repeal this law of nature and of God; and she fondly believes that ten millions of the Free People of the Union will allow her and her seceding brethren to open and shut the portals of this mighty region at their pleasure.   They may do so, and the swarming millions which throng the course of these noble streams and their tributaries may consent to exchange the charter which they hold from the God of Heaven, for a bit of parchment signed at Montgomery or Richmond; but if I may repeat the words which I have lately used on another occasion, it will be when the Alleghanies and the Rocky Mountains, which form the eastern and western walls of the imperial valley, shall sink to the level of the sea, and the Mississippi and the Missouri shall flow back to their fountains.

Such, Fellow-citizens, as I contemplate them, are the great issues before the country, nothing less, in a word, than whether the work of our noble Fathers of the Revolutionary and Constitutional age shall perish or endure; whether this great experiment in National polity, which binds a family of free Republics in one United Government—the most hopeful plan for combining the homebred blessings of a small State with the stability and power of great empire—shall be treacherously and shamefully stricken down, in the moment of its most successful operation, or whether it shall be bravely, patriotically, triumphantly maintained.   We wage no war of conquest and subjugation; we aim at nothing but to protect our loyal fellow-citizens, who, against fearful odds, are fighting the battles of the Union in the disaffected States, and to reëstablish, not for ourselves alone, but for our deluded fellow-citizens, the mild sway of the Constitution and the Laws.   The result cannot be doubted.   Twenty millions of freemen, forgetting their divisions, are rallying as one man in support of the righteous cause—their willing hearts and their strong hands, their fortunes and their lives, are laid upon the altar of the country.   We contend for the great inheritance of constitutional freedom transmitted from our revolutionary fathers.   We engage in the struggle forced upon us, with sorrow, as against our misguided brethren, but with high heart and faith, as we war for that Union which our sainted Washington commended to our dearest affections.   The sympathy of the civilized world is on our side, and will join us in prayers to Heaven for the success of our arms.

APPENDIX.

APPENDIX A, p. 9.

AFTER the remarks in the foregoing address, p. 9, were written, touching the impossibility, at the present day, of *repealing* the instrument by which in 1788 South Carolina gave her consent and ratification to the Constitution of the United States, I sought the opinion on that point of Mr. George Ticknor Curtis, the learned and accurate historian of the Constitution. It afforded me great pleasure to find, from the following letter, that my view of the subject is sustained by his high authority:

JAMAICA PLAINS,
Saturday Evening, *June* 8, 1861.

MY DEAR SIR: Since I came home, I have looked carefully at the ratification of the Constitution by South Carolina. The formal instrument, sent to Congress, seems to be much more in the nature of a Deed or Grant, than of an *Ordinance*. An ordinance would seem to be an instrument adopted by a public body, for the regulation of a subject that in its nature remains under the regulation of that body;—to operate until otherwise ordered. A Deed, or Grant, on the other hand, operates to pass some things; and unless there be a reservation of some control over the subject-matter by the Grantor, his cession is necessarily irrevocable. I can perceive no reason why these distinctions are not applicable to the cession of political powers by a People, or their duly authorized representatives. The question submitted to the People of South Carolina, by the Congress, was, Whether they would cede the powers of government embraced in an instrument sent to them, and called the Constitution of the United States. In other words, they were asked to make a Grant of those Powers. When, therefore, the duly authorized Delegates of the People of South Carolina executed an instrument under seal, declaring that they, " in the name and behalf" of that people, " assent to and ratify the said Constitution," I can perceive no propriety in calling this Deed an *Ordinance*. If they had adopted an instrument entitled, " An Act [or Ordinance] for the government of the People of South Carolina," and had gone on, in the body of the instrument, to declare that the Powers embraced in the Constitution of the United States should be exercised by the agents therein provided, until otherwise ordered, there would have been something left for a repeal to operate upon. But nothing like this was done, and everybody knows that such a ratification could not have been accepted.

There are those, as you are well aware, who pretend that the most absolute and unrestricted terms of cession, which would carry any other subject entirely out of the grantor, do not so operate when the subject of the grant is political sovereignty. But a political school which maintains that a deed is to be construed in one way when it purports to convey one description of right, such as political sovereignty, and in another way when it purports to convey a right of another kind, such as property, would hold a very weak brief in any tribunal of jurisprudence, if the question could be brought to that arbitrament. The American people have been very much accustomed to treat political grants, made by the sovereign power without reservation, as irrevocable conveyances and executed contracts; and although they hold to the right of revolution, they have not yet found out how a deed, absolute on its face, is to be treated in point of law, as a repealable instrument, because it deals with political rights and duties. If any court in South Carolina were now to have the question come before it, whether the laws of the United States are still binding upon their citizens, I think they would have to put their denial upon the naked doctrine of *revolution;* and that they could not hold that, as matter of law and regular political action, their ratification deed of May 23d, 1788, is "repealed" by their late ordinance. Most truly and respectfully yours,

GEO. T. CURTIS.

MR. EVERETT.

APPENDIX B, p. 22.

Hon. REVERDY JOHNSON to Mr. EVERETT.

BALTIMORE, 24th June, 1861.

MY DEAR MR. EVERETT.

I have your note of the 18th, and cheerfully authorize you to use my name, as you suggest.

The letter I read in the speech which I made in Frederick, should be conclusive evidence that, at its date, Mr. Calhoun denied the right of secession, as a constitutional right, either express or implied.

But, in addition to this, I had frequent opportunities of knowing that this was his opinion. It was my good fortune to be a member of the Senate of the United States, whilst he was one of its greatest ornaments, for four years, from 1845, until I became a member of Gen. Taylor's administration, and during two sessions (I think 1846 and 1847) I lived in the same house with him. He did me th' honor to give me much of his confidence, and frequently his nullification doctrine was the subject of conversation. Time and time again have I heard him, and with ever increased surprise at his wonderful acuteness, defend it on Constitutional grounds, and distinguish it, *in that respect*, from the doctrine of Secession. This last he never, with me, placed on any other ground than that of revolution. This, he said, was to destroy the Government; and no Constitution, the work of sane men, ever provided *for its own destruction.* The other was to preserve it, was, practically, but to amend it, and in a constitutional mode. As you know, and he was ever told, I never took that view. I could see no more constitutional warrant for this than for the other, which, I repeat, he ever in all our interviews repudiated, as wholly indefensible as a constitutional remedy. His mind, with all its wonderful power, was so ingenious that it often led him into error, and at times to such an extent as to be guilty of the most palpable inconsistencies. His views of the tariff and internal improvement powers of the Government, are instances. His first opinions upon both were decided, and almost ultra. His earliest reputation was won as their advocate, and yet four years before his death he denounced both, with constant zeal and with rare power, and, whilst doing so, boldly asserted his uniform consistency. It is no marvel, therefore, with those who have observed his career and studied his character, to hear it stated now that he was the advocate of constitutional secession.

It may be so, and perhaps is so; but this in no way supports the doctrine, as far as it is rested on his authority. His first views were well considered and formed, without the influence of extraneous circumstances, of which he seemed to me to be often the victim.

Pure in private life and in motives, ever, as I believe and have always believed, patriotic, he was induced, seemingly without knowing it, in his later life, to surrender to section what was intended for the whole, his great powers of analysis and his extraordinary talent for public service. If such a heresy, therefore, as constitutional secession could rest on any individual name, if any mere human authority could support such an absurd and destructive folly, it cannot be said to rest on that of Mr. Calhoun.

With sincere regard, your friend,
REVERDY JOHNSON.

Hon. EDWARD EVERETT, Boston.

APPENDIX C, p. 31.

The number of fugitive slaves, from all the States, as I learn from Mr. J. C. G. Kennedy, the intelligent superintendent of the census bureau, was, in the year 1850, 1,011, being about one to every 3,165, the entire number of slaves at that time being 3,200,364, a ratio of rather more than $\frac{1}{30}$ of one *per cent*. This very small ratio was diminished in 1860. By the last census, the whole number of slaves in the United States was 3,949,-557, and the number of escaping fugitives was 803, being a trifle over $\frac{1}{50}$ of one *per cent*. Of these it is probable that much the greater part escaped to the places of refuge in the South, alluded to in the text. At all events, it is well known that escaping slaves, reclaimed in the free States, have in almost every instance been restored.

There is usually some difficulty in reclaiming fugitives of any description, who have escaped to another jurisdiction. In most of the cases of fugitives from justice, which came under my cognizance as United States Minister in London, every conceivable difficulty was thrown in my way, and sometimes with success, by the counsel for the parties whose extradition was demanded under the Webster-Ashburton treaty. The French Ambassador told me, that he had made thirteen unsuccessful attempts to procure the surrender of fugitives from justice, under the extradition treaty between the two governments. The difficulty generally grew out of the difference of the jurisprudence of the two countries, in the definition of crimes, rules of evidence, and mode of procedure.

The number of blacks living in Upper Canada and assumed to be all from the United States, is sometimes stated as high as forty thousand, and is constantly referred to, at the South, as showing the great number of fugitives. But it must be remembered that the manumissions far exceed in number the escaping fugitives. I learn from Mr. Kennedy that while in 1860 the number of fugitives was but 803, that of manumissions was 3,010. As the manumitted slaves are compelled to leave the States where they are set free, and a small portion only emigrate to Liberia, at least nine-tenths of this number are scattered through the northern States and Canada. In the decade from 1850 to 1860, it is estimated that 20,000 slaves were manumitted, of whom three-fourths probably joined their brethren in Canada. This supply alone, with the natural increase on the old stock and the new comers, will account for the entire population of the province.

A very able and instructive discussion of the statistics of this subject will be found in the Boston Courier of the 9th of July. It is there demonstrated that the assertion that the Northern States got rid of their slaves by selling them to the South, is utterly unsupported by the official returns of the census.

APPENDIX D, p. 37.

In his message to the Confederate Congress of the 29th April last, Mr. Jefferson Davis presents a most glowing account of the prosperity of the peculiar institution of the South. He states, indeed, that it was "imperilled" by Northern agitation, but he does not affirm (and the contrary, as far as I have observed, is strenuously maintained at the South) that its progress has been checked or its stability in the slightest degree shaken.

I think I have seen statements by Mr. Senator Hunter of Virginia, that the institution of slavery has been benefited and its interests promoted, since the systematic agitation of the subject began; but I am unable to lay my hand on the speech, in which, if I recollect rightly, this view was taken by the distinguished senator.

I find the following extracts from the speeches of two distinguished southern senators, in "The Union," a spirited paper published at St. Cloud, Minnesota:

It was often said at the North, and admitted by candid statesmen at the South, that anti-slavery agitation strengthened rather than weakened slavery. Here are the admissions of Senator Hammond on this point, in a speech which he delivered in South Carolina, October 24, 1858 :—

"And what then (1833) was the state of opinion in the South? Washington had emancipated his slaves. Jefferson had bitterly denounced the system, and had done all that he could to destroy it. Our Clays, Marshalls, Crawfords, and many other prominent Southern men, led off in the colonization scheme. The inevitable effect in the South was that she believed slavery to be an evil— weakness—disgraceful—nay, a sin. She shrunk from the discussion of it. She cowered under every threat. She attempted to apologize, to excuse herself under the plea—which was true—that England had forced it upon her; and in fear and trembling she awaited a doom that she deemed inevitable. But a few bold spirits took the question up—they compelled the South to investigate it anew and thoroughly, and what is the result? Why, it would be difficult to find now a Southern man who feels the system to be the lightest burden on his conscience; who does not, in fact, regard it as an equal advantage to the master and the slave, elevating both, as wealth, strength, and power, and as one of the main pillars and controlling influences of modern civilization, and who is not now prepared to maintain it at every hazard. *Such have been the happy results of this abolition discussion.* "So far *our gain has been immense* from this contest, savage and malignant as it has been."

And again he says :—

"The rock of Gibraltar does not stand so firm on its basis as our slave system. For a quarter of a century it has borne the brunt of a hurricane as fierce and pitiless as ever raged. At the North, and in Europe, they cried 'havoc,' and let loose upon us all the dogs of war. And how stands it now? Why, in this very quarter of a century our slaves have doubled in numbers, and each slave has more than doubled in value. The very negro who, as a prime laborer, would have brought $400 in 1828, would now, with thirty more years upon him, sell for $800."

Equally strong admissions were made by A. H. Stephens, now Vice-President of the "Confederacy," in that carefully prepared speech which he delivered in Georgia in July, 1859, on the occasion of retiring from public life. He then said :—

"Nor am I of the number of those who believe that we have sustained any injury by these agitations. It is true, we were not responsible for them. We were not the aggressors. We acted on the defensive. We repelled assault, calumny, and aspersion, by argument, by reason, and truth. But so far from the institution of African slavery in our section being weakened or rendered less secure by the discussion, *my deliberate judgment is that it has been greatly strengthened and fortified*—strengthened and fortified not only in the opinions, convictions, and consciences of men, but by the action of the Government."

Gen. Cadwallader.

DIARY.

......

DECEMBER 17, 1860.

—The South Carolina Convention met this day at Columbia, the capital of the State, General D. F. Jamieson in the chair, and passed a resolution to adjourn to Charleston, in consequence of the prevalence of the small-pox at Columbia, which was declared epidemic.

Dec. 18.—The bill for arming the State of North Carolina passed the Senate, after considerable debate, by a vote of forty-one to three.

The Commissioners from Alabama and Mississippi have arrived at Raleigh.—_Herald, Dec._ 19.

—Senator Crittenden, of Kentucky, offered a resolution in the Senate for certain amendments to the Constitution, which would practically reëstablish the Missouri Compromise, prevent the interference of Congress with slavery in the States, and provide for the faithful performance of the Fugitive Slave Law.—_N. Y. Times, Dec._ 19.

Dec. 19.—A meeting of members of the Georgia Legislature, favoring coöperation, was held at Milledgeville. A convention of Southern States desiring coöperation was urged, and an address to the people of South Carolina, Alabama, Mississippi, and Florida, was issued.— _Tribune, Dec._ 20.

—A bill has been introduced into the Legislature of North Carolina, providing that

"No ordinance of said Convention, dissolving the connection of the State of North Carolina with the Federal Government, or connecting it with any other, shall have any force or validity until it shall have been submitted to, and ratified by, a majority of the qualified voters of the State for members of the General Assembly, to whom it shall be submitted for their approval or rejection."—_Evening Post, Dec._ 20.

Dec. 19.—The Commissioner from Mississippi to Maryland addressed the citizens of Baltimore this evening. In the course of his remarks upon the intentions of the seceding States, he said:

"Secession is not intended to break up the present Government, but to perpetuate it. We do not propose to go out by way of breaking up or destroying the Union as our fathers gave it to us, but we go out for the purpose of getting further guaranties and security for our rights; not by a Convention of all the Southern States, nor by Congressional tricks, which have failed in times past, and will fail again. But our plan is for the Southern States to withdraw from the Union, for the present, to allow amendments to the Constitution to be made, guaranteeing our just rights; and if the Northern States will not make those amendments, by which these rights shall be secured to us, then we must secure them the best way we can. This question of slavery must be settled now or never. The country has been agitated seriously by it for the past twenty or thirty years. It has been a festering sore upon the body politic; and many remedies having failed, we must try amputation, to bring it to a healthy state. We must have amendments to the Constitution, and if we cannot get them we must set up for ourselves."

—The secession leaders at Charleston declare no more soldiers shall be sent to the forts in that harbor. A captain of a schooner landed some supplies there a few days since, and was terribly abused for it. He was told it would not be safe for any vessel to attempt it in future.

—The Governor of Maryland declined to receive the Commissioner from Mississippi to that State, setting forth his reasons in an elaborate Union letter.—(_See Document No._ 1.)

Dec. 20.—The news from Charleston is very unfavorable this morning.

"Civil war is imminent—peace is impossible," are the utterances which meet the ear on every side. There is here no longer any more hope of peace than of compromise, say the people. The speeches from northwestern representatives have taken us by surprise. Such flaming tirades against disunion, coupled with direct threats of coercion, were not expected from that quarter. It is not deemed impossible that the rich and saucy Northwest may join forces with the poor and starving East, and give the South some trouble, in the times now pressing upon us. The position of South Carolina is, however, so firmly taken, that though "one rose from the dead" to urge her retreat, she would not take one step backward.—*N. Y. Times*, Dec. 21.

—THE Secession Ordinance passed the Convention of South Carolina to-day by a unanimous vote.—(*Doc.* 2.)

As soon as its passage was known without the doors of the Convention, it rapidly spread on the street, a crowd collected, and there was immense cheering.

In the House of Representatives at Washington, Mr Garnet of Virginia announced the fact as follows: "Why, Sir, while your bill is under debate, one of the sovereign States of this Confederacy has, by the glorious act of her people, withdrawn, in vindication of her rights, from the Union, as the telegraph announced at 1½ to-day." [Here some three or four Southern members expressed approval by a slight clapping of hands. There was no other manifestation in the House.]

—THERE was an enthusiastic meeting at Memphis, Tennessee, this evening, to ratify the secession of South Carolina.

—THE Charleston *Mercury* discusses the necessity of providing for seacoast defence, and proposes to construct a half-sunken battery at the mouth of the river, with a block-house one hundred and fifty feet in the rear.

Dec. 20.—The secession of South Carolina was celebrated at Mobile by the firing of a hundred guns, and a military parade. There was great rejoicing. The bells rang merrily, and the people in the streets by hundreds expressed their joy at the secession. Many impromptu speeches were made, and the greatest excitement existed.

—IN the midst of a crowd of over three thousand people, collected in Secession Hall at Charleston this evening, the ordinance of secession was duly signed and sealed by the members of the Convention. The occasion was one of the greatest solemnity at some of its periods,

and of the wildest excitement at others.—*N. Y. Times*, Dec. 21.

Dec. 21.—At New Orleans a general demonstration of joy over the secession of South Carolina was made. One hundred guns were fired, and the pelican flag unfurled. Impromptu secession speeches were made by leading citizens, and the "Marseillais Hymn" and polkas were the only airs played. A bust of Calhoun was exhibited decorated with a cockade.

—SOUTH CAROLINA'S secession produced no sensation at Baltimore. People seemed relieved and cheerful, and the streets were gaily crowded, and business was better.—*Times*, Dec. 22.

—AT Wilmington, Del., one hundred guns were fired to-day in honor of the secession of South Carolina.—*Tribune*, Dec. 22.

—THE Convention of South Carolina adopted the declaration of causes justifying the secession of that State.—(*Doc.* 3.)

Dec. 22.—Senator Andrew Johnson was burned in effigy at Memphis, Tenn., to-day.

—THERE was a secession meeting in Ashland Hall, in Norfolk, Va. Disunion speeches were delivered by Colonel V. D. Grover and General John Tyler. The speeches were enthusiastically applauded.—*N. Y. Times*, Dec. 23.

—SENATOR CRITTENDEN, of Kentucky, made a speech this evening to the citizens of Washington, in which he advocated Union and the laws.

Dec. 22.—This evening the New England Society at New York celebrated the anniversary of the landing of the Pilgrims, by a dinner, toasts, and speeches. The reading of the sentiment, "The American Union; it must and shall be preserved," was received with unbounded applause. Among the speakers were the Vice President elect and Senator Seward. —(*Doc.* 4.)

—THE Charleston *Mercury* insists that the President will not reinforce the garrison at Fort Moultrie. "The reinforcement of the forts at this time and under present circumstances," says that paper, "means coercion— war.—When the forts are demanded and refused to be delivered up to those in whom is vested the title of eminent domain, and for whose protection and defence alone they were ceded and built up; and when, the Federal

Government showing a hostile purpose, it shall become necessary and proper for us to obtain possession, then it will be right for the world and Black Republicanism to expect that the State, by her authorities, will move in the premises. *The people will obey the call for war, and take the forts.*"

—GOVERNOR BUCKINGHAM, of Connecticut, in his proclamation for a day of fasting and prayer, urges upon the citizens of that State the propriety of a petition that the country may be carried through this crisis "in such a manner as shall forever check the spirit of anarchy, bring peace to a distracted people, and preserve, strengthen, and perpetuate our national Union."

Dec. 23.—This evening, Senator Toombs, of Georgia, assuming that there is no hope of compromise, telegraphed from Washington an address to the people of that State—(*Doc.* 5.)

—AT Petersburg, Va., a secession pole, one hundred feet high, erected yesterday on the most prominent street, amid the cheers from a large crowd, and bearing the palmetto flag, was sawed down this morning, just before the dawn of day, by an unknown party, and the flag carried off. There was great excitement when it was known.—*N. Y. Daily News, Dec.* 24.

—A COMPANY of eighty men arrived at Charleston from Savannah, and yesterday tendered their services to the Governor of the State, under the name of the Minute Men, or Sons of the South.—*Charleston Courier.*

—THE disbursing clerk in charge of the Indian Trust Fund, at Washington, was detected in embezzling a large amount of State bonds and coupons belonging to that fund. The sum is estimated at $830,000. The Secretary of State first discovered the defalcation, and telegraphed to Secretary Thompson (who was then in North Carolina as Commissioner from Mississippi to recommend secession) to return to Washington immediately. The Secretary arrived on Saturday evening, and had an interview with the President. In company with the Secretary of State, the Attorney-General, and District Attorney Ould, he then proceeded to make an investigation. Bailey, the defaulter, was absent from his office, and the key of the safe was missing; but entrance was obtained by force, and a large sum in bonds was found to have disappeared.

Godard Bailey, the defaulting clerk, has not been arrested; and it is supposed he has several accomplices, of whom the Washington police are in search.

Dec. 24.—Governor Pickens, agreeably to the ordinance of secession, issued a proclamation, proclaiming South Carolina a separate, sovereign, free, and independent State, with the right to levy war, conclude peace, negotiate treaties, leagues, or covenants, and do all acts whatever that rightly appertain to a free and independent State.—*Herald, Jan.* 1, 1861.

—A MASS meeting was held at New Orleans to ratify the nominations of the Southern Rights candidates for the Convention. It was the largest congregation of every party ever assembled in that city. Cornelius Fellows was President, and speeches were made by Charles M. Conrad, Charles Gayare, and others, advocating immediate secession, amid unbounded enthusiasm. The Southern Marseillaise was sung as the banner of the Southern Confederacy was raised, amid reiterated and prolonged cheers for South Carolina and Louisiana.—*National Intelligencer, Dec.* 25.

—THE election for delegates to the State Convention to meet January 7th, took place to-day. The separate State secession ticket was elected in Mobile by a thousand majority.

The election passed off quietly through the State. In many places there was no opposition; the secession ticket, in the whole State, has 50,000 majority.—*Times, Dec.* 25.

—GOVERNOR MOORE issued a proclamation, convening the Legislature of Alabama January 14th, to provide by State laws for any emergency that may arise from the action of the secession Convention called for January 7th.

—THE Speaker laid before the House of Representatives a letter signed by Messrs. McQueen, Bonham, Boyce, and Ashmore, members from South Carolina, to the effect that the act of secession passed by their State had dissolved their connection with that body, and that they should accordingly withdraw. The letter was laid on the table, and the Speaker directed the names of the South Carolina members to be retained on the roll, thus not recognizing the conduct of their State as severing their connection with the House.—(*Doc.* 6.)

—THE Richmond *Enquirer* of to-day announces that President Lincoln will be forced to relinquish Washington, and suggests the propriety of the prompt interposition of Maryland and Virginia to prevent Mr. Lincoln's inauguration at Washington, by taking possession of the capital without delay.

—EXCITEMENT at Pittsburgh, Pa., in consequence of a report that the artillery at the Alleghany arsenal was to be transferred to new forts in the southwest. A call is in circulation, addressed to the Mayor, to convene a meeting of the citizens to take action in the matter. The call is signed by prominent men of all parties. The feeling against allowing a gun to be removed south is almost unanimous.—*Evening Post, Dec.* 26.

Dec. 25.—The dispatches from Pittsburgh, that the arms in the arsenal there would not be allowed to be shipped, made a great sensation at Washington. The story was greatly enlarged. Northern men, including members of Congress, have telegraphed to the people to stand firm, and not allow the arsenals to be stripped of all arms.

Dec. 26.—Fort Moultrie was evacuated tonight. Previous to the evacuation, the guns were spiked and the carriages destroyed by fire. The troops have all been conveyed to Fort Sumter. Major Anderson states that he evacuated the fort in order to allay the discussion about that post, and at the same time strengthen his own position.—(*Doc.* 7.) The evacuation of the fort commenced a little after sundown. The men were ordered to hold themselves in readiness, with knapsacks packed, at a moment's notice; but up to the moment of their leaving had no idea of abandoning the post. They were reviewed on parade, and were then ordered to two schooners lying in the vicinity, where they embarked, taking with them all the necessaries, stores, &c., requisite in their evacuation.

Several trips were made during the night, and a great part of the provisions and camp furniture were transported under cover of night. The brightness of the moon, however, afforded but slight concealment to their movements, and in one of the trips, Lieutenant Davis in command, a schooner full of soldiers and baggage passed directly under the bow of the guard-boat Nina. The officer who made the statement expressed himself to be ignorant whether the watch on board the Nina discovered the movement or not; at all events, he

said, they did not signify any cognizance of the fact.—(*Doc.* 8.)—*Charleston Mercury, Dec.* 28.

—MESSRS. BARNWELL, ORR, and ADAMS, the Commissioners appointed by South Carolina to treat with the Federal Government, arrived in Washington to-day. This evening they have held a consultation with a few friends, among whom was Senator Wigfall, of Texas.—*Boston Post, Dec.* 27.

—IN the Convention at Charleston, Mr. Rhett offered the following ordinance:

First.—That the Conventions of the seceding slaveholding States of the United States unite with South Carolina, and hold a Convention at Montgomery, Ala., for the purpose of forming a Southern Confederacy.

Second.—That the said seceding States appoint, by their respective Conventions or Legislatures, as many delegates as they have representatives in the present Congress of the United States, to the said Convention to be held at Montgomery; and that on the adoption of the Constitution of the Southern Confederacy, the vote shall be by States.

Third.—That whenever the terms of the Constitution shall be agreed upon by the said Convention, the same shall be submitted at as early a day as practicable to the Convention and Legislature of each State, respectively, so as to enable them to ratify or reject the said Constitution.

Fourth.—That in the opinion of South Carolina, the Constitution of the United States will form a suitable basis for the Confederacy of the Southern States withdrawing.

Fifth.—That the South Carolina Convention appoint by ballot eight delegates to represent South Carolina in the Convention for the formation of a Southern Confederacy.

Lastly.—That one Commissioner in each State be elected to call the attention of the people to this ordinance.

Dec. 27.—A meeting of the citizens of Pittsburgh, Pa., was held, to give expression to the public indignation created by the removal of ordnance to the Southern forts. General William Robinson presided. Resolutions were adopted, declaring loyalty to the Union, deprecating any interference with the shipment of arms under government orders, however inopportune or impolitic the order might appear; deploring the existing state of things in connection with the administration of important departments of the public service, so as to have shaken confidence in the people of the free States; that, while Pennsylvania is on guard at the Federal capital, it is her special duty to look to the fidelity of her sons, and in that view call on the President as a citizen of this Commonwealth, to see that the public receive no detriment at his hands. It behooves the President to purge his cabinet of every man known to give aid and comfort to, or in any way countenancing the revolt of any State against the authority of the constitution and the laws of the Union.—*Evening Post, Dec.* 28.

—" CAPTAIN N. L. COSTE, U. S. R. Service, in command of the cutter William Aiken, betrayed his vessel into the hands of the State authorities of South Carolina.

" The crew, on being notified of the position of Captain Coste, under the State ordinance concerning the customs, promptly volunteered to remain under his command as an officer of South Carolina under that ordinance." [1]

—A MEETING was held this evening at Richmond, Va., to give expression of opinion on the present crisis. Several speeches were made, favoring prompt secession measures, and others advocating a resort to negotiation.—*Herald, Dec.* 29.

—THE Governor of South Carolina is tendered the services of troops from Georgia, Alabama, and different portions of Carolina.

Dec. 28.—Early this afternoon the palmetto flag was raised over the Custom House and Post Office at Charleston; and to-night Castle Pinckney and Fort Moultrie have been taken possession of by the South Carolina military. These forts are held under instructions from Governor Pickens, who authorizes their peaceable possession, for the protection of the government property. Castle Pinckney and Fort Moultrie were held by a very small force, which surrendered without collision.—*Times, Dec.* 29.

—AN enthusiastic Union meeting was held at Memphis, Tenn., to-day. It was addressed by Hon. Neill S. Brown and others. Resolutions were passed opposing separate State secession; against coercion; and favoring a Convention of the Southern States to demand their rights, and if refused to take immediate action. —*Phila. Press, Dec.* 29.

[1] See statement of Lieutenant Underwood, *N. Y. Times, Jan.* 9, 1861.

—THE citizens of Wilmington, Del., fired a salute of twenty-one guns in honor of Major Anderson and his heroic band.

—GOVERNOR HICKS' refusal to convene the Maryland Legislature for disunion purposes, is generally regarded at Washington with warm approbation, and creates great dismay among the disunionists who have urged it. The greater portion of the latter are said to be office-seekers, disappointed politicians, and rowdies, who seek plunder. A prominent gentleman, who has just seen Governor Hicks, says the rank and file of Maryland are true to him.—*Tribune, Dec.* 29.

Dec. 29.—Major Anderson is denounced by the Charleston papers. The *Courier* says:

" Major Robert Anderson, United States Army, *has achieved the unenviable distinction of opening civil war between American citizens by an act of gross breach of ·faith.* He has, under counsels of a panic, deserted his post at Fort Moultrie, and, under false pretexts, has transferred his garrison and military stores and supplies to Fort Sumter."

The *Mercury,* more temperately, says:

" Major Anderson alleges that the movement was made without orders and upon his own responsibility, and that he was not aware of such an understanding. He is a gentleman, and we will not impugn his word or his motives. But it is due to South Carolina and to good faith that the act of this officer should be repudiated by the Government, and that the troops be removed forthwith from Fort Sumter."—(*Doc.* 9.)

—JOHN B. FLOYD resigned his position as Secretary of War, owing to the refusal of the President to withdraw the Federal troops from the forts at Charleston.—(*Doc.* 10.)—*Baltimore Sun, Jan.* 1.

Dec. 30.—It is generally considered that Mr. Floyd has not resigned because of Major Anderson's patriotic course, *but merely used it as a pretext to conceal the real cause.* The whole country knows that his position, under the " trying circumstances," has not been a very agreeable one, especially during the last two weeks. The alleged cause of his leaving Mr. Buchanan is, that the latter refuses to recall or order back to Fort Moultrie the gallant Anderson. Floyd asserts that he, some time ago, promised the South Carolina seceders to leave things in the harbor of Charleston undisturbed

—in *statu quo ante bellum*—and that the President gave the same promise. This agreement having been broken by Major Anderson, he insisted upon his returning to Fort Moultrie; and, because the President was unwilling to give that order, he sent in his resignation.—*Phila. Press, Dec.* 31.

—THE South Carolina troops took possession of the arsenal at Charleston. The arsenal contains many thousand arms and military stores. Military preparations are actively and zealously progressing.—*Evening Post, Dec.* 31.

Dec. 31.—Strong fortifications have been ordered by the South Carolina Convention in and around Charleston harbor, to resist any reinforcements that may be sent to Major Anderson. Governor Pickens is in daily receipt of dispatches from the South, tendering men to defend South Carolina from invasion.

—THE scene in the Senate at Washington to-day was intensely exciting. Senator Benjamin, of Louisiana, who, it had been reported, would make a conciliatory speech, gave out that he would make a parting secession speech —an announcement which drew an immense audience. Senator Benjamin spoke calmly throughout, but the character of his speech at the close opened up to every one the new era in national affairs. His closing declaration, that the South could never be subjugated, was greeted by the galleries with disgraceful applause, screams, and uproar. It was evidently the act of persons who had purposely packed the galleries. For this demonstration the galleries were promptly cleared; but as the people passed out, remarks were current among the mob such as, "That's the talk"—"Now we will have war"—"Benjamin's a brick"— "D—n the abolitionists"—"Abe Lincoln will never come here."—*Times, Jan.* 1.

—GENERAL WOOL takes strong ground in favor of the Union, of sustaining Anderson in his position at Fort Sumter, and earnestly urges that a firm ground be adopted to put down rebellion.

He declares that if Fort Sumter be surrendered to the secessionists, in twenty days two hundred thousand men will be in readiness to take vengeance on all who would betray the Union into the hands of its enemies.—(*Doc.* 11.) —*Troy Times, Dec.* 31.

JANUARY 1, 1861.

The evidences of a purpose on the part of the secessionists to seize upon the public property and usurp the Government at its capital, have become so clear that energetic measures are taking to defeat their plans, and repress the treason. Now that the Administration begins to appreciate the necessity of preserving the Government, and manifests the purpose to repudiate the treasonable influences which have hitherto paralyzed its arm, the people are beginning to report facts exposing the violent plots concocting in the District and its neighborhood.

It is now well known that military companies have been organized and drilled for months past in Maryland and Virginia—some of them under the eye of an officer of the regular army —and that the distinct object of their organization is to aid in the seizure of Washington city in the interest of the disunionists, or the prevention by force of Lincoln's inauguration. Some of the less prudent of their leaders boast in private circles that they have five thousand well-armed and organized men ready to strike the blow instantly upon the concerted signal being given.—*Times, Jan.* 2.

—AT Charleston, the attitude of the Administration is regarded as warlike.

A censorship is exercised over the telegraph, and the city is nightly patrolled by the military. It is proposed to starve out the troops at Fort Sumter, and then attack them on rafts with the aid of batteries already erected. There is a battery of earthwork, logs, and sand, on the end of Sullivan's Island, and also one on Morris' Island.

Commander Pettigru, of Castle Pinckney, orders that no boat shall be allowed to approach the wharf-head without permission, under penalty of serious consequences in case of violation. The city river-front is carefully guarded. The Palmetto Guards, 100 strong, have charge of the arsenal under the palmetto flag, instead of the Federal flag.

Collector Colcock notifies ship-masters that all vessels from and for ports outside of South Carolina must enter and clear at Charleston.

The Columbia Artillery, numbering 50 men, arrived at 1 o'clock to-day, and proceeded to the harbor. They will use cannon belonging to Charleston.—*Boston Transcript, Jan.* 2.

—THE South Carolina Convention passed an ordinance to define and punish treason. It declares that in addition to that already declared treason by the General Assembly, treason against the State shall consist only in levying war against the State, adhering to its enemies, and giving them aid and comfort. The penalty is death without the benefit of the clergy.— *Evening Post, Jan. 2.*

Jan. 2.—The steam frigate *Brooklyn* and another vessel at Norfolk are ordered to be in readiness for immediate departure to Charleston. The secession leaders discovered the intention to start these vessels, and notified their sympathizers at Norfolk to have minute-men ready to seize them if they attempted to go to sea. The Administration is on the watch to prevent it.—*Commercial Advertiser.*

A letter received in Washington from Alabama, states the secession sentiment to be utterly uncontrollable; and says that, in the event of the firing of a single gun in opposition to disunion, "Mr Lincoln's life will not be worth a week's purchase."—*Boston Courier.*

—CAPTAIN CHARLES STONE, upon the recommendation of General Scott, is appointed to organize the militia of the District of Columbia. Captain Stone graduated at West Point at the head of his class, went into the Ordnance Corps, was a lieutenant in command of a battery at the siege of Vera Cruz; was brevetted for gallant conduct at Molina del Rey, and served on the entire line of operations from Vera Cruz to the city of Mexico, directly under the eye of General Scott, who expresses the highest confidence in his genius for command.—*Tribune.*

—INTELLIGENCE is received in Washington that Fort Sumter is besieged; that all Major Anderson's communications are cut off; that Fort Moultrie has been completely repaired and the guns remounted; and that every thing is in readiness to open a fire on Major Anderson. New batteries are being erected around him by the secessionists.—*N. Y. Times.*

—IN New York city an assembly of the people in the City Hall Park fire 100 guns in honor of Major Anderson.

—FIVE thousand citizens of Baltimore have signed a letter addressed to Governor Hicks, of Maryland, approving his course in refusing to convene the Legislature of that State. The list is headed by John P. Kennedy, Mr. Fillmore's

Secretary of the Navy, and comprises the names of nine-tenths of the business men of the city. Calls for public meetings to sustain the Governor are now being issued all over the State.—*Baltimore American.*

—GOVERNOR ELLIS, of North Carolina, dispatched troops to seize upon Fort Macon, at Beaufort, the forts at Wilmington, and the United States arsenal at Fayetteville.—*Times, Jan. 3.*

Jan. 3.—The order for the removal of guns from the Alleghany arsenal to southern forts is revoked by the War Department, under a decision of the Cabinet.

—FORT PULASKI, at Savannah, Ga., is taken possession of by State troops, by order of the Governor.

—A BOOK is opened in New York city, for the enrolment of volunteers to meet any demand which may be made by the Governor of the State for troops to aid in preserving the Union.—*Times, Jan. 4.*

—THE Florida State Convention assembled at Tallahassee.

—HON. H. DICKENSON, Commissioner from Mississippi, addresses both Houses of the Delaware Legislature, inviting Delaware to join a Southern Confederacy. The House, having heard him, passed unanimously the following resolution, in which the Senate concurred:

Resolved, That, having extended to Hon. H. Dickenson, Commissioner from Mississippi, the courtesy due him as a representative of a sovereign State of the Confederacy, as well as to the State he represents, we deem it proper and due to ourselves and the people of Delaware to express our unqualified disapproval of the remedy for the existing difficulties suggested by the resolutions of the Legislature of Mississippi.—*Philadelphia Ledger.*

—THE South Carolina Commissioners left Washington for Charleston, upon the President's declination to receive any further communication from them. They consider the abrupt termination of their business by the President an insult to themselves and their State, and treat it as a declaration of war.—*(Doc. 12.)*

—IN Washington, reports that armed bands were organizing to take possession of the capital before the votes for President and Vice-President are counted, meet with general credence. General Scott is actively engaged in the preparations to put down this mob.

Jan. 4.—Great excitement prevailed at Norfolk, Va., in consequence of the report that four companies of soldiers at Fortress Monroe had been ordered to Charleston.—*Balt. Sun.*

—It is stated in Washington, on the authority of a member of the Georgia delegation, that the United States revenue cutter *Dolphin* was fired upon and seized to-day, by the secessionists at Savannah. Upon the same statement in Georgia, the Governor issued an order for her release.—*Times, Jan.* 5.

—The South Carolina Convention appointed Hons. T. J. Withers, L. M. Keitt, W. W. Boyce, James Chesnut, Jr., R. B. Rhett, Jr., R. W. Barnwell, and C. G. Memminger, delegates to the General Congress of the seceding States.

—The United States arsenal at Mobile was taken by the secessionists at daylight this morning. It contained six stand of arms, 1,500 barrels of powder, 300,000 rounds of musket-cartridges, and other munitions of war. There was no defence.—*Evening Post, Jan.* 7.

—An appeal to the people of Florida, by the Charleston *Mercury*, to seize the forts and other defences at Pensacola and Key West, threatens the capture of the California treasure ships by letters of marque and privateers.—(*Doc.* 13.)

—Fast-day throughout the United States, by proclamation of the President. It is generally observed.—(*Doc.* 14.)

—Fort Morgan, at the entrance of Mobile Bay, was taken this morning by Alabama troops, and is now garrisoned by two hundred men.—*The Press, Jan.* 5.

—This evening a workingmen's meeting was held at Cincinnati, Ohio. Speeches were made, and resolutions adopted, declaring that the Union must be preserved in its integrity by the enforcement of the laws in every part of the Union, by whatever means may be necessary; that the remedy for all grievances can be had under the constitution, and that the only way to safety and peace is the maintenance of it.—*Troy Times.*

—At Schenectady a salute was fired in honor of Major Anderson and his brave men. National airs were performed amid cheers for Major Anderson and Secretaries Holt and Stanton.—*Albany Journal.*

—A meeting was held at Westchester, Pa., to enrol volunteers in the regiment of Chester county, to offer their services to the Government to maintain the constitution and enforce the laws.—*Evening Post. Jan.* 5.

—The following notice is served on residents of Charleston, indiscriminately :

Beat No 1, 16th Regiment, Regimental Parade.

Sir : You are hereby summoned to be and appear at the Citadel Square, properly armed and accoutred, according to law, on Wednesday next, at 1 o'clock P. M., precisely. An inspection of arms will take place at each parade. If you appear in pantaloons, blue or black coat, and black hat, arms and accoutrements in complete order will be furnished you at each parade on the ground ; if not, the law compels you to furnish yourself with a musket, bayonet, cartridge-box, bayonet-scabbard, with cross-belts, all in good order and fit for service, on one dollar fine for each defect.

Every person subject to military duty in this regiment, who removed from one beat to another, is required to report himself to the captains of the beats from which and to which he has removed, or be fined five dollars, besides all fines for the non-performance of military duty in both beats.

Court-martial held on defaulters at the Military Hall, Wentworth street, on the third Monday of December, at 12 o'clock M. By order of captain.

S. Vale Mallins, Corporal.

Jan. 5.—A large meeting was held at Norfolk, Va., this evening. Strong speeches were made, urging the citizens to arm themselves and place themselves in a state of defence for any emergency, which were loudly cheered.

Resolutions recommending the Legislature to organize thoroughly the military power of the State, and prepare for civil war should it occur ; scorning coercion ; and preparing to resist invasion, were unanimously adopted.—*National Intelligencer, Jan.* 7.

—Apprehensions of an attack on Washington are subsiding, in consequence of the measures already taken. General Carrington, of that city, has issued a call for a military organization for its defence.—(*Doc.* 15.)

—In the State Convention of Florida, assembled at Tallahassee, resolutions were offered declaring the right of Florida to secede, and the duty of the State to prepare for secession, made special order for the 7th.

—A RESOLUTION was unanimously adopted in the Missouri Senate, instructing the Committee on Federal Relations to report a bill calling a State Convention.—*Times.*

—STEAMSHIP Star of the West, Captain Mc-Gowan, cleared at New York for Havana and New Orleans. Two hundred and fifty artillerists and marines, with stores and ammunition, were put on board in the lower bay by steam-tug, and in the night the ship went to sea, supposed to be destined for Charleston.

—THE South Carolina Convention adjourned this morning, subject to the call of the president.—*Evening Post, Jan. 5.*

Jan. 6.—A meeting of citizens, irrespective of party, was held at Chicago, Ill., this evening. The resolutions adopted express love for the Union ; regard every attempt to rend it as the basest treason and most insane folly ; regard the Constitution of the United States as forming a union between the people of the several States, and intended to be perpetual ; and every attempt by a State to secede or annul the laws of the United States, is not only usurping the powers of the general Government, but aggression upon the equal rights of the other States ; that peaceable secession, if possible, must necessarily be a matter of agreement between the States, and until such agreement is made, the existing Government has no choice but to enforce the law and protect the property of the nation ; that in view of what is now transpiring in the Southern States, of threats to prevent the inauguration of a President, constitutionally elected, it is incumbent upon the loyal people of the several States to be prepared to render all their aid, military and otherwise, to the enforcement of the Federal laws ; that Major Anderson deserves the thanks of the country for the course pursued by him.—*Evening Post, Jan. 8.*

—A COMPANY of marines was put into Fort Washington, on the Potomac, 14 miles south of Washington city.

—FORTY tons of shot, shell, and powder, were forwarded from New York city by Adams' express for New Orleans ; reported to be destined for Mexico, but believed to be for Louisiana.

—SEVERAL volunteer companies of Washington were on parade, and upon dismissal were directed to carry their guns to their homes with forty rounds of ball-cartridges each.

—THE Alabama and Mississippi delegations in Washington held a conference, and telegraphed to the Conventions of their respective States, to advise immediate secession, as they consider that there is no prospect of a satisfactory adjustment. A caucus of Southern senators at Washington advocated separate and immediate secession.—*Times, Jan. 7.*

—GOVERNOR HICKS, of Maryland, published an address to the people of that State upon his refusal to convene the Legislature. It strongly opposes secession.—(*Doc.* 16.)

Jan. 7.—A variety of plans for capturing Fort Sumter have been devised, but as yet none have been put in practice. One man thought it might be taken by floating down to the fort rafts piled with burning tar-barrels, thus attempting to smoke the American troops out as you would smoke a rabbit out of a hollow. Another was for filling bombs with prussic acid and giving each of the United States soldiers a smell. Still another supposed that the fort might be taken without bloodshed by offering to each soldier ten dollars and a speaking to. And still another thought that by erecting a barricade of cotton bales, and arming it with cannon, a floating battery might be made, which, with the aid of Forts Moultrie and Johnson, and Castle Pinckney, together with redoubts thrown up on Morris' and Jones' Islands, and with further assistance of an armed fleet, an attack might be made on the fort, and at some convenient point a party of sharpshooters might be stationed, who would pick off the garrison, man by man, thus giving an opportunity to a party of infantry to scale the walls of the fort. Such a storming, however, could only be accomplished by an immense sacrifice of life ; and the only practicable mode of taking the fort would seem to be by a protracted siege, and by the unchristian mode of starving them.—*South Carolinian.*

—MAJOR ANDERSON's course was sustained in the House of Representatives to-day, by the following resolution, offered by Mr. Adrian, of New Jersey :

Resolved, That we fully approve the bold and patriotic act of Major Anderson in withdrawing from Fort Moultrie to Fort Sumter, and the determination of the President to maintain that fearless officer in his present condition ; and we will support the President in all constitutional measures to enforce the laws and preserve the Union.

—To-DAY the arrest of Senators Toombs and Wigfall, on the charges of treason, for sending dispatches to the South recommending the seizure of the forts, was spoken of in the Cabinet "jocularly."

—THE Alabama Convention organized at Montgomery, William M. Brooks in the chair. —*Times, Jan.* 8.

—THE Mississippi Convention organized at Jacksonville, A. J. Barry, of Lowndes, in the chair. It was resolved that a committee of fifteen be appointed by the president, with instructions to prepare and report, as speedily as possible, an ordinance of secession, providing for the immediate withdrawal of Mississippi from the Federal Union, with a view of establishing a new Confederacy, to be composed of the seceding States.— *Mobile Advertiser.*

—THE Governor of Virginia, in a message to the Legislature, in special session, condemns the hasty action of South Carolina, but opposes and says that " he will regard the attempt of the Federal troops to pass across Virginia for the purpose of coercing a Southern State, as an act of invasion which must be repelled."— *Times, Jan.* 8.

Jan. 8.—The *Southern Confederacy* (published at Atlanta, Ga.), a paper which has been fighting most gallantly for the Union and the laws, says of the late election for members of the Georgia Convention :

" It is a notable fact, that, wherever the 'Minute Men,' as they are called, have had an organization, those counties have voted, by large majorities, for immediate secession. Those that they could not control by persuasion and coaxing, *they dragooned and bullied, by threats, jeers, and sneers.* By this means thousands of good citizens were induced to vote the immediate secession ticket through timidity. Besides, the towns and cities have been flooded with sensation dispatches and inflammatory rumors, manufactured in Washington city for the especial occasion. To be candid, there never has been as much lying and bullying practised, in the same length of time, since the destruction of Sodom and Gomorrah, as has been in

the recent State campaign. The fault has been at Washington city ; from that cess-pool have emanated all the abominations that ever cursed a free people."

—THE Baltimore *Exchange* says " the whole population of Maryland is united in the desire to preserve the Union ; yet it may be that the people, by a blind and ill-advised course, may render the State obnoxious in future to the charge of having contributed, by her indecision and weakness, to the overthrow of the republic."—*Evening Post, Jan.* 8.

—GOVERNOR HICKS, of Maryland, in a letter to J. L. Curry, Commissioner from Alabama, says he regards coöperation between the slave States as an infraction of the Constitution, which he, as Governor of Maryland, swore to support. The people of that State are firm in their friendship for the Union, and will never swerve from it ; they have seen, with mortification and regret, the course taken by South Carolina ; for in their opinion it is better to use the Union for the enforcement of their rights than to break it up because of apprehensions that the provisions of the Constitution will be disregarded, and they will cling to it until it shall actually become the instrument of destruction to their rights and peace and safety. Disunion would be ruin to Maryland, and in the proposed Southern Confederacy she sees no refuge from the ills she must suffer in such an event. " Let us," says Governor Hicks, " have our rights in the Union, and through and by the Constitution."—*Baltimore Sun.*

—THE N. C. troops, and persons residing in the vicinity of Forts Caswell and Johnson, took possession of those defences this day.[1]

—SECRETARY THOMPSON resigned his place in the Cabinet, upon learning that the Star of the West had sailed from New York with troops.

—FROM Charleston it is announced that the messages to Fort Sumter cannot be delivered, as there is no communication between the fort and the city.

—THE Sub-Treasurer of Charleston has communicated to the Government, that the South Carolina authorities will not allow him to pay

[1] A correspondence on this subject took place immediately between Governor Ellis and Secretary Holt. The forts were surrendered and the State troops removed.— *Dec.* 17.

any more drafts, not even to pay Anderson's men. All the cash in his vaults is to be retained there.

—IT is ascertained that all the seceding States have drawn their quota of arms for 1861 in advance. The order from South Carolina was filled only a few days before the passage of the ordinance of secession.—*Commercial, Jan.* 8.

Jan. 9.—Mississippi State Convention passed the ordinance of secession. Delegations from South Carolina and Alabama were invited to seats in the Convention. They were greeted with applause. Efforts were made to postpone action, which were voted down. The fifteen delegates who opposed the ordinance will sign it to-morrow, making the vote unanimous.

Fireworks were displayed at the capitol in Jackson this evening. The excitement is intense.—*N. O. Picayune, Jan.* 10.

—AT half-past 7 A. M. the steamship Star of the West was signalled at the entrance of Charleston harbor. As she made her way toward Fort Sumter, a shot was sent across her bow from a battery on Morris' Island, when she displayed the United States flag, and was repeatedly fired into from the Morris' Island battery and from Fort Moultrie. Her course was then altered, and she again put to sea. Guns were run out at Fort Sumter, but none were fired. At 11 o'clock Major Anderson sent a flag with a communication to Governor Pickens, to inquire if this act had the sanction of the State Government; was informed that it had, and thereupon sent a special messenger to Washington with dispatches.—(*Doc.* 18.)

Jan. 10.—An intense excitement at Charleston, on account of a rumor that the sloop-of-war Brooklyn was dispatched for that place. Great preparations are made to receive her. The buoys in the harbor are removed, and threats are made to fire on the ship.

—A STEAM-TUG called the Aid left the wharf to-night for the purpose of reconnoitring. She is mounted with one gun, and is under the command of Lieut. Hamilton, formerly of the Federal navy.

—FORT MOULTRIE is being rapidly put in order by a large force of workmen. There are over forty South Carolina railroad hands actively and constantly employed under Mr. Bryant. Twenty hearty, strong negroes were sent down by the Rev. Mr. Prentiss and set to

work, and did work faithfully all night upon the ramparts.—*Charleston Courier, Jan.* 11.

Jan. 11.—To-day a party of Louisiana State troops, under command of Captain Bradford, took possession of the United States Marine Hospital, about two miles below New Orleans. The patients in the Hospital, numbering two hundred and sixteen, were ordered to be removed; those who are convalescent, immediately, and those who are confined to their beds, as soon as possible. The reason assigned for this inhuman action is that the authorities want the quarters for their own troops.

—A UNION meeting was held at Wilmington, N. C., this evening, which was attended by over one thousand persons.—*Evening Post, Jan.* 15.

—FLORIDA and Alabama adopted ordinances of secession; Florida passed her ordinance by a vote of 62 to 7, and Alabama by yeas 61, nays 39. The Alabama Convention was far from unanimous; a large part of that State is decidedly opposed to extreme measures.

The Alabama ordinance of secession calls upon the people of all the Southern States to meet in convention at Montgomery, on the 4th of February next, for the purpose of forming a provisional or permanent government. Immediately after the passage of the ordinance, an immense mass meeting was held in front of the capitol; a secession flag, presented by the women of Montgomery, was raised on the State House, cannon were fired, guns fired, etc., and in the evening the whole town was illuminated.—(*Doc.* 19.)—*Evening Post, Jan.* 12.

—JUDGE JONES, of the United States District Court, this afternoon announced from the windows of the court-room in the custom-house building, at Mobile, that the United States Court for the Southern District of Alabama was "adjourned forever."

Mr. George M. Brewer, of the same place, gave one hundred cords of wood for the use of the garrison at Fort Morgan, and proffered the services of twenty negro men as laborers on the works.—*Mobile Advertiser, Jan.* 12.

AT Richmond, Va., a banquet was given to John B. Floyd, late Secretary of the Navy. That gentleman made a speech, wherein he related a conversation with the President, which he claimed showed a breach of faith on the part of the latter, leading to the former's resignation. He also counselled resistance to Federal coercion. Speeches were made by Lieutenant-Governor Montague, Attorney-General Tucker, and others. The policy of the Legislature was severely commented upon.

—ABOLITIONISTS attempted to hold a meeting at Rochester, N. Y. It was broken up by citizens, and resolutions in favor of the Union were passed, and cheers given for General Scott and Major Anderson. A flag bearing the inscription, "No compromise with slavery," was not allowed to be suspended across Buffalo street. The authorities prevented a general riot.—*N. Y. Herald, Jan.* 12.

—BOTH branches of the New York Legislature adopted strong Union resolutions, tendering the assistance of the State to the President, and ordered them sent to the President, and the Governors of all the States.—(*Doc.* 20.)

Jan. 12.—The Star of the West arrived at New York, having failed to land her troops at Fort Sumter. The Captain reported that unexpected obstacles in the removal of buoys, lights, and ranges, which, though he arrived in the night, compelled him to wait till daybreak outside the harbor, rendered a successful entrance impossible.—(*Doc.* 21.)

—SENATOR SEWARD, in his place in the Senate, spoke upon the present troubles of the country, and avowed his "adherence to the Union, in its integrity and with all its parts; with his friends, with his party, with his State, or without either, as they may determine; in every event, whether of peace or of war; with every consequence of honor or dishonor, of life or death." He said that "Union is not less the body than liberty is the soul of the nation." The speech is denounced by both extremes, and is understood by the Southerners to mean "coercion," while the political friends of the Senator consider it a relinquishment of his principles.—*Times, Jan.* 13.

—FORT BARRANCAS and the navy yard at Pensacola, were seized. The late commandant of the navy yard, in a dispatch to Government, says:

"Armed bodies of Florida and Alabama troops appeared before the gate of the navy yard, and demanded possession. Having no means of resistance, I surrendered and hauled down my flag. They are now in possession."

A dispatch to the Florida senators announced the same as follows:

"We repaired down here and captured Fort Barrancas and navy yard, and then paroled the officers, granting them permission to continue to occupy their quarters. We are now in possession. This move was in consequence of the Government garrisoning Fort Pickens, which has before remained unoccupied. You will propose to the Administration, resuming the *status quo ante bellum* and we will immediately evacuate."

The Pensacola navy yard contains a hundred and fifty-six thousand dollars' worth of ordnance stores.—*Richmond Enquirer, Jan.* 14.

—ARTILLERY were ordered to Vicksburg by the Governor early this morning, to hail and question passing boats on the Mississippi river.

A salute of fifteen guns was fired last night at Jackson, on the reception of the news from Alabama and Florida. — *Raleigh Standard, Jan.* 14.

Jan. 13.—Governor Pickens, of South Carolina, sent to Washington for a balance of $3,000 due him as late Minister to Russia. The Department adjusted his accounts by sending him a draft on the Charleston Sub-Treasury, the money in which has been seized by the State.

Jan. 14.—Judge Smalley delivered a charge to the grand jury of the Federal court in New York, specifying what overt acts constitute treason.[1]

Jan. 15.—Major-General Sandford tendered the whole of the First Division New York State Militia to the Commander-in-Chief, to be ready for service in an hour's notice.

—COLONEL HAYNE, a Commissioner of South Carolina to Washington, was received by the President, and demanded the withdrawal of the garrison of Fort Sumter. He was requested to submit a written demand.

—THE United States Coast Survey schooner Dana, was seized by the Florida State authorities.—*The World.*

Jan. 16.—The names of William L. Yancey of Alabama, and James H. Hammond of South Carolina, appear in the Apalachicola *Times* of this day, as candidates for the presidency and vice-presidency of the Southern Confederacy.

---

[1] The *Evening Post* of the 14th of January contains this charge in full.

Jan. 18.—In the Massachusetts State Legislature to-day, a series of resolutions was passed by a unanimous vote, tendering to the President of the United States such aid in men and money as he may request, to maintain the authority of the general Government. The preamble to the resolution declares that the State of South Carolina, in seizing the fortifications of the Federal Government, the Post Office, Custom House, moneys, arms, munitions of war, and by firing upon a vessel in the service of the United States, has committed an act of war. The Senate passed a bill authorizing the increase of the volunteer military of the State.—*Boston Journal, Jan.* 19.

Jan. 19.—The State Convention of Georgia has adopted the secession ordinance by a vote of two hundred and eight against eighty-nine. —(*Doc.* 22.)

A motion to postpone the operation of the ordinance until the 3d of March was lost by about thirty majority.

Alexander H. Stephens and Herschel V. Johnson are among those who voted against the ordinance.

The ordinance of secession is ordered to be engrossed on parchment, and to be signed on Monday at noon.

Judge Linton Stephens says that, while he approves of the ordinance, he sees no reason for its adoption now. He therefore will not vote for or sign it.

Unusual demonstrations of approbation are being made at Milledgeville to-night in honor of the adoption of the ordinance, including the firing of cannon, the letting off of sky-rockets, the burning of torches, and music and speeches. —*Richmond Enquirer.*

Jan. 21.—Jefferson Davis, of Mississippi, withdrew from the Senate at Washington to-day. The ordinance of secession having passed the Convention of his State, he felt obliged to obey the summons, and retire from all official connection with the Federal Government.— (*Doc.* 23.)

—At the Brooklyn, N. Y., navy yard, the entire force was put under arms, and held in readiness to act immediately, through some apprehension of an attack by an organized force of persons in sympathy with secession. The guns of the North Carolina were shotted, and a portion of the Brooklyn city military was mustered to coöperate.—*Herald, Jan.* 22.

—The Georgia State Convention resolved, *unanimously :* .

" As a response to the resolutions of the Legislature of the State of New York, that this Convention highly approves of the energetic and patriotic conduct of the Governor of Georgia in taking possession of Fort Pulaski by the Georgia troops ; that this Convention request him to hold possession of said fort until the relations of Georgia with the Federal Government shall be determined, and that a copy of this resolution be transmitted to the Governor of the State of New York.—*Times, Jan.* 22.

—Wendell Phillips addressed the Twenty-eighth Congregational Society in Boston this afternoon on the " Political Lessons of the Hour." He declared himself to be a disunion man, and was glad to see South Carolina and other southern slave States had practically initiated a disunion movement. He hoped that all the slave States would leave the Union, and not stand upon the order of their going, but go at once. He denounced the compromise spirit manifested by Mr. Seward and Charles Francis Adams with much severity of language ; and there was an occasional stamping of feet and hissing, but no outbreak. Mr. Phillips was escorted home by a few policemen, and a great crowd pushing about him.—*Springfield Republican.*

—A Union meeting was held to-night at Trenton, N. J., Thomas J. Stryker, Cashier of the Trenton Bank, in the chair.

The Committee on Resolutions reported, deploring the state of the country ; recommending, as a means of settling differences, the adoption by the people of the Crittenden resolutions, or some other pacific measures, with such modifications as may be deemed expedient ; recommending the Legislature of New Jersey to pass a law to take a vote of the people, yes or no, on the Crittenden resolutions ; approving of the course of Virginia in appointing a Commission to go to Washington, and recommending the New Jersey Legislature to do the same.

Speeches were made by Judge Naar, C. W. Jay, and others.

Jan. 22.—Sherrard Clemens of Va. made a strong Union speech in the House of Representatives to-day.—(*Doc.* 24.)

Jan. 24.—The Charleston *Mercury* continues

the publication of anonymous incendiary appeals, intended to stir up the people to an attack on Fort Sumter. One, headed "Fort Sumter, the Bastion of the Federal Union," concludes with these words:

"No longer hoping for concessions, let us be ready for war, and when we have driven every foreign soldier from our shores, then let us take our place in the glorious Republic the future promises us. Border southern States will never join us until we have indicated our power to free ourselves—until we have proven that a garrison of seventy men cannot hold the portal of our commerce. The fate of the Southern Confederacy hangs by the ensign halliards of Fort Sumter."

—THE Toronto *Leader*, the Government paper of Canada, this morning says it is in a position to announce in the most positive terms that it is the intention of the English Government to acknowledge the independence of the Southern Confederacy as soon as it is formed.

—THE London *Times*, in an article on the disunion movement in America, asserts that the United States cannot "for many years be to the world what they have been."—(*Doc.* 25.)

—AN effort was made by the New York police to seize a quantity of fire-arms which were known to be shipped on board the steamer Montgomery. While the officers were searching on board for the arms, the captain ordered the vessel's fasts to be cut, and she steamed away from the pier, scarcely giving the policemen time to jump ashore. The five hundred muskets found on board the schooner Caspian were returned to the captain, the authorities being satisfied that the vessel was bound to Carthagena.—*Chicago Tribune.*

—THE United States arsenal at Augusta, Ga., was surrendered to the State authorities, upon the demand of Governor Brown.—*Baltimore Sun, Jan.* 25.

—THE Catawba Indians of South Carolina offered their services to Governor Pickens, and were accepted.—*Times, Jan.* 25.

Jan. 25.—A large Union mass meeting was held at Portland, Me., this evening; Chief Justice Shepley presided, and the meeting was addressed by many of the ablest speakers of all parties. Union resolutions were passed.

—A CORRESPONDENCE between Senator Toombs, of Georgia, and Fernando Wood, mayor of New York, relative to the seizure of arms by the police of that city, creates comment and surprise.—(*Doc.* 26.)

Jan. 26.—The Louisiana State Convention passed the ordinance of secession to-day, by a vote of one hundred and thirteen to seventeen. A delay ordinance was proposed yesterday, but was voted down by a large majority. A gold pen was given each member, with which to sign the ordinance of secession.—(*Doc.* 27.)—*Buffalo Courier.*

Jan. 27.—The Grand Jury at Washington made three presentments of Ex-Secretary Floyd, first, for maladministration in office; second, for complicity in the abstraction of the bonds; and third, for conspiracy against the Government.—*N. Y. Tribune.*

Jan. 29.—The United States revenue cutter Robert McClelland, Captain Breshwood (a Virginian), was surrendered at New Orleans to the State of Louisiana.—*Times, Feb.* 8.

—SECRETARY DIX's dispatch to Hemphill Jones, to "shoot on the spot" any one who attempts to "haul down the American flag" caused great enthusiasm.—(*Doc.* 28.)

Jan. 31.—The State of South Carolina, by her attorney-general, I. W. Hayne, offered to buy Fort Sumter, and declared that, "if not permitted to purchase, she would seize the fort by force of arms." The United States, in reply, asserted political rights superior to the proprietary right, and not subject to the right of "eminent domain."—*Times, Feb.* 9.

—The United States branch mint, and the custom-house at New Orleans, seized by the State authorities. In the mint were government funds to the amount of $389,000, and in the sub-treasury, $122,000—(*Doc.* 29.)—*Louisville Journal, Feb.* 2.

Feb. 1.—The Texas State Convention, at Galveston, passed an ordinance of secession, to be voted on by the people on the 23d of February, and if adopted, to take effect March 2.—(*Doc.* 30.)—*New Orleans Picayune, Feb.* 7.

Feb. 2.—The United States revenue cutter Lewis Cass, Capt. Morrison, a Georgian, was surrendered by the officer at Mobile to the State of Louisiana.—(*Doc.* 31.)—*N. Y. Times, Feb.* 6.

Feb. 4.—The Montgomery convention organized with Howell Cobb, president, and Johnson F. Hooper, secretary.—(*Doc.* 32.)

—The North Carolina House of Representatives passed unanimously a declaration that if reconciliation fails, North Carolina will go with the other slave States.—*Times, Feb.* 6.

Feb. 5.—The Peace Convention, at Washington, organized permanently, with Ex-president John Tyler in the chair; J C. Wright, of Ohio, secretary.—*Herald, Feb.* 6.

Feb. 8.—The Congress at Montgomery this evening unanimously agreed to a constitution and provisional government. They will go into immediate operation.—(*Doc.* 33.)—No propositions for compromise or reconstruction. After the vote on the constitution was taken, Jefferson Davis was elected President, and Alexander H. Stevens Vice-President of the Southern Confederacy, by the Congress.—(*Doc.* 34.)—*Commercial Advertiser.*

—Brigs W. R. Kibby and Golden Lead; barks Adjuster and C. Colden Murray; and schooner Julia A. Hallock, all owned in New York, were seized in the harbor of Savannah, by order of the Governor of Georgia, in reprisal for the seizure, in New York, of arms consigned to Georgia.—*Baltimore American.*

—The Little Rock arsenal, Arkansas, with 9,000 stands of arms, 40 cannon, and a large amount of ammunition, was surrendered to the State of Arkansas.—*N. Y. Times, Feb.* 11.

Feb. 9.—At Montgomery, Mr. Memminger presented a flag sent by some of the young ladies of South Carolina to the Convention.—(*Doc.* 35.)—*National Intelligencer.*

Feb. 10.—The New York vessels seized by the State of Georgia were released.—*Courier & Enquirer.*

Feb. 13.—Abraham Lincoln, of Illinois, and Hannibal Hamlin, of Maine, were declared by Vice-President Breckenridge, elected President and Vice President of the United States for the four years from March 4, 1861.—(*Doc.* 36.)—*Tribune, Feb.* 14.

—Eight thousand Sharp's rifle cartridges and 10,000 Sharp's rifle primers, were seized by the police in New York city on a Charleston steamer.—*Idem.*

Feb. 18.—Jefferson Davis was inaugurated President of the Southern Confederacy.—(*Doc.* 37.)

Feb. 19.—Old Fort Kearney, Kansas Territory, was taken possession of by the secessionists, and a secession flag raised. It was soon after retaken by a party of Unionists.—*Times, Feb.* 21.

Feb. 21.—The President of the Southern Confederacy nominated the following members of his Cabinet:

Secretary of State—Mr. Toombs.
Secretary of the Treasury—Mr. Memminger.
Secretary of War—Mr. L. Pope Walker.

They were confirmed.—*Tribune, Feb.* 22.

—Governor Brown, at Savannah, Ga., seized the ship Martha J. Ward, bark Adjuster, and brig Harold, all belonging to citizens of New York. They will be detained until the arms are delivered up by the State of New York.

—The Congress at Montgomery passed an act declaring the establishment of the free navigation of the Mississippi.—*Philadelphia Press, Dec.* 23.

Feb. 22.—The people of Charleston, S. C., celebrated Washington's birthday with great enthusiasm. The Pickens cadets paraded for the first time, and were presented to Governor Pickens by Lieutenant Magrath. The Governor made the company a brief address, urging upon its members the bright and shining example of Washington as deserving imitation. Subsequently a banner was presented to the Washington Light Infantry, and in the evening the company reassembled in Hibernian Hall, where it was addressed by Colonel Edward Carroll, in an oration of a rather sanguinary hue. Other companies also celebrated the day in their own way.—*Louisville Journal.*

—The Collector of Charleston gives official notice that all vessels from foreign States, except Texas, will be treated as "foreign vessels," and subjected to the port dues and other charges established by the laws of the Confederated States.—*Charleston Courier.*

Feb. 23.—President-elect Abraham Lincoln arrived in Washington. The published programme of his journey had been abandoned at Harrisburg, which city he left secretly last night.—(*Doc.* 38.)—*Commercial, Feb.* 23.

—United States property, to a great amount, together with the various army posts in Texas, were betrayed to that State by General Twiggs.—(*Doc.* 39.)—*Times, Feb.* 26.

Feb. 26.—Captain Hill, in command of Fort Brown, Texas, refused to surrender his post as ordered by General Twiggs, and engaged in preparations to defend it.—*Times, March* 6.

Feb. 27.—The Peace Convention submitted to the United States Senate a plan of adjustment involved in seven amendments to the Constitution of the United States.—(*Doc.* 40.) —*Herald, March* 4.

Feb. 28.—Mr. Corwin's report from the committee of thirty-three came up for final passage in Congress this morning. It was agreed to amid thunders of applause from the galleries and the floor. As the vote proceeded, the excitement was intense, and on the announcement of the result, the inexpressible enthusiasm of the members and the crowded galleries found vent in uproarious demonstrations. All feel that it is the harbinger of peace.—(*Doc.* 41.)— *Commercial, Feb.* 28.

March 1.—General Twiggs was expelled from the army of the United States. The following is the official order for his expulsion:

WAR DEPARTMENT,
ADJUTANT-GENERAL'S OFFICE,
WASHINGTON, March 1, 1861.

The following order is published for the information of the army:

" WAR DEPARTMENT, March 1, 1861.

" By the direction of the President of the United States, it is ordered that Brigadier-General David E. Twiggs be and is hereby dismissed from the army of the United States for his treachery to the flag of his country, in having surrendered on the 18th of February, 1861, on the demand of the authorities of Texas, the military posts and other property of the United States in his department and under his charge.

J. HOLT, Secretary of War.

" By order of the Secretary of War.

" S. COOPER, Adjutant-General."

—*Evening Post, March* 4.

—THE Secretary of War at Washington received a despatch from Major Anderson, in which he contradicts the statement that President Davis had been to Charleston. He says that the report that he had been sick is without a particle of foundation. He is in good health, as is also his little band of soldiers. Affairs in Charleston harbor are arriving at a point when further delay on their part will be impossible. Their extensive works of defence and attack are nearly if not quite completed.

The feeling between the authorities and Major Anderson continues to be friendly, and he is allowed all the facilities that he could expect. Fresh provisions and marketing are supplied in abundance. He experienced no difficulty in sending or receiving his mail matter. — *Washington Star.*

March 2.—The revenue cutter Dodge was seized in Galveston Bay, by order of the authorities of Texas. The officer in command resigned, as Breshwood did at New Orleans, and tendered his services to the rebels.—*Times, March* 6.

March 4.—Abraham Lincoln was inaugurated at Washington, sixteenth President of the United States. He kissed the thirty-four States of the Union as represented by thirty-four young ladies.

The inauguration procession proceeded to the east portico of the capitol, in front of which a platform had been erected. Every available space in the vicinity was packed with a curious crowd of spectators. Every thing being in readiness, Senator Baker, of Oregon, came forward and introduced Mr. Lincoln in these simple words: " Fellow-citizens: I introduce to you Abraham Lincoln, the President-elect of the United States of America." Mr. Lincoln then advanced to a small table, which had been placed for his accommodation, and proceeded to deliver his inaugural address, every word of which was distinctly heard on the outskirts of the swaying crowd. The oath of office was then administered to Mr. Lincoln by Chief Justice Taney; the procession was again formed, Mr. Lincoln was escorted to the White House, and was duly installed in the office of President of the United States.—(*Doc.* 42.)

—A STATE Convention declared Texas out of the Union and Governor Houston issued his proclamation to that effect.

March 5.—General Peter G. T. Beauregard, lately a major in the United States Engineer Corps, was ordered by Jefferson Davis, President of the Southern Confederacy, to proceed to Charleston and take command of the forces there assembled, and to be assembled for the investment of Fort Sumter.—*Herald, March* 7.

—IN the Texas State Convention, a letter was received from General Waul, enclosing a letter from the Secretary of War of the Confederate States, in relation to the military com-

ABRAHAM LINCOLN

PRESIDENT OF U.S.A.

A. Lincoln.

NEW YORK. G.P. PUTNAM.

plications in Texas. President Davis instructs the Secretary of War to say that he is disposed to assume every responsibility compatible with the relations of the Federal Government to Texas. Davis considers it due to international courtesy that the Government of the Confederate States (Texas included, after her withdrawal from the United States) should accord to the troops belonging to the Federal Government a reasonable time within which to depart from her territory. Should the Federal Government refuse to withdraw them, President Davis does not hesitate to say, that all the powers of the Southern Confederacy shall be promptly employed to expel them. General Waul says that the possibility of settling difficulties by a reconstruction of the old Union is never alluded to in the Congress, and that the proposal would receive about the same encouragement as a proposition to reannex Texas to the States of Mexico.—*Evening Post, March* 20.

—THE President's inaugural meets with a varied reception throughout the country. The South pronounces it warlike, while a greater portion of the North considers it conservative. —(*Doc.* 43.)

March 6.—Fort Brown, Texas, was finally surrendered by arrangement between Captain Hill and the Texas Commissioners.—*Galveston Civilian, March* 11.

March 9.—The Southern Confederacy Congress passed an act for the establishment and organization of the army of the Confederate States.—(*Doc.* 44.)—*Times, March* 15.

March 12.—The London *News* of to-day publishes a strong protest against a recognition of the Southern Confederacy by the British Government.—(*Doc.* 45.)

March 14.—The act, passed by the Florida Legislature, defining treason, became a law by the approval and signature of the Governor. It declares that in the event of any actual collision between the troops of the late Federal Union and those in the employ of the State of Florida, it shall be the duty of the Governor of the State to make public proclamation of the fact; and thereafter the act of holding office under the Federal Government shall be declared treason, and the person convicted *shall suffer death.*—*Evening Post, March* 26.

March 18.—Supplies were cut off from Fort Pickens and the fleet in the Gulf of Mexico.— (*Doc.* 46.)

March 20.—At about 7 o'clock this evening, Lieutenant Homer, in command of the Continentals, at drill was informed that there was a sloop lying at the wharf at the foot of Spanish alley in Mobile, which was laden with supplies for the United States fleet outside, between that place and Pensacola. A detachment of the company was on drill at the time, and Lieutenant Homer immediately ordered them down to the point mentioned, and then and there took charge of the little sloop Isabel. She was laden with beef, pork, barrels of eggs, etc. The person in charge acknowledged that these supplies were intended for the fleet outside.—*Mobile Tribune, March* 21.

—CORRESPONDENCE between Mr. Secretary Seward and the Commissioners from the Confederate States is published.—(*Doc.* 47.)

March 21.—A. H. Stephens, Vice-President of the "Confederate States" of the South, delivered a speech at Savannah, Ga. It is intended to be a vindication of the new features in the constitution, which has been adopted for their government.—(*Doc.* 48.)

March 22.—Governor Pettus, of Mississippi, in accordance with the order of the President of the Confederate States, issued a proclamation calling upon the organized military of the State for fifteen hundred infantry.—*Georgia Republic, March* 25.

—DR. Fox, of the United States navy, a special messenger from the Government to Major Anderson, reached Charleston and visited Fort Sumter by permission, in company with Captain Hartstein.

"Intercepted despatches"—by which we are to understand "stolen letters"—subsequently disclosed to the authorities in Charleston, it is said, that Mr. Fox employed this opportunity to devise and concert with Major Anderson a plan to supply the fort by force; and that this plan was adopted by the United States Government.—*Times, March* 23 *and April* 13.

—A MEETING was held at Frankfort, Ala., at which the following resolutions, among others of a similar character, were passed:

Resolved, That we approve the course pursued by our delegates, Messrs. Watkins and Steele, in convention at Montgomery, in not signing the so-called secession ordinance.

That secession is inexpedient and unnecessary, and we are opposed to it in any form, and the more so since a majority of the slave States have refused to go out, either by what is called "southern coöperation," or "precipitate secession;" and that the refusal to submit the so-called secession ordinance to the decision of the people is an outrage upon our right and liberty, and manifests a spirit of assumption, unfairness, and dictatorship.

Resolved, That our congressional nominee, if elected, is to represent us in the United States Congress, and not in the Congress of this so-called "Southern Confederacy."—*Tuscumbia North Alabamian.*

—THE Montgomery *Mail* protests against the word *stripes*:

."We protest against the word 'stripes,' as applied to the broad *bars* of the flag of our confederacy. The word is quite appropriate as applied to the Yankee ensign or a barber's pole; but it does not correctly describe the red and white divisions of the flag of the Confederate States. The word is *bars*—we have removed from under the stripes."—*World, April* 2.

March 25.—Colonel Lamon, a Government messenger, had an interview at Charleston with Governor Pickens and General Beauregard.—*Times, March* 26.

—THE rumors from Charleston are very conflicting concerning the evacuation of Fort Sumter. One report states that Major Anderson is strengthening his position; another, that he has received orders to evacuate the fort and report himself for duty at Newport barracks, and that the officers are packing their goods in expectation of immediate departure. The truth of the matter will probably be known in a day or two.—*Evening Post.*

March 28.—Governor Pickens, of South Carolina, sent a message to the convention of that State, informing it that six hundred men would be required to garrison the forts in Charleston harbor; besides giving other important details respecting the financial condition of the State.*

—THE actual vote of the State of Louisiana on secession is given by the New Orleans papers of to-day as follows: For secession, 20,448; against it, 17,296.—*World, April* 4.

* This message is printed complete in the New York *Tribune* of April 2, 1861.

March 30.—The Mississippi State Convention, at Jackson, ratified the Constitution of the Confederate States, by a vote of 78 to 7.—*Tribune, April* 1.

March 31.—It is asserted for the hundredth time, in apparently authoritative circles, that Fort Sumter will be evacuated on or before Wednesday next, April 3d.—*World, April* 1.

April 3.—Despatches were received in Washington to-day, confirming the reported reinforcement of Fort Pickens; and the Cabinet held a long session, without coming to any definite conclusion in regard to the long-mooted evacuation of Fort Sumter. One company of artillery left Washington for Fort Hamilton, and two more are to follow to-morrow. Unwonted activity also prevails in the navy, several vessels being rapidly fitted for service.—*World, April* 4.

—THE mortar batteries on Morris' Island, Charleston harbor, fired into an unknown schooner. She displayed the stars and stripes, and put to sea. A boat from Sumter with a white flag went out to her; nobody hurt. A shot had gone through her.—(*Doc.* 49.)

—ALL officers of the Southern Confederate army, on leave of absence, were ordered to their respective commands.—*Times, April* 5.

—THE South Carolina Convention ratified the Constitution of the Confederate States, by a vote of 114 to 16.—*Tribune, April* 6.

—THE Charleston correspondent writes:

"By the by, let us never surrender to the North the noble song, the 'Star-Spangled Banner.' It is southern in its origin; in sentiments, poetry and song; in its association with chivalrous deeds, it is ours; and the time, I trust, is not remote, when the broad stripes and brilliant stars of the confederate flag of the South will wave triumphantly over our capitol, Fortress Monroe, and every fort within our borders."—*Richmond Examiner.*

April 4.—The Virginia Convention adopted, in committee of the whole, several of the series of resolutions reported by the majority of the Committee on Federal Relations, and rejected, by the decisive vote of 89 to 45, a motion to substitute for one of the resolutions an ordinance of secession, to be submitted to the popular vote.—*World, April* 5.

—MANY rumors are in circulation to-day.

They appear to have originated from movements on the part of the United States troops, the reasons for which have not been communicated to the reporters at Washington as freely as the late Administration was in the habit of imparting Cabinet secrets. There can be no doubt that serious movements are on foot. The tone of the southern press for the last week, and the concentration of troops at Pensacola, indicate a determination to precipitate a conflict at Fort Pickens, probably with a view to hasten the secession movement in Virginia.—*Tribune, April* 5.

April 7.—General Beauregard issued an order, and sent a special messenger to Major Anderson, to give him an official notification that no further intercourse between Fort Sumter and the city would be permitted. — *Times, April* 9.

—THE steam transport Atlantic sailed under sealed orders from New York, laden with troops and provisions. Among the troops is Captain Barry's celebrated company of United States Flying Artillery. — *Commercial Advertiser, April* 8.

April 8.—Information having been given by the United States authorities to the authorities at Charleston that they desired to send supplies to Fort Sumter by an unarmed vessel, they were informed that the vessel would be fired upon and not permitted to enter the port. Official notification was then given by the United States Government that supplies would be sent to Major Anderson, peaceably if possible, otherwise by force. Lieutenant Talbot, attached to the garrison of Fort Sumter, and who accompanied the bearer of this despatch, was not permitted to proceed to his post.

—ORDERS were isssued to the entire military force of Charleston, held in reserve, to proceed to their stations without delay. Four regiments of a thousand men each were telegraphed for from the country.

Dr. Gibbs, surgeon-general, was ordered to prepare ambulances, and make every provision for the wounded.

—AT midnight Charleston was thrown into great excitement by the discharge of seven guns from Citadel square, the signal for all the reserves to assemble ten minutes afterwards.

Hundreds of men left their beds, hurrying to and fro towards their respective destinations.

In the absence of sufficient armories, at the corners of the streets, public squares, and other convenient points, meetings were formed, and all night the long roll of the drum and the steady tramp of the military, and the gallop of the cavalry resounding through the city, betokened the close proximity of the long-anticipated hostilities. The Home Guard corps of old gentlemen, who occupy the position of military exempts, rode through the city, arousing the soldiers, and doing other duty required by the moment.

United States vessels were reported off the bar. Major Anderson displayed signal lights during the night from the walls of Fort Sumter.—*Times, April* 10.

—THE State Department at Washington replied to-day to the Confederate State Commissioners, declining to receive them in their official capacity, but expressing deference for them as gentlemen. The Secretary expressed a peaceful policy on the part of the Government, declaring a purpose to defend only when assailed. —*Tribune, April* 9.

April 9.—Governor Curtin, of Pennsylvania, sent a special message to the Legislature to-day, urging the necessity of purchasing arms and reorganizing the military system of that State. —*Times, April* 10.

—JEFFERSON DAVIS made a requisition on the Governor of Alabama for 3,000 soldiers.— *Tribune, April* 10.

—THE Charleston *Mercury* of to-day announces war as declared. "Our authorities," it says, "yesterday evening received notice from Lincoln's Government, through a special messenger from Washington, that an effort will be made to supply Fort Sumter with provisions and that if this were *permitted*, no attempt would be made to reinforce it with men! This message comes simultaneously with a *fleet*, which we understand is now off our bar, waiting for daylight and tide to make the effort threatened.

"We have patiently submitted to the insolent military domination of a handful of men in our bay for over three months after the declaration of our independence of the United States. The object of that self humiliation has been to avoid the effusion of blood, while such preparation was made as to render it causeless and useless.

"It seems we have been unable, by discretion, forbearance, and preparation, to effect the desired object, and that now the issue of battle is to be forced upon us. The gage is thrown down, and we accept the challenge. We will meet the invader, and the God of Battles must decide the issue between the hostile hirelings of Abolition hate and Northern tyranny, and the people of South Carolina defending their freedom and their homes. We hope such a blow will be struck in behalf of the South, that Sumter and Charleston harbor will be remembered at the North as long as they exist as a people."

—STEAMERS Illinois and Baltic, in commission for United States Government, got to sea from New York. They discharged their pilots at 7.30 A. M., and sailed southwardly.—(*Doc.* 50.)

—UNITED STATES sloop-of-war Pawnee sailed from Norfolk at 6 P. M., with sealed orders.—*Times, April* 11.

April 10.—The floating battery, finished, mounted, and manned at Charleston, was taken out of the dock last evening, and anchored in the cove, near Sullivan's Island.

The people are not excited, but there is a fixed determination to meet the issue. The Convention has just adjourned, subject to the call of the president. Before adjourning, it passed resolutions approving the conduct of General Twiggs in resigning his commission and turning over the public property under his control to the authorities.

Governor Pickens was in secret session with the Convention. About 1,000 troops were sent to the fortifications to-day; 1,800 more go down to-morrow.

Messrs. Wigfall, Chesnut, Means, Manning, McGowan, and Boyleston, have received appointments in General Beauregard's staff. A large number of the members of the Convention, after adjournment, volunteered as privates. About 7,000 troops are now at the fortifications. The beginning of the end is coming to a final closing. Fort Sumter will be attacked without waiting for the fleet. Every thing is prepared against a land attack. The enthusiasm is intense, and the eagerness for the conflict, if it must come, unbounded.—*N. Y. Day Book.*

—THE officers of the District of Columbia militia were ordered to meet at 10 o'clock A. M.,

in consequence of information relative to a contemplated movement for the seizure of the city of Washington by the secessionists under Ben McCullough. Orders were issued for the militia to assemble at their armories.

Seven militia companies reported to General Scott, and between six and eight hundred of them volunteered for any service in which the President might desire them to act.—*Times, April* 11.

April 11.—The steamship Coatzacoalcos arrived at New York this morning, bringing home the Federal troops who were left in Texas without a commander, after the treason of General Twiggs.

—THE Government at Washington is acting on positive information in taking all possible precautionary measures for the defence of, and the maintenance of peace at, that point.

A company of military were marched inside the capitol to-night, and a picket of guards is stationed on each of the roads leading into the city. This was done on no new information, but is among the signs of the revolution. A military company has not been within the walls of the capitol before since the war of 1812.

The oath of fidelity was administered to several companies of volunteers to-day.—*World, April* 12.

—UNUSUAL activity now prevails in military circles in Pennsylvania. New companies are forming, and the old organizations are drilling frequently. The prospect of active service in the event of the breaking out of actual hostilities in the South, is exciting much discussion among the volunteer companies, and it is understood that several have already tendered their services to the Secretary of War, in case the Government should need their aid. It is also understood that in the event of an attack on the Government, the latter will make an early call upon Pennsylvania for men. Our volunteers labor under great disadvantages in respect to arms, and in a case of emergency many more men would be forthcoming than there are arms to place in their hands.—*Phila. Press.*

—THIS morning the Commissioners of the Confederate States left Washington. They are satisfied that no recognition of the Southern Confederacy will ever take place under the administration of President Lincoln. In their final communication they reflect severely on the Administration, taking the ground they have exhausted every resource for a peaceful solution of the existing difficulties, and that if civil war results, on the head of the Federal Government will rest the responsibility. They charge the Administration with gross perfidy, insisting that under the shelter of the pretext and assertion that Fort Sumter was to be evacuated, an immense armada has been despatched to provision and reinforce that fort. They repeat they had almost daily indirect assurances from the Administration that Fort Sumter was positively to be abandoned, and that all the Government's efforts were to be directed toward peace. The commissioners allege that the Government at Montgomery was earnestly desirous of peace; and that, in accordance with its instructions, as well as their own feelings, they left no means unexhausted to secure that much-desired end; but all their efforts having failed, they were now forced to return to an outraged people with the object of their mission unaccomplished; and they express the firm conviction that war is inevitable.—(*Doc.* 51.)— *World, April* 12.

—At 2 P. M. Colonel Chesnut and Major Lee, aids to General Beauregard, conveyed to Fort Sumter the demand that Major Anderson should evacuate that fort. Major Anderson replied at 6 P. M. that his "sense of honor and his obligations to his Government would prevent his compliance" with the demand. He informed the gentlemen verbally that he would be "starved out in a few days."

It was stated that there were at this time 7,000 men around Fort Sumter under arms, and 140 pieces of ordnance of heavy calibre in position and ready for use.—*Charleston Mercury.*

April 12.—At 1 A. M. a second deputation from General Beauregard conveyed to Fort Sumter the message that if Major Anderson would name the time when he would evacuate, and would agree not to fire in the mean time upon the batteries unless they fired upon him, no fire would be opened upon Fort Sumter. To this Major Anderson replied that he would evacuate at noon on the 15th, if not previously otherwise ordered, or not supplied, and that he would not in the mean time open his fire unless compelled by some hostile act against his fort or the flag of his Government. At 3.30 A. M. the officers who received this answer notified Major Anderson that the batteries under command of General Beauregard would open on Fort Sumter in one hour, and immediately left.

The sentinels in Sumter were then ordered from the parapets, the posterns were closed, and the men ordered not to leave the bombproofs until summoned by the drum.

At 4.30 A. M. fire was opened upon Fort Sumter from Fort Moultrie, and soon after from the batteries on Mount Pleasant, Cummings' Point, and the floating battery; in all 17 mortars and 30 large guns for shot—mostly columbiads. Meantime the garrison of Sumter took breakfast quietly at their regular hour, were then divided into three reliefs, each of which was to work the guns for four hours; and the fire of Sumter was opened at 7 A. M. from the lower tier of guns, upon Fort Moultrie, the iron battery on Cummings' Point, two batteries on Sullivan's Island, and the floating battery simultaneously. When the first relief went to work, the enthusiasm of the men was so great that the second and third reliefs could not be kept from the guns.

As the fire of the enemy became warm, it was found that there was no portion of the fort not exposed to the fire of mortars. Shells from every direction burst against the various walls. Cartridges soon run out; there were no cartridge bags, and men were set to make them out of shirts. There was no instrument to weigh powder, and this, with the absence of breech-sides and other implements necessary to point guns, rendered an accurate fire impossible.

Fire broke out in the barracks three times, and was extinguished. Meals were served at the guns. At 6 P. M. the fire from Sumter ceased. Fire was kept up from the enemy's batteries all night, at intervals of twenty minutes.—*Tribune, Times, and Herald, April* 13, 14, 15.

April 13.—Fire from the enemy's batteries was resumed at daylight, and from Fort Sumter at 7 A. M. At about 8 the officers' quarters in Sumter took fire from a shell, and the work at the guns was necessarily somewhat slackened, as nearly all the men were taken away to extinguish the flames. Shells from Moultrie and Morris' Island fell now faster than ever. Dense volumes of smoke still poured out of the barracks at 9, when the men were again sent to the guns. At 10 o'clock the halliards on the flag-staff were cut by a shell, and the flag ran down a little and stuck, so that it appeared to be displayed at half-mast. Several ships, one a large steamer, were in the offing at 10.30, and shots were fired at them from Morris' Island and Fort Moultrie. About 11 o'clock the fire in the barracks again burst forth fiercely. Three piles of hand-grenades and shells, placed ready for use, became heated by it and exploded at intervals. The day was oppressively warm, and the heat of the fire added, made the atmosphere of the fort almost insufferable. At 12 the whole roof of the barracks was in flames, and soon after men were set to work to take the powder out of the magazine, lest the heat should reach and explode it there. Ninety barrels were rolled out and the doors closed. The fire of Fort Sumter was now almost entirely relinquished, though from the other forts it was rather increased. Cartridges were nearly all gone, and owing to the flying sparks no more could be made. Smoke from the fire was blown into the fort so thickly that the men could not see one another. As the fire in the barracks spread from the officers' to the men's quarters, it became necessary to throw overboard the powder that had been taken from the magazines. All was thrown over but three barrels, which were wrapped around with wet cloths and left. From these the garrison was soon separated by the fire, and now only the cartridges in the guns were left. These were fired now and then to indicate that the fort was not silenced. Thus in truth the work was held while there was a cartridge to fire or powder enough accessible to make one. The flagstaff, which had been hit nine times, was cut at about 1, and the flag was then nailed to the cut piece, and so raised upon the ramparts. At this time both officers and men were compelled to lie flat upon their faces in the casemates, and hold wet cloths to their mouths to escape suffocation. Soon after Ex-Senator Wigfall came to the fort with a flag of truce, which he wished held up while he spoke; but the batteries did not respect it. He, however, represented himself as an aid of General Beauregard, and agreed for the evacuation of Fort Sumter. It was afterward learned that he had spoken falsely, and had no authority whatever from General Beauregard.

At 12.55 P. M. the flag of Fort Sumter was drawn down, and the fort was surrendered soon after upon honorable terms; the garrison to carry away the flag of the fort, and all company arms and property, and all private property; and all proper facilities to be afforded for their removal to any post in the United States the commander might elect.

No men were hurt in Sumter by the fire of the enemy. It is reported by the secessionists that no men were either killed or wounded upon their side.

A boat from the United States squadron outside, with a flag of truce, arrived at Morris' Island, with a request to be allowed to come and take Major Anderson and his forces.— (*Doc.* 52.)—*Tribune, Times, Herald, and World.*

—A DESPATCH from Montgomery, Ala., says that Fort Pickens was reinforced last night.— (*Doc.* 53.)

—To-DAY the President expelled from the Federal army, for refusing to act on a particular service, Captain William B. St. Johns, of the Third Infantry, and First Lieutenant Abner Smead, of the First Artillery.

—THE Legislature of Pennsylvania passed the war bill without amendment last evening. Previous to its passage, the news of the bombardment of Fort Sumter was announced, and produced a profound sensation. The bill appropriates five hundred thousand dollars for the purpose of arming and equipping the militia; authorizes a temporary loan; provides for the appointment of an Adjutant-General, Commissary-General, and Quartermaster-General, who, with the Governor, are to have power to carry the act into effect.—*Phila. Enquirer.*

—To-DAY the Virginia Commissioners were formally received by the President at Washington, when they presented the resolutions under which they were appointed.—(*Doc.* 54.)

—THE attack upon Fort Sumter, and its surrender, instead of depressing, fires and animates all patriotic hearts. One deep, strong, overpowering sentiment now sweeps over the whole community—a sentiment of determined, devoted, active loyalty. The day for the toleration of treason—treason to the Constitution! defiance to the laws that we have made!—has gone by. The people have discovered that what they deemed almost impossible has actually come to pass, and that the rebels are determined to break up this Government, if they can do it. With all such purposes they are de-

G.E.Perine.Sc.

Robert Anderson

MAJOR ROBERT ANDERSON. U.S.A.

(NOW BRIG. GEN. U.S.A.)

Entered according to act of Congress A D 1861 by G.P.Putnam in the Clerks office of the district court of the southern district of N.Y.

termined to make an end as speedily as may be.—(*Doc.* 55.)—*Times, April* 15.

—Bishop Lynch, Roman Catholic, at Charleston, S. C., celebrated the bloodless victory of Fort Sumter with a Te Deum and congratulatory address. In all the churches allusions were made to the subject.

The Episcopal Bishop, wholly blind and feeble, said it was his strong persuasion, strengthened by travel through every section of South Carolina, that the movement in which the people were engaged was begun by them in the deepest conviction of duty to God; and God had signally blessed their dependence on him. If there is a war, it will be purely a war of self-defence.—*Tribune, April* 16.

—General Beauregard, in general orders to-day, congratulates "the troops under his command on the brilliant success which has crowned their gallantry, by the reduction of the stronghold in the harbor of Charleston."—(*Doc.* 56.)

April 15.—Major Anderson evacuated Fort Sumter, going out with the proper honors to his flag. While the salute of fifty guns was being fired, a gun exploded, and killed one man and wounded four others. Major Anderson and his command were conveyed on board the Baltic steam transport.—*Times, April* 16.

—The President of the United States called by proclamation for 75,000 volunteers to suppress insurrectionary combinations; and commanded "the persons composing the combinations aforesaid to disperse and retire peaceably to their respective abodes within twenty days." In the same proclamation, an extra session of both Houses of Congress was called for the 4th of July.—(*Doc.* 57.)—*Times, April* 15.

—At Alexandria, Va., the publication of President Lincoln's proclamation has greatly increased the secession feeling. Business of all kinds is completely suspended. Merchants are engaged in discussing the probability of a prolonged sanguinary civil war. The impression is that the Virginia Convention will instantaneously pass the ordinance of secession, or call a Border State Convention.

—At Mobile, Ala., President Lincoln's response to the Virginia Commissioners is regarded as a declaration of war.

—At Richmond, Va., the President's proclamation is received with general execration.

The public mind is fearfully excited. The secessionists declare that nothing is more favorable to their cause, and that military men would sooner die than respond to such a call.

—At Wilmington, N. C., the proclamation is received with perfect contempt and indignation. The Union men openly denounce the Administration. The greatest possible unanimity prevails. There was great rejoicing there Saturday on the reception of the news of the reduction of Fort Sumter.—*Tribune, April* 16.

—Large Union meetings were held at Detroit, Mich., Westchester and Pittsburgh, Pa., Lawrence, Mass., and Dover, N. H. At Pittsburgh the meeting was opened by the Mayor, who introduced the venerable William Wilkinson. Mr. Wilkinson was made President of the meeting. About twenty-five Vice-Presidents were also appointed. Resolutions were adopted, declaring undying fealty to the Union, approving the course of the Legislative and Executive branches of the State Government in responding to the call of the President, disregarding all partisan feeling, and pledging their lives, fortunes, and sacred honor in the defence of the Union, and appointing a Committee of Public Safety.

A resolution approving the action of the Philadelphia banks in the prompt offer of money to the Government, was also passed.

The meeting was addressed by Judge Wilkins, Thomas M. Marshall, the Hon. P. C. Shannon, Dr. McCook, Ex-Governor Johnston, the Hon. A. W. Loomis, and other prominent citizens of all parties. The speeches elicited great applause.—*Tribune, April* 16.

—Governor Yates, of Illinois, issued a proclamation to convene the Legislature at Springfield, on the 23d of April, for the purpose of enacting such laws and adopting such measures as may be deemed necessary upon the following subject, to wit: The more perfect organization and equipment of the militia of the State, and placing the same upon the best footing, to render efficient assistance to the General Government in preserving the Union, enforcing the laws, protecting the property and rights of the people, and also the raising of such money, and other means, as may be required to carry on the foregoing objects.—*Commercial Advertiser.*

—A large meeting of citizens, irrespective of party, was held at Erie, Pa., this evening. Resolutions were adopted, pledging the hearts and hands of Erie city and county to maintain the integrity of the Government and honor of the flag.

The Wayne Guards, of Erie, and other companies, will offer their services to the Governor.—*Evening Post, April* 17.

—THIS afternoon, a coasting schooner was discovered lying in Newark Bay, with a palmetto flag flying at its masthead. A party of "glass-house boys" procured a boat, and proceeding to the vessel, ordered the captain to lower the flag and substitute in its place the Stars and Stripes. The captain refused, when they threatened to pitch him overboard and sink the vessel. The American flag was soon spread out to the breeze, when it was heartily cheered, and the palmetto was stowed away below.—*N. Y. Times.*

—AT Philadelphia the Union pledge is receiving the signature of all classes of citizens. It responds to the President's proclamation, and declares an unalterable determination to sustain the Government, throwing aside all differences of political opinion.

An excited crowd assembled this morning before the printing office on the corner of Fourth and Chestnut streets, where *The Palmetto Flag*, a small advertising sheet, is published, and threatened to demolish it. The proprietor displayed the American flag, and threw the objectionable papers from the windows; also, *The Stars and Stripes*, another paper printed at the same office, restoring the crowd to good humor. The crowd moved down to *The Argus* office in Third street, opposite Dock street, ordering that the flag should be displayed.

After visiting the newspaper offices and Government property, they marched in a body up Market street, bearing a flag. At all points on the route, well-known Union men were obliged to make all haste to borrow, beg, or steal something red, white, and blue, to protect their property with. Searches were made for the publication rooms of *The Southern Monitor;* but as that paper has suspended, the mob were unable to carry out their intention of destroying the forms. They satisfied themselves with breaking the signs to pieces. The ring-leaders were furnished with ropes with which to hang the editor if caught.

During the afternoon, General Patterson's mansion, corner of Thirteenth and Locust streets, was mobbed and threatened with destruction. A servant answered their call, and unfortunately slammed the door in their faces. The crowd became uproarious and violent, and made an attempt to force open the door. General Patterson finally appeared at the window, bearing the colors of the regiment. The crowd then moved away. It is understood that General Patterson, who is charged with secessionism, intends throwing up his commission.

They then visited General Cadwallader, who made a Union speech and threw out a flag. Several prominent Southerners, with secession proclivities, including Robert Tyler, have received warnings from a so-called Vigilance Committee.

The following is the speech that was made by Mayor Henry to the excited mob which threatened *The Palmetto Flag* building:

"*Fellow-Citizens:* By the grace of Almighty God, treason shall never rear its head or have a foothold in Philadelphia. [Immense cheering.] I call upon you as American citizens to stand by your flag and protect it at all hazards—at the point of the bayonet, if necessary; but, in doing so, remember the rights due your fellow-citizens and their private property. [Immense cheering.] That flag is an emblem of the Government, and I call upon all good citizens who love their country and its flag, to testify their loyalty by going to their respective places of abode, leaving to the constituted authorities of the city the task of protecting the peace, and preventing every act which could be construed into treason to their country."

The Mayor then hoisted the stars and stripes. —*Tribune, April* 16.

—SEVENTEEN vessels were seized in the port of New York from ports in southern States, their clearances being improper, and not signed by United States officers. They were fined $100 each, and some were held subject to forfeiture.—*World, April* 16.

—JEFFERSON DAVIS replies to President Lincoln's proclamation as follows:

"Fort Sumter is ours, and nobody is hurt. With mortar, Paixhan, and petard, we tender 'Old Abe' our *Beau—regard."* — *Charleston Mercury.*

—AT Albany, N. Y., popular sentiment grows stronger and stronger. Several prominent citizens, particularly among the young men, have sent in applications as volunteers, and some are already organizing companies among those who are friends at home. The capital has presented an unusual appearance all day, the whole building having been filled with citizens who have apparently left their business to gather at head-quarters, and watch eagerly the progress of events. The spirit of the masses is decidedly aroused, and from present indications Albany will be behind no city in the State or Union in evincing her patriotism and her determination, as the crisis has come, to stand firmly by the Government of the country, without pausing to charge upon any the responsibility of the present terrible events.—*Tribune.*

—FERNANDO WOOD, Mayor of New York, issued a proclamation, calling upon the people of the city to avoid turbulence and excitement, and to rally to the restoration of the Constitution and Union.—(*Doc.* 58.)

—AN enthusiastic Union meeting was held at Cleveland, Ohio. Speeches were made by Senator Wade and other prominent gentlemen. Resolutions were adopted to sustain the Government, approving of the President's call for volunteers, recommending the Legislature to make appropriations of men and money, and appointing a committee to ascertain the efficiency of the Cleveland militia. The greatest unanimity of feeling prevailed, and the speakers were constantly interrupted by wild cheers and responses. A similar meeting was held at Norwalk, Ohio.—*Buffalo Courier.*

—THE Directors of the Bank of Commerce, of Providence, R. I., advanced a loan of $30,000 to the State for aiding in the outfit of troops. Large offers from private citizens have also been made to Governor Sprague for a similar purpose. The Globe Bank tendered to the State a loan of $50,000.—*Tribune.*

—AN immense Union meeting was held at Troy, N. Y. Resolutions were adopted, sustaining the Government, and pledging the city to raise a regiment of volunteers. Hon. John A. Griswold presided, and Isaac McConihee, Jonas C. Heartt, Henry Ingraham, Judge Gould, and Judge Robinson were made Vice-Presidents. Secretaries were also appointed.

The meeting adjourned in a body to the residence of General Wool, where, on behalf of the citizens, an address was made by Martin J. Townsend, to which General Wool responded that his heart was rejoiced at this glorious demonstration of patriotism. Never, by any former compliment bestowed upon him, had he been thrilled by such a measure of joy. It is true that he had fought under the old flag, but he had done no more than his duty towards the best Government that ever existed. He had fought under the stars and stripes that were carried in triumph by Washington, and under which Jackson closed the second war for independence at New Orleans in a halo of glory. Will you permit that flag to be desecrated and trampled in the dust by traitors now? Will you permit our noble Government to be destroyed by rebels in order that they may advance their schemes of political ambition and extend the area of slavery? No, indeed, it cannot be done. The spirit of the age forbids it. Humanity and manhood forbid it, and the sentiments of the civilized world forbid it. My friends, that flag must be lifted up from the dust into which it has been trampled, placed in its proper position, and again set floating in triumph to the breeze. I pledge you my heart, my hand, all my energies to the cause. The Union shall be maintained. I am prepared to devote my life to the work, and to lead you in the struggle.—*Times, April* 17.

—THE Governor of Kentucky, in reply to Secretary Cameron's call for troops from that State, says:

"Your despatch is received. In answer, I say emphatically, Kentucky will furnish no troops for the wicked purpose of subduing her sister southern States.   B: MAGOFFIN."
                                    —*Louisville Journal.*

—AT New York, Philadelphia, Trenton, and other places, journals were compelled to display the American flag. Happily no damage was done to persons or property.—*Herald, Tribune, Times, World, April* 16.

April 16.—The Ringgold Flying Artillery, of Reading, Pa., Captain James McKnight, 180 men, with four field-pieces, received a requisition from the Governor this morning to set out this evening, at 6 o'clock, for Harrisburgh, a place of rendezvous for the first Pennsylvanians in the field.

There was a large and enthusiastic Government meeting at Tyrone, Blair county, to-night. Speeches were enthusiastically received. Ex-Senator Bigler arrived after the adjournment, and expressed himself unequivocally for the Government, and he was determined to sustain it to the last. Two military companies from Tyrone, two from Altoona, and two from Hollidaysburgh, will leave to-morrow for Harrisburgh.—*Times, April* 17.

—THE Mechanics', Elm City, Fairfield County, Thames, and other banks of Connecticut, voted large sums of money to assist in equipping the troops, and the support of their families.—*Idem.*

—GOVERNOR BUCKINGHAM, of Connecticut, issued a proclamation calling for volunteers, to rendezvous at Hartford.—*Idem.*

—THE session of the New York East Methodist Conference was opened by the following prayer:

" Grant, O God, that all the efforts now being made to overthrow rebellion in our distracted country, may be met with every success. Let the forces that have risen against our Government, and Thy law, be scattered to the winds, and may no enemies be allowed to prevail against us. Grant, O God, that those who have aimed at the very heart of the republic may be overthrown. We ask Thee to bring these men to destruction, and wipe them from the face of the country!"—*Tribune, April* 17.

—NEW HAMPSHIRE responds to the President's proclamation, and will furnish the troops required. The Concord Union Bank tendered a loan of $20,000 to the Governor, and all the Directors, with the Cashier, agree to contribute $100 each to the support of such families of the volunteers of Concord, as may fall in defending the flag of the country.—*N. H. Statesman.*

—A UNION meeting was held at the Hudson House, Jersey City, N. J., for the purpose of taking action to raise volunteers, whose services are to be tendered to the Federal Government. J. W. Scudder, Esq., was chosen President; two Vice-Presidents from each ward were also chosen, and C. H. Dummer acted as Secretary.

Stirring speeches were made by Dr. H. D. Holt, Hon. N. C. Slaight, Benjamin Van Riper, and John H. Low.

During the speaking, cheers were given for the Stars and Stripes, the Federal Government, Major Anderson, &c.

Benjamin Van Riper advocated the striking down of every northern man who advocated secession, and all traitorous newspapers.

Mr. John Low proposed that at some future period they call upon the proprietors of the *American Standard*, in Jersey City, " the editor of which had so much maligned the Government, and make them hoist the American flag, or make them leave the town." This proposition was received with tremendous cheering, and cries of " Let's do it to-night."—*Times, April* 17.

—FOUR regiments, ordered to report for service in Boston, Mass., commenced arriving there before 9 A. M. this morning, the companies first arriving not having received their orders until last night. Already about thirty companies have arrived, numbering over 1,700 men in uniform, and with these are several hundred who are importunate to be allowed to join the ranks.

The bark Manhattan, which arrived at Boston this forenoon from Savannah, had a secession flag hoisted. A crowd proceeded to the wharf, and compelled Captain Davis to take it down and hoist the stars and stripes.

The City Government of Lawrence, Mass., appropriated $5,000 for the benefit of the families of those who have volunteered to defend the country's flag.—*Boston Transcript.*

—ONE of the largest meetings ever held in Delaware was held this evening at Wilmington, the Mayor presiding. The following resolution was adopted unanimously:

Resolved, That we censure and condemn the course of Senator Bayard, in the United States Senate, for not advocating a compromise between the North and South, and that we feel confident that his course has placed us in a false position before the world; that we repudiate his teachings, as having an Anti-Union tendency, and are unworthy of a patriot and Delawarian.—*Times, April* 17.

—GOVERNOR LETCHER, of Virginia, in reply to the call of the President of the United States, refuses to furnish troops for the support of the Federal Government. In his letter to Secretary Cameron, he remarks:

" I have only to say that *the militia of Virginia will not be furnished to the powers at Washington for any such use or purpose as they have in view.* Your object is to subjugate the southern States, and a requisition made upon me for such an object—an object, in my judgment, not within the purview of the Constitution or the Act of 1795—will not be complied with. *You have chosen to inaugurate civil war, and having done so, we will meet it in a spirit as determined as the Administration has exhibited towards the South."—World, April 20.*

—Governor Ellis, of North Carolina, telegraphed the President that he could not respond to the call for troops, as he had doubts of his authority and right to do so.

A war bill, with an appropriation of $3,000,000, was passed in the New York Legislature, and signed by the Governor.

The Government of the Southern Confederacy called for 32,000 men ; 2,000 from Florida, and 5,000 from each of the other States.—*Times, April 17.*

—A large meeting of German workingmen was held at Newark, N. J., this evening. An attempt was made to disorganize the body, which was soon suppressed by earnest and loud repeated cries for the Constitution and the Union. Several speeches were made, and it was declared that the only hope for the workingmen was to be found in the preservation of the Government. The meeting broke up with cheers for the Union. This is a sample of the spirit which pervades the German population.

"The German Turners' Society," numbering about a hundred men, also met, and unanimously resolved to form a military corps of riflemen, and offer their services to the Government. They also resolved to send delegates to the various Turner associations in the State, and to recommend a plan of organization.—*Evening Post.*

April 17.—The steamship Star of the West was taken near Indianola, Texas, by the Galveston Volunteers, without resistance. She has on board eight to nine hundred barrels of provisions.

The steamer Habana has been purchased by the Southern Confederacy, and will be transformed into a war steamer. She will carry eight guns and one pivot gun.—*Times, April 22.*

—General Cass made a speech at Detroit, Michigan, on the occasion of the Board of Trade unfurling the national flag over their rooms. He is strongly in favor of supporting the Union, the Constitution, and the country's flag, under all circumstances. He said that, in a crisis like the present, it was the duty of every citizen to stand by the Government.—*Louisville Democrat.*

—Piqua, Ohio, to-day raised a company, and tendered its services to the Government.

A large and enthusiastic meeting was held last night at Michigan City, Ind. Democrats and Republicans are a unit for the Constitution and Union. Strong anti-secession resolutions were adopted, denouncing all as traitors whose views are not to sustain the Government. Salutes were fired to the Stars and Stripes, which were displayed in all parts of the city. A volunteer company was immediately organized. The first man who signed the roll is a prominent clergyman.

The first company of volunteers left Lafayette, Ind., for Indianapolis, at 2 o'clock P. M. to-day. They were escorted to the depot by the Lafayette Artillery ; and two companies are nearly full, who will follow in a few days. —*Buffalo Courier.*

—An excited secession meeting was held at Baltimore, Md. T. Parkin Scott occupied the chair, and speeches denunciatory of the Administration and the North were made by Wilson C. N. Carr, Wiliam Burns, president of the National Volunteer Association, and others.—*Baltimore Clipper, April 19.*

—The main entrance to the harbor of Norfolk, Va., was obstructed by the sinking of small boats by order of Governor Letcher.—*Idem.*

—Governor Letcher, of Virginia, issued a proclamation, in which the independence of the Confederate States is recognized, and all armed volunteers, regiments, or companies, are commanded to hold themselves in readiness for immediate orders, and to prepare for efficient service.—(*Doc. 59.*)

—A meeting, composed of all parties, was held at Middletown, Orange county, N. Y. Speeches were made, and great enthusiasm prevailed.—*Tribune, April 20.*

—The Virginia State Convention passed the "ordinance to repeal the ratification of the Constitution of the United States of America by the State of Virginia, and to resume all the rights and powers granted under said authorities."—(*Doc. 60.*)

—Further precautions were taken at Washington to guard against a sudden raid of the rebels upon the city. The Long Bridge across the Potomac was patrolled by a party of dragoons, and at night a detachment of artillery, with guns posted to sweep the bridge, kept guard on the Washington side. Intense excitement prevailed.—*Tribune.*

—JEFFERSON DAVIS issued a proclamation, offering to grant letters of marque and reprisal, to aid the Southern Confederacy "in resisting the wanton and wicked aggressions" of the Federal Government.—(*Doc.* 61.)

April 18.—Governor Harris, of Tennessee, replies to President Lincoln's call for two regiments of troops, by saying that "Tennessee will not furnish a single man for coercion, but fifty thousand, if necessary, for the defence of our rights or those of our Southern brothers."—*Louisville Democrat, April* 21.

—GOVERNOR JACKSON, of Missouri, answers Secretary Cameron by telling him that his "requisition is illegal, unconstitutional, revolutionary, inhuman, diabolical, and cannot be complied with." Missouri won't furnish a single man for such an unholy crusade.—*Charleston Mercury, April* 19.

—JOHN BELL, Niell S. Brown, Bailie Payton, and eight other citizens of Tennessee, issued an address calling upon the people of that State to maintain a position of independence in the present struggle, taking sides with the union and peace of the country against all assailants, whether from the North or the South.—(*Doc.* 61½.)

—THE Common Council of Boston appropriated $100,000 to provide for soldiers enlisting from Boston. The Lowell city government appropriated $8,000 for soldiers' families.—*Boston Journal.*

—AT Xenia, Ohio, $14,000 were subscribed to aid the volunteers. At noon Captain Tripp's company of one hundred men left Mount Vernon, Ind., for Indianapolis.—*Louisville Democrat, April* 21.

—THE *National Union*, published at Winchester, Ky., says:

"Mark, now, what we say: any attempt on the part of the Government of this State, or of any one else, to put Kentucky out of the Union by force, or using force to compel Union men in any manner to submit to an ordinance of secession, or any pretended resolution or decree, arising from such secession, is an act of treason against the State of Kentucky.

"It is, therefore, lawful to resist any such ordinance. We hope that we are now fully understood thus far."

A meeting at Chicago, Illinois, called for the purpose of sustaining the Government, was the largest and most enthusiastic ever held in the city. Speeches were made by prominent gentlemen of both parties. Stirring resolutions were adopted. $6,000 were subscribed for the support of the volunteers until taken charge of by the State.—*Free Press.*

—THE banks in Trenton, N. J., Chicago, Ill., Portland, Me., subscribed in support of the Federal Government. A meeting of the officers, representing all the Boston (Mass.) banks, was held this morning, when resolutions were adopted to loan the State of Massachusetts 10 per cent. on their entire capital for the defence of the Government. The capital of the Boston banks amounts to $38,800,000.—*Boston Transcript.*

—AT Pittsburgh, Pa., an intense war feeling prevails. Business is almost suspended. Immense crowds throng all the prominent streets, flags are floating everywhere, and the volunteer companies are all filled and departing eastward. Liberal subscriptions are being made for the comfort of volunteers and the support of their families. Recruiting is still going on, although there are more than enough for the requirements of the State to fill the Federal requisition. A Committee of Public Safety held a meeting to-day, and organized. A large quantity of powder which had been sent down the river, was intercepted at Steubenville, it being feared it would fall into the hands of the Secessionists. Ropes were suspended by lamp-posts last night, by unknown persons, labelled "Death to traitors." Some assaults have been made on persons who have expressed sympathy with the Secessionists.—*Philadelphia Press.*

—LIEUTENANT JONES, United States army, in command at Harper's Ferry with forty-three men, destroyed the arsenal at that place and retreated. He was advised that a force of 2,500 men had been ordered to take his post by Governor Letcher; and he put piles of powder in straw in all the buildings, and quietly waited the approach of the enemy. When his picket guard gave the alarm that 600 Virginians were approaching by the Winchester road, the men were run out of the arsenal and the combustibles fired. The people fired upon the soldiers, killing two, and rushed into the arsenal. All the works, munitions of war, and 15,000 stand of arms were destroyed.—(*Doc.* 62.)—*Times, April* 21.

Jeff. Davis.

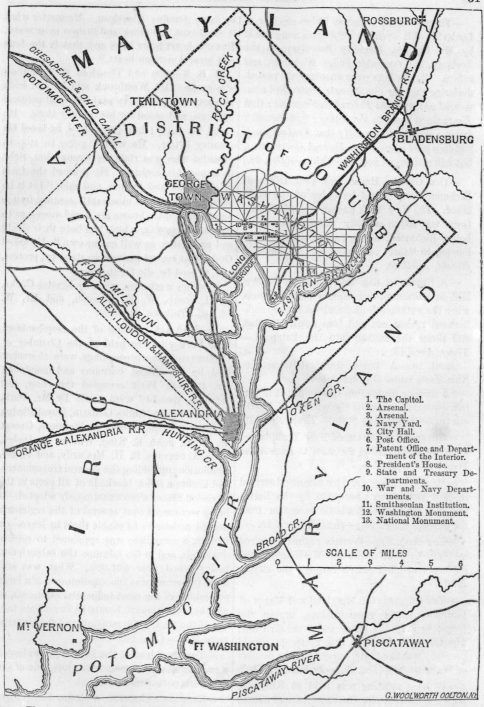

MARYLAND

ROSSBURG

CHESAPEAKE & OHIO CANAL

POTOMAC RIVER

ROCK CREEK

TENLYTOWN

DISTRICT OF COLUMBIA

WASHINGTON BRANCH R.R.

BLADENSBURG

GEORGE TOWN

WASHINGTON

7
10 8 9   5
13   6   4
12   11   2
          1

LONG BRIDGE

EASTERN BRANCH

FOUR MILE RUN

ALEX. LOUDON & HAMPSHIRE R.R.

ALEXANDRIA

OXEN CR.

ORANGE & ALEXANDRIA R.R.

HUNTING CR.

VIRGINIA

1. The Capitol.
2. Arsenal.
3. Arsenal.
4. Navy Yard.
5. City Hall.
6. Post Office.
7. Patent Office and Department of the Interior.
8. President's House.
9. State and Treasury Departments.
10. War and Navy Departments.
11. Smithsonian Institution.
12. Washington Monument.
13. National Monument.

BROAD CR.

SCALE OF MILES
0   1   2   3   4   5   6

POTOMAC RIVER

MARYLAND

MT. VERNON

FT. WASHINGTON

PISCATAWAY

PISCATAWAY RIVER

G. WOOLWORTH COLTON. N.Y.

The portion of the original District of Columbia lying west of the Potomac River was retroceded to the State of Virginia in 1846, and now forms the County of Alexandria.

We are indebted to the proprietors of the *N. Y. Tribune* for this map.

—There was an immense Union meeting at Louisville this evening. Speeches were made by Mr. Guthrie, formerly Secretary of the Treasury, the venerable Judge Nicholson, and others. Resolutions were unanimously passed, declaring that *the Confederate States had commenced war with the Federal Government;* that *Kentucky is loyal to the Union;* that *Secession is not a remedy for an evil;* that *Kentucky will not take part against the Federal Government,* but will maintain a neutral position.—(*Doc.* 63.)

—The Custom House and Post Office at Richmond were seized by order of the Governor. The New York packet steamer Jamestown was seized at City Point, sixty miles below Richmond, and a packet schooner belonging to Maine was taken at Richmond.— *Herald, April* 20.

—A Secession flag was raised on Federal Hill, in Baltimore, and saluted with a cannon, when the workmen from foundries in the neighborhood rushed out and tore down the flag, and threw the cannon into the Patapsco.— *Times, April* 19.

April 18.—A letter from Baltimore to New York, under this date, says :

" A serious disposition is manifested in certain quarters to obstruct the passage of Northern troops through the State.— *Times, April* 20.

—Governor Morgan, of New York, issued a proclamation calling for men to answer the President's requisition.

—Major Anderson and his command arrived in New York from Charleston by the Baltic, and met with an enthusiastic reception from the people.—(*Doc.* 64.)—*Herald, April* 19.

—The Sixth Massachusetts regiment arrived in New York *en route* for Washington, and made a triumphal march through the city.— *Ibid.*

—The Governor of Maryland and Mayor of Baltimore issued proclamations, urging the people to keep the peace and avoid civil war. The Governor declared that no troops should be sent from the State, except for the defence of Washington.—(*Doc.* 65.)—*Tribune, April* 20.

—A mass meeting was held at Kingston, N. Y., to sustain the Government and defend the Union. John B. Steele presided. In his speech, on taking the chair, he said :

" It must never be supposed that the flag could be desecrated without touching the soul of every genuine American. No matter what it must cost, the Stars and Stripes must wave. But one heart beats here, and that is the true and loyal American heart."

W. S. Kenyon and Theodore R. Westbrook also spoke. Mr. Westbrook said he laid aside all party lines, all party prejudices, all political opinions, and stood for his country alone. He loved his party ; but, thank God, he loved his country better. He wasn't going to stop to consider who was right or wrong ; but, right or wrong, his country. He grasped the folds of the Stars and Stripes, and said, " Let it be known that in the nineteenth century traitor hands and traitor hearts are found among us to disgrace that flag, which had been their shield and protection, as well as our own." He asked God might record his vow to stand by, protect, and, if need be, die for that flag.

Speeches were also made by Erastus Cooke, G. H. Sharp, W. H. Romeyn, and Mr. W. Chipp.— *Tribune, April* 20.

April 19.—A meeting of the merchants of New York city was held at the Chamber of Commerce. The proceedings were characterized by the utmost harmony and unanimity. Mr. Peletiah Perit occupied the chair, and patriotic speeches were made by Mr. Perit, George Opdyke, James Gallatin, Royal Phelps, S. B. Chittenden, Prosper M. Wetmore, George W. Blunt, John E. King, William E. Dodge, John A. Stevens, R. H. McCurdy, and others. Resolutions upholding the Federal Government, and urging a strict blockade of all ports in the secession States were unanimously adopted. It being announced that several of the regiments needed assistance to enable them to leave—on motion, a committee was appointed to receive donations, and in ten minutes the subscription had reached over $21,000. What was still more important was the appointment of a large committee of the most influential capitalists, to use their exertions to secure an immediate taking of the $9,000,000 remaining of the Government loan.—(*Doc.* 66.)

—The President of the United States issued a proclamation, announcing the blockade of the Southern ports.—(*Doc.* 67.)

—Sherrard Clemens, a strong Union man, and late member of Congress for Richmond, Va., is held as a prisoner at Richmond. He is still firm in his loyalty to the Government and his opposition to rebellion.—*Tribune, April* 19.

—AT Wilmington, Ohio, the first volunteer company, consisting of 125 men, organized to-day. Three thousand dollars were subscribed in one hour for the benefit of volunteers. Great enthusiasm prevails, and the work goes bravely on in raising both men and money. Another company is forming. A suspected Secessionist was seized this evening, and experienced some rough treatment.—*Louisville Democrat, April* 21.

—A RIFLE company was organized at Dayton, Ohio, under command of Captain Childs, consisting of 75 picked men. The company left Columbus at noon to-day, amid the cheers of a large crowd of citizens. Home guards are being formed. One company is to be formed of men over forty-five years old, under the command of Edward W. Davis.—*Idem.*

—REV. WARREN SWIFT, of Utica, N. Y., a Presbyterian minister of excellent abilities and wide-spread reputation, enlisted, and started for head-quarters this morning.—*Idem.*

—GENERAL SHERMAN, the State commandant at Galveston, Texas, issued an order enrolling "all citizens capable of bearing arms, not over sixty years of age, who do not enroll themselves into some one of the volunteer companies of the city by the 23d inst., in the militia. In case of being called into service they will be required to bring such arms as they may have, until they can be furnished by the State.

"The war has begun! It may reach our shores! Who in Texas will shrink from his duty in such a crisis? We invoke the spirit not only of 1776, but of 1836, to arouse from its slumber, and again assert the independence of Texas. The misrule of Black Republicanism would scarcely be less fatal to our interests than that of Mexican intolerance. We have shaken off the one; let us manfully repel the other."

The order is accompanied by other similar ones, necessary to carry it into effect. The alarm signal for the assembling of the city troops will be first a fire alarm, and secondly after an interval of one minute, six taps of the bell, to be repeated four times with intervals. —*N. O. Picayune, April* 23.

—IT is now learned by the return of the expedition to relieve Sumter, that a plan was perfected to throw in 300 men and supplies by boats at daylight on the 13th. This was frustrated, however, by the Baltic running upon Rattlesnake shoal on the night of the 12th.— *World, April* 19.

—MARYLAND, Delaware, and Pennsylvania, were added to the Military Department of Washington.—(*Doc.* 68.)—*Times, April* 25.

—A POSITIVE announcement "that General Scott had resigned his position in the army of the United States and tendered his sword to his native State—Virginia," was made at Montgomery. At Mobile, one hundred guns were fired in honor of his resignation.—*Charleston Mercury, April* 22.

—IMMENSE Union meetings were held last night at Auburn, Hudson, Ogdensburgh, Albion, Binghamton, and other towns and villages in western New York. Past political differences are forgotten, and the people are enthusiastic in support of the Administration.—*Troy Times.*

April 19.—At New York a large American flag, forty feet long by twenty wide, was flung out upon a flagstaff from a window in Trinity steeple, at a height of 240 feet. The chimes meanwhile played several airs appropriate to the occasion, among which were "Yankee Doodle," "the Red, White, and Blue," winding up with "All's well." The enthusiasm of the large concourse that had spontaneously gathered was most intense.

A flagstaff, with flag attached, was also run out of a window over the portico in front of St. Paul's Church.—*Tribune, April* 20.

—A PORTION of the Sixth Massachusetts, and the Seventh Pennsylvania, were attacked in the streets of Baltimore by a mob upon their passage through that city.

The Massachusetts Regiment occupied eleven cars. Upon their arrival at the President-street depot, the cars were permitted to leave with the troops still on board, and proceeded quietly through the streets of Baltimore, on their way to the depot at the other side of the town. But they had not gone more than a couple of blocks before the crowd became so dense that the horses attached to each car were scarcely able to push their way through. At this point the mob began to hoot and yell frightfully, and loud threats were uttered against the military. The troops, however, maintained a strict reserve, and the crowd then commenced to throw stones, brickbats, and other missiles, in a perfect shower, against the cars. Many of the troops were severely wounded in this manner. However, the first nine cars reached the depot, and departed for Washington. The remaining two cars of the train, with about 100 men, were thus cut off from the main body, and the men found themselves encompassed by an infuriated mob of over 8,000. These isolated cars were immediately attacked, and several of the soldiers had their muskets snatched from them. At this moment news came that the Philadelphia Volunteers had arrived, and the report excited the mob to a fearful degree. The road was now obstructed, and the soldiers alighted, formed a solid square, and advanced with fixed bayonets in double quick time, the Mayor of Baltimore at their head, all the while surrounded by the mob—now swelled to at least 10,000. The military behaved admirably, and still abstained from firing upon their assailants. The mob now commenced a perfect shower of missiles, occasionally varied by a random shot from a revolver or one of the muskets taken from the soldiers. The soldiers suffered severely from the immense quantity of stones, brickbats, paving-stones, &c.; the shots fired also wounded several. When two of the soldiers had been killed, and the wounded had been conveyed to the centre of the column, the troops at last, exasperated by the treatment they had received, commenced to return the fire singly, but at no one time did a platoon fire in a volley.

The volunteers, after a protracted and severe struggle, at last reached the depot, bearing with them in triumph their killed and wounded, and immediately embarked.

Two of the Massachusetts men were killed and eight wounded. Seven rioters were killed, and many wounded, but the number is not known. When information was received at the depot of this attack, the Pennsylvania regiment, which was unarmed, was sent back. Some were slightly wounded.—*Times, April* 20, 21,

The mob completely reigned in Baltimore after the attack.—All the gunshops were plundered. Other shops throughout the city were closed.—A public meeting was held in the afternoon, at which the Mayor and Gov. Hicks were present.—Secession sentiments prevailed.

The Mayor and Governor both notified the President that no more troops could pass through Baltimore unless they fought their way.—(*Doc.* 69.)—*Times, April* 21.

—BOSTON was terribly excited at the attack on the Massachusetts troops in Baltimore. The Government recognizes the similarity in the day and event suggested by the 19th of April, 1775, and those immortal memories which cluster around the men of Lexington and Concord.

The Governor sent the following despatch to the Mayor of Baltimore:

I pray you cause the bodies of our Massachusetts soldiers, dead in battle, to be immediately laid out, preserved in ice, and tenderly sent forward by express to me. All expenses will be paid by this Commonwealth.

JOHN A. ANDREW,
Governor of Massachusetts.
—(*Doc.* 70.)

At Fall River, Mass., a meeting was called on the reception of the news. Patriotic speeches were made, and the city government was instructed to appropriate $10,000 to fit out volunteers, and to pay each volunteer $20 per month in addition to the Government pay.— *Providence Journal.*

April 19.—The City Council of Philadelphia, this morning, at a special meeting, appropriated $1,000,000 to equip the volunteers and support their families during their absence from home. Fourteen thousand dollars were subscribed for the same purpose at Norwich, Conn.—*N. Y. Times.*

—THE Seventh Regt., N. Y. S. M., left for Washington amid the greatest enthusiasm. In every street an immense innumerable throng cheered them on their way. News of the fight in Baltimore was received before they left, and 48 rounds of ball-cartridge were served out.— (*Doc.* 71.)

Lieut. Jones, late in command of Harper's Ferry, arrived at Carlisle Barracks, Pa., having made a forced march the previous night of 30 miles from Harper's Ferry to Hagerstown.— *Times, April* 20.

—THE Rhode Island Marine Artillery passed through New York, on their way to the seat of war. These troops are officered by—Commanding Officer, Colonel Tomkins; Lieutenant Colonel, George C. Harkness; Captain, Benjamin F. Remington; Lieutenant, A. M. Tower; Lieutenant, Henry B. Brastow; Surgeon, Nathaniel Millar. They number 130 men, and carry with them 110 horses, eight guns of very heavy calibre, and the other requisite arms and ammunition. The horses are fine, spirited-looking animals, and appeared to be in that condition which will enable them to sustain a good deal of field hardship.—*Herald, April 20.*

—THE Eighth Regiment of Massachusetts Volunteers, under command of Colonel Timothy Munroe, passed through New York on their march to the south. It is composed of six companies: Newburyport Artillery, Newburyport Light Infantry, Gloucester Artillery, Lynn City Guards, Capt. Hundson, Lynn Light Infantry, Capt. Frazer, Lafayette Guards, Marblehead, Capt. Orne, all of Essex County, numbering twelve hundred. They are all picked men, those of Gloucester and Marblehead being stout and sturdy fishermen; those from Lynn and Newburyport chiefly shoemakers. Many of the members of the two Lynn companies served throughout the Mexican campaign. All of the men were in the best of spirits. Brig.-Gen. Benj. F. Butler and Quartermaster John Moran, of Boston, accompany the Regiment.—(*Doc.* 72.)—*N. Y. Tribune, April 20.*

April 20.—Last night a mob from Baltimore, lying in wait for the train from Philadelphia, at Canton, fired a pistol at the engineer, who stopped the train. The crowd, compelling the passengers to leave the cars, occupied the train, and forced the engineer to take them back to Gunpowder Bridge. There the train was stopped, and the crowd set fire to the draw of the bridge and waited till that portion was burned; returning to Bush River Bridge, the draw was likewise burned. The mob then returned to Canton Bridge and burned that. The train then conveyed the mob to the President-street station.—*Phila. Press.*

—THE Charleston Courier of to-day contains an account of the damage done by Fort Sumter to Fort Moultrie and the surrounding property. It says the fire was "terribly destructive, and, when viewed in connection with the fact that no life was lost, is the most extraordinary case ever recorded in history."—(*Doc.* 73.)

—A MASS meeting of citizens in support of the Union, the Constitution and the Government, was held in Union Square, New York City. It was called by leading citizens without distinction of party.—(*Doc.* 73½.)

—JOHN C. BRECKENRIDGE, Ex-Vice-President, addressed a large audience at Louisville, Ky., this afternoon, denouncing President Lincoln's proclamation as illegal, and saying that he could not make his 75,000 men efficient until after the meeting of Congress. He proposed that Kentucky present herself to Congress on the Fourth of July through her Senators and Representatives, and protest against the settlement of the present difficulties of the country by the sword—meanwhile that Kentucky call a State Convention to aid her Congressmen in presenting such a protest. Should that fail, however, it was the duty and the interest of Kentucky to unite her fortunes with the South. —*N. Y. Times, April 22.*

—THE Fourth Regiment of Massachusetts militia landed at Fortress Monroe, Va., from the steamer State of Maine.—(*Doc.* 74.)—*J. B. B. in the N. Y. Times, April 22.*

—THE citizens of Taunton, Mass., presented Major Robert Anderson a sword, "as an expression of their admiration of his courage, loyalty, and devotion to the country." The presentation was made by Capt. W. C. Lovering at the Brevoort House in New York.—*Tribune, April 22.*

—UNION meetings were held at Schenectady, Hudson, Utica, Waverley, and Dunkirk, N. Y.; Stockbridge, Mass.; Bridgeport, Conn.; Springfield and Chicago, Ill. During the proceedings at Chicago, at the suggestion of Judge Mannierre, the whole audience raised their right hands and took the oath of allegiance to the Union, repeating the oath after the Judge.—*Detroit Free Press.*

—A SOUTHERN merchant writes to a correspondent in New York:

"——, Tenn., April 20, 1861.

"Gentlemen: Our note to you for $187 12-100, due to-day, has not been paid.

"We deeply regret the necessity that impels us to say, *that during the existence of this war* we are determined to pay no notes due our northern friends."—*Evening Post.*

—THE St. Nicholas, a steamer plying between Washington and Baltimore, was seized at the former place this morning for prudential purposes.—*National Intelligencer.*

—HIRAM SIBLEY, President of the Western Union, and T. R. Walker, President, and J. D. Reid, Superintendent of the New York, Albany and Buffalo Telegraph Companies, issued orders that no messages, ordering arms or munitions of war, will be received by their companies unless for the defence of the Government of the United States, and endorsed by the Mayor of the City from which it proceeds. Messages in cypher, excepting despatches from the Press of the U. S. officers of the Government, will be refused.

The Toronto Globe of this morning has a long article on the relations between England and the United States, advocating a sincere and firm alliance, forgetting all past differences, and says that the North has a just cause; that the permanent good will of the American people is worth striving for, and hopes to see the rebellion put down and the traitors dealt with as they deserve.—*Louisville Democrat, April 21.*

April 20.—The Missourians seized the United States Arsenal at Liberty, Mo., and garrisoned it with 100 men. In the arsenal were 1,300 stand of arms, ten or twelve pieces of cannon, and quite an amount of powder.

Two thousand stand of arms were furnished the citizens of Leavenworth from the arsenal at Fort Leavenworth, and the commander at that post accepted the services of 300 volunteers to guard the arsenal pending the arrival of troops from Fort Kearney.—*Times, April 22.*

—The Council of Wilmington, Delaware, appropriated $8,000 to defend the city, and passed resolutions approving of the President's proclamation. Also, asking the Governor to issue a proclamation for the same purpose. The Brandywine bridges and all on the road between Susquehanna and Philadelphia are guarded, and workmen have been sent to repair the bridges destroyed on the Northern Central road.—*Phila. Enquirer.*

—Governor Curtin of Pennsylvania issued a proclamation calling a meeting of the State Legislature for the 30th of April, "to take into consideration and adopt such measures as the present emergencies may demand."—(*Doc.* 75.) —*Phila. Press.*

—A letter was received at Philadelphia from Governor Letcher, of Virginia, offering $30,000 to the patentee of the bullet mould. The reply was "no money can purchase it against the country."—*Evening Post.*

—An enthusiastic Union meeting was held at Middletown, Orange County, N. Y., this evening. The assemblage was presided over by Moses H. Corwin, a veteran of the war of 1812, and speeches were made by C. C. McQuoid, A. H.

Byington, Charles H. Van Wyck and others. Mr. Van Wyck announced the fact of his having "enlisted for the war," and with his company, just organized at Newburgh, he should proceed to Washington as a regular, *if he had to walk all the way.—Tribune, April 23.*

—The steamship, Star of the West, was taken into New Orleans as a prize to the Confederate States Government.—(*Doc.* 76.)

—Gosport Navy Yard, opposite Norfolk, Va., with stores, timber, munitions of war, etc., was burned by the U. S. officers in charge, to prevent its falling into the hands of the Secessionists, who occupied Norfolk and Portsmouth in force under Gen. Taliefero. The U. S. liners Pennsylvania, 74 guns; Delaware, 74; Co-

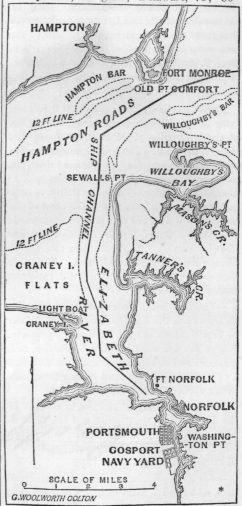

GOV. WILLIAM SPRAGUE of R.I.

Wm Sprague

NEW YORK. G.P.PUTNAM.

Entered according to act of Congress A.D.1861 by G.P.Putnam, in the clerks office of the district court for the southern district of N.Y.

lumbus, 74 ; steam frigate Merrimac, 44 ; frigate Raritan, 45 ; frigate Columbia, 44 ; sloop Germantown, 22 ; sloop Plymouth, 22 ; brig Dolphin, 8 ; a powder-boat, and the frigate United States, (in ordinary.) It being impossible to get them out of the harbor, they were scuttled, and were also fired.

The frigate Cumberland was towed out by the steam-tug Yankee. The value of the property destroyed is estimated at $50,000,000.— (*Doc. 77.*)—*Times, April* 24.

April 21.—The railroad between Philadelphia and Baltimore was taken possession of by the U. S. Government. Orders were given from the Navy Department at Washington to the officers of the various United States vessels, that all persons found sailing under Jefferson Davis' letters of marque and reprisal be treated as pirates. That the contumacious be *immediately hung from the yard-arms*, and the crew and the more penitent officers be placed in irons to await their trial as ocean brigands.—*Times, April* 21.

—THE people of Oswego and Rochester, N. Y., Toledo, Dayton, and Zanesville, Ohio, subscribed large sums of money for the support of the volunteers and their families; at the latter place, large property holders agreed to give rent free to volunteers during their absence.— *Albany Journal.*

—GENERAL SCOTT telegraphed to Senator Crittenden of Kentucky, as follows :

"I HAVE NOT CHANGED; HAVE NO THOUGHT OF CHANGING; ALWAYS A UNION MAN."—(*Doc.* 78.)

—GEORGE WILLIAM BROWN, mayor of Baltimore, Md., had a consultation with the President of the United States, in reference to the passage of northern troops through Baltimore. On his return from Washington, the Mayor submitted to the people a statement as to his interview with the President.—(*Doc.* 79.)

April 21.—The Worcester third battalion of Rifles, arrived at New York. They are commanded by Major Charles Devens, and number 200 men, officered as follows: Company A, Worcester City Guard, Capt. A. B. R. Sprague ; First Lieut., J. Pickett ; Second Lieut., O. Moulton ; Third Lieut., G. Egra.

Company C, Emmett Guard, Capt McConville ; First Lieut., F. McCafferty ; Second Lieut., M. O. Driscoll ; Third Lieut., T. O'Niel ; Fourth Lieut., — Melvin.—*Times, April* 22.

—A MASS meeting of citizens, numbering many thousands, was held in Boston, Mass., this forenoon, and was addressed by Fletcher Webster, Charles L. Woodbury, and many distinguished citizens. The meeting was to raise a regiment for Fletcher Webster, and was completely successful. The most intense enthusiasm prevailed among the crowd. The meeting continued till nearly night. It was a remarkable expression of the entire voice of our people.—*N. Y. Tribune, April* 22.

—THE First Regiment of Rhode Island Volunteers passed through New York, on their way to the South. Governor Sprague accompanies these troops, as commander in chief of the Rhode Island forces. His staff consists of Colonels Frieze, Goddard, Arnold, Capt. A. W. Chapin, Assistant Adjutant-General.—(*Doc.* 80.)

—THE Sixth, Twelfth, and Seventy-first Regiments, New York State Militia, left New York for Washington this day, (Sunday.) The people were early astir, and by 10 o'clock every available spot where a human being could stand, was occupied, throughout the entire length of Broadway ; and from near Canal-street to Grace Church, not only the sidewalks, but the whole of the street, was densely thronged. Every window, door, stoop, balcony, and house-top, were alive with human beings, of every age, sex, and condition, awaiting the marching of the Regiments, which it was known would depart during the day for the seat of Government, or other destination where their services might be required. It was some time after the bells had summoned the worshippers to their respective churches before the troops made their appearance. As they marched along, no language can do justice to the enthusiasm with which the assembled multitude greeted them. Cheers from ten thousand voices swelling in prolonged chorus, the waving of handkerchiefs by fair hands, the display of flags and streamers throughout the route of march, made the scene one of the most animated and exciting ever witnessed in the city.—*Times, April* 22.

April 21.—The United States branch mint at Charlotte, North Carolina, was seized by the State authorities. No resistance was offered. Colonel Bryce now holds it with a military force, under orders from Governor Ellis.—*N. Y. Evening Post, April* 29.

—Wendell Phillips delivered a discourse in Boston on the present rebellion. Some time ago he made a speech deprecating, in the most emphatic manner, any appeal to arms, as certain to result in the renewed and permanent triumph of slavery. The people of the North, he said, would not fight, and the first result of a military demonstration would be the complete surrender of the North, and the concession of everything that might be demanded at their hands.—(*Doc.* 81.)

April 21.—Andrew Johnson, U. S. Senator from Tennessee, passed through Lynchburg, Va., on his way from Washington to Tennessee. A large crowd assembled and groaned at him. They offered every indignity, and efforts were made to take him off the cars. Mr. Johnson was protected by the conductor and others. He denied sending a message asserting that Tennessee should furnish her quota of men.— *Commercial Advertiser, April* 26.

—The citizens of Baltimore were fearfully excited on account of a rumored descent upon them by Federal troops from Cockeysville, seventeen miles distant from the city; but at night the excitement subsided on receiving intelligence that the troops had been turned back to Harrisburg, Pa., by order of Gen. Scott.— *N. Y. Tribune, April* 26.

—In nearly all the churches in New York— and probably in a majority of churches throughout the country—the sermons of to-day were mainly in reference to the war. Many congregations have made the day an occasion for patriotic contributions for the outfit of volunteers, or for the support of their families. In the Church of the Puritans in Brooklyn, (although Mr. Beecher, the pastor, was absent, and the services were conducted by Rev. H. D. Northrup of Brooklyn,) a letter was read from the Thirteenth Regiment N. Y. S. M., asking for uniforms for recruits—and the response was a collection of about $1,100 for that patriotic purpose. In the Broadway Tabernacle, the pastor, Rev. J. P. Thompson, D. D., preached a sermon in the evening on "God's Time of Threshing." The choir performed "The Marseillaise" to a hymn composed for the occasion by the pastor. A collection was taken for the Volunteers' Home Fund amounting to $450— to which a member of the congregation afterwards added $100. Dr. Bethune's sermon was

from the text: "In the name of our God we will set up our banners." In Dr. Bellows' church the choir sang "The Star-Spangled Banner," which was vigorously applauded by the whole house. At Grace church (Episcopal) Dr. Taylor began by saying, "The Star-Spangled Banner has been insulted." The gallant Major Anderson and his wife attended service at Trinity. At Dr. McLane's Presbyterian church, Williamsburg, "The Star-Spangled Banner" was sung. Dr. T. D. Wells (Old-School Presbyterian) preached from the words: "He that hath no sword, let him buy one." Dr. Osgood's text was: "Lift up a standard to the people." Many of the churches—of all denominations— are sending some of their most active members to the field as volunteers.—*Independent, April* 25.

—The Fifth Regiment of Massachusetts Militia, Col. Lawrence, with the Boston Flying Artillery, Major Cook, left Boston for New York at 7 o'clock this morning. The Third Battalion of Rifles, Major Stevens, left Worcester last night for New York. Massachusetts has within six days responded to the President's proclamation, with five full regiments of infantry, a battalion of rifles, and a splendid corps of flying artillery. The artillery take six brass 6-pounders, with horses fully equipped.—*N. Y. Times, April* 22.

—A meeting of Californians was held in New York to take measures for the formation of a California Regiment. The meeting was organized by the nomination of J. C. Birdseye as chairman, and speeches were made, and resolutions sustaining the Union and the Government were adopted.—(*Doc.* 82.)

—The *Liverpool* (Eng.) *Times* publishes a remarkable article on the political troubles in the United States.—(*Doc.* 83.)

—The burial of the American flag was publicly celebrated at Memphis, Tennessee.—*N. Y. Express, April* 29.

April 22.—Several delegations of citizens of Maryland waited upon President Lincoln, to endeavor to procure some countermand of the order for troops to march to Washington. One delegation of thirty, from five "Young Men's Christian Associations" of Baltimore, had a prolonged interview, but made no impression upon him.—*N. Y. Times, April* 25.

—Gov. Hicks presented to the President a

communication again urging the withdrawal of troops from Maryland, a cessation of hostilities, and a reference of the national dispute to the arbitrament of Lord Lyons. To this the Secretary of State replied, that the troops were only called out to suppress insurrection, and must come through Maryland, as that was the route chosen for them by the Commander-in-Chief, and that our troubles could not be "referred to any foreign arbitrament."—(*Doc.* 84.)

April 22.—Robt. E. Lee, late of the United States Army, was nominated by the Governor and unanimously confirmed by the Convention as "Commander of the military and naval forces of Virginia."—*National Intelligencer, April* 27.

—The *Charleston Mercury* of this day says that "the officers of the army and navy of the Confederate States, and captains sailing under letters of marque, will greatly oblige the proprietors of that paper by furnishing sketches and incidents of the expected conflict between our gallant soldiers and their enemies.

"When supplied exclusively, a *liberal compensation* will be allowed."

—The United States Arsenal at Fayetteville, North Carolina, surrendered to the State authorities. It contains a large number of arms. —Governor Ellis, of North Carolina, called for 30,000 volunteers additional to the regular militia, and all the organized corps are under orders to be in readiness at a moment's notice. —*Boston Transcript, April* 29.

—Information was received by Gov. Curtin that Lieut. Jennifer, late of the United States Army, stationed at Carlisle Barracks, Pa., had fled from that place. Gov. Curtin, by aid of the telegraph facilities in his possession, succeeded in having him arrested at Hanover, in York County, Pa. It is said that Jennifer has been communicating information to the rebels as to the exact condition of things at Carlisle, and of the movements of Gov. Curtin's troops.—*N. Y. Times, April* 23.

—The N. Y. City Common Council passed an ordinance appropriating $1,000,000 for outfit and equipment and for the families of volunteers.—Several hundred uniforms made for the Southern army were seized at 4 Dey street, N. Y. City.—*Idem.*

—Gen. Thomas Jones, under instructions received from Governor Rector, seized at Napoleon, Arkansas, a large quantity of Government military supplies, consisting of one hundred and forty thousand ball cartridges, one hundred Maynard rifles, two hundred cavalry saddles, and five hundred sabres.—*Memphis Argus, April* 25.

April 22.—A meeting was held in Clarksburg, Harrison county, Virginia. Resolutions were adopted censuring severely the course pursued by Governor Letcher and the Eastern Virginians. Eleven delegates were appointed to meet delegates from other northwestern counties, to meet at Wheeling, May 13th, to determine what course should be pursued in the present emergency. Reports thus far received speak encouragingly of the Union sentiment in Western Virginia.—*National Intelligencer, April* 29.

—The Twenty-fifth Regiment of New York Militia arrived at New York from Albany. The regiment numbers over five hundred men, and is commanded by Colonel M. K. Bryan.— *N. Y. Tribune, April* 23.

—A meeting was held at Palace Garden, in New York, for the purpose of organizing a "Home Guard" of men over 45 years. The following Committee was appointed to carry out the objects of the meeting : Major A. M. Bininger, Col. Charles B. Tappen, Col. Burr Wakeman, Samuel Hotaling, Esq., and Judge Edmonds. Upwards of 300 names were enrolled.—*N. Y. Tribune, April* 25.

—The *Baltimore American* of this day contains a recapitulation of the killed and wounded during the riot that occurred at Baltimore on the 19th April.—(*Doc.* 85.)

—An embargo upon "provisions of any kind," and upon steamboats, was declared by the Mayor and Police Board of Baltimore.— (*Doc.* 86.)

—The *Charleston Mercury* of to-day, in an article headed "President Lincoln a Usurper," concludes that he will "deplore the 'higher-law' depravity which has governed his counsels. Seeking the sword, in spite of all moral or constitutional restraints and obligations, he may perish by the sword. He sleeps already with soldiers at his gate, and the grand reception-room of the White House is converted into quarters for troops from Kansas—border ruffians of Abolitiondom."

—At Lexington, Ky., between two and three hundred Union men assembled, raised the Stars and Stripes, and expressed their determination to adhere to them to the last. Speeches were made by Messrs. Field, Crittenden, Codey, and others. The most unbounded enthusiasm prevailed, and the speakers were greeted with great applause.—*Phila. Inquirer.*

—A LARGE and enthusiastic meeting of the residents of Chestnut Hill, Pa., and its vicinity, was held to "counsel together in the present alarming condition of the country, and take some steps to protect it from the assaults of traitors."—*Idem.*

April 22.—A. H. Stephens, Vice-President of the Southern Confederacy, arrived at Richmond, Va. In the evening he was serenaded, and made a speech, in which he said, that if the Federal Administration made war upon Maryland, the whole South would rally to her aid.— (*Doc.* 87.)

—A MEETING of the Bench and Bar of the city of New York, in view of the present crisis in the history of the country, was held at the Superior Court room, in that city. The judges and ex-judges of the different benches were present, and nearly every law firm in the city had its representative. Judge Daniel P. Ingraham presided; speeches were made, and patriotic resolutions were adopted.—(*Doc.* 88.)

—IN the evening a large meeting of the citizens of Westchester, N. Y., was held in Morrisania.—*N. Y. Tribune, April* 23.

—FATHER RAFINA, priest of the Montrose Avenue Catholic church, Williamsburg, N. Y., with his own hands raised the American flag upon the top of his church. The ceremony was witnessed by at least two thousand people, who greeted the glorious emblem with cheer after cheer as it waved majestically over the sacred edifice. The reverend father addressed the assemblage in a few appropriate remarks, which were received with marked enthusiasm.—*Idem.*

—UNION meetings were held at Geneva and Adams, N. Y. At Geneva, speeches were made by Judge Folger and others, and a large sum of money was subscribed and guaranteed for the families of the volunteers. At Adams the utmost enthusiasm prevailed.—*Albany Journal, April* 24.

—THE New York Seventh Regiment arrived at Annapolis, Md., and were joined there by the Eighth Massachusetts Regiment, with Gen. Butler in command.

An attack upon the School-ship Constitution was anticipated in Annapolis, and she was drawn out of the harbor.—*N. Y. Times, April* 25.

—SECRETARY CAMERON, in an official letter, conveyed the thanks of the Federal Government to Major Anderson for his conduct at Fort Sumter, as follows:—

WAR DEPARTMENT, WASHINGTON, April 22, 1861.

MAJOR ROBERT ANDERSON, *late Commanding Officer at Fort Sumter:*

MY DEAR SIR: I am directed by the President of the United States to communicate to you, and through you to the officers and men under your command at Forts Moultrie and Sumter, the approbation of the Government of your and their judicious and gallant conduct there; and to tender to you and them the thanks of the Government for the same.

I am, very respectfully,

SIMON CAMERON, Secretary of War.

—*National Intelligencer, April* 24.

April 22.—Gen. B. F. Butler, on board the steamer Maryland, off Annapolis, in special orders congratulates the troops upon the safety of the frigate Constitution, in the following language: "The purpose which could only be hinted at in the orders of yesterday, has been accomplished. The frigate Constitution has lain for a long time at this port substantially at the mercy of the armed mob which sometimes paralyzes the otherwise loyal State of Maryland. Deeds of daring, successful contests, and glorious victories, had rendered Old Ironsides so conspicuous in the naval history of the country, that she was fitly chosen as the school in which to train the future officers of the navy to like heroic acts. It was given to Massachusetts and Essex County first to man her; it was reserved to Massachusetts to have the honor to retain her for the service of the Union and the laws. This is a sufficient triumph of right—a sufficient triumph for us. By this the blood of our friends shed by the Baltimore mob is in so far avenged. The Eighth Regiment may hereafter cheer lustily upon all proper occasions, but never without orders. The old 'Constitution,' by their efforts, aided untiringly by the United States officers having her in charge, is now safely 'possessed, occupied, and enjoyed' by the Government of the United States, and is safe from all her enemies."—*N. Y. Tribune, April* 29.

April 23.—The *Montgomery* (Ala.) *Advertiser* of this day says :—Up to yesterday morning the following military companies of this State had responded to the proclamation of the Governor, calling for 3,000 and 5,000 volunteers, respectively, for the service of the Confederate States.. The list comprises fifty-one companies, which completes the requisition for 3,000, and furnishes eleven companies, or nearly a thousand men, in response to the last requisition for 5,000. There is no doubt but that in a few days the balance of the last 5,000 will be offered and accepted. Alabama has now actually in the field and ready to march about 5,400 troops. Notwithstanding this fact, the war fever has just begun to rage ; and, if necessary, we verily believe that the number could be increased to forty or fifty thousand in thirty days. There are perhaps twenty counties in the State that have not as yet furnished a man, but will certainly do so. Of these troops, two regiments have already been ordered to Virginia.

—John Bell and Edwin H. Ewing, at a public meeting held at Nashville, Tenn., declared themselves in the strongest and most emphatic terms for " resistance to the attempted subjugation of the South."—(*Doc.* 89.)

—Governor Moore, of Louisiana, issued an address, calling for 5,000 additional State troops. He says :—" The Government at Washington, maddened by defeat and the successful maintenance by our patriotic people of their rights and liberties against its mercenaries in the harbor of Charleston, and the determination of the Southern people forever to sever themselves from the Northern Government, has now thrown off the mask, and, sustained by the people of the non-slaveholding States, is actively engaged in levying war, by land and sea, to subvert your liberties, destroy your rights, and to shed your blood on your own soil. If you have the manhood to resist, rise, then, pride of Louisiana, in your might, in defence of your dearest rights, and drive back this insolent, barbaric force. Like your brave ancestry, resolve to conquer or perish in the effort ; and the flag of usurpation will never fly over Southern soil. Rally, then, to the proclamation which I now make on the requisition of the Confederate Government."

A number of parishes in Louisiana appropriated ten thousand dollars each for the support of the volunteers, and pledged themselves to pay fifty thousand dollars a year each as long as the war shall last.

A meeting of five hundred of the ladies of New Orleans, was held at the St. Charles Hotel, for the purpose of making arrangements for the holding of a fair to raise money for clothing the Louisiana volunteers.—*N. Y. Herald, April 26.*

—The Western Pennsylvania Regiment passed through Philadelphia for the seat of war. It consists of the following companies :—State Zouaves, Captain Seagrist ; Turner Rifles, Captain Emlen ; Seaborn Guards, Captain Winch ; Ringgold Rifles, Captain Lawrence ; Scott Artillery, Captain Medler ; Union Light Infantry, Captain Corley ; Columbia Infantry, Captain Brannan ; State Guards, Captain McDowell. The whole are under the command of Lieut. Col. P. C. Cress and Major R. B. Petriken.—*Phila. Inquirer, April 24.*

—The New Orleans papers are convinced from the language of the Northern press, and from every possible manifestation of public opinion, that " a very considerable proportion of the people at the North are actuated by an impulse of blind, irrational and insensate hatred towards the South."—(*Doc.* 90.)

—The First South Carolina Regiment of Volunteers left Charleston for the seat of war on the Potomac. As the troops left for the dépôt in groups, there was the warm, hearty shaking of hands, the friendly " God bless you," and the silent prayer of brothers, sisters, and mothers, offered up for the safety of South Carolina's gallant sons, who, after months of hard service in the camp, have nobly volunteered, at the shortest notice, and without even an opportunity to visit their homes, to march to the assistance of the Old Dominion, " the Mother of States and Statesmen," in the day of her trial.

The call made upon South Carolina has been promptly responded to. Gov. Pickens has been perfectly overwhelmed with offers of brigades, battalions, regiments, and companies, all desirous of being accepted as volunteers for Virginia. The reverence felt for her soil by South Carolinians is only equalled by the spirit and enthusiasm of the people to be the first to defend her, and, if necessary, with the best blood of the State.—*Charleston Courier, April 24.*—(*Doc.* 91.)

—An immense Union meeting was held at Brooklyn, N. Y. Robert J. Walker delivered an eloquent and forcible speech in defence of the Constitution and laws. Meetings were also held at Albion and Whitehall, N. Y., and Woodstock, Vt. At the latter, Senator Collamer spoke.—(*Doc.* 92.)

—The Eighth, Thirteenth, and Sixty-ninth Regiments of New York State Militia left New York for Washington.—(*Doc.* 93.)

—General B. F. Butler has taken military possession of the Annapolis and Elk Ridge Railroad in Maryland. Governor Hicks protests against the act, "as it will interfere with the meeting of the Legislature."—(*Doc.* 93½.)

—Sherman's celebrated battery, consisting of ninety men and eight howitzers, passed through Philadelphia, Pa., on the route to Washington. The train containing the troops stopped in Market street, between Fifteenth and Sixteenth, which was immediately observed by the ladies of Benton street, who rushed out and vied with each other in their attention to the weary soldiers. Bread, meat, pies, and cakes, were brought forward in goodly supplies, hundreds of girls running with hot dinners just from the ranges; bakers with baskets of bread and cakes; fruiterers with baskets of apples, oranges, &c., were quickly upon the ground. The men said that they were thirsty, and in a trice there were a dozen pretty girls handing up cups of water. After the battery had been thus refreshed, a collection was taken up, and the soldiers were supplied with enough segars and tobacco to last for some days. The military cheered continually for the ladies of Philadelphia, and as the train moved off, they gave nine hearty cheers for Philadelphia, the Union, the Constitution, and the success of the Federal arms in the South.—*Phila. Inquirer, April* 24.

April 24.—A remarkable feature in the present war excitement is the alacrity with which citizens of foreign birth or origin, and even those who are not naturalized at all, are hastening to the defence of the Government and the national flag. There is hardly a foreign country represented in the North, the children whereof are not organizing regiments and tendering their services to the Government.—*N. Y. Herald, April* 27.

—Rumors of an attack on Fort Pickens continue to receive credence in some quarters. The *Portsmouth* (Va.) *Transcript* of the 23d April says:—"Despatches received last night give important and glorious news. Fort Pickens was taken by the South. The loss on our side is said to be heavy. One despatch states the loss on the side of the South at 2,500 men; but the victory is ours."

Immediately after the above, the *Baltimore Sun* says that it is enabled to state "on the authority of a private despatch, received in this city last night, that the report of the battle is incorrect."

—The Twenty-fifth Regiment of N. Y. State Militia, from Albany, with a party of regulars and one hundred and seventy-five men of the Seventh New York Regiment left New York for the seat of war.—*N. Y. Tribune, April* 25.

—A volunteer company was organized at Sag Harbor, and $3,000 subscribed by the citizens for the benefit of the families of the volunteers.—*Idem, April* 26.

—Daniel Fish, gunmaker, of the city of New York, was arrested and handed over to the custody of the United States Marshal on a charge of treason, and misprision of treason, in having sent off large quantities of arms for the use of the Southern traitors. The correspondence and bills of lading found in his possession abundantly sustain the charge. A man calling himself Dr. Sabo, was also arrested, and is now in the hands of the United States authorities for recruiting men for the Southern navy. The papers which he used for the purpose were headed "United States of America," and purported to be authorized by the United States Collector and Naval Officer *of Charleston*. As there are no such officers at that port acting in behalf of the United States of America, it is evident that the intention was to enlist men under a false pretence, and, after getting them to Charleston, impress them into the service of the C. S. A.—*N. Y. Tribune, April* 25.

—Messrs. Hotchkiss & Sons, of Sharon, Connecticut, offered the Governor of their State a bronze rifled cannon, (16-pounder,) and all of their patent projectiles which can be fired from it during the war. Gov. Buckingham has accepted the gift. They also offered to produce additional rifled cannon and projectiles at cost.—*Idem.*

—Beriah Magoffin, Governor of Kentucky, issued a proclamation calling upon the State to place herself in a state of defence; and conven-

G.E.Perine. Sc.

Your obedient Servant
Benj. F. Butler

MAJ. GEN. BENJ. F. BUTLER.

NEW YORK. G.P.PUTNAM.

ing the Legislature on the 6th day of May, to take such action as may be necessary for the general welfare.—(*Doc.* 94.)

—The Navy Department at Washington signified its approbation of the loyalty, spirit, and good conduct of William Conway, an aged seaman, doing duty as Quartermaster in the Warrington Navy Yard, Florida, at the time of its surrender, in promptly and indignantly refusing to obey, when ordered by Lieutenant F. B. Renshaw to haul down the national flag.— *National Intelligencer, May* 3.

—THERE was an immense Union meeting at Detroit, Michigan. General Cass presided and delivered a short but effective speech.—(*Doc.* 95.)

—Two thousand federal troops are stationed at Cairo, Illinois. Of these, says the *Charleston Courier* of the 30th April, "fully three hundred are supposed to be negroes, and the remainder have been picked up from the gutters of Chicago, and among the Dutch. A force of one thousand firm-hearted Southern men would drive them from the place, if the attack was properly made."

—THE members of the Brown High School at Newburyport, Mass., raised the American flag near their school building in the presence of a large concourse of citizens. Patriotic speeches were made by Caleb Cushing and others.— (*Doc.* 96.)

—JOHN LETCHER, governor of Virginia, issued a proclamation authorizing the release of all private vessels and property seized by the State except the steamships Jamestown and Yorktown; advising the people to return to their usual avocations, promising them protection, and appealing to them "not to interfere with peaceable, unoffending citizens who preserve the peace and conform to our laws."—(*Doc.* 97.)

April 25.—Colonel Van Dorn of the State troops of Texas captured four hundred and fifty United States troops at Saluria.—(*Doc.* 98.)

—FORT SMITH, Arkansas, taken possession of by the State troops. About 12 o'clock at night a volunteer force of nearly three hundred men, under the command of Col. Solon Borland, landed at the wharf, when the post was formally surrendered by Capt. A. Montgomery to Gen. E. Burgvein, Adjutant-General of the State, who placed Col. Borland in charge. About an hour before their arrival Capt. Sturgis

left with his command, consisting of two cavalry companies. He took away the horses belonging to his command, and such supplies as he could transport. He is falling back on Fort Washita.

Capt. Montgomery and Major Gatlin were taken prisoners, and afterward released on parole. The Confederate flag was raised on the fort at 12 o'clock, amid the firing of cannon and the cheers of the people. After the review three cheers were given for the Arkansas citizen soldiery, three cheers for Jeff. Davis, and three cheers for Gov. H. M. Rector. The stock and property taken possession of is estimated to be of the value of $300,000.—*N. Y. Tribune, April* 26.

—THE Steam Transport Empire City, from Texas, arrived at New York, having on board the Third Regiment of Infantry and the Second Regiment of Cavalry, U. S. A., numbering six hundred men.—*N. Y. Herald, April* 26.

—AN enthusiastic meeting of the British residents of the city was held at New York. Speeches were made by S. M. Saunders, (the President,) Colonel Shepherd, Rev. H. N. Hudson, C. C. Leigh, and others.—*Idem.*

—A DEPUTATION of twenty Indians, headed by White Cloud, in behalf of the Sioux and Chippeways, arrived in New York. They tender to the United States, in behalf of themselves and 300 other warriors, their services against rebellion. Having heard that the Cherokees had sided with the rebels, they could not remain neutral, and, with a promptness worthy of imitation in high quarters, have come to offer their services in defense of the Government. They ask to be armed and led.

White Cloud is the interpreter of the Sioux, and is a man of intelligence and true patriotic ardor. He visited the Quartermaster's Department to-day, and addressed the soldiers being inspected there. He says, the men on the way are all good warriors, ranging from 18 to 40 years of age.—*N. Y. Tribune, April* 26.

—GEORGE LAW addressed a letter to the President of the United States, demanding of Government the opening of lines of communication between Washington and the North.—(*Doc.* 99.)

—GOVERNOR YATES of Illinois, in a special message to the Legislature of that State, gives the reasons that induced the armed occupation of Cairo city. He says, "That the transfer of part of the volunteer forces of this State to the city of Cairo was made in compliance with an order of the War Department, directing a force to be stationed at Cairo. Simultaneously with the receipt of the order, reliable information reached me of the existence of a conspiracy by disaffected persons in other states to seize upon Cairo and the southern portion of the Illinois Central Railroad, and cut off communication with the interior of the State. It was my desire that the honor of this service should have been given to the patriotic citizens of the counties in the immediate vicinity. But as these were not at that time organized and armed for patriotic duty, and the necessity for speedy action was imperative, the requisition was filled from companies previously tendered from other portions of the State."—*N. Y. Evening Post, April 29.*

—The Gulf City Guards, of Mobile, Ala., Capt. Hartwell, left that place for Virginia. The Register says:—This is a fine and gallant company, of the flower of Mobile. Verily has Mobile contributed 400 of her best and most chivalrous youth in the four companies that have gone North, and yet the demand for marching orders has not abated in the least. Companies are offering their services and others are forming. Mobile has 4,500 fighting men. We have about 1,000 in the field, and the balance are ready to march. About 5 o'clock, the Guards moved from the armory, and marched up Royal to Dauphin, and down Dauphin to the steamer Selma, on board of which boat they took passage to Montgomery.—*N. O. Picayune, April 28.*

—General Harney, on his way to Washington, was arrested by the Virginia authorities, at Harper's Ferry. He left Wheeling, Va., for the purpose of reporting himself at headquarters at Washington. Before the train reached Harper's Ferry it was stopped, and a number of troops mounted the platforms; whilst the train was moving slowly on, the troops passed through the cars, and the General being pointed out, he was immediately taken into custody. —*N. Y. Times, April, 28.*

—The Illinois troops struck a great blow at the secessionists of Missouri. Acting under orders from the President of the United States, an expedition of Illinois volunteers visited St. Louis, advanced upon the Federal Arsenal at that place, and brought away immense stores of artillery, ammunition, and small arms, which had been stored at that post by the Government.

The amount of Federal property thus secured from the hands of the Secessionists of Missouri is of great value. Among the articles recovered were 21,000 stand of small arms and a park of artillery. There was no fighting. The Illinois boys declare, in true Western style, that the "Secessionists are euchred."—(*Doc.* 100.)

—At New Orleans, the steamship Cahawba was seized by Capt. Shivers, of the Caddo Rifles. Arranging his plans, selecting four of his men, and taking them armed in cabs, he proceeded to the foot of St. Joseph street, where the Cahawba was lying. Arriving there, the men jumped out of the cabs, formed in line, and Capt. Shivers, accompanied by Judge Price, boarded the steamer. The deck watch asked what was wanted. Captain Shivers replied he wanted to see the officer in command of the Cahawba. The watchman proceeded to the first mate's room and announced the presence of a gentleman on board, who wanted to see him.

The mate came on deck, and Capt. Shivers politely told him to surrender the ship. The mate stated that the captain of the Cahawba was not on board, and therefore he had nothing to say. Capt. Shivers then ordered his men on board, put a guard fore and aft, and elsewhere, thus taking possession.—*N. O. Delta, April 25.*

The Cahawba was released soon after her seizure, by order of Gov. Moore, who had received orders from the Confederate Government prohibiting any obstruction to commerce in Southern ports.—*N. Y. Herald, April 27.*

—The second detachment of Rhode Island troops passed through New York on their way to Annapolis, Md. The officers of the detachment are:—Lieutenant-Colonel commanding, J. T. Pitman; Major, Joe. W. Bolsch; Lieutenants, Carl C. Harris, Eddy, Luther; Lieutenant Colonel, Charles C. H. Day; Surgeon, M. McKnight.

The troops are subdivided as follows:—First Light Infantry, Mechanics' Rifles, Westerly Rifles, Newport Artillery; Wesley Rifles; Providence Artillery, Cadets of Providence, East Greenwich detachment, and Pawtucket detachment. The troops are well armed, each company having eight of Burnside's self-breech-loading rifles. Their countenances are expressive of strong determination, and a glance at the texture of their hands will show plainly that they have come from the mechanical and hard working classes of Rhode Island. The women of Rhode Island are not behindhand in offering their services for their country. The volunteers bring along with them two very prepossessing young women, named Martha Francis and Katey Brownell, both of Providence, who propose to act as "daughters of the regiment," after the French plan.

As a proof of the patriotic spirit which animates the citizens of Rhode Island, it may be mentioned that a man named William Dean, who lost one arm in the Mexican war, is now a volunteer in this corps, being willing to lose another limb in defence of the honor of his country. The noble fellow carries his musket slung behind his back, but it is said when the hour comes for bloodier action he can use it with as good effect and expertness as if in possession of his natural appendages. The regiment also carries a flag which was borne through all the terrors of the Revolution. The uniform of the Regiment is light and comfortable; it consists of a blue flannel blouse, gray pants, and the army regulation hat.—*N. Y. Herald.*

—At Annapolis, Md., the grounds of the Naval Academy are now a military camp. Gen. Butler in command. The railroad between Annapolis and Washington is guarded with his troops. Tho track, which was destroyed by the rebels, has been relaid, and communication between the two cities is open. Gen. Butler has taken possession of the heights opposite Annapolis, and commanding that city.

The Maryland Legislature met to-day at Frederick. Gen. Butler says that if it passes an ordinance of secession, he will *arrest the entire body!*—*N. Y. Times, April* 27.

—The New York Seventh Regiment arrived at Washington, marched up Pennsylvania avenue to the President's house, and thence to the War Department. They were warmly applauded and hailed with great joy.—(*Doc.* 101).

—Governor Letcher of Virginia issued a proclamation, with accompanying documents, announcing the transfer of that State to the government of the Southern Confederacy, in advance of any expression of opinion by the people on the ordinance of secession passed on the 17th of April.—(*Doc.* 102.)

—A great Union meeting was held at Castleton, Vt. Over ten thousand persons were present. Speeches were made by P. W. Hyde, C. M. Willard, Willard Child, and others. Great enthusiasm prevailed. Forty-one men enrolled themselves as members of a volunteer company. The officers of the company are as follows: Captain, James Hope; First Lieutenant, John Howe; Second Lieutenant, Henry D. Noble.—*N. Y. Times, April* 27.

—Senator Douglas was publicly received by the Illinois Legislature, and made a patriotic speech, urging immediate action in support of the Government.—*Chicago Tribune, April* 26.

April 26.—Governor Brown of Georgia issued a proclamation prohibiting the payment of all debts to Northern creditors till the end of hostilities, and directing the payment of money into the State Treasury, to be refunded to depositors with interest at the end of the war.—*Montgomery Weekly Post, May* 1.

—The enthusiasm of the people at the West in rallying for the defence of the Union, far exceeds the expectations of the most sanguine Republicans. Throughout the entire Northwest there is a perfect unanimity of sentiment. Ten days ago, men who now cry, down with the rebels, were apologizing for the South—justifying its action, and wishing it success. Every town in Illinois is mustering soldiers, and many of the towns of five or six thousand inhabitants have two and three companies ready for action. Companies are also formed for drill, so that, in case of need, they will be prepared to march at any moment. Money is poured out freely as water, and ladies unite in making shirts, blankets, and even coats and pants for the soldiers. Arrangements have been made to take care of the families of the soldiers during their absence. All say, none shall fight the battles of their country at their own expense.—*Cor. Boston Transcript, May* 1.

—The steamer Daniel Webster from New York, arrived at the bar at the mouth of the Mississsipi, and received orders to return immediately for fear of seizure. The tug boat Tuscarora came alongside, and took four passengers off. The Webster left before the others could get ashore.—*N. Y. Commercial, May* 1.

—A meeting of the citizens of the Seventeenth Ward, N. Y., was held, to take action in behalf of the families of volunteers from that district.

B. R. Winthrop occupied the chair. Resolutions were adopted, and speeches were made by F. A. Conkling, Chauncey Schaeffer, John Cochrane and others.—*N. Y. Tribune, April* 27.

—A Union meeting at Bedford, Westchester county, N. Y., this afternoon, on the occasion of raising the flag, was addressed by Senator Hall, John Jay, Rev. M. Bogg, of the Episcopal Church, Rev. Mr. Ferris, Dr. Woodcock, Dr. Shores, Mr. Hart, Captain of the Bedford company, Mr. Brown, of the Croton Falls Company, and others.—*N. Y. Times, April* 27.

—John W. Ellis, governor of North Carolina, issued a proclamation calling an extra session of the General Assembly of the State, and deprecating the proclamation of President Lincoln asking for troops.—(*Doc.* 103.)

—The bridges over Gunpowder River on the Philadelphia, Wilmington and Baltimore Railroad were burned by the rebels of Baltimore. The bridge over Bush River, on the same route, was destroyed last evening about sundown.—*N. Y. Herald, April* 28.

—The Baltimore *Sun* of to-day, has a leader which seems to indicate that the conservative influence is gaining ground in that city. It emphatically declares that it is not a secession paper. It says that the passage of an ordinance of secession by the Legislature would be an arrogation of power not vested in it. It favors calling a State Convention, the delegates to be elected directly from the people. It denies the stories of violence to Union men at Baltimore. There is a great feeling among business men of the city for the re-establishment of trade, and silent conservatism is changing gradually to open Unionism.—*N. Y. Times, April* 27.

—A large meeting of the ladies of Syracuse, N. Y., was held, to organize for providing supplies for the volunteers. Mrs. E. W. Leavenworth was made president, Mrs. H. W. Chittenden, vice-president, and Mrs. J. B. Burnet, treasurer.

The Common Council of Buffalo, N. Y., yesterday appropriated $35,000 to equip the Sixty-fifth and Seventy-fourth Regiments.—*N. Y. Times, April* 27.

—The Seventh Regiment of New York took the oath to support the Constitution of the United States, at the War Department, in Washington; not a man flinched; the scene was most impressive.

—Moses Herrick of the Beverly Company, Eighth Massachusetts Regiment, met with an accident by the discharge of a gun.—*N. Y. Tribune, April* 29.

—The Federal Government is taking most energetic measures to carry out the blockade of the ports of the seceded States. All the available war vessels are put into service. Mercantile steamers are also taken up, and such as are not used for purposes of transportation are being fitted out as gunboats, to cruise off the coast and run up shallow waters.—*N. Y. Herald, April* 27.

—William Burton, governor of Delaware, issued a proclamation calling out volunteers to defend the Union.—(*Doc.* 104.)

—A meeting of the ladies of the congregation of Trinity church, and of St. Paul's, St. John's, and Trinity chapels, in New York, to the number of about one hundred and fifty, took place in the Sunday-school room, of St. John's chapel, for the purpose of providing articles for the hospitals and the use of the United States Army.—*N. Y. Courier & Enquirer, April* 27.

—The steam-tug Yankee, armed with two heavy guns, left New York to join the blockade of the Southern ports.—*N. Y. Commercial Advertiser, April* 27.

April 27.—Several new military departments were created by the subdivision of the military department of Washington.—(*Doc.* 105.)

—The Virginia *Sentinel* of to-day, says, "Our people must rest quiet upon the fact that the military preparations for our defence are under the direction of shrewd, skilful, indefatigable, experienced and patriotic officers. Our commanding general, Robert E. Lee, has long been the pride of the service, and he is supported by subordinates of acknowledged capacity and large experience.

"The plans of our Government are, of course, not suitable matter of public proclamation. Our military boards keep their own counsels, as it is obviously proper they should do. The people should patriotically abstain from even the attempt to unriddle them, for the wisest plans are often baffled by disclosure, however made. Let us trust with a generous confidence those to whose hands we have committed the conduct of affairs, and prepare ourselves to sustain them with all the power of a united and courageous people."

—FIVE men were arrested at the Navy-yard, at Washington, where they were employed, having been discovered filling bomb-shells with sand and sawdust, instead of the proper detonating material. They were confined in the Capitol, under guard of the Seventh Regiment. —*N. Y. Times, May* 1.

—THE Fifth and Eighth Massachusetts Regiments arrived at Washington yesterday morning, followed immediately by the Rhode Island forces.

This morning, about six o'clock, the Seventy-first New-York marched in from Annapolis Junction. It made a magnificent appearance as it swept down the Avenue, with its full bands playing. The men looked less fatigued than those of either of the other regiments, and were warmly commended by the citizens as they passed, and by the officers and men of the other regiments who were out to witness their entrance into the city. Next to the Massachusetts men they showed the greatest capacity to endure fatigue.—(*Doc.* 106.)—*The World, May* 1.

—SOUTHERNERS employed in the departments at Washington resigned and left for the South, refusing to take the prescribed oath of fealty to the Constitution of the United States.—(*Doc.* 107.)

—MESSRS. WINSLOW, LANIER & Co., of New York, offered Governor Morton of Indiana the sum of twenty-five thousand dollars for the purpose of arming and equipping the quota of volunteers from Indiana.—*N. Y. Com. Advertiser, April* 27.

—A NUMBER of residents of Virginia passed through Chambersburg, Pa., *en route* for the North. Many of them have left every thing behind, and are obliged to depend upon the charities of the people to continue their journey.

All who come from as far south as Richmond, could get out of the State only by a special permit from Governor Letcher. Their statements show that a reign of terror exists in the interior of Virginia. The mob everywhere appropriate to their own use whatever they may fancy; farmers are stopped on the road, their horses taken from them under the plea that they are for the defence of the South; granaries are searched, and every thing convertible for food for either man or beast carried off. This has been practiced to such an extent that along the northern border of Virginia a reaction is taking place, and instructions are being sent from Western Maryland, to the Delegates at Annapolis, that if they vote for secession the people will hang them on their return home. The news of the unanimous sentiment of the North, the prompt and decisive action on the part of the State Governments in enlisting men, has strengthened the Union men of Western Maryland and the border counties of Virginia.—*N. Y. Tribune, April* 28.

—A SUDDEN and wonderful change takes place in the sentiment of Maryland. The American flag was raised at Hagerstown, and extensive preparations are being made for further Union demonstrations.

Alleghany county has instructed its representatives that if they vote for secession, they will be hung on their return home. The Stars and Stripes are waving over Frederick City. The Home Guard refuse to parade unless its folds are displayed, and the tune of Yankee Doodle played. At the Clear Spring House the Stars and Stripes are waving, and the miners have sworn to resist secession to the death.—*N. Y. Courier & Enquirer, April* 28.

—THE steamer C. E. Hillman, from St. Louis, bound for Nashville, was abandoned by her officers previous to reaching Cairo, Illinois. The deserted steamer was found to contain one thousand kegs of powder, and other contraband articles.

At the same place, the steamer J. D. Perry, from St. Louis to Memphis, was brought to. Nothing of a contraband character being found on board, she was allowed to proceed on her trip.—*N. O. Picayune, April* 30.

—A SOUTHERN Rights meeting was held in Warsaw, Mo. Resolutions were unanimously adopted favoring immediate secession; requesting the Governor to repel any attempt of the Administration to march troops through Missouri for the purpose of making war on the Southern States, or to reinforce the forts and arsenals in Missouri; and complimenting the Governor for refusing to send Lincoln the quota of troops called for.—*N. O. Picayune, April* 30.

—S. H. NEEDHAM, a private in the Sixth Massachusetts regiment died this morning at Baltimore. He was struck on the back of the head with paving stones at the riot, having his skull fractured. He had spoken but a single word since then, which was in answer to a question whether he had a family, when he said "No."—*Boston Transcript, April* 29.

—A MEETING was held around the Washington Elm, at Cambridge, Mass., to give expression of the sentiments of the citizens of that vicinity upon the present troubles. John Sargent occupied the chair, and opened the meeting with a brief speech, in which he declared it to be the duty of every American to support the Government.—*Boston Sat. Express, April* 27.

—THE "New York Ladies' Relief Union" issued a circular suggesting "the importance of systematizing the earnest efforts now making by the women of New York for the supply of extra medical aid to the federal army, through the present campaign."—(*Doc.* 108.)

—THERE is one strong, deep-rooted determination in Massachusetts, which seems to pervade all classes, old and young; and that is—if the country needs their services, they will stand ready to answer to the order—"Forward—march!" The young men are all desirous of going to the war, *any how;* and the old men are equally desirous to march, IF NECESSARY.—*Boston Saturday Express, April* 27.

—GOVERNOR HICKS delivered a message to the Maryland Legislature. It briefly details the startling events which induced him to assemble that body.—(*Doc.* 109.)

—THE rebel army stationed at Richmond, numbers three thousand and seventy-two men, of which about six hundred are South Carolina troops under the command of Brig.-Gen. M. L. Bonham.—*Richmond Enquirer, April* 27, *and N. Y. Herald, April* 30.

—A NUMBER of French residents of New York held a meeting this afternoon for the purpose of taking measures with reference to the present state of the country. Messrs. Fremont, Quesne, and Faidu were appointed a Committee to conduct the proceedings. M. Victor Faidu stated the object of the meeting, and proposed that it be made preliminary to a general meeting of French citizens for their proper organization to participate in the present conflict—it was their duty to support the Government of the United States in this strife between human liberty and freedom against slavery and feudal oppression. M. Fremont offered resolutions tendering the support of French citizens to the United States, but he hoped that the government, if the contest was carried to the extreme,

would guarantee the total abolition of slavery. —*N. Y. Daily News, April* 29.

—PRESIDENT LINCOLN decided that the ports of Virginia and North Carolina should be included in the blockade of the Southern harbors and issued a proclamation to that effect.—(*Doc.* 110.)

—EDWARD EVERETT delivered an eloquent Union speech, at a flag raising in Chester Square, Boston, Mass.—(*Doc.* 111.)

—THE Harbor Police of New York seized six sloops in the harbor, laden with powder, which, it was supposed, was intended for the use of Secessionists. On the same day, Capt. Squires, of the Fifteenth Ward Police, seized several pairs of military pantaloons at the shop of a tailor in Ridge-street, who was recently in the employ of Newbeck & Co., No. 4 Dey-street, where 1,000 uniforms intended for the South, were recently seized.—*N. Y. Times, April* 29.

—THE reinforcement of Fort Pickens, is authoritatively announced to-day. It was accomplished on the night of Friday, April 12th, "without the firing of a gun or the spilling of one drop of blood."—(*Doc.* 112.)

April 28.—The Daylight, the first steamer direct from New York, *viâ* Potomac, reached Washington at 10 A. M. She found many lights out on the Virginia coast; and up the Chesapeake and Potomac, two light ships and many buoys destroyed by the rebels. The Daylight came without convoy; had no guns, except one howitzer, which Capt. Veile obtained from the Pocahontas, at the mouth of the Potomac. Capt. Veile and the 172 recruits for the New York Seventh Regiment, have the honor of the first passage up the Potomac.

—THE United States frigate Constitution arrived at New York from Annapolis, Md., having had a narrow escape from seizure by the rebels.

After the secession of Virginia, the demonstrations of the rebels became so apparent that it was deemed of the greatest importance to get her out over the bar. Her crew of twenty-five men and officers had been at their quarters with shotted guns night and day for four days. Troops were drilling on the shore; signals between them were constantly made out; large parties were around the ship to find her assailable point. She had four anchors and seven chains out, when the order came to get her over the bar.

The steamer Maryland, in General Butler's charge, came alongside; one anchor was hove up, for use, all the other chains were slipped, and the ship started at 9 A. M. drawing 20½ feet. There was then but 19 feet on the bar, and for some time it was doubtful if she would go, but by great exertion, by lighting and careening her, she was forced over. The captain, pilot, and engineers of the Maryland, which had been seized by General Butler, were very averse to do their duty, and it was only by putting them under a guard with revolvers, that they would proceed with the vessel.

After dragging her over the bar, the vessel grounded on the outer spit. About 10 P. M., information having been brought off that the channel outside the ship would be obstructed, kedges were laid out, and it was endeavored to warp the ship over the spit, part of the men being at the guns. The Maryland having been run aground by her officers during the warping, a squall came up and drove the ship ashore again. At daylight a steam tug from Havre de Grace came in sight, and was taken to tow the ship out. She was then taken in tow by the R. R. Cuyler, and brought to New York.—*N. Y. Commercial, April* 29.

—THE Fifth Regiment of New York State militia left New York on board the British steam transport Kedar, for Annapolis. This regiment is composed almost entirely of Germans, and is commanded by Colonel Schwartzwaelder. For some days past they have occupied 162 neat tents, precisely of the pattern furnished to the Hudson's Bay Indians, on the bare grounds of the Battery, where thousands of people visited them, and admired the excellent order and homelike appearance of their quarters.—(*Doc.* 113.)—*N. Y. Tribune, April* 29.

April 29.—A meeting of the Bar of Suffolk county was held at Boston, Mass., to consider the present situation of the country, and the measures necessary, when a blow is aimed at the existence of the Government, and the supremacy of law in the country. The meeting was numerously attended. Resolutions sustaining the Federal Government were adopted, and speeches were made by Judge Thomas, B. F. Hallet, J. C. Park, and others.—*Boston Transcript, April* 30.

—WILLIAM C. RIVES, Senator Hunter, Judge Brockenbrough, and Messrs. Preston and Camden, have been appointed by the Richmond Convention as delegates to the Montgomery Congress from Virginia.—*Montgomery* (Ala.) *Post, May* 1.

—BY order of Governor Harris of Tennessee, seventy-five thousand dollars' worth of Tennessee bonds and five thousand dollars in cash, belonging to the United States, which were in possession of the Collector at Nashville, were seized by the State authorities. The seizure was conditional, the property to be held in trust until the Government restores the property of the State and its citizens, involved in the seizure of the steamer Hillman by troops of the Federal Government.

The steamer Hillman was seized at Cairo, by the Illinois troops, on the 26th of April, because she was laden with munitions and other articles contraband of war.—*National Intelligencer, May* 7.

—THE *Charleston Mercury* of to-day contains the following:—" *To His Excellency Governor Pickens.*—Will you oblige the mothers, wives, and sisters of the Carolina troops, and appoint next Thursday as a day of Thanksgiving to Almighty God for the late bloodless victory.—ONE OF MANY."

—SEVERAL companies of the Third and Fourth Regiments of Georgia passed through Augusta for the expected scene of warfare—Virginia. Sixteen well-drilled companies of volunteers and one negro company, from Nashville, Tennessee, offered their services to the Confederate States.—*Charleston Mercury, April* 30.

—AT New Orleans, La., the steamships Texas, Tennessee, and the G. W. Hewes, the property of Charles Morgan, Esq., were taken possession of by order of Gov. Moore. Captain Warren of the steam-tug Tuscarora, who was arrested on the charge of having furnished information to the captain of the Daniel Webster, which caused him to leave this port, was released on giving bonds of two thousand dollars for his future loyal conduct. It is ascertained that the blame rests less upon him than upon the owners of the above-named steamers. —*N. O. Delta, April* 30.

—A MILITARY review took place at New Orleans, La. The city was one long military camp. Where the main body of troops appeared was not the only place to find the soldiers. They were in every section of the city, on the river and in the suburbs; in fact, New Orleans was completely under the control of military arms, within and around. It was one of those days that brought to memory the period of 1814. The streets, the house-tops, the windows, and balconies of every building were thronged with ladies, and at least thirty thousand persons witnessed a military pagent not equalled in this section of the South. The enthusiasm was immense, and beyond description.—(*Doc.* 115.)

—At Roxbury, Mass., a beautiful silk flag was presented, by the ladies of that city, to the volunteer company of Capt. Chamberlain. Hon. J. S. Sleeper presided, and the presentation address was made by Rev. Dr. George Putnam. The flag was placed in the hands of Capt. Chamberlain by a sweet little girl tastefully dressed in white, relieved by red and blue. Capt. Chamberlain knelt as he received the flag, and responded briefly in a voice choked with emotion. Capt. C.'s company stood before the platform in a hollow square, and responded with loud cheers to the patriotic sentiments which the occasion called forth.—*Boston Transcript, April* 30.

—Secession in Maryland was defeated by a direct vote in the House of Delegates of the State, of fifty-three against secession and thirteen for it. The State Senate published an address, signed by all its members, denying the intention of passing an ordinance of secession. —*N. Y. Times, April* 30.

—Ellsworth's Fire Zouaves left New York for Annapolis, Md. They were escorted to the boat by an immense body of brother firemen and citizens.—(Doc. 116.)

—Jefferson Davis sent a message to the Congress at Montgomery to-day. While reading in Congress, the allusion to Virginia was loudly cheered. A quotation from President Lincoln's proclamation advising the people of the South to retire to their homes within twenty days, was met with derisive laughter from the crowd in the galleries. Nearly all the members of Congress were present.— *Charleston Mercury, April* 30.—(Doc. 117.)

—Citizens of Weverton, Frederick Co., Maryland, in a letter to Governor Hicks, protest against the entrance of Virginia troops from Harper's Ferry into their State.—(Doc. 118.)

—There was an interesting display of patriotism by the young ladies of Brooklyn (N. Y.)

Heights Seminary. They unfurled a beautiful flag at their chapel, in Montague street, where speeches were made by Dr. West, the principal; Professor Washburne of Harvard Law School, and Rev. Dr. Storrs.

A preliminary meeting, to make arrangements for providing for the families of volunteers, was held at the Brooklyn Institute, Mayor Hall presiding. $2,500 was subscribed on the spot. Committees, composed of the most wealthy and active citizens were appointed to further the objects of the meeting.—*New York Times, May* 1.

—Virginia Ladies, resident in Washington, are constantly warned by their friends at home to leave that city before its inevitable destruction by the Southern army.—*N. Y. Herald, May* 1.

—A spontaneous Union meeting was held in East Baltimore, Md. 1,500 to 2,000 persons were present, and great enthusiasm was manifested. Strong Union resolutions were adopted, and the national banner was unfurled.

Regular daily communication between Baltimore and Philadelphia was fully reëstablished. —*N. Y. Herald, April* 30.

—Up to this day seventy-one thousand volunteers offered their services to Governor Dennison, of Ohio, to fill the thirteen regiments required by the Proclamation of President Lincoln.—*N. Y. Courier and Enquirer, April* 30.

—The American flag was raised upon the steeple of North Dutch church at New York. Nearly every church edifice and public building in the city is decorated in the same manner.—(*Doc.* 119.)—*Commercial Advertiser, April* 30.

April 30.—The Virginia Convention passed an ordinance to provide against the sacrifice of property, and to suspend proceedings in certain cases. It is to apply only to debts due non-residents, and not to those due the State. The ordinance is to remain in force until repealed or changed by the Convention or the General Assembly; and if not so repealed or changed, is to expire at the end of thirty days after the first day of the General Assembly.— *National Intelligencer, May* 7.

—The school-teachers of Boston, Mass., relinquished the following proportion of their salaries during the continuance of the national troubles:

Superintendent of Schools and Masters of Latin, English High and Girls' High and Normal Schools—25 per cent.

Masters of Grammar Schools and Sub-masters of Latin and English High Schools—15 per cent.

Sub-masters of Grammar Schools and Ushers of Latin and English High Schools—12½ per cent. Ushers of the Grammar Schools—10 per cent.

The aggregate of the percentage on the salaries will amount to between $12,000 and $13,-000.—*N. Y. World, May 3.*

—THE first cannon was cast in Nashville, Tenn., last Saturday, April 27.—*Charleston Mercury, May 3.*

—THE members of the New York Yacht Club met, and resolved to offer, through the Commodore, the services of all their yachts to the Government of the United States for any duty compatible with the qualities and dimensions of the vessels.—*N. Y. Tribune, May 2.*

—A. H. STEPHENS, Vice-President of the seceding States, arrived at Atlanta, Georgia, on his return from Virginia. He was received by a crowd of citizens, to whom he made a speech.—(*Doc.* 120.)

—THE New Jersey Legislature met, and Gov. OLDEN delivered his Message, recommending a loan of $2,000,000 for war purposes, and a State tax of $100,000 per annum; the thorough arming of the State, and the raising of four regiments additional to those called for, to be held subject to the call of the Government. He also recommended that provision be made for the defence of the Southern part of the State, either by fortified posts or by an intrenched camp.—*N. Y. Tribune, May 1.*

—DANIEL FISH, charged with selling guns to the South, was examined before the U. S. Commissioner and discharged.—*N. Y. Herald, May 1.*

—THE First Battalion of the Third Alabama Regiment left Montgomery this morning for Virginia.—Col. KERSHAW and staff, with Captains RICHARDSON, HASLES, and McMANNUS' companies of South Carolina troops arrived at Richmond, Va., this evening at 5 o'clock.—*Charleston Mercury, May 1.*

—GENERAL HARNEY is released by Governor Letcher of Virginia.

The Washington City Councils passed a series of resolutions, expressing the strongest devotion to the Union, and thanking the citizen soldiery of the North now there, for coming forward so promptly at the call of the Government.—*N. Y. Times, May 1.*

—THE *Toronto* (Canada) *Globe* of to-day, in a long article on American affairs, says that the North, by their impatience with reference to President Lincoln's policy, ignore the stupendous and delicate task he has before him, and will drive the country to anarchy and chaos.

It advocates strengthening Mr. Lincoln's hands, and to abstain from perplexing his councils.

The Leader, the Government organ, fears that Canada may become involved, and advocates an armed neutrality, and suggests that the Canadian Government represent to the imperial authorities the expediency of sending six or eight regiments of the line for the protection of the frontier.

—THE Palmetto Guard, Marion Artillery, and German Artillery returned from Morris' Island to Charleston, S. C. "Their brave and noble actions during the bombardment of Fort Sumter are not forgotten, we can assure them, but will ever live in grateful remembrance."—(*Doc.* 121.)—*Charleston News, May 1.*

—A UNITED States Armory is to be established at Rock Island, Ill., in the place of the one destroyed at Harper's Ferry.—*N. Y. Tribune, April 30.*

THE TWENTY-EIGHTH REGIMENT N. Y. S. M., composed of the best class of Germans, and commanded by Colonel Bennett, left Brooklyn, N. Y., for the seat of war. At 11 o'clock the last farewell was said; the Regiment formed, about 800 men, and headed by MEYERS' Band and a corps of drummers and fifers, they marched through Myrtle avenue and Fulton street to Fulton Ferry, where they embarked on board the ferry-boat *Nassau*, and were taken direct to the steamer *Star of the South*, then lying at Pier No. 36 North River. The streets through which they marched were lined with enthusiastic citizens to bid the troops God speed, and from nearly every house waved the Stars and Stripes and those other inspiring signals—white handkerchiefs. The troops were everywhere cordially received. At the foot of Fulton street a few brief farewells were said, and amid the booming of cannon and the cheers of the populace, the troops took their departure.

Fifty-seven recruits for Company G, Capt. THORNE, and a number for Capt. SPRAGUE's Company of the Thirteenth Regiment, went with the Twenty-eighth to join their Regiment at Annapolis.—(*Doc.* 122.)

—A MEETING of the Harvard Medical School was held in Cambridge, Mass., at which the following resolution was adopted:

Resolved, That we, the members of the Harvard Medical School, do here and now resolve ourselves into a volunteer medical corps, and as such do hereby tender our services to the Governor of this Commonwealth, to act in behalf of this State or country, in whatever capacity we may be needed.—*Boston Transcript, May* 1.

—CITIZENS of Philadelphia, representing all parties, addressed a congratulatory letter to Lieut.-General Scott.—(*Doc.* 123.)

—YESTERDAY the Louisiana Guards, and to-day the Montgomery Guards, left New Orleans for the seat of war in Virginia. The former company, previous to their departure, were presented with a beautiful flag by Mrs. A. H. Seaman at her residence.—*N. O. Delta, April* 30.

May 1.—The story of an armistice having been requested by Secretary Cameron was denied as follows:

WASHINGTON, Wednesday, May 1.
Simeon Draper, Esq., Chairman Union Defence Committee:

There is not a word of truth in any of the newspaper reports of the armistice made or proposed. That sort of business ended on the 4th of March.

F. W. SEWARD.
—*N. Y. Times, May* 2.

—A LARGE and enthusiastic meeting of the citizens of Wiscasset, Maine, was held, Wilmot Wood, Esq., presiding. Some spirited resolutions were unanimously passed; and it was recommended to the town to raise $5,000 for the support of families of volunteers who, under the command of Edwin M. Smith, Esq., were enrolled in a company for the defence of the Union.—*Boston Transcript, May* 7.

—THE Baptist State Convention of Georgia, submitted a communication to the Congress of the seceded States at Montgomery, endorsing, approving, and avowing support to, the Confederate Government, and requesting the said Government to proclaim a day of fasting and prayer, " that God will deliver us from the

power of our enemies, and restore peace to the country."—(*Doc.* 124.)

—THE governor of Connecticut sent a message to the legislature of that State, containing the following:—" Col. Samuel Colt, of Hartford, on the 25th of April last, offered to the executive his services in promoting the enlistment of a regiment of able-bodied men from the State for the war, and to furnish a sufficient number of his revolving breech rifles for their equipment. To this noble proposition I have replied, expressing my high appreciation of the patriotic offer, and assuring him that the tender of ten companies would at once be accepted, the troops organized into a regiment, the field officers appointed in harmony with the wishes of the regiment and the dignity of the State, and their services placed at the disposal of the General Government. These arms, which are the very latest improvements, with the saber bayonets, would sell in market to-day for over $50,000 in cash. Col. Colt is now actively engaged in enlisting a full regiment for the war, and also furnishing officers to drill and perfect the men in the use of the weapons at his own expense."—*The World, May* 3.

—GENERAL HARNEY, in a letter to Col. Fallon of St. Louis, gives an account of his arrest and subsequent release by the authorities of Virginia; declares that he will serve under no other banner than the one he has followed for forty years; denies the right of secession, and implores his fellow-citizens of Missouri not to be seduced by designing men to become the instruments of their mad ambition, and plunge the State into revolution.—(*Doc.* 125.)

—THE Albany (N. Y.) Burgesses Corps arrived at New York, and proceed to Washington to-morrow to join the Twenty-fifth regiment, N. Y. S. M.—(*Doc.* 126.)

—AN attempt was made to blow up the State Powder House, on Bramhall Hill, at Portland, Me., containing 1,000 kegs of powder, by building a fire at an air-hole outside. It was discovered, and extinguished.—*N. Y. Tribune, May* 2.

—GOV. BLACK of Nebraska, issued a proclamation, recommending a thorough volunteer organization throughout the Territory. He has supplied companies with arms and equipments, and seems determined to place Nebraska in the best possible condition of defence. —*Idem.*

GEN. SIMON CAMERON

SECRETARY OF WAR

NEW YORK, G.P. PUTNAM.

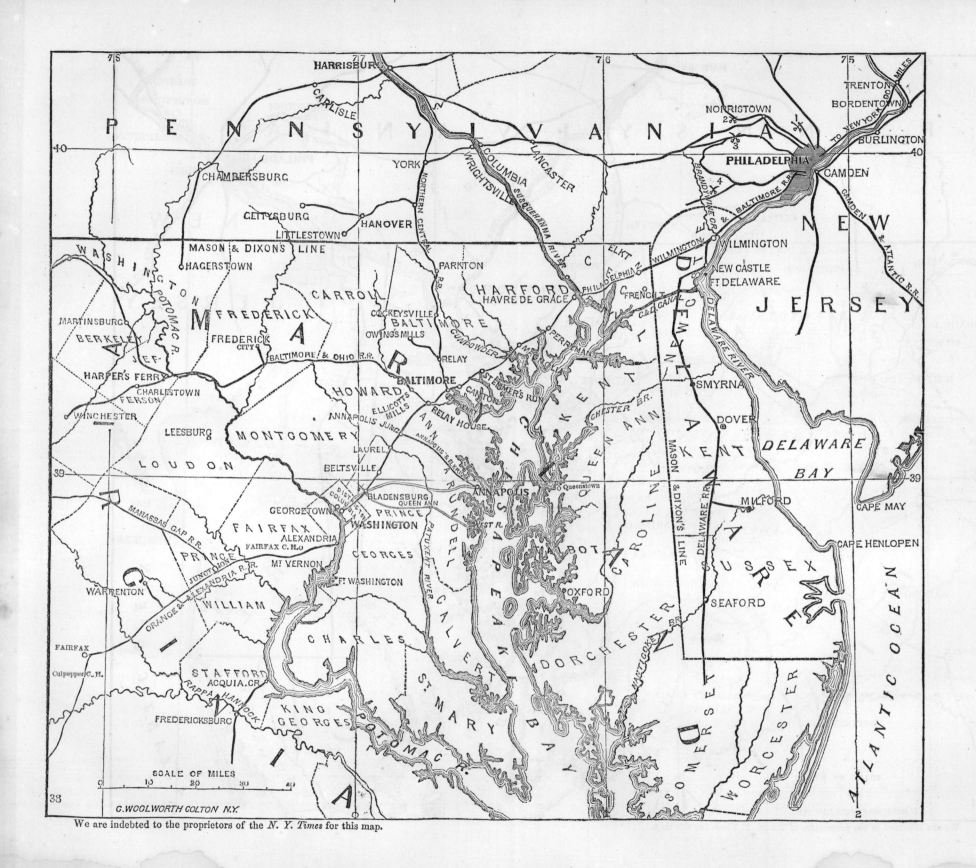

We are indebted to the proprietors of the *N. Y. Times* for this map.

—THE remains of the three Massachusetts soldiers who were killed in Baltimore, arrived at Boston in charge of private D. S. Wright, of the Sixth regiment, who was detailed by Col. Jones for the duty. The bodies were taken from the receiving tomb in Baltimore, under the supervision of Mayor Brown, and left Tuesday morning last. The fact was not generally known, but a large crowd gathered at the dépôt.

Gov. Andrew and staff, the executive council, with the divisionary corps of cadets as an escort, were present to receive the bodies. The coffins were covered with national flags, as were the hearses which bore them to Stone Chapel, under which they were deposited to await final and more public obsequies. On the route to the chapel the band played dirges, and the rapidly-gathered crowds uncovered as the procession moved past.—*Boston Transcript, May 2.*

—THE Montgomery (Ala.) *Weekly Post* of this day, says:—" There is no longer any doubt as to the position of General Scott. His general order of April 19 will satisfy the most skeptical. He will prove false to the mother which gave him birth."—(*See Doc.* 68, *p.* 78.)

—LIEUT. COLLIER, of the United States marines, attached to the Minnesota, raised the American flag to-day on the steeple of the Old South Church at Boston, Mass.

At noon the star-spangled banner was raised with great demonstration of enthusiasm from the post-office and custom-house at Baltimore, Md., by order of the newly-appointed officials. A large crowd assembled in front of the custom-house to witness the flag-raising. A new flag-staff was erected over the portico, and at precisely quarter to twelve, Captain Frazier, a veteran sea-captain of Fells Point, who was assigned the honor, drew up the flag, which, as it spread to the breeze, was greeted with tremendous applause, waving of hats, cheers for the Union and the old flag. The crowd then joined in singing the "Star-spangled Banner."—*N. Y. Commercial Advertiser, May 1.*

—WILLIAM GRAY, of Boston, Mass., gave ten thousand dollars for the benefit of the volunteers' families.—*N. Y. Times, May 2.*

—THE South Carolina College Cadets and the Washington Artillery returned to Charleston, S. C., from duty at the forts in the harbor of that place.—(*Doc.* 127.)

May 2.—The Sixty-ninth New York Regiment, (altogether composed of Irishmen,) under the command of Col. Corcoran, arrived at Washington, from the Annapolis Junction, Md., where, with the exception of one company which preceded them on Tuesday, they have been on duty for several days past.—*National Intelligencer, May 3.*

—GOVERNOR ANDREW, the Mayors of Lowell and Lawrence, and others, met at the State House, in Boston, Mass., for the purpose of identifying the bodies of the Massachusetts soldiers killed in Baltimore. Several articles which were the property of the deceased were exhibited, but failing to identify the bodies by these, the company proceeded to the vault beneath King's Chapel, where the coffins were opened. The first corpse was at once recognized as Sumner H. Needham of Lawrence, by two of his brothers. The second was recognized as that of Addison O. Whitney of the Lowell City Guards, by three of his intimate friends. He was reported as among the missing when the regiment reached Washington. He died from a shot in the left breast. He was a spinner in the Middlesex Mills, and has a sister at Lowell. The third body proved to be that of Luther C. Ladd of Lowell, also of the Lowell City Guards. He had not been heard from since the fight, but a letter was received from his brother in the regiment at Washington stating that he was missing. The body was identified by a brother-in-law of Ladd. He was about eighteen years of age, a machinist, and was born at Alexandria, N. H. He was shot in the thigh, and probably bled to death at once. His face was somewhat swollen, and gave evidence of rough usage.—*Boston Traveller, May 3.*

—THE mouth of James River, and Hampton roads are under strict blockade. The blockading vessels are the frigate Cumberland, steamships Monticello and Yankee, and three or four steam tugs.—*The World, May 4.*

—ELLSWORTH'S Regiment of Fire Zouaves arrived at Washington. Their march through the city was a complete ovation. They were greeted with great cheering and other demonstrations of enthusiasm. The splendid appearance of the regiment, both as to numbers and

DIARY—9

equipments, caused great surprise, and elicited universal praise.—*N. Y. Tribune, May 3.*

—THE adjourned meeting of merchants to take into consideration the action necessary in regard to the state license, was held at Wheeling, Va. The Committee made a report setting forth the law in reference to the matter, submitted a resolve to the effect that we are good citizens of the State of Virginia, and at the same time hold ourselves loyal citizens of the United States, and will maintain allegiance to the same as heretofore; that we are willing to pay a license tax so long as Virginia is in the United States, but we are not willing to pay revenue to the present usurped government at Richmond, which, without the consent of the people of Virginia, has assumed to absolve us from allegiance to the United States, recommending the merchants of Wheeling and Ohio county to withhold the payment of taxes for the present. The resolutions were unanimously adopted. A German announced that the commissioner of the revenue resigned to forward the patriotic undertaking.—*The World, May 3.*

—JUDGE CAMPBELL of the United States Supreme Court, who resides in Alabama, sent in his resignation. He is a Unionist, but feels bound to adhere to the fortunes of his State.— *N. Y. Tribune, May 3.*

THE Marine Artillery of Rhode Island (flying artillery) arrived in Washington having a battery of six pieces, apparently perfect, like all we have thus far seen from that gallant little State, in every appointment of military art that can give efficiency to this most effective arm of modern warfare. The battery is served by about one hundred and sixty men, who are experienced cannoneers, and who, we learn, have left behind them an equal number, ready at a moment's notice to tender their services to the Government. The Rhode Island regiment of infantry, twelve hundred strong, appeared also in the streets on parade, attracting universal admiration for the military precision of their movements and the fine soldiery bearing of both officers and men.

The Artillery made a visit to the President of the United States about five o'clock in the afternoon. He received them in front of the mansion, and was complimented in return by three hearty cheers as they passed in review. —*National Intelligencer, May 3.*

—THE *New Orleans Picayune,* of to-day, says: "We heard but recently of a united North to defend and preserve the Union—now we hear of a united North to subjugate the South. The change is rapid. It shows the increasing strength of those whose permanent success would be destructive of liberty. These are the enemies the South has to combat. A Southern victory at Washington would not only strike terror into their ranks, but go far towards releasing the good and estimable people of the North from a thralldom which has become as terrible as it is degrading. We hope to have the pleasure, ere many days, of chronicling the glorious achievement."

—THE national flag was hoisted over the Interior Department at Washington. It was enthusiastically greeted by the dense mass of spectators and by the Rhode Island regiment, whose appearance and drill, together with their music, elicited general praise. They were accompanied by Governor Sprague and suite in full uniform.

The President and Secretaries Seward and Smith were near the staff when the flag was raised, and having saluted it, they were in turn cheered.

The regiment, having re-entered the building where they are quartered, sung "Our Flag still Waves."—*N. Y. Evening Post, May 3.*

—THE religious press presents a singular and varied view of the political affairs of the United States.—(*Doc.* 128.)

May 3.—The American flag was elevated above the roof of the University at New York, by Captain Jones, late of Harper's Ferry, amid the enthusiastic cheers of a large collection of people.

Dr. Bethune made some remarks, taking occasion to make a fitting allusion to Major Anderson and Fort Sumter, which were received with repeated and enthusiastic cheering. He had looked over ancient history for a parallel to this deed of valor, but found none. The bravery shown by the three hundred Spartans at the Pass of Thermopylæ was well known; but there still was one coward among them. There was no coward among the men at Sumter. He had been present at a conversation with the gallant defender of the fort, when a gentleman remarked he regretted that the major had not blown up the fort, to which Major Anderson replied that it was better as it was. The ruined battlements and battle-scarred walls of Fort Sumter would be an everlasting shame and disgrace to the South Carolinians. At the conclusion of Dr. Bethune's remarks the "Star-spangled Banner" was sung, all the audience rising to their feet and joining in the chorus. Col. Baker and Capt. Jones also made short addresses.—*The World, May* 4.

—GOVERNOR LETCHER published a proclamation, saying that the sovereignty of the Commonwealth of Virginia having been denied, her territorial rights assailed, her soil threatened with invasion by the authorities of Washington, and every artifice employed which could inflame the people of the Northern States against her, it therefore becomes the solemn duty of every citizen of Virginia to prepare for the impending conflict.

To this end, and for these purposes, and with a determination to repel invasion, Governor Letcher authorizes the Commanding General of the military forces to call out, and cause to be mustered into service from time to time, as the public exigencies may require, such additional number of volunteers as he may deem necessary.—(*Doc.* 129.)

—THE First Regiment, Colonel Johnson; the Second, Col. Baker; the Third, Col. Napton; the Fourth, Col. Miller, of New Jersey Troops, with Brigadier-General Runyon and staff, left Bordentown for the seat of war, proceeding down the Delaware, *via* the Delaware and Chesapeake canal. The troops and stores are in a fleet of fourteen steam propellers, the W. Woodward, Henry Cadwalader, Octorora, Delaware, Raritan, Trenton, Patroon, F. W. Brune, Elizabeth, Franklin, Farmer, J. B. Molleson, Eureka, and Fanny Gardner.—*World, May* 4.

—UNION Ward meetings were held to night throughout Baltimore, Md., and resolutions were adopted to the following purport:—

That we cherish the Constitution and laws of the United States, and will devote our fortunes and lives to defend their integrity against all revolutionary or violent assaults; that we regret the violent attacks on the troops of the United States while peacefully marching through the city to protect the seat of Government, and indignantly repudiate making it a pretext to organize an armed mob, under the guise of a special police, to place the city in a hostile attitude to the General Government; declaring abhorrence at the attempt of the Legislature to inaugurate a military despotism by the bill for the creation of a Board of Public Safety; that the persons named for said Board have not the confidence of the people, and we protest against the whole measure as an invasion on the prerogatives of the Governor and a usurpation of the Executive power by the Legislature.—*N. Y. Tribune, May* 4.

—THE following notice was issued at Pittsburg, Pa., to-day: Shippers of goods in New York are hereby notified that all packages found to contain guns, pistols, powder, and other articles contraband of war, destined for the Southern States, will not be permitted to pass the city of Pittsburg.

By order of the Committee,
E. D. Gazzani, Chairman.
—*N. Y. Tribune, May* 4.

—A LETTER was received at New York giving information of a design to burn that city, the supply of water to be cut off at the time the city was fired. Philadelphia and Boston were also to be burned.—(*Doc.* 130.)

—FOURTEEN companies of Kentuckians from the border counties tendered their services to the Secretary of War through Colonel T. V. Guthrie. Ten were accepted with orders to encamp on the Ohio side of the river.—*Boston Transcript, May* 4.

—THE Connecticut legislature unanimously passed a bill appropriating $2,000,000 for the organization and equipment of a volunteer militia, and to provide for the public defence.—*N. Y. Tribune, May* 4.

—GOVERNOR JACKSON of Missouri, in a message to the legislature of that State, says the President of the United States in calling out the troops to subdue the seceded States, has threatened civil war, and his act is unconstitutional and illegal, and tending towards consolidated despotism. While he evidently justifies the action of the Confederate States in seceding, he does not recommend immediate secession, but holds the following language:

"Our interest and sympathies are identical with those of the slaveholding States, and necessarily unite our destiny with theirs. The similarity of our social and political institutions, our industrial interests, our sympathies, habits, and tastes, our common origin, territorial contiguity, all concur in pointing out our duty in regard to the separation now taking place between the States of the old federal Union." He further adds that "Missouri has at this time no war to prosecute. It is not her policy to make an aggression; but, in the present state of the country, she would be faithless to her honor, recreant to her duty, were she to hesitate a moment in making the most ample preparation for the protection of her people against the aggression of all assailants. I therefore recommend an appropriation of a sufficient sum of money to place the State at the earliest practicable moment in a complete state of defence."

In conclusion he says: "Permit me to appeal to you and through you to the whole people of the State, to whom we are all responsible, to do nothing imprudent or precipitate. We have a most solemn duty to perform. Let us then calmly reason one with another, avoid all passion and tendency to tumult and disorder, obey implicitly the constituted authorities, and endeavor ultimately to unite all our citizens in a cordial coöperation for the preservation of our honor, the security of our property, and the performance of all those high duties imposed upon us by our obligations to our families, our country, and our God."—*Louisville Journal, May 4.*

—PRESIDENT LINCOLN issued a proclamation calling into the service of the United States 42,000 volunteers for three years' service, and directing the increase of the regular army and navy of the United States.—(*Doc.* 131.)

—FOUR companies of volunteers left Buffalo, N. Y., for the rendezvous at Elmira. They were escorted to the depot by the Home Guard. Major Millard Fillmore, Ex-President, commanding in person. The Home Guard is composed of retired commissioned officers of the State Militia, and is being thoroughly drilled by Major Fillmore. About 150 members are already enrolled.—*N. Y. Tribune, May 4.*

—TWO associations of ladies of New Orleans were formed for aiding and equipping volunteers, and for making lint and bandages, and nursing the sick and wounded. The meetings were very large and enthusiastic.—*Baltimore Sun, May 7th.*

May 4.—A large Union meeting was held at Kingwood, Preston county, Va., when resolutions were adopted expressing unalterable opposition to the ordinance of secession, favoring a division of the State, and resolving to vote for

a delegate to the next session of Congress.—*National Intelligencer, May 11.*

—COMMODORE CHARLES STEWART, of the United States Navy, addressed a letter to George W. Childs of Philadelphia, furnishing him with the reminiscences of a conversation which passed between Com. Stewart and John C. Calhoun, in the year 1812, after the declaration of war against Great Britain by the Congress of the United States.—(*Doc.* 132.)

—THE artists of New York met at the rooms of Messrs. Kensett and Lang in that city. Mr. D. Huntingdon was called to the chair. Messrs. Kensett, Gray, and Lang embodied resolutions which were adopted by those present, expressing their desire to contribute to the relief of families of volunteers of the city of New York who are now serving in defence of government and law, and resolving that a committee be appointed to solicit contributions of pictures or other works of art, to be disposed of at public auction; said committee to have power, also, to receive moneys presented in aid of the fund. Messrs. Gray, Lang, Hubbard, Huntington, Stone, and Baker were named the committee, with full power to forward the plan proposed. —*N. Y. Evening Post, May 7.*

—THE Ithaca (N. Y.) volunteers arrived in New York on their way to the seat of war. They number one hundred and fifteen men, and are commanded by the following officers:— Captain, Jerome Rowe; First Lieutenant, James Tischner; Ensign, William O. Wyckoff; Orderly Sergeant, William Godley; Second Sergeant, Edwin C. Fulkenson; Third do., Edward Atwater; Fourth do., Dr. Tolbo; First Corporal, Leonard Atwater; Second do., Clinton McGill; Third do., James A. Dickinson; Fourth do., George Shepherd.—*N. Y. Herald, May 5.*

—THE Onondaga Regiment left Syracuse, N. Y., for Elmira. This is the first regiment organized under the new Volunteer bill of the State of New York. Ten full companies presented their muster-rolls to the Adjutant-General, not merely full, but with an excess of nearly one hundred men.—*N. Y. Tribune, May 5.*

—THE *New Orleans Delta* of to-day contains a full account of the numbers and condition of the rebel troops and defences in the vicinity of Fort Pickens; from which it appears that Gen. Bragg has under his command an army of over six thousand fighting men, besides a large force of laborers, sailors, and marines.—(*Doc.* 133.)

—THE Buena Vista Volunteers, from Philadelphia, Captain Powers, arrived at New York. They are to join Col. D. E. Sickles's regiment. These are men who went unarmed to Baltimore, and fought the Gorillas with their fists.— *N. Y. Tribune, May 5.*

—THE Phœnix Ironworks at Gretna, opposite Lafayette, New Orleans, cast the first gun for the Confederate Navy. It is an eight-inch Dahlgren shell, and has eight feet six inches bore.

The steamship Star of the West was put in commission as the receiving ship of the Confederate States Navy at New Orleans. She is stationed at the navy yard at Algiers, under the temporary command of Midshipman Comstock, for receiving sailors and marines now being enlisted for the navy.—*N. O. Picayune, May 5.*

—A COMMITTEE of the Maryland Legislature held an interview with President Lincoln. They admitted both the right and the power of the government to bring troops through Baltimore or the State, and to take any measures for the public safety which, in the discretion of the President, might be demanded either by actual or reasonably apprehended exigencies. They expressed their belief that no immediate effort at secession or resistance of the federal authority would be attempted by the Legislature or State authorities, and asked that, in this view, the State should, as long as possible, be spared the evils of a military occupation or a mere revengeful chastisement for former transgressions.

The President replied that their suggestions and representations should be considered, but that he should now say no more than that the public interests, and not any spirit of revenge, would actuate his measures.—*N. Y. Herald, May 5.*

—A UNION meeting was held at Wheeling, Va., Hon. Frank Pierpont, of Mason county, and George M. Porter, late member of the convention, addressed the people in able speeches, urging resistance to the secession ordinance, and favoring the division of the State. Resolutions were adopted approving the action of the merchants in refusing to pay taxes to the authorities at Richmond, denunciatory of the secession ordinance, and declaring adhesion to the stars and stripes.—*Boston Transcript, May 6.*

DIARY—10

—THE American flag was displayed from the tower of the First Baptist Church in Broome street, New York, with appropriate ceremonies. A large concourse of people listened to stirring speeches by President Eaton, of Madison University, Rev. Dr. Armitage, Rev. Mr. Webber, of Rochester, and Hon. W. D. Murphy, of the Oliver street church.

Dr. Armitage referred to the fact that the pastors of this First Baptist Church (a church which has existed more than a century) had all been noted for their zealous patriotism. One of the most eminent of them—Spencer H. Cone—had, in the war of 1812, himself gallantly defended that emblem of civil and religious liberty, the stars and stripes, at Fort McHenry; and at this moment members of this church are in the camp, equally ready to defend it against all aggression. No free government or constitutional liberty have ever been secured or perpetuated by any nation without the seal of its own blood. If the liberties thus purchased for us by our fathers, and the government which they founded—the best the world has ever seen—are to be insulted and trampled upon, shall we not strike down the traitor, even though he be one of the family— even though he be our own brother?

"I too," said Dr. Eaton, "am emphatically a man of peace, for I am a minister of the gospel of the Prince of Peace; but in this crisis, my friends, it is my firm conviction that the best and surest way to perpetuate the blessing is promptly to send down, if need be, half a million of men to those seditious brethren of ours, and compel them to keep the peace. We cherish no malice against them—God forbid. But their traitorous hands are now clutching the very life of our body politic, and we must use prompt and vigorous action in defence of our very national existence."—*N. Y. Evening Post, May 7.*

May 5.—Raleigh, North Carolina, is alive with soldiers, who have been pouring in at the call of the Governor. Sixteen companies, comprising twelve hundred men, rank and file, are encamped at the Fair Grounds, and there are several more quartered in other parts of the city. They are all fine looking, and in their eagerness to acquire military knowledge frequently have voluntary drills, not being satisfied with the three regularly appointed ones for each day.

Ten companies have been selected by the Governor to constitute the " First Regiment of North Carolina Volunteers," and an election of field officers has taken place, resulting in the selection of D. H. Hill, C. C. Lee, and J. H. Lane, respectively, to the offices of Colonel, Lieutenant-Colonel, and Major.—*Charleston Mercury, May* 11.

—THE Twenty-eighth New York Regiment (from Brooklyn) arrived at Washington by the steamer Star of the South. In the absence of Col. Bennett, detained at home by sickness, Lieut.-Col. E. Burns is in command. The other officers are Acting Lieut.-Col. W. R. Brewster; Adjutant, D. A. Bokee; Surgeon, P. B. Rice; Surgeon's Mates, Drs. Rappold and Prentice; Captain of Engineer Corps, Von Kumeke; Quartermaster, F. Steigier; Assistant Quartermaster, C. Menseh; Acting Paymaster, W. Mavelle; Chaplain, Mr. Zapt. They number about six hundred men, divided into ten companies, commanded by Captains Brewer, Baker, Campbell, Brandenberry, Beadle, Seeper, Ruegor, Wills, Kuhl, and Weaver. —*National Intelligencer, May* 7.

—BRIGADIER-GENERAL PHILIP ST. GEORGE COCKE commanding the "Potomac Department " of the State of Virginia, in orders issued to-day, says:

" The capital of the United States has never been threatened, and it is not now threatened. It is beyond and outside the limits of the free and sovereign State of Virginia."

If Gen. Cocke means to say that the " capital of the United States " has never been threatened *by him*, all credence will be given to his declarations under this head; but if it is intended to suggest that there have been no threats of attack from other quarters, sufficient to justify the precautionary measures taken by the Federal Government, his assurances cannot be received without casting discredit on men high in the confidence of the Confederate States, and on able and influential journals, heretofore understood to be the authentic exponents of Southern wishes and purposes.—(*Doc.* 134.)

—A BODY of Federal troops, under command of Gen. B. F. Butler, arrived at the Relay House, nine miles from Baltimore, took possession of the telegraph wires, planted eight howitzers on the viaduct, and invested the entire neighborhood. They encamped on the grounds of William Talbot, adjoining those of George W. Dobbin, on the west side of the Patapsco. This point is the junction of the Baltimore and Ohio road, and the Washington branch, and gives full command of the road to and from the West.—*The World, May* 6.

—THE women of Mobile organized themselves into a society to make sand bags for defence, lint and bandages for the wounded, clothes for the soldiers of the Confederate Army, to nurse the sick and wounded, and to seek out the families of those volunteers upon whose exertions their families are dependent for daily support.—*N. O. Picayune, May* 5.

May 6.—GOVERNOR HICKS, in response to an order of the Maryland Senate, inquiring if he consented to or authorized the burning of the bridges on the Northern Central, and the Baltimore, Wilmington, and Philadelphia railroad, said : " I have to say that I neither authorized nor consented to the destruction of said bridges, but left the whole matter in the hands of the Mayor of the city of Baltimore, with the declaration that I had no authority in the premises; that I was a lover of law and order, and could not participate in such proceedings."— *National Intelligencer, May* 10.

—THE six regiments demanded by the Federal Government of Indiana were raised and mustered into service and ready to march in a week after the call was made. They are now in camp, drilling daily, and living the regular soldier life. They would have been on the way to the post assigned them long ago if they had been armed. But up to this time, though the guns have come, the accoutrements are still behind.—*Indiana State Journal, May* 7.

—VIRGINIA was admitted into the Southern Confederacy in Secret Session of the Confederate Congress.—*N. Y. Times, May* 14.

—THE COMMITTEE appointed by the General Assembly of Maryland to visit President Lincoln and present him with a copy of the joint resolutions adopted by that body on the 2d of May, presented their report.—(*Doc.* 135.)

—THE town of Dorchester, Mass., voted $20,000 for the war, besides appropriating $20 per month to every married volunteer, and $15 to every single volunteer. This applies not only to citizens of Dorchester who enlist in the town or out, but to citizens of other towns who may enlist in Dorchester, provided their

MAJ. GEN. JOHN A. DIX, U.S.A.

From Photograph in possession of his family

NEW YORK, G.P. PUTNAM.

Entered according to act of Congress A.D. 1861 by G.P.Putnam, in the clerks office of the district court for the southern district of N.Y.

own towns do not make any provision for them.—*N. Y. Express, May 9.*

—GENERAL JOHN A. DIX, late Secretary of the Treasury, was appointed one of the four major-generals from the State of New York. General Dix is a native of New Hampshire, and is a son of the late Lieut.-Colonel Timothy Dix. He entered the United States Military Academy at West Point in 1812; was promoted ensign in 1814, and was subsequently promoted to a third lieutenancy in the twenty-first regiment of infantry. His subsequent rank of promotion is as follows:

Second lieutenant, March, 1814; transferred August 14, 1814, to artillery arm; returned same year in the re-organization of the army; adjutant, 1816; first lieutenant, March 18; aide-de-camp to Major-General Brown, 1816; transferred to First artillery, May, 1821; Third artillery, August, 1821; captain, August 25; resigned his commission in the army, December 31, 1828. He afterward filled the post of Adjutant-General of the State of New York, Secretary of State, and United States Senator from January, 1845 to 1849; Postmaster of New York in 1860–61; and was called to the post of Secretary of the Treasury, under James Buchanan, January 11, 1861.—*Commercial Advertiser, May 7.*

—THE First, Second, and Third regiments of New Jersey State Militia arrived at Washington. They constitute, with the Fourth, previously arrived, a brigade of 3,200 men, under the command of Gen. Theodore Runyon. His staff consists of Capt. J. B. Mulligan, Aid; Brigade-Major, A. V. Bonnell; Private Secretary and Special aid, C. W. Tollis.—*(Doc. 136.)*

—THE Arkansas Convention, by a vote of sixty-nine to one, passed an ordinance of secession from the Federal Union. The ordinance was unanimously ratified by the State.—*N. O. Picayune, May 7.*

—THE correspondence between Mr. Faulkner, late American Minister at Paris, and Secretary Seward, in relation to the recognition of the Southern Confederacy by the government of France, is published.—*(Doc. 137.)*

—THE *Washington Star* of this morning, speaking of the intended attack on Washington by the secessionists, says, "The scheme of the oligarchy was to have attacked this city sometime between daybreak of the 18th and day-

break of the 21st of April ultimo. They had been led to believe that the Virginia ordinance of secession would have been pushed through the Convention a few days before that was accomplished, (on the 17th,) and that the troops of that State would have been able to take Washington by surprise between the dates we have named above. The secret outside Convention that was assembled by the disunion Convention in Richmond on the 17th ultimo, was called to aid the scheme, and the raid on Harper's Ferry was to the end of aiding it also. That was contrived and carried out wholly by disunion revolutionary means; the Governor (Letcher) having declined to order it, or the raid on the Government property (the Navy Yard, &c.) in and near Norfolk. John Bell was doubtless in the conspiracy, we apprehend, as his change of front took place just in time to admit of his getting on what he foolishly supposed would be the winning side. The resignation of the large number of army and navy officers between the 18th and 21st of April, in a body, was doubtless also planned to embarrass the Government just previous to the contemplated attack upon the Federal Metropolis. The conspirators had no idea that the Government would prove more prompt and efficient in their measures of defence, than they in theirs of attack."

—PRESIDENT LINCOLN's letter to Governor Hicks of Maryland and Mayor Brown of Baltimore, dated on the day after the attack upon the Massachusetts troops, (April 19,) is published in full in the newspapers of to-day.—*(Doc. 138.)*

—THE Police Commissioners of St. Louis, Mo., formally demanded of Capt. LYON, the officer in command at the Arsenal, the removal of United States troops from all places and buildings occupied by them outside the Arsenal grounds. The Captain, as was doubtless expected, declined compliance with the demand, and the Commissioners have referred the matter to the Governor and Legislature. The Commissioners allege that such occupancy is in derogation of the Constitution and laws of the United States, and in rejoinder Capt. LYON replies, inquiring what provisions of the Constitution and laws were thus violated. The Commissioners, in support of their position, say that originally "Missouri had sovereign and exclusive jurisdiction over her whole territory," and had delegated a portion of her sovereignty to the

United States over certain tracts of land for military purposes, such as arsenals, parks, &c., and the conclusion implied, but not stated, is, that this is the extreme limit of the right of the United States Government to occupy or touch the soil of the sovereign State of Missouri.—*St. Louis Democrat, May* 7.

—AN important interview took place at Camp Defiance, Cairo, Ill., between Colonel Tilghman, commander of the Kentucky forces, and Colonel Prentiss in command at Cairo.—(*Doc.* 139.)

—THE act recognizing the existence of war between the United States and the seceding States, and concerning letters of marque prizes and prize goods, which had passed the Southern congress at Montgomery, was made public, the injunction of secrecy having been removed therefrom.—(*Doc.* 140.)

—A MEETING of the principal shipowners and commercial men of Maine was held at Augusta. It was summoned by Governor Washburn to take into consideration the state of the country, and the expediency of procuring a guard for the coast. Resolutions were adopted tendering the services of the shipowners to the Government, and pledging their ability to furnish thirty steam vessels within from 60 to 90 days, if required. George F. Patten, of Bath, John B. Brown, of Portland, and George W. Lawrence, of Warren, were appointed a committee to proceed to Washington and communicate to the Government the views of the merchants and shopkeepers of the State, and to urge the most vigorous action in the premises. The meeting embraced the leading shipowners of all parties, and the sentiment in favor of executing the laws was not only unanimous, but enthusiastic.—*Boston Transcript, May* 8.

May 7.—A serious riot occurred at Knoxville, Tenn., caused by hoisting a Union flag and the delivery of inflammatory speeches. About twenty shots were fired in all. A man named Douglas, a ringleader in the fight, was wounded, having received several shots. An outsider, named Bull, was mortally wounded.—*National Intelligencer, May* 11.

—JUDGE OGDEN of the County Court of Oyer and Terminer of Hudson County, N. J., delivered a charge to the Grand Jury, in which he defined the crime of treason as giving aid, comfort, and information to the enemy.

The Massachusetts First Regiment, which has been for several days at Boston waiting marching orders, on learning that the War Department would hereafter accept no troops for a less period than three years, unanimously offered their services to the Governor for the full term.

The New Jersey House of Assembly ordered to a third reading the bill to raise a war loan of $1,000,000. Resolutions of thanks to Governor Olden for his activity in raising troops, to President Lincoln for his energetic defence of the Union, and pledging New Jersey to stand by the Union with all her power, were introduced into the Senate by a democrat, and passed by a unanimous vote.—*N. Y. Tribune, May* 8.

—THE contributions of the people of the North for the war, during the last three weeks amount to the sum of $23,277,000. Pennsylvania leads the column with a free gift of $3,500,000. New York and Ohio have each given $3,000,000; Connecticut and Illinois each $2,000,000; Maine, $1,300,000; Vermont and New Jersey, each $1,000,000; Wisconsin and Rhode Island, $500,000; Iowa, $100,000. The contributions of the principal cities are: New York, $2,173,000; Philadelphia, $330,000; Boston, $186,000; Brooklyn, $75,000; Buffalo, $110,000; Cincinnati, $280,000; Detroit, $50,000; Hartford, $64,000.—(*Doc.* 141.)

—THE Twentieth Regiment of N. Y. S. M. from Ulster County, under the command of Colonel George W. Pratt, left New York for the seat of war.—(*Doc.* 142.)

—REVERDY JOHNSON addressed the Home Guard of Frederick, Md., upon the occasion of the presentation to them of a National flag from the ladies of that place. The population of the city was swelled by the addition of upwards of two thousand persons, who poured in from the surrounding towns and villages, sometimes in lengthy cavalcades of horses and vehicles, and again in companies of tens and fifties. Union cockades and badges were displayed in profusion upon the coats of the jubilant Union men, numbers of whom were decidedly ambitious in their ideas of patriotic personal adornment, wearing cockades as large as sun-flowers. The Stars and Stripes fluttered gaily from about forty different points, and, altogether, Frederick may be said to have donned her holiday suit for the occasion.

The scene of the presentation formalities was

the Court-house yard, where a stand, draped with the national colors, had been erected, and at the hour designated for the commencement of the ceremonies, was surrounded by two or three thousand persons, including the Brengle Guard, a body of about three hundred respectable citizens, principally aged and middle-aged men, organized for the purpose of home protection and defence.—(*Doc.* 143.)

—FOUR hundred Pennsylvania volunteers, escorted by three hundred regular United States troops from Carlisle barracks, arrived at Washington at 10 o'clock, on the evening of Thursday, April 18th, and bivouacked at the capitol.—*N. Y. Times, April* 19.

—ISHAM G. HARRIS, Governor, sent a message to the General Assembly of Tennessee, announcing the formation of a military league between that State and the Confederate States; submitting the plan of the league, the joint resolution ratifying it, and a "declaration of independence and ordinance dissolving the Federal relations between the State of Tennessee and the United States of America."—(*Doc.* 144.)

May 8.—The Salem, Mass., Zouaves arrived at Washington. They number 66 men, and are officered as follows: Captain, A. F. Devereux; 1st Lieutenant, G. F. Austin; 2d Lieutenant, E. A. P. Brewster; 3d Lieutenant, G. D. Putnam. They are armed with the Minié musket, and uniformed in dark blue jackets and pants, trimmed with scarlet braid, and red fatigue caps.—*National Intelligencer, May* 11.

—A PRIVATEER was captured at the mouth of the Chesapeake, by the steamer Harriet Lane. The officers and crew, with the exception of two seamen, escaped.—*Philadelphia Press, May* 9.

—THE *Richmond Examiner* of to-day demands a Dictator; it says: "No power in executive hands can be too great, no discretion too absolute, at such moments as these. *We need a Dictator.* Let lawyers talk when the world has time to hear them. Now let the sword do its work. *Usurpations of power by the chief,* for the preservation of the people from robbers and murderers, *will be reckoned as genius and patriotism by all sensible men in the world now,* and by every historian that will judge the deed hereafter."

—THE Fourth Pennsylvania Regiment from the county of Montgomery, arrived at Washington from Annapolis. It is commanded by the following officers:

Colonel, John F. Hartranft; Lieut. Col., Edward Schall; Major, Edwin Schall; Adjutant, Chas. Hunsicker; Quartermaster, Yerkes; Surgeon, Dunlop; Assistant-Surgeons, Christ and Rogers; Captains, Bolton, Schall, Chamberlain, Dunn, Snyder, Allabaugh, Amey, Brooke, Cooke, and Taylor.

The regiment numbers about 900, and comprises a fine body of hardy yeomanry and artisans, who left their fields and shops to rally in defence of the National Capital.—*National Intelligencer, May* 9.

—THE steam frigate Minnesota, the flag-ship of the blockading squadron, sailed from Boston, Mass.—*Boston Transcript, May* 8.

—A MEETING in aid of the volunteers from Roxbury, Mass., was held in that city. Speeches were made by Rev. J. E. Bartholomew, Edward Everett, and Alexander H. Rice.—(*Doc.* 145.)

—GENERAL BUTLER, at the Relay House, Md., promulgated special brigade orders concerning the several events that have occurred at the camp at that place since its formation.—(*Doc.* 146.)

May 9.—At 3 o'clock this afternoon the steamer Maryland, with other transports, arrived at Baltimore with 1,300 troops from Perryville. They consist of five companies of the 3d Infantry, regulars, Major Shepherd, 420 men; one company of Sherman's Battery of Light Artillery, with 6 pieces of cannon and 70 horses, under Major Sherman; and the 1st Regiment, ten companies, of Pennsylvania Artillery, Col. Patterson, armed with muskets, and numbering 800 men. They were landed at Locust Point, one of the termini of the Baltimore and Ohio Railroad, within half a mile of Fort McHenry, and there transferred on board of two trains of cars, which departed immediately.

Two hundred men were left to take charge of the horses, provisions and baggage, and these were to be forwarded at a later hour. The Mayor and Police Commissioners, with two hundred police, crossed in a ferry-boat to Locust Point, and were present at the debarkation.

The Harriet Lane stood off the point with her ports open. The transfer to the cars was accomplished without much difficulty, and there was no excitement other than that which proceeded from the curiosity of the people to witness the proceedings.

The track from Locust Point skirts the lower part of the city, and joins the main stem near Camden Station.—*N. Y. Tribune, May* 10.

—THE *Richmond Whig* says: "We beg to suggest to all Southern papers the propriety of omitting all mention of the movement of troops within our borders. A word to the wise."

"The caution is a good one, and might well be extended to correspondents, both private and public, by telegraph and by mail. The caution is the more necessary, because of our large daily correspondence with the people of the North, with whom we are unfortunately at war."—*N. O. Picayune, May* 10.

—THE Confederate Congress passed an act authorizing the President of the Southern Confederacy to raise such a force for the war as he may deem expedient.—(*Doc.* 147.)

—THE PALMETTO GUARD left Charleston, S. C., for Virginia. The company numbers eighty-five privates, and is commanded as follows:

Geo. B. Cuthbert, Captain; C. R. Holmes, First Lieutenant; T. S. Brownfield, Second Lieutenant; L. S. Webb, Third Lieutenant; Samuel Robinson, First Sergeant; J. E. Wright, Second Sergeant; G. M. LaLane, Third Sergeant; H. D. Hanahan, Fourth Sergeant; M. J. Darly, Fifth Sergeant; J. B. Boyd, First Corporal; J. E. Gaillard, Second Corporal; A. M. Brailsford, Third Corporal; DeSaussure Edwards, Fourth Corporal; J. E. Dutart, Fifth Corporal; E. W. Bellinger, Sixth Corporal; O. D. Mathews, Quartermaster; R. S. Miller, jr., Commissary.—*Charleston Mercury, May* 10.

—THE Cumberland, Pawnee, Monticello, and Yankee are enforcing the blockade off Fortress Monroe. The Yankee pursued an armed schooner up York River, but after proceeding a short distance was fired upon from a concealed battery, and compelled to return.

The steamers Philadelphia, Baltimore, Powhattan, and Mount Vernon, of the Acquia Creek line, recently taken possession of by the Federal Government, are cruising on the Potomac, all heavily armed. Southern troops are concentrating in the vicinity of Norfolk. An Alabama regiment of 1,100 men, and eighty cadets of the same State, have arrived, and encamped in the vicinity of Fort Norfolk.

The Virginians have five batteries erected in Norfolk harbor; one on Craney Island; one at Sandy Point; one at the Hospital; one near Fort Norfolk, and one on the Bluffs three miles from the Hospital.—*N. Y. Evening Post, May* 11.

—J. LAWRENCE KEESE, a private in the 8th Company of the 7th Regiment of New York, was accidentally shot at Washington. He was standing in front of his tent washing his hands, when a musket fell from a stack of arms within a few feet of him, and went off, the ball entering his side, passing through his lungs, and killing him almost instantly. He was a young man of fine talents, and greatly esteemed by his comrades.—*N. Y. Commercial, May* 10.

—TO-DAY was strictly observed as a fast-day at Wheeling, Va. Patriotic sermons were delivered in nine out of the twelve churches. The Methodist Church pulpit was decorated with the Stars and Stripes. Rev. Mr. Smith delivered an eloquent address. He said he would hold no fellowship with traitors. If there was a secessionist in his congregation he wanted him to leave. Other ministers prayed that the rebels might be subdued or wiped from the face of the earth.—*N. Y. Herald, May* 10.

—THE steamship Africa arrived at New York from England, bringing the first news of the impression produced in Europe by the reduction of Fort Sumter. The earliest feeling was one of the profoundest gloom and discouragement, but subsequent reflection suggested a probability, eagerly accepted, that hostilities would terminate with the opening act; and that, startled by the shock of arms, the Government and the separated States would have fresh dispositions for an amicable arrangement. The notion, founded on the fact that no lives had been lost, also became current; that the affair was merely a sham fight, arranged entirely to cover the evacuation from discredit, and save the reputation of Major Anderson. These ideas were indorsed generally by the journals, who, however, regarded the business as extremely enigmatic, and as needing further enlightenment before final judgment could be passed.—(*Doc.* 148.)

—Two companies of Southern volunteers from Baltimore, numbering sixty-five men,

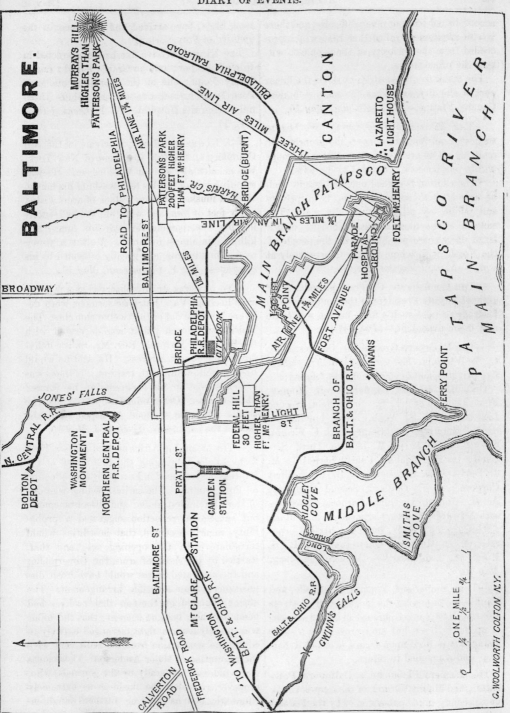

For the use of this map we are indebted to the proprietors of the *N. Y. Tribune.*

passed through Frederick, Md., on their way to Virginia. They were under the command of Capts. Wetmore and Price, and unarmed. They marched through the city protected by Gen. Shriver and the sheriff, and their appearance created deep excitement, but no outbreak. A company of about thirty-four volunteers left Frederick early this morning for Harper's Ferry, under the command of Captain Bradley T. Johnson.—*National Intelligencer, May* 11.

—THE First Regiment of Connecticut Volunteers left New Haven this morning for the seat of war.—*N. Y. Tribune, May* 10.

May 10.—The Confederate Secretary of War invested R. E. Lee with the control of the rebel forces of Va., by the following order:

MONTGOMERY, May 10, 1861.
To Major-Gen. R. E. Lee:

To prevent confusion, you will assume the control of the forces of the Confederate States in Virginia, and assign them to such duties as you may indicate, until further orders; for which this will be your authority.

I. P. WALKER, Secretary of War.
—*National Intelligencer, May* 15.

—THE Charleston *News* of this day contains the prayer of the Rev. James Bardwell, at the opening of the Tennessee Legislature on the 25th of April.—(*Doc.* 149.)

—IN addition to the new Military Departments of Washington, Annapolis, and Pennsylvania, the States of Ohio, Indiana, and Illinois will constitute a fourth, subdivided into several others, to be called the Department of the Ohio. Major-General McClellan, Ohio Volunteers, is assigned to its command; headquarters, Cincinnati.

The President, by general orders, directs that all officers of the army, except those who have entered service since 1st April, take and subscribe anew the oath of allegiance to the United States, as set forth in the 10th article of war.—*N. Y. Evening Post, May* 11.

—THE First Regiment of Vermont Volunteers, commanded by Colonel J. Wolcott Phelps, arrived at New York, and took up their quarters in the Park Barracks. This regiment consists of ten companies—77 men each—of hardy Green Mountain boys, whose stalwart frames and broad shoulders are the envy of all beholders. These ten companies were selected from

four different regiments. The uniform of the regiment is of gray cloth, each man being supplied with a heavy overcoat of the same material. One or two companies have a blue uniform instead of the gray. Each man wears a hemlock sprig in his hat. They are all supplied with new Minié muskets, but have no ammunition.

The men are nearly all Vermonters, there being scarcely a dozen foreigners in the regiment. They are all esteemed citizens at home, and nearly every one abandoned a profitable business to give his strong arm to his country. They have been encamped at Rutland, Vt., for the past eight days, completing their outfit, and when they came to strike their tents and take up the line of march, not a man was on the sick list. Their destination is Fort Monroe.

The character of the Green Mountain boys may be illustrated by the following incident: As the cars were leaving their camp-ground in Rutland, on the morning of the 9th instant, a private, in response to the cheers of the people, said: "The Vermont Regiment, citizens in peace, soldiers in war, give you the sentiment embodied in the charge of the Grecian matron to her son—*We will bring back our shields or be brought back upon them.*"—(*Doc.* 150.)

—THE Protestant Episcopal Diocese of Alabama adopted the following ordinance:

"Whereas, the Constitution of the Diocese of Alabama was adopted when the said Diocese actually was, on the presumption of its continuing to be, a part of the 'Protestant Episcopal Church in the United States;'

"And whereas, the State of Alabama is no longer a part of the United States:

"Therefore, it is hereby declared by this convention that the first article of the constitution of the Diocese, with all those canons, or portion of canons, dependent upon it, are null and void.

"It is furthermore declared that all canons, or portions of canons, both diocesan and general, not necessarily dependent upon the recognition of the authority of the Church in the United States, are hereby retained in force.

"This declaration is not to be construed as affecting faith, doctrine or communion."—*N. O. Picayune, May* 12.

—PRESIDENT LINCOLN issued a proclamation directing the commander of the forces of the United States on the Florida coast to permit no person to exercise any office or authority upon the islands of Key West, the Tortugas, and

Santa Rosa, which may be inconsistent with the laws and Constitution of the United States, authorizing him at the same time, if he shall find it necessary, to suspend there the writ of habeas corpus, and to remove from the vicinity of the United States fortresses all dangerous or suspected persons.—(*Doc.* 151.)

—CAPTAIN TYLER, of the Second Dragoons, commanding at Fort Kearney, fearing that a mob might take and turn against the garrison the ten twelve-pounder howitzers in his possession, spiked them. He had received orders to remove the pieces to Fort Leavenworth, but thought it unsafe to do so in the distracted state of the country. Threats had been made to take them from him.—*N. Y. Sun, May* 14.

—THE Second Regiment of Connecticut Volunteers, Colonel Terry, embarked from New Haven for Washington on the steamer Cahawba. They marched down Chapel street, escorted by a large body of citizens, cavalry, a body of old New Haven Grays, and by the Emmet Guard—making a very fine appearance. The whole city was alive with people, and the route of the procession was a grand array of flags.—*N. Y. Evening Post, May* 11.

—THE *London News* publishes an interesting article on the difficulties in the United States, and endeavors to indicate the position which the States under Jefferson Davis now occupy with relation to those under President Lincoln, and the status which both portions of the country now hold with relation to Great Britain and the rest of the world.—(*Doc.* 152.)

—THE steamer Pembroke sailed from Boston, Mass., for Fort Monroe, with reinforcements, including Capt. Tyler's Boston Volunteers, and a company from Lynn, under Capt. Chamberlain.—*N. Y. World, May* 11.

—THE Winans steam-gun was captured this morning. A wagon, containing a suspicious-looking box and three men, was observed going out on the Frederick road from Baltimore, and the fact being communicated to General Butler, at the Relay House, he despatched a scouting party in pursuit, who overtook the wagon six miles beyond the Relay House, at Ilchester. On examination it was found that the box contained the steam-gun. It was being taken to Harper's Ferry. The soldiers brought the gun and the three men back to the Relay House. The prisoners, one of whom was Dickenson, the

inventor of the gun, were sent to Annapolis.—*Baltimore American, May* 11.

—THE Diocesan Convention of Massachusetts passed resolutions in regard to the present state of affairs. One of them is as follows:—

Resolved, That the convention of clerical and lay delegates of the Protestant Episcopal Church in the diocese of Massachusetts do hereby express their heartfelt sympathy with the National Government in all right efforts to vindicate the authority of the Federal Union against " all sedition, privy conspiracy, and rebellion."— *Boston Advertiser, May* 11.

—THE Maryland Legislature passed a resolution, imploring the President of the United States to cease the present war.—(*Doc.* 153.)

—AT about 2 P. M., a sudden movement was made by the U. S. forces in St. Louis under Capt. Lyon, upon Camp Jackson, near that city, by which the camp was entirely surrounded in less than half an hour, and compelled to an unconditional surrender. A great mob followed the U. S. troops to the camp, and began a noisy demonstration against them, and to throw stones. One company received the order to fire, and did so. Twenty-two persons were killed, and many were wounded. The mob then dispersed. A large quantity of arms and munitions were taken in the camp, together with 639 prisoners.—(*Doc.* 154.)

May 11.—A great Union demonstration took place in San Francisco, Cal. Nothing like it was ever seen there before. Business was totally suspended; all the men, women and children of the city were in the streets, and flags waved everywhere. Three stands for speakers were erected, and Senator Latham and McDougall, General Sumner, General Shields, and others addressed vast audiences. The spirit of all the addresses, as well as of the resolutions adopted, was: the Administration must be sustained in all its efforts to put down secession and preserve the Union complete.

A procession marched through the principal streets, composed of thousands of men on horseback, in carriages and on foot, and embracing all the military and civic organizations of the city. All political parties joined in the demonstration.—*Alta Californian, May* 12.

—THE *Savannah Republican* of to-day says: " we have conversed with a gentleman who has just returned from the camp at Pensacola and brings the latest intelligence.

As details are not to be expected, we may state generally that the condition of the troops and fortifications is all that could be desired. Gen. Bragg has proved the very man for the work, and the volunteers lend a ready hand to carry out every order. Pickens is covered by our batteries on three sides. There are eight between the Navy-Yard and Fort Barrancas, four between the latter and the light-house, and a formidable mortar battery in the rear of Fort McRae. There is also a heavy mortar battery in the rear of Barrancas. All these works have been erected by the hands of the volunteers, and are armed with the very heaviest and best of artillery. The channel on a line between McRae and Pickens has been obstructed by sinking a number of small vessels. It was supposed that every thing would be complete by the middle of the coming week, after which we shall have a bombardment that will be worthy of record. Pickens must fall, and the more men they put in it the greater will be the destruction. Besides Pickens, the enemy have thrown up a battery on the island some five miles from the fort, which they are now engaged in arming for the struggle. Some hundred or more horses can be seen on the island, and seven ships of war and transports are lying off, something less than a mile from the shore."

—THE Fifth Regiment of N. Y. V. M. arrived at Washington from Annapolis, Md.—*National Intelligencer, May 13.*

—A LARGE meeting took place at Wheeling, Va. Hon. John S. Carlile and Frank Pierpont spoke. Mr. Carlile took ground in favor of separation from Eastern Virginia, and was rapturously applauded. He proclaimed that while there should be no coercion to go out, there should be none to prevent remaining in the Union. Virginia, he said, owed forty-nine millions of dollars; a debt incurred without benefit to Western Virginia; and he demanded to know by what right the citizens of this section should not be allowed to have an opinion of their own expressed and recognized in the State councils, when the question of allegiance was discussed. Allegiance was first due to the Federal Government if there was no interference with State rights.—*N. Y. Times, May 12.*

—THE First Regiment of Pennsylvania Infantry, under command of Colonel Lewis, arrived at Washington.—*N. Y. Tribune, May 12.*

—THIS afternoon, a large body of the Home Guards entered St. Louis, Mo., through Fifth street, from the Arsenal, where they had been enlisted during the day, and furnished with arms. On reaching Walnut street, the troops turned westward, a large crowd lining the pavement to witness their progress. At the corner of Fifth street the spectators began hooting, hissing, and otherwise abusing the companies as they passed, and a boy about fourteen years old discharged a pistol into their ranks. Part of the rear company immediately turned and fired upon the crowd, and the whole column was instantly in confusion, breaking their ranks, and discharging their muskets down their own line and among the people on the sidewalks. The shower of balls for a few minutes was terrible. Seven persons were killed, and a large number wounded. To allay the excitement and restore confidence to the people, Gen. Harney issued a proclamation to the people of St. Louis and the State, which was posted throughout the city, expressing deep regret at the state of things existing, pledging himself to do all in his power to preserve peace, and calling on the people and public authorities to aid him in the discharge of his duties. He says the military force under his command will only be used at the last extremity, and hopes he will not be compelled to resort to martial law, but simply states that the public peace must be preserved, and the lives of the people protected. He says he has no authority to change the location of the Home Guard quarters in the city, but to avoid all cause of circulation of the excitement, if called upon to aid the local authorities, will use the regular army in preference. In accordance with this proclamation, a battalion of regulars was sent to the city and placed under the direction of the Police Commissioners to act as a military police corps.— *N. Y. Times, May 13.*

—THE United States Steam Frigate Niagara arrived off the bar of Charleston, S. C., and began the blockade of that port.—(*Doc. 155.*)

—SIX companies of volunteers left Buffalo, N. Y., for the rendezvous at Elmira. Buffalo has so far sent to camp ten companies of volunteers. The Third Company of the Broome Co. N. Y. Volunteers, under command of Captain Peter Jay, took their departure from Binghamton, N. Y., for Elmira. They were addressed by the Hon. Daniel S. Dickinson, Tracy R. Morgan, and others. They vowed to stand by the Constitution and the Union as long as one star remained.—*N. Y. Times*, May 12.

—SCHOONER G. M. Smith, prize to the frigate Cumberland, arrived at New York in charge of prize-master Thos. Chisholm.—*Idem.*

May 12.—The Boston Rifle Company, numbering seventy-two men, now at Washington, is armed with the Whitney rifle and sabre bayonet, and is a reliable body of soldiers. The officers are: Capt., A. Dodd; First Lieut., C. Dodd; Second Lieut., C. G. Atwood; Third Lieut., G. A. Hicks; Fourth Lieut., J. Nason. The uniform is light blue pants, red shirt, dark gray overcoat, and fatigue cap.—*National Intelligencer, May 13.*

—GENERAL WM. S. HARNEY, commanding the military department of the West, at St. Louis, Mo., issued a proclamation declaring that the public peace *must be preserved*, and asking the people to return to their avocations, abstain from the excitement of heated discussions, and observe the laws of the local authorities.—(*Doc.* 156.)

—AN attempt was made at night to destroy the Monocacy Bridge, three miles from Frederick, Md., by a party from Point of Rocks. They cut the wires in the telegraph office, and threatened to kill the operator if he resisted. They then went to the bridge, but could not set fire to it, as it is all iron and stone.—*N. Y. Times, May 15.*

—THERE was a grand review at York, Penn., to-day. The Governor and many members of the Legislature were present. There were five regiments on the ground.

An attempt was made to tear up the track of the Northern Central Railroad, fourteen miles North of Baltimore. It was detected before much injury was done.—*N. Y. Times, May 13.*

—THE Connecticut Regiment, under the command of Colonel Alfred H. Terry, arrived at Washington.—(*Doc.* 157.)

—THE *New Orleans Picayune* of to-day says: "Books were opened yesterday at the Merchants' Exchange for subscriptions to stock in a propeller steamer to be fitted out as a privateer. Fifty thousand dollars have already been subscribed, and fifty thousand more are required. A fine chance is now presented to our enterprising citizens to embark in a venture which

cannot fail of yielding a handsome profit. The books will continue open in the back room of the Exchange, up stairs, until all the stock is taken."

—THE apportionment of the President's call for seventy-five regiments for three years was published.—(*Doc.* 158.)

May 13.—The Southern Baptist Convention, in session at Savannah, Ga., adopted a report of their committee on the state of the country, in which they hold "that the States once combined on this continent can no longer live together as one confederacy;" that the movement of Northern soldiers to sustain the Government is "an invasion designed to destroy whatever is dear in the heroic traditions of the South." They tender to the government at Montgomery their sympathy and confidence, and recommend the churches of the South to observe the first and second days of June as days of fasting, humiliation, and prayer. This report borrows additional interest from the fact that it comes from the pen of Dr. Richard Fuller of Baltimore, who made himself conspicuous, three or four weeks ago, as a member of that committee of young Christians who waited upon Mr. Lincoln to request that the Government of the United States would reconsider its order for the troops needed at Washington to come through Maryland.—(*Doc.* 159.)

—A UNION meeting was held in Martinsburgh, Berkeley county, Va. The gathering was large, and the greatest enthusiasm prevailed. Strong resolutions were adopted, and a protest entered against the warlike attitude which Virginia had assumed in opposition to the General Government. Eastern Virginia is not, as has been represented, unanimous for secession.—*Newark (N. J.) Advertiser, May 22.*

—SIX hundred troops from Georgia and Alabama arrived at Pensacola, the advance guard of 2,000 ordered there by General Bragg.—*Mobile Advertiser, May 15.*

—A PORTION of the Federal troops lately stationed at the Relay House on the Baltimore and Ohio Railroad, entered Baltimore. They arrived at the Camden station at seven and a half o'clock in the evening, disembarked in good order, and marched from the dépôt, piloted by Col. Hare and Capt. McConnell, down Lee street to Hanover, and thence to Montgomery, to Light, to Hamburgh, to Federal Hill, and, moving to the high ground surrounding the Observatory, stacked arms, and made preparations for rest.

The force was under command of Gen. Butler, and composed of a portion of the Boston Light Artillery, Major Cook; a strong detachment of the Sixth Massachusetts Regiment, Col. Jones; and about five hundred of the Eighth New York Regiment, Lieut.-Col. Waltenburgh.

On the route to the Hill, the streets were thronged with people, who greeted the military with cheers at every step, the ladies at the windows and the doors joining in the applause by waving their handkerchiefs. Arrived at their destination—which was unknown to the troops until they reached the place—they began to bestow themselves as comfortably as possible in the absence of tents. Their operations were seriously interrupted by a soaking shower that completely deluged the place, but, having become accustomed to camp life, they seemed to pay little attention to it. At a late hour large fires were built, somewhat dispelling the gloom of the place, and rendering the atmosphere more comfortable. The forces will be largely reinforced, and additional force is expected, who will immediately take possession of the commanding heights around Baltimore. Public Schoolhouse No. 10, corner of Warren and William streets, was taken possession of by the troops for the purpose of storing away their baggage and other articles likely to be injured by being exposed to the weather.—*Baltimore Clipper, May* 14.

—JUDGE GILES, of Baltimore, having issued a writ of *habeas corpus,* directing the delivery of a soldier at Fort McHenry, Major Morris, the commander at that post, refused to obey the writ, and gave his reasons in a published letter. —*N. Y. Evening Post, May* 14.—(*Doc.* 160.)

—EARLY this morning the steamer Pawnee was moored off the city of Alexandria, Va., so that her guns and mortars command the town. She has several of James's rifled cannon on board, which will throw grape, shell, hot shot or solid into any part of the town, and far beyond into the camp of an army that may be so imprudent as to pitch their tents in the suburbs of the city.—*N. Y. Herald, May* 14.

—THE Virginia Union Convention assembled at Wheeling, and organized, with Dr. J. W. Moss in the chair.—*Idem.*

—SENATOR BAYARD, of Delaware, issued an address to his constituents, called forth by the denunciations against him on his return from the South. He narrates the history of his journey, gives the motives which induced him to undertake it, and denies having been in consultation with the rebels in Montgomery. He proposes to rest on his past course, his general character, and his future life, and declares that he shall resign as soon as he is convinced that there is to be a war.—(*Doc.* 161.)

—MRS. SARAH SANFORD, a native of New Haven, Conn., and a graduate of the South Hadley Female Seminary, but for some time past an assistant teacher in a New Orleans Grammar School, was stripped naked and tarred and feathered in Lafayette Square, New Orleans, in the presence and amid the applause of an immense crowd of people. The assigned reason was abolition sentiments, expressed to her pupils, and by them repeated to their parents. Dr. Charles McQueen, recently from New Orleans, was an eye witness to the transaction.—*Buffalo Express.*

May 14.—Gen. Harney published an address to the people of Missouri, saying that the military bill recently passed by the Legislature is an indirect secession ordinance, manifestly unconstitutional, and ought not to be upheld by good citizens. He says, that whatever may be the termination of the present condition of things in respect to the Cotton States, Missouri must share the destiny of the Union, and all the power of the Government will be exerted to maintain her position.—(*Doc.* 162.)

—THE Confederate Congress requested President Davis, by resolution, to appoint a day of fasting and prayer.—(*Doc.* 163.)

—A LARGE and enthusiastic Union meeting was held in East Baltimore, Md., James T. Randolph presiding, assisted by a number of vice-presidents; patriotic resolutions were adopted, and addresses were delivered by John L. Thomas and John G. Wilmot, of Baltimore, and Dr. Strafford, of Caroline county, and received with every demonstration of approval.—(*Doc.* 164.)

—THERE was a great demonstration at Annapolis, Md., in honor of opening the branch railroad connecting Annapolis station and the pier of the Naval Academy, then just completed by the skilful engineer corps of the Thirteenth

New York Regiment. A long train of cars carried the Thirteenth Regiment on an excursion over the new road to a short distance beyond the city. They were accompanied with a full band of music, and as the train moved off a salute was fired from the Naval School. The regiment marched back to the city and much enthusiasm was manifested by citizens.—*National Intelligencer, May* 16.

—Ross WINANS was arrested at the Relay House, on the Baltimore and Ohio road, by the federal officers. Governor Hicks, with others, endeavored to have him released on security, but this was refused, and he was placed under guard.—*Phila. Press, May* 15.

—GOVERNOR ANDREW, in an address to the two branches of the Legislature of Massachusetts, delivered to-day, says :—

"This is no war of sections,—no war of North on South. It is waged to avenge no former wrongs, nor to perpetuate ancient griefs or memories of conflict. It is the struggle of the people to vindicate their own rights, to retain and invigorate the institutions of their fathers,—the majestic effort of a National Government to vindicate its power and execute its functions for the welfare and happiness of the whole,—and therefore while I do not forget, I will not name to-day that "subtle poison" which has lurked always in our national system —and I remember also at this moment, that even in the midst of rank and towering rebellion, under the very shadow of its torch and axe, there are silent but loyal multitudes of the citizens of the South who wait for the national power to be revealed and its protecting flag unfurled for their own deliverance.

"How shall I record the grand and sublime uprising of the people, devoting themselves— their lives—their all! No creative art has ever woven into song a story more tender in its pathos or more stirring to the martial blood than the scenes just enacted—passing before our eyes in the villages and towns of our dear old Commonwealth. Henceforth be silent, ye shallow cavillers at New England thrift, economy, and peaceful toil! Henceforth let no one dare accuse our northern sky, our icy winters, or our granite hills?

"'Oh what a glorious morning' was the exulting cry of Samuel Adams, as he, excluded from royal grace, heard the sharp musketry which on the dawn of the 19th of April, 1775,

announced the beginning of the War of Independence. The yeomanry, who in 1775, on Lexington Common and on the banks of Concord River, first made that day immortal in our annals, have found their lineal representatives in the historic regiment which on the 19th of April, 1861, in the streets of Baltimore, baptized our flag anew in heroic blood, when Massachusetts marched once more '*in the sacred cause of liberty and the rights of mankind.*'

"Grave responsibilities have fallen, in the Providence of God, upon the Government and the people;—and they are welcome. They could not have been safely postponed. They have not arrived too soon. They will sift and try this people, all who lead and all who follow. But this trial, giving us a heroic present to revive our past, will breathe the inspiration of a new life into our national character and reassure the destiny of the Republic. "*

—A SCHOONER was seized at the wharf in Baltimore, by a United States officer. She had a number of pikes, manufactured by Winans, and Minié rifles on board. She was taken over to the south side of the harbor, under Federal Hill, and a guard placed on board.—*N. Y. Times, May* 15.

—GEN. BUTLER issued a proclamation from his head-quarters on Federal Hill—in which he explains why Baltimore is occupied by the troops, and guarantees safety and protection to all citizens engaged in lawful pursuits.—(*Doc.* 165.)

—THOMAS H. HICKS, governor of Maryland, issued a proclamation calling for four regiments of troops "to serve within the limits of the State of Maryland, or for the defence of the capital of the United States."—(*Doc.* 166.)

—THE CONNECTICUT SECOND REGIMENT, numbering eight hundred men, arrived at Washington. They are handsomely uniformed, and have a complete camp equipage and about forty fine horses. They are armed (all save two companies, which have Minié muskets) with Sharpe's rifles and sabre bayonets.—(*Doc.* 167.)

—POSTMASTER-GENERAL BLAIR annulled the contract for carrying the mails between St. Louis and Memphis, owing to the forcible stoppage of the steamers by which they were conveyed. This is the first case under the law of

* GOVERNOR ANDREW'S address is printed in full in the *Boston Transcript, May* 14.

the last Congress which authorized a discontinuance of the mail in case of illegal obstruction.—*Boston Transcript, May* 15.

—GEN. BUTLER made a formal demand on the city authorities of Baltimore for the delivery of a quantity of arms stored in the warehouse of John S. Gittings, corner of Gay and Second streets. Marshal Kane refused to deliver up the arms without the officers produced an order from the Mayor.

Finally, after some altercation, an order was produced, and the arms were brought out, making fifteen dray-loads. About two-thirds of the fire-arms were carbines; the rest were flint-lock muskets. There was also a large quantity of pikes. A guard of Federal troops was placed over the arms, and, escorted by a large number of police, they were taken to the fort. A crowd of turbulent men and boys followed, yelling and hooting, for a portion of the distance. Some were armed with pistols, and there was an evident desire to commit violence, but all such demonstrations were restrained by the police. —*N. Y. Times, May* 15.

May 15.—A proclamation of neutrality with respect to the Secession rebellion is issued by Queen Victoria, in which all subjects of Great Britain are forbidden to enter the service of the contending parties, or to endeavor "to break a blockade lawfully and effectually established." —(*Doc.* 168.)

—THE bark Ocean Eagle, Capt. Luce, from Rockland, Me., with 3,144 casks of lime, consigned to Creevy & Farwell, was captured by the privateer steamer Calhoun, of New Orleans. —*N. O. Picayune, May* 17.

—Two yachts, belonging to private individuals, were formally accepted by the Government, and detailed for service by the Treasury Department. Their owners, James Gordon Bennett, jr., of New York, and T. P. Ives, of Providence, R. I., were commissioned as Lieutenants in the Revenue service, and ordered to their respective vessels as Lieutenants commanding.—*N. Y. Tribune, May* 16.

—BISHOP WHITTINGHAM, the head of the Episcopal Church in Maryland, addressed a circular to the several Episcopal clergymen of his diocese, forbidding hereafter the omission of the prayer for the President of the United States from the regular church service; which had been done by a few disunion persons under his jurisdiction.—(*Doc.* 169.)

—THE town of Potosi, in Washington county, Mo., was taken possession of, under orders of Gen. Lyon, by Captain Coles, of company A, Fifth Regiment, of United States volunteers.— (*Doc.* .)

May 16.—A letter upon the Virginia election was written by Senator Mason of that State, in which he says, that "the ordinance of secession" (not yet voted upon by the people of Virginia) "annulled the Constitution and laws of the United States within that State, and absolved the citizens of Virginia from all obligation and obedience to them;" and that if it be now rejected by the people, Virginia must "take sides," and "turn her arms against her Southern sisters." Moreover, that ordinance brought into Virginia several thousand soldiers of the Confederate army, and thus the faith of Virginia is pledged to it, for if it be rejected, their soldiers will merely have been entrapped. —(*Doc.* 170.)

—THE *Montgomery* (Ala.) *Advertiser*, of to-day, says that the various accounts about hundreds of letters of marque having been granted by the War Department of the Southern Confederacy, and that thousands of applications are already on file, is a gross error. Applications for that business are made to the collectors of the different ports, and not to the department at Montgomery, where none have been received. A number of applications have been made to the collectors of New Orleans, Mobile, and other Southern ports.

—GENERAL BUTLER was serenaded at the National Hotel in Washington, and in response made a happy speech upon the war, and the position of Massachusetts in it.—(*Doc.* 171.)

—UPON the opening of the U. S. Circuit Court at Boston, Judge Sprague charged the Grand Jury upon the crime of piracy.—(*Doc.* 172.)

—THE Second Regiment of Maine volunteer militia passed through New York, on their way to the seat of war. Previous to their departure the natives of Maine, resident in the city, presented the regiment with an American flag; the presentation being made at the City Hall, in the presence of thousands of enthusiastic spectators.—(*Doc.* 173.)

—A CORRESPONDENCE between Gov. Andrews of Mass., and Gen. Benjamin F. Butler, relative to the proposed suppression by the latter of a slave insurrection, is published.—(*Doc.* 174.)

—BRIGADIER-GENERALS Butler and McClellan were appointed Major-Generals.—*N. Y. News*, May 17.

—SECRETARY SEWARD declares it treason to accept from the government of a Southern State the proffered price of vessels previously seized. —(*Doc.* 174½.)

May 17.—In behalf of the Government of the United States, and the better to secure the peace of St. Louis, and promote the tranquillity of Missouri, United States warrants were issued for the search of places suspected to contain articles contraband of war. The warrants were placed in the hands of United States Marshal Rawlings, who proceeded, accompanied by a corps of United States soldiers, under Captain Sweeney, to the State Tobacco Warehouse on Washington Avenue, and to the Central Metropolitan Police Station on Chesnut street. At the former were found several hundred rifles, muskets, cavalry pistols, holsters, small boxes of ammunition; and at the latter place, Arnot's Building, two pieces of cannon, and several hundred rifles.—*St. Louis Democrat, May* 18.

—A SUBMARINE boat, or infernal machine supposed to be owned by the secessionists, was captured in Philadelphia.—(*Doc.* 175.)

—SURGEON-GENERAL GIBBES of the C. S. A., reports that no serious casualty occurred in the bombardment of Sumter to the Confederate forces. "Four trifling contusions at Fort Moultrie only; none at other posts."

The Virginia papers recommend Southerners to sing the Marseillaise.—*N. Y. Express, May* 20.

—THE Confederate Congress authorizes the issue of $50,000,000 in bonds, payable in twenty years, at an interest not exceeding eight per centum, and in lieu of bonds to issue $20,000,-000 in treasury notes, in small sums, without interest.—*N. Y. Herald, May* 19.

May 18.—Governor Brown, of Georgia, issued a proclamation, inhibiting the carrying of arms or accoutrements of any kind purchased by the State, beyond its limits, without his consent. This proclamation appears to relate to the informal departure of soldiers.

"Governor Brown," says the *Savannah Republican*, "may be technically right in this or-

der, but he has at least selected an unfortunate time for issuing it. From the beginning a misunderstanding seems to have existed between him and the Confederate authorities, to be found with no other State, and it is high time it had been brought to a close."—*N. Y. Commercial, May* 22.

—A PATRIOTIC demonstration took place in the town of Old Saybrook, Ct., made particularly interesting by the antiquity of the place, and its various revolutionary relics and reminiscences. A fine flagstaff was raised upon the spot which had given birth to the old Saybrook platform, and but a short distance from the old fort built by the first settlers of the place.

The services were prefaced by the raising of the flag by Deacon Sill, (91 years of age) a colonel of the war of 1812, and the patriarch of the place. A prayer and addresses were then made by the Rev. Messrs. McCall, Loper and Gallup; the intervals being appropriately filled by national songs admirably given by a club from a neighboring village. In conclusion, the old men of the village were called upon, and short and telling speeches were made.—*Boston Advertiser, May* 21.

—THE *Montgomery* (Ala.) *Mail* of to-day has the following paragraph in reference to Fort Pickens: "Having returned this morning from Pensacola, where we have been for several days, we can assure our readers that the reports going to show that a battle will soon occur at Fort Pickens are mere conjectures. Of the plans of any of those in command nothing is known outside of head-quarters. Our own impression, formed while in Pensacola, is that there will be no battle at all at Pickens, or at least that it is not now the intention of the Confederate authorities to attack it."

—ARKANSAS was by unanimous vote admitted a State of the Southern Confederacy, and its delegates to the Southern Congress. They are R. W. Johnson, of Pine Bluff; A. Rust, of Little Rock; A. H. Garland, of Little Rock; W. W. Watkins, of Carrollton; H. F. Thomasson, of Van Buren.—*N. Y. Times, May* 26.

—THREE merchants of Baltimore, Jerome A. Pendergrast, James Whiteford, and George McGowan, were arrested charged with riotous conduct in obstructing the track of the Baltimore and Ohio Railroad on the 19th of April, while the Massachusetts troops were *en route* to Washington. They were under indictment by the Grand Jury, and were admitted to bail.—*N. Y. Times*, May 26.

—THE military department of Virginia, to embrace eastern Virginia to the summit of the Blue Ridge, and the States of North Carolina and South Carolina, was created; Major-General Benjamin F. Butler was placed in command. —Rappahannock River was blockaded, which rendered perfect the blockade of Virginia.— *N. Y. Herald*, May 19.

—FOURTEENTH REGIMENT N. Y. S. M. from Brooklyn departed for Washington, amid great enthusiasm.—*Doc.* 176.

—THE Tug Yankee arrived in Philadelphia, having in tow three schooners loaded with tobacco, viz.: the Emily Ann, the Mary Willis, and the Delaware Farmer, belonging to and bound to Baltimore from Richmond. They surrendered to the Harriet Lane, and were ordered to Philadelphia by the flag officer of the Minnesota. Outside of Cape Henry the Mary Willis broke loose, and as the Yankee turned round to recover her, the Emily Ann got a lurch and sprung her mainmast. Her foremast had to be cut away to save her. The Emily Ann arrived at the wharf, leaking badly, and is being unloaded. Lieut. Bryant, of the Navy, who had the prizes in charge, stated that the ship North Carolina, in ballast, from Havre, and another ship, the Argo, had been seized and taken to New York. Twenty vessels had been detained by the fleet, including five tobacco schooners.—*Phila. Ledger*, May 19.

—AN expedition of New York troops sent to recapture the lightship, taken by the secessionists, brought it up to the Washington Navy Yard to-day.—They were fired into, but nobody was hurt.—*N. Y. Herald*, May 19.

May 19.—Shots were exchanged between the U. S. Steamers Freeborn and Monticello, and a rebel battery at Sewell's Point north of Elizabeth River, Virginia.—(*Doc.* 177.)

—Two schooners with secession troops on board were taken by U. S. steamer Freeborn, in the Potomac, 10 miles below Fort Washington.—*N. Y. World*, May 21.

THE rebels at Harper's Ferry, Md., were reinforced from the south. Two thousand troops arrived from Mississippi and two regiments from Alabama.—*N. Y. Herald*, May 21.

DIARY—9

—A MEETING of the New York Bible Society was held, in reference to supplying the Bible to all soldiers, who go to fight for the Federal Government. Wm. Allen Butler presided, and speeches were made by the president, Dr. Tyng, Dr. Hitchcock, and others.—(*Doc.* 178.)

—A BODY of 1,000 Virginians and South Carolinians from Harper's Ferry took a position on the Virginia side of the Potomac, opposite Williamsport, a town about seven miles from Hagerstown, Md. They there were in a situation to command the ferry at that spot.—*Phila. Press*, May 21.

May 20.—Mrs. Judge Daly, of New York, and a number of ladies associated with her, sent to the Sixty-ninth regiment 1,260 linen havelocks—a complement sufficient to supply the whole regiment.—*N. Y. Herald*, May 21.

—THE ship Argo, which was captured in Hampton Roads on Sunday afternoon, (May 19,) by the United States steam frigate Minnesota, arrived at New York in charge of a prize crew under command of Midshipman McCook and Clerk Elias W. Hall. The Argo was bound from Richmond, Virginia, for Bremen, and at the time of her seizure had on board $150,000 worth of tobacco.—*N. Y. Journal of Commerce*, May 21.

—AT precisely 3 o'clock P. M., by order of the Government, a descent was made by the United States Marshals upon every considerable telegraph office throughout the Free States, and the accumulated despatches of the twelvemonth past were seized. The object was to obtain evidence of the operations of the Southern rebels with their Northern accomplices, which the confidential telegrams passing between them could most certainly furnish. The seizures in all the principal cities were made at the same time so as to prevent the destruction of evidence which might have followed the receipt of a warning from any particular point. The whole matter was managed with the greatest secrecy, and so well planned that the project was a complete success. By this bold manœuvre the Government has obtained possession of a mass of evidence of the greatest importance. *N. Y. Tribune*, May 21.

—THE ordinance of secession was passed by the North Carolina State Convention, together with an ordinance ratifying and assenting to the Constitution of the Confederate States.— (*Doc.* 179.)

—ABRAM S. VOSBURGH, Colonel of the New York Seventy-first Regiment, died in Washington, D. C., of a pulmonary complaint.—*N. Y. Express*, May 20.

—GEN. BUTLER left Washington for Annapolis. The New York Second Regiment left New York for the seat of war.—(*Doc.* 180.)—*N. Y. Tribune*, May 21.

—Gov. MAGOFFIN, of Kentucky, issued a proclamation pretentiously in obedience to public sentiment, by which Kentucky virtually takes a position of neutrality, and in which its citizens are bidden to "so conduct themselves that the deplorable calamity of invasion may be averted."—(*Doc.* 181.)

—MILITARY maps of Virginia made for Gov. Letcher, from special surveys, were seized in Washington by the War Department.—*N. Y. Tribune*, May 21.

May 21.—Gen. Price, of the Missouri Militia, and Gen. Harney U. S. A., agreed upon a plan to maintain the public peace. Gen. Price pledged the whole power of the State officers to maintain order among the people of the State, and Gen. Harney declares that this object being assured, he can have no occasion as he has no wish, to make military movements, which might otherwise create excitement and jealousies which he most earnestly desires to avoid.—*Ohio Statesman*, May 22.

—THIS afternoon two companies, numbering 120 muskets, from the Philadelphia camp, composed of companies E and G under the command of Major McLane, went to Baltimore; proceeded to an unoccupied house near Green Mount Cemetery, and seized a large quantity of arms stored there, comprising 1,600 muskets, the boxes marked, " Virginia muskets," and 34 boxes containing 4,000 pikes, the boxes marked, "From Denmeads." The whole made twenty-six dray loads and were all taken to camp, and thence to Fort McHenry. The arms had been in the custody of the city authorities.—*Idem.*

—THE Second Regiment of Tennessee Volunteers, numbering 952 men, arrived at Richmond, Va., and went into camp at the head of Main street.—(*Doc.* 182.)

—THE ship General Parkhill of Liverpool, for Charleston, arrived at Philadelphia in charge of a prize crew of the Niagara. She was spoken off Cape Romain on the 12th, and ordered off. The next day she was captured in attempting to run the blockade. She is 600 tons with a general cargo, a large portion being salt. It is suspected that arms and munitions of war are concealed under the salt. She was commanded by Capt. Forbes, and had two secession flags flying.—*Philadelphia Press*, May 21.

—JEFFERSON DAVIS approved the act, passed at the session of the Southern Congress, prohibiting Southerners owing moneys to Northern merchants from paying the same, and compelling payment instead into the treasury of the seceded States.—(*Doc.* 183.)

—A COMPREHENSIVE and able article upon the present condition of affairs in the United States, is published in the *Cologne Gazette.*—(*Doc.* 184.)

—THE Confederate Congress in session at Montgomery, Ala., adjourned to meet at Richmond, Va., July 20th.—*N. Y. Herald*, May 28.

—A LETTER from Roxabelle, N. C., says:—The Chowan Association, by a unanimous vote, cut off all intercourse with the Bible Union, and recommended those owing subscriptions to withhold the same, deprecating any further agency of the Bible Union among the churches —another fruit of the reckless fanaticism of the Northern agitators. Unwilling to bow down to the Jehovah revealed by Moses and preached by Paul, they seek anti-slavery God. Nor are they unmindful in their ardent devoirs to the almighty dollar. Thousands have gone into the Bible Union treasury, annually for years past; but the steam is now stopped.—*N. Y. Express*, May 24.

—THE New School Presbyterian Assembly in session at Syracuse, N. Y., passed a series of resolutions upholding the Federal Government, the Constitution and laws.—*Albany Journal*, May 24.

—GEN. SAM. HOUSTON addressed the people of Independence, Texas, on the 10th of May last, on the occasion of a May festival. In the course of his remarks he took occasion to define his position in the present political crisis.—(*Doc.* 185.)

May 22.—The *Richmond* (Va.) *Whig* of to-day says: " We are not enough in the secrets of our authorities to specify the day on which Jeff. Davis will dine at the White House, and Ben. McCullough take his siesta in Gen. Sickles' gilded tent. We should dislike to produce any disappointment by naming too soon or too early a day; but it will save trouble if the gentlemen will keep themselves in readiness to dislodge at a moment's notice! If they are not smitten, however, with more than judicial blindness, they do not need this warning at our hands They must know that the measure of their iniquities is full, and the patience of outraged freedom is exhausted. Among all the brave men from the Rio Grande to the Potomac, and stretching over into insulted, indignant and infuriated Maryland, there is but one word on every lip: '*Washington;*' and one sentiment on every heart: vengeance on the tyrants who pollute the Capital of the Republic!"

—THERE was an exciting time in Passaic, N. J., on the occasion of raising the Stars and Stripes by the citizens of that locality. A handsome flag, donated by the scholars of the Passaic Academy, was raised upon that edifice, and one of much larger proportions was raised upon Passaic Heights. Eloquent and patriotic addresses were made by Rev. Marshall B. Smith and Thos. D. Haxsey, Esq., of Paterson. The Passaic Light Guard turned out in good numbers and saluted the flag with several rounds. —*N. Y. Commercial, May 24.*

—A CORRESPONDENT of the *Savannah* (Ga.) *Republican,* writing from Montgomery, Alabama, says: "It is feared that the blockade of Lincoln will seriously diminish the revenue, unless speedily raised, and if not, the government will have to resort to direct taxation, in order to provide for its support. The plan will prove acceptable to the people, and will be more effective than a mere dependence upon an uncertain income. Some one has suggested, though not officially, the project of levying a tax of four per cent. upon slaves; but, considering the average value of the slaves at present to be four hundred dollars, the income will not exceed thirty-six millions. The Secretary of War alone estimates for thirty-five millions, and it is probable that at least one hundred will be needed for disbursement this year. We may, therefore, confidently expect a system of direct taxation in case any inconvenience is experienced in collections of the customs revenue. The tariff will be reduced to an exceedingly low figure, and will expose, by its action, the monstrosities of its colleague, the Morrill tariff."

—MAJOR-GENERAL BUTLER and Staff arrived

at Fortress Monroe, and were received with the customary military honors. There was a grand

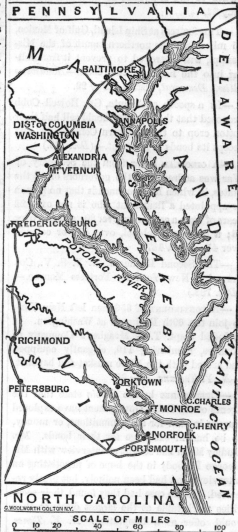

review of the troops in the evening, the parade-line, four thousand men, stretching across the parade-ground of the fortress. The spectacle was magnificent, and there was great enthusiasm among the men.

—A PARTY of Virginians attempted at night to capture a ferry-boat on the Potomac near Clear Spring, Md. Notice was given the Union men of Clear Spring, three miles distant, who turned out to guard the boat. During the night the Virginians seized the boat, and were fired upon by the guard, and when midway across had to abandon the prize and escape in a skiff. Two Virginians were shot. The ferry-boat returned to the Maryland shore.—*Y. N. Times, May 24.*

—THE fortress at Ship Island, Gulf of Mexico, 95 miles from the northern mouth of the Mississippi, was destroyed to prevent it from falling into the hands of the rebels.—*Handsboro (Miss.) Democrat, (Extra,) May 22.*

—IN a speech at Atlanta, Ga., Howell Cobb proposed that the planters should sell half their cotton crop to the Southern Confederacy, and accept its bonds in payment.—*(Doc. 186.)*

—A CIRCULAR letter from the Secretary of War was addressed to the governors of all the States, in which he recommends that no person be appointed a lieutenant who is not over 22 years of age; a captaincy, over 30; a major, over 35; a lieutenant-colonel, over 40; or colonel, over 45.—*(Doc. 187.)*

—THE Second Regiment, N. Y. S. V., Col. Carr, left New York for Fortress Monroe.—*(Doc. 188.)*

—A CONTINGENT of 350 men left New York to join the 69th Regiment at Washington. It included Capt. T. F. Meagher's Company of Zouaves, numbering 110, elegantly equipped and armed with the Minié musket and bayonet. —*N. Y. Tribune, May 23.*

—DESPATCHES by the *Persia* state that the agents of the Rebel Government have explored Europe in vain for arms, munitions, or money, to be had in exchange for their bonds. Mr. Dudley Mann had sought an interview with Mr. George Peabody in the hope of negotiating an interview, and had been politely, but firmly repulsed. In no case had they found their securities marketable at the largest discount they could offer as a temptation.—*N. Y. Times, May 23.*

—THE President and Cabinet attended the flag raising at the Post-office Department in Washington. Thousands of spectators were present. As the colors ascended, a lull in the breeze caused them for a moment to hug the staff. In a few seconds, however, the breeze freshened and caused the beautiful Stars and Stripes to float out for full fifty feet. The effect was electric. The host of spectators, the President, the Cabinet—all united in cheers. Mr. Lincoln, amidst the wildest enthusiasm of the mass, made a brief address.

He said that a few months ago the Stars and Stripes hung as listless and still all over the Union as the flag just raised, but in a short time they were caught up by the coming breeze and made to float over the whole loyal nation, and among millions who were now determined to keep the flag flying till the bitter end or until the restoration of peace and unity.

Speeches were also made by Mr. Blair, Mr. Seward, and Mr. Caleb B. Smith. The remarks of Mr. Seward were received with the most intense enthusiasm.—*N. Y. Commercial Advertiser, May 22.*

—THE steamer J. C. Swan was seized at Harlow's Landing, thirty miles below St. Louis, and brought to the St. Louis arsenal, by order of Gen. Lyon. This is the steamer that brought the arms from Baton Rouge, which were captured by Gen. Lyon, at Camp Jackson. Measures will be taken to effect the legal confiscation of the boat. About 5,000 pounds of lead, *en route* for the South, were also seized at Ironton, on the Iron Mountain Railroad, by order of Gen. Lyon. Some resistance was offered by a party of citizens, and several shots were fired on both sides, but nobody was hurt.—*(Idem.)*

—MAJOR-GENERAL SANDFORD was placed in command of the New York troops on duty at Washington.—*N. Y. Times, May 24.*

—AMONG the speakers at the annual meeting of the Wesleyan Mission Society in London, was Rev. Dr. McClintock, of New York. He improved the occasion to make a stirring appeal to the audience against the misrepresentations of the London *Times* about American affairs, and to set them right on the subject. His address was received with very great applause. At one passage, the whole audience rose to their feet, and cheered for the speaker, and for the cause of the Union which he was advocating.—*(Doc. 188½.)*

May 23.—A. H. Stephens arrived at Atlanta, Ga., on his return from Montgomery, and in response to a call of the citizens delivered a strong secession speech.—*(Doc. 189.)*

—GEN. BUTLER at Fortress Monroe, in a general order, announced the following staff: Capt. Grier Tallmadge, Assistant Quartermaster and Acting Assistant Adjutant-General, Capt. T. Bailey Myers; Acting Assistant Quartermaster, Capt. Peter Hagerty; and Second Lieut., George H. Butler; Major Richard S. Fay, Military Secretary.—*N. Y. Commercial, May 31.*

—THE Philadelphia *Evening Journal* of to-day says: "We have it from good authority that there are, at this time, about five hundred Indians stationed at Harper's Ferry, with the rebel, or traitor army. If this be the mode of warfare these blood-thirsty, *scalping* devils are to be brought into the fight, our friends in the South must not consider it all unkind if we accept the proffered services of the ten regiments of free negroes in Canada and the North, and send them down South. Our Governor refused to let one regiment of negroes pass through our State to go South to do battle, but if *Indians* are to be brought into the field by Jeff. Davis, the South may rely on it they will be met with a corresponding force of negroes, and they will increase their numbers as they pass through the country, by having the slaves join them."

—THE Advance Guard, Fifth Regiment, N. Y. Volunteers, Col. Duryea, embarked on board the steam transport Alabama, from New York, for Fortress Monroe.—(*Doc.* 190.)

—THE Mississippi, which sailed from Boston, Mass., this forenoon, returned to that place and anchored off the Navy Yard. She had proceeded but a few miles down the harbor, when it was discovered that in repairing the engines, about two inches of the delivery pipe, through which the water from the condensers was forced out of the side of the ship, had been cut out, and in its place a joint of gum and canvas substituted, when it should have been a slip joint of iron or other metal. The defective part gave way, pouring a flood of water into the ship, when the engines were immediately stopped and the anchor thrown out. Temporary repairs were made so that she was enabled to return, but she lost a 6,000 lb. anchor by the parting of a cable. Michael Quinn of Virginia, late Chief Engineer in the Navy, superintended the repairs of the Mississippi. He recently resigned, returned to Virginia, and his name was stricken from the Navy roll.—*N. Y. Tribune, May* 24.

—THE First and Second Regiments of the Ohio volunteers, numbering together eighteen hundred men, and under the command respectively of Colonels McCook and Wilson, reached Washington. It has been several weeks since they left home, having been in the mean time encamped in Pennsylvania—first at Lancaster, and afterwards near Philadelphia. They left the latter city early yesterday morning, on the railroad, coming by way of Baltimore.—(*Doc.* 190½.)

—AN immense dry-dock was anchored at night in the Pensacola channel east of Fort Pickens by the rebels, who had intended, however, to anchor it elsewhere. Gen. Brown, in command at the fort, forbade its further removal. Its anchorage between Forts Pickens and McRae was for some time contemplated.— *N. O. Delta, May* 24.

—A BATTERY of Whitworth guns, twelve-pounders, with ammunition and carriages complete, arrived in New York city, as a present to the Government from patriotic Americans abroad. The battery is consigned to Henry F. Spaulding, Samuel D. Babcock, and Henry A. Smythe, who have informed Secretary Cameron of its arrival, and that it is at the disposition of the Government. Each one of the guns bears the following inscription: "From loyal Americans in Europe, to the United States Government, 1861." Mr. R. G. Moulton, an American at present residing in Manchester, deserves great credit for his energetic efforts in raising funds for the purchase of this battery.—*N. Y. Times, May* 24.

—ONE of the secession flags displayed from the head-quarters of the "Grays," at Alexandria, Va., and within sight from Washington, was captured by two adventurous Union men—William McSpedon, of New York city, and Samuel Smith, of Queens County, N. Y.

—GEN. PATTERSON and staff arrived at Fort McHenry, Baltimore. Col. Vosburgh, late of the 71st N. Y. regiment, was buried in Greenwood Cemetery, L. I.—*N. Y. Times, May* 24.

—THE Third Connecticut Regiment arrived at Washington. It numbers over eight hundred men, all well drilled, and is commanded by Colonel J. Arnold.—(*Doc.* 191.)

—THE Alexandria (Va.) *Sentinel* of to-day, says: "The Washington Home Guard, Capt. Powell, took to-day 169 head of fine mutton, three miles above the chain bridge. They were appraised at $2.50 a head, and are impounded near this place. They had been purchased of some Virginia drover by the Georgetown butchers, and were to have been delivered by some party, who had undertaken to swim them across the river at so much a head. It has not been found out who it is in Virginia that is thus furnishing aid and comfort to her enemies. This company deserves great credit for the vigilance they have exercised in protecting the adjoining country from marauding bands of Lincoln's soldiery, as also to prevent disloyal Virginians from furnishing supplies to the enemy."

—JEFFERSON DAVIS issued instructions to privateers sailing under his letters of marque. —(*Doc.* 192.)

—GEN. BUTLER, desiring to know the precise lay of the land about Fortress Monroe, Va., concluded to pay a visit to the neighboring village of Hampton. Col. Phelps's regiment of Vermonters were detailed for the reconnoissance, and took up the march across the dyke and bridge leading from the Fortress to the Hampton side of the bay. Observing the movement, the rebels rushed down to the bridge, and, with combustibles ready, prepared to set fire to it. At this the advance guard of the Vermonters took the double quick step, and before the fire had made much headway were down on the burning bridge and rebels. The latter fled precipitately, and the former was soon rescued from destruction. A field-piece, which the rebels had planted in the neighborhood, was unceremoniously pitched into the bay. Gen. Butler pushed on and completed the reconnoissance, to the infinite disgust of the rebels, and, probably, of John Tyler in particular, whose villa is not far distant. The ground for the permanent encampment was selected on the farm of Mr. Segor at the end of the bridge, and to-morrow will be the first permanent occupation of the soil of Virginia, made by Capt. Carr's and Col. Phelps's Regiments, who will go into encampment there.—*N. Y. Tribune, May* 27.

—THE *Wheeling* (Va.) *Intelligencer* of to-day, says:—That the first belligerent issue between the "Union men" of Western Virginia and the "State troops" recognizing the authority of the Southern Confederacy, has been joined at the town of Clarksburg, in the county of Harrison. Two companies of the Confederate military having marched into that place on the 20th instant, the court-house bell was rung as a signal for the assemblage of the two "Union military companies" of Clarksburg, under the command of Captains A. C. Moore and J. C. Vance, who demanded that the "Confederate forces" should surrender their arms and dis-

band. After a brief parley the demand was complied with.

May 24.—Sergeant Butterworth, of the N. Y. Fire Zouaves, was shot by a sentry at Alexandria, Va., through his failure to give the word when challenged.—*N. Y. News, May* 27.

—AN attempt to poison the Union forces in Missouri, by means of arsenic in the bread, was betrayed by a negress.

The Missouri troops, organized under the requisition of Governor Jackson, refused to disband, according to the terms of agreement between General Harney and General Price.— *St. Louis Democrat, May* 24.

—THE STEUBEN VOLUNTEERS, 7th Regiment N. Y. S. V., departed from New York for the seat of war.—(*Doc.* 193.)

—ALL vessels belonging to the United States, which arrived at New Orleans, La., after the 6th inst., were formally seized by the Confederate States Marshal, in conformity with the act of the Confederate Congress in relation to privateering, which gave thirty days for all vessels in Southern ports to leave, but made no provision for vessels arriving after its passage.— *N. O. Picayune, May* 25.

—THE Senate of Kentucky passed resolutions that that State will not sever her connection with the National Government, nor take up arms for either belligerent party, but arm herself for the protection of peace within her borders, and tender her services as a mediator to effect a just and honorable peace.—*Ohio Statesman, May* 25.

JOHN LOTHROP MOTLEY published an article on the "Causes of the Civil War in America," in the *London Times* of this day.—(*Doc.* 146½.)

—JEFFERSON DAVIS issued at Montgomery, Ala., a proclamation appointing Thursday the 13th day of June, 1861, to be observed as a day of fasting and prayer by the people of the seceded States.—(*Doc* 194.)

—A GENERAL movement into Virginia was executed under the command of Gen. Mansfield. The N. Y. Seventh Regiment left their camp in Washington at 1:20 A. M., each man having sixty rounds of ball cartridge. They touched the "sacred soil of Virginia" at 4 A. M., landing at the Alexandria Bridge, near which they encamped. The New York Sixty-ninth and Twenty-eighth Regiments, with Lieut. Drummond's cavalry and a battery, passed the Chain

Bridge, below Georgetown, at about 1 A. M. They first took possession of the Loudon and Hampshire Railroad, seized the train, arrested the passengers, took the cars and engine, and captured one secession soldier, who was on board the train. The 69th then took position on the Orange and Manassas Gap Railroad, which runs out of Alexandria.

They took up some of the rails, and awaited in ambush the arrival of the train, which they supposed would leave Alexandria with the fugitives. When it came it was surrounded, and the train captured. About seven hundred persons were on board, including 300 men. The entire party were held as prisoners of war, and were kept as hostages for the fair treatment of any loyal citizens that may fall into the hands of the rebels. Two companies of the N. Y. Second, the N. Y. Fifth, Twelfth, Twenty-fifth, three companies of the New York Seventy-first and the N. Y. Fire Zouaves; the Rhode Island First, and the Rhode Island batteries; the Michigan Third; the New Jersey Fourth; three companies of an Ohio Regiment; one company Massachusetts Fifth; three companies of cavalry regular army; and twenty-five hundred District of Columbia troops, also participated in the movement on Virginia—making in all 13,000 men.—*N. Y. Times, May 25.*

A little before 5 o'clock A. M., the commander of U. S. steamer Pawnee, lying in the Potomac, off Alexandria, Va., sent a flag of truce to the rebel forces, giving them one hour in which to withdraw from the town. At five, the steamers Baltimore and Mount Vernon, with the N. Y. Fire Zouaves, made fast to the wharf. As the steamers approached, the rebel sentinels fired their guns in the air and retreated.

The Zouaves landed in good order in double quick time, each company forming on the street facing the river. Company E, Capt. Leveridge, was the first to disembark. It was at once detailed to destroy the railroad track leading to Richmond, which service was promptly performed. After detailing company E, Col. Ellsworth directed the adjutant to form the regiment, and then with his aid, Lieut. Winser, and a file of men, started for the telegraph office for the purpose of cutting the wires. They marched in double quick time up the street, and had proceeded three blocks, when the attention of Colonel Ellsworth was attracted by a large secession flag flying from the Marshall House

kept by J. W. Jackson. Col. Ellsworth entered the hotel, and meeting a man in the hall asked, "Who put that flag up?" The man answered, "I don't know; I am a boarder here." Col. Ellsworth, Lieut. Winser, the chaplain of the regiment, Mr. House, a volunteer aid, and the four privates, then went up to the roof, and Col. Ellsworth cut down the flag. The party returned down the stairs, preceded by private Francis E. Brownell of Company A. As they left the attic, the man who had said he was a boarder, but who proved to be the landlord, Jackson, was met in the hall having a double-barrel gun, which he levelled at Brownell. Brownell struck up the gun with his musket, when Jackson pulled both triggers, and the contents lodged in the body of Col. Ellsworth, entering between the third and fifth ribs. Col. Ellsworth was at the time rolling up the flag. He fell forward on the floor of the hall and expired instantly, only exclaiming "My God."

Private Brownell immediately levelled his musket at Jackson, and fired. The ball struck Jackson on the bridge of the nose, and crashed through his skull, killing him instantly. As he fell Brownell followed his shot by a thrust of his bayonet, which went through Jackson's body. The companions of Col. Ellsworth, seven in number, immediately posted themselves so as to command the halls of the hotel, and threatened to shoot the first man who showed his head outside of a door. In this way they stood for ten minutes. Their protracted absence alarmed Adjutant Leoser, who ordered Company A, Capt. Coyle, to search for the Colonel. The Company found their commander dead, and their comrades in possession of the hotel. They made a litter of muskets, and placing the body of the Colonel on it, returned to the boat, whence it was soon after taken to Washington.

Simultaneously with the landing of the Zouaves the first Michigan Regiment entered Alexandria by the road leading from Long Bridge, and proceeded direct to the railroad depot, of which they took possession, capturing a troop of rebel cavalry numbering one hundred, with their horses and equipments. All the heights which command Washington were occupied in this movement, and the construction of earthworks for batteries was immediately begun. Batteries were placed at each end of the two bridges which cross the Potomac. A portion of the New York troops were ordered towards the Manassas Gap Junction, and the New Jersey regiment was posted at the forks a mile from the Long Bridge. Numerous wagons, with camp equipage, went over about noon to the Federal troops in Virginia, and a great many men commenced work at the intrenchments.

Col. Ellsworth's body was taken to Washington and placed in the engine-house at the Navy Yard. The house was heavily draped with American flags, crape, and bouquets of flowers. It was guarded by the Zouaves, a company of the Seventy-first N. Y. regiment, and some regulars. Thousands of people assembled there to see the remains during the day, the President's family among the number. At seven o'clock Alexandria was comparatively quiet. But the Zouaves were anchored at night on a steamer in the river, to prevent them from avenging the death of Ellsworth. They were disposed to burn the town.—(*Doc.* 195.)

May 25.—Colonel Duryea's Zouaves arrived at Fortress Monroe, Va., this morning by the Alabama, and encamped near the Hampton Bridge, with the Vermont and Troy regiments. The Pembroke also arrived with two companies of Massachusetts troops. There are now about 6,000 men within or under the walls of the fortress. The Quaker City came up to the fortress with a rich prize this morning—the bark Winnifred, of Richmond, from Rio Janeiro, laden with coffee. Gen. Butler, accompanied by acting Adjutant-Gen. Tallmadge, and his aids, made a dashing reconnoissance several miles between the James and York Rivers. A picket guard of rebels fled on their approach.

Three fugitives, the property of Col. Mallory, commander of the rebel forces near Hampton, were brought in to Fortress Monroe by the picket guard yesterday. They represent that they were about to be sent South, and hence sought protection. Major Cary came in with a flag of truce, and claimed their rendition under the Fugitive Slave law, but was informed by Gen. Butler that, under the peculiar circumstances, he considered the fugitives contraband of war, and had set them to work inside the fortress. Col. Mallory, however, was politely informed that so soon as he should visit the fortress and take a solemn oath to obey the laws of the United States, his property would promptly be restored.—*N. Y. Tribune, May* 27.

—THE New Orleans *Picayune* of to-day says: "One week hence there will not be any available mode of letter or newspaper express or telegraphic communication between the Confederate and the United States. Our Postmaster-General has announced his determination to assume the discharge of the duties of his office on the 1st day of June. From that date all existing U. S. mail contracts, so far as we are concerned, will have been annulled. Meantime, the Washington Administration adopt the same policy, and to make non-intercourse thoroughly impossible, prohibit express companies from carrying express matter, inclusive of letters, across the Potomac River. By order of the commanding general U. S. A., at Washington, Adams' Express was opened on the 16th inst., and all such matter was stopped. Without mail or express communication with the North, and the carrying of mail matter by individuals being considered in the light of treasonable ' communication with the enemy,' in a few days we shall have but scant opportunity of enriching our columns with interesting intelligence from the other side of the border. We might get an occasional budget by the way of Havana, but we suppose it is intended by the despotic clique at Washington that the blockade shall prevent that. Won't it be queer to read, hereafter, the latest news from ' way down east,' *via* Paris and London?

" Well, we suppose we can stand it as well as they can on the other side of the line. Let us see who will first get tired of the embargo."

—THE First Regiment N. Y. Volunteers, Col. Allen, left New York for the seat of war. —(*Doc.* 196.)

—FUNERAL ceremonies over the body of Col. Ellsworth took place in Washington. The remains lay in state in the east room of the President's house for several hours. Owing to the immense throng of anxious gazers on the remains of the deceased, the funeral *cortége* delayed moving from the Executive Mansion till near 1 o'clock. All along the line of Pennsylvania avenue flags were displayed at half-mast and draped in mourning. Every available point, including the windows, balconies, and house-tops, was thronged with anxious and sorrowful gazers. Various testimonials of respect were paid. All the bells of the city were tolled, and the heads of the soldiers and troops uncovered. Several companies of the City Corps, followed by the New York Seventy-first Regiment, Marines, and the local Cavalry Corps, formed the military escort, with their arms reversed and colors shrouded. The hearse was followed by a detachment of Zouaves, one of whom, the avenger of Col. Ellsworth, carried the identical secession flag torn down by the deceased. Then followed the President, accompanied by Secretaries Seward and Smith, and the rest of the procession was composed of carriages, containing the captains of the Zouave Regiment. *N. Y. Times, May 26.*

May 26.—A letter from Major Sprague, U. S. A., giving an account of affairs in Texas, since the arrest of the federal troops in that locality, was published in the *Albany* (N. Y.) *Argus.*—(*Doc.* 197.)

—THE privateer Calhoun, Capt. Wilson, arrived at New Orleans, La., having in tow the following prizes: schooners John Adams and Mermaid, of Provincetown, Mass., and the brig Panama, of Boston, Mass.; all these are whalers, and have on board about 215 bbls. of sperm and black whale oil. They were taken about 20 miles from the passes; their crews number 63 men; and all of them told that these vessels had been whaling for some time and cruising in the Gulf.—*Natchez Courier, May 30.*

—THE *Mobile Register* of yesterday, after announcing the invasion of Virginia by the Federal troops, observes: "Servile insurrection is a part of their programme, but they expect no great amount of practical good to result therefrom—consequently, it is contended that *it would be a far better course of policy for the Abolitionists to murder the slaves and thus exterminate slavery.* A more monstrous proposition could not emanate from the most incarnate fiend among the damned. But infamous as it is it finds an advocate in the abolition press. The slaves are to be indiscriminately slaughtered, and when the last one is butchered, then it is thought the institution will cease to exist. The soul recoils in horror at the idea of an unscrupulous war upon the innocent and defenceless slave. The Syrian massacre of the Christians and all the crimes of its bloody participants pale before the proposed atrocities of the Black Republicans. Their masters, however, in this, as all other instances, will be their protectors and saviors. With this much of their published programme, we must not be surprised at any act or threat as the campaign advances."

—A CORRESPONDENT writes from Montgomery to the *New Orleans Delta:*—"The startling intelligence of the invasion of the soil of Virginia, and the actual occupation of Alexandria by United States forces, was received here last evening. The Cabinet, I am informed, immediately went into a procrastinated session. No event since the initiation of this revolution has ever created a sensation so profound, and so sorrowful. The mere taking of a deserted and exposed village, is in itself nothing; but when regarded as indicative of the future policy of the old Government, it at once becomes a question pregnant with great importance. Mr. Lincoln has declared in his proclamation, and at various other times reiterated the expression, that the only object his Government had in view, was the retaking and the reoccupation of what he asserted to be Government property; but now, in the face of this promise, which has gone before the world, he converts his Abolition horde into an army of invasion, and now occupies a city within the boundaries of our Republic. This Government has no longer an election. Its duty is now manifest to all. The nation must rise as a man and drive the hireling miscreants from a soil polluted by the foulness of their tramp. Virginia alone could speedily perform the work of expurgation, but *her* cause is now *our* cause, *her* battles *our* battles, and let the Government at large pour a continuous stream of men into Virginia, and preserve from dishonor that patriotic mother of States."

—THE rebel Congress passed an act to prohibit the exportation of cotton, except through Southern seaports.—(*Doc.* 198.)

—THIS afternoon at about 4 o'clock, Gen. McClellan, commanding the military department of Ohio, received information that two bridges had been burned near Farmington, on the B. & O. R. R., and that arrangements had been made to burn the others between that point and Wheeling. The general had been making arrangements to move on Grafton in force, but this intelligence caused him to hasten his movements. He returned at once to Cincinnati and issued telegraphic orders for an advance. One column was directed to move from

Wheeling and Bellaire, under command of Col. B. F. Kelly, 1st Virginia Volunteers; another from Marietta, on Parkersburg, under Col. Steedman, 14th Ohio Volunteers. These officers were directed to move with caution, and to occupy all the bridges, etc., as they advanced. A proclamation to Virginians, and address to the troops, were issued by Gen. McClellan simultaneously with the advance.—(*Doc.* 199.)

—THE First Regiment of New Hampshire Volunteers, Colonel Tappan, passed through New York on their way to the seat of war. The regiment left Camp Union, at Concord, yesterday morning. Its progress through Massachusetts and Connecticut was an ovation, crowds assembling at all the stations to give them a greeting.—(*Doc.* 200.)

—POSTMASTER-GENERAL BLAIR issued the following order:—"All postal service in the States of Virginia, North Carolina, South Carolina, Georgia, Florida, Alabama, Mississippi, Louisiana, Arkansas, and Texas, will be suspended from and after the 31st inst. Letters for offices temporarily closed by this order, will be forwarded to the dead letter office, except those for Western Virginia, which will be sent to Wheeling."—*Boston Transcript, May* 27.

May 27.—Emerson Etheridge, of Tennessee, addressed the citizens of Louisville, Ky., on the great questions which are dividing the South at the present time. He commenced his address with an allusion to the distracted condition of the country, congratulating himself and his audience that he stood upon Kentucky soil, a State that was yet loyal to the Union. He clearly proclaimed himself for his country, first, last, and forever. Having but recently come from a State in which anarchy reigned supreme, he could the better appreciate the blessings of political liberty which were yet vouchsafed to Kentuckians, and which he felt Kentuckians had the patriotism, the gallantry, and the power to perpetuate. He drew a picture of Kentucky in her proud position as a sister in the Union of the States, of her wealth, of her usefulness as an asylum for the oppressed of both sections of our unhappy and divided country, and of her grandeur in after days when she has safely outridden the storm which wrecked the frailer sisterhood around her. While he dealt deadly blows to the apologists of dissolution, he spoke cheering words of comfort and assurance to the friends of the Union. He was

withering in his denunciation of rebellion, powerful in argument, ready and illustrative in anecdote, and fervid and glowing in eloquence. —*Louisville Journal, May* 28.

—GEN. BEAUREGARD issued orders in Charleston, relinquishing command of the forces around Charleston to Col. R. H. Anderson.—*Augusta Chronicle, May* 28.

—IN the case of John Merryman, a secessionist arrested in Baltimore and detained a prisoner in Fort McHenry, a writ of *habeas corpus* was issued by Judge Taney, made returnable this day in the United States District Court. Gen. Cadwallader declined surrendering the prisoner till he heard from Washington, and an attachment was issued for Gen. Cadwallader. —*N. Y. Times, May* 28.

—THE United States steamer Brooklyn arrived off the Pass L'Outre bar at the mouth of the Mississippi, and commenced the blockade of that river.—*N. O. Picayune, May* 28.

—BRIGADIER-GENERAL McDOWELL, U. S. army, took command of the Union forces in Virginia, and relieved Major-General Sandford, N. Y. State Militia.—*N. Y. Herald, May* 28.

—GEORGE W. THOMPSON, one of the judges of the Circuit Court of the State of Virginia, issued a proclamation ordering the rebels in the western part of that State to disperse. Peculiar interest attaches to the document from the fact that one of Judge Thompson's sons, W. P. Thompson, a young lawyer, resident at Fairmont, is aide-de-camp to Gen. Thomas S. Haymond, commander of the confederate forces in Western Virginia, and the leader of the first company which marched on Grafton. Another of his sons is also a secessionist, and a private in the same company.—(*Doc.* 201.)

—THE blockade of Mobile (Ala.) harbor was commenced. The *Natchez Courier* of to-day says:—"Fort Morgan welcomed the blockading fleet by displaying the U. S. flag, with the Union down, from the same staff, and below the confederate flag."

—COL. A. DURYEA was placed in command of the camp near Fortress Monroe, by Major-General Butler.—(*Doc.* 202.)

—THE Twentieth N. Y. Volunteer Regiment left New York city for the seat of war.— (*Doc.* 203.)

—THE First Regiment of Virginia Volunteers, Col. Kelly, stationed at Wheeling, Va., left that place at 7 A. M., and moved towards Grafton. After their departure, the Sixteenth Ohio Regiment, 1,000 strong, stationed at Bellaire, Ohio, under command of Col. Irvine, crossed the Ohio and followed Col. Kelly's command. The Fourteenth Ohio Regiment, Col. Steadman, crossed the Ohio, at Marietta, about the same time, and occupied Parkersburg. At midnight the rebels evacuated Grafton in great haste.—(*Doc.* 204.)

—THE Washington Artillery of New Orleans, La., left that city for Virginia. Previous to their departure, they were addressed by the Rev. Dr. Palmer.—(*Doc.* 205.)

May 28.—The forty-seventh annual meeting of the American Baptist Missionary Union, was held in the Pierrepont Street Baptist Church, Brooklyn, Ex-Gov. Briggs, of Massachusetts, in the chair. The exercises were opened with prayer by the Rev. Dr. Welch. The Chairman then addressed the meeting at some length, setting forth the object for which they had assembled. In reference to the present state of the country, he said that soldiers were now to be seen in every direction, flags were floating from every window in every street, old and young were rallying round the standard of the Government to sustain order and law, but amid all this outburst of enthusiasm the Prince of Peace must not be deserted. He was sure that the cause of all our difference with the South was owing to their misapprehension of the sentiments of the North, and he believed that if the heart of the North could be unvailed to their brethren of the South, all our national troubles would cease at once. Speaking of the charge made against the North by the Rev. Dr. Fuller of Baltimore—that the bad men of the North, the pastors, the churches, and the politicians, all united in crying for blood—for the blood of the Southern people, he inquired if this was the case? The congregation at once responded a vigorous " No." " No," said he, a more cruel, more unfounded charge never issued from the mouth of man. He denied that any such sentiments as Dr. Fuller had imputed to the North were entertained by Northern Christians. He hoped that the Union would place their sentiments on this subject on record, that the world might judge between truth and error.—*N. Y. Tribune, May* 29.

—THE Ninth New York Regiment, which was the first to offer their services to the Gov-

ernment, arrived at Washington. Having enlisted for three years, they lose their identity as State militia, and at once enter service as United States troops. Eight hundred of them are fully uniformed, and will prove a valuable acquisition to the regular army.—(*Doc.* 206.)— *National Intelligencer, May* 29.

—A NEW military department is formed by Gen. Scott, out of that portion of Virginia lying east of the Alleghanies and north of James River, exclusive of Fortress Monroe and vicinity, and Brigadier-General McDowell is appointed to its command. His staff consists of Colonel P. Stone, Fourteenth Infantry, who has recently rendered inestimable services in organizing the District of Columbia Militia; Captain B. O. Tyler, Brevet Captain James B. Fry, and Lieutenant Putnam, of the Topographical Engineers. —*N. Y. Herald, May* 29.

—THE blockade of the port of Savannah was initiated by the U. S. gunboat Union.—*Savannah Republican, May* 31.

—BRIGADIER-GENERAL PIERCE, Massachusetts Militia, was appointed to succeed Gen. Butler, promoted. He left for Washington immediately. Col. Waite, Major Sprague, and the other officers who were captured in Texas, and liberated on parole not to serve against the Confederate States, reached Washington, and reported to the War Department. Col. Lefferts, at Battalion Drill, took the sentiment of the Seventh N. Y. S. M., about remaining until ordered home by Government, their time having expired. Furloughs were offered to all who wished, but only five out of 1,225 asked for them.—*N. Y. Times, May* 29.

—IN the case of Gen. Cadwallader, whose arrest for contempt of Court was ordered, the Marshal reported that, on going to Fort McHenry, he was refused admittance.—(*Doc.* 207.)

—THE Chautauqua Volunteers, under the command of Capt. James M. Brown, left Jamestown, New York, for active service.—*Chautauqua Democrat, May* 29.

—IN the English House of Commons, a debate on British relations with America took place, being opened by a communication from Lord John Russell concerning the blockade. Lord John stated that Lord Lyons had properly said to Admiral Milne that the blockade, if sufficient, must be respected. Mr. T. Duncombe spoke with some warmth on the treatment which British subjects received in the Southern States, and commented with great severity on the piratical offer of $20 per head offered by the rebels for every person killed on board an American vessel. The debate was further continued by Mr. B. Osborne, Mr. Bright, Mr. Gregory, and Mr. Bouverie. Mr. Gregory treated the reported offer spoken of as a newspaper rumor, and declared that he should, on the 7th, press his motion for the acknowledgment of the " Confederate States."—(*Doc.* 207½.)

—JUDGE HALL's charge to the grand jury at Rochester, N. Y., on the law of treason, was published.—*N. Y. World, May* 28.

—Two letters from Edward Bates, Attorney-General of the United States, to John Minor Botts of Virginia, were made public.—(*Doc.* 208.)

—THE assertion of the Governor of Georgia, that property of citizens of that State found in the State of New York is forcibly taken from its owners, is denied in a letter published this day, signed by the officers of seven New York banks.—(*Doc.* 209.)

—THE Rochester Regiment, Colonel Quimby, and the Syracuse Regiment, Colonel Walrath, left Elmira, N. Y., for the seat of war.—*Buffalo Courier, May* 31.

—THE Garibaldi Guard, under the command of Colonel D'Utassy, left New York for the seat of war.—(*Doc.* 210.)

May 29.—A mass meeting of leading members of the Baptist Church was held at Brooklyn, N. Y., for the purpose of giving formal expression to their feelings, as a religious community in the present crisis, and to record their attachment to the Union, and their determination to uphold the efforts of the Federal Government, in behalf of the Constitution.—(*Doc.* 211.)

—THE Brooklyn, Capt. Poore, entered the Mississippi River, below New Orleans, and sent out a number of boats, strongly manned with armed men, to board the ships lying on the bar, to acquaint them of the terms of the blockade. After some discussion, it was agreed that the ships on the bar should have fourteen days to go out. Capt. Poore also made a full survey and soundings of the river.—*N. O. Delta, May* 31.

—A STATEMENT of the Geographical arrangements of the army of the United States, corrected to date, is published.—(*Doc.* 212.)

—PRESIDENT DAVIS reached Richmond this morning, accompanied by his nephew, Mr. Joseph Davis, Col. Northrop, of the Confederate Army, and Col. Wigfall. Gov. Letcher and the Executive Council met and received the President at Petersburg. An immense assemblage welcomed his arrival at Richmond, with the most enthusiastic demonstrations of delight. The President, in a brief address, thanked the multitude for the hearty reception given him. —*N. O. Delta, May* 30.

—TO-DAY the American flag was raised over the late residence of Lieutenant-General Scott, at Elizabethtown, N. J., in the presence of about five thousand people. When the flag was given to the breeze, the "Star-Spangled Banner" was sung, the vast concourse of people joining the chorus, producing a fine effect. Mayor Burnett presided, and speeches were made by William F. Day and Rev. Hobart Chetwood, which were received with great applause.—*N. Y. Commercial, May* 30.

—THE correspondence in relation to the establishment of a department of nurses, and the acceptance of the services of Miss Dix, by the Secretary of War, is published.—(*Doc.* 213.)

—THE *New Orleans True Delta* of this day contains the following:—" We have again and again received information of the motions and sentiments of vagabond free persons of color, upon whom it would be well that the police should keep an eye. These men are without ostensible means of earning a livelihood, and *are, by many degrees, too familiar with our slave population, instilling into their minds sanguine notions of the ' good time' to be experienced* in the event of Lincoln's hoped-for success over the Southern people. The lake end of the Pontchartrain Railroad is infested with persons of this character, *who exhibit a remarkable shrewdness* in broaching their pestiferous hints and suggestions. The city also affords rendezvous, at which there are gathered knots of these vagabonds at unseasonable hours. Of course the localities are selected with a view to privacy and remoteness from the inquisitive eyes of the watchman. Careful espionage may bring to light the object of these nocturnal consultations."

—THE Twentieth, Twenty-first, and Twenty-fourth Regiments of Pennsylvania militia left Philadelphia for Chambersburg.—*N. Y. Commercial, May* 30.

Engraved by J.C.Buttre.

J.C. Fremont.

MAJ. GEN. JOHN C. FREMONT.

—COLONEL MANN's Regiment of Pennsylvania militia, arrived at Easton, Pa., and went into camp.—(Doc. 214.)

—THE American citizens in Paris favorable to the Union breakfasted together in the Hotel du Louvre. About one hundred and fifty attended, of whom one-third were ladies, including the wife of General Scott. Mr. Cowdin presided. Resolutions were adopted, pledging the meeting to maintain the Union under any circumstances. Mr. Dayton, the U. S. Minister, said that, since his arrival in France, he could detect no unfriendly feeling on the part of France to the United States, and certainly no French citizen would be found among the privateersmen. He expressed the conviction that the rebellion would be put down. Cassius M. Clay spoke at length, and was emphatic in his comments on the conduct of England in recognizing Southern belligerent rights. He declared that if ever the flag of England was associated with the black flag of the South, the Star-Spangled Banner of the United States and the tri-color of France would be seen together against her, for France had not forgotten St. Helena. Hon. Anson Burlingame spoke on the same topic. Col. Fremont was next called upon, and was received with enthusiasm. He made a quiet and moderate speech. He regretted the fanatical war, and felt confident it would end in the triumph of truth and justice. He had been called back to America, and would lose no time in responding. He was ready to give his best services to his country. Rev. Dr. McClintock followed. He said he did not attach any importance to the mutterings of the English press. The people of England had not yet spoken, and when they did speak, their voices would not be found on the side of piracy and slavery. Capt. Simons, of the U. S. Army, said he was on his way home, in obedience to the summons of Gen. Scott. Mr. Haldeman, Minister to Vienna, and Rev. Mr. Thayer, also spoke. All the speakers evinced not the slightest doubt of the final triumph of the North.— *Galignani's Messenger, May 30.*

—THE *London News*, of this date, contains a remarkable article on the "War in America."—(Doc. 214½.)

May 30.—N. P. Banks, of Massachusetts, was appointed a Major-General, and Robert C. Schenck, of Ohio, a Brigadier-General in the Army. The eminent intelligence, energy, and activity of these distinguished citizens render their appointment signally judicious and fortunate.—*National Intelligencer, June 1.*

—THE Twelfth, Onondaga, and the Thirteenth, Rochester, N. Y., Regiments, commanded by Colonels Mulrath and Trumby, left Elmira for Washington. The Buffalo and Cayuga Regiments escorted them to the depot. An immense crowd was present to witness their departure.—*N. Y. Commercial, May 30.*

—THE *New Orleans Delta* of to-day says: "Henceforth all the cotton and other produce of the South destined for foreign markets must go from our seaports. So it has been determined by our Congress at Montgomery. The only exemption under the law is in favor of the trade between Mexico and Northwestern Texas. This is a wise measure. The threat of the Northern journals to force our shipments of produce to the North by a blockade of our seaports is thus promptly met, and their scheme defeated. Now, let us see who can stand the embargo longest. Our cotton and tobacco planters can go on and gather the immense crops which this season promises, and store them in their barns and warehouses, only sending to the ports what may be necessary to pay expenses, and which our friends from abroad insist upon having, and will take all the risk of buying and sending abroad. Meantime, what with two crops of corn, and any quantity of other produce, we can maintain a very comfortable existence. The negroes not being hurried to take off the crops, will have a very easy time of it. Their truck patches will supply them with an abundance of good vegetables. Their only trouble is that they can't go to the war and help their young masters to wallop the Abolitionists. This is rather hard upon them, especially as every plantation and household will have one or more of their race to represent them in battle. 'Old Wirginny' is the dance ground of our negroes, and to fight for it is their highest ambition. One of our negro acquaintances asked us a few days ago to intercede with his master to allow him to go on with one of our volunteer companies to the scene of war, stating that he wanted to fight for the graves of his ancestors, and he could not understand why his master should object to his going, when the Massachusetts people had placed a negro in command of one of their divisions. The story of General But-the Government, and taken to the Washington Navy-Yard.—*Boston Transcript, May 31.*

—At Acquia Creek, 55 miles below Washington on the Potomac, the U. S. gun-boat Freeborn, Capt. Ward, opened fire about 10 A. M., on the shells fell into the batteries. The fire from the earthwork batteries ceased in a short time, but a terrific fire was kept up from the main battery on the hill. The boats hauled off at 10 minutes of 12.—(*Doc.* 220.)

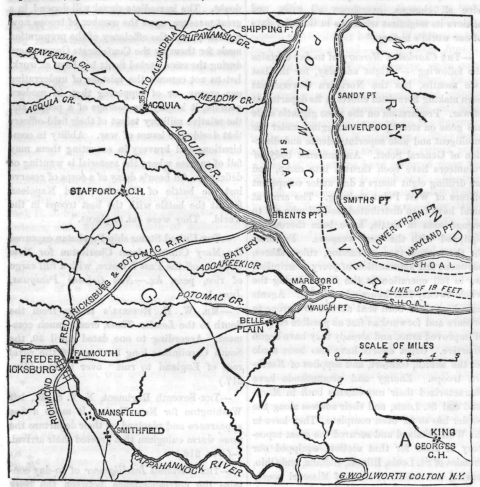

SCALE OF MILES

G. WOOLWORTH COLTON N.Y.

ferry-boat Page, lying at the depot of the Richmond, Fredericksburg, and Potomac Railroad. A second round was fired at the depot building, and a third across the bow of the Page. Three batteries on shore, two in the earthwork, near the depot, and a third from the hill above, immediately opened on the Freeborn, when the gun-boat Anacosta came to her assistance. As soon as the vessels had fixed their range they fired with marked effect. The Anacosta took up a position and played upon the depot with rapidity, firing thirteen shells, three of them taking effect and causing much consternation among the rebels. Several of the Freeborn's

June 1.—The bombardment of the rebel batteries at Acquia Creek was re-begun, at 11 30 A. M., by the U. S. gun-boats Freeborn and Pawnee. The firing on shore was scarcely as spirited at any time as on the day before. The heights were abandoned, the guns apparently having been transferred to the earthworks at the railroad termination, to replace the battery silenced there on the 31st ult. This railroad battery was otherwise repaired. The Freeborn approached to within about two miles from the shore, and fired four or five shots, when the Pawnee entered into the conflict, taking a position nearer to the land. For the first two hours, the fire from the shore batteries was sharp, but was returned with more expedition by the Pawnee. During the engagement, she fired 160 shells, one of which was seen to explode immediately over the heads of the Confederates who were working the battery. The observer, through a telescope, saw numbers of bodies of them carried away on wagons. During that time the shore movements were faster than at any other. The Freeborn lodged three shells in succession in the beach battery, perceptibly damaging the works, which had the effect of greatly diminishing the fire. The Freeborn received two shot, one of which passed through the cabin, damaging some of the crockery, but not the vessel, except making a passage through the bulwarks of slight consequence. The Pawnee received eight or nine shot, but all too high to inflict much damage. One struck her main-topsail yard, which was thereby unslung; another grazed the mizzenmasthead and passed through the hammock nettings. It is the opinion of the officers on board, that had the rebels been provided with good gunners, the vessels might probably have been sunk. Some of the Confederates' shots passed over the masthead to the Maryland shore. After five hours of incessant fire the gun-boats hauled off owing to the fatigue of the men, the day being very warm. During the last hour of the engagement only two or three shots were thrown from the shore, and the gunners were seen stealthily now and then to emerge from the concealment, and hastily load and fire a single gun. The railroad depot and buildings on the shore at Aquia Creek are all destroyed. The damage to the beach battery is not considered permanent, as the Confederates can soon repair it.—*N. Y. Times, June 3.*

—ABOUT daylight, Company B, of the second U. S. Cavalry, 47 privates, under Lieutenant Tompkins and Second Lieutenant Gordon, and three members of the New York Fifth Regiment, Quartermaster Fearing, Assistant Quartermaster Carey, and Adjutant Frank, reconnoitring within 300 yards of Fairfax Courthouse, by the Winchester road, were fired on by two of a picket of the Virginia troops. They captured the picket and then entered the village from the North side, and were fired on from the Union Hotel and from many houses, and from platoons behind fences. They charged down the principal street upon the mounted

riflemen whom they dispersed, and then wheeled about and instantly charged back, and were then met by two considerable detatchments, with a field-piece. Turning, they cut through a third detachment in the rear, and left the village bringing with them five prisoners, and killing throughout the engagement, as the officer in command thought, twenty-seven men. Two of the United States cavalry are missing, two are killed, and Assistant Quartermaster Carey, of the New York Fifth Regiment, is wounded in the foot. Lieutenant Tompkins had two horses shot under him, the last one falling on his leg, injuring it slightly.*—*(Doc. 221.)—Washington Star, June 1.*

—THE secession forces on the upper Potomac, attempted to take possession of the ferryboat lying opposite Williamsport, for the purpose, as is conjectured, of removing into "Falling Waters," a point four miles below, where there is a considerable number of secession troops stationed, who doubtless intended by means of the boat to cross to the Maryland side on a marauding expedition. The Union company at Williamsport, as soon as they observed the opposite party possessing themselves of the boat, ordered them to desist, which they refused to do; whereupon the Union guns opened fire upon them, which was returned, and a brisk fire was kept up on both sides for about an hour. Three or four secessionists were wounded, one seriously. None were killed or wounded on the Federal side.—*N. Y. Evening Post, June 3.*

—SHORTLY before 12 o'clock last night a skirmish took place at Arlington Mills, near Alexandria, between Capt. Brown's company of Zouaves and Capt. Roth's, Company E, of the Michigan Regiment, and a scouting party of nine Virginians. The Zouaves had just arrived to relieve the Michigan troops, and had posted sentinels when the Virginians attacked them. The Federal troops drove them away. One Zouave was killed and another wounded.

* Upon other authority it is said that the only one killed in the rebel camp was Capt. John Q. Marr, of the Warrenton Rifles. He heard the troops coming up and ordered them to halt. They replied that they were Capt. Powell's Cavalry Company. Capt. Marr then ordered his men to arms, when the United States Dragoons fired a volley, killing the captain. Instantly the rebels rushed out in undress, and in a disordered condition, and fired on the cavalry at random. Capt. Marr was a member of the Virginia State Convention, and a member elect of the Legislature from Fauquier County.—*N. Y. Times, June 2.*

DIARY—10

It is supposed one rebel was killed or wounded, as in the retreat he was carried off. The rebels retired in the woods during the night, and this morning took a hand-car and left for parts unknown.—*N. Y. Commercial, June 2.*

—At night word came into the camp of the Twenty-eighth New York Regiment, that the two dragoons missing from Company B, which made the sally on Fairfax Court-house this morning, were captured by the rebels, and were to be hung. Company B was immediately summoned from their quarters, and mounting, rode up to the Court-house, and having by some means ascertained the precise location of their comrades, made a dash through the village, and recovered the two men, whom they brought back in triumph to the camp.

Of the five Confederate prisoners taken at the Court-house one is a son of the late Major Washington of the Army. He said he did not want to fight against the United States, and made amends by taking the oath of allegiance. —*N. Y. Times, June 3.*

—The big guns were planted at Cairo, Ill., and the first thirty-two pound ball was sent booming down the Mississippi, a warning to all traitors to keep at a respectable distance. Great satisfaction was expressed throughout the camp that these heavy guns were at length in place. The firing over, a whole regiment of nearly a thousand men, detailed for the day, sprang to their shovels and wheelbarrows, and the work of completing the breastworks went gaily on. The levee itself forms an excellent breastwork, behind which, now that Bird's Point is fortified, the soldiers would be perfectly protected, and with Sharp's rifles they could mow down whole regiments, if the steamers that bore them escaped the artillery and effected a landing.—*National Intelligencer, June 13.*

—Jefferson Davis was serenaded at Richmond, and addressed the assembled crowd. To a person who wanted to hear something about Buena Vista, he said that they "would make the battle-field of Virginia another Buena Vista, and drench it with blood more precious than that which flowed there." Gov. Wise also addressed the crowd, and told them to arm with any thing they could get, and to take a lesson from John Brown.—*(Doc. 222.)*

—There is published an order of the Post-master General of the Southern Confederacy, by which the postmasters throughout the rebel States are ordered to "retain" the stamps, locks, etc., of the various offices—the property of the United States.—*(Doc. 223.)*

—L. W. Bliss, Acting Governor of Jefferson Territory, proclaimed the neutrality of that Territory, and forbid the payment of any debts or future dues to the United States or any body else outside the Territory; but he generously offered to receive payment for all debts due to outsiders into the Territorial Treasury, and give his notes for it on interest at ten per cent. —*(Doc. 224.)*

—The address of the Central Committee of Northwestern Virginia to the people of that locality, is published in full.—*(Doc. 225.)*

June 2.—Three thousand men, of Indiana, Ohio, and Virginia volunteers, the whole under command of Col. Crittenden, of Indiana, were assembled on the parade ground at Grafton, Va., in the afternoon, and informed in general terms that they were to start on a forced march that night. They were then supplied with ammunition and one day's rations, and dismissed. The men were full of ardor, expecting that they were going direct to Harper's Ferry. At eight o'clock they were again assembled, and took up the line of march on the road leading southward. A heavy rain soon commenced to fall, and continued all night.—*N. Y. Times, June 6.*

—About midnight a squad of secession cavalry made a dash at the outposts of the Twenty-eighth New York Regiment, and fired upon them. The alarm was instantly sounded and the regiment turned out, and a scouting party despatched in pursuit of the enemy, who retreated. The fire was returned by the outposts of the Twenty-eighth, with what effect is not known, as the night was exceedingly dark. No damage whatever was done by the enemy.—*N. Y. Times, June 3.*

—The Seventy-ninth Regiment, N. Y. S. M., Lieut.-Col. S. M. Elliott, commanding, left New York for Washington, accompanied by a body of recruits of the Seventy-first and Ninth N. Y. Regiments.—*(Doc. 226.)*

—Gen. Twiggs was appointed Major-General in the Confederate army, and accepted the rank. He will command the military district of Louisiana.—*Natchez Courier, June 4.*

—Senator Rousseau, a member of the upper house of the legislature of Kentucky, delivered a strong Union speech before that body on the 21st of May last. The senator exposes the folly of attempting to preserve a neutral attitude in the present crisis, and boldly tells many very plain truths to the secessionists of Kentucky.— (*Doc.* 227.)

June 3.—Quartermaster T. Bailey Myers arrived at New York from Fortress Monroe, bringing from that quarter a secession flag as a present to the Union Defence Committee. The flag was captured at Hampton village, near the fort, and when taken was flying from its staff on the *roof of John Tyler's country residence.* Lieutenant Duryea, the colonel's son, let down the traitorous emblem, and ran up the Stars and Stripes, which are now flying. The scouting detachment brought in the secession colors to head-quarters, and they were forwarded by Major-General Butler. The flag is a dirty looking affair of red, white, and blue flannel, with eight stars. It is roughly made, the sewing having been done by half-taught fingers. —*N. Y. Commercial Advertiser, June* 4.

—Gen. Beauregard arrived at Manassas Junction, and assumed command of the rebel forces there.—*N. Y. Times, June* 6.

—At night twelve volunteers from Camp Lincoln, near Leavenworth, Kansas, headed by Sergeant Decurin, of the Elwood Guards, armed with Minié rifles and revolvers, marched to Iatan, Mo., fourteen miles above Leavenworth city, and crossed in skiffs to capture a secession flag. When asked their purpose, Decurin demanded the flag by the authority of the United States. The flag was hauled down, and the party started on their return, when they were fired at by the secessionists, and the fire was returned. Three of the volunteers were wounded, one severely.—*N. Y. World, June* 6.

—At 1 a. m., the Union force from Grafton, approached Philippi, a little town on the Monongahela, 20 miles south of Grafton, occupied by 1,500 rebels. Scouts went forward to reconnoitre, a favorable report was received, and the troops advanced about 5 a. m., and were fired at by the sentinels on duty, who appeared to be the only men on the alert. The camp, however, was immediately aroused, and before it was reached by our troops three companies of riflemen advanced to meet them, and delivered a volley as Col. Kelly's regiment turned the corner of a street. They then turned and retreated towards the main body. At this fire several of our men were slightly wounded, and Col. Kelly received a ball in the side. The regiment pressed on, and was quickly followed by the Indiana and Ohio regiments. When the column got within range of the main body of the enemy, the latter delivered a straggling fire, and then at once broke and fled. It was a complete rout. The Union troops delivered a volley with good effect at the enemy, and then charged upon them at full run. The enemy took the direction of Leedsville, ten miles further south. Col. Crittenden ordered the Ohio regiment to stay and guard the town, and the other two regiments continued the pursuit. They returned after daylight, with several prisoners. The secessionists had no idea of being attacked. They had no intrenchments, and had only set the ordinary guard. One or two of the Federal troops were killed. The loss of the secessionists, so far as known, is sixteen killed, a large number wounded, and ten prisoners. Some twenty-five of Col. Kelly's men were wounded, but none dangerously. The amount of ammunition captured was not large, but there was a lot of camp kettles and provisions, and miscellaneous camp equipage, that fell into the hands of the federal troops; also seventeen horses. Col. Kelly's wound was not mortal.—(*Doc.* 228.)

—Stephen A. Douglass, Senator of the United States from Illinois, died at Chicago at ten minutes past nine o'clock in the morning. —*Buffalo Courier, June* 4.

—The Fourteenth Regiment, Colonel Johnson, and the Fifteenth, Colonel Oakford, of Pennsylvania Volunteers, arrived at General Patterson's camp at Chambersburg from Lancaster.—*National Intelligencer, June* 6.

—The British Government decided not to allow the entry of privateers into any of their ports. This was announced by Lord John Russell in Parliament, saying that Government had determined to prohibit privateers from bringing prizes into any British port. It was also stated that France intended adhering to the law which prohibits privateers remaining in port over twenty-four hours.—(*Doc.* 229.)

—The border State Convention met at Frankfort, Kentucky.—*N. Y. Tribune, May* 27.

—MAJOR-GENERAL PATTERSON, from headquarters at Chambersburg, Pa., issued a proclamation announcing to the soldiers that "they would soon meet the insurgents."—(*Doc.* 230.)

—THE First Regiment Scott Life Guard and the Third Regiment N. Y. S. V., left New York city for Fortress Monroe.—(*Doc.* 231.)

June 4.—The *Memphis Bulletin* of to-day contains the following: "Persons having slaves at home, whose services can be dispensed with for the next ten or fifteen days, would do a great kindness to the volunteers at Randolph, by sending negro men to that point. The volunteers should be drilled, and the fortifications, on which they have labored so long and faithfully, should be finished by negroes."

—A MAN named Fletcher, living in Columbia township, Randolph County, Ark., divulged last week a plot to the citizens which he had discovered among the negroes in that vicinity. The plot contemplated the murder of several citizens who they supposed had money, and then making their way to the free States. An investigation led to the development of the fact that certain negroes had proposed to give Fletcher $20 each to take them to a free State, announcing that their plan contemplated the murder of citizens, the possession of their means, and their final escape to the North. The negroes implicated by Fletcher, twenty in number, were arrested. A white man named Percifield, found guilty of being an instigator in the affair, was hung, as was also Fletcher, who was connected with Percifield.—*Memphis (Tenn.) Avalanche, June* 5.

—ELIAS HOWE, JR., of New York, the sewing machine millionaire, presented each field and staff officer of the Massachusetts Fifth Regiment, at the seat of war, with a stallion fully equipped for service.—*N. Y. Express.*

—THE Tenth Regiment N. Y. Volunteers, National Zouaves, Colonel McChesney, left their encampment at Sandy Hook for Fortress Monroe. Previous to their departure they paraded through the city of New York, where they received a flag.—*N. Y. Sun, June* 5.

—THE *Savannah Republican* of to-day has the following: "*Notice to the Press.*—We are requested by the military authorities of the Confederate States to urge upon our brethren of the press throughout the South the importance of abstaining from all specific allusions to the movement of troops. The very wisest plans of the Government may be thwarted by an untimely or otherwise injudicious exposure."

A directly opposite policy appears to prevail at the North. Not only is every movement of the Federal troops heralded abroad with lightning speed for the "sensation press," but it would seem as if the news-gatherers have access to the records of the Departments, so as to enable them to proclaim in advance every plan and purpose of the Government, whether great or small.—*National Intelligencer, June* 13.

—NOAH L. FARNHAM, late Lieutenant-Colonel of the Regiment of Fire Zouaves of New York, was appointed Colonel of that Regiment, in place of the late Colonel Ellsworth.—*N. Y. World, June* 5.

—JUDGE TANEY'S written opinion in the *habeas corpus* case of Merriman, was published in the Washington *National Intelligencer* of this date. It is simply a protest against the suspension of the writ by the President of the United States. The Judge argues that Congress alone has the legal authority to suspend this privilege, and that the President cannot "in any emergency, or in any state of things," authorize its suspension.

—TEN Regiments of foot, with Doubleday's, Dodge's, and Seymour's batteries of flying artillery and five hundred dragoons, were in camp around Chambersburg, Pa.—Thirty-two men arrived at Williamsport, Md., from Berkley Co., Va., whence they had fled to avoid impressment into the rebel army.—A new Collector was appointed for Louisville, Kentucky, with orders to prohibit the shipment South of provisions, *via* that port.—*N. Y. Herald, June* 5.

—A PROCLAMATION dated Fort Smith, Arkansas, and signed "W. F. Rector, Asst. Adjutant-General," says, "the authority of the United States has ceased upon this frontier."—(*Doc.* 232.)

—THE *Natchez (Miss.) Courier* of this day has the following: "A wise and salutary law was passed by the Confederate Congress, before its adjournment, prohibiting, during the existence of the blockade of any of the Southern ports by the United States Government, the exportation of any raw cotton or cotton yarn except through the seaports of the Confederate States. The penalty for a violation of the law is the forfeiture of the cotton or yarn so attempted to be exported, as also fine or imprisonment for the person violating it. Every steamboat or railroad car, used with the consent of the person owning or in charge of it for the purpose of violating the act, is also forfeited. This law completely blocks the Lincoln scheme. The Administration's idea was, that if Southern ports were blockaded, the cotton would go by inland routes to Northern seaports for exportation. Great Britain and France will now have to go without cotton, or else raise the Lincoln blockade."—(See Doc. p. 292.)

—MAJOR-GENERAL PRICE (rebel) of Missouri, issued a proclamation "to prevent all misunderstanding of his opinions and intentions," and expressed the desire "that the people of Missouri should exercise the right to choose their own position" in the contest.—(Doc. 233.)

June 5.—A demand was served upon Messrs. Daniel J. Foley & Bros., Baltimore, by Mr. Bonifant, the United States Marshal, under instructions from Mr. Cameron, Secretary of War, calling for the immediate delivery into the possession of the Marshal of all the powder of the Hazard Powder Company, Connecticut, stored in the powder-house of the company at Lower Canton. The amount of the powder on hand was about 3,500 kegs, or 60,000 pounds, valued at $16,000. The agents turned the powder over to the Marshal, who took an inventory of the same. A similar demand, from the same source, was made upon Messrs. A. L. Webb & Bro., Baltimore, agents for the Messrs. Dupont's powder works, Delaware. The demand was complied with, and the powder on hand, a small amount, turned over into the possession of the United States.—Baltimore Sun, June 6.

—GENERAL BEAUREGARD issued a proclamation from Mannassas Junction, giving an extravagant picture of the deplorable consequences to be expected from an invasion of the Federal forces.—(Doc. 234.)

—AT Williamsport a Baltimorean, named Dewitt C. Reuch, swore he could whip the whole Union force, and that he had killed at least one man in the attack upon the Massachusetts Regiment in Baltimore. His friends tried to get him away and put him on a horse, when he drew a revolver and fired two shots at individuals and three into the crowd. Three shots were returned, all taking effect, killing him instantly.—Philadelphia Ledger, June 7.

—THROUGHOUT all the counties of Virginia, within forty or fifty miles of Harper's Ferry, a levy of militia is being now made by draft. All the men between eighteen and fifty years of age, not physically incapable of doing military duty, are enlisted, and three-tenths of the whole are to be mustered into the field. The names are placed in one box, and as many numbers—from one to ten (repeated)—are placed in another box. When a name is drawn forth a number is also drawn; and if it be either No. 1, 2, or 3, the person is "elected" a soldier into the disunion army. Otherwise he escapes immediate service.—Washington Star, June 6.

—THE Ninth Regiment N. Y. V., Colonel Hawkins, left New York for Fortress Monroe.—(Doc. 235.)

—THE Richmond (Va.) Whig of to-day announces that after to-day no passports will be issued to persons leaving the State, and no one will be admitted to the State except for reasons of peculiar force; also, that the Tennessee volunteers in Virginia are authorized to vote on the ordinance of the secession of Tennessee, although stationed in Virginia.—A Bank Convention, held at Atlanta, Ga., recommended that all the Southern banks, railroads, and tax collectors, receive the Treasury notes of the Confederacy as currency, and both States, cities, and corporations having coupons payable at New York, to appoint the place of payment South.—N. Y. Herald, June 10.

—ABOUT eight o'clock this morning the steamer Harriet Lane, under the command of Capt. Faunce, United States Navy, proceeded up the James River, from Fortress Monroe, as far as the mouth of the Nasemond, for the purpose of reconnoitring and looking out for batteries. It was not long before she observed a large and heavy battery planted upon the point, which is nearly opposite Newport News Point, and about five miles distant. The steamer opened fire, which was briskly returned by the batteries, and for nearly a half hour the action continued. It was found that but one gun of the steamer could reach the battery, the guns of which being heavier easily reached the former, and several shot struck her. During the affair the most intense excitement prevailed, and hundreds of soldiers ascended the ramparts and roof of the Hygeia Hotel, for the purpose of looking at the scene. The Lane returned in an hour after the action, and made an official report to Com. Pendergrast of the squadron. Lieut. Duncan, of the Harriet Lane, states that the fight was pretty hot. The steamer threw several shells into the battery with much accuracy. The battery was well served, the damage to the cutter having been inflicted with a 34-pounder rifled cannon. It was at first thought that no battery existed at the place where the fight occurred, and the Harriet Lane was sent to ascertain if the report was true. She found out that one did exist, and that seven guns were mounted upon it, and hence the attempt made to dislodge them.—*National Intelligencer, June* 8.

—A LETTER from Cassius M. Clay to the *London Times*, in relation to the civil war in America, is published in the United States. Mr. Clay says that the rebellion can be subdued, but that it is not the intention of the U. S. Government to subjugate the Southern States; that only rebels will be punished; that it is the interest of England to support the Government; and that it is unwise for England to venture to sow seeds of discord, for she is far from secure from home revolution or foreign attack in the future. In conclusion Mr. Clay claims that England is the natural ally of the United States.—(*Doc.* 236.)

—THE people of Wheeling, Va., were greatly astounded upon learning that Major A. Loring had been arrested by United States officers. He was taken to the Baltimore and Ohio Railroad depot, where he remained until 7 o'clock, when the train left for Grafton. Major Loring's arrest was occasioned by certain papers found upon the person of W. J. Willey, who was captured after the skirmish at Phillippa, and who is charged with leading the party who destroyed the bridges on the Baltimore and Ohio Railroad, between Wheeling and Grafton.—(*Doc.* 237.)

—THE U. S. Marshal took possession of the gun factory of Messrs. Merrill & Thomas, in Baltimore, and seized all the breech-loading muskets in the establishment. Intimation was given that ample employment would soon be given to the establishment in the manufacture of arms for the Government.—*N. Y. Express, June* 5.

June 6.—Gov. Pickens of South Carolina issued a proclamation saying:—"I have understood that many good people have been remitting funds to creditors in Northern States. In the existing relations of the country such conduct is in conflict with public law, and all citizens are hereby warned against the consequences."—*N. Y. Tribune, June* 14.

—THIS evening the Town Guard of Harrodsburg, Ky., were attracted to the Spring Grounds by a noise in that direction. When they came near the old shooting gallery they heard voices responding to one who seemed to be officiating as an officer. Surrounding the building, they pushed open the door, and lo! an assembly of Knights of the Golden Circle *in masks!* One of the Guard, on entering, knocked off the mask of one of the Knights; and a lawyer and secessionist stood forth. No examination of the arcana was made, a majority of the Guards being secessionists. Several Virginia gentlemen were in Harrodsburg that night.—*Louisville Journal, June* 14.

—THE Nineteenth N. Y. Regiment, Colonel Clark commander, left Elmira for Washington, via Harrisburg. An immense concourse of people witnessed the departure. Great enthusiasm prevailed.—*N. Y. Herald, June* 7.

—A MEETING was held at the Cooper Institute, in New York, for the purpose of securing the co-operation of citizens in the endeavor to provide for the religious wants of volunteers. Wm. E. Dodge, Esq., presided, and addresses were made by Rev. Drs. Tyng and Hitchcock, after which the following resolutions were adopted:

Resolved, That in the opinion of this meeting the project of the Young Men's Christian Association, to provide for the religious wants of the Volunteers, is worthy of public confidence and co-operation, and that we commend the same to the support of the churches and the community.

Resolved, That Messrs. William E. Dodge, Wilson G. Hunt, Benj. F. Maniere, Benj. W. Bonney, and Alexander W. Bradford, be appointed a committee to receive donations in furtherance of the proposed object, to be expended under the supervision of the army committee of the Young Men's Christian Association.—*N. Y. Commercial, June* 7.

—A SECESSION camp at Ellicott's Mills, in

Kentucky, ten miles distant from Cairo, Ill., was dispersed by two companies sent thither by General Prentiss. Colonel Wickliffe protested against the act as an invasion of the soil of Kentucky; to which Gen. Prentiss said, in reply, that the act had been prompted by a letter claiming protection for the Union men there. He declared his intention also to send troops any place needed for the protection of loyal citizens.—*National Intelligencer, June 8.*

—In the New York Chamber of Commerce it was *Resolved,* That the Executive Committee of this Chamber, after consultation with and subject to the approval of Col. Anderson, or his second in command, cause to be prepared a suitable medal for each of the soldiers and non-commissioned officers of the late garrison of Fort Sumter, and to have them presented at as early a day as possible, at the expense of this Chamber.

By amendment the resolution was made to include the garrison of Fort Pickens under Lieutenant Slemmer, and the officers of both garrisons.—*N. Y. Tribune, June 7.*

—Thirty-five of the prisoners captured at Alexandria, took the oath of allegiance with cheerful alacrity; and were discharged.—*Washington Star, June 7.*

June 7.—The Engineer Corps of the Sixty-ninth Regiment of New York, with Company B, of the Second Cavalry, took five prisoners and a drove of cattle, fifty in number, which were on their way to the secession forces.—*N. Y. World, June 10.*

—An express messenger arrived at New Orleans from Mr. Adolphe Ducros's plantation, at the mouth of Bayou Bienvenu, which empties into Lake Borgne, with information to Maj.-Gen. Twiggs, that two fishermen had reported the arrival of two small war steamers in Lake Borgne, one carrying three guns, and the other a long pivot gun forward. The fishermen stated that the steamers lay off in the lake, and that night before last they sent two boats towards the mouth of the bayou, as was supposed, for taking soundings. Gen. Twiggs ordered Major Taylor, in command of the barracks, to proceed immediately to Martello Tower, at the mouth of Bayou Bienvenu, with a company of infantry, to garrison the tower, which contains several heavy mounted guns, for the protection of this avenue to the city. This point is but ten miles from New Orleans in a direct line, and a little over fifteen by the Mexican Gulf Railroad. It is celebrated for being the point at which the British landed their troops in the war of 1813–'14.—*New Orleans Picayune, June 8.*

—The Tenth Regiment, of New York, arrived at Fortress Monroe.—*N. Y. Times, June 9.*

—The tents at Camp McClure, Chambersburg, Pa., were struck at six o'clock A. M., and the line of march taken up soon afterwards for Brown's Mill, near Green Castle, and eight miles distant from Camp McClure. The force in motion was Brig.-Gen. Thomas' command, was headed by him, and included the U. S. Cavalry, (recently from Texas,) 4 companies, the Philadelphia City Troop, and the 2 companies of artillerists, commanded by Captains Doubleday and Seymour, McMullin's Independent Rangers, the Twenty-third Regiment, Col. Dare, the Twenty-first Regiment, Col. Ballier, and the Sixth Regiment, Col. Nagle. The line was nearly 2 miles in length. The men all had their knapsacks closely slung to prevent jolting, and had evidently prepared themselves, so far as their knowledge taught them, for a long march.—*Idem.*

—The Indiana Regiment of Zouaves, Col. Wallace, fully armed and equipped, passed through Cincinnati, Ohio, en route for Cumberland, Md. They made a splendid appearance, and were enthusiastically received.—*Ohio State Journal, June 8.*

—Colonel Corcoran, of the Sixty-ninth N. Y. Regiment, with a detachment of one hundred men, proceeded to Ball's Corner, 5 miles beyond the lines in Virginia, where he arrested a party of five secessionists, one wearing the uniform of a secession sergeant; one, named Richard Meitch, an employé at the capital as watchman, and one named Ball, a rich farmer, on whom was found a muster roll of a rebel company, and in whose house were found arms, bedding, and cooking utensils for a company of at least fifty men. Nine hundred dollars in gold were also found, but returned by the mistaken generosity of the sergeant, to Ball's wife, without the Colonel's knowledge until after their return to the camp.—*N. Y. Times, June 8.*

—The New York Nineteenth Regiment, from Elmira, commanded by Col. Clark, and the

Third Maine Regiment Volunteers, Col. Howard, arrived at Washington.—(*Doc.* 238.)

—A CREW of 402 seamen, ordinary seamen, and landsmen, left the receiving-ship North Carolina at Brooklyn, for Portsmouth, N. H., where they will constitute a ship's company for the United States frigate Santee, which, after lying in various positions at the Navy Yard for half a century, has been put in commission for blockade service. The Advance Brigade of Federal troops, under Col. Thomas, reached Greencastle, thirteen miles south of Chambersburg, Pa.— *N. Y. World, and N. Y. Times, June* 8.

June 8.—The bridges at Point of Rocks and Berlin, on the Potomac River, were burned by order of Johnston, the rebel general. Neither of them were railroad bridges.—*N. Y. Herald, June* 10.

—THE sanitary commission was authorized by the Secretary of War, and approved by the President. Its aim is to help, by cautious suggestion, in the laborious and extraordinary exigencies of military affairs, when the health of the soldiers is a matter of the most critical importance. The commission consists of the Rev. Dr. Bellows, Prof. A. D. Bache, LL. D., Prof. Wolcott Gibbs, M. D., Prof. Jeffries Wyman, M. D., W. H. Van Buren, M. D., Dr. S. G. Howe, Dr. Wood, U. S. A., Col. Cullum, U. S. A., and Major Shiras, U. S. A.—*N. Y. Commercial, June* 10.

—SOME disunion troops from Leesburg, Va., burnt four bridges on the Alexandria, Loudon, and Hampshire Railroad, at Tuscarora, Lycoline, Goose Creek, and Beaver Dams, being the balance of the bridges from Leesburg to Broad Run.—*N. Y. World, June* 15.

—THE ceremony of the presentation of a Confederate flag, from the ladies of Baltimore to the members of the Maryland Guard, now in Virginia, took place in the Capitol grounds, at Richmond, Va. Mrs. Augustus McLaughlin, the wife of one of the officers of the late United States Navy, who brought the flag from Baltimore, concealed as only a lady knows how, was present, and received the compliments of a large number of ladies and gentlemen who surrounded her upon the steps of the monument, from which the address was made. The presentation speech was made by the Hon. J. M. Mason. Accompanying the flag is the inscription : "The ladies of Baltimore present this flag of the Confederate States of America to the soldiers composing the Maryland Regiment, now serving in Virginia, as a slight testimonial of the esteem in which their valor, their love of right, and determination to uphold true constitutional liberty, are approved, applauded, and appreciated by the wives and daughters of the monumental city."—(*Doc.* 239.)—*Richmond Dispatch, June* 10.

—Gov. HICKS, of Maryland, issued a proclamation calling upon all persons having arms belonging to that State, to surrender them.— (*Doc.* 240.)

—THIS morning a detachment of Federal troops from Annapolis, on one of the steamers of the Ericsson line, made their appearance in Miles River, and landed at the ferry, the nearest point to Easton, Md. On landing they proceeded to arrest Messrs. Thomas and William Holliday, whom they compelled to inform them where the armory for the safe-keeping of the guns was located. They also arrested Charles G. Kerr, Esq., late of the Exchange newspaper, and a Mr. Roberts, and several others. The military then proceeded on their search for arms, and succeeded in finding a number of muskets, and several iron field-pieces, all of which they put on the steamer and removed to Annapolis. Two of the old iron field-pieces were some time since removed from Cambridge, where they were planted for the defence of that place in the war of 1814. Before going to Miles River Ferry they stopped at the farm of Capt. Ogle Tilghman, a few miles below, but did not find the proprietor at home. They reported to Mrs. T. that they were from Richmond, and had come for the purpose of offering arms to the inhabitants, at the same time asking if there were any in the house. There were none but the private arms of Capt. T., which they did not disturb. While the detachment was drawn up on the boat, one of the soldiers placed the muzzle of his musket under his chin for a rest for his head, when the weapon accidentally discharged. The ball passed out through the top of his head, killing him instantly, and then passed through the hurricane deck in close proximity to two soldiers who were there. The detachment consisted of 250 men of the N. Y. 13th Regiment, under Col. Abel Smith.—*Baltimore Sun, June* 11.

—GENERAL T. A. MORRIS, commanding the United States troops at Phillippi, issued a proclamation announcing that Western Virginia is now free from the enemies to her peace, the United States forces having routed the secessionists at Philippi, causing them to flee for refuge to the passes of the mountains; and he therefore calls upon all loyal Virginians to come to the support of the United States Government, and serve in defence of their own soil.—(*Doc.* 241.)

—THE New Orleans *Catholic Standard* says: "Let no Southern child be educated outside the limits of the Confederate States. We have excellent schools and colleges at Richmond and Norfolk in Virginia; at Charleston and Columbia in South Carolina; at Savannah and Augusta in Georgia; at St. Augustine in Florida; at Mobile in Alabama; at Bay St. Louis, Pass Christian, Sulphur Springs, Vicksburg, and Natchez in Mississippi; at Fort Smith, Helena, and Little Rock in Arkansas; at Marksville, and Memphis in Tennessee; at Galveston, New Braunfels, San Antonio, Brownsville, and Liberty in Texas; and at St. Michael's Grand Coteau, Vermillionville, Thibodeaux, Donaldsonville, Natchitoches, Avoyelles, Alexandria, Shreveport, Iberville, Algiers, and New Orleans in Louisiana. The social bonds between us and the Catholics at the North have been severed by them. We acknowledge them no longer as our countrymen. They and their institutions have no claims upon us."

—THE Burlington (Vt.) *Times*, of this date, contains an extended narrative of the movements of the First Vermont Regiment at Fortress Monroe and its vicinity.—(*Doc.* 242.)

—ADDRESSES to the People of the United States and to the people of Kentucky, signed by J. J. Crittenden, Jas. Guthrie and others, members of the Border State Convention, lately in session at Frankfort, Ky., were published. Only the States of Kentucky and Missouri were represented; one gentleman was irregularly present from Tennessee. To the people of the United States the Convention says that, "in its opinion, the obligation exists to maintain the Constitution of the United States and to preserve the Union unimpaired;" and suggests that something "ought to be done" to quiet "apprehension within the slave States that already adhere to the Union." To the people of Kentucky they say that the proper course for that State "to pursue, is to take no part in the controversy between the

Government and the seceded States but that of mediator and intercessor," and ask if this "is not an attitude worthy of a great people." —(*Doc.* 243.)

June 9.—A detachment of the Rhode Island Regiment finished building a floating bridge on the Potomac, near Georgetown, by which thousands of men could be transported across in a few hours. Capt. Medlar, Provost-marshal of Alexandria, seized army supplies consisting of uniforms and cavalry swords, to the value of fifteen hundred dollars.—*N. Y. World*, *June* 10.

—Two prisoners were captured yesterday by four privates of Company B, Michigan Regiment, one mile this side of Berks Station, and thirteen miles from Alexandria, Va., on the Orange and Alexandria Railroad. One of the prisoners is a corporal in a cavalry company, and the other a private in the Governor's Guards of Richmond, which is also a cavalry company. The Michigan men while scouting approached near Berks Station, when they saw a number of stacks of muskets. They put back and were pursued by the two cavalry, but sought refuge in ambush, and succeeded in capturing their prisoners and brought them to Alexandria, where they are treated with exceeding kindness. They appear to be quite contented, and one of them, who is a physician, is writing a statement of his experience. The names of the prisoners are Dr. Thomas M. Flemming and Samuel Green.

Seven thousand yards of cassinet and other military goods were seized at the Adams Express office to-day, consigned to Point of Rocks, via Alexandria and Loudon Railroad, valued at about $10,000.

Expedition, the first number of the soldiers' newspaper, printed by the Pennsylvania Fifth Regiment, appeared this evening. It is printed in fine style on the old Alexandria *Sentinel* press, and is full of interesting information regarding the condition of the soldiers, &c. It is edited by Lieutenant Ely, of Lebanon county. Several columns are devoted to German literature.—*N. Y. Courier & Enquirer*, *June* 10.

—IN the last number of the Danville (Ky.) *Review*, Rev. Dr. Breckinridge discusses the southern rebellion in temperate but forcible language. He traces the origin and progress of the insurrection, and demonstrates not only that the rebel leaders are bent upon the accomplishment of selfish ends, but that the latent loyalty of the masses of the southern people needs but the protection of the Federal Government to be able to assert itself, to the utter discomfiture of Jeff. Davis and his fellows. Dr. Breckinridge is the uncle of the late Vice-President of the United States.—*N. Y. Evening Post, June 22.*

—ALL day the Naval Brigade, under the direction of a company of United States marines, were engaged off Fortress Monroe, Va., practising the management of eight or ten scows, each carrying twenty-four oars, and capable of transporting 130 men each, besides the rowers. When this marine drill was concluded every oar was carefully muffled, and the scows, manned each by a coxswain and twenty-six rowers from the Naval Brigade, glided out from the fort, and rowed in the harbor to the mouth of Hampton River, and up the stream. At about midnight they were moored on the hither shore in Hampton, and just below the remains of the bridge destroyed in the rebel retreat two weeks previously. The stream at that point is from sixty to one hundred yards in width. In the afternoon orders were given for a concerted movement of forces from Newport News, and from the camps at Fortress Monroe, against a position that the rebels had taken up at or near Great Bethel, in York county, a place about 12 miles northwest of Fortress Monroe. In accordance with the terms of the order three companies of Duryea's regiment, under Capt. Kilpatrick, went forward from Hampton on the Bethel road at 10 P. M., and soon after the remainder of Duryea's regiment, and the New York Third, Col. Townsend, followed, and were ferried over Hampton Creek by the boats of the Naval Brigade previously taken round from Fortress Monroe. Meantime, 5 companies, each from the Vermont First Regiment, and the Massachusetts Fourth, under Lieut.-Col. Washburne; six companies of the N. Y. Seventh, Col. Bendix, and a squad of regulars with 2 howitzers, under Lieut. Greble, moved forward from the position at Newport News, to form a junction on the road with the men from Fortress Monroe.

June 10.—At 1 A. M. the 3 companies of the New York Fifth, under Capt. Kilpatrick, reached New Market Bridge, and there waited for the main body of the Fifth, which came up at 3 A. M., when the whole regiment started

forward for Little Bethel, where they arrived about daylight, and encountered a picket guard of the enemy, which was taken. Shortly after Duryea's regiment passed onward toward Little Bethel, the force from Newport News came up the road from that place, and took the road from Hampton to Bethel, not far behind the Fifth; but they left at the junction of the roads, under Col. Bendix, a rear guard of one hundred and seventy men and one field-piece, with the order to hold this position at all hazards. This order anticipated the possibility that a rebel force might get in the rear of the Federal troops and cut off the retreat. Almost immediately after, the Third N. Y. Regiment came up the Hampton road. It was still dark, and their colors could not be seen. Their approach also was over a ridge, and as General Pierce and staff, and Colonel Townsend and staff, in a body, rode in advance of their troops, and without any advance guard thrown out, as customary, to reconnoitre, they appeared from Col. Bendix's position to be a troop of cavalry. It was known that the Federal force had no cavalry, and the fire of this rear guard was poured into the advancing body, at the distance of a quarter of a mile. But the road in which the Third was marching was a little below the level of the land along the edge, and was bordered on either side by fences which served as a partial cover, and hence the fire was comparatively harmless. Ten men were wounded by it, and one killed. The Third fell back and formed upon a hill near the road, and Gen. Pierce sent a hurried message to Fortress Monroe for support, in accordance with which the N. Y. First and Second, Cols. Allen and Carr, were sent forward. Col. Duryea, admonished by the fire in his rear that something was wrong, also brought his regiment back. Daylight soon divulged the true state of the case, and the force was organized, and Brig.-Gen. Pierce of Mass. assumed the command.

Gen. Pierce determined to push on in advance, and the force moved in the following order:—Col. Duryea with the N. Y. Fifth; Lieut.-Col. Washburne, with the companies from Newport News, and Greble's battery; Col. Townsend, with the N. Y. Third; Col. Allen, with the N. Y. First; and Col. Carr, with the N. Y. Second. When the fire of Col. Bendix's command was delivered, that force was stationed very near to the outlying camp of the enemy, who at once took the alarm, and got away. Thus the rebels at Great Bethel were informed of the advance of a superior force, and sent back to their head-quarters at Yorktown for re-inforcements. When the column reached Little Bethel it was fired upon from a house which was consequently burned, and communicated its flames to several others. The Federal forces had finally reached a place in the outskirts of Great Bethel, where the road along which they moved is crossed by a marshy stream called Back River. Until recently this stream was spanned by a bridge known as the County Bridge; this had been destroyed by the rebels, and almost before its destruction was noticed, a heavy fire was opened upon the Federal troops from two masked batteries mounting rifled cannon upon the further bank of the stream. Fortunately this first fire was not very accurate, and the missiles carried nearly a mile beyond the position the troops occupied. Then came a discharge of musketry. Thus surprised, the Federal troops were thrown into some disorder; but were soon rallied, and formed with the artillery in the centre, (upon the road,) and the infantry upon the right, and left partially covered in woods. In this position the enemy's fire was returned at a distance of one hundred yards. Under cover of this fire an attempt was made to carry the enemy's works by a charge, and Capts. Winslow, Bartlett, and Killpatrick of the Fifth, charged with their commands in front; Captain Denike, and Lieut. Duryea, (son of Col. Duryea,) and about two hundred of the Troy Rifles upon the right, Col. Townsend with his men to the left. The enemy were forced out of the first battery, all the forces were rapidly advancing, and every thing promised a speedy victory, when 250 of the Vermont men, with Lieut.-Col. Washburne, on the extreme left were mistaken for the enemy by Col. Townsend, who thereupon ordered his men to fall back. The Zouaves in front thus left unsupported also fell back, and the advantage so bravely gained was thus forfeited; upon consultation it was deemed impossible to flank the rebel position, and as after half an hour's experiment the fire of the light howitzers and musketry was found utterly ineffective against the enemy, who was well supplied with rifled cannon, the order to retreat was given, and the force was brought off in good order. Casualties in the Federal army were (as far as known)—killed, 13; wounded,

30. Several were missing. Of the wounded, 10, and of the dead, 1, were the loss by the error on the road when Col. Bendix fired into the N. Y. Third. Among the killed were Lieut. Greble, of the regular service, in command of the artillery, and Major Theodore Winthrop, aid to Gen. Butler. Of the Confederate loss, little is known. It is stated by the *Charleston Mercury* at 17 killed. The enemy is thought to have had at least 10 guns in battery, and is known to have had 2,200 men. The retreat of the Federal forces was necessarily very slow and tedious, many almost falling back and with difficulty made to keep their places. All expected that the rebels had flanked around into Hampton, and would fight them at the ferry. The rear of the entire force was covered by the howitzers, which charged upon the pursuing cavalry until they fell back toward the batteries. The news of the retreat arrived at Hampton long before the troops, and the ferry transports were all moored along the shore by the order of Gen. Butler, who was on the Monroe-ward side of the stream. When at last the poor soldiers came in and saw their way safe, a shout of joy sprang from the ranks and many of them sang most heartily. The wounded and dead, with a few exceptions, had been gathered up, and were carried by the weary retreating force and in the baggage wagons.—(*Doc.* 244.)

—THIS evening the propeller Resolute, Capt. Budd, arrived at the Navy Yard, at Washington, together with the propeller Young America seized by the Cumberland at Old Point, and now in the service of the Government. Last Saturday night Capt. Budd, with a boat's crew of five men, went into Briton's Bay, and seizing the schooner Somerset at Leonardtown, towed her out into the Potomac, where they fired her, the schooner burning to the water's edge. On Monday morning master's-mate Fuller, with a boat's crew of four, went on board the schooner William Sampson, lying at the shore, about five miles above Acquia Creek, and burnt her also, completely destroying her. The owner and his plantation hands stood on shore at the time, but thought it prudent to say nothing. Neither of the vessels were loaded, and were in a very bad condition through want of repairs, and as it was well-known that they had been carrying provisions, &c., over to the Virginians, their fate was very soon decided.—*National Intelligencer, June* 13.

—Major-General Banks was detailed to the command of the Department of Annapolis, and established his head-quarters at Baltimore, Md.—*N. Y. Herald, June 10.*

—Three battalions of the District of Columbia Volunteers passed through Georgetown, D. C., and at about the same time the Second Connecticut, First New Hampshire, and New York Ninth Regiments broke camp and proceeded by the Rock Creek Road. The two forces were to unite at Tenlytown, three miles above Georgetown. Their destination is supposed to be Edward's Ferry, on the Potomac. The latter point is about thirty miles from Georgetown, and an equal distance from Harper's Ferry and Washington. In the morning Capt. Owens proceeded with the District troops, and about forty of the Second Texas cavalry went in the same direction. In addition to camp equipage and intrenching tools, they were provisioned for twelve days. Large trains of wagons crossed into Virginia at the Government Ferry at Georgetown throughout the day, indicating, it is supposed, that one or more regiments on that side have received orders to march. One of the Ohio regiments, it is expected, will soon take up its line of march to follow Col. Stone's column.—Hon. John Cochran of New York was authorized by the Secretary of War to have mustered for immediate service, under a United States Commission, for three years, a regiment of infantry, to be commanded by himself as Colonel.—*Washington Star, June 10.*

—The Fourth Connecticut Regiment over 1,000 strong, completely armed and equipped, left Hartford, Conn., for Jersey City on board steamers City of Hartford and Granite State. Four military companies turned out to escort them, and at least 10,000 persons witnessed their departure, which took place amid the greatest enthusiasm and firing of cannon.— (*Doc. 245.*)

June 11.—Lieut. Slemmer, late in command of Fort Pickens, had a handsome reception at Independence Hall, Philadelphia. A military procession, consisting of Col. Small's Regiment of ten companies, preceded by a drum corps and a brass band, playing Hail Columbia, escorted the Lieutenant and his aged father-in-law from the Continental Hotel to the Hall, where Mayor Henry addressed him in behalf of the Councils and people of the city in happy terms,

saying, among other things: "It is for that firm maintenance of the Constitution and its laws that your fellow-citizens have assembled this day to greet you with their applause and admiration. It is in support of that Constitution that Philadelphia has sent her sons by thousands to the tented field, and will, if the necessity arises, pour forth hosts of brave and willing men to battle in this great cause. Permit me to express the sincere wishes of your fellow-citizens for the restoration of that health which has been materially impaired by your arduous services, and with it to convey the assurance that they will regard with interest each new laurel that will adorn your future career."

To this Lieut. Slemmer replied: "Mr. Mayor and Councils of Philadelphia, I thank you very heartily for your expression of esteem and approval. When I stood almost alone, with a handful of men on Santa Rosa Island, it was the thought of just such sympathy as you have here expressed which made the performance of that duty a more welcome task. Enemies were around us, but we felt that we were not alone; for we knew that the whole North in heart, soul, and prayers was with us. Gentlemen, I would like to have seen the end of that little piece of work before coming among you; but having waited patiently for four long months, my men, who so nobly stood around me in darkness and peril, having become diseased through confinement and want of proper food, I concluded that the best thing for them and the country would be to bring them North where they might recruit their strength so as to enter again those stirring scenes where soon every soldier will be needed."—*National Intelligencer, June 15.*

—In the Maryland Legislature in session at Frederick, Mr. McKaig presented a report from the Commissioners appointed by the Legislature to visit Montgomery. Accompanying this was a paper from Jefferson Davis expressing his gratification to hear that the State of Maryland was enlisted on the side of peace and reconciliation, and *avowing his perfect willingness for a cessation of hostilities*, and a readiness to receive any proposition for peace from the United States Government.—(*Doc. 246.*)

—Colonel Wallace, with his Indiana regiment, proceeded from Cumberland, Md., about forty miles into Virginia, to a place called

MAJ. GEN. GEO B. Mc CLELLAN, U.S.A.

Geo B McClellan
Maj Genl USA

NEW YORK, G.P.PUTNAM.

Romney, where he surprised a body of about five hundred armed rebels. They showed fight, and a brisk little battle followed, resulting in the rout of the rebels. Colonel Wallace pursued them, killing two, and wounding one of them sure, as that number was left on the field. Some of the killed and wounded among the rebels were conveyed away in the flight. Only one of Colonel Wallace's men was wounded, none killed. The Indiana boys seized a considerable amount of arms, ammunition, some horses, and provisions. Colonel Wallace then returned with his force to Cumberland, instead of holding Romney, which is on the route towards Harper's Ferry, and about fifty miles from the latter place.—*Baltimore American, June* 14.

June 12.—The Second Regiment Missouri Volunteers, Col. Siegel, went up the Pacific Railroad from St. Louis, and occupied the line as far as the Gasconade River in order to prevent further damage by the rebels. They met with no opposition from the traitors in that section.—*N. Y. Herald, June* 20.

—THE steamer City of Alton, with two companies of Col. Oglesby's Regiment and a squad of artillery-men, with two field-pieces, made an excursion from Cairo, Ill., down the Mississippi, five miles below Columbus, Kentucky, to-day. On returning, when near Columbus, some machinery of the boat broke, and the boat drifted ashore. While the machinery was repairing, the captain of the boat, with three of his crew, went ashore and cut down a secession flag which was flying on the shore, and brought it to Cairo. No attempt was made to prevent their taking the flag. Passengers, who have arrived from Columbus since the City of Alton left, say, that great excitement prevailed among the citizens, and that locomotives and cars were immediately despatched to Union city to convey rebel troops to Columbus. No rebel troops were seen by the excursionists between Cairo and Columbus.—*Louisville Courier, June* 15.

—GOVERNOR JACKSON of Missouri issued a proclamation rehearsing the so-called grievances inflicted by the Federal Government, which, he said, were designed to reduce Missouri to the same condition as Maryland. He accused the Federal authorities of fostering the inauguration of revolution and civil war for the overthrow of the State Government, and called 50,000 State militia into active service for the protection of the lives, liberty, and property of the citizens.—(*Doc.* 247)

—A MAN was discovered in an attempt to poison some of the soldiers of the Second Michigan Regiment at Washington by offering them water to drink, in which strychnine was deposited. He was immediately arrested.—*N. Y. World, June* 13.

—THE state-room of William Trappman, a passenger on board the steamer America, which left Boston for Liverpool to-day, was visited and searched on the suspicion that he was a bearer of despatches from the Confederate Government. He produced papers showing that he was Prussian Consul at Charleston, and also a bearer of despatches from Lord Lyons to the British Government. Nothing of an objectionable character was found in his possession, and he was released. Subsequently a despatch was received from the War Department authorizing his arrest on the charge of treason, but the steamer had in the meantime sailed.—*Boston Post, June* 13.

—THE Western Virginia Convention met yesterday at Wheeling, and after effecting a temporary organization adjourned till ten o'clock this morning. About forty counties were represented on the basis of their representation in the Legislature. Arthur J. Boreman, of Wood county, was chosen permanent chairman, and delivered a patriotic address on taking his seat. He reviewed the ordinance of secession passed by the Richmond convention, and exhorted the delegates to firm, decided, and thorough action. The delegates were then sworn in. The programme of the convention seems to be the formation of a provisional government for the whole State; the deposition of the present State authorities, and the entire reörganization of the municipal Government.

Mr. Carlile offered a resolution, which was unanimously adopted, thanking Gen. McClelland for sending troops to Western Virginia; commending the gallant troops at Philippa, and complimenting the bravery of Col. Kelly of the First Virginia Regiment.—*N. Y. Commercial Advertiser, June* 12.

—THE Louisville *Journal* of to-day contains the following: "A facetious account has been given of Gov. Rector's response to President Lincoln's demand for troops, ('Nary one—see you d—d first.') We find the genuine despatch embodied in his message to the Legislature, as follows:

"Executive Office,
Little Rock, Ark., April 22, 1861.

"*Hon. Simon Cameron, Secretary of War, Washington City, D. C.:*

"In answer to your requisition for troops from Arkansas, to subjugate the Southern States, I have to say that none will be furnished. The demand is only adding insult to injury.

"The people of this Commonwealth are freemen, not slaves, and will defend to the last extremity their honor, lives, and property against northern mendacity and usurpation.

"Henry M. Rector,
Governor of Arkansas."

June 13.—By proclamation of Jefferson Davis, this day was observed as a fast-day throughout the States in rebellion against the U. S. Government.—*N. Y. Times, June* 2.

—The United Turner Rifles, Twentieth Regiment N. Y. S. V., Colonel Max Weber, left New York for Fortress Monroe and the army of Southeastern Virginia. In their march through the city they were drawn up in front of the City Hall, where a flag was presented to them by Samuel B. Ruggles, in behalf of Mrs. Charles E. Strong and other ladies of New York.—(*Doc.* 248.)

—Brigadier-General Schenck has been assigned to the Second Michigan Regiment now in Washington. He is thus attached to the Military Department of Washington, the chief of which is General Mansfield.—Conflicting statements having been made, it is proper to say—while Major-General Banks superseded General Cadwalader in command of the Department at Annapolis, the latter has been assigned to command a new division to coöperate with General Patterson in the progressing actions against Harper's Ferry.—*Rochester Union, June* 14.

—The steamer Iatan, with the Second Battalion of the First Regiment of Missouri volunteers, under command of Lieutenant Colonel Andrews, one section of Totten's light artillery and two companies of regulars, under Captain Lathrop, and the steamer J. C. Swon, with the First Battalion of the First Regiment, under Colonel Blair, and another section of Totten's battery, and a detachment of pioneers, and General Lyon and staff, numbering 1,500 men all told, left St. Louis for some point up the Missouri River, supposed to be Jefferson city. They had horses, wagons, and all necessary camp equipage, ammunition, and provisions for a long march.—*Louisville Journal, June* 14.

—The troops which started from Washington on Monday, left the vicinity of Tenlytown the next day, and are now beyond Rockville; the National Rifles, under Major Smead, the Slemmer Guards, Capt. Knight, and the Cameron Guards, accompanied by Capt. Magruder's battery of U. S. Artillery, with three field-pieces, being in advance. The troops have taken the river route, and will be followed immediately by the First Pennsylvania and New York Ninth Regiments, which were at Rockville on Tuesday. What is called the river route is the road which diverges from the Frederick Road outside of Rockville, and passes through Poolesville direct to Edwards' Ferry and on to Leesburg, Va. For several weeks past the Edwards' Ferry route has been a general thoroughfare for secessionists from Maryland, and also for military stores, provisions, etc. The Fifth Battalion D. C. Volunteers took boats at the Chain Bridge yesterday morning at eight o'clock, and proceeded towards Edwards' Ferry. This battalion is commanded by Lieut.-Col. Everett.—*Washington Star, June* 12.

—The Third Michigan Regiment, numbering 1,040 men, left Grand Rapids this morning for the seat of war. They are a fine body of men fully armed, equipped, and ready for service.—*N. Y. Commercial Advertiser, June* 13.

—The Sixth Regiment N. Y. S. V., Colonel William Wilson's Zouaves, left New York for Fort Pickens. Previous to its departure the regiment was presented with a set of colors by the ladies of the Relief Committee.—(*Doc.* 249.)

—A portion of Montgomery's men, under Capt. Jamison, armed with Sharp's rifles and revolvers, reached Wyandotte, Kansas, from Lawrence under orders from Col. Mitchell. Montgomery, with several hundred mounted men, will at once take possession of the Kansas side of the Missouri line, so as to be ready to meet Gov. Jackson's forces whenever they make a movement from Independence towards Kansas City. The militia and volunteer companies are ready to march to the order, as soon as the orders are sent.—*St. Louis Democrat, June* 18.

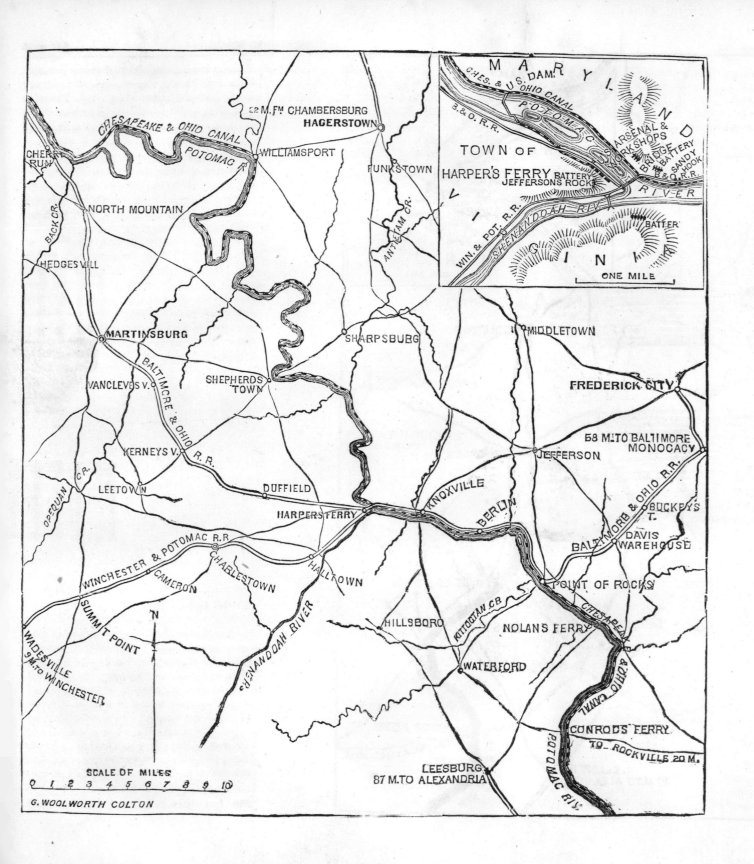

—THE largest meeting ever known in Dover, Delaware, was held there to-day. Chancellor Harrington presided. The following, among other resolutions, was adopted unanimously :

Resolved, That, considering the sentiments embodied in the foregoing resolution, incompatible with the views of James A. Bayard, now Senator, as expressed in his last speech in the Senate, and his recent addresses to the people of Delaware, we most respectfully request him to resign.

Not less than three thousand persons were at the meeting, and great enthusiasm prevailed. A resolution was also passed requesting the Governor to call the Legislature together.— *Rochester Union, June 14.*

—AN attack was made by the rebels on the outpost of the Pennsylvania Fifth regiment at Alexandria, in which a private of company G was wounded in the arm. His arm was amputated.—*N. Y. Commer. Advertiser, June 14.*

—GEN. BEAUREGARD ordered the Fairfax Court-House Company, Capt. Ball, recently prisoners in Washington, to leave the State of Virginia, because they took the oath of allegiance to the United States. Those of them who may be induced to violate it, will, of course, be excepted from the operation of this order.— *N. Y. World, June 15.*

June 14.—A signal balloon was seen at a considerable elevation over beyond the chain bridge, on the Leesburgh Road, at night, supposed to have been sent up by the rebels, for the purpose of communicating intelligence to secessionists in or near Washington.— *Washington Star, June 15.*

—A LITTLE fight occurred near Seneca's Mill, on the Maryland side of the Potomac, 28 miles above Washington. Lieut.-Col. Everett, in command of three companies of District Volunteers, 200 men, (a detachment of Col. Stone's column,) started in canal boats from Georgetown, D. C., and were obliged to leave after a few miles up, the rebels having cut the dam. At Seneca the detachment was fired upon by 100 cavalry, on the Virginia side of the river. Col. Everett marched his men into the dry bed of the canal, and, sheltered by the opposite bank, returned the cavalry fire. Shots were exchanged for some time across the Potomac, a distance of seven-eighths of a mile. None of Col. E.'s men were injured. Two Virginia troopers

were shot, one thought to be killed, as well as the commander, supposed to be Capt. Shreves. Upon the fall of their leader, the cavalry retreated. During the fight bullets were flattened on stones near our men, who lay down in perfect shelter.—*N. Y. Express, June* 17.

—JOHN A. DIX, Major-General of the New York State forces, was appointed Major-General in the army of the United States.—*N. Y. Tribune, June* 14.

—AT Rochester, N. Y., a flag was raised upon the court-house. The ceremonies were commenced with a prayer by the Rev. Dr. Dewey, followed by the hoisting of the flag, during the playing of the " Star-Spangled Banner." Speeches were then made by Judge John C. Chumasero, Roswell Hart, and H. B. Ensworth. —*Rochester Express, June* 14.

—ON the representation of certain Irishwomen of Alexandria, that their husbands, who had never been naturalized, and were therefore British subjects, had been impressed into the rebel service, Lord Lyons instructed the British consul at that point to make an investigation, and, if satisfied of the truth of the statements, to demand their release of the commanding general.—*N. Y. World, June* 15.

—HARPER'S FERRY, Md., was finally evacuated by the Confederate forces. This step had so often been predicted, and denied with such confident assertions of the impregnable fortifications erected there and of the determination of the Confederate leaders to make it the chosen point for a desperate stand, that the first reports were received with doubts and incredulity. Confirmatory statements, however, of the withdrawal of pickets from all points above and below the Ferry, of the burning of the railroad bridge, and the destruction of provisions they were unable to carry off, finally not only confirmed the evacuation, but gave to it somewhat of the aspect of a hurried retreat. The troops left in two columns—one column going toward Winchester with the intention of joining the force at Manassas Junction ; the other retreating through Loudon county toward Leesburg. Before leaving Harper's Ferry the Confederates destroyed all the public property in the vicinity. The fine bridge, including the Winchester span, over one thousand feet in length, was burnt. An attempt was made to blow up the piers. The Government Armory buildings were burnt.

The machinery had previously been removed to Richmond. The railroad bridge at Martinsburg and the turnpike bridge over the Potomac at Shepherdstown were also destroyed.—*Baltimore American, June* 15.—(*Doc.* 264.)

—Gov. JACKSON, of Missouri, having learned that Gen. Lyon was on the way to attack him at Jefferson city, evacuated that place. Soon after sunrise but few of the rebels were to be found in the town. Orders were given by Governor Jackson for the destruction of the Moreau Bridge, four miles down the Missouri, and Gen. Sterling Price attended to the demolition of the telegraph. All the cars and locomotives that could be used were taken by the rebels in their flight, and as fast as they crossed streams they secured themselves from pursuit by burning the bridges. They were quite cautious in concealing their place of destination from the loyal men of Jefferson, but certain remarks made it pretty certain that they were bound for Booneville, forty miles above, and one of the strongest secession towns in the State.—*N. Y. Herald, June* 20.

June 15.—Privateer No. 1—of the Confederate States—(the Savannah) captured May 3d, by U. S. brig Perry, arrived in the port of New York.—(*Doc.* 251.)

—THE obstructions of the Baltimore and Ohio Railroad at Point of Rocks, Md., were removed, and the road was re-opened to Harper's Ferry for the first time this morning since the occupation and obstruction of the road by the secessionists. The immense boulder, weighing about one hundred tons, thrown from the Point of Rocks upon the road by the Confederate troops, was removed last night by blasting, and the track now passes over its crushed fragments, which served to fill up the depression in the bed of the road, caused by its fall. An immense mass of the rock projects into the canal, leaving sufficient space, however, for the passage of the canal boats. The culverts which were attempted to have been blown up are now fully repaired, the solid character of the work rendering the attempted destruction but partial in extent.—*Baltimore American, June* 15.

—THE First Massachusetts Regiment, under the command of Colonel Cowdin, left Boston for the seat of war.—(*Doc.* 252.)

—JEFFERSON CITY, Mo., was occupied by Gen. Lyon, in command of the Union force, who was warmly welcomed by the mass of the citizens. Gen. Lyon there learned that Gov. Jackson and the whole military and civil government of the State had fled to Booneville, forty miles above, and that they have not far from fifteen hundred men there, the most of them armed with their own rifles and shot-guns, six or eight iron cannon, and are throwing up earthworks to protect the town from attack, both by river and by land.—*N. Y. Herald, June* 20.

—AN experiment with Sawyer's American rifled cannon was made at the Rip Raps, in Hampton Roads. Seven of eleven 48-pound

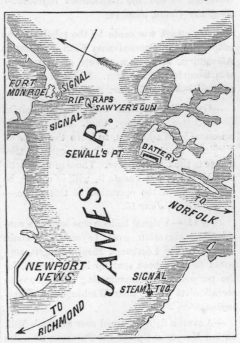

shells exploded a short distance from the rebel camp, on Sewall's Point, and one of them over their intrenchments. It created a sensation among the secessionists. A house near the secession banner displayed a white flag.—*N. Y. Times, June* 18.

June 16.—This afternoon J. G. Morrison, Jr., and several of his friends, unfurled the Star-Spangled Banner on the Maryland abutment of the bridge lately destroyed at Harper's Ferry. The cherished symbol of the Union was hailed with delight by the people of Harper's Ferry, and particularly by the women, who flocked to the opposite bank and saluted it by

Yours truly
N. Lyon.

NEW YORK, G.P. PUTNAM.

the waving of handkerchiefs and other manifestations of joy.—*Baltimore American, June* 20.

—GENERAL JOSEPH H. LANE, of Kansas, was appointed a Brigadier-General in the army of the United States.—*N. Y. Tribune, June* 20.

—A RECONNOISSANCE of the Loudon and Hampshire Railroad, in Va., was made under Col. Powers, accompanied by the First Regiment of Connecticut troops. All the bridges were found safe, and the train returned. When two miles east of Vienna, a man in ambush fired on the train, wounding George Busbee, of the Connecticut Life Guards. Gen. Tyler was standing beside the wounded man, on an open car. The shot was evidently intended for him. The train was stopped as soon as possible, and the companies were divided to scour the woods, and search the neighboring farm-houses, etc., to make a circuit of a mile. Two men were arrested, named Walker and McMills, in the house of the latter. All the evidence that could be obtained, tended towards criminating Walker, who, with the other prisoner and a negro witness, was brought to Alexandria. The train was within three miles of 900 rebel troops, and six miles of Fairfax Court House, where, it is understood, there are 2,500 troops, besides recent arrivals.—*N. Y. Times, June* 17.

June 17.—A letter from Cronstadt, Russia, written by the mate of a ship, says: "There is a Charleston ship lying alongside of us that hoisted the flag of the Confederate States, and for so doing I understand that the captain was arrested and placed in the guard-house of the Russian officers. They would not acknowledge or in any way recognize the flag of the rebels."—*Boston Journal, July* 12.

—LIEUT. GEORGE H. BUTLER with others proceeded from Fortress Monroe to Big Bethel to bring away the remains of Major Winthrop. At Little Bethel a picket took their message to Colonel Magruder, who sent Captain Kilsen, of Louisiana, to receive them. Two hours after Colonel Magruder came, and they were handsomely received. With Colonel Magruder were Colonel De Russy, brother of the Chief of the Engineers at Fortress Monroe, Colonel Hill, of North Carolina, and other late officers of the army. None of Lieutenant Butler's party were permitted to go near the batteries. The body of Major Winthrop was taken up by Colonel Magruder's men and escorted to the wagon by

a force of three hundred, who fired a volley. Most of them had shot guns. An escort was offered to Hampton, but Lieutenant Butler declined it. Colonel Magruder and others spoke in the highest terms of Major Winthrop's bravery. He was distinctly seen for some time leading a body of men to the charge, and had mounted a log and was waving his sword and shouting to his men to "Come on!" when a North Carolina drummer-boy borrowed a gun, leaped on the battery, and shot him deliberately in the breast. He fell nearer to the enemy's works than any other man went during the fight. He wore the sword of Colonel Wardrop of the Massachusetts Third, and it was supposed that it was Colonel Wardrop who fell. The sword was sent to North Carolina as a trophy. —*N. Y. Evening Post, June* 19.

—IN the Wheeling (Va.) Convention Mr. Dorsey, of Monongalia, moved that the Declaration of Independence be put upon its passage, calling for the yeas and nays. It was unanimously adopted: Yeas, 56—not a vote in the negative. Thirty members were absent on leave, and the Declaration was signed by fifty-six, the same number as signed the National Declaration of Independence.—(*Doc. 256.*)

—THREE hundred Federal troops, under Capt. Gardner, of the Pennsylvania First Regiment, had a skirmish at Edwards' Ferry, with a considerable force of secessionists. The fight lasted nearly three hours, when the rebels fled, having had fifteen to twenty of their number killed and wounded, one private in Capt. Gardner's command was killed, and three or four were wounded slightly. The fight occurred from across the river. The attack was made by the enemy with a view to taking possession of the Ferry. The news was brought to Washington by Capt. Gardner's First Lieutenant, who was engaged in the action.—*N. Y. Times, June* 20.

—THIS morning, at St. Louis, Mo., a part of Col. Kallman's Regiment of reserve corps were returning from the North Missouri Railroad, when opposite the Recorder's Court-room on Seventh street, between Olive and Locust, a company near the rear of the column suddenly wheeled and discharged their rifles, aiming chiefly at the windows of the Recorder's Court and the second story of an adjoining house, killing four citizens, mortally wounding two, and slightly injuring one. The statements regarding the cause of the firing were very conflicting —one being that a pistol shot was fired from the window of a house on the corner of Seventh and Locust, which took effect in the shoulder of one of the captains, when he gave word to fire; another, that a soldier accidentally discharged his rifle in the ranks, at which the whole company became frightened and discharged a full volley into the crowd on the sidewalk and windows of houses. The Recorder's Court was in session, crowded with prisoners and spectators. Police officer Pratt was shot in the side, and died in ten minutes. Deputy Marshal Frauzo received three balls in the legs and arms. The window just behind Recorder Peers' desk was riddled with bullets, and broken glass scattered over his desk.—*Sandusky Register, June 18.*

—IN honor of the day—the anniversary of the battle of Bunker Hill—the Charlestown City Guard, comprising two companies of the Massachusetts Fifth, gave a grand entertainment at their camp near Alexandria, Va. Under the pleasant shade of a luxuriant grove long tables were spread with dainties quite unusual in that part of the land. Many of the dishes were furnished by the generous ladies of Massachusetts, and vividly recalled the good living of that dear old State—ever true to liberty and constitutional law. The edibles disposed of, sentiments were the order of the hour. The memory of Warren was appropriately toasted, and there were a dozen patriotic speeches from the officers and friends of the Guard, which, coming from the shadow of the solid column commemorating the glory of Warren and his heroic comrades, always honor the day with peculiar enthusiasm. At this time, and in sight of the spot where Ellsworth —who has been well denominated the Warren of the great struggle in which we are now involved—gave his life a willing sacrifice to his country, the proceedings of this afternoon were exceedingly fitting — and honorable to the Guard.

At Boston, Mass., the anniversary was observed with more than usual manifestations of patriotism. At the monument in Charlestown there was a civic and military gathering. The Stars and Stripes were raised on a flag-staff about 40 feet above the shaft, making the height 260 feet from the ground. Gov. Andrew and others made eloquent speeches appropriate to the occasion.— *Washington Star, June 20.*

—GEN. LYON issued a strong proclamation, pointing out the determined efforts of the Governor and Legislature to force the State out of the Union, and the unconstitutionality of the military bill. He rehearsed the result of the conference with Governor Jackson, and stated that attempts to execute the provisions of the military bill had imposed most exasperating hardships on peaceful and loyal citizens, with persecutions and proscriptions of those opposed to its provisions. Complaints of these acts, he said, had been received by him as commander of the Federal forces, and also sent to Washington with appeals for relief from Union men who, in many instances, had been driven from the State. He gave his orders received from the President, stating that it devolved upon him to stop them summarily by the forces under his command, with such aid as might be required from Kansas, Iowa, and Illinois.— (*Doc. 257.*)

—AN expedition of 300 Zouaves, commanded by Lieutenant-Colonel Warren, and accompanied by Capt. Smith, of the United States Topographical Corps, left Fortress Monroe to make a reconnoissance in the vicinity of Big Bethel and up the route to Yorktown.—*N. Y. Times, June 19.*

—AT 4 P. M., as a train with telegraph constructors and 660 of the First Ohio Regiment went up the Loudon and Hampshire Railroad, Va., they were fired upon by a rebel battery stationed on a hill at a curve in the road, near Vienna, a small station about 15 miles from Alexandria. The battery consisted of three 6-pounders, and was worked by a company from Alexandria. Its first fire was very destructive. The men were immediately brought out of the car and formed and returned the fire, when, by some mismanagement the train returned to Alexandria and left them. They were however brought off in good order. Six were killed and nine wounded. Two of the wounded subsequently died. The rebels also had six killed. The rebel battery was supported by 800 infantry and 200 cavalry. Directly after the retreat of the Ohio troops, a regiment of South Carolinians, with a battery of six pieces, arrived upon the scene of action. Shortly after their appearance, an alarm was raised by the supposed approach of a large body of Union troops, when the whole rebel force beat a sudden retreat through Vienna, in the direction of Fairfax Court House. A resident of Vienna, who saw them pass two hours after the action, estimated them at two thousand.—(*Doc.* 258.)

—NEAR Independence, Missouri, a detachment of Union troops, under Captain Stanley, with a flag of truce, visited the camp of the State troops to ascertain the purposes of Captain Holloway, the rebel officer. During the conference Captain Stanley suspected movements were being made with the design of attacking him, and ordered his detachment to retreat. While retreating they were fired on by the State troops, at an order given by a private; but their fire was so irregular they killed their own commander, Captain Holloway, and J. B. Clanahan, and severely wounded several more of their own men. Captain Stanley's men did not fire, they having received orders not to do so under any circumstances. Captain Stanley retreated to Kansas City and reported the affair, when Captain Prince, with a strong body of troops, attacked and routed the State forces, capturing thirty horses and a large quantity of baggage.—*N. Y. Herald, June* 20.

—GEN. LYON left Jefferson City, Mo., for Booneville. He landed four miles below the town and opened a heavy cannonade against the rebels, who retreated and dispersed into an adjacent wood, whence, hidden by brushes and trees, they opened a brisk fire on our troops. General Lyon then ordered a hasty retreat to the boats; and the rebels, encouraged by this movement, rallied and followed the troops into a wheatfield, and were thus drawn from cover. General Lyon halted, faced his troops about, and, bringing the whole force of his artillery to bear, opened a murderous fire on the rebels, many of whom were killed, and the balance fled in all directions, leaving their arms on the field. General Lyon then moved forward and took possession of Booneville. Governor Jackson viewed the battle from a distant hill, and fled for parts unknown after the defeat of his forces. General Price was not in the battle, and his absence is thus accounted for: Sunday morning the pickets brought a report that seven steamboats were coming up the river with Union troops. A consultation was immediately had between Gov. Jackson and Gen. Price, and the Governor ordered the State troops to disband, they not being able to sustain themselves

against such force. General Price then went home; the troops, however, were determined to have a fight. Col. Marmaduke then became disaffected, and resigned. A few hours later the report about the steamboats proved untrue, and the Governor ordered the troops to prepare for resistance, appointing Mr. Little to command.—There is no reliable account as to the number of killed, wounded, or taken prisoners, though the killed are stated at 300. It is stated that General Lyon's force had the State troops in a position where they could have killed them in large numbers. He ordered the firing to cease, and halted to make them prisoners.—*St. Louis Republican, June* 18.—(*Doc.* 258½.)

—COL. BOERNSTEIN, commanding the Federal force at Jefferson City, Mo., issued a proclamation establishing a Provisional Government in consequence of the absence of the proper authorities. He promised protection to life and property, and urged the Union men, four companies, to assist him.—(*Doc.* 259.)

—THE First Regiment of Massachusetts Volunteers, pioneers of the three years' enlistments from that State, arrived at Washington and took quarters in Woodward's buildings, Pennsylvania avenue. The regiment numbers 1,050 men, and is fully provided with camp equipage— Sibley and Wall tents, army wagons, &c. The uniform is the standard gray, furnished by the State—the muskets the Springfield rifle.

General Patterson crossed the Potomac at Williamsport, and marched down the Virginia banks of the Potomac towards Harper's Ferry. —*National Intelligencer, June* 18.

June 18.—Gen. Lyon issued another proclamation to the people of Missouri from his camp at Booneville. He released the prisoners taken in the late engagement, in consideration of their youth and of the deceit that had been practised upon them, simply requiring their pledge not again to bear arms against the United States. His proclamation warned all persons against presuming upon a like clemency in future, as the continuance of treason would certainly render harsh measures necessary.— (*Doc.* 260.)

—THE Federal force at Hagerstown and Williamsport, Md., comprise the Pennsylvania 1st, 2d, 3d, 7th, 11th, 13th, and 24th Regiments, together with the First Rhode Island Regiment, two Regiments of United States Regulars, and seven hundred United States Cavalry. Included in this formidable body are Capt. Doubleday's corps and McMullen's Company of Philadelphia Rovers. The portion of the force which forded the river at Williamsport were under command of Gen. Thomas, and comprised the two regiments of regulars and about six hundred of the Rhode Islanders. The men waded through the stream generally up to their hips in water, and occasionally up to their arms. Their passage on the occasion is said to have been a very imposing and spirited spectacle. The men dashed into the stream singing "Dixie" and other popular camp airs with great *vim* and enthusiasm. —*National Intelligencer, June* 20.

—NEAR Conrad's Ferry, Maryland, the rebels practised upon the Federal troops from the opposite side of the Potomac with three or four 6-pounders. Their fire was returned from the rifle pieces of some twenty picked marksmen, who in the course of their firing brought down one of the enemy's gunners. The distance across is so great, however, that even rifled muskets are of little avail except by chance shots.—*N. Y. Evening Post, June* 18.

—THE TWENTY-SEVENTH PENNSYLVANIA REGIMENT, (mostly Germans,) Colonel Einstein, about one thousand strong, passed through Baltimore, Md., on the route to the seat of war. They are well armed and equipped, and have entered the service with the spirit of true soldiers. Whilst at Camden, opposite Philadelphia, where they encamped for some time, they were treated with great kindness by the people of that city.—(*Doc.* 261.)

—A BALLOON ascension for military purposes took place at Washington. The elevation attained was not very great, though it was perfectly satisfactory as an experiment. The aëronauts were Prof. Lowe, Gen. Burns, of the Telegraph Company, and H. C. Robinson, operator. The balloon was connected with the War Department by telegraph. The first message ever telegraphed from a balloon was then sent to the President of the United States by Prof. Lowe. It was as follows:

BALLOON ENTERPISE, WASHINGTON, June 17.

To THE PRESIDENT OF THE UNITED STATES:

SIR:—This point of observation commands an area nearly fifty miles in diameter. The city, with its girdle of encampments, presents a superb scene. I take great pleasure in sending you this first despatch ever telegraphed from an aërial station, and in acknowledging my indebtedness to your encouragement for the opportunity of demonstrating the availability of the science of aëronautics in the military service of the country.

Yours respectfully,

T. S. C. LOWE.

—AN official order from the Duke of Newcastle, forbidding privateers to enter the ports of Canada, was published in the Montreal (Canada) papers.—(*Doc.* 262.)

—THE Fourteenth Regiment N. Y. S. V. passed through New York City *en route* for the Seat of War.—The Eighteenth Regiment N. Y. Volunteers left Albany.—(*Doc.* 263.)

—CAPT. BUDD, commanding the United States steamer Resolute, arrived at Washington, bringing as a prize the schooner Buena Vista, seized in the St. Mary's River. He captured two other vessels—namely, the schooner Bachelor and the sloop H. Day. The former had disregarded a warning given several days ago, and had deceived Captain Rowan by false statements, and was found on the Maryland side, opposite Matthias Point, at a place where it was convenient for crossing. They belonged to the same owner. —*N. Y. Commercial Advertiser, June* 19.

DOCUMENTS AND NARRATIVES.

DOC. I.—REPLY OF THE GOVERNOR OF MARYLAND TO THE COMMISSIONER FROM MISSISSIPPI.

STATE OF MARYLAND, EXECUTIVE CHAMBER,
ANNAPOLIS, Dec. 19, 1860.

SIR : Your letter of the 18th instant informs me that you have been appointed by the Governor of Mississippi, in pursuance of a resolution of her Legislature, a Commissioner to the State of Maryland, and that the occasion of your mission is "the present crisis in the national affairs of this country, and the danger which impends the safety and rights of the Southern States, by reason of the election of a sectional candidate to the office of President of the United States, and upon a platform of principles destructive of our constitutional rights and which, in the opinion of the State of Mississippi, calls for prompt and decisive action, for the purpose of our protection and future security."

You also inform me that Mississippi desires the co-operation of her sister States of the South in measures necessary to defend our rights ; and to this end, you desire to know whether I will convene the Legislature of Maryland for the purpose of counselling with the constituted authorities of the State of Mississippi, and at what time it may be expected our General Assembly will be called for that purpose.

In the conversation I had with you this morning, you were good enough to explain more fully the views and intentions of Mississippi in this matter—her desire that our Legislature should also appoint Commissioners to meet those of other Southern States ; and that action at once be had by all the Southern States for the formation of a new Government among themselves.

The position of Maryland, as a small Southern Border State, renders the exercise of any power I may possess, for the purpose indicated by you, a matter of very grave importance.

Our State is unquestionably identified with the Southern States, in feeling and by the institutions and habits which prevail among us. But she is also conservative, and, above all things devoted to the Union of these States under the Constitution. Her people will use all honorable means to preserve and perpetuate these. I think I know the sentiments of her citizens in this matter, and that I am not mistaken when I say that, almost unanimously, they intend to uphold that Union, and to maintain their rights under it—that they believe these last will yet be admitted and secured ; and that not until it is certain they will be respected no longer—not until every honorable, Constitutional, and lawful effort to secure them is exhausted—will they consent to any effort for its dissolution.

The people of Maryland are anxious that time be given, and an opportunity afforded, for a fair and honorable adjustment of the difficulties and grievances of which they, more than the people of any other Southern State have a right to complain. And, in my opinion, if the people of this Union really desire its continuance and perpetuity, such adjustment may be effected. I hope and believe it will be effected—and promptly. And until the effort is found to be in vain, I cannot consent, by any precipitate or revolutionary action, to aid in the dismemberment of this Union.

When I shall see clearly that there is no hope of such adjustment, and am convinced that the power of the Federal Government is to be perverted to the destruction instead of being used for the protection of our rights—then, and not till then, can I consent so to exercise any power with which I am invested, as to afford even the opportunity for such a proceeding.

Whatever powers I may have I shall use only after full consultation, and in fraternal concert, with the other Border States; since we and they, in the event of any dismemberment of the Union, will suffer more than all others combined.

I am now in correspondence with the Governors of those States, and I await with solicitude for the indications of the course to be pursued by them. When this is made known to me, I shall be ready to take such steps as our duty and interest shall demand, and I do not doubt the people of Maryland are ready to go with the people of those States for weal or woe.

I fully agree with all that you have said as to the necessity for protection to the rights of the South ; and my sympathies are entirely with the gallant people of Mississippi, who stand ready to resent any infringement of those rights. But I earnestly hope they will act with prudence as well as with courage.

Let us show moderation as well as firmness, and be unwilling to resort to extreme measures until necessity shall leave us no choice.

I am unable to inform you when the Legislature of this State will be called together, for until I can perceive the necessity for such a step I am not willing to awake the apprehension and excite the alarm which such a call at the present time could not fail to create.

I have the honor to be, with great respect, your obedient servant,
THOS H. HICKS.

HON. A. H. HANDY, Commissioner of Mississippi.

Doc. 2.—SECESSION ORDINANCE OF SOUTH CAROLINA.

An Ordinance to Dissolve the Union between the State of South Carolina and other States united with her under the compact entitled the Constitution of the United States of America:

We, the people of the State of South Carolina, in Convention assembled, do declare and ordain, and it is hereby declared and ordained, that the ordinance adopted by us in Convention, on the 23d day of May, in the year of our Lord 1788, whereby the Constitution of the United States of America was ratified, and also all Acts and parts of Acts of the General Assembly of this State ratifying the amendments of the said Constitution, are hereby repealed, and that the union now subsisting between South Carolina and other States under the name of the United States of America is hereby dissolved.

The ordinance was taken up and passed by a unanimous vote of 169 members, at 1¼ o'clock.

The following is a summary of the debate on the passage of the ordinance:

Mr. MAGRATH—I think the special matter of the ordinance should be immediately considered. To my understanding there is no Collector of the Port nor Postmaster now within the limits of South Carolina. What you have done to-day has extinguished the authority of every man in South Carolina deriving authority from the General Government. I am in favor of this body making such provisional arrangements as may be necessary in the interval which may exist between this moment and the time when the Legislature may act. I am not, however, to be implicated as sanctioning the idea that there is no lawful authority within the limits of the State except the General Government.

Mr. GREGG—After South Carolina abrogated the Constitution of the United States, are its laws still in force? I think not. All the laws of Congress fall instantly to the ground on the act of Secession.

Mr. CHEVES—As an immense chasm will be made in the law, and as it is necessary to avoid inconvenience to the people, we must make some temporary arrangements to carry on the Government.

Mr. GREGG—There is no law on the subject of the collection of the duties in South Carolina now. We have now accomplished the work after forty years.

Mr. HAYNE—The Congress of the United States is no longer our Government. It will be for our Legislature to say what laws of the United States shall be continued and what not. The simple act of secession does not abrogate all the laws. We have a great many laws on our statute books which were passed by the Governor and the Privy Council.

Mr. GREGG—The Congressional laws for the collection of revenue are for the support of the Federal Government at Washington, and all our Post-office laws fall on our dissolution with that Government.

Mr. MILES—We have to deal with facts and stern realities. We must prevent confusion, anarchy, and the derangement of our Government affairs. Things must for the present remain in *statu quo,* or confusion will arise.

Mr. HAYNE—Sudden action is injurious.

Mr. CHESNUT—Two questions are involved—power and duty. We must preserve our people, not only from inconveniences, but chaotic condition. We must revivify such laws as will best preserve us from calamities. As to duty, will you turn the ship of State adrift? what will become of the officers?

Mr. MASEYCK—There is no duty for the Collector of the Port to do. The Post-office has been swept off. My opinion is that the present system of postal arrangements is a nuisance. The public can be better served by private parties between cities like Philadelphia and New York, one cent instead of three, and between less important ten or more cents.

Mr. CALHOUN—We have pulled a temple down that has been built three-quarters of a century. We must clear the rubbish away to reconstruct another. We are now houseless and homeless, and we must secure ourselves against storms.

Mr. DUNKIN—If that ordinance be passed things will go on in the Custom-house and Post-office exactly as now, until other arrangements can be made by this Convention. There is nothing in the Ordinance to affect the dignity, honor, and welfare of the State of South Carolina. We must keep the wheels of the Government going. The Constitution of the United States is not entirely abrogated by the Ordinance. What is legal tender in the payment of debts? Is it not gold and silver of the United States? In the case of clearing and entry of vessels, we are very liable to have the same confiscated.

Mr. CARROLL—The present revenue would be continued till an act of the Legislature authorized otherwise.

Mr. BROWN—There is no longer communication with the Government from which we are just separated.

Mr. DUNKIN—The spirit of the ordinance must be temporarily sustained till we treat with the General Government.

Mr. GREGG—The President of the United States has thrown down the gauntlet in his Message. He has said that it was his duty to collect the revenue, and that he would do it. On one side the Federal Government claims the right and declares its intention to execute the power of collecting revenue in our ports; on the other side, we have declared that we are free. I desire no compromise. Is it necessary to maintain the fifteen to thirty per cent. duties imposed by the Congress of the United States? Should these duties continue to be levied our people will suffer a terrible calamity. For carrying the mails let the present contracts be assumed by South Carolina instead of the United States.

Mr. RHETT—This great revolution must go on with as little danger as possible to the country. By making the Federal agents ours, the machinery will move on. The Federal laws of taxation must not exist over us. I trust that the present system of taxation has fallen forever.

Mr. BARNWELL—We have seceded from the United States, and established our independence. We can't allow the United States to exercise authority over us any more. Let postal convenience be sacrificed if necessary. There never was any thing purchased worth having, unless it cost a sacrifice.

Mr. MASEYCK said, in regard to the mail, all restrictions must be removed. Let us appoint our officers. Let the Collector of the Port battle with the difficulties as they come.

—*New York Times,* Dec. 21, 1860.

Doc. 3.—DECLARATION OF CAUSES WHICH INDUCED THE SECESSION OF SOUTH CAROLINA.

The people of the State of South Carolina in Convention assembled, on the 2d day of April, A. D. 1852, declared that the frequent violations of the Constitution of the United States by the Federal Government, and its encroachments upon the reserved rights of the States, fully justified this State in their withdrawal from the Federal Union; but in deference to the opinions and wishes of the other Slaveholding States, she forbore at that time to exercise this right. Since that time these encroachments have continued to increase, and further forbearance ceases to be a virtue.

And now the State of South Carolina having resumed her separate and equal place among nations, deems it due to herself, to the remaining United States of America, and to the nations of the world, that she should declare the immediate causes which have led to this act.

In the year 1765, that portion of the British Empire embracing Great Britain undertook to make laws for the Government of that portion composed of the thirteen American Colonies. A struggle for the right of self-government ensued, which resulted, on the 4th of July, 1776, in a Declaration, by the Colonies, "that they are, and of right ought to be, FREE AND INDEPENDENT STATES; and that, as free and independent States, they have full power to levy war, conclude peace, contract alliances, establish commerce, and to do all other acts and things which independent States may of right do."

They further solemnly declared that whenever any "form of government becomes destructive of the ends for which it was established, it is the right of the people to alter or abolish it, and to institute a new government." Deeming the Government of Great Britain to have become destructive of these ends, they declared that the Colonies "are absolved from all allegiance to the British Crown, and that all political connection between them and the State of Great Britain is, and ought to be, totally dissolved."

In pursuance of this Declaration of Independence, each of the thirteen States proceeded to exercise its separate sovereignty; adopted for itself a Constitution, and appointed officers for the administration of government in all its departments—Legislative, Executive and Judicial. For purposes of defence they united their arms and their counsels; and, in 1778, they entered into a League known as the Articles of Confederation, whereby they agreed to intrust the administration of their external relations to a common agent, known as the Congress of the United States, expressly declaring, in the first article, "that each State retains its sovereignty, freedom and independence, and every power, jurisdiction and right which is not, by this Confederation, expressly delegated to the United States in Congress assembled."

Under this Confederation the War of the Revolution was carried on; and on the 3d of September, 1783, the contest ended, and a definite Treaty was signed by Great Britain, in which she acknowledged the Independence of the Colonies in the following terms:

"ARTICLE 1. His Britannic Majesty acknowledges the said United States, viz.: New Hampshire, Massachusetts Bay, Rhode Island and Providence Plantations, Connecticut, New York, New Jersey, Pennsylvania, Delaware, Maryland, Virginia, North Carolina, South Carolina and Georgia, to be FREE, SOVEREIGN, AND INDEPENDENT STATES; that he treats with them as such; and, for himself, his heirs and successors, relinquishes all claims to the government, propriety, and territorial rights of the same and every part thereof."

Thus were established the two great principles asserted by the Colonies, namely, the right of a State to govern itself; and the right of a people to abolish a Government when it becomes destructive of the ends for which it was instituted. And concurrent with the establishment of these principles, was the fact, that each Colony became and was recognized by the mother country as a FREE, SOVEREIGN AND INDEPENDENT STATE.

In 1787, Deputies were appointed by the States to revise the articles of Confederation; and on 17th September, 1787, these Deputies recommended, for the adoption of the States, the Articles of Union, known as the Constitution of the United States.

The parties to whom this constitution was submitted were the several sovereign States; they were to agree or disagree, and when nine of them agreed, the compact was to take effect among those concurring; and the General Government, as the common agent, was then to be invested with their authority.

If only nine of the thirteen States had concurred, the other four would have remained as they then were—separate, sovereign States, independent of any of the provisions of the Constitution. In fact, two of the States did not accede to the Constitution until long after it had gone into operation among the other eleven; and during that interval, they each exercised the functions of an independent nation.

By this Constitution, certain duties were imposed upon the several States, and the exercise of certain of their powers was restrained, which necessarily impelled their continued existence as sovereign states. But, to remove all doubt, an amendment was added, which declared that the powers not delegated to the United States by the Constitution, nor prohibited by it to the States, are reserved to the States respectively, or to the people. On the 23d May, 1788, South Carolina, by a Convention of her people, passed an ordinance assenting to this Constitution, and afterwards altered her own Constitution to conform herself to the obligations she had undertaken.

Thus was established, by compact between the States, a Government with defined objects and powers, limited to the express words of the grant. This limitation left the whole remaining mass of power subject to the clause reserving it to the States or the people, and rendered unnecessary any specification of reserved rights. We hold that the Government thus established is subject to the two great principles asserted in the Declaration of Independence; and we hold further, that the mode of its formation subjects it to a third fundamental principle, namely, the law of compact. We maintain that in every compact between two or more parties, the obligation is mutual; that the failure of one of the contracting parties to perform a material part of the agreement, entirely releases the obligation of the other; and that, where no arbiter is provided, each party is remitted to his own judgment to determine the fact of failure, with all its consequences.

In the present case, that fact is established with certainty. We assert that fourteen of the States have deliberately refused for years past to fulfil their constitutional obligations, and we refer to their own statutes for the proof.

The Constitution of the United States, in its fourth Article, provides as follows:

"No person held to service or labor in one State under the laws thereof, escaping into another, shall, in consequence of any law or regulation therein, be discharged from such service or labor, but shall be delivered up, on claim of the party to whom such service or labor may be due."

This stipulation was so material to the compact that without it that compact would not have been made. The greater number of the contracting parties held slaves, and they had previously evinced their estimate of the value of such a stipulation by making it a condition in the Ordinance for the government of the territory ceded by Virginia, which obligations, and the laws of the General Government, have ceased to effect the objects of the Constitution. The States of Maine, New Hampshire, Vermont, Massachusetts, Connecticut, Rhode Island, New York, Pennsylvania, Illinois, Indiana, Michigan, Wisconsin, and Iowa, have enacted laws which either nullify the acts of Congress, or render useless any attempt to execute them. In many of these States the fugitive is discharged from the service of labor claimed, and in none of them has the State Government complied with the stipulation made in the Constitution. The State of New Jersey, at an early day, passed a law in conformity with her constitutional obligation; but the current of Anti-Slavery feeling has led her more recently to enact laws which render inoperative the remedies provided by her own laws and by the laws of Congress. In the State of New York even the right of transit for a slave has been denied by her tribunals; and the States of Ohio and Iowa have refused to surrender to justice fugitives charged with murder, and with inciting servile insurrection in the State of Virginia. Thus the constitutional compact has been deliberately broken and disregarded by the non-slaveholding States; and the consequence follows that South Carolina is released from her obligation.

The ends for which this Constitution was framed are declared by itself to be "to form a more perfect union, to establish justice, insure domestic tranquillity, provide for the common defence, promote the general welfare, and secure the blessings of liberty to ourselves and our posterity."

These ends it endeavored to accomplish by a Federal Government, in which each State was recognized as an equal, and had separate control over its own institutions. The right of property in slaves was recognized by giving to free persons distinct political rights; by giving them the right to represent, and burdening them with direct taxes for, three-fifths of their slaves; by authorizing the importation of slaves for twenty years; and by stipulating for the rendition of fugitives from labor.

We affirm that these ends for which this Government was instituted have been defeated, and the Government itself has been destructive of them by the action of the non-slaveholding States. Those States have assumed the right of deciding upon the propriety of our domestic institutions; and have denied the rights of property established in fifteen of the States and recognized by the Constitution; they have denounced as sinful the institution of Slavery; they have permitted the open establishment among them of societies, whose avowed object is to disturb the peace and eloin the property of the citizens of other States. They have encouraged and assisted thousands of our slaves to leave their homes; and those who remain, have been incited by emissaries, books, and pictures, to servile insurrection.

For twenty-five years this agitation has been steadily increasing, until it has now secured to its aid the power of the common Government. Observing the *forms* of the Constitution, a sectional party has found within that article establishing the Executive Department, the means of subverting the Constitution itself. A geographical line has been drawn across the Union, and all the States north of that line have united in the election of a man to the high office of President of the United States whose opinions and purposes are hostile to Slavery. He is to be intrusted with the administration of the common Government, because he has declared that that "Government cannot endure permanently half slave, half free," and that the public mind must rest in the belief that Slavery is in the course of ultimate extinction.

This sectional combination for the subversion of the Constitution has been aided, in some of the States, by elevating to citizenship persons who, by the supreme law of the land, are incapable of becoming citizens; and their votes have been used to inaugurate a new policy, hostile to the South, and destructive of its peace and safety.

On the 4th of March next this party will take possession of the Government. It has announced that the South shall be excluded from the common territory, that the Judicial tribunal shall be made sectional, and that a war must be waged against Slavery until it shall cease throughout the United States.

The guarantees of the Constitution will then no longer exist; the equal rights of the States will be lost. The Slaveholding States will no longer have the power of self-government, or self-protection, and the Federal Government will have become their enemy.

Sectional interest and animosity will deepen the irritation; and all hope of remedy is rendered vain, by the fact that the public opinion at the North has invested a great political error with the sanctions of a more erroneous religious belief.

We, therefore, the people of South Carolina, by our delegates in Convention assembled, appealing to the Supreme Judge of the world for the rectitude of our intentions, have solemnly declared that the Union heretofore existing between this State and the other States of North America is dissolved, and that the State of South Carolina has resumed her position among the nations of the world, as separate and independent state, with full power to levy war, conclude peace, contract alliances, establish commerce, and to do all other acts and things which independent States may of right do.

Doc. 4.—SPEECH OF SENATOR SEWARD,
NEW YORK, DEC. 22.

Fellow-citizens: My friend, Mr. Evarts, I believe, is acting as Chairman of Committee here, or President, or something of that sort—I do not exactly understand what. Coming a stranger as I do to the Astor House [laughter] I am put under *duresse* as soon as I get here, and am brought down from my own private room to this place. That is all I know about myself or you either [laughter]; but I find you here, and Mr. Evarts with his mallet in his hand. I suppose it means that he is something like a presiding officer or speaker, or something of that kind. Mr. Draper has intimated to me that you're all Yankees, [A voice—"Yes, we are,"] and I thought it as likely as not that you were. Therefore, I suppose that I might as well set all doubt about myself at rest at once, and anticipate all your inquiries. I left Auburn this morning at 9 o'clock, after breakfast; I got here at rather a late hour, for rather a late dinner. [A voice—"Did you come by the express train?"] I came by the express train. Nothing particular happened me on the way [roars of laughter] except that I might as well anticipate the *Express* on Monday morning, as I did not anticipate the *Express* last Monday morning, by saying that I met Thurlow Weed in the cars. [Laughter.]

A voice—"What did he say?"

Mr. Seward—There the Yankee comes out at once. A gentleman asks me what he said. Now I am not a Yankee. There is no New England blood in me, and I do not answer impertinent questions. [Laughter.] I will not tell what he said to me. I will only tell what I said to him, and that was that I repudiated—all compromises whatsoever, which New York, Pennsylvania, and New England could not stand upon. I learned from him that he had been in Springfield, in the State of Illinois. I suppose you would all like to know what he told me he learned there. [Laughter, and shouts of "Yes."] I will give you the best satisfaction I can. He prints a newspaper called the *Evening Journal*. He is a man of truth, I believe; and if he is, and wants to tell what he learned, you can get it in his newspaper. [Laughter.] But I have somehow got off from the direct course of my argument. I began to tell you about myself, and, somehow or other, I have got to telling about Mr. Weed and his journey to Springfield. I may as well go on in this indirect way till I get back to my direct road. I met the Governor going up to Albany. He did not tell me exactly, but I had a strong suspicion, from his appearance generally, and from some hints which he dropped, that Charles Stetson, of the Astor House, would probably be Inspector General of the State of New York. [Laughter.] I judge so because the Governor asked me my opinion about Mr. Stetson. I told him that, as a tavern keeper, I did not know a great deal in his favor, but that as a military officer, I thought he had no superior [roars of laughter], and that if it should turn out that the State of Florida should invade the State of New York in these troubles of ours, I did not know any better man to send out to meet them than Charles Stetson [uproarious laughter], who would disarm them of all hostility by bringing them in to a supper like this at the Astor House.

Fellow-citizens—he continued, in a more serious tone—these are extraordinary things that are happening in our day. I remember that it was the men of New England, who lived only two or three times as long ago as I have lived, and as my friend Mr. Joseph Grinnell has lived, whom I am glad to see here. I hope he is sounder in his politics than he was the last time I heard of him. [Laughter.] I hope he is as sound as his brother Moses. It is only twice as long ago as we have lived, I say, since these men of New England invented the greatest political discovery in the world—the confederation of republican states. The first confederation of republican states in America was the invention of New England. I have always admired and respected the people of New England for that great discovery, which, after having been put into successful operation in the colonies of Massachusetts Bay and Plymouth, and Connecticut and New Haven, came ultimately, after having been sanctioned by the wisdom and experience of Dr. Franklin, to be adopted by the people of the thirteen British colonies on this continent, south of the St. Lawrence. It has been reserved for our day, and for this very hour, to see an innovation of another kind, of an opposite nature, by a portion of our countrymen residing south of the Potomac. The Yankees invented confederation. The people of South Carolina have invented secession. The wisdom of the latter is now to be tried in comparison with the experience of the former. At the first glance it exhibits this singular anomaly—that of a state which has in the Senate of the United States two seats, and in the House of Representatives six members, each of them paid $3,000 a year out of a treasury to which they contribute only a small part—a state consisting of 700,000 people of all conditions, and of whom 274,000 are white, going out of the Union, to stand by itself, and sending to the Congress of the United States three commissioners to stand outside of the bar to negotiate for their interests, and to be paid by herself, instead of having two senators and six representatives in Congress, on an equality with all the other states. This is the experiment that is to be tried by states on this continent—whether they will find it wiser to occupy seats within the Congress of the United States, and to have their representatives paid by the United States for coming there; or, in lieu of that, to send Commissioners to present their claims and their rights at the bar of the United States, without the privilege of voting on their own claims, and to be paid for by the states themselves. This is the last political invention of the times. I need not say to you that I do not think it is likely to be followed by many other states on this continent, or to be persevered in long, because it is manifestly very much inferior to the system that already exists. The State of South Carolina desires to go out. Just at this moment I am going back to Washington for the purpose of admitting the State of Kansas in; and I venture to say that for every state on this continent that will go out of the Union, there stand already waiting at least two states that will be glad to come in and take their place. [Loud cheers.] They will do so for this simple reason—that every state on the continent of North America will be a democratic or republican state. You, gentlemen of New England, do not like always to hear the word democratic. I will, therefore, use the word republican. No republican state on this continent or any other can stand alone. That is an impossibility. And the reason is a simple one. So much liberty, so much personal independence, such scope to emulation and ambition, as a free republic gives, where universal suffrage exists, are too much for any one state, standing alone, to maintain. Therefore it is, as you have seen, that the moment it was thought that secession had commenced in this great national confederacy of ours, you begin to hear at once of secession, not only in South Carolina, but of secession in California, secession in New England, and lastly, you begin to hear of secession of New York city and Long Island from the State of New York. [Laughter.] They are right in all this. Dissolve this American Union, and there is not one state that can stand without renewing perpetually the process of secession until we are brought to the condition of the States of Central America—pitiful states, unable to stand alone. No, gentlemen, republican states are like the sheaves in the harvest field. Put them up singly, and every gust blows them down; stack them together, and they defy all the winds of heaven. [Tumultuous applause.] And so you have seen that these thirteen republican states all came to the conviction, each of them that it could not stand alone; and the thirteen came together, and you have seen other states added to them. The state of Michigan, the state of Indiana, of Illinois, the state of Wisconsin, the state of Iowa and the state of Louisiana—what under heaven kept each of these states from setting up for itself and becoming independent? Nothing, but that it could not stand alone. And they are ready to be united to other republican states on this continent. So it was with Texas. She was independent. Why did she not remain so? You know how much it tried us to admit her into the Union; but it tried her much harder to stay out as long as she did. Why is not Kansas content to remain out? Simply because of the sympathy and the interest which makes it needful that all republican states on this continent shall be united in one. Let South Carolina, let Alabama, let Louisiana—let any other state go out, and while they are rushing out you will see Canada and all the Mexican States rushing in to fill up the vacuum. [Loud applause.] It is the wisdom discovered by our fathers which is all concentrated in these three words of such pregnant meaning—*E Pluribus Unum*. [Loud applause.] There is no such thing as one, separate from the many, in republican states. [Continued applause.] And now, fellow-citizens, I will speak one word concerning the anomalous condition of our affairs produced by this disposition of some of the American states to secede from the Union. It has taken, as it ought to have taken, the American people and the world by surprise. Why has it taken them by surprise? Because it is unwise and unnatural. It is wise that all the republican states of this continent should be confederated. It is unwise that any of them should attempt to separate. And yet it ought not to have taken us by surprise. Whoever could have imagined that a machine so complicated, so vast, so new, so untried, as this confederated system of republican states, should be exempt from the common lot of states which have figured in the history of the world? A more complex system of government was never devised—never conceived of among men. How strange it is, how unreasonable it is, that we should be surprised that a pin may drop out of this machinery and that the wheel should drag, or that the gudgeon should be worn until the wheel should cease to play with the regular action! How could we expect to subsist for a period of seventy years exempt from the necessity of repairing our political system of government? Every state in this Union

is just like the federal Union—a republic. It has its constitution, and its regular system of action. No state is more than seventy years old, and there is not in any one state of this Union a constitution which is more than twenty-five years old; and so certain has it become that no state can adopt a constitution which will last for more than twenty-five years without being repaired and renewed, that in our own state the constitution which we adopted twenty years ago contains a provision that next year, without any appeal to the people whatever, a convention shall come together in the state of New York and make a new constitution. Is it strange, then, that this complex system of our government should be found, after a lapse of seventy years, to work a little rough, a little unequal, and that it should require that the engineer should look at the machinery to see where the gudgeon is worn out, and to see that the main wheel is kept in motion? A child can withdraw a pin from the mightiest machine and arrest all its motion, and the engineer cannot see it when it is being done; but if the engine be rightly devised and strongly constructed, the engineer has only to see where the pin has fallen out and replace it, and the machine will then go on stronger and more vigorous than ever. [Applause.] We are a family of thirty-three states, and next Monday I hope that we shall be a family of thirty-four. [Cheers.] Would it not be strange, in a family of thirty-four members, if there should not, once in the course of a few years, be one or two, or three or four, or five of the members who would get discontented, and want to withdraw awhile, and see how much better they could manage their fortunes alone? I think there is nothing strange in this. I only wonder that nobody has ever withdrawn before, to see how much better they could get along on their own book, than they get along in this plain, old-fashioned way under the direction of Uncle Sam. They say that, while I was a boy, Massachusetts and some of the New England States got the same idea of contumacy for the common parent and want of affection for the whole family, and got up a Hartford Convention. [Laughter.] I hope you do not think this personal. [No, no.] Somebody in Massachusetts—I do not know who—tried it. All I know about it is, that for the first twenty years of my political life, although I was a democrat—a Jeffersonian—born and dyed in the faith of the Republican fathers, somehow or other, because I happened to become a whig, I was held responsible for the Hartford Convention. [Laughter.] And I have made this singular discovery in contrasting those times with the present; that, whereas, when Massachusetts or any New England State, gets in a pet and proposes to go out of the Union, the democratic party all insist that it is high treason, and ought to be punished by coercion; when one of the slave states gets into the same fret, and proposes to go out of the Union, the democratic party think it exceedingly excusable, and have doubts whether—she ought not be helped out of the Union, and whether we ought not to give her a good dowry besides. [Laughter.] Now, gentlemen, my belief about all this is, that whether it is Massachusetts or South Carolina, or whether it is New York or Florida, it would turn out the same way in each case. There is no such thing in the book, no such thing in reason, no such thing in philosophy, and no such thing in nature, as any state existing on the continent of North America outside of the United States of America. I do not believe a word of it ; and I do not believe it, for a good many reasons. Some I have already hinted at; and one is, because I do not see any good reason given for it. The best reason I see given for it is, that the people of some of the southern states hate us of the free states very badly, and they say that we hate them, and that all love is lost between us. Well, I do not believe a word of that. On the other hand, I do know for myself and for you, that, bating some little differences of opinion about advantages, and about proscription, and about office, and about freedom, and about slavery and all those which are family difficulties, for which we do not take any outsiders in any part of the world into our councils on either side, there is not a state on the earth, outside of the American Union, which I like half so well as I do the state of South Carolina—[cheers]—neither England, nor Ireland, nor Scotland, nor France, nor Turkey ; although from Turkey they sent me Arab horses, and from South Carolina they send me nothing but curses. Still, I like South Carolina better than I like any of them ; and I have the presumption and vanity to believe that if there were nobody to overhear the state of South Carolina when she is talking, she would confess that she liked us tolerably well. I am very sure that if anybody were to make a descent on New York to-morrow—whether Louis Napoleon, or the Prince of Wales, or his mother [laughter], or the Emperor of Russia, or the Emperor of Austria, all the hills of South Carolina would pour forth their population for the rescue of New York. [Cries of " Good," and applause.] God knows how this may be. I do not pretend to know, I only conjecture. But this I do know, that if any of those powers were to make a descent on South Carolina, I know who would go to her rescue. [A voice— "We'd all go."] We would all go—everybody. [" That's so," and great applause.] Therefore they do not humbug me with their secession. [Laughter.] And I do not think they will humbug you ; and I do not believe that, if they do not humbug you and me, they will much longer succeed in humbugging themselves. [Laughter.] Now, fellow-citizens, this is the ultimate result of all this business. These states are always to be together—always shall. Talk of striking down a star from that constellation. It is a thing which cannot be done. [Applause.] I do not see any less stars to-day than I did a week ago, and I expect to see more all the while. [Laughter.] The question then is, what in these times—when people are laboring under the delusion that they are going out of the Union and going to set up for themselves—ought we to do in order to hold them in. I do not know any better rule than the rule which every good father of a family observes. It is this. If a man wishes not to keep his family together, it is the easiest thing in the world to place them apart. He will do so at once if he only gets discontented with his son, quarrels with him, complains of him, torments him, threatens him, coerces him. This is the way to get rid of the family, and to get them all out of doors. On the other hand, if you wish to keep them, you have got only one way to do it. That is, be patient, kind, paternal, forbearing, and wait until they come to reflect for themselves. The South is to us what the wife is to her husband. I do not know any man in the world who cannot get rid of his wife if he tries. I can put him in the way to do it at once. [He has only got two things

to do. One is to be unfaithful to her. The other is to be out of temper with her. I do not know a man on earth who—even though his wife was as troublesome as the wife of Socrates—cannot keep his wife if he wants to do so ; all that he needs is, to keep his own virtue and his own temper. [Applause.] Now, in all this business I propose that we shall keep our own virtue, which, in politics, is loyalty, and our own temper, which, in politics, consists in remembering that men may differ, that brethren may differ. If we keep entirely cool and entirely calm, and entirely kind, a debate will ensue which will be kindly in itself, and it will prove very soon either that we are wrong—and we shall concede to our offended brethren—or else that we are right, and they will acquiesce and come back into fraternal relations with us. I do not wish to anticipate any question. We have a great many statesmen who demand at once to know what the North propose to do—what the Government proposes to do—whether we propose to coerce our southern brethren back into their allegiance. They ask us, as of course they may rightfully ask, what will be the value of fraternity which is compelled ? All I have to say on that subject is, that so long ago as the time of Sir Thomas More, he discovered, and set down the discovery in his writing, that there were a great many schoolmasters, and that while there were a very few who knew how to instruct children, there were a great many who knew how to whip them. [Laughter.] I propose to have no question on that subject, but to hear complaints, to redress them if they ought to be redressed, and if we have the power to redress them ; and I expect them to be withdrawn if they are unreasonable, because I know that the necessities which made this Union exist, for these states, are stronger to-day than they were when the Union was made, and that those necessities are enduring, while the passions of men are short lived and ephemeral. I believe that secession was stronger on the night of the 6th of November last, when a President and Vice-president who were unacceptable to the Slave States were elected, than it is now. That is now some fifty days since, and I believe that every day's sun which set since that time, has set on mollified passions and prejudices, and that if you will only give it time, sixty days' more suns will give you a much brighter and more cheerful atmosphere. [Loud and long continued applause.]

Doc. 5.—TOOMBS' ADDRESS, Dec. 23, 1860.

I came here to secure your constitutional rights, and to demonstrate to you that you can get no guarantee for those rights from your Northern confederates. The whole subject was referred to a Committee of Thirteen in the Senate. I was appointed on the Committee, and accepted the trust. I submitted propositions, which, so far from receiving decided support from a single member of the Republican party of the Committee, were all treated with derision or contempt. A vote was then taken in the Committee on amendments to the Constitution proposed by Hon. J. J. Crittenden, and each and all of them were voted against unanimously by the Black Republican members of the Committee. In addition to these facts, a majority of the Black Republican members of the Committee declared distinctly that they had no guarantees to offer, which was silently acquiesced in by the other members. The Black Republican members of this Committee of Thirteen are representative men of the party and section, and, to the extent of my information, truly represent them.

The Committee of Thirty-three on Friday adjourned for a week, without coming to any vote, after solemnly pledging themselves to vote on all the propositions then before them on that day. It is controlled by the Black Republicans, your enemies, who only seek to amuse you with delusive hope until your election, that you may defeat the friends of secession. If you are deceived by them, it shall not be my fault. I have put the test fairly and frankly. It is decisive against you now. I tell you, upon the faith of a true man, that all further looking to the North for security for your constitutional rights in the Union ought to be instantly abandoned. It is fraught with nothing but ruin to yourselves and your posterity. Secession by the 4th day of March next should be thundered from the ballot-box by the unanimous vote of Georgia on the 2d day of January next. Such a voice will be your best guarantee for liberty, security, tranquillity, and glory.   R. TOOMBS.

Doc. 6.—LETTER OF SOUTH CAROLINA CONGRESSMEN TO THE SPEAKER OF THE HOUSE OF REPRESENTATIVES.

SIR : We avail ourselves of the earliest opportunity since the official communication of the intelligence, of making known to your honorable body that the people of the State of South Carolina, in their sovereign capacity, have resumed the powers heretofore delegated by them to the Federal Government of the United States, and have thereby dissolved our connection with the House of Representatives. In taking leave of those with whom we have been associated in a common agency, we, as well as the people of our Commonwealth, desire to do so with a feeling of mutual regard and respect for each other—cherishing the hope that in our future relations we may better enjoy that peace and harmony essential to the happiness of a free and enlightened people.

JOHN McQUEEN,
Dec. 24.   M. L. BONHAM,
W. W. BOYCE,
J. D. ASHMORE,
To the SPEAKER of the House of Representatives.

Doc. 7.—EVACUATION OF FORT MOULTRIE.

It was given out yesterday at Fort Moultrie, on Sullivan's Island, that an attack was expected to be made upon it by the people of this city, and that therefore it would be necessary to remove the wives and children of the men to a more secure place. Accordingly three schooners were engaged, which hauled up to the Fort wharf and loaded with what was supposed by the few persons resident on the island, to be the bedding and furniture of the men's families. It was given out that these vessels were to land their passengers and their goods at Fort Johnson, on James Island ; and they hoisted sail and apparently steered for that point.

On last night, at about half-past nine o'clock, the entire force, with the exception of about six or eight men, embarked on board of their own row boats, and proceeded to Fort Sumter, which they garrisoned at once, and where they met the persons who had left in the schooners, with many munitions of war which they had surreptitiously taken from Fort Moultrie. The few men left at the fortification last night, under the command of Captain Foster, as soon as the evacuation had taken place, at once commenced the *spiking of the guns, the cutting down of the flag-staff,* and the *burning of the gun-carriages,* the smoke of which could be seen this morning from our wharves.

Fort Moultrie in a mutilated state, with useless guns, and flames rising in different portions of it, will stand to show the cowardly conduct of the officers who had charge of it, and who in times of peace basely deserted their post and attempted to destroy a fortification which is surrounded with so many historical reminiscences that the arm of the base scoundrel who would have ruined it should have dropped from its socket.

The schooners, we are informed, although pretending to sail for Fort Johnson, stood off and on until nightfall when they put into the wharf at Fort Sumter. We feel an anxiety to know the names of these vessels and their captains, and shall endeavor to find them out.

About half-past seven o'clock last evening two heavy discharges from Fort Moultrie, were heard in the city, and was the object of considerable talk, and the news of this morning satisfied us that it must have been the signal of the debarkation of the troops.—*Charleston News,* Dec. 27.

Doc. 8.—FORTS SUMTER AND MOULTRIE.

" In order to ascertain truthful statements of the actual damage done to the forts, of the causes of the movement, and of the state of affairs generally, reporters were despatched to the scene during the forenoon. On the way across the harbor, the hoisting of the American flag from the staff of Fort Sumter, at precisely 12 o'clock, gave certain indication that the stronghold was occupied by the troops of the United States. On a nearer approach the fortress was discovered to be occupied, the guns appeared to be mounted, and sentinels were discovered on duty, and the place to give every sign of occupancy and military discipline. The grim fortress frowned defiance on every side ; the busy notes of preparation resounded through its unforbidding recesses, and everything seemed to indicate the utmost alacrity in the work on hand.

" Turning towards Fort Moultrie, a dense cloud of smoke was seen to pour from the end facing the sea. The flagstaff was down, and the whole place had an air of desolation and abandonment quite the reverse of its busy look one week ago, when scores of laborers were engaged in adding to its strength all the works skill and experience could suggest.

" In the immediate vicinity of the rear or landside entrance, however, greater activity was noticeable. At the time of our visit, a large force of hands had been summoned to deliver up their implements for transportation to Fort Sumter. Around on every side were the evidences of labor in the fortification of the work. In many places, a portion of the defences were strengthened by every appliance that art could suggest or ingenuity devise; while, in others, the uncompleted works gave evidences of the utmost confusion. On all hands the process of removing goods, furniture, and munitions was yet going on. The heavy guns upon the ramparts of the fort were thrown down from their carriages and spiked. Every ounce of powder and every cartridge had been removed from the magazines; and, in fact, every thing like small arms, clothing, provisions, accoutrements, and other munitions of war had been removed off and deposited—nothing but heavy balls and useless cannon remained.

"The entire place was, to all appearances, littered up with the odds, ends, and fragments of war's desolation. Confusion could not have been more complete had the late occupants retired in the face of a besieging foe. Fragments of gun carriages, &c., broken to pieces, bestrewed the ramparts. Sand bags, and barrels filled with earth, crowned the walls, and were firmly imbedded in their bomb-proof surface, as an additional safeguard—and notwithstanding the heterogeneous scattering of materials and implements, the walls of the fort evinced a vague degree of energy in preparing for an attack. A ditch some fifteen feet wide and about the same in depth surrounds the entire wall on three sides. On the south side, or front, a glacis has been commenced and prosecuted nearly to completion, with a rampart of sand bags, barrels, &c.

"On one side of the fort a palisade of Palmetto logs is extended around the ramparts as a complete defence against an escalading party. New embrasures have been cut in the walls so as to command the faces of the bastion and ditch. These new defences are all incomplete, and are evidence of the haste with which they were erected. Considering the inferior force, in point of numbers, under his command, Major Anderson had paid particular attention to strengthening only a small part of the fort.

"A greater portion of the labor expended was spent upon the citadel or centre of the west point of the position. This he had caused to be strengthened in every way; loop-holes were cut and every thing was so arranged that in case a well-concerted attack was made, he would have retired from the outer bastions to the citadel, and afterwards blow up the other portions of the fort. For this purpose mines had already been sprung, and trains had been laid ready for the application of the match. The barrack rooms and every other part of the fort that was indefensible would have gone at a touch.

"On the ramparts of the fort fronting Fort Sumter, were nine eight-inch columbiads, mounted on wooden carriages. As soon as the evacuation of the fort was complete, the carriages of these guns were fired, and at the time of visiting the fort yesterday, were nearly consumed, and the guns thereby dismounted. These guns, as well as those constituting the entire armament of the fortress, were spiked before it was abandoned. This is the only damage done the fortification, further than cutting down the flagstaff, and the breaking up of ammunition wagons to form ramparts on the walls of the fort."—*Charleston Courier*, Dec. 28.

DOC. 9.—MAJOR ANDERSON'S MOVEMENT.

We must own that the news of the transaction in Charleston harbor was learned by us yesterday with a prouder beating of the heart. *We could not but feel once more that we had a country*—a fact which has been to a certain degree in suspense for some weeks past. What is given up for the moment is of no consequence, provided the one point stands out clear, that *the United States means to maintain its position, where its rights exist, and that its officers, civil and military, intend to discharge their duty.* The concentration of the disposable force in Charleston harbor in a defensible post, is thus a bond of union. It is a decisive act, calculated to rally the national heart. * * We are not disposed to allow the Union to be broken up for grievances of South Carolina, which might be settled within the Union; and if there is to be any fighting, we prefer it within, rather than without. The abandonment of Fort Moultrie was obviously a necessary act, in order to carry into effect the purpose contemplated with such an inferior force as that under the command of Major Anderson.—*Boston Courier*.

If anybody ever doubted Major Anderson's eminent military capacity, that doubt must be dispelled by the news that we publish in another column. Of his own accord, without orders from Washington, but acting on the discretion which an officer in an independent command always possesses. Major Anderson, commander of the defences of Charleston harbor, transports his troops to the key of his position, Fort Sumter, against which no gun can be laid which is not itself commanded by a 10-inch columbiad in the embrasures of that octagon citadel. This rapid, unexpected manœuvre has disconcerted treason, and received the highest military commendation in the country.

Brave Major of Artillery, true servant of your country, soldier of penetrating and far-seeing genius, when the right is endangered by fraud or force, at the proper time the needed man is always provided. The spirit of the age provides him, and he always regards the emergency. WASHINGTON, GARIBALDI, ANDERSON.—*Boston Atlas and Bee*.

The announcement of the evacuation of Fort Moultrie and the occupation of Fort Sumter, was received with various expressions of opinion; but the predominant one was a feeling of admiration for the determined conduct and military skill of Col. ANDERSON in abandoning an indefensible position, and, by a strategetic *coup de main* which has reversed the whole position of affairs, transferring his force to Fort Sumter, the strongest of the Charleston fortifications, and the key of its defences. Col. ANDERSON is believed to have acted in this matter without special orders, but as he has charge of all the forts, the disposition of the force under his command is a matter in regard to which he may be supposed to have full authority.—*Baltimore American*.

Concerning the object of the movement of Major ANDERSON, we can, as at present informed, say little. But whether he acted in pursuance of orders from head-quarters, or consulted merely his own judgment, the step he has taken must be conceded to have been a wise and prudent one. He could not, with the force under his command, have defended both Fort Moultrie and Fort Sumter; and by retiring to the one which is not only the strongest in itself, but is the key of the position, he has rendered an attack upon his post less probable than it was before, and has placed himself in a better situation to resist it.—*Baltimore Exchange.*

Doc. 10.—SECRETARY FLOYD TO THE PRESIDENT.

War Department, Dec. 29, 1860.

Sir: On the morning of the 27th inst. I read the following paper to you in the presence of the Cabinet:

Counsel Chamber, Executive Mansion.

Sir: It is evident now from the action of the Commander of Fort Moultrie, that the solemn pledges of the Government have been violated by Major Anderson. In my judgment but one remedy is now left us by which to vindicate our honor and prevent civil war. It is in vain now to hope for confidence on the part of the people of South Carolina in any further pledges as to the action of the military. One remedy is left, and that is to withdraw the garrison from the harbor of Charleston. I hope the President will allow me to make that order at once. This order, in my judgment, can alone prevent bloodshed and civil war.

(Signed.)
John B. Floyd,
Secretary of War.

I then considered the honor of the Administration pledged to maintain the troops in the position they occupied, for such had been the assurances given to the gentlemen of South Carolina who had a right to speak for her. South Carolina, on the other hand, gave reciprocal pledges that no force should be brought by them against the troops or against the property of the United States. The sole object of both parties in these reciprocal pledges was to prevent a collision and the effusion of blood, in the hope that some means might be found for a peaceful accommodation of the existing troubles, the two Houses of Congress having both raised Committees looking to that object. Thus affairs stood until the action of Major Anderson, taken unfortunately while the Commissioners were on their way to this capital on a peaceful mission looking to the avoidance of bloodshed, has complicated matters in the existing manner. Our refusal or even delay to place affairs back as they stood under our agreement, invites a collision and must inevitably inaugurate civil war. I cannot consent to be the agent of such calamity. I deeply regret that I feel myself under the necessity of tendering to you my resignation as Secretary of War, because I can no longer hold it under my convictions of patriotism, nor with honor, subjected as I am to a violation of solemn pledges and plighted faith.

With the highest personal regard,
I am most truly yours,
John B. Floyd.
To His Excellency the President
of the United States.

THE PRESIDENT'S REPLY.

Washington, Dec. 31, 1860.

My Dear Sir: I have received and accepted your resignation of the office of Secretary of War; and not wishing to impose upon you the task of performing its mere routine duties, which you have so kindly offered to do, I have authorized Postmaster-

general Holt to administer the affairs of the Department until your successor shall be appointed.

Yours, very respectfully,
James Buchanan.
Hon. John B. Floyd.

Doc. 11.—GENERAL WOOL'S LETTERS TO A FRIEND IN WASHINGTON.

Troy, December 31, 1860.

My Dear Sir:—South Carolina, after twenty-seven years—Mr. Rhett says thirty years—of constant and increasing efforts by her leaders to induce her to secede, has declared herself out of the Union; and this, too, without the slightest wrong or injustice done her people on the part of the government of the United States. Although she may have seized the revenue cutter, raised her treasonable Palmetto flag over the United States Arsenal, the Custom-house, Post-office, Castle Pinckney, and Fort Moultrie, she is not out of the Union, nor beyond the pale of the United States. Before she can get out of their jurisdiction or control, a re-construction of the constitution must be had *or civil war ensue.* In the latter case it would require no prophet to foretell the result.

It is reported that Mr. Buchanan has received informally the Commissioners appointed by the rebels of South Carolina to negotiate for the public property in the harbor of Charleston, and for other purposes. It is also reported that the President disapproved of the conduct of Major Anderson, who, being satisfied that he would not be able to defend Fort Moultrie with the few men under his command, wisely took possession of Fort Sumter, where he could protect himself and the country from the disgrace which might have occurred, if he had remained in Fort Moultrie. Being the commander in the harbor, he had the right to occupy Fort Sumter, an act which the safety of the Union as well as his own honor demanded. It is likewise stated that apprehensions are entertained that Major Anderson will be required to abandon Fort Sumter and re-occupy Fort Moultrie. There can be no foundation for such apprehensions; for surely the President would not surrender the citadel of the harbor of Charleston to rebels. Fort Sumter commands the entrance, and in a few hours could demolish Fort Moultrie. So long as the United States keeps possession of this fort, the independence of South Carolina will only be in name and not in fact. If, however, it should be surrendered to South Carolina, which I do not apprehend, *the smothered indignation of the free states would be roused beyond control.* It would not be in the power of any one to restrain it. *In twenty days two hundred thousand men would be in readiness to take vengeance on all who would betray the Union into the hands of its enemies.* Be assured that I do not exaggerate the feelings of the people. They are already sufficiently excited at the attempt to dissolve the Union, for no other reason than that they constitutionally exercised the most precious right conferred on them, of voting for the person whom they considered the most worthy and best qualified to fill the office of President. Fort Sumter therefore ought not, and I presume will not, be delivered over to South Carolina.

I am not, however, pleading for the free States, for they are not in danger, but for the Union and the preservation of the cotton States. Those who sow the wind may expect to reap the whirlwind. The leaders of South Carolina could not have noticed that we live in an age of progress, and that all Christendom is making rapid strides in the march of civilization and freedom. If they had, they would have discovered that the announcement of every victory obtained by the hero of the nineteenth century, Garibaldi, in favor of the oppressed of Italy, did not fail to electrify every American heart with joy and gladness. "Where liberty dwells there is my country," was the declaration of the illustrious Franklin. This principle is too strongly implanted in the heart and mind of every man in the free States, to be surrendered because South Carolina desires it in order to extend the area of slavery. With all christianized Europe and nearly all the civilized world opposed to slavery, are the Southern States prepared to set aside the barriers which shield and protect their institutions under the United States government? Would the separation of the South from the North, give greater security to slavery than it has now under the Constitution of the Union? What security would they have for the return of runaway slaves? I apprehend none ; whilst the number of runaways would be greatly augmented, and the difficulties of which slaveholders complain would be increased ten-fold. However much individuals might condemn slavery, the Free States are prepared to sustain and defend it as guarantied by the Constitution.

In conclusion, I would avoid the bloody and desolating example of the Mexican States. I am now, and forever, in favor of the Union, its preservation, and the rigid maintenance of the rights and interests of the States, individually as well as collectively. Yours, &c., JOHN E. WOOL.

GENERAL WOOL TO GENERAL CASS, BEFORE THE RESIGNATION OF THE LATTER.

[Private.] TROY, Dec. 6, 1860.

MY DEAR GENERAL : Old associations and former friendship induce me to venture to address to you a few words on the state of the country. My letter is headed "private," because I am not authorized to address you officially.

I have read with pleasure the President's Message. South Carolina says she intends to leave the Union. Her representatives in Congress say she has already left the Union. It would seem that she is neither to be conciliated nor comforted. *I command the Eastern Department*, which includes South Carolina, Georgia, Florida, Alabama, and Mississippi. You know me well. I have ever been a firm, decided, faithful, and devoted friend of my country. *If I can aid the President to preserve the Union I hope he will command my services. It will never do for him or you to leave Washington without every star in this Union is in its place.* Therefore, no time should be lost in adopting measures to defeat those who are conspiring against the Union. Hesitancy or delay may be no less fatal to the Union than to the President or your own high standing as a statesman.

It seems to me that troops should be sent to Charleston to man the forts in that harbor. You have eight companies at Fort Monroe, Va. *Three or four of these companies should be sent, without a moment's delay, to Fort Moultrie.* It will save the Union and the President much trouble. It is said Doc. —12

that to send at this time troops to that harbor would produce great excitement among the people. That is nonsense, when the people are as much excited as they can be, and the leaders are determined to execute their long meditated purpose of separating the state from the Union. So long as you command the entrance to the city of Charleston, South Carolina cannot separate herself from the Union. Do not leave the forts in the harbor in a condition to induce an attempt to take possession of them. It might easily be done at this time. If South Carolina should take them it might, as she anticipates, induce other states to join her.

Permit me to entreat you to urge the President to send at once three or four companies of artillery to Fort Moultrie. The Union can be preserved, but it requires firm, decided, prompt and energetic measures on the part of the President. He has only to exert the power conferred on him by the Constitution and laws of Congress, and all will be safe, and he will prevent a civil war, which never fails to call forth all the baser passions of the human heart. If a separation should take place, you may rest assured blood would flow in torrents, followed by pestilence, famine, and desolation, *and Senator Seward's irrepressible conflict will be brought to a conclusion much sooner than he could possibly have anticipated.* Let me conjure you to save the Union, and thereby avoid the bloody and desolating example of the states of Mexico. A separation of the States will bring with it the desolation of the cotton States, which are unprepared for war. Their weakness will be found in the number of their slaves, with but few of the essentials to carry on war, whilst the free States will have all the elements and materials for war, and to a greater extent than any other people on the face of the globe.

Think of these things, my dear General, and save the country, and save the prosperous South from pestilence, famine, and desolation. Peaceable secession is not to be thought of. Even if it should take place, in three months we would have a bloody war on our hands.

Very truly your friend, JOHN E. WOOL.

Hon. LEWIS CASS, Secretary of State,
Washington, D. C.
—*Troy Times*, Dec. 31.

Doc. 12.—THE CORRESPONDENCE BETWEEN THE SOUTH CAROLINA COMMISSIONERS AND THE PRESIDENT OF THE UNITED STATES.

WASHINGTON, Dec. 20, 1860.

SIR: We have the honor to transmit to you a copy of the full powers from the Convention of the people of South Carolina, under which we are "authorized and empowered to treat with the Government of the United States for the delivery of the forts, magazines, light-houses, and other real estate, with their appurtenances, in the limits of South Carolina; and also for an apportionment of the public debt, and for a division of all other property held by the Government of the United States, as agent of the Confederated States, of which South Carolina was recently a member, and generally to negotiate as to all other measures and arrangements proper to be made and adopted in the existing relation of the parties, and for the continuance of peace and amity between this Commonwealth and the Government at Washington."

In the execution of this trust it is our duty to furnish you, as we now do, with an official copy of the Ordinance of Secession, by which the State of South Carolina has resumed the powers she delegated to the Government of the United States, and has declared her perfect sovereignty and independence.

It would also have been our duty to have informed you that we were ready to negotiate with you upon all such questions as are necessarily raised by the adoption of this Ordinance, and that we were prepared to enter upon this negotiation, with the earnest desire to avoid all unnecessary and hostile collision, and so to inaugurate our new relations as to secure mutual respect, general advantage, and a future of good will and harmony, beneficial to all the parties concerned.

But the events of the last twenty-four hours render such an assurance impossible. We came here the representatives of an authority which could, at any time within the past sixty days, have taken possession of the forts in Charleston harbor, but which, upon pledges given in a manner that we cannot doubt, determined to trust to your honor rather than to its own power. Since our arrival here an officer of the United States, acting as we are assured, not only without, but against your orders, has dismantled one fort and occupied another—thus altering to a most important extent, the condition of affairs under which we came.

Until these circumstances are explained in a manner which relieves us of all doubt as to the spirit in which these negotiations shall be conducted, we are forced to suspend all discussion as to any arrangement by which our mutual interests may be amicably adjusted.

And, in conclusion, we would urge upon you the immediate withdrawal of the troops from the harbor of Charleston. Under present circumstances, they are a standing menace which renders negotiation impossible, and, as our recent experience shows, threatens speedily to bring to a bloody issue questions which ought to be settled with temperance and judgment. We have the honor to be,

Very respectfully, your obedient servants,

R. W. BARNWELL,
J. H. ADAMS,   } Commissioners.
JAS. L. ORR,

To the PRESIDENT of the United States.

THE PRESIDENT'S REPLY.

WASHINGTON CITY, Dec. 30, 1860.

GENTLEMEN : I have had the honor to receive your communication of 28th inst., together with a copy of " your full powers from the Convention of the people of South Carolina," authorizing you to treat with the Government of the United States, on various important subjects therein mentioned, and also a copy of the Ordinance, bearing date on the 20th inst., declaring that " the Union now subsisting between South Carolina and other States, under the name of the United States of America, is hereby dissolved."

In answer to this communication, I have to say that my position as President of the United States was clearly defined in the message to Congress, on the 3d inst. In that I stated that, " apart from the execution of the laws, so far as this may be practicable, the Executive has no authority to decide what shall be the relations between the Federal Government and South Carolina. He has been invested with no such discretion. He possesses no power to change the relations hitherto existing between them, much less to acknowledge the independence of that State. This would be to invest a mere executive officer with the power of recognizing the dissolution of the Confederacy among our thirty-three sovereign States. It bears no resemblance to the recognition of a foreign *de facto* government—involving no such responsibility. Any attempt to do this would, on his part, be a naked act of usurpation. It is, therefore, my duty to submit to Congress the whole question in all its bearings.

Such is my opinion still. I could, therefore, meet you only as private gentlemen of the highest character, and was entirely willing to communicate to Congress any proposition you might have to make to that body upon the subject. Of this you were well aware. It was my earnest desire that such a disposition might be made of the whole subject by Congress, who alone possess the power, as to prevent the inauguration of a civil war between the parties in regard to the possession of the Federal forts in the harbor of Charleston ; and I, therefore, deeply regret that, in your opinion, " the events of the last twenty-four hours render this impossible." In conclusion, you urge upon me " the immediate withdrawal of the troops from the harbor of Charleston," stating that " under present circumstances they are a standing menace, which renders negotiation impossible, and, as our recent experience shows, threaten speedily to bring to a bloody issue questions which ought to be settled with temperance and judgment."

The reason for this change in your position is, that since your arrival in Washington, " an officer of the United States acting, as we (you) are assured, not only without, but against your (my) orders, has dismantled one fort and occupied another—thus altering to a most important extent the condition of affairs under which we (you) came." You also allege that you came here " the representatives of an authority which could, at any time within the past sixty days, have taken possession of the forts in Charleston harbor, but which, upon pledges given in a manner that we (you) cannot doubt, determined to trust to your (my) honor rather than to its power."

This brings me to a consideration of the nature of those alleged pledges, and in what manner they have been observed. In my Message of the 3d of December last, I stated, in regard to the property of the United States in South Carolina, that it " has been purchased for a fair equivalent, by the consent of the Legislature of the State, for the erection of forts, magazines, arsenals, &c., and over these the authority ' to exercise exclusive legislation,' has been expressly granted by the Constitution to Congress. It is not believed that any attempt will be made to expel the United States from this property by force ; but if in this I should prove to be mistaken, the officer in command of the forts has received orders to act strictly on the defensive. In such a contingency, the responsibility for consequences would rightfully rest upon the heads of the assailants." This being the condition of the parties, on Saturday, 8th December, four of the Representatives from South Carolina, called upon me, and requested an interview. We had an earnest conversation on the subject of these forts, and the best means of preventing a collision between the parties, for the purpose of sparing the effusion of blood. I suggested, for prudential reasons, that it would be best to put in writing what they said to me verbally. They did so, accordingly, and on Monday morning, the 10th inst., three of them presented to me a paper signed by all the Representatives from South Carolina, with a single exception, of which the following is a copy:

To His Excellency James Buchanan, President of the United States.

In compliance with our statement to you yesterday, we now express to you our strong convictions that neither the constituted authorities, nor any body of the people of the State of South Carolina, will either attack or molest the United States forts in the harbor of Charleston, previously to the act of the Convention, and we hope and believe not until an offer has been made through an accredited representative, to negotiate for an amicable arrangement of all matters between the State and the Federal Government, provided that no reinforcements shall be sent into those forts, and their relative military status shall remain as at present.

John McQueen,
M. L. Bonham,
W. W. Boyce,
Lawrence M. Keitt.

Washington, Dec. 9, 1860.

And here I must, in justice to myself, remark that at the time the paper was presented to me, I objected to the word "provided," as it might be construed into an agreement on my part, which I never would make. They said that nothing was further from their intention—they did not so understand it, and I should not so consider it. It is evident they could enter into no reciprocal agreement with me on the subject. They did not profess to have authority to do this, and were acting in their individual character. I considered it as nothing more, in effect, than the promise of highly honorable gentlemen to exert their influence for the purpose expressed. The event has proven that they have faithfully kept this promise, although I have never since received a line from any one of them, or from any member of the convention on the subject. It is well known that it was my determination, and this I freely expressed, not to reinforce the forts in the harbor, and thus produce a collision, until they had been actually attacked, or until I had certain evidence that they were about to be attacked. This paper I received most cordially, and considered it as a happy omen that peace might be still preserved, and that time might be thus given for reflection. This is the whole foundation for the alleged pledge.

But I acted in the same manner as I would have done had I entered into a positive and formal agreement with parties capable of contracting, although such an agreement would have been on my part, from the nature of my official duties, impossible. The world knows that I have never sent any reinforcements to the forts in Charleston harbor, and I have certainly never authorized any change to be made "in their relative military status." Bearing upon this subject, I refer you to an order issued by the Secretary of War, on the 11th inst. to Maj. Anderson, but not brought to my notice until the 21st inst. It is as follows:

Memorandum of Verbal Instructions to Major Anderson, First Artillery, commanding Fort Moultrie, S. C.

You are aware of the great anxiety of the Secretary of War that a collision of the troops with the people of this State shall be avoided, and of his studied determination to pursue a course with reference to the military force and forts in this harbor, which shall guard against such a collision. He has, therefore, carefully abstained from increasing the force at this point, or taking any measures which might add to the present excited state of the public mind, or which would throw any doubt on the confidence he feels that South Carolina will not attempt by violence to obtain possession of the public works, or interfere with their occupancy.

But as the counsel and acts of rash and impulsive persons may possibly disappoint these expectations of the Government, he deems it proper that you should be prepared with instructions to meet so unhappy a contingency. He has therefore directed me, verbally, to give you such instructions.

You are carefully to avoid every act which would needlessly tend to provoke aggression, and for that reason you are not, without necessity, to take up any position which could be construed into the assumption of a hostile attitude; but *you are to hold possession of the forts in the harbor, and if attacked, you are to defend yourself to the last extremity.* The smallness of your force will not permit you, perhaps, to occupy more than one of the three forts, but an attack on, or attempt to take possession of either of them, will be regarded as an act of hostility, and you may then put your command into either of them which you may deem most proper to increase its power of resistance. *You are also authorized to take similar steps whenever you have tangible evidence of a design to proceed to a hostile act.*

D. P. Butler, Assistant Adjutant-General.

Fort Moultrie, S.C., Dec. 11, 1860.

This is in conformity to my instructions to Major Buell.   John B. Floyd, Secretary of War.

These were the last instructions transmitted to Major Anderson before his removal to Fort Sumter, with a single exception, in regard to a particular which does not in any degree affect the present question. Under these circumstances it is clear that Major Anderson acted upon his own responsibility, and without authority, unless, indeed, he had "tangible evidence of a design to proceed to a hostile act" on the part of South Carolina, which has not yet been alleged. Still he is a brave and honorable officer, and justice requires that he should not be condemned without a fair hearing.

Be this as it may, when I learned that Major Anderson had left Fort Moultrie and proceeded to Fort Sumter, my first promptings were to command him to return to his former position, and there to await the contingencies presented in his instructions. This would only have been done with any degree of safety to the command by the concurrence of the South Carolina authorities. But before any step could possibly have been taken in this direction, we received information that the "Palmetto flag floated out to the breeze at Castle Pinckney, and a large military force went over last night (the 27th) to Fort Moultrie." Thus the authorities of South Carolina, without waiting or asking for any explanations, and doubtless believing, as you have expressed it, that the officer had acted not only without but against my orders, on the very next day after the night when the removal was made, seized by a military force two of the Federal forts in the harbor of Charleston, and have covered them under their own flag instead of that of the United States.

At this gloomy period of our history, startling events succeed each other rapidly. On the very day, the 27th instant, that possession of these two forts was taken, the Palmetto flag was raised over the Federal Custom-house and Post-office in Charleston ; and on the same day every officer of the Customs—Collector, Naval Officer, Surveyor, and Appraiser—resigned their offices.—And this, although it was well known from the language of my message that, as an executive officer, I felt myself bound to collect the revenue at the port of Charleston, under the existing laws. In the harbor of Charleston we now find three forts confronting each other, over all of which the Federal flag floated only four days ago ; but now, over two of them, this flag has been supplanted, and the Palmetto flag has been substituted in its stead. It is under all these circumstances that I am urged immediately to withdraw the troops from the harbor of Charleston, and am informed that without this negotiation is impossible. This I cannot do—this I will not do. Such an idea was never thought of by me in any possible contingency. No such allusion had been made in any communication between myself and any human being. But the inference is that I am bound to withdraw the troops from the only fort remaining in the possession of the United States in the harbor of Charleston, because the officer there in command of all of the forts thought proper, without instructions, to change his position from one of them to another.

At this point of writing, I have received information by telegraph from Capt. Humphreys, in command of the arsenal at Charleston, that "it has to-day (Sunday, the 30th) been taken by force of arms." It is estimated that the munitions of war belonging to this arsenal are worth half a million of dollars.

Comment is needless. After this information, I have only to add, that whilst it is my duty to defend Fort Sumter, as a portion of the public property of the United States, against hostile attacks, from whatever quarter they may come, by such means as I possess for this purpose, I do not perceive how such a defence can be construed into a menace against the city of Charleston. With great personal regard I remain, yours very respectfully,

JAMES BUCHANAN.

To Hon. ROBERT W. BARNWELL, JAMES H. ADAMS, JAMES L. ORR.

SECOND LETTER OF THE COMMISSIONERS TO THE PRESIDENT.

WASHINGTON, D. C., Jan. 1, 1861.

SIR : We have the honor to acknowledge the receipt of your letter of the 30th December, in reply to a note addressed by us to you, on the 28th of the same month, as Commissioners from South Carolina.

In reference to the declaration with which your reply commences, that your "position as President of the United States was already defined in the message to Congress of the 3d instant ; " that you possess " no power to change the relations heretofore existing between South Carolina and the United States," " much less to acknowledge the independence of that State," and that consequently you could meet us only as private gentlemen of the highest character, with an entire willingness to communicate to Congress any proposition we might have to make—we deem it only necessary to say that the State of South Carolina having, in the exercise of that great right of self-government which underlies all our political organizations, declared herself sovereign and independent, we, as her representatives, felt no special solicitude as to the character in which you might recognize us. Satisfied that the State had simply exercised her unquestionable right, we were prepared, in order to reach substantial good, to waive the formal considerations which your constitutional scruples might have prevented you from extending. We came here therefore expecting to be received as you did receive us, and perfectly content with that entire willingness, of which you assured us, to submit any proposition to Congress which we might have to make upon the subject of the independence of the State. The willingness was ample recognition of the condition of public affairs, which rendered our presence necessary. In this position, however, it is our duty both to the State which we represent and to ourselves, to correct several important misconceptions of our letter, into which you have fallen.

You say : " It was my earnest desire that such a disposition might be made of the whole subject by Congress, who alone possess the power, to prevent the inauguration of a civil war between the parties in regard to the possession of the Federal forts in the harbor of Charleston ; and I therefore deeply regret that in your opinion the events of the last twenty-four hours render this impossible." We expressed no such opinion ; and the language which you quote as ours, is altered in its sense by the omission of a most important part of the sentence. What we did say was, " But the events of the last twenty-four hours render such an assurance impossible." Place that "assurance," as contained in our letter, in the sentence, and we are prepared to repeat it.

Again, professing to quote our language, you say : " Thus the authorities of South Carolina, without waiting or asking for any explanation, and doubtless believing, as you have expressed it, that the officer had acted not only without but against my orders," &c. We expressed no such opinion in reference to the belief of the people of South Carolina. The language which you have quoted was applied solely and entirely to our assurances obtained here, and based, as you well know, upon your own declaration—a declaration which, at that time, it was impossible for the authorities of South Carolina to have known. But, without following this letter into all its details, we propose only to meet the chief points of the argument.

Some weeks ago the State of South Carolina declared her intention, in the existing condition of public affairs, to secede from the United States. She called a Convention of her people to put her declaration in force. The Convention met and passed the Ordinance of Secession. All this you anticipated, and your course of action was thoroughly considered in your Annual Message. You declared you had no right, and would not attempt, to coerce a seceding State, but that you were bound by your constitutional oath, and would defend the property of the United States within the borders of South Carolina if an attempt was made to take it by force. Seeing very early that this question of property was a difficult and delicate one, you manifested a desire to settle it without collision. You did not reinforce the garrison in the harbor of Charleston. You removed a distinguished and veteran officer from the command of Fort Moultrie because he attempted to increase his supply of ammunition. You refused to send additional troops to the same garrison when applied for by the officer appointed to succeed him. You accepted the resignation of the oldest and most eminent member of your Cabinet, rather than allow the garrison to be strengthened. You compelled an officer stationed at Fort Sumter to return immediately to the arsenal forty muskets which he had taken to arm his men. You expressed not to one, but to many, of the most distinguished of our public characters, whose testimony will be placed upon the record whenever it is necessary, your anxiety for a peaceful termination of this controversy, and your willingness not to disturb the military status of the forts, if Commissioners should be sent to the Government, whose communications you promised to submit to Congress. You received and acted on assurances from the highest official authorities of South Carolina, that no attempt would be made to disturb your possession of the forts and property of the United States, if you would not disturb their existing condition until the Commissioners had been sent, and the attempt to negotiate had failed. You took from the members of the House of Representatives a written memorandum that no such attempt should be made, "provided that no reinforcements should be sent to those forts, and their relative military status shall remain as at present." And although you attach no force to the acceptance of such a paper—although you "considered it as nothing more in effect than the promise of highly honorable gentlemen"—as an obligation on one side, without corresponding obligation on the other—it must be remembered (if we were rightly informed) that you were pledged, if you ever did send reinforcements, to return it to those from whom you had received it, before you executed your resolution. You sent orders to your officers, commanding them strictly to follow a line of conduct in conformity with such an understanding. Besides all this, you had received formal and official notice from the Governor of South Carolina that we had been appointed Commissioners, and were on our way to Washington. You knew the implied condition under which we came; our arrival was notified to you, and an hour appointed for an interview. We arrived in Washington on Wednesday, at 3 o'clock, and you appointed an interview with us at 1 the next day. Early on that day, (Thursday,) the news was received here of the movement of Major Anderson. That news was communicated to you immediately, and you postponed our meeting until 2½ o'clock on Friday, in order that you might consult your Cabinet. On Friday we saw you, and we called upon you then to redeem your pledge. You could not deny it. With the facts we have stated, and in the face of the crowning and conclusive fact that your Secretary of War had resigned his seat in the Cabinet, upon the publicly avowed ground that the action of Major Anderson had violated the pledged faith of the Government, and that unless the pledge was instantly redeemed, he was dishonored, denial was impossible; you

did not deny it. You do not deny it now, but you seek to escape from its obligation on the grounds, first, that we terminated all negotiation by demanding, as a preliminary, the withdrawal of the United States troops from the harbor of Charleston; and, second, that the authorities of South Carolina, instead of asking explanation, and giving you the opportunity to vindicate yourself, took possession of other property of the United States. We will examine both.

In the first place, we deny positively that we have ever in any way made any such demand. Our letter is in your possession; it will stand by this on record. In it we informed you of the objects of our mission. We say that it would have been our duty to have assured you of our readiness to commence negotiations, with the most earnest and anxious desire to settle all questions between us amicably and to our mutual advantage, but that events had rendered that assurance impossible. We stated the events, and we said that until some satisfactory explanation of these events was given us, we could not proceed; and then, having made this request for explanation, we added: "And in conclusion, we would urge upon you the immediate withdrawal of the troops from the harbor of Charleston. Under present circumstances they are a standing menace, which renders negotiation impossible," &c. "Under present circumstances!" What circumstances? Why, clearly the occupation of Fort Sumter and the dismantling of Fort Moultrie by Major Anderson, in the face of your pledges, and without explanation or practical disavowal. And there is nothing in the letter which would, or could, have prevented you from declining to withdraw the troops, and offering the restoration of the status to which you were pledged, if such has been your desire. It would have been wiser and better, in our opinion, to have withdrawn the troops; and this opinion we urged upon you; but we demanded nothing but such an explanation of the events of the last twenty-four hours as would restore our confidence in the spirit with which the negotiations should be conducted. In relation to this withdrawal of the troops from the harbor, we are compelled, however, to notice one passage of your letter. Referring to it, you say: "This I cannot do. This I will not do. Such an idea was never thought of by me in any possible contingency. No allusion to it had ever been made in any communication between myself and any human being."

In reply to this statement, we are compelled to say, that your conversation with us left upon our minds the distinct impression, that you did seriously contemplate the withdrawal of the troops from Charleston harbor. And in support of this impression, we would add, that we have the positive assurance of gentlemen of the highest possible public reputation and the most unsullied integrity—men whose name and fame, secured by long service and patriotic achievements, place their testimony beyond cavil—that such suggestions had been made to and urged upon you by them, and had formed the subject of more than one earnest discussion with you. And it was this knowledge that induced us to urge upon you a policy, which had to recommend it its own wisdom and the might of such authority. As to the second point, that the authorities of South Carolina, instead of asking explanations, and giving you the opportunity to vindicate yourself, took possession of other property of the

United States, we would observe: 1. That even if this were so, it does not avail you for defence, for the opportunity for decision was afforded you before these facts occurred. We arrived in Washington on Wednesday; the news from Major Anderson reached here early on Thursday, and was immediately communicated to you. All that day men of the highest consideration—men who had striven successfully to lift you to your great office—who had been your tried and true friends through the troubles of your administration, sought you and entreated you to act—to act at once. They told you that every hour complicated your position. They only asked you to give the assurance that if the facts were so—that if the commander had acted without and against your orders, and in violation of your pledges—that you would restore the status you had pledged your honor to maintain. You refused to decide. Your Secretary at War, your immediate and proper adviser in this whole matter, waited anxiously for your decision, until he felt that delay was becoming dishonor. More than twelve hours passed, and two Cabinet meetings had adjourned, before you knew what the authorities of South Carolina had done; and your prompt decision at any moment of that time would have avoided the subsequent complications. But, if you had known the acts of the authorities of South Carolina, should that have prevented your keeping your faith? What was the condition of things? For the last sixty days you have had in Charleston harbor, not force enough to hold the forts against an equal enemy. Two of them were empty—one of those two the most important in the harbor. It could have been taken at any time. You ought to know better than any man that it would have been taken, but for the efforts of those who put their trust in your honor. Believing that they were threatened by Fort Sumter especially, the people were with difficulty restrained from securing, without blood, the possession of this important fortress. After many and reiterated assurances, given on your behalf, which we cannot believe unauthorized, they determined to forbear, and in good faith sent on their Commissioners to negotiate with you. They meant you no harm—wished you no ill. They thought of you kindly, believed you true, and were willing, as far as was consistent with duty, to spare you unnecessary and hostile collision. Scarcely had these Commissioners left than Major Anderson waged war. No other words will describe his action. It was not a peaceful change from one fort to another; it was a hostile act in the highest sense, and only justified in the presence of a superior enemy, and in imminent peril. He abandoned his position, spiked his guns, burned his gun-carriages, made preparations for the destruction of his post, and withdrew, under cover of the night, to a safer position. This was war. No man could have believed (without your assurance) that any officer could have taken such a step, "not only without orders, but against orders." What the State did was in simple self-defence; for this act, with all its attending circumstances, was as much war as firing a volley; and war being thus begun, until those commencing it explained their action and disavowed their intention, there was no room for delay; and even at this moment while we are writing, it is more than probable, from the tenor of your letter, that reinforcements are hurrying on to the conflict, so that when the first gun shall be fired, there will

have been on your part one continuous, consistent series of actions, commencing in a demonstration essentially warlike, supported by regular reinforcements and terminating in defeat or victory. And all this without the slightest provocation; for, among the many things which you have said, there is one thing you cannot say—you have waited anxiously for news from the seat of war, in hopes that delay would furnish some excuse for this precipitation. But this "tangible evidence of a design to proceed to a hostile act, on the part of the authorities of South Carolina," which is the only justification of Major Anderson you are forced to admit, "has not yet been alleged." But you have decided, you have resolved to hold, by force, what you have obtained through our misplaced confidence; and by refusing to disavow the action of Major Anderson, have converted his violation of orders into a legitimate act of your executive authority. Be the issue what it may, of this we are assured, that, if Fort Moultrie has been recorded in history as a memorial of Carolina gallantry, Fort Sumter will live upon the succeeding page as an imperishable testimony of Carolina faith.

By your course, you have probably rendered civil war inevitable. Be it so. If you choose to force this issue upon us, the State of South Carolina will accept it, and, relying upon Him who is the God of Justice as well as the God of Hosts, will endeavor to perform the great duty which lies before her hopefully, bravely, and thoroughly.

Our mission being one for negotiation and peace, and your note leaving us without hope of a withdrawal of the troops from Fort Sumter, or of the restoration of the *status quo* existing at the time of our arrival, and intimating, as we think, your determination to reinforce the garrison in the harbor of Charleston, we respectfully inform you that we purpose returning to Charleston to-morrow afternoon.

We have the honor to be, Sir, very respectfully your obedient servants.

R. W. BARNWELL,
J. H. ADAMS,   } Commissioners.
JAMES L. ORR,

To His Excellency the President of the United States.

The following is the indorsement upon the document:

EXECUTIVE MANSION, 3½ o'clock, Wednesday. This paper, just presented to the President, is of such a character that he declines to receive it.

Doc. 13.—THE MERCURY'S APPEAL.

To our friends in Florida we would respectfully pass a word. There are two powerful strongholds and most important points of military offence and defence in Florida—Pensacola and Key West. The States both of Georgia and Alabama have wisely taken time by the forelock, and put themselves in possession of such fortresses as lie within their borders, simply because they do not choose that their territories should be occupied, their commerce cut off, and the lives of their people put in jeopardy, by General Scott's, or Mr. Buchanan's despotic theory of the powers and duties of the executive officer of a consolidated, vulgar mobocracy. They have chosen to ward off violence and outrage by a timely precaution. If any thing could tend to demonstrate to the Executive at Washington the folly of attempting the blockading of southern ports, it would be the late action of Georgia and Alabama in regard to their forts. Yet it is impossible to tell to what extremities folly and desperation may drive men. In this view, it is important for the people of Florida to reflect that there are, perhaps, no fortresses along our whole southern coast more important than those of Florida. These forts can command the whole Gulf trade. And should Mr. Buchanan carry out what appears to be his present plan, he certainly must desire to hold possession of these forts. He may thus, with the assistance of war-steamers, block up the whole Gulf. But let Florida hold these forts, and the entire aspect of affairs is changed. Such vessels, in time of war, will have no port of entry, and must be supplied in every way from a very long distance, and that at sea; while the commerce of the North in the Gulf *will fall an easy prey to our bold privateers; and California gold will pay all such little expenses on our part.*

We leave the matter for the reflection and decision of the people of Florida.—*Charleston Mercury.*

Doc. 14.—A RECOMMENDATION TO THE PEOPLE OF THE UNITED STATES.

Numerous appeals have been made to me by pious and patriotic associations and citizens, in view of the present distracted and dangerous condition of our country, to recommend that a day be set apart for humiliation, fasting and prayer throughout the Union. In compliance with their request, and my own sense of duty, I designate

FRIDAY, THE 4TH DAY OF JANUARY, 1861,

for this purpose, and recommend that the people assemble on that day, according to their several forms of worship, to keep it as a solemn fast.

The Union of the States is at the present moment threatened with alarming and immediate danger—panic and distress of a fearful character prevail throughout the land—our laboring population are without employment, and consequently deprived of the means of earning their bread—indeed, hope seems to have deserted the minds of men. All classes are in a state of confusion and dismay; and the wisest counsels of our best and purest men are wholly disregarded.

In this, the hour of our calamity and peril, to whom shall we resort for relief but to the God of our Fathers? His omnipotent arm only can save us from the awful effects of our own crimes and follies—our own ingratitude and guilt towards our Heavenly Father.

Let us, then, with deep contrition and penitent sorrow, unite in humbling ourselves before the Most High, in confessing our individual and national sins, and in acknowledging the justice of our punishment. Let us implore Him to remove from our hearts that false pride of opinion which would impel us to persevere in wrong for the sake of consistency, rather than yield a just submission to the unforeseen exigencies by which we are now surrounded. Let us, with deep reverence, beseech Him to restore the friendship and good will which prevailed in former days among the people of the several States, and, above all, to save us from the horrors of civil war and "blood guiltiness." Let our fervent prayers ascend to His throne, that He would not desert us

in this hour of extreme peril, but remember us as He did our fathers in the darkest days of the Revolution, and preserve our constitution and our Union —the work of their hands—for ages yet to come. An Omnipotent Providence may overrule existing evils for permanent good. He can make the wrath of man to praise Him, and the remainder of wrath He can restrain. Let me invoke every individual, in whatever sphere of life he may be placed, to feel a personal responsibility to God and his country for keeping this day holy, and for contributing all in his power to remove our actual and impending difficulties.   JAMES BUCHANAN.

WASHINGTON, Dec. 14, 1860.

Doc. 15.—CARRINGTON'S CALL.

"*To the Public:* Whereas, the militia of the district is not organized, and threats have been made that the President-elect shall not be inaugurated in Washington, and there is reason therefore to apprehend that on the 4th of March next our city may be made the scene of riot, violence, and bloodshed; and, whereas, the undersigned believes that the honor of the nation and our city demands that the President-elect shall be inaugurated in the national metropolis, and that the young men of Washington City are determined not to desert their homes in the hour of danger, but to maintain their ground and defend their families and friends, in the Union and on the side of the constitution and the laws, therefore, the undersigned earnestly invites all who concur with him in opinion, and who are not now connected with some military company, to join with him in forming a temporary military organization, with a view of preserving peace and order in our midst on the 4th of March next, or whenever the emergency requires it—and for that purpose to unite with the volunteer companies of our city, which have, in a spirit of gallantry and patriotism worthy of our imitation, pledged themselves to the cause of the Union, the constitution, and the laws. It is proper to state that I take this step after consultation with friends in whom I have the greatest confidence. It is not my object to interfere with my brother officers of the militia—the organization proposed is to be purely volunteer, for the purpose above stated, in which I am willing to serve in any capacity. I make the proposition not as one of the generals of the militia, but as a citizen of Washington, who is prepared to defend his home and his honor, at the peril of his life.

Jan. 5, 1861.   "EDWARD C. CARRINGTON."

Doc. 16.—EXTRACT FROM GOV. HICKS' ADDRESS.

I firmly believe that a division of this Government would inevitably produce civil war. The secession leaders in South Carolina, and the fanatical demagogues of the North, have alike proclaimed that such would be the result, and no man of sense, in my opinion, can question it. What could the Legislature do in this crisis, if convened, to remove the present troubles which beset the Union? We are told by the leading spirits of the South Carolina Convention that neither the election of Mr. Lincoln nor the non-execution of the Fugitive Slave law, nor both combined, constitute their grievances. They declare that the real cause of their discontent dates as far back as 1833. Maryland and every other State in the Union, with a united voice, then declared the cause insufficient to justify the course of South Carolina. Can it be that this people, who then unanimously supported the cause of Gen. Jackson, will now yield their opinions at the bidding of modern secessionists? I have been told that the position of Maryland should be defined so that both sections can understand it. Do any really understand her position? Who that wishes to understand it can fail to do so? If the action of the Legislature would be simply to declare that Maryland is with the South in sympathy and feeling; that she demands from the North the repeal of offensive, unconstitutional statutes, and appeals to it for new guarantees; that she will wait a reasonable time for the North to purge her statute-books, as to do justice to her Southern brethren, and, if her appeals are vain, will make her common cause with her sister border States in resistance to tyranny if need be, it would only be saying what the whole country well knows, and what may be said much more effectually by her people themselves, in their meetings, than by the Legislature, chosen eighteen months since, when none of these questions were raised before them. That Maryland is a conservative Southern State all know who know any thing of her people or her history. The business and agricultural classes, planters, merchants, mechanics, and laboring men; those who have a real stake in the community, who would be forced to pay the taxes and do the fighting, are the persons who should be heard in preference to excited politicians, many of whom, having nothing to lose from the destruction of the Government, may hope to derive some gain from the ruin of the State. Such men will naturally urge you to pull down the pillars of this "accursed Union," which their allies at the North have denominated a "covenant with hell." The people of Maryland, if left to themselves, would decide, with scarcely an exception, that there is nothing in the present causes of complaint to justify immediate secession; and yet, against our judgments and solemn convictions of duty, we are to be precipitated into this revolution, because South Carolina thinks differently. Are we not equals? Or shall her opinions control our actions? After we have solemnly declared for ourselves, as every man must do, are we to be forced to yield our opinions to those of another State, and thus in effect obey her mandates? She refuses to wait for our counsels. Are we bound to obey her commands? The men who have embarked in this scheme to convene the Legislature, will spare no pains to carry their point. The whole plan of operations, in the event of the assembling of the Legislature, is, as I have been informed, already marked out, the list of ambassadors who are to visit the other States is agreed on, and the resolutions which they hope will be passed by the Legislature, fully committing this State to secession, are said to be already prepared. In the course of nature, I cannot have long to live, and I fervently trust to be allowed to end my days a citizen of this glorious Union. But should I be compelled to witness the downfall of that Government inherited from our fathers, established, as it were, by the special favor of God, I will at least have the consolation, at my dying hour, that I neither by word nor deed assisted in hastening its disruption. (Signed) THOMAS H. HICKS.

Doc. 17.—CORRESPONDENCE BETWEEN GOV. ELLIS AND SECRETARY HOLT.

JANUARY 12, 1861.

SIR:—Reliable information has reached this Department, that, on the 8th inst., Forts Johnson and Caswell were taken possession of by State troops and persons resident in that vicinity, in an irregular manner.

Upon receipt of this information I immediately issued a military order requesting the forts to be restored to the authorities of the United States, which orders will be executed this day.

My information satisfies me that this popular outbreak was caused by a report, very generally credited, but which, for the sake of humanity, I hope is not true, that it was the purpose of the administration to *coerce* the Southern States, and that troops were on their way to garrison the Southern ports and to begin the work of subjugation. This impression is not yet erased from the public mind, which is deeply agitated at the bare contemplation of so great an indignity and wrong; and I would most earnestly appeal to your Excellency to strengthen my hands in my efforts to preserve the public order here, by placing it in my power to give public assurance that no measures of force are contemplated towards us.

Your Excellency will pardon me, therefore, for asking whether the United States forts will be garrisoned with United States troops during your administration.

This question I ask in perfect respect, and with an earnest desire to prevent consequences which I know would be regretted by your Excellency as much as myself.

Should I receive assurance that no troops will be sent to this State prior to the 4th of March next, then all will be peace and quiet here, and the property of the United States will be fully protected as heretofore. If, however, I am unable to get such assurances, I will not undertake to answer for the consequences.

The forts in this State have long been unoccupied, and their being garrisoned at this time will unquestionably be looked upon as a hostile demonstration, and will, in my opinion, certainly be resisted.

Secretary HOLT responded, under date of Jan. 15:

"Your letter of the 12th inst., addressed to the President of the United States, has by him been referred to this Department, and he instructs me to express his gratification at the promptitude with which you have ordered the expulsion of the lawless men who recently occupied Forts Johnson and Caswell. He regards this action on the part of your Excellency as in complete harmony with the honor and patriotic character of the people of North Carolina, whom you so worthily represent.

"In reply to your inquiry, whether it is the purpose of the President to garrison the forts of North Carolina during his administration, I am directed to say that they, in common with the other forts, arsenals, and other property of the United States, are in the charge of the President, and that if assailed, no matter from what quarter or under what pretext, it is his duty to protect them by all the means which the law has placed at his disposal. It is not his purpose to garrison the forts to which you refer at present, because he considers them entirely safe, as heretofore, under the shelter of that law-abiding sentiment for which the people of North Carolina have ever been distinguished. Should they, however, be attacked or menaced with danger of being seized or taken from the possession of the United States, he could not escape from his constitutional obligation to defend and preserve them. The very satisfactory and patriotic assurance given by your Excellency justifies him, however, in entertaining the confident expectation that no such contingency will arise."

Doc. 18.—CORRESPONDENCE BETWEEN MAJ. ANDERSON AND GOV. PICKENS.

To His Excellency the Governor of South Carolina:

SIR: Two of your batteries fired this morning on an unarmed vessel bearing the flag of my Government. As I have not been notified that war has been declared by South Carolina against the United States, I cannot but think this a hostile act, committed without your sanction or authority. Under that hope I refrain from opening a fire on your batteries. I have the honor, therefore, respectfully to ask whether the above-mentioned act—one which I believe without parallel in the history of our country or any other civilized Government—was committed in obedience to your instructions, and notify you, if it is not disclaimed, that I regard it as an act of war, and I shall not, after reasonable time for the return of my messenger, permit any vessel to pass within the range of the guns of my fort. In order to save, as far as it is in my power, the shedding of blood, I beg you will take due notification of my decision for the good of all concerned,—hoping, however, your answer may justify a further continuance of forbearance on my part.

I remain, respectfully,
ROBERT ANDERSON.

GOV. PICKENS' REPLY.

GOV. PICKENS, after stating the position of South Carolina towards the United States, says that any attempt to send United States troops into Charleston harbor, to reinforce the forts, would be regarded as an act of hostility; and in conclusion adds, that any attempt to reinforce the troops at Fort Sumter, or to retake and resume possession of the forts within the waters of South Carolina, which Major ANDERSON abandoned, after spiking the cannon and doing other damage, cannot but be regarded by the authorities of the State as indicative of any other purpose than the coercion of the State by the armed force of the Government; special agents, therefore, have been off the bar to warn approaching vessels, armed and unarmed, having troops to reinforce Fort Sumter aboard, not to enter the harbor. Special orders have been given the commanders at the forts not to fire on such vessels until a shot across their bows should warn them of the prohibition of the State. Under these circumstances the Star of the West, it is understood, this morning attempted to enter the harbor with troops, after having been notified she could not enter, and consequently she was fired into. This act is perfectly justified by me.

In regard to your threat about vessels in the harbor, it is only necessary for me to say, you must be the judge of your responsibility. Your position in the harbor has been tolerated by the authorities of the State, and while the act of which you complain is in perfect consistency with the rights and duties of the State, it is not perceived how far the conduct you propose to adopt can find a parallel in the history of any country, or be reconciled with any other purpose than that of your Government imposing on the State the condition of a conquered province.

F. W. PICKENS.

SECOND COMMUNICATION FROM MAJOR ANDERSON.

To His Excellency Governor Pickens:

SIR: I have the honor to acknowledge the receipt of your communication, and say, that under the circumstances I have deemed it proper to refer the whole matter to my Government, and intend deferring the course I indicated in my note this morning until the arrival from Washington of such instructions as I may receive.

I have the honor also to express the hope that no obstructions will be placed in the way, and that you will do me the favor of giving every facility for the departure and return of the bearer, Lieut. T. TALBOT, who is directed to make the journey.

ROBERT ANDERSON.

ATTACK ON THE STAR OF THE WEST.

"About half-past six o'clock yesterday (Wednesday) morning, the steamer General Clinch discovered the steamship Star of the West and signalled the fact of her approach to the occupants of the battery on Morris Island. As soon as the signals were seen by those on guard there, Morris Island was astir with men at their posts before the orders could be given them to prepare for action. They remained in anxious suspense, but ready for what they believed was sure to come, a volley from Fort Sumter. The Star of the West rounded the point, took the ship channel inside the bar, and proceeded straight forward until opposite Morris Island, about three-quarters of a mile from the battery. A ball was then fired athwart the bows of the steamer. The Star of the West displayed the stars and stripes. As soon as the flag was unfurled the fortification fired a succession of shots. The vessel continued on her course with increased speed; but two shots taking effect upon her, she concluded to retire. Fort Moultrie fired a few shots at her, but she was out of their range. The damage done to the Star of the West is trifling, as only two out of seventeen shots took effect upon her. Fort Sumter made no demonstration, except at the port-holes, where the guns were run out bearing on Morris Island."—*Charleston Courier, Jan. 10.*

Doc. 19.—THE ALABAMA ORDINANCE OF SECESSION.

AN ORDINANCE TO DISSOLVE THE UNION BETWEEN THE STATE OF ALABAMA AND OTHER STATES, UNITED UNDER THE COMPACT AND STYLE OF THE UNITED STATES OF AMERICA.

Whereas, The election of Abraham Lincoln and Hannibal Hamlin to the offices of President and Vice-President of the United States of America, by a sectional party, avowedly hostile to the domestic institutions, and peace and security of the people of the State of Alabama, following upon the heels of many and dangerous infractions of the Constitution of the United States, by many of the States and people of the Northern section, is a political wrong of so insulting and menacing a character, as to justify the people of the State of Alabama in the adoption of prompt and decided measures for their future peace and security.

Therefore, be it declared and ordained, by the people of the State of Alabama, in convention assembled, that the State of Alabama now withdraws from the Union, known as the United States of America, and henceforth ceases to be one of the said United States, and is and of right ought to be a sovereign independent State.

SEC. 2. And be it further declared and ordained by the people of the State of Alabama in convention assembled, that all powers over the territories of said State, and over the people thereof, heretofore delegated to the Government of the United States of America, be, and they are hereby, withdrawn from the said Government, and are hereby resumed and vested in the people of the State of Alabama.

And as it is the desire and purpose of the people of Alabama, to meet the slaveholding States of the South who approve of such a purpose, in order to frame a revisional as a permanent Government, upon the principles of the Government of the United States, be it also resolved by the people of Alabama, in convention assembled, that the people of the States of Delaware, Maryland, Virginia, North Carolina, South Carolina, Florida, Georgia, Mississippi, Louisiana, Texas, Arkansas, Tennessee, Kentucky and Missouri, be and they are hereby invited to meet the people of the State of Alabama, by their delegates in convention, on the 4th day of February next in Montgomery, in the State of Alabama, for the purpose of consultation with each other, as to the most effectual mode of securing concerted, harmonious action in whatever measures may be deemed most desirable for the common peace and security.

And be it further resolved, That the President of this convention be and he is hereby instructed to transmit forthwith a copy of the foregoing preamble, ordinance and resolutions to the Governors of the several States named in the said resolutions.

Done by the people of Alabama, in convention assembled, at Montgomery, this 11th day of January, 1861.

The preamble, ordinance and resolutions were adopted by Ayes 61, Nays 39.

CELEBRATION IN MOBILE.

Yesterday was the wildest day of excitement in the annals of Mobile. The whole people seemed to be at the top point of enthusiasm from the time that the telegraphic announcement of the passage of the secession ordinance in the convention was received, until the hour when honest men should be abed. To add, if possible, to the excitement, the news of the secession of our sister State of Florida was received simultaneously with that of the withdrawal of Alabama.

Immediately on the receipt of the news, an immense crowd assembled at the "secession pole," at the foot of Government-street, to witness the spreading of the Southern flag, and it was run up amid the shouts of the multitude and the thunders of cannon. One hundred and one guns for Alabama and fifteen for Florida were fired, and after remarks from Dr. Woodcock, Mr. Lude, and other gentlemen, the crowd repaired to the Custom House, walking in procession with a band of music at the head, braying the warlike notes of the "Southern Marseillaise."

Arrived at the Custom House, a lone star flag was waved from its walls amid enthusiastic shouts. The balcony of the Battle House, opposite, was thronged with ladies and gentlemen, and the street was crowded with excited citizens. Standing upon the steps of the Custom House, brief and stirring addresses were delivered by Dr. Woodcock, Gen. Niel Robinson, Gen. Lawler, Gen. Butler, Dr. Lyle, Robert H. Smith, Mayor Withers, and Hon. George N. Stewart.

It was announced that a despatch had been received from the Governor, to the effect that he expected that Mobile would raise a hundred thousand dollars for the defence of the city. Gen. Robinson and Gen. Lawler immediately put down their names for a thousand dollars each, Dr. Lyle, of Mississippi, for two hundred and fifty, and other gentlemen for other sums. A committee was appointed to canvass the city and obtain subscriptions.

The military paraded the streets. The Cadets were out in force, bearing the splendid flag which was presented them the day previous, and is a most gorgeous banner, and, with the Independent Rifles, marched to Bienville Square, where they fired continuous salvos of musketry.

The demonstration at night was worthy the magnitude of the event celebrated. The display was of the most brilliant description. During the whole day the "busy sound of hammers" on all sides gave note of preparation for illumination; and when night fell, the city emerged from darkness into a blaze of such glory as could only be achieved by the most recklessly extravagant consumption of tar and tallow. The broad boulevard of Government-street was an avenue of light, bonfires of tar-barrels being kindled at intervals of a square's distance along its length, and many residences upon it were illuminated. The Court House and other buildings at the intersection of Royal-street shone with a plenitude of candles.

Royal street was a gorgeous gush of light, the great front of the Battle House and other buildings being a perfect conflagration of illumination. All the newspaper offices were, of course, numbered among the *illuminati* of the occasion. Dauphin-street, for many squares, was a continuous blaze of light, and the buildings around Bienville Square rivalled each other in taste and magnificence of display. With a choice epicureanism of triumph and rejoicing, the Custom House was illuminated by a fair show of patriotic candles—Ossas of insult being thus piled on Pelions of injury to Uncle Sam.

In the remote, unfrequented streets of the city, as well as in the more prominent avenues of business or residence, frequent illuminated buildings could be seen dispersing the gloom of night from about them. Rockets blazed and crackers popped, and the people hurrahed and shouted as they never did before. The streets, as light as day, were overflowed with crowds of ladies who had turned out to see the display. Many of the designs of illuminatory work were exceedingly tasteful and beautiful. The "Southern Cross" was a favored emblematic pattern, and gleaming in lines of fire, competed with the oft-repeated "Lone Star" for admiration and applause from the multitude. In short, the occasion seemed several Fourth of Julys, a number of New Year's eves, various Christmases, and a sprinkling of other holidays all rolled into one big event. While we write, at a late hour, some enthusiastic orator is haranguing a shouting multitude from the steps of the Custom House, and all the juvenile fireworks of China and the other Indies seem to be on a grand burst of combined explosion, startling the ear of night with their mimic artillery of gratulation.

—*Mobile Advertiser*, Jan. 12.

Doc. 20.—N. Y. STATE RESOLUTIONS.

Whereas, The insurgent State of South Carolina, after seizing the Post Offices, Custom House, moneys and fortifications of the Federal Government, has, by firing into a vessel ordered by the Government to convey troops and provisions to Fort Sumter, virtually declared war ; and,

Whereas, The forts and property of the United States Government in Georgia, Alabama and Louisiana have been unlawfully seized, with hostile intentions ; and,

Whereas, Their Senators in Congress avow and maintain their treasonable acts ; therefore,

Resolved, That the Legislature of New York is profoundly impressed with the value of the Union, and determined to preserve it unimpaired ; that it greets with joy the recent firm, dignified and patriotic Special Message of the President of the United States, and that we tender to him, through the Chief Magistrate of our own State, whatever aid in men and money may be required to enable him to enforce the laws and uphold the authority of the Federal Government ; and that, in the defence of the Union, which has conferred prosperity and happiness upon the American people, renewing the pledge given and redeemed by our fathers, we are ready to devote our fortunes, our lives, and our sacred honor.

Resolved, That the Union-loving citizens and representatives of Delaware, Maryland, Virginia, North Carolina, Kentucky, Missouri and Tennessee, who labor with devoted courage and patriotism to withhold their States from the vortex of secession, are entitled to the gratitude and admiration of the whole people.

Resolved, That the Governor be respectfully requested to forward, forthwith, copies of the foregoing resolutions to the President of the Nation, and the Governors of all the States of the Union.

—*N. Y. Times*, Jan. 12.

Doc. 21.—CAPT. McGOWAN'S REPORT.

STEAMSHIP STAR OF THE WEST,
 NEW YORK, Saturday, Jan. 12, 1861.

M. O. ROBERTS, ESQ.—SIR : After leaving the wharf on the 5th inst., at 5 o'clock P. M., we proceeded down the Bay, where we hove to, and took on board four officers and two hundred soldiers, with their arms, ammunition, &c., and then proceeded to sea, crossing the bar at Sandy Hook at 9 P. M. Nothing unusual took place during the passage, which was a pleasant one for this season of the year.

We arrived at Charleston Bar at 1.30 A. M. on the 9th inst., but could find no guiding marks for the Bar, as the lights were all out. We proceeded with caution, running very slow and sounding, until about 4 A. M., being then in 4½ fathoms water, when we discovered a light through the haze which at that time covered the horizon. Concluding that the lights were on Fort Sumter, after getting the bearings of it, we steered to the S. W. for the main ship-channel, where we hove to, to await daylight, our lights having all been put out since 12 o'clock, to avoid being seen.

As the day began to break, we discovered a steamer just in shore of us, who, as soon as she saw us, burned one blue light and two red lights as signals, and shortly after steamed over the bar and into the ship-channel. The soldiers were now all put below, and no one allowed on deck except our own crew. As soon as there was light enough to see, we crossed the bar and proceeded on up the channel, (the outer bar buoy having been taken away,) the steamer ahead of us sending off rockets, and burning lights until after broad daylight, continuing on her course up nearly two miles ahead of us. When we arrived about two miles from Fort Moultrie, Fort Sumter being about the same distance, a masked battery on Morris Island, where there was a red Palmetto flag flying, opened fire upon us—distance, about five-eighths of a mile. *We had the American flag flying at our flagstaff at the time, and soon after the first shot, hoisted a large American Ensign at the fore.* We continued on under the fire of the battery for over ten minutes, several of the shots going clear over us. One shot just passed clear of the pilot-house, another passed between the smoke-stack and walking beams of the engine, another struck the ship just abaft the fore-rigging and stove in the planking, while another came within an ace of carrying away the rudder. At the same time there was a movement of two steamers from near Fort Moultrie, one of them towing a schooner, (I presume an armed schooner,) with the intention of cutting us off. Our position now became rather critical, as we had to approach Fort Moultrie to within three-quarters of a mile before we could keep away for Fort Sumter. A steamer approaching us with an armed schooner in tow, and the battery on the island firing at us all the time, and having no cannon to defend ourselves from the attack of the vessels, we concluded that, to avoid certain capture, or destruction, we would endeavor to get to sea. Consequently we wore round and steered down the channel, the battery firing upon us until the shot fell short. As it was now strong ebb tide, and the water having fallen some three feet, we proceeded with caution, and crossed the bar safely at 8.50 A. M., and continued on our course for this port, where we arrived this morning after a boisterous passage. A steamer from Charleston followed us for about three hours, watching our movements.

In justice to the officers and crews of each department of the ship, I must add that their behavior while under the fire of the battery reflected great credit on them.

Mr. Brewer, the New York pilot, was of very great assistance to me in helping to pilot the ship over Charleston Bar, and up and down the channel.

Very respectfully, your obedient servant,

JOHN McGOWAN, Captain.

—*Times*, Jan. 14.

Doc. 22.—GEORGIA SECESSION ORDINANCE.

AN ORDINANCE TO DISSOLVE THE UNION BETWEEN THE STATE OF GEORGIA AND OTHER STATES UNITED WITH HER UNDER THE COMPACT OF GOVERNMENT ENTITLED THE CONSTITUTION OF THE UNITED STATES.

We, the people of the State of Georgia, in Convention assembled, do declare and ordain, and it is hereby declared and ordained, that the ordinances adopted by the people of the State of Georgia in convention in 1788, whereby the Constitution of the United States was assented to, ratified and adopted, and also all acts and parts of acts of the General Assembly ratifying and adopting amendments to the said Constitution, are hereby repealed, rescinded and abrogated.

And we do further declare and ordain that the Union now subsisting between the State of Georgia and other States, under the name of the United States, is hereby dissolved, and that the State of Georgia is in full possession and exercise of all those rights of sovereignty which belong and appertain to a free and independent State.

Doc. 23.—SPEECH OF JEFFERSON DAVIS ON LEAVING THE SENATE.

I rise for the purpose of announcing to the Senate that I have satisfactory evidence that the State of Mississippi, by solemn ordinance in convention assembled, has declared her separation from the United States. Under these circumstances, of course, my functions terminate here. It has seemed to be proper that I should appear in the Senate and announce that fact, and to say something, though very little, upon it. The occasion does not invite me to go into the argument, and my physical condition will not permit it, yet something would seem to be necessary on the part of the State I here represent, on an occasion like this. It is known to Senators who have served here, that I have for many years advocated, as an essential attribute of State sovereignty, the right of a State to secede from the Union. If, therefore, I had not believed there was justifiable cause—if I had thought the State was acting without sufficient provocation— still, under my theory of government, I should have felt bound by her action. I, however, may say I think she had justifiable cause, and I approve of her acts. I conferred with the people before that act was taken, and counselled them that if they could not remain, that they should take the act. I hope none will confound this expression of opinion with the advocacy of the right of a State to remain in the Union, and disregard its constitutional obligations by nullification. Nullification and secession are indeed antagonistic principles. Nullification is the remedy which is to be sought and applied, within the Union, against an agent of the United States, when the agent has violated constitutional obligations, and the State assumes for itself, and appeals to other States to support it. But when the States themselves, and the people of the States, have so acted as to convince us that they will not regard our constitutional rights, then, and then for the first time, arises the question of secession in its practical application. That great man who now reposes with his fathers, who has been so often arraigned for want of fealty to the Union, advocated the doctrine of nullification, because it preserved the Union. It was because of his deep-seated attachment to the Union that Mr. Calhoun advocated the doctrine of nullification, which he claimed would give peace within the limits of the Union, and not disturb it, and only be the means of bringing the agent before the proper tribunal of the States for judgment. Secession belongs to a different class of rights, and is to be justified upon the basis that the States are sovereign. The time has been, and I hope the time will come again, when a better appreciation of our Union will prevent any one denying that each State is a sovereign in its own right. Therefore, I say I concur in the act of my State, and feel bound by it. It is by this confounding of nulli-

fication and secession that the name of another great man has been invoked to justify the coercion of a seceding State. The phrase "to execute the law," as used by General Jackson, was applied to a State refusing to obey the laws and still remaining in the Union. I remember well when Massachusetts was arraigned before the Senate. The record of that occasion will show that I said, if Massachusetts, in pursuing the line of steps, takes the last step which separates her from the Union, the right is hers, and I will neither vote one dollar nor one man to coerce her, but I will say to her, "God speed!" Mr. Davis then proceeded to argue that the equality spoken of in the Declaration of Independence was the equality of a class in political rights, referring to the charge against George III. for inciting insurrection, as proof that it had no reference to the slaves. But we have proclaimed our independence. This is done with no hostility or any desire to injure any section of the country, nor even for our pecuniary benefit, but from the high and solid foundation of defending and protecting the rights we inherited, and transmitting them unshorn to our posterity. I know I feel no hostility to you Senators here, and am sure there is not one of you, whatever may have been the sharp discussion between us, to whom I cannot now say, in the presence of my God, I wish you well. And such is the feeling, I am sure, the people I represent feel towards those whom you represent. I, therefore, feel I but express their desire, when I say I hope and they hope for those peaceful relations with you, though we must part, that may be mutually beneficial to us in the future. There will be peace if you so will it, and you may bring disaster on every part of the country, if you thus will have it. And if you will have it thus, we will invoke the God of our fathers, who delivered them from the paw of the lion, to protect us from the ravages of the bear; and thus putting our trust in God, and our own firm hearts and strong arms, we will vindicate and defend the rights we claim. In the course of my long career, I have met with a great variety of men here, and there have been points of collision between us. Whatever of offence there has been to me, I leave here. I carry no hostile feelings away. Whatever of offence I have given, which has not been redressed, I am willing to say to Senators in this hour of parting, I offer you my apology for any thing I may have done in the Senate; and I go thus released from obligation, remembering no injury I have received, and having discharged what I deem the duty of man, to offer the only reparation at this hour for every injury I have ever inflicted.

[As the Senators from Florida, Alabama and Mississippi were about to retire from the Senate, all the Democratic Senators crowded around them and shook hands with them. Messrs. Hale and Cameron were the only Republican Senators that did so.]

—Herald, Jan. 22.

Doc. 24.—SHERRARD CLEMENS' SPEECH.

He thanked God that he was permitted, after a long sickness, to take his stand upon that floor in renovated health, at a time when his services might prove most valuable to his constituents. He would not now speak in passion. It would not befit the solemn and portentous issues of the hour. They were in the midst of great events. It might be that they were in the dying days of the Republic, and he would not therefore utter, even in a whisper, one word which might tend to bring down the impending avalanche upon the quiet homes of the people. He would at the same time speak as a Southern man, identified with all the interests of the South. He would speak as a Western Virginian, and as the custodian of those who were not old enough to know the perils to which they were exposed, by those who were now riding on the crest of the popular wave, but who were, nevertheless, destined to sink into the very trough of the sea to a depth so unfathomable that not a bubble would ever rise, to mark the spot where they went so ignominiously down. Well might those who had inaugurated the revolution which was now stalking over the land, cry out with uplifted hands for peace, and deprecate the effusion of blood. It was the inventor of the guillotine who was its first victim, and the day was not far off when they would find among their own people, those who would have to rely upon the magnanimity of that population, whom they had most cruelly outraged and deceived. He had not the heart to enter into a detail of the arguments, or to express the indignant emotions, which rose to his lips for utterance. But before God, and in his inmost conscience he believed that Slavery would be crucified, should this unhappy controversy end in a dismemberment of the Union. If not crucified, it would carry the death-rattle in its throat. It remained to be seen whether treason could be carried out with the same facility with which it has been plotted. There was a holy courage among the minority of every State that might be for the time overwhelmed. Lazarus was not dead, but slept; and ere long the stone would be rolled away from the mouth of the tomb, and they would witness all the glories of a resurrection. It would not be forgotten, that among the clans of Scotland, beacon fires used to be lit by concerted signals from crag to crag, in living volumes of flame, yet expiring even in its own fierceness, and sinking into ashes as the fagots which fed them were consumed. To such a picture as that might be likened a rebellion such as political leaders sometimes excite for a brief hour; but the fires of rebellion burnt out with the fagots, and all was cold and dark again. There was a striking contrast between such a movement, between such a rebellion as he alluded to, and the uprising of the masses of the people in vindication of violated rights. As great a difference as there was between Snug, the joiner, and Bottom, the weaver, who "could roar you as fierce as a lion, or coo you as gently as a sucking-dove." One was the stage-trick of a political harlequin, the other was a living reality—the one was a livid and fitful flame, the other was a prairie on fire, finding in every step of its progress food for its all-ravening maw. In the present emergency, before this political conspiracy, it might be that he would stand alone with his colleague, (Mr. Wilson.) Let it be so. He sought no office. His political race was very nearly voluntarily run. History would record the proceeding of this turbulent period, and time—the gentle but infallible arbiter of all things earthly—would decide the truth. Upon that he would take his stand. They lived in an age of political paradoxes. Broad, expansive love of country had become a diseased sentimentality. Patriotism had become a starveling birdling, clinging with unfledged wings around the nest of twigs where it was born. A statesman must now not only narrow his mind and give up to party what was meant for mankind, but he must recede as submissively as a blind horse in a bark mill to every perverted opinion which sits, whip in hand, on the revolving shaft, at the end of which he is harnessed. To be a diamond of the first water, he must stand in the Senate House of his country, and in the face of a forbearing people, glory in being a traitor and a rebel. He must solemnly proclaim the death of the nation to which he had sworn allegiance, and with the grave stolidity of an undertaker, invite its citizens to their own funeral. He must dwarf and provincialize his patriotism to the State on whose local passion he thrives, to the country where he practises court, or to the city where he flaunts in all the meretricious dignity of a Doge of Venice. He can take an oath to support the Constitution of the United States, but he can enter with honor into a conspiracy to overthrow it. He can, under the sanctity of the same oath, advise the seizure of forts and arsenals, dockyards and ships, and money belonging to the Union, whose officer he is, and find a most loyal and convenient retreat in State authority and State allegiance. He was ready to laugh in their faces if they only told him that, before the time when he was "muling and puking in his nurse's arms," there lived a very obscure person named GEORGE WASHINGTON, who, before he died, became eminent by perpetrating the immortal joke of advising the people of the United States, that it was of infinite moment, that they should properly estimate the immense value of their national Union —that they should cherish a cordial, habitual and immovable attachment to it—that they should watch its preservation with jealous anxiety, discountenance whatever might suggest a suspicion that it could in any event be abandoned, and indignantly frown down the first dawning attempt to alienate any portion of the country from the rest, or to enfeeble the sacred ties which linked together its various parts. WASHINGTON saw into the future, and discovered that disastrous period in our history against which he warned his countrymen when he told them to "beware of geographical parties." These extreme parties, North and South, had at last met. Their differences had been created and carried on by systematic perversions of each other's aims and objects. In the North it had been represented that the South desired and intended to monopolize with slave territory all the public lands, and to drive therefrom free labor, to convert every free State into common ground for the recapture of colored persons as slaves who were free, and to put the Federal Government in all its departments under the control of a slave oligarchy. These and all other stratagems that could be resorted to aroused antagonistic feelings, which were welded with turbulent passions. As they planted so they reaped. Now that victory had been won by the Republican party, and the Government must be administered upon national policy; the fissures in the ground occupied by them became apparent, and hence there would necessarily be a large defection in its ranks among the more ultra of its adherents, who were, as a general thing, ideal, speculative, and not practical men. Out of actual power, a party was apt to be radical. Vest it with power, and it became conservative. This was the ordeal through which the Republican, like all other parties, was now passing, and he hoped for the peace of the country, and the triumph of practical, rather than ideal policy and measures. Herein consisted the almost insuperable difficulty of coming to any feasible adjustment upon the existing discontents. The bulk of politicians, North and South, were bound by a past record and past professions. They were, in fact, thinking all the while "what Mrs. Grundy would say." The people themselves understood the cause of the difficulty, and if they but once interfered, the country would be saved. What was the difficulty now? He appealed whether it was not that in the hands of ultras, North and South, the slaveholder had been used as a shuttledore, who, for purposes utterly dissimilar, had been banded from South Carolina to Massachusetts, and from Massachusetts back again to South Carolina, until now the last point of endurance had been reached? Every violent word uttered North had been sent South, and the South had responded in the spirit. The abolitionist himself had been granted an audience in every Southern city, at every Southern political meeting, and the most violent insulting, agrarian speeches repeated even in the hearing of the slaves themselves. Was it not humiliating to confess, that the very people who would burn in effigy, if not at the stake, a postmaster who would dare to distribute a copy of abolition speeches, honor as among their chief defenders the candidates who could quote the most obnoxious passages from all who had made Southern politics a vast hot-bed for the propagation of abolition sentiments? The two great sections of the nation stood at that moment towards each other like two encamped armies, waiting the orders to engage. The patriot planned, deplored, and appealed, but found little succor in the only quarter whence succor could come. The abolitionist revelled in the madness of the hour. He saw the cracks in the iceberg at last. To him the desert and the battle-field were alike welcome. He had knelt down in the desert with the camels, for a speck in the far distance showed that the simoom was coming. He looked into the future as into a dark cloud in the morning, when nothing but the early lark was on the wing. But soon history, like the light of the eastern horizon, would curtain back that cloud, and paint in blood's ruddiest tints field and forest, hamlet and city, the very mountains to their pine-crowned tops, and the great ocean itself, as an ensanguined flood, where brother contending with brother should find a nameless sepulchre. No anaconda, with his filthy folds around the banyan tree, threw out the venomous tongue and yearned with fiercer passion for the crushed bone and the pulpy flesh than he, the abolitionist, now expectant of his prey, yearned for this long-proposed repast. Well might he cry that the day of jubilee had come. Well might he marshal his hosts to the last great war of sections and of races. Defeated, stigmatized, insulted, scoffed at, ostracized and gibbeted by his countrymen, he now gloated over the most fearful of all retributions. His deadliest foes in the South had now struck hands in a solemn league of kindred designs, and with exultant tramp, stolidly marched, adorned, like a Roman ox, with the garlands of sacrifice, to their eternal doom. At this moment, when a sudden frenzy had struck blind the Southern people, this picture could not even be realized in all its horrors. When he looked at his country, and its present distracted and desolate condition, and its possible fate, he felt almost ready to close the quick accents of speech, and allow the heart to sink down voiceless in its despair. He would refer them to the words of LLOYD GARRISON, and demand what answer would be given to them. Mr. CLEMENS then referred to an article in the *Liberator*,

which appeared a few days after the secession of South Carolina, in which GARRISON said that "the last covenant with death was annulled, and the agreement with hell broken, by the action of South Carolina herself;" closing with an appeal to Massachusetts, ending with the words, "How stands Massachusetts at this hour in reference to the Union?—in an attitude of hostility." Mr. CLEMENS then quoted from a speech of WENDELL PHILLIPS, delivered in the Music Hall, at Boston, a few days ago, in which PHILLIPS declared, "We are Disunionists, not for any love of separate confederacies," &c., ending with a reference to South Carolina, "and Egypt will rejoice that she has departed." The people had, therefore, arrayed against them these knights of a new crusade. The Constitution of the United States was the sanctified Jerusalem against which their deluded cohorts battled. They contended that the only mode to overthrow slavery was to overthrow the constitution. These men claimed that their allegiance was only due to the States wherein they lived. They claimed to be States' rights men of the strictest sect, and they would wield the legislative power of the State for the extinction of slavery, as South Carolina professed to wield it for the perpetuation of slavery. In this crisis it was meet that Massachusetts, so largely partaking of the common glory in the past—Massachusetts, where the first blood for American liberty had been shed—should rise superior to the convulsions of the hour, and give an earnest at least that the spirit of conciliation, of inter-State comity, of fraternal affection, was not yet wholly lost. As the worn traveller in the midst of the snows of the Alps lingered with delighted gaze upon the friendly light which peered from the windows of the convent where from the desolation of the storm around him he might at last find repose, so did he hail the little gleam of hope in the future. Mr. CLEMENS gave statistics of population and slavery in the Border States and in the Gulf States, for the purpose of showing, as he said, that there was an irreversible law of population governing the question, and that the South wanted population and capital rather than territory. If secession were allowed to be carried out, he would show them a Southern Confederacy from which every man would turn back affrighted and pale, because it would be on the bloody hand that his rights of property would have to depend. Slavery cannot expand rapidly, either within the Union or without the Union, so long as slaves remained at their present high prices. The only mode by which slavery could ever expand, was to reduce the price, and have a new source of supply. That was, in fact, the real design of the coast States. Mr. CLEMENS, in proof of this, referred to all the Southern Conventions of late years, and cited the admissions of Messrs. MILES, BONHAM, McRAE, and CRAWFORD, in the House, to show that the object was the re-opening of the slave-trade. Suppose, said he, that they do not get, out of the Union, this equality which they now claim? That is a little problem in the Rule of Three, which will be ciphered out if these events are much longer pending. The Border Slave States might as well be prepared first as last for the realization of the truth. But where was slavery to expand? If the South left the Union, she would never get as much of the present territory as he could grasp in his hand. A war of thirty years would never get it back, nor could there ever be extorted from the North a treaty giving the same guarantees to slavery that it now had. Where was slavery to expand? Not to Central America, for England exercised sovereignty over one-half her domain. Not to Mexico, for England had caused the abolition of slavery there also. Their retiring confederates ought not to forget the events of 1834, when GEORGE THOMPSON, the English abolitionist, was sent to enlighten the dead conscience of the American people. In this connection he cited a letter from THOMPSON to MURRELL, of Tennessee, in which was this sentence: "The dissolution of the Union is the object to be kept steadily in view." In the event of a Southern Confederacy, there will be, besides the African slave-trade, other elements of discord and agitation. Slavery was the great ruling interest of the extreme States, while the other States had other great interests which could not be lightly abandoned. It would be for the interest of the coast States to have free trade in manufactured goods; but how would that operate on the mechanical and manufacturing industry of Missouri, Kentucky, Virginia, Maryland and Delaware? There would be, therefore, in the proposed Union, an antagonism quite as great as there ever has been in this. But if manufactories were to be protected and encouraged in the Border Slave States, their white population would increase so fast that they would be but nominally Slave States, and would finally become Free States. He appealed to the North to guarantee by constitutional enactments the principle secured by the decision of the Supreme Court in the Dred Scott case. Let us feel, he said, that we have a country to save instead of a geographical section to represent. Let us act as men, and not as partisans, and the old Constitution, now in the trough of the sea, with battered masts and sails, will weather the storm.

—*Times*, Jan. 23.

Doc. 25.—THE DISUNION MOVEMENT.

Never for many years can the United States be to the world what they have been. Mr. Buchanan's message has been a greater blow to the American people than all the rants of the Georgian Governor or the "ordinances" of the Charleston Convention. The President has dissipated the idea that the States which elected him constitute one people. We had thought that the Federation was of the nature of a nationality; we find it is nothing more than a partnership. If any State may, on grounds satisfactory to a local convention, dissolve the union between itself and its fellows; if discontent with the election of a President, or the passing of an obnoxious law by another State, or, it may be, a restrictive tariff, gives a State the "right of revolution," and permits it to withdraw itself from the community, *then the position of the American people with respect to foreign Powers is completely altered.* It is strange that a race whose patriotic captiousness when in the society of Europeans is so remarkable, should be so ready to divide and to give up the ties of fellow-citizenship for a cause which strangers are unable to appreciate. Still stranger is it that a chief magistrate, who would have plunged the world in war rather than a suspicious craft should be boarded by English officers after it had displayed the Stars and Stripes, or would have done battle against despots for any naturalized refugee from Continental Europe, should, without scruple, and against the advice of his own Secretary of State, declare the Federal Union dissolved whenever a refractory State chooses to secede.

It may well be imagined that the American people have been taken by surprise, both by the suddenness and violence of the outcry for secession, and by the ready concessions of the President. From the day the message appeared it was evident that South Carolina no longer formed part of the Union. The State had, by every organ which it possessed—by its Senators, its Representatives, by the voice of the Press, of the great slaveowners, and of the multitude—declared its resolution to secede. Only courage like that of General Jackson could have quelled the "Gamecock State," as we perceive some of its admirers call it. But there was a middle path between civil war and such an instant recognition as Mr. Buchanan thought advisable. As one charged with the duty of upholding the Federal power, he might have easily used the authority vested in him to delay the movement, and give the Union and South Carolina itself time for reflection. Mr. Cass would, probably, deprecate holding a State by force, but he still declined to remain in the cabinet of the statesman who would not reinforce Fort Moultrie, and assert, during the short remainder of his term of office, the supremacy of the constitution. But as things went the action of South Carolina was predetermined. On the 20th of December that State seceded from the Union by an unanimous vote, and by this time has probably gained possession of all the Federal property within its borders, and established a post-office and custom-house of its own. The instruments which the Carolinians drew up on this occasion are singular and almost amusing. The philosophy and phraseology of the Declaration of Independence of 1776 are imitated. Whole paragraphs are copied from that famous document. The thoughts and style of Jefferson were evidently influenced by the great writers of his age, and we may trace Montesquieu and Rousseau in every line of his composition. It is rather interesting to see his language, which denounced King George's violation of the social compact, used by a conclave of frantic negro-drivers to stigmatize the conduct of those who will not allow a Southern gentleman to bring his "body servant" into their territory. South Carolina, however, has shown wisdom in thus taking high ground. People are generally taken at the value which they set on themselves, and Carolina does right to play the part of outraged patience and indignant virtue. She has declared, in the language of the Fathers of the Republic, that the Federal Union no longer answers the ends of its foundation by insuring the happiness and prosperity of South Carolina, and that the conduct of several States having been a violation of the compact made by all, South Carolina resumes her rights as a sovereign community, and will make war or peace, conclude treaties, or establish commerce, independently of the Government at Washington.

This bold course has its natural effect on the exciteable slaveowners. The secession of South Carolina has been received everywhere with enthusiasm. It may, perhaps, be said that the other States have feigned an approbation which they do not feel, in order to bring the North to terms by the menace of a Southern Republic. But, whether from feeling or policy, the secession cry was just at its loudest at the close of the year. It was looked upon as certain that six or seven States would separate from the Union in the first days of 1861. Georgia leads the van. The ordinance of secession was looked upon as already passed. The North Carolina Legislature had read a second time the bill for arming the State. Alabama had voted, by a large majority, in favor of secession. In Virginia, the oldest, the most conservative, and the most cautious of the Slave States, we are told that the secession feeling was gaining ground. State conventions are to meet in Florida on the 3d of January, in Alabama on the 7th, in Texas on the 9th, in Georgia on the 9th, and in Louisiana on the 23d; and our correspondent believes that "there will be a majority in each of them in favor of immediate and separate secession." Hence in a few days more the United States of America, as the world has hitherto known them, will cease to exist.

But now comes the most singular part of this history. Till within a few weeks hardly any body in this country believed in the dissolution of the Union. People thought that instincts of patriotism and private interest would prevail, and that the Yankees and the Southerners would quarrel harmoniously for many years to come. The event seems to be against these anticipations, and Englishmen are content to look on in silence and wonder. Not so the Americans. While every mail is bringing news of fiery speeches and the planting of palmetto trees, the almost universal tone of private letters is that there is nothing in it at all. South Carolina cannot secede, or if she does she must come back again. The other States only want to make terms and to come back into the Union after having extorted new concessions as the price of reconciliation. The wish may be father to the thought, but that such is the thought is to be learnt from the most cursory glance at the American newspapers. The course of proceeding is to be as follows: South Carolina, Alabama, Mississippi, Florida, Texas, perhaps Louisiana, are to separate, form a federation of their own, and then treat on equal terms with those who remain faithful to Mr. Lincoln. The Northern Slave States, with Virginia and North Carolina at their head, are to act as mediators, and enforce concessions by the threat of joining the Southern league, which would then number fifteen Slave States, with a vast territory, and the prospect of conquering all the riches of Mexico. The President, it is whispered, is in favor of compromise; Gov. Seward is in favor of compromise; in short, now that the loss of Southern wealth threatens them, great numbers of the stanchest Anti-Slavery men are in favor of compromise. What the terms of the compromise shall be of course remains in doubt. The hope of the democratic party in the North is that the slaveholders will not be too exacting, or insist on the repeal of the personal liberty acts, by which some of the Abolitionist States have nullified the Fugitive Slave act. Many of the Republicans are anxious to revive the Missouri compromise, by which slavery will be prohibited in any part of the United States territory north of 36° 30'. But as the abolition of this compromise and the assertion of the slaveowners' right to carry negroes into any part of the territory is a recent and very great victory, it is hardly likely that the South will concede this. No one in this country can pretend to judge of the event; but this we may conclude from the tone of American discussion, that the North will not be too rigid, and that the slaveowners will receive what all but the most rabid of them will consider satisfaction. Gov. Seward, who first spoke of the "irrepressible conflict" which was impending, now prophesies peace and harmony at no distant day, while many

of his most intimate friends have given their adhesion to the scheme of compromise brought forward by Mr. Crittenden. But whatever may be the final result, we may expect to hear shortly that other States have followed the example set by South Carolina.

—*London Times*, Jan. 9.

Doc. 26.—CORRESPONDENCE BETWEEN SENATOR TOOMBS AND MAYOR WOOD.

MILLEDGEVILLE, Jan. 24, 1861.

To His Honor Mayor Wood:

Is it true that any arms intended for and consigned to the State of Georgia have been seized by public authorities in New York? Your answer is important to us and to New York. Answer at once.
R. TOOMBS.

To this the Mayor returned the following answer:

Hon. Robert Toombs, Milledgeville, Ga.:

In reply to your dispatch, I regret to say that arms intended for and consigned to the State of Georgia, have been seized by the Police of this State, but that the City of New York should in no way be made responsible for the outrage.

As Mayor, I have no authority over the Police. If I had the power I should summarily punish the authors of this illegal and unjustifiable seizure of private property. FERNANDO WOOD.

—*N. Y. Times*, Jan. 26.

Doc. 27.—LOUISIANA SECESSION ORDINANCE.

"AN ORDINANCE TO DISSOLVE THE UNION BETWEEN THE STATE OF LOUISIANA AND THE OTHER STATES UNITED WITH HER, UNDER THE COMPACT ENTITLED THE CONSTITUTION OF THE UNITED STATES OF AMERICA:

"We, the people of the State of Louisiana, in Convention assembled, do declare and ordain, and it is hereby declared and ordained that the ordinance passed by the State of 22d November, 1807, whereby the Constitution of the United States of America and the amendments of said Constitution were adopted, and all the laws and ordinances by which Louisiana became a member of the Federal Union, be, and the same are hereby repealed and abrogated, and the Union now subsisting between Louisiana and the other States, under the name of the United States of America, is hereby dissolved.

"We further declare and ordain, that the State of Louisiana hereby resumes the rights and powers heretofore delegated to the Government of the United States of America, and its citizens are absolved from allegiance to the said Government, and she is in full possession of all the rights and sovereignty that appertain to a free and independent State.

"We further declare and ordain, that all rights acquired and vested under the Constitution of the United States, or any act of Congress, or treaty, or under laws of this State not incompatible with this ordinance, shall remain in force, and have the same effect as though this ordinance had not passed."

A resolution was reported to the Convention that the following be added to the ordinance:

"We, the people of Louisiana, recognize the right of free navigation of the Mississippi River and tributaries by all friendly States bordering thereon, we also recognize the right of the ingress and egress of the mouths of the Mississippi by all friendly States and Powers, and hereby declare our willingness to enter into stipulations to guarantee the exercise of those rights."

Doc. 28.—THE CUTTER McCLELLAND.

The following statement in relation to the surrender of the revenue cutter *Robert McClelland*, is derived from an official source:

On the 19th of January, four days after Secretary Dix took charge of the Treasury Department, he sent Mr. Wm. Hemphill Jones, Chief Clerk in the First Comptroller's Office, to New Orleans and Mobile, to save, if possible, the two cutters on service there. Captain Morrison, a Georgian, in command of the *Lewis Cass* at Mobile, must have surrendered her before Mr. Jones' arrival. On the 29th of January, the Secretary received, in relation to the other, the following telegraphic dispatch from Mr. Jones:

NEW ORLEANS, Jan. 29, 1861.
Hon. J. A. Dix, Secretary of Treasury: Capt. Breshwood has refused positively in writing, to obey any instructions of the Department. In this I am sure he is sustained by the Collector, and believe acts by his advice. What must I do?
W. H. JONES, Special Agent.

To this dispatch Secretary Dix immediately returned the following answer, before published:

TREASURY DEPARTMENT, Jan. 29, 1861.
W. HEMPHILL JONES, New Orleans: Tell Lieut. Caldwell to arrest Capt. Breshwood, assume command of the cutter, and obey the order through you. If Capt. Breshwood, after arrest, undertakes to interfere with the command of the cutter, tell Lieut. Caldwell, to consider him as a mutineer, and treat him accordingly. If any one attempts to haul down the American flag, shoot him on the spot.
JOHN A. DIX, Secretary of the Treasury.

This dispatch must have been intercepted both at Montgomery and New Orleans, and withheld from Mr. Jones, and the treason of Captain Breshwood was consummated by means of a complicity on the part of the telegraph line within the States of Alabama and Louisiana. (See Doc. 31.)

—*N. Y. Times*, February 8.

Doc. 29.—THE MINT AT NEW ORLEANS.

The Louisiana Convention, after having taken possession of the United States Sub-Treasury at New Orleans, passed the subjoined ordinance, authorizing the payment therefrom of certain Government drafts:

Whereas, The State of Louisiana has taken under its control the funds deposited in the late Sub-Treasury of the United States at New Orleans, but considering it just that certain drafts drawn against the same should be paid;

Therefore, be it ordained by the people of the State of Louisiana in convention assembled, That the State depositary of said funds be, and he is authorized to pay all drafts drawn in the legitimate course of disbursement by the disbursing officers of the United States on the funds heretofore deposited in the Sub-Treasury of the United States at New Orleans, to

Doc.—13

the credit of said officers respectively: *Provided*, That no draft shall be paid except out of the balance standing to the credit of the officer drawing the same: *And, provided, further*, That the aggregate amount of drafts hereby authorized to be paid shall not exceed the sum of $306,592 80.

Be it further ordained, That the State depositary aforesaid be, and he is hereby authorized to pay all outstanding drafts drawn by the United States prior to the passage of the ordinance of secession, against the funds heretofore deposited in the Sub-Treasury of the United States at New Orleans, to the credit of the public revenue of the United States, *Provided*, that the aggregate amount of said drafts shall not exceed the sum of $146,226 74; but no transfer drafts on the bullion fund shall be recognized or paid.

Be it further ordained, That the sum of $31,164 44, standing to the credit of the Post Office Department on the books of the late Sub-Treasurer of the United States, at New Orleans, is hereby held subject to draft of the United States, in payment of postal services, until otherwise ordered by this convention or the General Assembly of the State.

Doc. 30.—THE TEXAS ORDINANCE OF SECESSION.

AN ORDINANCE TO DISSOLVE THE UNION BETWEEN THE STATE OF TEXAS AND THE OTHER STATES UNDER THE COMPACT STYLED "THE CONSTITUTION OF THE UNITED STATES OF AMERICA."

Sec. 1. Whereas, the Federal Government has failed to accomplish the purposes of the compact of union between these States, in giving protection either to the persons of our people upon an exposed frontier, or to the property of our citizens; and whereas, the action of the Northern States is violative of the compact between the States and the guarantees of the Constitution; and, whereas, the recent developments in federal affairs make it evident that the power of the Federal Government is sought to be made a weapon with which to strike down the interests and property of the people of Texas and her sister slaveholding States, instead of permitting it to be, as was intended—our shield against outrage and aggression—therefore, "We, the people of the State of Texas, by delegates in the Convention assembled, do declare and ordain that the ordinance adopted by our Convention of delegates on the fourth (4th) day of July, A.D. 1845, and afterwards ratified by us, under which the Republic of Texas was admitted into the Union with other States, and became a party to the compact styled 'The Constitution of the United States of America' be, and is hereby repealed and annulled."

That all the powers which, by the said compact, were delegated by Texas to the Federal Government are resumed. That Texas is of right absolved from all restraints and obligations incurred by said compact, and is a separate sovereign State, and that her citizens and people are absolved from all allegiance to the United States or the Government thereof.

Sec. 2 The ordinance shall be submitted to the people of Texas for their ratification or rejection, by the qualified voters, on the 23d day of February, 1861; and unless rejected by a majority of the votes cast, shall take effect and be in force on and after the 2d day of March, A.D. 1861. Provided that in the representative district of El Paso said election may be held on the 18th day of February, 1861.

Done by the people of the State of Texas, in convention assembled, at Austin, the 1st day of February, A.D. 1861.

Doc. 31.—A REPORT FROM SECRETARY DIX.

Secretary Dix sent a report to the House of Representatives, in answer to Mr. Sickles' resolution of inquiry, showing the following state of facts:

"*First.*—The impediments to commerce by usurping control of the ports of Mobile, Charleston, Pensacola and New Orleans.

"*Second.*—The control of commerce of the Mississippi Valley, by requiring the duties on all goods entered at New Orleans for delivery at St. Louis, Nashville, Louisville, and Cincinnati, to be paid to the State of Louisiana.

"*Third.*—The seizure by Louisiana of all United States moneys, as well as those of private depositors in the mint and sub-treasury at New Orleans and other places.

"*Fourth.*—The seizure of revenue cutters, by arrangement between their commanders and the collectors of Mobile, New Orleans and Charleston.

"*Fifth.*—The expulsion of the sick and invalid patients at the United States Hospital at New Orleans, in order to provide accommodation for Louisiana troops."

Mr. Dix says it is believed that duties on imports continue to be collected in the ports of entry established in South Carolina, Georgia, Alabama, Louisiana and Florida, and that vessels are entered and cleared in the usual manner; but so far as the department has been advised, the collectors assume to perform their duties under the authority of the States in which they reside, and hold and reserve the duties, subject to the same authority.

Speaking of the general subject, Mr. Dix says:

"Throughout the whole course of encroachment and aggression, the Federal Government has borne itself with a spirit of paternal forbearance, of which there is no example in the history of public society; waiting in patient hope that the empire of reason would resume its sway over those whom the excitement of passion has thus far blinded, and trusting that the friends of good order, wearied with submission to proceedings which they disapproved, would at no distant day rally under the banner of the Union, and exert themselves with vigor and success against the prevailing recklessness and violence."

T. Hemphill Jones, the special agent appointed to secure the revenue cutters McClelland and Lewis Cass from seizure by the Louisiana secessionists, reports to the Treasury Department that he arrived in New Orleans in pursuance of his instructions on the 26th January. He found Captain Breshwood, of the McClelland, after a long search, and handed him the following order:

NEW ORLEANS, Jan. 29, 1861.

SIR:—You are hereby directed to get the United States revenue cutter McClelland, now lying here, under way immediately, and proceed with her to New York, where you will await the further instructions of the Secretary of the Treasury. For my authority to make this order you are referred to the letter of the Secretary, dated the 19th inst., and handed you personally by me.

Very respectfully,
WM. HEMPHILL JONES,
Special Agent.

To Capt. J. G. BRESHWOOD, commanding U. S. revenue cutter Robert McClelland.

Breshwood conferred with Collector Hatch of New Orleans, and then returned the following answer, flatly refusing to obey the order:

U. S. REVENUE CUTTER ROBERT MCCLELLAND,
NEW ORLEANS, January 29, 1861.

SIR: Your letter, with one of the 19th of January from the Hon. Secretary of the Treasury, I have duly received, and in reply refuse to obey the order.

I am, Sir, your obedient servant,
JOHN G. BRESHWOOD, Captain.

To WM. HEMPHILL JONES, Esq., Special Agent.

Mr. Jones's report continues:

Believing that Captain Breshwood would not have ventured upon this most positive act of insubordination and disobedience of his own volition, I waited upon the Collector at the Custom House, and had with him a full and free conversation upon the whole subject. In the course of it, Mr. Hatch admitted to me that he had caused the cutter to be brought to the city of New Orleans by an order of his own, dated January 15, so that she might be secured to the State of Louisiana, although at that time the State had not only not seceded, but the Convention had not met, and in fact did not meet until eight days afterwards. This, I must confess, seemed to me a singular confession for one who at that very time had sworn to do his duty faithfully as an officer of the United States; and on intimating as much to Mr. Hatch, he excused himself on the ground that in these revolutions all other things must give way to the force of circumstances. Mr. Hatch likewise informed me that the officers of the cutter had long since determined to abandon their allegiance to the United States, and cast their fortunes with the independent State of Louisiana. In order to test the correctness of this statement, I addressed another communication to Captain Breshwood, of the following tenor:

NEW ORLEANS, January 29, 1861.

SIR: By your note of this date I am informed that you refuse to obey the orders of the honorable Secretary of the Treasury. As, on accepting your commission, you took and subscribed an oath faithfully to discharge your duties to the Government, and as you well know, the law has placed the revenue cutters and their officers under the entire control of the Secretary of the Treasury, I request you to advise me whether you consider yourself at this time an officer in the service of the United States.

Very respectfully,
WM. HEMPHILL JONES, Special Agent.

To Captain BRESHWOOD.

To this letter I never received any reply. I then repaired again on board the cutter, and asked for the order of the Collector bringing her to New Orleans. The original was placed in my possession, of which the following is a copy. And here it may be proper to observe, that the order is written and signed by the Collector himself:

CUSTOM HOUSE, NEW ORLEANS,
COLLECTOR'S OFFICE, Jan. 15, 1861.

SIR: You are hereby directed to proceed forthwith

under sail to this city, and anchor the vessel under your command opposite the United States Marine Hospital, above Algiers.

Very respectfully, your obedient servant,
F. H. HATCH, Collector.

To Captain J. G. BRESHWOOD, United States Revenue Cutter McClelland, Southwest Pass, La.

Defeated at New Orleans, Mr. Jones then took his way to Mobile, to look after the Lewis Cass. Her Captain (Morrison) could not be found, but Mr. Jones discovered in the cabin the following letter, which explains the surrender of that vessel:

STATE OF ALABAMA, COLLECTOR'S OFFICE,
MOBILE, January 30, 1861.

SIR: In obedience to an ordinance recently adopted by a convention of the people of Alabama, I have to require you to surrender into my hands, for the use of the State, the revenue cutter Lewis Cass, now under your command, together with her armaments, properties and provisions on board the same. I am instructed also to notify you, that you have the option to continue in command of the said revenue cutter, under the authority of the State of Alabama, in the exercise of the same duties that you have hitherto rendered to the United States, and at the same compensation, reporting to this office and to the Governor of the State. In surrendering the vessel to the State, you will furnish me with a detailed inventory of its armaments, provisions and properties of every description. You will receive special instructions from this office in regard to the duties you will be required to perform. I await your immediate reply.

Very respectfully, your obedient servant,
T. SANFORD, Collector.

To J. J. MORRISON, Esq., Captain Revenue Cutter Lewis Cass, Mobile, Ala.

Mr. Jones concludes his report with the statement, that he made a final and unsuccessful effort to recover the McClelland, but, failing in the attempt, he retraced his steps to Washington.

—*Evening Post*, Feb. 22.

Doc. 32.—DELEGATES TO THE MONTGOMERY CONVENTION, ALABAMA, FEB. 4.

ALABAMA.

Robert H. Smith,	Richard W. Walker,
Colin J. McRae,	John Gill,
W. R. Chilton,	S. F. Hale,
David P. Lewis,	Thomas Fearn,

J. L. M. Curry.

FLORIDA.

Jackson Morton,	J. Patton Anderson,

James Powers.

GEORGIA.

Robert Toombs,	Howell Cobb,
Francis Barton,	Augustus R. Wright,
Martin Crawford,	Thomas R. Cobb,
Judge Nesbitt,	Augustus Keenan,
Benjamin Hill,	A. H. Stephens.

LOUISIANA.

John Perkins, Jr.,	A. Declomet,
C. M. Conrad,	E. Sparrow,
Duncan F. Kenner,	Henry Marshall.

MISSISSIPPI.

Wiley P. Harris,	Walker Brooke,
W. S. Wilson,	W. S. Barry,
A. M. Clayton,	J. T. Harrison,

J. A. P. Campbell.

NORTH CAROLINA.

J. L. Bridgers,	M. W. Ransom,

Ex-Gov. Swann.

SOUTH CAROLINA.

T. J. Withers,	W. W. Boyce,
R. B. Rhett, Jr.,	James Chestnut, Jr.,
L. M. Keitt,	R. W. Barnwell,

G. G. Memminger.

Doc. 33.—CONSTITUTION OF THE CONFEDERATED STATES.

THE TITLE OF THE CONSTITUTION FOR THE PROVISIONAL GOVERNMENT OF THE CONFEDERATED STATES OF AMERICA.

The Preamble reads as follows:

"We, the deputies of the sovereign and independent States of South Carolina, Georgia, Florida, Alabama, Mississippi and Louisiana, invoking the favor of Almighty God, do hereby, in behalf of these States, ordain and establish this Constitution for the provisional government of the same, to continue one year from the inauguration of the President, or until a permanent constitution or confederation between the said States shall be put in operation, whichsoever shall first occur."

The seventh section, first article, is as follows:

"The importation of African negroes from any foreign country other than the slaveholding States of the United States, is hereby forbidden, and Congress is required to pass such laws as shall effectually prevent the same."

Article second—"Congress shall also have power to prohibit the introduction of slaves from any State not a member of this Confederacy."

Article fourth of the third clause of the second section says:

"A slave in one State escaping to another shall be delivered up on the claim of the party to whom said slave may belong, by the executive authority of the State in which such slave may be found; and in case of any abduction or forcible rescue, full compensation, including the value of the slave, and all costs and expenses, shall be made to the party by the State in which such abduction or rescue shall take place."

Article sixth of the second clause says:

"The Government hereby instituted shall take immediate steps for the settlement of all matters between the States forming it, and their late confederates of the United States, in relation to the public property and public debt at the time of their withdrawal from them, these States hereby declaring it to be their wish and earnest desire to adjust every thing pertaining to the common property, common liabilities, and common obligations of that Union, upon principles of right, justice, equity, and good faith."

The tariff clause provides that "the Congress shall have power to lay and collect taxes, duties, imposts, and excises for revenue necessary to pay the debts and carry on the Government of the Confederacy, and all duties, imposts, and excises shall be uniform throughout the Confederacy."

All the other portions of the Constitution are almost identical with the Constitution of the United States.

—*Commercial Advertiser.*

Doc. 34.—SOUTHERN OPINIONS.

The *Charleston Mercury* thus discusses the power of the Southern Congress:

In the first place, has this convention any authority to elect a President and Vice-President of the Southern Confederacy? Excepting in Mississippi, it is doubtful whether any other State convention in the South thought of any such project. What good can result from this convention assuming to elect the President and Vice-President of the Confederacy, without at the same time electing the Senators and Representatives of the Congress? Mississippi has already exercised the right to elect her Senators and Representatives to the Congress.— Surely the other States should exercise the same right. It will not do for her to appoint her Representatives by her convention, and then come here and appoint ours besides.

But there is a graver matter than its absurdity behind this scheme. Is it any thing else than the policy of reconstructing the Union? Take the Constitution of the United States as it is, with all its constructive powers, and get the frontier States in the Confederacy with us, and will the Constitution ever be altered? And if not altered, will we not have the same battle to fight over again with them, after a few years, which we have been compelled to fight with the Northern States? But will a Southern confederacy exist at all with such a policy? Will not all the Northern States come again into a Union with us? Why should they not? They are satisfied with the Constitution of the United States as it is, open to their interpretation. It establishes a capital despotism under their power. Of course they will seek to reconstruct the Union. And will it not be done? Yes, certainly, under this scheme. After all, we will have run a round circle, and end where we started.

The Augusta (Ga.) *Chronicle* recommends the Hon. A. H. Stephens as provisional President, because he bears no "stain of the prevalent corruption," and because he is "Southern by birth and education, patriotic beyond question, calm, sound, and mature in judgment, with a reputation that was national when we had a nation, and a favorite, at one time or another, with all parties."

Such a nomination, the *Chronicle* says, would reconcile the feelings of our friends at the North, and also the Union men of the South. It then says:

Disguise it as we may, the greatest danger to the new confederacy arises, not from without, not from the North, but *from our own people.* We have only to refer to recent speeches in Congress, such as those of Clemens, Etheridge, and Nelson, to show that the indications are growing stronger *that organized if not armed opposition to the new order of things may arise in States or parts of Southern States* not vitally interested in the Slavery question. Such discontent is to be allayed if possible.

Our position has ever been that *all* the Southern States should unite in action, and we have advocated separate action and an independent State Government by Georgia only because we saw no hope for **united** action by all the Southern States. We have invariably been consistent in our desire for coöperation. When our hopes seemed about to fail, and separate State action was an "accomplished fact," we thought it better that Georgia, powerful in resources beyond any of her neighbors, rich and prosperous, should set up for herself, and not link her fortunes to a confederacy ruled by disorganizing charlatans, without the talent to construct, though potent to destroy; governed by chimerical schemers, without a particle of practical common sense or business knowledge, in which she would have to bear more than her share of the burdens, and incur more than her proportion of the financial and commercial disadvantages. But with Stephens at the helm (for he has brains) Georgia and the South are safe.

Doc. 35.—MEMMINGER'S SPEECH.

I conceive, Mr. President, this a fitting occasion to discharge a commission which has been entrusted to me by some of my constituency of South Carolina. I have before me a flag which some of the young ladies of South Carolina present to this Congress, as a model flag for the Confederate States of America. This flag, as it will be seen upon inspection, embraces the idea of a cross—a blue cross on a red field.

Now, Mr. President the idea of a cross no doubt was suggested to the imagination of the young ladies, by the beauteous constellation of the Southern cross, which the great Creator has placed in the Southern heavens, by way of compensation for the glorious constitution at the north pole. The inauguration of the young ladies was doubtless inspired by the genius of Dante, and the scientific skill of Humboldt. But sir, I have no doubt that there was another idea associated with it, in the minds of the young ladies—a religious one; and although we have not seen in the heavens the "*in hoc signo vinces*" written upon the labarum of Constantine, yet the same sign has been manifested to us upon the tablets of the earth; for we all know that it has been by the aid of revealed religion, that we have achieved over fanaticism the victory which we this day witness; and it is becoming on this occasion that the debt of the South to the cross, should be thus recognized.

I have also, Mr. President, another commission from a gentleman of taste and skill, in the city of Charleston, who offers another model, which embraces the same idea of a cross, but upon a different ground. The gentleman who offers this model, appears to be more hopeful than the young ladies. They offer one with seven stars, six for the States already represented in this Congress, and the seventh for Texas, whose deputies, we hope, will soon be on their way to join us. He offers a flag which embraces the whole fifteen States. God grant that this hope may be realized, and that we may soon welcome their stars, to the glorious constellation of the Southern confederacy! (Applause.)

Mr. Miles—I move that a committee of one from each State be appointed to report upon a flag for the Confederate States of America. Adopted.

The States were called, and the following committee was announced:—Messrs. Shorter, of Alabama; Morton, of Florida; Barton, of Georgia; Sparrow, of Louisiana; Harris of Mississippi; and Miles, of South Carolina.

Doc. 36.—COUNTING THE VOTE.

A message was sent to the Senate, informing them that the House was now waiting to receive them, so that in a joint body the electoral votes of the President and Vice President may be opened and the result announced.

After a short interval the Senators, preceded by their officers, were announced.

The members of the House immediately rose, and remained standing till the Senators took seats in a semi-circular range, in front of the clerk's desk.

Vice President Breckinridge was conducted to the right of the Speaker, and the tellers, viz:—Senator Trumbull and Representatives Washburn, of Illinois, and Phelps, took seats at the Clerk's desk.

When order was restored, Vice President BRECKINRIDGE rose and said:—

"We have assembled, pursuant to the constitution, in order that the electoral votes may be counted, and the result declared, for President and Vice President for the term commencing on the 4th of March, 1861, and it is made my duty under the constitution, to open the certificates of election in the presence of the two Houses; and I now proceed to the performance of that duty.

Vice President Breckinridge then opened the package containing the electoral vote of Maine, and handed it to the tellers, when the certificate thereof was read, the Secretary of the Senate making a note thereof.

The electoral votes of New Hampshire, Massachusetts, Rhode Island, Connecticut, Vermont, and New York were similarly disposed of.

Senator DOUGLAS suggested, and no objection was made, that the formal part of the certificates, and the names of the electors, be omitted from the reading.

The reading of the vote of South Carolina was productive of good-humored excitement.

The reading of all the electoral votes having been completed, the tellers reported the result:

Whereupon the Vice President, rising, said:

ABRAHAM LINCOLN, of Illinois, having received a majority of the whole number of electoral votes, is duly elected President of the United States for the four years commencing on the 4th of March, 1861:

And that HANNIBAL HAMLIN, of Maine, having received a majority of the whole number of electoral votes, is duly elected Vice President of the United States for the same term.—*Commercial Advertiser.*

Doc. 37.—INAUGURAL OF JEFFERSON DAVIS.

Gentlemen of the Congress of the Confederate States of America, Friends and Fellow-Citizens:

Called to the difficult and responsible station of Chief Executive of the Provisional Government which you have instituted, I approach the discharge of the duties assigned me with an humble distrust of my abilities, but with a sustaining confidence in the wisdom of those who are to guide and aid me in the administration of public affairs, and an abiding faith in the virtue and patriotism of the people. Looking forward to the speedy establishment of a permanent government to take the place of this, and which by its greater moral and physical power will be better able to combat with the many difficulties which arise from the conflicting interests of separate nations, I enter upon the duties of the office to which I have been chosen, with the hope that the beginning of our career as a confederacy may not be obstructed by hostile opposition to our enjoyment of the separate existence and independence which we have asserted, and which, with the blessing of Providence, we intend to maintain.

Our present condition, achieved in a manner unprecedented in the history of nations, illustrates the American idea that governments rest upon the consent of the governed, and that it is the right of the people to alter and abolish governments whenever they become destructive to the ends for which they were established. The declared compact of the Union from which we have withdrawn was to establish justice, ensure domestic tranquillity, provide for the common defence, promote the general welfare, and secure the blessings of liberty to ourselves and our posterity; and when in the judgment of the sovereign States now composing this confederacy, it has been perverted from the purposes for which it was ordained, and ceased to answer the ends for which it was established, a peaceful appeal to the ballot-box declared that, so far as they were concerned, the government created by that compact should cease to exist. In this they merely asserted the right which the Declaration of Independence of 1776 defined to be inalienable. Of the time and occasion of its exercise they as sovereigns were the final judges, each for itself. The impartial, enlightened verdict of mankind will vindicate the rectitude of our conduct; and He who knows the hearts of men will judge of the sincerity with which we labored to preserve the government of our fathers in its spirit.

The right solemnly proclaimed at the birth of the States, and which has been affirmed and reaffirmed in the bills of rights of the States subsequently admitted into the Union of 1789, undeniably recognizes in the people the power to resume the authority delegated for the purposes of government. Thus the sovereign States here represented, proceeded to form this confederacy; and it is by the abuse of language that their act has been denominated revolution. They formed a new alliance, but within each State its government has remained. The rights of person and property have not been disturbed. The agent through whom they communicated with foreign nations is changed, but this does not necessarily interrupt their international relations. Sustained by the consciousness that the transition from the former Union to the present confederacy has not proceeded from a disregard on our part of our just obligations or any failure to perform every constitutional duty, moved by no interest or passion to invade the rights of others, anxious to cultivate peace and commerce with all nations, if we may not hope to avoid war, we may at least expect that posterity will acquit us of having needlessly engaged in it. Doubly justified by the absence of wrong on our part, and by wanton aggression on the part of others, there can be no cause to doubt the courage and patriotism of the people of the confederate States will be found equal to any measures of defence which soon their security may require.

An agricultural people, whose chief interest is the export of a commodity required in every manufacturing country, our true policy is peace, and the freest trade which our necessities will permit. It is alike our interest and that of all those to whom we would sell and from whom we would buy, that there should be the fewest practicable restrictions upon the interchange of commodities. There can be but little rivalry between ours and any manufacturing or navigating community, such as the northeastern States of the American Union. It must follow, therefore, that mutual interest would invite good will and kind offices. If, however, passion or lust of dominion should cloud the judgment or inflame the ambition of those States, we must prepare to meet the emergency and maintain by the final arbitrament of the sword the position which we have assumed among the nations of the earth.

We have entered upon a career of independence, and it must be inflexibly pursued through many years of controversy with our late associates of the Northern States. We have vainly endeavored to secure tranquillity and obtain respect for the rights to which we were entitled. As a necessity, not a choice, we have resorted to the remedy of separation, and henceforth our energies must be directed to the conduct of our own affairs, and the perpetuity of the confederacy which we have formed. If a just perception of mutual interest shall permit us peaceably to pursue our separate political career, my most earnest desire will have been fulfilled. But if this be denied us, and the integrity of our territory and jurisdiction be assailed, it will but remain for us with firm resolve to appeal to arms and invoke the blessing of Providence on a just cause.

As a consequence of our new condition, and with a view to meet anticipated wants, it will be necessary to provide a speedy and efficient organization of the branches of the Executive department having special charge of foreign intercourse, finance, military affairs, and postal service. For purposes of defence the Confederate States may, under ordinary circumstances, rely mainly upon their militia; but it is deemed advisable in the present condition of affairs, that there should be a well instructed, disciplined army, more numerous than would usually be required on a peace establishment. I also suggest that, for the protection of our harbors and commerce on the high seas, a navy adapted to those objects will be required. These necessities have, doubtless, engaged the attention of Congress.

With a Constitution differing only from that of our fathers in so far as it is explanatory of their well known intent, freed from sectional conflicts, which have interfered with the pursuit of the general welfare, it is not unreasonable to expect that the States from which we have recently parted may seek to unite their fortunes to ours, under the government which we have instituted. For this your Constitution makes adequate provision, but beyond this, if I mistake not, the judgment and will of the people are, that union with the States from which they have separated is neither practicable nor desirable. To increase the power, develop the resources, and promote the happiness of the Confederacy, it is requisite there should be so much homogeneity that the welfare of every portion would be the aim of the whole. Where this does not exist antagonisms are engendered which must and should result in separation.

Actuated solely by a desire to preserve our own rights, and to promote our own welfare, the separation of the Confederate States has been marked by no aggression upon others, and followed by no domestic convulsion. Our industrial pursuits have received no check, the cultivation of our fields progresses as heretofore, and even should we be involved in war there would be no considerable diminution in the production of the staples which have constituted our exports, in which the commercial world has an interest scarcely less than our own. This common interest of producer and consumer can only be intercepted by an exterior force which should obstruct its transmission to foreign markets, a course of conduct which would be detrimental to manufacturing and commercial interests abroad.

Should reason guide the action of the government from which we have separated, a policy so detrimental to the civilized world, the Northern States included, could not be dictated by even a stronger desire to inflict injury upon us; but if it be otherwise, a terrible responsibility will rest upon it, and the suffering of millions will bear testimony to the folly and wickedness of our aggressors. In the meantime there will remain to us, besides the ordinary remedies before suggested, the well known resources for retaliation upon the commerce of an enemy.

Experience in public stations of a subordinate grade to this which your kindness has conferred, has taught me that care and toil and disappointments are the price of official elevation. You will see many errors to forgive, many deficiencies to tolerate; but you shall not find in me either want of zeal or fidelity to the cause that is to me the highest in hope and of most enduring affection. Your generosity has bestowed upon me an undeserved distinction, one which I neither sought nor desired. Upon the continuance of that sentiment, and upon your wisdom and patriotism, I rely to direct and support me in the performance of the duties required at my hands.

We have changed the constituent parts but not the system of our government. The Constitution formed by our fathers is that of these Confederate States. In their exposition of it, and in the judicial construction it has received, we have a light which reveals its true meaning. Thus instructed as to the just interpretation of that instrument, and ever remembering that all offices are but trusts held for the people, and that delegated powers are to be strictly construed, I will hope by due diligence in the performance of my duties, though I may disappoint your expectation, yet to retain, when retiring, something of the good will and confidence which will welcome my entrance into office.

It is joyous in the midst of perilous times to look around upon a people united in heart, when one purpose of high resolve animates and actuates the whole, where the sacrifices to be made are not weighed in the balance, against honor, right, liberty, and equality. Obstacles may retard, but they cannot long prevent the progress of a movement sanctioned by its justice and sustained by a virtuous people. Reverently let us invoke the God of our fathers to guide and protect us in our efforts to perpetuate the principles which by his blessing they were able to vindicate, establish, and transmit to their posterity; and with a continuance of His favor ever gratefully acknowledged, we may hopefully look forward to success, to peace, to prosperity.

Doc. 38.—PRESIDENT LINCOLN'S JOURNEY.

A dispatch from Harrisburg, Pa., to the N. Y. Times, dated Feb. 23, 8 A. M., says:—

Abraham Lincoln, the President-elect of the United States, is safe in the capital of the nation. By the admirable arrangement of General Scott the country has been spared the lasting disgrace, which would have been fastened indelibly upon it, had Mr. Lincoln been murdered upon his journey thither, as he would have been, had he followed the programme as announced in papers, and gone by the Northern Central railroad to Baltimore.

On Thursday night after he had retired, Mr. Lincoln was aroused and informed that a stranger desired to see him on a matter of life or death. He declined to admit him unless he gave his name, which he at once did. Such prestige did the name carry that while Mr. Lincoln was yet disrobed, he granted an interview to the caller.

A prolonged conversation elicited the fact, that an organized body of men had determined that Mr. Lincoln should not be inaugurated, and that he should never leave the city of Baltimore alive, if, indeed, he ever entered it.

The list of the names of the conspirators presented a most astonishing array of persons high in Southern confidence, and some whose fame is not confined to this country alone.

Statesmen laid the plan, bankers indorsed it, and adventurers were to carry it into effect. They understood Mr. Lincoln was to leave Harrisburg at 9 o'clock this morning by special train, and the idea was, if possible, to throw the cars from the road at some point where they would rush down a steep embankment and destroy in a moment the lives of all on board. In case of the failure of this project their plan was to surround the carriage on the way from depot to depot in Baltimore, and assassinate him with dagger or pistol shot.

So authentic was the source from which the information was obtained, that Mr. Lincoln, after counselling his friends, was compelled to make arrangements which would enable him to subvert the plans of his enemies.

Greatly to the annoyance of the thousands who desired to call on him last night, he declined giving a reception. The final council was held at 8 o'clock.

Mr. Lincoln did not want to yield, and Col. Sumner actually cried with indignation; but Mrs. Lincoln, seconded by Mr. Judd and Mr. Lincoln's original informant, insisted upon it, and at 9 o'clock Mr. Lincoln left on a special train. He wore a Scotch plaid cap and a very long military cloak, so that he was entirely unrecognizable. Accompanied by Superintendent Lewis and one friend, he started, while all the town, with the exception of Mrs. Lincoln, Col. Sumner, Mr. Judd, and two reporters, who were sworn to secrecy, supposed him to be asleep.

The telegraph wires were put beyond reach of any one who might desire to use them.

At one o'clock the fact was whispered from one to another, and it soon became the theme of the most excited conversation. Many thought it a very injudicious move, while others regarded it as a stroke of great merit.

THE FEELING IN BALTIMORE.

The prevailing feeling excited by Mr. Lincoln's quiet passage through Baltimore, was one of relief and of gratification, though expressions of disappointed curiosity were frequently heard. The injudicious determination of certain political friends of the President-elect in this city to mark his arrival

with a public demonstration, had excited a spirit of stern opposition, which it was feared would manifest itself in acts which, though designed directly to rebuke the ill-advised zeal of the parties referred to, might yet have been misconstrued into a personal affront to the President-elect, and so have reflected discreditably upon the good repute of Baltimore. The action, therefore, of Mr. Lincoln, in disappointing alike the purposes of his political friends and the public curiosity, was a simple and practical avoidance of what might have been an occasion of disorder and of mortification to all interested in the preservation of the good name of our city.

Ample precautions were adopted to guard against any violation of the public peace. A large police force was detailed for duty at the depot, and to protect the President and his suite on their passage through the streets, against the turbulent pressure of the crowds which he experienced in other cities on his route hither; and these measures of Marshal Kane, even if they had failed to restrain any expression of disapprobation, would certainly have secured Mr. Lincoln from insult, had such been intended.

On the arrival of the cars and the appearance on the platform of the Baltimore Republican committee, they were received with groans and hootings. A rush was made at William E. Beale and Francis S. Corkran, but they were protected by the police, and neither of them were injured further than knocking their hats over their eyes. The following was the committee: William G. Snethen, chairman; Judge William L. Marshall, L. Blumenberg, of Gaystreet; William E. Beale. Hon. Judge Palmer, of Frederick, was with the party.

Mrs. Lincoln and her three sons proceeded to the residence of Col. John S. Gittings, president of the Northern Central railway, at Mount Vernon Square, having accepted an invitation tendered to them on their way to this city, so as to relieve them from the crowd and excitement. They left the cars, we learn, at the junction of Charles-street, where Mr. Gittings's carriage was in waiting for them, and were in a few minutes enjoying the quiet of his spacious mansion, while crowds were gaping for a sight of them at the depot.

One fellow in the crowd at Calvert station, who was known as a violent Republican, had his hat knocked off a dozen times by the rowdies.

—*Baltimore American.*

At 15 minutes to one o'clock a mighty heaving and surging in the multitude at the north entrance of the depot, proclaimed some fresh excitement, and in a few moments the York accommodation train entered the depot, followed by an excited crowd, which mistook it for the special train of the President-elect and suite. As soon as the train stopped, the crowd leaped upon the platforms, and mounted to the tops of the cars like so many monkeys, until like a hive of bees they swarmed upon them—shouting, hallooing, and making all manner of noises. The officers in charge of the train appeared, and the crowd, discovering their error, recoiled, a little chop-fallen, but prepared for another excitement.

After it became apparent to the multitude that the President-elect had indeed escaped their attentions, they turned about to bestow them upon such of his humbler constituents as they recognized in their midst. These attentions were exhibited in a system of crowding and squeezing exceedingly unpleasant to those upon whose persons the "pressure" was brought to bear.

* * * * * *

Had we any respect for Mr. Lincoln, official or personal, as a man, or as President-elect of the United States, his career and speeches on his way to the seat of government would have cruelly impaired it; but the final escapade by which he reached the capital would have utterly demolished it, and overwhelmed us with mortification. As it is, no sentiment of respect of whatever sort with regard to the man suffers violence on our part, at any thing he may do. He might have entered Willard's Hotel with a "head spring" and a "summersault," and the clown's merry greeting to Gen. Scott, "Here we are!" and we should care nothing about it personally.

We do not believe the Presidency can ever be more degraded by any of his successors, than it has been by him, even before his inauguration; and so, for aught we care, he may go to the full extent of his wretched comicalities. We have only too much cause to fear that such a man, and such advisers as he has, may prove capable of infinitely more mischief than folly when invested with power. A lunatic is only dangerous when armed and turned loose; but only imagine a lunatic invested with authority over a sane people and armed with weapons of offense and defence. What sort of a fate can we anticipate for a people so situated? And when we reflect that fanaticism is infested with like fears, suspicions, impulses, follies, flights of daring and *flights* of cowardice common to lunacy itself, and to which it is akin, what sort of a future can we anticipate under the presidency of Abraham Lincoln?
—*Baltimore Sun.*

THE CONSPIRACY TO ASSASSINATE PRESIDENT LINCOLN.

Some of Mr. Lincoln's friends having heard that a conspiracy existed to assassinate him on his way to Washington, set on foot an investigation of the matter. For this purpose they employed a detective of great experience, who was engaged at Baltimore in the business some three weeks prior to Mr. Lincoln's expected arrival there, employing both men and women to assist him. Shortly after coming to Baltimore, the detective discovered a combination of men banded together under a solemn oath to assassinate the President elect. The leader of the conspirators was an Italian refugee, a barber, well known in Baltimore, who assumed the name of *Orsini*, as indicative of the part he was to perform. The assistants employed by the detective, who, like himself, were strangers in Baltimore City, by assuming to be secessionists from Louisiana and other seceding States, gained the confidence of some of the conspirators, and were intrusted with their plans. It was arranged in case Mr. Lincoln should pass safely over the railroad to Baltimore, that the conspirators should mingle with the crowd which might surround his carriage, and by pretending to be his friends, be enabled to approach his person, when, upon a signal from their leader, some of them would shoot at Mr. Lincoln with their pistols, and others would throw into his carriage hand-grenades filled with detonating powder, similar to those used in the attempted assassination of the Emperor Louis Napoleon. It was intended that in the confusion which should result

from this attack, the assailants should escape to a vessel which was waiting in the harbor to receive them, and be carried to Mobile, in the seceding State of Alabama.

Upon Mr. Lincoln's arrival in Philadelphia upon Thursday, the 21st of February, the detective visited Philadelphia, and submitted to certain friends of the President-elect, the information he had collected as to the conspirators and their plans. An interview was immediately arranged between Mr. Lincoln and the detective. The interview took place in Mr. Lincoln's room, in the Continental Hotel, where he was staying during his visit in Philadelphia.

Mr. Lincoln, having heard the officer's statement, informed him that he had promised to raise the American flag on Independence Hall on the next morning—the morning of the Anniversary of Washington's Birthday—and that he had accepted the invitation of the Pennsylvania Legislature to be publicly received by that body in the afternoon of the same day. "Both of these engagements," said he, with emphasis, "I will keep if it costs me my life. If, however, after I shall have concluded these engagements, you can take me in safety to Washington, I will place myself at your disposal, and authorize you to make such arrangements as you may deem proper for that purpose."

On the next day, in the morning, Mr. Lincoln performed the ceremony of raising the American flag on Independence Hall, in Philadelphia, according to his promise, and arrived at Harrisburg on the afternoon of the same day, where he was formally welcomed by the Pennsylvania Legislature. After the reception, he retired to his hotel, the Jones House, and withdrew with a few confidential friends to a private apartment. Here he remained until nearly 6 o'clock in the evening, when, in company with Col. Lamon, he quietly entered a carriage without observation, and was driven to the Pennsylvania Railroad, where a special train for Philadelphia was waiting for him. Simultaneously with his departure from Harrisburg, the telegraph wires were cut, so that his departure, if it should become known, might not be communicated at a distance.

The special train arrived in Philadelphia at 10¾ o'clock at night. Here he was met by the detective, who had a carriage in readiness into which the party entered, and were driven to the depot of the Philadelphia, Wilmington and Baltimore Railroad.

They did not reach the depot until 11¼ o'clock; but, fortunately for them, the regular train, the hour of which for starting was eleven, had been delayed. The party then took berths in the sleeping car, and without change of cars, passed directly through to Washington, where they arrived at the usual hour, 6½ o'clock, on the morning of Saturday the 23d. Mr. Lincoln wore no disguise whatever, but journeyed in an ordinary travelling dress.

It is proper to state here that, prior to Mr. Lincoln's arrival in Philadelphia, Gen. Scott and Senator Seward, in Washington, had been apprised, from independent sources, that imminent danger threatened Mr. Lincoln in case he should publicly pass through Baltimore; and accordingly a special messenger, Mr. Frederick W. Seward, a son of Senator Seward, was despatched to Philadelphia, to urge Mr. Lincoln to come direct to Washington, in a quiet manner. The messenger arrived in Philadelphia late on Thursday night, and had an interview with the President-elect, immediately subsequent to his interview with the detective. He was informed that Mr. Lincoln would arrive by the early train on Saturday morning, and, in accordance with this information, Mr. Washburn, member of Congress from Illinois, awaited the President-elect at the depot in Washington, whence he was taken in a carriage to Willard's Hotel, where Senator Seward stood ready to receive him.

The detective travelled with Mr. Lincoln under the name of E. J. Allen, which name was registered with the President-elect's on the book at Willard's Hotel. Being a well-known individual, he was speedily recognized, and suspicion naturally arose that he had been instrumental in exposing the plot which caused Mr. Lincoln's hurried journey. It was deemed prudent that he should leave Washington two days after his arrival, although he had intended to remain and witness the ceremonies of inauguration.

The friends of Mr. Lincoln do not question the loyalty and hospitality of the people of Maryland, but they were aware that a few disaffected citizens who sympathized warmly with the Secessionists, were determined to frustrate, at all hazards, the inauguration of the President-elect, even at the cost of his life.

The characters and pursuits of the conspirators were various. Some of them were impelled by a fanatical zeal which they termed patriotism, and they justified their acts by the example of Brutus, in ridding his country of a tyrant. One of them was accustomed to recite passages put into the mouth of the character of *Brutus*, in Shakspeare's play of "Julius Cæsar." Others were stimulated by the offer of pecuniary reward. These, it was observed, staid away from their usual places of work for several weeks prior to the intended assault. Although their circumstances had previously rendered them dependent on their daily labor for support, they were during this time abundantly supplied with money, which they squandered in bar-rooms and disreputable places.

After the discovery of the plot, a strict watch was kept by the agents of detection over the movements of the conspirators, and efficient measures were adopted to guard against any attack which they might meditate upon the President-elect until he was installed in office.

Mr. Lincoln's family left Harrisburg for Baltimore, on their way to Washington, in the special train intended for him. And as, before starting, a message announcing Mr. Lincoln's departure and arrival at Washington had been telegraphed to Baltimore over the wires, which had been repaired that morning, the passage through Baltimore was safely effected.

The remark of Mr. Lincoln, during the ceremony of raising the flag on Independence Hall on Friday morning, that he would assert his principles on his inauguration, although he were to be assassinated on the spot, had evident reference to the communication made to him by the detective on the night preceding.

The names of the conspirators will not at present be divulged. But they are in possession of responsible parties, including the President.

The number originally ascertained to be banded together for the assassination of Mr. Lincoln was twenty; but the number of those who were fully apprised of the details of the plot became daily smaller as the time for executing it drew near.

Some of the women employed by the detective went to serve as waiters, seamstresses, &c., in the families of the conspirators, and a record was regularly kept of what was said and done to further their enterprise. A record was also kept by the detective of their deliberations in secret conclave, but, for sufficient reasons, it is withheld for the present from publication. The detective and his agents regularly contributed money to pay the expenses of the conspiracy.

—Albany Evening Journal.

Doc. 39.—TWIGGS' TREASON.

The following is a list of the property given up to the State of Texas by Gen. Twiggs:

1,800 mules, valued at $50 each	$90,000
500 wagons, valued at $140 each	70,000
950 horses, valued at $150 each	142,500
500 harness, valued at $50 each	25,000
Tools, wagon materials, iron, nails, horse and mule shoes	250,000
Corn (at this port)	7,000
Clothing	150,000
Commissary stores	75,000
Ordnance stores	400,000
Total	$1,209,500

Exclusive of public buildings to which the Federal Government has a title. Much of the property is estimated at the original cost, its value in Texas being much greater, and worth to the State at least a million and a half of dollars.

—San Antonio Herald, Feb. 23.

Doc. 40.—PLAN OF THE PEACE CONVENTION.

ARTICLE 13.

Section 1. In all the present territory of the United States north of the parallel of 36° 30′ of north latitude, involuntary servitude, except in punishment of crime, is prohibited. In all the present territory south of that line, the *status* of persons held to involuntary service or labor, as it now exists, shall not be changed; nor shall any law be passed by Congress or the Territorial Legislature to hinder or prevent the taking of such persons from any of the States of this Union to said territory, nor to impair the right arising from said relation; but the same shall be subject to judicial cognizance in the Federal courts, according to the course of the common law. When any Territory north or south of said line, within such boundary as Congress may prescribe, shall contain a population equal to that required for a member of Congress, it shall, if its form of Government be republican, be admitted into the Union on an equal footing with the original States, with or without involuntary servitude, as the constitution of such State may provide.

Sec. 2. No territory shall be acquired by the United States, except by discovery, and for naval and commercial stations, depots, and transit routes, without the concurrence of a majority of all the Senators from States which allow involuntary servitude, and a majority of all the Senators from States which prohibit that relation; nor shall territory be acquired by treaty, unless the votes of a majority of the Senators from each class of States hereinbefore mentioned be cast as a part of the two-thirds majority necessary to the ratification of such treaty.

Sec. 3. Neither the constitution nor any amendment thereof, shall be construed to give Congress power to regulate, abolish, or control within any State the relation established or recognized by the laws thereof touching persons held to labor or involuntary service therein, nor to interfere with or abolish involuntary service in the District of Columbia without the consent of Maryland, and without the consent of the owners, or making the owners who do not consent just compensation; nor the power to interfere with or prohibit representatives and others from bringing with them to the District of Columbia, retaining, and taking away, persons so held to labor or service; nor the power to interfere with or abolish involuntary service in places under the exclusive jurisdiction of the United States, within those States and Territories where the same is established or recognized; nor the power to prohibit the removal or transportation of persons held to labor or involuntary service in any State or Territory of the United States to any other State or Territory thereof, where it is established or recognized by law or usage; and the right during transportation, by sea or river, of touching at ports, shores, and landings, and of landing in case of distress, shall exist; but not the right of transit in or through any State or Territory, or of sale or traffic, against the laws thereof. Nor shall Congress have power to authorize any higher rate of taxation on persons held to labor or service than on land. The bringing into the District of Columbia of persons held to labor or service, for sale, or placing them in depots to be afterwards transferred to other places for sale as merchandise, is prohibited.

Sec. 4. The third paragraph of the second section of the fourth article of the constitution shall not be construed to prevent any of the States, by appropriate legislation, and through the action of their judicial and ministerial officers, from enforcing the delivery of fugitives from labor to the person to whom such service or labor is due.

Sec. 5. The foreign slave trade is hereby forever prohibited; and it shall be the duty of Congress to pass laws to prevent the importation of slaves, coolies, or persons held to service or labor, into the United States and Territories from places beyond the limits thereof.

Sec. 6. The first, third, and fifth sections, together with this section, of these amendments, and the third paragraph of the second section of the first article of the constitution, and the third paragraph of the second section of the fourth article thereof, shall not be amended or abolished without the consent of all the States.

Sec. 7. Congress shall provide by law that the United States shall pay to the owner the full value of his fugitive from labor, in all cases where the marshal, or other officer, whose duty it was to arrest such fugitive, was prevented from so doing by violence or intimidation from mobs or riotous assemblages, or when, after arrest, such fugitive was rescued by like violence or intimidation, and the owner thereby deprived of the same; and the acceptance of such payment shall preclude the owner from further claim to such fugitive. Congress shall provide by law for securing to the citizens of each State the privileges and immunities of citizens in the several States.

—N. Y. Herald.

Doc. 41.—CORWIN'S AMENDMENT.

The amendment to the twelfth section of the constitution, offered at Washington by Mr. Corwin, reads as follows:

"No amendment shall be made to the constitution, which will authorize or give Congress power to abolish or interfere, within any State, with the domestic institutions thereof, including that of persons held to labor or servitude by the laws of said State."

—Tribune.

Doc. 42.—INAUGURAL OF ABRAHAM LINCOLN.

Fellow-citizens of the United States:

In compliance with a custom as old as the Government itself, I appear before you to address you briefly, and to take, in your presence, the oath prescribed by the Constitution of the United States to be taken by the President, before he enters on the execution of his office.

I do not consider it necessary, at present, for me to discuss those matters of administration about which there is no special anxiety or excitement. Apprehension seems to exist among the people of the southern States, that, by the accession of a Republican Administration, their property and their peace and personal security are to be endangered. There has never been any reasonable cause for such apprehension. Indeed, the most ample evidence to the contrary has all the while existed, and been open to their inspection. It is found in nearly all the published speeches of him who now addresses you. I do but quote from one of those speeches, when I declare that "I have no purpose, directly or indirectly, to interfere with the institution of slavery in the States where it exists." I believe I have no lawful right to do so; and I have no inclination to do so. Those who nominated and elected me, did so with the full knowledge that I had made this, and made many similar declarations, and had never recanted them. And, more than this, they placed in the platform, for my acceptance, and as a law to themselves and to me, the clear and emphatic resolution which I now read:

"*Resolved,* that the maintenance inviolate of the rights of the States, and especially the right of each State to order and control its own domestic institutions according to its own judgment exclusively, is essential to that balance of power on which the perfection and endurance of our political fabric depend; and we denounce the lawless invasion by armed force of the soil of any State or Territory, no matter under what pretext, as among the gravest of crimes."

I now reiterate these sentiments; and in doing so I only press upon the public attention the most conclusive evidence of which the case is susceptible, that the property, peace, and security of no section are to be in anywise endangered by the now incoming Administration.

I add, too, that all the protection which, consistently with the constitution and the laws, can be given will be cheerfully given to all the States when lawfully demanded, for whatever cause, as cheerfully to one section as to another.

There is much controversy about the delivering up of fugitives from service or labor. The clause I now read is as plainly written in the constitution as any other of its provisions:

"No person held to service or labor in one State under the laws thereof, escaping into another, shall, in consequence of any law or regulation therein, be discharged from such service or labor, but shall be delivered up on claim of the party to whom such service or labor may be due."

It is scarcely questioned that this provision was intended by those who made it for the reclaiming of what we call fugitive slaves; and the intention of the lawgiver is the law.

All members of Congress swear their support to the whole Constitution—to this provision as well as any other. To the proposition, then, that slaves whose cases come within the terms of this clause "shall be delivered up," their oaths are unanimous. Now, if they would make the effort in good temper, could they not, with nearly equal unanimity, frame and pass a law by means of which to keep good that unanimous oath?

There is some difference of opinion whether this clause should be enforced by national or by state authority; but surely that difference is not a very material one. If the slave is to be surrendered, it can be of but little consequence to him or to others by which authority it is done; and should any one, in any case, be content that this oath shall go unkept on a merely unsubstantial controversy as to how it shall be kept?

Again, in any law upon this subject, ought not all the safeguards of liberty known in the civilized and humane jurisprudence to be introduced, so that a free man be not, in any case, surrendered as a slave? And might it not be well at the same time to provide by law for the enforcement of that clause in the Constitution which guaranties that "the citizens of each State shall be entitled to all the privileges and immunities of citizens in the several States?"

I take the official oath to-day with no mental reservations, and with no purpose to construe the Constitution or laws by any hypercritical rules; and while I do not choose now to specify particular acts of Congress as proper to be enforced, I do suggest that it will be much safer for all, both in official and private stations, to conform to and abide by all those acts which stand unrepealed, than to violate any of them, trusting to find impunity in having them held to be unconstitutional.

It is seventy-two years since the first inauguration of a President under our national Constitution. During that period fifteen different and very distinguished citizens have in succession administered the executive branch of the government. They have conducted it through many perils, and generally with great success. Yet, with all this scope for precedent, I now enter upon the same task, for the brief constitutional term of four years, under great and peculiar difficulties.

A disruption of the Federal Union, heretofore only menaced, is now formidably attempted. I hold that in the contemplation of universal law and of the Constitution, the Union of these States is perpetual. Perpetuity is implied, if not expressed, in the fundamental law of all national governments. It is safe to assert that no government proper ever had a provision in its organic law for its own termination. Continue to execute all the express provisions of our national Constitution, and the Union will endure forever, it being impossible to destroy it except by some action not provided for in the instrument itself.

Again, if the United States be not a government proper, but an association of States in the nature of a contract merely, can it, as a contract, be peaceably unmade by less than all the parties who made it? One party to a contract may violate it—break it, so to speak; but does it not require all to lawfully rescind it? Descending from these general principles we find the proposition that in legal contemplation the Union is perpetual, confirmed by the history of the Union itself.

The Union is much older than the Constitution. It was formed, in fact, by the Articles of Association in 1774. It was matured and continued in the Declaration of Independence in 1776. It was further matured, and the faith of all the then thirteen States expressly plighted and engaged that it should be perpetual, by the Articles of Confederation, in 1778; and, finally, in 1787, one of the declared objects for ordaining and establishing the Constitution was to form a more perfect Union. But if the destruction of the Union by one or by a part only of the States be lawfully possible, the Union is less than before, the Constitution having lost the vital element of perpetuity.

It follows from these views that no State, upon its own mere motion, can lawfully get out of the Union; that resolves and ordinances to that effect, are legally void; and that acts of violence within any State or States against the authority of the United States, are insurrectionary or revolutionary, according to circumstances.

I therefore consider that, in view of the Constitution and the laws, the Union is unbroken, and, to the extent of my ability, I shall take care, as the Constitution itself expressly enjoins upon me, that the laws of the Union shall be faithfully executed in all the States. Doing this, which I deem to be only a simple duty on my part, I shall perfectly perform it, so far as is practicable, unless my rightful masters, the American people, shall withhold the requisition, or in some authoritative manner direct the contrary.

I trust this will not be regarded as a menace, but only as the declared purpose of the Union that it will constitutionally defend and maintain itself.

In doing this there need be no bloodshed or violence, and there shall be none unless it is forced upon the national authority.

The power confided to me *will be used to hold, occupy, and possess the property and places belonging to the Government*, and collect the duties and imposts; but beyond what may be necessary for these objects there will be no invasion, no using of force against or among the people anywhere.

Where hostility to the United States shall be so great and so universal as to prevent competent resident citizens from holding the Federal offices, there will be no attempt to force obnoxious strangers among the people that object. While the strict legal right may exist of the Government to enforce the exercise of these offices, the attempt to do so would be so irritating, and so nearly impracticable withal, that I deem it better to forego for the time the uses of such offices.

The mails, unless repelled, will continue to be furnished in all parts of the Union.

So far as possible, the people everywhere shall have that sense of perfect security which is most favorable to calm thought and reflection.

The course here indicated will be followed, unless

current events and experience shall show a modification or change to be proper; and in every case and exigency my best discretion will be exercised according to the circumstances actually existing, and with a view and hope of a peaceful solution of the national troubles, and the restoration of fraternal sympathies and affections.

That there are persons, in one section or another, who seek to destroy the Union at all events, and are glad of any pretext to do it, I will neither affirm nor deny. But if there be such, I need address no word to them.

To those, however, who really love the Union, may I not speak, before entering upon so grave a matter as the destruction of our national fabric, with all its benefits, its memories, and its hopes? Would it not be well to ascertain why we do it? Will you hazard so desperate a step, while any portion of the ills you fly from, have no real existence? Will you, while the certain ills you fly to, are greater than all the real ones you fly from? Will you risk the commission of so fearful a mistake? All profess to be content in the Union if all constitutional rights can be maintained. Is it true, then, that any right, plainly written in the Constitution has been denied? I think not. Happily the human mind is so constituted, that no party can reach to the audacity of doing this.

Think, if you can, of a single instance in which a plainly-written provision of the Constitution has ever been denied. If, by the mere force of numbers, a majority should deprive a minority of any clearly-written constitutional right, it might, in a moral point of view, justify revolution; it certainly would, if such right were a vital one. But such is not our case.

All the vital rights of minorities and of individuals are so plainly assured to them by affirmations and negations, guaranties and prohibitions in the Constitution, that controversies never arise concerning them. But no organic law can ever be framed with a provision specifically applicable to every question which may occur in practical administration. No foresight can anticipate, nor any document of reasonable length contain, express provisions for all possible questions. Shall fugitives from labor be surrendered by national or by state authorities? The Constitution does not expressly say. Must Congress protect slavery in the Territories? The Constitution does not expressly say. From questions of this class, spring all our constitutional controversies, and we divide upon them into majorities and minorities.

If the minority will not acquiesce, the majority must, or the government must cease. There is no alternative for continuing the government but acquiescence on the one side or the other. If a minority in such a case, will secede rather than acquiesce, they make a precedent which in turn will ruin and divide them, for a minority of their own will secede from them whenever a majority refuses to be controlled by such a minority. For instance, why not any portion of a new confederacy, a year or two hence, arbitrarily secede again, precisely as portions of the present Union now claim to secede from it? All who cherish disunion sentiments are now being educated to the exact temper of doing this. Is there such perfect identity of interests among the States to compose a new Union as to produce harmony only, and prevent renewed seces-

sion? Plainly, the central idea of secession is the essence of anarchy.

A majority held in restraint by constitutional check and limitation, and always changing easily with deliberate changes of popular opinions and sentiments, is the only true sovereign of a free people. Whoever rejects it, does, of necessity, fly to anarchy or to despotism. Unanimity is impossible; the rule of a majority, as a permanent arrangement, is wholly inadmissible. So that, rejecting the majority principle, anarchy or despotism in some form is all that is left.

I do not forget the position assumed by some that constitutional questions are to be decided by the Supreme Court, nor do I deny that such decisions must be binding in any case upon the parties to a suit, as to the object of that suit, while they are also entitled to very high respect and consideration in all parallel cases by all other departments of the government; and while it is obviously possible that such decision may be erroneous in any given case, still the evil effect following it, being limited to that particular case, with the chance that it may be overruled and never become a precedent for other cases, can better be borne than could the evils of a different practice.

At the same time the candid citizen must confess that if the policy of the government upon the vital questions affecting the whole people is to be irrevocably fixed by the decisions of the Supreme Court, the instant they are made, as in ordinary litigation between parties in personal actions, the people will have ceased to be their own masters, unless having to that extent practically resigned their government into the hands of that eminent tribunal.

Nor is there in this view any assault upon the court or the judges. It is a duty from which they may not shrink, to decide cases properly brought before them; and it is no fault of theirs if others seek to turn their decisions to political purposes. One section of our country believes slavery is right and ought to be extended, while the other believes it is wrong and ought not to be extended; and this is the only substantial dispute; and the fugitive slave clause of the constitution, and the law for the suppression of the foreign slave trade, are each as well enforced, perhaps, as any law can ever be in a community where the moral sense of the people imperfectly supports the law itself. The great body of the people abide by the dry legal obligation in both cases, and a few break over in each. This, I think, cannot be perfectly cured, and it would be worse in both cases after the separation of the sections than before. The foreign slave trade, now imperfectly suppressed, would be ultimately revived, without restriction, in one section; while fugitive slaves, now only partially surrendered, would not be surrendered at all by the other.

Physically speaking we cannot separate—we cannot remove our respective sections from each other, nor build an impassable wall between them. A husband and wife may be divorced, and go out of the presence and beyond the reach of each other, but the different parts of our country cannot do this. They cannot but remain face to face; and intercourse, either amicable or hostile, must continue between them. Is it possible, then, to make that intercourse more advantageous or more satisfactory after separation than before? Can aliens make treaties easier than friends can make laws? Can treaties be more faithfully enforced between aliens than laws can among friends? Suppose you go to war, you cannot fight always; and when, after much loss on both sides and no gain on either, you cease fighting, the identical questions as to terms of intercourse are again upon you.

This country, with its institutions, belongs to the people who inhabit it. Whenever they shall grow weary of the existing government, they can exercise their constitutional right of amending, or their revolutionary right to dismember or overthrow it. I cannot be ignorant of the fact that many worthy and patriotic citizens are desirous of having the national Constitution amended. While I make no recommendation of amendment, I fully recognize the full authority of the people over the whole subject, to be exercised in either of the modes prescribed in the instrument itself, and I should, under existing circumstances, favor, rather than oppose, a fair opportunity being afforded the people to act upon it.

I will venture to add, that to me the convention mode seems preferable, in that it allows amendments to originate with the people themselves, instead of only permitting them to take or reject propositions originated by others not especially chosen for the purpose, and which might not be precisely such as they would wish either to accept or refuse. I understand that a proposed amendment to the Constitution (which amendment, however, I have not seen) has passed Congress, to the effect that the Federal Government shall never interfere with the domestic institutions of States, including that of persons held to service. To avoid misconstruction of what I have said, I depart from my purpose not to speak of particular amendments, so far as to say that, holding such a provision to now be implied constitutional law, I have no objection to its being made express and irrevocable.

The chief magistrate derives all his authority from the people, and they have conferred none upon him to fix the terms for the separation of the States. The people themselves, also, can do this if they choose; but the Executive, as such, has nothing to do with it. His duty is to administer the present government as it came to his hands, and to transmit it unimpaired by him to his successor. Why should there not be a patient confidence in the ultimate justice of the people? Is there any better or equal hope in the world? In our present differences is either party without faith of being in the right? If the Almighty Ruler of nations, with his eternal truth and justice, be on your side of the North, or on yours of the South, that truth and that justice will surely prevail by the judgment of this great tribunal, the American people. By the frame of the Government under which we live, this same people have wisely given their public servants but little power for mischief, and have with equal wisdom provided for the return of that little to their own hands at very short intervals. While the people retain their virtue and vigilance, no administration, by any extreme wickedness or folly, can very seriously injure the Government in the short space of four years.

My countrymen, one and all, think calmly and well upon this whole subject. Nothing valuable can be lost by taking time. If there be an object to hurry any of you, in hot haste, to a step which you would never take deliberately, that object will be frustrated by taking time; but no good object can be frustrated by it.

Such of you as are now dissatisfied still have the old Constitution unimpaired, and on the sensitive point, the laws of your own framing under it; while the new administration will have no immediate power, if it would, to change either.

If it were admitted that you who are dissatisfied hold the right side in the dispute, there is still no single reason for precipitate action. Intelligence, patriotism, Christianity, and a firm reliance on Him who has never yet forsaken this favored land, are still competent to adjust, in the best way, all our present difficulties.

In your hands, my dissatisfied fellow-countrymen, and not in mine, is the momentous issue of civil war. The government will not assail you. You can have no conflict without being yourselves the aggressors. You have no oath registered in Heaven to destroy the government; while I shall have the most solemn one to "preserve, protect, and defend" it.

I am loath to close. We are not enemies, but friends. We must not be enemies. Though passion may have strained, it must not break our bonds of affection.

The mystic cords of memory, stretching from every battle-field and patriot grave to every living heart and hearthstone all over this broad land, will yet swell the chorus of the Union, when again touched, as surely they will be, by the better angels of our nature.

Doc. 43.—THE INAUGURAL ADDRESS.

HOW IT IS RECEIVED.

The Baltimore papers discuss the tone of Mr. Lincoln's Inaugural Address. The *American* regards the address with favor.

"The tone of the speech is pacific; that is to say, Mr. Lincoln avows his determination to preserve peace, so far as it may be done, in the performance of his duty as he understands it. He denies that he has the power to recognize the right or the fact of secession, and therefore denies that he has the liberty to refrain from the performance of what would be plain obligations if no such right or fact had been assumed to exist. While, therefore, he announces his intention to collect the revenue and to possess and defend the forts, he distinctly declares that he will do these things in such a manner as to avoid the necessity for strife, if it is possible to do so. It is perfectly evident, from the whole tenor of his Address, *that he does not intend to be the aggressor*, if peace may not be preserved.

"No one will deny that he has met the issues presented with a firmness and frankness that are in themselves commendable. He does not expect to be misunderstood, and he foreshadows his policy with a directness that provides for no future evasions or change of programme. It is hardly probable that the citizens of the Southern Confederacy have waited for this Inaugural with the expectation that it was to contain a relinquishment of United States authority in the seceded states, or a promise to recognize the government there set up; and if they have, it is not probable that the Address will leave them in doubt upon this subject.

"Whatever may be the differences of opinion

throughout the country upon the various subjects of which the address treats, it will be very generally received as an honest and outspoken avowal of the policy of the new administration. It is certain that it furnishes no pretext for disunion that has not existed since the November election."

The Baltimore *Sun* denounces the Address as "sectional and mischievous," and adds that "if it means what it says, it is the knell and the requiem of the Union, and the death of hope."

The Baltimore *Exchange* says, "the measures of Mr. Lincoln mean war."

The Baltimore *Patriot* believes, with the *American*, that Mr. Lincoln means to avoid aggression, and adds:

"The reasoning and expositions of the Inaugural, in the virtues of patience, forbearance, &c., apply as well to Mr. Lincoln as to the people of the several States, and as he expects the people to exercise those virtues, so must he allow the people to expect that he will apply the counsel to himself, as well as to them. In this there is *another assurance of pacificatory purposes, and of the intention to enforce the laws, as nearly as possible, in conformity with the will of the whole people.* This position is greatly strengthened by the appeal to the Almighty Ruler of Nations, with his eternal truth and justice, as the great appellate tribunal of the American people. We make this observation in reference to Mr. Lincoln as an enlightened and conscientious statesman, and not as an educated and conscientious fanatic. In the character of the statesman, he will wisely and judiciously apply the law he is obliged to enforce as a sufficient instrument for the accomplishment of its purposes, without any appeal to the higher law of the fanatics, which is subversive of all human law and government, and impels the submission of all human thought and consideration and action to the whim or notion of an individual man."

In Virginia the secessionists denounce it as a warlike document, and threaten immediate secession and fight.

In the seceding States intense excitement was created by the reception of the Address.

In North Carolina, the Inaugural was favorably received by the Unionists, who regarded it as a hopeful indication of the peace policy of the administration.

The St. Louis *Democrat* says: "We can only say this morning, that it meets the highest expectations of the country, both in point of statesmanship and patriotism, and that its effect on the public mind cannot be other than salutary in the highest degree."

The St. Louis *Republican* says: "We hoped for a more conservative and more conciliatory expression of sentiments; much will depend upon the putting in practice of the ideas advanced that will test the question—be it one of expediency or right—whether the forts can be held or retaken and the revenues collected without bloodshed."

The Boston *Post* is pleased. It says:

"The conservatives will be glad to see, at this time, the opening avowals of the Address. The pledge not to interfere with slavery in the States; the denunciation of lawless invasions of those States; the avowal to protect slavery in case of a servile insurrection; the promise to carry into effect the fugitive slave obligation, seem to come up to the requirements of the Constitution. Nor is this all. Towards the conclusion the President returns to the

subject, and further manifests his desire to conciliate, by frankly endorsing the Corwin amendment to the Constitution, which has just received a two-thirds vote of both branches of Congress."

Doc. 44.—SYNOPSIS OF THE CONFEDERATE STATES' ARMY BILL.

SEC. 1. Enacts, that from and after the passage of the act, the military establishment of the Confederate States shall be composed of one corps of engineers, one corps of artillery, six regiments of infantry, one regiment of cavalry, and of the staff department already established by law.

2. The Corps of Engineers shall consist of one colonel, four majors, five captains, one company of sappers, miners, and pioneers, consisting of ten sergeants or master-workmen, ten corporals or overseers, two musicians, and thirty-nine privates of the first-class, or artificers, and thirty-nine men of second-class, or laborers—making in all one hundred.

3. Said company shall be officered by one captain and as many lieutenants, taken from the line of the army, as the President may deem necessary.

4. Duties of the colonel of the Engineer Corps prescribed.

5. The artillery corps shall consist of one colonel, one lieutenant-colonel, ten majors, and forty companies of artillerists and artificers; and each company shall consist of one captain, two first lieutenants, one second lieutenant, four sergeants, four corporals, two musicians and seventy privates; also one adjutant to be selected by the colonel from the first lieutenants, and one sergeant-major to be selected from enlisted men of the corps.

6. Each regiment of infantry shall consist of one colonel, one lieutenant-colonel, one major and ten companies. Each company shall consist of one captain, one first lieutenant, two second lieutenants, four sergeants, four corporals, two musicians and ninety privates; and to each regiment there shall be one adjutant, and one sergeant-major.

7. The cavalry regiment shall consist of one colonel, one lieutenant-colonel, one major and ten companies. Each of which shall consist of one captain, one first lieutenant, two second lieutenants, four sergeants, four corporals, one farrier, one blacksmith, two musicians and sixty privates; also, of one adjutant and one sergeant-major.

8. There shall be four brigadier-generals, entitled to one aid-de-camp each.

9. All officers of the army shall be appointed by the President, by and with the advice and consent of the Congress; and the rank and file shall be enlisted for not less than three nor more than five years.

10. All officers are required to stand a creditable military examination.

11 and 12. Promotions in the army shall be made according to seniority and ability.

13. The pay of the brigadier-general is $3,612 per year, and his aid-de-camp (in addition to his pay as lieutenant) the sum of $35 per month.

14. Monthly pay of the officers of the Corps of Engineers: colonel, $210; majors, $162; captains, $140; lieutenants serving with sappers and miners will receive the pay of cavalry officers of the same grade.

15. The monthly pay of the colonel of the artillery corps is $210; lieutenant-colonel, $185; majors,

$150; and when serving on ordnance duty, $162; captains, $130; lieutenants, $90; second lieutenants, $80. The adjutant, in addition to his pay as lieutenant, the sum of $10 per month. Officers serving in the light artillery, or performing ordnance duty, shall receive the same pay as officers of cavalry in the same grade.

16. The monthly pay of officers in the infantry regiment. Colonels, $195; lieutenant-colonels, $170; majors, $150; captains, $130; lieutenants, $90; second lieutenants, $80; and the adjutant, in addition to his pay as lieutenant, $10 per month.

17. The monthly pay of officers of cavalry: Colonel, $210; lieutenant-colonel, $185; major, $162; captains, $140; first lieutenant, $100; second lieutenants, $90; and the adjutant $10 per month in addition to his pay as lieutenant.

18. The pay of officers of the general staff (except those of the medical department,) will be the same as officers of cavalry of the same grade. The annual salary of the surgeon-general is $3,000, with fuel and quarters; monthly pay of surgeons of ten years' service in that grade, $200; a surgeon of less time service, $162; assistant-surgeon of ten years' service, $150; assistant-surgeon of five years' service, $130, and for assistant of less than five years' service, $110.

19. There shall be allowed, in addition to the pay herein before provided, to every commissioned officer, except the surgeon-general, $9 per month for every five years' services, and to the officers of the army of the United States who have resigned, or may resign, to be received into the service of The Confederate States, this additional pay shall be allowed from the date of their entrance into the former service. There shall also be an additional monthly allowance to every general officer commanding in chief a separate army actually in the field, the sum of $100.

20. The pay aforesaid shall be in full of all allowances, except forage, fuel, quarters, and travelling expenses, while travelling under orders, etc., etc.

21. Allows forage to officers, etc.

22. Monthly pay of enlisted men: Sergeants or master workmen of engineer corps, $34; corporals or overseers, $20; privates of first-class or artificers, 17; privates of second-class, or laborers, and musicians, $13; sergeant-major of cavalry, $21; first sergeant, $20; sergeants, $17; corporals, farriers, and blacksmiths, $13; musicians, $13; privates, $12; first sergeants, $20; sergeants, $17; corporals and artificers, $13; musicians, $12; and privates, $11. Non-commissioned officers, artificers, musicians, and privates serving in light batteries shall receive the same pay as those of cavalry.

23. The President is authorized to enlist all master workmen necessary to the ordnance service, not exceeding one hundred men, and at salaries ranging from $13 to $34 per month.

24. Each enlisted man shall receive one ration per day and clothing.

25. Refers to commutation of rations.

26. The Secretary of War is directed to prescribe the duties of every department of service.

27. Requires Quartermasters and Commissaries to give bonds.

28. Prohibits any officer from being interested in purchases made for the army.

29. The rules and articles of war of the United States, with slight exceptions, adopted by the Congress of the Confederate States.

30. The President is directed to call into service only so many of the troops herein provided for as he may deem necessary.

31. Repeals all conflicting laws.

The law is quite long, and hence the reason of the analysis, which will doubtless be more satisfactory to readers generally than the perusal of the entire law.

Below is a tabular statement of the number and grade of officers and men:

Rank.	Engineer Corps.	Artillery.	Infantry.	Cavalry.	Total.
Colonels	1	1	6	1	9
Lieutenant-Colonels	—	1	6	1	8
Majors	4	10	6	1	21
Number of Companies	—	40	60	10	110
Captains	5	40	60	10	115
First Lieutenants	—	80	60	10	150
Second Lieutenants	—	40	120	20	180
Sergeants	10	160	240	40	450
Corporals	10	160	240	40	450
Privates	78	2,800	5,400	600	8,878
Farriers	—	—	—	4	4
Blacksmiths	—	—	—	4	4
Musicians	2	80	240	20	342
Adjutants	—	1	6	1	8
Sergeant Majors	—	1	6	1	8

Total ....,.....10,737
Add Brigadier-Generals............................ 4
Aids to Brigadier-Generals........................ 4

—N. Y. Herald.

Doc. 45.—AN ENGLISH PROTEST AGAINST SOUTHERN RECOGNITION.

Mr. Gregory has given notice that on an early day he will call the attention of her Majesty's government to the expediency of a prompt recognition of the Southern Confederacy of America. *There is no occasion for Mr. Gregory or any one else to be anxious to get our government to acknowledge the so-called Southern Confederacy of American States.* The practice of the British government in such cases is firmly established and well understood, viz., to recognize all *de facto* governments, irrespective of opinions, origin, or any circumstance but the fact of being the actually established ruling power. If ever and whenever that happens with the Southern States, which now professes to be a confederacy, there can be no doubt about their being recognized by all the European powers; and by England, with the utmost certainty and distinctness. *But the case has not reached this stage; and it is very far from reaching it.* The secession leaders who have assumed office do not pretend to be more than a provisional body; *no appeal has been made to the people of their States;* none of the constitutional conditions of republican organization have as yet been complied with; and none of the antecedents which were specified by the founders of the republic as justifying rebellion have occurred. The movers in the case have begged the question in regard to the right of secession; and there has as yet been no opportunity of reply on the other side. The whole matter remains for treatment; and, in the most democratic country in the world, the great body of the people has been silent during a whole winter of crisis, from actual want of opportunity to declare their opinion and will. There can be no recognition from without of any new claims put forth in such an interval; and *the American nation has a right to expect from its foreign allies patience to wait till the people have spoken and taken their course of action.*

The inauguration address of the Provisional President of the South was intended to produce just such an effect as it seems to have produced on Mr. Gregory's mind. *This audacious parody on the Declaration of Independence might*, it was evidently thought, catch the ear of Americans, to whom that Declaration is as familiar as the Lord's Prayer; and it might entrap the imagination of foreigners who might not have paid sufficient attention to the course of American affairs to detect its inapplicability. One does not look for extreme accuracy or for any impartiality in political manifestoes issued by revolutionary officials, on their first attempt to rule the people they have raised; but *it may be doubted whether in any European conflict within this revolutionary century any document has appeared more impudently false than Mr. Jefferson Davis's Address.* It is so incredible that he and any hearers qualified for political action can be self-deceived to such a point as to believe what he was saying, that we can only suppose the object to be to lead the ignorant people about them by the sound of familiar and venerated words, trusting to their inability to perceive the baselessness of the thoughts. If the poor whites of the Southern section, who constitute nearly three-fourths of the white population, can really be led by such an address as this to fancy themselves resisting oppression, and establishing free government under the special blessing of Heaven, in imitation of their fathers ninety years ago, they are indeed fit only for such subjection to oligarchical government as has long been, and still will be, required of them.

In citing the familiar and venerable statement of the Declaration of Independence, as to the causes which justify rebellion, and the principles on which the resulting polity should be framed and organized, Mr. Jefferson Davis pronounced the most crushing condemnation of his own case, in terms of the keenest irony. The staunchest Republican of the North might have taken up the same parable as the aptest speech he could make. The Philadelphia patriots exhibited the long course of oppressions the colonies had endured before they lost patience, and the actual extremities of injury they underwent before they raised a hostile flag. In the present case the Southern party has enjoyed thirty years' possession of the Federal Government—thirty years of domination over the whole Union—during which they have altered the laws, undermined the Constitution, carved out territory, restricted liberty and created license, for their own sectional objects and interests. So much for the long oppression which has driven them to resistance. And what outrage roused the reluctant men of peace at last? What was the Stamp Act of the present occasion? It was the loss of an election, a constitutional election, conducted in a regular and orderly way.

—*London News*, March 12.

Doc. 46.—BRAGG'S ORDER.

The order of Major-General Bragg, cutting off supplies from the United States fleet off Pensacola:

Headquarters Troops Confederate States, ?
Near Pensacola, Fla., *March* 18, 1861. ?

The Commanding-General learns with surprise and regret that some of our citizens are engaged in the business of furnishing supplies of fuel, water

and provisions to the armed vessels of the United States now occupying a threatening appearance off this harbor.

That no misunderstanding may exist on this subject, it is announced to all concerned that this traffic is strictly forbidden, and all such supplies, which may be captured in transit to said vessels, or to Fort Pickens, will be confiscated.

The more effectually to enforce this prohibition, no boat or vessel will be allowed to visit Fort Pickens or any of the United States naval vessels without special sanction.

Col. John H. Forney, Acting Inspector-General, will organize an efficient Harbor Police for the enforcement of this order. By command of Brigadier-General   Braxton Bragg.

Robert C. Wood, jr. Asst. Adjt. Gen.

—*Times*, March 23.

Doc. 47.—CORRESPONDENCE BETWEEN MR. SEWARD AND THE CONFEDERATE COMMISSIONERS.

The following is the correspondence between the Secretary of State and the Commissioners from the Confederate States:—

Messrs. Forsyth and Crawford to Mr. Seward, opening Negotiation and stating the Case.

Washington City, March 12, 1861.

Hon. Wm. H. Seward, Secretary of State of the United States:

Sir:—The undersigned have been duly accredited by the government of the Confederate States of America as Commissioners to the government of the United States, and in pursuance of their instructions have now the honor to acquaint you with that fact, and to make known, through you, to the President of the United States, the objects of their presence in this Capital.

Seven States of the late federal Union having, in the exercise of the inherent right of every free people to change or reform their political institutions, and through conventions of their people, withdrawn from the United States and reassumed the attributes of sovereign power delegated to it, have formed a government of their own. The Confederate States constitute an independent nation, *de facto* and *de jure*, and possess a government perfect in all its parts and endowed with all the means of self-support.

With a view to a speedy adjustment of all questions growing out of this political separation, upon such terms of amity and good will as the respective interests, geographical contiguity, and future welfare of the two nations may render necessary, the undersigned are instructed to make to the government of the United States overtures for the opening of negotiations, assuring the Government of the United States that the President, Congress, and people of the Confederate States earnestly desire a peaceful solution of these great questions; that it is neither their interest nor their wish to make any demand which is not founded in strictest justice, nor do any act to injure their late confederates.

The undersigned have now the honor in obedience to the instructions of their government, to request you to appoint as early a day as possible, in order that they may present to the President of the United States the credentials which they bear and the objects of the mission with which they are charged. We are, very respectfully,

Your obedient servants,
JOHN FORSYTH,
MARTIN J. CRAWFORD.

THE REPLY OF MR. SEWARD.

Memorandum.

DEPARTMENT OF STATE,
WASHINGTON, March 15, 1861.

Mr. John Forsyth, of the State of Alabama, and Mr. Martin J. Crawford, of the State of Georgia, on the 11th inst., through the kind offices of a distinguished Senator, submitted to the Secretary of State their desire for an unofficial interview. This request was, on the 12th inst., upon exclusively public consideration, respectfully declined.

On the 13th inst., while the Secretary was preoccupied, Mr. A. D. Banks, of Virginia, called at this Department, and was received by the Assistant Secretary, to whom he delivered a sealed communication, which he had been charged by Messrs. Forsyth and Crawford to present the Secretary in person.

In that communication Messrs. Forsyth and Crawford inform the Secretary of State that they have been duly accredited by the Government of the Confederate States of America as Commissioners to the government of the United States, and they set forth the objects of their attendance at Washington. They observe that seven States of the American Union, in the exercise of a right inherent in every free people, have withdrawn, through conventions of their people, from the United States, re-assumed the attributes of sovereign power, and formed a government of their own, and that those Confederate States now constitute an independent nation *de facto* and *de jure*, and possess a government perfect in all its parts and fully endowed with all the means of self-support.

Messrs. Forsyth and Crawford, in their aforesaid communication, thereupon proceeded to inform the Secretary that, with a view to a speedy adjustment of all questions growing out of the political separation thus assumed, upon such terms of amity and good will as the respective interests, geographical contiguity and the future welfare of the supposed two nations might render necessary, they are instructed to make to the government of the United States overtures for the opening of negotiations, assuring this government that the President, Congress and people of the Confederate States earnestly desire a peaceful solution of these great questions, and that it is neither their interest nor their wish to make any demand which is not founded in strictest justice, nor do any act to injure their late confederates.

After making these statements, Messrs. Forsyth and Crawford close their communication, as they say, in obedience to the instructions of their government, by requesting the Secretary of State to appoint as early a day as possible, in order that they may present to the President of the United States the credentials which they bear and the objects of the mission with which they are charged.

The Secretary of State frankly confesses that he understands the events which have recently occurred, and the condition of political affairs which actually exists in the part of the Union to which his attention has thus been directed, very differently

Doc.—14

from the aspect in which they are presented by Messrs. Forsyth and Crawford. He sees in them, not a rightful and accomplished revolution and an independent nation, with an established government, but rather a perversion of a temporary and partisan excitement to the inconsiderate purposes of an unjustifiable and unconstitutional aggression upon the rights and the authority vested in the federal government, and hitherto benignly exercised, as from their very nature they always must so be exercised, for the maintenance of the Union, the preservation of liberty, and the security, peace, welfare, happiness, and aggrandizement of the American people. The Secretary of State, therefore, avows to Messrs. Forsyth and Crawford that he looks patiently but confidently for the cure of evils which have resulted from proceedings so unnecessary, so unwise, so unusual, and so unnatural, not to irregular negotiations, having in view new and untried relations with agencies unknown to and acting in derogation of the Constitution and laws, but to regular and considerate action of the people at those States, in co-operation with their brethren in the other States, through the Congress of the United States, and such extraordinary conventions, if there shall be need thereof, as the federal Constitution contemplates and authorizes to be assembled.

It is, however, the purpose of the Secretary of State on this occasion not to invite or engage in any discussion of these subjects, but simply to set forth his reasons for declining to comply with the request of Messrs. Forsyth and Crawford.

On the 4th of March inst., the newly elected President of the United States, in view of all the facts bearing on the present question, assumed the executive Administration of the Government, first delivering, in accordance with an early, honored custom, an Inaugural Address to the people of the United States. The Secretary of State respectfully submits a copy of this address to Messrs. Forsyth and Crawford.

A simple reference to it will be sufficient to satisfy those gentlemen that the Secretary of State, guided by the principles therein announced, is prevented altogether from admitting or assuming that the States referred to by them have, in law or in fact withdrawn from the Federal Union, or that they could do so in the manner described by Messrs. Forsyth and Crawford, or in any other manner than with the consent and concert of the people of the United States, to be given through a national convention, to be assembled in conformity with the provisions of the Constitution of the United States. Of course the Secretary of State cannot act upon the assumption or in any way admit that the so-called Confederate States constitute a foreign Power, with whom diplomatic relations ought to be established.

Under these circumstances, the Secretary of State, whose official duties are confined, subject to the direction of the President, to the conducting of the foreign relations of the country, and do not at all embrace domestic questions or questions arising between the several States and the federal government, is unable to comply with the request of Messrs. Forsyth and Crawford, to appoint a day on which they may present the evidences of their authority and the objects of their visit to the President of the United States. On the contrary, he is obliged to state to Messrs. Forsyth and Crawford that he has no authority nor is he at liberty to recognize them as diplomatic agents, or hold correspondence or other communication with them.

Finally, the Secretary of State would observe that, although he has supposed that he might safely and with propriety have adopted these conclusions without making any reference of the subject to the Executive, yet so strong has been his desire to practise entire directness and to act in a spirit of perfect respect and candor towards Messrs. Forsyth and Crawford, and that portion of the Union, in whose name they present themselves before him, that he has cheerfully submitted this paper to the President, who coincides generally in the views it expresses, and sanctions the Secretary's decision declining official intercourse with Messrs. Forsyth and Crawford.

Doc. 48.—SPEECH OF A. H. STEPHENS.

Mr. Mayor and Gentlemen of the Committee, and Fellow-citizens—For this reception you will please accept my most profound and sincere thanks. The compliment is doubtless intended as much, or more, perhaps, in honor of the occasion, and my public position in connection with the great events now crowding upon us, than to me personally and individually. It is, however, none the less appreciated by me on that account. We are in the midst of one of the greatest epochs in our history. The last ninety days will mark one of the most memorable eras in the history of modern civilization.

[There was a general call from the outside of the building for the speaker to go out, that there were more outside than in.

The Mayor rose and requested silence at the doors, that Mr. Stephens' health would not permit him to speak in the open air. Mr. Stephens said he would leave it to the audience whether he should proceed in-doors or out. There was a general cry of in-doors, as the ladies, a large number of whom were present, could not hear outside.

Mr. Stephens said that the accommodation of the ladies would determine the question, and he would proceed where he was. At this point the uproar and clamor outside, was greater still for the speaker to go out on the steps. This was quieted by Col. Lawton, Col. Foreman, Judge Jackson and Mr. J. W. Owens going out and stating the facts of the case to the dense mass of men, women, and children who were outside, and entertaining them in short, brief speeches.

Mr. Stephens all this while quietly sitting down until the furore subsided.]

Mr. Stephens rose, and said, When perfect quiet is restored I shall proceed; I cannot speak as long as there is any noise or confusion. I shall take my time; I feel as though I could spend the night with you, if necessary. [Loud applause] I very much regret that every one who desires cannot hear what I have to say, not that I have any display to make or any thing very entertaining to present, but such views as I have to give, I wish all not only in this city, but in this State, and throughout our Confederated Republic, could hear, who have a desire to hear them.

I was remarking that we are passing through one of the greatest revolutions in the annals of the world—seven States have, within the last three months, thrown off an old Government and formed a new. This revolution has been signally marked, up to this time, by the fact of its having been accomplished without the loss of a single drop of blood. [Applause.] This new Constitution, or form of government, constitutes the subject to which your attention will be partly invited.

In reference to it, I make this first general remark: It amply secures all our ancient rights, franchises, and privileges. All the great principles of Magna Charta are retained in it. No citizen is deprived of life, liberty, or property, but by the judgment of his peers, under the laws of the land. The great principle of religious liberty, which was the honor and pride of the old Constitution, is still maintained and secured. All the essentials of the old Constitution, which have endeared it to the hearts of the American people, have been preserved and perpetuated. [Applause.] Some changes have been made—of these, I shall speak presently. Some of these I should have preferred not to have seen made, but these perhaps meet the cordial approbation of a majority of this audience, if not an overwhelming majority of the people of the Confederacy. Of them, therefore, I will not speak. But other important changes do meet my cordial approbation. They form great improvements upon the old Constitution. So, taking the whole new Constitution, I have no hesitancy in giving it as my judgment, that it is decidedly better than the old. [Applause.] Allow me briefly to allude to some of these improvements. The question of building up class interests, or fostering one branch of industry to the prejudice of another, under the exercise of the revenue power, which gave us so much trouble under the old Constitution, is put at rest forever under the new. We allow the imposition of no duty with a view of giving advantage to one class of persons, in any trade or business, over those of another. All, under our system, stand upon the same broad principles of perfect equality. Honest labor and enterprise are left free and unrestricted in whatever pursuit they may be engaged in. This subject came well-nigh causing a rupture of the old Union, under the lead of the gallant Palmetto State, which lies on our border, in 1833.

This old thorn of the tariff, which occasioned the cause of so much irritation in the old body politic, is removed forever from the new. [Applause.] Again, the subject of internal improvements, under the power of Congress to regulate commerce, is put at rest under our system. The power claimed by construction under the old Constitution, was at least a doubtful one—it rested solely upon construction. We of the South, generally apart from considerations of Constitutional principles, opposed its exercise upon grounds of expediency and justice. Notwithstanding this opposition, millions of money, in the common Treasury, had been drawn for such purposes. Our opposition sprung from no hostility to commerce, or all necessary aids for facilitating it. With us it was simply a question, upon *whom* the burden should fall. In Georgia, for instance, we had done as much for the cause of internal improvements as any other portion of the country, according to population and means. We have stretched out lines of railroads from the seaboard to the mountains, dug down the hills and filled up the valleys, at a cost of not less than $25,000,000. All this was done to open up an outlet for our products of the interior, and those to the west of us, to reach the marts of the world. No State was in greater need of such facilities than Georgia; but we had not asked that these works should be made by appropriations out of the common treasury. The cost of the grading, the superstructure and equipments of our roads was borne by those who entered upon the enterprise. Nay, more—not only the cost of the iron, no small item in the aggregate cost, was borne in the same way, but we were compelled to pay into the common treasury several millions of dollars for the privilege of importing the iron after the price was paid for it abroad. What justice was there in taking this money, which our people paid into the common Treasury on the importation of our iron, and applying it to the improvement of rivers and harbors elsewhere?

The true principle is to subject commerce of every locality to whatever burdens may be necessary to facilitate it. If the Charleston harbor needs improvement, let the commerce of Charleston bear the burden. If the mouth of the Savannah river has to be cleared out, let the sea-going navigation which is benefited by it bear the burden. So with the mouths of the Alabama and Mississippi rivers. Just as the products of the interior—our cotton, wheat, corn, and other articles—have to bear the necessary rates of freight over our railroads to reach the seas. This is again the broad principle of perfect equality and justice. [Applause.] And it is specially held forth and established in our new Constitution.

Another feature to which I will allude, is that the new Constitution provides that Cabinet Ministers and heads of Departments shall have the privilege of seats upon the floor of the Senate and House of Representatives—shall have a right to participate in the debates and discussions upon the various subjects of administration. I should have preferred that this provision should have gone further, and allowed the President to select his constitutional advisers from the Senate and House of Representatives. That would have conformed entirely to the practice in the British Parliament, which, in my judgment, is one of the wisest provisions in the British Constitution. It is the only feature that saves that Government. It is that which gives it stability in its facility to change its administration. Ours, as it is, is a great approximation to the right principle.

Under the old Constitution, a Secretary of the Treasury, for instance, had no opportunity, save by his annual reports, of presenting any scheme or plan of finance or other matter. He had no opportunity of explaining, expounding, enforcing or defending his views of policy; his only resort was through the medium of an organ. In the British Parliament the Premier brings in his budget, and stands before the nation responsible for its every item. If it is indefensible, he falls before the attacks upon it, as he ought to. This will now be the case, to a limited extent, under our system. Our heads of Departments can speak for themselves and the Administration in behalf of its entire policy, without resorting to the indirect and highly objectionable medium of a newspaper. It is to be greatly hoped, that under our system we shall never have what is known as a Government organ. [Rapturous applause.]

[A noise again arose from the clamor of the crowd outside, who wished to hear Mr. STEPHENS, and for some moments interrupted him. The Mayor rose and called on the police to preserve order. Quiet being restored, Mr. S. proceeded.]

Another change in the Constitution relates to the length of the tenure of the Presidential office. In the new Constitution it is six years instead of four, and the President rendered ineligible for a re-election. This is certainly a decidedly conservative change. It will remove from the incumbent all temptation to use his office or exert the powers confided to him for any objects of personal ambition. The only incentive to that higher ambition which should move and actuate one holding such high trusts in his hands, will be the good of the people, the advancement, prosperity, happiness, safety, honor, and true glory of the Confederacy. [Applause.]

But not to be tedious in enumerating the numerous changes for the better, allow me to allude to one other—though last, not least: the new Constitution has put at rest *forever* all the agitating questions relating to our peculiar institutions—African slavery as it exists among us—the proper *status* of the negro in our form of civilization. *This was the immediate cause of the late rupture and present revolution.* JEFFERSON, in his forecast, had anticipated this, as the "rock upon which the old Union would split." He was right. What was conjecture with him, is now a realized fact. But whether he fully comprehended the great truth upon which that rock *stood* and *stands*, may be doubted. *The prevailing ideas entertained by him and most of the leading statesmen at the time of the formation of the old Constitution were, that the enslavement of the African was in violation of the laws of nature; that it was wrong in principle, socially, morally and politically.* It was an evil they knew not well how to deal with; but the general opinion of the men of that day was, that, somehow or other, in the order of Providence, the institution would be evanescent and pass away. This idea, though not incorporated in the Constitution, was the prevailing idea at the time. The Constitution, it is true, secured every essential guarantee to the institution while it should last, and hence no argument can be justly used against the constitutional guarantees thus secured, because of the common sentiment of the day. *Those ideas, however, were fundamentally wrong. They rested upon the assumption of the equality of races. This was an error.* It was a sandy foundation, and the idea of a Government built upon it—when the "storm came and the wind blew, it *fell*."

Our new Government is founded upon exactly the opposite ideas; its foundations are laid, its cornerstone rests, upon the great truth that the negro is not equal to the white man; that slavery, subordination to the superior race, is his natural and moral condition. [Applause.] *This, our new Government, is the first, in the history of the world, based upon this great physical, philosophical, and moral truth.* This truth has been slow in the process of its development, like all other truths in the various departments of science. It is so even amongst us. Many who hear me, perhaps, can recollect well that this truth was not generally admitted, even within their day. The errors of the past generation still clung to many as late as twenty years ago. Those at the North who still cling to these errors with a zeal above knowledge, we justly denominate fanatics. All fanaticism springs from an aberration of the mind; from a defect in reasoning. It is a species of insanity. One of the most striking characteristics of insanity, in many instances, is, forming correct conclusions from fancied or erroneous premises; so with the *anti-slavery* fanatics: their conclusions are right if their premises are. They assume that the negro is equal, and hence conclude that he is entitled to equal privileges and rights, with the white man. If their premises were correct, their conclusions would be logical and just; but their premises being wrong, their whole argument fails. I recollect once of having heard a gentleman from one of the Northern States, of great power and ability, announce in the House of Representatives, with imposing effect, that we of the South would be compelled, ultimately, to yield upon this subject of slavery; that it was as impossible to war successfully against a principle in politics, as it was in physics or mechanics. That the principle would ultimately prevail. That we, in maintaining slavery as it exists with us, were warring against a principle—a principle founded in nature, the principle of the equality of man. The reply I made to him was, that upon his own grounds we should succeed, and that he and his associates in their crusade against our institutions would ultimately fail. The truth announced, that it was as impossible to war successfully against a principle in politics as well as in physics and mechanics, I admitted, but told him it was he and those acting with him who were warring against a principle. They were attempting to make things equal which the Creator had made unequal.

In the conflict thus far, success has been on our side, complete throughout the length and breadth of the Confederate States. It is upon this, as I have stated, our social fabric is firmly planted; and I cannot permit myself to doubt the ultimate success of a full recognition of this principle throughout the civilized and enlightened world.

As I have stated, the truth of this principle may be slow in development, as all truths are, and ever have been, in the various branches of science. It was so with the principles announced by Galileo —it was so with Adam Smith and his principles of political economy. It was so with Harvey, and his theory of the circulation of the blood. It is stated that not a single one of the medical profession, living at the time of the announcement of the truths made by him, admitted them. Now, they are universally acknowledged. May we not therefore look with confidence to the ultimate universal acknowledgment of the truths upon which our system rests? It is the first Government ever instituted upon principles in strict conformity to nature, and the ordination of Providence, in furnishing the materials of human society. Many Governments have been founded upon the principles of certain classes; but the classes thus enslaved, were of the same race, and in violation of the laws of nature. Our system commits no such violation of nature's laws. The negro by nature, or by the curse against Canaan, is fitted for that condition which he occupies in our system. The architect, in the construction of buildings, lays the foundation with the proper material—the granite—then comes the brick or the marble. The substratum of our society is made of the material fitted by nature for it, and by experience we know that it is the best, not only for the superior but for the inferior race, that it should be so. It is, indeed, in conformity with the Creator.

It is not for us to inquire into the wisdom of His ordinances or to question them. For His own purposes He has made one race to differ from another, as He has made "one star to differ from another in glory."

The great objects of humanity are best attained, when conformed to his laws and degrees, in the formation of Governments as well as in all things else. Our Confederacy is founded upon principles in strict conformity with these laws. This stone which was rejected by the first builders "*is become the chief stone of the corner*" in our new edifice. [Applause.]

I have been asked, what of the future? It has been apprehended by some, that we would have arrayed against us the civilized world. I care not who or how many they may be, when we stand upon the eternal principles of truth we are obliged and must triumph. [Immense applause.]

Thousands of people, who begin to understand these truths, are not yet completely out of the shell; they do not see them in their length and breadth. We hear much of the civilization and christianization of the barbarous tribes of Africa. In my judgment, those ends will never be obtained but by first teaching them the lesson taught to Adam, that "in the sweat of thy brow shalt thou eat bread," [applause,] and teaching them to work, and feed, and clothe themselves.

But to pass on. Some have propounded the inquiry, whether it is practicable for us to go on with the Confederacy without further accessions. Have we the means and ability to maintain nationality among the Powers of the earth? On this point I would barely say, that as anxious as we all have been, and are, for the Border States, with institutions similar with ours, to join us, still we are abundantly able to maintain our position, even if they should ultimately make up their minds not to cast their destiny with ours. That they ultimately will join us, be compelled to do it, is my confident belief; but we can get on very well without them, even if they should not.

We have all the essential elements of a high national career. The idea has been given out at the North, and even in the Border States, that we are too small and too weak to maintain a separate nationality. This is a great mistake. In extent of territory we embrace 564,000 square miles and upwards. This is upwards of 200,000 square miles more than was included within the limits of the original Thirteen States. It is an area of country more than double the territory of France or the Austrian Empire. France, in round numbers, has but 212,000 square miles. Austria, in round numbers, has 248,000 square miles. Ours is greater than both combined. It is greater than all France, Spain, Portugal and Great Britain, including England, Ireland, and Scotland, together. In population, we have upwards of 5,000,000, according to the census of 1860; this includes white and black. The entire population, including white and black, of the original Thirteen States, was less than 4,000-000 in 1790, and still less in 1776, when the independence of our fathers was achieved. If they, with a less population, dared maintain their independence against the greatest power on earth, shall we have any apprehension of maintaining ours now?

In point of material wealth and resources, we are greatly in advance of them. The taxable property of the Confederate States cannot be less than $22,-000,000,000. This, I think I venture but little in saying, may be considered as five times more than the colonies possessed at the time they achieved their independence. Georgia alone possessed last year, according to the report of our comptroller-general, $672,000,000 of taxable property. The debts of the seven Confederate States sum up in the aggregate less than $18,000,000; while the existing debts of the other of the late United States sum up in the aggregate the enormous amount of $174,000,-000. This is without taking into the account the heavy city debts, corporation debts, and railroad debts, which press, and will continue to press, a heavy incubus upon the resources of those States. These debts, added to others, make a sum total not much under $500,000,000. With such an area of territory—with such an amount of population—with a climate and soil unsurpassed by any on the face of the earth—with such resources already at our command—with productions which control the commerce of the world—who can entertain any apprehensions as to our success, whether others join us or not.

It is true, I believe, I state but the common sentiment, when I declare my earnest desire that the border States should join us. The differences of opinion that existed among us anterior to secession related more to the policy in securing that result by coöperation than from any difference upon the ultimate security we all looked to in common.

These differences of opinion were more in reference to policy than principle, and as Mr. Jefferson said in his inaugural, in 1801, after the heated contest preceding his election, there might be differences in opinion without differences on principle, and that all, to some extent, had been Federalists and all Republicans; so it may now be said of us, that whatever differences of opinion as to the best policy in having a coöperation with our border sister Slave States, if the worst come to the worst, that as we were all coöperationists, we are now all for independence, whether they come or not. [Continued applause.]

In this connection, I take this occasion to state that I was not without grave and serious apprehensions that if the worst came to the worst, and cutting loose from the old Government would be the only remedy for our safety and security, it would be attended with much more serious ills than it has been as yet. Thus far we have seen none of those incidents which usually attend revolutions. No such material as such convulsions usually throw up has been seen. Wisdom, prudence, and patriotism have marked every step of our progress thus far. This augurs well for the future, and it is a matter of sincere gratification to me that I am enabled to make the declaration of the men I met in the Congress at Montgomery (I may be pardoned for saying this) an abler, wiser, a more conservative, deliberate, determined, resolute, and patriotic body of men I never met in my life. [Great applause.] Their works speak for them; the Provisional Government speaks for them; the constitution of the permanent Government will be a lasting monument of their worth, merit, and statesmanship. [Applause.]

But to return to the question of the future. What is to be the result of this revolution?

Will every thing, commenced so well, continue as it has begun? In reply to this anxious inquiry I can only say, it all depends upon ourselves. A young man starting out in life on his majority, with health, talent, and ability, under a favoring Providence, may be said to be the architect of his own fortunes. His destinies are in his own hands. He may make for himself a name of honor or dishonor, according to his own acts. If he plants himself upon truth, integrity, honor, and uprightness, with industry, patience, and energy, he cannot fail of success. So it is with us: we are a young Republic, just entering upon the arena of nations; we will be the architect of our own fortunes. Our destiny, under Providence, is in our own hands. With wisdom, prudence, and statesmanship on the part of our public men, and intelligence, virtue, and patriotism on the part of the people, success, to the full measure of our most sanguine hopes, may be looked for. But if we become divided—if schisms arise—if dissensions spring up—if factions are engendered—if party spirit, nourished by unholy personal ambition, shall rear its hydra head, I have no good to prophesy for you. Without intelligence, virtue, integrity, and patriotism on the part of the people, no Republic or representative government can be durable or stable.

We have intelligence, and virtue, and patriotism. All that is required is to cultivate and perpetuate these. Intelligence will not do without virtue. France was a nation of philosophers. These philosophers became Jacobins. They lacked that virtue, that devotion to moral principle, and that patriotism which is essential to good government. Organized upon principles of perfect justice and right—seeking amity and friendship with all other powers—I see no obstacle in the way of our upward and onward progress. Our growth by accessions from other States, will depend greatly upon whether we present to the world, as I trust we shall, a better government than that to which they belong. If we do this, North Carolina, Tennessee, and Arkansas can not hesitate long; neither can Virginia, Kentucky, and Missouri. They will necessarily gravitate to us by an imperious law. We made ample provision in our constitution for the admission of other States; it is more guarded, and wisely so, I think, than the old Constitution on the same subject, but not too guarded to receive them as fast as it may be proper. Looking to the distant future, and perhaps not very distant either, it is not beyond the range of possibility, and even probability, that all the great States of the north-west shall gravitate this way as well as Tennessee, Kentucky, Missouri, Arkansas, &c. Should they do so, our doors are wide enough to receive them, *but not until they are ready to assimilate with us in principle.*

The process of disintegration in the old Union may be expected to go on with almost absolute certainty. We are now the nucleus of a growing power, which, if we are true to ourselves, our destiny, and our high mission, will become the controlling power on this continent. To what extent accessions will go on in the process of time, or where it will end, the future will determine. So far as it concerns States of the old Union, they will be upon no such principle of *reconstruction* as now spoken of, but upon *reorganization* and new assimilation. [Loud applause.] Such are some of the glimpses of the future as I catch them.

But at first we must necessarily meet with the inconveniences, and difficulties, and embarrassments incident to all changes of government. These will be felt in our postal affairs and changes in the channels of trade. These inconveniences, it is to be hoped, will be but temporary, and must be borne with patience and forbearance.

As to whether we shall have war with our late confederates, or whether all matters of difference between us shall be amicably settled, I can only say, that *the prospect for a peaceful adjustment is better, so far as I am informed, than it has been.*

The prospect of war, is at least not so threatening as it had been. The idea of coercion shadowed forth in President LINCOLN'S inaugural, seems not to be followed up thus far so vigorously as was expected. Fort Sumter, it is believed, will soon be evacuated. What course will be pursued towards Fort Pickens, and the other forts on the Gulf, is not so well understood. It is to be greatly desired that all of them should be surrendered. Our object is *Peace,* not only with the North, but with the world. All matters relating to the public property, public liabilities of the Union when we were members of it, we are ready and willing to adjust and settle, upon the principles of right, equality, and good faith. War can be of no more benefit to the North, than to us. The idea of coercing us, or subjugating us, is utterly preposterous. Whether the intention of evacuating Fort Sumter, is to be received as an evidence of a desire for a peaceful solution of our difficulties with the United States, or the result of necessity, I will not undertake to say. I would fain hope the former. Rumors are afloat, however, that it is the result of necessity. All I can say to you, therefore, on that point is, keep your armor bright, and your powder dry. [Enthusiastic applause.]

The surest way to secure peace, is to show your ability to maintain your rights. The principles and position of the present Administration of the United States—the Republican Party—present some puzzling questions. While it is a fixed principle with them, never to allow the increase of a foot of Slave Territory, they seem to be equally determined not to part with an inch " of the accursed soil." Notwithstanding their clamor against the institution, they seem to be equally opposed to getting more, or letting go what they have got. They were ready to fight on the accession of Texas, and are equally ready to fight now on her secession. Why is this? How can this strange paradox be accounted for? There seems to be but one rational solution—and that is, notwithstanding their professions of humanity, they are disinclined to give up the benefits they derive from slave labor. Their philanthropy yields to their interest. The idea of enforcing the laws, has but one object, and that is a collection of the taxes, raised by slave labor to swell the fund necessary to meet their heavy appropriations. The spoils is what they are after—though they come from the labor of the slave. [Continued applause.]

Mr. STEPHENS reviewed at some length the extravagance and profligacy of appropriations by the Congress of the United States for several years past, and in this connection took occasion to allude to another one of the great improvements in our new Constitution, which is a clause prohibiting Congress from appropriating any money from the Treasury except by a two-thirds vote, unless it be for some object which the Executive may say is necessary to carry on the Government.

When it is thus asked for and estimated, he continued, the majority may appropriate. This was a new feature.

Our fathers have guarded the assessment of taxes, by insisting that representation and taxation should go together. This was inherited from the mother country, England. It was one of the principles upon which the Revolution had been fought. Our fathers also provided in the old Constitution that all appropriation bills should originate in the Representative branch of Congress ; but our new Constitution went a step further, and guarded not only the pockets of the people, but also the public money, after it was taken from their pockets.

He alluded to the difficulties and embarrassments which seemed to surround the question of a peaceful solution of the controversy with the old Government. How can it be done? is perplexing many minds. The President seems to think that he cannot recognize our independence, nor can he, with and by the advice of the Senate, do so. The Constitution makes no such provision. A general Convention of all the States has been suggested by some.

Without proposing to solve the difficulty, he barely made the following suggestion :

That as the admission of States by Congress under the Constitution was an act of legislation, and in the nature of a contract or compact between the States admitted and the others admitting, *why should not this contract or compact be regarded as of like character with all other civil contracts—liable to be rescinded by mutual agreement of both parties?* The seceding States have rescinded it on their part. Why cannot the whole question be settled, if the North desire peace, simply by the Congress, in both branches, with the concurrence of the President, giving their consent to the separation, and a recognition of independence? This he merely offered as a suggestion, as one of the ways in which it might be done with much less violence to constructions of the Constitution than many other acts of that Government. [Applause.] The difficulty has to be solved in some way or other—this may be regarded as a fixed fact.

Several other points were alluded to by Mr. S., particularly as to the policy of the new Government towards foreign nations, and our commercial relations with them. Free trade, as far as practicable, would be the policy of this Government. No higher duties would be imposed on foreign importations than would be necessary to support the Government upon the strictest economy.

In olden times the olive branch was considered the emblem of peace, we will send to the nations of the earth another and far more potential emblem of the same, the Cotton Plant. The present duties were levied with a view of meeting the present necessities and exigencies, in preparation for war, if need be; but if we have peace, and he hoped we might, and trade should resume its proper course, a *duty of ten per cent. upon foreign importations, it was thought, might be sufficient to meet the expenditures of the Government.* If some articles should be left on the free list, as they now are, such as breadstuffs, &c., then, of course, duties upon others would have to be higher—but in no event to an extent to embarrass trade and commerce. He concluded in an earnest appeal for union and harmony, on the part of all the people in support of the common cause, in which we were all enlisted, and upon the issues of which such great consequences depend.

If, said he, we are true to ourselves, true to our cause, true to our destiny, true to our high mission, in presenting to the world the highest type of civilization ever exhibited by man—there will be found in our Lexicon no such word as FAIL.

Mr. STEPHENS took his seat amid a burst of enthusiasm and applause, such as the Athenæum has never had displayed within its walls, within "the recollection of the oldest inhabitant."

—*Savannah Republican.*

Doc. 49.—THE VESSEL FIRED INTO AT CHARLESTON.

The vessel fired into from the forts on Morris Island has arrived at Savannah. The schooner is the R. H. Shannon, Capt. Monts, of Boston, and she was bound for this city with a cargo of ice, consigned to A. Haywood. On Wednesday she was shrouded for many hours in a dense fog, during which she drifted through mistake over the Charleston bar. Soon after the fog lifted, the captain, not knowing his whereabouts, found himself nearly abreast of the fort on Morris Island, and while cogitating over his latitude and longitude, he was greeted with a salute from the fort. He immediately ran up his colors—the stars and stripes—but that demonstration seemed an unsatisfactory answer to their summons. Several shot (thirty-two's) were fired into his rigging, one of which passed through his mainsail and another through his topsail. In the midst of his dilemma, not knowing where he was or the object of this hostile demonstration, a boat from Fort Sumter came to his relief, and being made acquainted with the facts, he lost no time in putting to sea. The schooner suffered no material damage from the shots, though one of them came most uncomfortably near the head of one of the crew. Capt. M. thinks there is no mistake about the Morris Island boys being excellent marksmen.

—*Savannah Republican,* April 5.

Doc. 50.—THE UNITED STATES FLEET AT CHARLESTON.

The following list embraces the names, with armaments and troops, of the fleet despatched from New York and Washington to Charleston harbor, for the relief of Fort Sumter:—

VESSELS OF WAR.

Steam sloop-of-war Pawnee, Captain S. C. Rowan, 10 guns and 200 men. The Pawnee sailed from Washington, with sealed orders, on the morning of Saturday, April 6.

Steam sloop-of-war Powhatan, Captain F. D. Porter, 11 guns and 275 men. The Powhatan sailed from the Brooklyn Navy Yard on Saturday afternoon, April 6.

Revenue cutter Harriet Lane, Captain J. Faunce, 5 guns and 96 men. On Saturday, April 6, the Harriet Lane exchanged her revenue flag for the United States navy flag, denoting her transfer to the Government naval service, and sailed suddenly on last Monday morning, with sealed orders.

THE STEAM TRANSPORTS.

Atlantic, 358 troops, composed of Companies A and M of the Second artillery, Companies C and H of the Second infantry, and Company A of sappers and miners from West Point. The Atlantic sailed from the stream at 5 o'clock on Sunday morning last, April 7.

Baltic, 160 troops, composed of Companies C and D, recruits, from Governor's and Bedloe's islands. The Baltic sailed from Quarantine at 7 o'clock on Tuesday morning last, April 9.

Illinois, 300 troops, composed of Companies B, E, F, G and H, and a detachment from Company D, all recruits from Governor's and Bedloe's islands, together with two companies of the Second infantry, from Fort Hamilton. The Illinois sailed from Quarantine on Tuesday morning at 6 o'clock.

THE STEAMTUGS.

Two steamtugs, with a Government official on each, bearing sealed despatches, were also sent. The Yankee left New York on Monday evening, 8th, and the Uncle Ben on Tuesday night.

THE LAUNCHES.

Nearly thirty of these boats—whose services are most useful in effecting a landing of troops over shoal water, and for attacking a discharging battery when covered with sand and gunny bags—have been taken out by the Powhatan and by the steam transports Atlantic, Baltic and Illinois.

RECAPITULATION.

VESSELS.	GUNS.	MEN.
Sloop-of-war Pawnee	10	200
Sloop-of-war Powhatan	11	275
Cutter Harriet Lane	5	96
Steam transport Atlantic	—	353
Steam transport Baltic	—	160
Steam transport Illinois	—	300
Steamtug Yankee	Ordinary crew.	
Steamtug Uncle Ben	Ordinary crew.	
Total number of vessels		8
Total number of guns (for marine service)		26
Total number of men and troops		1,380

It is understood that several transports are soon to be chartered, and despatched to Charleston with troops and supplies.

—*N. Y. Herald.*

Doc. 51. — CONFEDERATE COMMISSIONERS' FINAL LETTER TO SECRETARY SEWARD.

WASHINGTON, April 9, 1861.

Hon. Wm. H. Seward, Secretary of State of the United States, Washington.

The " memorandum"* dated Department of State, Washington, March 15, 1861, has been received through the hands of Mr. J. T. Pickett, Secretary to this Commission, who, by the instructions of the undersigned, called for it on yesterday at the Department.

In that memorandum you correctly state the purport of the official note addressed to you by the undersigned on the 12th ult. Without repeating the contents of that note in full, it is enough to say here that its object was to invite the Government of the United States to a friendly consideration of the relation between the United States and the seven States lately of the Federal Union, but now separated from it by the sovereign will of their people, growing out of the pregnant and undeniable fact that those people have rejected the authority of the United States and established a Government of their own. Those relations had to be friendly or hostile. The people of the old and new Governments, occupying contiguous territories, had to stand to each

* See Document 47.

other in the relation of good neighbors, each seeking their happiness and pursuing their national destinies in their own way, without interference with the other, or they had to be rival and hostile nations. The Government of the Confederate States had no hesitation in electing its choice in this alternative. Frankly and unreserved, seeking the good of the people who had intrusted them with power, in the spirit of humanity, of the Christian civilization of the age, and of that Americanism which regards the true welfare and happiness of the people, the Government of the Confederate States, among its first acts, commissioned the undersigned to approach the Government of the United States with the olive branch of peace, and to offer to adjust the great questions pending between them in the only way to be justified by the consciences and common sense of good men who had nothing but the welfare of the people of the two Confederacies at heart.

Your Government has not chosen to meet the undersigned in the conciliatory and peaceful spirit in which they are commissioned. Persistently wedded to those fatal theories of construction of the Federal Constitution always rejected by the statesmen of the South, and adhered to by those of the Administration school, until they have produced their natural and often predicted result of the destruction of the Union, under which we might have continued to live happily and gloriously together, had the spirit of the ancestry who framed the common Constitution, animated the hearts of all their sons, you now, with a persistence untaught and uncured by the ruin which has been wrought, refuse to recognize the great fact presented to you of a complete and successful revolution; you close your eyes to the existence of the Government founded upon it, and ignore the high duties of moderation and humanity which attach to you in dealing with this great fact. Had you met these issues with the frankness and manliness with which the undersigned were instructed to present them to you and treat them, the undersigned had not now the melancholy duty to return home and tell their Government and their countrymen, that their earnest and ceaseless efforts in behalf of peace had been futile, and that the Government of the United States meant to subjugate them by force of arms. Whatever may be the result, impartial history will record the innocence of the Government of the Confederate States, and place the responsibility of the blood and mourning that may ensue upon those who have denied the great fundamental doctrine of American liberty, that "governments derive their just powers from the consent of the governed," and who have set naval and land armaments in motion to subject the people of one portion of the land to the will of another portion. That that can never be done while a freeman survives in the Confederate States to wield a weapon, the undersigned appeal to past history to prove. These military demonstrations against the people of the seceded States are certainly far from being in keeping and consistency with the theory of the Secretary of State, maintained in his memorandum, that these States are still component parts of the late American Union, as the undersigned are not aware of any constitutional power in the President of the United States to levy war without the consent of Congress, upon a foreign people, much less upon any portion of the people of the United States.

The undersigned, like the Secretary of State, have no purpose to "invite or engage in discussion" of the subject on which their two Governments are so irreconcilably at variance. It is this variance that has broken up the old Union, the disintegration of which has only begun. It is proper, however, to advise you that it were well to dismiss the hopes you seem to entertain that, by any of the modes indicated, the people of the Confederate States will ever be brought to submit to the authority of the Government of the United States. You are dealing with delusions, too, when you seek to separate our people from our Government and to characterize the deliberate, sovereign act of the people as a "perversion of a temporary and partisan excitement." If you cherish these dreams you will be awakened from them and find them as unreal and unsubstantial, as others in which you have recently indulged. The undersigned would omit the performance of an obvious duty were they to fail to make known to the Government of the United States that the people of the Confederate States have declared their independence with a full knowledge of all the responsibilities of that act, and with as firm a determination to maintain it by all the means with which nature has endowed them as that which sustained their fathers when they threw off the authority of the British crown.

The undersigned clearly understand that you have declined to appoint a day to enable them to lay the objects of the mission with which they are charged, before the President of the United States, because so to do would be to recognize the independence and separate nationality of the Confederate States. This is the vein of thought that pervades the memorandum before us. The truth of history requires that it should distinctly appear upon the record that the undersigned did not ask the Government of the United States to recognize the independence of the Confederate States. They only asked audience to adjust, in a spirit of amity and peace, the new relations springing from a manifest and accomplished revolution in the Government of the late Federal Union. Your refusal to entertain these overtures for a peaceful solution, the active naval and military preparation of this Government, and a formal notice to the commanding general of the Confederate forces in the harbor of Charleston, that the President intends to provision Fort Sumter by forcible means, if necessary, are viewed by the undersigned, and can only be received by the world, as a declaration of war against the Confederate States; for the President of the United States knows that Fort Sumter cannot be provisioned without the effusion of blood. The undersigned, in behalf of their Government and people, accept the gage of battle thus thrown down to them; and appealing to God and the judgment of mankind for the righteousness of their cause, the people of the Confederate States will defend their liberties to the last against this flagrant and open attempt at their subjugation to sectional power.

This communication cannot be properly closed without adverting to the date of your memorandum. The official note of the undersigned, of the 12th March, was delivered to the Assistant Secretary of State on the 13th of that month, the gentleman who delivered it, informing him that the Secretary of this Commission would call at 12 o'clock, noon, on the next day, for an answer. At the appointed hour, Mr. Pickett did call, and was informed by the

Assistant Secretary of State that the engagements of the Secretary of State, had prevented him from giving the note his attention. The Assistant Secretary of State then asked for the address of Messrs. Crawford and Forsyth, the members of the Commission then present in this city, took note of the address on a card, and engaged to send whatever reply might be made to their lodgings. Why this was not done it is proper should be here explained. The memorandum is dated March 15, and was not delivered until April 8. Why was it withheld during the intervening twenty-three days? In the postscript to your memorandum you say it "was delayed, as was understood, with their (Messrs. Forsyth and Crawford's) consent." This is true; but it is also true that on the 15th of March Messrs. Forsyth and Crawford were assured by a person occupying a high official position in the Government, and who, as they believed, was speaking by authority, that Fort Sumter would be evacuated within a very few days, and that no measure changing the existing *status* prejudicially to the Confederate States, as respects Fort Pickens, was then contemplated, and these assurances were subsequently repeated, with the addition that any contemplated change as respects Pickens, would be notified to us. On the 1st of April we were again informed that there might be an attempt to supply Fort Sumter with provisions, but that Gov. Pickens should have previous notice of this attempt. There was no suggestion of any reënforcements. The undersigned did not hesitate to believe that these assurances expressed the intentions of the Administration at the time, or at all events of prominent members of that Administration. This delay was assented to, for the express purpose of attaining the great end of the mission of the undersigned, to wit: A pacific solution of existing complications. The inference deducible from the date of your memorandum, that the undersigned had, of their own volition and without cause, consented to this long hiatus in the grave duties with which they were charged, is therefore not consistent with a just exposition of the facts of the case. The intervening twenty-three days were employed in active unofficial efforts, the object of which was to smooth the path to a pacific solution, the distinguished personage alluded to coöperating with the undersigned; and every step of that effort is recorded in writing, and now in possession of the undersigned and of their Government. It was only when all these anxious efforts for peace had been exhausted, and it became clear that Mr. Lincoln had determined to appeal to the sword to reduce the people of the Confederate States to the will of the section or party whose President he is, that the undersigned resumed the official negotiation temporarily suspended, and sent their Secretary for a reply to their official note of March 12.

It is proper to add that, during these twenty-three days, two gentlemen of official distinction as high as that of the personage hitherto alluded to aided the undersigned as intermediaries in these unofficial negotiations for peace.

The undersigned, Commissioners of the Confederate States of America, having thus made answer to all they deem material in the memorandum filed in the Department on the 15th of March last, have the honor to be, JOHN FORSYTH,
MARTIN J. CRAWFORD,
A. B. ROMAN,

A true copy of the original by one delivered to

Mr. F. W. Seward, Assistant Secretary of State of the United States, at 8 o'clock in the evening of April 9, 1861.
Attest, J. T. PICKETT,
Secretary, &c., &c.

MR. SEWARD IN REPLY TO THE COMMISSIONERS, ACKNOWLEDGES THE RECEIPT OF THEIR LETTER, BUT DECLINES TO ANSWER IT.

DEPARTMENT OF STATE, ?
WASHINGTON, April 10, 1861. $

Messrs. Forsyth, Crawford, and Roman, having been apprised by a memorandum which has been delivered to them, that the Secretary of State is not at liberty to hold official intercourse with them, will, it is presumed, expect no notice from him of the new communication which they have addressed to him under date of the 9th inst., beyond the simple acknowledgment of the receipt thereof, which he hereby very cheerfully gives.

A true copy of the original received by the Commissioners of the Confederate States, this 10th day of April, 1861.
Attest, J. T. PICKETT,
Secretary &c., &c.
—*Tribune*, April 19.

Doc. 52.—FORT SUMTER CORRESPONDENCE.

The following is the correspondence immediately preceding the hostilities:
CHARLESTON, April 8.
L. P. WALKER, Secretary of War:
An authorized messenger from President Lincoln, just informed Gov. Pickens and myself that provisions will be sent to Fort Sumter peaceably, or otherwise by force.
G. T. BEAUREGARD.

MONTGOMERY, 10th.
Gen. G. T. BEAUREGARD, Charleston:
If you have no doubt of the authorized character of the agent who communicated to you the intention of the Washington Government, to supply Fort Sumter by force, you will at once demand its evacuation, and if this is refused, proceed in such a manner as you may determine, to reduce it. Answer.
L. P. WALKER, Sec. of War.

CHARLESTON, April 10.
L. P. WALKER, Secretary of War:
The demand will be made to-morrow at 12 o'clock.
G. T. BEAUREGARD.

MONTGOMERY, April 10.
Gen. BEAUREGARD, Charleston:
Unless there are especial reasons connected with your own condition, it is considered proper that you should make the demand at an early hour.
L. P. WALKER, Sec. of War.

CHARLESTON, April 10.
L. P. WALKER, Secretary of War, Montgomery:
The reasons are special for 12 o'clock.
G. T. BEAUREGARD.

HEADQUARTERS, PROVISIONAL ARMY, C. S. A. ?
CHARLESTON, S. C., April 11, 1861—2 P. M. $

SIR: The Government of the Confederate States has hitherto forborne from any hostile demonstration against Fort Sumter, in the hope that the Government of the United States, with a view to the amicable adjustment of all questions between the two Governments, and to avert the calamities of war, would voluntarily evacuate it. There was reason at one time to believe that such would be the course pursued by the Government of the United States; and under that impression my Government has refrained from making any demand for the surrender of the fort.

But the Confederate States can no longer delay assuming actual possession of a fortification commanding the entrance of one of their harbors, and necessary to its defence and security.

I am ordered by the Government of the Confederate States to demand the evacuation of Fort Sumter. My Aids, Colonel Chesnut and Captain Lee, are authorized to make such demand of you. All proper facilities will be afforded for the removal of yourself and command, together with company, arms, and property, and all private property, to any post in the United States which you may elect. The flag which you have upheld so long and with so much fortitude, under the most trying circumstances, may be saluted by you on taking it down.

Colonel Chesnut and Captain Lee will, for a reasonable time, await your answer.

I am, sir, very respectfully,
Your obedient servant,
G. T. BEAUREGARD,
Brigadier-General Commanding.
Major ROBERT ANDERSON, Commanding at Fort Sumter, Charleston Harbor, S. C.

HEADQUARTERS, FORT SUMTER, S. C. }
April 11th, 1861. }

GENERAL: I have the honor to acknowledge the receipt of your communication demanding the evacuation of this fort; and to say in reply thereto that it is a demand with which I regret that my sense of honor and of my obligations to my Government prevent my compliance.

Thanking you for the fair, manly, and courteous terms proposed, and for the high compliment paid me,

I am, General, very respectfully,
Your obedient servant,
ROBERT ANDERSON,
Major U. S. Army, Commanding.

To Brigadier-General G. T. BEAUREGARD, commanding Provisional Army, C. S. A.

MONTGOMERY, April 11.

Gen. BEAUREGARD, Charleston:

We do not desire needlessly to bombard Fort Sumter, if Major ANDERSON will state the time at which, as indicated by him, he will evacuate, and agree that, in the mean time, he will not use his guns against us, unless ours should be employed against Fort Sumter. You are thus to avoid the effusion of blood. If this or its equivalent be refused, reduce the fort as your judgment decides to be most practicable.

L. P. WALKER, Sec. of War.

HEADQUARTERS, PROVISIONAL ARMY, C. S. A. }
CHARLESTON, April 11, 1861—11 P. M. }

MAJOR: In consequence of the verbal observations made by you to my Aids, Messrs. Chesnut and Lee, in relation to the condition of your supplies, and that you would in a few days be starved out if our guns did not batter you to pieces—or words to that effect;—and desiring no useless effusion of blood, I communicated both the verbal ob-

servation and your written answer to my communication to my Government.

If you will state the time at which you will evacuate Fort Sumter, and agree that in the mean time you will not use your guns against us, unless ours shall be employed against Fort Sumter, we will abstain from opening fire upon you. Colonel Chesnut and Captain Lee are authorized by me to enter into such an agreement with you. You are therefore requested to communicate to them an open answer.

I remain, Major, very respectfully,
Your obedient servant,
G. T. BEAUREGARD,
Brigadier-General Commanding.
Major ROBERT ANDERSON, Commanding at Fort Sumter, Charleston Harbor, S. C.

HEADQUARTERS, FORT SUMTER, S. C. }
2.30 A. M., April 12, 1861. }

GENERAL: I have the honor to acknowledge the receipt of your second communication of the 11th inst., by Col. Chesnut, and to state, in reply, that cordially uniting with you in the desire to avoid the useless effusion of blood, I will, if provided with the proper and necessary means of transportation, evacuate Fort Sumter by noon on the 15th instant, should I not receive, prior to that time, controlling instructions from my Government, or additional supplies; and that I will not, in the mean time, open my fire upon your forces, unless compelled to do so by some hostile act against this fort, or the flag of my Government by the forces under your command, or by some portion of them, or by the perpetration of some act showing a hostile intention on your part against this fort, or the flag it bears.

I have the honor to be, General,
Your obedient servant,
ROBERT ANDERSON,
Major U. S. A. Commanding.
To Brigadier-General G. T. BEAUREGARD, Commanding Provisional Army, C. S. A.

FORT SUMTER, S. C. }
April 12, 1861, 3.20 A. M. }

SIR: By authority of Brigadier-General Beauregard, commanding the Provisional Forces of the Confederate States, we have the honor to notify you that he will open the fire of his batteries on Fort Sumter in one hour from this time.

We have the honor to be, very respectfully,
Your obedient servants,
JAMES CHESNUT, jr.
Aide-de-Camp.
STEPHEN D. LEE,
Captain S. C. Army and Aide-de-Camp.
Major ROBERT ANDERSON, United States Army, Commanding Fort Sumter.

—Charleston Mercury, April 19.
—Times, April 13.

THE BOMBARDMENT.

On Thursday the demand to surrender the fort was made and declined, all the officers having been consulted by Major Anderson in regard to the summons. At about 3 o'clock on Friday morning notice was given us that fire would be opened on us in one hour unless the demand to surrender was instantly complied with. Major Anderson resolved not to return fire until broad daylight, not wishing to waste any of his ammunition. Fire was opened upon us from all points at once. To our astonishment a masked battery of heavy columbiads opened upon us from the part of Sullivan's Island near the floating battery, of the existence of which we had not the slightest intimation. It was covered with brush and other material, which completely concealed it. It was skilfully constructed and well secured; seventeen mortars firing 10-inch shell, 33 heavy guns, mostly columbiads, being engaged in the assault. The crash made by those shots against the walls was terrific, and many of the shells took effect inside the fort. We took breakfast at 6½ o'clock, leisurely and calmly, after which the command was divided into three reliefs, equally dividing the officers and men. The first relief was under the command of Capt. Doubleday, of the Artillery, and Lieut. Snyder, of the Engineer corps. This detachment went to the guns and opened fire upon the Cumming's Point battery, Fort Moultrie, and Sullivan's Island. The iron battery was of immense strength, and most of our shots struck and glanced off again. The fire was so terrific on the parapet of Sumter that Maj. Anderson refused to allow the men to man the guns. Had they been permitted to do so every one of them would have been sacrificed. Fort Moultrie was considerably damaged by our cannonading, a great many of our shots having taken effect on the embrasures. Several shots are known to have penetrated the floating battery; but little damage was done to it.

The reliefs were changed every four hours. We succeeded in dismounting two of the guns on Cumming's Point battery. A new English gun which was employed by the enemy, was fired with great accuracy. Several of its shots entered the embrasures of Sumter, one of them slightly wounding four men. The full effect of our firing we have been unable to ascertain, having nothing to rely upon but the reports of the enemy. Our men owed their safety to the entirely extraordinary care exercised by the officers in command. A man was kept constantly on the look-out, who would cry "shot" or "shell" at every shot the enemy made, thus affording our men ample opportunity to seek shelter. The workmen were at first rather reluctant to assist the soldiers in handling the guns, but they gradually took hold and rendered valuable assistance. But few shots were fired before every one of them was desperately engaged in the conflict.

We had to abandon one gun on account of the close fire made upon it. Hearing the fire renewed with it, I went to the spot. I there found a party of workmen engaged in serving it. I saw one of them stooping over, with his hands on his knees, convulsed with joy, while the tears rolled down his powder-begrimmed cheeks. "What are you doing here with that gun?" I asked. "Hit it right in the centre," was the reply, the man meaning that his shot had taken effect in the centre of the floating battery.

The aim of the enemy was principally directed at our flag-staff, from which proudly waved the Stars and Stripes. After two days' incessant firing, the flag-staff was finally shot away.

The effect of the enemy's shot on the officers' quarters particularly, was terrific. One tower was so completely demolished that not one brick was left standing upon the other. The barracks caught fire on the first day several times, and were put out several times by Mr. Hart, of New York, a volunteer, who particularly distinguished himself for his coolness and bravery, assisted by others. Half a mil-

lion dollars will hardly suffice to repair the damages to the fort. On the second day it caught fire from a 10-inch shell, the danger to be encountered in the attempt to extinguish it being so great that the Major concluded not to attempt it. The effect of the fire was more disastrous than we could have supposed. The subsequent shots of the enemy took more effect in consequence; the walls were weakened, and we were more exposed. The main gates were destroyed by the fire, thus leaving us exposed to the murderous fire of the enemy. Five hundred men could have formed on the gorge and marched on us without our being able to oppose them. The fire surrounded the fort on all sides. Fearful that the walls might crack, and the shells pierce and prostrate them, we commenced taking the powder out of the magazine before the fire had fully enveloped it. We took 96 barrels of powder out, and threw them into the sea, leaving 200 barrels in. Owing to a lack of cartridges, we kept five men inside the magazine, sewing as we wanted them, thus using up our shirts, sheets, blankets, and all the available material in the fort. When we were finally obliged to close the magazine, and our material for cartridges was exhausted, we were left destitute of any means to continue the contest. We had eaten our last biscuit thirty-six hours before. We came very near being stifled with the dense livid smoke from the burning buildings. The men lay prostrate on the ground, with wet handkerchiefs over their mouths and eyes, gasping for breath. It was a moment of imminent peril. If an eddy of wind had not ensued, we all, probably, should have been suffocated. The crashing of the shot, the bursting of the shells, the falling of walls, and the roar of the flames, made a pandemonium of the fort. We nevertheless kept up a steady fire. Toward the close of the day ex-Senator Wigfall made his appearance at the embrasure with a white handkerchief on the end of a sword, and begged for admittance. He asked to see Major Anderson. While Wigfall was in the act of crawling through the embrasure, Lieut. Snyder called out to him, "Major Anderson is at the main gate." He passed through the embrasure into the casemate, paying no attention to what the Lieutenant had said. Here he was met by Capt. Foster, Lieut. Mead, and Lieut. Davis. He said: "I wish to see Major Anderson; I am Gen. Wigfall, and come from Gen. Beauregard."

He then added in an excited manner, "Let us stop this firing. You are on fire and your flag is down. Let us quit."

Lieut. Davis replied, "No, Sir, our flag is not down. Step out here and you will see it waving over the ramparts."

"Let us quit this," said Wigfall. "Here's a white flag, will anybody wave it out of the embrasure?"

One of the officers replied, "That is for you to do, if you choose."

Wigfall responded, "If there is no one else to do it, I will," and jumping into the embrasure waved the flag toward Moultrie. The firing still continued from Moultrie and the batteries of Sullivan's Island. In answer to his repeated requests one of the officers said "one of our men may hold the flag," and Corporal Binghurst jumped into the embrasure. The shot continuing to strike all around him, he jumped down again, after having waved the flag a few moments, and said, "Damn it, they don't respect this flag, they are firing at it."

Wigfall replied, "They fired at me two or three times, and I stood it; and I should think that you might stand it once."

Wigfall then said, "If you will show a white flag from your ramparts they will cease firing."

Lieut. Davis replied, "If you request that a flag shall be shown there while you hold a conference with Major Anderson, and for that purpose alone, it may be done."

At this point Major Anderson came up. Wigfall said, "I am Gen. Wigfall, and come from Gen. Beauregard, who wishes to stop this."

Major Anderson, rising on his toes, and coming down firmly upon his heels replied, " Well, Sir."

"Major Anderson," said Wigfall, "you have defended your flag nobly, Sir. You have done all that is possible for men to do, and Gen. Beauregard wishes to stop the fight. On what terms, Major Anderson, will you evacuate this Fort?"

Major Anderson's reply was, "Gen. Beauregard is already acquainted with my only terms."

"Do I understand that you will evacuate upon the terms proposed the other day?"

"Yes, Sir, and on those conditions only," was the reply of the Major.

"Then, Sir," said Wigfall, " I understand, Major Anderson, that the fort is to be ours?"

"On those conditions only, I repeat."

"Very well," said Wigfall, and he retired.

A short time afterward a deputation, consisting of Senator Chesnut, Roger A. Pryor, Capt. Lee, and W. Porcher Miles, came from Gen. B., and had an interview with Major Anderson; when it came out that Wigfall had no "authority to speak for Gen. Beauregard, but acted on his own hook." "Then," said Lieut. Davis, "we have been sold," and Major Anderson, perceiving the state of the case, ordered the American flag to be raised to its place.

The deputation, however, requested him to keep the flag down till they could communicate with Gen. Beauregard, as matters were liable to be complicated. They left, and between two and three hours after, the garrison meanwhile exerting themselves to extinguish the fire, another deputation came from Gen. Beauregard, agreeing to the terms of evacuation previously proposed, and substantially to the proposals of Wigfall. This was Saturday evening. That night the garrison took what rest they could. Next morning the Isabel came down and anchored near the fort. The steamer Clinch was used as a transport to take the garrison to the Isabel, but the transfer was too late to allow the Isabel to go out by that tide.

The terms of evacuation were that the garrison should take all its individual and company property, that they should march out with their side and other arms with all the honors, in their own way and at their own time; that they should salute their flag, and take it with them.

The enemy agreed to furnish transports, as Major Anderson might select, to any part of the country, either by land or water. When the baggage of the garrison was all on board of the transport, the soldiers remaining inside under arms, a portion were told off as gunners to serve in saluting the American flag. When the last gun was fired, the flag was lowered, the men cheering. At the fiftieth discharge there was a premature explosion, which killed one man instantly, seriously wounded another, and two more not so badly. The men were then formed and marched out, the band playing "Yankee Doodle," and "Hail to the Chief."

Vast crowds of people thronged the vicinity. Remaining on board the Isabel that night, the next morning they were transferred to the Baltic, this operation taking nearly the whole day.

On Tuesday evening they weighed anchor and stood for New York.

ANOTHER ACCOUNT.

On Thursday, the 11th of April, three of Gen. Beauregard's aids appeared at Fort Sumter, and brought a communication which stated that he had refrained from making any hostile demonstration, with the hope of finally obtaining the fort by a treaty, etc. But orders having been received from Jefferson Davis to demand of Major Anderson, in the name of the Southern Confederacy, its surrender or evacuation, Major Anderson replied that he was sorry a request had been made which he could not grant; that he had already gone as far as his sense of duty and his sense of honor would allow. Major Anderson also mentioned to one of his aids, aside and unofficially, that the garrison was out of provisions, having nothing but pork; that they could probably manage to live till Monday, the 15th. The aids carried this reply to Gen. Beauregard, who telegraphed it to Jefferson Davis, and also the remark that Major Anderson was nearly starved out.

The next morning, at half-past 1 o'clock, the aids came down with another communication from Gen. Beauregard to the effect that he had learned that the garrison was nearly starved out, and desired to know of Major Anderson on what day he would evacuate the fort; that Gen. Beauregard would allow him to evacuate and take him to any port in the United States, provided he would agree not to fire upon the batteries unless Fort Sumter should be fired upon.

[Query.—Does this fact show that the despatches to Major Anderson had been opened, and, knowing that an attempt to put provisions into the fort would soon be made, the boats coming in could be fired into, while Major Anderson would be precluded from protecting them?]

Major Anderson replied that he would be obliged to evacuate by Monday, the 15th, before noon, provided Fort Sumter or the flag that it bore was not fired upon. Councils of war were held immediately after the receipt of these two communications, which were unanimous in favor of the answer that was returned. The deputy which brought the second communication consisted of Major Lace, Col. Chism, Roger A. Pryor, Senator Chesnut, and others. Major Anderson's reply was considered by them for fifteen or twenty minutes, when they returned an answer that the batteries would open their fires in one hour. This was at 3½ o'clock on Friday morning. After this reply the deputy of Gen. Beauregard immediately left.

The sentinels were immediately removed from the parapets of Fort Sumter, the posterns closed, the flag drawn up, and an order sent to the troops not to leave the bomb proofs, on any account, until summoned by the drum. At 4.30 a. m. one bombshell was thrown at Sumter, bursting immediately over the fort. After the pause of a few moments the firing became general on the part of the batteries of the Secessionists, doing the greatest credit to the artillerists. The command did not return a single shot until the men had had their breakfast.

As the number of men was so small, and the garrison so nearly exhausted by the several months of siege which they had gone through, it was necessary to husband their strength. The command was therefore divided into three relief, or equal parties, who were to work the different batteries by turns, each four hours.

The first relief opened upon the iron batteries at Cumming's Point, at a distance of 1,600 yards, the iron floating battery, distant 1,800 or 2,000 yards at the end of Sullivan's Island, the enfilading battery on Sullivan's Island, and Fort Moultrie. This was at 7 o'clock in the morning, Capt. Doubleday firing the first gun, and all the points named above being opened upon simultaneously. For the first four hours the firing was kept up with great rapidity; the enthusiasm of the men, indeed, was so great that the second and third reliefs could not be kept from the guns. This accounts for the fact that double the number of guns were at work during the first four hours than at any other time.

Shells burst with the greatest rapidity in every portion of the work, hurling the loose brick and stone in all directions, breaking the windows, and setting fire to whatever woodwork they burst against. The solid shot firing of the enemy's batteries, and particularly of Fort Moultrie, was directed at the barbette guns of Fort Sumter, disabling one ten-inch-columbiad, (they had but two,) one eight-inch columbiad, one forty-two pounder, and two eight-inch sea-coast howitzers, and also tearing a large portion of the parapet away. The firing from the batteries on Cumming's Point was scattered over the whole of the gorge, or rear, of the fort. It looked like a sieve. The explosion of shells, and the quantity of deadly missiles that were hurled in every direction and at every instant of time, made it almost certain death to go out of the lower tier of casemates, and also made the working of the barbette, or upper uncovered guns, which contained all our heaviest metals, and by which alone we could throw shells, quite impossible. During the first day there was hardly an instant of time that there was a cessation of the whizzing of balls, which were sometimes coming half a dozen at once. There was not a portion of the work which was not seen in reverse (that is, exposed by the rear) from mortars.

On Friday, before dinner, several of the vessels of the fleet beyond the Bar were seen through the port-holes. They dipped their flag. The command ordered Sumter's flag to be dipped in return, which was done, while the shells were bursting in every direction. [The flagstaff was located in the open parade, which is about the centre of the open space within the fort.] Sergeant Hart saw the flag of Fort Sumter half-way down, and, supposing that it had been cut by the enemy's shot, rushed out through the fire to assist in getting it up. Shortly after it had been re-raised, a shell burst and cut the halyards, but the rope was so intertwined around the halyards, that the flag would not fall.

The cartridges were exhausted by about noon, and a party was sent to the magazines to make cartridges of the blankets and shirts, the sleeves of the latter being readily converted into the purpose desired. Another great misfortune was, that there was not an instrument in the fort by which they could weigh powder, which of course destroyed all attempt at accuracy of firing. Nor had they tangent scales, breech sides, or other instruments with which to point a gun.

When it became so dark as to render it impossible to see the effect of their shot, the port-holes were closed for the night, while the batteries of the secessionists continued their fire the whole night.

During Friday, the officers' barracks were three times set on fire by the shells, and three times put out under the most galling and destructive firing. This was the only occasion on which Major Anderson allowed the men to expose themselves without an absolute necessity. The guns on the parapet—which had been pointed the day before—were fired clandestinely by some of the men slipping up on top.

The firing of the rifled guns from the iron battery on Cumming's Point became extremely accurate in the afternoon of Friday, cutting out large quantities of the masonry about the embrasures at every shot, throwing concrete among the cannoneers, and slightly wounding and stunning others. One piece struck Sergeant Kearnan, an old Mexican war veteran, striking him on the head and knocking him down. Upon being revived, he was asked if he was hurt badly. He replied: "No; I was only knocked down temporarily," and he went to work again.

Meals were served at the guns of the cannoneers, while the guns were being fired and pointed. The fire commenced in the morning as soon as possible.

During Friday night the men endeavored to climb the flag-staff, for the purpose of fastening new halliards, the old ones having been cut by the shot, but found it impossible. The flag remained fast.

For the fourth time the barracks were set on fire early on Saturday morning, and attempts were made to put it out. But it was soon discovered that red-hot shot were being thrown into the fort with the greatest rapidity, and it became evident that it would be impossible to put out the conflagration. The whole garrison was then set at work, or as many as could be spared, to remove the powder from the magazines, which was desperate work, rolling barrels of powder through the fire.

Ninety odd barrels had been rolled out through the flames, when the heat became so great as to make it impossible to get out any more. The doors were then closed and locked, and the fire spread and became general. The wind so directed the smoke as to fill the fort so full that the men could not see each other, and with the hot, stifling air, it was as much as a man could do to breathe. Soon they were obliged to cover their faces with wet cloths in order to get along at all, so dense was the smoke and so scorching the heat.

But few cartridges were left, and the guns were fired slowly; nor could more cartridges be made, on account of the sparks falling in every part of the works. A gun was fired every now and then only to let the fleet and the people in the town know that the fort had not been silenced. The cannoneers could not see to aim, much less where they hit.

After the barracks were well on fire, the batteries directed upon Fort Sumter increased their cannonading to a rapidity greater than had been attained before. About this time, the shells and ammunition in the upper service-magazines exploded, scattering the tower and upper portions of the building in every direction. The crash of the beams, the roar of the flames, the rapid explosion of the shells, and the shower of fragments of the fort, with the blackness of the smoke, made the scene indescribably terrific and grand. This continued for several hours. Meanwhile, the main gates were burned down, the chassis of the barbette guns were burned away on the gorge, and the upper portions of the towers had been demolished by shells.

There was not a portion of the fort where a breath of air could be got for hours, except through a wet cloth. The fire spread to the men's quarters, on the right hand and on the left, and endangered the powder which had been taken out of the magazines. The men went through the fire and covered the barrels with wet cloths, but the danger of the fort's blowing up became so imminent, that they were obliged to heave the barrels out of the embrasures. While the powder was being thrown overboard, all the guns of Moultrie, of the iron floating battery, of the enfilade battery, and the Dahlgren battery, worked with increased vigor.

All but four barrels were thus disposed of, and those remaining were wrapped in many thicknesses of wet woollen blankets. But three cartridges were left, and these were in the guns. About this time the flag-staff of Fort Sumter was shot down, some fifty feet from the truck, this being the ninth time that it had been struck by a shot. The man cried out, "The flag is down; it has been shot away!" In an instant, Lieut. Hall rushed forward and brought the flag away. But the halliards were so inextricably tangled, that it could not be righted; it was, therefore, nailed to the staff, and planted upon the ramparts, while batteries in every direction were playing upon them.

A few moments after, and a man was seen with a white flag tied to his sword, and desiring admission. He was admitted through an embrasure. In a great flurry, he said he was Gen. Wigfall, and that he came from Gen. Beauregard, and added that he had seen that Sumter's flag was down. Lieut. Davis replied, "Oh, sir! but it is up again." The cannonading meanwhile continued. Gen. Wigfall asked that some one should hold his flag outside. Lieut. Davis replied, "No, sir! we don't raise a white flag. If you want your batteries to stop, you must stop them." Gen. Wigfall then held the flag out of an embrasure. As soon as he had done so, Lieut. Davis directed a corporal to relieve him, as it was Gen. Wigfall's flag. Several shots struck immediately around him while he was holding it out, when he started back, and putting the flag in Wigfall's face, said, "D——n it; I won't hold that flag, for they don't respect it. They struck their colors, but we never did." Wigfall replied, "They fired at me three or four times, and I should think you ought to stand it once." Wigfall then placed the white flag on the outside of the embrasure, and presented himself to Major Anderson, and said that Gen. Beauregard was desirous that blood should not be unnecessarily shed, and also stated that he came from Gen. Beauregard, who desires to know if Major Anderson would evacuate the fort, and that if he would do so he might choose his own terms.

After a moment's hesitation Maj. Anderson replied that he would go out on the same terms that he (Maj. Anderson) had mentioned on the 11th. Gen. Wigfall then said: "Very well; then it is understood that you will evacuate. That is all I have to do. You military men will arrange every thing else on your own terms." He then departed, the white flag still waving where he had placed it, and the stars and stripes waving from the flag-staff which had become the target of the rebels.

Shortly after his departure Maj. Lee, the Hon. Porcher Miles, Senator Chesnut, and the Hon. Roger A. Pryor, the staff of Gen. Beauregard, approached the fort with a white flag, and said they came from Gen. Beauregard, who had observed that the flag had been down and raised again a few minutes afterward. The General had sent over, desiring to know if he could render any assistance, as he had observed that the fort was on fire. (This was perhaps a delicate mode of asking for a surrender.) Maj. Anderson, in replying, requested them to thank Gen. Beauregard for the offer, but it was too late, as he had just agreed with Gen. Beauregard for an evacuation. The three, comprising the deputy, looked at each other blankly, and asked with whom? Maj. Anderson, observing that there was something wrong, remarked that Gen. Wigfall, who had just left, had represented himself to be aide of Gen. Beauregard, and that he had come over to make the proposition.

After some conversation among themselves, they said to Maj. Anderson that Wigfall had not seen Gen. Beauregard for two days. Maj. Anderson replied that Gen. Wigfall's offer and its acceptance had placed him in a peculiar position. They then requested him to place in writing what Gen. Wigfall had said to him, and they would lay it before Gen. Beauregard.

Before this reached Gen. Beauregard, he sent his Adjutant-general and other members of his staff, including the Hon. Roger A. Pryor and Gov. Manning, proposing the same conditions which Major Anderson had offered to go out upon, with the exception only of not saluting his flag. Major Anderson said that he had already informed Gen. Beauregard that he was going out. They asked him if he would not accept of the terms without the salute. Major Anderson told them, No; but that it should be an open point.

At this interview a rather amusing incident occurred. The Hon. Roger A. Pryor of Virginia, being very thirsty, and seeing something in a glass that looked very much like a cocktail, without any remark, took a large tumblerfull. The surgeon, observing it, said to him, "Col. Pryor, did you drink any of that?" Pryor, looking very pale answered, "Yes, quite an amount; a good deal." The surgeon said it was poison. Pryor turned paler yet, and asked what he should do. The surgeon told him to go with him to the hospital.

The last that was seen of Pryor by the officers—he was going out leaning upon the surgeon's arm, presenting a somewhat comical appearance, as he was dressed in a colored shirt, large spurs, belt and sword, with revolver and bowie knife. The doctor gave the great bowie-knife hero a dose of ipecac, which produced the desired effect. Pryor did not express himself as having had a peculiarly pleasant visit to Fort Sumter.

Gen. Beauregard sent down to say that the terms had been accepted, and that he would send the Isabel or any other vessel at his command to convey Major Anderson and the troops to any port in the United States which he might elect.

The evacuation took place about 9½ o'clock on Sunday morning, after the burial with military honors of private Daniel Hough, who had been killed by the bursting of a gun. The men had been all the morning preparing cartridges for the purpose of firing a salute of one hundred guns. This done, the embarkation took place, the band meanwhile playing Yankee Doodle.

No braver men ever lived than the defenders of Fort Sumter, and when all showed such lofty courage and patriotism it would be invidious to make distinctions; but the ardor and endurance of musician Hall of Company E was remarked by every man in Sumter, and the company intend to present him with a testimonial. He was at the firing of the first guns, and fought on all day, and would not accept either of the three reliefs. He was up at the first shot the next day, and worked without cessation till night. His example and words of cheer had great effect. This is the more worthy of remark as he belonged to the musicians, and he was not obliged to enter into the engagement at all.

MINUTES OF AN OFFICER IN FORT SUMTER.

We passed Friday night without firing. A shot or shell came against our walls about every fifteen minutes during the night. We placed a non-commissioned officer and four men at each salient embrasures; partly expecting the boats from the fleet outside, and partly expecting a boat attack from the enemy.

Our own shells and rampart grenades caught fire from the burning of the quarters, and exploded among us in every direction, happily without doing any injury.

The officers were engaged in moving barrels of powder with the flames around them, in tearing down a burning platform near the magazine, and in rescuing public property from the burning buildings, with our own shells and those of the enemy bursting among us.

The interior of the fort is a scene of frightful desolation; it is indescribable.

Mr. Hart, a volunteer from New York, particularly distinguished himself in trying to put out the flames in the quarters, with shells and shot crashing around him. He was ordered away by Major Anderson, but begged hard to be permitted to remain and continue his exertions.

When the building caught fire, the enemy commenced firing hot shot.

Mr. Sweaner of Baltimore was badly wounded in three places by a piece of shell.

Many of the South Carolina officers who came into the fort on Saturday, who were formerly in our service, seemed to feel very badly at firing upon their old comrades and flag.

Commander Hartstene acted like a brother. He was very active in offers of service, and when he went aboard the lighter he ran up the American flag over us. He took charge of the men left behind wounded by the accident. He asked Capt. Doubleday to procure a small piece of our flag for him.

Our flag has several shell-holes through it.

AN IMPROMPTU ACCOUNT OF THE SIEGE OF SUMTER.

While the reporters were seated at a table, busily engaged in transcribing the various statements they had received from the officers of Maj. Anderson's command, an officer who had previously stood quietly in the back-ground, suddenly addressed them in a most emphatic manner, substantially as follows; " Gentlemen of the press, I earnestly entreat that you will clearly set before our countrymen at the North the fact that *Fort Sumter was not evacuated while there was a cartridge to fire, or powder enough left to make one with.* Never did famished men work more bravely than those who defended that fortress, knowing, as they did, that if successfully defended and held by them, there was not even a biscuit left to divide among them. They never would have left it while a protecting wall stood around them, had they been provided with provision and ammunition. Every man was true and faithful to his post, and the public may be assured that hunger and want of ammunition alone caused us to leave Fort Sumter. We were all exposed to a most terrible fire from all quarters, and it was only by exercising the utmost care that the officers were enabled to preserve the men from a terrible slaughter. You may further state, Gentlemen, that Fort Sumter is hardly worth the holding; had there been the full fighting complement of men within its walls, the fort would not have afforded suitable protection for one-half of them. The enemy's shot rained in upon and about us like hail, and more men in Sumter would only have made more havoc. As it was, we are fortunate in having escaped without the loss of one of those brave men who were willing to die for the flag which waved over them. It was a painful sight to all to see the Stars and Stripes finally hauled down, but we all felt that we had done our duty, and must submit. The fort was not surrendered, but evacuated almost upon our own terms."

—*Tribune*, April 19.

OPINIONS OF THE PRESS.

Fort Sumter is lost, but freedom is saved. There is no more thought of bribing or coaxing the traitors who have dared to aim their cannon balls at the flag of the Union, and those who gave their lives to defend it. It seems but yesterday that at least two-thirds of the journals of this city were the virtual allies of the Secessionists, their apologists, their champions. The roar of the great circle of batteries pouring their iron hail upon devoted Sumter, has struck them all dumb. It is as if one had made a brilliant and effective speech, setting forth the innocence of murder, and having just bidden adieu to the cheers and the gas-light, were to be confronted by the gory form and staring eyes of a victim of assassination, the first fruit of his oratorical success. For months before the late Presidential election, a majority of our journals predicted forcible resistance to the government as the natural and necessary consequence of a Republican triumph; for months since they have been cherishing and encouraging the Slaveholder's Rebellion, as if it were a very natural and proper proceeding. Their object was purely partisan—they wished to bully the Republican Administration into shameful recreancy to Republican principle, and then call upon the people to expel from power a party so profligate and cowardly. They did not succeed in this; they *have* succeeded in enticing their Southern *protegés* and some time allies into flagrant treason.

There cannot be a rational doubt that every man who aided or abetted the attack on Fort Sumter is involved in the guilt of treason. That all the besiegers of Forts Sumter and Pickens have incurred the penalty of treason—which is death—is indisputable.

Most of our journals lately parading the pranks of the Secessionists with scarcely disguised exultation, have been suddenly sobered by the culmination of the slaveholding conspiracy. They would evidently like to justify and encourage the traitors further, but they dare not; so the Amen sticks in their throat. The aspect of the people appals them. Democrat as well as Republican, Conservative and Radical, instinctively feel that the guns fired at Sumter were aimed at the heart of the American Republic. Not even in the lowest groggery of our city would it be safe to propose cheers for Beauregard and Gov. Pickens. The Tories of the Revolution were relatively ten times as numerous here as are the open sympathizers with the Palmetto Rebels. It is hard to lose Sumter; it is a consolation to know that in losing it we have gained a united people. Henceforth, the loyal States are a unit in uncompromising hostility to treason, wherever plotted, however justified. Fort Sumter is temporarily lost, but the country is saved. Live the Republic!

No blame is imputed to Major Anderson by the Administration, and no whisper affecting his fidelity and loyalty is tolerated. He acted upon a necessity contemplated by his orders, which was to yield the fort in case he should be encompassed by an overwhelming force, or reduced to an extremity by the want of provisions. According to information which reached here recently, his supplies were expected to be exhausted last Tuesday, and hence the extraordinary efforts which were made here to recruit his enfeebled garrison. Major Anderson himself endeavored to get rid of the laborers who had been employed in the fort, for the purpose of restricting the consumption to his actual military command; but the State authorities refused to permit their departure, and these additional mouths were thus imposed upon his limited stock of provisions. In view of the threatened contingency, an attempt was made to communicate with him on the 4th inst., conveying discretion to abandon the fort, if, in his judgment, it could not be held until supplies could be forwarded. But that and other despatches were intercepted, which put the Secessionists in full possession of the exact circumstances of his condition, and enabled General Beauregard to time his operations, as they were subsequently developed. Then the order cutting off his purchases in the Charleston market was made. The despatch which Lieutenant Talbot took down repeated this discretion, but also announced to him that a vessel with supplies, supported by several ships of war, would be sent to his relief. That despatch could not be delivered, and its general character was anticipated by the instructions of the government, which had been feloniously appropriated before. It will thus be seen, that the Revolutionists were fully informed, not only of the state of the garrison, but of the policy of the government in every essential particular. With their immense force, and numerous batteries, and considering that the storm had dispersed the fleet which had been sent to Major Anderson's relief, or, at least prevented their co-operation, the result is not surprising. —*New York Tribune.*

At all events, the reduction of Fort Sumter and this manifesto of President Lincoln are equivalent to a declaration of war on both sides, between the Confederate and the United States. In a conflict of this sort, there can be but two parties—a Northern and a Southern party; for all other parties will cease to exist. The political principles, organizations and issues which have divided our country and our people, in various shapes and forms, since the treaty of our independence with England, will all be very soon overwhelmed in the sweeping changes of a civil war. It would be folly now to argue what might, could, would, or should, have been done by Southern fire-eaters and Northern disorganizers in 1854, 1860, or by Mr. Buchanan, or by Mr. Lincoln, or by the late session of Congress. Civil war is upon us, and the questions which now supersede all others are: What are the consequences now before us? Where is this war to end? and how and when? What is our duty under this warlike condition of things? and what are the movements and the conditions necessary to change this state of war to a state of peace?

These questions will irresistibly impress themselves upon the mind of every thinking man, north and south. Earnestly laboring in behalf of peace, from the beginning of these sectional troubles down to this day, and for the maintenance of the Union through mutual concessions, we do not even yet utterly despair of arresting this civil war before it shall have passed beyond the reach of reason.

—*N. Y. Herald.*

The "irrepressible conflict" started by Mr. Seward, and endorsed by the Republican party, has at length attained to its logical, foreseen result. That conflict, undertaken "for the sake of humanity," culminates now in inhumanity itself, and exhibits the afflicting spectacle of brother shedding brother's blood.

Refusing the ballot before the bullet, these men, flushed with the power and patronage of the Federal Government, have madly rushed into a civil war, which will probably drive the remaining Slave States into the arms of the Southern Confederacy, and dash to pieces the last hope for a reconstruction of the Union.

To the gallant men, who are so nobly defending the flag of their country within the walls of Fort Sumter, the nation owes a debt of eternal gratitude —not less than to the equally gallant and patriotic spirits, who, in like obedience to the demands of duty, are perilling their lives and shedding their blood in the heroic, but, as yet, unsuccessful endeavor to afford them succor. But, to the cold-blooded, heartless demagogues, who started this civil war—themselves magnanimously keeping out of the reach of bodily harm—we can only say, you must find your account, if not at the hands of an indignant people, then in the tears of widows and orphans. The people of the United States, it must be borne in mind, petitioned, begged and implored these men, who are become their accidental masters, to give them an opportunity to be heard, before this unnatural strife was pushed to a bloody extreme, but their petitions were all spurned with contempt, and now the bullet comes in to decide the issue!

—*N. Y. Express.*

The curtain has fallen upon the first act of the great tragedy of the age. Fort Sumter has been surrendered, and the stars and stripes of the American Republic give place to the felon flag of the Southern Confederates. The defence of the fortress did honor to the gallant commander by whom it was held, and vindicated the Government under which he served. Judging from the result, it does not seem to have been the purpose of the Government to do any thing more. The armed ships which accompanied the supplies took no part in the contest. Whatever may have been the reason for it, their silence was probably fortunate. They could scarcely have forced their way through the heavy batteries which lined the coast, nor could their participation in the fight have changed the result. The preparations of the enemy were too complete, and their forces too numerous, to warrant any hope of success with the number of guns at our command. The fort was bravely defended. It has fallen without loss of life—the ships are on the spot to enforce the blockade of Charleston harbor—Fort Pickens, according to a despatch from Montgomery, has already been reinforced—and every thing is ready for unrolling the next and the far more terrible scene of this great drama.

The Government of the United States is prepared to meet this great emergency, with the energy and courage which the occasion requires, and which the sentiment of the nation demands. The President issues his proclamation to-day, convening Congress for the 4th of July, and calling for *seventy-five thousand volunteers* for the defence of the Union, and the protection of the rights and the liberties of the American people. The people will respond to this demand with alacrity and exultation. They ask nothing better than to be allowed to fight for the Constitution which their fathers framed. Whatever may have been their political differences, there has never been a moment when they were not ready to sink them all in devotion to their common country, and in defence of their common flag. The President's proclamation will be hailed with an enthusiasm which no event of the last twenty years has called forth—with a high-hearted determination to exterminate treason, which will carry terror into the hearts of the Confederates, who have conspired for the destruction of the freest and best government the world has ever seen. —*N. Y. Times.*

The spirit which has been manifested since the assault upon Fort Sumter commenced shows that the anomaly we have too long witnessed, of peace upon one side, and war upon the other, will very speedily be destroyed. Henceforth we shall no longer strive to see how little we can do to strengthen forts, to maintain armies, to fit out fleets, to enforce the laws, and protect the honor of the nation, but how much. We will no longer seek to tie the hands of the Government—to cripple its powers—to unman and degrade it—to strengthen and encourage treason, and to dishearten and humiliate loyalty. The issue is now made up—either this great Republic or its desperate adversaries must be overthrown; and may God defend the right!

Henceforth each man, high and low, must take his position as a patriot or a traitor—as a foe or a friend of his country—as a supporter of the flag of the stars and stripes or of the rebel banner. The contest which is impending will doubtless be attended with many horrors; but all the facts show that it has been forced upon us as a last resort; and war is not the worst of evils. Since the startling events of the last five months have been succeeded by a brutal bombardment of a fort erected at vast expense for the defence of Charleston harbor, which would have been peaceably evacuated if the rebels

had not insisted upon the utter humiliation of the Government, and since the Secretary of War of the Southern Confederacy has threatened to capture Washington, and even to invade the Northern States, while a formal declaration of hostilities is about to be made by the Confederate Congress, we should be wanting in every element of manhood, be perpetually disgraced in the eyes of the world, and lose all self-respect, if we did not arouse to determined action to re-assert the outraged dignity of the nation.

—*Phila. Press.*

Were the Confederate States now a foreign foe, and we had declared war against them, with the *status* of Sumter as it was in the present case, we should regard them as the veriest fools and cowards, had they failed to make the attack before reinforcements could arrive, and so to secure the advantages of their position. And by this estimate they must be judged in this thing. For although the administration at Washington does not regard them as a foreign foe, yet the Confederate States constitute a nation, with its independence declared, and therefore they regard the United States as a foreign foe. In the attack upon Sumter they have done just what the United States would have done with respect to England at the opening of the Revolutionary war; just what any nation would do under the same circumstances. And in fact they have done that thing, which, had they not done, they would have been the subject of scoff and ridicule up and down the whole gamut of Black Republican insolence. The questions which now arise are all with respect to the future. The inflamed and warlike spirit accredited to the Northern cities and free States generally, must not be taken into the account, or we shall plunge into a prolonged, sanguinary, and indecisive conflict, in which the border States will soon become the "dark and bloody ground." A war of conquest and subjugation against the Southern Confederacy, will terminate in inevitable disaster, whatever may be the actual termination of the strife. Such a war must begin, as it has really been anticipated, by a positive purpose on the part of the administration at Washington to reduce the Southern States to political inequality in the Union. Consequently, the alternative of submission to this administration at any time, includes assent to political inequality, and the recognition of a power which has avowed an "irrepressible conflict" with Southern institutions. Whatever successes may attend the United States, therefore, as against the Confederate States, the end must be the recognition of independence of the latter, or the holding them by military power. In the latter case all union is at an end; peace and harmony will be unattainable; and the utter prostration of all business will continue indefinitely. On the other hand, the recognition of the independence of the Confederate States will at once end the strife, restore public confidence, and relieve the enterprises of industry and capital from the embarrassment which now hinders their prosperity, and must in the end overwhelm them with calamity.

—*Baltimore Sun.*

Doc. 53.—THE FIRST DEFEAT OF THE REBELS.

IT is evident that General Scott has once more beaten the enemies of his country by mere force of his admirable stratagetical genius. To do so, he has, as was necessary, suffered not only traitors, but loyal men, to rest under a misapprehension.

Those who remember the impatience with which the American public watched his apparent inaction at one period of the Mexican war, will not have forgotten the shout of admiration which went up from the people, when it was at last discovered that the supposed inaction had been in reality the wisest and shrewdest action; and that by the most masterly display of military strategy he had outwitted the enemy, and obtained a splendid victory, when nought but defeat and disaster stared our army in the face.

He who reads and compares carefully the despatches from Charleston, Montgomery, and Washington, in this morning's journals, can not avoid the gratifying conclusion that that which looks at first blush like a disaster to the government, is in reality but the successful carrying out of an admirable plan of military operations. Before this, the traitors see themselves caught in the toils. In fact, it seems to have sickened the chief traitor, Davis, already; for Montgomery despatches relate that when the news from Charleston came, and the mob serenaded Davis and Walker, "the former was not well and did not appear;" and even his secretary was costive of words, and "declined to make a speech."

The facts which tend to the conclusion we have pointed out, may be summed up as follows:

General Scott has been averse to the attempt to reënforce Fort Sumter. He saw that it would cost men and vessels, which the Government could not spare just now.

As an able general, he saw that Sumter and Charleston were points of no military importance, and would only need valuable men to hold, if we took them—with no adequate advantage gained.

He saw that the two keys of the position were Fort Pickens in the Gulf, and Washington, the capital.

He knew that Davis had not generalship to perceive that on the 4th of March, and for some weeks afterward, it would have been almost impossible for the Federal Government to defend Washington against such a force as the traitors had already collected before Sumter, and which could be marched at any time on a capital not yet prepared for defence—not yet even purged of traitors.

His plans, based on these facts, were at once laid. By every means in his power, he concentrated the attention of traitors and loyal men on Sumter. He must have seen with infinite satisfaction the daily increasing force gathered at Charleston, while the Government lost no time in strengthening the capital. Every hour the traitors spent before Sumter gave them only more surely into the hands of their master.

To make assurance doubly sure, he pretended to leave Fort Pickens in the lurch. It was said to be in danger, when Scott knew that a formidable force was investing it. Men feared that all would be lost by the inaction of the Government, when it was never more shrewdly energetic.

At last Washington was reasonably safe. Forces were gathered. Once more our brave old General saw himself with means in his hands. Then came the armament, popularly believed to be destined for Sumter. The Government said not a word—only asked of the traitors the opportunity to send its

own garrison a needed supply of food. They refused, and—fearing the arrival of the Federal fleet —drunk and besotted with treason, and impatient to shed the blood of loyal soldiers, they made the attack.

Scarce had they begun when they saw, with evident terror, ships hovering about the harbor's mouth; they plied their cannon in desperate haste; but no ship came in to Anderson's help. What was the matter?

Made bold by the furious thirst for blood, they dared the ships to come in. But no ship offered its assistance to Anderson. More, the guns of Sumter were only directed at the works of the traitors, and Major Anderson evidently tried to fire in such a manner as not to kill men. He did not even try a few bombs on the city, though it is certain, from a letter of one of his own officers, that his guns would reach beyond the centre of Charleston.

What was the matter? Beauregard must have thought the Government officers both fools and cowards. When his own boats were sailing unharmed about the harbor, between Sumter and Moultrie, bearing his orders, was it possible that the forces outside could stand apathetic, while a brave garrison was being done to death? When the battle was to the death, would a shrewd officer neglect to divert his enemy's attention by firing his city?

If it seemed mysterious to us, waiting on Saturday with breathless suspense, it must have seemed incomprehensible to any cool head in the traitor camp.

Still no ships came in—and, in fact, the reports state that only three or four small vessels remained in the offing. After forty hours' cannonade, in which not one man is killed, Major Anderson, an officer of undoubted courage and honor, runs up a white flag, surrenders the fort, and becomes the guest of General Beauregard. Let no man hastily cry traitor! He only obeyed his orders. He made an honorable defence. He took care to shed no blood. He "gave orders not to sight men, but to silence batteries."

Meantime, while the rebels are ignorantly glorifying the victory of five thousand men over eighty, what news comes from Montgomery? The telegraph in the hands of the rebels says:

"Fort Pickens was reënforced last night."

"It is understood that Charleston harbor is blockaded."

Despatches from Lieut. Slemmer, captured by the rebels, gave Davis the first intimation of his defeat? No wonder the rebel chief was "sick," and went to bed! No wonder that his Secretary, Walker, declined to make a speech!

And what from Washington? These significant paragraphs:

"The report that Anderson has surrendered, and is the guest of General Beauregard, has been communicated to the President. The latter was not surprised, but, on the contrary, remarked, 'The supply vessels could not reach him, and he did right.' When he was told that the report was that nobody was injured in Fort Sumter, he seemed very much gratified, and remarked that he regretted that Major Anderson could not be supplied, as that was all he needed.

"The next act in the play will represent a scene at Fort Pickens, in Pensacola harbor."

The position of affairs is this: Charleston is blockaded. Fort Pickens is reënforced by troops which the traitors foolishly believed were destined for Sumter. Washington is secure beyond peradventure. The traitors have, without the slightest cause, opened the war they have so long threatened. The country is roused to defend its assailed liberties, and gathers enthusiastically about the Government, and treason has been checkmated at the first blow it struck. Let them keep Sumter a few weeks.

Let no man cry traitor to Major Anderson! Let no one fear for the energy of the Administration. Let us thank God that brave old General Scott remains to give his loyal heart and wise head to his country's service!

—*Evening Post.*

Doc. 54.—THE PRESIDENT'S SPEECH TO THE VIRGINIA COMMISSIONERS.

To Hon. Messrs. PRESTON, STUART, and RANDOLPH:

GENTLEMEN: As a committee of the Virginia Convention, now in session, you present me a preamble and resolution in these words:

Whereas, in the opinion of this Convention, the uncertainty which prevails in the public mind as to the policy which the Federal Executive intends to pursue towards the seceded States, is extremely injurious to the industrial and commercial interests of the country, tends to keep up an excitement which is unfavorable to the adjustment of the pending difficulties, and threatens a disturbance of the public peace; therefore,

Resolved, That a committee of three delegates be appointed to wait on the President of the United States, present to him this preamble, and respectfully ask him to communicate to this Convention the policy which the Federal Executive intends to pursue in regard to the Confederate States.

In answer I have to say, that having, at the beginning of my official term, expressed my intended policy as plainly as I was able, it is with deep regret and mortification I now learn there is great and injurious uncertainty in the public mind as to what that policy is, and what course I intend to pursue. Not having as yet seen occasion to change, it is now my purpose to pursue the course marked out in the inaugural address. I commend a careful consideration of the whole document as the best expression I can give to my purposes. As I then and therein said, I now repeat, "The power confided in me will be used to hold, occupy, and possess property and places belonging to the Government, and to collect the duties and imports; but beyond what is necessary for these objects there will be no invasion, no using of force against or among the people anywhere." By the words "property and places belonging to the government," I chiefly allude to the military posts and property which were in possession of the government when it came into my hands. But if, as now appears to be true, in pursuit of a purpose to drive the United States authority from these places, an unprovoked assault has been made upon Fort Sumter, I shall hold myself at liberty to repossess it, if I can, like places which had been seized before the Government was de-

volved upon me; and in any event I shall, to the best of my ability, repel force by force. In case it proves true that Fort Sumter has been assaulted, as is reported, I shall, perhaps, cause the United States mails to be withdrawn from all the States which claim to have seceded, believing that the commencement of actual war against the Government justifies and possibly demands it. I scarcely need to say that I consider the military posts and property situated within the States which claim to have seceded, as yet belonging to the Government of the United States as much as they did before the supposed secession. Whatever else I may do for the purpose, I shall not attempt to collect the duties and imposts by any armed invasion of any part of the country; not meaning by this, however, that I may not land a force deemed necessary to relieve a fort upon the border of the country. From the fact that I have quoted a part of the inaugural address, it must not be inferred that I repudiate any other part, the whole of which I reaffirm, except so far as what I now say of the mails may be regarded as a modification.*

Doc. 55.—THE FEELING IN THE CITY OF NEW YORK.

FROM the first announcement that hostilities had actually commenced in Charleston Harbor, and that Major Anderson's garrison of sixty or seventy men were sustaining and replying as best they could, to a fierce bombardment from a force more than one hundred times their number, down to the moment it was announced that he was compelled to strike his flag, the feeling that stirred the people as one man, here, and so far as we can learn, elsewhere also, was too deep, too strong, and will be too enduring, to be characterized by the term excitement. Never have we seen anything like it. While the keen sagacity of the public mind readily detected the absurdity and downright falsehood of many of the despatches, yet those received on Friday night, created a sharp relish for more; consequently, Saturday morning, all the forenoon, and throughout the whole day, business was forsaken or limited to the briefest necessity. At the Stock Board cheers were given for Major Anderson, and the Government stocks stiffened with renewed determination to stand by the country. As despatch after despatch came, like bombs from an enemy's battery, the feeling was depressed or elated according to their character.

The announcement that Fort Sumter was on fire sounded like a knell as well as an impossibility. It was a silly, unnecessary falsehood, or else some calamity had happened within the walls of Fort Sumter, on which it was based. It caused forebodings. "Where is the fleet?" was on all lips. That there had been some unlucky miscarriage, as the public mind had conceived its objects, was quite plain. Finally came the report that the stars and stripes would soon come down, and, later, that they had actually given place to the flag of Rebellion; when, in spite of doubts, and the strong inclination to disbelief, particularly of the statement that, notwithstanding the bombardment had continued nearly

* The fact that the secessionists opened the fight at Charleston before any attempt was made by the Government to reinforce or supply Fort Sumter, is viewed here as an attempt on their part to coerce the Government, and puts the responsibility upon them.—*New York Herald, April* 14.

thirty-six hours, "nobody was hurt," on either side, the feeling reached its climax. It did not find vent in extraordinary manifestations, but crystallized in a deep-seated conviction that a contest had been inaugurated, and an issue joined that would not be suffered to go by default. No compromise now with Rebellion, is the universal sentiment. If there were differences before, there cannot be said to be any now.

Yesterday the churches throughout the city were crowded to overflowing, many persons attending in order to hear what might be disseminated from the pulpit, in regard to the war which had been inaugurated.

While the discourses of some of the preachers made direct and extended allusion to the great event in their churches, it was referred to in the prayers and lessons of the day. Others, doubtful of the authenticity of the news, abstained from any reference to the subject.

During the progress of one of the Fourth-avenue cars down-town, Capt. Miller, with a friend, was quietly discussing the affairs of Government, when their conversation was interrupted by a gentlemanly-looking person, who attributed all the trouble to the " D—d Black Republicans." Capt. Miller, who is a member of the church, but nevertheless a fighting man, turned suddenly upon the individual and said: " Now, look here, Mr., you're a stranger to me, but if you want to join in conversation with me you must come in the character of a gentleman." Stranger suddenly discovered that he had arrived at his destination.

On Saturday evening, a gentleman in the crowd that gathered on Printing-House Square was disposed to rejoice over the news, and expressed the opinion that it was the best way to bring about a settlement. "Settlement did you say, my friend?" responded a six-footer, whose peculiarity of speech indicated that he was raised somewhere in the vicinity of the Green Mountains, "I will tell you what, there is just one way to get a settlement, provided this news is true, and that is by one side or the other getting whipped!" The cheers of the crowd showed how heartily the sentiment was responded to.

Three men, apparently laborers, who were alone reading the despatches as they came, when information came that Anderson had hauled down the American Flag, were so affected that they wept.

As an evidence of the feeling among the representative men of our city, we will state that Commodore Vanderbilt informed our reporter last night that no application had been made to him by the Government in reference to his steamships; but he said, MY STEAMSHIPS ARE AT THE DISPOSAL OF THE GOVERNMENT.

—N. Y. *Tribune*, April 15.

THE RESURRECTION OF PATRIOTISM.

The incidents of the last two days will live in History. Not for fifty years has such a spectacle been seen, as that glorious uprising of American loyalty which greeted the news that open war had been commenced upon the Constitution and Government of the United States. The great heart of the American people beat with one high pulsation of courage, and of fervid love and devotion to the great Republic. Party dissensions were instantly hushed; political differences disappeared, and were as thoroughly forgotten as if they had never existed; party bonds flashed into nothingness in the glowing flame of patriotism ;—men ceased to think of themselves or their parties,—they thought only of their country and of the dangers which menace its existence. Nothing for years has brought the hearts of all the people so close together,—or so inspired them all with common hopes, and common fears, and a common aim, as the bombardment and surrender of an American fortress.

We look upon this sublime outburst of public sentiment as the most perfect vindication of popular institutions,—the most conclusive reply to the impugners of American loyalty, the country has ever seen. It has been quite common to say that such a Republic as ours could never be permanent, because it lacked the conditions of a profound and abiding loyalty. The Government could never inspire a patriotic instinct, fervid enough to melt the bonds of party, or powerful enough to override the selfishness which free institutions so rapidly develop. The hearts of our own people had begun to sink within them, at the apparent insensibility of the public to the dangers which menaced the Government. The public mind seemed to have been demoralized,—the public heart seemed insensible to perils which threatened utter extinction to our great Republic. The secession movement, infinitely the most formidable danger which has ever menaced our Government, was regarded with indifference and treated as merely a novel form of our usual political contentions. The best among us began to despair of a country which seemed incompetent to understand its dangers, and indifferent to its own destruction.

But all this is changed. The cannon which bombarded Sumter awoke strange echoes, and touched forgotten chords in the American heart. American Loyalty leaped into instant life, and stood radiant and ready for the fierce encounter. From one end of the land to the other—in the crowded streets of cities, and in the solitude of the country—wherever the splendor of the Stars and Stripes, the glittering emblems of our country's glory, meets the eye, come forth shouts of devotion and pledges of aid, which give sure guarantees for the perpetuity of American Freedom. War can inflict no scars on such a people. It can do them no damage which time cannot repair. It cannot shake the solid foundations of their material prosperity,—while it will strengthen the manly and heroic virtues, which defy its fierce and frowning front.

It is a mistake to suppose that War,—even Civil War,—is the greatest evil that can afflict a nation. The proudest and noblest nations on the earth have the oftenest felt its fury, and have risen the stronger, because the braver, from its overwhelming wrath. War is a far less evil than degradation,—than the national and social paralysis which can neither feel a wound nor redress a wrong. When War becomes the only means of sustaining a nation's honor, and of vindicating its just and rightful supremacy, it ceases to be an evil and becomes the source of actual and positive good. If we are doomed to assert the rightful supremacy of our Constitution by force of arms, against those who would overthrow and destroy it, we shall grow the stronger and the nobler by the very contest we are compelled to wage.

We have reason to exult in the noble demonstration of American loyalty, which the events of the last few days have called forth from every quarter of the country. Millions of freemen rally with exulting hearts, around our country's standard. The great body of our people have but one heart and one purpose in this great crisis of our history. Whatever may be the character of the contest, we have no fears or misgivings as to the final issue.

—*N. Y. Times*, April 16.

Doc. 56—GEN. BEAUREGARD'S GENERAL ORDERS.

HEADQUARTERS PROVISIONAL ARMY, C. S. A., }
CHARLESTON, S. C., April 14. }
General Orders, No. 20.]

THE Brigadier-general Commanding is happy to congratulate the troops under his command, on the brilliant success which has crowned their gallantry, privations, and hardships, by the reduction of the stronghold in the harbor of Charleston. This feat of arms has been accomplished after a severe cannonading of about thirty-three hours, in which all the troops have indicated, by their daring and bravery, that our cause must and shall triumph.

Fort Sumter, which surrendered yesterday about 1:45 P. M., will be evacuated at 9 o'clock A. M. to-day, and to show our magnanimity to the gallant defenders, who were only executing the orders of their government, they will be allowed to evacuate upon the same terms which were offered to them before the bombardment commenced. Our success should not lull us into a false security, but should encourage us in the necessary preparations to meet a powerful enemy, who may at any time attempt to avenge this, their first check in the present contest.

The commandants of batteries will promptly send in their reports through the proper channels, giving a journal of the firing of their batteries against Fort Sumter, and of the fire of Fort Sumter against their batteries; furnishing the name of those who particularly distinguished themselves, and other incidents relative thereto, in order that the general commanding may be able to make known to the Confederate States' Government, in a proper manner, their bravery and gallantry.

The General is highly gratified to state that the troops, by their labor, privations, and endurance at the batteries, and at their posts, have exhibited the highest characteristics of tried soldiers and he takes the occasion to thank all, his staff, the regulars, the volunteers, the militia, the naval forces, and the numerous individuals who have contributed to the surrender of Fort Sumter.

By order of Brigadier-General Beauregard,

D. R. JONES, Assistant Adjutant General.

—*Charleston Mercury.*

Doc. 57.—A PROCLAMATION.

By the President of the United States.

WHEREAS, the laws of the United States have been for some time past and now are opposed, and the execution thereof obstructed, in the States of South Carolina, Georgia, Alabama, Florida, Mississippi, Louisiana, and Texas, by combinations too powerful to be suppressed by the ordinary course of judicial proceedings, or by the powers vested in the marshals by law: now, therefore, I, ABRAHAM LINCOLN, President of the United States, in virtue of the power in me vested by the Constitution and the laws, have thought fit to call forth, and hereby do call forth, the militia of the several States of the Union to the aggregate number of 75,000, in order to suppress said combinations and to cause the laws to be duly executed.

The details for this object will be immediately communicated to the State authorities through the War Department. I appeal to all loyal citizens to favor, facilitate, and aid this effort to maintain the honor, the integrity, and existence of our national Union, and the perpetuity of popular government, and to redress wrongs already long enough endured. I deem it proper to say that the first service assigned to the forces hereby called forth, will probably be to repossess the forts, places, and property which have been seized from the Union; and in every event the utmost care will be observed, consistently with the objects aforesaid, to avoid any devastation, any destruction of, or interference with, property, or any disturbance of peaceful citizens of any part of the country; and I hereby command the persons composing the combinations aforesaid, to disperse and retire peaceably to their respective abodes, within twenty days from this date.

Deeming that the present condition of public affairs presents an extraordinary occasion, I do hereby, in virtue of the power in me vested by the Constitution, convene both houses of Congress. The Senators and Representatives are, therefore, summoned to assemble at their respective Chambers at twelve o'clock, noon, on Thursday, the fourth day of July next, then and there to consider and determine such measures as, in their wisdom, the public safety and interest may seem to demand.

In witness whereof, I have hereunto set my hand, and caused the seal of the United States to be affixed.

Done at the City of Washington, this fifteenth day of April, in the year of our Lord, one thousand eight hundred and sixty-one, and of the independence of the United States the eighty-fifth.

ABRAHAM LINCOLN.

By the President.

WILLIAM H. SEWARD, Secretary of State.

The following is the form of the call on the respective State Governors for troops, issued through the War Department:

SIR:—Under the Act of Congress for calling out the Militia to execute the laws of the Union, to suppress insurrection, to repel invasion, &c., approved February 28, 1795, I have the honor to request your Excellency to cause to be immediately detailed from the militia of your State the quota designated in the table below, to serve as infantry or riflemen for a period of three months, unless sooner discharged. Your Excellency will please communicate to me the time at about which your quota will be expected at its rendezvous, as it will be met as soon as practicable by an officer or officers to muster it into service and pay of the United States. At the same time the oath of fidelity to the United States will be administered to every officer and man. The mustering officers will be instructed to receive no man under the rank of commissioned officer, who is in years apparently over 45 or under 18, or who is not in physical strength and vigor. The quota for each State is as follows:

Maine	1	Virginia	3
New Hampshire	1	North Carolina	2
Vermont	1	Kentucky	4
Massachusetts	2	Arkansas	1
Rhode Island	1	Missouri	4
Connecticut	1	Ohio	13
New York	17	Indiana	6
New Jersey	4	Illinois	6
Pennsylvania	16	Michigan	1
Delaware	1	Iowa	1
Tennessee	2	Minnesota	1
Maryland	4	Wisconsin	1

It is ordered that each regiment shall consist, on an aggregate of officers and men, of 780. The total thus to be called out is 73,391. The remainder to constitute the 75,000 men under the President's proclamation will be composed of troops in the District of Columbia.

— *World and N. Y. Times.*

OPINIONS OF THE PRESS.

To the simple, dignified, calm, but firm Proclamation of the President of the United States, the loyal States of this Union will respond, "In the name of God, Amen;" and not only 75,000, but five times 75,000 men will be ready to come forward to meet this rampant, insolent rebellion in arms of South Carolina and the States confederated with her in treason, and put it down. This rebellion has wantonly and without provocation, inaugurated civil war, and its first blow has been successful; but even its victory will bring down upon its head a signal defeat and terrible retribution in the end, for it will rouse the loyal States from a forbearance under insult and defiance unparalleled in the history of any Government; and with right for their cause, and force and means able to maintain it, the hour will soon come when South Carolina and her Confederates in Treason will rue the day when, with a spirit worthy of Lucifer, they undertook to break up the best and most beneficent Government on the face of the earth. We have firm trust in God that it will be so.

—*Courier and Enquirer.*

The Government of the United States is prepared to meet this great emergency with the energy and courage which the occasion requires, and which the sentiment of the nation demands. The President issues his proclamation to-day, convening Congress for the 4th of July, and calling for seventy-five thousand volunteers for the defense of the Union, and the protection of the rights and the liberties of the American people. The people will respond to this demand with alacrity and exultation. They ask nothing better than to be allowed to fight for the Constitution which their fathers framed. Whatever may have been their political differences, there has never been a moment when they were not ready to sink them all in devotion of their common flag. The President's Proclamation will be hailed with an enthusiasm which no event of the last twenty years has called forth—with a high-handed determination to exterminate treason, which will carry terror into the hearts of the Confederates, who have conspired for the destruction of the freest and best Government the world has ever seen.

—*N. Y. Times.*

On one point, so far as we have been able to ascertain, perfect unanimity exists among our moneyed men—the Government must be sustained. Every one deplores the terrible calamity which has befallen the Republic. But there is no desire among the merchants or capitalists of New York to shirk the issue, or to evade the responsibilities of the contest. Upon New York will devolve the chief burden of providing ways and means for the war; our financial community accept the duty, and will perform it. This view we find to be universal among moneyed men, including many whose sympathies have heretofore been with the South. If the Government prove true to the country, it need not feel any uneasiness about money. In the opinion of our leading bankers, a hundred millions, over and above the receipts of the Government from customs and land sales, if necessary to defray the expenses of the war for a year from this date, could be readily borrowed in Wall street, at a rate of interest certainly not exceeding that which France and England paid for the money which they borrowed for the Russian war. If for the purpose of bringing the war to an end, and settling this controversy of ours forever, a further sum be requisite, it will be forthcoming. Wall street, so far as we can judge, is ready to sustain the Government heartily and liberally.

—*N. Y. Herald.*

The Confederate Traitors have commenced the war, they have been so long preparing for without obstruction, and their first prize in fight (having previously confined themselves to stealing, under pretense of peace) has been the capture of Fort Sumter and sixty men by a force of five thousand, with nineteen heavy batteries. This inglorious success will cost them dear. Inexcusably and wantonly taking up the offensive, they have at once cut themselves off from all honest sympathy, even in the South, and kindled a patriotic rage that envelopes all parties and all classes throughout the Union States henceforth. The President has issued his proclamation calling out 75,000 men to put down the rebellion, and convening Congress on the Fourth of July. Gov. Morgan of this State, will at once call out a contingent of 25,000 men, and Gov. Curtin of Pennsylvania will do the same. New regiments are already forming rapidly, in anticipation of the proclamation.

—*N. Y. Sun.*

It is now for the people of New England, especially, and of the great North-West, who have so earnestly demanded a vigorous policy, to prove the sincerity of their zeal by rallying to the support of the Government in this hour of its peril. Treason has boldly lifted up its head; it has marshaled its hosts; it has bid impudent defiance to the Government; it has cannonaded and taken a celebrated fortress; its Secretary of War has had the insolence to make a public boast that the Secession flag will float over the national capital before the 1st of May. These rebels and desperadoes have given unmistakable proofs of their earnestness. They must now be checked, or anarchy and misrule will sweep over the whole country like a destructive deluge. Fellow-citizens of the Free States, this is the hour to prove your loyalty—to test your patriotism—to earn the gratitude of your country.

—*N. Y. World.*

The President's proclamation proves him worthy to be the head of the nation. His honest words find an echo in millions of loyal hearts this day. Only these words were needed to seal the speedy doom of treason. To-day, who is not for the Union is against it. To-day he whose heart does not throb, and whose blood does not stir with patriotic fire is a vile traitor. The rebels have chosen war. They have done their best to slay a loyal garrison. Without a single cause of complaint, they have turned their arms against the Union and against the lives of loyal citizens. From to-day dates the extermination of treason from the land. The people will not rest, the nation will not be satisfied, while a traitor is left in arms.

—Evening Post.

It is too late now for concession or compromise; government or anarchy is the only alternative left to us. Forbearance has been useless, and has been construed into evidence of fear or feebleness. It has also excited the cupidity of the rebels, and fostered their aggressive designs. It is no longer with them the assertion of the mere right of secession or separation from the Union. Their avowed purpose is the overthrow of Constitutional Government. With men thus minded it is useless to reason. No compromises will satisfy them; no concessions arrest their anarchical and wicked purposes. They, a small minority of the people, demand that the majority must recognize them as masters, and give up every thing to them—the archives and property and administration of the Government, our Constitution, our flag, our laws, our free institutions—all that, as freemen, is dear to us. To such a demand, freemen, lovers of constitutional government and constitutional rights, can make but one answer. And when the rebel minority that make it try to enforce it by the cannon and the sword, to the cannon and the sword the loyal majority must of necessity also make their appeal, and will do it. The majority have never sought, have never desired—nay, they have studiously avoided—a resort to war. It has been forced upon them. In honor, and in self-defence, they cannot refuse the alternative.

—Commercial Advertiser.

A few words more—as to what we think the President should do, (and the words are more valuable from an opponent than if from a friend,) because acts thus advised by an opponent cannot be complained of, if adopted. *First :* Not another mail should be sent to South Carolina. Twice has our flag been fired upon there, without direct or immediate, overwhelming necessity, and South Carolinians, by their own act, cease to be our countrymen. *Second :* Not another gun, cannon, revolver, or pound of powder should be permitted to go to the seceding States. The President of the United States, through his revenue officers, should instantly estop their exportation, and States should stop their inter-transit trade. *Third :* The Port of Charleston ought to be instantly blockaded. There may be no law for it, but South Carolina has put herself out of the protection of any law of ours. She does not respect us, and we cannot be expected to respect her.

—N. Y. Express.

"Take your places in line." The American flag trails in the dust. There is from this hour no longer any middle or neutral ground to occupy. All party lines cease. Democrats, Whigs, Americans, Republicans, and Union men, all merge into one or two parties—patriots or traitors. For ourselves, we are not prepared for either or any form of government which the imagination might suggest as possible or probable to follow in the wake of a republic. We are for the Government as

handed down to us by our fathers. It was consecrated in blood, and given to us as a sacred legacy. It is ours to live by, and, by the blessing of God, it shall be ours to die by. We will have it and none other. We have no political feuds or animosities to avenge ; we know no cause save to wipe an insult from our flag, and to defend and maintain an assailed Government and a violated Constitution. We care not who is President, or what political party is in power, so long as they support the honor and the flag of our country, we are with them; those who are not are against us, against our flag, and against our Government. "Take your places in line."

—Philadelphia Enquirer.

Henceforth each man, high and low, must take his position as a patriot or a traitor—as a foe or a friend of his country—as a supporter of the flag of the stars and stripes or of the rebel banner. All doubts and hesitation must be thrown to the winds; and with the history of the past spread before us, we must choose between maintaining the noble fabric that was reared by our wise and brave ancestors, under which we have enjoyed so much liberty and happiness, and openly joining the rash, reckless, despotic, cruel, and villanous band of conspirators, who have formed a deep laid and desperate plot for its destruction. The contest which is impending will doubtless be attended with many horrors, but all the facts show that it has been forced upon us as a last resort; and war is not the worst of evils. Since the startling events of the last five months have been succeeded by a brutal bombardment of a fort erected at vast expense for the defence of Charleston harbor, which would have been peaceably evacuated if the rebels had not insisted upon the utter humiliation of the Government ; and since the Secretary of War of the Southern Confederacy has threatened to capture Washington, and even to invade the Northern States, while a formal declaration of hostilities is about to be made by the Confederate Congress,—we should be wanting in every element of manhood be perpetually disgraced in the eyes of the world, and lose all self-respect, if we did not arouse to determined action to re-assert the outraged dignity of the nation.

—Phila. Press.

In this lamentable condition of affairs, what is the duty of the Administration ? We know not what course it has marked out for itself, or what sufficient preparations are made by it to hold its position securely in Washington. The Administration ought to be best advised of its danger and what is required of it in this emergency, and possibly has taken measures which it may deem sufficient for its security. It has sounded the military of the States which can be depended upon for defence, and has got offers of aid. But this force ought at once to be called into the service of the United States, and hurried on to Washington city as if an attack were certain every moment. Fifty thousand volunteers should be called into the service of the National Government, and be so placed that they could, under any circumstances, be within a few hours' reach of the capital. Ten thousand of them should be placed in that city, whether Maryland and Virginia like it or not. A proclamation should be issued calling upon all the Union men of the country, North and South, to hold themselves in readiness to support the Government and the laws. An army of observation should be established at available points, to strike wherever a blow will tell the best the moment that the Secession Rebels make a single aggressive movement against the Government.

—Philadelphia Ledger.

The present presents the most momentous period in the world's history. For many years past the people of the United States have been engaged with a purpose, to exhibit to the nations of the earth the feasibility of a Republican form of Government; for as many years, thus far, the so-called experiment has proved successful, but it is to be now determined whether our supposed success was real or fancied. We are among those who believe, if properly managed, there is strength enough in a Republican form of Government to make it self-sustaining. Let us now test the question; let the strong arm of the law be seen and felt; let the authority of the Government be earnestly asserted; let every right and power of the nation be presented in its own defence, and then let European despotism mock at us if they dare.

—Philadelphia News.

The Secession leaders are relying very largely upon the first shock of battle for the promotion of a general Secession feeling in the Southern States. They ought, however, to consider that the sympathies of honest and sensible men are not likely to go with the wrong-doers. If the General Government commit any wrong or outrage upon South Carolina or Florida, it will be condemned; but if a United States vessel shall be fired into and her men slain for a mere attempt to take food to the Government's troops in the Government's own forts, and if war shall grow out of the collision, no spirit of Secession or rebellion will be created thereby this side the cotton line. Such at least is our opinion, founded upon our conviction that the great mass of our fellow-citizens are sensible and patriotic and just. Who that loves his country would see it humiliated and its honor trampled on?

—Louisville Journal.

The authorities at Washington are now for raising seventy-five thousand troops, and fancy they will do exploits. They ought to reflect that the few they can spare to the South go far from home, into an intensely hostile country, and to them most unpropitious climate. They will have, after the excitement is over, little heart in the business. There will be no laurels to win. The rest of mankind will give them no credit. Even England and France deplore the strife, and offer prayers that it may cease. Every patriot will feel ashamed of the fratricidal war. They will meet an enemy skilled in war, as proud and vain as ever trod a battle-field—an enemy fighting for his home and his firesides, and who can bring into the field any number of fighting men that he may need. We say *any* number, and it is true—one hundred thousand if needed. If they doubt it, they can try the experiment, and it will be another Fort Sumter experiment.

We don't doubt the bravery of the North; but in this contest they will lack the stimulus of their foes, and meet their equals at great disadvantage. Then there is a sentiment in this country that all just governments are founded on the consent of the governed. If a whole tier of States seek other arrangements in government; if their old government is odious to them, and they seek a release from it, and resist with determination the old government, what shall be done about it? There is our Declaration of Independence, and the strong expressions of States when they entered the Union, which, if they do not recognize the right of secession, squint so much that way that they are easily applied to that purpose. It is an odious task to force a government on an unwilling people. Resistance becomes exalted into a patriotic virtue. No matter how little cause really provokes the resistance. How easy it is to inflame the South against this conduct of coercion! What, they will say, is the motive? Is it any love for us that all this blood is shed to retain us in the same Union? No, they will say; they hate us! They abhor slavery and slaveholders! They tried to keep us out of the Union, and they swear it as a part of their religion that they will have no more Slave States! Why do they wish to retain us, but to play the tyrant over us? Why are they not ready to let us go in peace? They preach against us, pray against us, and what do they want with us but to subjugate us—to indulge their preaching and prayer at our expense?

The terms now used in all these irrepressible prints are, rebels, traitors, and the empty threats to punish them. The bluster and gasconade about having a government, only reminds men of George III., who used empty words after they had lost their meaning. We say nothing about the similarity of the cases upon their merits. George & Co. thought the Colonies had no more reason than the Southern States now have; and the latter think they have more reason to rebel than their fathers had, and they know that these threats against them are more imbecile than the threat of His Majesty against the Colonies.

Depend upon it, Messrs. Lincoln & Co., you are wasting treasure and blood to no purpose. All your professions of peace will count nothing. You talk like enemies and act like them. Even these border Slave States, who have stood by their government, who feel a patriotic attachment to the Union their fathers made, are unheeded. Their advice disregarded, and their wise counsels spurned. They ask for peace most earnestly, as essential to a restoration of confidence and salvation of the Union; and Lincoln & Co. call for troops, and are mustering armies, when all the effect will be to gratify their own resentment and make the breach incurable. They mistake altogether our government and people. No power can restore a State to this Union but its people.

—Louisville Democrat.

"We learn that seventy-five thousand troops, the full number called for by the President's proclamation, have been tendered in this State alone, and that one hundred thousand are probably prepared to do military duty. Our people are all alive with patriotism and honest bravery. They will never let the Government languish or go down for want of support."

The quota of six regiments called for from Illinois was full last Saturday night, and enough additional companies were offered to make six regiments more. Altogether, up to Monday night, one hundred and twenty-five companies were offered to the Governor. Of these, sixty were accepted, twenty-five were accepted conditionally, and the remainder ordered to hold themselves in readiness. The work of recruiting still goes on.

—Cleveland Leader.

There is one direction where we can scarcely look for the tears that blind us. When we see the whole-hearted, unselfish devotion of our Northern people, we thank God that we have a country. We thank God for mothers that cheer on their sons, for young wives that have said "go" to their husbands, for widows who have given their *only* sons. It is our solemn belief that, since the proclamation of the President, there has been in this country more earnest, unselfish heroism, more high-minded self-devotion, in one week than in years of ordinary life.

—Independent.

THE UPRISING OF THE COUNTRY.

Let no one feel that our present troubles are deplorable, in view of the majestic development of nationality and patriotism which they have occasioned. But yesterday we were esteemed a sordid, grasping, money-loving people, too greedy of gain to cherish generous and lofty aspirations. To-day vindicates us from that reproach, and demonstrates that, beneath the scum and slag of forty years of peace, and in spite of the insidious approaches of corruption, the fires of patriotic devotion are still intensely burning. The echoes of the cannon fired at Sumter have barely rolled over the Western hills ere they are drowned in the shouts of indignant freemen, demanding to be led against the traitors who have plotted to divide and destroy the country. Party lines disappear—party cries are hushed or emptied of meaning—men forget that they were Democrats or Republicans, in the newly aroused and intense consciousness that they are Americans. The ordeal now upon us may cost our country many lives and much treasure, but its fruits will be richly worth them all. But few weeks have elapsed since babbling demagogues were talking of an Eastern, a Central, a North-western, and a Pacific, as well as a South-western and a Border-State Confederacy: let them now be silent a little, and note the cost of dividing the Union barely once before they talk further of shivering it into five or six fragments. The experience will be conclusive. Let but this trial be surmounted, and no one will again plot the dissolution of the Union for at least half a century.

We feel confident that the President's call for seventy-five thousand militia from all the loyal States will be responded to within thirty days by proffers of more than one hundred thousand from the Free States alone, and that this number can be doubled upon a mere suggestion that the additional number is desired. Any number that may be required will step forward as fast as they may be called for, even though it should be judged best to confront the Secessionists on their frontier with half a million men.

But the Rebels also can muster men enough, while they are as yet far ahead of us in arms and munitions; their weak point is that of finance. With a notorious and abusive champion of Repudiation at their head, they cannot borrow a dollar outside of their own limits, and their first loan of fifteen millions will exhaust the resources of their banks. That sum will just about suffice to put one hundred thousand men in the field in fighting array; it will be utterly exhausted before they shall have been two months on foot. Their banks are already two-thirds broken, and their notes selling slowly in our Northern cities at fifty per cent. of their face: whence are their next funds to be obtained? How are they to defend their two thousand miles of mainly exposed sea-coast and navigable inlets against an undisputed naval ascendency, without more men and unlimited supplies of money?

It is a plain case that they must hurry matters or succumb, and that they must make an immediate dash at our weakest point, the Federal Metropolis. If Jeff. Davis and Beauregard are not on the Potomac within sixty days, their rebellion will stand exposed a miserable failure. They must back their allies in North Carolina and Virginia by a prompt display of force and daring, to which end all their energies must first be directed. We do not believe they will even stop to reduce Fort Pickens if it should be so held as to compel them to besiege it in form. *They cannot wait;* we can; and they will show that they cannot, by a speedy advance on Washington, unless they shall despair of success, and desist from serious effort altogether.

It is cheering then, to know that Washington will be defended by ten thousand men before the close of this week, and that the number will be doubled the next, and quadrupled the week after. That will be enough until we have tidings that Virginia has seceded and Jeff. Davis is this side of the Roanoke: thenceforth the number of volunteers pouring into Washington for its defence, will be limited only by the ability of the Northern and Western railroads to convey them.

We have a civil war on our hands—there is no use in looking away from the fact. For this year, the chief business of the American people must be proving that they have a Government, and that Freedom is not another name for Anarchy. Hundreds of thousands must be temporarily drawn away from peaceful and productive avocations until this point is settled—drawn away just at the time when labor is wanted to sow and plant for the ensuing harvest. But those who will be left behind must work the harder and plant the more, since years of war are usually years of dear bread. Farmers! employ all the help you can pay, and put in all the crops for which you can seasonably and thoroughly prepare the ground, for a season of scarcity is probably at hand. Let each do his best toward preparing for it.

—N. Y. Tribune, April 17.

A despatch from Washington says that the President will to-day issue a proclamation, calling upon the loyal States for seventy-five thousand militia to aid the General Government in enforcing the laws and recapturing the forts and other public property seized by the revolutionists. We have no doubt the call will be responded to with a good deal of alacrity. We doubt, however, whether as many men will be as willing to enlist in the army as are anxious to hold office under the Government.

—Buffalo Courier.

Of all the wars which have disgraced the human race, it has been reserved for our own enlightened nation to be involved in the most useless and foolish one. What advantage can possibly accrue to any one from this war, however prolonged it might be? Does any man suppose that millions of free white Americans in the Southern States, who will soon be arrayed against us, can be conquered by any efforts which can be brought against them? Brave men, fighting on their own soil, and as they believe, for their freedom and dearest rights, can never be subjugated. The war may be prolonged until we are ourselves exhausted, and become an easy prey to military despotism or equally fatal anarchy; but we can never conquer the South. Admit, if you please, that they are rebels and traitors; they are beyond our reach. Why should we destroy ourselves in injuring them?

Who are to fight the battles of sectional hatred in this sad strife? The Seceders will fight; but will the Abolitionists, who have combined with them to overthrow the Union, make themselves food for powder? If this could be so; if ten thousand picked fire-eaters of either side could be arrayed against each other, and would fight, until, like the Kilkenny cats, all were destroyed, the country would be the better for it. But while the Secessionist defends himself, the Abolitionist will sneak in the back ground, leaving those to do the fighting who have no interest in the bloody strife, no hatred against their brethren. The best we can hope is, that, at the end of a fearful struggle, when the country becomes tired of gratifying the spirit of fanaticism, we shall have a peace, through a treaty in which both sides must make sacrifices, but each must agree to respect the rights of the other. How much better to make such a treaty now, before further blood is shed, before worse hatreds are engendered.

— *Utica (N. Y.) Observer.*

To-day come the tidings that the President has made a call upon the Governors of the several States for seventy-five thousand men, and intimates that if more are offered they will be accepted. Prominent men at Washington are leaving for their respective States, to aid in the organization of the troops. In ten days Lincoln will probably have two hundred thousand volunteers at his disposal. With this force he will be enabled to prosecute the John Brown schemes of his party for a time with vigor, and perhaps with success.

— *Patterson (N. J.) Reporter.*

Seventy-five thousand men have been called for, and the War Department will make known the details of the service to the State authorities. We have no doubt that the demands of the Federal Executive will be responded to by the States on which they may be made. It is the imperative duty of all good citizens to desire to see the laws obeyed and all the constitutional obligations of the States fulfilled. None but those who invoke a "higher law," as the rule and guide of their actions, will hesitate to do what the Constitution and the laws require them to do. *Nevertheless, it is to be expected that there will be but little cheerfulness manifested in the obedience to a call which is intended to array in arms citizens of States connected by such numerous ties as have so recently bound together the people of this dissevered Confederacy.* Painful as has been the suspense in which the President's dubious and vacillating course has held the public mind, it is much more so to find the last lingering hope of peace dispelled by this sudden call to arms under circumstances so embarrassing and humiliating.

— *Trenton (N. J.) True American.*

We earnestly pray that the war may be averted. If the Border States, upon the action of which the whole question hinges, determine to remain in the Union, we cannot doubt that they will require a pacific policy to be pursued. If they join the already seceded States, then, as the point to be determined will be whether upon a mere sectional issue the North will fight with the South, the whole question will be presented in a new aspect, and we cannot but believe that cool reflection will then also demonstrate the necessity of a pacific policy. We leave the question at present for the development of future events.

— *Boston Courier.*

Democrats of Maine! The loyal sons of the South have gathered around Charleston as your fathers of old gathered about Boston in defence of the same sacred principles of liberty—principles which *you* have ever upheld and defended with your vote, your voice, and your strong right arm. Your sympathies are with the defenders of the truth and the right. Those who have inaugurated this unholy and unjustifiable war are no friends of yours, no friends of Democratic Liberty. Will you aid them in their work of subjugation and tyranny?

When the Government at Washington calls for volunteers or recruits to carry on the work of subjugation and tyranny under the specious phrase of "enforcing the laws," "retaking and protecting the public property" and "collecting the revenue," let every Democrat fold his arms and bid the minions of tory despotism do a tory despot's work. Say to them fearlessly and boldly, in the language of England's great Lord, the Earl of Chatham, whose bold words in behalf of the struggling Colonies of America, in the dark hours of the Revolution, have enshrined his name in the heart of every friend of freedom and immortalized his fame wherever the name of liberty is known—say in his thrilling language: "If I were a Southerner, as I am a Northerner, while a foreign troop was landed in my country, I would never lay down my arms—*never, never, never!*"

— *Bangor (Me.) Union.*

The President has issued his proclamation calling Congress to meet on the 4th of July. Also calling for 75,000 volunteers to aid in carrying on a conflict with the South. The news already received from the Border States indicates that they will leave the Union, and that the war will be between nineteen free and fifteen slave States.

Could this war policy possibly save the Union and promote the welfare of the people, we could look upon it with more complacency. But as it must inevitably more completely divide the Union and injure the interests of the whole country, we believe it to be an unwise and unsafe policy. To march soldiers into the Southern country to contend with armies and yellow fever—and to end in no good, but much evil, does not seem to be a discreet or a righteous policy.

A bloody conflict may be continued with the South for weeks, for months, or for years. At its close a compromise must be made no more favorable to the North than was the Crittenden compromise. But the evils of the unnecessary strife will continue into the long years of the future, and be felt by millions. No good whatever can come out of the shocking conflict.

War has been commenced. Its origin is the negro agitation. Let the friends of the agitation point out the spot where a slave has been benefited if they can. Great evils have come. Where are the benefits?

— *Hartford (Ct.) Times.*

President Lincoln has called an extra session of Congress, to meet on the 4th of July, and the measure will undoubtedly receive the approval of the people in all the loyal States.

We dislike to believe that the sole wish of the President is to be supplied with the means of prosecuting a war against the South, and that Congress will be asked to do nothing more than pass force bills and raise money for their execution.

A war based upon a spirit of revenge, or a disposition to subjugate the States now assuming an attitude of rebellion, will not long be tolerated by the people. *If we have no nobler purposes than to gratify our passions, we shall soon witness a sudden and overwhelming reaction all over the North, and the Governments of Europe will interfere to bring our quarrels to a close.*

We must not long embarrass the commerce of the country. England looks to the South for cotton, and will not, for any length of time, permit the blockading of Southern ports.

The refusal of the Black Republican leaders to yield any thing of their contemptible party creed has weakened, and is still weakening the Government. The Border States would have been as firmly bound to the Union as Rhode Island herself, if Congress had adopted Crittenden's resolutions, or even the proposition of the Peace Conference at its recent session.

In the free States there is a population of nearly 20,000,000 of souls. In the seven Confederate States there are less than 3,000,000 of white inhabitants. Even if all the Border Slave States should be against us, the difference in point of numbers would be as two to one. Under these circumstances the Christian world looks to us for a magnanimous, not to say generous policy. We must be liberal toward the South, in all things, where liberality can be deemed a virtue, or we shall become a hissing and by-word in every civilized community.

Starting with these reflections, which seem to us true and appropriate, what shall we say of the duty of Congress? Is it not to make such offers to the revolted States as will give reasonable men there assurances of their safety in the Union's keeping? Is it not to do what alone can allay the fears of those thousands who are now ready to fight against us, because dreading their own subjugation and degradation? Is it not to remove, so far as it is in our power, the apprehensions of good men that we mean to wage a sectional warfare which shall end only in the overthrow of their institutions? Is it not to satisfy the world, by generous acts, that we still love forbearance and peace; that we do not willingly array brother against brother.

We say, let Congress, on the first day of the session, *put the Government right*, and *put the North right*, on the questions which have led to this quarrel. *Deny it who may, we began this controversy. We began this interference with State rights. We have been for thirty years the aggressors. We have produced, by our own wilfulness and bigotry, by our exhibitions of hatred and affected superiority, the very state of things from which the country is now suffering.* Let Congress turn the tide which is now setting against us in the minds of thinking men. Let a fair, reasonable, liberal, honorable compromise be offered at once, and let the offer be kept before the South until the controversy is brought to an end. —*Providence Daily Post.*

Men of all parties, possessing intelligence, pa-

triotism and independence of character, have been adverse to the political expediency of any attempt to reinforce Sumter; and when the proposition was made to abandon that fortification, upon the urgent request of General Scott, the measure was hailed with joy as a peace-offering. We have never attempted to justify the Secessionists, any more than we have attempted to vindicate the clamors of Black Republicanism; but we have simply disapproved of a line of policy on the part of the administration of President Lincoln, which, if carried out, must entail upon our country all the horrors of a civil war. We did not believe such a policy would restore that Union, but expressed our opinion that it would forever defeat its reconstruction. Seriously impressed with the belief that our opinions upon these subjects were the reflection of the sentiments of the people of the country, we have given utterance to them. But for so doing we have received from Republican officials and others in this community coarse abuse and defamation. Events have demonstrated how well founded were our opinions. The attempt has been made at provisioning Sumter, and what is the result? Fort Sumter is captured by the Southern Confederacy— the Administration is defeated in the first onset. The Southern Confederacy has the prestige of victory. Has this defeat demonstrated that we *have a Government?* On the contrary, it has clearly demonstrated that fanaticism and imbecility rule at Washington. Overriding and disregarding the counsels of Gen. Scott, the Administration first declares for war, and then, when told by Gen. Scott that Sumter could not be relieved with a less force than 20,000 men, sends forth an armada of four or five vessels, and less than one-fourth of the number of men required to insure success. In disregarding the advice of Gen. Scott, President Lincoln has entailed upon the country the disgrace of a defeat in the first onset.

But the past is past, and cannot be recalled. As a choice between two evils, we would have preferred separation to civil war. The "powers that be" have chosen the latter alternative, and the destinies and honor of our country are in the hands of a weak and imbecile man, the tool of a party which has, ever since its organization, been arrayed in hostility to the Constitution and to the perpetuity of the Union. As it is, Abolition fanaticism bids fair to involve our whole country in the horrors of a civil war—a war in which brother must meet brother in the deadly conflict. While we will stand by the honor and integrity of our political institutions and civil authorities to the fullest extent required of loyal citizens, we do not feel to rejoice at the dark clouds which seem to be settling over our country. We will leave to Abolition fanatics the pleasure of rejoicing over the downfall of the Union, and the substitution of the evils of war for the pursuits of peace.

—*Auburn Democrat.*

Doc. 58.—PROCLAMATION BY THE MAYOR.

MAYOR'S OFFICE, NEW YORK, April 15, 1861.

TO THE PEOPLE OF THE CITY OF NEW YORK:

As Chief Magistrate, representing the whole people, I feel compelled at this crisis to call upon them to avoid excitement and turbulence. Whatever may be or may have been individual positions

or opinions on questions of public policy, let us remember that our country now trembles upon the brink of a precipice, and that it requires a patriotic and honest effort to prevent its final destruction. Let us ignore the past, rising superior to partisan considerations, and rally to the restoration of the Constitution and the Union as they existed in the days and in the spirit of our fathers. Whether this is to be accomplished by fratricidal warfare or by concession, conciliation and sacrifice, men may differ, but all will admit that here at least harmony and peace should prevail. Thus may we, under the guidance of Divine Providence, set an example of peace and good will throughout our extended country. In this spirit and with this view, I call upon the people of New York, irrespective of all other considerations or prejudices, to unite in obedience to the laws, in support of the public peace, in the preservation of order and in the protection of property.   FERNANDO WOOD, Mayor.
                                    —*Tribune*, April 16.

Doc. 59.—GOV. LETCHER'S PROCLAMATION.

WHEREAS seven of the States, formerly composing a part of the United States, have, by authority of their people, solemnly resumed the powers granted by them to the United States, and have framed a Constitution and organized a Government for themselves, to which the people of those States are yielding willing obedience, and have so notified the President of the United States by all the formalities incident to such action, and thereby become to the United States a separate, independent and foreign power; And whereas the Constitution of the United States has invested Congress with the sole power to "declare war," and until such declaration is made, the President has no authority to call for an extraordinary force to wage offensive war against any foreign power; and whereas, on the 15th inst., the President of the United States, in plain violation of the Constitution, issued a proclamation calling for a force of seventy-five thousand men, to cause the laws of the United States to be duly executed over a people who are no longer a part of the Union, and in said proclamation threatens to exert this unusual force to compel obedience to his mandates; And whereas the General Assembly of Virginia, by a majority approaching to entire unanimity, declared at its last session, that the State of Virginia would consider such exertion of force as a virtual declaration of war, to be resisted by all the power at the command of Virginia; and subsequently, the convention now in session, representing the sovereignty of this State, has reaffirmed in substance the same policy, with equal unanimity; And whereas the State of Virginia deeply sympathizes with the Southern States, in the wrongs they have suffered, and in the position they have assumed; and having made earnest efforts peaceably to compose the differences which have severed the Union, and having failed in that attempt, through this unwarranted act on the part of the President; and it is believed that the influences which operate to produce this proclamation against the seceded States will be brought to bear upon this commonwealth, if she should exercise her undoubted right to resume the powers granted by her people, and it is due to the honor of Virginia that an improper exercise of force against her people

should be repelled; Therefore, I, John Letcher, Governor of the Commonwealth of Virginia, have thought proper to order all armed volunteer regiments or companies within this State forthwith to hold themselves in readiness for immediate orders, and upon the reception of this proclamation to report to the adjutant-general of the State their organization and numbers, and prepare themselves for efficient service. Such companies as are not armed and equipped will report that fact, that they may be properly supplied.

{ L. S. }   In witness whereof, I have hereunto set my hand and caused the seal of the commonwealth to be affixed, this 17th day of April, 1861, and in the eighty-fifth year of the commonwealth.   JOHN LETCHER.
                                    —*The World.*

Doc. 60.—VIRGINIA'S ORDINANCE OF SECESSION.

THE following is the "ordinance to repeal the ratification of the Constitution of the United States of America, by the State of Virginia, and to resume all the rights and powers granted under said constitution," which passed the State Convention on the 17th of April, 1861:

The people of Virginia, in the ratification of the Constitution of the United States of America, adopted by them in convention, on the 25th day o June, in the year of our Lord one thousand seven hundred and eighty-eight, having declared that the powers granted under the said constitution were derived from the people of the United States, and might be resumed whensoever the same should be perverted to their injury and oppression, and the Federal Government having perverted said powers, not only to the injury of the people of Virginia, but to the oppression of the Southern slaveholding States;

Now, therefore, we, the people of Virginia, do declare and ordain, that the ordinance adopted by the people of this State in convention on the twenty-fifth day of June, in the year of our Lord one thousand seven hundred and eighty-eight, whereby the Constitution of the United States of America was ratified, and all acts of the General Assembly of this State ratifying or adopting amendments to said constitution, are hereby repealed and abrogated; that the Union between the State of Virginia and the other States under the constitution aforesaid is hereby dissolved, and that the State of Virginia is in the full possession and exercise of all the rights of sovereignty which belong and appertain to a free and independent State. And they do further declare that said Constitution of the United States of America is no longer binding on any of the citizens of this State.

This ordinance shall take effect and be an act of this day, when ratified by a majority of the votes of the people of this State, cast at a poll to be taken thereon, on the fourth Thursday in May next, in pursuance of a schedule hereafter to be enacted.

Done in convention in the city of Richmond, on the seventeenth day of April, in the year of our Lord, one thousand eight hundred and sixty-one, and in the eighty-fifth year of the Commonwealth of Virginia.

A true copy,   JNO. L. EUBANK,
                        Secretary of Convention.

SECESSION OF VIRGINIA.

The announcement that the Convention of Virginia had passed an Ordinance of Secession, was received with the most universal and profound satisfaction. There are no longer in Virginia two parties. The Union men and the Secessionists are arrayed in a solid band of brotherhood under the flag of Virginia. The only rivalry is which shall do and suffer most in defence of our common honor against the monstrous despotism at Washington. LINCOLN's Proclamation has accomplished the union of all parties in Virginia and the South. The Ordinance of Secession is the answer of the Convention to that Proclamation, and the action of the Convention is but the echo of the people's will. The old Union, for which our fathers fought and bled, has been wilfully sacrificed by a Black Republican despot, and he now seeks to wrench from us our Liberty and Independence. Virginia, which led the van in the war of '76, now meets him on the threshold. She has been slow to act, but she will be slower still to retrace her steps. The Union has lost its brightest planet, but it will henceforth beam as a star of the first magnitude in the purer, brighter, and grander constellation of the Southern Cross.

—Richmond Dispatch.

Doc. 61.—PROCLAMATION BY JEFFERSON DAVIS.

Whereas, ABRAHAM LINCOLN, the President of the United States has, by proclamation, announced the intention of invading this Confederacy with an armed force, for the purpose of capturing its fortresses, and thereby subverting its independence, and subjecting the free people thereof to the dominion of a foreign power; and *whereas* it has thus become the duty of this Government to repel the threatened invasion, and to defend the rights and liberties of the people by all the means which the laws of nations and the usages of civilized warfare place at its disposal;

Now, therefore, I, JEFFERSON DAVIS, PRESIDENT OF THE CONFEDERATE STATES OF AMERICA, do issue this my Proclamation, inviting all those who may desire, by service in private armed vessels on the high seas, to aid this Government in resisting so wanton and wicked an aggression, to make application for commissions or Letters of Marque and Reprisal, to be issued under the Seal of these Confederate States.

And I do further notify all persons applying for Letters of Marque, to make a statement in writing, giving the name and a suitable description of the character, tonnage, and force of the vessel, and the name and place of residence of each owner concerned therein, and the intended number of the crew, and to sign said statement and deliver the same to the Secretary of State, or to the Collector of any port of entry of these Confederate States, to be by him transmitted to the Secretary of State.

And I do further notify all applicants aforesaid that before any commission or Letter of Marque is issued to any vessel, the owner or owners thereof, and the commander for the time being, will be required to give bond to the Confederate States, with at least two responsible sureties, not interested in such vessel, in the penal sum of five thousand dollars; or if such vessel be provided with more than one hundred and fifty men, then in the penal sum of ten thousand dollars, with condition that the owners, officers, and crew who shall be employed on board such commissioned vessel, shall observe the laws of these Confederate States and the instructions given to them for the regulation of their conduct. That they shall satisfy all damages done contrary to the tenor thereof by such vessel during her commission, and deliver up the same when revoked by the President of the Confederate States.

And I do further specially enjoin on all persons holding offices, civil and military, under the authority of the Confederate States, that they be vigilant and zealous in discharging the duties incident thereto; and I do, moreover, solemnly exhort the good people of these Confederate States, as they love their country, as they prize the blessings of free government, as they feel the wrongs of the past and these now threatened in aggravated form by those whose enmity is more implacable because unprovoked, that they exert themselves in preserving order, in promoting concord, in maintaining the authority and efficacy of the laws, and in supporting and invigorating all the measures which may be adopted for the common defence, and by which, under the blessings of Divine Providence, we may hope for a speedy, just, and honorable peace.

In testimony whereof, I have hereunto set my hand, and caused the Seal of the Confederate States to be affixed, this *seventeenth* day of April, 1861.

By the President,
(Signed)   JEFFERSON DAVIS.

R. TOOMBS, Secretary of State.

The *Charleston Mercury* of the 19th April, in referring to this proclamation, says: "To avoid any misunderstanding and prevent comment arising from the supposition that the President intends to assume the authority and responsibility of issuing these himself, without the action of Congress, we would say that the proclamation is merely a *preparatory* indication of what he intends to recommend to Congress, and what we have no doubt Congress will do and ought to do, in the event that war becomes *inevitable.* The secession of Virginia and the frontier Southern States may command the peace even from the silly fanatics who at present rule Washington. The South does not want war. We stand on the defensive. But if the Northern Government choose to have war, they can and will have it, they may rest assured."

Doc. 61½.—ADDRESS TO THE PEOPLE OF TENNESSEE.

IN the perilous times upon which our country is thrown, we trust it will not be deemed presumptuous or improper in us to express to our fellow-citizens our united opinion as to the duty of the State in this dire emergency.

We are threatened with a civil war, the dreadful consequences of which, if once fully inaugurated, no language can depict. In view of such consequences we deem it the duty of every good citizen to exert his utmost powers to avert the calamities of such a war. The agitation of the slavery question, combined with party spirit and sectional animosity, has at length produced the legitimate fruit. The present is no time to discuss the events of the past. The awful presence is upon us, and the portentous future is hanging over us. There has been a collision, as is known to you, at Fort Sumter, between the forces of the seceded States and those of the National Government, which resulted in the capture of the fort by the army of the Confederate States. In view of this event and of other acts growing out of the secession of seven of the Southern States, the President has issued his proclamation calling out the militia of the States of the Union to suppress what the Proclamation designates a "combination too powerful to be suppressed by the ordinary course of judicial proceedings, or by the powers vested in the Marshals by law."

Tennessee is called upon by the President to furnish two regiments, and the State has, through her Executive, refused to comply with the call. This refusal of our State, we fully approve. We commend the wisdom, the justice, and the humanity of the refusal. We unqualifiedly disapprove of secession, both as a constitutional right and as a remedy for existing evils; we equally condemn the policy of the Administration in reference to the seceded States. But while we, without qualification, condemn the policy of coercion as calculated to dissolve the Union forever and to dissolve it in the blood of our fellow-citizens, and regard it as sufficient to justify the State in refusing her aid to the Government, in its attempt to suppress the revolution in the seceded States, we do not think it her duty, considering her position in the Union, and in view of the great question of the peace of our distracted country, to take sides against the Government. Tennesse has wronged no State or citizen of this Union. She has violated the rights of no State, north or south. She has been loyal to all where loyalty was due. She has not brought on this war by any act of hers. She has tried every means in her power to prevent it. She now stands ready to do any thing within her reach to stop it. And she ought, as we think, to decline joining either party. For in so doing, they would at once terminate her grand mission of peace-maker between the States of the South and the General Government. Nay, more; the almost inevitable result would be the transfer of the war within her own borders—the defeat of all hopes of reconciliation, and the deluging of the State with the blood of her own people.

The present duty of Tennessee, is to maintain a position of independence—taking sides with the Union and the peace of the country against all assailants, whether from the North or South. Her position should be to maintain the sanctity of her soil, from the hostile tread of any party.

We do not pretend to foretell the future of Tennessee, in connection with the other States, or in reference to the Federal Government. We do not pretend to be able to tell the future purposes of the President and Cabinet in reference to the impending war. But should a purpose be developed by the Government of overrunning and subjugating our brethren of the seceded States, we say unequivocally, that it will be the duty of the State to resist at all hazards, at any cost, *and by arms*, any such purpose or attempt. And to meet any and all emergencies, she ought to *be fully armed*, and we would respectfully call upon the authorities of the State to proceed at once to the accomplishment of this object.

Let Tennessee, then, prepare thoroughly and efficiently for coming events. In the meantime, let her, as speedily as she can, hold a Conference with her sister slaveholding States yet in the Union, for the purpose of devising plans for the preservation of the peace of the land. Fellow-citizens of Tennessee, we entreat you to bring yourselves up to the magnitude of the crisis. Look in the face impending calamities. Civil war—what is it? The bloodiest and darkest pages of history answer this question. To avert this, who would not give his time, his talents, his untiring energy—his all? There may be yet time to accomplish every thing. Let us not despair. The Border Slave States may prevent this civil war; and why shall they not do it?

NEIL S. BROWN,　　　　S. D. MORGAN,
RUSSELL HOUSTON,　　JOHN S. BRIEN,
E. H. EWING,　　　　　ANDREW EWING,
C. JOHNSON,　　　　　JOHN H. CALLENDER,
JOHN BELL,　　　　　BAILIE PEYTON.
R. J. MEIGS,

NASHVILLE, April 18, 1861.

　　　　　　　　　　　　—*Louisville Journal.*

Doc. 62.—LIEUT. JONES' OFFICIAL REPORT.

CARLISLE BARRACKS, Pa., April 20, 1861.

The Assistant Adjutant-General, Head-quarters Army, Washington, D. C.:

SIR: Immediately after finishing my despatch of the night of the 18th inst., I received positive and reliable information that 2,500 or 3,000 State troops would reach Harper's Ferry in two hours, from Winchester, and that the troops from Halltown, increased to 300, were advancing, and even at that time—a few minutes after 10 o'clock—within 20 minutes' march of the Ferry. Under these circumstances, I decided the time had arrived to carry out my determination, as expressed in the despatch above referred to, and accordingly gave the order to apply the torch. In three minutes, or less, both of the Arsenal buildings, containing nearly 15,000 stand of arms, together with the carpenters' shop, which was at the upper end of a long and connected series of workshops of the Armory proper, were in a complete blaze.

There is every reason for believing the destruction was complete.

After firing the buildings, I withdrew my command, marching all night, and arrived here at 2¼ P. M. yesterday, where I shall await orders.

Four men were missing on leaving the Armory, and two deserted during the night.

I am, Sir, very respectfully, your obedient serv't,

R. JONES, First Lieut. R. M. Rifles,
Commanding Dept. Rect.

Doc. 63.—MEETING AT LOUISVILLE, KY.

MR. GUTHRIE'S SPEECH.

THE Hon. James Guthrie rose amid tremendous cheering. He said: Fellow-citizens, my voice is not very strong, and I fear it cannot be heard all over this great assemblage, but I will try to make it heard. Events press upon us with haste, and we scarcely know what is to come next. When Mr. Lincoln was elected President we all felt that the remedy for a sectional President was in the Union and under the Constitution. We knew we had a Senate against him, and hoped that we had the House against him; and there would have been if all men had stood at their posts as Kentucky has stood. But certain States chose to take the remedy into their own hands, and dissolve their connexion with the Union; South Carolina first, and then seven other States followed. They have organized a separate Government, and one exercising governmental authority. Louisville spoke early, decidedly, and firmly against a sectional party in the Union, and under the Constitution. We had a Legislature called; we have had a Peace Conference at Washington, and both failed; the result of the deliberations of both Houses of Congress failed to find a remedy for secession. The Peace Conference at Washington was equally unsuccessful in solving this dangerous question. Mr. Lincoln was inaugurated. He gave us his inaugural. It was construed as an inaugural of peace and as an inaugural of war. His chosen friends did not know how to take it, and his opponents were divided as to its meaning. I suspected it; for, like the serpent, it spoke with a forked tongue! [Cheers.] Then the troops were to be withdrawn from Fort Sumter, and then not, but were to be furnished with supplies only. Now, in the action of the Southern Confederacy and that of Mr. Lincoln, the friends of both parties find excuses for them; but when it was the peace of the country, and the saving it from war and bloodshed, then there should have been no interference of etiquette to prevent such a dreadful calamity. Kentucky spoke as her statesmen have always spoken, of conciliation, peace, harmony, and a final settlement. But war has been inaugurated; Fort Sumter has fallen. The President has issued a proclamation calling for 75,000 men; but he has not told us what he was going to do with them! Is he going to retake Fort Sumter? Is he going to defend Fort Pickens? If so, why does he congregate them at Washington? I was at Washington when Lincoln came, and it was like a beleaguered city. We heard sounds of martial music, the tramp of armed men, and the roll of artillery! And now Lincoln wants 75,000 men, where every other President has lived like an American citizen, as we have lived, and walked, in perfect security among his fellow-citizens. We learn from the telegraph that State after State is tendering men and money. Is the party now in possession of the Government going to conquer the seven seceding States, and hold them as subjugated provinces? If they are, Lincoln should, like an honest man, have told us in his inaugural, and some say he is an honest man. In all these free States sending men and money, we hear no voice of peace, and after his legions have drowned the South in carnage, is there to be no peace? What is the end of all wars—peace! No free people were ever conquered until they were exterminated. Why shall not the people of America have peace before, rather than after war, when its desolating influence has blighted the land? I want Kentucky to take her stand for peace—[Cheers,]—and appeal to that still small voice in the North crying for peace. There are religious men from habit, education and from profession, whose hearts, when Kentucky calls for peace, will be reached, and whose voice will reach the powers that be, and we will have peace. What a spectacle we present! A people that have prospered beyond

example in the records of time; free and self-governed, without oppression, without taxation to be felt, are now going to cut each other's throats; and why? Because Presidents Lincoln and Davis couldn't settle the etiquette upon which the troops were to be withdrawn from Fort Sumter. Kentucky is a State in this matter, on the border of the Ohio, with six or seven hundred miles of coast bordering upon Ohio, Indiana and Illinois—States with whom we have ever lived in peace and good fellowship. We have no quarrel with them, and they must have none with us. We have asked the South to stay their hands, for we had a great stake in this Government, and they have not. We plead with Lincoln for peace, and have not been hearkened to. Shall we be hearkened to in the din of arms? There will be a time when Kentucky's voice, if she stands firm on her own soil, fighting with neither section—will be heard by millions of people of the free States, who will hearken to us and say: "Why should there be strife between us and you?" I have always counselled against inconsiderate measures. We are not situated to meet even our border friends in arms. How long would it take to make the northern bank of the Ohio bristle with men and bayonets and cannon hostile to us? Let us stand boldly and fearlessly, as is characteristic of Kentuckians, and cry peace! Hold fast to that we know to be good, and let these men who want to make the experiment of secession go as individual amateurs and find congenial spirits for their work. [Cheers.] I will leave to other gentlemen to dilate upon all those subjects. We have men who want us out at once. Does not that inaugurate war? Does not that begin to create men of the Northern border into foes? Keep up your relations of trade and commerce and good fellowship; stand firm by the cause and heed the counsels of men who have ever counselled peace and harmony and attendant prosperity. This thing of breaking the links of a Government under which we have prospered, is a hard thing to do. It prostrates the labor of the husbandman as it has prostrated the business of merchants. How much better will the business be if war is inaugurated? I tell you that you need not believe the telegraphic reports. I know the hearts and sentiments and feelings that will come forth and battle in the free States for us! If the North comes to ravage our land, we will meet them as Kentuckians always meet their foes. We will meet them as Kentuckians should meet them, so long as there is a tree for a fortification, or a foot of land for a freeman to stand upon. [Applause.] I am for holding fast to that she knows to be good, and for her standing firm for right, and for abiding events as heroes should do. Why should a man be scared by the first danger and fly into still greater peril? You were startled at the reports from Cincinnati; last evening Louisville was excited; to-day you are reconciled, for there was nothing in the reports. You will hear of great battles, but you will often hear of great battles that were never fought. Now, I don't believe that the overruling Providence that was with us through the Revolution, in the councils of the framers of this Government, and has been with us ever since, has deserted us, and I hope He has chosen Kentucky to be the great mediator for the restoration of peace and the preservation of our country.

The Hon. Nat Wolfe, from the Committee on Resolutions, reported the following preamble and resolutions, which were adopted with hardly a dissenting voice:

Events of commanding importance to the future safety and honor of Kentucky have occurred which call for action on the part of her citizens; and every consideration of self-interest, and every dictate of wisdom and patriotism must prompt our State to maintain most resolutely her position of loyalty. Situated on the border of the Slave States, with 700 miles of territory exposed to the hostile attack, should the Union be divided into two separate sovereignties, and with but one million of population to oppose the four or five millions of the States contiguous to her, which might become unfriendly, Kentucky owes it to herself to exercise a wise precaution before she precipitates any course of action which may involve her in an internecine war. She has no reason to distrust the present kindly feelings of the people who reside on the north bank of the Ohio River, long her friendly neighbors, and connected by a thousand ties of consanguinity; but she must realize the fact that if Kentucky separates from the Federal Union and assumes her sovereign powers as an independent State, that Ohio, Indiana, and Illinois, remaining loyal to the Federal Union, must become her political antagonists. If Kentucky deserts the Stars and Stripes, and those States adhere to the flag of the Union, it seems impossible to imagine a continuance of our old friendly relations when constantly-recurring causes of irritation could not be avoided. It is from no fear that Kentucky would not always prove herself equal to the exigencies of any new position she might see proper to assume, and from no distrust of the bravery of her sons, that these suggestions are made; but as, "when in the course of human events it becomes necessary for one people to dissolve the political bands which have connected them with another, a decent respect to the opinions of mankind requires that they should declare the causes which impel them to the separation," so an equal necessity exists that we should not dissolve those bands with our friends and neighbors without calling to our aid every suggestion of prudence, and exhausting every effort to reconcile difficulties, before taking steps which cannot be retraced, and may lead to exasperation, collisions, and eventual war; therefore be it

Resolved, 1. That, as the Confederate States have, by overt acts, commenced war against the United States, without consultation with Kentucky and their sister Southern States, Kentucky reserves to herself the right to choose her own position, and that while her natural sympathies are with those who have a common interest in the protection of Slavery, she still acknowledges her loyalty and fealty to the Government of the United States, which she will cheerfully render until that Government becomes aggressive, tyrannical, and regardless of our rights in slave property.

2. That the National Government should be tried by its acts, and that the several States, as its peers in their appropriate spheres, will hold it to a rigid accountability, and require that its acts should be fraternal in their efforts to bring back the seceding States, and not sanguinary or coercive.

3. That, as we oppose the call of the President for volunteers for the purpose of coercing the seceding States, so we oppose the raising of troops in this State to coöperate with the Southern Confederacy, when the acknowledged intention of the latter is to march upon the City of Washington and capture the Capitol, and when, in its march thither, it must pass through States which have not yet renounced their allegiance to the Union.

4. That secession is a remedy for no evil, real or imaginary, but an aggravation and complication of existing difficulties.

5. That the memories of the past, the interests of the present, and the solemn convictions of future duty and usefulness in the hope of mediation, prevent Kentucky from taking part with the seceding States against the General Government.

6. That " the present duty of Kentucky is to maintain her present independent position, taking sides not with the Administration, nor with the seceding States, but with the Union against them both, declaring her soil to be sacred from the hostile tread of either, and if necessary, to make the declaration good with her strong right arm."

7. That to the end Kentucky may be prepared for any contingency, "we would have her arm herself thoroughly at the earliest practicable moment," by regular legal action.

8. That we look to the young men of the Kentucky State guard, as the bulwarks of the safety of our Commonwealth, and that we conjure them to remember that they are pledged equally to fidelity to the United States and Kentucky.

9. That the Union and the Constitution, being mainly the work of Southern soldiers and statesmen, in our opinion furnish a surer guaranty for "Southern Rights " than can be found under any other system of government yet devised by men.

The Hon. Archie Dixon then spoke as follows:

MR. DIXON'S SPEECH.

Turning to the flag which graced the stand, he said:

Fellow-Citizens: Whose flag is that which waves over us? To whom does it belong? Is it not yours, is it not our own Stars and Stripes, and do we mean ever to abandon it? That flag has ever waved over Kentucky soil with honor and glory. It is our flag —it is my flag—it is Kentucky's flag! When that flag is trailed in the dust and destroyed, I pray Heaven that the earth may be destroyed with it, for I do not wish, and I trust I shall never look upon its dishonor. It is our flag—ours while we have a country and a Government. I shall never surrender that flag. I have loved it from boyhood, and have watched it everywhere, and imagine it in this dark hour still waving amid the gloom, and feel that its stars will still shine forth in the smoke of battle, and lead our country back to honor and glory! Why is our country so stricken down, and why is our glory shaded in gloom—our Constitution and Government destroyed? What cause has brought about all this difference between the North and the South? Some say it was the Territories. Some say the Government wars on the South; that Mr. Lincoln was elected as a sectional candidate, and on a principle of hostility to an institution of the South. It is true. But has the _Government_ ever warred on the South? This contest should be with Mr. Lincoln, and not with that flag—with the Union! It is Lincoln and his party who are the enemies of the country—they are the foes of the Constitution. [Cheers.] It is that party of the North whose purpose is to sever the States. It is with them that we should war, and not with the Government—the Union under which we have been so prosperous. Look to the history of the country and tell me, has the Government ever made war on the South? I boldly affirm it that the amendment to the Constitution, which affects Southern interests, has been made at the instance of Southern men. Was not the act of 1850 enacted at the instance of Southern men, and was it not framed and advocated by our own immortal statesman—Kentucky's noble and gallant Clay? The principle upon which all our Territories have been organized holds that people who owned slaves might take them there, and the Territories could be admitted as Slave States. Those acts thus providing are still in force. The South asked for the repeal of the Missouri Compromise, and it was done. What next? Even since the inauguration of Mr. Lincoln, his party has given sanction to three new Territories under the same existing laws. All have the right to take their slaves there. What, then, is the cause of our difficulty? Look at it clearly. Is it the tariff? Was it not made as the South wanted it, and was it not South Carolina who changed it? Did not the General Government change the then existing value of silver and gold for the benefit of the South? We were told the other day that if Lincoln was elected his intention was to destroy Slavery. Did he not declare that the Fugitive Slave law should be enforced? How has it been done? Were not five slaves only lately taken from Chicago and delivered to their owners? He declares he will enforce the laws, and not interfere with Slavery. Then why this war? I will tell you why. Because Mr. Lincoln has been elected President of the country, and Mr. Davis could not be, and therefore a Southern Confederacy was to be formed by Southern demagogues, and now they are attempting to drag you on with them. That is the plain state of the case. Demagogues at the North and demagogues at the South have divided the country; they would strike the dagger to the hearts of their brothers; they inaugurated the civil war now raging, and wish to drag you on with them. I say, for my part, I am not to be forced. I will not be driven to desert my country and my country's flag, nor turn to strike my dagger at her heart, but ever stand forward to defend her glory and her honor. What are we to do with South Carolina and her seceded sisters? Do you mean to tell me they will come back? What if you give them over, will they ever come back? They have turned their backs on their country, and now they want you to march with them. In a just cause I will defend our State at every point and against every combination; but when she battles against the law and the Constitution, I have not the heart—I have not the courage to do it! I cannot do it—I will not do it! Never! strike at that flag of our country—follow Davis to tear down the Stars and Stripes, the eagle which has soared so high aloft as the emblem of so mighty a nation—give up that flag for the Palmetto—strike that eagle from his high place and coil around the stars the rattlesnake! The serpent stole into the garden of Eden and whispered treason to Heaven in the ear of Eve. And now the serpent would seduce us from our allegiance to our country. Were it possible for him to coil himself around the flag, I would tear him from the folds and crush him beneath my feet. The rattlesnake for the eagle! If you follow the serpent your fate will be as Adam's. Measureless woe, for all generations, has been that fate. Hell

was created because of that treason to Heaven, and if we follow after the serpent our fate will be to sink into the hell of Secession. This is the fate which befalls you if you follow Davis. But you must take a position. One side advises us to go out, while some say remain in the Union. They tell us that we are bound to fight, no matter how we decide. Kentucky is always ready to fight. She was born to fight when necessary, and when the soil of Kentucky is stained with blood, and the spirit of her sons aroused, let her enemies tremble! But she should ever fight upon the right side. But why is the Union broken up? Is it not because Lincoln is President? How long is his rule to last? In the history of nations, what is four years? How soon will he be dragged down and another and a better man raised to his high place? The American people are powerful when they are aroused to action, but they should act calmly. Now they are wild with excitement and act without judgment. What would we do if invaded? We would fly from house to house and rush together, but would we be in any capacity to defend ourselves? Calmness and not excitement should characterize us. Seven States have seceded, and the General Government attempts to enforce the laws. The war commences and blood is shed, and forces are ready arrayed against each other in hostile action. If we move out, what is our fate? Who is to defend? How are you to defend yourself if you go out of the Union? If you do, you at once declare war against the Union—you oppose the Stars and Stripes. We have a million of white population resident in a State only separated by the Ohio River from Indiana, Illinois, and Ohio, with a population of five millions. Through each State are numerous railroads, able to transport an army in a few days to our doors. What roads have we but those to Nashville and Lexington? And what can we do with them? In sixty days the North can pour an army of one hundred thousand men upon every part of us. What can we do? The State could raise perhaps sixty thousand men for her defence, but what can they do? Can they save your State and your city? From the heights beyond the river they can bombard your city and destroy it. They can cut off all communication with the South, and every foot of Kentucky soil eventually become desecrated by the invader. Can the South help you? She has got more than enough to do to defend herself, for the North can with her fleet cut off all communication with the outside world, and by the Mississippi River with Western States, and actually starve the South into subjection. One hope for Kentucky remains—stand still, with the Border States, and defy invasion from either side. My sympathies are wholly with the South, but I am not prepared to aid her in fighting against our Government. If we remain in the Union we are safe; if we go out we will be invaded; if we hold as we are we are safe, if we go out we will be overpowered. There is but one position to assume for honor and safety, and that position taken we can save the country. Another point: If an army invades us can we save, can we protect, our homes and families? When, in our city, the sentinel struts the streets, and we are powerless before him, who is to protect our families? Those who have plenty of money can flee, but what is the poor man to do? He will have to fight. Think of it—who is to protect them then from brutality and shame, our

Doc.—16

city from pillage and destruction? And it will surely befall us if we do not stand by our flag. We do not mean to submit to Lincoln. He has commanded us to send troops. We send word that Kentucky will not do it. Will he compel us? Let him not dare it! Let him not rouse the sleeping lions of the Border States. She sleeps now—still and quiet, but it is not from lack of strength, courage, or power. She waits for the assault. Let it come, and, roused, she will crush the power that assails, and drag Mr. Lincoln from his high place. Can he make Kentucky help him kill? He has a right to demand troops, and he did. Glendower could, as he said, call spirits from the vasty deep, but would they come when they were called? Will the troops from Kentucky come at his call? No, they will never lend themselves to such a cause. But, Kentucky will stand firm with her sister Border States in the centre of the Republic, to calm the distracted sections. This is her true position, and in it she saves the Union and frowns down Secession. Let us wait for reason to resume her seat. Let us not fight the North or South, but firm in our position tell our sister Border States that with them we will stand to maintain the Union, to preserve the peace, and uphold our honor, and our flag, which they would trail in the dust. We will rear ourselves as a rock in the midst of the ocean, against which the waves, lashed by sectional strife, in fury breaking, shall recoil and overwhelm those who have raised them! If we give up the Union, all is lost. There will then be no breakwater, but instead, Kentucky will be the battle-ground—the scene of a conflict between brethren—such a conflict as no country has yet witnessed. But if we take the true stand, the tide of war and desolation will be rolled back on both sides. If we must fight, let us fight Lincoln and not our Government. To go out of the Union is to raise a new issue with the North and turn the whole country against you. The ship of state is one in which we *all* sail, and when thus launched into the ocean, and about to founder because part of the crew rebel against the commander, it is the duty of all, unhesitatingly, to aid and save. Safety demands that we stand by the flag, by the Government, by the Constitution! In the distance you hear the shouts of men and the roaring of cannon. The foemen are gathering for the dreadful conflict, and when you cut loose from the Union it is to take a part. But you are secure from both as long as you remain neutral. You are to determine now. Examine all the points; look where you are going before you take the step that plunges you into ruin, and, calmly reasoning, free from excitement, determine to stand forever by the country, the Constitution, and the Stars and Stripes, and be still the mightiest nation the world ever saw.

Judge Nicholas made a beautiful, eloquent, and patriotic speech, which was greatly applauded, and closed by offering a series of resolutions, the last of which, as follows, was adopted, the balance being withdrawn :

Resolved, That we hail in Major Robert Anderson, the gallant defender of Fort Sumter against overwhelming odds, a worthy Kentuckian, the worthy son of a patriot sire, who has given so heroic an example of what ought always to be the conduct of a patriot soldier, in the presence of the armed assailants of his country's flag; that he, his officers, and men, have well earned the admiration and gratitude of the nation.

Judge Bullock was generally called for, and responded in a clear, forcible, and logical speech, indorsing the spirit of the preamble and resolutions adopted, and urging Kentucky to pursue the course laid down in them as the safest, wisest, and most noble for the first-born of the Union. His speech was characterized by that eloquence of diction so well known as an attribute of Judge Bullock's oratorical efforts. He was frequently interrupted in the course of his remarks by cheers and applause.

The Hon. John Young Brown followed in a speech unsurpassed in power and brilliancy. This gifted young orator rehearsed the history of the last Congress, the efforts for compromise, the surrender by the Republicans of the fundamental idea of the Chicago platform, in the positive non-extension of Slavery in the formation of the new Territories. He held his audience spell-bound, as it were, for more than an hour, as he poured out burning words of indignation upon those who have brought the country into its present unfortunate condition, or depicted the horrors of civil war. He earnestly urged the neutrality of Kentucky in the present crisis, as the best and most practicable position for Kentucky to maintain her integrity in the Union, and to mediate between the antagonistic sections.

The meeting, which was entirely orderly, adjourned after giving rounds of cheers for the Union and for the American flag.

—*Louisville Journal,* April 21.

Doc. 64.—MAJOR ANDERSON'S DESPATCHES TO THE WAR DEPARTMENT.

STEAMSHIP BALTIC, }
Off Sandy Hook, April 18, 1861. }

Hon. S. Cameron, Secretary of War, Washington, D. C :—

Sir :—Having defended Fort Sumter for thirty-four hours, until the quarters were entirely burned, the main gates destroyed by fire, the gorge wall seriously injured, the magazine surrounded by flames, and its door closed from the effects of the heat, four barrels and three cartridges of powder only being available, and no provisions but pork remaining, I accepted terms of evacuation, offered by General Beauregard, being the same offered by him on the 11th inst., prior to the commencement of hostilities, and marched out of the fort Sunday afternoon, the 14th inst., with colors flying and drums beating, bringing away company and private property, and saluting my flag with fifty guns.

ROBERT ANDERSON,
Major First Artillery.

—*Times.*

Doc. 65.—PROCLAMATION OF THE GOVERNOR OF MARYLAND.

TO THE PEOPLE OF MARYLAND.

The unfortunate state of affairs now existing in the country has greatly excited the people of Maryland.

In consequence of our peculiar position, it is not to be expected that the people of the State can unanimously agree upon the best mode of preserving the honor and integrity of the State, and of maintaining within her limits that peace so earnestly desired by all good citizens.

The emergency is great. The consequences of a rash step will be fearful. It is the imperative duty of every true son of Maryland to do all that he can to arrest the threatened evil. I therefore counsel the people, in all earnestness, to withhold their hands from whatever may tend to precipitate us into the gulf of discord and ruin gaping to receive us.

I counsel the people to abstain from all heated controversy upon the subject, to avoid all things that tend to crimination and recrimination, to believe that the origin of our evil day may well be forgotten now by every patriot in the earnest desire to avert from us its fruit.

All powers vested in the Governor of the State will be strenuously exerted, to preserve the peace and maintain inviolate the honor and integrity of Maryland.

I call upon the people to obey the laws, and to aid the constituted authorities in their endeavors to preserve the fair fame of our State untarnished.

I assure the people that no troops will be sent from Maryland, unless it may be for the defence of the national capital.

It is my intention in the future, as it has been my endeavor in the past, to preserve the people of Maryland from civil war; and I invoke the assistance of every true and loyal citizen to aid me to this end.

The people of the State will in a short time have the opportunity afforded them, in a special election for Members of the Congress of the United States, to express their devotion to the Union, or their desire to see it broken up.

TH. H. HICKS,
Governor of Maryland.

BALTIMORE, April 18, 1861.

PROCLAMATION OF THE MAYOR OF BALTIMORE.

MAYOR'S OFFICE, April 18, 1861.

I HEARTILY concur in the determination of the Governor to preserve the peace and maintain inviolate the honor and integrity of Maryland, as set forth in the above proclamation, and will earnestly co-operate with his efforts to maintain peace and order in the city of Baltimore.

And I cannot withhold my expression of satisfaction at his resolution that no troops shall be sent from Maryland to the soil of any other State. The great questions at issue must, in the last resort, be settled by the people of the city and State for themselves at the ballot box, and an opportunity for a free expression of their opinions will speedily be afforded at the approaching Congressional election.

If the counsels of the Governor shall be heeded we may rest secure in the confidence that the storm of civil war which now threatens the country will at least pass over our beloved State and leave it unharmed; but if they shall be disregarded, a fearful and fratricidal strife may at once burst forth in our midst.

Under such circumstances, can any good citizen doubt for a moment, the course which duty and honor alike require him to pursue?

GEO. WM. BROWN,
Mayor.

Doc. 66.—RESOLUTIONS OF THE N. Y. CHAMBER OF COMMERCE.

Whereas, Our country has, in the course of events, reached a crisis unprecedented in its past history, exposing it to extreme dangers, and involving the most momentous results; and *Whereas,* The President of the United States has, by his Proclamation, made known the dangers which threaten the stability of Government, and called upon the people to rally in support of the Constitution and laws; and *Whereas,* The merchants of New York, represented in this Chamber, have a deep stake in the results which may flow from the present exposed state of national affairs, as well as a jealous regard for the honor of that flag under whose protection they have extended the commerce of this city to the remotest part of the world; therefore,

Resolved, That this Chamber, alive to the perils which have been gathering around our cherished form of Government and menacing its overthrow, has witnessed with lively satisfaction the determination of the President to maintain the Constitution and vindicate the supremacy of Government and law at every hazard. [Cheers.]

Resolved, That the so-called secession of some of the Southern States having at last culminated in open war against the United States, the American people can no longer defer their decision between anarchy or despotism on the one side, and on the other liberty, order, and law under the most benign Government the world has ever known.

Resolved, That this Chamber, forgetful of past differences of political opinion among its members, will, with unanimity and patriotic ardor, support the Government in this great crisis: and it hereby pledges its best efforts to sustain its credit and facilitate its financial operations. It also confidently appeals to all men of wealth to join in these efforts. [Applause.]

Resolved, That while deploring the advent of civil war which has been precipitated on the country by the madness of the South, the Chamber is persuaded that policy and humanity alike demand that it should be met by the most prompt and energetic measures; and it accordingly recommends to Government the instant adoption and prosecution of a policy so vigorous and resistless, that it will crush out treason now and forever. [Applause.]

Resolved, That the proposition of Mr. Jefferson Davis to issue letters of marque to whosoever may apply for them, emanating from no recognized Government, is not only without the sanction of public law, but piratical in its tendencies, and therefore deserving the stern condemnation of the civilized world. It cannot result in the fitting out of regular privateers, but may, in infesting the ocean with piratical cruisers, armed with traitorous commissions, to despoil our commerce and that of all other maritime nations. [Applause.]

Resolved, That in view of this threatening evil, it is, in the opinion of this Chamber, the duty of our Government to issue at once a proclamation, warning all persons, that privateering under the commissions proposed will be dealt with as simple piracy. It owes this duty not merely to itself, but to other maritime nations, who have a right to demand that the United States Government shall promptly discountenance every attempt within its borders to legalize piracy. It should, also, at the earliest moment, blockade every Southern port, so as to prevent the egress and ingress of such vessels. [Immense applause.]

Resolved, That the Secretary be directed to send copies of these resolutions to the Chambers of Commerce of other cities, inviting their co-operation in such measures as may be deemed effective in strengthening the hands of Government in this emergency.

Resolved, That a copy of these resolutions, duly attested by the officers of the Chamber, be forwarded to the President of the United States.

BLOCKADE RESOLUTIONS.

Whereas, War against the Constitution and Government of these United States has been commenced, and is carried on by certain combinations of individuals, assuming to act for States at the South claiming to have seceded from the United States ; and

Whereas, Such combinations have officially promulgated an invitation for the enrollment of vessels, to act under their authorization, and, as so-called " privateers," against the flag and commerce of the United States ; therefore,

Resolved, by the Chamber of Commerce of the State of New York, That the United States Government be recommended and urged to blockade the ports of such States, or any other State that shall join them, and that this measure is demanded for defence in war, as also for protection to the commerce of the United States against these so-called " privateers " invited to enrol under the authority of such States.

Resolved, That the Chamber of Commerce of the State of New York pledges its hearty and cordial support to such measures as the Government of the United States may, in its wisdom, inaugurate and carry through in the blockade of such ports.

—*The World*, April 20.

Doc. 67.—A PROCLAMATION,

BY THE PRESIDENT OF THE UNITED STATES OF AMERICA.

Whereas an insurrection against the Government of the United States has broken out in the States of South Carolina, Georgia, Alabama, Florida, Mississippi, Louisiana, and Texas, and the laws of the United States for the collection of the revenue cannot be efficiently executed therein conformably to that provision of the Constitution which requires duties to be uniform throughout the United States :

And *whereas* a combination of persons, engaged in such insurrection, have threatened to grant pretended letters of marque to authorize the bearers thereof to commit assaults on the lives, vessels, and property of good citizens of the country lawfully engaged in commerce on the high seas, and in waters of the United States :

And *whereas* an Executive Proclamation has been already issued, requiring the persons engaged in these disorderly proceedings to desist therefrom, calling out a militia force for the purpose of repressing the same, and convening Congress in extraordinary session to deliberate and determine thereon :

Now, therefore, I, ABRAHAM LINCOLN, President of the United States, with a view to the same purposes before mentioned, and to the protection of the

public peace, and the lives and property of quiet and orderly citizens pursuing their lawful occupations, until Congress shall have assembled and deliberated on the said unlawful proceedings, or until the same shall have ceased, have further deemed it advisable to set on foot a Blockade of the ports within the States aforesaid, in pursuance of the laws of the United States and of the laws of nations in such cases provided. For this purpose a competent force will be posted so as to prevent entrance and exit of vessels from the ports aforesaid. If, therefore, with a view to violate such Blockade, a vessel shall approach, or shall attempt to leave any of the said ports, she will be duly warned by the Commander of one of the blockading vessels, who will indorse on her register the fact and date of such warning ; and if the same vessel shall again attempt to enter or leave the blockaded port, she will be captured and sent to the nearest convenient port, for such proceedings against her and her cargo as prize as may be deemed advisable.

And I hereby proclaim and declare, that if any person, under the pretended authority of said States, or under any other pretence, shall molest a vessel of the United States, or the persons or cargo on board of her, such person will be held amenable to the laws of the United States for the prevention and punishment of piracy.

By the President,   ABRAHAM LINCOLN.

WILLIAM H. SEWARD, *Secretary of State.*

WASHINGTON, April 19, 1861.

Doc. 68—GENERAL ORDERS—No. 3.

HEAD-QUARTERS OF THE ARMY, }
WASHINGTON, April 19, 1861. }

THE Military Department of Washington is extended so as to include, in addition to the District of Columbia and Maryland, the States of Delaware and Pennsylvania, and will be commanded by Major-Gen. PATTERSON, belonging to the volunteers of the latter State.

The Major-General will, as fast as they are mustered into service, post the volunteers of Pennsylvania all along the railroad from Wilmington, Del., to Washington City, in sufficient numbers and in such proximity as may give a reasonable protection to the lines of parallel wires, to the road, its rails, bridges, cars and stations.

By command :   WINFIELD SCOTT.

E. D. TOWNSEND, Assistant Adjutant-General.

Doc. 69—THE BALTIMORE RIOT.

MAYOR'S OFFICE, April 19, 1861.

SIR : This will be presented to you by the Hon. H. Lenox Bond, Geo. W. Dobbin and Jno. C. Brune, esqs., who will proceed to Washington by an express train, at my request, in order to explain fully the fearful condition of our affairs in this city. The people are exasperated to the highest degree by the passage of troops, and the citizens are universally decided in the opinion that no more troops should be ordered to come.

The authorities of the city did their best to-day to protect both strangers and citizens, and to prevent a collision, but in vain ; and but for their great efforts a fearful slaughter would have occurred.

Under these circumstances, it is my solemn duty to inform you that it is not possible for more soldiers to pass through Baltimore, unless they fight their way at every step.

I therefore hope and trust, and most earnestly request, that no more troops be permitted or ordered by the Government to pass through the city. If they should attempt it, the responsibility for the bloodshed will not rest upon me. With great respect, your obedient servant,

GEO. WM. BROWN, Mayor.

To His Excellency ABRAHAM LINCOLN, President of the United States:

I have been in Baltimore since Tuesday evening, and co-operated with Mayor Brown in his untiring efforts to allay and prevent the excitement and suppress the fearful outbreak as indicated above, and I fully concur in all that is said by him in the above communication. Very respectfully, your obedient servant,

THOMAS HICKS, Governor of Maryland.

To His Excellency President LINCOLN.

DESPATCH FROM THE PRESIDENT.

Mayor Brown received a despatch from President Lincoln this morning, stating that no more troops would pass through this city.

MAYOR'S OFFICE, Baltimore, April 19.

To His Excellency the President of the United States:

SIR:—A collision between the citizens and the northern troops has taken place in Baltimore, and the excitement is fearful. Send no more troops here. We will endeavor to prevent all bloodshed. A public meeting of citizens has been called, and the troops of the State and the city have been called out to preserve the peace. They will be enough.

Respectfully:

THO. H. HICKS, Governor.
GEO. WM. BROWN, Mayor.

The following correspondence then took place between the governor and mayor and John W. Garrett, Esq., president of the Baltimore and Ohio Railroad:

MAYOR'S OFFICE, CITY HALL,
BALTIMORE, April 19, 1861.

JOHN W. GARRETT, Esq., President Baltimore and Ohio Railroad:

SIR:—We advise that the troops now here be sent back to the borders of Maryland. Respectfully,

GEO. WM. BROWN.
THOS. H. HICKS.

By order of the Board of Police.

CHAS. HOWARD, President.

BALTIMORE AND OHIO RAILROAD,
BALTIMORE, April 19.

To his Excellency, THOMAS H. HICKS, Governor; His Honor, GEO. W. BROWN, Mayor of Baltimore, and CHAS. HOWARD, Esq., President of the Board of Police Commissioners:

I have the honor to acknowledge the receipt of your communication of this date, in which you "advise that the troops here be sent back to the borders of Maryland." Most cordially approving the advice, I have instructed by telegraph the same to the Philadelphia, Wilmington and Baltimore Rail-

road Co., and this company will act in accordance therewith. Your obedient servant,

JOHN W. GARRETT, President.

The following note accompanies the correspondence :

Gov. Hicks and Mayor Brown have advised that the Rhode Island and Massachusetts volunteers (who were delayed at President Street) *be returned to Philadelphia.*

It is also understood that no more troops will be carried by the Baltimore and Ohio Railroad.

—*Baltimore Clipper, extra,* April 19.

THE RATTLESNAKE'S FANGS.

THE eighty-sixth anniversary of the fight at Lexington was signalized, at Baltimore yesterday, by the first blood shed north of Charleston in the great Pro-Slavery Disunion Rebellion. The Massachusetts soldiery passing quietly and inoffensively through that city, in obedience to the orders of their Government, were assaulted by a vast Disunion mob, which first obstructed the Railroad, then blocked up the streets through which they were compelled to march, and passing rapidly from hooting and yelling to throwing showers of paving-stones, they at last wore out the patience of the troops by shooting three of them dead, and wounding several others, when the soldiers fired back, and stretched a few of the miscreants on the ground. The mob then gave way sufficiently to allow the defenders of their country's Government and flag to push on to the depot of the Baltimore and Ohio Railroad, where they took the cars provided for them, and proceeded quietly to Washington.

That the villains who fomented this attack are at once traitors and murderers, no loyal mind can doubt. There is no pretence that Maryland has seceded from the Union—on the contrary, the most desperate efforts to plunge her into the abyss of rebellion have proved abortive. She is among the States whose authorities, though sorely tried, stand firmly by the Government and Flag of the Union. Yet, in full view of this fact, the Baltimore secessionists held a great public meeting on Thursday morning, and were harangued by their leaders in the most exciting and treasonable language. One of them, Wilson N. C. Carr, announced himself as ready and willing to shoulder his musket for the defence of Southern homes and firesides. His interrogatory whether the 75,000 minions of Lincoln should pass over the soil of Maryland to subjugate our sisters of the South was answered with deafening shouts of "No, never." Such was the direct and calculated incitement to the murderous attack of yesterday. We rejoice to add that it resulted in the triumph of Loyalty and the Union, and in the necessary proclamation of Martial Law.

In every instance of collision between the Unionists and the secessionists up to this moment, the latter have not only been the aggressors, but the wanton, unprovoked, murderous aggressors. How much longer is this to go on? What can martial law in Baltimore be worth if the traitors who instigated this assassination be not dealt with according to law? If the authorities of Maryland do not suppress these murderous traitors, the United States will be compelled to occupy Baltimore with a force sufficient to preserve order and keep the way open to the city of Washington. This is no time for half measures.

—*N. Y. Tribune.*

Doc. 70.—CORRESPONDENCE BETWEEN GOV. ANDREW AND MAYOR BROWN.

"BALTIMORE, April 20, 1861.

"_The Hon. John A. Andrew, Governor of Massachusetts:_

"SIR:—No one deplores the sad events of yesterday in this city more deeply than myself, but they were inevitable. Our people viewed the passage of armed troops to another State through the streets as an invasion of our soil, and could not be restrained. The authorities exerted themselves to the best of their ability, but with only partial success. Governor Hicks was present, and concurs in all my views as to the proceedings now necessary for our protection. When are these scenes to cease? Are we to have a war of sections? God forbid. The bodies of the Massachusetts soldiers could not be sent out to Boston, as you requested—all communication between this city and Philadelphia by railroad, and with Boston by steamers, having ceased; but they have been placed in cemented coffins, and will be placed with proper funeral ceremonies in the mausoleum of Greenmount Cemetery, where they shall be retained until further directions are received from you. The wounded are tenderly cared for. I appreciate your offer, but Baltimore will claim it as her right to pay all expenses incurred. Very respectfully, your obedient servant,

"GEO. W. BROWN, Mayor of Baltimore."

To this the following reply was returned by the Governor:

"_To His Honor Geo. W. Brown, Mayor of Baltimore:_

"DEAR SIR:—I appreciate your kind attention to our wounded and our dead, and trust that at the earliest moment the remains of our fallen will return to us. I am overwhelmed with surprise that a peaceful march of American citizens over the highway to the defence of our common capital should be deemed aggressive to Baltimoreans. Through New York the march was triumphal.

"JOHN A. ANDREW,
"Governor of Massachusetts."

—_Evening Post._

Doc. 71.—DEPARTURE OF THE NEW YORK SEVENTH REGIMENT.

THE intelligence that the Seventh Regiment, the "crack" Regiment, the almost adored military body of New York, would leave for Washington, created an excitement scarcely surpassed by any thing that has transpired since the first news of the attack on Fort Sumter. Although it was announced that 3 P. M. was the time for the assembling of the Regiment at their Armory, over Tompkins Market, Broadway was the scene of gathering for hundreds of people long before noon. The march of the second instalment of Massachusetts troops, early in the forenoon, was but an incentive to their patriotism. If they had to wait many hours, as indeed they had, they were prepared to stand on the tip-toe of expectation till their favorite Regiment passed, even if nightfall came. The aspect of Broadway was very gay indeed. Minus the firing of pistols and the explosion of Chinese crackers, it was many Fourth-of-Julys rolled into one. The Stars and Stripes were everywhere, from the costliest silk, twenty, thirty, forty feet in length,

to the homelier bunting, down to the few inches of painted calico that a baby's hand might wave. It would be invidious to say from what buildings the National flag was displayed, because it would be almost impossible to tell from what buildings it did not wave, and never, if flags can be supposed to be animated with any of the feelings of their owners, with a purer devotion to the Union. Evidently, all political partisanship was cast aside. But the gayest, and in this respect, the most remarkable thoroughfare was Cortlandt-street. Lafayette-place, where the Regiment was to form previous to marching, was very attractively dressed—a huge flag being displayed from the Astor Library, among numerous others from private buildings. But Cortlandt-street showed a gathering of flags, a perfect army of them. They were not, in that comparatively brief space from Broadway to the Jersey City Ferry, to be numbered by dozens or by scores: every building seemed like "Captains of Fifties." It was flag, flag, from every window from the first floor to the roof, from every doorway,—in short, it was flag, flag,—and of quite large sizes, too, till the wearied eye refused the task of counting them. Such was the display along the route of the "Seventh." Such is and will be the route for all noble troops entering our City from the New England States.

Around the Armory of the Seventh Regiment crowds gathered at an early period of the day, and moved on, only to be replaced by other crowds. So the excitement was kept up, till towards three o'clock the throng became stationary. It was, by no means, an ordinary crowd. Well-dressed ladies, men whose checks can be honored at the best Banks for as many dollars as would build a church of excellent architecture, were among them. They were about to witness the departure of the Seventh Regiment, too probably, to the battle-field. Though the flags waved gaily over them, their faces wore a grave look—not sad exactly, but it was no time for mirth.

From all quarters the members of the Regiment, in full fatigue dress, with their knapsacks and blankets, kept pouring into the Armory. Guards at the doors kept the crowd, who had no business inside, from entering, but the building was filled to its utmost, notwithstanding, by the members, their relatives and friends. There were many touching scenes of farewell-taking, but these were merely episodes. Mothers, wives, sisters, will weep on such occasions, but there was no faltering among the men. A heartier shake of the hand than usual, to a friend,—a warmer kiss—let it be reverentially said—to a wife or mother, and the manhood of the soldier grew the greater, and he trussed his knapsack the tighter to his back as he gave the last adieu.

They formed in Lafayette-place about 4 P. M., in the presence of an immense crowd, each window of each building being filled with such fair applauders as might cheer the heart of the forlornest bachelor, if there was any such among those noble soldiers. Once in line, they proceeded through Fourth-street to Broadway, down that great thoroughfare to Cortlandt-street, and across the ferry, in boats provided for the purpose, to Jersey City. The line of march was a perfect ovation. Thousands upon thousands lined the sidewalks. It will be remembered as long as any of those who witnessed it live to talk of it, and beyond that, it will pass into the recorded history of this fearful struggle. The

Regiment was escorted by a band of Zouaves, who volunteered for the occasion. Their gay uniform and peculiar step revived the excitement that had begun somewhat to droop among the crowd that had waited for hours, the Regiment not reaching the Park till 5½ o'clock. After the Zouaves came a strong body of police, and after the police, THE REGIMENT. Not as on festival days, not as on the reception of the Prince of Wales, but nobly and sternly, as men who were going to the war. Hurried was their step, not so regular as on less important occasions. We saw women, we saw men shed tears as they passed. Amidst the deafening cheers that rose, we heard cries of "God bless them." And so along Broadway, and through Cortlandt-street, under its almost countless flags, the gallant Seventh Regiment left the City.

The excitement in Jersey City, long before they had crossed the ferry, was scarcely less intense, and when they landed there, they found they were by no means in a foreign State. It seemed that all the people of the sister city had turned out. It was a reënaction of what their fellow-townsmen and townswomen had done for them. White handkerchiefs, waved by ladies' hands, were as numerous as the dog-wood blossoms in Spring, and it was proved that a Jerseyman can raise as hearty a cheer as the best New Yorker. And so it was till all were fairly disposed of in the cars, and the cars moved off.

—N. Y. Times.

OFFICERS OF THE SEVENTH REGIMENT.

The following is a list of the officers of the Seventh Regiment:

Colonel—Marshal Lefferts.
Lieutenant-Colonel—William A. Pond.
Major—Alexander Thaler.
Adjutant—J. H. Libenau.
Engineer—E. L. Viele.
Surgeon—T. M. Cheeseman; Surgeon's Mate, J. C. Dalton, Jr.
Chaplain—Rev. S. H. Weston.
Quartermaster—L. W. Winchester.
Assistant-Quartermaster—G. W. Brainard.
Paymaster—Meredith Howland.
Commissary—William Patten.
Ordnance Officer—John A. Baker.
Military Secretary—C. T. McClenachan; and the non-commissioned staff, eight officers.

FIRST COMPANY—Captain, William P. Bensell; First Lieutenant, James H. Hewett; Second Lieutenant, James E. Harway, five sergeants, six corporals, and 90 privates.

SECOND COMPANY—Captain, E. W. Clark; First Lieutenant, N. L. Farnham; Second Lieutenant, Edward Bernard; five sergeants, six corporals, and 120 privates.

THIRD COMPANY—Captain, James Price; First Lieutenant, J. J. Wickstead; Second Lieutenant, George T. Haws; five sergeants, six corporals, and 100 men.

FOURTH COMPANY—Captain, William H. Riblet; First Lieutenant, William Gurney; Second Lieutenant, John W. Bogert; five sergeants, six corporals, and 100 men.

FIFTH COMPANY—Captain W. A. Speaight; First Lieutenant, F. Millard; Second Lieutenant, J. F. Cook; five sergeants, six corporals, and about 100 men.

SIXTH COMPANY—Captain, B. M. Nevers, Jr.;

First Lieutenant, R. F. Halsted; Second Lieutenant, J. B. Young; five sergeants, six corporals, and 100 men.

SEVENTH COMPANY—Captain, John Monroe; First Lieutenant, John P. Schermerhorn; Second Lieutenant, John D. Moriarity; five sergeants, seven corporals, and about 100 men.

THE COMPLETE FORCE.

Non-commissioned staff,	8
Government staff,	11
Field officers,	8
Artillery corps, 54 men, 2 howitzers, 2 officers, 2 sergeants,	61
Engineer corps—2 men, 2 officers, 2 sergeants,	29
Recruits in fatigue dress,	175
Company 1—63 men, 3 officers, 4 sergeants,	70
Company 2—100 men, 3 officers, 5 sergeants,	108
Company 3—70 men, 3 officers, 5 sergeants,	78
Company 4—82 men, 3 officers, 5 sergeants,	90
Company 5—54 men, 3 officers, 5 sergeants,	62
Company 6—80 men, 3 officers, 5 sergeants,	88
Company 7—60 men, 1 officer, 5 sergeants,	66
Company 8—78 men, 3 officers, 5 sergeants,	86
Band—40 pieces,	40
Drum corps,	12
Total,	985

—N. Y. Tribune.

Doc. 72.—THE EIGHTH REGIMENT OF MASSACHUSETTS.

THE staff officers of the Regiment are as follows: Timothy Monroe of Lynn, Colonel; Edward W. Hinks of Lynn, Lieutenant-Colonel; Andrew Elwell of Gloucester, Major; C. M. Merritt of Lynn, Sergeant-Major; E. A. Ingalls of Lynn, Quartermaster; H. E. Monroe of Lynn, Quartermaster's Sergeant; R. G. Asher of Lynn, Paymaster; Dr. B. B. Breed of Lynn, Surgeon; Warren Tapley of Lynn, Surgeon's Mate; John T. Cole of Lynn, Regiment Clerk.

On the route of the Regiment at the Jersey City depot, an affecting incident occurred. Col. Monroe being loudly called for, appeared, surrounded by Gen. Butler, Quartermaster-General John Moran, Col. Hinks, and the rest of the staff. A. W. Griswold, Esq., a prominent member of the New York bar, stepped forward, holding in his hand a magnificent silk flag, mounted on a massive hickory staff. He addressed the commandant of the 8th Regiment as follows:

Col. Monroe—Sir, you are from Massachusetts; "God bless you!" Her sons everywhere are proud of her history, and, while her armies are commanded by such officers as are now at their head, we have faith in her future. As a son of Massachusetts, I beg to present this standard as a token of my appreciation of the cause in which you are engaged. I confide it to your keeping. "Stand by it."

Col. Monroe responded with the following appropriate and eloquent remarks;

"As a son of Massachusetts, I receive it from a son of her soil, and I will defend it, 'God help me.'"

The cheering which followed was deafening—nine cheers were proposed and given for the flag, and at that moment 800 hardy troops, just arrived from the sacred precincts of Bunker Hill, vowed solemnly to defend that flag with their lives and honor.

The flag is made of silk; heavy crimson tassels hanging from the spear of the staff.

—*Tribune*, April 20.

Doc. 73.—FORT MOULTRIE.

THE raking fire from Fort Sumter against Fort Moultrie was terribly destructive, and when viewed in connection with the fact that no life was lost, is the most extraordinary case ever recorded in history. As you enter, the eye falls upon the battered walls of the archway, with openings in some places large enough for windows. In other places may be seen the hanging splinters of the rafters, large pieces of ceiling seemingly about to drop, while the holes in the roof throw a clear light over the scene of destruction, which renders it painfully impressive. It would be an almost impossible task to count the number of balls discharged at this devoted fortress. All of the officers' quarters were battered with seven, eight, or ten balls, which penetrated the whole depth of the building. The western wall on the upper balcony was entirely shot away. The barracks were almost entirely destroyed. The furnace for heating hot shot was struck four times, the flag of the Confederate States received three shots, and the Palmetto flag four—a rather singular and peculiar circumstance, when viewed in connection with the seven Confederate States. The merlons of sand-bags, &c., remain unbroken.

On the outside walls we counted over one hundred shots. Laborers were engaged in clearing away fallen bricks, &c. It will be necessary to pull down the old walls and rebuild anew. Even the beds and bedding in the officers' quarters and the men's barracks were cut and torn into splinters and shreds. Had it not been for the bomb-proof shelter, the loss of life would no doubt have been appalling. One shell entered the brick wall of Major Ripley's bedroom, ran down the wall, and burst on the bureau immediately over the head of the bed. Our limited time prevented us from visiting the battery to the north of Fort Moultrie. We learn, however, that though many of the buildings around it had been struck several times, and fences, trees, &c., cut away, the battery sustained no injury.

THE BUILDINGS DAMAGED.

The following were the houses destroyed or damaged :

Mr. Henry Oetjen's house, a two-story frame dwelling, almost in range of the Floating Battery. This was completely riddled.

Mrs. Gilman's summer residence, partially destroyed.

Mrs. Brown's house, in front of the Enfilade Battery. This was removed previous to the cannonading.

Mr. George M. Coffin's summer residence nearly destroyed.

Mr. Smith's house partially destroyed.

Mrs. C. Fitzsimon's house received seven shots, and is mostly destroyed.

Mr. Gervais's house, back of Fort Moultrie, almost riddled.

Mr. Benjamin Mordecai's house, badly damaged.

Mr. T. Savage Heyward's house, badly damaged.

Mr. F. P. Elford's house—roof battered in and weather-boarding torn off.

Mr. Thomas Farr Capers's house was struck several times.

Mr. Copes's house, in front of the Enfilade Battery, was removed by order of the authorities.

The Moultrie House received four shots, one cutting away one of the main pillars, and making a clean breach through the building from one end to the other.

The other shots have damaged the walls and ceiling to a very considerable extent. Fortunately, no one was in at the time.

Mr. James M. Caldwell's house received several shots.

Mr. David Briggs's house was badly shattered.

Mr. Ross's house received one shot.

Mrs. Fillette's house was damaged by a shell, which burst on the roof and broke through the window.

The fence in front of the Presbyterian Church was shot away, but the church is uninjured.

The railroad track in front of Fort Moultrie was also torn up by the shot and shell.

The small building, formerly used as the Quartermaster's Department, United States Army, was very badly shattered, and large portions of the wall cut away.

Several other houses were struck with one or more balls, tearing off the weather-boarding and shattering the roofs. The largest number of the houses, however, are untouched. Providentially no hot shot was thrown from Sumter—probably from the fact that the garrison had no fuel. Many of those whose houses have been battered esteem it more fortunate than otherwise, and have determined to allow the buildings to remain, as far as possible, in the condition in which they were found after the battle, as a memento of the glorious 12th and 13th days of April, 1861.

—*Charleston Courier*, April 20.

Doc. 73½.—MEETING AT UNION SQUARE, NEW YORK, MAY 20, 1861.

THE Rev. Dr. Spring, of the Brick Church, of the city, was invited to offer the opening prayer. The venerable gentleman, before offering prayer, said:—

I think myself very happy, Mr. President and fellow-citizens, that, as a native-born American, as a son of one of the revolutionary officers, as a member of Christ's church and one of His ambassadors, I am permitted to bear my testimony in favor of this noble cause. My past views on the agitated questions of the country are well known to those of you who are familiar with the press. I have seen no occasion to alter them; I adhere to them now. But the question now is not between slavery and anti-slavery—between republicanism and democracy; it is between law and anarchy—between government and mere phantoms, that sink into nothingness compared with the main question of government or no government in this favored country. And, Sir, it is that my feeble voice, in the behalf of that church which I represent, may be heard to-day, that I cheerfully accept the invitation to open this meeting with prayer. When I think of the little band of men who took such a noble part in the struggle at Fort Sumter, maintaining the flag of their country while burning fires were about them —(referring to Major Anderson and the other officers present)—I feel cheered. (Cheers.) Your faces here to-day cheer me. The dead lips of that Father of his Country speak to you and to me!

And what do they say?—"United we stand—divided we fall." Let us lift up our hearts to Almighty God for His presence and blessing.

PRAYER.

Almighty God, Creator of the heavens and the earth, the Infinite One, we are Thy creatures; Thou the Infinite and Eternal Creator, the King Eternal, Immortal and Invisible; the Great Emperor of heaven and of earth, doing Thy counsel in the armies of heaven and amid all the inhabitants of this lower world. We know we are unworthy; as a people we have to confess our sins before Thee, and come to Thy throne in the name of Jesus Christ, the great Mediator, who is Himself the Prince of the kings of the earth, that we might have an interest in Thy pardoning mercy, and under the blessings of our God and our fathers' God, we address ourselves to the exercises of this day and to the struggle to which Thy holy Providence calls us. Oh, God of our fathers, remember this favored land. We have reason to thank Thee for the spirit and success which Thou didst impart to our fathers in the revolutionary struggle; and may some of that spirit of our revered fathers and sainted mothers come down to their descendants on such occasions as this; and may that portion of the people of this land who, in the spirit of revolt, have gone from us, understand that we are but one people. Oh, God, we commit the cause in which the noble men—young men and men of middle age—have gone forth to fight the battles of this country and resist the aggressions of the foe, to Thy care, to Thy favor, to Thy providence, to Thy protection. Smile upon them and upon us, through Christ our Redeemer. Amen. (Responses of "Amen.")

These preliminaries having been arranged, the meeting was formally organized as follows:—

Mr. McCurdy put in nomination for President Mr. John A. Dix.

The following list of officers was then put in nomination, and acceded to:—

VICE-PRESIDENTS.

W. B. Astor,	Robt. Ray,	Erastus Brooks,
Greene C. Bronson,	Benj. L. Swan,	Joseph Schleigman,
Peter Cooper,	John Q. Jones,	Schuyler Livingston
W. M. Evarts,	David Hoadley,	W. H. Osborn,
W. C. Bryant,	Robt. J. Taylor,	A. A. Vanderpoel,
Pelatiah Perit,	Jas. N. Phelps,	W. W. De Forrest,
Geo. Bancroft,	Jas. Low,	A. B. Baylis,
John A. King,	John Ewen,	Elnathan Thorne,
Moses Taylor,	Jas. A. Briggs,	W. B. Maclay,
James Boorman,	John D. Jones,	Fred. Kapp,
Stewart Brown,	Wm. C. Bryce,	Anson Herrick,
John J. Phelps,	Henry F. Vail,	Theodore Fowler,
R. B. Minturn,	Frederick Bronson,	Daniel Leroy,
Henry Grinnell,	F. A. Conkling,	S. L. Mitchill,
O. D. F. Grant,	A. J. Williamson,	Augustus Schell,
W. E. Dodge,	D. H. Arnold,	Chas. Christmas,
Watts Sherman,	Geo. Folsom,	J. B. Varnum,
Edwin Crosswell,	Andrew Carrigan,	Wm. Hall,
L. G. B. Cannon,	A. C. Kingsland,	Chas. A. Secor,
John D. Wolfe,	Isaac Ferris,	John T. Hoffman,
Seth B. Hunt,	J. Anchincloss,	Hamilton Fish,
Edwin Dobbs,	M. Franklin,	Luther Bradish,
Joseph Stuart,	D. R. Martin,	Fernando Wood,
R. H. McCurdy,	Wm. Chauncey,	A. T. Stewart,
Joseph W. Alsop,	H. B. Chaflin,	Morris Ketchum,
E. E. Morgan,	Wm. Bryce,	Jonathan Sturges,
Willis Blackstone,	A. S. Hewitt,	J. J. Astor,
Nath. Hayden,	S. B. Althause,	John Cochran,
John Lloyd,	Peter Lorillard,	Alex. Duncan.
Chas. H. Russell,		

SECRETARIES.

J. Smith Homans,	D. D. Lord,	George A. Vogel,
John Bigelow,	C. H. Marshall, Jr.,	Fletcher Westray,
John T. Johnston,	Jas. G. De Forest,	Charles B. Norton.
Sheppard Gandy,		

SPEECH OF THE HON. JOHN A. DIX.

On taking the chair, the President said:—

Fellow-Citizens:—We have come together to express our determination to uphold the authority of the Government and to maintain inviolate the honor of the country. The circumstances under which we are assembled are calculated to fill any patriotic heart with the deepest concern. For the first time in our day civil strife has broken out in the bosom of our prosperous and happy country, and has been pushed by unscrupulous men to the extremity of war and bloodshed. With no provocation whatever from the Federal Government they turned their arms in fraternal hatred against it, even when it was administered by those who were actuated by the most friendly dispositions toward them. But I do not doubt, when the present excitement shall have passed away, when those who have thus arrayed themselves against the Government of the country shall have learned from a disastrous experience that their true interest lies in peace, all will concede, on a review of the past in a spirit of fairness and moderation, that there was no just ground for alienation. (Cheers.) But, fellow-citizens, I feel that all such considerations are inappropriate to the hour. The time for action has come. Practical issues are upon us, to be dealt with under a just sense of the responsibilities they have brought with them. The Constitution of the United States has been spurned and repudiated. The authority of the Government has been resisted by military force. The flag of the Union has been insulted, in more than one instance torn down, and even trampled under foot. Most of us were born, and all of us have lived in prosperity and peace under the protection of the constitution; we have regarded our allegiance to the Union as second only to our religion in the sanctity of its obligations; and we have venerated the national standard, under which Washington and Jackson and the host of gallant men who were their companions in arms, or who followed in their footsteps, achieved undying honors for themselves and their country. (Enthusiastic applause.) We should be more or less men if we could look with indifference on these outrages on all we hold most dear. There is no justification for the cause of the Confederate States in overturning within their limits the authority of the Federal Government. They have no excuse for it. This is no time for elaborate argument. Let me say in a word, that no respectable defence of the right of secession has ever fallen under my notice. No man contends that there is any warrant for it in the constitution. There is but one way for a State to go out of the Union—the way in which all came in—by the concurrence of the common authority. In no other manner can the terms of separation be agreed on. (We don't want to separate.) Whatever preliminary action there may be, it must come to this conclusion at last. It is an omitted case in our political compact. The framers of the constitution did not contemplate the dissolution of the Union. They framed the Government for themselves and their posterity. The repudiation of its authority by one of its members was not foreseen or provided for. It is a case which cannot be reached by the powers vested in Congress or in the Executive; and the States are necessarily remitted to the exercise of their united sovereignty for the solution of a problem which concerns the existence of all. It was for this reason that a Committee, of which I was Chairman, in an address to our Southern brethren, adopted at a meeting in Pine-street, in December last, recommended that the States should meet together for consultation, and if they could not settle their difficulties amicably and preserve the Union, that they should arrange the terms of separation, and save the country from the horrors civil war. We implored them to pause, in order to give us time for an effort to restore harmony and fraternal feeling. We appealed to them in language of entreaty, which would have been humiliating if it had not been addressed to brethren of the same political family. To this appeal, enforced by the concurrence of eminent citizens of this State, who had always been the most strenuous advocates of Southern rights, the States to which it was addressed responded by setting the authority of the Union at defiance, by seizing the public forts and arsenals, by seducing federal officers from their allegiance, and in one instance by confiscating the treasure of the Government. For months those outrages were submitted to, with no effort on the part of the Government to resent or punish them, in the hope that, under the guidance of better counsels, those who committed them would return to their allegiance. This forbearance, unexampled in the history of nations, and falsely interpreted into a pusillanimous surrender of its authority by the Federal Government, had only the effect of invigorating the spirit of resistance, until at last the slender force in Fort Sumter was attacked—some 6,000 or 7,000 men against 100—and compelled, after a heroic resistance, to evacuate it. (Cheers for Fort Sumter.) The gallant commander of that handful of loyal men who sustained this unequal contest is before you. (Tremendous cheers for Major Anderson.) There hangs the flag under which they upheld the honor of their country ; and its tattered condition shows the desperate defence they made. (Enthusiastic cheering.) It is under these circumstances that the General Government has appealed to the country to come to its support. (We will! we will!) It would have been treacherous to its trust if it had not determined to uphold the authorities confided to it. And here, fellow-citizens, it is important that we should clearly understand the position of the late Administration, on this question. It is due to this Administration as well as the last, that we should all understand it. I shall be very brief, but I must ask your close attention for the few moments that will be needed. On the 3d of December last, in his Annual Message to Congress, the late President made a strong and unanswerable argument against the right of secession. He also indicated his purpose to collect the revenue and defend the forts in South Carolina. In a special message to Congress on the 8th of January he declared (I use the language of the message) "the right and the duty to use military force defensively against those who resist the federal officers in the execution of their legal functions and against those who assail the property of the Federal Government, is clear and undeniable." (Cries of "Good for him," and loud cheering.) The authorities of South Carolina were repeatedly warned that, if they assailed Fort Sumter, it would be the commencement of civil war, and they would be responsible for the consequences. (Cheers.) The last and most emphatic of these warnings is contained in the admirable answer of Mr. Holt, Secretary of War, to Mr. Hayne, the Commissioner from South Carolina, on the 6th of February. It is

in these words :—"If, with all the multiplied proof which exists of the President's anxiety for peace, and of the earnestness with which he has pursued it, the authorities of that State shall assault Fort Sumter and peril the lives of the handful of brave and loyal men shut up within its walls, and thus plunge our common country into the horrors of civil war, then upon them and those they represent must rest the responsibility." (Enthusiastic applause, and waving of hats.) I believe the letter from which I have read this extract has never been published, for I, as a member of the Administration at the time it was written, have a right to say that it had the cordial approval of the late President, and all his constitutional advisers. (Cheers for General Dix.) And this brings me to the point I wish to make. I violate no confidence in making it. It is this :—If South Carolina had tendered war to the late Administration as she has to this—I mean by a hostile and deadly assault—it would have been unanimously accepted. (Prolonged cheering.) I repeat, then, that this Administration has done no more than its duty. Nay, I believe, that self-preservation rendered necessary what it has done. I have no doubt that the Confederate leaders at Montgomery have entertained, and still entertain, the design of marching upon Washington to overthrow the Government, taking its place and presenting itself to the nations of the world as the true representative of the people of the United States. (Cries of "Never, never ; they can't do it.") Against this usurpation and fraud, if it shall be attempted, I trust we shall contend with all the strength God has given us. (Cries of " We will.") I am for supporting the Government. I do not ask who administers it. It is the Government of my country, and as such I shall give it in this extremity all the support in my power. I regard the pending contest with the secessionists as a death struggle for constitutional liberty and law—a contest which, if successful on their part, could only end in the establishment of a despotic government, and blot out, wherever they were in the ascendant, every vestige of national freedom. You know, fellow-citizens, that I have always been in favor of adjusting controversies between the States by conciliation, by compromise, by mutual concession—in a word, in the spirit in which the constitution was formed. Whenever the times shall be propitious for calm consultation they will find me so still. But until then, let us remember that nothing could be so disastrous, so humiliating and so disreputable to us all as to see the common Government overthrown or its legitimate authority successfully resisted. Let us, then, rally with one heart, to its support. I believe it will act with all the moderation and forbearance consistent with the preservation of the great interests confided to it. There is no choice left but to acquiesce in its surrender to revolutionary leaders, or to give it the means it needs for defence, and for self-preservation and for the assertion of its authority, holding it responsible for their legitimate use. Fellow-citizens, we stand before the statue of the Father of his Country. The flag of the Union which floats over it hung above him when he presided over the Convention by which the constitution was framed. The great work of his life has been rejected, and the banner by which his labors were consecrated has been trampled in the dust. If the inanimate bronze in which the sculptor has shaped his image could be changed to the living form which led the armies of the Revolution to victory, he would command us, in the name of the hosts of patriots and political martyrs who have gone before, to strike for the defence of the Union and the constitution.

Mr. Dix closed his remarks amid the most enthusiastic applause.

The Chairman then read the following resolutions, which were unanimously adopted:—

Whereas, the Union of the States, under the guidance of Divine Providence, has been the fruitful source of prosperity and domestic peace to the country for nearly three-quarters of a century; and

Whereas, the constitution, framed by our Revolutionary fathers, contains within itself all needful provisions for the exigencies of the Government, and, in the progress of events, for such amendments as are necessary to meet new exigencies; and

Whereas, an armed combination has been formed to break up the Union, by throwing off the obligations of the constitution, and has, in several of the States, carried on its criminal purpose, and, finally, by assaulting Fort Sumter, a fortress of the United States occupied by a slender but heroic garrison, and capturing it by an overwhelming force after a gallant defence, thus setting the authority of the Government at defiance, and insulting the National Flag; and

Whereas, the Government of the United States, with an earnest desire to avert the evils of civil war, has silently submitted to these aggressions and insults with a patient forbearance unparalleled in the annals of history, but has at last deemed it due to the public honor and safety to appeal to the people of the Union for the means of maintaining its authority, of enforcing the execution of the laws, and of saving our country from dismemberment and our political institutions from destruction; therefore,

Resolved, That the Declaration of Independence, the war of the Revolution, and the Constitution of the United States have given origin to this Government, the most equal and beneficent hitherto known among men; that under its protection the wide expansion of our territory, the vast development of our wealth, our population, and our power, have built up a nation able to maintain and defend before the world the principles of liberty and justice upon which it was founded; that by every sentiment of interest, of honor, of affection and of duty, we are engaged to preserve unbroken for our generation, and to transmit to our posterity, the great heritage we have received from heroic ancestors; that to the maintenance of this sacred trust we devote whatever we possess, and whatever we can do, and in support of that Government under which we are happy and proud to live, we are prepared to shed our blood and lay down our lives.

Resolved, That the founders of the Government of the United States have provided, by the institution of the Supreme Court, a tribunal for the peaceful settlement of all questions arising under the constitution and the laws; that it is the duty of the States to appeal to it for relief from measures which they believe unauthorized; and that attempts to throw off the obligations of the constitution, and to obtain redress by an appeal to arms, can be considered in no other light than as levying war against the United States.

Resolved, That the Constitution of the United States, the basis and the safeguard of the Federal Union, having been framed and ratified by the original States, and accepted by those which subsequently became parties to it, is binding upon all; and that any resumption by any one of them of the rights delegated to the Federal Government, without first seeking a release from its obligations through the concurrence of the common sovereignty, is unauthorized, unjust to all the others, and destructive of all social and political order.

Resolved, That when the authority of the Federal Government shall have been re-established, and peaceful obedience to the constitution and laws prevail, we shall be ready to confer and co-operate with all loyal citizens throughout the Union, in Congress or in Convention, for the consideration of all supposed grievances, the redress of all wrongs, and the protection of every right, yielding ourselves, and expecting all others to yield, to the will of the whole people as constitutionally and lawfully expressed.

Resolved, That it is the duty of all good citizens, overlooking past differences of opinion, to contribute by all the means in their power to maintain the Union of the States, to defend the constitution, to preserve the national flag from insult, and uphold the authority of the Government against acts of lawless violence, which, if longer unresisted, would inevitably end in breaking down all the barriers erected by our fathers for the protection of life, liberty and property, and involve the country in universal anarchy and confusion.

Resolved, That a committee of twenty-five, to be nominated by the President, be appointed by this meeting to represent the citizens in the collection of funds and the transaction of such other business in aid of the movements of the Government as the public interests may require.

SPEECH OF DANIEL S. DICKINSON.

FELLOW CITIZENS—I was invited to speak on this occasion—in the language of the call—to the people, without distinction of party, and I avail myself, with alacrity, of the invitation. This morning I travelled two hundred miles in order to be present. (Cheers.) We are cast on perilous times. The demon of discord has inaugurated his terrible court, and it becomes us as a great people to act in a manner becoming this Government and people. In a somewhat extended service I have entertained my own views of what each section of this confederacy owed to the other. Through a spirit of forbearance, fraternity and friendship, I had hoped, notwithstanding there might be subjects of irritation, that the healing influence of time and the recollection of the great names and greater memories of the Revolution would call back all to their duty, that all might be harmonized, and that we might all march on together like brethren to a great and common destiny. (Cheers.) But while we were revelling in these dreams a fortress has been attacked and reduced, or evacuated. The flag of the country has been insulted, public property seized, and civil war exists this day by the action of those who should be and are our sister States—by those who are our brethren. In this great crisis it is no time to inquire for causes remote and distant; it is no time to inquire who holds the helm of the ship of State; it is no time to inquire what interest or section placed him there. The only question is, does he steer the ship between the Scylla and Charybdis which threaten our Union, according to the lights of the constitution? If he does, he is to be sustained. (Cheers.) I shall not pursue this matter in an angry spirit. I would make every effort to bring back every wandering lamb to the fold again. I would not levy war for aggression—I would levy it for defensive peace. (Cheers.) I would not do it to despoil others. I would arm, and that in a manner becoming this Government and people, not for aggression, I repeat, but for defence—for the purpose of retaining our honor and dignity, not only at home, but among the nations of the earth. (Cheers.) The most brilliant successes that ever attended the field of battle could afford me no pleasure; because I cannot but reflect that of every one who falls in this unnatural strife, be it on one side or on the other, we must, in our sober moments, exclaim,—

> Another sword has laid him low,
> Another, and another's;
> And every hand that dealt a blow—
> Ah, me! it was a brother's.

But we are called upon to act. There is no time for hesitation or indecision—no time for haste and excitement. It is a time when the people should rise in the majesty of their might, stretch forth their strong arm and silence the angry waves of tumult. It is time the people should command peace. (Cheers.) It is a question between union and anarchy—between law and disorder. All politics for the time being are and should be committed to the resurrection of the grave. The question should be, "Our country, our whole country, and nothing but the country." (Cheers.)

> 'Tis not the whole of life to live
> Nor all of death to die.

We should go forward in a manner becoming a great people. But six months since, the material elements of our country were never greater. To-day, by the fiat of madness, we are plunged in distress and threatened with political ruin, anarchy and annihilation. It becomes us to stay the hands of this spirit of disunion. The voice of the Empire State can be potential in this unnatural strife. (Cheers.) She has mighty power for union. She has great wealth and influence, and she must bring forward that wealth and exert that influence. She has numerous men and she must send them to the field, and in the plenitude of her power command the public peace. This is a great commercial city —one of the modern wonders of the earth. With all the great elements that surround her, with her commercial renown, with her architectural magnificence, with her enterprise and energy, she is capable of exercising a mighty power for good in silencing the angry waves of agitation. (Cheers.) While I would prosecute this war in a manner becoming a civilized and a Christian people, I would do so in no vindictive spirit. I would do it as Brutus set the signet to the death-warrant of his son— "Justice is satisfied, and Rome is free." (Cheers.) I love my country; I love this Union. It was the first vision of my early years; it is the last ambition of my public life. Upon its altar I have surrendered my choicest hopes. I had fondly hoped that in approaching age it was to beguile my solitary hours, and I will stand by it as long as there is a Union to stand by—(cheers)—and when the ship of the Union shall crack and groan, when the skies lower and threaten, when the lightnings flash, the thunders roar, the storms beat and the waves run mountain-high, if the ship of State goes down, and the Union perishes, I would rather perish with it than survive its destruction. (Loud cheers.) I love that flag, with all its stars and stripes—that flag of my fathers—that flag that is known and honored throughout the earth, wherever civilization has travelled. I love it still; I would say, with the British peer, "With all thy faults I love thee still." Let us, my friends, stay up the hands of Union men in other sections of the country. How much have they sacrificed of advantage, of national wealth, of political promotion! Let us aid them and cheer them on. Let us, my fellow-citizens, rally round the flag of our country, rendered illustrious by the gallant Anderson. (Cheers.) In the spirit of peace and forbearance he waved it over Fort Sumter. The pretended authorities of South Carolina and the other Southern States attacked him because they seemed to consider him a kind of minister plenipotentiary. Let us maintain our flag in the same noble spirit that animated him, and never desert it while one star is left. (Cheers.) If I could see my bleeding, torn, maddened and distracted country once more restored to quiet and lasting peace under those glorious stars and stripes, I could almost be ready to take the oath of the infatuated leader in Israel—Jephtha—and swear to sacrifice the first living thing that I should meet on my return from victory. (Loud cheers.)

SPEECH OF SENATOR BAKER, OF OREGON.

The majesty of the people is here to-day to sustain the Majesty of the Constitution—(cheers)—and I come, a wanderer from the far Pacific, to record my oath along with yours of the great Empire State. (Applause and three cheers for Baker.) The hour for conciliation has passed, the gathering for battle is at hand; and the country requires that every man shall do his duty. (Loud cheers.) Fellow-citizens, what is that country? Is it the soil on which we tread? Is it the gathering of familiar faces? Is it our luxury and pomp and pride? Nay, more than these, is it power and might and majesty alone? No, our country is more, far more than all these. The country which demands our love, our courage, our devotion, our heart's blood, is more than all these—(loud applause)—our country is the history of our fathers —our country is the tradition of our mothers—our country is past renown—our country is present pride and power—our country is future hope and destiny—our country is greatness, glory, truth, constitutional liberty—above all, freedom forever! (Enthusiastic cheers.) These are the watchwords under which we fight; and we will shout them out till the stars appear in the sky, in the stormiest hour of battle. (Cheers.) I have said that the hour for conciliation is past. It may return; but not to-morrow, nor next week. It will return when that tattered flag (pointing to the flag of Fort Sumter) is avenged. (Prolonged and enthusiastic cheers.) It will return when rebel traitors are taught obedience and submission. It will return when the rebellious confederates are taught that the North, though peaceable, are not cowardly—though forbearing, are not fearful. (Cheers.) That hour of conciliation will come back when again the ensign of the Republic will stream over every rebellious fort of every Confederate State. (Renewed cheers.) Then, as of old, the ensign of the pride and power, and dignity and majesty, and the peace of the Republic will return. (Loud applause.) Young men of New York—young men of the United

States—you are told this is not to be a war of aggression. In one sense that is true; in another, not. We have committed aggression upon no man. In all the broad land, in their rebel nest, in their traitor's camp, no truthful man can rise and say that he has ever been disturbed, though it be but for a single moment, in life, liberty, estate, character, or honor. (Cheers and cries of "That's so.") The day they began this unnatural, false, wicked, rebellious warfare, their lives were more secure, their property more secure, by us—not by themselves, but by us—guarded far more securely than any people ever have had their lives and property secured from the beginning of the world. (Applause.) We have committed no oppression, have broken no compact, have exercised no unholy power; have been loyal, moderate, constitutional, and just. We are a majority of the Union, and we will govern our own Union, within our own constitution, in our own way. (Cries of "Bravo," and applause.) We are all democrats. We are all republicans. We acknowledge the sovereignty of the people within the rule of the constitution; and under that constitution and beneath that flag, let traitors beware. (Loud cheers.) In this sense, then, young men of New York, we are not for a war of aggression. But in another sense, speaking for myself as a man who has been a soldier, and as one who is a senator, I say, in the same sense, I am for a war of aggression. I propose to do now as we did in Mexico—conquer peace. (Loud and enthusiastic applause.) I propose to go to Washington and beyond. (Cheers.) I do not design to remain silent, supine, inactive—nay, fearful—until they gather their battalions and advance their host upon our borders or in our midst. I would meet them upon the threshold, and there, in the very State of their power, in the very atmosphere of their treason, I propose that the people of this Union dictate to these rebels the terms of peace. (Loud cheers.) It may take thirty millions; it may take three hundred millions. What then? We have it. (Cries of "Good," and applause.) Loyally, nobly, grandly do the merchants of New York respond to the appeals of the Government. It may cost us seven thousand men. It may cost us seventy-five thousand men in battle; it may cost us seven hundred and fifty thousand men. What then? We have them. (Renewed cheering.) The blood of every loyal citizen of this Government is dear to me. My sons, my kinsmen, the young men who have grown up beneath my eye and beneath my care, they are all dear to me; but if the country's destiny, glory, tradition, greatness, freedom, government, written constitutional government—the only hope of a free people—demand it, let them all go. (Enthusiastic cheers.) I am not here now to speak timorous words of peace, but to kindle the spirit of manly, determined war. I speak in the midst of the Empire State, amid scenes of past suffering and past glory; the defences of the Hudson above me; the battle-field of Long Island before me, and the statue of Washington in my very face—(loud and enthusiastic cheers)—the battered and unconquered flag of Sumter waving in his hands, which I can almost now imagine trembles with the excitement of battle. (Great enthusiasm.) And as I speak, I say my mission here to-day is to kindle the heart of New York for war—short, sudden, bold, determined, forward war. (Applause.) The Seventh regiment has gone. (Three cheers for the

Seventh regiment.) Let seventy and seven more follow. (Applause.) Of old, said a great historian, beneath the banner of the cross, Europe precipitated itself upon Asia. Beneath the banner of the constitution let the men of the Union precipitate themselves upon disloyal, rebellious Confederate States. (Tremendous applause.) A few more words, and I have done. (Cries of "Go on," "You're the man," "We'll hear you till night.") Let no man underrate the dangers of this controversy. Civil war, for the best of reasons upon the one side, and the worst upon the other, is always dangerous to liberty—always fearful, always bloody; but, fellow-citizens, there are yet worse things than fear, than doubt and dread, and danger and blood. Dishonor is worse. (Prolonged cheers.) Perpetual anarchy is worse. States forever commingling and forever severing are worse. (Renewed cheers.) Traitors and Secessionists are worse. To have star after star blotted out—(Cries of "Never! never!")—to have stripe after stripe obscured—(cries of "No! no!")—to have glory after glory dimmed—to have our women weep and our men blush for shame throughout generations yet to come—that and these are infinitely worse than blood. (Tremendous cheers.) People of New York, on the eve of battle allow me to speak as a soldier. Few of you know, as my career has been distant and obscure, but I may mention it here to-day, with a generous pride, that it was once my fortune to lead your gallant New York regiment in the very shock of battle. (Applause.) I was their leader, and upon the bloody heights of Cerro Gordo I know well what New York can do when her blood is up. (Loud applause, and "three cheers for Baker.") Again, once more, when we march, let us not march for revenge: As yet we have nothing to revenge. It is not much that where that tattered flag waved, guarded by seventy men against ten thousand; it is not much that starvation effected what an enemy could not compel. (Prolonged applause.) We have as yet something to punish, but nothing, or very little, to revenge. The President himself, a hero without knowing it—and I speak from knowledge, having known him from boyhood—the President says:—"There are wrongs to be redressed, already long enough endured." And we march to battle and to victory because we do not choose to endure this wrong any longer. (Cheers.) They are wrongs not merely against us; not against you, Mr. President; not against me, but against our sons and against our grandsons that surround us. They are wrongs against our ensign—(cries of "That's so," and applause)—they are wrongs against our Union; they are wrongs against our Constitution; they are wrongs against human hope and human freedom; and thus, if it be avenged, still, as Burke says: "it is a wild justice at last," and we will revenge them. While I speak, following in the wake of men so eloquent, so conservative, so eminent, so loyal, so well known—even while I speak, the object of your meeting is accomplished; upon the wings of the lightning it goes out throughout the world that New York, the very heart of a great city, with her crowded thoroughfares, her merchants, her manufacturers, her artists—that New York, by one hundred thousand of her people, declares to the country and to the world that she will sustain the Government (applause) to the last dollar in her treasury —to the last drop of your blood. (Renewed cheers.) The national banners leaning from ten thousand windows in your city to-day proclaim your affection and reverence for the Union. You will gather in battalions,

> Patient of toil, serene amidst alarms,
> Inflexible in faith, invincible in arms ;

and as you gather, every omen of present concord and ultimate peace will surround you. The ministers of religion, the priests of literature, the historians of the past, the illustrators of the present, capital, science, art, invention, discoveries, the works of genius—all these will attend us in our march, and we will conquer. And if, from the far Pacific, a voice feebler than the feeblest murmur upon its shore may be heard to give you courage and hope in the contest, that voice is yours to-day ; and if a man whose hair is gray, who is well-nigh worn out in the battle and toil of life, may pledge himself on such an occasion and in such an audience, let me say, as my last word, that when, amid sheeted fire and flame, I saw and led the hosts of New York as they charged in contest upon a foreign soil for the honor of your flag ; so again, if Providence shall will it, this feeble hand shall draw a sword, never yet dishonored—not to fight for distant honor in a foreign land, but to fight for country, for home, for law, for government, for constitution, for right, for freedom, for humanity, and in the hope that the banner of my country may advance, and wheresoever that banner waves, there glory may pursue and freedom be established. (Loud and prolonged applause.)

[Lieutenant Hall, of Fort Sumter, was here introduced to the audience, and made his bow amidst enthusiastic cheers.]

ROBERT J. WALKER'S SPEECH.

I received the request to address you but a few hours since, and being wholly unprepared, shall therefore detain you but a few moments. This greatest popular meeting ever assembled in the history of the world, has a deep significance. The hundred thousand freemen whom I now address, have assembled here for a great and glorious purpose. It is a sublime spectacle, and the greatest epoch in the history of the world. The question is, shall this Union be maintained and perpetuated, or shall it be broken and dissolved? (Cries of "Never.") No question so important has ever occurred in the history of our race. It involves not only the fate of this great country, but the question of free institutions throughout the world. The case of self-government is now on trial before the forum of our country and of the world. If we succeed and maintain the Union, free institutions, under the moral force of our example, will ultimately be established throughout the world ; but if we fail, and our Government is overthrown, popular liberty will have made its last experiment, and despotism will reign triumphant throughout the globe. Our responsibilities are fearful. We have a solemn duty to perform—we are this day making history. We are writing a book whose pages can never be erased—it is the destiny of our country and of mankind. For more than seventy years this Union has been maintained, and it has advanced our country to a prosperity unparalleled in the history of the world. (Applause.) The past was great, but the future opened upon prospects beyond the power of language to describe. But where are we now ? The world looks on with scorn and derision. We have, it is said, no government—a mere voluntary association of independent States—a debating society, or a moot court, without any real power to uphold the laws or maintain the constitution. We have no country, no flag, no Union ; but each State at its pleasure, upon its own mere whim or caprice, with or without cause, may secede and dissolve the Union. Secession, we are told, is a constitutional right of each State, and the constitution has inscribed its own death-warrant upon its face. If this be so, we have indeed, no government, and Europe may well speak of us with contempt and derision. This is the very question we are now to solve—have we a government, and has it power to maintain its existence ? This question is not for the first time presented to the consideration of the American people. It arose in 1832, when South Carolina nullified the revenue laws of the Union, and passed her secession ordinance. In that contest I took a very active part against the doctrines of nullification and secession, and upon that question, after a struggle of three years, I was elected by Mississippi as a Senator of the United States. A contest so prolonged and violent had never before been witnessed in this country. It was fought by me in every county of the State under the banner of the Union. The sentiments contained in the many speeches then made by me, and then published, are the opinions I now entertain. They are all for the Union and against secession, and they are now the opinions of thousands of Union men of the South, and of Mississippi. (Applause.) These opinions are unchanged, and deeply as I deplore our present situation, it is my profound conviction that the welfare, security, and prosperity of the South can only be restored by the re-establishment of the Union. I see, in the permanent overthrow of the Union, the utter ruin of the South and the complete prostration of all their interests. I have devoted my life to the maintenance of all their constitutional rights and the promotion of their happiness and welfare ; but secession involves them and us in one common ruin. The recognition of such a doctrine is fatal to the existence of any government—of the Union—it is death—it is national suicide. (Applause.) This is the question now to be decided—have we a Union—have we a flag—are the stars and stripes a reality or a fiction—have we a government, and can we enforce its laws, or must the whole vanish whenever any one State thinks proper to issue the despotic mandate ? Is the Union indissoluble, or is it written on the sand, to be swept away by the first angry surge of State or sectional passion which may sweep over it ? It was the declared object of our ancestors to found a perpetual Union. The original articles of confederation, by all the States, in 1778, declared the Union to be "perpetual," and South Carolina (with all the States) then plighted her solemn faith that "the union of the States shall be perpetual." And in modifying these articles by the formation of the constitution in 1787, the declared object of that change was to make "the Union more perfect." But how more perfect, if the Union is indissoluble in 1787, but might at any moment be destroyed by any one State after the adoption of the constitution ? No, my countrymen, secession is not a constitutional right of any one State. It is war—it is revolution—and can only be established on the ruins of the constitution and of the Union. We must resist and subdue it, or our Government will be but an organized anarchy, to be surely succeeded, as anarchy ever has been, by military despotism. This, then, my fellow-citizens, is the last great contest for the liberties of our country and of the world. (Applause.) If we are defeated, the last experiment of self-government will have failed and we will have written with our own hands the epitaph of human liberty. We will have no flag, we will have no government, no country, and no Union ; we will cease to be American citizens, and the despots of Europe will rejoice in the failure of the great experiment of republican institutions. The liberties of our country and of the world will have been intrusted to our care, and we will have dishonored the great trust and proved ourselves traitors to the freedom of our country and of mankind. This is not a sectional question—it is not a Northern or a Southern question. It is not a question which concerns our country only, but all mankind. It is this, Shall we by a noble and united effort sustain here republican institutions, or shall we have secession and anarchy to be succeeded by despotism, and extinguish forever the hopes of freedom throughout the world ? God grant you, my dear countrymen, courage, and energy, and perseverance, to maintain successfully the great contest. You are fighting the last great decisive battle for the liberties of our country and of mankind—faint not, falter not, but move onward in one great column for the maintenance of the constitution and the Union. Remember it was a Southern man, a noble son of Kentucky, (Major Anderson,) who so gloriously sustained the flag of our country at Fort Sumter, and never surrendered that flag. He brought it with him to New York, and there it is, held in the hands of Washington, in that marble column now before us representing the Father of his Country, and whose lips now open and urge us, as in his Farewell Address, to maintain the constitution and the Union. And now, whilst I address you, the news comes that the city of Washington, founded by the Father of his Country and bearing his sacred name, is to be seized by the legions of disunion. Never. Never must or shall this disgrace befall us. That capital must and shall be defended, if it requires every Union man in America to march to its defence. And now, then, fellow-citizens, a desperate effort is made to make this a party question—a question between Democrats and Republicans. Well, fellow-citizens, I have been a Democrat all my life, and never scratched a democratic ticket, from Constable up to President, but say to you this is no party question. (Cheers.) It is a question of a maintenance of the Government and the perpetuation of the Union. The vessel of State is rushing upon the breakers, and, without asking who may be the commander, we must all aid in her rescue from impending disaster. When the safety of my country is involved, I will never ask who is President, nor inquire what may be the effect on parties of any particular measure. Much as I love my party, I love my country infinitely more, and must and will sustain it at all hazards. Indeed, it is due to the great occasion here frankly to declare that, notwithstanding my earnest opposition to the election of Mr. Lincoln, and my disposition most closely to scrutinize all his acts, I see thus far nothing to condemn in his efforts to maintain the Union. And now, then, my countrymen, one word more before I close. (Cheers.) I was trained in devotion to the Union by a patriot sire, who fought the battles of liberty during the war of the Revolution. My life has been given to the support of the Union. I never conceived a thought or wrote or uttered a word, except in its defence. And now, let me say, that this Union must, will, and shall be perpetuated ; that not a star shall be dimmed or a stripe erased from our banner ; that the integrity of the Government shall be preserved, and that, from the Atlantic to the Pacific, from the lakes of the North to the Gulf of Mexico, never shall be surrendered a single acre of our soil, or a drop of its waters. (Loud and long continued cheering.)

LETTER OF ARCHBISHOP HUGHES.

The Chairman then read the following letter from Archbishop Hughes, amid loud applause :—

NEW YORK, April 20, 1861.

DEAR SIR :—Unable to attend the meeting at Union Square in consequence of indisposition, I beg leave to state my sentiments on the subject of your coming together, in the following words :—

Ministers of religion and ministers of peace, according to the instructions of their Divine Master, have not ceased to hope and pray that peace and Union might be preserved in this great and free country. At present, however, that question has been taken out of the hands of the peacemakers, and it is referred to the arbitrament of a sanguinary contest. I am not authorized to speak in the name of any of my follow-citizens. I think so far as I can judge, there is the right principle among all those whom I know. It is now fifty years since, a foreigner by birth, I took the oath of allegiance to this country under its title of the United States of America. (Loud cheers.) As regards conscience, patriotism, or judgment, I have no misgiving. Still desirous of peace, when the Providence of God shall have brought it, I may say that since the period of my naturalization I have none but one country. In reference to my duties as a citizen, no change has come over my mind since then. The Government of the United States was then, as it is now, symbolized by a national flag, popularly called "The Stars and Stripes." (Loud applause.) This has been my flag, and shall be to the end. (Cheers.) I trust it is still destined to display in the gales that sweep every ocean, and amid the gentle breezes of many a distant shore, as I have seen it in foreign lands, its own peculiar waving lines of beauty. May it live and continue to display these same waving lines of beauty whether at home or abroad, for a thousand years and afterwards as long as Heaven permits, without limit of duration.

JOHN HUGHES, Archbishop of New York.

MAYOR WOOD'S SPEECH.

FELLOW-CITIZENS :—The President has announced that Colonel Baker, the gentleman who has so eloquently addressed you to-day, proposes to raise a New York brigade, if the State will bear the expense of outfit (cheers) ; and here, as Mayor of this city, so far as I have the power to speak, I pledge for the corporation that sum. (Loud applause, and cries of "good !") When I assumed the duties of the office I have now the honor to hold, my official oath was that I would support the Constitution of the United States and the Constitution of the State of New York ; and I imply from that that it is not only my duty, as it is consistent with my principles and sense of right, to support the constitution, but the Union, the Government, the laws and the flag. (Loud cheers.) And, in the discharge of that duty, I care not what past political associations may be severed. I am willing to give up all past prejudices and sympathies, if in conflict with the honor and interest of my country in this great crisis. (Applause.) I am willing to say here that I throw myself entirely into this contest with all my power and with all my might. (Loud cheers.) My friends, the greatest man next to Washington, that this country has ever produced—Andrew Jackson—has said that "the Union must and shall be preserved"—(cheers)—and in that connection he has said, and it is directly pertinent to the present contest, "the Union must and shall be preserved—peaceably if we can, but forcibly if we must." (Enthusiastic applause.) There are those of us who have heretofore held antagonist positions to what is supposed to be the policy and the principles of this Administration, who are willing to accept that noble declaration of the sacred Jackson, as a resort to force upon this occasion. (Prolonged cheers, and cries of " That's so ! " " Good ! ") Why, gentlemen, what is the nature of your Government? Ours is a government of opinion expressed through the laws. The laws being made by the people, through their representatives, are simply the expressions of popular sentiment ; and the administrators of the laws should be maintained in the exercise of all legal authority. (Cheers.) I have always advocated a strong Executive power; because, to be efficient it requires ample authority, and under our form of Government, the agent being merely the exponent of the popular will, he should be provided with every means to maintain that will. Thus in maintaining the Government, we maintain ourselves, our inalienable rights and the basis of free institutions. It is true that individuals retain the right of independent criticism, and at the ballot box have an opportunity to exercise this right ; yet we are all bound to abide by the result. These views are pertinent to the occasion, so far as the people of the city and State of New York are concerned. (Applause.) This city is a portion of the State, and this State retians its position as one of the United States of America. (Loud cheers.) Therefore we must stand by the Government, we must obey the laws, we must respect official authority, we must respond with alacrity to the calls of patriotism, and so long as we may have the strength, support the constitution and the Union. (Applause.) In accordance, then, with these views, I have no hesitation in throwing whatever power I may possess in behalf of the pending struggle. If a military conflict is necessary, and that military authority can be exercised under the constitution and consistently with the laws, dreadful as the alternative may be, we have no recourse except to take up arms. (Cheers, and cries of "We will do it.") In times of great peril great sacrifices are required. When the human frame is upon the verge of death, every effort of skill and the most desperate experiments are resorted to to preserve life and prevent dissolution. This may be said to be an apt illustration of the present condition of the body politic. In the expression of these views, which I design to be understood as a public proclamation in favor of maintaining the authority of government as such, " peaceably if we can but forcibly if we must," (renewed cheering,) I desire also to be understood as taking back no sentiment I have ever uttered on the political issues of the day. (Cries of "Good for you.") If the Presidential election was to be held over again to-morrow, my vote and my sentiments would be unchanged ; nor am I to be regarded as countenancing or justifying mob law or violence. The people themselves have elected or established tribunals for the adjudication of offences against the laws, and all of us are restrained and must conform thereto. Every man's opinion is to be respected ; and he who denies to a fellow-citizen the right of independent thought violates the first principles of republicanism and strikes a blow at the theory of our Government. (Loud applause.) My friends, it has been said here to-day that your flag has been insulted. Aye ! not only has your flag been insulted, but the late Secretary of War, assuming to represent the Confederate States, has said that the confederate flag shall wave over your Capitol before the first of May. (Groans.) And, more than that, that the confederate flag shall fly over Faneuil Hall in Boston. (Cries of "Never," groans and hisses.) My friends, before that banner can fly over Faneuil Hall in Boston, it must be carried over the dead body of every citizen of New York. (Enthusiastic applause.) In behalf of you I am prepared to say here, and, through the press, to our friends of the South, that before that flag shall float over the national capitol, every man, woman, and child would enlist for the war. (Renewed cheers, and cries of "That they will.") Gentlemen, I have no voice, although the heart, to address you longer. (Cries of "Go on.") Abler and more eloquent men that myself are here. I can only say, therefore, that I am with you in this contest. We know no party now. (Cheers.) We are for maintaining the integrity of the national Union intact. We are for exhausting every power at our command in this great, high, and patriotic struggle— (cheers)—and I call upon every man, whatever may have been his position heretofore, whatever may be his individual sympathy now, to make one great phalanx in this struggle, that we may, in the language of the eloquent Senator who preceded me, proceed to "conquer peace." (Loud applause.)

My friends, it has been already announced by the Chairman that the Baltic and other vessels at the foot of Canal-street are ready to take five thousand men to-morrow to the capital of Washington. I urge a hearty response to that call, that New York may speak trumpet-tongued to the people of the South. (Enthusiastic applause.)

SPEECH OF EX-GOVERNOR HUNT.

Mr. President and Fellow-Citizens—A profound sense of duty impels me to take a brief part in your deliberations at this trying crisis in our national history. At no period since the darkest hours of the Revolution has the republic been involved in dangers appealing so emphatically to the patriotism and wisdom of the people. It has been my constant hope that the controversies which have disturbed the harmony of the two great sections of our country might find a peaceful and constitutional solution, that the voice of reason and patriotism would finally prevail over the turbulence of excited passions, and above all, that we might be spared the agonizing spectacle of a great and free people destroying the richest inheritance ever bestowed upon mankind, in unnatural and fratricidal strife. But, Mr. President, we are compelled to deal with the stern realities before us. The past is beyond recall. It belongs to history. The present is no time for reviving former controversies or discussions. We must meet the issue which is forced upon us. Let us remember only that we have a country to serve, a constitution to defend, and a national Union to cherish and uphold. On one side we behold our national. Government struggling for the maintenance of its constitutional authority ; on the other a formidable combination of discontented States, arrayed in open and disloyal resistance. Whatever differences of opinion may exist touching the causes of the attempted subversion of the federal power, I am sure you will all agree that they are not such as to furnish a sufficient justification for the States which seek to renounce and annul the national compact. Our constitution makes ample provisions for the redress of grievances, and who shall say that the people, on a direct appeal to their patriotism and sense of justice, would not be found faithful to its principles and true to its spirit and design? Instead of revolution or secession we have at least the right to demand that an honest effort should be made to settle differences within the Union, and according to the principles of the constitution. This is the only mode consistent with reason or compatible with the public safety. Amid the present distractions and dangers I cannot but feel that it is the duty of every true citizen to uphold and maintain the Government of the United States. Come what may, we must stand by our country and support the Union in its integrity. You and I, Mr. President, have sworn more than once to support the Constitution of the United States. I consider that oath perpetually binding; but if it were blotted out, the obligations of loyalty and patriotic fidelity to the Government under which we live would demand our best efforts for its preservation. Why should we not support the constitution? It has made us a great and powerful people —prosperous at home, respected abroad, and conferring upon our citizens everywhere a larger share of liberty and happiness than has fallen to the lot of any other nation on earth. While the country is convulsed by violence and dissension, it is not pretended that the Government, in its action, had invaded the constitutional rights of any of its members, or given any adequate cause for resistance to its rightful authority. Yet so rapid has been the progress of disaffection that the national capital is in danger of armed invasion and seizure. Sir, the capital of this Union must be defended at all hazards; and I hope to see the preparations for that purpose on a scale fully commensurate with the magnitude of the danger. Let the force be sufficient, if not to prevent, then to repel any assault on the seat of Government. I cannot even yet believe that the attempt will be made. The men of the South ought to know that the men of the North will not permit the capital to be wrested from the legitimate national functionaries without a struggle such as this continent has never seen. If the time has not gone by, I would make a last appeal to Virginia not to permit any hostile invasion of the federal district. Can she forget that it bears the august name of her own Washington, and that it was he who dedicated its soil to the national Union, to be held as a sacred trust by the United States? It is consecrated ground. It is guarded by the most sacred and venerable recollections. Let no impious hand be laid upon the temple of American liberty and nationality. Any attempt to make the city of Washington the theatre of bloody civil conflict would be alike treasonable, fratricidal, and sacrilegious, and could not fail to arouse a spirit of intense, unappeasable vengeance. Whatever else may come, I pray to Heaven that this land may be spared the woes which are inevitable if the possession of the capital is to be determined by the arbitrament of the sword. I yet indulge the hope that this Union is to be perpetual. That hope is dearer to me than life, and I will be found among the last to relinquish it. We may well pause before admitting the idea that the people of the North and South have be-

Doc —17

come so incurably alienated, or that there is such incompatibility of interest and feeling that they can no more dwell together in peace, under a common government. If we should ever be forced to the conclusion that a separation is inevitable or desirable, there are regular and pacific methods in which the question may be submitted to the people, in whom the sovereign power resides, for their solemn deliberation and verdict, in view of their obligations to themselves and their posterity. We are bound to make every effort which wisdom can devise or patriotism suggest to avert the calamities of a final dissolution of the Union. If a national convention could be invoked in a constitutional mode and enabled to deliberate in peace, undisturbed by the clash of arms, is it too much to hope that it might result in a satisfactory solution of our present troubles? I feel, Mr. President, that I have some right to appeal to the Union men of the South, and to invoke them to join hands with us in one more patriotic effort to preserve our common nationality. In these unhappy dissensions I have been an humble advocate of moderation and forbearance; in my love of country, discarding all geographical distinctions, and contending for a faithful observance of the constitutional rights of both sections. Knowing full well that a large portion of the Southern people were earnestly devoted to the national constitution in all their efforts to uphold it from the assaults of its enemies, the warmest affections of my heart have been with them. While abhorring the spirit of disunion and secession, I have cherished and still feel an ardent attachment for the loyal Union men of the Southern States. I have loved them as brethren, and am not willing to be disjoined from them, now or hereafter. Overborne as they are in many of the States by the resistless torrent of popular frenzy and delusion, may they still stand firm in their loyalty, and be prepared to aid in the noble work of pacification. Let them not believe that the mass of the Northern people are their enemies or desire their subjugation; nor should it be assumed that the Federal Government intends to reduce them to dishonorable submission by force of arms. Notwithstanding the irritations engendered by past controversies, the national heart of the North is still sound, and its prevailing desire at the present moment is that our Union may be preserved and perpetuated, in the spirit of the fathers, as a bond of peace and affection between the people of all the States, for the common benefit and security of both sections. It is this sentiment of nationality, now thoroughly aroused, which prompts our people to step forth with patriotic ardor and enthusiasm to pledge their lives and fortunes for the support and defence of the Federal Government in all its constitutional vigor. While they feel themselves bound by the highest considerations of patriotism to sustain the executive arm in defence of the national supremacy, they are not actuated by a spirit of aggression towards their fellow-citizens of the South. They look to the Government to act with firmness in defence of its just rights and prerogatives, yet with kindness and moderation towards the people of every State; and if compelled to draw the sword with one hand for the preservation of its authority, it should ever be ready to tender with the other the olive branch of peace and conciliation.

I believe these are the sentiments which animate you all on the present occasion, and which this impressive demonstration of the popular will is intended to embody and express. In manifesting your attachment to the Government founded by our fathers, and your undying devotion to that national flag, under whose ample folds we have steadily marched onward in an unexampled career of greatness and renown, you aim only to attest your affection for the Union, and your determination to stand by your country, and your whole country, one and indivisible. For myself, I can only say that my whole heart is with you, in every effort for the maintenance of our national Union and constitution. Let every patriot, in this trying hour, range himself on the side of his country and give a prompt and cheerful support to every measure of Government, which may be necessary to vindicate its rightful power and integrity. My fellow-citizens, we must not despair of the republic. I pray that the God of our fathers, who has so signally favored and sustained our country in times past, may dispel the clouds which darken the horizon, and ever continue to protect the majestic fabric of American Union and nationality.

SPEECH OF WM. M. EVARTS.

Mr. Chairman and Gentlemen: I regard this as a business meeting commencing the greatest transaction that this generation of men have seen. We stand here the second generation from the men who declared our independence, fought the battles of the Revolution, and framed our constitution. The question for us to decide is, whether we are worthy children of such men—whether our descendants shall curse us as we bless our fathers. (Cheers.) Gentlemen, you have got something more to do than you have done hitherto—something more than merely to read the glorious history of the past; you have got to write a history for the future that your children will either glory in or blush for. (Loud cheers.) When Providence puts together the 19th of April, 1776, when the first blood was shed at Lexington, and the 19th of April, 1861, when the first blood was shed at Baltimore, I tell you it means something. (Loud cheers.) When that statue of Washington sustains in its firm hands the flagstaff of Fort Sumter, I tell you it means something. (Three cheers were here given for the flag and Major Anderson.) There is but one question left, and that is, whether you mean something too. (Cheers, and responses of "Yes, we do.") If you mean something, do you mean enough? Do you mean enough of time, of labor, of money, of men, of blood, to seal and sanction the glories of the future of America? (Cheers.) Your ancestors fought for and secured independence, liberty and equal rights. Every enemy of liberty, independence, and equal rights has told you that those ideas are inconsistent with government. It is for you to show that government of the people means that the people shall obey the government. (Cheers.) Having shown what the world never saw till the Declaration of Independence was made—what a people which governs itself can do in peace, you are to show what a people which governs truly means to accomplish, when it wages war against traitors and rebels. (Cheers.) Each man here is fighting his own quarrel and protecting the future of his children. With these sentiments, you need no argument and no suggestion to carry you through this conflict. You are to remember your fathers and care for your children. (Cheers.)

LETTER OF THE HON. JAMES T. BRADY.

The following letter was here read, from James T. Brady:

UNITED STATES CIRCUIT COURT, }
PHILADELPHIA, April 19, 1861. }

WM. M. EVARTS, ESQ.:—My Dear Sir—I have been in this city since Saturday, engaged as counsel in a case, the trial of which is proceeding while I write, and there is little prospect of its being finished until about Wednesday next. It will be impossible for me to attend the meeting in New York to-morrow, which I am invited to address, and I must content myself with expressing briefly what I think in reference to the present crisis. I am sure that no one more deeply than I deplores the present critical and excited condition of the country. In common with millions of our people I mourn over the prospect of a civil war, the occurrence of which cannot but awaken the most poignant sorrow in the heart of every man who desires the ascendency of democratic principles and the continued existence of free government. It is useless to speculate about the causes which have produced this lamentable state of affairs. No questions as to inferior political subjects can now be debated, and all other considerations are inferior to the inquiry as to what is the duty of the American people at this alarming juncture. I cannot, within the limits of a letter thus hastily written, give my views of the means adopted or omitted in any quarter, by which our present condition has been produced or might have been avoided; but I repeat what on recent occasions I have felt called upon to state, that my country is the United States of America—by that name I hope and believe it will ever be known—to it, by that name, my allegiance is entirely due, and shall always be cheerfully given, and I can imagine no contingency which could ever lead me to withdraw one particle of my love or devotion from that flag which waved over the head of Washington in the grandest moments of his grandest triumph, and upon which no power on earth has hitherto been able to affix defeat or dishonor. I have always loved the Southern people reflectingly, as well as naturally sympathized with them, and been ever ready and willing, with the utmost zeal and ability, to aid in maintaining all their rights in our confederacy under the Federal Constitution. I am not prepared to admit that even the most ardent son of South Carolina could, in this respect, have been more sincere or earnest than I. But in no view, even of the doctrines asserted by that State, have I been able to discover any just cause for the secession movement now progressing under circumstances so dangerous and deplorable. If prudent and wise counsels had prevailed, I think this movement would never have attained its present point; but the fact cannot be disguised or evaded that several of our States have, so far as they could effect that result, withdrawn from the Union and formed a Southern confederacy. The great question, worthy the most cautious reflection of all our statesmen, and arousing the anxiety of our whole people is, how can the Union be restored to its integrity, and its old attractions be reproduced? If, however, that most desirable result cannot be accomplished, and the new confederacy insists upon its separate organization, it is very plain that the loyal States should and must continue their association and adhere to the Constitution, title, and purposes of the Union established by the great, good, and patriotic men of the past. If the Southern people insist upon having a country and a name—a government and a destiny distinct from ours, and no just measures can prevent this consequence—I, for one, submit to the event, however lamentable. But I cannot go with the South, away from my home and institutions—away from the Government and Constitution, and I cannot consent that any portion of our territory, property, or honor shall be wrested from us by force. Beyond this, at present, I am not prepared to go. I deem it absurd to hope for any wrong to attempt any coercion of the seceding States into remaining with us; but at the same time, I think we have a right to the forts and all other lawful property of the United States of America, and that the forcible seizure of any part of them by the South was without any justification whatever. I am sorry to observe in presses of different political opinions, expressions strongly calculated, and in some cases, I fear, intended to foment between the South and the North a more angry and sanguinary feeling than already exists. While we should entertain and express, with proper firmness, a due appreciation of the duties which the nation has a right to see us discharge, we should also be careful not to increase the difficulty of removing the obstacles to a restoration of good feeling among the various States. I do not flatter myself that these views have the importance which some friends seem to think my opinions might at this moment possess. But in the present, as in all previous instances affecting my course in public, I freely and fully define my position. I pray heaven that some means may yet be devised to prevent our brethren shedding each other's blood, and that all of us who reside on American soil may be restored to that condition so happily expressed by the great man who demanded and predicted for us one country, one constitution, one destiny. That this beneficent issue may occur through the holy influences of peace and the kindly offices of fraternity, is my profound aspiration. But within the limits and to the extent, crudely stated in what I have already written, I say to my fellow-citizens of New York city that I shall cling while life remains to the name and fame of the United States of America, sharing its government and glory, and abiding with resignation any perils or adversity that may fall upon us, hoping ever that, from any and every trial, it may come forth with no part of its just rights impaired, and no portion of its power or prosperity diminished. That this may be the sentiment of all the States still loyal to the Union, and serve as their guide in all the future, is the fervent hope and confident expectation of him, who, without departing in any respect from the political principles he has ever entertained, feels it an imperative duty to avow unwavering and undying fidelity to his country. JAMES T. BRADY.

The President announced the following persons as members of the Committee of Finance:

Moses Taylor,	Edwards Pierrepont,
Moses H. Grinnell,	Richard M. Blatchford,
Royal Phelps,	Alexander T. Stewart,
William E. Dodge,	Hamilton Fish,
Greene C. Bronson,	Samuel Sloan,
William M. Evarts,	John Jacob Astor,
John J. Cisco,	Wm. F. Havemeyer,
James T. Brady,	Charles H. Russell,
Simeon Draper,	Rudolph A. Witthaus,
James S. Wadsworth,	Charles H. Marshall,
Isaac Bell,	Prosper M. Wetmore,
James Boorman,	Robert H. McCurdy.
Abiel A. Low,	

On motion, the name of Hon. John A. Dix was added to the committee.

Mr. S. B. Chittenden offered the following resolution, which was unanimously adopted amid hearty cheers:

Resolved, That New York adopts the widows and children of her citizens who may fall in the defence of the Union.

SPEECH OF HON. R. C. SCHENCK, OF OHIO.

MEN OF NEW YORK—Let me inform you that I meet you here to-day, as it were, by accident, but that does not, at the same time, debar me from the privilege of being one of yourselves; therefore, I have no apology to make on this head. (Hear, hear.) I also meet you as an American, and in this respect I am one of yourselves, as I said before. (Applause.) On this ground I know you, and in knowing you, and finding myself in your company, I feel at home —yes, perfectly at home. (Loud cheers.) I live in Ohio; but it is not New York or Ohio we are now trying—that is not the question—that is not the subject which has brought us together this day. The great question—the vitally important question —which we have to consider is, whether we are citizens or not; and in being citizens, we are also to inquire whether we have become refractory and have need of chastisement. (Loud cheers, and cries of "Chastise the South.") You are aware of the chastisement that was endeavored to be administered to the men of Massachusetts. These brave men had passed through your streets to the capital; you see such men passing through every day as they did, and more are yet to follow. I was in Boston when those brave men, who were so barbarously assailed, left for the seat of war; I witnessed her population blessing them, and bidding them God speed, and cordially wishing success to their brave artillery. (Loud cheers.) Therefore, I cannot speak of New York more than of another. The lines are now broken, yet we feel here, as citizens, bound to support the law. God send that this may be the case; but, before we turn against the constitution, let us stand up nobly and die, and if blood naturally must flow, let it flow in defence of the Union. (Great cheers.) There is no middle ground now between the parties. They have assumed the offensive, and we must act on the defensive. (Cheers and cries of "We will.") We must be either on the one side or the other! It has come to that, and we cannot now evade it. (Hear, hear.) The responsibility is now upon you to vindicate the honor and dignity of your institutions, and from this you cannot escape. Those States which obey the law, are the only ones now you are bound to maintain and keep. We are here to-day in their behalf, and I am glad to state that we are here without distinction of party. (Applause.) We know neither Republicans, Democrats, Bell-Everett men, nor any other; but we are here to state, and to proclaim strongly and loudly, that we shall stand by the Union to the last, and support it against those who would attempt to overthrow it. (Loud and long continued cheers.) This platform we are determined to stand upon, and all other platforms placed in antagonism to it shall be broken away like the grass before the fire of the mountain prairies. (Tremendous cheers.) I ask you to look at those thirteen stripes (pointing to the flag on the bust of Washington) which wave in your midst. They are the thirteen planks you are called upon this day to stand on, and God grant that it may be made an enduring platform, where we can all stand together! (Hear and cheers.) I am about to return to the State of Ohio, or the State they call Buckeye. (Loud laughter.) I have not time to say much more to you now. (Loud cries of "Go on, we are not tired of you yet.") Talk is not the matter in these times, it is action. (Applause.) Then I call upon you, the men of New York, to act as you have ever done; I implore you to act as men; do your duty to your country and to yourselves. If eloquence were needed, that eloquence is to be found in your numbers, in the mighty array which I now see before me. (Loud cheers.) The fire that at present burns in your patriotic hearts tells me that you will never permit the Constitution of the United States to be frittered away. (Loud cheers, and cries of "No, never.") I am going home to assist in supporting the glorious flag of our Union, that banner which was never yet tarnished; and, if possible, to re-unite the United States of America. ("Hear," and cheers.) In conclusion, I would say, let us be determined to be a nation of freemen; and if it be that we cannot again be a united people, I hope that we shall ever hold firmly and sacredly the principles of our glorious constitution as framed and cemented by those who were the framers of this great and mighty Union. The speaker concluded amid rounds of applause.

The CHAIRMAN here came forward and said he had received a telegraphic despatch from Governor Morgan, which he would read to the meeting.

Mr. CHARLES H. RUSSELL also presented himself to the meeting, and stated that he had received a telegraphic message from Governor Morgan calling upon them to supply four additional regiments, and two also of volunteers.

The CHAIRMAN read another telegraphic despatch, which stated that the Seventh regiment had reached Philadelphia in safety; that they were on their way to Annapolis, and would proceed from thence at once to Washington, not touching at all at Baltimore. This intelligence was received with deafening plaudits.

MR. CHITTENDEN'S SPEECH.

FELLOW-CITIZENS AND FELLOW-COUNTRYMEN—My name was not on the programme of this great meeting as a speaker, and consequently I have no right here. But in what I do say to you I will not occupy your time more than two or three minutes. (Hear, hear.) I have been, for the last seventeen years, an humble merchant in your city among the great merchants of New York; and whatever I have achieved during those seventeen years, I am willing to devote to the great cause which has brought us all together here this day. (Tremendous cheering.) I look upon this epoch in the history of this great country as one of the most important which has ever occurred on the face of the earth. I ask was there ever such a meeting as this assembled before in defence of the Union flag? What are all the great men of New York here for?—one hundred thousand men? Of what use is all the money in the banks? Why, these are, comparatively speaking, nothing when contrasted with the distress which has happened to the United States of America. (Hear, hear.) The Union, however, we must defend; and although future generations may have to refer to the history of this day, it will be with pride and gratification that they will learn that we met to defend the flag of our Union.

(Loud cheers.) The merchants of New York were enterprising men, and the merchants of New York when they spoke out it was not without reason. They have the sinews of war, and they have prepared to willingly distribute it. (Applause.) The steamer Baltic will as fast as possible convey many brave men to the scene of action—to the battle-field; and their helpless women and children will be left behind. These noble and gallant men leave all behind them for the good of their country. But they leave us, knowing that their wives and children will be taken care of. (Loud cheers.) These are the sentiments of the New York people; and I am proud and glad to say that, according to the resolution which you have just a little while ago heard read, the people of New York will adopt them. (Renewed and long continued applause.)

MR. CALEB LYON'S SPEECH.

FELLOW-CITIZENS :—This surging sea of upturned faces, these stalwart arms, and honest and patriotic hearts, betoken the greatness of this occasion endorsed, as it is, by the merchant princes upon my right and upon my left, representing the commerce, the wealth and the intelligence of the Empire City of the Empire State. (Applause.)

Endurance has ceased to be a virtue. We come here for the sacred purpose of laying all that our hearts hold dear upon the altar of our country; to vindicate her constitution, to uphold her laws, and to support her legitimately constituted authorities, with our influence, with our property, and, if need be, with our lives.

Years ago, there went forth Peter the Hermit who, with undaunted zeal, advocated the conquest of the holy sepulchre from the hands of the usurping infidel; but his thrilling eloquence of the wrongs, indignities, and insults never fell upon the ear of such an ocean audience as this. He labored for a dead idea; we contend for a living truth—for that Washington who led to victory our armies, who consolidated our Government, who supported our constitution, who gave vitality to our laws, whose Mt. Vernon sepulchre is desecrated, and in the hands of the insurrectionists, and the capital he founded is now threatened by impious assault!

It now devolves upon us, fellow-citizens, to rally and stop these parricidal hands, and take part in the great crusade by which that sepulchre, the capital, and the country can alone be saved. Are you ready? (Cries of, "We are!")

Men of New York! your great awakening tells the South of no single soul's sympathy for secession; it will tell her that the North is a perfect unit upon the doctrine that our Government is not a confederacy, but a union, for good or ill, for weal or woe, present and future, perpetual, indivisible, and eternal. (Cheers.) From the balls that struck Fort Sumter, like the dragon's teeth that were sown in classic days upon the shores of the Euxine, from which sprang armed warriors, are our volunteers rising in serried thousands from the snow-clad shores of the St. Lawrence to the fertile valleys of the Susquehannah, from the forests of Chatauque to the Highlands of the Hudson, begirt with the panoply of right. I say, let our brethren of the South pause, ere the crevassed Mississippi River turns the States of Mississippi and Louisiana into dismal swamps, and New Orleans to a wilderness of waters. Let them pause ere northern chivalry devastates the shores of South Carolina, and makes the site of Charleston what the desert of Sahara now is, in remembrance of her infamous and cowardly attack of nineteen batteries and nine thousand men, upon an unfinished fortification, garrisoned by seventy ill-ammunitioned and hungry soldiers, and for every drop of loyal Massachusetts blood spilled in the streets of Baltimore, other blood alone can wash it away in rivulets just as warm and red. Yesterday we said farewell to the glorious Seventh Regiment, the flower of this city's soldiery, its household guards. Words can feebly describe the unanimity with which they mustered for their country's service. The lover left his betrothed, the husband his bride, the father his new-born babe, the merchant his counting room, the mechanic his shop, the student his books, the lawyer his office, and the parson his church, as one man, the entire regiment responding to that love of country worthy of the better days of the Republic, many more of them gone, doubtless, to return no more ; and if they fall, theirs will be the proud Lacedemonian's epitaph, "They died in the defence of their country and its laws." It is said that when General Jackson came to die, he told his spiritual adviser that there was one sin of omission that lay heavily on his soul. "What is it?" softly inquired the devoted minister. The old General roused his departing energies, and exclaimed, "It is that I did not hang Calhoun." His reason was prophetic. John C. Calhoun, having sowed the seeds of nullification, whose blossoms were secession, and the fruit fraternal bloodshed and civil war !—*facilis descensus Averni !*—we are now called upon to teach the people of the South a salutary lesson of submission to the Constitution, and obedience to the laws. [Cheers.]

They who now see only seven of Uncle Sam's stars (and those would be Pleiades) will clearly see the whole thirty-four ere this war is finished ; and they who choose but three stripes of Uncle Sam's bunting, (and those laid the wrong way,) will feel the force of the whole thirteen ere the campaign is ended. Before us are the ball-broken flag-staff and tattered colors, speaking in trumpet tones of the treachery of South Carolina. That flag, whose dazzling folds have crystallized the love of a thousand heroes in our hearts, is destined to float once more over the ramparts of Sumter, before we will listen to the voice of peace. I feel that the spirit that is here is the spirit of 1776, it is that of 1812, it is that of a sublime instinct of self-preservation rising up to perpetuate the grandest nationality of freemen the world has ever known. [Cheers.]

When after ages shall open the volume of history to the illuminated page lighted by this day's sun, let it be said that in her darkest hour New York knew her duty and was equal to the occasion, and volunteered without stint her treasure and her blood. [Enthusiastic cheers.]

The stand No. two was located opposite the Everett House. The meeting was called to order by Mr. Samuel Sloane, who nominated Ex-Governor Fish for President, which nomination was ratified with great enthusiasm. The following Vice Presidents were appointed :—

W. H. Aspinwall, Wm. Whitlock, Jr., G. S. Bedford,
Cornel's Vanderbilt, N. Ludlam, Wm. M. Richards,
James T. Brady, J. J. Roosevelt, W. C. Rhinelander,
Daniel Lord, Isaac Seymour, Thomas Tileston,
Sheppard Knapp, J. McLeod Murphy, Jno. A. Kennedy,
Wm. A. Booth, A. R. Wetmore, O. A. Brownson,

Jno. F. Butterworth, Wm. G. Lambert, Jas. W. Underhill,
F. S. Winston, A. W. Bradford, Bernard Kelly,
Jno. C. Hamilton, W. S. Hatch, E. H. Ludlow,
Denning Duer, W. P. Lee, Thos. J. Barr,
J. A. Westervelt, Erastus C. Benedict, A. M. White,
Wm. H. Stewart, C. Newbold, James Bryce,
C R. Robert, W. H Appleton, R. C. Root,
George S. Robbins, Jno. E. Williams, D. B. Fearing,
Richard Patrick, Richard Irvin, Wm. McMurray,
Robert T. Haws, William Tucker, John R. Brady,
John S. Giles, Val. G. Hall, Henry Hilton,
John H. Hall, James Marsh, W. F. Havemeyer,
George Griswold, Horace Webster, Jas. Gallatin,
Ezra Nye, D. A. Cushman, W. B. Crosby,
George Law, A. C. Richards, F. B. Cutting,
Fred. Foster, Tim'y P. Chapman, Dan. F. Tiemann,
H. B. Raymond, Chas. P. Kirkland, J. S. Bosworth,
L. B. Woodruff, Jno. Dimon, T. B. Stillman,
Solomon Banta, Samuel Hotaling, Geo. T. H. Davis,
Morgan Jones, Richard Warren, W. Curtis Noyes,
George Young, George Jones, James Lenox,
D. P. Maurice, Geo. T. Olyphant, B. R. Winthrop,
Horace Greeley, B. Cornell, D. D. Field.
Dan. E. Devlin,

The presiding officer said :—Fellow-citizens, we desire to commence this meeting with prayer by the Rev. Dr. Vinton.

The reverend gentleman stepped forward, and delivered the following prayer :—

PRAYER OF DR. VINTON.

O, Almighty God, Creator of all men, high and mighty, whose kingdom ruleth over all—whose power no creature dare resist—thou art the protector of those who trust in thee. We come before thee to confess our own sins and the sins of our nation, and to declare our confidence in thee as our light and our salvation. O God, we have heard with our ears and our fathers have declared unto us the noble works thou didst in their days, and in the old time before them. Let the shield of thy omnipotent care be extended over the United States of America to defend the constitution and to perfect the union of the people. Be the ruler of our rulers and the counsellor of our legislators, so that they may guide our feet into the ways of peace. Inspire the people with a spirit to think and to do that which is right. Thou hast proclaimed throughout the land—"Prepare war, wake up the mighty men, let all the men of war draw near, let them come up, beat your plough-shares into swords, and your pruning hooks into spears—let the weak say, I am strong." A loving patriotism has yielded the pride and treasures of the family to protect the State. A religious loyalty has animated and nerved society to whatever it valued in social desire to uphold the government of the United States, as a divine institution ordained by God for good. Bless and prosper the courage and piety that have been thus displayed to defend them who with their lives in their hands maintain the cause of our country. God's strength of our life cover their heads in the day of battle. Be Thou the Ruler and Guide of all, that they may so pass through the things temporal, that they lose not the things eternal. O God, bring again peace in our time, and allay all passions, prejudice, and pride. May Thy spirit descend upon the great congregation of Thy people, inspire the orators to speak the truth in love, and bow our hearts in obedience to duty as Christians and fellow-citizens, as loyalists and patriots, as sinners saved in a common salvation through Jesus Christ, to whom with the Father and the Holy Ghost be praise now and forever. Amen.

SPEECH OF HAMILTON FISH.

My fellow-citizens, I shall not detain you longer than to express my appreciation of the position conferred upon me of presiding over a meeting of patriots convened to declare their intention to uphold the government, to maintain and support the constitution and the cause of the United States. We have fallen, indeed, on troublous times. Rebellion is abroad; treason attempts to overthrow the work of patriots, and it is for you, for us, to say the work that has been made shall stand. (Voices, " It shall.") Yes, stand it will, in spite of traitors, in spite of rebellion. Thank God, I look now upon a multitude that knows no party divisions—no Whigs, Democrats or Republicans. (A voice, " We are all Americans and for the Union." Great cheering.) There is no party but the Union. The only distinction now, until this contest shall be settled, till order shall be established, is that of citizen or traitor. (Voices, " Down with them." Great applause.)

SPEECH OF JOHN COCHRANE.

FELLOW-CITIZENS :—No ordinary events have notified you to assemble, nor ordinary circumstances have convened you upon this spot. Another of the periods in human affairs which constitute the epochs of history has transpired; and summoned by the emergency from their usual vocations the people have congregated here to-day to take order upon that which so intimately affects them. Since the construction of our government hitherto has its controlling policy been determined and applied through the instrumentality of political parties. To be sure, the vital functions of these parties have uniformly been derived from the people, as the source of all political power; yet the favorite method of asserting its sovereignty, most usually preferred by public opinion, has been that which embraces party organization and party discipline. Accordingly we have seen great public measures when proposed either adopted or defeated under the auspices and by the strength of political divisions. The clamors of conflicting opinions have at various times proceeded from the various organizations which prompted them. The Federalist at one time contended with the Republican; at another the Democrat struggled for political ascendency with an opposition variously designated, as expediency or the irresistible conflict of some political necessity conferred the various titles of National Republican, Whig, or Republican. These progressive changes you will not, fellow-citizens, fail to perceive were characteristic of the difficulties which prevailed among the citizens of a common country respecting the method of guiding its destiny. They were but the internal distinctions adopted among men occupying together the common position of one government and one country, and devoting their whole energies, whatever their conflicting opinions upon incidental questions, to the advancement and prosperity of that government and that country. Such hitherto has been the attitude of our political parties towards each other, and such their relations to the country, whose best interests each and all aspired to consult. It is not singular, therefore, that when government and country are imperilled the divisions of party should disappear, and that their memory should be regarded but as an incentive to a more cordial and general co-operation for the general welfare. But yesterday and the commotions of party strife characterized our councils and imparted vigor to our political contest. Then, with a constitution unimpeached and a government unimpaired, the struggle for ascendency contributed to political divisions. But

to-day, party zeal has subsided and party emulation ceased; for to-day our country demands the efforts of all her children. To-day, the people and the whole people have cast aside the attributes of the political partisan, and in an unbroken array have assembled to express their unanimous condemnation of the practices by which the public peace has been violated, and the public weal endangered. (Cheers.) Events of dire import signal to us the approach of war—not the war constituted of resistance to the hostile tread of an invading foe, and laden with the consequences only of foreign aggression resented, and foreign attack resisted—but a war inflamed by the passions, waged by the forces, and consisting of the conflict of citizens, brothers and friends. It is true that the problem of the future must baffle the most comprehensive wisdom, and compel the patriot into painful anxiety for the fate that awaits us. Yet we are not forbidden to extract from the past whatever consolations rectitude of purpose and a discreet conduct allow, and to summon their inspiration to our alliance and aid. It is not my purpose, fellow-citizens, to weary you with the recapitulation of the party differences, the conflict of which, while constituting our past political history at the same time shaped the question so long, so pertinaciously, and so fearfully debated between the North and the South, I need not direct your attention to those acts which seem necessarily to constitute the preliminaries to the bloody arbitrament that is upon us, and the consideration of which, however brief, cannot fail to manifest the patience and forbearance with which conflict has been shunned and the evils of war sought to be averted. Nearly all that need be submitted upon this point is directly pertinent to the recent and coercive attitude of the citizens very generally of the city of New York. Upon the revolutionary action of the seven Gulf States there occurred here an access of desire that every honorable means should be employed to induce their retention to the confederation of States in this Union. If this could not be attained, it was still hoped that a considerate policy might retain the border slave States, and thus possess us of the means of an ultimate restoration of its former integrity to the Union. Thus, though the property of the United States had been seized, its jurisdiction violated, and its flag assailed, yet it was by very many still thought wiser to refrain from hostility and to court renewed national harmony, through the milder methods of conciliation and compromise. Accordingly many, actuated by such motives, established themselves firmly in the policy of such concessions as, satisfactory to the Union sentiment of the border slave States, would, in their opinion, recommend themselves also to the judgment of the Northern people. I believe that a very large portion of our fellow-citizens entertained similar views, and were quite willing to advance towards any settlement of our sectional difficulties, not so much in the sense of remedial justice to the South as in that of an effectual method of restoring the Union. For myself, I may say that while actuated by such views, I have never supposed that the requirements of the border slave States would exact what a Northern opinion would not grant; nor, while affirming my belief that Northern patriotism would resist the infraction of Southern rights, did I for an instant imagine that I could be understood as including secession, and the seizure of the property of the

United States among them. Whatever the constitution has secured to the South, that there has been an abiding wish throughout the North to confirm; and although there have been and are differences of opinion as to the extent of Southern constitutional rights, yet I have never understood the disciples of any Northern political school to advocate those that were not affirmed by its party platform to be strictly of a constitutional character. But strenuous as were these efforts to disembarrass by coercion, even for the execution of the laws, the friendly intervention of the border slave States in behalf of a disrupted confederacy, their authors have been baffled, and their dearest hopes extinguished by the active hostility of South Carolina. Her attack upon Fort Sumter was simply an act of war. The right of property and the jurisdiction thereof, continued in the United States, and its flag denoted a sovereignty perfect and unimpaired. (Applause.) The cannon ball which first visited these battlements in hostile career violated that sovereignty and insulted that flag. It was the coercion which, at the North, had been deprecated for the sake of the Union and suspended, that was thus commended by the South to the North. The ensigns of government, and the emblems of national honor, were systematically assailed; and the adhering States were reduced to the attitude and compelled to the humiliation of an outraged nationality. Nor was this all. Menaces, so authentic as to merit the attention accorded to facts, marked the national capital for attack. Hostilities, with this object, were concerted against the government, and received the open approbation of the revolutionary leaders. In truth, the scene of war against the States represented by the government at Washington, which opened with the bombardment of Fort Sumter, has gradually developed into the fearful proportions of an organized invasion of their integral sovereignty. Such has been the gradual, nay, the almost imperceptible progress from initiatory violence to federal rights to the levying war upon the federal government. And now, fellow-citizens, it seems to me that no profound reflection is necessary to perceive that the posture of affairs which united so many of the Union loving men of the North against the policy of a coercion, supposed to be fraught with the danger of permanent dissolution, is not the same with that which represents the seceded States in open war to the constitution and the government. The considerations which deprecated the coercion of the South, address themselves with equal force against the coercion of the North. That which was opposed because of its anticipated injury to efforts at adjustment, becomes far more objectionable in its positive initiation of hostilities against the constitution and laws. The tramp of war is heard in our streets. The fearful note of preparation rises above the din of daily life, and mingles with our busy thoughts the solemnities of approaching conflict. Let us not deceive ourselves. It is no gala occasion—that which receives our attention. Confident as we are, many are the sad experiences which war reserves for those subjected to its stern necessities; and ere the strife ceases, terminate as it may, we must expect the reverses which have generally characterized the experience of all belligerents. But through all the coming scenes there will expand the pervading sense of the rectitude of those who strive for the rights of government and of country—the comforting reflection, that in a war which afflicts so many of our dearest affections, we at least

were not the aggressors. Nor should a success productive of subjugation of any portion of our fellow-citizens be contemplated among the possibilities of the future. The contest so unhappily inaugurated, is directed to the establishment of the authority of the government and the vindication of its flag. It is to be hoped that, as for the attainment of such an object men of all parties have disregarded political divisions, so that men without exception will accept the first opportunity to welcome returning peace upon the basis of one constitution and one country. Still if that national reconstruction, which unfortunately has hitherto baffled every patriotic and peaceful effort, shall neither be attainable by any other method, our resistance to aggression, now conducted to the issue of arms, will at least have asserted our national dignity and have prevented the inexpressible humiliation of national dismemberment and desolation accomplished at the expense of the degradation of the North. Should final separation prove inevitable notwithstanding every effort for a return to the peaceful repose of an undivided republic, we shall at least have entitled ourselves to the invaluable self respect founded in the consciousness of laws maintained, and honor vindicated. (Cheers.) The summons which the chief executive has proclaimed for military aid has appealed to the patriotism of the entire North. As at a single bound, thousands have responded, and other thousands await the call which shall require them also to arm in the common cause. (Cheers.) I cannot find that the magistrate's power is to be circumscribed now by constitutional scruples, or restrained by the doubts of constitutional power. The action which threatens the subversion of the government is confessedly revolutionary, and avows its justification in the imprescriptable right of self-preservation. Now, I think that it cannot be questioned that an effort to overthrow a government, by a portion of its citizens, on the plea of self-preservation, conclusively remits the government assailed to resistance upon the same rights; and that all means are justifiable for the suppression of revolution which it is conceded may be employed in its behalf. Many of the Southern States, disregarding the fundamental law which united them under the government of the Union, have armed themselves against its constitution, and wage unprovoked war against its citizens. They propose thus, by an appeal to the transcendent law of nature—the law that human happiness and the safety of society are the objects to which all institutions and all governments must be sacrificed—to justify their efforts at revolution, and to disrupt the confederation. I do not perceive that the resistance of such an effort is to be criticized in the spirit of strict constitutional construction; but that the same law which guides the revolution, should and must also apply to all efforts to oppose it, viz.:—the law which commands the employment of any force and in the best manner calculated to repress the movement which menaces the happiness, and is believed to be destructive of the safety of the people. I cannot doubt that in case of an emergency, proportionately formidable, the whole body of the community threatened, might upon the plea of self-preservation, arise in immediate resistance of the danger without reference to the provisions of constitutional law. Such an act would doubtless be referable to the magnitude of the danger, and be justifiable by a law above and beyond all compacts whatever. But it is needless, fellow-citizens, to pursue this theme further. The hour bears its events, and is fraught with its lessons. We are in the midst of revolution—not the revolution of the rhetorician, invoked to swell his periods, and to impress an audience; but the revolution of facts, the revolution of war. We have assembled to resist its wild career, and, if possible, to restore a distracted country once more to the authority of law and to the peace of orderly and constitutional government. To such an effort we summon the assistance of all good men. To such an effort we bring our party predilections and political associations, and sacrifice them all in the presence of our countrymen upon the altar of our common country. To such an effort we devote our energies and our means, all the while hoping and acting for the restoration of peace and the reunion of a severed confederacy; but still remembering that should the unhappy time arrive when final separation becomes inevitable, our affections and our efforts are due to the geographical section to which we belong—that our future is inseparable from the future of the North. (Cheers.) In the mean time the path of duty and honor conducts in but one direction—consists with but one course. It brings us, one and all, to the support of the government, the maintenance of the constitution, and the execution of the laws. (Applause.) Thousands are they who tread therein, and their motto is our country, and our whole country—in every event our country. (Loud cheering.)

SPEECH OF HIRAM KETCHUM.

FELLOW-CITIZENS:—Whoever attempts to address his fellow-citizens at this time should, in my judgment, well weigh and consider the words that he utters. They should not be words of irritation or of anger, but words which indicate a settled purpose and determination. Our first duty, my fellow-citizens, on this occasion, is to banish all thoughts of difference between ourselves. (A voice, "Good.") We are to forget that we have had any controversy among ourselves. (A voice, "They are forgotten.") We must come up as one united people. (A voice, "So we will.") And for what should we be united? My fellow-citizens, the great principle which lies at the foundation of our institutions is that the people are capable of self-government, that the majority of the people must rule. (Cheers for the people.) That their will, constitutionally expressed, is the law of the land: that the minority must submit to the majority. (Applause, and "That is so.") It is upon that principle, my fellow-citizens, that our whole institutions of liberty rest. It is that principle, for which the flag of our country is the emblem, and it is upon that principle that we must take our stand. That is the Fort Sumter which we must defend. (Applause.) We must resist to the death if necessary, all who would assail or attempt to destroy the principle of popular liberty. (Applause.) It is that principle which our fathers through the Revolution maintained, through a war of seven years, which they established by the formation of the constitution under which we live. It is that principle which has attracted to our shores thousands and millions of persons from foreign countries to come here, and they have sworn allegiance to this government, to this constitution. They will never violate that oath—the millions who have come here from foreign lands. (Cheers.) Yes, there are multitudes here who have taken that oath. There are millions in this country who have taken that oath. (A voice, "And will keep it, too.") They have taken it upon the Evangelists of Almighty God, they have taken it upon the cross, and they will stand by

it. (A voice, "We will.") And do you suppose that it is less obligatory upon them than it is upon us, who have sucked in that obligation with our mothers' milk? ("Good," and applause.) Now, my friends, I am going to show you, before I sit down, that the war now is in defence of that principle. The assault is upon that principle. The batteries of the enemy are directed against the principle of popular government—the principle that the people shall rule by the majorities; and that I propose, in a very few words, to demonstrate to you before I take my seat. Now, my friends, what are the facts? We have lately had an election of President and Vice-President of the United States. There were those among us—and I was of that number—that did not wish to see the Republican party prevail. Every ward and every election district in this city signified its wish that the Republican party should not prevail. Now, our fellow-citizens at the South have, therefore, supposed that they could rely upon the city of New York to sympathize with them in their rebellion. ("No, never.") What was the principle? We came up to say—"All your grievances can be redressed in the Union and under the Constitution and at the ballot-box." We gave a fair trial, and we were defeated; and what then? Did we justify anybody to go outside of the Constitution—("No")—and to break up the Government? Have we not been defeated time and again? I have been defeated; my party has been defeated time and again. I have known what it was to be defeated when I advocated Henry Clay as President of the United States, and I have known what it was to shed scalding tears over that defeat. But did we authorize him to rebel against my country? ("No.") Has it not been our practice, my fellow-citizens, I submit to you, to have free discussion, free press, and an animated and free canvass? But when the question was settled, the minority always submitted. Is not that American law? ("Yes, and it will be.") Have you not seen parties come here time and again at the polls, angry, severe, and anxious, and have you not seen them the next day, after the ballot was counted, shake hands? (Laughter and applause.) That is American law. ("Yes, it is.") That is American feeling. ("That's so.") We say, "We got beat, and we, as the minority, yield. At the next election we will try you again." (Applause.) That is our law; and now, when I went into this last canvass, and tried, as I did, according to the best of my ability, to defeat the election of Abraham Lincoln,—("And so did I,")—believing that the success of that party would be injurious to the country, when it was over, and I was defeated, what remained but to give up, to submit to the majority of the people, and to sustain the President who was elected by the majority, (applause;) and had I any thought that those people with whom I was acting were going to rebel against the Government, I never would have acted with them for one moment. ("No, nor I.") The three hundred and twenty thousand men in the State of New York, who came up and voted with the South, never would have voted with her if they had supposed that these men were going to rebel against the Government of the country. ("That is so!" "Bravo!" Applause.) Now, my friends, what do we hear? Why, when the election is over, they who have entered the contest and had the fight have had a fair chance at the ballot-box, have had a fair controversy in the canvass. And what do they say? Because we have not succeeded, we will break up this

Government. ("They cannot do it!" "Never!") This glorious Government, this Government which has stood more than seventy years, and brought such prosperity and such blessings upon the people as was never known in the history of the world— ("That's so")—which has enabled us to prosper— which has built up this great city—which has founded institutions of learning, and schools, and benevolent institutions, and enabled the poor man to educate his children, and to grow up and be somebody in the land—these institutions are now to be crushed. And why? Because they did not succeed at an election. Is that the talk? ("No.") What would Henry Clay have said to his followers if they had said, We have not elected you, and now we will break up the nation? He would have said, Get out of my sight. What would Jackson or anybody have said? What would any American have said, because we have not succeeded in this election, we will go out of the Union? Will that do? ("No.") Well, now, gentlemen, these people have made war upon this great, this cherished, this glorious principle, which has thus far conducted us to renown, to the happiness which we now enjoy, and made our flag, which is the emblem of this principle, known, respected, honored and feared all over the civilized world, and has never been dishonored except by these rebels. (Great applause.) Now, my friends, what I want is that you shall every man this day take the oath inwardly in your own consciences that you will maintain this principle of republican liberty. (Applause.) That is the fortress. That flag (pointing to the American flag) is the emblem of republican liberty; and you, my fellow-citizens of foreign birth, who have sworn to support the Constitution, and you, my fellow-citizens, born on the soil, who are equally bound to support that Constitution, I want you to stand up for the principle for which our fathers fought for seven years —for the principle that the people are capable of self government, and that the majority shall rule. And now let us see what has been done on the other side. They tell you that they have the right of revolution. Every people, when oppressed beyond endurance, have a right of revolution. When the people of this country were oppressed by Great Britain, they exercised the right of revolution; but what did they do first? They saw that there were no other means of redress but by revolution. Then our friends at the South, whom some of us here have aided to redress their grievances, can they say that their grievances, such as they complain of, cannot be redressed without a revolution? ("No.") Why, my friends, at this very election which made Abraham Lincoln President of the United States, the very people that put that party into power in the executive department of the country, put the majority and the representatives of the people in both branches of the Legislature in the hands of the opposition. ("That is so.") They would have had, if they had stayed in the House of Representatives, now to come into existence, thirty majority, and they would have had a majority in the Senate. They would have had, as they have, the Supreme Court on their side; and now, my friends, what could they complain of? ("Nothing.") Some of us believe that when the four years commenced they would have had a majority if they had only given the time, and only given the room for free discussion; but they could not wait. Having a majority in the branches of the Legislature, if the President had done what he said he was going to do, they could have restrained him;

but they must break away from this Union; they must destroy this Government, and now what comes to pass? We now find that this is the result of a conspiracy; a conspiracy which has been formed secretly for years by designing political men to overturn the Government of this country. ("That is so.") Now let us see. I have said that they mean to overthrow popular Government, let us see if I cannot prove it. They have attempted to form a Government; they have attempted to form a Union. They have made a Constitution; have they submitted it to the people? ("No, they dare not.") When the Constitution of the United States was formed, what was the process? ("It was submitted to the people.") The process was this, my friends: A convention met and formed this Constitution; a convention properly chosen met and formed it, and then this Constitution was reported to the Congress of the United States. Then the Congress ordered the people in each State to choose representatives and to form conventions; and then the Constitution was to be submitted to these conventions, debated freely without fear; and then, and not till then, until the will of the people had been ascertained—not till then, did it become the Constitution of the people of the United States. That is the way that the Constitution under which we live, which we have sworn to defend, was formed. It is the Constitution of the people, made by the whole people for the whole of the people, and can only be abolished and altered in the way that the people themselves have directed in the instrument itself. Now, what is the other course? They rush into a convention hastily and in a passion, and, after a heated conflict, they rush into a convention. They send delegates, and these delegates meet, form a Constitution without having any power given to them, because the question simply was, "Shall we secede?" They met, they formed a convention, and they made a new Constitution, and there are efforts made to have it submitted to the people, and they won't submit it to the people; they have never submitted it to the people; they dare not submit it to them. It is not the people's Government. They do not mean to have a people's Government. They mean to have a military despotism which shall rule the people. ("That's so." Applause. "Never.") And now, my friends, there are thousands and tens of thousands of good Union men in these very States which profess to have seceded. There are thousands and tens of thousands there who think as you and I think here to-day, but they dare not utter their sentiments. They would be hanged by the neck if they uttered their sentiments. They would be put down by villains; and now it is for their sake as well as ours, it is for the sake of the liberty of this Union, and for the liberty of the people, that we contend this day. (Great cheers.) Now, my friends, there are those who will follow me, but let me leave this impression strong on your minds, that we make no war, we have not been the aggressors. We stand by the Constitution and the principles of our fathers. We stand by popular liberty; we stand by the right of the people to make their own laws by the majority of their votes, and that is the principle which they have attacked and which they mean to destroy, and which, by the blessing of God, we mean to defend to the last—(great applause)—defend in argument, defend in the press, defend on the stump, defend with our lives. (Tremendous applause.) Fellow-citizens, I leave the subject. I leave you to contemplate upon it. I leave you to decide whether this Government shall stand for the benefit of mankind—for the benefit of our posterity—for the benefit of those who may seek the blessings of liberty from foreign shores, I leave you to decide. With you, with the people themselves, it is to determine this great question, and I cannot doubt what will be the determination. We will stand by our Constitution and our laws, and we will enforce our Constitution and our laws (Applause.)

SPEECH OF HENRY J. RAYMOND.

Fellow-Americans and brethren, in the cause of human liberty I never felt more at a loss for words, I never felt more the poverty of human language, than at this moment. But what need that I should say any thing to you, when the occasion speaks trumpet-tongued to every American heart? While armed rebellion is upon us, and while responsive echoes come from every loyal heart—while blood of loyal citizens has been shed in the Monumental City for no other crime than because they were on their way to defend the capital of the republic from lawless invasion—what need of words, then, while events like these are around us? There is but one sentiment abroad, and there is no need of appeal, for every heart beats responsive to the demands of the Constitution and the liberties which that Constitution secures and protects. We live and have been living in an age of revolution. Europe has rocked to and fro and surged under the tread of armed men, fighting for what? To beat down oppressive Governments that warred upon human rights and trampled their people under foot. Here on this continent, where liberty is in the possession of the Government, where human rights are respected, where the laws and the Constitution are made by the people—here on this continent we find treason and rebellion rampant. What is the spectacle presented to us to-day? Armed rebellion aiming to overthrow and tread under foot the Constitution and Government of the country. For what purpose? To vindicate human rights? No! Human rights are safe with the Government. This is a Government of the people, and cannot overthrow the liberties it fosters and protects, for our liberties rest in the hearts of the people, and the people themselves are the rulers of the nation. And now what our duty is in this emergency, is the only question asked, and in considering that we need no arguments and no party appeals. I, fellow-citizens, helped to put this Government into power; but God destroy me at once if I would not, the moment the Administration proved hostile to the Constitution, desert it and make way with it. We ask but one thing of the Administration—that it protect the Government committed to its care. We demand that of them; and if they do not perform that duty, we will put off from them. (Cheers.) Why, the Government of the country is but the agent of the people; and if the Government cannot defend the liberties of the people, the people will prove able to take care of their own liberties. (Applause.) The capital of our country is in danger. (Cries of "No.") Yes, in a danger that I fear we do not sufficiently appreciate—which I fear that the Government does not properly appreciate or understand. What is the state of the case to-day? Virginia, the mother of statesmen, and the mother of traitors too. (Cheers.) Virginia has long been pretending to be holding back in this crisis, and standing aloof from the contest, for the purpose of restoring peace. But what is the fact as now manifested? She stands forth at the head of this great rebellion. Twenty-five hundred men appeared yesterday at Harper's Ferry, not to find muskets which Floyd had intended for their use, thank God, but to take possession of the useless armory. And where did they come from? They came from Richmond. And with what purpose? To arm themselves, and to arm some fifteen thousand other Secessionists, and then to take the capital of Washington on the rear. (Cheers.) Need I call upon you to go to the rescue? (Cries of "We will.") That is the talk; that is the duty of American freemen. We are not to stand here urging action, while the Constitution is in danger, and the capital of the republic threatened with flames. If we consider our liberties worth preserving—if we have any veneration for the Constitution—if the memory of Washington is still enthroned in our hearts as the founder of our liberties—let us be up and doing. (Cheers.) Let me give you this piece of information: I understand since I came here that General Scott has sent word to this city that the capital is in danger, and that volunteers are wanted, orders or no orders. (Enthusiastic cries of "We will all go, every man of us.") Now, I have another piece of information to give you, that the steamer Baltic will be at the wharf to-morrow morning to take as many volunteers as may choose to go. (Loud cheers.) The people have resolved that the Government shall be preserved, and they must and shall preserve it.

At this time the speaker was interrupted by many voices crying out—"At what time will the Baltic leave?"

Mr. RAYMOND—At 10 o'clock, I learn, from the foot of Canal street. (Three cheers were given for General Scott, and three for the Baltic.) Fellow-citizens, I believe that we have a Government at Washington on which we can rely, and worthy of preserving. If the Government proves false to the country, why, we will drive them from their places, and put men in their places who will take care of the Government. Thousands will rise and rush to the rescue of the capital, and to keep it from the possession of the rebels who have made piracy their watchword, and who commenced their present work with plunder, and who have adopted as a basis of their action and of their power, plunder and arson, and with the weapons stolen from the Government have aimed an assassin blow at the heart of the republic. What we want is, that a terrible blow be struck, and that it will be felt by those who have strongly provoked it. They have already ascertained that they cannot longer trust to one great hope they had in their enterprise. They had counted confidently on the divisions of the North. They believed that they would be perfectly safe in marching an army to Washington, and that in doing so they would receive support from this city. This reliance of theirs only shows them now how little they understood what the American heart is made of, whether that heart beats in the city of New York or in the Western prairies. It shows they know nothing of liberty, or the impulses of liberty. It shows that they know nothing of the attachment of the people to the Government—to that Government under which we have grown great, and mighty, and prosperous—a Government which gave to the South itself its only title to consideration among the nations of the earth. I have nothing further to say but what I have already announced, that the Baltic sails to-morrow; and I trust that you will all rush to the rescue, and preserve the capital, and prevent its falling into the hands of the barbarians—

(laughter and cheers)—who threaten to destroy it. The South may rest assured that the enterprise undertaken by her cannot succeed, and cannot long run on. They will learn that it is one thing to take a people and a Government by surprise, but that it is quite another thing to wage a war of despotism over thirty millions of people. What have the Secessionists done towards human liberty? What sort of a Government have they established? A Government of force, a Government of despotism. Jefferson Davis is to-day as pure and as unmitigated and complete a despot over those he rules, as any who sits upon any throne of Europe. (Applause, and cries of "That's so." Three groans were then given for Davis.) If he gets possession of Washington—(cries of "Don't you be alarmed at that")—if he is allowed to form a Government, it will be such a Government as the people will have as little to do with as possible. (Cries of "He can't do that.") No; but if he gets possession of the capital, one hundred thousand men will rush to the rescue and sweep rebellion from the headquarters of the Government. He (Davis) will find that the heart of the American people is irrevocably fixed upon preserving the republic. (Cheers.) I heard an anecdote to-day from Major Anderson—(cheers for Anderson)—which may interest you, and at the same time illustrate this position. During the attack on Fort Sumter, a report came here that the flag on the morning of the fight was half-mast. I asked him if that was true, and he said there was not a word of truth in the report. He said that during the firing one of the halyards was shot away, and the flag in consequence dropped down a few feet. The rope caught in the staff, and could not be reached, so that the flag could not be either lowered or hoisted; and, said the Major, "God Almighty nailed that flag to the flagmast, and I could not have lowered it if I tried." (Immense cheering.) Yes, fellow-citizens, God Almighty has nailed that resplendent flag to its mast, and if the South dares to march upon Washington, they will find that that cannot be taken down. No, not by all the powers they can collect. No! they will find that that sacred sword which defends and strikes for human rights—that sword which Cromwell wielded, and which our fathers brought into the contest, and which made us a nation—will be taken once more from its scabbard to fight the battle of liberty against rebellion and treason. (Vehement cheering.) As I have already said, the Baltic will be at the foot of Canal street to-morrow morning to take volunteers to serve the country, whether they have orders or not. (Cries of "We'll go.") I would advise you not to go without arms. (Cries of "Where will we get them?") I have already made the announcement of the sailing, and now I am requested to make another. You may have seen in the morning papers that Governor Hicks, of Maryland, said that he would endeavor to prevent the passage of troops through Baltimore. I desire to say for him, that he has stood in the breach long months in Maryland, and he has done more to preserve the Union than any other man in the Southern States, and he is entitled to the warm gratitude of all for arresting rebellion on its very first tide, and when it was sweeping the whole South to destruction. (Three cheers were given with great unanimity for Governor Hicks.) If they could have once secured a State Convention in Maryland, they would have had everything their own way. State Conventions are old tricks of despotism. Whenever any thing despotic

was to be carried out against the will of the people, State Conventions have always been the convenient instrument used, for they assumed to be the representatives of the people, and having sovereign power, did just as they pleased. Take the case of Virginia. The Convention was elected by the people to stand by the Union; yet it goes into secret session, and then resolves to make an attack upon the national capital, to seize the seat of Government, and to burn down the bridges between Baltimore and Philadelphia. Maryland had no such standpoint for rebellion—she stood firm, and Governor Hicks has held the State to its moorings in the Union, and he deserved the thanks of the North. Governor Hicks had said that he would endeavor to prevent the passage of troops, simply that he might, in that way, prevent needless bloodshed, while, at the same time, he would not interfere with measures necessary for the defence of the capital. A message has just been put into my hands, stating that the President had conceded that no more troops should be brought through Maryland, if Governor Hicks would pledge the State not to interfere with the passage of troops up the Potomac—thus leaving a quiet path to Washington by water. I trust in Heaven that before three days, aye, before two days, that at least 50,000 men will be concentrated at the capital of the country to protect it from the hands of traitors. (Cheers, and cries of "What about the Seventh Regiment?") They were in Philadelphia this morning, and it was determined that they would be sent on by water; but I believe the Seventh kicked against it, and were anxious to go through Baltimore. (Immense cheering.) The Seventh Regiment, they would recollect, paid a visit to Baltimore, at which time they received the courtesies and hospitalities of their fellow-soldiers there, and they were anxious to see whether these same men had become their enemies and the enemies of the country at the same time. The Seventh was the pet regiment of New York, and well it deserves to be. They were a band of noble, gallant young men, who would stand by their country to the last extremity. I would have been glad if the Seventh had first gone on, that they might have opened the way for their comrades. But there is a Providence which presides over these movements. Look at this one single instance of Providential arrangement. The Massachusetts Regiment, on the 19th April, 1861, were assailed and two of their number killed, simply because they were on their way to protect the Federal capital. The first blood of the Revolution came from Massachusetts, on the streets of Lexington, and now we find that on the anniversary of the battle of Lexington, which inaugurated and sanctified the revolution of our fathers, the blood of a Massachusetts man has been shed to inaugurate the revolution now upon us. (Vehement cheering.) But if Massachusetts has had the glory of giving her blood the first in this cause, if she can now claim the high honor of being the first to shed her blood in defence of the Constitution, she shall not be left alone in the contest to preserve it. (Loud cheers.) A despatch has been just received by Major-General Sandford from Colonel Lefferts, of the Seventh, stating that his command would leave Philadelphia by rail for Havre de Grace—(great cheering)—where they would embark on board a steamer to Annapolis, to go thence to Washington by rail. You may rely upon it, while we are here assembled to respond to the Constitution, our brethren of the Seventh are on the soil of Washington, ready to fight, and, if necessary, die for it. (Three cheers were given for the Seventh Regiment, during which Mr. R. sat down.)

SPEECH OF RICHARD O'GORMAN, ESQ.

FELLOW-CITIZENS :—This is not the time for many words. Speech should be like the crisis, short, sharp, and decisive. What little I have to say will be shortly said. I am an Irishman—(Cheers for O'Gorman)—and I am proud of it. I am also an American citizen, and I am proud of that. (Renewed applause.) For twelve years I have lived in the United States, twelve happy years, protected by its laws, under the shadow of its constitution. When I assumed the rights of citizenship, I assumed, too, the duties of a citizen. When I was invested with the rights which the wise and liberal constitution of America gave to adopted citizens, I swore that I would support the Constitution, and I will keep my oath. (Tremendous cheering, and a voice, "You would not be an Irishman if you did not.") This land of mine, as well as of yours, is in great danger. I have been asked what side I would take; and I am here. (Cheers.) No greater peril ever assailed any nation. Were all the armies and all the fleets of Europe bound for our shores to invade us, it would not be half so terrible a disaster as that we have to face now. Civil war is before us. We are threatened not with subjugation, but disintegration, utter dissolution. The nation is crumbling beneath our feet, and we are called to save it. Irish born citizens, will you refuse? ("No, no.") This quarrel is none of our making: no matter. I do not look to the past. I do not stop to ask by whose means this disaster was brought about. A time will come when history will hold the men who have caused it to a heavy account; but for us, we live and act in the present. Our duty is to obey, and our duty is to stand by the Constitution and the laws. (Applause.) I saw to-day the officers of the Sixty-ninth Irish regiment, and they are ready. (Cheers for Col. Corcoran.) Fellow-citizens, if there be any men in these United States, who look to this war with any feeling of exultation, I take no part with them. I look to it with grief, with heartfelt grief. It is, after all, a fratricidal war; it is a war that nothing but inevitable necessity can excuse, and the moment that inevitable necessity ceases, the moment peace can be attained—for peace is the only legitimate end of any war.—I pray to God that it may cease and we be brothers and friends again. Some of the gentlemen who preceded me to-day have said that traitors have sprung from Virginia. O, fellow-citizens, when you passed that statue—the statue of the Father of his Country—and saw that serene, calm face, and that hand raised, as it were, in benediction over this people, forget not that Washington was a son of Virginia. The South has been deceived, cruelly deceived, by demagogues; they have had false news from this side, and that has deceived them. They did not know, we did not know it ourselves, what a fund of loyalty, what stern hearty allegiance there was all through this land for the Constitution and the Union. Fellow-citizens, the cloud that lowers over us now will pass away. There may be storm; it may be fierce and disastrous, but trust me that storm was needed to clear and purify the political atmosphere. We are passing through an inevitable political and national crisis. We could not go on as we were going on. A sea of corruption was swelling all around us, and threatened to engulph honor, reputation, and the good name of the nation and of individuals. That stagnant water stirs, but trust me, it is an angel

that has touched the waters. ("Good.," and applause.) An angel hand has touched them and turned the fœtid stream into a healing balm. That angel is patriotism, that walks the land in majesty and power. (Applause.) And were nothing else gained by this terrible struggle than the consciousness that we have a nation and a national spirit to support it, I would still say that this ordeal that we are going through will not be all in vain. (Cheers.) For me, fellow-citizens, as far as one man can speak I recognize but one duty. I will keep my oath, I will stand as far as in me lies by the Constitution and the laws. Abraham Lincoln is not the President of my choice; no matter, he is the President chosen under the Constitution and the laws. The government that sits in Washington is not of my choice, but it is *de facto* and *de jure* the government, and I recognize none other. That flag is my flag, and I recognize none other but that one. (Bravo and applause.) Why, what other flag could we have? It has been set by the hands of American science over the frozen seas of the North; it is unrolled where by the banks of the Amazon the primeval forests weave their tangled hair. All through the infant struggles of the republic under its consecrated folds men poured out their life blood with a liberal joy to save this country. ("And will again.") All through the Mexican war it was a sign of glory and of hope. Fellow-citizens, all through Europe, when down-trodden men look up and seek for some sign of hope, where do they look but to that flag, the flag of our Union? (Great applause.) I deprecate this war; I do hope that it will cease, but it is war. That flag must not be allowed to trail in the dust, not though the hand that held it down is a brother's. I have done. (Voices "Go on, go on.") All I can say is, that, with all the men that honestly go out to fight this fight, my sympathies go with them. I trust it will be fought out in an honorable and chivalrous manner, as becomes men that are fighting to-day with those that may be their friends to-morrow. But if there cannot be peace, if war must be, then for the Constitution and the Union I am, and may God defend the right. (Tremendous cheering.)

SPEECH OF IRA P. DAVIS.

He said he had a difficult task to perform in addressing them after the eloquent speaker who had just left the stand. Yet, as a citizen, and as an American, and as one whose father fought at Lexington, he was before them that day to do his duty. He would call their attention to a few facts to illustrate the principle involved in this great question. The Government of the United States was based on the principle that all power is inherent in the people; that at any time the people can alter, amend, or, if they pleased, totally abrogate the Government. But while this right was recognized, it was still their duty to observe the sacredness of contracts. The people of Great Britain, of France, and other nations of the world, with whom we have made treaties through our lawful counsellors, recognize the people living on the continent, within certain jurisdictions, as a nation. And though the people here might, if they pleased, change the character of the Government, yet the Government of these countries would hold them responsible within these districts, to fulfil their contracts and treaties—to live up to the contracts they had made. So was it with the people of those States. The Federal Government was nothing more than the executor of the contracts entered into by the thirty-four States of the Union as a nation, and though the people of any one of those States were disposed to change the character and form of the Government, yet that would not annul the contracts entered into by them with the General Government, or with the other States throughout the General Government. They possessed Constitutional methods of changing the form by which their contracts with the General Government should be fulfilled. There was no way of dissolving the contracts except by mutual consent —(cheers)—or by fulfilling these contracts. So the Southern States might, if they pleased, alter and change the form of their Constitution; but if they desired to retreat from their association with the North and West and East, they must present their grievances to the people of all the States, the people themselves being the only tribunal to decide the question involved. They must present their grievances to the people, and the people, after being duly convened, would, through the legitimate officers, proceed in a legal, Constitutional manner, to change that Constitution; and they must abide their time, and must wait till that process has been gone through. They could not dissolve their union with these States —they could not be allowed to bring that evil upon the country. He concurred with a previous speaker, that many of these Southern demagogues were misled. They had looked to New York with her 30,000 Democratic majority to back them up in their traitorous designs; but they little knew the heart of the great Democracy. They underrated your honesty, they underrated your nobility of character. The men that they hoped would aid them, will in thousands and tens of thousands march to the defence of the capital. As a citizen and as a Democrat he had labored hard against the election of the powers that be. He had labored as hard as his humble ability would permit, to prevent the election of Mr. Lincoln; but, so help me God, as a citizen and as a lover of my country, I will defend his administration so long as he holds his seat. (Loud cheers.) He held that they were not only all bound to support the President and the Constitution and the confederacy of these States as expressed through the State Legislatures by every man who has exercised the right of suffrage; they were bound to support the party that succeeded to office. Were these men to enter into the political arena with a chance of winning and none at all of losing? By the very fact that they had exercised the right of suffrage made them bound to submit to the decision of the majority. (Cheers.) It was a great insult to say that they were threatened by a band of desperadoes who underrated their character and endeavored to bring them down to their own level. Short speeches were now called for. They were called upon to support the Constitution and to maintain the President in his call, and to urge upon him the knowledge of the fact that he will have a million of men, if necessary, to carry out the Government and to punish the traitors who would raise their traitorous swords to overturn it. The true way to deal with the crisis was to nip the treason in its bud, by sending forth such a body of soldiers as would paralyze those men with terror. That was the only way. The South had had months to arm, and they had been collecting arms for years past. It was not because they were defeated at the late election they should become dissatisfied, and attempt to break up the Government. ("That's so," and cheers.) Those base connivers, those traitors who had assailed the flag of the Union, had been plotting the over-throw of the Government for years past. Their conduct at the Charleston Convention proved that unmistakably. Their object in breaking up the Convention was to throw the election into the hands of the Republicans, so that they might have a pretext for disunion. (Cheers.) The action now taken was not with any view of subjugation, but merely to maintain law and order and to support the Government. They were engaged in working out the great problem of popular Government. It was long thought that the people could not govern themselves, but they had shown the practicability of it. The Government was placed in a position of great danger; but if they passed through this ordeal, they will more clearly and gloriously prove the success of popular Government. (Cheers.)

SPEECH OF PROFESSOR MITCHELL.

Professor MITCHELL was introduced, and, fired with nervous eloquence and patriotism, he infused the same spirit into his auditors. He spoke as follows:—I am infinitely indebted to you for this evidence of your kindness. I know I am a stranger among you. ("No," "No.") I have been in your State but a little while; but I am with you, heart and soul, and mind and strength, and all that I have and am belongs to you and our common country, and to nothing else. I have been announced to you as a citizen of Kentucky. Once I was, because I was born there. I love my native State, as you love your native State. I love my adopted State of Ohio, as you love your adopted State, if such you have; but, my friends, I am not a citizen now of any State. I owe allegiance to no State, and never did, and, God helping me, I never will. I owe allegiance to the Government of the United States. A poor boy, working my way with my own hands, at the age of twelve turned out to take care of myself as best I could, and beginning by earning but $4 per month, I worked my way onward until this glorious Government gave me a chance at the Military Academy at West Point. There I landed with a knapsack on my back, and, I tell you God's truth, just a quarter of a dollar in my pocket. There I swore allegiance to the Government of the United States. I did not abjure the love of my own State, nor of my adopted State, but all over that rose proudly triumphant and predominant my love for our common country. And now to-day that common country is assailed, and, alas! alas! that I am compelled to say it, it is assailed in some sense by my own countrymen. My father and my mother were from Old Virginia, and my brothers and sisters from Old Kentucky. I love them all; I love them dearly. I have my brothers and friends down in the South now, united to me by the fondest ties of love and affection. I would take them in my arms to-day with all the love that God has put into this heart; but if I found them in arms, I would be compelled to smite them down. You have found officers of the army who have been educated by the Government, who have drawn their support from the Government for long years, who, when called upon by their country to stand for the Constitution and for the right, have basely, ignominiously and traitorously either resigned their commissions, or deserted to traitors, rebels, and enemies. What means all this? How can it be possible that men should act in this way? There is no question but one. If we ever had a Government and Constitution, or if we ever lived under such, have we ever recognized the supremacy of right? I say, in God's name, why not recognize it now? Why not to-day? Why not forever? Suppose those friends of ours from old Ireland, suppose he who has made himself one of us, when a war should break out against his own country, should say, "I cannot fight against my own countrymen," is he a citizen of the United States? They are no countrymen longer when war breaks out. The rebels and the traitors in the South we must set aside; they are not our friends. When they come to their senses, we will receive them with open arms; but till that time, while they are trailing our glorious banner in the dust, when they scorn it, condemn it, curse it, and trample it under foot, then I must smite. In God's name I will smite, and as long as I have strength I will do it. (Enthusiastic applause.) O, listen to me, listen to me! I know these men; I know their courage; I have been among them; I have been with them; I have been reared with them; they have courage; and do not you pretend to think they have not. I tell you what it is, it is no child's play you are entering upon. They will fight, and with a determination and a power which is irresistible. Make up your mind to it. Let every man put his life in his hand, and say, "There is the altar of my country; there I will sacrifice my life." I, for one, will lay my life down. It is not mine any longer. Lead me to the conflict. Place me where I can do my duty. There I am ready to go, I care not where it leads me. My friends, that is the spirit that was in this city on yesterday. I am told of an incident that occurred, which drew the tears to my eyes, and I am not much used to the melting mood at all. And yet I am told of a man in your city who had a beloved wife and two children, depending upon his personal labor day by day for their support. He went home and said, "Wife, I feel it is my duty to enlist and fight for my country." "That's just what I've been thinking of, too," said she; "God bless you! and may you come back without harm! but if you die in defence of the country, the God of the widow and the fatherless will take care of me and my children." That same wife came to your city. She knew precisely where her husband was to pass as he marched away. She took her position on the pavement, and finding a flag, she begged leave just to stand beneath those sacred folds and take a last fond look on him whom she, by possibility, might never see again. The husband marched down the street; their eyes met; a sympathetic flash went from heart to heart; she gave one shout, and fell senseless upon the pavement, and there she lay for not less than thirty minutes in a swoon. It seemed to be the departing of her life. But all the sensibility was sealed up. It was all sacrifice. She was ready to meet this tremendous sacrifice upon which we have entered, and I trust you are all ready. I am ready. God help me to do my duty! I am ready to fight in the ranks or out of the ranks. Having been educated in the Academy, having been in the army seven years; having served as commander of a volunteer company for ten years, and having served as an adjutant-general, I feel I am ready for something. I only ask to be permitted to act; and in God's name give me something to do.

[The scene that followed the close of Professor MITCHELL's eloquent and patriotic remarks baffles description. Both men and women were melted to tears, and voices from all parts of the vast mutitude re-echoed the sentiments of the speaker, and every one seemed anxious to respond to the appeal to rush to the defence of the country.]

REMARKS OF SAMUEL HOTALING.

The next speaker was Mr. SAMUEL HOTALING, who called upon the citizens of New York to defend their flag, their homes, and the blessed heritage which our ancestors left us. He had been a farmer and a merchant, and he was now ready to be a soldier. This meeting is mainly held to stimulate us to action and to arms. We must shoulder our muskets and take our place, carry our swords to the Capitol at Washington, and even to Texas, for the protection of our friends and our country. The speaker went on to say that the motto of the rebels was Captain Kidd piracy. They were a band of traitors to their country and to their oaths; and what could we expect from thieves like them? He said he had never been a rabid abolitionist, but it was his opinion that Providence was as much at work now as He was when the children of Israel in Egypt received their emancipation under Moses.

He believed that in five years this warfare would produce such bankruptcy and starvation in the Southern States, that their white laboring people and their slaves would go into a state of anarchy, bloodshed, and San Domingo butchery, and that within that period the seceded States would petition the Federal Government for aid and money to transmit their butchering Africans among themselves across the Atlantic ocean to the land of their fathers.

Mr. HALLECK then called upon all young men to enroll as volunteers, and to proceed to Washington to strengthen the Seventh Regiment. As for himself, he felt as if he would leave his wife and four children to go to Washington and take whatever part was necessary to maintain the Government. (Cheers.) He had voted against the party coming into office; but now, so help me God, I will do all I can to aid the Administration to the uttermost. He had come from the mighty Niagara, and he would assure them that in Western New York thousands of young men were prepared to enrol themselves to fight for the Union and the Constitution.

At Stand No. 3, located on the northwest side of Union Square, the meeting was called to order by Mr. Richard Warren, who nominated Mr. Wm. F. Havemeyer as Chairman of the meeting.

The following gentlemen acted as Vice-Presidents:

Jno. A. Stevens,	Isaac Bell, Jr.,	James G. Bennett,
R. A. Witthaus,	Dan. P. Ingraham,	R. B. Connolly,
R. M. Blatchford,	W. M. Vermilye,	Paul Spofford,
Elijah F. Purdy,	J. L. Aspinwall,	Smith Ely, Jr.,
Samuel B. Ruggles,	Richard Schell,	O. Ottendorfer,
James Owen,	Fred. Lawrence,	M. B. Blake,
S. B. Chittenden,	J. G. Vassar,	Francis S. Lathrop,
Thos. C. Smith,	J. G. Pierson,	Henry Pierson,
August. F. Schwab,	John H. Swift,	Isaac Delaplaine,
Wm. Lyell,	Allan Cummings,	Richard O'Gorman,
Chas. P. Daly,	Geo. B. DeForest,	Peter M. Bryson,
W. H. Hays,	W. C. Alexander,	Charles W. Sanford,
Samuel D. Babcock,	Augt. Weisman,	Charles Aug. Davis,
A. V. Stout,	H. D. Aldrich,	Henry E. Davies,
Geo. R. Jackson,	R. L. Kennedy,	Josiah Sutherland,
Jno. T. Agnew,	R. Mortimer,	Anth'y L. Robinson,
Francis Hall,	Horatio Allen,	James W. White,
Thos. A. Emmett,	Norman White,	M. H. Grinnell,
Wm. Allen Butler,	Geo. T. Hope,	Geo. Opdyke,
Edwin Hoyt,	Ogden Haggerty,	G. C. Verplanck,
Jno. E. Devlin,	John Wadsworth,	R. L. Stuart,
James W. Beekman,	Josiah Oakes,	Jas. S. Wadsworth,
P. M. Wetmore,	Loring Andrews,	Simeon Draper,
Geo. S. Coe,	F. L. Talcott,	J. Punnett,
N. Knight,	Alfred Edwards,	Robt. J. Dillon,
Jno. A. C. Gray,	John Jay,	Samuel Sloan,
Cyrus Curtiss,	Martin Bates,	Jno. C. Greene,
Henry A. Smythe,	W. H. Webb,	Jno. McKeon,
David Thompson,	J. G. Brooks,	Royal Phelps.
T. H. Faile,		

Mr. HAVEMEYER, on taking the chair, made a few brief remarks, observing that in the course of his life he never had supposed that he would be called upon to perform the duty which all present were called upon to perform this day.

Mr. Havemeyer then introduced the Rev. Mr. PRESTON, who read a short prayer.

Mr. Witthaus was called upon to act as Secretary of the meeting, and a list of Vice-Presidents was read and adopted.

The resolutions were then read by Mr. RICHARD WARREN, and were adopted by a unanimous vote. During these proceedings the crowd in the square, fronting the stand, had augmented by tens of thousands, and the greatest degree of enthusiasm prevailed everywhere. The excitement increased at the appearance of Major Anderson on the platform, accompanied by Messrs. Simeon Draper and Police Superintendent Kennedy. The gallant Major was introduced to the Germans by Mr. Draper. The first speaker introduced was Mr. Coddington, and while he was speaking, Captain Foster and Dr. Crawford, the Surgeon of Fort Sumter, arrived on the platform. They were introduced by Mr. Warren, and were received with vociferous cheers. These gentlemen, as also Major Anderson previously, soon left the stand, and the speaker was permitted to proceed with the discourse.

SPEECH OF DAVID S. CODDINGTON.

FELLOW-CITIZENS:—The iron hail at Fort Sumter rattles on every Northern breast. It has shot away the last vestige of national and personal forbearance. A loaf of bread on its way to a starving man was split in two by a shot from his brother. You might saturate the cotton States with all the turpentine of North Carolina; you might throw upon them the vast pine forests of Georgia, then bury the Gulf storm's sharpest lightning into the combustible mass, and you would not redden the Southern horizon with so angry a glow as flashed along the Northern heart when the flames of Fort Sumter reached it. To-day, bewildered America, with her torn flag and her broken charter, looks to you to guard the one, and restore the other. How Europe stares and liberty shudders, as from State after State that flag falls, and the dream breaks! Hereafter Southern history will be as bare as the pole from which the sundered pennant sinks, and treason parts with the last rag that concealed its hideousness. I know how common and how easy it is to dissolve this Union in our mouths. Dangerous words, like dangerous places, possess a fearful fascination, and we sometimes look down from the heights of our prosperity with an irresistible itching to jump off. This spectre of disunion is no new ghost, born of any contemporary agitation. For years it has been skulking semi-officially about the Capitol. Through the whole range of our parliamentary history every great question, from a tariff to a Territory, has felt its clammy touch. Did it not drop its death's head into the tariff scales of '33, hoping to weigh the duties down to a conciliation level? did it not shoot its ghastly logic into the storm of '20, and frighten our soundest statesmanship into that crude calm called the Missouri Compromise? did it not sit grinning upon the deck of all our naval battles, hoping to get a turn at the wheel, that it might run the war of 1812 upon a rock? did it not stand up upon the floor of the first Congress and shake its bony fingers in the calm face of Washington? and did not our fathers, who stood unmoved the

shock of George the Third's cannon, shudder in the presence of this spectre, when they thought how the infant republic might be cast away upon its bleak and milkless breast? Then it was a thin, skulking, hatchet-faced ghost. At last, fed upon the granaries of Northern and Southern fanaticism, it has come to be a rotund, well fed, corpulent disaster. Southern passion may put on the war-paint; Southern statesmanship may attempt to organize a pique into an empire, to elevate a sulk into a sacrament, by marrying disappointment to revolution, and reducing a temporary constitutional minority into a hopeless organic political disaster. They may even propose in solemn convention to abolish the Fourth of July, and throw all its patriotic powder into the murderous arsenal of fratricidal conflict; but they cannot, except through self-destruction, permanently disrupt our nationality. Talk of the wise statesmanship of the South! Had they allowed Kansas to become a free State they would have been in possession of the national government at this moment. Although the repeal of the Missouri Compromise awoke the North from its deep sleep upon the slave question, yet the most economical outlay of prudence would have continued them in possession of the government for an indefinite future. Then Mexico would have been possible, without the awful leap which copies her morals without the possibility of possessing her territories. South Carolina once lived upon a potato to rout a king, and she is fast going back to that immortal vegetable, in order to crown a fallacy. Our republicanism means the whole nation, or it means nothing. Together, the parts temper each other; asunder, the aristocracy of the slave power makes equality a myth, and the free radical North less safely democratic. If Abraham Lincoln has inaugurated a crash; if George Washington is to be no longer known as the successful contender for a combined and self-regulating nationality; if Bishop Berkeley's star of empire has crumbled away into belligerent asteroids, and we are to fall, like Cæsar, at the base of this black Pompey's pillar, we shall at least go into this holy battle for the Constitution, with no law broken and no national duty unfulfilled. We have not stolen a single ship, or a pound of powder, or a dollar of coin to sully the sacred tramp with which patriotism pursues robbery and rebellion. All the ills of the South could have been remedied within the Constitution—all their wrongs righted by the victory of future votes. Shall I tell you what secession means? It means ambition in the Southern leaders and misapprehension in the Southern people. Its policy is to imperialize slavery; and to degrade and destroy the only free republic in the world. It is a fog of the brain and a poison at the heart. Dodging the halter, it walks in a volcano which must explode whenever the tempestuous shock of Northern invasion shall render slavery impossible. The day that Southern statesmanship turned pirate, Southern slavery lost its last hold on Northern forbearance. God forbid that servile war should ever be on our consciences; but what power could restrain the frenzied passion of continuously provoked multitudes, when the taste of blood has brutalized their march? We have not come here to talk about any man's party creed. We have not come to seek the falling fruits of patronage, but to save the beautiful and wide-spreading tree upon which all our blessings grow. Party and partyisms are dead; only grim, black powder is alive now. Who talks of Tammany or Mozart Hall? Who haunts the coal-hole or the wood-pile, when our souls' fuel is on fire for flag and country? Did not Washington fight seven years, break ice on the Delaware, break bones and pull triggers on Monmouth field, send ten thousand bleeding feet to where no blood ever comes, and pass from clouds of smoke to archways of flowers —for what? That States should defy their best guardian, which is the nation, insult history and make republicanism impossible? Here, in this city of our love and pride, this cradle of the civil life of Washington, where despotism sheathed its last sword and constitutional liberty swore its first oath; where steam first boiled its way to a throne, and art and commerce and finance, and all the social amenities marshalled their forces to the sweet strain of the first inaugural—here, where government began and capital centres, is the sheet anchor of American loyalty. Nothing so disappoints secession as the provoking fidelity of New York to the Constitution. From the vaults of Wall-street, Jefferson Davis expected to pay his army, and riot in all the streets and in all towns and cities of the North to make their march a triumphant one. Fifty thousand men to-day tread on his fallacy. Gold is healthy, gold is loyal, gold is determined; it flows easy, because the war is not to subjugate or injure any one, but to bring back within the protecting folds of the Constitution an erring and rebellious brother,—a brother whom we have trusted and toasted, fought with side by side on the battle field, voted for at the ballot-box, showered with honor after honor upon his recreant head, while that brother was poisoning the milk in his mother's breast, striking a parricidal blow at the parental government which has protected and prospered us all as no people were ever so prospered and protected. Heretofore, in our differences, we have shouldered ballots instead of bayonets. With a quiet bit of paper in our hands we have marched safely through a hundred battles about tariff, bank, anti-liquor, anti-rent, and all those social and political questions about which a free people may amicably differ. If slavery cannot be appeased with the old life of the ballot, depend upon it the bayonet will only pierce new wounds in its history. We have heretofore kept all our lead moulded into type, that peaceably and intellectually we might enter the Southern brain, until passion and precipitation have forced us to melt down that type into a less friendly visitor. Kossuth says that bayonets think; and ours have resolved in solemn convention to think deeply, act promptly, and end victoriously. Do you wonder to-day to see that flag flying over all our reawaked national life, no longer monopolized by mast-head, steeple, or liberty-pole, but streaming forth a camp signal from every private hearthstone, breaking out in love pimples all down our garments, running like wild vine flowers over whole acres of compact anxious citizens? Why has that tender maiden turned her alabaster hands into heroic little flagstaffs, which, with no loss of modesty, unveils to the world her deep love of country? Do you see that infant show off its playthings, tottering under rosettes and swathed in the national emblem by foreboding parents, who would protect its growth with this holy talisman of safety? Do you see, too, those grave old citizens, sharpened by gain-seeking, and sobered with law-expounding, invade their plain exterior with peacock hues, which proclaim such tenacity to a flag that has fanned, like an angel's wing, every form of our prosperity and pride? It seems hard for philosophy to divine how any section of the country, so comprehensively prosperous, could allow a mean jealousy of another portion, a little more wealthy and populous, to so hurry it on into rebellion, not against us, but a common Government and a common glory, to which both are subject and both should love. Does not each State belong to all the States, and should not all the States be a help and a guide to each State? Louisiana's sugar drops into Ohio's tea-cup; and should not every palace built on Fifth-avenue nod its head amicably to whatever cotton receipts its bills? Over-pride of locality has been the scourge of our nationality. When our thirty-one stars broke on the north star, did not Texas, as well as Pennsylvania, light up the bleak Arctic sky? When the old flag first rose over the untouched gold of California, did not Georgia and New York join hands in unveiling the tempting ore? Virginia has seceded and carried my political fathers with it—Washington and Jefferson. The State has allowed their tombs to crumble, as well as their principles. Outlaw their sod! Who will dare to ask me for my passport at the grave of Washington?

SPEECH OF FREDERIC KAPP.

If I understand you rightly, Mr. President, your object in inviting German speakers to this large meeting is to prove by their addresses that in respect to the present crisis there is no difference of opinion in any class of our population, that a unanimity of feeling prevails in the hearts of all citizens, adopted as well as native, and that the same just and patriotic indignation swells the breast of every lover of his country against the unscrupulous traitors who are trying to set up a government of their own by perjury, theft, and plunder. It has often been said, and I am sorry to confess not without some share of truth, that wherever there are two Germans together there are three different opinions among them. I am, however, happy to tell you that is not so in the face of the danger which now threatens to break up the national government. I see around me old German democrats and republicans—men belonging to every variety of parties, at home and in this country. But the past differences are forgotten, and as long as the present crisis will last, I am sure all will unanimously co-operate for the same end, namely:—for the preservation of this great republic, which is as dear to the Germans as to any other men. Although I am not authorized to speak for others, I feel confident that I do but express the sentiments of every German in this country when I say that we are unanimously for the adoption of the most energetic means against the fiendish attempts of our common foe. Fellow-citizens, let us not deceive ourselves; the present struggle requires prompt action and powerful means to overcome it. The stronger we prepare ourselves, the better we shall be able to defeat the purposes of the enemies of this Union, and who are at the same time the enemies to the cause of universal civilization and liberty. The internecine war now raging here is not only a private affair of America; it is a question of the highest importance to the whole civilized world, which expects that we will crush anarchy in its inception. We have to prove that civil liberty, with all its blessings, is not only an experiment—not a mere passing state of political being, which lasts only so long as it is not assailed either by a military or the slaveholder's despotism, but that it a power self-sustaining, and interwoven with our natures and with our whole national existence. Liberty is precarious, and we would not be worthy of it unless we have sense and spirit enough to defend it. Let us prove ourselves adequate to the expectations of the friends of liberty in the old world as well as in the new, whose eyes are fixed upon us. The two powers which have grown up side by side in the United States from the beginning, self-government and slavery, stand now face to face against each other. It is now for the first time in the history of the world, that slavery in its worst developments, makes a revolution against the morals and ethics of society; that it tries to found a State on all that is mean, contemptible, and unsound in human nature. But such a State cannot and will not last. If justice and liberty do not form its basis, it is doomed from the first day of its existence. But it will not disappear of itself; it must be swept away by us, and, as peaceful means will not do, we must use iron means, and we must send to these sinners against human nature our arguments with twelve-pounders and mortars. As my eyes are glancing over this majestic assembly, majestic as well by its numbers as by its enthusiasm, I perceive at once that every one of you, fellow-citizens, understands his duty, and that every one of you will be ready for your country's call. This call will be war—and nothing but war—until our arms shall have won a glorious triumph, and our flag shall float again victorious from the Potomac to the Rio Grande. (Great cheering.)

SPEECH OF MR. OTTO SACKENDORF.

If I had prepared a speech, I would not be able to recite it in the presence of such a jubilation, the booming of the cannons and the shouts, which have greeted the hero of Fort Sumter. But I will recite to you the verses of our national poet, Theodor Körner, who said that when the people rises there will be no coward found to sit idle, and who called the man a contemptible enervated fellow who would not be in the ranks of the defenders of his country, when that country called him. You do not look like cowards. (Cries of "No, no!") You look like brave fellows. (Cheers.) What are platforms, what are parties; there is a higher sentiment prevailing, and no political clique shall divide us. We are now gathered here in purpose of discussing a measure of the government. We know what we are about; there can be no doubt about it. We see the object when we see the heroes of Fort Sumter, when we hear the sound of the guns! Who is blind or deaf enough not to see that we have to shoulder the musket and to go into the holy war for our adopted country. Not the union of parties, but the union of strength is it, what we want. We have not left our country in which we have been persecuted, and from which we are exiled, in order that we might have the same *mizere* repeated here. It was not for nothing that we have left there the recollections of our younger years, the playmates and our fellow-warriors in the fight for freedom. We have got in this country that freedom for which we have fought in vain on the other side of the Atlantic Ocean, and we will show that we are worthy of that new fatherland by defending its rights against the fiendish aggressions of ruthless rebels, who threaten the existence of this republic. Democrats and republicans, remember the danger in which the country is, and take the musket to avert the danger for now and forever. (Mr. S. was most heartily cheered when he left the stand.)

SPEECH OF HUGO WESENDONCK.

He observed that the Germans were disposed to show their thankfulness to this country. It was in

Doc.—18

the German character to be thankful. Some of those present had come here and gained positions, and those who had not, had gained the privilege to be free men and independent citizens. For this they ought to be thankful. There was a particular reason for them to be patriots, and this was because they were naturally republicans—not republicans in the political meaning in this country, but in the real sense of the term. The political parties were now entirely out of question, and one party had probably made as many mistakes as the other. We were republicans now, and as such all present ought to stand by our country. The despots of Europe were anxiously and hopefully watching the movements in this country. So far, we had insisted upon the republican form of government as the only one which is right and calculated to make a people happy. Let all those present stand by our flag. There were other reasons why it should be done; it was this. The war against the North was a war against human liberty. The question was now, whether they (the Germans) would stand by the side of liberty, or by the side of oppression. The government of the Union had long been very lenient and discreet, but it had exhausted its patience. Patience had ceased to be a virtue. There was no question now whether war or no war; war had been wantonly and deliberately forced upon us, and they (the Germans) were ready for war. Mr. Wesendonck created coniderable enthusiasm among the thousands of Germans present.

After he had finished his speech in English, he continued in German, and remarked:—It has often been asked why we make war against the South? War cannot last forever, and the South can be exterminated, but not subjugated. But this is not the question; we have to punish rebellion, and the victory will be on the side of the North. To be sure, the North was very slow; the South had had six months for preparation; they have taken a firm position; have armed themselves with all implements of modern warfare, and have the advantage of time. Mr. Lincoln has been blamed because he was too indulgent; but there was something which he had to take into consideration, namely, public opinion. Why? We have now the North as a unit, and we can quietly look on and be sure of success, if we fight for our rights with that tenacity of purpose which always has characterized the Germans. We have the advantage of money and numbers, and we will have the same enthusiasm to the end which we have to-day. Patriotism is not shown on one single day only; we must have perseverance, even if we should be defeated in the beginning; we must finally vanquish, because we are the defenders of liberty, humanity, and right. There is no doubt but that we shall carry this war to the last extremity, because we want to give the rights to the South which are due to them; but we want some rights for ourselves, too. We have no opposition to it if the South introduces restraints within its own borders; but they shall not dare to intrude upon our rights; if they do so, we will whip them. They shall not break down our palladium. Liberty and the South will always be in an irrepressible conflict, although by no fault of their own. There is a discrepancy in these two words. The South have made all their institutions themselves, but the climate has made them to some extent. There are good men in the South; and although I do not want to reproach the South, I declare that liberty and Southern institutions always will be in an irrepressible conflict. This war is no great misfortune for their country, because at the end of it the air will be purified, and we shall have a sound body, instead of one subject to the symptoms of reversion. We shall have it by sacrifices of money, work, and life, and the Union will exist now as ever; and the North will be victorious. It has often been asserted that the almighty dollar was the only thing Americans cared about; but it is evident there is something higher in existence, and it wanted only the emergency to prove it. Who had seen the gallant Seventh Regiment marching yesterday, when called by their country, along Broadway, who does not understand that the love of liberty is predominant over every other thing, and can never be extinguished? There was no aristocracy about America or the Seventh Regiment. The merchant, the laborer, all classes went to work for the same great cause. One idea elevated them, one wish and one action—that is, the re-establishment of the Union; and, as they do, let us not look back upon the party; let us face future danger and future victory. If you do this, my fellow-citizens, then the future will be ours.

SPEECH OF GUSTAVUS STRUVE.

Mr. STRUVE was the President of the Garibaldi Committee, which sent Mr. Reventioro to Garibaldi to bring him money and assistance. He said:— When we took the sword in our hands thirteen years ago, we did it on purpose of founding a republic, the ideal of which was America. We have arrived here, but the storms which have cast us upon this shore have not ceased yet, and again we have to fight for our ideal, which has been attacked by the enemy of freedom and civilization, by the slaveholding tyrant, the lickspittle of European despots, who thinks he can tear down this sacred flag. But we will carry this flag high in our hands, where those rebels never can reach it. We shall hold it more sacred, higher and more united than in Germany. In Germany, disunion was our curse; but in this country we are united with all people, who have found an asylum in their glorious country, and before all with the sons of the patriotic founders of the great republic which has adopted us. The same spirit which lived in us in 1848 is still living in us; it lives in me and you, in every one of us. The question is now between secession and Union, between liberty and slavery. Wherever we stand, if not on the side of Union and liberty, and we mean to defend it to-day as we did in the battle-fields of 1848. Brethren, nothing can help to-day but the sword, and you are going to take that sword, to live or die freemen, as we have been all during our life. Let us act, not speak. The freedom which is our palladium, shall be defended by he brave sons of Germany.

[Mr. Struve seemed highly impressed with the object of his speech, and was repeatedly interrupted by the enthusiastic cheers of the crowd, which gave three other cheers for the gentleman when he left.]

SPEECH OF RICHARD WARREN.

He was a Minute Man, said Mr. WARREN, and having been called to say a few words to the Germans, he would give them his welcome and fellowship. He asked them to stand by this country, this new country of theirs. The cowardly acts perpetrated on Fort Sumter made the heart of every American, cemented with German strength, shout, Shame! shame! Shame! shame! would be said by every German in the Old World, when the news would get to them. To-day, what sight was this? The Almighty God looked down upon us. The spirit of Washington seemed to animate that statue yonder, as if to say to us, to be faithful to our country. If he (the speaker) had ten sons, they all should go and defend the country. German citizens—no more Germans, but American citizens—urged the speaker, stand to your home that you have adopted. There were more men there to-day than this South Carolina had. (Applause.) Come on, come on, Jefferson Davis; if you would, you would be hung. Tremble, traitors, as traitors have to tremble when the freemen of the country speak. Mr. Warren wound up with a eulogy on Major Anderson and his brave men, and he was enthusiastically cheered by the Germans.

SPEECH OF IGNATZ KOCH.

Mr. IGNATZ KOCH said:—It was the duty to go into the fight against the South. When the Germans left their country bleeding and covered with wounds received in the struggle for liberty, when thousands of the brave fellows were killed, they swore that liberty would be the war-cry of the future time. When the Germans came over to this country, the Americans did not understand them, and thought it was all the same whether a man was a German or a Dutchman; one reverend gentleman said in Mr. Koch's presence, that Hamburg was the capital of Dutchland! They were understood now by the Americans, and it was conceded that the Germans knew something else beside lager beer, and that they knew nothing better than freedom. In Germany there were good prospects for a republic, and nobody had destroyed them but the Germans themselves. This shall not be done with the second fatherland. The Germans had elected the present President, Mr. Lincoln, a man of liberal ideas, energy, and sincerity of purpose; while Mr. Buchanan—(cries of, "No politics!") The orator finished his remarks by asking for "three chairs for the Union!" by which he probably meant "cheers," as the Union is not so tired yet as to want three chairs.

SPEECH OF SOLOMON L. HULL.

He alluded to the fact that yesterday (Friday) being the anniversary of the battle of Lexington, when the first blood was spilled in the Revolution, on that day the first blood was spilled in this war. Yesterday those noble grandsons of those who were engaged in the former struggle, were the first who spilled their blood in this war. Massachusetts was in the field, and New York would follow suit. Throughout the Revolution New York and Massachusetts fought side by side, and they would do the same in this war. This was a fearful crisis. Our enemy pretended to be fearful fighters, having had six months' preparation, but our men would meet them. The speaker made allusion to the events at Baltimore, and the report that the gallant Seventh Regiment had forced their way through the mob. (Cheers.) The news was not precise as yet, but he would say, that if the Baltimoreans had spilt one drop of blood of that gallant New York regiment, the resentment to follow would be terrible. (Tremendous applause.) I am just informed, said the speaker, that the rebels attacked them with brickbats, that the noble regiment forced their way through, and that three hundred of the insurgents were lying weltering in their gore. [This information, although a mere report, caused immediately an immense excitement.]

SPEECH OF MR. O. O. OTTENDORFER.

This address was delivered by Mr. OSWALD OTTENDORFER, editor of the New York *Staats Zeitung:* In his introductory remarks he alluded to the occasion which had given rise to such an unparalleled and truly sublime display of enthusiasm and patriotic feeling. He maintained that we were here to save the groundwork of our institutions, in the acknowledgment of our lawful authorities, in the regard for the result of an election agreeable to a Constitution so universally admitted to be the pillars of our political existence, the bulwark of our liberties and our prosperity. Take away these pillars, or suffer their disintegration, and the whole proud structure will tumble into atoms. Look around, or peruse the pages of the history of the country, and tell us what is the secret of our progress and success? Political parties have contributed to the advancement of the country by means of the application of such principles, which in their opinion could be made instrumental to the furtherance of our general welfare. But this display of the activity and powers of parties could never have been successful without fealty to the cardinal principle, that every lawful election carries with it the duty of abeyance in its results, and that only from a strict adherence to this obligation and usage a party can maintain its ascendency, and command the confidence of the people. Unconditional obedience to self-created laws, and implicit respect for the decision of the popular will, were the fruitful sources of party power and prestige not alone, by the reasons which have led the whole civilized world at once to admire our system, and to fear or cheer our progress. The proof of the capability of man for self-government—as made apparent from our example—was gaining ground among the lovers of liberty of all nations, and presented an ever-active stimulus to our own people to contribute to its reassertion and confirmation. At this very hour we are here assembled for the very same object. As to the ways and means through which that end is to be reached, contrary opinions have not failed to be maintained, and in particular as to the recognition of the result of our late Presidential election. Such has been the case, and has been a fruitful source of evils of various descriptions. The refusal of such recognition in some parts of the country, the obstinate resistance to the constitutionally created authority, the stubborn denial of established and fundamental truths, the rejection of every conciliatory proposition, and many other shapes of opinion, found their adherents; and with some it was difficult to reason at all, or to persuade them that the application of power or the resort to revolution was not always the safest way to adjust difficulties or to retrieve wrongs. It is not long since that every shape and variety of opinions have found their adherents among our people. Everybody understood perfectly well, that the maintenance of our lawful authorities was imperative and indispensable; very few, however, agreed as to the manner in which that end was to be achieved, and how in particular the pending revolution which had given rise to a renewal of all these diversities of opinions, was to be treated; but on one point all agreed, namely, that obedience to the constitutional powers was to be exacted at all events, either by means of persuasion or by force. Our meeting here is proof to the fact, that patriotism and loyalty have conquered prejudice and alienation, and that all are united in one common purpose, the maintenance of the authority of our Government, the protection of our flag and property, and the correction of palpable errors, that have been the consequence of the machinations of men disloyal and inimical alike to the Union, and to their best interests and welfare. The events of the last few days have convinced all of us of the futility of the application of any further conciliatory measures, and that the people of the United States see nothing left them beyond an appeal to the ultima ratio, force; and in order to uphold the very existence of the nation, and to perpetuate the blessings of that Union under which we all alike, ourselves and the revolutionists, have prospered in so unprecedented a degree. But if force is once to be applied, let us do it vigorously, and without faltering and hesitation. As it is, we see no other alternative before us to secure to our posterity the blessings of the Union, than by asserting its indissolubility with arms in hand. [The speaker, who was vociferously cheered, again and again excused himself from continuing his remarks any further on account of indisposition, and withdrew amidst hearty plaudits.]

At Stand No. 4, situated at the southwest corner of Union Square, the meeting was called to order by Mr. ROYAL PHELPS, who nominated Mr. Moses H. Grinnell as Chairman.

Fellow-citizens, said Mr. PHELPS, I have been requested to call this meeting to order by nominating a presiding officer. At political meetings it is not always an easy task to name a chairman who will satisfy all; but this is not a political meeting—this is a patriotic meeting, called for the purpose of supporting our legally elected President (Abraham Lincoln), our Constitution, and our flag. For this purpose I know of no one who will give greater satisfaction to you than the old, well-known, and highly respected merchant, Mr. Moses H. Grinnell. (Cheers.) Those in favor of having Mr. Grinnell as our presiding officer will please say "Aye." A tremendous "aye" was the response, and amid enthusiastic cheering, Mr. Grinnell assumed the duties of President of the meeting.

Mr. GRINNELL now said the next thing in order would be the nomination of Vice-Presidents, and the following list was accordingly read:—

VICE-PRESIDENTS.

James Harper,	Robert C. Goodhue,	Wm. H. Neilson,
Wm. V. Brady,	J. Van Buren,	F. B. Spinola,
C. V. S. Roosevelt,	Joseph Battelle,	Thos. Commerford,
A. R. Eno,	C. Vanderbilt Cross,	W. S. Herriman,
Edward J. Jaffray,	Samuel R. Betts,	S. W. Roosevelt,
Eli White,	F. Marquand,	Thomas Denny,
M. O. Roberts,	Joseph Hoxie,	J. D. Morgan,
George Briggs,	Philip Hamilton,	George Jones,
Simeon Baldwin,	C. G. Conover,	Henry G. Norton,
W. J. Peck,	B. F. Manierre,	Joseph P. Norris,
Thomas Adams,	J. H. McCunn,	John H. Smylie,
Willard Parker,	J. J. T. Stranahan,	Corn. K. Garrison,
Jas. Watson Webb,	Henry K. Bogert,	Daniel Parish,
A. A. Low,	Charles King,	Thos W. Clarke,
Charles Partridge,	John Stewart,	Wm. H. Leonard,
Luke Kiernan,	James Humphrey,	Geo. G. Barnard,
U. A. Murdock,	George F. Thomas,	Lewis B. Woodruff,
Charles Butler,	Wm. Jellinghaus,	James Bowen,
W. C. Wetmore,	G. W. Burnham,	Thomas C. Acton,
Hiram Ketchum,	Edward Minturn,	S. S. Wyckoff,
Lathrop Sturges,	W. E. Warren,	J. D. Ingersoll,
B. W. Bonney,	Theo. Glaubensklee	John Harper,
Fred. Schuchardt,	Samuel T. Tisdale,	B. F. Beekman,
John J. Cisco,	James G. King,	W. H. Townsend,
J. Sampson,	Gerard Hallock,	Ph. Frankenheimer
Edward Haight,	James W. Gerard,	E. J. Wilson,
Henry Coullard,	Edward Larned,	John Ward,
John Moncreif,	W. G. Sprague,	James W White,
Wm. H. Johnson,	Edwds Pierrepont,	John H. Lyell.
C. P. Leverich,	George J. Fox,	

The foregoing were unanimously adopted as the Vice-Presidents of the meeting, as were also the following names as

SECRETARIES.

George W. Ogston, V. B. Denslow, Nath. Coles,
Samuel Hall, David Adee, Frank S. Allen,
Thomas Thornell, E. L. Winthrop, J. Wyman Jones.
John A. Ryerson,

The meeting having now been fully organized, Rev. Dr. VERMILYEA offered the following prayer, the vast crowd standing with uncovered heads, and the most impressive silence being preserved:—

PRAYER OF REV. DR. VERMILYEA.

Infinite and adorable God! Thou art the all-powerful Creator, and in Thy providence Thou rulest over the nations and to the ends of the earth. We bow in presence of Thine awful majesty to supplicate Thy guidance and help amidst the agitations and perils of our beloved country. Wicked and designing men have plotted treason, and have now excited the passions of a portion of the people to levy war against that Constitution and Government Thou didst enable our fathers to establish; and blood has been shed in the causeless strife. Bring to nought, we beseech Thee, the counsels of the traitors, and restore amity to the people and peace and prosperity to the afflicted land. For this purpose give calm wisdom and inflexible decision to Thy servant, the President of the United States, and all his counsellors. May they shrink from no needful responsibility, but adopt promptly and execute firmly such means as may be most effectual in speedily enforcing the laws, maintaining the Constitution and Government, and punishing the disobedient. Bless the Army and Navy of the United States. May they be, what they were designed to be, the bulwark and defence of the country in this hour of trial. If it may be, spare further effusion of blood; but if not, then grant, O God, a heart of adamant to every officer and soldier and seaman, and help those who go forth to fight our battles for us, each man to do his duty. Bless the Governor and officers of this State, and the body of the people who, after long fraternal forbearance, are now risen to assert the majesty of law, and uphold the best Government the world has ever seen. Give us perfect unity, and let all party diversities be hushed and forgotten. May the whole faithful portion of the people, now forced into this struggle for our political life and freedom, determine with fixed purpose never to falter nor give over until law and the Government are effectually vindicated and sustained. Though it may be for months or for years, though disaster and defeat may come, may they have the fortitude to suffer and the courage to persevere until this end is attained; for in it we believe are bound up the interests of freedom and of constitutional Government in this land and the world over, now and for generations yet unborn. Mercifully look upon this great city. Inspire its people in this sharp emergency with a spirit of obedience to law, and aid its magistrates in the preservation of social order among us. Let all classes realize the responsibility of this solemn crisis, and each one be submissive and gird himself to the work that may be required of him. Thus we pray most humbly and fervently, O our God. We acknowledge Thy supremacy; we look to Thee for Thy divine blessing. Thou who didst give success to our fathers in their day, give success to our righteous cause. Help us to support

the powers that be, which are ordained of God. Spare blood, if it may be. Speedily end this needless and unnatural warfare, and bring in peace and good-will over the whole land. We ask—we implore these blessings—for the sake of Thy Son, Jesus Christ, our adorable Saviour. Amen.

At the conclusion of the prayer, Rev. Dr. VERMILYEA said he desired to say a few words. I was, said he, born a citizen of this city, under the Stars and Stripes, and here I spent the greater part of my life. I cannot fight, but I can pray, and I have prayed most fervently for the success of our cause, and for constitutional liberty; and now I will read to you the following brief document:—

NEW YORK, April 20, 1861.

CARPENTER & VERMILYEA—Pay to the order of Hon. John A. Dix one hundred dollars to aid in furnishing men and means to uphold the Constitution and Government of our country against treason and rebellion.
$100. THOS. E. VERMILYEA.

The reading of this brief but expressive document was greeted with cheers.

MR. GRINNELL'S REMARKS.

Mr. GRINNELL said that this was a meeting of American citizens without distinction of party; it was a meeting of citizens without respect to former political issues, a meeting impelled by one impulse and one purpose—the preservation of our country's integrity and the Constitution under which we live. (Applause.) Gentlemen, said Mr. G., a crisis has arrived; the arm of the traitor has been raised against this Union. That arm must be broken down. (Enthusiastic applause.) Blood—yes, yesterday the blood of Massachusetts was shed. Yesterday, the anniversary of the glorious battle of Lexington, the grandchildren of those who fought there, and whose blood was the first that was shed in our Revolution—yesterday, my friends, the blood of their children was spilled in the streets of Baltimore. (Sensation.) Now, I say, the time has come when you and I, the young, the old and the middle-aged, must do their duty like men. Let no man stand aside. Let him who wants physical strength pour out his advice, and his money, if he have any to give. To you, young gentlemen, who have the bone and the sinew in you, supported by conscientious feelings of the duty you owe to your country—to you we look to stand by those Stars and Stripes. (Cheers.) We are all in the same boat,—(Cries of, "That's so,")—and we know only one pilot and one guide; and that is, the Constitution, and the God who reigns over all. (Applause.) Gentlemen, I will not take up your time any longer; you have so many eloquent speakers to address you, that I will not detain you.

The resolutions which were read at Stand No. 1, and all the others, were also read here and adopted with the most unbounded enthusiasm. Those parts referring to Major Anderson's defence of Fort Sumter, and to the preservation intact of the Union, were applauded and cheered to the echo. The whole series were put to the vote, and passed with the greatest unanimity.

You have heard, said Mr. Grinnell, the resolutions; do you all second them? (Cries of "Yes, yes.")

Then adopt them with three cheers. ("Aye, aye," and tremendous cheers.)

At this point of the proceedings Major Anderson came upon the stand, arm-in-arm with Mr. Simeon Draper, and when brought to the front of the platform such a cheer as went up from that vast multitude was never heard before. It must have gladdened the heart of the hero of Fort Sumter. Three cheers thrice repeated were given for him, and he was obliged to go to the rear of the stand and show himself; there he was greeted with a similar demonstration. It was at least five minutes before quiet could be restored, and the meeting allowed to proceed. In the meantime crowds swarmed around the gallant Major, and nearly shook the hands off him in the warmth of their friendship.

SPEECH OF WILLIAM CURTIS NOYES, ESQ.

I have never before had reason to speak anywhere under circumstances of such extraordinary solemnity. The most eloquent speaker that could address you has just presented himself in the person of Major Anderson. (Loud cheers and applause, which lasted several minutes.) He has just come from the smoke and flame of the fiery furnace, kindled by a band of faithless traitors. (Loud cheers, and three groans for the traitors.) You have just sent from among your midst nearly one thousand men, the flower of the city of New York, to resent the insult to your flag. (Loud applause.) You have sent them to resent the insult to your flag, and the greater insult, namely, an insult to the Constitution and the laws of your country; and you know that if those men are permitted to make their progress to Washington, and southward, they will tell a tale of which New York may justly be proud. (Cheers.) Your assembling here proves that you, young men, and, I hope, some of us old men, are ready to follow their example, shoulder their muskets, put on their knapsacks and their fatigue dresses—not their fancy dresses—and march to the rescue of the Constitution and the country. (Loud cheers.) Yesterday was the anniversary of the battle of Lexington. The blood of Massachusetts was the first to be shed on that anniversary,—(three cheers for Massachusetts,)—yesterday, in the putting down of this rebellion. (Cheers.) John Clarke, one of the heroes of the battle of Lexington, wrote in his almanac, opposite that day, "This is the inauguration of the liberty of the American world." (Cheers.) I beg you to mark the phrase, "The inauguration of the liberty of the American world." Not, a fragment of it—not of the Northern States—not of a portion of this great Union, but of "the liberty of the American world"—the whole Union. (Loud cheers.) This Union will go on, notwithstanding this rebellion, until that prophecy, uttered eighty years ago and upwards, is fulfilled. (Cheers.) We are not in the midst of revolution. We are in the midst of rebellion. There never was a more beneficent, a more benign Government, than that of the United States, since time began. (Loud applause.) Never! (Cheers.) It has borne so gently always—(three loud cheers for the Government of the United States) —it has borne so gently always upon the shoulders of the people, that they have hardly known it— scarcely felt it. Nothing has been oppressive or unjust, and no tyranny has been offered in any in-

stance, north or south. Now, my fellow-citizens, this is a rebellion against a faultless, not only a faultless, but a forbearing Government. (Applause.) Let us see for a moment. For months, nay, for years, the destruction of this Union has been plotted to a certain degree, until almost the entire generation has been educated in the infernal doctrines of a traitor now sleeping in his grave, and who endeavored thirty years ago to dissolve this Union. (Three groans for John C. Calhoun.) It has not been because the Government was unkind or unjust in its operation, but it was because that man was disappointed in his unhallowed, unholy, and damnable ambition. And now his followers are going forward and carrying out the doctrines, and under the pretext of the election that did not suit them, they immediately seceded from the Union, and have inaugurated a bloody, causeless war. (A voice, "That's so.") You are called upon, and I think the whole people of this country are called on, to put down these traitors, to restore the condition of the country to its ordinary purity, and drive these traitors, if it may be, into the sea. (Loud cheers.) I have said that we have a forbearing Government. Was there ever an instance of greater forbearance than this Government has exercised? (Cries of "No! no!") Never! Even under the administration of Mr. Buchanan they were permitted to go on —permitted to prepare for war—to organize an army —to steal our public fortresses, our public treasury, and everything that was necessary for the freedom of their country South, and not a hand was raised against them. (A voice, "Buchanan is a traitor.") I was going on to say, in connection with his forbearance, that he had dishonest traitors in his Cabinet, who were stealing from the Treasury, and arming themselves against the Government, and there was only one—the hero of Detroit—who stood up against it. (Three cheers for General Cass.)

At this juncture, Captain Foster, of the Engineer Corps, and Dr. Crawford, both of whom were with Major Anderson in Fort Sumter, appeared on the stand, and were introduced by the President to the assemblage. They bowed their acknowledgments, were received with deafening cheers, and, having conversed with some of the gentlemen on the platform, retired.

Mr. NOYES resumed as follows:—The only objection that I have to Dr. Crawford, is that he administered an antidote to Mr. Pryor. I wish the antidote had been administered first, and something else afterwards. (Loud laughter and cheers.) I was saying that there was only one true patriot in the Cabinet of Mr. Buchanan, and he left the moment he discovered the perfidious conduct of his associates. Let him be, as he deserves to be, forever embalmed in your recollections, and in those of a grateful posterity. (Loud applause.) He has retired to his own home, but he has retired with public gratitude, which will follow him to his last moment. I said we had a forbearing Government. After Fort Sumter was taken possession of by Major Anderson, the Government were still supine; and even after the inauguration of Mr. Lincoln, if any thing could have been done, nothing was done, to prevent the closing round of the men in that brave fortress, and round the braver hearts in it. Seventeen or eighteen batteries were prepared, as soon as ready, to pour out fire upon it. Was there ever a greater instance of forbearance than this? Never! And the moment they discovered it was to be relieved, in provisions only, that instant they sought to murder every man in that hopeless garrison. Our Government then was forbearing. Our Government has been kind. But what is the character of the Government that has been inaugurated, claiming to be the Government of the Confederate States? What is the character of that Government? I call your attention to a single instance. They have inaugurated a wholesale system of piracy on the entire commerce of the country. (Applause.) That is what they have done, and that is the character of the measures which they will adopt in all the war which is to go on. Now, what is the duty of the Administration under such circumstances? (Shouts of "Shoot them! shoot them!") Let us see how they speak of the national flag, that idol of your hearts, which every one of us has adored from the moment his eyes first saw the light. Let us see how they speak of the national flag. Here is a speech of Gov. Pickens, delivered immediately after Fort Sumter had surrendered. This Governor of South Carolina, the pupil of Mr. Calhoun, under the tutorship of Jefferson Davis, thus speaks of our flag —a flag which was never trailed in the dust before, and which has maintained its integrity with unflinching courage, and was never with a stain before. He says:—

"I hope on to-morrow, Sabbath though it be, that under the protection of Providence, and under the orders of General Beauregard, commander of our forces from the Confederate States, you shall have the proud gratification of seeing the Palmetto flag raised upon that fortress, and the Confederate flag of these free and independent States side by side with it; and there they shall float forever, in defiance of any power that man can bring against them. (Applause.) We have humbled the flag of the United States; and as long as I have the honor to preside as your Chief Magistrate, so help me God, there is no power on this earth shall ever lower from that fortress those flags, unless they be lowered and trailed in a sea of blood. (Vociferous applause.) I can here say to you, it is the first time in the history of this country that the Stars and Stripes have been humbled. It has triumphed for seventy years, but to-day, on the 13th day of April, it has been humbled, and humbled before the glorious little State of South Carolina. (Applause.) The Stars and Stripes have been lowered before your eyes this day, but there are no flames that shall ever lower the flag of South Carolina while I have the honor to preside as your Chief Magistrate."

Now I give one response to that, and I ask you to respond to it:—

Forever float that standard sheet,
　Where breathes the foe but falls before us:
With freedom's soil beneath our feet,
　And freedom's banner waving o'er us.

(Loud and continued cheers.)

SPEECH OF SENATOR SPINOLA.

There is no more glorious cause under which we could assemble than that which calls us together—the cause of our country. War under any circumstances is to be regretted, and more particularly it is to be mourned over when we find such a war as is now upon us; but it has come, and there is only one thing left for us to do, and that is, our duty. It is for you to say whether you will meet these traitors and drive them into the ocean. (Cries of "Yes," "Yes.") God in His mercy gave you this country, and Washington gave you the Constitution under which we live. Both have been intrusted to you for safety and perpetuation. Will you take care of them, or will you not? ("We will, we will.") Before coming upon this stand I circuited this park, and as I walked by the statue of Washington on the other side, and saw the flag of Fort Sumter, torn and tattered as it is—torn and tattered, but not dishonored—I gloried in that flag. I gloried in Anderson and his little band of thirty-five gunners, who kept off for so many hours thirty thousand treason-mongers of South Carolina, who were not able even to make them strike that flag. (Cheers.) We must not stop now to inquire what has produced this war. You must only inquire as to the proper means to meet and carry it on successfully, and to finish it at the earliest moment. To accomplish this, let the Northmen rally in their might, and these traitors shall meet an end more ignominious than that which fell upon the traitor Arnold. (Applause.) Familiar to every man within the sound of my voice is the fact that our men have been interrupted in their way to the Federal capital. Let not those "Blood Tubs" provoke us to too great an extent, or we will make the city of Baltimore suffer terribly. We will leave nothing but a smouldering ruin where Baltimore now stands. (Tremendous cheering.) The great leading avenue to the Federal capital shall be kept open under all circumstances. No power on earth shall close it. Jefferson Davis says for the first time in three-quarters of a century the American flag has been humbled. He lied when he said so. (Applause.) There is not blood enough in his body to humble it. (Renewed applause.) Jefferson Davis and Cobb have filled their pockets at the public expense, and, having robbed the republic, have endeavored to destroy it. May God's mercy rest upon them until they wither away from the respect of mankind! (Cheering.) My countrymen, revolution under some circumstances is justifiable, but only when the rights of the people have been invaded, and when the iron heel of despotism has crushed them to the earth; but here in this instance no wrong has been perpetrated, no outrage has been committed, except in the dirty imagination of political demagogues in the cotton States. (Cheers.) And they seek to break up this Government. But let me tell you, they shall not do it. (Cheers.) Men have died for the liberties of their fellow-men. Go to Ireland, and you will there behold the grave of her patriot martyr, Emmet, who perished on the scaffold because he desired to give to his countrymen the same liberty we now enjoy. And if a patriot was thus treated for trying to gain the independence of his native land, what should be done with the traitor who seeks to destroy the freedom of his country, and to bring it to destruction? (Cries of "Hang him.") Hanging is too good for him. A more severe but certain punishment should await him; but a single jerk, and it is all over with him. Our Government, my friends, must not falter in this hour of our emergency. Every nerve must be brought into action, and every action must deal a blow of death to every traitor. (Cheers.) The Potomac should be lined with gunboats, and every time that one of these vagabonds appears upon its banks, he should be blown to the devil without mercy. (Cheers and laughter. A voice, "Yes, and without the benefit of clergy.") My friend says, "without the benefit of clergy;" to that I say, Amen! This war may be a long one, but it is to be a victorious one to you. Some men ask, "Can we coerce them back into the Union?" I don't say we can, but we can conquer them; and when we do so, every dollar of property in those States shall be confiscated for the benefit of the great Northern army. Those fine plantations shall belong to the Northern soldier, and with Northern men we shall repeople those States. This may be bold talk, but it is true, and it is certain to take place. I am still for peace, if it can be had. We have waited with all patience for it. They have fired upon our flag, and we will never suffer it to be fired upon with impunity. We may as well let them know now as hereafter, that the reward we will mete out to them for their treason shall be, committing their homes to the flames, and their own carcasses to the eagles of America. (Cheers.)

SPEECH OF DAVID DUDLEY FIELD.

This is not a time for words, but for deeds. Our Union is assailed: that Union which was created after so many years of patient labor, of common suffering, and common glory. Our Constitution is defied: that Constitution which Washington, Franklin, Madison, Hamilton, and their compatriots made, and which has served us so well in peace and in war. Our liberties are menaced: those liberties which we inherited from our brave and suffering fathers, and which we received as an inheritance to be transmitted intact to our children. The symbol of our country's strength and honor: that flag which our countrymen have borne over so many lands and seas, has been insulted and trampled. Our fortresses, arsenals, mints, custom-houses, hospitals, have been seized. The roads to our national capital have been obstructed, and our own troops, marching to its succor, molested and stopped; every form of contumely and insult has been used towards us. The foundations of Government and society are rocking around us. Truly, my fellow-citizens, this is no time for words—we must act, act now, act together, or we are lost. This is no occasion to inquire into the causes of this awful state of things. All hands, all hearts, all thoughts, should be concentrated upon the one great object of saving our country, our Union, our Constitution—I had almost said, our civilization. If we fail in this great emergency, if we allow a single source of discord to intrude into our counsels, if we do not give to our glorious land, in this hour of its peril, our substance, our labors, and our blood, we shall prove ourselves most degenerate children. A great conspiracy has been forming and extending for many years to overthrow this Government; the people have only now believed its existence; it was something so monstrous as to be incredible, till an armed rebellion has overcome eight States, and seems to be spreading over more; a military despotism has obtained control of eight millions of people, and is knocking at the gates of the capital. Therefore arm yourselves; for this contest is to be decided by arms; let every man arm himself. None capable of bearing arms can be spared. It is not 30,000 that this State must get ready, but 300,000. Arm yourselves by land and sea; rally to the support of the Government; give your counsel and your strength to the constituted authorities, whom the votes of the people and the laws of the land have placed in power. Never give up. Never despair. Never shrink. And from this darkness and gloom, from the smoke and flame of battle, we shall, with God's blessing, come out purified as by fire, our love of justice increased, the foundations of our institutions more firmly cemented, and the blessings of liberty more certainly secured to ourselves and our posterity. Every motive that can influence men is present to us this day —love of honor and love of right—the history of the heroic past, the vast interests of the present and the future of all the millions that for ages shall inhabit this continent.

SPEECH OF JUDGE THOMPSON.

FELLOW-COUNTRYMEN,—In 1832, the State of South Carolina attempted to nullify the action of the Federal Government upon the questions affecting our revenue laws. Fortunately, Andrew Jackson was then President of the United States. Himself the very impersonation of republican democracy, he was also at that period surrounded by loyal majorities in both the Senate and House of Representatives. In that emergency the old hero at once determined to defend the Constitution and uphold the laws. Both branches of Congress stood firmly by the side of the people's chosen chief, who proclaimed, in words which cannot die—"The Union must and shall be preserved!" (Tumultuous applause.) True, South Carolina had aided to swell the majority by which he was placed amongst the foremost rulers of the nations of the earth—nevertheless, his fidelity and patriotism, his devotion to the Constitution which he had sworn to support, raised him above the reach and beyond the stretch of mere party feeling, and prompted him to lose sight of everything that might tend to seduce him from the service of the country he loved so well. Thus it was that the prompt, statesmanlike, and energetic action of the Federal authorities in that memorable and trying crisis, most effectually suppressed the spirit of rebellion which then menaced the peace of the country and the stability of our cherished institutions; and the determined announcement of Jackson to preserve the Union at all hazards, was responded to by the united voice of every hamlet, village, town, and city throughout the limits of our blessed land. Since then Columbia's sons have ever made the heavens ring with music to the inspired words:—

> Then a song for our Union—the watchword recall
>   Which gave the republic her station.
> United we stand—divided we fall—
>   It made and preserved us a nation.
> The union of lakes, the union of lands,
>   The union of States none can sever;
> The union of hearts, the union of hands,
>   And the flag of our Union for ever and ever,
>   The flag of our Union for ever! (Great cheering.)

After the lapse of thirty peaceful years—years of unexampled national prosperity—20,000,000 of freemen, in this hour of our country's peril, again are chaunting the magic words:—

> The flag of our Union forever and ever,
> The flag of our Union forever!—(Cheers.)

The decisive and vigorous policy of the hero of New Orleans gave peace and harmony to the country at once, and proved to the world that whether fighting under Washington or Scott, against a foreign enemy, or under Jackson or Lincoln (cheers) against domestic foes, the people of this enlightened land have a government which is invincible against assaults and attacks, let them come from without or from within. The spirit of rebellion again rears its hideous head amongst the citizens of the sunny South; and as it was met by Jackson thirty years ago, so is it now being met by President Lincoln. (Cheers.) Now, as then, though we differ upon questions of domestic politics—whether we favor or oppress the internal doctrines and platforms upon which Jackson or Lincoln was elected—nevertheless, we are all agreed that "The Union must and shall be preserved!" The speaker proceeded in an eloquent strain, favoring the energetic enforcement of the laws, and the Constitution upon which they rest. He had always been a democrat, yet he would forget his party proclivities, and join heart and hand in the work of suppressing insurrection, and in vindicating the supreme majesty of the law. He closed by saying:—My heart's desire and prayer to high Heaven is, that as God was on the side of our fathers in the trying days of the Revolution, so may He now stand by the sacred cause of their sons in these days of disloyalty and rebellion! And now that the horrors of civil war are upon us, may the conflict continue till the death-rattle shall seize upon the palsied throat of dying Treason and Disunion! (Loud applause.)

REMARKS OF EX-JUDGE PIERREPONT.

FELLOW-CITIZENS—What does all this mean. Is it that our Southern brethren have been trampled upon and their rights invaded? (Cries of "No no.") Let me tell you, fellow-countrymen, what it is. Every Southern traitor hates a Northern working-man and says that he should be a slave. They hate the man who works honestly for the support of his family, and say he ought to be a slave. They make war upon you because they want a despotic government and power. They want to place the power in the hands of a few. If they succeed they will build up a military despotism. Next will follow an empire, and lords and ladies and an aristocracy will be the order. (Cries of "Never.") They say that we are cowards, that we won't say any thing in reply; but be ready. (Immense applause and cheers.)

SPEECH OF THOMAS C. FIELDS.

FELLOW-CITIZENS—No sight could more enliven the heart of a man who would be true to his country, than the one which is now presented around this square to-day. It is in the city of New York that we find that every man lays aside his business and his prejudices and comes as an honest man to lay upon the altar of his country the offering he has for its defence. (Cheers.) I may say that the great heart of the city of New York throbs lively to-day when the news comes teeming from the telegraph that her citizen soldiers, her sons, have been impeded in their progress to the national capital by obstructions placed in the way by the rebels to our country, and traitors to the Constitution. Fellow-citizens, there is hardly one within the sound of my voice but must feel the responsibility which rests upon us as men and as citizens of this great metropolis of the nation. But let us not forget in this, the hour of trial to our country, there should be but one feeling amongst us, and that feeling of devotion, entirely the defence of our flag and the protection and perpetuity of our Government. Will it be said of us, the most enlightened nation on the face of the earth, that in this, the nineteenth century, we, within almost the period of a man's life, should be found ungrateful to the recollections of the past, unmindful of the present, and forgetful of the duty which we owe to our country? Believe it not, fellow-countrymen, that this country of ours is not to endure for more than the lifetime of a man. I believe that it has had a past history, and I tell you it is to have a future life. Why, this very Government,

as has been justly observed, is a kind and beneficent one, and so kind and beneficent in its operation that we hardly knew that we lived under one. There was no restraint or restriction upon us, and we were not burthened by taxation. Let us teach our Southern brethren that they must yield to the requirements of the Constitution; that they must redress their grievances, if they have any, within the Constitution and according to the provisions calculated and approved of for their redress; and until they are willing to submit to that arbitration—until they are willing to bring their grievances and lay them before a jury of their country, before the people of the United States—I say, until that hour they are our enemies, and they must be treated as such. Now, fellow-citizens—and it lingers on my tongue in saying so—they are our enemies, and it is our duty to oppose them and compel them to conform to the principles of the Constitution. We have arrived at the hour of trial, and I ask you all to bear yourselves firmly in the struggle which is before us in meeting these men, who are freemen like yourselves. You must remember at all times that we have but one object in view. We must lay aside all selfish feelings, and struggle to accomplish that end which will best secure to us our liberties, and tend to secure the liberty of all mankind. We would be recreants to ourselves—to the standard which history has given us—if we did not at this time come up as one man in the cause of our country. As I said before, every consideration should be laid aside in support of the flag whose stripes denote the past of our freedom, and whose stars show the brightness of our future greatness. (Loud cheers.) Press onward, fellow-countrymen, if necessary, but let it be done quickly. Let the spirit of our ancestors—let the spirit of freedom in the North—awaken. Let them come in as one man, and let us crush out this monster. (Vociferous cheers.) Yes, this monster rebellion, which seeks to find a lodgment among our people. (Cheers.) Press them out, I say. Press them out once, and do it well, and that will be their end. (Loud and continued cheers.)

SPEECH OF W. J. A. FULLER.

FELLOW-CITIZENS:—This is no time for set speeches. Fine phrases, rhetorical flourishes and rounded periods, are not what the people want. There is more eloquence in the words "I enlist" than in the combined utterances of all the orators in the nation. What man, by words, could inspire such military enthusiasm and ardent patriotism as did the roll of the drum and tread of the New York "Imperial Guard," the gallant Seventh, as it marched through our streets yesterday? But earnest words are necessary to incite the government to vigorous action. I am rejoiced at this opportunity of addressing you, because I can through the reported speech attempt to diffuse an energy into the government corresponding to the enthusiasm of the people. The Government has, by lying supinely on its back and hugging closely the delusive phantoms of concession and compromise, permitted treason to run riot in the land and bind it hand and foot. See with what delight the people hailed the first evidence of action. The proclamation of the President, which was a brave and good one, was issued on Monday morning last. Its effect upon a patient, forbearing, and long suffering people was like the blast upon Roderick's bugle horn—'twas worth a thousand men. It was like the presence of Napoleon at the head of his army, which the combined despots of Europe were wont to estimate as a reinforcement of one hundred thousand men. It was the first trumpet-note of freedom. Its echoes reverberated among the hills of peaceful and happy New England, across the fertile valleys of the Susquehanna and the Genesee, and over the broad prairies of the West, sweeping them like their own destructive fires, until the dying cadences were lost, mingling with the pæans of rejoicing that came answering back to us from that last and brightest star in liberty's greatest constellation. Never before was a Government so cordially sustained by the people. They have responded to this call upon their patriotism with a loyalty, a devotion and enthusiasm which has no parallel in history. Nobly have the people done their duty. It remains for the Government to do theirs—to do the will of the people. The paper blockade is well. Let the Government see that it immediately becomes efficient, especially at the mouth of the Mississippi. Let the Government forever discard its "do little and drift along" policy, and give the people action, action—prompt, vigorous, energetic, crushing, bloody, and decisive. Let it quit searching musty law tomes for precedents. Make precedents. The idea of the government being harnessed down by the iron bands of formula and delay when dealing with revolutionists, traitors, and rebels, is criminal and absurd. *Inter arma leges silent.* When Gen. Jackson threatened to hang Calhoun, he was told by his Attorney-General that there was no law for it. His reply was, "If you can't find law for me, I will appoint an Attorney-General who can." If the Government will adopt a vigorous policy the law for every thing it does will be found in the hearts of the people. The eyes of the people are upon the Government. They cannot wait its tardy action. They will reward energy, and will hold it to a strict accountability for imbecility. The war will be short and decisive; or long, disastrous, and without permanent results, unless the Government does its whole duty. The time for defensive warfare has passed, and the time for aggressive action has come. The strongest defence is counter attack. Carry the war literally into Africa, by marching upon Virginia. Liberate the Africans, if need be, to crush out this most unnatural rebellion. Take military control of all the avenues leading to Washington, north, south, east, and west. In Baltimore are loyal men, but if they are not strong enough to quell the rebels in their midst, the government must do it for them. The transit through Baltimore must be kept unobstructed, even if it be necessary to lay the city in ashes and inscribe upon its monuments:—"Here stood the Monumental City." If the government yields to the clamors of a mob or even to the "urgent requests" of the Mayor and Governor not to send troops through the city, it will lose the hearty confidence and support of the people which it now enjoys, and be disgraced in the eyes of the nation and the world. Suppose a request had been made to the Emperor Napoleon under similar circumstances, would he have heeded it? He would have said, as he did when somewhat similarly placed, "My soldiers want bread and wine; if you do not supply it immediately, I will." It is hardly necessary to add, that the provisions were supplied. The Government should at once plant batteries along the entire southern bank of the Potomac, and not wait for the rebels to do it, and point their cannon against the capital. It should lay in ashes those cities, whether on the sea-coast or in the interior, whose citizens attempt, in any way, to interfere with our navy or our army in the execution

of the commands of the Government. The mails South should all be stopped. The telegraph, railroad, and every leading avenue of communication to the South should be under a military control sufficiently strong to stop all communication. The rebels should be left in outer darkness, to wrangle and fight among themselves. Cairo should at once be made a military post. Not a word of intelligence, not a pound of provisions, no supplies of any kind, should be permitted to pass the military border which the Government ought immediately to establish. In short, all transit and communication of every kind southward should be stopped. But I will not enlarge upon suggestions as to the policy of the Government. I only wish that it may know that the people demand action. Deeds, not words, are what the people now expect. The flag which is the emblem of their nationality has been derided, defied, trampled upon, and trailed in the dust by traitors. The honor of that flag must be sustained; the insult must be washed out in blood. Nothing else can restore its tarnished lustre. A flag is the representation of history, the emblem of heroic daring and of brave deeds. The associations of a flag alone make it sacred. Who sees the tri-color of France, without thinking of Napoleon and the army of Italy, of Marengo and Austerlitz, of Moscow and Waterloo? No man can read of the strife of Lexington and Concord, whose heart does not thrill with emotion at this glorious baptism of the Stars and Stripes. No man can see the banner of the republic, now waving in triumph from Bunker's height, and not with startled ear and glowing breast hear the din of the conflict, behold the fierce repulse of advancing squadrons, and the flames of burning Charlestown. No man, even from the sunny South, can be at Saratoga, and not tread with exultant step and throbbing heart the ground where the Star-spangled Banner first successfully rolled back the tide of British power and aggression. No man can think of that sacred emblem trailing in blood through the snows of Valley Forge, or across the frozen Delaware, or amid the swamps of Carolina, and not weep that the patriotism of the Jaspers, the Sumters, and the Marions, no longer burns upon their native altars; and so through the long and dark hours of that dreary struggle—the gallant defence of Moultrie, at Cowpens and Eutaw Springs—at a "time which tried men's souls," when the strong became weak, the hopeful despondent, the bold grew timid, and the tattered ensign seemed but a funereal pall or winding-sheet to envelop the nakedness of a forlorn cause, until it covered, as with a brilliant mantle of glory and redemption, the new-born republic at Yorktown—that sacred flag was upborne on many a hard-fought field, and carried in triumph through many an unequal contest. Although not yet in the prime of manhood, I have roamed much in my day; and wherever I have been, any association that awakened recollections of the land of my birth was peculiarly pleasing. But especially were my feelings kindled into enthusiasm when that silent appeal was made to my patriotism, by beholding "the gorgeous ensign of the republic," so long "known and honored throughout the world." When I gazed upon its ample folds, floating to the breeze, and spreading the broad wings of its protection over our citizens in remotest seas, I felt a thrill of pleasure which experience only can know, and which language would fail to describe. I have seen its Stars and Stripes waving in Polar seas, and beheld its graceful folds fluttering in the light winds of torrid climes;

and, at home or abroad—ashore or afloat—on the stormy seas of high latitudes, or beneath the summer skies of the tropics—whenever and wherever my eyes have beheld that flag, I have gazed upon it with feelings of exultation and of pride, and thanked God, from the bottom of my heart, that I was an American citizen. I love, more than ever, that "Star-spangled Banner," now that a few of its stars are temporarily obscured;

May it continue to wave
O'er the land of the free and the home of the brave :

To achieve this consummation so devoutly to be wished, the rebels and traitors who have defied and insulted that flag must be taught a severe lesson. In the name of God and humanity—in the name of that God above us, laying His requirements upon us, and in the name of that humanity around us, bound to us by a relationship which nothing can sever or annul, the people call upon the Government to make this lesson of rebellion short, terrible, and lasting.

The meeting on Stand No. 5 was organized by the unanimous appointment of Egbert Benson, Esq., as Chairman, and Thos. Williams as Secretary.

Joseph P. Simpson, Esq., was then introduced as the first speaker, and received with loud applause. He said :—

Fellow-Citizens—I am very proud to be here before you on this important and momentous occasion. I am proud that you are here, for I believe you are friends to your country, friends to this noble Union of ours. In the war of 1812 I was in the active service of our country, and I performed all the duty that was required of me there. (Cheers.) I had a brother who was on board of Commodore McDonough's ship, on the beautiful Lake Champlain, and who fought bravely and successfully in vindication of the cause of freedom. (Applause.) I see before me here to-day, in this vast assembly, many who are hard-working men. Let me say to you, my friends, that I can sympathize with you all, for I have been a hard-working man myself. More than sixty-four years ago I went an apprentice-boy into a workshop to earn my living. Therefore I know what it is to be a working man; I can feel for a man who has to work for his living; and I tell you, that in order to secure a living, we must sustain our country. (Cheers.) There is no better nation upon earth than this nation. There is no people that have secured such liberty, and privileges, and blessings, as this people have enjoyed. And now, what is it, fellow-citizens, that brings us here? Oh, my heart bleeds, my spirit mourns, that I have lived to see the day when a reckless, unthinking, and—I hate to say the word—a disloyal people, a people who are untrue to their country, have raised their arms against the liberty of this great nation. I say, fellow-citizens, stand firm by your country.

At this point a tremendous excitement among the crowd, and shouts of "Cheers for the hero of Fort Sumter!" announced that Major Anderson was approaching. Accompanied by Simeon Draper and Superintendent Kennedy, he was conducted upon the stand, and introduced to the vast assembly amid the wildest enthusiasm. Subsequently, Captain Foster and Dr. Crawford, from Fort Sumter, were also introduced, and received with great cheering. Soon after being presented, they retired from the platform.

Mr. Simpson resumed :—I know, my friends, that I am not so much an object of interest as that noble man, Major Anderson, who well deserves all the honor that is accorded him. Let me say to you, continue to love the Stars and Stripes as you have loved that noble ensign in the past. It is that flag which has floated, and now floats over this nation, and which has carried its fame to every sea and every land. So I say, fellow-citizens, cleave to the Stars and Stripes. (Cries of "We will.") And further, let me say, look out for traitors among us, who would sell their birthright for a mess of pottage. (Cries of "Yes, yes.") Stand by the honor of your country and your country's flag, and, if needs be, buckle on your armor, and go forth to defend it against any and all assailants, let them come from whatever quarter they may; and, old as I am—seventy-four years of age—I am ready to go with you. (Cheers.)

SPEECH OF GEN. APPLETON, OF MASSACHUSETTS.

This mighty gathering of the patriotic citizens of the great city of New York speaks in no equivocal language. It is not in my power to give it greater significance. It is meet that you should thus assemble; it is fit and proper that the multitudes of this great city should convene together to consult upon matters concerning the public welfare. Every thing dear to humanity, every thing dear to our social relations, every thing important touching our past history and our national concerns, is involved in the issue now before the country. (Cheers.) It is, my friends, a matter most deeply to be deplored, that a country so vast in its territory, so great in all its resources, so grand in the glorious liberty which Heaven has vouchsafed to it, should be placed in peril. But such is the fact. The stability of our national Government, the very existence of our country, is threatened. Because, if you have no Constitution, you have no country that is worth defending. (Applause.) What is liberty without law, without order? I know full well that those States which have seceded pretend that they had a right to withdraw from the Union, and to assert their separate independence. Well, if that be true, if States have the right to go off at their own will and pleasure, then the position which we assume that the Union is indivisible, is wrong, and we have no right to interfere with them. But mark you, my friends, is not our Government a Government of the people of the whole country? (Cries of "Yes," "Yes.") Why did our fathers undertake to establish our present Constitution? It was because, under the old Confederation, there was such a variety of interests in the several States, that there could be no harmonious action for the benefit of the whole country; and so those wise and patriotic statesmen of our earlier history assembled together for the purpose of forming a more perfect Union, and establishing a better form of Government, which should be a Government over the whole country, free and independent. It was the work of the people of all the separate States. And let me say to you, that if the Government which was then established, if the Constitution which was then formed, contemplated any such contingency as the withdrawal of a portion of the people, then all the work of our fathers in framing that Constitution was a farce, and amounted to nothing practical at all. (Applause.) But the fact remains true, that this is one Government, one and indivisible. (Cheers.) If such were not the case, then the efforts put forth upon so many occasions by the immortal Clay and Webster, to secure the perpetuity of this Government and all our interests and liberties, were utterly in vain. And since we were constituted one Government, I say those individuals who have broken off from us, and pretended to have established another Government, are—

(A Voice, "Traitors.")

Mr. APPLETON—Yes, they are traitors, and were guilty of a crime of the greatest atrocity. Although I did not come forward to claim your attention for any great length of time, when I know there are other speakers better qualified to interest you, there is one fact to which I wish to advert, that tends to aggravate the criminality of those States which have seceded from the Union. It is this: At the time they seceded, our country was in a state of the greatest prosperity; therefore there was no reason which would satisfy any rational mind to justify that act. Had we not sustained the transportation of the mails in those States? Had we not built the forts within their limits, and in every way provided for their defence, and, in the case of some, actually purchased their territory? It was under these circumstances, so aggravating, so unprovoked, so unjustifiable, that they have gone off; and now it devolves upon all the people of our land to lend their influence, their lives, their sacred honors—to use all the means in their power to perpetuate our Constitution and our Government. (Cheers.) Remember, my friends, that you have inherited from your fathers a glorious legacy; you have inherited from them a Constitution which is justly considered the most glorious upon earth. To these young men before me who have inherited these glorious privileges, who have inherited the liberty they so richly enjoy, let me say, when the occasion occurs, lend your personal effort, lend your strength and vigor, lend your lives, if need be, to preserve the honor and integrity of your country. (Cheers.) These old men upon this platform have all served their country in her hour of trial in the past—(cheers)—and they now call upon you to unite in her defence at the present moment of her peril. War, I know, is a great evil; but there are other evils greater than war. It were better that we should perish, than see our glorious country destroyed forever. O, think of it! The loss of our rich inheritance, the loss of all the glorious privileges and liberties we enjoy! Let us all unite, then, in saying, in the language of John Adams, "Live or die, sink or swim, we go for our country and for its blessed liberties." (Cheers.)

SPEECH OF MR. ABBOTT.

Mr. ABBOTT, a veteran of 1812, was next introduced to the multitude, who received him with loud demonstrations of applause.

He said that in the year 1812, this great nation reposed in quiet. They then had their commerce shut out from any foreign power, an armament of vessels on the ocean, besides thousands of adopted citizens. Well, the war ensued. He had been everywhere in that war with General Scott—(cheers) —consequently he had seen the Stars and Stripes floating proudly in the breeze, enveloped in smoke, while the shot from cannons knocked the earth from beneath their feet. (Applause.) But now the question was, Shall we have a Government?—(A voice,

"And stand by it?")—and shall the Government be supported? (Cries of "Yes, yes," and cheers.) Or shall history write the extinction of the best Government that has ever existed on this earth? ("No, no," and loud cheers.) Did all of them answer in the negative? ("Yes, yes.") Now, how should the Government be supported? By strong arms and brave hearts. (Cheers, and cries of "We have got them.") He saw them before him. Oh, if it were necessary for him to go with them and fight, old as he was, he would not hesitate a single moment. (Cheers.) But, although his heart was young and his whole soul enlisted in the cause, yet his limbs were withered and aged; but he saw smiling, firm faces enough around him, which proved to him that there were men enough in the city to go out and battle with the foe. (Cheers.) He wished to remark to them, that the present issue was more desperate, the cause more important, than in the former war to which he had just alluded. He never saw, during the war of 1812, the extreme enthusiasm and excitement which now prevailed in this city. Who among them did not feel his blood run chill when he heard of the manner in which their flag had been treated, in being fired upon by a foe uprising from their own country? Therefore he urged them on to the contest. He begged of them to be firm, and to remember that they might not die in the battle-field. If they did die, they would die with honor. (Cheers.)

The CHAIRMAN here rose, and said that beautiful and inspiring air, "The Star-Spangled Banner"— (cheers)—would now be sung, and he hoped all who could would join in the chorus. The song was then sung by thousands of voices in the most enthusiastic and thrilling manner.

SPEECH OF C. H. SMITH.

FELLOW-COUNTRYMEN—(Loud cheering, which lasted for several minutes.) Fellow-countrymen—for on this occasion I know of no one here but my fellow-countrymen—we are assembled to-day in the glorious cause of our country. (Cheers.) There is no question of politics to-day to divide you and me. It makes no difference where you or I was born, though I hail this city as my birthplace, and you may have been born in old Ireland, or in Germany. (Loud cheers.) They had assembled in one common brotherhood, to take measures for the protection of that glorious old flag which had been borne through the Revolution of '76, baptized in the blood of our forefathers, and sacred to the memory of liberty and popular institutions. (Applause.) I tell you, my countrymen, to-day, that this is no child's play. It is a question of manhood, of freedom, of liberty, and of popular Government. (Cheers.) The question is, Shall we be overridden by those who have assailed us for the last fifty years—by those who, the very moment their hands are taken from the public pocket, presume to insult our flag, and try to conquer us? Shall we submit to that? (Loud cries of "No, no.") We are not men if we submit to it. We would deserve to be what they have driven all their lives—black slaves—if we submit to it. We won't submit to it. (Several voices, "Bravo! bravo!") We won't submit; and to-day the common sentiment that thrills the common heart of the North is, Our country and our country's flag. (Tremendous cheering.) Born on this island, which contains to-day one million of souls, in all the pride of my birthplace—my forefathers having fought for that glorious flag—to-day I say, "My country, one, undivided, and inseparable. I know no North, no South, no East, no West—nothing but my country and my country's flag." (Immense cheering, and waving of ladies' handkerchiefs.)

The Chairman here interrupted the speaker to say, it had been just stated to him that Washington, their noble capital, was in danger; and as the steamship Baltic lay at the foot of Canal street, for the purpose of taking away volunteers to-morrow morning, he wanted five thousand of them to go at 7 o'clock in the morning. "Now, then," said the speaker, "who will go?" (The question was answered by hundreds in a breath, who cried out lustily, "We'll all go; we'll all go.") "There are four regiments," he continued, "to sail to-morrow for Baltimore. Those who want to serve their country, let them come forward and enroll themselves to protect the flag of their country." (Cheers.)

Mr. Smith resumed—I remember these old gentlemen—(the Veterans)—and on every occasion I have met them when they appeared in public. They have been pleased to call me their young friend. Not so young, perhaps, as to make a great distinction, but yet their friend forever. In those I recognize men who have stood up in the face of the British cannon—who have listened to the whizzing of thousands of bullets, and all for the glory and freedom of our common country. (Cheers.) And in these brave old remnants of the Revolution I am proud to say that I have relatives to-day. An uncle of mine is now on this stand who has fought for the glory of his country, and is still ready to render his services, if needs be, in that country's cause. Even Roger A. Pryor, of Virginia, who got so sick after having taken a brandy cock-tail at Fort Sumter—the scion of one of the noblest families in Virginia—even Roger A. Pryor, with that dose of ipecac in his stomach, does not boast of such blood in his veins as this common plebeian born on Manhattan Island. What a ridiculous figure Pryor must have cut with that magazine of revolvers and bowie-knives surrounding the upper part of his hips. Now, we want a good square fight this time. We have, as I said before, on this island one million of souls. We have one hundred thousand voters, and every one of them is a fighting man. (Cheers.) If it is necessary, then, you and I will leave our wives and families, believing there is public corporate spirit enough in this city to support them while we are fighting for our country. (Cheers.) We will go down South and show them that though we were born north of Mason and Dixon's line, though we have cold winters, we have warm hearts and red blood in our veins. (Tumultuous cheering.) This is the time to try men's souls. Show me your traitor to-day, and I will show you the rope that is spun to hang him. (Great applause.) There is no time now for mealy mouths to talk. The summer soldiers, they may forsake the cause of freedom, but he who stands up firmly deserves the love and thanks of men and women both. (Cheers.) These were the motives which actuated the Revolutionary patriots. These are the words which exalted every American heart when the soldiers of the Revolution went to New Jersey to fight the battles

of Monmouth and Trenton. (Applause.) And to-day the same words thrill every heart. This is no time for mealy mouths—no time for milk-and-water men—no time for summer soldiers—fighting is the business of the day. Who will fight? I will. Will you? (Great cheering, and cries of "Yes, yes!") It is not the muscle in the street brawl that is now required; it is the heart and will—the love of liberty—the feeling that we are men. (Cheers.) No man who has cracked his whip over a nigger's shoulders shall crack it over us. (Cheers.) There is no oligarchy here. You men, with your rough felt hats—you with your cloth caps that cost two-and-sixpence—you with your silky hat that cost five dollars—you with your Grand street, Chatham street, or Broadway make of clothes—there is no distinction between us. We are all men, we are fighting for liberty. (Boisterous cheering.) It is not a question of money nor class, but one of free institutions, popular government, and manhood. (Cheers.) Let you and I, then, prove ourselves worthy of the name of Americans. No matter where you were born, "We believe these truths to be self-evident, that all men are created equal; that they are endowed by their Creator with certain inalienable rights, amongst which are life, liberty, and the pursuit of happiness." We have a glorious Union cemented with the blood of our fathers, to fight for, and we say, as they said, when they fought for it—"the Union, one and forever—one and inseparable." (Loud cheering.) There can be no secession. There is but one common sentiment actuating the North. It is no sectional thing on our part. Major Anderson, though he was forced by untoward circumstances to yield, did not allow the flag of his country to be disgraced; and whenever any American thinks of defending that flag, let him remember Major Anderson, and let no influences force him to yield one jot or tittle from that flag, from which no star shall be struck, not a stripe taken. Let no circumstances force him to yield to any domestic traitor or any foreign foe. (Cheers.)

REMARKS OF EDMOND BLANKMAN.

He came there, he said, as a looker-on; but when he heard the patriotic speeches of old men, ready to die for their country, he had something to say. With his fellow-citizens he had a strong right arm to use always for his country and its flag. (Cheers.) He asked them, his friends—he asked the ladies present, who were there in that assemblage, who did not love the glorious Stars and Stripes? (Applause and cries of "None, none.") Their brethren of the South might say that they would reduce the Capital to ashes, but in return to them he said this—Let them do their spite—let them level the city to the ground—let them despoil its beautiful edifices—and let them if they would, pull down that magnificent statue of their Washington, and he said, that from the ashes of our ruins would arise the glorious and great Constitution of our forefathers, phœnix-like, in all its integrity—the safeguard and protection of our future posterity.

After an eloquent appeal to the patriotism of the American people, the speaker closed his remarks, and the proceedings terminated.—N. Y. Herald, April 21, 24.

Many eloquent and patriotic speeches were made from the balconies of buildings on the south side of Union square, and amid a very large concourse of ladies and gentlemen. From the balcony of Haughwout's building, the remarks of the Rev. Dr. GEORGE W. BETHUNE and ex-Ald. DOUGLASS of Brooklyn elicited and stirred the right vein, and long and enthusiastic cheers were given by the listening crowd.

It was impossible to put a sudden stop to such enthusiasm. Ten thousand people lingered around the square, and were addressed by stump speakers from balconies at half a dozen or more different places, from the steps of houses, from the regular stands, from the tops of pillars at the entrances of the Park, and Union square did not become quiet until darkness came on, and reminded the people of other matters beside the Union. Large companies of volunteers continued, however, to parade up and down the streets, some of them having no less than five hundred adherents, and the numbers were constantly increasing.

Doc. 74.—THE FOURTH REGIMENT OF MASSACHUSETTS.

THE 4th Regiment, 2d Brigade, 1st Division, Massachusetts Volunteer Militia, left Boston at 8¼ p. m., on Wednesday, 17th April. It comprises 500 rank and file, divided into nine companies, and is officered as follows: Colonel Commandant, Abner B. Packard; Lieutenant-Colonel, Hawkes Fearing, jr.; Major, H. O. Whittemore; Adjutant, Henry Walker; Quartermaster, Wm. M. Carruth; Paymaster, Wm. D. Atkinson, jr.; Surgeon, Henry M. Saville; Surgeon's Mate, Wm. Lyman Foxon.—*N. Y. Tribune, April* 20.

Doc. 75.—GOVERNOR CURTIN'S PROCLAMATION, APRIL 20.

Whereas, an armed rebellion exists in a portion of the States of this Union, threatening the destruction of the national Government, periling public and private property, endangering the peace and security of this Commonwealth, and inviting systematic piracy; and *whereas*, adequate provision does not exist by law to enable the Executive to make the military power of the State as able and efficient as it should be for the common defence of the State and the General Government, and

Whereas, An occasion so extraordinary requires prompt legislative power—

Therefore, I, by virtue of the power vested in me, do hereby convene the General Assembly of this Commonwealth, and require the members to meet at their respective Houses at Harrisburg, on Tuesday, April 30th, at noon, there to take into consideration and adopt such measures in the premises as the present exigencies may demand.

ANDREW G. CURTIN.

Doc. 76.—THE CAPTURE OF THE STAR OF THE WEST, APRIL 20.

THE expedition for the capture of the vessel composed of about 80 men, under command of Col. Van Dorn, hurriedly organized in Galveston, Tex., was made up of men from the Galveston Artillery and the Island City Rifles; the Guards are Irish, and the Rifles are a German company. The party arrived at Indianola on Wednesday, and kept all ready, apparently in no manner interested in the active preparations going on for the debarkation of the United States soldiers, which was effected by the aid of the steamship Fashion, acting as a lighter to remove the men to the Star of the West, which lay outside.

About half-past 9 o'clock at night Col. Van Dorn and his band quietly got on board the Gen. Rusk, and made out to the Star of the West.

When the Rusk got within hailing distance, the captain of the United States vessel sang out to know who was approaching. Van Dorn replied:

"The General Rusk, with troops on board."

The answer was correct to the letter, and very readily impressed the captain of the Star of the West that he was about taking on board his own men. His blissful ignorance of his visitors' identity and designs was not suffered to remain long.

The vessels were made fast, without any suspicion on one side or any demonstration on the other. Then, swift as the lightning, the Texan band was over the bulwarks and in virtual possession of the vessel. No effort was made at resistance, for it would have been absurd; and comprehending in an instant how matters were, the commander "gave up the ship" with the best grace he could muster.

The vessel was put about for Galveston, and left Col. Van Dorn there.

The next news we may have of that enterprising officer will be that he has taken the U. S. troops prisoners, or else that there has been a fight.—*N. O. True Delta.*

Doc. 77.—BURNING OF GOSPORT NAVY-YARD.

PORTSMOUTH, Va., Sunday Morning, April 21, 1861.

THE Pawnee, with the Commodore's flag at her peak, and about six hundred trusty men aboard, cast off from the dock of Fort Monroe, about 7 o'clock on Saturday evening. The crowded parapets of the fort sent a loud and hearty cheer to the departing ship, which was answered with an exulting huzza from her populous deck. The night was bright and still, and the moon, at half-full, shed abundant light on land and sea. The Pawnee steamed up the Roads toward Norfolk, easily passing between the sunken vessels with which the channel was intended to be blocked, and about 8¼ entered the Gosport Harbor. Her coming was not unexpected, and as she glided to her place at the dock, the men on the Pennsylvania and the Cumberland, several hundred in number, greeted her with a volley of cheers that echoed and reëchoed, till all of Norfolk and Portsmouth must have heard the hail. The men of the Pennsylvania fairly outdid themselves, in their enthusiasm on this occasion. They clambered into the shrouds, and not only answered to the "three cheers," but volunteered "three times three," and gave them with a hurricane of heartiness. This intense feeling on their part is easily explicable. They have been a long time almost imprisoned on shipboard, on a ship imbedded in the river, motionless and helpless, and subject to *promises* from the Secessionists of speedy demolition. In the advent of the Pawnee they saw deliverance from such durance, and they exulted with tremendous emphasis.

All Portsmouth and Norfolk were thoroughly aroused by the arrival of the Pawnee. They did not expect her, and were not prepared for her. They were seized with trepidation, thinking, perhaps, she had come, and along with the Cumberland and Pennsylvania, meant to bombard the towns for having obstructed the channel, and for having, the night before, rifled the United States magazine, just below Norfolk, of about 4,000 kegs of powder. Being utterly defenceless and quite terrified, the Secessionists made no protest against the Pawnee's presence, nor did they venture too near the Navy-yard.

The Pawnee made fast to the dock, and Col. Wardrop marched out his regiment, and stationed them at the several gates of the Navy-yard to oppose the entrance of any forces from without, in case any attempt to enter should be made. Having adopted this precaution, the Commodore set the marines on the Pennsylvania, the Cumberland, the Pawnee, and in the yard, to work. All the books and papers, the archives of the establishment, were transferred to the Pawnee.

Every thing of interest to the Government to preserve on the Pennsylvania, was transferred to the Cumberland. On this latter, it was also said, a large amount of gold from the Custom-house at Norfolk, had been in good time placed. Having made safe every thing that was to be brought away, the marines were next set to work to destroy every thing on the Pennsylvania, on the Cumberland, and in the yard, that might be of immediate use in waging war upon the Government. Many thousand stands of arms were destroyed. Carbines had their stocks broken by a blow from the barrels, and were thrown overboard. A large lot of revolvers shared the like fate. Shot and shell by thousands went with hurried plunge to the bottom. Most of the cannon had been spiked the day and night before. There were at least 1,500 pieces in the yard—some elegant Dahlgren guns, and Columbiads of all sizes.

It is impossible to describe the scene of destruction that was exhibited. Unweariedly it was continued from 9 o'clock until about 12, during which time the moon gave light to direct the operations. But when the moon sank behind the western horizon, the barracks near the centre of the yard were set on fire, that by its illumination the work might be continued. The crackling flames and the glare of light inspired with new energies the destroying marines, and havoc was carried everywhere, within the limits of orders. But time was not left to complete the work. Four o'clock of Sunday morning came, and the Pawnee was passing down from Gosport harbor with the Cumberland, the coveted prize of the Secessionists, in tow—every soul from the other ships and the yard being aboard of them, save two. Just as they left their moorings, a rocket was sent up from the deck of the Pawnee. It sped high in air, paused a second, and burst in shivers of many-colored lights. And as it did so, the well-set trains at the ship-houses, and on the decks of the fated vessels left behind, went off as if lit simultaneously by the rocket. One of the ship-houses contained the old New York, a ship thirty years on the stocks, and yet unfinished. The other was vacant; but both houses and the old New York burnt like tinder. The vessels fired were the Pennsylvania, the Merrimac, the Germantown, the Plymouth, the Raritan, the Columbia, the Dolphin. The old Delaware and Columbus, worn out and dismantled seventy-fours, were scuttled and sunk at the upper docks on Friday.

I need not try to picture the scene of the grand conflagration that now burst, like the day of judgment, on the startled citizens of Norfolk, Portsmouth, and all the surrounding country. Any one who has seen a ship burn, and knows how like a fiery serpent the flame leaps from pitchy deck to smoking shrouds, and writhes to their very top, around the masts that stand like martyrs doomed, can form some idea of the wonderful display that followed. It was not 30 minutes from the time the trains were fired till the conflagration roared like a hurricane, and the flames from land and water swayed, and met, and mingled together, and darted high, and fell, and leaped up again, and by their very motion showed their sympathy with the crackling, crashing roar of destruction beneath. But in all this magnificent scene, the old ship Pennsylvania was the centre-piece. She was a very giant in death, as she had been in life. She was a sea of flame, and when "the iron had entered into her soul," and her bowels were consuming, then did she spout from every port-hole of every deck, torrents and cataracts of fire that to the mind of Milton would have represented her a frigate of hell pouring out unremitting broadsides of infernal fire. Several of her guns were left loaded, but not shotted, and as the fire reached them, they sent out on the startled and morning air minute guns of fearful peal, that added greatly to the alarm that the light of the conflagration had spread through the surrounding country. The Pennsylvania burnt like a volcano for five hours and a half before her mainmast fell. I stood watching the proud but perishing old leviathan as this sign of her manhood was about to come down. At precisely 9½ o'clock, by my watch, the tall tree that stood in her centre tottered and fell, and crushed deep into her burning sides, whilst a storm of sparks flooded the sky.

As soon as the Pawnee and Cumberland had fairly left the waters, and were known to be gone, the gathering crowds of Portsmouth and Norfolk burst open the gates of the navy-yard and rushed in. They could do nothing, however, but gaze upon the ruin wrought. The Commodore's residence, left locked but unharmed, was burst open, and a pillage commenced, which was summarily stopped. As early as six o'clock, a Volunteer Company had taken formal possession in the name of Virginia, and run up her flag from the flag-staff. In another hour, several companies were on hand, and men were at work unspiking cannon, and by 9 o'clock they were moving them to the dock, whence they were begun to be transferred, on keels, to points below, where sand batteries were to be built. Notwithstanding the effort to keep out persons from the yard, hundreds found their way in, and spent hours in wandering over its spacious area, and inspecting its yet stupendous works, and comparing the value of that saved with that lost.

There was general surprise expressed that so much that was valuable was spared. The Secessionists forgot that it was only the *immediate agencies* of war that it was worth while to destroy. Long before the workshops and armories, the foundries, and ship-wood left unharmed can bring forth new weapons of offence, this war will be ended. And may be, as of yore, the Stars and Stripes will float over Gosport Navy-yard. All that is now spared will then be so much gained!

The Secessionists are excessively chagrined by this movement. The vessels were sunk in the entrance of the harbor expressly to catch the Cumberland and other valuable ships of war. The act was done by Gov. Letcher's order; and the despatch to Richmond, announcing the execution of the scheme, exultingly proclaimed: "Thus have we secured for Virginia three of the best ships of the Navy"—alluding to the Cumberland, Merrimac, and Pennsylvania.

But they have lost all, and ten millions of dollars' worth of property besides. The Cumberland has been piloted successfully between the seven sunken vessels, and now floats proudly in front of Fort Monroe, with her great war guns thrust far out of her sides, as if hungering and hunting for prey. It will be a hard thing for Norfolk and Portsmouth to fill their harbors with ships while she lies here in the gateway.

As usual when a set of people are foiled, the officer in command gets heaps of censure. It is so in this case. Gen. Taliaferro, who was put in command at Norfolk by Gov. Letcher, is riddled by sarcasm and ridicule. He is charged with being imbecile and a drunkard. It is said that he was dead asleep (or dead drunk) at 6 o'clock on Sunday morning, and with difficulty was aroused at that hour to be told that the Navy-yard was sacked and on fire! Gen. Taliaferro will be superseded immediately, or the Virginians here will revolt.

I will send you, in this letter, as there is no mail leaving here this evening, such accounts as the Norfolk papers of the morning may contain of this burning. It only remains to say that by 8 o'clock Sunday morning the Pawnee lay off comfortably near Fort Monroe, where towards night she was joined by the Cumberland, who took more time to get out. Your correspondent waited to see the dying embers of Gosport Navy-yard.

Much excitement has prevailed in Norfolk and Portsmouth all day for the following cause: Two officers from the Pawnee—one a son of Com. Rodgers and the other a Capt. Wright of the Massachusetts Volunteers—were left in the Navy-yard, and were to come to the ship in a small boat. From the quickness and fierceness of the fire they were cut off and bewildered, and made to the Norfolk shore. It was broad daylight when they landed, and being in uniform they were instantly arrested as prisoners. It was with difficulty their lives were saved from the populace. It was stated during the day that Com. Paulding had sent up word if they were not released he would come up and blow the towns to pieces. This appalled the timid, and many fled to the woods; but the mass remained and went bravely to work planting cannon below the towns to oppose the ships. The prisoners are not surrendered.

—N. Y. Times, April 26.

Doc. 78.—WHERE GEN. SCOTT STANDS.

In the course of a speech delivered in Ohio Senator Douglas said:

"Gentlemen, I have been requested by so many different ones to make a statement in response to the inquiries that are propounded to me, that I do so as a matter of justice to an eminent patriot.

"I have been asked whether there is any truth in the rumor that Gen. Scott was about to retire from the American army. It is almost profanity to ask that question. ("Good, good," and three cheers for Gen. Scott.) I saw him only last Saturday. He was at his desk, pen in hand, writing his orders for the defence and safety of the American Capital. (Cheers.) Walking down the street, I met a distinguished gentleman, a member of the Virginia Convention, whom I knew personally, and had a few minutes' conversation with him. He told me that he had just had an interview with Lieut.-Gen. Scott; that he was chairman of the committee appointed by the Virginia Convention to wait upon Gen. Scott, and tender him the command of the forces of Virginia in this struggle.

"Gen Scott received him kindly, listened to him patiently, and said to him : 'I have served my country under the flag of the Union for more than fifty years, and as long as God permits me to live, I will defend that flag with my sword ; even if my own native State assails it.' (Tremendous applause and three more cheers for Gen. Scott.) I do not pretend that I am precisely accurate in the language used, but I know I am in the idea, and I have given the language as nearly as I could repeat it. I have felt it due to him and to the country to make this statement, in view of the reports that have been circulated, and the repeated inquiries made of me since my arrival here to-day."

—*N. Y. Times.*

GENERAL SCOTT'S VIEWS.

Some allusions having been made to the annexed paper, both in the public prints and in public speeches, and some misapprehensions of its character having thereby got abroad, we have obtained a copy of it for publication, in order that our readers may see what it is. They will find in it a fresh evidence of the veteran general's devotion to his country as a citizen, and of his forecast as a soldier.

Views suggested by the imminent danger (October 29, 1860) of a disruption of the Union by the secession of one or more of the Southern States.

To save time the right of secession may be conceded, and instantly balanced by the correlative right, on the part of the Federal Government, against an *interior* State or States, to re-establish by force, if necessary, its former continuity of territory.—[Paley's Moral and Political Philosophy, last chapter.]

But break this glorious Union by whatever line or lines that political madness may contrive, and there would be no hope of reuniting the fragments except by the laceration and despotism of the sword. To effect such result the intestine wars of our Mexican neighbors would, in comparison with ours, sink into mere child's play.

A smaller evil would be to allow the fragments of the great Republic to form themselves into new Confederacies, probably four.

All the lines of demarcation between the new Unions cannot be accurately drawn in advance, but many of them approximately may. Thus, looking to natural boundaries and commercial affinities, some of the following frontiers, after many waverings and conflicts, might perhaps become acknowledged and fixed :

1. The Potomac river and the Chesapeake Bay to the Atlantic. 2. From Maryland, along the crest of the Alleghany (perhaps the Blue Ridge) range of mountains, to some point in the coast of Florida. 3. The line from say the head of the Potomac to the west or northwest, which it will be most difficult to settle. 4. The crest of the Rocky Mountains.

The Southeast Confederacy would, in all human probability, in less than five years after the rupture, find itself bounded by the first and second lines indicated above, the Atlantic and the Gulf of Mexico, with its capital at say Columbia, South Carolina. The country between the second, third, and fourth of those lines would, beyond a doubt, in about the same time, constitute another Confederacy, with its capital at probably Alton or Quincy, Illinois. The boundaries of the Pacific Union are the most definite of all, and the remaining States would constitute the Northeast Confederacy, with its capital at Albany.

It, at the first thought, will be considered strange that seven Slaveholding States and parts of Virginia and Florida should be placed (above) in a new Confederacy with Ohio, Indiana, Illinois, &c ; but when the overwhelming weight of the great Northwest is taken in connection with the laws of trade, contiguity of territory, and the comparative indifference to freesoil doctrines on the part of Western Virginia, Kentucky, Tennessee, and Missouri, it is evident that but little if any coercion, beyond moral force, would be needed to embrace them ; and I have omitted the temptation of the unwasted public lands which would fall entire to this Confederacy—an appanage (well husbanded) sufficient for many generations. As to Missouri, Arkansas, and Mississippi, they would not stand out a month. Louisiana would coalesce without much solicitation, and Alabama, with West Florida, would be conquered the first winter from the absolute need of Pensacola for a naval depot.

If I might presume to address the South, and particularly dear Virginia—being " native here and to the manor born "—I would affectionately ask, will not your slaves be less secure, and their labor less profitable under the new order of things than under the old ? Could you employ profitably two hundred slaves in all Nebraska, or five hundred in all New Mexico ? The right, then, to take them thither would be a barren right. And is it not wise to

" Rather bear the ills we have
Than fly to others that we know not of " ?

The Declaration of Independence proclaims and consecrates the same maxim : " Prudence, indeed, will dictate that Governments long established should not be changed for light and transient causes." And Paley, too, lays down as a fundamental maxim of statesmanship, " never to pursue national *honor* as distinct from national *interest ;* " but adds : " This rule acknowledges that it is often necessary to assert the honor of a nation for the sake of its interests."

The excitement that threatens secession is caused by the near prospect of a Republican's election to the Presidency. From a sense of propriety as a soldier, I have taken no part in the pending canvass, and, as always heretofore, mean to stay away from the polls. My sympathies, however, are with the Bell and Everett ticket. With Mr. Lincoln I have had no communication whatever, direct or indirect, and have no recollection of ever having seen his person; but cannot believe any unconstitutional violence, or breach of law, is to be apprehended from his administration of the Federal Government.

From a knowledge of our Southern population it is my solemn conviction that there is some danger of an early act of rashness preliminary to secession, viz., the seizure of some or all of the following posts: Forts Jackson and St. Philip in the Mississippi, below New Orleans, both without garrisons; Fort Morgan, below Mobile, without a garrison; Forts Pickens and McRea, Pensacola harbor, with an insufficient garrison for one; Fort Pulaski, below Savannah, without a garrison; Forts Moultrie and Sumter, Charleston harbor, the former with an insufficient garrison, and the latter without any; and Fort Monroe, Hampton roads, without a sufficient garrison. In my opinion all these works should be immediately so garrisoned as to make any attempt to take any one of them, by surprise or *coup de main*, ridiculous.

With the army faithful to its allegiance, and the navy probably equally so, and with a Federal Executive, for the next twelve months, of firmness and moderation, which the country has a right to expect—*moderation* being an element of power not less than *firmness*—there is good reason to hope that the danger of secession may be made to pass away without one conflict of arms, one execution, or one arrest for treason.

In the mean time it is suggested that exports should remain as free as at present; all duties, however, on imports, collected, (outside of the cities,*) as such receipts would be needed for the national debt, invalid pensions, &c., and only articles contraband of war be refused admittance. But even this refusal would be unnecessary, as the foregoing views eschew the idea of invading a seceded State.

NEW YORK, October 29, 1860. WINFIELD SCOTT.

Lieut.-General Scott's respects to the Secretary of War to say—

That a copy of his " Views, &c.," was despatched to the President yesterday, in great haste; but the copy intended for the Secretary, better transcribed, (herewith,) was not in time for the mail. General S. would be happy if the latter could be substituted for the former.

It will be seen that the " Views " only apply to a case of secession that makes a *gap* in the present Union. The falling off say of Texas,

* In forts or on board ships of war. The great aim and object of this plan was to gain time—say eight or ten months—to await expected measures of conciliation on the part of the North, and the subsidence of angry feelings in the opposite quarter.

Doc.—19

or of all the Atlantic States, from the Potomac south, was not within the scope of General S.'s provisional remedies.

It is his opinion that instructions should be given, at once, to the commanders of the Barrancas, Forts Moultrie and Monroe, to be on their guard against surprises and *coups de main*. As to *regular approaches* nothing can be said or done, at this time, without volunteers.

There is one (regular) company at Boston, one here, (at the Narrows,) one at Pittsburg, one at Augusta, Ga., and one at Baton Rouge—in all five companies only, within reach, to garrison or reinforce the forts mentioned in the " Views."

General Scott is all solicitude for the safety of the Union. He is, however, not without hope that all dangers and difficulties will pass away without leaving a scar or painful recollection behind.

The Secretary's most obedient servant,

October 30, 1860. W. S.
—*National Intelligencer*, January 18, 1861.

Doc. 79.—STATEMENT OF MAYOR BROWN.

BALTIMORE, April 21.

MAYOR BROWN received a despatch from the President of the United States at 3 o'clock A. M., (this morning,) directed to himself and Governor Hicks, requesting them to go to Washington by special train, in order to consult with Mr. Lincoln for the preservation of the peace of Maryland. The Mayor replied that Governor Hicks was not in the city, and inquired if he should go alone. Receiving an answer by telegraph in the affirmative, his Honor, accompanied by George W. Dobbin, John C. Brune, and S. T. Wallis, Esqs., whom he had summoned to attend him, proceeded at once to the station. After a series of delays, they were enabled to procure a special train about half-past seven o'clock, in which they arrived at Washington about ten.

They repaired at once to the President's house, where they were admitted to an immediate interview, to which the Cabinet and Gen. Scott were summoned. A long conversation and discussion ensued. The President, upon his part, recognized the good faith of the City and State authorities, and insisted upon his own. He admitted the excited state of feeling in Baltimore, and his desire and duty to avoid the fatal consequences of a collision with the people. He urged, on the other hand, the absolute, irresistible necessity of having a transit through the State for such troops as might be necessary for the protection of the Federal Capital. *The protection of Washington, he asseverated with great earnestness, was the sole object of concentrating troops there, and he protested that none of the troops brought through Maryland were intended for any purposes hostile to the State, or aggressive as against the Southern States.* Being now unable to bring them up the Potomac in security, the Government must either bring them through Maryland or abandon the capital.

He called on Gen. Scott for his opinion, which the General gave at length, to the effect that troops might be brought through Maryland, without going through Baltimore, by either carrying them from Perryville to Annapolis, and thence by rail to Washington, or by bringing them to the Relay House on the Northern Central Railroad, and marching them to the Relay House on the Washington Railroad, and thence by rail to the Capital. If the people would permit them to go by either of these routes uninterruptedly, the necessity of their passing through Baltimore would be avoided. If the people would not permit them a transit thus remote from the city, they must select their own best route, and, if need be, fight their way through Baltimore, a result which the General earnestly deprecated.

The President expressed his hearty concurrence in the desire to avoid a collision, and said that no more troops should be ordered through Baltimore if they were permitted to go uninterrupted by either of the other routes suggested. In this disposition the Secretary of War expressed his participation.

Mayor Brown assured the President that the city authorities would use all lawful means to prevent their citizens from leaving Baltimore to attack the troops in passing at a distance; but he urged, at the same time, the impossibility of their being able to promise any thing more than their best efforts in that direction. The excitement was great, he told the President; the people of all classes were fully aroused, and it was impossible for any one to answer for the consequences of the presence of Northern troops anywhere within our borders. He reminded the President also that the jurisdiction of the city authorities was confined to their own population, and that he could give no promises for the people elsewhere, because he would be unable to keep them if given. The President frankly acknowledged this difficulty, and said that the Government would only ask the city authorities to use their best efforts with respect to those under their jurisdiction.

The interview terminated with the distinct assurance on the part of the President that no more troops would be sent through Baltimore unless obstructed in their transit in other directions, and with the understanding that the city authorities should do their best to restrain their own people.

The Mayor and his companions availed themselves of the President's full discussion of the day to urge upon him respectfully, but in the most earnest manner, a course of policy which would give peace to the country, and especially the withdrawal of all orders contemplating the passage of troops through any part of Maryland.

On returning to the cars, and when just about to leave, about 2 P. M., the Mayor received a despatch from Mr. Garrett, announcing the approach of troops to Cockeysville, and the excitement consequent upon it in the city. Mr. Brown and his companions returned at once to the President, and asked an immediate audience, which was promptly given. The Mayor exhibited Mr. Garrett's despatch, which gave the President great surprise. He immediately summoned the Secretary of War and Gen. Scott, who soon appeared, with other members of the Cabinet. The despatch was submitted. The President at once, in the most decided way, urged the recall of the troops, saying that he had no idea they would be there to-day, lest there should be the slightest suspicion of bad faith on his part in summoning the Mayor to Washington, and allowing troops to march on the city during his absence; he desired that the troops should, if it were practicable, be sent back at once to York or Harrisburg. Gen. Scott adopted the President's views warmly, and an order was accordingly prepared by the Lieutenant-General to that effect, and forwarded by Major Belger, of the army, who accompanied the Mayor to this city. The troops at Cockeysville, the Mayor was assured, were not brought there for transit through the city, but were intended to be marched to the Relay House, on the Baltimore and Ohio Railroad. They will proceed to Harrisburg, from there to Philadelphia, and thence by the Chesapeake and Delaware Canal, or by Perrysville, as Major General Patterson may direct.

This statement is made by authority of the Mayor, and Messrs. George W. Dobbin, John C. Brune, and S. T. Wallis, who accompanied Mr. Brown, and who concurred with him in all particulars in the course adopted by him in the two interviews with Mr. Lincoln.

GEORGE WM. BROWN, Mayor.

—*National Intelligencer,* April 23.

Doc. 80.—GOV. SPRAGUE'S RHODE ISLANDERS.

THIS Regiment consists of 10 Companies, of 102 rank and file each, commanded by the following officers: Colonel, A. E. Burnside; Lieutenant-Colonel, Joseph Story Pitman; Major, J. S. Slocum; Adjutant, Charles H. Merriman; Quartermaster, Cyrus G. Dyer; Quartermaster-Sergeant, E. M. Jencks; Paymaster, Henry T. Sissen; Sergeant-Major, John P. Shaw. The Company officers are as follows:

Company A—Captain, Arthur F. Dexter; First Lieutenant, Addison H. White; Second Lieutenant, G. Frank Low; Ensign, Charles F. Topliff.

Company B—Captain, Nicholas Van Slyck; First Lieutenant, Nelson Vaill; Second Lieutenant, James E. Hidden; Ensign, James E. Bailey.

Company C—Captain, William W. Brown; First Lieutenant, Luther C. Warner; Second

Lieutenant, Zephaniah Brown; Ensign, Albert C. Eddy.

Company D—Captain, Nathaniel W. Brown; First Lieutenant, Sylvester R. Knight; Second Lieutenant, Charles R. Dennis; Ensign, Henry A. Prescott.

Company E—Captain, Stephen R. Bucklin; First Lieutenant, William R. Walker; Second Lieutenant, Lucian B. Stone; Ensign, Levi Tower.

Company F—Captain, Geo. W. Tew; First Lieutenant, Wm. A. Stedman; Second Lieutenant, Benj. L. Slocum; Ensign, James H. Chappell.

Company G—Captain, David A. Peloubet; First Lieutenant, Albert G. Bates; Second Lieutenant, Edward Luther, jr.; Ensign, John L. Bushee.

Company H—Captain, Charles W. H. Day; First Lieutenant, Joseph Brooks, jr.; Second Lieutenant, Earl C. Harris; Ensign, Asa A. Ellis.

Company J—Captain, Henry C. Card; First Lieutenant, Wm. H. Chapman; Second Lieutenant, James Babcock; Ensign, J. Clark Barber.

Company K—Captain, Peter Simpson; First Lieutenant, Thomas Steere; Second Lieutenant, John A. Allen; Ensign, George H. Grant.

Battery of Light Artillery—Captain, Charles H. Tompkins; First Lieutenant, Wm. H. Reynolds; Second Lieutenant, Benj. F. Remington, jr.; Third Lieutenant, Augustus M. Tower; Fourth Lieutenant, Henry B. Brastow; Surgeon, Nathaniel Miller. (This battery is now at Easton, Pa.)

Medical Staff—Surgeon Wheaton and Asst. Surgeons Rivers and Carr.

Chaplain—Augustus Woodbury.

The Regimental Band contains 22 musicians. The uniform of the Regiment consists of the regulation hat, a loose blue blouse, and gray pantaloons. A plain leather belt around the waist sustains the cartridge-box, the bayonet, and six-barrelled revolver, with which each man is armed. The officers are distinguished by a small gold strap on the shoulders; they wear a sash and a long sabre, and a revolver supported by a plain belt. Seven companies are armed with long-range rifle muskets and bayonets, and three with United States rifles and sword-bayonets. Six men in each company are armed with the Burnside's breech-loading rifle for sharp shooting. Each man carries strapped diagonally across his back a large red blanket, which has a striking effect. The men are from 20 to 30 years of age, are in robust health and finest spirits, and filled with the most ardent devotion to their officers. The regiment was enrolled, uniformed, drilled, and ready for service in three days.

Col. Burnside and many of the officers of the regiment, and of Gov. Sprague's staff, have served with distinction in Mexico.

Moses Jenkins, a private in this regiment, is a gentleman worth one million dollars. When the regiment was organized he destroyed his ticket for a passage to Europe that he might remain to fight in defence of the flag of his country.

The Rev. Augustus Woodbury resigned his charge unconditionally; the trustees refused at first to accept his resignation. The Rev. gentleman was so determined, however, that they decided to receive his resignation, to supply his place, and to continue his salary, and presented him $100.

Many of the officers and men are wealthy, members of rich houses in Newport and Providence, and all are of the best blood of Rhode Island.

The Regimental Band is the celebrated American Band of Providence, and contains some of the first musicians of that city.

One of the men, in conversation with our reporter, stated that, "All Rhode Island is after us, as fast as they can be organized and equipped."

The Providence Journal of Saturday says: "Those who have been disappointed in getting places in the Rhode Island Regiment need not feel discouraged. Another and still another will doubtless be called for. There will be room for 3,000 men from Rhode Island."

—N. Y. Tribune, April 22.

Doc. 81.—DISCOURSE OF WENDELL PHILLIPS, April 21.

"Therefore, thus saith the Lord: Ye have not hearkened unto me in proclaiming liberty every one to his brother, and every man to his neighbor; behold, I proclaim a liberty for you, saith the Lord, to the sword, to the pestilence, and to the famine."—Jer. xxxiv. 17.

Many times this winter, here and elsewhere, I have counselled peace—urged, as well as I knew how, the expediency of acknowledging a Southern Confederacy, and the peaceful separation of these thirty-four States. One of the journals announces to you that I come here this morning to retract these opinions. No, not one of them! [Applause.] I need them all—every word I have spoken this winter—every act of twenty-five years of my life, to make the welcome I give this war hearty and hot. Civil war is a momentous evil. It needs the soundest, most solemn justification. I rejoice before God to-day for every word that I have spoken counselling peace; and I rejoice with an especially profound gratitude, that for the first time in my anti-slavery life, I speak under the Stars and Stripes, and welcome the tread of Massachusetts men marshalled for war. [Enthusiastic cheering.] No matter what the past has been or said; to-day the slave asks God for a sight of this banner, and counts it the pledge of his redemption. [Applause.] Hitherto it may have meant what you thought, or what I did; to-day, it represents Sovereignty and Justice. [Renewed applause.] The only mistake that I made, was in supposing Massachusetts wholly choked with cotton dust and cankered with gold. [Loud cheering.] The South thought her patience and generous willingness for peace were cowardice; to-day shows the mistake. She has been sleeping on her arms since '76, and the first cannon shot brings her to her feet with the war-cry of the Revolution on her lips. [Loud cheers.] Any man who loves either liberty or manhood, must rejoice at such an hour. [Applause.]

Let me tell you the path by which I, at least, have trod my way up to this conclusion. I do not acknowledge the motto, in its full significance, "Our country, right or wrong." If you let it trespass on the domain of morals, it is knavish and atheistic. But there is a full, broad sphere for loyalty; and no war-cry ever stirred a generous people that had not in it much of truth and right. It is sublime, this rally of a great people to the defence of what they think their national honor! A "noble and puissant nation rousing herself like a strong man from sleep, and shaking her invincible locks." Just now, we saw her "reposing, peaceful and motionless; but at the call of patriotism, she ruffles, as it were, her swelling plumage, collects her scattered elements of strength, and awakens her dormant thunders."

But how do we justify this last appeal to the God of Battles? Let me tell you how I do. I have always believed in the sincerity of Abraham Lincoln. You have heard me express my confidence in it every time I have spoken from this desk. I only doubted sometimes whether he were really the head of the Government. To-day he is at any rate Commander-in-chief.

The delay in the action of Government has doubtless been necessity, but policy also. Traitors within and without made it hesitate to move till it had tried the machine of the Government just given it. But delay was wise, as it matured a public opinion definite, decisive, and ready to keep step to the music of the Government march. The very postponement of another session of Congress till July 4, plainly invites discussion—evidently contemplates the ripening of public opinion in the interval. Fairly to examine public affairs, and prepare a community wise to coöperate with the Government, is the duty of every pulpit and every press.

Plain words, therefore, now, before the nation goes mad with excitement, is every man's duty. Every public meeting in Athens was opened with a curse on any one who should not speak what he really thought. "I have never defiled my conscience from fear or favor to my superiors," was part of the oath every Egyptian soul was supposed to utter in the Judgment Hall of Osiris, before admission to Heaven. Let us show, to-day, a Christian spirit as sincere and fearless. No mobs in this hour of victory, to silence those whom events have not converted. We are strong enough to tolerate dissent. That flag which floats over press or mansion at the bidding of a mob, disgraces both victor and victim.

All winter long I have acted with that party which cried for peace. The anti-slavery enterprise to which I belong, started with peace written on its banner. We imagined that the age of bullets was over; that the age of ideas had come; that thirty millions of people were able to take a great question, and decide it by the conflict of opinions; and, without letting the ship of State founder, lift four millions of men into Liberty and Justice. We thought that if your statesmen would throw away personal ambition and party watch-words, and devote themselves to the great issue, this might be accomplished. To a certain extent, it has been. The North has answered to the call. Year after year, event by event, has indicated the rising education of the people,—the readiness for a higher moral life, the patience that waits a neighbor's conversion. The North has responded to the call of that peaceful, moral, intellectual agitation which the anti-slavery idea has initiated. Our mistake, if any, has been that we counted too much on the intelligence of the masses, on the honesty and wisdom of statesmen as a class. Perhaps we did not give weight enough to the fact we saw, that this nation is made up of different ages; not homogeneous, but a mixed mass of different centuries. The North *thinks*—can appreciate argument—it is the Nineteenth Century—hardly any struggle left in it but that between the working class and the money kings. The South *dreams*—it is the thirteenth and fourteenth century—baron and serf—noble and slave. Jack Cade and Wat Tyler loom over the horizon, and the serf rising calls for another Thierry to record his struggle. There the fagot still burns which the Doctors of the Sorbonne called, ages ago, "the best light to guide the erring." There men are tortured for opinions, the only punishment the Jesuits were willing their pupils should look on. This is, perhaps, too flattering a picture of the South. Better call her, as Sumner does, "the Barbarous States." Our struggle, therefore, is no struggle between different ideas, but between barbarism and civilization. Such can only be settled by arms. [Prolonged cheering.] The Government has waited until its best friends almost suspected its courage or its integrity; but the cannon shot against Fort Sumter has opened the only door out of this hour. There were but two. One was Compromise; the other was Battle. The integrity of the North closed the first; the generous forbearance of nineteen States closed the other. The South opened this with cannon shot, and Lincoln shows himself at the door. [Prolonged and enthusiastic cheering.] The war, then, is not aggressive, but in self-defence, and Washington has become the Thermopylæ of Liberty and Justice. [Applause.] *Rather than surrender it, cover every square foot of it with a living body,* [loud cheers;] *crowd it with a million of men, and empty every bank vault at the North to pay the cost.* [Renewed cheering.] Teach the world once for all, that North America belongs to the Stars and Stripes, and under them no man shall wear a chain. [Enthusiastic cheering.] In the whole of this conflict, I have looked only at Liberty—only at the slave. Perry entered the battle of the Lakes with "DON'T GIVE UP THE SHIP," floating from the masthead of the Lawrence. When with his fighting flag he left her crippled, heading north, and mounting the deck of the Niagara, turned her bows due west, he did all for one purpose —to rake the decks of the foe. Acknowledge secession, or cannonade it, I care not which; but "proclaim Liberty throughout all the land unto all the inhabitants thereof." [Loud cheers.]

I said, civil war needs momentous and solemn justification. Europe, the world, may claim of us, that before we blot the nineteenth century by an appeal to arms, we shall exhaust every means to keep the peace; otherwise, an appeal to the God of Battles is an insult to the civilization of our age; it is a confession that our culture and our religion are superficial, if not a failure. I think that the history of the nation and of the Government both, is an ample justification to our own times and to history for this appeal to arms. I think the South is all wrong, and the Administration is all right. (Prolonged cheering.) Let me tell you why. For thirty years, the North has exhausted conciliation and compromise. They have tried every expedient, they have relinquished every right, they have sacrificed every interest, they have smothered keen sensibility to national honor, and Northern weight and supremacy in the Union; have forgotten they were the majority in numbers and in wealth, in education and strength; have left the helm of the Government and the dictation of policy to the Southern States. For all this, the conflict waxed closer and hotter. The Administration that preceded this was full of traitors and thieves. It allowed the arms, ships, money, military stores of the North to be stolen with impunity. Mr. LINCOLN took office robbed of all the means to defend the constitutional rights of the Government. He offered to withdraw from the walls of Sumter every thing but the flag. He allowed secession to surround it with the strongest forts which military science could build. The North offered to meet in convention her sister States, and arrange the terms of peaceful separation. Strength and right yielded every thing—they folded their hands—waited the returning reason of the mad insurgents. Week after week elapsed, month after month went by, waiting for the sober second-thought of two millions and a half of people. The world saw the sublime sight of nineteen millions of wealthy, powerful, united citizens allowing their flag to be insulted, their rights assailed, their sovereignty defied and broken in pieces, and yet waiting with patient, brotherly, magnanimous kindness, until insurrection, having spent its fury, should reach out its hand for a peaceful arrangement. Men began to call it cowardice, on the one hand; and we, who watched closely the crisis, feared that this

effort to be magnanimous would demoralize the conscience and the courage of the North. We were afraid that, as the hour went by, the virtue of the people, white-heat as it stood on the 4th day of March, would be cooled by the temptations, by the suspense, by the want and suffering, that were stalking from the Atlantic to the Valley of the Mississippi. We were afraid the Government would wait too long, and find, at last, that instead of a united people, they ere deserted, and left alone to meet the foe.

At this time, the South knew, recognized, by her own knowledge of constitutional questions, that the Government could not advance one inch towards acknowledging secession; that when ABRAHAM LINCOLN swore to support the Constitution and laws of the United States, he was bound to die under the flag of Fort Sumter, if necessary. (Loud applause.) They knew therefore, that the call on the Administration to acknowledge the Commissioners of the Confederacy was a delusion and a swindle. I know the whole argument for secession. Up to a certain extent, I accede to it. But no Administration that is not a traitor, can ever acknowledge secession. (Cheers.) The right of a State to secede, under the Constitution of the United States—it is an absurdity; and ABRAHAM LINCOLN knows nothing, has a right to know nothing, but the Constitution of the United States. (Loud cheers.) The right of a State to secede, as a revolutionary right, is undeniable; but it is the nation that is to recognize that; and the nation offered, in broad convention, at the suggestion of Kentucky, to meet the question. The offer was declined. The Government and the nation, therefore, are all right. (Applause.) They are right on Constitutional law; they are right on the principles of the Declaration of Independence. (Cheers.)

Let me explain this more fully, for this reason: because—and I thank God for it, every American should be proud of it—you cannot maintain a war in the United States of America against a constitutional or a revolutionary right. The people of these States have too large brains and too many ideas to fight blindly—to lock horns like a couple of beasts, in the sight of the world. (Applause.) Cannon think in this Nineteenth Century; and you must put the North in the right—wholly, undeniably, inside of the Constitution and out of it—before you can justify her in the face of the world; before you can pour Massachusetts like an avalanche through the streets of Baltimore, (great cheering,) and carry Lexington and the 19th of April south of Mason and Dixon's Line. (Renewed cheering.) Let us take an honest pride in the fact that our Sixth Regiment made a way for itself through Baltimore, and were the first to reach the threatened capital. In the war of opinions, Massachusetts has a right to be the first in the field.

I said I knew the whole argument for secession. Very briefly let me state the points. No

Government provides for its own death; therefore there can be no constitutional right to secede. But there is a revolutionary right. The Declaration of Independence establishes what the heart of every American acknowledges, that the people—mark you! THE PEOPLE!—have always an inherent, paramount, inalienable right to change their Governments, whenever they think—whenever *they* think—that it will minister to their happiness. That is a revolutionary right. Now, how did South Carolina and Massachusetts come into the Union? They came into it by a Convention representing the people. South Carolina alleges that she has gone out by Convention. So far, right. She says that when the *people* take the State rightfully out of the Union, the right to forts and national property goes with it. Granted. She says, also, that it is no matter that we bought Louisiana of France, and Florida of Spain. No bargain made, no money paid between us and France or Spain, could rob Florida or Louisiana of her right to re-model her Government whenever the people found it would be for their happiness. So far, right. THE PEOPLE—mark you! South Carolina presents herself to the Administration at Washington, and says, "There is a vote of my Convention, that I go out of the Union." "I cannot see you," says ABRAHAM LINCOLN. (Loud cheers.) "As President, I have no eyes but constitutional eyes; I cannot see you." (Renewed cheers.) He was right. But MADISON said, HAMILTON said, the Fathers said, in 1789, "No man but an enemy of liberty will ever stand on technicalities and forms, when the essence is in question." ABRAHAM LINCOLN could not see the Commissioners of South Carolina, but the North could; the nation could; and the nation responded, "If you want a Constitutional Secession, such as you claim, but which I repudiate, I will waive forms—let us meet in convention, and we will arrange it." (Applause.) Surely, while one claims a right within the Constitution, it may without dishonor or inconsistency meet in convention—even if finally refusing to be bound by it. To decline doing so is only evidence of intention to provoke war. Every thing under that instrument is peace. Every thing under that instrument may be changed by a National Convention. The South says, "No!" She says, "If you don't allow me the constitutional right, I claim the revolutionary right." The North responds—"When you have torn the Constitution into fragments, I recognize the right of the people of South Carolina to model their Government. Yes, I recognize the right of the three hundred and eighty-four thousand white men, and four hundred and eighty-four thousand black men, to model their Constitution. Show me one that they have adopted, and I will recognize the revolution. (Cheers.) But the moment you tread outside of the Constitution, the black man is not three-fifths of a man—he is a whole one." (Loud cheering.)

Yes, the South has a right to secede; the South has a right to model her Government; and the moment she will show us four millions of black votes thrown even against it, I will acknowledge the Declaration of Independence is complied with (Loud applause)—that the people, south of Mason and Dixon's line, have remodeled their government to suit themselves: and our function is only to recognize it.

I say, the North had a right to assume this position. She did not. She had a right to ignore revolution until this condition was complied with; and she did not. She waived it. In obedience to the advice of MADISON, to the long history of her country's forbearance, to the magnanimity of nineteen States, she waited; she advised the Government to wait. Mr. LINCOLN, in his inaugural, indicated that this would be the wise course. Mr. SEWARD hinted it in his speech, in New York. The London *Times* bade us remember the useless war of 1776, and take warning against resisting the principles of Popular Sovereignty. The *Tribune*, whose unflinching fidelity and matchless ability, make it, in this fight, "the white plume of Navarre," has again and again avowed its readiness to waive forms and go into convention. We have waited. "We said, any thing for peace." We obeyed the magnanimous statesmanship of JOHN QUINCY ADAMS. Let me read you his advice, given at the "Jubilee of the Constitution," to the New York Historical Society, in the year 1839, he says: Recognizing this right of the *people* of a State—mark you, not a State, the Constitution knows no States; the right of revolution knows no States; it knows only THE PEOPLE. Mr. ADAMS says: "The PEOPLE of each State in the Union have a right to secede from the Confederated Union itself.

"Thus stands the RIGHT. But the indissoluble link of union between the people of the several States of this Confederated Nation is, after all, not in the *right*, but in the *heart*.

"If the day should ever come (may Heaven avert it) when the affections of the people of these States shall be alienated from each other —when the fraternal spirit shall give way to cold indifference, or collisions of interest shall fester into hatred, the bands of political association will not long hold together parties no longer attracted by the magnetism of conciliated interests and kindly sympathies; and far better will it be for the people of the disunited States to part in friendship from each other, than to be held together by constraint. Then will be the time for reverting to the precedents which occurred at the formation and adoption of the Constitution, to form again a more perfect Union, by dissolving that which could no longer bind, and to leave the separated parts to be reunited by the law of political gravitation to the centre."

The North said "Amen," to every word of it. They waited. They begged the States to meet them. They were silent when the cannon-shot pierced the flag of the *Star of the West*. They said "Amen," when the Government offered to let nothing but the bunting cover Fort Sumter. They said "Amen," when LINCOLN stood alone, without arms, in a defenceless Capital, and trusted himself to the loyalty and forbearance of thirty-four States.

The South, if the truth be told, *cannot* wait. Like all usurpers, they dare not give time for the people to criticize their title to power. War and tumult must conceal the irregularity of their civil course, and smother discontent and criticism at the same time. Besides, bankruptcy at home can live out its short term of possible existence only by conquest on land and piracy at sea. And, further, only by war, by appeal to popular frenzy, can they hope to delude the Border States to join them. War is the breath of their life.

To-day, therefore, the question is, by the voice of the South, "Shall Washington or Montgomery own the continent?" And the North says, "From the Gulf to the Pole, the Stars and Stripes shall atone to four millions of negroes whom we have forgotten for seventy years; and before you break the Union, we will see that justice is done to the slave." (Enthusiastic and long continued cheers.)

There is only one thing that those cannon shot in the harbor of Charleston settled, and that is, that there never can be a compromise. (Loud applause.) We Abolitionists have doubted whether this Union really meant Justice and Liberty. We have doubted the honest intention of nineteen millions of people. They have said, in answer to our criticism,—"We believe that the Fathers meant to establish justice. We believe that there are hidden in the armory of the Constitution weapons strong enough to secure it. We are willing yet to try the experiment, "Grant us time." We have doubted, derided the pretence, as we supposed. During these long and weary weeks, we have waited to hear the Northern conscience assert its purpose. It comes at last. (An impressive pause.) Massachusetts blood has consecrated the pavements of Baltimore, and those stones are now too sacred to be trodden by slaves. (Loud cheers.)

You and I owe it to those young martyrs, you and I owe it, that their blood shall be the seed of no mere empty triumph, but that the negro shall teach his children to bless them for centuries to come. (Applause.) When Massachusetts goes down to that Carolina fort to put the Stars and Stripes again over its blackened walls, (enthusiasm,) she will sweep from its neighborhood every institution that hazards their ever bowing again to the Palmetto. (Loud cheers.) All of you may not mean it now. Our fathers did not think in 1775 of the Declaration of Independence. The Long Parliament never thought of the scaffold of CHARLES the First, when they entered on the struggle; but having begun, they made thorough work. (Cheers.) It is an attribute of the Yankee blood—Slow to fight, and fight once. (Renewed cheers.) It was a holy war, that for Independence: this is a holier and the last—that for Liberty. (Loud applause.)

I hear a great deal about Constitutional Liberty. The mouths of the Concord and Lexington guns have room for only one word, and that is LIBERTY. You might as well ask Niagara to chant the Chicago Platform, as to ask how far war shall go. War and Niagara thunder to a music of their own. God alone can launch the lightnings, that they may go and say, Here we are. The thunder-bolts of His throne abase the proud, lift up the lowly, and execute justice between man and man.

Now, let we turn one moment to another consideration. What should the Government do? I said "thorough" should be its maxim. When we fight, we are fighting for Justice and an Idea. A short war and a rigid one, is the maxim. Ten thousand men in Washington! it is only a bloody fight. Five hundred thousand men in Washington, and none dare come there but from the North. (Loud cheers.) Occupy St. Louis, with the millions of the West, and say to Missouri, "You cannot go out!" (Applause.) Cover Maryland with a million of the friends of the Administration, and say, "We must have our Capital within reach. (Cheers.) If you need compensation for slaves taken from you in the convulsion of battle, here it is. (Cheers.) Government is engaged in the fearful struggle to show that '89 meant Justice, and there is something better than life in such an hour as this." And, again, we must remember another thing—the complication of such a struggle as this. Bear with me a moment. We put five hundred thousand men on the banks of the Potomac. Virginia is held by two races, white and black. Suppose those black men flare in our faces the Declaration of Independence. What are we to say? Are we to send Northern bayonets to keep slaves under the feet of JEFFERSON DAVIS? (Many voices—"No," "never.") In 1842, Gov. WISE, of Virginia, the symbol of the South, entered into argument with QUINCY ADAMS, who carried Plymouth Rock to Washington. (Applause.) It was when JOSHUA GIDDINGS offered his resolution stating his Constitutional doctrine that Congress had no right to interfere, in any event, in any way, with the Slavery of the Southern States. Plymouth Rock refused to vote for it. Mr. ADAMS said (substantially,) "If foreign war comes, if civil war comes, if insurrection comes, is this beleaguered capital, is this besieged Government to see millions of its subjects in arms, and have no right to break the fetters which they are forging into swords? No; the war power of the Government can sweep this institution into the Gulf." (Cheers.) Ever since 1842, that statesmanlike claim and warning of the North has been on record, spoken by the lips of her most moderate, wisest, coolest, most patriotic son. (Applause.)

When the South cannonaded Fort Sumter, the bones of ADAMS stirred in his coffin. (Cheers.) And you might have heard him, from that granite grave, at Quincy, proclaim to the nation, "The hour has struck! Seize the thunderbolt God has forged for you, and annihilate the system which has troubled peace for seventy years!" (Cheers.) Do not say that it is a cold-blooded suggestion. I hardly ever knew Slavery to go down in any other circumstances. Only once, in the broad sweep of the world's history, was any nation lifted so high that she could stretch her imperial hand across the Atlantic, and lift, by one peaceful word, a million of slaves into Liberty. God granted that glory only to our mother-land.

How did French Slavery go down? How did the French slave trade go down? When Napoleon came back from Elba, when his fate hung trembling in the balance, and he wished to gather around him the sympathies of the liberals of Europe, he no sooner set foot in the Tuileries than he signed the edict abolishing the slave trade against which the Abolitionists of England and France had protested for many years in vain. And the trade went down, because Napoleon felt that he must do something to gild the darkening hour of his second attempt to clutch the sceptre of France. How did the slave system go down? When, in 1848, the Provisional Government found itself in the Hotel de Ville, obliged to do something to draw to itself the sympathy and liberal feeling of the French nation, they signed an edict —it was the first from the rising republic— abolishing the death penalty and Slavery. The storm which rocked the vessel of State almost to foundering, snapped forever the chain of the French slave. Look, too, at the history of Mexican and South American emancipation; you will find that it was, in every instance, I think, the child of convulsion.

That hour has come to us. So stand we to-day. The Abolitionist who will not now cry, when the moment serves, "Up boys, and at them," is false to liberty. (Great cheering.) (A voice—"So is every other man.") Say not it is a hard lesson. Let him who fully knows his own heart and strength, and feels, as he looks down into his child's cradle, that he could stand and see that little nestling borne to Slavery and submit—let him cast the first stone. But all you, whose blood is wont to stir over Naseby and Bunker Hill, will hold your peace, unless you are ready to cry with me—*Sic Semper Tyrannis!* So may it ever be with tyrants. (Loud applause.)

Why, Americans, I believe in the might of nineteen millions of people. Yes, I know that what sowing-machines, and reaping-machines, and ideas, and types, and school-houses cannot do, the muskets of Illinois and Massachusetts can finish up. (Cheers.) Blame me not that I make every thing turn on Liberty and the slave. I believe in Massachusetts. I know that free speech, free toil, school-houses and ballot-boxes

are a pyramid on its broadest base. Nothing that does not sunder the solid globe can disturb it. We defy the world to disturb us. (Cheers.) The little errors that dwell upon our surface, we have medicine in our institutions to cure them all. (Applause.)

Therefore there is nothing left for a New-England man, nothing but that he shall wipe away the stain that hangs about the toleration of human bondage. As WEBSTER said at Rochester, years and years ago, "If I thought that there was a stain upon the remotest hem of the garment of my country, I would devote my utmost labor to wipe it off." (Cheers.) To-day that call is made upon Massachusetts. That is the reason why I dwell so much on the slavery question. I said I believed in the power of the North to conquer; but where does she get it? I do not believe in the power of the North to subdue two million and a half of Southern men, unless she summons justice, God, and the negro to her side; (cheers,) and in that battle we are sure of this—we are sure to rebuild the Union down to the Gulf. (Renewed cheering.) In that battle, with that watchword, with those allies, the thirteen States and their children will survive—in the light of the world, a nation which has vindicated the sincerity of the Fathers of '87, that they bore children, and not peddlers, to represent them in the nineteenth century. (Repeated cheers.) But without that—without that, I know also, we shall conquer. Sumter annihilated compromise. Nothing but victory will blot from history that sight of the Stars and Stripes giving place to the Palmetto. But without justice for inspiration, without God for our ally, we shall break the Union asunder; we shall be a Confederacy, and so will they. This war means one of two things—emancipation or disunion. (Cheers.) Out of the smoke of the conflict there comes that—nothing else. It is impossible there should come any thing else. Now, I believe in the future and permanent union of the races that cover this Continent from the Pole down to the Gulf. One in race, one in history, one in religion, one in industry, one in thought, we never can be permanently separated. Your path, if you forget the black race, will be over the gulf of disunion,—years of unsettled, turbulent, Mexican and South American civilization back through that desert of forty years to the Union which is sure to come.

But I believe in a deeper conscience, I believe in a North more educated than that. I divide you into four sections. The first is the ordinary mass, rushing from mere enthusiasm to

> "A battle whose great aim and scope
> They little care to know,
> Content like men at arms to cope,
> Each with his fronting foe."

Behind that class stands another, whose only idea in this controversy is sovereignty and the flag. The seaboard, the wealth, the just-converted hunkerism of the country, fill that class.

Next to it stands the third element, the people; the cordwainers of Lynn, the farmer of Worcester, the dwellers on the prairie—Iowa and Wisconsin, Ohio and Maine—the broad surface of the people who have no leisure for technicalities, who never studied law, who never had time to read any further into the Constitution than the first two lines—" Establish *Justice* and secure *Liberty*." They have waited long enough; they have eaten dirt enough; they have apologized for bankrupt statesmen enough; they have quieted their consciences enough; they have split logic with their abolition neighbors long enough; they are tired of trying to find a place between the forty-ninth and forty-eighth corner of a constitutional hair, (laughter ;) and now that they have got their hand on the neck of a rebellious aristocracy, in the name of the PEOPLE they mean to strangle it. That, I believe, is the body of the people itself. Side by side with them stands a fourth class—small, but active—the Abolitionists, who thank God that he has let them see His salvation before they die. (Cheers.)

The noise and dust of the conflict may hide the real question at issue. Europe may think—some of us may—that we are fighting for forms and parchments, for sovereignty and a flag. But really, the war is one of opinion; it is Civilization against Barbarism—it is Freedom against Slavery. The cannon shots against Fort Sumter was the yell of pirates against the DECLARATION OF INDEPENDENCE: the war-cry of the North is its echo. The South, defying Christianity, clutches its victim. The North offers its wealth and blood in glad atonement for the selfishness of seventy years. The result is as sure as the Throne of God. I believe in the possibility of Justice, in the certainty of Union. Years hence, when the smoke of this conflict clears away, the world will see under our banner all tongues, all creeds, all races—one brotherhood; and on the banks of the Potomac, the Genius of Liberty, robed in light, four and thirty stars for her diadem, broken chains under her feet, and an olive branch in her right hand. (Great applause.)

—*N. Y. Times*, April 23.

Doc. 82.—MEETING OF CALIFORNIANS, APRIL 22.

THE Californians assembled in the large room of the Metropolitan Hotel. The meeting was organized by the call of J. C. BIRDSEYE, Esq., to the Chair. The following gentlemen were nominated Vice-Presidents : William T. Coleman, C. K. Garrison, J. Y. Hallett, D. L. Ross, Capt. Folger, E. Leonard, Eugene Kelly, J. P. Wentworth, S. W. Bryant, Minor Frink, W. S. Denio, Col. E. D. Baker, Charles Watrous, D. W. Cheeseman, Samuel Gamege, Col. Keutzer, Capt. F. Martin, Ira P. Rankin, S. P. Parker, Hon. James Satterlee. These gentlemen are all resident Californians on a temporary visit to this

City. The Secretaries appointed were MILLARD B. FARROLL, J. J. ARRINGTON, and ROSE FISH, Esqs.

The President, Mr. BIRDSEYE, stated that the object of the meeting was to enable Californians to do their duty, equally with the men of other States, in response to the call of the Chief of the Nation. It was the duty of Californians to show what the popular response of California would be when, as a State, she answers the appeal of the country in its hour of danger. The proposition now was to raise here in New York a Californian regiment to aid the Government. There were a number of Californians in New York, who would contribute large sums of money for that purpose. What Californians would do in their own State was one thing, what they should do here was another. But California would ever be true to the Union.

Col. BAKER was called upon to address the meeting. He said he had had the honor to address an enthusiastic meeting on Saturday at Union Square, that he was quite hoarse and could not do much talking. It was the time for action, and not for talking. The country demanded fighting men. The question alone was, how many men and how much money could be provided. For his part, he (the speaker) would do his duty. It had been represented that California was not true to the Union. If she is not, we (said the Colonel) will make her so. What are wanted are fighting men—men who can handle a knapsack and dig an intrenchment, and defend it when it is dug. He (the speaker) thought that 800 men might be raised in this City to form a California Regiment. Old as he was, there were some red drops in his heart which would not, if necessary, be spared on such an occasion.

Dr. GILPIN, Ex-Governor of Nevada Territory, followed. The present war, he said, was a war for human rights, and for posterity in all time. It was to establish the great principle that labor shall be free. Never in the history of the human race had a more sacred opportunity offered itself to draw the sword in behalf of human freedom. He was about to depart beyond the Rocky Mountains, but he would delay his departure while the Capital of his country was in danger, hoping to find a place, even as a private, in the ranks of those who were prepared to defend the American flag.

Mr. PARKES, the recently appointed Postmaster of San Francisco, was the next speaker. The Administration, he said, had given him an office, but he was willing to stay here to sustain the Administration. If danger threatened steamers from California, as it undoubtedly did—steamers coming here with specie, and with the wives and children of Californians—they must be protected. He knew that the captains of those vessels, rather than let that specie fall into the hands of enemies, would cast it overboard. He thought, in the present crisis, that all California steamers ought to be armed. A committee of five was appointed to draft resolutions. An Executive Committee of five was also appointed to raise a California Regiment.

Mr. Ross Fish, of Maryland, made a most patriotic speech. Col. Baker was appointed commander of the regiment; after which the following resolutions were read and unanimously adopted :

Whereas, The integrity and perpetuity of the Government of the United States has been and is seriously threatened and assailed by the open revolt of a large portion of the people of several States of the Union, and

Whereas, There has been no just cause for this action either on the part of the Government itself or the people, and

Whereas, The Government and the people have borne and forborne, until such a period has been reached that longer forbearance will assuredly result in the total disruption and destruction of our Republican form of government, and now the Government, sustained by the people, proposes to quell the unjust and unholy rebellion, and restore peace and prosperity to the country once more ; therefore,

Resolved, That we, as residents of the American States and Territories of the Pacific coast, have a common interest with the people of the other sections of our country in the defence and preservation of the Government of our Fathers.

Resolved, That we pledge our lives, our fortunes, and our sacred honor to do all that in us lies, to maintain the dignity of the Government and uphold the flag of our country all over this broad land, and all over the world, wherever it may be legitimately unfurled.

Resolved, That we will use our best efforts to raise a regiment, or as large a body of troops as can be called together in New York, to be composed of men from the Pacific coast, and others who choose to join them, whose services shall be offered to the Government for the maintenance of the majesty and supremacy of the Constitution and the laws, and the suppression of rebellion wherever it may exist.

Resolved, That the Californians on the Atlantic coast form themselves into a regiment for the maintenance of the Constitution and Union, and with reference to carrying out the objects of this meeting, and maintaining the inviolability of the Stars and Stripes.

The meeting then adjourned, after giving three enthusiastic cheers " and a tiger " for the Union.

—*N. Y. Times,* April 22.

Doc. 83.—OPINION OF THE LIVERPOOL TIMES.

The latest accounts from America are ominous in the extreme, and it is greatly to be feared that the North and the South will, after all, come to blows. We had hoped a different result, and we hope so still, but it is useless to disguise the feeling which prevails not less in New York than in Charleston, that a deadly collision is impending—a fratricidal war imminent. For this melancholy state of things people in Europe were not prepared. The tone of the new President's inaugural address pointed to war; but his subsequent conduct has been at variance with this belief, and hopes were entertained that, as the South could not be again seduced into the Union, she would not be coerced. We may receive, at any hour or any day, intelligence that the deadly conflict has begun; and once commenced, there is no telling how long it may continue, or where it may end.

America, in this hour of her fate, can be said to owe little to the judgment of her Presidents —the last or the present. Mr. Buchanan's ill-omened message to Congress, at the end of his term, was a direct incentive to the breaking up of the Federal compact; and now we have the pacific policy which followed Mr. Lincoln's accession to office cast aside, and a policy of force substituted which may end in destruction of thousands of lives and the flowing of rivers of blood. Matters had proceeded to such a pass that a pacific solution of the difficulty was the only reasonable and proper one. It may be that the accounts which have reached us are exaggerated and unreliable ; but when the business men of New York look on civil war as imminent, and when the capital of the South is moved by a similar belief, we, in England, have no alternative but to accept the probability, however much we may deplore it.

As war, then, between the two Republics seems to be regarded as certain, the question that remains to be asked is, what will the principals gain by it? It is evident that President Lincoln has neither an army nor a navy at hand to make the South submit; and it is equally certain that the South is even more anxious than the North to test it by a trial of strength. The old Government has certainly one alternative to which it may resort ; but it is so terrible in conception, and would prove so malignant in practice, that we will do Mr. Lincoln the justice of expressing our disbelief in his ever having recourse to it. *The South is so strong on its own ground that no amount of Federal force which can be brought into the field, within any reasonable period, would stand a chance of success ;* but the Washington Government might readily make the slaves the instruments of vengeance, by putting arms into their hands to be turned against their masters. A servile war, thus inaugurated, would probably be one of the bloodiest and fiercest in the whole records of mankind, and, while the men of the South were engaged in putting it down, their seaboard might be scoured, their cities ravaged, their property confiscated or destroyed, by the Unionist party. An extreme and desperate alternative like this would test the strength of the South ; *but the probability is that, even against such accumulated difficulties and odds, the South would ultimately triumph.* But what would be the feeling that such an act would leave behind? The contempt with which the white planter regards his black slave would be substituted for the most malignant hatred towards his own color and his own countrymen in the other sections of the Republic—an animosity would be engendered that time could not soften nor circumstances mollify, and the foundation would be laid for internecine wars more furious and destructive than any which the Republicans ever waged against the Red Indians of the prairies. We cannot, as we have said, suppose that Mr. Lincoln and his supporters, after their recent declarations, would have recourse to this *diabolical policy ;* and yet, short of it, we can see no reasonable prospects of success in soliciting an encounter with the South. Three or four millions of black auxiliaries, pressed into the service of the Washington Cabinet, might turn the scale—but at what a price!

If civil war has really commenced between the North and the South, *we hope that the representatives of England and France at Washington have been instructed by their respective governments to tender their aid as mediators before the struggle has roused all the fierce passions which if continued for any length of time, are certain to be called into play.* Both nations wish well to the American people: both are alike interested in the general prosperity of the country in every latitude; and both are impelled towards it by the strongest sympathy that can animate friendly nations. This seems to us the last resource before the sword is drawn and the scabbard thrown away, and probably the suggestion would meet the approval of that large class in both extremes of the country which must look with horror and dismay at the prospect of men and brothers cutting each other's throats under circumstances so fearfully provocative of vengeance.

—*Liverpool Times,* April 20.

Doc. 84.—LETTER FROM SECRETARY SEWARD TO GOV. HICKS.

DEPARTMENT OF STATE, April 22, 1861.

His Excellency Thos. H. Hicks, Governor of Maryland.

SIR: I have had the honor to receive your communication of this morning, in which you inform me that you have felt it to be your duty to advise the President of the United States to order elsewhere the troops then off Annapolis, and also that no more may be sent through Maryland; and that you have further suggested that Lord LYONS be requested to act as mediator between the contending parties in our country, to prevent the effusion of blood.

The President directs me to acknowledge the receipt of that communication, and to assure you that he has weighed the counsels which it contains with the respect which he habitually cherishes for the Chief Magistrates of the several States, and especially for yourself. He regrets, as deeply as any magistrate or citizen of the country can, that demonstrations against the safety of the United States, with very extensive preparations for the effusion of blood, have made it his duty to call out the force to which you allude.

The force now sought to be brought through Maryland is intended for nothing but the defence of this Capital. The President has necessarily confided the choice of the national highway which that force shall take in coming to this city, to the Lieutenant-General commanding the Army of the United States, who, like his only predecessor, is not less distinguished for his humanity, than for his loyalty, patriotism, and distinguished public service.

The President instructs me to add that the national highway thus selected by the Lieutenant-General has been chosen by him, upon consultation with prominent magistrates and citizens of Maryland, as the one which, while a route is absolutely necessary, is furthest removed from the populous cities of the State, and with the expectation that it would, therefore, be the least objectionable one.

The President cannot but remember that there has been a time in the history of our country when a General of the American Union, with forces designed for the defence of its Capital, was not unwelcome anywhere in the State of Maryland, and certainly not at Annapolis, then, as now, the Capital of that patriotic State, and then, also, one of the Capitals of the Union.

If eighty years could have obliterated all the other noble sentiments of that age in Maryland, the President would be hopeful, nevertheless, that there is one that would forever remain there and everywhere. That sentiment is that no domestic contention whatever, that may arise among the parties of this Republic, ought in any case to be referred to any foreign arbitrament, least of all to the arbitrament of an European monarchy.

I have the honor to be, with distinguished consideration, your Excellency's most obedient servant, WILLIAM H. SEWARD.

—*National Intelligencer,* April 23.

Doc. 85.—THE BALTIMORE RIOT.

THE following is a recapitulation of the killed and wounded during the collision, April 19th:

Citizens Killed.—Robert W. Davis, Philip S. Miles, John McCann, John McMahon, Wm. R. Clark, James Carr, Sebastian Gies, Wm. Malloney, Michael Murphy.

Citizens Wounded.—James Myers, mortally —— Coney, Wm. Ree, boy unknown.

Soldiers Killed.—Two, unknown.

Soldiers Wounded.—S. H. Needham, Michael Green, D. B. Tyler, Edward Colwin, H. W. Danforth, Wm. Patch; three unknown.

The total killed is nine citizens and two soldiers; wounded, three citizens and eight soldiers. —*Baltimore American,* April 22.

The *Washington Star* says: The wounded of the Massachusetts soldiers in the fight at Baltimore on Friday, are as follows: Company C, Stoneham Light Infantry—Capt. J. H. Dyke, ball wound in the head; left in Baltimore, and supposed to have died since; Henry Dyke, ball wound in the leg; W. H. Young, hit with a brickbat on the arm; Stephen Flanders, bad wound with a brickbat on the head; H. Perry, brickbat wound on the knee; John Fortier, wounded on the head with a stone; C. L. Gill, a bad wound on the knee from the breech of a gun; John W. Pennall, knocked on the head with a brickbat; John Kempton, several bad bruises on the legs and arms from paving-stones; Morris Meade, wounded on the leg by a brickbat; Lieut. James Wroe, two side cuts on the head from brickbats; Daniel Brown, the third finger of the left hand shot off. Company D, Lowell—C. H. Chandler, wounded on the head by a brick. Company I, Lawrence—V. G. Gingrass, ball through the arm; Alonzo Joy, two fingers shot off; Sergeant G. J. Dorall, cut on the head with a brickbat; of this company five or six are left in Baltimore, and the nature of their wounds is not known. Company D—W. H. Lamson, struck on the eye and back of the head with paving stones, and other severe bruises on the body. Charles Stinson, Company C, nose broken with a brick. Company D—Ira W. Moore, badly wounded on the left arm with brickbats; George Alexander, back of the head and neck badly cut with a brick.

The *Star* adds: "All the above, except Capt. Dyke, are at the Washington Infirmary, under the charge of Surgeon Smith, of their own regiment, and Dr. J. S. Smith, Surgeon to the D. C. Volunteers, who has kindly volunteered his services as assistant. A considerable number of citizens of Massachusetts temporarily residing here, have formed themselves into an association to aid by money and other means in relieving troops sent here from that State, whenever assistance may be required."

Doc. 86.—AN EMBARGO AT BALTIMORE.

The following order appears in the Baltimore papers of April 23:

BALTIMORE, April 22, 1861.

It is ordered by the Mayor and the Board of Police that *no provisions of any kind be transferred from the City of Baltimore* to any point or place, from this time, until further orders, without special permission.

The execution of this order is intrusted to Col. I. R. TRIMBLE.

The following order has been issued:

It being deemed necessary for the safety and protection of the city, that no steamboat be permitted to leave our harbor without the sanction of the city authorities, I hereby, by authority of the Mayor and Board of Police, direct that no steamboat shall leave the harbor without my permit.

I. R. TRIMBLE, Commanding.

N. Y. Times, April 25.

Doc. 87.—SPEECH OF A. H. STEPHENS AT RICHMOND, VA., APRIL 22.

The distinguished gentleman was introduced to the throng by Mayor Mayo, and received with hearty cheers. In response, Mr. Stephens returned his acknowledgments for the warmth of the personal greeting, and his most profound thanks for it as the representative of the Confederate States. He spoke of the rejoicing the secession of Virginia had caused among her Southern sisters. Her people would feel justified if they could hear it as he had. He would not speak of the States that were out, but those who were in. North Carolina was out, and did not know exactly how she got out. The fires that were blazing here he had seen all along, his track from Montgomery to Richmond. At Wilmington, N. C., he had counted on one street twenty flags of the Confederate States. The news from Tennessee was equally cheering—there the mountains were on fire. Some of the States still hesitated, but soon all would be in. Tennessee was no longer in the late Union. She was out by resolutions of her popular assemblies in Memphis and other cities. Kentucky would soon be out; her people were moving. Missouri—who could doubt the stand she would take?—when her Governor, in reply to Lincoln's insolent proclamation, had said:— "You shall have no troops for the furtherance of your illegal, unchristian, and diabolical schemes!" Missouri will soon add another star to the Southern galaxy. Where Maryland is you all know. The first Southern blood has been shed on her soil, and Virginia would never stand by and see her citizens shot down. The cause of Baltimore is the cause of the whole South.

He said the cause we were engaged in was that which attached people to the Constitution of the late United States—it was the cause of civil, religious, and constitutional liberty. Many of us looked at the Constitution as the anchor of safety. In Georgia the people had been attached to the previous Union, but the Constitution which governed it was framed by Southern talent and understanding. Assaults had been made on it ever since it was established. Lately a latitudinous construction had been made by the North, while we of the South sought to interpret it as it was—advocating strict construction, State rights, the right of the people to rule, &c. He spoke of all the fifteen Southern States as advocating this construction. To violate the principles of the Constitution was to initiate revolution; and the Northern States had done this.

The constitution framed at Montgomery discarded the obsolete ideas of the old Constitution, but had preserved its better portion, with some modifications, suggested by the experience of the past; and it had been adopted by the Confederate States, who would stand by it. The old Constitution had been made an engine of power to crush out liberty; that of the Confederate States to preserve it. The old Constitution was improved in our hands, and those living under it had, like the phœnix, risen from their ashes.

The revolution lately begun did not affect alone property, but liberty. He alluded to Lincoln's call for 75,000 volunteers, and said he could find no authority in the old Constitution for such a flagrant abuse of power. His second proclamation had stigmatized as pirates all who sailed in letters of marque; this was also in violation of the Constitution, which alone gave Congress that power.

What had the friends of liberty to hope for? Beginning in usurpation, where would he end? You are, however, said he, no longer under the rule of this tyrant. With strong arms and stout hearts you have now resolved to stand in defence of liberty. The Confederate States have but asserted their rights. They believed that their rulers derived their just powers from the consent of the governed. No one had the right to deny the existence of the sovereign right of secession. Our people did not want to meddle with the Northern States—only wanted the latter to leave them alone. When did Virginia ever ask the assistance of the General Government?

If there is sin in our institutions, we bear the blame, and will stand acquitted by natural law, and the higher law of the Creator. We stand upon the law of God and Nature. The Southern States did not wish a resort to arms after secession. Mr. Stephens alluded to the negotiations between Major Anderson and the authorities of the Confederate States, to demonstrate the proposition. History, he said, if rightly written, will acquit us of a desire to shed our brother's blood.

The law of necessity and of right compelled us to act as we did. He had reason to believe that the Creator smiled on it. The Federal flag was taken down without the loss of a single life. He believed that Providence would be with us and bless us to the end. We had appealed to the God of Battles for the justness of our cause. Madness and folly ruled at Washington. Had it not have been so, several of the States would have been in the old Union for a year to come. Maryland would join us, and may be, ere long, the principles that Washington fought for might be again administered in the city that bore his name.

Every son of the South, from the Potomac to the Rio Grande, should rally to the support of Maryland. If Lincoln quits Washington as ignominously as he entered it, God's will will have been accomplished. The argument was now exhausted. Be prepared; stand to your arms—defend your wives and firesides. He alluded to the momentous consequences of the issue involved. Rather than be conquered, let every second man rally to drive back the invader. The conflict may be terrible, but the victory will be ours. Virginians, said he, you fight for the preservation of your sacred rights —the land of PATRICK HENRY—to keep from desecration the tomb of WASHINGTON, the graves of MADISON, JEFFERSON, and all you hold most dear.

—*Richmond Dispatch*, April 23.

Doc. 88.—MEETING OF THE NEW YORK BAR, APRIL 22.

JUDGE EDMONDS called the meeting to order, and nominated for presiding officer the Hon. Daniel P. Ingraham, of the Supreme Court. The motion was acceded to amid loud cheers.

Mr. Charles E. Whitehead put in nomination the following list of Vice-Presidents:

Hon. Samuel R. Betts, Hon. Thos. W. Clerke,
Hon. J. J. Roosevelt, Hon. C. P. Daly,
Hon. John T. Hoffman, Hon. Greene C. Bronson,
Hon. Daniel Lord.

William Allen Butler put in nomination the following list of Secretaries:

Gilbert Dean, E. W. Stoughton,
Hon. Chas. A. Peabody, Richard O'Gorman.

These nominations were acceded to unanimously.

Three cheers were called for the American flag, and responded to enthusiastically.

Judge Edmonds said: In behalf of the Committee of Arrangements I offer the following resolutions for the consideration of the meeting. I am admonished by the Committee that I must make no speech. The time for speeches has gone by. The time for action has arrived, [loud cheers,] and I am, therefore, instructed to call upon this meeting of intelligent and patriotic men to act, and not to talk. I read the resolutions:

In all periods of the history of our people, the lawyer has been preëminently true to the cause of civil liberty, the supremacy of the law, and the integrity of constitutions; and it becomes the members of the profession, whether members of the Bench, practitioners at the Bar, or our students and clerks, to rally in the defense of our dearly cherished institutions, against the felonious assaults now made upon them. And the members of the profession in the City of New York, and those connected with them in the administration of justice, acknowledging the high obligations of fidelity to the Union and the Constitution, in every emergency and against every assault, and feeling the imperative call upon them in the impending crisis to take immediate and effective action as a profession, it is by them

Resolved, That an executive committee of fifteen be appointed to collect and receive subscriptions from the members of the profession and all connected with them, to be applied by them for the purposes of national defence and in aid of those of our brethren who are or may be called into active service, or the families of those who fall or may be disabled in the service, and generally to do every act in behalf of the Bar that may be necessary to carry into effect the general purposes of this meeting.

Resolved, That we hold ourselves in readiness whenever requested, in behalf of any member of this Bar, who may be in service in the Army or Navy of the United States, to assume and perform for his benefit any professional business he may have in charge, and without expense to him.

Resolved, That the members of the profession in the City of New York will stand by the Union, the Constitution, and the supremacy of the laws, in every and any emergency; and to that they pledge their means and personal efforts, as well against aggression from abroad as against efforts at home; and they hold it to be their solemn duty in this emergency to coöperate with the public authorities, State and National, civil and military, in preserving peace and good order, in maintaining good government, in sustaining the Constitution and the legal authorities of the land, in protecting the homes and firesides of our people.

Resolved, That we recognize in the contest in which we are engaged no parallel in the history of the world. Aiming at no acquisition of territory, prompted by no ambition for distinction or power, and impelled by no angry passions, the people of the United States are warring for freedom only against wanton aggressions upon all the institutions which have secured that freedom to us. In such a contest, where the wisdom of the past can afford us no adequate guide, it becomes the lawyer, regardless of the obscurity which so often settles upon moral courage amid the blaze of martial renown, to be firm, true, calm, and active in every emergency, and by a generous self-sacrifice evince at once the ardor and purity of his patriotism. To such a line of conduct we dedicate ourselves, and invite our brethren throughout the State to associate and coöperate with us.

David Dudley Field moved the adoption of the resolutions.

The Hon. Charles P. Kirkland said: Before these resolutions are adopted I desire to say, six months since I lost my very dear eldest son. I have but two left, and the youngest 19 years of age. Both started yesterday for Washington in the 71st Regiment. [Loud cheers].

The resolutions were adopted amid loud cheers.

Subscription papers were at once circulated in the audience, during which the President announced the following gentlemen as the Executive Committee:

Hon. John W. Edmonds,	Hon. Wm. H. Leonard,
Hon. Joseph S. Bosworth,	Hon. Henry Hilton,
Hon. Edwards Pierrepont,	Daniel Lord,
Henry Nicoll,	Dorman P. Eaton,
Wm. Fullerton,	Rich'd O'Gorman,
Luther R. Marsh,	Alex. Hamilton, Jr.,
Wm. Allen Butler,	Gilbert Dean,

John T. C. Smidt.

The work of receiving subscriptions then commenced in good earnest—the first sums subscribed being $500, and even these were increased in the latter part of the meeting, when the effort was made to bring the aggregate up to a stated amount.

The sums subscribed made an aggregate of over $25,000.

Throughout, the proceedings were characterized by the most noble feelings of patriotism; and many pleasant episodes occurred, a few of which are as follows:

The Hon. E. P. Cowles stated that he had equipped a son in the First Regiment, but he desired to contribute in addition $100.

Mr. E. H. Owen had sent a son to the war, and he desired to subscribe $100.

The Hon. John Slosson said he had equipped his only son and sent him on to the field. The firm of Schell, Slosson, & Hutchins had contributed $500, to which he would add $100 for himself. He had also three nephews in the service.

Richard Busteed had equipped a nephew and an adopted son, who were now on their way to the scene of conflict. In addition, he subscribed $350.

E. W. Chester said he had not $500 to contribute, but his partner had gone with the 71st Regiment, leaving his wife and family to his care. That should be his contribution. [Applause.]

The Hon. J. H. McCunn, City Judge, in addition to contributing $500 to help equip his own regiment, subscribed $100 to the fund of this meeting.

Judge Pierrepont said that an Englishman desired to contribute his share, $100. He was Mr. Charles Edwards. [Applause.]

A gentleman called attention to the fact that a military company was now being organized among the members of the Bar.

Judge Edmonds said he would revive the recollection that he was once Colonel of a Regiment. [Three cheers for Col. Edmonds were called for and responded to amid loud cheers and laughter.] He would only say that he was about to organize a regiment again, and those who were willing to join in such an organization for home consumption he would like to have remain when the meeting should adjourn. [Applause.] He was 60 and odd years old, but in his ashes were glowing youthful fires. [Cheers.]

Mr. Tom Bennett said he was an Englishman; that he had been endeavoring to get his countrymen together, but had not succeeded. He was now ready to join any other regiment and fight. [Cheers for Bennett.]

Mr. Haynor said he had no means to contribute, but he was ready to shoulder his musket and go wherever he was required. He had a large family, but he knew they would be taken care of. [Applause.] He had an only son, and he, too, was ready to unite with a regiment, to do his duty to his country. [Cheers.]

Ex-Judge Birdsall said he had but limited means, but he gave $25 to the fund, and within a week should be in the field himself. (Applause.)

Nat. Waring said that he had already fitted out three young men in Brooklyn, would now contribute $25, and if it were necessary he would go himself. (Applause.)

The Hon. Stephen B. Cushing, late Attorney-General, said that a son and clerk he had already sent to the war, and his partner was about to leave as colonel of an entire regiment.

Mr. Choate stated that Mr. Fullerton had appropriated $500 for the support of the Newburgh Company, which his nephew commanded, and he now added to this fund $100. (Loud cheers.)

Henry Freeman Lay, a law clerk, contributed $5, and announced that he had joined the Zouaves as a drummer.

Malcom Campbell subscribed $100. He wrote on a slip of paper, which was read to the meeting, that his feelings were too intense to permit him to speak; but before the end of the week he should be in Washington ready to do whatever duty was assigned him.

John Chetwood said that a boy of 15 years, James Riley, had enlisted as a drummer. He subscribed $100 in his name.

Mr. Russell said that on Saturday morning, to his great surprise, his partner, Mr. Mileham Hoffman, son of Judge Hoffman, walked out of their office to enlist for Washington. (Cheers.)

Mr. Chauncey Schaffer, who had been attending an impromptu meeting in the adjoining Court-room, said: We have imposed fines for the cause to the amount of $1,000, and the work is going on. It affords me pleasure to say that more than a dozen names have been enrolled for active service among the young members of the profession, who, while disclaiming to be masters of the science, were positive that they had learned how to charge. (Laughter.)

At this point, the contributions were announced to have reached $17,000.

A gentleman stated that intelligence had been received from Philadelphia to the effect that the bar of that city had a meeting to-day, with the purpose of raising $20,000 on the spot. (Applause.)

It was determined at once that however astute "Philadelphia lawyers" might be, New York lawyers would have to exceed their figure.

W. R. & S. H. Stafford, it was announced, had sent two of their clerks to the field, and now added their contribution of $100.

Two young practitioners, both grandsons of Noah Webster, Charles C. and W. W. Fowler, contributed $25 each.

The subscription having reached near $20,000, it was suggested that the amount must be made to equal that of the merchants, and a new enthusiasm was aroused, and soon the amount reached over $25,000.

Mr. Busteed said that so far as the action of the merchants was concerned, he had been informed by Mr. Wm. G. Lambert that the honored merchants of New York, as the result of the meeting of the Chamber of Commerce, had written to the President that they would furnish him with a hundred millions of dollars if it was necessary (loud cheers,) and that to sustain the Government, they had pledged themselves as sacredly as had the Fathers of the Revolution.

It was announced, also, that Mr. Birney, of the firm of Birney & Prentice, was also raising a regiment, and had been commissioned.

Mr. Evarts made a similar statement in reference to the Hon. Daniel E. Sickles.

—N. Y. Tribune, April 23.

Doc. 89.—JNO. BELL AND EDWIN H. EWING.

Hon. John Bell spoke for about three-quarters of an hour, stating in effect that so far as present duties and responsibilities are concerned, the past is a sealed book. The time for action and unity of action in the South had arrived, and he was for standing by the South, and defending the South, all the South, against the unnecessary, aggressive, cruel, unjust, and wanton war which is being forced upon us. He recounted at some length the efforts which he had made in the past, and especially with the present Administration, to avert this war, and the hopes he had cherished for the preservation of peace; but those hopes had now vanished, and our duty was to defend ourselves and to make common cause with all our sister slaveholding States against a common invading foe. He advocated a strong and effective military league or union among all slaveholding States for the successful prosecution of the war. He declared that Tennessee had, in effect, dissolved her relations with the Federal Union, and though he had hoped and labored to the last to preserve the Union first, and second, if separation was inevitable, to make it peaceable, he now abandoned all such hope, and his voice was clear and loud to every Tennesseean—to arms! to arms! He counselled the most effective and energetic public measures to secure the best organization possible of the military strength of the State.

Mr. Bell was followed by Hon. Edwin H. Ewing, who declared that in his opinion the Union between the North and the South was at an end forever, and he had no hope of its restoration. He regarded this as a war of subjugation, and he would never consent to such a domination as was attempted to be established over us. He was for a most vigorous prosecution of the war. He denied that the Federal Administration is the United States of America, or that Washington was the rightful seat of Government. The District of Columbia was carved out of Southern territory, and they ought not to be permitted to hold an island in our own country. He was therefore for taking it. He was for unity of action among all the

States of the South under any military leader who was best qualified to lead them. He said that though Mr. Jefferson Davis had not been a favorite with him as a politician, he believed him to be as able and competent a military commander as there is in the South, and he was for marching under him, or any other man, against the invaders of Southern soil. His cry was, "To arms! to arms!" not only to resist the invasion of our own soil, but that of any of the Southern States. He had no thought of accepting the poor privilege of being swallowed up at last.

Hon. Andrew Ewing followed, declaring, in the strongest and most emphatic terms, for resistance to the attempted subjugation of the South. He was for the whole South standing as a unit.

—Nashville Banner, April 24.

Doc. 90.—OPINIONS OF THE NEW ORLEANS PRESS.

THE sectional prejudice among thousands which, until recent events, had laid dormant and inert, has been roused to active demonstration by the fiendish tactics of Black Republican journals. These have so mingled the most violent denunciation of the South and its institutions with frantic appeals in behalf of the Union and the American flag, as to stir up the ignorant masses to a pitch of uncontrollable excitement, and to fill them with vindictive and malignant hostility. If these fomenters of strife were permitted to direct the policy of the United States Government, a war of extermination against the South should be waged. All their counsels tend to this object; and, as they appear to be gradually obtaining the ascendency with the Lincoln Administration, it may be that before the lapse of many months the conflict will really assume the hideous character they desire to impart to it.

—N. O. Bee, April 27.

Public sentiment in the South has become a unit. Never before was there such unanimity on any question as now exists in the Confederate States; and in those slave States that are not yet technically within them, almost the same unanimity is manifested. The coercive policy of the Black Republican Government has produced what nothing else could have done. It has obliterated all mere party differences in the Southern States, and brought all men upon the same platform of resistance to such coercion. The conservative sentiments of the border slave States are rapidly giving way before the crazy efforts at subjugation of the usurping despotism at Washington City. That power seems to have entirely forgotten that there is a legislative body known as Congress, for it is arrogating to itself as much authority as Louis Napoleon or the Emperor of Russia ever exercised. The Republican Cabinet has been converted into an oligarchy, wielding unlimited authority. Genuine Republican theory and practice appear to be completely lost sight of. The Lincoln Cabinet, instead of merely carrying into effect the laws that Congress passes, makes laws of its own, or rather proceeds to make war upon the Confederate States without any law. Why don't Mr. Lincoln fulminate a decree declaring Congress abolished, and himself and his friends in perpetual authority, with power to do just what they like, law or no law? He might as well do this, as to do what he is doing.

—N. O. Bulletin, April 27.

The Bulletin also says that while the South is a unit, public opinion in the North appears to be settling down into a determination to support the war measures of the Lincoln Administration. Among the journals which still resist the tremendous pressure of fanaticism, and denounce the insane policy of the coercionists, the Bulletin mentions the Bangor Union, and the Argus, Maine; the New York Daily News and New York Day Book, and the Greensburg (Pa.) Democrat. We believe the Boston Courier might be added to the list, and perhaps Medary's paper, the Crisis, in Ohio. Of course the opposition of these journals is utterly incapable of checking or modifying the war current in the North. Nothing can do that but some terrible reverse to the Northern arms. Nothing but downright force and physical terror can achieve a moral triumph over the brutal instincts of fanaticism.

The *N. O. Crescent*, referring to an article in the Toronto (Canada) Leader, observes:

The Leader says it is "too late now for the North to adopt the only statesmanlike policy—to recognize secession as a fact, and act accordingly." We think not. We think the North may save itself much of disaster, much of national disgrace and dishonor, millions of money and seas of blood, by promptly recognizing at this time, the independence of the Confederate States. It is all that we have ever asked. We have asked only that we be recognized as a separate nationality, and all questions connected with our future relations and our former joint possession of national property to be settled by peaceable negotiation. What we demanded at first we will eventually have, just so sure as fate—except that, since this inhuman and unnatural war has been precipitated upon us, the North will lose much that it might otherwise have preserved.

The *Picayune* speaks of the utter contempt and disregard of laws and Constitutional forms manifested in the recent proceedings of the Lincoln Administration. With the cry of the Constitution and the enforcement of the law on its lying lips, it violates both, and proceeds to inaugurate a bitter and bloody war with the preposterous avowal that it is not making war, but only taking measures to "disperse" a mob and put down a riot.

—N. O. Delta, April 27.

Doc. 91.—THE FIRST SOUTH CAROLINA REGIMENT.

The following are the officers of the South Carolina troops:

M. L. Bonham, Brigadier-General; Col. W. C. Moragne, Deputy Adjutant-General; Col. W. D. Simpson, Division Inspector-General; Col. A. P. Aldrich, Quartermaster; Col. R. B. Boyleston, Commissary; Col. J. N. Lipscomb, Paymaster; Col. J. McF. Gaston, Brigade Surgeon; Major S. W. Nelson; Major E. S. Hammond; Major S. W. Melton.

FIRST REGIMENT SOUTH CAROLINA VOLUNTEERS.

Maxcy Gregg, Colonel; D. H. Hamilton, Lieutenant-Colonel; Augustus M. Smith, Major.

The regiment is composed of the Richland Rifles, of Columbia, Capt. Miller; Darlington Guards, Capt. McIntosh; Edgefield Rifles, Capt. Dean; Union District Volunteers, Capt. Gadberry; Edgefield Guards, Capt. Merriweather; Monticello Guards, Capt. Davis; Rhett Guards, of Newberry, Capt. Walker; and Richardson Guards, of Charleston, Capt. Axson.

All of these troops were on service in Charleston harbor during the late bombardment, but freely and enthusiastically accepted service in the campaign opening on the banks of the Potomac, without visiting their homes. Before leaving, the ladies of Charleston presented them a new flag, which the Courier describes as follows:

It is made of blue silk, with silk tassels, the staff surmounted by a golden cross. On one side is the Palmetto tree, elegantly worked with white floss silk. An oak vine, of the same beautiful texture, surrounds the Palmetto, intertwined with laurel leaves. The trimming is also white silk. Two elegant standards, of white silk, with golden fringe, accompany the flag. They bear on them the inscription, "First Regiment South Carolina Volunteers, 1861."

—*N. O. Picayune*, April 28.

Doc. 92.—SPEECH OF HON. ROBERT J. WALKER, April 23.

This is a sublime spectacle upon which our country and the world are now gazing. Deplorable as is this rebellion, it has solved the disputed question, that the people of this Republic are competent for self-government; that we can not only administer our affairs in peace, and bring foreign wars to a successful conclusion, but that we are able also to perform the far more difficult task of suppressing rebellion within our limits. (Loud cheers.) On this question we are a united people, from the southern boundary of my native State of Pennsylvania, to the lakes of the North, and within these latitudes from the Atlantic to the Pacific.

There are no two parties here to-day. There is but one party—the party for the Union, which proclaims with one voice its stern determination to sustain the flag of our country, to replace it upon every fort within our limits, to carry it back into every harbor, and compel it to float by the arms of freemen in each and every one of our thirty-four States. (Loud and long-continued applause.) Mr. Walker said this was the third campaign in which he had been engaged in fighting the hydra of secession and disunion, and contended for the maintenance and perpetuation of the Union. The first was when South Carolina proceeded to nullify the laws of Congress in 1832, and secede from the Union. A native of Pennsylvania, he had emigrated to the State of Mississippi, and during three years he fought in that contest against nullification and secession, until (on the 8th of January, 1836) he was elected by the Union Jackson Democratic Party of Mississippi to the Senate of the United States. In that contest, which continued during three years with extreme violence, he addressed more than one hundred meetings with the flag of the Union unfolded over him, and wearing another similar flag of the Stars and Stripes around him as a sash, presented to him by the Union ladies of Mississippi. (Great cheering.) To show that the principles of that contest were the same as those now involved, he would read a few short extracts from his first speech at the opening of this campaign, delivered at Natchez, Mississippi, on the first Monday of January, 1833, as printed in the Mississippi *Journal* of that date.

Here Mr. Walker read the following extracts from an old and tattered and torn newspaper:

"Never, fellow-citizens, did I rise to address you with such deep and abiding impressions of the awful character of that crisis which involves the existence of the American Union. No mortal eye can pierce the veil which covers the events of the next few months, but we do know that the scales are now balancing in fearful equipoise—Liberty and Union in the one hand, Anarchy and Despotism in the other. Which shall preponderate is the startling question, to which we must all now answer. Already one bright, one kindred star is sinking from the banner of the American Union—the very fabric of our Government is rocking on its foundations; one of its proudest pillars is now moving from beneath the glorious arch, and soon may we all stand amid the broken columns and upon the scattered fragments of the Constitution of our once united and happy country.

"Whilst, then, we may yet recede from the brink of that precipice on which we now stand, whilst we are once more convened as citizens of the American Union, and have still a common country; whilst we are yet fondly gazing, perhaps for the last time, upon that banner which floated over the army of WASHINGTON, and living beneath that Constitution which bears his sacred name, let us at least endeavor to transmit to posterity, unimpaired, that Union cemented by the blood of our forefathers.

"Gov. Hayne, of Carolina, in his late proclamation, inquires if that State was linked to the

Union, 'in the iron bonds of a perpetual Union.'

"These bonds were not of iron, or Carolina would never have worn them, but they are the enduring chains of peace and union. One link could not be severed from this chain, united in all its parts, without an entire dissolution of all the bonds of Union; and one State cannot dissolve the Union among all the States. Yet Carolina admits this to be the inevitable consequence of the separation of that State, for in the address of her Convention she declares that 'the separation of South Carolina would inevitably produce a general dissolution of the Union.' Has the Government of the Union no power to preserve itself from destruction, or must we submit to 'a general dissolution of the Union,' whenever any one State thinks proper to issue the despotic mandate? It was the declared object of our ancestors, the hope of their children, that they had formed 'a perpetual Union." The original compact of Carolina with her sister States, by which the Confederacy was erected, is called 'Articles of Confederation and *perpetual Union*.'

"In the 13th article of this Confederacy it is expressly declared that 'the Union shall be perpetual,' and in the ratification of this compact, South Carolina united with her sister States in declaring, 'and we do further solemnly plight and engage the faith of our respective constituents' 'that the Union shall be perpetual;' and may she now withdraw the pledge, without a violation of the compact? By the old Confederacy, then, the Union was perpetual, and the declared object of the Constitution was, 'to form a more perfect union' than that existing under the former Confederacy. Now, would this union be more perfect under the new than the old Confederacy, if, by the latter, the union was perpetual, but under the former limited in its duration at the will of a single State.

"My hope is in the people; I believe they are not 'tyrants' by choice or 'necessity,' and that in every State they would sustain their representatives in preserving the Union; from the poor man's cottage they would come forward and say, you did well to prefer Union and liberty to dollars and cents—they are the only inheritance we received from our fathers, the only legacy we can bequeath to our children, and you have saved the priceless heritage—and if any by their vote should say, dissolve the Union rather than reduce the revenue, and this last, fairest fabric of human liberty should crumble in the dust, the withering curses of unnumbered millions would blast his peace and blacken his memory, and his only epitaph would be, *here lies a destroyer of the American Union*. Let not Carolina's ordinance delay your action. The Union party in Carolina, cheered by the voice of the nation, may become the majority, and sweep that ordinance from the records of the State. Repealed or not, it must not repeal the Union, or prevent the execution of its laws. Let Congress, let every State Legislature, and the people of every county, fix the seal of reprobation upon the doctrines of nullification and secession, and doom them never more to disturb the harmony of the people, and shake the pillars of the American Union. Let the present Congress adjust the tariff, and they will stand next in the grateful recollection of the American people to the Congress of '76, that gave us Liberty and Union, and this preserved them. They will return in triumph to their constituents; not the triumph of party, but of the Union. The day this act of peace and concord shall be passed, should be celebrated as a national jubilee. Tyrants will cease to predict the downfall of the American Union, for it will stand firm and unbroken, a rock of adamant, imperishable though faction's storms have beat upon its brow, though mad ambition's volcanic fires have burnt around it, yet no human power could move it from the everduring basis of the affections of a free, united, and a happy people."

Mr. WALKER said so important was it to sustain these great principles, that he begged leave to quote much higher authority than his own in favor of these great doctrines. On the 2d of May, 1836, Hon. CHARLES J. INGERSOLL, member of Congress from Philadelphia, visited the venerable JAMES MADISON, then Ex-President of the United States. On his return to the Federal city, Mr. INGERSOLL published the result of this interview in the *Daily Washington Globe*. On reference to that publication, it will be found that Mr. MADISON fully indorsed this speech of mine against nullification and secession; and further declared that it contained the only true representation, not only of his own opinions, but those of Mr. JEFFERSON, on these great questions. (Enthusiastic applause.) Mr. WALKER said, this is a death struggle in which we are engaged. If the doctrine of secession prevails, we never can have any Government, any Union, any flag, or any country, but anarchy will be inaugurated, to be succeeded by despotism. If, however, as he (Mr. WALKER) said he fully believed, this doctrine of secession shall be forever suppressed by our success in this contest, we will emerge stronger than ever from the trial, and our Government more respected than ever, at home or abroad, and retaining every State and Territory intact. (Loud applause.)

Mr. WALKER said his second campaign in the defence of the Union was in Kansas, as the Governor of that Territory. He said that he went there upon the urgent and oft-repeated solicitation of the President, upon the express condition that the Lecompton Constitution, so called, should be submitted to the prior vote of the people for ratification or rejection. But for that pledge which he (Mr. WALKER) gave to the people of Kansas, civil war would have been inaugurated in Kansas early in June, 1857. This principle was right in itself in all cases; but it was indispensably necessary in

Kansas, because a large majority of the counties of the Territory had been actually disfranchised in electing delegates to the Convention assembled to frame the Constitution, not one of which counties had given or could give a single ballot in the election of delegates. This vital defect in the organization of the Convention, could be secured only by submitting their action to the ratification or rejection of the people of Kansas in every county of the Territory. And it was the rejection of that principle, the great principle of popular liberty, that has caused our present disasters. (Loud cheers.)

Mr. WALKER said that all previous elections in Kansas before his arrival there had been wretched mockeries. Large armies from an adjacent State had marched into the Territory, and seized the polls and the ballot boxes, displaced the regular judges, placed their sergeants and corporals in their stead, and elected their satellites to the Legislature. They intended to accomplish the same result in the election in October, 1857, by military force. But he, (Mr. WALKER,) as Governor of the Territory, had then assembled a large army composed of the forces of the United States in Kansas. He (Mr. WALKER) had accompanied this army to the frontiers. He posted it at all important points on the line dividing Kansas from Missouri, and announced his determination to defend the ballot boxes of Kansas from external aggression by the whole force of the army of the United States. This movement was successful. The ballot box was thus defended from aggression, and the first peaceable election was held in Kansas. But those who had thus been defeated by the voice of the people, were not satisfied with the result. Having failed to seize the polls again by force, they resorted to frauds and forgeries unparalleled in the history of the world. You have seen, fellow-citizens, the substituted Cincinnati Directory for the returns of the vote of the people. You have seen the pretended returns at Oxford, where the names of the clerks and judges were forged, substituting 1,900 votes, where nineteen only were given. You have seen the pretended returns from McGee County, a vile forgery upon their face, where no election was holden, and not a vote given; and yet where more than 1,200 fictitious ballots were returned to me. These forgeries were all transparent. They were clear upon their face. They were not returned; they were not sworn to by the judges and clerks of the election, as required by law. They were as perfect a nullity as if a mere newspaper had been thrown at me for my adoption. These forgeries were rejected by me; and the result was that the party opposed to Slavery in Kansas, constituting nine-tenths of the people, succeeded, and elected their Territorial legislature—the first which ever represented the voice of the people of Kansas. (Loud cheers.)

For thus insisting that the Lecompton Constitution, so called, should be submitted to the prior vote of the people, and for thus rejecting those forged and simulated, so called, returns, I was bitterly denounced in the South by the very men who have organized the present rebellion. But, fellow-citizens, though the President and Cabinet fell from their positions, and deserted the pledges which they had given —though the South was apparently united to a unit against me, and recreant cravens from the North were united with them, I maintained my position to the last, and never ceased to denounce this unparalleled outrage upon the rights of a free people. I felt, gentlemen, and so declared, that the promulgation of such doctrines was calculated to destroy the Union, and opposed them at all times to the utmost extent of my humble abilities. If the course then adopted by me in Kansas had been pursued, this disunion project could never have been successfully inaugurated. (Loud cheers.) Thus ended my second campaign in defence of the Constitution and the Union.

And, now, gentlemen, I have entered upon the third campaign in defence of the same great principles. This campaign, gentlemen, I feel, will be the last, for the people are united as one man, and are all prepared to pour out their life-blood as freely as water from a goblet in defence of the flag of our country. This contest, I believe, will be of short duration; but, whether of long continuance or not, it will never terminate until the flag of the Union waves in triumph over Fort Sumter, and all our other fortifications and harbors, and over every other acre of our soil and every drop of all our waters from the Atlantic to the Pacific, from the lakes of the North and the St. Lawrence to the Gulf of Mexico, throughout every State and Territory of the Union.

—N. Y. Times.

Doc. 93.—DEPARTURE OF THE 8th, 13th, AND 69th N. Y. REGIMENTS.

EIGHTH REGIMENT.

THE members of the 8th Regiment, Col. Geo. Lyons, and the recruits belonging thereto, took position in Sixteenth and Seventeenth streets.

The regiment did not move before 4 o'clock. The delay was said to have been occasioned by some misunderstanding in reference to the change in the order regarding the guns. It appears that an order had been received to the effect that the Grey Troup should leave the howitzers and take six 6-pounders. The Governor had been telegraphed for permission to take horses and harness, and they had to wait for a reply. At length the order for the horses and harness was received, and immediately operations were set on foot for starting.

A large body of friends of the regiment walked ahead of the procession. These included about one hundred of the G. L. Fox Guard. All along the line, on Broadway, down to Canal street, the windows of the various stores, and the sidewalks, were crowded with ladies and children, all desirous of seeing the departure of the Washington Greys for the field of battle; many of them with well-tried hearts were comforting each other with an indefinite variety of patriotic sentiments. The regiment was greeted with the most vociferous cheering all the way down to Pier No. 36 North River, where they embarked, being 1,000 in number, on board the steamship Alabama.

The crowd on the dock, and also on Pier No. 35, was immense. The members of the regiment, including the recruits, were in most excellent spirits, and as the ship moved away from the wharf, at about 7 o'clock, and the immense assemblage on the wharf sent forth their cheers and "tigers," the soldiers fired their revolvers in the air.

In Hudson street, the Grey troop, numbering 100 men, with a battery of six 6-pounders and thirty-six horses, turned down and proceeded to Pier No. 13, where they embarked on board the steamship Montgomery. The preparation for the embarkation of the horses had to be made, the ship's water had to be taken in, and other work had to be done; but all hands were put to work, and it was completed in good time. The Montgomery sailed from her wharf about 10 o'clock.

OFFICERS OF THE EIGHTH REGIMENT.

Regimental Officers.—George Lyons, Colonel; Chas. G. Waterbury, Lieutenant Colonel; Obadiah Wintworth, Major; D. B. Kuler, jr., Adjutant; Alderman Charles G. Cornell, Quartermaster; A. C. Smith, jr., Commissary; M. H. Cushman, Paymaster; Foster Swift, M. D., Surgeon; Thos. Rutter, Chaplain.

Company A.—James O. Johnston, Captain; Arthur Woods, 1st Lieutenant; Geo. W. Day, 2d Lieutenant.

Company B.—Thomas Sweeney, Captain; Chas. A. Enos, 1st Lieutenant; M. Wall, 2d Lieutenant.

Company C.—Burgur, Captain; John Appleton, 1st Lieutenant; Richard Dunphy, 2d Lieutenant.

Company D.—E. D. Lawrence, Captain; Isaac Cohen, 1st Lieutenant; Vacant, 2d Lieutenant.

Company E.—M. Griffin, Captain; Alonzo Dutch, 1st Lieutenant; Chas. T. Hurlburt, 2d Lieutenant; G. L. Fox, 3d Lieutenant.

Company F.—Leander Buck, Captain; D. A. Allen, 1st Lieutenant; James Dimond, 2d Lieutenant.

Company G.—Wm. T. Carr, Captain; J. G. Schiele, 1st Lieutenant; Henry S. Decker, 2d Lieutenant.

Company H.—Samuel N. Gregory, Captain; Samuel N. Burrill, 1st Lieutenant; Wm. G. Halsey, 2d Lieutenant.

Troop I.—Artillery, six guns; J. M. Varian, Captain; Robert Brown, 1st Lieutenant; —— Burns, 2d Lieutenant; —— Carpenter, 3d Lieutenant.

Engineers.—Wm. Walton, Captain.

THE SIXTY-NINTH REGIMENT.

The 69th Regiment is composed entirely of Irishmen. Col. Corcoran, who is in command, is exceedingly popular with his countrymen, and this popularity was enhanced at least 50 per cent. by the triumphant manner in which he emerged from the troubles which surrounded him. When the 69th offered its services to the Government, the Court-Martial which had been summoned to try the Colonel for disobedience of orders was dismissed, and he was restored to his command. This victory touched the Irish heart, and no sooner did he issue a call for volunteers than his recruiting office was besieged by applicants who were anxious to serve their country under his orders. Had the Colonel been called upon for an entire brigade he could have supplied them in the same time and with less trouble than he has furnished 1,000 men. Up to Monday night, 6,500 names had been enrolled in his regiment. On Tuesday morning the 69th was ordered to assemble at their armory, No. 42 Prince street, to receive their equipments previous to their departure.

At an early hour the entire street was taken possession of by the regiment and its friends, and the distribution of muskets, blankets, etc., commenced. In front of Col. Corcoran's dwelling, No 5 Prince street, a large truck, loaded with blankets, was stationed, and the recruits were required to file by this truck one by one. The rush at this point was perfectly tremendous, so eager were the men to obtain their equipments. The Captain of each company was stationed on the vehicle; and here the acceptance or rejection of the recruits occurred.

Passing the blanket wagon, where a blanket was thrown at the accepted ones, they were passed to another man, who seized their head covering and crowned them with the regimental cap. Still another individual placed a musket in their hands, while others furnished them with a tin plate, knife, fork, and tin cup. It was not until 2 o'clock in the afternoon that all the men were equipped, after which the companies were formed, and accompanied by the enthusiastic crowd, marched to Great Jones street, from which point the regiment were to start. For several hours there had been an assemblage of men, women, and children in Broadway, mostly Irish, which had effectually driven every vehicle from that thoroughfare. Housetops and windows were crowded with enthusiastic women, who waved their handkerchiefs incessantly to the crowd beneath. Several Irish civic societies, comprising about 2,000 persons, with waving banners—the harp of Erin kissing the Stars and Stripes—had formed in procession in Broadway, as an escort, and patiently waited for the regiment to move.

About 3 o'clock the order to march was received, and the entire procession, civic and military, moved down Broadway. The march was a perfect triumph for the Irish citizens, vindicating their loyalty and patriotism in a most substantial manner. Col. Corcoran, who arose from a bed of sickness to accompany his regiment, was nearly killed by kindness. He occupied a carriage with one or two friends, and it became necessary for the police to protect him from the crowd which pressed upon him from all sides.

When the procession arrived at Pier No. 4 North River, where the James Adger was waiting to receive them, an attempt was made to shut off the crowd and prevent their passing the gates, but the efforts of the police were unavailing. The throng pressed in, and soon the pier was a scene of the utmost confusion. The soldiers were forced from the ranks, and speedily becoming identified with the crowd had to fight their way to the steamer's gang-plank. For at least an hour the rush of soldiers and citizens towards the steamer, was terrific. Patriotic Irishmen were determined to bid their friends good-bye, and in their efforts to do so were knocked down and trampled under foot, kicked, bayoneted, and otherwise maltreated; but they heeded it not. Regaining their feet with a "hurrah for the 69th" they again entered the contest. Several soldiers were served in the same manner, others lost their muskets or caps in the scramble; but all eventually got on board alive.

At 6½ o'clock the Adger steamed away from the dock amid the most uproarious cheering. If the friends of the Jeff. Davis Government ever reckoned upon any assistance from the Irish population of the North, the display of yesterday must convince them that they were mistaken. The harp of Erin floats beside the Stars and Stripes in perfect union, and will do so throughout the present struggle. If more troops are needed by the Government the Irish of this city will furnish five times the number they already have done. The following are the officers of the 69th regiment:

Colonel, Michael Corcoran; Lieutenant-Colonel, Robert Nugent; Major, James Bagley; Surgeon, Robert Johnson; Assistant-Surgeon, —— Kiernan; Assistant-Surgeon, Patrick Nolan; Engineer, J. B. Kirker; Chaplains, D. Sullivan and the Rev. Mr. Mooney; Captains, James Haggerty, Thomas Lynch, Jas. Kavanagh, Thomas Clark, Patrick Kelly, J Bresslen, F. Duffy, James Kelly, and Coonan.

Mrs. Judge Daly presented the gallant fellows with a beautiful silken standard of the National colors.

THIRTEENTH REGIMENT.

The 13th Regiment embarked amid the most intense enthusiasm of the citizens of Brooklyn, who congregated by thousands, lining the streets from the City Hall to the Armory, in Cranberry-street, near Henry-street, to see them off. It was announced that the regiment would take up the line of march at 8 o'clock, A. M. Long before that hour the neighborhood of the Armory was filled with an almost impenetrable mass of human beings, nearly every one of whom had friends or near relatives in the regiment. Many ladies were there—the wives, sisters, and daughters of the soldiers. These were permitted to enter the Armory during the latter part of the day.

The old members of the regiment had all been provided with arms and equipments, but the new recruits, comprising by far the largest portion of the force, were devoid of nearly everything excepting shoes and other articles of clothing; the great requisites, muskets, knapsacks, blankets, &c., were missing. All was bustle and confusion. Carts were sent to New York for muskets, and about noon they arrived. The other equipments came along by degrees, and were furnished to the men. It was then discovered that there were not enough of equipments for the number of men enrolled. The officer in command had only one course to pursue in this exigency, and that was to send those recruits who could not be provided to the arsenal, there to await further orders. The total number equipped was about 450, including officers and musicians. About 200 were compelled to remain behind. It is understood that they will be equipped and sent on.

After all necessary details had been arranged, the companies marched out and formed in line on Cranberry-street. It was then three o'clock, P. M. The street was kept clear by the police, under direction of Inspector Folk, and after the inspection of the command by Acting Brigade Inspector S. A. Dodge, the drums beat, the band struck up a patriotic strain, and the regiment marched to Fulton-street, and thence to the Fulton ferry. The crowd of spectators was immense. Every available space was occupied, every door-step and every window was filled. The enthusiasm was unbounded. Cheer after cheer rent the air as the noble fellows marched along.

The head of the regiment reached the ferry at 4 o'clock, and in a few minutes thereafter the men had all embarked on board the ferry-boat Atlantic, which had been especially provided for the purpose by the ferry company.

As the regiment was marching on board, the band struck up "The Girl I Left Behind Me;" and when the boat had moved out of the slip, they played "Auld Lang Syne."

The Napper Tandy Light Artillery, Capt. Smith, was stationed on the city wharf, and fired a salute of 34 guns. A vast concourse had assembled at the foot of the street, and as the boat came in view the most tremendous cheers rent the air.

The troops were taken on board the Marion, lying in the North River.

The following is a list of the officers:

Colonel, Abel Smith; Lieutenant-Colonel, R. B. Clarke; Major, (vacant); Quartermaster, A Garrison; Paymaster, Boyd; Surgeon, Chase; Chaplain, The Rev. Mr. Lee; Commissary, Street; Sergeant-Major, J. H. Rosenquest; Quartermaster's Sergeant, Vail; Sergeant-of-the-Guard, Cheshire; Commissary Sergeant, Wetmore; Ordinance Sergeant, Carpenter; Right General Guide, Sherman; Left General Guide, Nash; Assistant Surgeon, Allingham; Colonel's Secretary, Brockway. Company Officers—A, Capt. Sullivan, Lieut. Mead; B, Capt. Sprague, Lieuts. Hay and McKee; C, Capt. Morgan, Lieut. Dodge; D, Capt. Balsden, Lieuts. Strong and Bennett; E, Capt. Jones, Lieut. Richards; F, Capt. Betts, Lieuts. Morton and Betts; G, Capt. Thorne, Lieuts. Johnson and Woodward. Engineer Corps, Sergeant Briggs.

Company F, is composed exclusively of firemen, attached to Victory Engine Company No. 13, and a very hardy set of men they are. Their uniforms consist of felt hats, black fire coats, drab pants and red shirts. Their muskets are most formidable-looking weapons. The dress of the main portion of the regiment is gray throughout.

It was expected that the regiment would march to the City Hall to be inspected; and thousands of persons gathered in the vicinity; but they were greatly disappointed, when after waiting all day they ascertained that the regiment had marched direct to the boat by the shortest route. The colors of the regiment are borne by Ensign Bromell of Company E.

—*N. Y. Tribune*, April 24.

Doc. 93½.—GOV. HICKS AND GEN. BUTLER.

THE correspondence between the Governor of Maryland and the commander of the Massachusetts troops:

EXECUTIVE CHAMBER, ANNAPOLIS, }
Friday, April 23, 1861. }

To Brig. Gen. B. F. Butler:

SIR: Having, by virtue of the powers vested in me by the Constitution of Maryland, summoned the Legislature of the State to assemble on Friday, the 26th instant, and Annapolis being the place, in which, according to law, it must assemble; and having been credibly informed that you have taken military possession of the Annapolis and Elk Ridge Railroad, I deem it my duty to protest against this step; because, without at present assigning any other reason, I am informed that such occupation of said road will prevent the members of the Legislature from reaching this city.

Very respectfully yours,
THOMAS H. HICKS.

To which Gen. BUTLER replied as follows:

HEAD-QUARTERS U. S. MILITIA, }
ANNAPOLIS, Md., April 23, 1861. }

To His Excellency Thomas H. Hicks, Governor of Maryland:

You are credibly informed that I have taken possession of the Annapolis and Elk Ridge Railroad. It might have escaped your notice, but at the official meeting which was had, between your Excellency and the Mayor of Annapolis, and the Committee of the Government

and myself, as to the landing of my troops, it was expressly stated as the reason why I should not land, that my troops could not pass the railroad because the company had taken up the rails, and they were private property. It is difficult to see how it can be, that if my troops could not pass over the railroad one way, the members of the Legislature could pass the other way. I have taken possession for the purpose of preventing the execution of the threats of the mob, as officially represented to me by the Master of Transportation of the railroad in this city, "that if my troops passed over the railroad, the railroad should be destroyed."

If the Government of the State had taken possession of the road in any emergency, I should have long hesitated before entering upon it; but as I had the honor to inform your Excellency in regard to another insurrection against the laws of Maryland, I am here armed to maintain those laws, if your Excellency desires, and the peace of the United States, against all disorderly persons whatsoever. I am endeavoring to save and not to destroy; to obtain means of transportation, so that I can vacate the Capital prior to the sitting of the Legislature, and not be under the painful necessity of incumbering your beautiful city while the Legislature is in session.

I have the honor to be, very respectfully,
Your Excellency's obedient servant,
B. F. BUTLER, Brig.-Gen.

Doc. 94.—PROCLAMATION OF GOV. MAGOFFIN, APRIL 24.

RECENT events are of so startling a character as to render it imperatively necessary that the Legislature of Kentucky be again convened in extraordinary session. It is now apparent that the most energetic measures are being resorted to by the Government at Washington to prosecute a war upon an extended scale with the seceded States. Already large sums of money and supplies of men are being raised in the Northern States for that purpose. The tread of armies is the response which is being made to the measures of pacification which are being discussed before our people; whilst up to this moment we are comparatively in a defenceless attitude.

Whatever else should be done, it is, in my judgment, the duty of Kentucky, without delay, to place herself in a complete position for defence. The causes for apprehension are now certainly grave enough to impel every Kentuckian to demand that this be done, and to require of the Legislature of the State such additional action as may be necessary for the general welfare. To this end, I now call upon the members of the General Assembly to convene at the Capitol in Frankfort, on the 6th day of May, 1861.

In testimony whereof I, Beriah Magoffin, Governor of the Commonwealth of Kentucky,

have hereunto subscribed my name and caused the seal of the Commonwealth to be affixed. Done at the city of Frankfort, the 24th day of April, 1861, and in the sixty-ninth year of the Commonwealth. B. MAGOFFIN.
By the Governor.
THOS. B. MONROE, Secretary of State.
By JAS. W. TATE, Assistant Secretary.
—*N. O. Picayune*, April 28.

DOC. 95.—SPEECH OF GENERAL CASS AT DETROIT, APRIL 24, 1861.

FELLOW-CITIZENS:—I am sorry you have not selected a chairman to preside over your assemblage more accustomed to such a task and more competent to fulfil it than I am. But while feeling my incompetency, I am encouraged by the hope that I shall find in your kind regard an excuse for any errors I may commit—believing it is my duty, while I can do but little, to do all I can to manifest the deep interest I feel in the restoration to peace and good order and submission to the law of every portion of this glorious Republic.

I cannot take this seat without contrasting the situation in which I now find myself with that in which I was placed on this very spot almost fifty years ago.

Then, in the days of our weakness, we were subjected to dishonorable capitulation brought about by the imbecility of the leader; while now, in the days of our strength, neither treason nor weakness can permanently affect the holy cause to which all hands and hearts are pledged. (Applause.) Then our contest was a legitimate war waged with a foreign foe; our war to-day is a domestic one, commenced by and bringing in its train acts which no right feeling man can contemplate without most painful regret. But a few short months since, and we were the first and happiest nation on the face of the globe. In the midst of this prosperity, without a single foe to assail us, without a single injury at home caused by the operations of the Government to affect us, this glorious Union, acquired by the blood and sacrifices of our fathers, has been disowned and rejected by a portion of the States composing it,—Union which has given us more blessings than any previous Government ever conferred upon man.

Here, thank God—its ensign floats proudly and safely—(applause)—and no American can see its folds spread out to the breeze without feeling a thrill of pride at his heart, and without recalling the splendid deeds it has witnessed in many a bloody contest, from the day of Bunker's Hill to our time. (Applause.) And that flag, your worthy Mayor has, by the direction of the municipal authority, hung upon the dome above us. The loyal American people can defend it, and the deafening cheers which meet us to-day are a sure pledge that they *will* defend it. (Applause.) A stern determination to do so is evinced by the preparations and patriotic devotion which are witnessed around us, and in the echoes which are brought here by every wind that blows.

You need no one to tell you what are the dangers of your country, nor what are your duties to meet and avert them. There is but one path for every true man to travel, and that is broad and plain. It will conduct us, not indeed without trials and sufferings, to peace and to the restoration of the Union. He who is not *for* his country is *against* her. (Applause.) *There is no neutral position to be occupied.* It is the duty of all zealously to support the Government in its efforts to bring this unhappy civil war to a speedy and satisfactory conclusion, by the restoration, in its integrity, of that great charter of freedom bequeathed to us by WASHINGTON and his compatriots. His ashes, I humbly trust, will ever continue to repose in the lowly tomb at Mt. Vernon, and in the United States of America, (applause,) which he loved so well, and did so much to found and build up. Manifest your regard for his memory by following, each with the compass of his power, his noble example and restore his work as he left it, by devoting heart, mind, and deed to the cause. (Loud-continued cheering.)
—*N. Y. Times*, April 29.

DOC. 96.—SPEECH OF CALEB CUSHING. APRIL 24, 1861.

GENERAL CUSHING said that he cordially participated in the present patriotic manifestations. Long may this glorious flag wave above our heads, the banner of victory and the symbol of our national honor! Our dear country now indeed demands the devotion of all people; for the dire calamity of civil war is upon us. He had labored hitherto for many years earnestly and in good faith at least, first for the conservation of the Union, and then to avert the evils of fratricidal war; and of what he might have said in that relation he had nothing now to retract. But the day of discussion had passed, and that of action had arrived. He had before him the question, which had occurred to public men in other countries, where political convulsions divided friend from friend, and brother from brother, and sometimes arrayed them against one another in hostile camps and in deadly strife. What in such a case is the dictate of duty? Should we retire into safe seclusion in a foreign country, to return in better times, to wear the honor of freedom, like Hyde? Or should we remain to confront the perils of our lot, like Falkland or Vane? The latter course, if not the safer one, is at any rate the most courageous one. He (Mr. C.) chose so to act. He was a citizen of the United States, owing allegiance to the Constitution, and bound by constitutional duty to support its Government. And he should do so. He was a son of Massachusetts, attached to her by ties of birth and affection, and from which neither friend nor foe should sever him. He would yield to no man in faithfulness to the Union, or in zeal for the maintenance of the laws and the constitutional authorities of the Union; and to that end he stood prepared, if occasion should call for it, to testify his sense of public duty by entering the field again at the command of the Commonwealth or of the Union."

Abstract of Newburyport Herald: in Nat. Intelligencer,
April 30,

Doc. 97.—GOV. LETCHER'S PROCLAMATION.

WHEREAS, in the emergency which was supposed to exist during the past week, arising from information that an invasion of the rivers of the State was about to be made, and the movements of the vessels of the United States with troops into the waters of this Commonwealth and the unusual destruction of public property by the agents of that Government, both at Harper's Ferry and at the Gosport Navy Yard, gave ample reason for such belief; and whereas, under such circumstances, sundry vessels in the waters of the James River, the Rappahannock, York, and Potomac Rivers, and their tributaries, have been seized and detained by the authorities of the State, or officers acting under patriotic motives without authority, and it is proper that such vessels and property should be promptly restored to the masters in command or to the owners thereof, therefore, I, JOHN LETCHER, Governor of the Commonwealth, do hereby proclaim that all private vessels and property so seized or detained, with the exception of the steamers Jamestown and Yorktown, shall be released and delivered up to the said masters or owners. Proper Navy officers have been assigned to each of the rivers of the State herein mentioned, with orders to release such vessels and property, and give certificates for damages incurred by the seizure and detention.

I feel it my duty, furthermore, to advise the people of the Commonwealth (not in the Military service of the State) to return to their usual avocations, in connection with the trade and commerce of the country, assuring them protection and defence. If war is to be inaugurated by an attempt to invade this Commonwealth, or to use coercion against the Southern Confederate States, a contingency dependent on the action of the Government of the United States, it shall be met and conducted by this Commonwealth upon principles worthy of civilized nations and of this enlightened age. I appeal to all our people not to interfere with peaceable, unoffending citizens or others who preserve the peace and conform to our laws, and I do hereby especially discountenance all acts of seizure of private property without authority of law, and require that order shall be restored, and that all the laws be administered and executed by the tribunals especially assigned for the purpose.

{ L. S. } Given under my hand as Governor, and under the seal of the Commonwealth at Richmond, 24th of April, 1861, and in the 85th year of the Commonwealth.

JOHN LETCHER.

By the Governor.
GEORGE W. MUNFORD,
Secretary of the Commonwealth.

The following officers of the State Navy are assigned to the duties required by this proclamation:

For James River—Captain Cooke and Commander Tucker.

For Potomac River—Captain Forrest, Lieutenant Semmes.

For Rappahannock River—Lieutenant Davis.

For York River—Commander J. L. Henderson and Lieut. S. S. Maury.

—*Richmond Inquirer.*

Doc. 98.—CAPTURE OF U. S. TROOPS BY COL. VAN DORN, AT SALURIA.

COL. VAN DORN arrived at Indianola with about 800 Texas volunteers, on Wednesday afternoon, 24th April, and having taken possession of the U. S. steamers Fashion and United States, and the propeller Mobile, without delay placed his forces on them, and about nine o'clock at night, came down to Saluria and anchored within about half a mile of the schooners having on board the U. S. troops, numbering 450, under the command of Major C. C. Sibley, 3d Infantry; Adjutant-Lieutenant Phillips, 1st Infantry; Ass't Surgeons Lynde and Byrne, Capts. Granger and Wallace, 1st Infantry; Capt. Bowman, 3d Infantry; Capt. Jordan, 8th Infantry; Lieut. Green, 1st Infantry, and Lieuts. Hopkins and Lay, 3d Infantry. The troops consisted of the band of the 1st Infantry, and Companies G and K of that Regiment, Companies A, F, and I, 3d Infantry, and Companies A and D of the 8th Infantry. Capt. Wallace had his lady and child, and Dr. Lynde his two children, on board the vessels. Notwithstanding some thirty-five soldiers and their wives had been left on shore, there were some ten or twelve women and children on board.

About three o'clock in the afternoon a severe norther sprang up, and a heavy sea raged from that time till the afternoon of Thursday. Nevertheless, at about six o'clock on that morning, Col. Van Dorn sent a message to Major Sibley requesting an interview at such point as might be convenient. Accordingly, the parlor of Judge Hawes, on Saluria Island, was selected, and at ten o'clock the parties met.—The commission on the part of the U. S. Army consisted of Major Sibley and his two senior officers, Capts. Wallace and Granger; and on the part of the Confederate States, Col. Van Dorn. At about 12 o'clock M., the conference ended in the surrender of the entire command as prisoners of war—the officers to be released on parole, and the men on their oaths that they would not take up arms against the Southern Confederacy,—surrendering their arms and all company property; such of the men and officers to be received into the Confederate army as may desire it; private property not to be molested; the soldiers not to be permitted to leave the State except by way of Galveston and the Mississippi River.

At one o'clock, P. M., the steamer Gen. Rusk, Capt. Leon Smith, having on board Gen. E. B. Nichols with 150 volunteers from Galveston, appeared off the bar. She came to near the pilot house, and upon the pilot coming on board learned the good news of the surrender which was then being carried into execution without a resort to the use of arms. Before the Rusk crossed the bar the officers on board, with their glasses, could distinctly see the troops on the two schooners, as also the three steamers with steam up having on board soldiers, (the Texas volunteers,) and as they could not suppose Col. Van Dorn had had time to concentrate his forces there, the conclusion with them was that the U. S. troops had been reinforced from the west by companies known to be coming down, and, consequently, that the men on the Rusk had a pretty fair prospect of a fight.

The Rusk remained at anchor until 10 o'clock, P. M., when she went up to Indianola, put out her mails, and went down to Saluria at sun-up yesterday morning, when, after taking on board Capt. W. R. Bradfute, bearer of dispatches from Major Van Dorn to Montgomery, as well as a considerable number of passengers, crossed the bar at 10 o'clock, and came into this port at 12 o'clock last night.

The 450 United States troops who had surrendered were on the schooners Horace and Urbana in charge of Col. Van Dorn when the Rusk left last night. They had gone down the bay on these schooners with a view of being embarked on the Fashion, but this steamer was deemed unseaworthy, and the United States was not in a much better condition, while the propeller Mobile was too small for their accommodation. It is expected that they will go on shore again to-day, and that most of them will enlist in the army of the Confederate States.

We see from Gen. Nichols' report to Gen. Sherman, that in less than an hour after the Rusk took position so as to command the schooners with the U. S. troops on board, he reported himself to Col. Van Dorn, and received in reply, that the surrender had just been agreed on.

Major Larkin Smith, who, we believe, was second in command at Indianola, resigned immediately on hearing of the secession of Virginia; and we learn his example was followed by some six or eight other United States officers.

—*Galveston (Texas) News,* April 27.

Doc. 99.—GEORGE LAW'S LETTER.

New-York, April 25, 1861.

To the President of the United States— *Sir:* The people of the Free States have now been for some time cut off from communication with the capital of their country, by a mob in the city of Baltimore. The troops of the General Government have been attacked and shot down by the mob, in their passage through that city in pursuance to the orders of the Government. The lines of communication have been destroyed, and the authority of the General Government has been set at defiance. This state of things has been permitted to continue for nearly a week, and our troops going to the capital have been delayed, and have had to find their way by irregular and circuitous routes, very much to their inconvenience. Citizens of the Free States have either been prevented altogether from visiting the capital or from returning thence to their homes, or have been compelled to run the gauntlet, been subjected to all sorts of insult and danger, and have had to resort to the most circuitous routes by private conveyance, and at exorbitant expense. All facilities by mail and telegraph have been cut off by the same unlawful assemblage in Baltimore and other parts of Maryland, at a time when free communication is so much required between the Free States and Washington.

The public mind is already excited to the highest point that this state of things has been so long tolerated; and the people are determined that free and uninterrupted communication with the seat of Government shall be immediately established, not by circuitous routes, but by the direct lines of communication that they have heretofore travelled over. And it *is demanded of Government that they at once take measures to open and establish those lines of communication, and that they protect and preserve them from any further interruption. Unless this is done, the people will be compelled to take it into their own hands, let the consequence be what they may, and let them fall where they will.* It is certainly most desirable that this be done through the regularly constituted authorities at Washington; and the Government is earnestly desired to act without delay.

There is entire unanimity of feeling on the part of the people of the Free States to sustain the Government and maintain the Union.

I trust, Mr. President, that this letter will not be received unkindly, as, in writing it, I simply do what I feel it to be my duty as a citizen to do in this extraordinary state of things.

I have the honor to be, sir, your most obedient servant, George Law.

—*N. Y. Tribune,* April 26.

Doc. 100.—HOW THE ARMS WERE TAKEN FROM THE ST. LOUIS ARSENAL.

Captain James H. Stokes, of Chicago, late of the regular army, volunteered to undertake the perilous mission, and Governor Yates placed in his hands the requisition of the Secretary of war for 10,000 muskets. Captain Stokes went to St. Louis, and made his way as rapidly as possible to the arsenal. He found it surrounded by an immense mob, and the postern gates all closed. His utmost efforts to penetrate the crowd were for a long time unavailing. The requisition was shown. Captain Lyon doubted the possibility of executing it. He said the arsenal was surrounded by a thousand spies, and every movement was watched and reported to the headquarters of the Secessionists, who could throw an overpowering force upon them at any moment. Captain Stokes represented that every hour's delay was rendering the capture of the arsenal more certain, and the arms must be moved to Illinois now or never. Major Callender agreed with him, and told him to take them at his own time and in his own way. This was Wednesday night, 24th April.

Capt. Stokes had a spy in the camp, whom he met at intervals in a certain place in the city. On Thursday he received information that Gov. Jackson had ordered two thousand armed men down from Jefferson city, whose movements could only contemplate a seizure of the arsenal, by occupying the heights around it, and planting batteries thereon. The job would have been an easy one. They had already planted one battery on the St. Louis levee, and another at Powder Point, a short distance below the arsenal. Capt. Stokes immediately telegraphed to Alton to have the steamer *City of Alton* drop down to the arsenal landing about midnight. He then returned to the arsenal, and commenced moving the boxes of guns, weighing some three hundred pounds each, down to the lower floor.

About 700 men were employed in the work. He then took 500 Kentucky flint-lock muskets, which had been sent there to be altered, and sent them to be placed on a steamer as a blind to cover his real movements. The Secessionists nabbed them at once, and raised a perfect Bedlam over the capture. A large portion of the outside crowd left the arsenal when this movement was executed; and Capt. Lyon took the remainder, who were lying around as spies, and locked them up in the guard-house. About 11 o'clock the steamer *City of Alton* came alongside, planks were shoved out from the windows to the main deck, and the boxes slid down. When the 10,000 were safely on board, Capt. Stokes went to Capt. Lyon and Major Callender, and urged them, by the most pressing appeals, to let him empty the arsenal. They told him to go ahead and take whatever he wanted. Accordingly, he took 10,000 more muskets, 500 new rifle carbines, 500 revolvers, 110,000 musket cartridges, to say nothing of the cannon and a large quantity of miscellaneous accoutrements, leaving only 7,000 muskets in the arsenal to arm the St. Louis volunteers.

When the whole were on board, about 2 o'clock on Friday morning the order was given by the captain of the steamer to cast off. Judge of the consternation of all hands when it was found that she would not move. The arms had been piled in great quantities around the engines to protect them against the battery on the levee, and the great weight had fastened the bows of the boat firmly on a rock, which was tearing a hole through the bottom at every turn of the wheels. A man of less nerve than Capt. Stokes would have gone crazy on the spot. He called the arsenal men on board, and commenced moving the boxes to the stern.

Fortunately, when about two hundred boxes had been shifted, the boat fell away from the shore, and floated in deep water. "Which way?" said Captain Mitchell, of the steamer. "Straight to Alton, in the regular channel," replied Captain Stokes. "What if we are attacked?" said Captain Mitchell. "Then we will fight," said Captain Stokes. "What if we are overpowered?" said Captain Mitchell. "Run her to the deepest part of the river, and sink her," replied Captain Stokes. "I'll do it," was the heroic answer of Capt. Mitchell; and away they went past the secession battery, past the entire St. Louis levee, and on to Alton, in the regular channel, where they arrived at five o'clock in the morning.

When the boat touched the landing, Capt. Stokes, fearing pursuit by some two or three of the Secession military companies by which the city of St. Louis is disgraced, ran to the market-house and rang the fire-bell. The citizens came flocking pell-mell to the river, in all sorts of habiliments. Capt. Stokes informed them of the situation of things, and pointed out the freight cars. Instantly, men, women, and children boarded the steamer, seized the freight, and clambered up the levees to the cars. Rich and poor tugged together with might and main for two hours, when the cargo was all deposited in the cars, and the train moved off, amid their enthusiastic cheers, for Springfield.

—*Chicago Tribune*, April 29.

Doc. 101.—THE SEVENTH REGIMENT.—

HOW IT GOT FROM NEW YORK TO WASHINGTON.

The Capitol, Washington, }
Saturday, April 27, 1861. }

We are here. Those three words sum up as much as Napier's "Peccavi," when he took Scinde, and we all feel somewhat as Mr. Cæsar Augustus must have felt when he had crossed the Rubicon.

It is almost unnecessary for me to detail to you the events of the day on which we left New York. The indefatigable efforts of that ubiquitous and persevering individual, the reporter, has left me little to do. Nevertheless, the scene at the armory on Friday was one to be commemorated. For the first time since its formation, the Seventh Regiment left its native city on active service. All day long, from an early hour in the morning, young men in uniforms or civilian's dress, might have been seen hurrying up and down Broadway, with anomalous-looking bundles under their arms. Dandies, who were the pride of club windows, were not above brown paper parcels; military tailors were stormed and taken with considerable loss—to the pocket. Delmonico, calm and serene, superintended sandwiches which were destined for the canteen. People in the streets looked with a sort of regretful admiration at the gray uniforms hurrying by. Hardware stores were ransacked of revolvers. A feverish excitement throbbed through the city—the beating of that big Northern pulse, so slow, so sure, and so steady.

At 3 o'clock, P. M., we mustered at the Armory, against which there beat a surge of human beings like waves against a rock. Within, all was commotion. Fitting of belts, wild lamentations over uniforms expected but not arrived. Hearty exchanges of comradeships between members of different companies, who felt that they were about to depart on a mission which might end in death. Here and there flickered Spring bonnets, which inclosed charming faces, as the calyx enfolds the flower; and, let me tell you, that on the faces of many of those dear blossoms there hung drops of mournful dew. At last the regiment was formed in companies, and we marched. Was there ever such an ovation? When Trajan returned conqueror, dragging barbaric kings at his chariot-wheels, Rome vomited its people into the streets, and that glorious column, that will be ever immortal, was raised. But what greeted the Emperor at his outset? The marble walls of Broadway were never before rent with such cheers as greeted us when we passed. The faces of the buildings were so thick with people, that it seemed as if an army of black ants were marching, after their resistless fashion, through the city, and had scaled the houses. Handkerchiefs fluttered in the air like myriads of white butterflies. An avenue of brave, honest faces smiled upon us as we passed, and sent a sunshine into our hearts that lives there still. In a prominent position stood Major Anderson, who saluted us, and was welcomed as such a man should be welcomed. And so on to the ferry.

Swift through New Jersey—against which no sneer be uttered evermore. All along the track shouting crowds, hoarse and valorous, sent to us, as we passed, their hopes and wishes. When we stopped at the different stations, rough hands came in through the windows, apparently unconnected with any one in particular until you shook them, and then the subtle magnetic thrill told that there were bold hearts beating at the end. This continued until night closed, and, indeed, until after midnight.

Within the cars the sight was strange. A thousand young men, the flower of the North, in whose welfare a million of friends and relatives were interested, were rushing along to conjectured hostilities with the same smiling faces that they would wear going to a "German" party in Fifth avenue. It was more like a festivity than a march. Those fine old songs, the chorusses of which were familiar to all, were sung with sweet voice. We were assured many times, in melodious accents, that "the whiskey bottle was empty on the shelf," and several individuals of that prominent, but not respectable class known as "bummers," were invited to "meet us on Canaan's happy shore." The brave old Harvard song of "Upi dee" was started, and, shameful to say, Mr. Longfellow's "Excelsior" seemed naturally to adapt itself to the 'tune. I do not think that "the pious monks of St. Bernard" would have been edified, had they heard themselves alluded to in that profane music.

Our arrival at Philadelphia took place at 4 o'clock. We slept in the cars, awaiting orders from our Colonel, but at daylight hunger—and it may be thirst—becoming imperious, we sallied out, and roamed about that cheerless neighborhood that surrounds the depot. Close by there was a small wooden shanty—let us say an Irish palace—which was presently filled by arid soldiers. The prog in the larder of this sumptuous residence was, I regret to say, limited. I did not even see the traditional pig about, although heaven knows he would have been appropriate enough. Finding that we were likely to remain for some time in the city —although under the impression that we were to go straight through to Baltimore—we wandered away from the Desert of the Depot and descended on civilized quarters. The superintendent of the Deaf and Dumb Asylum was a man for the emergency. He provided a handsome breakfast for all such members of the Seventh as chose to partake of it, and we commanded beefsteak on our fingers, and ordered tea by sign-manual. Great numbers of our regiment, being luxurious dogs, went down to the Continental and Girard hotels, where they campaigned on marble floors, and bivouacked on velvet couches. They are such delicate fellows, the Seventh Regiment! Further on you will see what those delicate hands have done.

We, of course, were entirely ignorant of our route, or how we were going. The general feeling of the regiment was in favor of pushing our way *coute qui coute* straight through Baltimore. Rumors came along that the city was in arms. The Massachusetts troops had to fight their way through, killing eighteen and losing two men. This seemed only to stimulate our boys, and the universal word was Baltimore. But as it turned out afterwards, we were under a wise direction, and the policy of our Colonel, to whom we perhaps are altogether indebted for bringing us safe here, was, I presume, to avoid all unnecessary collision, and bring his regiment intact into Washington. The rails were reported to have been torn up for forty miles about Baltimore, and as we were summoned for the defence of the Capital, it follows, according to reason, that if we could get there without loss we would better fulfil our duty. As it happened afterwards, we had to run through more peril than Baltimore could have offered.

There seemed but little enthusiasm in Philadelphia. A city that washes every morning with soap and water is not easily roused into excitement. The Quaker placidity still prevails, and when you add to this the majestic stolidity on the German element, it is not wonderful that the Capital of the Keystone State should not be uproarious. Still let me do Philadelphia justice. I understand that the people were out in large numbers to see us enter, but our delay disappointed them, and they went home. During our stay a lethargic decorum prevailed. The prim beavers of the citizens were glossy and self-possessed. We came and went without a reception or demonstration.

There was one peculiar difference that I noticed existing between the Massachusetts regiments that we met in Philadelphia and our men. The Massachusetts men—to whom all honor be given for the splendid manner in which they afterwards acted in a most trying situation—presented a singular moral contrast to the members of the Seventh. They were earnest, grim, determined. Badly equipped, haggard, unshorn, they yet had a manhood in their look that hardships could not kill. They were evidently thinking all the time of the contest into which they were about to enter. Their gray, eager eyes seemed to be looking for the heights of Virginia. With us, it was somewhat different. Our men were gay and careless, confident of being at any moment capable of performing, and more than performing, their duty. They looked battle in the face with a smile, and were ready to hob-nob with an enemy and kill him afterwards. The one was courage in the rough; the other was courage burnished. The steel was the same in both, but the last was a little more polished.

On April 20, at 4.20, P. M., we left the Philadelphia dock, on board the steamer Boston. The regiment was in entire ignorance of its destination. Some said we were going back to New York, at which suggestion there was a howl of indignation. Others presumed that we were going to steam up the Potomac—a course which was not much approved of, inasmuch that we were cooped up in a kind of river steamer that a shot from the fort at Alexandria might sink at any moment. We, however—to make use of a familiar expression—"went it blind," and the faces did not smile the less because our object was unknown.

It was on board of this steamer that "Joe" came out. You, of course, don't know who "Joe" is. Well, you may rest contented, because he will always remain "Joe" to you. I may, without transgression, however, give you his typograph. I will put him in position, level the lens, and—here he is. Imagine a well-built young fellow of about 21, with mercury instead of blood in his veins, ever on the move, with a sort of quaint, joyous humor

seething from him, as if he was always at boiling point. Joe's two specialties, like a winnowing machine that I once saw, are work and chaff. During the evening on board the steamer he distributed himself generally about, with a merry word and a joke for every one. What number of bad puns he made, or what horrible conundrums he made, my exhausted and horrified memory refuses to recall; suffice it to say, that laughter and good-humor followed in his wake, as the white foam smiles astern of some sharp little cutter going before the wind.

The first evening, April 20, on board the Boston, passed delightfully. We were all in first-rate spirits, and the calm, sweet evenings that stole on us as we approached the South, diffused a soft and gentle influence over us. The scene on board the ship was exceedingly picturesque. Fellows fumbling in haversacks for rations, or extracting sandwiches from reluctant canteens; guards pacing up and down with drawn bayonets; knapsacks piled in corners, bristling heaps of muskets, with sharp, shining teeth, crowded into every available nook; picturesque groups of men lolling on deck, pipe or cigar in mouth, indulged in the *dolce far niente*, as if they were on the blue shores of Capri rather than on their way to battle; unbuttoned jackets, crossed legs, heads leaning on knapsacks, blue uniforms everywhere, with here and there a glint of officers' red lighting up the foreground—all formed a scene that such painters as the English Warren would have revelled in.

I regret to say that all was not rose-colored. The steamer that the Colonel chartered had to get ready at three or four hours' notice, he having changed his plans, in consequence of the tearing up of the rails around Baltimore. The result was that she was imperfectly provisioned. As the appetites of the men began to develop, the resources of the vessel began to appear. In the first place, she was far too small to accommodate a thousand men, and we were obliged to sleep in all sorts of impossible attitudes. There is an ingenious device known to carpenters as "dove-tailing," and we were so thick that we had positively to dove-tail, only that there was very little of the dove about it; for when perambulating soldiers stepped on the faces and stomachs of the sleepers, as they lay on deck, the greeting that they received had but little flavor of the olive branch.

Notwithstanding that we found very soon that the commissariat was in a bad way, the men were as jolly as sandboys. I never saw a more good-humored set of men in my life. Fellows who would at Delmonico's have sent back a *turban de volaille aux truffes* because the truffles were tough, here cheerfully took their places in file between decks, tin plates and tin cups in hand, in order to get an insufficient piece of beef and a vision of coffee. But it was all merrily done. The scant fare was seasoned with hilarity; and here I say to those people in New York who have sneered at the

Seventh Regiment as being dandies, and guilty of the unpardonable crimes of cleanliness and kid gloves, that they would cease to scoff and remain to bless, had they beheld the square, honest, genial way in which these military Brummells roughed it. Farther on you will see what they did in the way of endurance and activity.

April 21 was Sunday. A glorious, cloudless day. We had steamed all night, and about 10 o'clock were in the vicinity of Chesapeake Bay. At 11 o'clock, A. M., we had service read by our chaplain, and at 1, P. M., we were seven miles from the coast. The day was calm and delicious. In spite of our troubles with regard to food—troubles, be it understood, entirely unavoidable—we drank in with delight the serenity of the scene. A hazy tent of blue hung over our heads. On one side the dim thread of shore hemmed in the sea. Flights of loons and ducks skimmed along the ocean, rising lazily, and spattering the waves with their wings as they flew against the wind, until they rose into air, and, wheeling, swept into calmer feeding grounds. Now and then the calm of the hour was broken with the heavy tramp of men, and the metallic voice of the corporal of the guard relieving his comrades. At 5 o'clock, P. M., we passed a light-ship and hailed her, our object being to discover whether any United States vessels were in the neighborhood waiting to convoy us up the Potomac River. We had heard that the forts at Alexandria were ready to open upon us if we attempted to pass up, and our steamer was of such a build that, had a shell or shot struck it, we would have been burned or drowned. It therefore behooved us to be cautious. The answers we got from the light-ship and other vessels that we hailed in this spot were unsatisfactory, and although the feelings of the men were unanimous in wishing to force the Potomac, wiser counsels, as it proved, were behind us, and we kept on. About this time a curious phenomenon occurred. Some men in the regiment who have fine voices—and their name is legion—had been singing, with all that delicious effect that music at sea produces, several of the finest psalms in our liturgy. The ocean softens and delicately repeats sound, and those airs, trembling and sliding along the almost unrippled surface of the sea, were so melodious, that if the Southern Cerberi had heard them, they would have slumbered at the gates of their own hell. While we were singing, the moon swung clear into air, and round her white disk was seen three circles, clear and distinct—*red, white, and blue!* The omen was caught by common instinct, and a thousand cheers went up to that heaven that seemed in its visible signs to manifest its approval of the cause in which we were about to fight. All this time we were entirely ignorant of where we were going. The officers kept all secret, and our conjectures drifted like a drifting boat. On the morning of the 22d we were in sight of Annapolis, off which

the Constitution was lying, and there found the Eighth Regiment of Massachusetts volunteers, on board the Maryland. They were aground, owing, it is supposed, to the treachery of the captain, whom they put in irons, and wanted to hang. I regret to say that they did not do it. During the greater portion of that forenoon we were occupied in trying to get the Maryland off the sandbar on which she was grounded. From our decks we could see the men in file trying to rock her, so as to facilitate our tugging. These men were without water and without food, were well conducted and uncomplaining, and behaved, in all respects, like heroes. They were under the command of Col. Butler, and I regret that that gentleman did not care more for the comforts of men whose subsequent pluck proved that nothing was too good for them. During the endeavors to get the Maryland afloat, we had some idle time on our hands, and your humble servant employed some of it in "composing" a Seventh Regiment song, which is now in rehearsal by the vocalists of the corps.[*]

On the afternoon of the 22d we landed at the Annapolis dock, after having spent hours in trying to relieve the Maryland. For the first time in his life your correspondent was put to work to roll flour-barrels. He was entrusted with the honorable and onerous duty of transporting stores from the steamer to the dock. Later still he descended to the position of mess servant, when, in company with gentlemen well known in Broadway for immaculate kids, he had the honor of attending on his company with buckets of cooked meat and crackers. The only difference between him and Co. and the ordinary waiter being, that the former were civil.

After this I had the pleasing duty of performing three hours of guard duty on the dock with a view to protect the baggage and stores. It was monotonous—being my first guard—but not unpleasant. The moon rose calm and white. A long dock next to the one on which I was stationed stretched away into the bay, resting on its numerous piles, until it looked in the clear moonlight like a centipede. All was still and calm, until at certain periods the guard challenged persons attempting to pass. There was a holy influence in the hour, and somehow the hot fever of anxiety that had been over us for days seemed to pass away under the touch of the magnetic fingers of the night.

We were quartered in the buildings belonging to the Naval School at Annapolis. I had a bunking-place in what is there called a fort, which is a rickety structure, that a lucifer match would set on fire, but furnished with imposing guns. I suppose it was merely built to practice the cadets, because as a defence it is worthless. The same evening boats were sent off from the yard, and towards nightfall the Massachusetts men landed, fagged, hungry,

[*] See song entitled "The Seventh," at page 17, Poetry and Incidents.

thirsty, but indomitable. At an early hour there was a universal snore through the Naval School of Annapolis.

The two days that we remained at Annapolis were welcome. We had been without a fair night's sleep since we left New York, and even the hard quarters we had there were a luxury compared to the dirty decks of the Boston. Besides, there were natural attractions. The grounds are very prettily laid out, and in the course of my experience I never saw a handsomer or better bred set of young men than the cadets. They number about ——, only twenty having left the school owing to political conviction. The remainder are sound Union fellows, eager to prove their devotion to the flag. After spending a delightful time in the Navy School, resting and amusing ourselves, our repose was disturbed, at 9, P. M., April 23, by rockets being thrown up in the bay. The men were scattered all over the grounds; some in bed, others walking or smoking, all more or less undressed. The rockets being of a suspicious character, it was conjectured that a Southern fleet was outside, and our drummer beat the roll-call to arms. From the stroke of the drum, until the time that every man, fully equipped and in fighting order, was in the ranks, was exactly, by watch, *seven minutes.* It is needless to say any thing about such celerity—it speaks for itself. The alarm, however, proved to be false, the vessels in the offing proving to be laden with the Seventy-first and other New York regiments; so that, after an unpremeditated trial of our readiness for action, we were permitted to retire to our virtuous couches, which means, permit me to say, a blanket on the floor, with a military overcoat over you, and a nasal concert all around you, that, in noise and number, outvies Musard's celebrated *concerts monstres.*

On the morning of the 24th of April we started on what afterwards proved to be one of the hardest marches on record. The Secessionists of Annapolis and the surrounding district had threatened to cut us off in our march, and even went so far as to say that they would attack our quarters. This, of course, was the drunken Southern ebullition. A civilian told me that he met in the streets of Annapolis two cavalry soldiers who came to cut our throats without delay, but as each brave warrior was endeavoring to hold the other up, my friend did not apprehend much danger.

A curious revulsion of feeling took place at Annapolis, and indeed all through Maryland, after our arrival.

The admirable good conduct which characterizes the regiment, the open liberality which it displays in all pecuniary transactions, and the courteous demeanor which it exhibits to all classes, took the narrow-minded population of this excessively wretched town by surprise. They were prepared for pillage. They thought we were going to sack the place. They found, instead, that we were prepared and willing to pay liberal prices for every thing, and that even patriotic presentations were steadily refused. While we were in the Navy School, of course all sorts of rumors as to our operations were floating about. It surprised me that no one suggested that we were to go off in a balloon; however, all surmises were put to an end by our receiving orders, the evening of the 23d, to assemble in marching order next morning. The dawn saw us up. Knapsacks, with our blankets and overcoats strapped on them, were piled on the green. A brief and insufficient breakfast was taken, our canteens filled with vinegar and water, cartridges distributed to each man, and after mustering and loading, we started on our first march through a hostile country.

Gen. Scott has stated, as I have been informed, that the march that we performed from Annapolis to the Junction is one of the most remarkable on record. I know that I felt it the most fatiguing, and some of our officers have told me that it was the most perilous. We marched the first eight miles under a burning sun, in heavy marching order, in less than three hours; and it is well known that, placing all elementary considerations out of the way, marching on a railroad track is the most harassing. We started at about 8 o'clock, A. M., and for the first time saw the town of Annapolis, which, without any disrespect to that place, I may say, looked very much as if some celestial schoolboy, with a box of toys under his arm, had dropped a few houses and men as he was going home from school, and that the accidental settlement was called Annapolis. Through the town we marched, the people unsympathizing, but afraid. They saw the Seventh for the first time, and for the first time they realized the men that they had threatened.

The tracks had been torn up between Annapolis and the Junction, and here it was that the wonderful qualities of the Massachusetts Eighth Regiment came out. The locomotives had been taken to pieces by the inhabitants, in order to prevent our travel. In steps a Massachusetts volunteer, looks at the piece-meal engine, takes up a flange, and says coolly, "I made this engine, and I can put it together again." Engineers were wanted when the engine was ready. Nineteen stepped out of the ranks. The rails were torn up. Practical railroad makers out of the regiment laid them again, and all this, mind you, without care or food. These brave boys, I say, were starving while they were doing this good work. What their Colonel was doing, I can't say. As we marched along the track that they had laid, they greeted us with ranks of smiling but hungry faces. One boy told me, with a laugh on his young lips, that he had not eaten any thing for thirty hours. There was not, thank God, a haversack in our regiment that was not emptied into the hands of these ill-treated heroes, nor a flask that was not at their disposal. I am glad to pay them tribute here, and mentally doff my cap.

Our march lay through an arid, sandy, tobacco-growing country. The sun poured on our heads like hot lava. The Sixth and Second companies were sent on for skirmishing duty, under the command of Captains Clarke and Nevers, the latter commanding as senior officer. A car, on which was placed a howitzer, loaded with grape and canister, headed the column, manned by the engineer and artillery corps, commanded by Lieut. Bunting. This was the rallying point of the skirmishing party, on which, in case of difficulty, they could fall back. In the centre of the column came the cars laden with medical stores, and bearing our sick and wounded, while the extreme rear was brought up with a second howitzer, loaded also with grape and canister. The engineer corps, of course, had to do the forwarding work. New York dandies, sir—but they built bridges, laid rails, and headed the regiment through that terrible march. After marching about eight miles, during which time several men caved in from exhaustion, and one young gentleman was sunstruck and sent back to New York, we halted, and instantly, with the Divine instinct which characterizes the hungry soldier, proceeded to forage. The worst of it was there was no foraging to be done. The only house within reach was inhabited by a lethargic person, who, like most Southern men, had no idea of gaining money by labor. We offered him extravagant prices to get us fresh water, and it was with the utmost reluctance we could get him to obtain us a few pailfuls. Over the mantel-piece of his miserable shanty I saw—a curious coincidence—the portrait of Col. Duryea, of our regiment.

After a brief rest of about an hour, we again commenced our march; a march which lasted until the next morning—a march than which in history, nothing but those marches in which defeated troops have fled from the enemy, can equal. Our Colonel, it seems, determined to march by railroad, in preference to the common road, inasmuch as he had obtained such secret information as led him to suppose that we were waited for on the latter route. Events justified his judgment. There were cavalry troops posted in defiles to cut us off. They could not have done it, of course, but they could have harassed us severely. As we went along the railroad we threw out skirmishing parties from the Second and Sixth companies, to keep the road clear. I know not if I can describe that night's march. I have dim recollections of deep cuts through which we passed, gloomy and treacherous-looking, with the moon shining full on our muskets, while the banks were wrapped in shade, and each moment expecting to see the flash and hear the crack of the rifle of the Southern guerilla. The tree frogs and lizards made a mournful music as we passed. The soil on which we travelled was soft and heavy. The sleepers lying at intervals across the track made the march terribly fatiguing. On all sides dark, lonely pine woods stretched away, and high

over the hooting of owls or the plaintive petition of the whip-poor-will rose the bass commands of Halt! Forward, march!—and when we came to any ticklish spot, the word would run from the head of the column along the line, "Holes," "Bridge, pass it along," &c.

As the night wore on the monotony of the march became oppressive. Owing to our having to explore every inch of the way, we did not make more than a mile or a mile and a half an hour. We ran out of stimulants, and almost out of water. Most of us had not slept for four nights, and as the night advanced our march was almost a stagger. This was not so much fatigue as want of excitement. Our fellows were spoiling for a fight, and when a dropping shot was heard in the distance, it was wonderful to see how the languid legs straightened, and the column braced itself for action. If we had had even the smallest kind of a skirmish the men would have been able to walk to Washington. As it was, we went sleepily on. I myself fell asleep walking in the ranks. Numbers, I find, followed my example; but never before was there shown such indomitable pluck and perseverance as the Seventh showed in that march of twenty miles. The country that we passed through seemed to have been entirely deserted. The inhabitants, who were going to kill us when they thought we daren't come through, now vamosed their respective ranches, and we saw them not. Houses were empty. The population retired into the interior, burying their money, and carrying their families along with them. They, it seems, were under the impression that we came to ravage and pillage, and they fled as the Gauls must have fled when Attila and his Huns came down on them from the North. As we did at Annapolis, we did in Maryland State. We left an impression that cannot be forgotten. Every thing was paid for. No discourtesy was offered to any inhabitant, and the sobriety of the regiment should be an example to others. I have now to finish without bringing our journey up to here. But let that rest for my next letter. I wish, however, before I conclude, to state that nothing could have been more effective or energetic than the movements of the Engineer Corps, to whom we were indebted for the rebuilding of a bridge in an incredibly short space of time.

The secret of this forced march, as well as our unexpected descent on Annapolis, was the result of Col. Lefferts' judgment, which has since been sustained by events. Finding that the line along the Potomac was closed, and the route to Washington by Baltimore equally impracticable, he came to the conclusion that Annapolis, commanding, as it did, the route to the Capital, must of necessity be made the basis of military operations. It was important to the Government to have a free channel through which to transport troops, and this post presented the readiest means. The fact that since then all the Northern troops have passed through the line that we thus opened, is a sufficient comment on the admirable judgment that decided on the movement. It secured the integrity of the regiment, and saved lives, the loss of which would have plunged New York into mourning. Too much importance cannot be attached to this strategy. To it the Seventh Regiment is indebted for being here at present intact and sound. For the present, adieu.

F. J. O'B.
—N. Y. Times.

Doc. 102.—GOV. LETCHER'S PROCLAMATION.

By the Governor of Virginia.—A Proclamation.

WHEREAS the Convention of this Commonwealth has, on this the 25th day of April, 1861, adopted an ordinance "for the adoption of the Constitution of the Provisional Government of the Confederate States of America;" and has agreed to a "Convention between the Commonwealth of Virginia and the Confederate States of America," which it is proper should be made known to the people of this Commonwealth and to the world:

Therefore, I, John Letcher, Governor of the Commonwealth of Virginia, do hereby publish and proclaim that the following are authentic copies of the ordinance and convention aforesaid.

[L. S.] Given under my hand as Governor, and under the seal of the Commonwealth at Richmond, this twenty-fifth of April, one thousand eight hundred and sixty-one, and in the eighty-fifth year of the Commonwealth.   JOHN LETCHER.

By the Governor.
GEORGE W. MUNFORD,
Secretary of the Commonwealth.

An ordinance for the adoption of the Constitution of the Provisional Government of the Confederate States of America.

We, the delegates of the people of Virginia in Convention assembled, solemnly impressed by the perils which surround the Commonwealth, and appealing to the Searcher of hearts for the rectitude of our intentions in assuming the grave responsibility of this act, do by this ordinance, *adopt and ratify* the Constitution of the Provisional Government of the Confederate States of America, ordained and established at Montgomery, Alabama, on the eighth day of February, eighteen hundred and sixty-one; provided that this ordinance shall cease to have any legal operation or effect if the people of this Commonwealth, upon the vote directed to be taken on the ordinance of secession passed by this Convention, on the seventeenth day of April, eighteen hundred and sixty-one, shall reject the same.

A true copy.   JNO. L. EUBANK, Secretary.

Convention between the Commonwealth of Virginia and the Confederate States of America.

The Commonwealth of Virginia, looking to a speedy union of said Commonwealth and the other Slave States with the Confederate States of America, according to the provisions of the Constitution for the Provisional Government of said States, enters into the following temporary convention and agreement with said States, for the purpose of meeting pressing exigencies affecting the common rights, interests, and safety of said Commonwealth and said Confederacy.

1st. Until the union of said Commonwealth with said Confederacy shall be perfected, and said Commonwealth shall become a member of said Confederacy, according to the Constitutions of both Powers, the whole military force and military operations, offensive and defensive, of said Commonwealth, in the impending conflict with the United States, shall be under the chief control and direction of the President of said Confederate States, upon the same principles, basis, and footing as if said Commonwealth were now, and during the interval, a member of said Confederacy.

2d. The Commonwealth of Virginia will, after the consummation of the union contemplated in this Convention, and her adoption of the Constitution for a Permanent Government of said Confederate States, and she shall become a member of said Confederacy under said Permanent Constitution, if the same occur, turn over to said Confederate States all the public property, naval stores, and munitions of war, etc., she may then be in possession of, acquired from the United States, on the same terms and in like manner as the other States of said Confederacy have done in like cases.

3d. Whatever expenditures of money, if any, said Commonwealth of Virginia shall make before the Union under the Provisional Government, as above contemplated, shall be consummated, shall be met and provided for by said Confederate States.

This Convention, entered into and agreed to in the city of Richmond, Virginia, on the twenty-fourth day of April, 1861, by Alexander H. Stephens, the duly authorized Commissioner to act in the matter for the said Confederate States, and John Tyler, William Ballard Preston, Samuel McD. Moore, James P. Holcombe, James C. Bruce, and Lewis E. Harvie, parties duly authorized to act in like manner for said Commonwealth of Virginia; the whole subject to the approval and ratification of the proper authorities of both Governments respectively.

In testimony whereof, the parties aforesaid have hereto set their hands and seals the day and year aforesaid and at the place aforesaid, in duplicate originals.

ALEXANDER H. STEPHENS, [Seal,]
Commissioner for Confederate States.

JOHN TYLER,   [Seal,]
WM. BALLARD PRESTON,   [Seal,]
S. McD. MOORE,   [Seal,]
JAMES P. HOLCOMBE,   [Seal,]
JAMES C. BRUCE,   [Seal,]
LEWIS E. HARVIE,   [Seal,]
Commissioners for Virginia.

Approved and ratified by the Convention of Virginia, on the 25th day of April, 1861.

JOHN JANNEY, President.

JNO. L. EUBANK, Secretary.
—National Intelligencer.

Doc. 103.—PROCLAMATION OF GOV. ELLIS, APRIL, 1861.

WHEREAS, by proclamation of Abraham Lincoln, President of the United States, followed by a requisition of Simon Cameron, Secretary of War, I am informed that the said Abraham Lincoln has made a call for seventy-five thousand men, to be employed for the invasion of the peaceful homes of the South, and for the violent subversion of the liberties of a free people, constituting a large part of the whole population of the late United States ; and, *whereas*, this high-handed act of tyrannical outrage is not only in violation of all Constitutional law, utter disregard of every sentiment of humanity and Christian civilization, and conceived in a spirit of aggression unparalleled by any act of recorded history, but is a direct step toward the subjugation of the whole South, and the conversion of a free republic, inherited from our fathers, into a military despotism, to be established by worse than foreign enemies on the ruins of our once glorious Constitution of equal rights :

Now, therefore, I, John W. Ellis, Governor of the State of North Carolina, for these extraordinary causes, do hereby issue this, my Proclamation, notifying and requesting the Senators and members of the House of Commons of the General Assembly of North Carolina, to meet in special session at the Capitol, in the City of Raleigh, on Wednesday, the 1st day of May next. And I furthermore exhort all good citizens throughout the State to be mindful that their first allegiance is due to the sovereignty which protects their homes and dearest interests, as their first service is due for the sacred defence of their hearts, and of the soil which holds the graves of our glorious dead.

United action in defence of the sovereignty of North Carolina, and of the rights of the South, becomes now the duty of all.

—N. Y. Tribune, April 26.

Doc. 104.—PROCLAMATION OF THE GOVERNOR OF DELAWARE, APRIL 26, 1861.

WHEREAS, a requisition has been made upon the undersigned, as Executive of the said State of Delaware, by the Secretary of War, for one regiment, consisting of seven hundred and eighty men, to be immediately detached from the militia of this State, "to serve as infantry or riflemen for the period of three months, unless sooner discharged ;" and, whereas, the laws of this State do not confer upon the Executive any authority enabling him to comply with such requisition, there being no organized militia nor any law requiring such organization ; and whereas, it is the duty of all good and law-abiding citizens to preserve the peace and sustain the laws and government under which we live, and by which our citizens are protected :

Therefore I, William Burton, Governor of the said State of Delaware, recommend the formation of volunteer companies for the protection of the lives and property of the people of this State against violence of any sort to which they may be exposed. For these purposes such companies, when formed, will be under the control of the State authorities, though not subject to be ordered by the Executive into the United States service—the law not vesting in him such authority. They will, however, have the option of offering their services to the general government for the defence of its capital and the support of the Constitution and laws of the country.

WILLIAM BURTON.
—N. Y. Herald, April 28.

Doc. 105.—NEW MILITARY DEPARTMENTS.

WAR DEPARTMENT,
ADJUTANT-GENERAL'S OFFICE,
WASHINGTON, April 27, 1861.

1. THE Military Department of Washington will include the District of Columbia, according to its original boundary, Fort Washington and the country adjacent, and the State of Maryland as far as Bladensburgh, inclusive. Colonel J. K. F. Mansfield, Inspector-General, is assigned to the command ; head-quarters at Washington City.

2. A new Military Department, to be called the Department of Annapolis, head-quarters at that city, will include the country for twenty miles on each side of the railroad from Annapolis to the City of Washington, as far as Bladensburgh, Maryland. Brigadier-General B. F. Butler, Massachusetts Volunteers, is assigned to the command.

3. A third department, called the Department of Pennsylvania, will include that State, the State of Delaware, and all of Maryland not embraced in the forgoing departments. Major-General Patterson to command ; head-quarters at Philadelphia, or any other point he may temporarily occupy.

4. Brevet-Colonel C. F. Smith having been relieved by Colonel Mansfield, will repair to Fort Columbus, N. Y., and assume the duties of Superintendent of the Recruiting Service, to which he was assigned in Special Orders No. 80, of March 15. Major Heintzelman, on being relieved at Fort Columbus, will repair to this city, and report for duty to the Department Commander.

5. Fort Adams, Rhode Island, is hereby placed temporarily under the control of the Secretary of the Navy, for the purpose of the Naval Academy now at Annapolis, Md.

The necessary transfer of property will be made by the departments interested. By order.

L. THOMAS, Adjutant-General.

—*National Intelligencer,* May 1.

Doc. 106.—LETTERS FROM THE N. Y. SEVENTY-FIRST REGIMENT.

WASHINGTON, April 27.

WE have just arrived at Washington after a week of very hard work and quite a scarcity of provisions on the way. I am writing in our quarters in the building erected for the Inauguration ball. On Sunday, the day of our departure, we stood in Bond street with our knapsacks about five hours; the march down Broadway was therefore excessively tiresome.

Our ship, R. R. Cuyler, was a sight to behold; she was very filthy, redolent of decayed meat, bilge-water, &c. The men in two or three hours became clamorous for their rations, which, when furnished, were found to consist of two sea-biscuits and a chunk of salt pork, and the rations continued so for the remainder of the voyage. Our beds were wooden bunks in the back part of the ship. I patronized my bunk the first night, but on Monday and Tuesday nights I took to the deck. On Wednesday morning we disembarked at Annapolis, and remained there till about half-past four o'clock on Thursday morning, (having been roused at three,) when we started on our march for the junction, without any breakfast, and marched till eleven o'clock, making eight or nine miles.

We then had our *dinner,* consisting of two sea-biscuits and as much water as one *could get.* We started again in two hours, marching all the time with our muskets and knapsacks, and went nine or ten miles, and stopped in a large open lot, the whole regiment, about one thousand men. At one end of the lot was a large woody marsh. Just as we were about to resume our march at 7 o'clock in the evening, we heard two or three Indian whoops coming from different parts of this march. It had before been reported that we were to be attacked if we continued our march that (Thursday) evening, and this of course strengthened our suspicions. It was now beginning to grow dark, and we were formed in hollow square to resist any attack that might be made.

About nine o'clock skirmishers were sent forward, and a short time afterwards the main body again started. We had eight or nine miles to go before reaching the railroad for Washington. I forgot to say that the reason we were obliged to walk was, that the railroad track had been torn up. (It is now clear all the way through, and in possession of the Government.) My feelings were none of the pleasantest as we defiled past the thick bushes and trees on each side of the road, and in the dark; the men were silent, all expecting at any moment to hear the muskets of lurking enemies on either side of us, but there was no flinching. In this way we marched three or four miles,

stopping every few minutes to listen for the bugle of our skirmishers; it took about four hours for those miles. We then came upon the camp of the Rhode Island regiment, under the lead of Gov. Sprague, and a fine noble set of men they are, generous as possible.

On hearing from us that we were lacking in rations, every man of them opened his ration-bag and gave us as much as we could carry. We left their encampment and kept on our way on the railroad track, and arrived at the Junction at four o'clock on the morning of Friday, after having marched continually for twenty-four hours, and walked twenty-eight miles. That's what I call a forced march for one thousand men. When we left the camp of the Rhode Islanders, where they begged us to stay all night, and furnished us coffee and bread, we were induced to march on the rest of the way to the Junction by the expectation that we should there receive coffee and biscuit, and have a nice shelter for the night. When we reached there nothing of the kind was to be found; there was not a particle of any thing to be had in the place until about nine o'clock in the morning, and then it was as much as a man's life was worth to attempt to get what there was. Imagine a thousand men in such a place, with no certainty when they could get off, there being only one engine on the road— you can conceive the state of things! We were all indignant that no better provision had been made for us by the Government, but there are many apologies for the neglect, and those who come after us will have no such suffering.

About seven o'clock Friday evening the cars from Washington came for us; the whole regiment had entered them, and were patiently waiting to be off, when we were all ordered out again and marched back to the field we came from, an eighth of a mile from the cars. There we were drawn up in martial order with two other regiments that had arrived, and we expected to camp in the field all night, but at about half-past ten we were ordered back to the cars, and there waited until early this morning, (Saturday,) when we finally started, and arrived at Washington without accident. An expected attack from five thousand men from Baltimore, reported to be coming down with four field-pieces, was the cause of our being ordered out of the cars at the Junction.

I should have said that on the Cuyler the eating was perfectly disgusting—the junk was served out to the men from *the hands of the cook.* I could not touch it for two days; the third day I became reconciled to it, and now I believe myself capable of eating any thing. The scramble for water was of course terrific, after the salt junk; the water was of the dirtiest kind imaginable, filled with all sorts of specks —but I became accustomed to this also. I do not think that hereafter I shall complain about dirty water, molasses, or any thing else, that may have a *few hairs, croton bugs,* or any such thing in it.

At the Junction, where there was so little to eat, I determined to find something; accordingly I walked a mile to a little cottage, where I found a negro and his wife supplying some other members of my regiment with bacon, milk, hoecake, &c. I took my seat at the table with the rest, and took a dirty plate, a quarter full of fragments, left by one who had just eaten from it. I asked the negro to clean it; he evidently not understanding the meaning of the word "clean," filled up the plate just as it was, and I, though not liking to eat what had been left by my predecessor, was too hungry to hesitate long about it.

I am going this afternoon to get cleaned up, having brushed my hair but once and washed my face but three times, and not having had my boots off night or day, since I left New York last Sunday.

NAVY-YARD, Sunday, April 28—10¼ A. M.

At half-past three o'clock yesterday afternoon we were ordered to the Navy-Yard. It is considered here a post of honor, and it is said Gen. Scott sent us here because he considered us a very hardy regiment. Our company is now quartered on a steamboat lying off the yard, till our barracks are cleaned and fixed; we shall probably get into them to-morrow.

On all our march from Annapolis we saw only forty or fifty houses, and those most miserable. We met with one Secessionist, who we asked for a pail of water for the thirsting soldiers; he replied, "I won't give you any water, if I die for it." We saw no more of that kind; all others whom we saw on that route seemed to be very friendly, waved their handkerchiefs, and did what they could for us; they were all destitute of provisions, the Seventh Regiment having preceded us the day before.

I have just received the most *interesting* intelligence—*we are to have roast beef for dinner*.

If my letter is perfectly wandering and disconnected, excuse it, as I am writing in a very inconvenient place, in the midst of such a noise that I can scarcely hear myself speak; small darkies crying out "Shine your boots for half a dime with the *Union* polish;" and soon others, "Here's the latest news from New York —New York *Herald, twenty-five cents*.

But we are all well, notwithstanding our sufferings, and we are sustained by the conviction that we are actuated by the spirit of a pure and a holy patriotism, and that our course is approved by all the good on earth, and by our Father in Heaven.   C. P. KIRKLAND, Jr.

Extract of a letter from a sergeant in the Seventy-first New York regiment to his wife.

"WASHINGTON NAVY-YARD, }
Sunday, April 28th. {

"We arrived here yesterday, after a week of terrible labor and privation, but I am happy to say, in the enjoyment of good health. Not a single case of sickness has yet come to my knowledge. We embarked on the R. R. Cuyler,

with over nine hundred men; and, after a voyage of three days, without rest, without food—except in small quantity and poor quality —without good water, and with seven hundred and fifty men afflicted with the most distressing sea-sickness—we arrived at Annapolis on Wednesday, about noon.

"Here I partook of the first real food I had tasted, consisting of oysters and crackers. We stayed at Annapolis, getting what rest we could, (I did not get any, as I was sergeant of the guard, and had to march on the relief every hour all night,) until two o'clock Thursday morning, when we were ordered to march for Annapolis Junction, about thirty miles distant. We got off about 4, A. M., and marched for eight hours, when we halted for two hours and were served with rations, consisting of two hard crackers only. We started again about 2, P. M., and marched six hours more till about 8, P. M., when we again halted and partook of corned beef, very little of it, and that little very tough, and a hard cracker.

"The entire march was made with our muskets and heavily-laden knapsacks, through sand six or eight inches deep, and the thermometer from 75 to 80. At this spot we had an alarm, and were drawn up in hollow square with muskets loaded; but the alarm proved false. We started again at 10, P. M., and arrived at the Junction at 3, A. M., of Friday, the 26th, having marched thirty miles in about twenty-four hours, our only food being three hard crackers and a piece of tough meat. Here we were stowed away like sardines in a miserable, rickety old wooden building, which had evidently been used as a bowling-alley. We remained here (and without any food, except one pig, which was bought by our company and roasted in the woods and distributed, as far as it would go, among the men) till about 7, P. M., when we got on board the cars for Washington.

"After getting comfortably seated, and, as we thought, about to start, dispatches were received that five thousand Baltimoreans, with a corps of four hundred and fifty artillerymen, were on their way to attack us. 'Attention, battalion—disembark,' was the order given, and promptly obeyed by the regiment, which was drawn up in a line of battle in a field close by, and we were ordered to sleep on our arms. We remained here about three hours, when we again took the cars, (this alarm also having proved false,) and between two and three o'clock on the morning of Saturday, the 27th, we started for Washington, where we arrived at seven o'clock. We were marched to the City Hall, and took up our quarters in the large wooden building erected for the Inauguration ball last month.

"Here we stayed till 3, P. M., when we marched to the Navy-Yard; we are quartered till to-morrow on a steamboat lying near; we then go into barracks in the Navy-Yard, and remain during our stay. Yesterday, in Washington, we had a bath and a good dinner of beefsteak and potatoes, which, after our sufferings from hunger, you will suppose was very acceptable. If I could have foreseen what I had to endure, I certainly should have made arrangements to be relieved at least from the want of food and from the knapsack. Keep up your spirits and have no apprehensions for us. We make our sacrifices cheerfully, as we know that our cause is the cause of our country, a holy cause; and that Providence smiles upon it."

—*N. Y. Commercial, and N. Y. Evening Post*, May 3.

Doc. 107.—THE WASHINGTON OATH.

THE following is the oath which so many of the United States clerks refused to take at Washington—60 or 70 of the number resigning in consequence of the demand that it should be administered. Mr. Chase, Secretary of the Treasury, declined to administer the oath, upon the ground that an oath to support the Constitution of the United States was all-sufficient for a loyal citizen. Those, he said, who would not obey that would break any other. His purpose was much commended by another Cabinet officer—the Secretary of War, we believe—and prevented a large number of resignations. It was particularly obnoxious to certain Union men of Maryland and Virginia, who regarded it as a doubt of their fidelity. The oath reads thus:

I, A. B., at the present time in the United States service as a Clerk, do solemnly swear that I will support, protect, and defend the Constitution and Government of the United States against all enemies, whether domestic or foreign, and that I will bear true faith and loyalty to the same as established by the Constitution and laws; and further, that I do this with a full determination and pledge, without any mental reservation or evasion, to perform in good faith all the duties which may be legally required of me, so help me God.

COUNTY OF WASHINGTON, } To wit.
District of Columbia.   }

Sworn to and subscribed before me, this —— day of April, 1861.   C. D., (J. P.)
—*N. Y. Express*, May 1.

Doc. 108.—ADDRESS TO THE WOMEN OF NEW YORK, APRIL 27, 1861.

To the Women of New York, and especially to those already engaged in preparing against the time of Wounds and Sickness in the Army:

THE importance of systematizing and concentrating the spontaneous and earnest efforts now making by the women of New York for the supply of extra medical aid to our army through its present campaign, must be obvious to all reflecting persons. Numerous societies, working without concert, organization, or head —without any direct understanding with the official authorities—without any positive in-

structions as to the immediate or future wants of the army—are liable to waste their enthusiasm in disproportionate efforts, to overlook some claims and overdo others, while they give unnecessary trouble in official quarters, by the variety and irregularity of their proffers of help or their inquiries for guidance.

As no existing organization has a right to claim precedence over any other, or could properly assume to lead in this noble cause, where all desire to be first, it is proposed by the undersigned, members of the various circles now actively engaged in this work, that the women of New York should meet in the Cooper Institute, on Monday next, at 11 o'clock, A. M., to confer together, and to appoint a General Committee, with power to organize the benevolent purposes of all into a common movement.

To make the meeting practical and effective, it seems proper here to set forth briefly the objects that should be kept in view. The form which woman's benevolence has already taken, and is likely to take, in the present crisis, is, first, the contribution of labor, skill, and money in the preparation of lint, bandages, and other stores, in aid of the wants of the Medical Staff; second, the offer of personal service as nurses.

In regard to the first, it is important to obtain and disseminate exact official information as to the nature and variety of the wants of the army; to give proper direction and proportion to the labor expended, so as to avoid superfluity in some things and deficiency in others; and to this end, to come to a careful and thorough understanding with the official head of the Medical Staff, through a Committee having this department in hand. To this Committee should be assigned the duty of conferring with other associations in other parts of the country, and, especially, through the press, to keep the women of the loyal States everywhere informed how their efforts may be most wisely and economically employed, and their contributions of all kinds most directly concentrated at New York, and put at the service of the Medical Staff. A central depot would, of course, be the first thing to be desired.

In regard to the second form of benevolence —the offer of personal service as nurses—it is felt that the public mind needs much enlightenment, and the overflowing zeal and sympathy of the women of the nation a careful channel, not only to prevent waste of time and effort, but to save embarrassment to the official staff, and to secure real efficiency in the service. Should our unhappy war be continued, the army is certain to want the services of extra nurses, not merely on account of the casualties of the field, but of the camp diseases originating in the exposure of the soldiery to a strange climate and to unaccustomed hardships. The result of all the experience of the Crimean war has been to prove the total uselessness of any but picked and skilled women in this department of duty. The ardor and zeal of all other women should therefore be concentrated on finding, preparing, and sending bands of women, of suitable age, constitution, training, and temperament, to the army, at such points and at such times as they may be asked for by the Medical Staff.

A central organization is wanted, therefore, to which all those desiring to go as nurses may be referred, where a Committee of Examiners, partly medical and partly otherwise, may at once decide upon the fitness of the candidate. Those accepted should then at once be put under competent instruction and discipline, (for which it is understood a thorough school will be opened at once by the Medical Faculty of the city,) and, as occasion offers, the best prepared, in successive order, be sent, under proper escort, to the scene of war, as they are wanted.

It is felt that all who want to go, *and are fitted to go*, should have in their turn a fair chance to do so, and are not unlikely to be wanted, sooner or later. Of these many may be rich and many poor. Some may wish to go at their own charges, and others will require to be aided as to their expenses, and still others for the loss of their time. But the best nurses should be sent irrespective of these distinctions, as only the best are economical on any terms.

It will at once appear that, without a central organization, with proper authority, there can be no efficiency, system, or discipline in this important matter of nurses; and there can be no organization, to which a cheerful submission will be paid, except it originates in the common will, and becomes the genuine representative of all the women of New York, and of all the existing associations having this kind of aid in view. It is obvious that such an organization will require generous contributions, and that all the women of New York, and of the country, not otherwise lending aid, will have a direct opportunity of giving support to the object so near their hearts through the treasury of this common organization.

To consider this matter deliberately, and to take such common action as may then appear wise, we earnestly invite the women of New York, and the Pastors of the Churches, with such medical advisers as may be specially invited, to assemble for counsel and action, at the Cooper Institute, on Monday morning next, at 11 o'clock.

Mrs. Gen. Dix, Mrs. H. Fish, Mrs. L. C. Jones, Mrs. E. Robinson, Mrs. W. Kirkland, Mrs. Wm. H. Aspinwall, Mrs. R. Minturn, Mrs. J. B. Johnson, Mrs. Judge Roosevelt, Mrs. A. Bininger, Mrs. W. C. Bryant, Mrs. R. L. Stuart, Mrs. D. D. Field, Mrs. W. Astor, jr., Mrs. M. Grinnell, Mrs. H. B. Smith, Mrs. R. Hitchcock, Mrs. F. Marberry, Mrs. S. F. B. Morse, Mrs. Judge Daly, Mrs. C. Swords, Miss Marquand, Mrs. G. Holbrooke, Mrs. D. Adams, Mrs. H. Baylis, Mrs. H. W. Bellows, Mrs. Stuart Brown, Mrs. Ellis, Mrs. J. D. Wolfe, Mrs. A. Potter, Mrs. Walker, Mrs. Elisha Fish, Mrs. C. A. Seward, Mrs. Dr. Osgood, Mrs. Griffin, Mrs. J. Sherwood, Mrs. S. H. Tyng, Mrs. Capt. Shumway, Mrs. Edw. Bayard, Mrs. James Jones, Mrs. Judge Betts, Mrs. Wm. Ward, Mrs. H. E. Eaton, Mrs. W. C. Evarts, Mrs. Judge Bonney,

Mrs. G. L. Schuyler, Mrs. Peter Cooper, Mrs. T. Tileston, Mrs. F. S. Wiley, Mrs. H. Webster, Mrs. Moffat, Mrs. S. J. Baker, Mrs. R. Gracie, Mrs. M. Catlin, Mrs. Chandler, Mrs. B. R. Winthrop, Mrs. G. Stuyvesant, Mrs. Geo. Curtis, Mrs. A. R. Eno, Mrs. W. F. Carey, Mrs. A. Hewitt, Mrs. Dr. Peaslee, Mrs. R. Campbell, Mrs. H. K. Bogart, Mrs. Chas. Butler, Mrs. C. E. Lane, Mrs. M. D. Swett, Mrs. R. M. Blatchford, Mrs. L. W. Prudgham, Mrs. A. W. Bradford, Mrs. W. H. Lee, Mrs. Parke Godwin, Mrs. H. J. Raymond, Mrs. S. L. M. Barlow, Mrs. J. Auchincloss, Miss Minturn, Mrs. M. Trimble, Mrs. S. B. Collins, Mrs. R. H. Bowne, Mrs. B. R. McIlvaine, Mrs. N. Lawrence, Mrs. John Reid, Mrs. C. Newbold, Mrs. J. B. Collins, Mrs. J. C. Smith, Mrs. P. Spofford, Mrs. C. W. Field, Mrs. P. Townsend, Mrs. L. Baker, Mrs. L. M. Rutherford, Mrs. Charles King.

—N. Y. *Tribune, April 27th.*

Doc. 109.—MESSAGE OF GOVERNOR HICKS.

BALTIMORE, April 27, 1861.

GENTLEMEN OF THE SENATE AND HOUSE OF REPRESENTATIVES:—The extraordinary condition of affairs in Maryland has induced me to exercise the constitutional prerogative vested in the Governor, to summon the Legislature in special session, in the hope that your wisdom may enable you to devise prompt and effective means to restore peace and safety to our State. I shall detail briefly the startling events which have induced me to summon you together, and which have so suddenly placed us in the state of anarchy, confusion, and danger, from which I sincerely trust you may be able to extricate us. Believing it to be the design of the administration to pass over our soil troops for the defence of the city of Washington, and fearing that the passage of such troops would excite our people and provoke a collision, I labored earnestly to induce the President to forego his purpose. I waited upon him in person, and urged the importance of my request. I subsequently communicated with him and his Cabinet by special dispatches, entreating an abandonment of his designs. To all my requests I could get but the reply that Washington was threatened with attack; that the Government had resolved to defend it; that there was no other way of obtaining troops than by passing them over the soil of Maryland, and that the military necessity of the case rendered it impossible for the Government to abandon its plans, much as it desired to avoid the dangers of a collision. My correspondence with the authorities at Washington is therewith submitted. The consequences are known to you. On Friday last a detachment of troops from Massachusetts reached Baltimore, and was attacked by an irresponsible mob, and several persons on both sides were killed. The Mayor and Police Board gave to the Massachusetts soldiers all the protection they could afford, acting with the utmost promptness and bravery. But they were powerless to restrain the mob. Being in Baltimore at the time, I coöperated with the Mayor to the fullest extent of my power in his efforts. The military of the city were ordered out to assist in the preservation of the peace. The railroad companies were requested by the Mayor and myself to transport no more troops to Baltimore city, and they promptly acceded to our request. Hearing of the attack upon the soldiers, the War Department issued orders that no more troops would pass through Baltimore city provided they were allowed to pass outside its limits. Subsequently a detachment of troops were ascertained to be encamped at or near Cockeysville, in Baltimore county. On being informed of this, the War Department ordered them back. Before leaving Baltimore, Colonel Huger, who was in command of the United States arsenal at Pikesville, informed me that he had resigned his commission. Being advised of the probability that the mob might attempt the destruction of this property, and thereby complicate our difficulties with the authorities at Washington, I ordered Colonel Petherbridge to proceed with sufficient force and occupy the premises in the name of the United States Government, of which proceeding I immediately notified the War Department. On Sunday morning last I discovered that a detachment of troops, under command of Brigadier-General Benjamin F. Butler, had reached Annapolis in a steamer, and had taken possession of the practice-ship Constitution, which during that day they succeeded in getting outside of the harbor of Annapolis, where she now lies. After getting the ship off, the steamer laid outside the harbor, and was soon joined by another steamer having on board the Seventh Regiment, from New York city. Brigadier-General Butler addressed me, asking for permission to land his forces. It will be seen from the correspondence herewith submitted, that I refused my consent. The Mayor of Annapolis also protested. But both steamers soon afterward landed and put off with the troops. Subsequently other large bodies of troops reached here in transports, and were landed. I was notified that the troops were to be marched to Washington. They desired to go without obstruction from our people, but they had orders to go to Washington, and were determined to obey those orders. In furtherance of their designs they took military possession of the Annapolis and Elk Ridge Railroad, in regard to which act I forwarded to Brigadier-General Butler the protest, and see the reply herewith submitted. On Wednesday morning the two detachments landed, and took up the line of march for Washington. The people of Annapolis, though greatly exasperated, acting under counsel of the most prudent citizens, refrained from molesting or obstructing the passage of the troops through the city. Seriously impressed with the condition of affairs, and anxious to avoid a repetition of events similar to those which had transpired in Baltimore, I deemed it my duty to make another appeal at Washington. Accordingly I sent a special messenger to

Washington, with a dispatch to the administration, advising that no more troops be sent through Maryland; that the troops at Annapolis be sent elsewhere, and urging that a truce be offered with a view of a peaceful settlement of existing difficulties by mediation. I suggested that Lord Lyons, the British Minister, be requested to act as mediator between the contending parties. The result of the mission will be seen from the correspondence herewith submitted. These events have satisfied me that the War Department has concluded to make Annapolis the point for landing troops, and has resolved to open and maintain communication between this place and Washington. In the brief time allowed, it is impossible for me to go more into detail. The documents accompanying this message places before you all the information possessed by me. I shall promptly communicate such other information as may reach me. Notwithstanding the fact that our most learned and intelligent citizens admit the right of the Government to transport its troops across our soil, it is evident that a portion of the people of Maryland are opposed to the exercise of that right. I have done all in my power to protect the citizens of Maryland, and to preserve peace within our borders. Lawless occurrences will be repeated, I fear, unless prompt action be taken by you. It is my duty to advise you of my own convictions of the proper course to be pursued by Maryland in the emergency which is upon us. It is of no consequence now to discuss the causes which have induced our troubles. Let us look to our distressing present and to our portentous future. The fate of Maryland, and perhaps of her sister border slave States, will undoubtedly be seriously affected by the action of your honorable body. Therefore should every good citizen bend all his energies to the task before us, and therefore should the animosities and bickerings of the past be forgotten, and all strike hands in the bold cause of restoring peace to our State and to our country. I honestly and most earnestly entertain the conviction that the only safety of Maryland lies in preserving a neutral position between our brethren of the North and of the South. We have violated no right of either section. We have been loyal to the Union. The unhappy contest between the two sections has not been commenced or encouraged by us, although we have suffered from it in the past. The impending war has not come by any act or any wish of ours. We have done all we could to avert it. We have hoped that Maryland and other border slave States, by their conservative position and love for the Union, might have acted as mediators between the extremes of both sections, and thus have prevented the terrible evils of a prolonged civil war. Entertaining these views, I cannot counsel Maryland to take sides against the general Government until it shall commit outrages on us which would justify us in resisting its authority. As a consequence, I can give no other counsel than that we shall array ourselves for Union and peace, and thus preserve our soil from being polluted with the blood of brethren. Thus, if war must be between the North and South, we may force the contending parties to transfer the field of battle from our soil, so that our lives and property may be secure.

It seems to me that, independently of all other considerations, our geographical position forces us to this, unless we are willing to see our State the theatre of a long and bloody civil war, and the consequent utter destruction of every material interest of our people, to say nothing of the blood of brave men and innocent women and children, which will cry out from our soil for vengeance upon us, if we fail to do all that in us lies to avert the impending calamity.

The course I suggest has all the while been the sole groundwork of my policy; and but for the excitement prevailing among our people during the past few days, I believe the object I have kept steadily in view during my administration would have been consummated. If it has failed, I have the full consciousness that, throughout the whole of my harassing and painful incumbency of the gubernatorial chair, I have labored honestly and faithfully for the peace, the safety, and the interests of Maryland, and of our common country. This consciousness has fully sustained me in all my troubles, and has enabled me to endure patiently all the cruel, unmerited, and heartless attacks that have been made upon my integrity. I have also comfort in the conviction that my policy has been sustained by a large majority of the people, and nothing that has transpired since the recent lamentable occurrence within our State has shaken that conviction. A momentary frantic excitement took the place of reason and good judgment, and men for the time threw aside all prudent thoughts of the future in the burning desire to avenge what they considered wrongs. I submit my suggestions to your wisdom, and I appeal to you not only as devoted citizens of Maryland, but as husbands and fathers, to allow that prudence and Christianlike temper, so honorable to all men, to guide your counsels; and I implore you not to be swayed by the passions which seem to be so fully aroused in our midst to do what the generations to come after us will ever deplore. In conclusion, gentlemen, I ask your indulgence, if I have omitted to present to you any other matter of interest in connection with the important subject which you are summoned to consider. The short time I have had in which to prepare this communication, and the turmoil and excitement around me, may have caused omissions; but, if so, they will be promptly supplied when indicated by you.

T. HALLIDAY HICKS.
—*N. Y. Herald*, April 28.

Doc. 110.—BLOCKADE OF NORTH CAROLINA AND VIRGINIA.

BY THE PRESIDENT OF THE UNITED STATES OF AMERICA.

WHEREAS, for the reasons assigned in my proclamation of the 19th instant, a blockade of the ports of the States of South Carolina, Georgia, Florida, Alabama, Louisiana, Mississippi and Texas, was ordered to be established; and whereas, since that date public property of the United States has been seized, the collection of the revenue obstructed, and duly commissioned officers of the United States, while engaged in executing the orders of their superiors, have been arrested and held in custody as prisoners, or have been impeded in the discharge of their official duties, without due legal process, by persons claiming to act under authority of the States of Virginia and North Carolina, an efficient blockade of the ports of these States will therefore also be established.

In witness whereof, I have hereunto set my hand, and caused the seal of the United States to be affixed.

Done at the city of Washington, this 27th day of April, in the year of our Lord one thousand eight hundred and sixty-one, and of the independence of the United States the eighty-fifth.

By the President, ABRAHAM LINCOLN.
WILLIAM H. SEWARD, Secretary of State.
—*N. Y. Evening Post*, April 29.

Doc. 111.—SPEECH OF EDWARD EVERETT, AT CHESTER SQUARE, BOSTON, APRIL 27, 1861.

FELLOW-CITIZENS AND FRIENDS: The great assemblage that I see around me, the simple but interesting ceremonial with which the flag of our country has been thrown to the breeze, the strains of inspiring music, the sweet concert of these youthful voices, the solemn supplication of the reverend clergyman which still fills our ears—all these proclaim the deep, patriotic sentiment, of which that flag is the symbol and expression. Nay, more, it speaks for itself. Its mute eloquence needs no aid from my lips to interpret its significance. Fidelity to the Union blazes from its stars; allegiance to the Government, beneath which we live, is wrapped within its folds.

We set up this standard, my friends, not as a matter of idle display; but as an expressive indication that in the mighty struggle which has been forced upon us, we are of one heart and one mind, that the government of the country must be sustained. We are a law-abiding, quiet-loving community. Our time, our thoughts, our energies, are habitually devoted to the peaceful arts by which states grow and prosper; but upon an issue in which the life of the country is involved, we rally as one man to its defence. All former differences of opinion are swept away; we forget that we have ever been partizans; we remember only that we are Americans, and that our country is in peril.

And what is it that has kindled this quiet and peace-loving community to the present unexampled excitement—a patriotic unanimity not witnessed even in 1776? Why is it, that the flag of the country—always honored, always beloved—is now, all at once, worshipped, I may say, with the passionate homage of this whole people? Why does it float, as never before, not merely from arsenal and masthead, but from tower and steeple, from the public edifices, the temples of science, the private dwelling, in magnificent display of miniature presentiment? Let Fort Sumter give the answer. When on this day fortnight, the 13th of April, (a day forever to be held in inauspicious remembrance, like the *dies Alliensis* in the annals of Rome,) the tidings spread through the land that the standard of United America, the pledge of her union, and the symbol of her power, for which so many gallant hearts had poured out their life-blood, on the ocean and the land, to uphold, had, in the harbor of Charleston, been, for a day and a half, the target of eleven fratricidal batteries, one deep, unanimous, spontaneous feeling shot with the tidings through the bosom of twenty millions of freemen, that its outraged honor must be vindicated.

And oh, fellow-citizens, if, aloof as we are from the immediate danger of the conflict, sheltered in our comfortable homes, with the objects of our affection around us, we can refuse our support to the Constitution, the Laws, and the Government, in whose defence those seventy brave men, for thirty frightful hours, without sleep, almost without food, compelled to draw the breath of Heaven into their lungs through moistened handkerchiefs, stood faithful and undaunted beneath the iron storm bursting from above, and the raging fires around them, we shall deserve ourselves, on some disastrous day, to pass through a like fiery ordeal.

—*Boston Transcript*, April 30.

Doc. 112.—REINFORCEMENT OF FORT PICKENS.

U. S. Steam Sloop Brooklyn, at anchor off }
Pensacola Bar, Sunday, April 21, 1861. }

Huzza! We have done it. We have satisfactorily settled one important question that has long been agitating the public mind, and that is, whether we were able to reinforce Fort Pickens or not. I have the great pleasure of assuring you this was accomplished between the hours of 11 and 12 o'clock on the night of Friday, the 12th inst., without the firing of a gun, or the spilling of one drop of blood. The manner in which it was successfully done is briefly as follows: A bearer of dispatches arrived from Washington during the day, bringing the orders we had so long anxiously looked for, and as soon as it became dark we began work with a good will, and in earnest. At first the marines from the frigate Sabine and the sloop St. Louis came on board our vessel, and immediately after the accomplishment of this, the anchor was hoisted by the jolly old salts with the merry chant of—

General Jackson won the day
Heave, yea ho!
At New Orleans, the people say;
Yeo, heave yeo!

We ran as close to the shore as possible for us to do, came to anchor, and without a moment's delay, lowered the boats and filled them with troops.

At 11 o'clock, Lieut. Albert N. Smith, of Massachusetts, being in command, they started on their mission, not knowing whether they were facing eternity, or whether they would live to see the light of another day. As they left the side of the vessel, many a "May God cause you to succeed," came from the lips of the loyal men by my side. If I live a thousand years, I shall not forget the feelings I had when I saw those brave fellows shake hands with all their old comrades, and, as a tear would now and then glisten in the gloom, but be instantly wiped away by a clenched hand, I felt they all knew their danger, and, knowing it, dared to face it with that true courage eminently worthy of all praise, and may they receive it!

The party were instructed to send up signals should they be attacked, and I do assure you never were there keener eyes than ours on that eventful night, as we peered into the darkness, momentarily expecting to see a rocket pierce the midnight gloom; but none appeared. While we were thus anxiously awaiting some evidence of the success or non-success of their mission, a boat is hailed—a faint answer comes back, "Lieut. Smith and the boats' crews," and in whispering tones we hear the news, "they have been successful"—brother officers shake hands, and give Lieut. Smith that praise justly deserved by him. They went around inside of the harbor, passed under the guns of Forts McRae and Barrancas without being heard, and safely landed all the troops without interruption.

This being so successfully accomplished, it was almost instantly concluded to attempt it again, and so orders were given that all the marines in the squadron should take to their boats, preparatory to being put into the fort; this being quickly done, the steamer Wyandotte took them in tow, and towed them as far as she could go, where they left her, and pulled into the harbor, taking the same course the first party had, and in good time reached the fort, and safely landed all that were in the boats. Just as day was breaking, we saw from our deck the boats shoving off from the beach, and when they returned to us, our anchor was instantly "up," and we steaming to our old anchorage, with very different sensations than we had when we started for the work. Thus, you see, the Brooklyn has accomplished what she was sent here for, viz.: the reinforcement of Fort Pickens, in spite of their General Bragg, their horde of murderous traitors, and the threats that oceans of blood would be spilled if even the attempt was made. We have done it. It also proves that my views of the entire practicability of such a scheme were very correct.

On Tuesday, the 15th, we were delighted to see the splendid steamer Atlantic sailing into our midst, and we were completely overjoyed when it was ascertained that she was laden with troops, horses, batteries, ammunition, stores, &c., &c., for the fort. The next day the frigate Powhattan arrived, and yesterday the Illinois came among us, laden the same as the Atlantic was; all the forces brought by these transports, together with the guns, ammunition, stores, &c., &c., have been safely transferred to the fort, giving it a thousand or more troops, and, together with the fleet outside, making it impregnable; in fact, with our present force, we think we can hold it against the entire South. The number of rebels in this vicinity is about 6,000, and they are constantly at work erecting batteries along the beach, and fortifying their positions in every way they can. We expect to get some pretty hard knocks in case of an encounter, but may God protect them when our dogs of war are let loose, and are speeding their implements of death.

—*N. Y. Tribune*, April 25—29.

Doc. 113.—OFFICERS OF THE FIFTH N. Y. REGIMENT.

COLONEL, Schwarzwaelder; Lieutenant-Colonel, L. Burger; Major, Van Ausburg; Adjutant, Paul Frank; Engineer, J. Dodge; Quartermaster, M. Fearing; Assistant-Quartermaster, —— Corrle; Paymaster, —— Stenway; Assistant-Paymaster, —— Fielder; Surgeon, Dr. Hasse; Assistant-Surgeon, Dr. Rosa. Company A—Captain, Gerdes; First-Lieutenant, Neander; Second do., Brettman. Company B —Captain, Heitmann; First Lieutenant, Held; Second do., Manver. Company C—Captain, Betgeman; First Lieutenant, Wakle; Second do., Brunjes. Company D—Captain, Mayer; First Lieutenant, Sackersdorff; Second do., ——. Company E—Captain, Nickel; First Lieutenant, Lensifer; Second do., Maun. Company F—Captain, Happendeimer; First Lieutenant, Aberle; Second do., Bungert. Company G—Captain, Luke; First Lieutenant, Jauer; Second do., Keis. Company H—Captain, Barlock; First Lieutenant, Kaltenparr; Second do., Leonpard. Company K—Engineer Corps—Captain, Dodge; First Lieutenant, Schloemer; Orderly Sergeant, Kirmuel; Non-Commissioned Staff—Calour, Beaness, Ernst, and Acker; Right Guide, Leonard; Left Guide, Michaelis; Drum Major, Berchet.

—*N. Y. Times*, April 29.

Doc. 114.—SPEECH OF VICE-PRESIDENT HAMLIN. APRIL 29, 1861.

MR. PRESIDENT, AND WOMEN OF NEW YORK. —In a time like the present, which is one of action rather than words, and in such a presence, there is, indeed, an embarrassment in the language I might use to express my thoughts. The cold logic of the head would hardly seem to do justice to the occasion, while the warm and generous impulses of the heart might be obnoxious on the charge of boasting, which is neither an evidence of patriotism nor courage. And still, if I can say a single word—for which none but myself will be responsible—to aid or cheer you in the rugged path of duty, I am willing to contribute that word. (Applause.) We present to-day such a spectacle as the world has never witnessed in any age or country. In all the loyal States there beats in men and women's bosoms but one single heart. (Applause). And that heart beats in vindication of our common country and the liberty we inherited from our fathers. (Applause.) We have differed in opinions upon the passing questions of the hour, for they are passed, and they are a sealed book. Let the dead bury the dead. (Applause.) We are to-day forgetful of the past. We live with the stirring present around us only in bright hopes of the future, and in the discharge of the duties that devolve upon us depends that future. Why is it that you, women, in such vast numbers from this Empire City, have gathered from your humble and your luxurious homes? Why is it? Why is it, but that you feel as men feel, that all that we have and all that is valuable in life is at stake and is imperilled? (Applause.) There is nothing, from the stirring mart of commerce up to all the endearments that cluster around the domestic altar, that is not in the issue. Of what use is commerce in all its ramifications—of what use is home with all its endearments, without it is guarded and protected by the law. All these are assailed by those who are attempting to subvert the government under which we live. The Stars, which are the hopes, and the Stripes, which are the emblems of liberty, have been ignominiously dishonored; our public property and our fortifications have been assailed and taken by rebels from their rightful owners; and the government under which we live is threatened with subversion. These are the things that have stirred the hearts of men and women until all are united. (Applause.) These are the things that have brought you together here—these the causes which have united us all as one. And let me say, there is no other course to pursue now but the vindication of the integrity of the government under which we live. (Applause.) It is a false philanthropy —it is a false humanity—that shall falter now in this trying hour of trouble. (Applause.) The safety of the republic consists in the energy and efficiency of the government. (Applause.) The loyalty of the people is unquestioned. Destruction only is with those who falter. These are stirring times, and now we must test the question, whether we have or have not a government? To abandon that great question now is to abandon all. (Applause.) In one sense of the word there is some truth in the allegation that the contest is a sectional one. In the broader and more comprehensive view it is not so. It is a question of government or no government. That is the true question which we have to settle—whether we have a government, whether we received that government from our fathers, and shall perpetuate it to those who come after us? (Applause.) That is the question, however variously sections may array themselves upon either side. How we are cheered along the pathway of our duty by the kind and cordial aid which woman gives! You have met here for the purpose of perfecting more thoroughly an organization which shall be of incalculable benefit to the cause. Your sons, your husbands, your brothers, who have gone forth to battle for all that you hold dear and valuable to you, will be sustained in the hour of conflict and in the hour of pain, when they know that their mothers and sisters are devoting their best energies to give them comfort, whatever their condition or wherever they may be. (Applause.) Our grand cause, and the prayers that will go up to heaven for them and for their cause, will stimulate them in the hour of battle, and after it shall pass away. (Applause.) God bless you, women of New York! Rome in the days of her culminated power never witnessed scenes like these. The world has never seen it. Here palatial parlors are devoted to the manufacture of useful and necessary articles for sons, brothers and fathers, who have gone to the war. (Applause.) You have met here to systematize your work and to invite the co-operation of others throughout the land. Let me tell you they will come from every green hillside and every valley all over New England, my home, and from every loyal State. (Loud applause.) They will coöperate with you; they will form one grand central point, pour in their contributions, and send to you those who are competent to alleviate the sufferings of the sick and wounded. (Applause.) They will co-operate with you, with their humble hands and their means—will join with you in their prayers to Heaven, to aid that cause which all know to be so just. And with your coöperation—with your prayers and appealing to the God of Heaven, for the rectitude of our purpose and the purity of our cause, we know liberty shall be perpetuated in our land.

—*N. Y. Herald*, April 30.

Doc. 115.—REVIEW AT NEW ORLEANS.

At 5 o'clock in the morning, in every quarter of the city, could be seen artillery, cavalry and infantry soldiers, all ready for some active duty.

At 10 o'clock the grand review took place on Canal street. The line of the review was nearly a mile in length, reaching from the levee to Rampart street. Some three or four thousand of our city soldiers made up the long and crowded lines, their uniforms of varying colors, and their burnished bayonets and accoutrements, their flags, giving them a gay and most imposing appearance. Outside of the space cleared for the review the crowd was perfectly compact. Through the courtesy of the storekeepers, ladies had admission to their windows and verandahs. The street was never, on any occasion, more greatly crowded or more splendidly embellished by the presence of the soldiers and the fair sex.

Gen. James Trudeau, whose staff was a prominent feature before the multitude—this being its first parade—was composed of Brigade Inspector, Maj. Alex. Trudeau; First Aid-de-Camp, Capt. Jas. R. Currell; Paymaster, Capt. Geo. Eustis; Quartermaster, Capt. Phil. Buchanan; Assistant Aids, Captains Conrad, Burthe, and Forstall. This legion consists principally of the Orleans battalion of Artillery, the Chasseurs-a-Pied, the Orleans Guard battalion, the Esplanade Guards, the Louisiana Cadets, the Garibaldi Rifles, and the German and other companies.

Gen. Tracy's brigade, the right resting on Camp street, was composed of a squadron (two companies) of cavalry, a battalion of artillery, and two regiments of infantry; the Plaquemine Rangers, a new company, and fine body of men, Capt. Villere commanding; the Jefferson Light Guards, Capt. Guy Dreux; the battalion of Washington Artillery, with eight field-pieces under detachments as light artillery, their legitimate service, and four companies as infantry. The artillery detachments of the Washington Artillery were under the command of Capt. Harry Isaacson, and the infantry companies under Capt. Voorhies—all under command of Major J. B. Walton.

The Continental Guards, Louisiana Grays, Chalmette Guards, Calhoun Guards, Sarsfield Rifles, De Soto Rifles, Delta Rifles, Southern Cadets, Second Company of Orleans Cadets, Bienville Rifles, and other companies, constituted the infantry of this brigade.

The Bienville Guards, Bienville Rifles, and a splendid looking body of men from Algiers, (whose title we did not learn,) appeared in citizen's dress, their uniforms being not yet ready, though they had their guns, and they were none the less admirable for want of their uniforms.

The Orleans Artillery battalion had eight brass pieces, each piece attended by a detachment, and the rest of the battalion marching as infantry. These and the Orleans Guard battalion, were the largest and the most splendid feature of the turn-out. The Orleans Guard turned out no less than 527 muskets.

These troops, together with numerous others, whose titles we did not obtain, all numbering about 4,000, forming into line, the right to the river and the left on Rampart street, the review took place. His Excellency, Governor Thomas O. Moore, attended by Major-General John L. Lewis and the usual full cortege of staff officers, rode past and inspected the long line, the companies presenting arms, the bands playing and the colors unfurled, as they passed; many persons amid the dense throng of spectators cheering the Governor as he passed, he appearing in his simple dress of a planter.

The review over, the brigades formed in procession and marched around Canal street, up town to Julia street, and as far down as Esplanade street. The immense multitude on Canal street dispersed, and divisions of the multitude flocked to meet the procession and get a nearer view of it as it wound its way through the city. Between 2 and 3 o'clock the march ended, and the companies separated and proceeded to their respective armories.

A more glorious day was seldom seen anywhere, the enthusiastic desire being so great to witness and participate in this pageantry.

—*N. O. Delta*, April 30.

Doc. 116.—DEPARTURE OF THE N. Y. FIREMEN ZOUAVES, April 29th.

It was generally supposed that this regiment would have left on Sunday, but owing to the non-arrival of rifles for this corps, the departure was indefinitely postponed. However, the anxiously looked-for arms came to hand this morning, and orders were immediately issued for the embarkation. The following is a list of officers of the regiment: Colonel, E. E. Ellsworth; Lieutenant-Colonel, Noah L. Farnham; Major, John A. Cregier. Companies and captains: A, John Coyle; B, Edward Burns; C, Michael C. Murphy; D, John Downing; E, John B. Leverick; F, William H. Burns; G, Michael A. Tagan; H, William Hackett; I, John Wildey; J, Andrew D. Purtell.

The head-quarters, Devlin's new store, Canal street, previous to their departure, presented a scene of extraordinary activity and excitement. The men were in the highest animal spirits, and all seemed happy at the prospect of soon having a set-to with the Secessionists. The men were marched by companies into the basement. Each man was there armed with a Sharpe's rifle. When on board the *Baltic* they were presented with a bowie-knife about sixteen inches long, (which can be fastened to the rifle, and used as a bayonet,) and a revolver.

At 1 o'clock the men formed into line in Canal street. A stand of colors was there presented to the regiment by Mr. W. H. Wickham, on behalf of the New York Fire Department. Col. Ellsworth was surrounded by his staff; they all remained uncovered while Mr. Wickham made the following speech:

Col. Ellsworth: The Board of Representatives of the New York Fire Department of this City have caused to be prepared this stand of colors to present to your regiment, composed of the firemen of New York and our associates. As President of the Fire Department, I now perform that duty. Take them, place them in the midst of your gallant band, and wherever the fight is the thickest, and the bullets fly the fastest, let these banners be borne, and may you and your comrades, in the hour of trial and battle, remember the proud motto emblazoned upon them:

"The Star-spangled Banner in triumph shall wave."

Let this be your war-cry as you rush to the onset. Let it nerve your arms and fire your ranks. Wave it in triumph only, and do you bring it back, Sir, though it be tattered and torn in the fight.

Old associates, remember, on every battle-field, and in every trial, that the thousands here around you, have placed in your hands a mighty charge. Go forth from this hour, and swear by that flag to live, for that flag to die.

The people have high hopes of you. You have established a character for noble daring, which has received the admiration and tribute of the people.

When the fire-bell rings in the night the citizen rests securely, for he knows that the New York Firemen are omnipotent to arrest the progress of destruction. You are now to exhibit your gallantry, your energies, in another field.

You are called to quench the flames of rebellion, and we know that whether in the midst of burning cities, or in the tented field, you will sustain your own high character, and these banners will ever wave in triumph, even though it be in the midst of ruins.

Our hearts are with you, at all times and in every place. Spring with the same alacrity to the performance of your duty, at the call of the bugle, as though the old familiar note of the fire-trumpet fell upon your ear. Do this, and you will succeed. Let no man's heart fail him; be firm, be united, be true to each other, have confidence in your commanders and yourselves, and when you return, we will rejoice with you over the glories you have won, and weep with you over those that may have fallen.

Col. Ellsworth said in reply, that his acquaintance with the men had been brief, but he thoroughly understood their feelings, and he was sure that, as long as one of them lived, that flag would never be disgraced. He was taking his command away without any drill, and he might almost say unformed; nevertheless, they were determined to do their duty, and he hoped to return with those colors as pure and unstained as they are now.

Col. Ellsworth then took the flags from the hands of Mr. W. H. Wickham, who handed them to the color-sergeant, who in his turn placed them in the charge of the regiment.

Mrs. John Jacob Astor, Jr., then stepped from a carriage and took up a position in front of the regiment. She was accompanied by

Gen. Dix, bearing the colors, who, on Mrs. Astor's behalf, said: "Colonel ELLSWORTH: I have been requested by the donor of the colors about to be presented to you, to read to you her letter of presentation. I have accepted the service with the greatest of pleasure, and I regard it as an honor second only to that of commanding such a regiment as I see before me, and of marshalling it under a flag presented by so graceful and patriotic a donor." The General then read the following letter from Mrs. Astor:

COL. ELLSWORTH—*Sir:* I have the honor of presenting the accompanying colors to the First Regiment New York Zouaves. In delivering the ensign of our nation into the charge of the brave men under your command, I am happy in the confidence that I intrust it to men whose heads are moved by a generous patriotism to defend it, and whose hearts feel now more deeply than they have ever done that the honor of their country's flag is sacred and precious to them as their own.

Accustomed as we are to think of them in the discharge of their ordinary duties with grateful sympathy and a well-founded pride, these feelings grow stronger the solemn moment when they are going from us to engage in a new and still more perilous service. I pray, Sir, that Heaven's gracious protection may be over you, and over these, to preserve and bring you back in safety to those whose hearts will follow you each day with prayer, and with a hopeful expectation of being gladdened through your success.

Believe me yours, with much respect and true regard,　　　　　　　AUGUSTA ASTOR.

Col. Ellsworth made a suitable reply.

Three cheers were then given for the presentations, three for the Commissioners of the New York Fire Department, and three more for the Chief Engineer.

Gen. Wool, who is staying at the St. Nicholas, reviewed the men as they passed. Each man, as he went by the veteran general, cheered him most lustily. The regiment was escorted to the boat by about 5,000 firemen, many of whom carried banners. Upon the one carried by Company 30 was inscribed,

"If our Country calls, the rest are ready."

The regiment, after leaving Canal street, marched up Broadway to Bond street, then down the Bowery to the Astor House, from thence up Broadway, and down Canal, at the foot of which street the steamer *Baltic* was lying.

PRESENTATION OF COLORS AT THE ASTOR HOUSE.

Calling a halt at the Astor House, Col. Ellsworth's regiment had another stand of colors presented to them from the ladies of the Astor House. Mr. Charles Stetson, Jr., who made the presentation, said on behalf of the ladies:

COL. ELLSWORTH and officers of the Fire Zouaves:—I am requested by the ladies of this house to present to your command, the Fire Zouaves of New York, this stand of colors. They will be your battle flags; and those whose fair hands have wrought them know, from the past history of the New York Fire Department, in the great cause of liberty and integrity of the Government these emblems will be manfully sustained. On behalf of the ladies I bid you and your command God speed, their eyes will follow you, and their prayers will be rendered up for you.

In reply, Col. Ellsworth said: Mr. STETSON, I beg of you to return our thanks to the ladies of the Astor House, and assure them for us that we would rather die than commit any act that would bring disgrace upon this flag. They would remember the fair donors with a great deal of gratitude, and he hoped that it would not be long before his regiment paraded again before them in front of the Astor House.

The *Baltic* was lying at the foot of Canal street. The friends and acquaintances of the men who were going off crowded the dock. The regiment marched on board the boat to the tune of "The Red, White and Blue." Many of the men joined in the chorus as they marched along the gangway. All seemed elated at the prospect of a speedy departure. At last the order was given for all those who were not going to go on shore. Hurried adieus were made; women were weeping, and strong stern men were embracing one another with an affection absolutely touching. A few revolutions of the paddle-wheels brought the *Baltic* into the middle of the stream, and amidst the firing of salutes from the various steamers in port, and the cheers of an immense concourse of persons, she steamed quietly away seawards.

When the regiment was in front of the Astor House, an order was handed to Col. Ellsworth from Gen. Sandford, who made an objection to the departure of the regiment on account of their being more than 770 men. It appears that there are about 101 men in every company of this regiment; by law there ought only to be 77, so Gen. Sandford put his veto on the departure of this regiment. Messrs. Kelly, Stetson and Delatour formed themselves into a committee, and waited on Gen. Sandford, to get him to remove his veto. He could do nothing, but referred them to Gen. Wool, who, upon the case being represented to him, immediately took the responsibility on his own shoulders, and allowed the Firemen Zouaves to start for Annapolis.

—*N. Y. Times,* April 30.

DOC. 117.—MESSAGE OF JEFFERSON DAVIS, APRIL 29, 1861.

Gentlemen of Congress:—It is my pleasing duty to announce to you that the Constitution framed for the establishment of a permanent government of the Confederate States of America has been ratified by the several conventions of each of those States which were referred to to inaugurate the said Government in its full proportions and upon its own substantial basis of the popular will.

It only remains that elections should be held for the designation of the officers to administer it.

There is every reason to believe that at no distant day other States, identical in political principles and community of interests with those which you represent, will join this Confederacy, giving to its typical constellation increased splendor—to its government of free, equal and sovereign States, a wider sphere of usefulness, and to the friends of constitutional liberty a greater security for its harmonious and perpetual existence.

It was not, however, for the purpose of making this announcement that I have deemed it my duty to convoke you at an earlier day than that fixed by yourselves for your meeting.

The declaration of war made against this Confederacy, by Abraham Lincoln, President of the United States, in his proclamation, issued on the 15th day of the present month, renders it necessary, in my judgment, that you should convene at the earliest practicable moment to devise the measures necessary for the defence of the country.

The occasion is, indeed, an extraordinary one. It justifies me in giving a brief review of the relations heretofore existing between us and the States which now unite in warfare against us, and a succinct statement of the events which have resulted to the end, that mankind may pass intelligent and impartial judgment on our motives and objects.

During the war waged against Great Britain by her colonies on this continent, a common danger impelled them to a close alliance, and to the formation of a Confederation by the terms of which the colonies, styling themselves States, entered severally into a firm league of friendship with each other for their common defence, the security of their liberties, and their mutual and general welfare, binding themselves to assist each other against all force offered to, or attacks made upon them, or any of them, on account of religion, sovereignty, trade, or any other pretence whatever.

In order to guard against any misconstruction of their compact, the several States made an explicit declaration in a distinct article—that each State retain its sovereignty, freedom and independence, and every power of jurisdiction and right which is not by this said Confederation expressly delegated to the United States in Congress assembled under this contract of alliance.

The war of the Revolution was successfully waged, and resulted in the treaty of peace with Great Britain in 1783, by the terms of which the several States were each by name recognized to be independent.

The articles of confederation contained a clause whereby all alterations were prohibited, unless confirmed by the Legislatures of every State after being agreed to by the Congress; and in obedience to this provision, under the resolution of Congress of the 21st of February, 1787, the several States appointed delegates for the purpose of revising the articles of confederation, and reporting to Congress and the several Legislatures such alterations and provisions therein as shall, when agreed to in Congress, and confirmed by the States, render the Federal Constitution adequate to the exigencies, of the Government, and the preservation of the Union.

It was by the delegates chosen by the several States under the resolution just quoted, that the Constitution of the United States was formed in 1787, and submitted to the several States for ratification, as shown by the seventh article, which is in these words: "The ratification of the conventions of nine States shall be sufficient for the establishment of this Constitution between the States so ratifying the same."

I have italicised certain words in the resolutions just made for the purpose of attracting attention to the singular and marked caution with which the States endeavored in every possible form to exclude the idea that the separate and independent sovereignty of each State was merged into one common government or nation; and the earnest desire they evinced to impress on the Constitution its true character—that of a compact between independent States—the Constitution of 1787, however, admitting the clause already recited from the articles of confederation, which provided in explicit terms that each State reclaimed its sovereignty and independence.

Some alarm was felt in the States, when invited to ratify the Constitution, lest this omission should be construed into an abandonment of their cherished principles, and they refused to be satisfied until amendments were added to the Constitution, placing beyond any pretence of doubt the reservation by the States of their sovereign rights and powers not expressly delegated to the United States by the Constitution.

Strange, indeed, must it appear to the impartial observer, that it is none the less true that all these carefully worded clauses proved unavailing to prevent the rise and growth in the Northern States of a political school which has persistently claimed that the Government set above and over the States, an organization created by the States, to secure the blessings of liberty and independence against foreign aggression, has been gradually perverted into a machine for their control in their domestic affairs.

The creature has been exalted above its Creator—the principals have been made subordinate to the agent appointed by themselves.

The people of the Southern States, whose almost exclusive occupation was agriculture, early perceived a tendency in the Northern States to render a common government subservient to their own purposes by imposing burthens on commerce as protection to their manufacturing and shipping interests.

Long and angry controversies grew out of these attempts, often successful, to benefit one section of the country at the expense of the other, and the danger of disruption arising from this cause was enhanced by the fact that the Northern population was increasing, by emigration and other causes, more than the population of the South.

By degrees, as the Northern States gained preponderance in the National Congress, self-interest taught their people to yield ready assent to any plausible advocacy of their right as majority to govern the minority. Without control, they learn to listen with impatience to the suggestion of any constitutional impediment to the exercise of their will, and so utterly have the principles of the Constitution been corrupted in the Northern mind that, in the inaugural address delivered by President Lincoln in March last, he asserts a maxim which he plainly deems to be undeniable, that the theory of the Constitution requires, in all cases, that the majority shall govern. And in another memorable instance the same Chief Magistrate did not hesitate to liken the relations between States and the United States to those which exist between the country and the State in which it is situated, and by which it was created.

This is the lamentable and fundamental error in which rests the policy that has culminated in his declaration of war against these Confederate States.

In addition to the long-continued and deep-seated resentment felt by the Southern States at the persistent abuse of the powers they had delegated to the Congress for the purpose of enriching the manufacturing and shipping classes of the North at the expense of the South, there has existed for nearly half a century another subject of discord, involving interests of such transcendent magnitude as at all times to create the apprehension in the minds of many devoted lovers of the Union that its permanence was impossible.

When the several States delegated certain powers to the United States Congress, a large portion of the laboring population were imported into the colonies by the mother country. In twelve out of the fifteen States, negro slavery existed, and the right of property existing in slaves was protected by law; this property was recognized in the Constitution, and provision was made against its loss by the escape of the slave.

The increase in the number of slaves by foreign importation from Africa was also secured by a clause forbidding Congress to prohibit the slave trade anterior to a certain date, and in no clause can there be found any delegation of power to the Congress to authorize it in any manner to legislate to the prejudice, detriment or discouragement of the owners of that species of property, or excluding it from the protection of the Government.

The climate and soil of the Northern States soon proved unpropitious to the continuance of slave labor, while the reverse being the case at the South, made unrestricted free intercourse between the two sections unfriendly.

The Northern States consulted their own interests by selling their slaves to the South and prohibiting slavery between their limits. The South were willing purchasers of property suitable to their wants, and paid the price of the acquisition, without harboring a suspicion that their quiet possession was to be disturbed by those who were not only in want of constitutional authority, but by good faith as vendors, from disquieting a title emanating from themselves.

As soon, however, as the Northern States, that prohibited African slavery within their limits, had reached a number sufficient to give their representation a controlling vote in the Congress, a persistent and organized system of hostile measures against the rights of the owners of slaves in the Southern States was inaugurated and gradually extended. A series of measures was devised and prosecuted for the purpose of rendering insecure the tenure of property in slaves.

Fanatical organizations, supplied with money by voluntary subscriptions, were assiduously engaged in exciting amongst the slaves a spirit of discontent and revolt. Means were furnished for their escape from their owners, and agents secretly employed to entice them to abscond.

The constitutional provision for their rendition to their owners was first evaded, then openly denounced as a violation of conscientious obligation and religious duty. Men were taught that it was a merit to elude, disobey, and violently oppose the execution of the laws enacted to secure the performance of the promise contained in the constitutional compact. Often owners of slaves were mobbed and even murdered in open day solely for applying to a magistrate for the arrest of a fugitive slave.

The dogmas of the voluntary organization soon obtained control of the Legislatures of many of the Northern States, and laws were passed for the punishment, by ruinous fines, and long-continued imprisonment in gaols and penitentiaries, of citizens of the Southern States who should dare ask of the officers of the law for the recovery of their property. Emboldened by success, on the theatre of agitation and aggression, against the clearly expressed constitutional rights of the Congress, Senators and Representatives were sent to the common councils of the nation, whose chief title to this distinction consisted in the display of a spirit of ultra fanaticism, and whose business was not to promote the general welfare, or ensure domestic tranquillity—but to awaken the bitterest hatred against the citizens of sister States by violent denunciations of their institutions.

The transactions of public affairs was impeded by repeated efforts to usurp powers not delegated by the Constitution, for the purpose of impairing the security of property in slaves, and reducing those States which held slaves to a condition of inferiority.

Finally, a great party was organized for the purpose of obtaining the administration of the Government, with the avowed object of using its power for the total exclusion of the slave States from all participation in the benefits of the public domain acquired by all the States in common, whether by conquest or purchase, surrounded them entirely by States in which slavery should be prohibited, thus rendering the property in slaves so insecure as to be comparatively worthless, and thereby annihilating in effect property worth thousands of millions of dollars.

This party, thus organized, succeeded in the month of November last in the election of its candidate for the Presidency of the United States.

In the meantime, under the mild and genial climate of the Southern States, and the increasing care for the well-being and comfort of the laboring classes, dictated alike by interest and humanity, the African slaves had augmented in number from about six hundred thousand, at the date of the adoption of the constitutional compact, to upwards of four millions.

In a moral and social condition they had been elevated from brutal savages into docile, intelligent, and civilized agricultural laborers, and supplied not only with bodily comforts, but with careful religious instruction, under the supervision of a superior race. Their labor had been so directed as not only to allow a gradual and marked amelioration of their own condition, but to convert hundreds of thousands of square miles of the wilderness into cultivated lands covered with a prosperous people. Towns and cities had sprung into existence, and it rapidly increased in wealth and population under the social system of the South.

The white population of the Southern slaveholding States had augmented from about 1,250,000, at the date of the adoption of the Constitution, to more than 8,500,000 in 1860, and the productions of the South in cotton, rice, sugar and tobacco, for the full development and continuance of which the labor of African slaves was and is indispensable, had swollen to an amount which formed nearly three-fourths of the export of the whole United States, and had become absolutely necessary to the wants of civilized man.

With interests of such overwhelming magnitude imperiled, the people of the Southern States were driven by the conduct of the North to the adoption of some course of action to avoid the dangers with which they were openly menaced. With this view, the Legislatures of the several States invited the people to select delegates to conventions to be held for the purpose of determining for themselves what measures were best to be adopted to meet so alarming a crisis in their history.

Here it may be proper to observe that, from a period as early as 1798, there had existed in all of the States of the Union a party almost uninterruptedly in the majority, based upon the creed that each State was, in the last resort, the sole judge as well of its wrongs as of the mode and measures of redress. Indeed, it is obvious that under the law of nations this principle is an axiom as applied to the relations of independent sovereign States, such as those which had united themselves under the constitutional compact.

The Democratic party of the United States repeated, in its successful canvass in 1836, the deduction made in numerous previous political contests, that it would faithfully abide by, and uphold the principles laid down in the Kentucky and Virginia Legislatures of 1799, and that it adopts those principles as constituting one of the main foundations of its political creed.

The principles thus emphatically announced embrace that to which I have already adverted —the right of each State to judge of and redress the wrongs of which it complains. Their principles were maintained by overwhelming majorities of the people of all the States of the Union at different elections, especially in the election of Mr. Jefferson in 1805, Mr. Madison in 1809, and Mr. Pierce in 1852. In the exercise of a right so ancient, so well established, and so necessary for self-preservation, the people of the Confederate States in their conventions determined that the wrongs which they had suffered, and the evils with which they were menaced, required that they should revoke the delegation of powers to the Federal Government which they had ratified in their several conventions. They consequently passed ordinances resuming all their rights as sovereign and independent States, and dissolved their connection with the other States of the Union. Having done this, they proceeded to form a new compact among themselves by new articles of confederation, which have been also ratified by conventions of the several States, with an approach to unanimity far exceeding that of the conventions which adopted the Constitutions of 1787. They have organized their new government in all its departments. The functions of the executive, legislative and judicial magistrates are performed in accordance with the will of the people, as displayed not merely in a cheerful acquiescence, but in the enthusiastic support of the government thus established by themselves; and but for the interference of the Government of the United States, this legitimate exercise of a people to self-government has been manifested in every possible form.

Scarce had you assembled in February last, when, prior even to the inauguration of the chief-magistrate you had elected, you expressed your desire for the appointment of commissioners, and for the settlement of all questions of disagreement between the two governments upon principles of right, justice, equity and good faith.

It was my pleasure as well as my duty to coöperate with you in this work of peace. Indeed, in my address to you on taking the oath of office, and before receiving from you the communication of this resolution, I had said that "as a necessity, not as a choice, we have resorted to the remedy of separating, and henceforth our energies must be directed to the conduct of our own affairs, and the perpetuity of the Confederacy which we have formed. If a just perception of mutual interest shall permit us to peaceably pursue our separate political career, my most earnest desire will then have been fulfilled."

It was in furtherance of these accordant views of the congress and the executive, that I made choice of three discreet, able and distinguished citizens, who repaired to Washington. Aided by their cordial coöperation and that of the Secretary of State, every effort compatible with self-respect and the dignity of the Confederacy was exhausted before I allowed myself to yield to the conviction that the Government of the United States was determined to attempt the conquest of this people, and that our cherished hopes of peace were unobtainable.

On the arrival of our commissioners in Washington on the 5th of March, they postponed, at the suggestion of a friendly intermediator, doing more than giving informal notice of their arrival. This was done with a view to afford time to the President of the United States, who had just been inaugurated, for the discharge of other pressing official duties in the organization of his administration, before engaging his attention in the object of their mission.

It was not until the 12th of the month that they officially addressed the Secretary of State, informing him of the purpose of their arrival, and stating in the language of their instructions their wish to make to the Government of the United States overtures for the opening of negotiations, assuring the Government of the United States that the president, congress, and people of the Confederate States desired a peaceful solution of these great questions—that it was neither their interest nor their wish to make any demand which is not founded on the strictest principles of justice, nor to do any act to injure their late confederates.

To this communication no formal reply was received until the 8th of April. During the interval, the commissioners had consented to waive all questions of form, with the firm resolve to avoid war if possible. They went so far even as to hold, during that long period, unofficial intercourse through an intermediary, whose high position and character inspired the hope of success, and through whom constant assurances were received from the Government of the United States of its peaceful intentions—of its determination to evacuate Fort Sumter; and

further, that no measure would be introduced changing the existing status prejudicial to the Confederate States; that in the event of any change in regard to Fort Pickens, notice would be given to the commissioners.

The crooked path of diplomacy can scarcely furnish an example so wanting in courtesy, in candor and directness, as was the course of the United States Government toward our commissioners in Washington. For proof of this I refer to the annexed documents marked, taken in connection with further facts which I now proceed to relate.

Early in April the attention of the whole country was attracted to extraordinary preparations for an extensive military and naval expedition in New York and other Northern ports. These preparations commenced in secrecy, for an expedition whose destination was concealed, and only became known when nearly completed, and on the 5th, 6th, and 7th of April, transports and vessels of war with troops, munitions and military supplies, sailed from northern ports bound southward.

Alarmed by so extraordinary a demonstration, the commissioners requested the delivery of an answer to their official communication of the 12th of March, and the reply dated on the 15th of the previous month, from which it appears that during the whole interval, whilst the commissioners were receiving assurances calculated to inspire hope of the success of their mission, the Secretary of State and the President of the United States had already determined to hold no intercourse with them whatever—to refuse even to listen to any proposals they had to make, and had profited by the delay created by their own assurances, in order to prepare secretly the means for effective hostile operations.

That these assurances were given, has been virtually confessed by the Government of the United States, by its act of sending a messenger to Charleston to give notice of its purpose to use force if opposed in its intention of supplying Fort Sumter.

No more striking proof of the absence of good faith in the confidence of the Government of the United States toward the Confederacy can be required, than is contained in the circumstances which accompanied this notice.

According to the usual course of navigation, the vessels composing the expedition, and designed for the relief of Fort Sumter, might be looked for in Charleston harbor on the 9th of April. Yet our commissioners in Washington were detained under assurances that notice should be given of any military movement. The notice was not addressed to them, but a messenger was sent to Charleston to give notice to the Governor of South Carolina, and the notice was so given at a late hour on the 8th of April, the eve of the very day on which the fleet might be expected to arrive.

That this manœuvre failed in its purpose was not the fault of those who controlled it. A heavy tempest delayed the arrival of the expedition, and gave time to the commander of our forces at Charleston to ask and receive instructions of the government. Even then, under all the provocation incident to the contemptuous refusal to listen to our commissioners, and the treacherous course of the Government of the United States, I was sincerely anxious to avoid the effusion of blood, and directed a proposal to be made to the commander of Fort Sumter, who had avowed himself to be nearly out of provisions, that we would abstain from directing our fire on Fort Sumter if he would promise to not open fire on our forces unless first attacked. This proposal was refused. The conclusion was, that the design of the United States was to place the besieging force at Charleston between the simultaneous fire of the fleet. The fort should, of course, be at once reduced. This order was executed by Gen. Beauregard with skill and success, which were naturally to be expected from the well-known character of that gallant officer; and, although the bombardment lasted some thirty-three hours, our flag did not wave over the battered walls until after the appearance of the hostile fleet off Charleston.

Fortunately not a life was lost on our side, and we were gratified in being prepared. The necessity of an useless effusion of blood by the prudent caution of the officers who commanded the fleet, in abstaining from the evidently futile effort to enter the harbor for the relief of Major Anderson, was spared.

I refer to the report of the Secretary of War, and the papers accompanying it, for further particulars of this brilliant affair.

In this connection I cannot refrain from a well-deserved tribute to the noble State, the eminently soldierly qualities of whose people were conspicuously displayed. The people of Charleston for months had been irritated by the spectacle of a fortress held within their principal harbor as a standing menace against their peace and independence—built in part with their own money—its custody confided with their long consent to an agent who held no power over them other than such as they had themselves delegated for their own benefit, intended to be used by that agent for their own protection against foreign attack. How it was held out with persistent tenacity as a means of offence against them by the very Government which they had established for their own protection, is well known. They had beleaguered it for months, and felt entire confidence in their power to capture it, yet yielded to the requirements of discipline, curbed their impatience, submitted without complaint to the unaccustomed hardships, labors and privations of a protracted siege, and when at length their patience was relieved by the signal for attack, and success had crowned their steady and gallant conduct, even in the very moment of triumph they evinced a chivalrous regard for the feelings of the brave but unfortunate officer who had been compelled to lower his flag.

All manifestations or exultations were checked in his presence. Their commanding general, with their cordial approval and the consent of his government, refrained from imposing any terms that would wound the sensibility of the commander of the fort. He was permitted to retire with the honors of war, to salute his flag, to depart freely with all his command, and was escorted to the vessel on which he embarked with the highest marks of respect from those against whom his guns had so recently been directed.

Not only does every event connected with the siege reflect the highest honor on South Carolina, but the forbearance of her people and of this government from making any harangue of a victory obtained under circumstances of such peculiar provocation, attest to the fullest extent the absence of any purpose beyond securing their own tranquillity, and the sincere desire to avoid the calamities of war.

Scarcely had the President of the United States received intelligence of the failure of the scheme which he had devised for the reinforcement of Fort Sumter, when he issued the declaration of war against this Confederacy, which has prompted me to convoke you. In this extraordinary production, that high functionary affects total ignorance of the existence of an independent government, which, possessing the entire and enthusiastic devotion of its people, is exercising its functions without question over seven sovereign States—over more than five millions of people—and over a territory whose area exceeds five hundred thousand square miles.

He terms sovereign States "combinations too powerful to be suppressed in the ordinary course of judicial proceedings, or by the powers vested in the marshals by law."

He calls for an army of seventy-five thousand men to act as the posse comitatus in aid of the process of the courts of justice in States where no courts exist, whose mandates and decrees are not cheerfully obeyed and respected by a willing people.

He avows that the first service to be assigned to the forces which have been called out will not be to execute the processes of courts, but to capture forts and strongholds situated within the admitted limits of this Confederacy, and garrisoned by its troops, and declares that this effort is intended to maintain the perpetuity of popular government.

He concludes by commanding the persons composing the "combinations" aforesaid, to wit: the five millions of inhabitants of these States, to retire peaceably to their respective abodes within twenty days.

Apparently contradictory as are the terms of this singular document, one point was unmistakably evident. The President of the United States calls for an army of 75,000 men, whose first service was to be to capture our forts. It was a plain declaration of war which I was not at liberty to disregard, because of my knowledge that under the Constitution of the United States the President was usurping a power granted exclusively to the congress.

He is the sole organ of communication between that country and foreign powers. The law of nations did not permit me to question the authority of the Executive of a foreign nation to declare war against this Confederacy. Although I might have refrained from taking active measures for our defence, if the States of the Union had all imitated the action of Virginia, North Carolina, Arkansas, Kentucky, Tennessee and Missouri, by denouncing it as an unconstitutional usurpation of power to which they refuse to respond, I was not at liberty to disregard the fact that many of the States seemed quite content to submit to the exercise of the powers assumed by the President of the United States, and were actively engaged in levying troops for the purpose indicated in the proclamation. Deprived of the aid of congress, at the moment I was under the necessity of confining my action to a call on the States for volunteers for the common defence, in accordance with the authority you had confided to me before your adjournment.

I deemed it proper further to issue a proclamation, inviting applications from persons disposed to aid in our defence in private armed vessels on the high seas, to the end that preparations might be made for the immediate issue of letters of marque and reprisal, which you alone, under the constitution, have the power to grant.

I entertain no doubt that you will concur with me in the opinion, that in the absence of an organized navy, it will be eminently expedient to supply their place with private armed vessels, so happily styled by the publicists of the United States the militia of the sea, and so often and justly relied on by them as an efficient and admirable instrument of defensive warfare.

I earnestly recommend the immediate passage of a law authorizing me to accept the numerous proposals already received.

I cannot close this review of the acts of the Government of the United States without referring to a proclamation issued by their President under date of the 19th inst., in which, after declaring that an insurrection has broken out in this Confederacy against the Government of the United States, he announces a blockade of all the ports of these States, and threatens to punish as pirates all persons who shall molest any vessel of the United States under letters of marque issued by this government. Notwithstanding the authenticity of this proclamation, you will concur with me that it is hard to believe that it could have emanated from a President of the United States.

Its announcement of a mere paper blockade is so manifestly a violation of the law of nations, that it would seem incredible that it could have been issued by authority; but conceding this to be the case, so far as the Executive is concerned, it will be difficult to satisfy the people of these States that their late confederates will sanction its declarations—will determine to ignore the usages of civilized nations, and will inaugurate a war of extermination on both sides, by treating as pirates open enemies acting under the authority of commissions issued by an organized government.

If such proclamation was issued, it could only have been published under the sudden influence of passion, and we may rest assured that mankind will be spared the horrors of the conflict it seems to invite.

For the details of the administration of the different departments, I refer to the reports of the secretaries of each, which accompany this message.

The State Department has furnished the necessary instructions for those commissioners who have been sent to England, France, Russia and Belgium, since your adjournment, to ask our recognition as a member of the family of nations, and to make with each of these powers treaties of amity and commerce.

Further steps will be taken to enter into like negotiations with the other European Powers, in pursuance to resolutions passed at your last session.

Sufficient time has not yet elapsed since the departure of these commissioners for the receipt of any intelligence from them.

As I deem it desirable that commissioners or other diplomatic agents should also be sent at an early period to the independent American Powers south of our Confederacy, with all of whom it is our interest and earnest wish to maintain the most cordial and friendly relations, I suggest the expediency of making the necessary appropriations for that purpose.

Having been officially notified by the public authorities of the State of Virginia that she had withdrawn from the Union and desired to maintain the closest political relations with us which it was possible at this time to establish, I commissioned the Hon. Alex. H. Stephens, Vice-President of the Confederate States, to represent this government at Richmond.

I am happy to inform you that he has concluded a convention with the State of Virginia, by which that honored Commonwealth, so long and justly distinguished among her sister States, and so dear to the hearts of thousands of her children in the Confederate States, has united her power and her fortunes with ours and become one of us. This convention, together with the ordinance of Virginia adopting the Provisional Constitution of the Confederacy will be laid before you for your constitutional action.

I have satisfactory assurances from other of our late confederates that they are on the point of adopting similar measures; and I cannot doubt that, ere you shall have been many weeks in session, the whole of the slaveholding States of the late Union will respond to the call of honor and affection, and by uniting their fortune with ours, promote our common interests and secure our common safety.

In the Treasury Department, regulations have been devised and put into execution for carrying out the policy indicated in your legislation, on the subject of the navigation of the Mississippi River, as well as for the collection of the revenue on the frontier.

Free transit has been secured for vessels and merchandise passing through the Confederate States, and delay and inconvenience have been avoided as far as possible.

In organizing the revenue service for the various railways entering our territory, as fast as experience shall indicate the possibility of improvement in these regulations, no effort will be spared to free commerce from all unnecessary embarrassments and obstructions.

Under your act authorizing a loan, proposals were issued inviting subscriptions for five millions of dollars, and the call was answered by the prompt subscription of eight millions by our own citizens, and not a single bid was made under par.

The rapid development of the purpose of the President of the United States to invade our soil, capture our forts, blockade our ports, and wage war against us, induced me to direct that the entire subscription should be accepted. It will now become necessary to raise means to a much larger amount to defray the expenses of maintaining our independence and repelling invasion.

I invite your special attention to this subject, and the financial condition of the Government, with the suggestion of ways and means for the supply of the treasury, will be presented to you in a separate communication.

To the department of Justice you have confided not only the organization and supervision of all matters connected with the courts of justice but also those connected with patents and with the bureau of the public printing.

Since your adjournment all the courts, with the exception of those of Mississippi and Texas, have been organized by the appointment of marshals and district attorneys, and are now prepared for the exercise of their functions. In the two States just named the gentlemen confirmed as judges declined to accept the appointment, and no nominations have yet been made to fill the vacancies.

I refer you to the report of the Attorney-General, and concur in his recommendation for immediate legislation, especially on the subject of patent rights. Early provision should be made to secure to the subjects of foreign nations the full enjoyment of their property in valuable inventions, and to extend to our own citizens protection not only for their own inventions, but for such as may be assigned to them or may hereafter be assigned by persons not alien enemies.

The patent office business is much more extensive and important than had been anticipated. The applications for patents, although confined under the laws exclusively to citizens of our Confederacy, already average seventy per month, showing the necessity for the prompt organization of a bureau of patents.

The Secretary of War, in his report and accompanying documents, conveys full information concerning the forces, regular, volunteer, and provisional, raised and called for under the several acts of Congress—their organization and distribution; also, an account of the expenditures already made, and the further estimates for the fiscal year ending on the 18th of February, 1862, rendered necessary by recent events.

I refer to the report, also, for a full history of the occurrences in Charleston harbor, prior to, and including the, bombardment and reduction of Fort Sumter, and of the measures subsequently taken for common defence on receiving the intelligence of the declaration of war against us, made by the President of the United States.

There are now in the field at Charleston, Pensacola, Forts Morgan, Jackson, St. Philip and Pulaski, 19,000 men, and 16,000 are now en route for Virginia. It is proposed to organize and hold in readiness for instant action, in view of the present exigencies of the country, an army of 100,000 men. If further force be needed the wisdom and patriotism of the Congress will be confidently appealed to for authority to call into the field additional numbers of our noble spirited volunteers, who are constantly tendering their services far in excess of our wants.

The operations of the Navy Department have been necessarily restricted by the fact that sufficient time has not yet elapsed for the purchase or construction of more than a limited number of vessels adapted to the public service. Two vessels have been purchased and manned, the Sumter and McRea, and are now being prepared for sea, at New Orleans, with all possible despatch. Contracts have also been made at that city, with two different establishments, for the casting of ordnance—cannon, shot and shell —with the view to encourage the manufacture of these articles, so indispensable for our defence, at as many points within our territory as possible. I call your attention to the recommendation of the Secretary for the establishment of a magazine and laboratory for the preparation of ordnance stores and the necessary appropriation required for that purpose.

Hitherto such stores have been prepared at the navy yards, and no appropriation was made at your last session for this object.

The Secretary also calls attention to the fact that no provision has been made for the payment of invalid pensions to our citizens. Many of these persons are advanced in life—they have no means of support—and by the secession of these States have been deprived of their claims against the Government of the United States.

I recommend the appropriation of the sum

necessary to pay these pensioners as well as those of the army, whose claim can scarcely exceed $20,000 per annum.

The Postmaster-General has already succeeded in organizing his department to such an extent as to be in readiness to assume the direction of our postal affairs on the occurrence of the contingency contemplated by the act of 15th March, 1861, or even sooner if desired by Congress.

The various books and circulars have been prepared, and measures taken to secure supplies of blanks, postage stamps, stamped envelopes, mail bags, locks, keys, &c.

He presents a detailed classification and arrangement of the clerical force and asks for its increase.

An Auditor of the Treasury for this Department is necessary, and a plan is submitted for the organization of his bureau.

The great number and magnitude of the accounts of this department require an increase of the clerical force in the accounting branch of the treasury. The revenues of this department are collected and distributed in modes peculiar to itself, and require a special bureau to secure a proper accountability in the administration of its finances.

I call your attention to the additional legislation required for this department—to the recommendation for changes in the law fixing the rates of postage on newspapers and sealed packages of certain kinds, and specially to the recommendation of the Secretary, in which I concur, that you provide at once for the assumption by him of the control of our entire postal service.

In the military organization of the States, provision is made for Brigadier and Major-Generals, but in the army of the Confederate States the highest grade is that of a Brigadier-General; hence it will no doubt sometimes occur that, where troops of the Confederacy do duty with the militia, the General selected for the command and possessed of the views and purposes of this Government, will be superseded by an officer of the militia, not having the same advantages.

To avoid contingencies in the least objectionable manner, I recommend that additional rank be given to the General of the Confederate army, and concurring in the policy of having but one grade of Generals in the army of the Confederacy, I recommend that the law of its organization be amended so that the grade be that of General.

To secure thorough military education, it is deemed essential that officers should enter upon the study of their profession at an early period of life, and have elementary instruction in a military school.

Until such school shall be established it is recommended that cadets be appointed and attached to companies until they shall have attained the age and shall have acquired the knowledge to fit them for the duties of lieutenants.

I also call your attention to an omission in the law organizing the army, in relation to military chaplains, and recommend that provision be made for their appointment.

In conclusion, I congratulate you on the fact that in every portion of our country there has been exhibited the most patriotic devotion to our common cause. Transportation companies have freely tendered the use of their lines for troops and supplies.

The Presidents of the railroads of the Confederacy, in company with others who control lines of communication with States that we hope soon to greet as sisters assembled in convention in this city, have not only reduced largely the rates heretofore demanded for mail service and conveyance of troops and munitions, but have voluntarily proffered to receive their compensation at their reduced rates in the bonds of the Confederacy, for the purpose of leaving all the resources of the Government at its own disposal for the common defence.

Requisitions for troops have been met with such alacrity that the numbers tendering their services have in every instance greatly exceeded the demand. Men of the highest official and social position are serving as volunteers in the ranks. The gravity of age, the zeal of youth, rival each other in the desire to be foremost in the public defence, and though at no other point than the one heretofore noticed have they been stimulated by the excitement incident to actual engagement and the hope of distinction for individual deportment, they have borne, what for new troops is the most severe ordeal, patient toil, constant vigil, and all the exposure and discomfort of active service with a resolution and fortitude such as to command the approbation and justify the highest expectation of their conduct when active valor shall be required in place of steady endurance.

A people thus united and resolute cannot shrink from any sacrifice which they may be called on to make, nor can there be a reasonable doubt of their final success, however long and severe may be the test of their determination to maintain their birthright of freedom and equality as a trust which it is their first duty to transmit unblemished to their posterity.

A bounteous Providence cheers us with the promise of abundant crops.

The fields of grain which will, within a few weeks, be ready for the sickle, give assurance of the amplest supply of food, whilst the corn, cotton, and other staple productions of our soil afford abundant proof that up to this period the season has been propitious.

We feel that our cause is just and holy.

We protest solemnly, in the face of mankind, that we desire peace at any sacrifice, save that of honor.

In independence we seek no conquest, no

aggrandizement, no cession of any kind from the States with which we have lately confederated. All we ask is to be let alone—that those who never held power over us shall not now attempt our subjugation by arms. This we will, we must resist, to the direst extremity.

The moment that this pretension is abandoned, the sword will drop from our grasp, and we shall be ready to enter into treaties of amity and commerce that cannot but be mutually beneficial.

So long as this pretension is maintained, with a firm reliance on that Divine Power which covers with its protection the just cause, we will continue to struggle for our inherent right to freedom, independence, and self-government.

JEFFERSON DAVIS.

MONTGOMERY, April 29, 1861.

—*N. O. Picayune*, May 2.

Doc. 118.—THE WEVERTON LETTER.

WEVERTON, Frederick Co., Md., April 29, 1861.

To Gov. HICKS:—At a meeting held in Weverton, by the citizens of Washington and Frederick Counties, the following memorial was agreed to, and ordered to be presented to your Excellency, by a Committee appointed for that purpose:

Whereas, since the occupation of Harper's Ferry by the troops of Virginia, a number of soldiers have at different times crossed over into our State, and, under pretence of obtaining arms, have disturbed the peace of the neighborhood, and outraged the feelings of citizens by searching private dwellings; and whereas the citizens of Sandy Hook, Weverton, and vicinity, protesting against the right of troops from Virginia invading our soil for such unfriendly purposes, do hereby beseech your Excellency to adopt such measures as, in your good judgment, will be sufficient to prevent any repetition of similar outrages.

We, furthermore, would especially state that troops making search informed us that they had obtained permission from your Excellency to search the private dwellings above stated to the extent of twenty miles in the territory of this State. We mention this in order to get a refutation of such a slanderous report, as we believe it wholly without foundation.

HENRY MORTINIER, Chairman.
ALFRED SPENCER, Sec.

—*N. Y. Tribune*, May 1.

Doc. 119.—A SIGN OF THE TIMES.

THE historian of our day will not fail to mention, for the edification of the men of future ages, (would that those of the present might be calm enough to derive the same instructive lesson from it!) the fact that the glorious old flag which was once "the flag of our Union," in truth as well as in name, floats boldly to the breezes of Heaven, *above* the cross of Christ,

whom our fathers reverently worshipped as "King of kings and Lord of lords." Pride and hatred now rise above humility and love, and the harsh notes of fratricidal war quite drown the gentle voice from Heaven, "Peace on earth, good will toward men."

Those of us who profess and call ourselves Christians, used but lately to place the cross of Christ above every thing else; but there is something *now* above that cross. Ought it to remain in such a proud, and, as it certainly must seem to every calm and humble Christian mind, a God-defying position? *Vide* the top of Grace Church steeple. God grant that Christian passers-by may look up and think, and learn a good lesson from such a significant sign of the times.

—*N. Y. News*, April 29.

Doc. 120.—SPEECH OF A. H. STEPHENS AT ATLANTA, GA., APRIL 30, 1861.

MY FELLOW-CITIZENS:—I think the country may be considered safe, since your interest in its welfare has brought you out at this hour of the night. I have just returned from a mission to old Virginia. It will be gratifying to you, I know, to state that she is not only out of the Union, but *she is a member of the Southern Confederacy, and has sent delegates to our Congress, now assembled.* North Carolina will have her delegates with us, also, in a few days. Her Legislature meets to-morrow, and I doubt not *she will be out of the Union before Saturday night.* The fires which first kindled the old Mecklenburgh Declaration of Independence are again burning throughout all her domains. From all that we have learned in the last few days, Tennessee will soon put herself on the side of the South, and be a new star in our shining galaxy. The news is also good from Kentucky, though I have nothing official from there. A few of her public men are trying to put the brakes down on her people; but they seem unwilling to submit any longer. From Missouri the news is most cheering, and Arkansas will soon be with us.

But the best of all is, that Maryland—gallant little Maryland—right under the guns of LINCOLN, and the threats of BLAIR, to make it a Free State, if the blood of the last white man has to be shed in accomplishing it—*has resolved, to a man, to stand by the South!* She will be arrayed against Abolitiondom, and cling to the South: and if she has not delegates with us now, she is in open defiance of LINCOLN and his Government, and will soon be with us, even by revolution. The cause of Baltimore is the cause of us all, from the Atlantic to the Rio Grande. Her hands must be held up, and triumph must be assured to her.

You have probably seen it stated that overtures of peace had been made by Lord LYONS, and, perhaps, by other parties. I tell you it is not true, and is only intended to deceive you. It is also said that the Lincoln Government has done so. This may be true; but if it is, it is all for treachery, as they gave traitorous assurances to our Commissioners at Washington. For weeks they were kept there under the most positive assurances of a pacific policy and intentions towards us—all with the basest motives that can actuate a treacherous heart. If peace propositions are made by them now, I conjure you not to trust them for a single moment—they only intend to deceive and betray—to lull your energies and suspicions, till they secure some cowardly advantage.

Our enemies say that they only want to protect the public property; and yet I have it from unquestioned authority that they have mined all the public buildings in Washington—the Capitol and all the other Departments—for the purpose of destroying them. They have called out 75,000 men, they say to protect the public property now in their possession, and to retake and protect that which they have been forced to give up; yet, wherever they are now, they have prepared to destroy the property, and have destroyed, or attempted to destroy, all that we have compelled them to relinquish, because of their intentions to use it for the purpose of subjugating us. Sumter was mined to be blown up on leaving it. Much of the property was burned up at Harper's Ferry, in hastily vacating that place; and an attempt was made to burn up not only all the public property, on leaving Gosport Navy Yard, but the whole city of Norfolk. This is one of the most remarkable instances on record where Providence was on our side. Plans were laid to burn up the Navy Yard and the whole city. The incendiary fires were lighted; and, if their intentions had succeeded, such a conflagration had never been witnessed on this continent, and would have been second only to the burning of Moscow; but, just at the critical moment, before the ravages had extended, the wind turned! The winds of Heaven turned, and stayed the spread of the devouring element. The same wind that kind Heaven sent to keep off the fleet at Charleston till Sumter was reduced, came to the relief of Norfolk at the critical moment. Providence was signally on our side. They attempted to blow up the Dock, the most expensive one on the continent—but there was a break in the train they had laid, and it failed. They attempted to burn down the old *Pennsylvania*, *Germantown*, and the *Merrimac*. They set the match, while they endeavored to get out of the way of their intended destruction; but the vessels sunk before the fire caught—another remarkable instance of the interposition of Providence on our behalf, and the strongest evidence of our rectitude. We were right at first, are right now, and shall keep ourselves right to the end.

What is to take place before the end, I know not. A threatening war is upon us, made by those who have no regard for right! We fight for our homes, our fathers and mothers, our wives, brothers, sisters, sons, and daughters, and neighbors! *They for* MONEY! The hirelings and mercenaries of the North are all hand to hand against you.

As I told you when I addressed you a few days ago, Lincoln may bring his seventy-five thousand soldiers against us; but seven times seventy-five thousand men can never conquer us. We have now Maryland and Virginia, and all the Border States with us. We have ten millions of people with us, heart and hand, to defend us to the death. *We can call out a million of people, if need be; and when they are cut down, we can call out another, and still another,* until the last man of the South finds a bloody grave, rather than submit to their foul dictation. But a triumphant victory and independence, with an unparalleled career of glory, prosperity and progress, await us in the future. *God is on our side, and who shall be against us?* None but His omnipotent hand can defeat us in this struggle.

A general opinion prevails that Washington city is soon to be attacked. On this subject I can only say, our object is peace. We wish no aggressions on any one's rights, and will make none. But *if Maryland secedes*, the District of Columbia will fall to her by reversionary right—the same as Sumter to South Carolina, Pulaski to Georgia, and Pickens to Alabama. When we have the right we will demand the surrender of Washington, just as we did in the other cases, and will enforce our demands at every hazard and at whatever cost. And here let me say that our policy and conduct from the first have been right, and shall be to the last. I glory in this consciousness of our rectitude.

It may be that "whom the gods would destroy, they first make mad." But for Lincoln's wicked and foolish war proclamation, the border States—some of them at least, would still have lingered in the hope that the Administration and its designs were not so basely treacherous as that document has shown them to be. Tennessee and other States would have lingered for some time. Now, all the slave States are casting in their lot with us, and linking their destinies with ours. We might afford to thank Lincoln a little for showing his hand. It may be that soon the Confederate flag with fifteen stars will be hoisted upon the dome of the ancient Capitol. If so, God's will be done is my prayer. Let us do nothing that is wrong. Let us commit our cause into His hand—perform our whole duty, and trust in Him for the crowning results.

I have many things I would like to say to you, but my strength will not admit, even if it were necessary for your encouragement—but it is not. I find that you are fully up to the music, that you thoroughly comprehend our condition, and are resolved to do your whole duty. I find our people everywhere are alive to their interests and their duty in this crisis. Such a degree of popular enthusiasm was never before seen in this country. I find my fellow-citizens all along the railroad line eager to hear the news, and to speed our glorious cause with their services. This is the fifth speech which I have made since I left home this evening at 6 o'clock. In my town, yesterday, a meeting was held, a company was organized, and their services tendered to our government. A flag was made in two hours by our patriotic ladies and presented to the company, and $2,200 was raised to equip the company and take care of the needy families of soldiers who may go off to fight for our country.

My friends, *forget not the soldier!* Send him contributions to make him comfortable while he is in the service. Take care of his family while he is absent. Employ your hands and your substance in doing works of charity in this day of your country's trial. If any should fall in the battle, remember the orphan and the widow, and take care of them. God will bless you in the noble performances of a patriotic duty.

My fellow-citizens, I must close these remarks. I am gratified to meet you to-night. I am gratified that Georgia and all the South is a unit. I rejoice to be able to tell you the welcome news that Virginia is a unit. Nearly every single member of her Convention will sign her Ordinance of Secession. And now, with my best wishes, I bid you good-night.

His speech was rapturously applauded throughout; and, as he retired, three cheers for Stephens were given with a will.

In a few moments, in response to earnest solicitations, he again came on the platform, and said:

"The news from Washington is very interesting. It has been stated in the newspapers—first, that the Virginia troops had occupied Arlington Heights, just across the Potomac from the President's house; and again, that Lincoln's troops had occupied that point. My information is that both these statements are incorrect. Lincoln, however, has occupied Georgetown Heights. He has from fifteen to twenty thousand soldiers stationed in and about Washington. Troops are quartered in the capitol, who are defacing its walls and ornaments with grease and filth, like a set of vandal hordes. The new Senate chamber has been converted into a kitchen and quarters—cooking and sleeping apparatus having actually been erected and placed in that elegant apartment. The Patent Office is converted into soldiers' barracks, and is ruined with their filth. The Post-Office Department is made a storehouse for barrels of flour and bacon. All the departments are appropriated to base uses, and despoiled of their beauty by those treacherous destructive enemies of our country. Their filthy spoliations of the public buildings, and works of art at the Capital, and their preparations to destroy them, are strong evidence to my mind that they do not intend to hold or defend the place; but to abandon it, after hav-

ing despoiled and laid it in ruins. Let them destroy it—savage-like—if they will. We will rebuild it. We will make the structures more glorious. Phœnix-like, new and more substantial structures will rise from its ashes. Planted anew, under the auspices of our superior institutions, it will live and flourish throughout all ages."

—*Atlanta (Ga.) Confederacy,* May 2.

Doc. 121.—THE PALMETTO GUARD, MARION ARTILLERY, AND GERMAN ARTILLERY.

THE companies passed by the *Mercury* office, with flags flying, and bands playing "Dixie," and looking, notwithstanding their hard service on Morris Island, in better trim than when, weeks ago, they took their departure.

The Marion Artillery, Capt. King, and German Artillery, Company A, Capt. Nohrden, marched to the Gun Shed, where they were dismissed, and proceeded to their several homes to make glad many hearts that have felt desolate during their absence.

The Palmetto Guard, Capt. Cuthbert—the heroes of the renowned Stevens' iron battery—marched to Military Hall, where a collation was in waiting, provided by the mothers, wives, and sisters of the members of the company. After a long term of camp life, the luxuries prepared by the ladies were most heartily enjoyed, and the source from which the supplies had been provided, gave an additional relish to the entertainment.

Many off-hand speeches were made, and toasts and sentiments sparkling with good humor, wit and patriotism, were abundant. Among the speakers were C. H. Stevens, Esq., immortalized as the founder of the iron battery, and bravely manned by the Guard; Major Ellison Capers, Captain Cuthbert, and Wm. B. Carlisle, Esq.

The mothers, wives, sisters and sweethearts of the Palmetto Guard, have contributed the sum of two hundred dollars for the purpose of presenting the company with a gold medal in commemoration of the memorable battle of Fort Sumter. The medal has been manufactured by Messrs. Spencer & Teague, where it may be seen to-day. The presentation will take place to-morrow, Major Ellison Capers, having been commissioned by the ladies on their part to present it.

Where every man has proved himself first among the fearless and the brave, it may seem invidious to mention any one in particular; but the subjects of the following have been such universal favorites with the company, that we feel confident no exceptions will be taken. Cadet George M. Lalane, of the Citadel Academy, hastened, at the first signal of alarm, to serve his native State, and proffered his services to the Palmetto Guard. With this company he has been on steady active service as corporal since December 27, and, being thoroughly familiar with military tactics and drill, he had the honor of acting as drill-sergeant most of the time. As a truly well-earned and merited compliment to this young gentleman, the Board of Visitors of the Citadel Academy have caused the following to be registered on the record book of that Institution:

"The efficiency and soldierly bearing of Cadet Lalane, during the affair of Fort Sumter, is highly commended by the Board of Visitors."

A younger brother, Paul B. Lalane—only in his thirteenth year—had the honor of being in the iron battery on the memorable 12th and 13th, and of firing seventeen guns with powerful effect during the bombardment. The youthful hero, from his reckless bravery and daring during the siege, has become the pet of the company, and is now their regularly appointed marker, he having acted in this capacity on the parade yesterday.

While fighting for our country's cause is necessary, the Palmetto Guard will not remain idle. They have volunteered their services for Virginia, and, towards the close of the week, will again buckle on the knapsack for the march. Without the border of their native Carolina, may their victories be as complete and as bloodless as that achieved on their own Palmetto shores.

The following is the list of officers of the Palmetto Guard who were in the fight on the 12th and 13th days of April, 1861: George B. Cuthbert, Captain; C. R. Holmes, First Lieutenant; T. S. Brownfield, Second Lieutenant; G. L. Buist, Third Lieutenant; T. L. Bissell, First Sergeant; J. B. Bissell, Second Sergeant; W. D. Gaillard, Third Sergeant; B. C. Webb, Fourth Sergeant; L. S. Webb, Fifth Sergeant; R. J. Brownfield, Sixth Sergeant; Samuel Robertson, First Corporal; J. E. Wright, Second Corporal; George Lalane, Third Corporal; G. B. Dyer, Fourth Corporal; J. M. Rhett, Fifth Corporal; E. W. Macbeth, Sixth Corporal.

—*Charleston Mercury*, May 1.

Doc. 122.—THE TWENTY-EIGHTH REGIMENT, N. Y. S. M.

The officers of this regiment are as follows: Col. Bennett, (who will remain at home until he recovers from severe injuries received by being thrown from a wagon;) Lieut.-Col. Burns, commanding; Surgeon, Rice. Company A, Capt. Bruer, Lieuts. Waudelt and Horn; Company B, Capt. Becke, Lieuts. Warmuth and Hoffman—(the last-named has resigned;) Company C, Capt. Campbell, (Lieuts. vacant;) Company D, Capt. Brandenburg, Lieuts. Bensler and Kramer; Company E, Capt. Beadle, Lieuts. Altanbrand and Bergemen; Company F, Capt. Schepper, Lieuts. Wenner and Breneisen; Company G, Capt. Reeger, Lieuts. Berger and Fox; Company H, Capt. Wills, Lieuts. Dowling and Schaeffer; Company I, Capt. Kiehl, Lieuts. Markert and Obernier; Company K, Capt. Weber, Lieuts. Moring and Kinow; Engineer Corps, Capt. Von Kameke. Capt. Thomas C. Clines, of Company C, is detailed for the recruiting service.

Chaplain, Rev. Mr. Zapt, of the Union Avenue German Lutheran Church.

—*N. Y. Times*, May 1.

Doc. 123.—LETTER TO GENERAL SCOTT.

PHILADELPHIA, April 30, 1861.

To Lieut.-Gen. Winfield Scott, General-in-Chief of the Army of the United States.

SIR:—The shock of a civil war in our beloved country, whose history, for more than half a century, has been illustrated, not less by your wisdom and patriotism than the splendor of your achievements in arms, will, we trust, justify this letter to you, even though it be a departure from usage.

We are your fellow-citizens of the United States. We are devotedly attached to our country. Her renown is precious to us. It is our richest inheritance, and we had fondly hoped to transmit it to our children, untarnished, as it came to us from our fathers.

In the civil strife which has just lighted up our land with an unnatural and deadly glare, we do not stop to inquire into the soundness of conflicting opinions as to the origin of the deplorable controversy. It is enough for us to know that the beloved and glorious flag of our Federal Union has been assailed, and we ask no further questions. In such a crisis, we are for sustaining, to any and every extent, the constituted authorities of the Union, believing, in the language of Mr. Jefferson, that, "*The preservation of the General Government in its whole constitutional vigor, is the sheet-anchor of our peace at home and safety abroad.*" While the Government stands by the flag, we stand by the Government. In this determination we obliterate, for the time being, all traces of party difference, by which many of us have been heretofore widely separated.

As citizens of Philadelphia—a city which, we are sure, must be endeared to your recollections, as it is to ours, by some of the proudest memories of the era of Independence—where the Declaration was signed—where the Constitution was signed, and from whence our illustrious founder issued to his countrymen his immortal Farewell Address—we adopt this mode of testifying our admiration, and offering you our deep-felt thanks for your great services to your country, in this hour of her extremest peril—services which will rival in immortality, and, we trust, in their triumphant results, your early and subsequent renown in the second and third great wars of the United States.

At a time like this, when Americans, distinguished by the favor of their country, entrenched in power, and otherwise high in influence and station, civil and military, are renouncing their allegiance to the flag they have sworn to support, it is an inexpressible source of consolation and pride to us to know that the General-in-Chief of the army remains like an impregnable fortress at the post of duty and glory, and that he will continue to the last to uphold that flag, and defend it, if necessary, with his sword, even if his native State should assail it.

That your career of rare distinction may be prolonged for many years of continued usefulness to your country, and happiness to yourself, and that you may live to see that great country once more in the enjoyment of the prosperity and renown among nations, to which your wisdom in council and your sword in battle have so largely contributed, is the anxious, earnest hope of those who here unite in tendering to you, not only the assurances of their profound respect, but what we believe you will value as highly, the spontaneous tribute of loyal American hearts.

We have the honor to remain,
With the highest consideration, dear sir,
Your friends and fellow-citizens,
ALEXANDER HENRY, HOR. BINNEY,
RICHARD VAUX, W. M. MEREDITH,
THEO. CUYLER, C. MACALESTER,
and others.
—*Phila. Press.*

Doc. 124.—THE BAPTIST CONVENTION OF GEORGIA.

ATHENS, Ga., April 29, 1861.

SIR:—I have the honor of transmitting to you the accompanying resolutions, unanimously passed on Saturday last, by the Baptist Convention of the State of Georgia, with the request that you will present them to the Congress over which you preside.

That God will direct and bless the councils of the Congress of the Confederate Government, is the prayer of the Baptist Convention of the State of Georgia, and of none more sincerely than your Obedient servant,
H. M. CRAWFORD,
HOWELL COBB, Chairman of Committee.
President of Congress.

At a meeting of the Georgia Baptist Convention, the following preamble and resolutions were unanimously passed:

Whereas, The State Convention of Georgia, in the legitimate exercise of her sovereignty, has withdrawn from the Confederacy known as the United States of America, and, for the better maintenance of her rights, honor, and independence, has united with other States in a new Confederacy, under the title of The Confederate States of America; and

Whereas, Abraham Lincoln is attempting, by force of arms, to subjugate these States, in violation of the fundamental principle of American liberty; therefore,

Resolved, by the members of the Baptist Convention of the State of Georgia, That we consider it to be at once a pleasure and a duty to

avow that, both in feeling and principle, we approve, indorse, and support the government of the Confederate States of America.

Resolved, That while this Convention disclaims all authority, whether ecclesiastical or civil, yet as citizens we deem it a duty to urge the union of all the people of the South in defence of the common cause, and to express the confident belief that in whatever conflict the madness of Mr. Lincoln and his Government may force upon us, the Baptists of Georgia will not be behind any class of our fellow-citizens in maintaining the independence of the South by any sacrifice of treasure, or of blood.

Resolved, That we acknowledge with devout thanksgiving to Almighty God, the signal favor with which, up to this time, He has blessed our arms and our policy, and that the Baptist churches of this State be requested to observe the first and second days of June next, as days of fasting and prayer, that God will deliver us from all the power of our enemies, and restore peace to our country.

Resolved, That the Confederate Government be requested to invite the churches of all denominations within the Confederacy to unite in observing said days of prayer and fasting.

Resolved, That copies of these resolutions be sent to President Davis, the Confederate Congress, and the governor of Georgia.
—*N. Y. Tribune,* May 8.

Doc. 125.—GENERAL HARNEY'S LETTER.

WASHINGTON, May 1, 1861.

MY DEAR SIR:—The report of my arrest at Harper's Ferry, by persons assuming to act under authority of the State of Virginia, has no doubt reached you. Upon my arrival at Richmond, under military escort, Governor Letcher immediately directed my release, with assurances disavowing the act of his subordinates, and expressing regret at their mistake or abuse of his authority. The kind attention and civility received from him, from the escort that accompanied me, and other distinguished citizens of Virginia, and esteemed friends whom I there met, compensated for any personal trouble or annoyance; yet I cannot but feel deep mortification and regret that our country should be in a condition to expose any one to such an incident. It has furnished occasion for mistake or misrepresentation in respect to my views and sentiments, which a sense of duty requires to be promptly corrected. No better mode occurs to me than by a letter addressed to yourself, as an esteemed personal friend.

It has been represented through the public press that I was a willing prisoner to the State of Virginia; that I designed to resign my commission in the United States army, throw off my allegiance to the Federal Government, and join the forces of the Confederate States.

Forty two years I have been in the military service of the United States, and have followed during all that time but one flag—the flag of the Union. I have seen it protecting our frontiers, and guarding our coasts, from Maine to Florida; I have witnessed it in the smoke of battle, stained with the blood of gallant men, leading on to victory; planted upon the strongholds, and waving in triumph over the capital of a foreign foe. My eyes have beheld that flag affording protection to our States and Territories on the Pacific, and commanding reverence and respect from hostile fleets and squadrons, and from foreign governments, never exhibited to any other banner on the globe. Twenty stars, each representing a State, have been added to that banner during my service, and under its folds I have advanced from the rank of lieutenant to that which I now hold. The Government, whose honors have been bestowed upon me, I shall serve the remainder of my days. The flag, whose glories I have witnessed, shall never be forsaken by me while I can strike a blow for its defence. While I have breath, I shall be ready to serve the Government of the United States, and be its faithful loyal soldier.

Without condemning, or in any degree criticizing the course other persons have deemed proper to pursue in the present juncture, my line of duty is plain to my own heart and judgment. The course of events that have led to the deplorable condition in which our country now stands has been watched by me with painful interest. Perceiving that many of my fellow-citizens in the Southern States were discontented with the Government, and desired some change to protect them from existing evils, my feelings have been strongly averse to coercion, and anxious for some compromise or arrangement that would restore peace and harmony. The provisions of the Federal Constitution afforded, in my judgment, ample means of redress through a Convention of all the States, which might adopt amendments that would reconcile all differences, or if that could not be accomplished, might provide for peaceful separation in a manner becoming friends and brethren. So long as this hope of peaceful settlement of our troubles could be indulged, I have felt it to be the wise duty of the general Government to bear with patience outrages that no other government could have endured, and to forbear any exertion of force until the last hope departed. But when the Confederate States with seven thousand men, under cover of strong fortifications or impregnable batteries, assailed a starving garrison of seventy men in Fort Sumter, compelled the banner of the United States to be lowered, and boasted of its dishonor before the world, the state of the question was immediately changed. Instead of the Government coercing States, demanding redress of grievances by constitutional means, the case was presented of revolutionists waging war against their Government, seeking an overthrow by force of arms, assailing public property by overwhelming force, laboring to destroy the lives of gallant officers and soldiers, and dishonoring the national flag. The question now before us, is, whether the Government of the United States, with its many blessings and past glories, shall be overthrown by the military dictatorship lately planted and now bearing sway in the Confederate States? My hand cannot aid in that work.

Finding ourselves in a state of civil war, actually existing or fast approaching, some of my brethren in arms, citizens of seceding States, and for whom I have the highest personal respect, have considered it their duty to throw up their commissions and follow their States. In that view of duty I cannot concur. As an officer of the army and a citizen of the United States, I consider my primary allegiance to be due to the Federal Government, and subordinate to that is my allegiance to the State. This, as you are aware, has been the concurring opinion of the most eminent jurists of this country. It was the judgment of the Court of Appeals of South Carolina in the case of Hunt, where the subject was discussed with matchless ability. In that case, the highest court of South Carolina deliberately decided that the soldier's and citizen's primary duty of allegiance is due to the United States Government, and not to the government of his State. Of late it has been contended that the allegiance due by a citizen to the Federal Government, was dissolved when his State secedes from the Union. Into that snare many have fallen. But in my judgment there is and can be no such right as secession of a State by its own act. The Government of the Union can only be dissolved by the concurrence of the States that have entered into the federal compact. The doctrine of secession is destructive to all government, and leads to universal anarchy.

But, supposing States may secede and destroy the Government whenever the fancy takes those who are strong enough to set up any arbitrary power in the State, Missouri, the State of my residence, has not seceded, and secession would, in my opinion, be her ruin. The only special interest of Missouri, in common with the Confederate States, is slavery. Her interest in that institution is now protected by the Federal Constitution. But if Missouri secedes, that protection is gone. Surrounded on three sides by free States, which might soon become hostile, it would not be long until a slave could not be found within her borders. What interest could Missouri then have with the cotton States, or a Confederacy founded on slavery and its extension? The protection of her slave property, if nothing else, admonishes her never to give up the Union. Other interests of vast magnitude can only be preserved by a steadfast adherence and support of the United States Government. All hope of a Pacific railroad, so deeply interesting to St. Louis and the whole State, must vanish with the Federal Government. Great manufacturing and commercial interests with which the cotton States can have no sympathy, must perish in case of secession, and from her present proud condition of a powerful thriving State, rapidly developing every element of wealth and social prosperity, Missouri would dwindle to a mere appendage and convenience for the military aristocracy established in the cotton States. Many other considerations might be offered to show that secession would be ruin to Missouri. And I implore my fellow-citizens of that State not to be seduced by designing men to become the instruments of their mad ambition, by plunging the State into the vortex of revolution.

Whether governed by feelings inspired by the banner under which I have served, or by my judgment of duty as a citizen, or by interest as a resident and property-owner in Missouri, I feel bound to stand by the Union, and, remaining in the Union, shall devote myself to the maintenance of the Federal Government, and the perpetuation of its blessings to posterity.　　　　Yours truly,

WM. S. HARNEY.

COLONEL JOHN O. FALLON, St. Louis.

—*N. Y. Herald*, May 6.

Doc. 126.—ALBANY BURGESSES CORPS.

THERE are 82 members, two drummers, and one fifer, besides the officers and non-commissioned officers, who equipped and armed themselves at their own expense before offering their services to the governor.

They are furnished with the regulation musket, case bayonet, knapsacks, haversacks, canteens, &c. Their uniform is a blue cap, light blue overcoat trimmed with red, plain blue frock coat, light blue pants with a broad white stripe down the side.

The following are the officers and non-commissioned officers:

Capt., H. Kingsley; 1st Lieutenant, J. C. Cook; 2d Lieutenant, W. D. Mahoney; Orderly Sergeant, H. C. Haskell; 2d, J. Vischer; 3d, T. Padlow; 4th, N. Van Antwerp; 1st Corporal, W. Vanderlip; 2d, Chas. Latham; 3d, C. F. Clapp; 4th, W. M. Netterville.

—*N. Y. Tribune*, May 2.

Doc. 127.—SOUTH CAROLINA COLLEGE CADETS.

THE following is a list of the officers: Captain, John H. Gary; First Lieutenant, E. D. Rogers; Second Lieutenant, Tredell Jones; Third Lieutenant, L. Watts; Ensign, J. S. Dupont; First Sergeant, S. M. Richardson; Second Sergeant, V. C. Habersham; Third Sergeant, J. M. Irvy; Fourth Sergeant, W. J. Gary; First Corporal, R. W. B. Elliott; Second Corporal, R. DeTreville Elliott; Third Corporal, R. M. Anderson; Fourth Corporal, J. J. Tripp; Fifth Corporal, J. G. McCall; Sixth Corporal, James Watts.

WASHINGTON ARTILLERY.

The following is a list of the officers: Captain, G. H. Walter; First Lieutenant, W. S.

Henry; Second Lieutenant, James Salvo; Third Lieutenant, W. G. Whilden; Fourth Lieutenant, W. S. Horsey; First Sergeant, P. S. Pelot; Second Sergeant, James Porter; Third Sergeant, Joseph Buck; Fourth Sergeant, Wm. Roberts; First Corporal, White; Second Corporal, Roy; Third Corporal, Owens; Fourth Corporal, Cook; Fifth Corporal, Wilbur.

—*Charleston News*, May 1.

Doc. 128.—THE RELIGIOUS PRESS ON THE WAR.

[*From the Baltimore True Union.*]

A HEAVY pall of sickening sadness shrouds our hearts as we rise from a glance over our " religious " exchanges. If there was anywhere to be expected a spirit of peace and conciliation in this awful hour, it certainly ought to have been looked for in the conductors of the Christian press. But alas! with few exceptions on both sides, they " breathe out threatenings and slaughter," and goad on the people to a furious, suicidal war.

The *Christian Secretary*, of Connecticut, says: " If we have a civil war and fight for five, ten, or twenty years, and drench our soil in fraternal blood, until, exhausted and worn out, both sides cry for peace, the same questions will come up for settlement that we first split on, and they will be just as difficult to arrange *then* as *now*. It has appeared to us that it would be better to settle these difficulties *before* fighting than *afterwards*, for we could see nothing that could be *gained* by the fight, but much that would be lost. Had the Government given up these forts, convened Congress and urged upon that body the imperative necessity of calling a National Convention for the purpose of a peaceable settlement of our difficulties, we believe the whole thing might have been settled without a resort to arms.

" Our prayer is that peace between the sections may be speedily restored. If the South won't live with us as a *united* people, then by all means let us live in harmony as two separate nations."

The *Witness*, of Indiana, says:—" After months of indignities borne by our Government from some of the Southern States—after she had endured dishonor and afflictions which need not be repeated, for they are fresh in every mind, she is now hunted by armed troops, the men of her own raising, and arms of her own making, and with them she is fiercely threatened to be stabbed, nay, perhaps is stabbed at this very writing to her heart! But, thank Heaven, she is not dead, nor is she mortally wounded! The United States of America is yet a Government endowed with all the capabilities of life and self-defence which have so long made her ' stars and stripes ' the glory of her name, and the banner of her citizens among all the nations of the earth. If she should be wounded by her own children which she has nourished and brought up, her wounds will speedily heal, for she is instinct with life.

—The North do not war on the South, but they defend their country's flag to the man and to the death. There is no disunion here; together we stand in the name of our country and of our God."

The *Christian Chronicle*, of Philadelphia, publishes a letter from a Massachusetts correspondent, containing the following statement: "The *peace* men have all been transformed into *men of war*. Even the ministers of the Gospel deem it proper on the Sabbath to stimulate the patriotism of their people and even bid them to imitate their own examples in volunteering to take the sword; and the consciousness of the righteousness of their cause and the undoubted favor of the God of Battles makes all hearts strong and even joyful.

"There is one prayer often to be heard on the lips of Christian men—'Pray God it may be a death-blow to slavery!' I doubt not that in those who have never felt any thing of the kind before, there will be generated an hostility to slavery of the most uncompromising nature. Nothing is more common than to hear the determination expressed—to oppose the recognition of slavery on the part of the General Government in future—to follow the counsel of our English friends, and 'pluck from the flag those blood-rotted strands,' and to make 'freedom national,' and 'slavery sectional,' to the fullest extent."

The *Watchman and Reflector* has an article on "The Doom of Slavery," in which it predicts that "if the conflict is protracted a single year, Virginia will be lost to slavery." "Virginia too must become the seat of war, and with fifty or a hundred thousand free-men encamped on her soil, and every part of the State convulsed with agitation and turmoil, slavery cannot maintain its existence."

It alludes to the collision between the mob and the soldiers in Baltimore, and adds: "But the mobocracy may as well be quiet. Baltimore is now at the mercy of our guns, and Maryland is one of the most vulnerable States in the Union."

The *Mississippi Baptist*, after describing the war policy of President Lincoln with reference to the Confederate States, adds: "If he carries out this policy fully, we see no alternative but a general war, a war both by sea and land; a war which will carry desolation, carnage, and blooodshed wherever the contending forces meet in battle array.—President Davis has a policy as well as President Lincoln, a policy which he will as assuredly carry out,—a policy which he indicated in his speeches before his inauguration, and in his inaugural address; a policy, in which he will be supported by the Congress of the Confederate States, and by thousands of the brave hearts and stout hands of the people of those States.

"And not only the Confederate States will sustain him, but thousands of the citizen soldiery of the border slave States will rush to his aid. And what will be the alternate result

of the deadly conflict that must ensue no mortal can conjecture. One thing is certain, revolutions never move backwards. Once the tide begins to move it will rush on with increased impetuosity, breaking over every barrier in the way of its onward progress. Once relieve passion from the restraints of reason and conscience, and arouse the feelings of bitter resentment which a long series of oppression has excited, and there will be no bounds to the excesses that will be the unavoidable result.

"But, it may be asked, may not all this be avoided?

"Which question is answered as follows:

"Now, we say, let the Congress and the Executive of the United States cease offensive operations against the Confederate States, and evacuate the forts within their borders, and then enter into a treaty of alliance, offensive and defensive, with the Government, and the dreadful alternative of a sanguinary, desolating conflict will be avoided, otherwise, we fear the war has but just begun."

The *Biblical Recorder*, of North Carolina, shows the unanimity of purpose existing on both sides, and says: "What then? Will Mr. Lincoln and his cabinet pursue to the bitter, bloody end their fiendish purpose? Can the madness of fanaticism go so far? We hope not. Surely reason will return in time to avert so direful a catastrophe. But if war must come, and we can have a united South, we entertain no fears as to the result. The conflict may be long and bloody; many evils and much suffering may be inflicted; commerce may be crippled, and many brave men lie down in death on the battle-field, but victory and peace will at last be ours. Men conscious of right, and fighting for their liberties, their honor, their homes, and all that they hold dear, cannot be subdued. When the North shall have learned this by sad experience, we shall have peace, and, freed from the shackles which have hitherto held us, we shall enter upon a career as glorious as can be found in the annals of the world.

"The South has been slow to assume her present position. It was only after she had patiently submitted for long years to aggression and insult, repeated and aggravated, that she consented to break up the old nationality. Now confiding in the justice of her cause, and looking to the Ruler of the Universe, she can calmly and hopefully await the result."

The *Tennessee Baptist* is strongly in favor of "secession." Rev. J. R. Graves, its principal editor, just returned from a journey through the South, says:—I learned something more about the politics of the masses of Mississippi and Louisiana. I had read in certain newspapers that the people in Louisiana are sound Union men at heart, and that secession is the work of politicians. So far as I travelled in Mississippi and Louisiana I found the people thoroughly secessionists—those who voted the "coöperative ticket" are now firmly fixed in sentiment.

You may write it down as a settled fact to be reckoned from, that these States will never form an alliance again with the Abolition States of the North—never while the world stands. An army of a million soldiers could not force them back. They will die to a man first, save, perhaps, here and there one who has neither " cotton nor negroes to fight for," and who would be glad to see no one better off than himself. Party lines are now annihilated. There is no longer any Whig or Democrat, Southern man and Yankee, but "Southern Confederacy men."

Tennesseeans are now called upon to decide whether they will fight the South or the North.

We rejoice to see the change the political mind of Tennessee is undergoing—*Nashville is overwhelmingly for secession to-day.* All the men I left Union men, I find now thinking with me, *save one—i. e.,* all I have yet conversed with. I learn that a similar change of opinion is universal, except in the mountainous districts of Tennessee. I regard that the fate of Tennessee is determined by the next vote that is cast for Governor. Whoever the man may be, let him be for a United South.

Union men of Tennessee, with few exceptions, are among the very foremost in the call for arming the State, and resisting the machinations of the Black Republican tyrant and his conclave at Washington.

The *Christian Index,* of Georgia, throws the whole blame of the war "upon Lincoln and his advisers;" says that upon the part of the South it is a war to maintain the right "of sovereignty pertaining to each State of the old Union and of the new Confederacy," in which "we are but defending our firesides, our families, our honor, and our independence." After speaking of the apparent policy of the United States Government, the editor adds:

" The tendency of these movements will be to bring Virginia and Maryland into the Southern Confederacy, and also Kentucky and Tennessee, and perhaps Arkansas; and if Lincoln persists in his coercive policy, President Davis will have no other alternative but to conquer a peace by attacking Washington city, and, on the tented field proving the superiority of Southern to Northern prowess.

" Thus will we force the ill-advisers of Mr. Lincoln to acknowledge and recognize our secession; we will compel an equitable division of the national property; and while the North will sink at once to the position of a third-rate power of the earth, we, from our Capitol at Washington city, will cause ourselves to be regarded as the valiant American Government that, by martial supremacy, asserted its right to a place among the first nations of the earth, and which, by its liberal policy towards other nations, and its possession of King Cotton, will but bind to itself in friendship all other countries, and which, by the enlightenment, religion, urbanity, and high-toned principles of its

people, will claim and receive the respect, admiration, and esteem of the world."

The *South Western Baptist,* of Alabama, says:

Well, the war is upon us! We have exhausted every effort for peace which duty and honor demand. Our peace offerings are spurned, our commissioners sent home from Washington with the insulting declaration that they cannot be received, and now the roar of artillery on our Southern borders announces the purblind policy of an abolitionized government, bent on the ruin of the country as well as its own! Let it come! " In the name of our God, we will set up our banners;" and by the blessing of Him who ruleth in the armies of heaven, the sword will never be sheathed until the last invader shall be driven from our shores. The battle of New Orleans, fought by Southern soldiers, commanded by Southern officers, may suggest to these hirelings of Mr. Lincoln what Southern men can and will do when their wives and children are behind them and an invading foe is before them. Let no man's heart fail him for fear. The spirit of our people is aroused, and hundreds of thousands stand ready to fly to the standard of our Southern Confederacy to maintain its integrity or perish in the attempt. " Let us play the man for our people, and for the cities of our God, and the Lord do what seemeth him good." Let prayer be made without ceasing unto God, and the result is not doubtful.

The *Methodist Protestant,* of Baltimore, says:

We make no pretensions to statesmanship, we are no cabinet officer, we know little of state-diplomacy, but we think we know enough of Christ and his religion to be certain that war, and especially civil war, is a most cruel and wicked thing. It is anti-Christian, and a nation like ours ought not engage in it. Moral force at an era of civilization like that in which we live, ought to be able to settle State difficulties. The points of national honor upon which men dwell so eloquently, are as likely to be overrated as the points of personal honor in the ordinary duel. And what is this war likely to be? A gigantic duel between the two sections, North and South. A duel between brothers. Both are to be injured, cruelly. Sorrow unspeakable is to be carried into the bosoms of innocent connections—and then, when mutual satisfaction IN BLOOD shall have been rendered, amicable relations will be established, and history will find material for another story of wrong and outrage, or the recital of successive battles, of victories and defeats, leaving the quarrel at the end, just where it was at the beginning—a thing to be settled by peaceful diplomacy.

The *Examiner,* of New York, says:

War is an evil from which peace-loving patriots have prayed God to save their beloved country. But there are worse evils than war, and one of them would be a subversion of the ancestral freedom of a great people, by the slavery-propagandist Confederacy which has made Montgomery the seat of its malign power. War, to prevent such a catastrophe, rises to the dignity of virtue acceptable to God.

Again, after denouncing the capture of Fort Sumter as "an uncalled-for attack," "an aggressive war on the Government and people of the United States," it continues:

In maintaining itself against this aggressive war, and in punishing its authors, the National Government will receive the hearty and united support of all loyal and right-minded men. We abhor war in all its forms—but if it must come, it could never be met by the American people with a more determined resolution, or with a deeper consciousness of right, than when it comes in the hateful guise of secession, and slavery extension. Long has the Government forborne to act, lest it might provoke some hostile measure. Its endurance has been beyond all the precedents of history. It must now arouse in its hitherto slumbering might, and assert its determination to rule the country. Already are thousands flocking to its standard from every constitutional State. Its cause is as righteous as ever summoned a people to arms. On it, we need not say, depends the life of the country. It appeals with the fullest power to the deepest sentiments of every patriotic heart—to the proud recollections of our national past—to the priceless interests that lie enwrapped in our hitherto happy Republic—to the undying loyalty that clings to our glorious, but insulted flag—to the sympathies we cherish for oppressed and outraged humanity—to the pride we have taken in American civilization, and the faith we have kept in the capacities and destinies of American freedom.

The *New York Chronicle* says:

A single blow has cut the Gordian knot which the North has been so anxious to untie peacefully. The question is now as simple as it before was complicated. The life or death of the Government established by our fathers, is the mighty stake for which the game of war is henceforth to be played.

We want peace, we all want peace. We are willing to make many sacrifices—to forbear much, and suffer much, to obtain it, but there are some things we may not endure, and some sacrifices we may not make. Great principles have sometimes to pass through the fiery furnace, and we have only to accept whatever sacrifices that ordeal may bring; not vindictively, not in the spirit of revenge for real or fancied wrongs, but simply as a stern duty which, as loyal men, without being recreant to every sentiment of justice and Christian principle, we cannot ignore or evade.

There is but one feeling now through the North. It is for vigorous, energetic and decisive measures, not for aggressive warfare, for no one here contemplates or desires it, but because the best peace measure now is the exhibition of such strength on the part of the Govern-

ment as will prevent further aggressive measures on the part of the South.

The *Watchman and Reflector*, of Boston, Mass., says:

We bitterly deplore the necessity of war. As Christian journalists we have counselled forbearance till it has ceased to be a virtue. We have hoped that our brethren of the South, while renouncing allegiance to the national Government, would refrain from any attack on its armed troops. But delay has only aggravated treason, forbearance has emboldened their movements, and civil war is now inevitable. There can be no doubt of the ultimate result. The North has ample resources of men and money. It has the undivided command of the sea for transportation of troops, and a network of railroads for conveyance of armies and provisions by land. If it were needful, a million of men could be mustered in the field in three months. The South is full of enthusiasm, and its people are chivalric and impetuous, but with few monetary resources, and no credit, and no navy, it must yield at length to superior force.

The North, too, we must believe, is in the right. It will have on its side the sympathy of the civilized world, and we may hope, also, the favor and protection of Almighty God. On Him we must wait in humble prayer and strong faith, and to him must we look for guidance and deliverance.

Doc. 129.—PROCLAMATION BY GOVERNOR LETCHER, May 3, 1861.

The sovereignty of the Commonwealth of Virginia having been denied, her territorial rights assailed, her soil threatened with invasion by the authorities at Washington, and every artifice employed which could inflame the people of the Northern States and misrepresent our purposes and wishes, it becomes the solemn duty of every citizen of this State to prepare for the impending conflict. These misrepresentations have been carried to such an extent that foreigners and naturalized citizens who, but a few years ago, were denounced by the North and deprived of essential rights, have now been induced to enlist into regiments for the purpose of invading this State, which then vindicated those rights and effectually resisted encroachments which threatened their destruction. Against such a policy and against a force which the Government at Washington, relying upon its numerical strength, is now rapidly concentrating, it becomes the State of Virginia to prepare proper safeguards.

To this end and for these purposes, and with a determination to repel invasion, I, JOHN LETCHER, Governor of the Commonwealth of Virginia, by authority of the Convention, do hereby authorize the commanding-general of the military forces of this State, to call out, and to cause to be mustered into the service of Virginia, from time to time, as the public exigencies may require, such additional number of volunteers as he may deem necessary.

To facilitate this call, the annexed Schedule will indicate the places of rendezvous at which the companies called for will assemble upon receiving orders for service.

Given under my hand as Governor, and under the seal of the Commonwealth, [L. S.] at Richmond, this 3d day of May, 1861, and in the 85th year of the Commonwealth.

JOHN LETCHER.

By the Governor.
GEORGE W. MUNFORD,
Secretary of the Commonwealth.

SCHEDULE.

The following places of rendezvous are designated as the point at which companies called from the annexed counties will assemble: Harper's Ferry, Staunton, Alexandria, Warrenton, Culpepper C. H., Gordonsville, Lynchburg, Abingdon, Fredericksburg, King George, Gloucester Point, West Point, Norfolk, Smithfield, Petersburg, Buffalo, Barbourville, Charleston, Parkersburg, Moundsville, Grafton, and Richmond.

—*Charleston Evening News*, May 6.

Doc. 130.—NEW YORK TO BE BURNED.

NEW YORK, May 3.

A WEEK or two since, Mr. Kennedy, Superintendent of Police of New York, received information of a design to burn the city, the supply of water to be cut off at the time the city was fired. A guard was placed over the mains of the aqueduct in the two counties through which they run, and was made so strong that no attempt to cut the pipe could be successfully made. Since then full evidence of the design has been obtained, and additional evidence that the cities of Philadelphia and Boston were included in the list. The leaders of the enterprise were well-known secessionists, some of whose names are now in possession of the police, but whose voices have been silenced by the recent uprising of the people. The whole police force has been on the alert since the first intimation of the probability of the attempt being made. Here is a letter received last evening from a source entitled to consideration :

LOUISVILLE, April 30, 1861.

Sir :—I have travelled four hundred miles to be able safely to mail this letter. A thoroughly organized plot is now in progress of execution to burn New York, Philadelphia, and Boston. A portion of the men assigned to your city are already in your midst, and others are on their way. *I know what I say to be true.* I dare not tell you how I know, for that would lead to my inevitable detection, the consequences of which you can readily guess.

The intention is to fire the three cities simultaneously, at as many places as possible, and at the same hour at night. This is to be done the night before the attack on Washington. * * * * * * has the direction of the whole plot. One hundred and twenty-five men have been assigned to your city and Brooklyn, and eighty to each of the others. This is not a movement of the Government, though known to Davis. At first he discouraged it, but since Lincoln's proclamation, he has withdrawn his opposition. The men intrusted with the execution of the plot all belong to the inner temple of the Knights of the Golden Circle.

The plan has been maturing for two months past, but did not include New York until within a week or ten days. The men assigned to Boston and Philadelphia have been at their posts for a week, but the determination to include New York has caused a delay, and now the time will depend upon how soon Davis is to attack Washington. I have told you not all that I know, but all that I can with safety to myself. The chances are you will disregard this warning; but I feel that I have at least discharged my duty. * * * * * * I am not your friend—I am one of the most unrelenting of your enemies; but I am an open, and, I hope, honorable foe. I expect to fight you to the death, but not with lucifer matches and camphene. Do not do the people of the South the injustice to believe that one out of ten among them would for a moment sanction this hell-begotten scheme. It is foreign to their nature. * *

—*N. Y. News*, May 4.

Doc. 131.—A PROCLAMATION

By the President of the United States.

WASHINGTON, Friday, May 3, 1861.

WHEREAS, existing exigencies demand immediate and adequate measures for the protection of the national Constitution and the preservation of the national Union by the suppression of the insurrectionary combinations now existing in several States for opposing the laws of the Union and obstructing the execution thereof, to which end a military force in addition to that called forth by my Proclamation of the fifteenth day of April in the present year, appears to be indispensably necessary, now, therefore, I, Abraham Lincoln, President of the United States, and Commander-in-Chief of the Army and Navy thereof, and of the militia of the several States, when called into actual service, do hereby call into the service of the United States forty-two thousand and thirty-four volunteers, to serve for a period of three years, unless sooner discharged, and to be mustered into service as infantry and cavalry. The proportions of each arm and the details of enrolment and organization will be made known through the Department of War; and I also direct that the regular army of the United States be increased by the addition of eight regiments of infantry, one regiment of cavalry, and one regiment of artillery, making altogether a maximum aggregate increase of 22,714 officers and enlisted men, the details of which increase will also be made known through the Department of War; and I further direct the enlistment, for not less than one nor more than three years, of 18,000 seamen, in addition to the present force, for the naval service of the United States. The details of the enlistment and organization will be made known through the Department of the Navy. The call for volunteers, hereby made, and the direction of the increase of the regular army, and for the enlistment of seamen hereby given, together with the plan of organization adopted for the volunteers and for the regular forces hereby authorized, will be submitted to Congress as soon as assembled.

In the mean time I earnestly invoke the coöperation of all good citizens in the measures hereby adopted for the effectual suppression of unlawful violence, for the impartial enforcement of constitutional laws, and for the speediest possible restoration of peace and order, and with those of happiness and prosperity throughout our country.

In testimony whereof, I have hereunto set my hand, and caused the seal of the United States to be affixed.

Done at the City of Washington this third day of May, in the year of our Lord one thousand eight hundred and sixty-one, and of the Independence of the United States the eighty-fifth.   ABRAHAM LINCOLN.

By the President.
  WILLIAM H. SEWARD, Secretary of State.

Doc. 132.—LETTER FROM COMMODORE STEWART.

"BORDENTOWN, May 4, 1861.

"MY DEAR SIR: Agreeably to your request I now furnish you with the reminiscences of a conversation which passed between Mr. John C. Calhoun and myself in the latter part of December, 1812, after the declaration of war by the Congress of the United States against Great Britain on the 18th of June previous.

"On the assembling of Congress, in the early part of December, I found that an important portion of the leading democratic members of Congress had taken up their quarters at Mrs. Bushby's boarding-house, among whom was Mr. Calhoun, a new member from South Carolina—and I believe this was his first appearance in the House of Representatives. In consequence of this I took Lieutenant Ridgley, my confidential officer, and the first lieutenant of the frigate Constitution, of which vessel I then held the command, and was preparing for sea at the Washington Navy Yard, left our lodgings at Strother's, and obtained board at Mrs. Bushby's with them. Ridgley was a witty and able talker, who could aid me in demonstrating the

necessity for, and the high policy of a formidable naval force wherewith to carry on the war with England, which I considered could only be done with effect through her being victoriously struck at on an element over which she deemed herself sole mistress. This appeared to me to constitute her most tender point.

"By this movement I found myself judiciously located to enable me to urge upon Congress any patriotic measures which seemed best calculated to meet and discomfit the self-sufficiency and arrogance of our oppressive enemy.

"Mr. Calhoun's age, I thought, approximated my own, which was thirty-four; and being a man of the highest order of talent, and representing a State in our Union which scarce ever permitted themselves to be represented by inferior ability in the national councils, I could not have commenced my object with one more fitted for the purpose I had in view. He was also a high-minded and honorable man, kind and friendly as well as open and confiding to those he deemed worthy. We soon formed an intimacy, and I frequently had long conversations with him on the war, the subjects relating thereto, and matters growing out of its existence —the navy being the most prominent—the gunboats, the merchants' bonds then on the tapis in Congress, and other matters of political or minor interest. One evening I struck on the divided views of our sectional interests of the war—stated to him that the opposite feelings on this subject had puzzled me exceedingly, and asked him how it was that the planting States were so strongly and so decidedly in favor of the war, while the commercial States were so much opposed to it. With this latter section of our country it seemed to me that the punishment of England, through the medium of war, ought to meet their highest approbation and call for their greatest efforts, as they were the greatest sufferers, through her instrumentality and power over our commercial affairs, since 1792, which were so arrogantly urged by plunder and impressment on the highway of nations, while the southern portion of the Union had felt but little in comparison. I observed, with great simplicity, 'You in the South and Southwest are decidedly the aristocratic portion of this Union; you are so in holding persons in perpetuity in slavery; you are so in every domestic quality; so in every habit in your lives, living, and actions; so in habits, customs, intercourse, and manners; you neither work with your hands, heads, nor any machinery, but live and have your living, not in accordance with the will of your Creator, but by the sweat of slavery, and yet you assume all the attributes, professions, and advantages of democracy.'

"Mr. Calhoun replied: 'I see you speak through the head of a young statesman, and from the heart of a patriot, but you lose sight of the politician and the sectional policy of the people. I admit your conclusions in respect to us southrons. That we are essentially aristocratic I cannot deny, but we can and do yield much to democracy. This is our sectional policy; we are from necessity thrown upon and solemnly wedded to that party, however it may occasionally clash with our feelings for the conservation of our interests. It is through our affiliation with that party in the middle and western States that we hold power; but when we cease thus to control this nation through a disjointed democracy, or any material obstacle in that party which shall tend to throw us out of that rule and control, we shall then resort to the dissolution of the Union. The compromises in the Constitution, under the circumstances, were sufficient for our fathers; but, under the altered condition of our country from that period, leave to the South no resource but dissolution; for no amendments to the Constitution could be reached through a convention of the people under their three-fourths rule.' I laughed incredulously, and said, 'well, Mr. Calhoun, ere such can take place, you and I will have been so long *non est* that we can now laugh at its possibility, and leave it with complacency to our children's children, who will then have the watch on deck.'

"Alas, my dear sir, how entirely were the views of that 'young headed statesman' circumscribed by the patriot feelings of his heart. What he then thought an impossibility for human hands to effect, for ages on ages to come, he now sees verified to the letter as predicted by that far-seeing statesman, John C. Calhoun. Even this noble republic is disrupted, its Constitution rent into shreds and tatters, by party follies and the wickedness of its people's selfishness. Had they but inherited a moiety of the virtues of their fathers, who bled and impoverished themselves through a long and bloody war to establish the independence and liberty, welfare and happiness of their posterity for all time to come; had they worshipped the true and living God instead of the 'almighty dollar,' they would not now have beheld the millions of patriots arming for the strife against traitors to their country, to the Constitution and the laws, once more to baptize in blood, for liberty's sake, the blessings which rational liberty accords under our Union. Had a prophet arisen in 1812, and predicted as John C. Calhoun did, nothing short of divine inspiration could have given credence to his foreshadowings. Alas, I have lived to see its accomplishment! He has gone to the tomb of his fathers, the pride of his section, honored for his talents and for his efforts in council, while your humble servant still lingers on the brink, under the national anathema of degradation, as a reward for many years of faithful services; which degradation was accorded him simultaneously with his reaching the head of the service to which his whole life had been devoted. You see, my dear sir, I have no disposition to 'bury my light under a bushel,' but will ever be ready to accord justice to whom justice is due. Thus in death we show the ruling passion stronger than in life, and as it is with individuals, so it is with nations—

the blackest spot found in the heart is ingratitude.

"Accept the assurances of my regard and esteem.

"CHARLES STEWART.

"George W. Childs, Esq., Philadelphia."

—*N. Y. Evening Post*, May 10.

Doc. 133.—THE REBEL ARMY AT PENSACOLA.

HEAD-QUARTERS, LOUISIANA REGIMENT, }
WARRINGTON, April 27, 1861. }

I MADE an excursion yesterday around the semicircle of the bay which girds Fort Pickens, with a view of inspecting the batteries and encampments of General Bragg's army. This semicircle commences at the Navy Yard and terminates at the Water Battery beyond McRae. At short intervals for two miles and a half there is an uninterrupted line of batteries along this semicircle. More are being erected daily by the zealous and active volunteers. It is amazing the quantity of work they do, and the rapidity with which they are drilled into good artillerists. The army is divided as follows: the extreme right of Bragg's position, including Fort McRae, is held by the Mississippians, whose encampment I visited yesterday. Col. Chalmers commands this division of the line. We found the Colonel in his marquee, over head and ears in the business of his command. He is a young but very active, intelligent, and zealous officer, and is rapidly reducing his wild, fearless, and sagacious warriors into good discipline. The eagerness of the Mississippi boys for a fight renders camp duty rather wearisome to them, but Col. Chalmers is determined to profit by the example of Jeff. Davis, who made the Mississippians in Mexico as efficient and well-disciplined as they were brave and impetuous, by the strictness of his discipline. The Mississippians, the two regiments of Col. Chalmers and Col. Phillips, are encamped in a very pretty location in the pine woods, within a quarter of a mile of the bay, and with a fine stream of fresh water flowing through the camp. Their encampment presents a very picturesque aspect, and was quite *en regle* in all its arrangements. Col. Chalmers's report for the day, of the two regiments, showed 1,628 men ready for duty. Four of the companies of Col. Phillips, the Second or Southern Regiment, were stationed in Fort McRae, under Capt. Joe Davis, of Canton, nephew of the President, a very intelligent and gallant officer. Besides these there are three independent Mississippi artillery companies, which are placed in charge of batteries. They are Capt. Carr's Jackson Artillery, 63; Capt. Lovell's Quitman Artillery, of Natchez, 75; Capt. Tull's Vicksburg Artillery company, 60; making in all 1,826 Mississippians who are enrolled in this army!

Next to the Mississippians are the Alabamians, who have two regiments encamped on the left of the Mississippians. They are divided into a regiment commanded by Col. Clayton, of 10 companies—800 men; and a battalion of 8 companies—600 men—under Lieut.-Col. Steadman. Several of the Alabama companies are assigned to batteries; one of them, under Lieut. Howard, having charge of the two 10-inch gun battery. The Alabamians are much cut up in their encampments and occupy a large space in the line. On their left are the Georgia Regiment, Col. Ramsey, 10 companies —750 men. This regiment, with the Alabama Regiment, and Capt. Girardey's artillery company in charge of the redoubt in the rear of Fort Barrancas, and battalion 63, make up the second division, commanded by Col. Clayton. The extreme left, extending from the Hospital to a point beyond the Navy Yard, is the division which Col. Gladden commands, and consists of the Florida Regiment, Col. Anderson, 620; of Major Lary's Georgia Battalion, 350; of Capt. Lee's artillery company, 114—composed entirely of artisans and mechanics; and of 1st Battalion of the Louisiana Regiment, 520, Col. Adams; the Zouaves, 505, Lieut.-Col. Coppens; and the Marines, 109.

The army of Gen. Bragg may, therefore, be thus stated accurately:

Brigadier-General Commanding, Braxton Bragg; Inspector-General, J. H. Forney; Chief of Engineers, W. H. Stevens; Chief of Ordnance, W. R. Boggs; Adjutant-General, R. C. Wood; Aids, George D. Garner, Thomas Ellis; Surgeon-General, A. J. Foard; Quartermaster, L. A. O'Bannon; Chief of Subsistence, T. W. Jones.

FIRST DIVISION—COL. J. R. CHALMERS.

1st Mississippi Regiment, Col. Chalmers,	787
2d Mississippi Regiment, Col. Phillips,	841
Quitman Artillery, Capt. Lovell,	75
Vicksburg Artillery, Capt. Tull,	60
Judson Artillery, Capt. Carr,	63
	1,826

SECOND DIVISION—COL. CLAYTON.

1st Alabama Regiment, Col. Clayton,	800
2d Alabama Battalion, Lieut.-Col. Steadman,	600
1st Georgia Regiment, Col. Ramsey,	760
	2,160

THIRD DIVISION—COL. GLADDEN.

One regiment Louisiana Infantry—two battalions.

1st Battalion, Lieut. Col. Adams, (regulars,) 6 companies,	620
Battalion of Zouaves, Lieut.-Col. Coppens.	505
Georgia Battalion, Major Lary,	350
1st Florida Regiment, Col. Anderson,	615
Ind. Artillery Company of Savannah, Capt. Lee,	114
	2,194

TROOPS AT PENSACOLA UNDER MAJOR BRADFORD.

2d Battalion of First Louisiana Regiment:

Louisiana Guards, Capt. Todd,	103
Crescent Rifles, Capt. Fisk,	92
Shreveport Greys, Capt. Beard,	138
Grivot Guards, Capt. Rightor,	92
Orleans Cadets, Capt. Dreux, (detached).	103
	528

Total number of troops, ...6,708

Though some of the regiments are quite deficient in the drill, I do not believe that a better and more efficient body of fighting men could be assembled in any part of the world. They compose the very best class of our Southern people, ardent, earnest, and resolute young men. They can never be conquered, or even defeated; they may be destroyed and annihilated; but when the Lincolnites subdue the country or the people which he has undertaken to subjugate, as long as we have such men to fight our battles, the spoils of his victory will be a blasted and desolated country and an extinct people. A. W.

—Special Correspondence of the *New Orleans Delta.*

Doc. 134.—"THE ATTACK ON WASHINGTON."

On the 12th of April last the honorable Mr. Walker, Secretary of War of the Confederate States, held the following language at Montgomery, Alabama:

"No man, he said, could tell where the war this day commenced would end, but he would prophesy that *the flag which now flaunts the breeze here would float over the dome of the old Capitol at Washington before the first of May.* Let them try Southern chivalry and test the extent of Southern resources, and it might float eventually over Faneuil Hall itself."

Such being the publicly avowed belief of the Secretary of War of the Confederate States, we quote in illustration of similar "threats," the following excerpts taken from leading Southern journals, merely premising that we could greatly add to their number if it were essential to the purpose:

From the Richmond Enquirer, of April 13.

ATTENTION, VOLUNTEERS!—Nothing is more probable than that President Davis will soon march an army *through North Carolina and Virginia to Washington.* Those of our volunteers who desire to join the Southern army as it shall pass through our borders, had better organize at once for the purpose, and keep their arms, accoutrements, uniforms, ammunition, and knapsacks in constant readiness.

From the New Orleans Picayune, of April 18.

The first fruits of a Virginia secession will be the removal of Lincoln and his Cabinet, and whatever he can carry away, to the safer neighborhood of Harrisburg or Cincinnati—perhaps to Buffalo or Cleveland.

From the Vicksburg (Miss.) Whig, of April 20.

Major Ben McCullough has organized a force of five thousand men *to seize the Federal Capital the instant the first blood is spilled.* The Montgomery Advertiser says this intelligence is from a Virginia gentleman now in Washington city, who had it direct from McCullough's own lips.

From the Richmond (Va.) Examiner, of April 23.

The capture of Washington city is perfectly within the power of Virginia and Maryland, if Virginia will only make the proper effort by her constituted authorities; nor is there a single moment to lose, *the entire population pant for the onset; there never was half the unanimity among the people before, nor a tithe of the zeal upon any subject that is now manifested to take Washington,* and drive from it every Black Republican who is a dweller there.

From the mountain tops and valleys to the shores of the sea *there is one wild shout of fierce resolve to capture Washington city* at all and every human hazard. The filthy cage of unclean birds must and will assuredly be purified by fire. The people are determined upon it, and are clamorous for a leader to conduct them to the onslaught. That leader will assuredly rise, aye, and that right speedily.

From the Goldsboro' (N. C.) Tribune, of April 24.

We understand that Duncan K. McRae, Esq., who came here last night, bears a special order for one regiment of North Carolina troops to march to the city of Washington. They are to be ready in forty-eight hours from the notice. This is by order of Gov. Ellis.

To have gained Maryland is to have gained a host. It insures Washington city, and the ignominious expulsion of Lincoln and his bodyguard of Kansas cut-throats from the White House. *It makes good the words of Secretary Walker at Montgomery in regard to the Federal Metropolis.* It transfers the lines of battle from the Potomac to the Pennsylvania border.

From the Raleigh (N. C.) Standard, of April 24.

North Carolina will send her full quota of troops to unite in the attack on Washington city. Our streets are alive with soldiers and officers, many of the latter being here to tender their companies to the Governor. Washington city will soon be too hot to hold Abraham Lincoln and his Government. *North Carolina has said it, and she will do all she can to make good her declaration.*

From the Eufaula (Ala.) Express, of April 25.

With independent Virginia on one side and the secessionists of Maryland (who are doubtless in the majority) on the other, our policy at this time *should be to seize the old Federal Capital* and take old Lincoln and his Cabinet pris-

Documents—14

oners of war. Once get the Heads of the Government in our power, and we can demand any terms we see fit, and thus, perhaps, avoid a long and bloody contest.

From the Wilmington (N. C.) Daily Journal, of April 27.

A correspondent writing from Georgetown, (S. C.) under date of April 26th, makes inquiry about a report that had got afloat there that three regiments of troops had left North Carolina to join Lincoln. What an idea! When North Carolina troops join old Abe it will be at the point of the bayonet, and he at the sharp end. When North Carolina regiments *go to Washington, and they will go,* they will stand side by side with their brethren of the South. What fool could have put in circulation such a report!

From the Milledgeville (Ga.) Southern Recorder, of April 30.

The government of the Confederate States *must possess the city of Washington.* It is folly to think it can be used any longer as the headquarters of the Lincoln Government, as no access can be had to it except by passing through Virginia and Maryland. The District of Columbia cannot remain under the jurisdiction of the United States Congress without humiliating Southern pride and defeating Southern rights. Both are essential to greatness of character, and both must coöperate in the destiny to be achieved.

The correspondent of the *Charleston Courier* wrote from Montgomery, Alabama, under date of the 28th ultimo, as follows:

"The aspect of Montgomery at this time is any thing but peaceful, and, with the presence of so many troops in the capitol at once, the people are beginning to realize the fact that we are in the midst of war, as well as to feel assured that vigor and energy characterize the Administration. In the churches to-day, prayers were offered for the success of our arms during the war. *The desire for taking Washington, I believe, increases every hour, and all things, to my thinking, seem tending to this consummation.* We are in lively hope that before three months roll by, the government, congress, departments, and all, will have removed to the present Federal Capital."

A correspondent of the *Baltimore Exchange*, writing from Montgomery (Alabama) under date of April 20, immediately after the receipt of the telegraphic intelligence announcing the attack of the Baltimore mob on the Massachusetts troops, communicated the following:

"In the evening bonfires were built in front of the Exchange Hotel, and from the vast crowd which assembled, repeated cheers were given for the loyal people of Baltimore. Hon. Roger A. Pryor, of Virginia, had arrived in the city in the afternoon, and as soon as it was known, there were loud calls for him. His reception was most enthusiastic, and some minutes elapsed before he could commence his remarks. He made a brief but very eloquent address, full of spirit. *He is in favor of marching immediately on Washington, and so stated, to which the crowd responded in deafening and prolonged cheers.*"

At the "flag presentation" which preceded the departure of the second regiment of South Carolina for Richmond, the following remarks were made by Colonel Kershaw on taking the colors:

"Sergeant Gordon, to your particular charge is committed this noble gift. Plant it wherever honor calls. If opportunity offers, let it be the first to *kiss the breeze of heaven from the dome of the capitol at Washington.*"

—*National Intelligencer*, May 9.

Doc. 135.

COMMISSIONERS' REPORT

TO THE MARYLAND LEGISLATURE.

To the Honorable General Assembly of Maryland:—The undersigned commissioners have the honor to report to the General Assembly of Maryland that they waited in person on the President of the United States on the 4th inst., and presented him with a copy of the joint resolutions adopted by your honorable body on the 2d inst. They were received by the President with respectful courtesy, and made such representations as were necessary to convey to him the sense of the General Assembly of Maryland, in relation to the occupation of the Capital of the State by federal troops, and the forcible seizure of property of the State and of private citizens on the Annapolis Railroad, and on the Washington Branch and the Baltimore and Ohio Railroad; and in this connection his attention was called to the suspension of intercourse between Baltimore and Washington, and of all parts of the State, with Annapolis, and the indignity put upon the State while still in the federal Union, by such an interference with the private rights of its citizens, and by such an occupation of its soil and ways of communication by the Federal Government. Full explanations were exchanged between the undersigned and the Secretary of War and Secretary of State, who were present and participated in the discussion, as to the facts and circumstances rendered necessary by the extraordinary incidents accompanying the passage of the federal troops through Maryland *en route* to the city of Washington, and especially in reference to these acts of the authorities of the city of Baltimore, which arrested the progress of the troops by the railroads leading from Pennsylvania and Delaware into Maryland, and of the opposition to the landing of the troops subsequently at Annapolis by the Governor of the State, and in conjunction with the action of the authorities of the State. The hostile feeling manifested by the people to the passage of

these troops through Maryland was considered and treated with entire frankness by the undersigned, who, while acknowledging all the legal obligations of the State to the Federal Government, set forth fully the strength of the sympathy felt by a large portion of our people for our Southern brethren in the present crisis. Although many of the instances and circumstances referred to were regarded in different lights by the undersigned and the Federal Government, even to the extent of a difference of opinion as to some of the facts involved, yet in regard to the general principle at issue, a concurrence of opinion was reached. The President concurred with the undersigned in the opinion that so long as Maryland has not taken, and was not about taking, a hostile attitude to the Federal Government, that the executive military occupation of her ways of communication, and the seizure of the property of her citizens, would be without justification; and what has been referred to in this connection, so far as it occurred, was treated by the Government as an act of necessity and self-preservation. The undersigned did not feel themselves authorized to enter into any engagement with the Federal Government to induce it to change its relations to the State of Maryland, considering it proper under the circumstances to leave the entire discretion and responsibility of the existing state of things to that Government, making such representations as they deem proper to vindicate the moral and legal aspects of the question, and especially insisting on its obligation to relieve the State promptly from restraint and indignity, and to abstain from all action in the transportation of troops that can be regarded as intended for chastisement or prompted by resentment. The undersigned are not able to indicate to what extent or to what degree the executive discretion will be exercised in modifying the relations which now exist between the State of Maryland and the Federal Government, and in the particular matter of the commercial communication between the city of Baltimore and the other part of the country, brought to the attention of the General Assembly by the Mayor and City Council of Baltimore; but they feel authorized to express the opinion that some modification may be expected. The undersigned feel painfully confident that a war is to be waged to reduce all the seceding States to allegiance to the Federal Government, and that the whole military power of the Federal Government will be exerted to accomplish that purpose; and though the expression of this opinion is not called for by the resolution of your honorable bodies, yet, having had the opportunity to ascertain its entire accuracy, and because it will explain much of the military preparations and movements of the troops through the State of Maryland, it is proper to bring it to your attention.

OTHO SCOTT,
ROBERT M. McLANE,
WM. J. ROSS.

—*N. Y. Herald*, May 7.

May 6, 1861.

Doc. 136.
OFFICERS OF THE N. J. TROOPS.

FIRST REGIMENT.—Col. Commanding, A. J. Johnson; Lieut. Col., James Peckell; Major, Wm. I. Mikels; Adjutant, Joseph Trawin; Quartermaster, T. F. Ketchum. Captains—Company A, John Britzinghoffer. Company B, W. S. Tibson. Company C, Thos. Q. Martin. Company D, H. O. Beach. Company E, W. B. Provost. Company F, H. Bowden. Company G, H. F. Stanford. Company H, Wm. Reynolds. Company I, John. H. Higginson. Company K, C. W. Johnson.

SECOND REGIMENT.—Colonel, Baker; Lieut.-Col., Speer; Surgeon, Quidour; Assistant do., Longstaff; Quartermaster, Drinkerhoff; Quartermaster's Sergeant, Hill; Adjutant, Van Rippen. Company A, Capt. Van Rippen. Company B, Capt. Hoffer. Company C, Capt. Grain. Company D, Capt. Lillendhal. Company E, Capt. Van Buskirk. Company F, Capt. Tonnelle. Company G, Capt. Ramsay. Company H, (Zouaves,) Capt. Babcock. Company I, Capt. Van Vorhees. Company K, Captain Dunning.

THIRD REGIMENT.—Wm. Napton, Colonel; Stephen Moore, Lieutenant-Colonel; James S. Yard, Major; James D. McIntosh, Adjutant; M. H. Beaumont, Quartermaster; E. F. Taylor, Surgeon; E. J. Marsh, Assistant Surgeon; J. L. Janeway, Chaplain. Company A, J. A. Yard, Captain; S. S. Gould, 1st Lieutenant; C. Ewing, 2d Lieutenant. Company B, D. Pierson, Captain; J. J. Cladeck, 1st Lieutenant; C. Mandeville, 2d Lieutenant. Company C, J. P. Lykens, Captain; J. W. Neal, 1st Lieutenant; J. R. Beatty, 2d Lieutenant. Company D, D. S. Mulford, Captain; F. S. Mills, 1st Lieutenant; H. K. Zehner, 2d Lieutenant. Company E, A. W. Angel, Captain; A. H. Slack, 1st Lieutenant; J. M. Bunnell, 2d Lieutenant. Company F, J. H. Smith, Captain; G. H. Green, 1st Lieutenant; A. L. Bills, 2d Lieutenant. Company G, V. W. Mount, Captain; J. T. Cottrell, 1st Lieutenant; W. H. Spain, 2d Lieutenant. Company H, George A. Allen, Captain; J. Gordon, 1st Lieutenant; M. Wychoff, 2d Lieutenant. Company I, S. R. Huselton, Captain; T. M. Stout, 1st Lieutenant; W. W. Abbott, 2d Lieutenant. Company K, W. Castner, Captain; S. Roff, 1st Lieutenant; G. M. Stelle, 2d Lieutenant. Non-commissioned staff officers, J. Anderson, Serjeant-Major; T. C. Stryker, Quartermaster-Sergeant.

FOURTH REGIMENT.—Staff: Col., Miller; Lieut.-Col., Straub; Quartermaster, Linton; Paymaster, Davis; Adjutant, Hatch; Surgeon, Woolston; Assistant Surgeon, Satterthwaith. Company A, Cook Rifles, Captain Perine, Bordentown. Company B, Captain Gale. Company C, Stockton Cadets, Captain Jackson; Company D, Gloucester Guard, Capt. Stratford. Company E, Camden Artillery, Capt.

Mickle. Company F, (flag company,) Camden Zouaves, Captain Hunt. Company G, Cook Rifles, Captain Cunningham. Company H, Anderson Guards, Captain Lear. Company I, Johnson Guards, Salem, Captain Dinneghson. Company K, Marion Rifles, Captain Burling.

The whole brigade, with its four pieces of artillery, arrived at Annapolis on Sunday, May 5th, in twenty-eight hours from Trenton, and proceeded direct for Washington. It is stated that the fourteen transports, with a strong convoy, Commander F. R. Loper, made a splendid appearance, steaming in two lines down the Chesapeake. They had been greeted by a great Union demonstration as they passed along the Chesapeake and Delaware Canal. They are armed with the Miniè musket, but are to have the Miniè rifle and sword-bayonet. The splendid stand of colors brought with them was presented to the regiment by the High School in Washington street, Newark, just prior to their departure for Washington. This regiment is composed of some of the best men in the State, and in athletic appearance, as well as general soldierly deportment, are a credit to the country.

—*National Intelligencer*, May 7, 8.

Doc. 137.
DIPLOMATIC CORRESPONDENCE.

MR. FAULKNER TO MR. SEWARD.

LEGATION OF THE UNITED STATES, }
PARIS, April 15, 1861. }

Honorable Wm. H. Seward, Secretary of State:

SIR: I called to-day upon M. Thouvenel, at the Ministry of Foreign Affairs, and was promptly admitted to an interview. Agreeably to your request, I handed to him a copy of the Inaugural Address of President Lincoln, and added that I was instructed by you to say to him, that it embraced the views of the President of the United States upon the difficulties which now disturbed the harmony of the American Union, and also due exposition of the general policy which it was the purpose of the Government to pursue, with a view to the preservation of domestic peace and the maintenance of the federal Union. Here M. Thouvenel asked if there was not some diversity of opinion in the Cabinet of the President as to the proper mode of meeting the difficulties which now disturbed the relations of the States and General Government. I replied, upon that point I had no information; under our system the Cabinet was an advising body: its opinions were entitled to weight, but did not necessarily compel the action of the President; the executive power was, by the Constitution, vested exclusively in the President. I said that I was further instructed to assure him that the President of the United States entertains a full confidence in the speedy restoration of harmony and unity of the Government by a firm, yet just and liberal policy, coöperating with the deliberate and loyal action of the American people. M. Thouvenel expressed his pleasure at the assurance. I further said the President regretted that the events going on in the United States might be productive of some possible inconvenience to the people and subjects of France, but he was determined that those inconveniences shall be made as light and transient as possible, and so far as it may rest with him, that all strangers who may suffer any injury from them shall be indemnified. I said to him that the President thought it not impossible an appeal would be made before long by the Confederate States to foreign powers, and among others to the Government of France, for the recognition of their independence; that no such appeal having yet been made, it was premature and out of place to discuss any of the points involved in that delicate and important inquiry; but the Government of the United States desired the fact to be known that whenever any such application shall be made, it will meet with opposition from the minister who shall then represent that Government at this court. I said to him that my mission at this court would soon terminate, and I should have no official connection with the question which it was anticipated might arise upon the demand of the Confederate States for recognition of their independence; that my place would soon be supplied by a distinguished citizen of the State of New Jersey, a gentleman who possessed the confidence of the President, who fully sympathized in his public views, and who would doubtless come fully instructed as to the then wishes and views of the Government of the United States, and that the only request which I would now make, and which would close all I had to say in the interview, was that no proposition recognizing the permanent dismemberment of the American Union shall be considered by the French Government until after the arrival and reception of the new Minister accredited by the United States to this Court. M. Thouvenel, in reply, said that no application had yet been made to him by the Confederate States in any form for the recognition of their independence; that the French Government was not in the habit of acting hastily upon such questions, as might be seen by its tardiness in recognizing the new kingdom of Italy; that he believed the maintenance of the federal Union in its integrity was to be desired for the benefit of the people of the North and South, as well as for the interests of France; and the Government of the United States might rest well assured that no hasty or precipitate action would be taken on that subject by the Emperor, But while he gave utterance to these views, he was equally bound to say that the practice and usage of the present century had fully established the right of de facto governments to recognition when a proper case was made out for the decision of foreign powers. Here the official interview ended. The conversation was then further protracted by an inquiry from M. Thouvenel, when the new tariff would go into operation,

and whether it was to be regarded as the settled policy of the Government? I told him that the first day of the present month had been prescribed as the period when the duties would take effect; that I had not yet examined its provisions with such care as would justify me in pronouncing an opinion upon its merits; that it was condemned by the commercial classes of the country; and that I had no doubt from the discontent manifested in several quarters that the subject would engage the attention of Congress at its next meeting, and probably some important modifications would be made in it. The finances of the Government were at this time temporarily embarrassed, and I had no doubt the provisions of the new tariff were adopted with a view, although probably a mistaken one, of sustaining the credit of the Treasury as much as of reviving the protective policy. He then asked me my opinion as to the course of policy that would be adopted toward the seceding States, and whether I thought force would be employed to coerce them into submission to federal authority. I told him that I could only give him my individual opinion, and that I thought force would not be employed; that ours was a government of public opinion, and although the Union unquestionably possessed all the ordinary powers necessary for its preservation, as had been shown in several partial insurrections which had occurred in our history, yet that the extreme powers of the Government could only be used in accordance with public opinion, and that I was satisfied that the sentiment of the people was opposed to the employment of force against the seceding States. So sincere was the deference felt in that country for the great principles of self-government, and so great the respect for the action of the people, when adopted under the imposing forms of State organization and State sovereignty, that I did not think the employment of force would be tolerated for a moment, and I thought the only solution of our difficulties would be found in such modifications of our constitutional compact as would invite the seceding States back into the Union, or a peaceable acquiescence in the assertion of their claims to a separate sovereignty. M. Thouvenel expressed the opinion that the employment of force would be unwise, and would tend to a further rupture of the Confederacy by causing the remaining southern States to make common cause with the States which had already taken action on the subject.

I am, very respectfully, your obedient servant,
CHARLES J. FAULKNER.

MR. SEWARD TO MR. DAYTON.

DEPARTMENT OF STATE,
WASHINGTON, May 4, 1861.

SIR: The despatches of your predecessor, Nos. 117, 119 and 120, have been received. The latter, acknowledging the receipt of your letter of recall, and announcing his intended return, requires no especial notice. No. 117 bears the date of 5th of April last. It contains only an exposition of Mr. Faulkner's views of the policy which this Government ought to pursue in regard to the disturbed condition of affairs at home, but at the same time gives us no information concerning the state of affairs in France.

The instructions heretofore transmitted to you, will show you the President's views on the subject Mr. Faulkner has discussed, and these will be your guide, notwithstanding any different opinion your predecessor may have expressed or left on record at Paris.

No. 119 bears date of the 15th April last, and contains a report of an official conversation, and also of an unofficial one, held between Mr. Faulkner and M. Thouvenel. In the former conversation, M. Thouvenel asked Mr. Faulkner whether there is not some diversity of opinion in the Cabinet of the President as to the proper mode of meeting the difficulties which now disturb the relations of the States and the General Government. Mr. Faulkner, in reply, said that he had no information on the subject. The matter is of no great moment, yet it is desirable that there be no misapprehensions of the true state of the Government in the present emergency. You may, therefore, recall that conversation to M. Thouvenel's memory, and then assure him explicitly that there is no difference of opinion whatever between the President and his constitutional advisers, or among those advisers themselves, concerning the policy that has been pursued and which is now prosecuted by the Administration in regard to the unhappy disturbances existing in the country. The path of Executive duty has thus far been too plainly marked out by stern necessity to be mistaken, while the solemnity of the great emergency, and the responsibility it involved, have extinguished in the public councils every emotion but those of loyalty and patriotism. It is not in the hands of this Administration that this Government is to come to an end at all, much less for want of harmony in devotion to the country. M. Thouvenel's declaration that the United States may rest well assured that no hasty or precipitate action will be taken on the subject of the apprehended application of the insurrectionists for a recognition of the independence of the so-called Confederate States, is entirely satisfactory, although it was attended by a reservation of views concerning general principles applicable to cases that need not now be discussed. In the unofficial conversation, Mr. Faulkner says that he himself expressed the opinion that force would not be resorted to to coerce the so-called seceding States into submission to the Federal authority, and that the only solution of the difficulties would be found in such modifications of the constitutional compact, as would invite the seceding States back into the Union, or a peaceable acquiescence in the assertion of their claim to a separate sovereignty. The

time when these questions had any pertinency or plausiblity, has passed away. The United States waited patiently while their authority was defied in turbulent assemblies and insidious preparations, willing to hope that mediation, offered on all sides, would conciliate and induce the disaffected parties to return to a better mind, but the case is now altogether changed. The insurgents have instituted revolution with open, flagrant, deadly war, to compel the United States to acquiesce in the dismemberment of the Union. The United States have accepted this civil war as an inevitable necessity. The constitutional remedies for all the complaints of the insurgents are still open to them, and will remain so. But, on the other hand, the land and naval forces of the Union have been put into activity to restore the Federal authority and save the Union from danger.

You cannot be too decided or too explicit in making known to the French Government that there is not now, nor has there been, nor will there be any—the least—idea existing in this Government of suffering a dissolution of this Union to take place in any way whatever. There will be here only one nation and one government, and there will be the same republic and the same constitutional Union that have already survived a dozen national changes and changes of government in almost every other country. These will stand hereafter, as they are now, objects of human wonder and human affection. You have seen, on the eve of your departure, the elasticity of the national spirit, the vigor of the national Government, and the lavish devotion of the national treasures to this great cause. Tell M. Thouvenel, then, with the highest consideration and good feeling, that the thought of a dissolution of this Union, peaceably or by force, has never entered into the mind of any candid statesman here, and it is high time that it be dismissed by statesmen in Europe.

I am, sir, respectfully, your obedient servant,

WM. H. SEWARD.

To WILLIAM L. DAYTON, Esq., &c. &c.

—N. Y. Evening Post, May 6.

Doc. 138.

PRESIDENT LINCOLN'S LETTER TO THE MARYLAND AUTHORITIES.

WASHINGTON, April 20, 1861.

Governor Hicks and Mayor Brown:

GENTLEMEN: Your letter by Messrs. Bond, Dobbin and Brune, is received. I tender you both my sincere thanks for your efforts to keep the peace in the trying situation in which you are placed. For the future, troops *must* be brought here, but I make no point of bringing them *through* Baltimore.

Without any military knowledge myself, of course I must leave details to General Scott. He hastily said this morning, in presence of these gentlemen, " March them *around* Balti-more, and not through it."

I sincerely hope the general, on fuller re-flection, will consider this practical and proper, and that you will not object to it. By this a collision of the people of Baltimore with the troops will be avoided, unless they go out of the way to seek it. I hope you will exert your influence to prevent this. Now and ever, I shall do all in my power for peace, consistently with the maintenance of Government.

Your obedient servant,
A. LINCOLN.
—*N. Y. Evening Post*, May 6.

Doc. 139.
INTERVIEW BETWEEN COLONELS TILGHMAN AND PRENTISS.

HEADQUARTERS, CAMP DEFIANCE, }
CAIRO, Ill., May 6, 1861. }

COLONEL LLOYD TILGHMAN, commanding the western division of Kentucky Militia, including Paducah and Columbus, places that have been considered as menacing our troops here, called, in company with Colonel Wickliffe, of Ken-tucky, upon Colonel Prentiss, commandant at this place. The following is the substance of their interview :

Colonel Tilghman—" I have visited you, sir, for the purpose of a little official intercourse with reference to the late questions which have excited the people of Kentucky, and to culti-vate, as far as in my power, peaceful relations. Some portions of the public press have erro-neously used the name of Kentucky, the name of her organized militia under my command, and my own name, in referring to the hostile movement of troops against you from Tennes-see." (Colonel Tilghman referred to an article in the Louisville *Journal*, which stated that hostile movements from Tennessee could go through Kentucky only by the aid of troops under Colonel Tilghman's command. He char-acterized the statement in severe terms, and said that Kentucky was still in the Union, and had no stronger wish than to remain so.)

Colonel Prentiss—" I can hardly express, gentlemen, how gratifying it is to me to find these the sentiments of all the leading men I have met from your side of the river. I assure you that, so far as I understand the sentiments of my State, my command and myself, those friendly feelings are cordially reciprocated. We must, however, when we understand that cer-tain points in either Kentucky, Tennessee, or Missouri are menacing us, prepare to defend them."

Colonel Tilghman—" Let me say, in defer-ence to Tennessee, that, so far as her authorities and official acts are concerned, she was, three days ago, in the Union. I have just come from there, where, in an official capacity, I defined to them, firmly and effectually, the policy of my State. She has a mercurial population, like every State, that is hard to control. But I feel

fully authorized to say in deference to Govern-or Harris, with whom I had an interview, and in deference to the State of Tennessee, that there are no hostile menaces toward you."

Colonel Prentiss—" I want you to under-stand me that, in designating certain points as hostile and menacing, I am far from including the whole State. As to Memphis, *I am reliably informed that bodies are arming and drilling with a proposed destination to some place North ; and I will say to you frankly, that we are prepared for the attack and await it.* But I am inclined to think they are the mob, with-out official encouragement."

Colonel Tilghman—" Yes, sir, I feel author-ized to express that view of it. The press ought to be restrained in its ready circulation of errors. There is not a word of truth in the statement of there being 12,000 men at Padu-cah for invasion ; or, as to the concentration of troops in any part of Kentucky under my control. As to the recent arrival of arms at Columbus, they were the property of the State. This, as her right, Illinois cannot raise any ob-jection to. Kentucky has her own rights to defend, and no State can do it more powerfully. She is a warm and generous friend, but a hearty enemy. We do not wish war. We are now electing our representatives to Congress, with the intention of holding out the olive branch. But the commerce of Kentucky is large, and our people do not understand how much of it is to be interrupted *in transitu.* They feel that they cannot ship a barrel of flour without being subjected to this system of *espionage,* which is entirely inadmissible."

Colonel Prentiss—" I am instructed to seize no property unless I have information that such property consists of munitions of war, destined to the enemies of the United States Govern-ment."

Colonel Tilghman—" Then you would not consider munitions of war shipped to Ken-tucky, under her authority, as contraband ? "

Colonel Prentiss—" That would depend up-on the point whether Columbus is arming and menacing us."

Colonel Tilghman—" They have not been and are not, allow me to say."

Colonel Prentiss—" Then I have been mis-informed. Generally, there would be no deten-tion of munitions of war destined to the au-thorities of Kentucky."

Colonel Tilghman—" The position I wish to assume is, that Kentucky is the peer of Illinois, and would not consent to any thing of the kind, under any pretence. Kentucky probably would never consent to the blockade of the Ohio."

Colonel Prentiss—" But if, as you say, Ken-tucky is a loyal State, she would have to allow the blockading of the Ohio. I assure you Illi-nois would allow it, if required by the General Government. Kentucky has not done her full duty to the Government. She has not fur-nished her quota of troops upon the demand of the President, in defence of the national flag ;

and this shows we are right in apprehending certain disaffected and disloyal communities which rule to some extent the sentiment of the State."

Colonel Tilghman—"I frankly acknowledge that you have the advantage of me there. But after my intercourse with you, and reassuring you of the groundlessness of your fears in my official capacity, it would be very inconsistent with your previous intimations, for you to credit counter rumors. My dear sir, there are not organized fifty men in Western Kentucky, outside of my command."

Colonel Prentiss—"As soon as our force is completely organized here, I intend to visit the other side."

Colonel Tilghman—"We shall receive you with every kindness. The position of Illinois and Kentucky relatively is very delicate, and on that account allow me to say that I hope you will continue in command here. Affairs must be managed on both sides with calmness. I think there is hardly a man in a hundred in the State of Kentucky but would fight for the old Constitution as interpreted by the Supreme Court. I am highly gratified at this interview, and I hope to see yourself and staff over there some day."

—*Chicago Tribune*, and *N. Y. Evening Post*, May 11.

Doc. 140.
ACT RECOGNIZING A STATE OF WAR.
[BY "CONFEDERATE" CONGRESS.]

THE following Act, recognizing the existence of war between the United States and the States in rebellion, was published May 6, 1861:

Whereas, The earnest efforts made by this government to establish friendly relations between the Government of the United States and the Confederate States, and to settle all questions of disagreement between the two governments upon principles of right, justice, equity, and good faith, have proved unavailing, by reason of the refusal of the Government of the United States to hold any intercourse with the commissioners appointed by this government for the purposes aforesaid, or to listen to any proposal they had to make for the peaceful solution of all causes of difficulties between the two governments; and *whereas*, the President of the United States of America has issued his proclamation, making requisition upon the States of the American Union for 75,000 men, for the purpose as therein indicated of capturing forts, and other strongholds within the jurisdiction of, and belonging to, the Confederate States of America, and has detailed naval armaments upon the coasts of the Confederate States of America, and raised, organized, and equipped a large military force to execute the purpose aforesaid, and has issued his other Proclamation, announcing his purpose to set on foot a blockade of the ports of the Confederate

States; and *whereas*, the State of Virginia has seceded from the Federal Union, and entered into a convention of alliance, offensive and defensive, with the Confederate States, and has adopted the Provisional Constitution of the said States, and the States of Maryland, North Carolina, Tennessee, Kentucky, Arkansas, and Missouri have refused, and it is believed that the State of Delaware and the inhabitants of the Territories of Arizona and New Mexico, and the Indian Territory south of Kansas, will refuse to coöperate with the Government of the United States in these acts of hostilities and wanton aggression, which are plainly intended to overawe, oppress, and finally subjugate the people of the Confederate States; and, *whereas*, by the acts and means aforesaid war exists between the Confederate States and the Government of the United States, and the States and Territories thereof, excepting the States of Maryland, North Carolina, Tennessee, Kentucky, Arkansas, Missouri, and Delaware, and the Territories of Arizona, and New Mexico, and the Indian Territory south of Kansas: Therefore,

SECTION 1. *The congress of the Confederate States of America do enact*, That the President of the Confederate States is hereby authorized to use the whole land and naval force of the Confederate States to meet the war thus commenced, and to issue to private armed vessels commissions, or letters of marque and general reprisal, in such form as he shall think proper, under the seal of the Confederate States, against the vessels, goods and effects of the Government of the United States, and of the citizens or inhabitants of the States and Territories thereof, except the States and Territories hereinbefore named. *Provided*, however, that property of the enemy (unless it be contraband of war) laden on board a neutral vessel, shall not be subject to seizure under this Act; *and provided further*, that vessels of the citizens or inhabitants of the United States now in the ports of the Confederate States, except such as have been, since the 5th of April last, or may hereafter be, in the service of the Government of the United States, shall be allowed thirty days after the publication of this Act to leave said ports and reach their destination; and such vessels and their cargoes, excepting articles contraband of war, shall not be subject to capture under this Act, during said period, unless they shall have previously reached the destination for which they were bound on leaving said ports.

SEC. 2. That the President of the Confederate States shall be and he is hereby authorized and empowered to revoke and annul at pleasure all letters of marque and reprisal which he may at any time grant pursuant to this Act.

SEC. 3. That all persons applying for letters of marque and reprisal, pursuant to this Act, shall state in writing the name, and a suitable description of the tonnage and force of the vessel, and the name and place of residence of each owner concerned therein, and the intended number of the crew ; which statement shall be signed by the person or persons making such application, and filed with the Secretary of State, or shall be delivered to any other officer or person who shall be employed to deliver out such commissions, to be by him transmitted to the Secretary of State.

SEC. 4. That, before any commission or letters of marque and reprisal shall be issued as aforesaid, the owner or owners of the ship or vessel for which the same shall be requested, and the commander thereof for the time being, shall give bond to the Confederate States, with at least two responsible sureties, not interested in such vessel, in the penal sum of five thousand dollars ; or if such vessel be provided with more than one hundred and fifty men, then in the penal sum of ten thousand dollars ; with condition that the owners, officers and crew, who shall be employed on board such commissioned vessel, shall and will observe the laws of the Confederate States, and the instructions which shall be given them according to law, for the regulation of their conduct ; and will satisfy all damages and injuries which shall be done or committed contrary to the tenor thereof, by such vessel, during her commission, and to deliver up the same when revoked by the President of the Confederate States.

SEC. 5. That all captures and prizes of vessels and property shall be forfeited, and shall accrue to the owners, officers and crews of the vessels by whom such captures and prizes shall be made ; and, on due condemnation had, shall be distributed according to any written agreement which shall be made between them : and if there be no such written agreement, then one moiety to the owners, and the other moiety to the officers and crew, as nearly as may be, according to the rules prescribed for the distribution of prize money by the laws of the Confederate States.

SEC. 6. That all vessels, goods, and effects, the property of any citizen of the Confederate States, or of persons resident within and under the protection of the Confederate States, or of persons permanently within the territories, and under the protection of any foreign prince, government or state in amity with the Confederate States, which shall have been captured by the United States, and which shall be recaptured by vessels commissioned as aforesaid, shall be restored to the lawful owners, upon payment by them of a just and reasonable salvage, to be determined by the mutual agreement of the parties concerned, or by the decree of any court having jurisdiction, according to the nature of each case, agreeably to the provisions established by law. And such salvage shall be distributed among the owners, officers, and crews of the vessels commissioned as aforesaid, and making such capture, according to any written agreement which shall be made between them ; and in case of no such agree-

ment, then in the same manner and upon the principles hereinbefore provided in case of capture.

SEC. 7. That before breaking bulk of any vessel which shall be captured as aforesaid, or other disposal or conversion thereof, or of any articles which shall be found on board the same, such captured vessel, goods or effects, shall be brought into some port of the Confederate States, or of a nation or state in amity with the Confederate States, and shall be proceeded against before a competent tribunal ; and after condemnation and forfeiture thereof, shall belong to the owners, officers and crew of the vessel capturing the same, and be distributed as before provided ; and in the case of all captured vessels, goods and effects, which shall be brought within the jurisdiction of the Confederate States, the District Courts of the Confederate States shall have exclusive, original cognizance thereof, as in civil causes of admiralty and maritime jurisdiction ; and the said courts or the courts, being courts of the Confederate States, into which such causes shall be removed, and in which they shall be finally decided, shall and may decree restitution, in whole or in part, when the capture shall have been made without just cause. And if made without probable cause, may order and decree damages and costs to the party injured, for which the owners and commanders of the vessels making such captures, and also the vessels, shall be liable.

SEC. 8. That all persons found on board of any captured vessels, or on board any recaptured vessels, shall be reported to the collector of the port in the Confederate States in which they shall first arrive, and shall be delivered into the custody of the marshal of the district, or some court or military officer of the Confederate States, or of any State in or near such port, who shall take charge of their safe keeping and support, at the expense of the Confederate States.

SEC. 9. That the President of the Confederate States is hereby authorized to establish and order suitable instructions for the better governing and directing the conduct of the vessels so commissioned, their officers and crews, copies of which shall be delivered, by the collector of the customs, to the commanders, when they shall give bond as before provided.

SEC. 10. That a bounty shall be paid by the Confederate States of $20 for each person on board any armed ship or vessel belonging to the United States at the commencement of an engagement, which shall be burnt, sunk or destroyed by any vessel commissioned as aforesaid, which shall be of equal or inferior force, the same to be divided as in other cases of prize money—and a bounty of $25 shall be paid to the owners, officers and crews of the private armed vessels, commissioned as aforesaid, for each and every prisoner by them captured and brought into port, and delivered to an agent authorized to receive them, in any port of the

Confederate States; and the Secretary of the Treasury is hereby authorized to pay or cause to be paid to the owners, officers, and crews of such private armed vessels, commissioned as aforesaid, or their agent, the bounties herein provided.

SEC. 11. That the commanding officer of every vessel having a commission, or letters of marque and reprisal, during the present hostilities between the Confederate States and the United States, shall keep a regular journal, containing a true and exact account of his daily proceedings and transactions with such vessel and the crew thereof; the ports and places he shall put into, or cast anchor in; the time of his stay there, and the cause thereof; the prizes he shall take, and the nature and probable value thereof; the times and places, when and where taken, and in what manner he shall dispose of the same; the ships or vessels he shall fall in with; the times and places, when and where he shall meet with them, and his observations and remarks thereon; also, of whatever else shall occur to him, or any of his officers or marines, or be discovered by examination or conference with any marines or passengers of, or in any other ships or vessels, or by any other means, touching the fleets, vessels and forces of the United States; their posts and places of station and destination, strength, numbers, intents and designs; and such commanding officer shall immediately on his arrival in any port of the Confederate States, from or during the continuance of any voyage or cruise, produce his commission for such vessel, and deliver up such journal, so kept as aforesaid, signed with his proper name and handwriting, to the collector or other chief officer of the customs at or nearest to such port; the truth of such journal shall be verified by the oath of the commanding officer for the time being; and such collector or other chief officer of the customs shall, immediately on the arrival of such vessel, order the proper officer of the customs to go on board and take an account of the officers and men, the number and nature of the guns, and whatever else shall occur to him on examination, material to be known; and no such vessel shall be permitted to sail out of port again until such journal shall have been delivered up, and a certificate obtained under the hand of such collector or other chief officer of the customs that she is manned and armed according to her commission; and, upon delivery of such certificate, any former certificate of a like nature which shall have been obtained by the commander of such vessel shall be delivered up.

SEC. 12. That the commanders of vessels having letters of marque and reprisal as aforesaid, neglecting to keep a journal as aforesaid, or wilfully making fraudulent entries therein, or obliterating the record of any material transactions therein, where the interest of the Confederate States is concerned, or refusing to produce and deliver such journal, commission, or

certificate pursuant to the preceding section of this act, then and in such cases the commissions or letters of marque and reprisal of such vessels shall be liable to be revoked; and such commander respectively shall forfeit for every such offence the sum of $1,000, one moiety thereof for the use of the Confederate States, and the other to the informer.

SEC. 13. That the owners or commanders of vessels having letters of marque and reprisal as aforesaid, who shall violate any of the acts of congress for the collection of the revenue of the Confederate States, and for the prevention of smuggling, shall forfeit the commission or letters of marque and reprisal, and they and the vessels owned or commanded by them shall be liable to all the penalties and forfeitures attaching to merchant vessels, in like cases.

SEC. 14. That on all goods, wares, and merchandise captured and made good and lawful prizes of war, by any private armed ship having commission or letters of marque and reprisal under this act, and brought into the Confederate States, there shall be allowed a reduction of 33⅓ per cent. on the amount of duties imposed by law.

SEC. 15. That five per centum on the net amount (after deducting all charges and expenditures) of the prize money arising from captured vessels and cargoes, and on the net amount of the salvage of vessels and cargoes recaptured by the private armed vessels of the Confederate States, shall be secured and paid over to the collector or other chief officer of the customs at the port or place in the Confederate States at which such captured or recaptured vessels may arrive, or to the consul or other public agent of the Confederate States, residing at the port or place, not within the Confederate States, at which such captured or recaptured vessels may arrive. And the moneys arising therefrom shall be held, and are hereby pledged by the government of the Confederate States as a fund for the support and maintenance of the widows and orphans of such persons as may be slain, and for the support and maintenance of such persons as may be wounded and disabled on board of the private armed vessels commissioned as aforesaid in any engagement with the enemy, to be assigned and distributed in such manner as shall hereafter be provided by law.

—Charleston Mercury, May 8.

Doc. 141.

PATRIOTIC CONTRIBUTIONS TO MAY 7, 1861.

Albany, N. Y........	$46,000	Burlington, N. J.....	$4,000
Auburn, N. Y.......	4,000	Bordentown, N. J....	3,000
Abington, Mass......	5,000	Bradford, Vt.........	2,000
Amesbury, Mass.....	5,000	Bridgetown, N. J....	1,000
Acton, Mass........	5,000	Bedford, Mass.......	2,000
Boston, Mass........	186,000	Bennington, Vt....	10,600
Brooklyn, N. Y......	75,000	Barre, Mass..........	2,000
Bridgeport, Ct.......	31,000	Braintree, Mass......	2,000
Burlington, Vt.......	3,000	Bedford, N. Y.......	1,000
Bath, Me............	10,000	Brunswick, Me......	1,000
Batavia, N. Y.......	4,000	Binghamton, N. Y....	10,000
Buffalo, N. Y........	110,000	Connecticut, State...2,000,000	

Cincinnati	$280,000	Newark, N. J	$136,000
Charlestown, Mass	10,000	New Haven, Ct	30,000
Chicago, Ill	20,000	Norwich, Ct	13,000
Circleville, Ohio	2,000	New London, Ct	10,000
Clinton, Ill	5,000	New Brunswick, N. J.	2,000
Cohasset, Mass	1,000	Needham, Mass	3,000
Clinton, N. Y	1,000	Newtown, Mass	3,000
Concord, Mass	4,000	N. Andover, Mass	3,000
Concord, N. H	10,000	Noblesville, Ind	10,000
Canandaigua, N. Y	7,000	Newbury, Mass	3,000
Canton, Mass	5,000	Newburyport, Mass	4,000
Cass County, Ind	6,000	Ohio, State	3,000,000
Cam. & Am. R. R. Co.	10,000	Oswego, N. Y	13,000
Detroit, Mich	50,000	Ottawa, Ill	10,000
Dunkirk, N. Y	20,000	Pennsylvania, State.	3,500,000
Dover, N. H	10,000	Philadelphia	330,000
Damariscotta, Me	3,000	Plymouth, Mass	2,000
Elizabeth, N. J	11,000	Poughkeepsie, N. Y..	10,000
Elkhart, Ind	8,000	Piqua, Ohio	20,000
Erie, Pa	25,000	Paterson, N. J	10,000
Evansville, Ind	15,000	Portland, Me	31,000
Fall River, Mass	10,000	Princeton, N. J	2,000
Flemington, N. J	5,000	Palmyra, N. Y	6,000
Fond du Lac, Wis	4,000	Quincy, Mass	10,000
Gloucester, Mass	10,000	Rhode Island, State..	500,000
Glen Falls, N. Y	10,000	Rochester	69,000
Great Falls, N. H	10,000	Rockland, Me	10,000
Greensburg, Ind	2,000	Salem, Mass	15,000
Georgetown, Mass	5,000	Stowe, Mass	2,000
Galena, Ill	1,000	Schenectady, N. Y	2,000
Hudson, N. Y	4,000	Seneca Falls, N. Y	3,000
Hamilton, Ohio	1,000	Stockbridge, Mass	3,000
Hoboken, N. J	2,000	Sycamore, Ill	4,000
Hornellsville, N. Y	1,000	St. Albans, Vt	10,000
Hartford, Conn	64,000	Sag Harbor, N. Y	3,000
Harrisburg, Pa	5,000	Sar. Springs, N. Y	2,000
Illinois, State	2,000,000	Southboro', Mass	2,000
Indiana, State	1,000,000	Syracuse, N, Y	34,000
Iowa, State	100,000	Salisbury, Mass	5,000
Ithaca, N. Y	10,000	Shelburne, Vt	1,000
Indianapolis, Ind	5,000	Schuylkill Co., Pa	30,000
Ipswich, Mass	4,000	Sutton, Mass	6,000
Jersey City. N. J	32,000	Troy, N. Y	48,000
Janesville. Wis	6,000	Toledo, Ohio	5,000
Kenton, Ohio	2,000	Taunton, Mass	40,000
Keene, N. H	10,000	Utica, N. Y	20,000
Lynn, Mass	10,000	Upper Sandusky, O..	5,000
Lockport, N. Y	2,000	Vermont, State	1,000,000
Lawrence, Mass	5,000	Wisconsin, State	225,000
Lowell, Mass	8,000	Weymouth, Mass	5,000
London, Ohio	1,000	Wilmington, Ohio	3,000
Lancaster, Pa	5,000	Waynesville, Ohio	2,000
Lebanon County, Pa.	10,000	Waltham, Mass	5,000
Maine, State	1,300,000	West Cambridge,Mass.	10,000
Michigan, various pl's.	50,000	Woodstock, Vt	1,000
Milwaukee, Wis	31,000	Watertown, N. Y	3,000
Marblehead, Mass	5,000	Warsaw, N. Y	3,000
Malden, Mass	2,000	Watertown, Mass	2,000
Madison, Ind	6,000	Waterford, N. Y	8,000
Mount Holly, N. J	3,000	Westboro', Mass	8,000
Morristown, N. J	3,000	West Troy. N. Y	7,000
Mystic, Ct	7,000	Woburn, Mass	5,000
Madison, Wis	9,000	Warsaw, N. Y	3,000
Marlboro'. Mass	10,000	Woodbury, Ct	5,000
Marshfield, Mass	5,000	Webster, Mass	4,000
New York, State	3,000,000	Xenia, Ohio	14,000
New York, City	2,173,000	Zanesville, Ohio	3,000
New Jersey, State	1,000,000		

Total.................................$23,277,000

—*N. Y. Tribune,* May 8.

Doc. 142.

DEPARTURE OF THE 20TH REGIMENT, OF ULSTER CO., N. Y., MAY 7, 1861.

THE Twentieth Regiment, Colonel G. W. Pratt, of Ulster county, arrived in New York on Sunday evening, the 28th of April, and were stationed at the Park barracks. They came for the purpose of going to Washington, via steamship, but no provisions had been made for their transportation.

The regiment mustered 781 men, when they arrived, recruits to the number of twenty came on subsequently, and 300 at least might have been added from the Highlands, had not the order "to stop recruiting" been forwarded.

On Sunday afternoon, May 5, a special order was received, ordering the Twentieth Regiment to return to their homes, as no more regular militia would be accepted; advices from Washington only calling for volunteers to serve for two years.

This order caused great consternation among the rank and file. They had enlisted in the hope of being engaged in the impending conflict, and expected to see actual service. Many of them had given up lucrative positions, left homes and families for the purpose of manifesting their patriotism for their country, and sustain the honor and integrity of the American flag. At seven o'clock, on the following evening, a special order was received from Washington, ordering them to at once proceed to the Capital.

When this news was imparted to the troops a scene of genuine enthusiasm ensued; cheer upon cheer rang upon the air; the President, the Governor, General Scott, Colonel Pratt, and in fact every name the troops could think of, was wildly cheered.

Colonel Pratt was deeply affected at the enthusiasm manifested by his men, and took no measures to check their outbursts of joy. After order was restored, the commandant made a few pithy remarks, thanking his regiment for the manner in which they had undergone disappointments, and congratulated them on the prospect of having an opportunity of showing of what material the Ulster county boys are composed. He said that his regiment would come back covered with glory. He also exonerated the State authorities from all blame in keeping them back, and said that the principal reason for their being ordered home was the great number of organized regiments of militia offering, by which the Government was forced to decline one-half the tenders.

A few encouraging words to the men, and the Colonel concluded by giving orders to be in marching order as soon as possible.

The celerity with which the camp was placed in marching order is one of the very best evidences of what might be expected of this regiment in actual service. The train could not leave owing to the storm, and the men again bivouacked.

At reveille the men were already in trim ready to take arms and march. A hearty and substantial breakfast was partaken of, and all the arrangements made necessary for the comfort of the troops. The order to form in line was given at eight o'clock.

After inspection by the officers and several military celebrities, who had assembled to witness their departure, the line of march was taken up, and the command wheeled out of the west gate of the Park, and filed down Broadway to Cortlandt street to the ferry. The officers were mounted on splendid chargers, and the general appearance of the regiment elicited considerable praise from the spectators. At the depot a train was in readiness to take the troops to Philadelphia.

Field Officers.—Colonel, George W. Pratt; Lieutenant Colonel, Hiram Schoonmaker; Major, Theodore B. Yates.

Staff Officers.—Adjutant, J. B. Hardenburgh; Engineer, D. T. Van Buren; Hospital Surgeon, (assigned to duty in the brigade,) A. Crispell; Surgeon, C. Leonard Ingersoll; Assistant Surgeon, Robert Longham; Quartermaster, John S. Giffin; Paymaster, P. T. Overbaugh; Commissary, W. Sonnsby; Chaplain, Rev. H. H. Reynolds.

Non-commissioned Staff.—Quartermaster Sergeant, P. F. Hasbrouck; Sergeant of Infantry, W. Webster Shaffer; Drum-Major, Geo. Myers; Fife-Major, A. Goller.

Line Officers.—Company A, of Cairo, Greene county, First Lieutenant, A. G. Barker, commanding; Second Lieutenant, James Stevens.

Company B, of Kingston, Captain G. H. Sharpe; First Lieutenant, Jacob Sharpe; Second Lieutenant, Cornelius Houghtaling.

Company C, of Kingston, Captain, J. Rudolph Tappen; First Lieutenant, Walter W. Van Ranselaer; Second Lieutenant, Peter S. Voorhees.

Company D, of Shokan, Ulster county, Captain, David Winne; First Lieutenant, John Hussy; Second Lieutenant, John W. Schoonmaker.

Company E, of Ellensville, Ulster county, Captain, William Lent; First Lieutenant, Jacob A. Blackman; Second Lieutenant, Nicholas Sahen.

Company F, of Rondout, Ulster county, Captain, P. J. Flynn; First Lieutenant, Edward O'Reilly; Second Lieutenant, John Murray.

Company G, of Saugerties, Captain, J. S. Oakley; First Lieutenant, J. Tallmadge Hendricks; Second Lieutenant, Sylvanus W. Miller.

Company H, of Rondout, Ulster county, Captain, John Duenbocker; First Lieutenant, Jerrie McIntire; Second Lieutenant, Lawrence Stocker.

Company K, (right flank company), Captain, James McArdle; First Lieutenant, Warren A. Mansfield; Second Lieutenant, Samuel W. Greene; Junior Lieutenant, William Cunningham.

N. Y. Com. Advertiser, May 7, & *N. Y. Herald,* April 30.

Doc. 143.
SPEECH OF REVERDY JOHNSON, AT FREDERICK, MD., May 7, 1861.

Mr. Johnson appeared upon the stand shortly before four o'clock, and, after an eloquent and fervent prayer by Rev. B. H. Creager, spoke as follows:

I am before you by the request of the patriotic Ladies of your city to present in their behalf a standard, the work of their hands, which they desire to intrust to your custody and protection. With this request I comply with the truest pleasure.

In this existing crisis of our country's fate every indication of a national, patriotic spirit is hailed with joy by every loyal heart. And when, as in this instance, it is exhibited by those whose thoughts are instinctively pure, having no partisan motives to influence them, no partisan prejudices to gratify, no petty ambition to subserve, no interest other than in their country's prosperity and good name, we rejoice at it even the more from a conviction that it must tend to strengthen the resolves of the loyal, encourage the hopes of the desponding, and bring to a pause the plottings of the rebellious.

Before doing the mere act I am delegated to perform, I hope you will consider the occasion as justifying a few thoughts as to the duty and interest of our State in the present emergency. In the original causes which have produced it she, thank God, had no share. Amongst the foremost and bravest in winning our independence; amongst the truest and wisest in forming our Government, and amongst the first in adopting it, her sons have uniformly given it a faithful and zealous support. No treasonable thought, so far as we know, ever entered the mind of one of them; certainly no threat of treason was ever whispered by them. They ever felt the immense advantage of the Union; they saw evidenced by every thing around them the blessings it conferred upon Maryland and upon all: prosperity unexampled, a national power increasing every year with a rapidity and to a degree never before witnessed in a nation's history, and winning for us a name challenging the respect and admiration of the world. They saw in the extent of the country, and the differences of climate and habits, elements of strength rather than of weakness, and apprehended therefore no parricidal efforts in any quarter to destroy the Government. If occasionally murmurs of dissatisfaction were heard elsewhere, they were attributed to the whining disposition of some and the disappointed ambition of others. They were ridiculed, subjected to no other punishment, but left to stand as "monuments of the safety with which error of opinion may be tolerated where reason is left free to combat it." No "whiskey insurrection" ever occurred within our borders; no ordinance of nullification was ever threatened by us; and, if we continue true to patriotic duty, no ordinance of secession, direct or indirect, open or covert, will ever be adopted by those in authority, or, if madly adopted, be tolerated by the people.

To this steadfast attachment to the Union we are not only bound by gratitude to the noble ancestry by whose patriotic wisdom it was bequeathed to us, and by the unappreciable blessings the bequest has conferred upon us, but by the assurance, which the most stolid intellect can hardly fail to feel, that its destruction would not only, and at once deprive us of all these, but precipitate us into irreparable ruin. In this ruin all would more or less participate, but our geographical position would make it to us immediate and total. A peaceable disseverance the good and great men who have heretofore guided our public councils ever predicted to be impossible. The proclamations now trumpeted through the land, the marshalling of hosts by thousands and tens of thousands, the whitening of our waters with an immense naval marine, the blockade of ports, the prostration of commerce, the destruction of almost all civil employment, the heated tone of the public press of all sections, belching forth the most bitter enmity, all, all testify to the truth of the prediction. How this is to result, Heaven alone knows.

But to my mind one thing is certain. The Government by no single act of its own, has given cause for resistance to its rightful authority. The powers which it was exercising at the moment when rebellion began to muster its "armies of pestilence," were clearly conferred upon it by the Constitution. And if the Executive, then just legally chosen, had meditated any illegal policy, the friends of constitutional rights were numerous enough in Congress, had they remained at their posts, as they were bound to do by their oaths and their duty to the holy cause of Constitutional Government, successfully and peaceably to have thwarted it.

The professed especial friends of Southern rights, instead of this, rudely shot from their spheres, and, under the utterly ridiculous claim of constitutional right, advised State secession. Madmen—if not worse—they desecrated, too, in support of this dogma, the name of Calhoun. He may have committed political errors—who has not? His doctrine of nullification was certainly one, in the judgment of all his great compeers, sanctioned by almost the entire country, but he never maintained the nonsensical heresy of rightful secession. On the contrary, long after that of the short-lived nullification, in February, 1844, writing to his "political friends and supporters" refusing to permit his name to be presented before the then approaching Baltimore Convention, he said:

"That each State has the right to act as it pleases in whatever relates to itself exclusively no one will deny; *but it is a perfectly novel doctrine that any State has such a right when she comes to act in concert with others in reference to what concerns the whole.* In such cases it is the plainest dictate of common sense that whatever affects the whole should be regulated by the *mutual consent of all, and not by the discretion of each.*"

That great philosophical statesman understood, as in another letter of the 3d of July, 1843, he invites his countrymen to understand "in all its great and beautiful proportions, the noble political structure reared by the wisdom and patriotism of our ancestors, and to have the virtue and the sense to preserve and protect it," and declared it the "duty of the Federal Government, under the guarantees of the Constitution, *promptly to suppress physical force as an element of change,* and to keep wide open the door for the free and full action of all the moral elements in its power."

The truth is, and I regret sincerely to believe it, that fear of a violation of Southern rights was with the prompters of the rebellion but a pretence.

What they have done and are still doing at the sacrifice of the nation's welfare, and of the welfare of their own section, exerting every nerve to accomplish, was and is but to retain official power, which they fancied was passing from them. Look at the usurped government at Montgomery. The mention of names is unnecessary—they are destined to an unhappy immortality. Those who plotted the seizure of forts, arsenals, mints, navy-yards, custom-houses, the admitted property of the United States, seducing soldiers and sailors from their sworn allegiance—using the very Senate chamber, dedicated and sacred to duty, as a spot from which to issue their treacherous telegrams—are there to be seen all in power, actual or prospective. The fact too clearly tells the revolting story. Men long enjoying public honors, earning through many years of service a national fame, owning their renown because of the world-wide fame of a glorious Government, are striving, day and night, to reduce it to dishonor and destruction. Thank God, our consolation is that the effort, however pregnant with the present calamity, will fall short of its horrid aim. They may "as well strike at the heavens with their arms" as lift them against the "American Union."

That the end must fail, who can doubt? The recent census furnishes pregnant proof of this. It shows that the Free States have a population of males between eighteen and forty-five of 3,778,000, and all the Slave States only 1,655,000, and the seceding States, excluding Virginia, but 531,000; and if to this vast difference of men is added that of wealth, inventive skill, habits of industry, and the absence of any element of domestic danger, the disparity is infinitely greater. In a struggle between such hosts—which may God in his mercy avert—who can fail to see what must be the end?

But to our State these facts teach a lesson that all can understand. If mad and wicked enough to attempt it, what could we do to resist this immense power on our borders? Call on the South? Make our State the battle-field? How long could the entire South, if flying to our succor, remain with and aid us? They might assist in drenching our land with blood; they might witness with us our desolation, but that doom in such a contest it would be. They would be driven back within their own limits and we left alone in our calamity, to be rendered the more acute when, as we should, we awoke to the insanity and crime which occasioned it. Looking, therefore, to interest alone, adherence to the Government is our clear policy. But when, as in my judgment it obviously is, that policy is demanded by the most obvious demands of patriotic duty, we should not hesitate one moment in adopting and abiding by it.

Let those who have produced the rebellion exclusively share its certain adverse fate. Let them not, by specious promises of assistance and future prosperity, swerve us from our allegiance. They are even now promising themselves comparative exemption from the perils of the struggle. A recent Secretary, after having used his high position to produce the result, and by his grossly ignorant or faithless measures bankrupt the Treasury, is now addressing the people of his immediate section to persuade them that the coming war and its horrors will be kept far from them, and confined to the Border States. Let us, as far as ours is concerned, be wise enough to frustrate this cowardly policy. If to gain their traitorous views war is to be waged, let them bear its entire brunt. Let us not be their deluded victims.

What is there in the modern history of South Carolina which should recommend her teachings to Maryland? What is there in the intellects of the Rhetts, the Yanceys, the Cobbs, and *id genus omne*, to make them our leaders? They did all they could to achieve the election of Mr. Lincoln, and hailed its accomplishment with undissembled delight. They thought they saw in it the realization of their long-cherished hopes—the precipitation of the Cotton States into a revolution; and then fancied exemption from the worst of the perils—and they now seek to effect it—in the intervention of the other Slave States between them and the danger. Short-sighted men, they never anticipated the calamities already upon them, and the greater certain to follow. Besides relying on the fact just stated, they also counted securely on a large and influential support in the Free States. Little did they know the true patriotic heart of the land. The first gun fired on the nation's flag raised that feeling in the Northern heart. That gun, fired without cause, and upon a noble garrison about to be starved into a surrender, by being, through timidity or a worse cause, left in that condition, caused every man able to bear arms to rush to the support of the Government. Where, in the past, the South could count its friends by thousands and hundreds of thousands, not one is now to be found. The cry is the Government must be sustained—the flag must be vindicated. Heaven forbid that the duty of that vindication should be forgotten by Maryland! A temporary cause may have made it prudent in a part of the State (I have not the heart to name the locality) to suppress it. It may have happened that the Stripes, so often borne by her sons to victory or a proud death, were justly esteemed the national emblem to outrage, which the constituted authorities (though before justly boastful of their power to preserve the peace, as they had before faithfully done) were unable to prevent or quell, and were immediately made to share the fate of the re-

bellious standard. But it is not less true that there is in every true Maryland bosom a devoted attachment to the national emblem, which will cause every man of us, whenever and wherever hearing the inspiring sounds, to unite in the chorus of our national anthem, " Oh long may it wave, o'er the land of the free and the home of the brave."

Though not especially impulsive, I cannot imagine how an American eye can look upon that standard without emotion. The twenty stars added to the first constellation tell its proud history, its mighty influence, and its unequalled career. Are these now to be forgotten and lost? Tell me not that this is sentiment. Sentiment, to be sure it is, but it is one that purifies and animates and strengthens the national heart. God may be worshipped (I make the comparison with all proper reverence) in the open field, in the stable—but is there no virtue in the cathedral? Does not the soul turn its thoughts heavenwards the moment its sacred threshold is crossed? This too is sentiment, but it is one that honors our nature, and proves our loyalty to the Almighty.

So it is with our national emblem. The man who is dead to its influence is in mind a fool or in heart a traitor. It is this emblem I am the honored organ now to present to you. I need not commend it to your constant, vigilant care; that, I am sure, it will ever be your pride to give it. When, if ever your hearts shall despond—when, if ever you shall desire your patriotism to be specially animated, throw it to the winds, gaze on its beautiful folds, remember the years and the fields over which, from '76 to the present time, it has been triumphantly borne; remember how it has consoled the dying and animated the survivor; remember that it served to kindle even to a brighter flame the patriotic ardor of Washington—went with him through all the struggles of the Revolution, consoled him in defeat, gave to victory an additional charm, and that his dying moments were consoled and cheered by the hope that it would forever float over a perpetual Union, and you at once feel its almost holy influence and swear to stand by and maintain it till life itself shall be no more.

Here it is, citizen soldiers. It is now yours, and with the assurance of its fair donors that they commit it to brave and loyal hands, and with their prayers for your individual happiness —for the restoration of our Government to its recent peaceful and glorious unity, and its continuance as such forever.

—*National Intelligencer*, May 11.

Doc. 144.
THE TENNESSEE LEAGUE.
MESSAGE OF GOVERNOR HARRIS.

EXECUTIVE DEPARTMENT, }
NASHVILLE, May 7, 1861. }

Gentlemen of the Senate and House of Representatives: By virtue of the authority of your joint resolution, adopted on the 1st day of May, instant, I appointed Gustavus A. Henry, of the county of Montgomery, Archibald O. W. Totten, of the county of Madison, and Washington Barrow, of the county of Davidson, "Commissioners, on the part of Tennessee, to enter into a military league with the authorities of the Confederate States, and with the authorities of such other slaveholding States as may wish to enter into it; having in view the protection and defence of the entire South against the war that is now being carried on against it."

The said commissioners met the Hon. Henry W. Hilliard, the accredited representative of the Confederate States, at Nashville on this day, and have agreed upon and executed a military league between the State of Tennessee and the Confederate States of America, subject, however, to the ratification of the two governments, one of the duplicate originals of which I herewith transmit for your ratification or rejection. For many cogent and obvious reasons, unnecessary to be rehearsed to you, I respectfully recommend the ratification of this league at the earliest practicable moment.

Very respectfully,

ISHAM G. HARRIS.

CONVENTION BETWEEN THE STATE OF TENNESSEE AND THE CONFEDERATE STATES OF AMERICA.

The State of Tennessee, looking to a speedy admission into the Confederacy established by the Confederate States of America, in accordance with the constitution for the provisional government of said States, enters into the following temporary convention, agreement, and military league with the Confederate States, for the purpose of meeting pressing exigencies affecting the common rights, interests, and safety of said States and said Confederacy.

First: Until the said State shall become a member of said Confederacy, according to the constitutions of both powers, *the whole military force and military operations, offensive and defensive, of said State, in the impending conflict with the United States, shall be under the chief control and direction of the President of the Confederate States* upon the same basis, principles, and footing as if said State were now and during the intervals a member of the said Confederacy. Said force, together with those of the Confederate States, is to be employed for the common defence.

Second: The State of Tennessee will, upon becoming a member of said Confederacy, under the permanent constitution of said Confederate States, if the same shall occur, *turn over to said Confederate States all the public property, naval stores, and munitions of war* of which she may then be in possession, acquired from the United States, on the same terms and in the same manner as the other States of said Confederacy have done in like cases.

Third: Whatever expenditures of money, if any, the said State of Tennessee shall make before she becomes a member of said Confed-

eracy, shall be met and provided for by the Confederate States.

This convention, entered into and agreed on in the city of Nashville, Tennessee, on the seventh day of May, A. D. 1861, by Henry W. Hilliard, the duly authorized Commissioner to act in the matter for the Confederate States, and Gustavus A. Henry, Archibald W. O. Totten, and Washington Barrow, commissioners duly authorized to act in like manner for the State of Tennessee. The whole subject to the approval and ratification of the proper authorities of both governments, respectively.

In testimony whereof, the parties aforesaid have herewith set their hands and seals, the day and year aforesaid, in duplicate originals.

HENRY W. HILLIARD, [Seal.]
Commissioner for the Confederate States of America.

GUSTAVUS A. HENRY, [Seal.]
A. O. W. TOTTEN, [Seal.]
WASHINGTON BARROW, [Seal.]
Commissioners on the part of Tennessee.

JOINT RESOLUTION RATIFYING THE LEAGUE.

Whereas, A military league, offensive and defensive, was formed on this the 7th of May, 1861, by and between A. O. W. Totten, Gustavus A. Henry, and Washington Barrow, Commissioners on the part of the State of Tennessee, and H. W. Hilliard, Commissioner on the part of the Confederate States of America, subject to the confirmation of the two governments:

Be it therefore resolved by the General Assembly of the State of Tennessee, That said league be in all respects ratified and confirmed, and the said General Assembly hereby pledges the faith and honor of the State of Tennessee to the faithful observance of the terms and conditions of said league.

The following is the vote in the Senate on the adoption of the league:

YEAS.—Messrs. Allen, Horn, Hunter, Johnson, Lane, Minnis, McClellan, McNeilly, Payne, Peters, Stanton, Thompson, Wood, and Speaker Stovall.

NAYS. — Messrs. Boyd, Bradford, Hildreth, Nash, Richardson, and Stokes.

Absent and not voting—Messrs. Bumpass, Mickley, Newman, Stokely, and Trimble.

The following is the vote in the House:

YEAS.—Messrs. Baker of Perry, Baker of Weakley, Bayless, Bicknell, Bledsoe, Cheatham, Cowden, Davidson, Davis, Dudley, Ewing, Farley, Farrelly, Ford, Frazie, Gantt, Guy, Havron, Hart, Ingram, Jones, Kenner, Kennedy, Lea, Lockhart, Martin, Mayfield, McCabe, Morphies, Nall, Hickett, Porter, Richardson, Roberts, Shield, Smith, Sewel, Trevitt, Vaughn, Whitmore, Woods, and Speaker Whitthorne.

NAYS.—Messrs. Armstrong, Brazelton, Butler, Caldwell, Gorman, Greene, Morris, Norman, Russell, Senter, Strewsbury, White of

Davidson, Williams of Knox, Wisener, and Woodard.

Absent and not voting—Messrs. Barksdale, Beaty, Bennett, Britton, Critz, Doak, East, Gillespie, Harris, Hebb, Johnson, Kincaid of Anderson, Kincaid of Claiborne, Trewhitt, White of Dickson, Williams of Franklin, Williams of Hickman, and Williamson.

AN ACT TO SUBMIT TO A VOTE OF THE PEOple a Declaration of Independence, and for other purposes.

SECTION 1. *Be it enacted by the General Assembly of the State of Tennessee*, That, immediately after the passage of this Act, the Governor of this State shall by proclamation, direct the sheriffs of the several counties in this State to open and hold an election at the various voting precincts in their respective counties on the 8th day of June, 1861; that said sheriffs, or in the absence of the sheriffs, the coroner of the county, shall immediately advertise the election contemplated by this Act; that said sheriffs appoint a deputy to hold said election for each voting precinct, and that said deputy appoint three judges and two clerks for each precinct, and if no officer shall from any cause attend any voting precinct, to open and hold said election, then any justice of the peace, or, in the absence of a justice of the peace, any respectable *freeholder* may appoint an officer, judges, and clerks to open and hold said election. Said officers, judges, and clerks, shall be sworn as now required by law, and who, after being so sworn, shall open and hold an election, open and close at the time of day and in the manner now required by law in elections for members to the General Assembly.

SEC. 2. *Be it further enacted*, That at said election the following declaration shall be submitted to a vote of the qualified voters of the State of Tennessee, for their ratification or rejection:

DECLARATION OF INDEPENDENCE AND ORDINANCE DISSOLVING THE FEDERAL RELATIONS BETWEEN THE STATE OF TENNESSEE AND THE UNITED STATES OF AMERICA.

First: We, the people of the State of Tennessee, waiving an expression of opinion as to the abstract doctrine of secession, but asserting the right as a free and independent people to alter, reform, or abolish our form of Government in such manner as we think proper, do ordain and declare that all the laws and ordinances by which the State of Tennessee became a member of the Federal Union of the United States of America, are hereby abrogated and annulled, and that all obligations on our part be withdrawn therefrom; and we do hereby resume all the rights, functions, and powers which by any of said laws and ordinances were conveyed to the Government of the United States, and absolve ourselves from all the obligations, restraints, and duties incurred thereto; and do hereby henceforth become a free, sovereign, and independent State.

Second: We furthermore declare and ordain, that Article 10, sections 1 and 2 of the Constitution of the State of Tennessee, which requires members of the General Assembly, and all officers, civil and military, to take an oath to support the Constitution of the United States, be and the same are hereby abrogated and annulled, and all parts of the Constitution of the State of Tennessee, making citizenship of the United States a qualification for office, and recognizing the Constitution of the United States as the supreme law of this State, are in like manner abrogated and annulled.

Third: We furthermore ordain and declare, that all rights acquired and vested under the Constitution of the United States, or under any act of Congress passed in pursuance thereof, or under any laws of this State, and not incompatible with this ordinance, shall remain in force and have the same effect as if this ordinance had not been passed.

SEC. 3. *Be it further enacted*, That said election shall be by ballot, that those voting for the Declaration and Ordinance shall have written or printed on their ballots "Separation," and those voting against it, shall have written or printed on their ballots "No Separation." That the clerks holding said election, shall keep regular scrolls of the voters as now required by law in the election of members to the General Assembly; that the clerks and judges shall certify the same with the number of votes for "Separation," and the number of votes "No Separation." The officer holding the election, shall return the same to the sheriff of the county, at the county seat, on the Monday next after the election. The sheriff shall immediately make out, certify, and send to the Governor the number of votes polled, and the number of votes for "Separation," and the number "No Separation," and file one of the original scrolls with the Clerk of the County Court; that upon comparing the vote by the Governor in the office of the Secretary of State, which shall be at least by the 24th day of June, 1861, and may be sooner if the returns are all received by the Governor, if a majority of the votes polled shall be for "Separation," the Governor shall, by his proclamation, make it known, and declare all connection by the State of Tennessee with the Federal Union dissolved, and that Tennessee is a free, independent government, free from all obligations to, or connection with the Federal Government. And that the Governor shall cause "the vote by counties" to be published, the number for "Separation," and the number "No Separation," whether a majority votes for "Separation," or "No Separation."

SEC. 4. *Be it further enacted*, That in the election to be held under the provisions of this act upon the Declaration submitted to the people, all volunteers and other persons connected with the service of this State qualified to vote for members of the Legislature in the counties where they reside, shall be entitled to vote in any county in the State where they may be in active service, or under orders, or on parole at the time of said election; and all other voters shall vote in the county where they reside, as now required by law in voting for members to the General Assembly.

SEC. 5. *Be it further enacted*, That at the same time, and under the rules and regulations prescribed for the election hereinbefore ordered, the following ordinance shall be submitted to the popular vote. To wit:

An Ordinance for the adoption of the Constitution of the Provisional Government of the Confederate States of America:

We, the people of Tennessee, solemnly impressed by the perils which surround us, do hereby adopt and ratify the Constitution of the Provisional Government of the Confederate States of America, ordained and established at Montgomery, Alabama, on the 8th day of February, 1861, to be in force during the existence thereof, or until such time as we may supersede it, by the adoption of a permanent Constitution.

SEC. 6. *Be it further enacted*, That those in favor of the adoption of said Provisional Constitution, and thereby securing to Tennessee equal representation in the deliberations and councils of the Confederate States, shall have written or printed on their ballots the word "Representation;" opposed, the words "No Representation."

SEC. 7. *Be it further enacted*, That, in the event the people shall adopt the Constitution of the Provisional Government of the Confederate States at the election herein ordered, it shall be the duty of the Governor forthwith to issue writs of election for delegates to represent the State of Tennessee in the said Provisional Government. That the State shall be represented by as many delegates as it was entitled to members of Congress to the recent Congress of the United States of America, who shall be elected from the several Congressional Districts as now established by law, in the mode and manner now prescribed for the election of Members of Congress of the United States.

SEC. 8. *Be it further enacted*, That this act shall take effect from and after its passage.

W. C. WHITTHORNE,
Speaker of the House of Representatives.

B. L. STOVALL,
Speaker of the Senate.

Passed *May* 6, 1861.

—*Nashville Banner*, May 8.

THE ORDINANCE PASSED.

The deed is done! And a black deed it is—the Legislature of Tennessee, in secret session, passed an ordinance of secession—voting the State out of the Federal Union, and changing the federal relations of a State, thereby affecting, to the great injury of the people, their most important earthly interests. The men who did this deed in secret conclave, were elected two years ago, and they were elected and sworn to support the Constitution of the United States, and the obligations of that oath must rest upon them until their successors are elected. They have dared to pass an ordinance that is really unconstitutional, unjustifiable, and is, upon the whole, a vile act of usurpation. That they say that the extraordinary emergency of the times demanded this outrage, will not do with those of us who know the State of Tennessee has not been oppressed, and is not invaded by a hostile foe, and is not likely to be unless we invite or provoke an attack. It has been the policy of all usurpers, in all ages, to excuse themselves for the exercise of arbitrary power, intended at once to oppress the people and to deprive them of their liberties.

The apology for doing this deed in secret session is, that it would not do to act with open doors, and thereby let the United States Government know what was transpiring. This is only a pretext for this act—it was to prevent *the People of Tennessee* from knowing what vile work they were engaged in, and applying the remedy. They did not want the real people to read the speeches of Union men delivered in that body, who gave reasons, numerous and strong, why Tennessee should not go into Jeff. Davis's repudiating Confederacy. But unprincipled politicians have resolved upon governing the people, and to induce them to submit, they must keep them in the dark as to their vile schemes.

In June, we are called upon to vote for or against this Ordinance of Secession, and all trains of evil, such as enormous taxes, and the raising of fifty thousand troops! Will the people ratify it, or will they reject it? Let every man, old and young, halt and blind, contrive to be at the polls on that day. If we lose then, our liberties are gone, and we are swallowed up by a military despotism more odious than any now existing in any monarchy of Europe!

—*Knoxville Whig*, May 11.

TENNESSEE SECEDED.

Tennessee is disenthralled at last. Freedom has again crowned her with a fresh and fadeless wreath. She has broken through the meshes of tyranny. She has shaken off the shackles which tyrants and usurpers were fastening upon her that they might reduce her to helpless and hopeless bondage. She has left a Union in which she was no longer an equal. She has dissolved her connection with States bent on her subjugation and destruction. She has thrown off the yoke of a Government prostituted to the vile purposes of injustice and oppression. Nobly has she asserted her independence and vindicated her sovereignty.

She has taken her place in the Southern constellation. She has added another star to the flag of the Confederate States, which floats over the dome of her capitol, the proud and unsullied emblem of Southern nationality. She has united her destiny with a sisterhood of

States, identified with her in sympathies, in interests, and institutions—with the new born republic of the South, which, like another Mars, has sprung into existence full armed—a young giant, whose tread is already on the pathway of victory and national renown; whose prowess, power, and resources challenge the recognition of civilized nations, and to whom a future of unexampled prosperity and glory has already opened.

We congratulate Tennessee and the Confederate States upon the mutual good fortune of this auspicious alliance. She brings into the new republic the rich dowry of her unsullied patriotism, her ancestral valor, and her mighty and varied resources, while from it she receives the protection and respectability of a powerful and rising nationality.

We hail this decisive step of Tennessee, as the glorious realization of patriotic hopes, long and fondly cherished by us, amid the gloom of discouragement and despondency, as the fruition of years of struggle, and toil, and anxious, and often despairing effort, in the cause of Southern rights.

There is a moral sublimity in the triumph of a great cause that stirs the deepest emotions of the soul. Not in the narrow spirit of political partisanship have we battled in this cause, but as a son of the South, prompted alone by an ardent desire for her safety, her freedom, and her honor. The exultant pleasure of this triumph is enhanced by the reflection that it is shared by all classes of our fellow-citizens alike, without reference to former party distinctions; all past political prejudices being obliterated by the noble and irrepressible patriotism which now animates and unites all Tennesseeans in the common cause of their State and section.

This important change in the political relations of Tennessee creates new and weighty duties and responsibilities, while it awakens new hopes and aspirations. At this moment they urge her to instant and strenuous action. The advent of the new republic has invoked the red thunderbolts of war upon its devoted head. It is no sooner born than it is called upon to defend its right to exist. It seems destined to pass through the fiery ordeal of the fiercest and bloodiest strife which, perhaps, history has yet recorded.

The faithless, meddling, and overbearing North, foiled in her long-cherished scheme of sectional domination, usurpation, and tyranny, by the unexpected revolt of the South, gnashes her teeth, and threatens the extermination of her victim. Her people are frenzied with rage; the hell-born passions of avarice, hate, and revenge, sway her infuriated mobs, thirsting for the blood of a people from whom they have received only benefits and favors. A spirit of wild and bloody atrocity, akin to that which raged in the French Revolution, has seized the entire Northern people, extinguishing at once all the sentiments of Christianity, and the feelings of humanity. Schemes of fiendish cruelty,

at which hell itself might turn pale and stand aghast, and demons blush, are now discussed and approved by the sleek and sanctimonious clergy of the North. Even woman, repressing the instinctive humanity and tenderness of her nature, clamors for the massacre of Southern women and children. An imbecile, but perfidious and atrocious Government, leads this wild and bloody raid upon the south. Its armies are now mustering and advancing upon us, with the insolent boast upon their lips that they will either subjugate or exterminate us.

Such are the black and threatening clouds of danger, charged with the lightnings of destruction, which now darken the horizon of the Southern Republic. Tennessee, in this tremendous crisis, will do her entire duty. Great sacrifices are demanded of her, and they will be cheerfully made. Her blood and treasure are offered without stint at the shrine of Southern freedom. She counts not the cost at which independence must be bought. The gallant volunteer State of the South, her brave sons now rushing to the standard of the Southern Confederacy, will sustain by their unflinching valor and deathless devotion, her ancient renown achieved on so many battle fields. In fact our entire people—men, women, and children—have engaged in this fight, and are animated by the single, heroic, and indomitable resolve to perish rather than submit to the despicable invader now threatening us with subjugation. They will ratify the ordinance of secession, amid the smoke and carnage of battle; they will write out their endorsement of it with the blood of their foe—they will enforce it at the point of the bayonet and the sword.

Welcome, thrice welcome, glorious Tennessee, to the thriving family of Southern Confederate States!　　—*Memphis Avalanche*, May 6.

Doc. 145.

ADDRESS OF EDWARD EVERETT,

AT ROXBURY, MASS., MAY 8, 1861.

Mr. Chairman, Ladies, and Gentlemen:—The object which brings us together, even if it had not been so satisfactorily stated and so persuasively enforced by the gentlemen who have preceded me, sufficiently explains itself. At the call of the President, seconded with the most praiseworthy and almost unexampled energy by the Governor of Massachusetts, a numerous force of volunteers has patriotically hastened to the defence of the Capital of the United States, threatened with invasion. The war, for a long time, though in profound peace secretly prepared for, has been openly commenced by the South, by the seizure of the undefended forts, arsenals, dockyards, mints, and custom houses of the United States, and the plunder of the public property contained in them, in flagrant violation of the law of the land, if the South is still in the Union, and equally flagrant violation of every principle of international law, if she is out of the Union.

But even these acts of treason and rebellion, for such they are, are thrown in the shade by that last unutterable outrage upon the flag of the Union, at Fort Sumter, (a fort which no more belongs to South Carolina than it does to New York or Massachusetts,) which has rallied twenty millions of freemen as one man to its defence.

Following up the unprovoked and unrighteous war thus inaugurated, a formidable military force, portions of which have been long organized and trained, is now supposed to be advancing on Washington, under a most able and energetic leader, who has the oath of God upon his conscience to support the Constitution, as a Senator of the United States, an office which he has not resigned. Of the nature of this war, in a constitutional point of view, I shall presently say a word. I will now only remark, that, if accounts from the South can be trusted, larger military forces than were ever before arrayed on the soil of America, are now on their march northward or concentrating in Virginia, to assault, and if possible, capture, and failing that, to lay in ashes, the city baptized with the sacred name of the Father of his country, the Capital of the Union, the seat of its government, the depository of its archives, and, as such, the heart, if I may so say, of the body politic.

While this formidable movement is in progress in front, the Government has been assailed in the rear, between the Capital of the Union and the loyal States of the North (from which alone, the Constitution, I grieve to say, in this hour of its extreme peril, is receiving support against open hostility, and treacherous neutrality, not less dangerous than open hostility,) by a ferocious and bloodthirsty mob, audaciously warring against the Government and its defenders with brickbats, paving-stones, and all the other cowardly weapons of the assassin, by burning bridges and tearing up railroads and cutting telegraph wires, as if it was not enough to commit murder and treason, unless war is waged at the same time against the noblest works of civilization and the most beneficent structures of peace. In this unexampled warfare, Providence, as in 1775, has accorded to Massachusetts the tearful glory of furnishing the first martyrs in the cause of the country, and, what would before have been thought impossible, has crowned even the 19th of April with new wreaths of immortal fame.

In this state of things the President of the United States has called upon the people to rally to the rescue of the national Capital, and to the defence of the Government of the country. Wide as the summons has gone forth, it has been obeyed, with an alacrity and unanimity that knows no parallel in our history; and the volunteers of Massachusetts have been the first in the field. Unwarlike in their habits and tastes, a full proportion of them in our recent keen but already forgotten party divisions, entertaining, as I have ever done, the kindliest

feelings toward the South, they have hurried from the lawyer's office, from the counting-room, from the artist's studio, in instances not a few from the pulpit; they have left the fisher's line upon the reel, the plough in the furrow, the plane upon the work-bench, the hammer on the anvil, the form upon the printing press,—there is not a mechanical art nor a useful handicraft that has not its experts in these patriotic ranks,—some at a moment's notice, all with unhesitating promptitude, and *they have left their families behind them.* These last words, fellow-citizens, tell the whole story; these words are the warrant under which this meeting is held. They have left behind them their wives, their children, their aged parents, their dependent relatives of every degree; in many cases, no doubt, those whose only reliable resource for their daily bread was in the stout arms, which have been called away to the defence of the menaced Union.

Well, my friends, these families must not suffer in the absence of their heads and supporters. The Government will no doubt compensate its defenders as liberally as the nature of the case admits. But every one knows that the soldier's pay is no adequate substitute for the earnings of a prosperous livelihood, even in the humblest branches of industry. The deficiency must be made up by the towns of which these brave volunteers are citizens, acting in their corporate capacity, and by efforts like that which you initiate this evening. In a word, it is absolutely necessary, that in one way or another, by public and private liberality, the means of liberal assistance for the families that need it, should be provided by those that remain at home. This is a duty in which all of every age and condition, and of either sex, must coöperate; and I rejoice to see, that the gentler sex is, as usual, setting us the example of industry and zeal, in this patriotic work. The rich must contribute of their abundance, and those of moderate means from their competence, till our brethren, who take their lives in their hands, in this righteous cause, are strengthened and cheered by the assurance, that those dearer to them than their lives will be cared for at home.

If any arguments were necessary to urge us to the performance of this duty, they would be found, and that of the most powerful and persuasive character, in the nature and character of the war which the South is waging upon us. And here a state of things presents itself which posterity will be slow to credit. On the last anniversary of our national independence, at the invitation of my fellow-citizens of Boston, I had occasion to undertake a defence of the United States Government, in its practical operation, against an attack made upon it, with considerable ability, in the British House of Lords. In this effort I claimed—honestly and conscientiously claimed, and, as I have reason to think, with the concurrence of my fellow-citizens, of all parties, throughout the country, that, under our constitution and laws, we had enjoyed a prosperity and made a progress, not merely in the utilitarian, but in the intellectual and refined arts of life, without an example in the world.

I said nothing of the unhappy sectional controversy that was raging the country, not because I was insensible to its dangerous character, but because nothing was said about it in the speech to which I undertook to reply. The general truth of my description of the prosperity of the country, and the genial and fostering influence of our Constitution and Laws, was as generally admitted at the South as at the North. No longer ago than the 14th of last November, Mr. Stephens, of Georgia, now Vice-President of the Southern Confederacy, and a gentleman of first rate intelligence, in a public speech at Milledgeville, declared it as his " settled conviction," that the present Government of the United States, though not without its defects, " comes nearer the objects of all good government than any other on the face of the earth." He pronounced it " a model republic, the best that the history of the world gives us any account of; " and he asked in triumph, " Where will you go, following the sun in his circuit round the globe, to find a government that better protects the liberties of the people, and secures to them the blessings which we enjoy ? "*

This, you will observe again, was the language of a very leading Southern statesman, the second officer of the new Confederacy, no longer ago than last November; and, in truth, the South had and has greater cause than any other part of the Union, to be satisfied with the Government under which she lives and on which she is making war. Respected abroad as an integral portion of one of the greatest powers of the earth, mainly in virtue of the navy of the Union, of which the strength resides at the North, the South, almost exclusively agricultural in her pursuits, derives from her climate a profitable monopoly of four great staple products—one of them the most important single article in the commerce of the world; while, in consequence, chiefly of the political sympathy with each other which pervades the slaveholding States, she has ever enjoyed a monopoly scarcely less complete of the Government of the country.

At this moment, and though numbering but a third part of the free population of the Union, if she had not most unjustifiably withdrawn her members of Congress, she would have had in her interest a majority in the Senate, in the House of Representatives, and in the Judiciary. For fifty-six out of the seventy-two years, the Presidents of the United States have been either Southern men or Northern men in whom the South has confided. For the first time, last November, a President was chosen who received no electoral votes from the South, but

that President has given the most distinct assurances that he has contemplated no encroachments on the constitutional rights of the South, as, indeed, lacking a majority of both houses, it is impossible that he should make any such encroachments, had he ever so ardently desired it. Such is the Government in its relations with the South; such the circumstances under which she thinks herself justified in revolting against it.

I say "revolting against it," although Mr. Jefferson Davis, in his inaugural address, declares it an abuse of language to call it a "revolution." I cannot go into that argument at this late hour, nor would it be appropriate to the occasion to do so; but I believe it to be as demonstrable as any proposition of Euclid, that this doctrine of "secession," that is, the constitutional right of a State to sever at will her connection with the Union, is, if possible, still more unfounded, still more fallacious, than that of its ill-omened and now universally discredited predecessor, "Nullification," which was crushed, never to rise again, thirty years ago, by the iron mace of Webster, in the Senate of the United States.

I will only say at present, that this monstrous pretended right of "secession," though called a "reserved right," is notoriously nowhere *expressly* reserved in the Constitution, although every one feels that nothing but an express reservation, in the plainest terms, would be a sufficient ground for claiming such a stupendous power. What is maintained by the politicians of the secession school is, that the right may be inferred from one of the amendments to the Constitution, by which it is provided that "the powers not delegated to the United States by the Constitution, or prohibited to the States, are reserved to the States respectively, or the people." It is to maintain a subtile and sophistical, and utterly unwarrantable inference from this amendment, that the South is now striving to break up the Government, and if resisted in that unhallowed attempt, to drench the country in blood.

But I am willing to stake the great issue on this amendment. The Constitution does expressly delegate to the United States all the powers of a sovereign State, with respect to international and interstate affairs; the whole war power; the whole admiralty power; the whole commercial power; the whole financial power; the power to regulate and dispose of the public territory; the power over the Indians, over the post-office and post-roads; over the army, the navy, the dockyards, the arsenals. All these powers and many others are expressly delegated to the United States, and as expressly prohibited to the individual States. The Constitution of the United States (to which the people of South Carolina assented on the 2d of May, 1788, as much as they ever assented to their State constitution) distinctly provides that no State shall keep troops or ships of war, or issue letters of marque and reprisal, or enter

---

* See Speech of A. H. Stephens, Nov. 14, 1861, *seq.*

into any treaty, alliance, or *confederation ;* and yet in the face of this express delegation of powers to the United States, and their express prohibition to the States, the seceding States have undertaken to exercise them all; have entered into a " confederation," raised an army, issued letters of marque and reprisal, and plunged into a war against the government, which every magistrate and officer among them was under oath to support, and all in virtue of having first uttered the magic words, " we secede." The history of the world does not furnish another such monstrous usurpation!

Such is the nature and foundation of the war in which we are engaged. As you perceive, it is for the very existence of the Government, it is a contest in which no good citizen can remain neutral. I am often asked how long I think it will last; but that is a question the South alone can answer. She makes the war; she has seized by surprise such of the strongholds of the country as she was able; she has possessed herself of the Navy-Yard at Norfolk, which guards the entrance to Chesapeake Bay; of Harper's Ferry, which commands one of the great highways from the Ohio River to the Atlantic Ocean; and, above all, of the mouth of the Mississippi, the outlet of the most extensive system of internal communication on the face of the globe. There will, in my judgment, never be peace, till the flag of the Union again floats from every stronghold from which it has been stricken down.

Do you think, fellow-citizens, that Ohio, Indiana, and Illinois will allow their most direct communication with the seaboard to be obstructed, at the pleasure of an alien State, at Harper's Ferry? Do you imagine that Eastern Pennsylvania and Southern New York, whose tributary waters flow through the Susquehanna into Chesapeake Bay, to say nothing of the Delaware and Chesapeake Canal, will tolerate a foreign master in Hampton Roads? Above all, do you believe that the Giant of the West will accept his pathway to the Gulf of Mexico as a privilege granted by this mushroom Confederacy? Yes, they will submit to this degrading yoke, they will acknowledge this galling usurpation; but it will be when the Alleghanies shall bow their imperial heads to the level of the sea, and the current of the Mississippi and the Missouri shall flow backward to the Rocky Mountains.

My friends, I deprecate war,—no man more so; and, of all wars, I most deprecate a civil war. And this, if prosecuted by the South in the spirit in which she has commenced it, will be what the stern poet of the civil wars of Rome called a *bellum plusquam civille,*—a more than civil war. I deprecate, more than I can express, a war with the South. You know my political course. Logan, the Indian chief, mournfully exclaimed, " Such was my love for the whites, that my countrymen pointed at me as I passed, and said, 'Logan is the friend of the white men!'" I have been pointed at for

years as the friend of the South. For maintaining what I deemed her constitutional rights, I have suffered no small portion of obloquy, and sacrificed the favor of a large portion of the community in which I was born, and which, from my youth up, I have endeavored to serve laboriously, dutifully, and affectionately. I was willing, while this ill-starred movement was confined to the States of the extreme South, and they abstained from further aggression, that they should go in peace.

This course, I thought, would retain the border States, and bring back the seceders in a year or two, wearied and disgusted with their burdensome and perilous experiment. Such I understand to have been, in substance, the programme of the Administration. But the South has willed it otherwise. She has struck a parricidal blow at the heart of the Union; and to sustain her in this unnatural and unrighteous war is what my conscience forbids. Neither will I remain silent, and see this majestic framework of government, the noblest political fabric ever reared by human wisdom, prostrated in the dust to gratify the disappointed ambition of a few aspiring men, (for that Mr. Vice-President Stephens bravely told his fellow-citizens last November was the cause of " a great part of our troubles,") and this under cover of a sophistical interpretation of the Constitution, at war alike with common sense, with contemporary history, and the traditions of the Government; unsupported by a single authority among the framers of the Constitution, and emphatically denounced by Mr. Madison their leader and chief.

What then remains, fellow-citizens, but that we should without unchristian bitterness toward our misguided countrymen, meet calmly and resolutely the demands of the crisis; that we should perform the duty of good citizens with resolution and steadiness; that we should cordially support the Government of the country in the difficult position in which it is placed; that we should cheer and encourage the brave men who have obeyed its call by a generous care of their families; and to sum it all in one word, come weal or woe, that we should stand by the flag of the Union!

—*Boston Transcript,* May 9.

Doc. 146.

GENERAL BUTLER'S ORDERS.

Head-quarters, Relay House, May 8, 1861.

The General in command congratulates the troops upon the promptness with which they have moved and occupied their present position, which he believes to be impregnable against any force which may be brought against it. The position of Major Cooke's battery commanding the viaduct, with his section in position commanding the railroad to Harper's Ferry, supported by the strong detachment of Colonel Jones' regiment at the Relay House, renders all movements by the railroad entirely within our command. The same guns command with grape and canister the ford below the iron works, while the extended pickets of Colonel Lyons fully protect the rear.

The General has been thus particular in describing his position, so that each portion of the force might know how to conduct in case of an attack which it only requires vigilance to foil. The General takes this opportunity publicly as he has done privately to thank Lieutenants Fox and Shilley, of the Eighth regiment, for their coolness, promptitude, and zeal in arresting one Spencer, who was uttering in the presence of the troops at the Relay House the atrocious sentiment that—" We [meaning himself and brother rebels] acted rightly toward the Massachusetts troops three weeks ago Friday." And saying " that the murderous mob who killed our friends there were right in their action; and that the same men were preparing to give us a warm reception on our return." For these treasonable speeches substantially admitted by him in his written examination, Spencer has been arrested and sent to Annapolis, where he will be properly dealt with.

Two incidents of the gravest character marked the progress of yesterday. Charles Leonard, private of Company G, Eighth Regiment, of New York, was accidentally killed instantaneously by the discharge of a musket, from which he was drawing the charge. He was buried with all the honors, amidst the gloom and sorrow of every United States soldier at this post, and the tender sympathies of many of the loyal inhabitants in our neighborhood.

It is fitting that we pause here, even in the discharge of our present solemn duties, to drop a tear upon the grave of a fellow-soldier, a friend and brother. A pure patriot, he gave up home for his country; a heroic, conscientious soldier, he died in the act of discharging his duty; and, although he was not stricken by the hand of death amid the clangor of arms, and in the heat of contest, yet his death was no less glorious because he met it in the quiet performance of his military duty. As a citizen he took up arms at his country's call; as a private soldier he sought only to fight in her ranks, and he met his death in support of that flag which we all revere and love. The first offering of New York of the life of one of her sons upon the country's altar, his blood mingling on the soil of Maryland with that of the Massachusetts men murdered at Baltimore, will form a new bond of union between us and all loyal States; so that, without need of further incentive to our duty, we are spurred on by the example of the life and death of Leonard.

The other matter to which the General desires to call the attention of the troops is this: Wishing to establish the most friendly relations between you and this neighborhood, the General invited all venders of supplies to visit our camp and replenish our somewhat scanty commissariat. But to his disgust and horror he finds well-authenticated evidence that a private

in the Sixth regiment has been poisoned by means of strychnine administered in the food brought into the camp by one of these peddlers. I am happy to be informed that the man is now out of danger. This act, of course, will render it necessary for me to cut off all purchases from unauthorized persons.

Are our few insane enemies among the loyal men of Maryland, prepared to wage war upon us in this manner? Do they know the terrible lesson of warfare they are teaching us? Can it be that they realize the fact that we can put an agent with a word into every household armed with this terrible weapon? In view of the terrible consequences of this mode of warfare, if adopted by us from their teaching, with every sentiment of devotional prayer, may we not exclaim, " Father, forgive them, they know not what they do."

Certain it is that any other such attempt, reasonably authenticated as to the person committing it, will be followed by the swiftest, surest, and most condign punishment.

Colonels Lyons, Jones, and Major Cooke are charged with the execution of this order so far as relates to their several commands, and they will promulgate the same by causing it to be read distinctly at the head of each company at morning roll call.

By order of B. F. Butler, Brig.-Gen. Commanding.

EDWARD G. PARKER, Lieut. Col., Aide-de-Camp.

—N. Y. Herald, May 10.

Doc. 146½.

CAUSES OF THE CIVIL WAR.

A LETTER TO THE LONDON TIMES BY JOHN LOTHROP MOTLEY.

THE *de facto* question in America has been referred at last to the dread arbitrament of civil war. Time and events must determine whether the " great Republic " is to disappear from the roll of nations, or whether it is destined to survive the storm which has gathered over its head. There is, perhaps, a readiness in England to prejudge the case; a disposition not to exult in our downfall, but to accept the fact; for nations, as well as individuals, may often be addressed in the pathetic language of the poet,—

" Donec eris felix, multos numerabis amicos ; Tempora cum fuerint nubila, nullus erit."

Yet the trial by the ordeal of battle has hardly commenced, and it would be presumptuous to affect to penetrate the veil of even the immediate future. But the question *de jure* is a different one. The right and the wrong belong to the past, are hidden by no veil, and may easily be read by all who are not wilfully blind. Yet it is often asked why have the Americans taken up arms? Why has the United States Government plunged into what is sometimes called " this wicked war "? Especially it is thought amazing in England that the President should have recently called for a great army of volunteers and regulars, and that the inhabitants of the Free States should have sprung forward as one man at his call, like men suddenly relieved from a spell. It would have been amazing had the call been longer delayed. The national flag, insulted and defied for many months, had at last been lowered, after the most astonishing kind of siege recorded in history, to an armed and organized rebellion; and a prominent personage in the Government of the Southern Confederacy is reported to have proclaimed amid the exultations of victory that before the 1st of May the same cherished emblem of our nationality should be struck from the capitol at Washington. An advance of the " Confederate troops" upon that city; the flight or captivity of the President and his Cabinet; the seizure of the national archives, the national title deeds, and the whole national machinery of foreign intercourse and internal administration, by the Confederates; and the proclamation from the American palladium itself of the Montgomery Constitution in place of the one devised by Washington, Madison, Hamilton, and Jay—a constitution in which slavery should be the universal law of the land, the corner-stone of the political edifice—were events which seemed for a few days of intense anxiety almost probable.

Had this really been the result, without a blow struck in defence of the national Government and the old Constitution, it is certain that the contumely poured forth upon the Free States by their domestic enemies, and by the world at large, would have been as richly deserved as it would have been amply bestowed. At present such a catastrophe seems to have been averted. But the levy in mass of such a vast number of armed men in the Free States, in swift response to the call of the President, shows how deep and pervading is the attachment to the Constitution and to the flag of Union in the hearts of the 19,000,000 who inhabit those States. It is confidently believed, too, that the sentiment is not wholly extinguished in the 9,000,000 white men who dwell in the Slave States, and that, on the contrary, there exists a large party throughout that country who believe that the Union furnishes a better protection for life, property, law, civilization, and liberty, than even the indefinite extension of African slavery can do.

At any rate, the loyalty of the Free States has proved more intense and passionate than it had ever been supposed to be before. It is recognized throughout their whole people that the Constitution of 1787 had made us a nation. The efforts of a certain class of politicians for a long period had been to reduce our Commonwealth to a Confederacy. So long as their efforts had been confined to argument, it was considered sufficient to answer the argument; but, now that secession, instead of remaining a topic of vehement and subtle discussion, has

expanded into armed and fierce rebellion and revolution, civil war is the inevitable result. It is the result foretold by sagacious statesmen almost a generation ago, in the days of the tariff "nullification." "To begin with nullification," said Daniel Webster in 1833, "with the avowed intention, nevertheless, not to proceed to secesssion, dismemberment, and general revolution, is as if one were to take the plunge of Niagara, and cry out that he would stop half way down." And now the plunge of secession has been taken, and we are all struggling in the vortex of general revolution.

The body politic, known for 70 years as the United States of America, is not a Confederacy, not a compact of sovereign States, not a copartnership; it is a Commonwealth, of which the Constitution drawn up at Philadelphia by the Convention of 1787, over which Washington presided, is the organic, fundamental law. We had already had enough of a confederacy. The thirteen rebel provinces, afterwards the thirteen original independent States of America, had been united to each other during the revolutionary war by articles of confederacy. " *The said States* hereby enter into a firm *league* of friendship *with each other*." Such was the language of 1781, and the league or treaty thus drawn up was ratified, not by the *people* of the States, but by the State Governments,—the legislative and executive bodies namely, in their corporate capacity.

The continental Congress, which was the central administrative board during this epoch, was a diet of envoys from sovereign States. It had *no power* to act *on individuals*. It could not *command* the States. It could move only by requisitions and recommendations. Its functions were essentially diplomatic, like those of the States-General of the old Dutch Republic, like those of the modern Germanic Confederation.

We were a league of petty sovereignties. When the war had ceased, when our independence had been acknowledged in 1783, we sank rapidly into a condition of utter impotence, imbecility, anarchy. We had achieved our independence, but we had not constructed a nation. We were not a body politic. No laws could be enforced, no insurrections suppressed, no debts collected. Neither property nor life was secure. Great Britain had made a treaty of peace with us, but she scornfully declined a treaty of commerce and amity; not because we had been rebels, but because we were not a state—because we were a mere dissolving league of jarring provinces, incapable of guaranteeing the stipulations of any commercial treaty. We were unable even to fulfil the conditions of the treaty of peace and enforce the stipulated collection of debts due to British subjects; and Great Britain refused in consequence to give up the military posts which she held within our frontiers. For 12 years after the acknowledgment of our *independence* we were mortified by the spectacle of foreign soldiers occupying a long chain of fortresses south of the great lakes and upon our own soil. We were a confederacy. We were sovereign States. And these were the fruits of such a confederacy and of such sovereignty. It was, until the immediate present, the darkest hour of our history. But there were patriotic and sagacious men in those days, and their efforts at last rescued us from the condition of a confederacy. The "Constitution of the United States" was an organic law, enacted by the sovereign people of that whole territory which is commonly called in geographies and histories the United States of America. It was empowered to act directly, by its own legislative, judicial, and executive machinery, upon every individual in the country. It could seize his property, it could take his life, for causes of which itself was the judge. The States were distinctly prohibited from opposing its decrees or from exercising any of the great functions of sovereignty. The Union alone was supreme, "any thing in the constitution and laws of the States to the contrary notwithstanding." Of what significance, then, was the title of "sovereign" States, arrogated in later days by communities which had voluntarily abdicated the most vital attributes of sovereignty? But, indeed, the words "sovereign" and "sovereignty" are purely inapplicable to the American system. In the Declaration of Independence the provinces declare themselves "free and independent States," but the men of those days knew that the word "sovereign" was a term of feudal origin. When their connection with a time-honored feudal monarchy was abruptly severed, the word "sovereign" had no meaning for us. A sovereign is one who acknowledges no superior, who possesses the highest authority without control, who is supreme in power. How could any one State of the United States claim such characteristics at all, least of all after its inabitants, in their primary assemblies, had voted to submit themselves, without limitation of time, to a constitution which was declared supreme? The only intelligible source of power in a country beginning its history *de novo* after a revolution, in a land never subjected to military or feudal conquest, is the will of the people of the whole land as expressed by a majority. At the present moment, unless the Southern revolution shall prove successful, the United States Government is a fact, an established authority. In the period between 1783 and 1787 we were in chaos. In May of 1787 the convention met in Philadelphia, and, after some months' deliberation, adopted, with unprecedented unanimity, the project of the great law, which, so soon as it should be accepted by the people, was to be known as the Constitution of the United States.

It was not a compact. Who ever heard of a compact to which there were no parties? or who ever heard of a compact made by a single party with himself? Yet the name of no State is mentioned in the whole document; the States

themselves are only mentioned to receive commands or prohibitions, and the "people of the United States" is the single party by whom alone the instrument is executed.

The Constitution was not drawn up by the States, it was not promulgated in the name of the States, it was not ratified by the States. The States never acceded to it, and possess no power to secede from it. It "was ordained and established" over the States by a power superior to the States—by the people of the whole land in their aggregate capacity, acting through conventions of delegates expressly chosen for the purpose within each State, independently of the State Governments, after the project had been framed.

There had always been two parties in the country during the brief but pregnant period between the abjuration of British authority and the adoption of the Constitution of 1787. There was a party advocating State rights and local self-government in its largest sense, and a party favoring a more consolidated and national government. The National or Federal party triumphed in the adoption of the new government. It was strenuously supported and bitterly opposed on exactly the same grounds. Its friends and foes both agreed that it had put an end to the system of confederacy. Whether it were an advantageous or a noxious change, all agreed that the thing had been done.

"In all our deliberations (says the letter accompanying and recommending the Constitution to the people) we kept steadily in view that which appeared to us the greatest interest of every true American, the *consolidation of our Union*, in which is involved our prosperity, safety, perhaps *our national existence*."—*Journal of the Convention*, 1 Story, 368.

And an eloquent opponent denounced the project for this very same reason—

"That this is a consolidated Government (said Henry), is demonstrably clear. The language is 'we, the people,' instead of 'we, the States.' It must be one great, consolidated national Government of the people of all the States."

And the Supreme Court of the United States, after the Government had been established, held this language in an important case, "Gibbons *v.* Ogden:"—

"It has been said that the States *were* sovereign, were completely independent, and were connected with each other by a league. This is true. But when these allied sovereignties converted their league into a Government, when they converted their Congress of Ambassadors into a Legislature, empowered to enact laws, the whole character in which the States appear underwent a change."

There was never a disposition in any quarter, in the early days of our constitutional history, to deny this great fundamental principle of the Republic.

"In the most elaborate expositions of the Constitution by its friends (says Justice Story), its character *as a permanent form* of government, as a fundamental law, as a supreme rule, which no State was at liberty to disregard, to suspend, or to annul, was constantly admitted and insisted upon."—1 Story, 325.

The fears of its opponents, then, were that the new system would lead to a too strong, to an overcentralized Government. The fears of its friends were that the central power of theory would prove inefficient to cope with the local or State forces, in practice. The experience of the last thirty years, and the catastrophe of the present year, have shown which class of fears were the more reasonable.

Had the Union thus established in 1787 been a confederacy, it might have been argued, with more or less plausibility, that the States which peaceably acceded to it might at pleasure peaceably secede from it. It is none the less true that such a proceeding would have stamped the members of the convention—Washington, Madison, Jay, Hamilton, and their colleagues—with utter incompetence; for nothing can be historically more certain than that their object was to extricate us from the anarchy to which that principle had brought us.

" *However gross a heresy it may be* (says the Federalist, recommending the new Constitution) to maintain that a party to a compact has a right to revoke that compact, the doctrine has had respectable advocates. The *possibility* of such a question shows the necessity of laying the foundation of our national Government deeper than in the mere sanction of delegated authority. The fabric of American empire ought to rest on the solid basis of the consent of the people."

Certainly, the most venerated expounders of the Constitution—Jay, Marshall, Hamilton, Kent, Story, Webster—were of opinion that the intention of the convention to establish a permanent, consolidated Government, a single commonwealth, had been completely successful.

" The great and fundamental defect of the Confederation of 1781, (says Chancellor Kent,) which led to its eventual overthrow, was that, in imitation of all former confederacies, it carried the decrees of the Federal Council to the States in their sovereign capacity. The great and incurable defect of all former Federal Governments, such as the Amphictyonic, Achæan, and Lycian Confederacies, and the Germanic, Helvetic, Hanseatic, and Dutch Republics, is that they were *sovereignties over sovereignties.* The first effort to relieve the people of the country from this state of national degradation and ruin came from Virginia. The general convention afterwards met at Philadelphia in May, 1787. The plan was submitted to a convention of delegates chosen by the people at large in each State for assent and ratification. Such a measure was laying the foundations of the fabric of our national polity where alone they ought to be laid,—on the broad consent of the people."—1 Kent, 225.

It is true that the consent of the people was given by the inhabitants voting *in* each State; but in what other conceivable way could the people of the whole country have voted? " They assembled in the several States," says Story ; " but where else could they assemble ? "

Secession is, in brief, the return to chaos from which we emerged three-quarters of a century since. No logical sequence can be more perfect. If one State has a right to secede to-day, asserting what it calls its sovereignty, another may, and probably will, do the same to-morrow, a third on the next day, and so on, until there are none left to secede from. Granted the premises that each State may peaceably secede from the Union, it follows that a county may peaceably secede from a State, and a town from a county, until there is nothing left but a horde of individuals all seceding from each other. The theory that the people of a whole country in their aggregate capacity are supreme, is intelligible ; and it has been a fact, also, in America for 70 years. But it is impossible to show, if the people of a State be sovereign, that the people of a county, or of a village, and the individuals of the village, are not equally sovereign, and justified in " resuming their sovereignty " when their interests or their caprice seems to impel them. The process of disintegration brings back the community to barbarism, precisely as its converse has built up commonwealths— whether empires, kingdoms, or republics—out of original barbarism. Established authority, whatever the theory of its origin, is a fact. It should never be lightly or capriciously overturned. They who venture on the attempt should weigh well the responsibility that is upon them. Above all they must expect to be arraigned for their deeds before the tribunal of the civilized world and of future ages—a court of last appeal, the code of which is based on the Divine principles of right and reason, which are dispassionate and eternal. No man, on either side of the Atlantic with Anglo-Saxon blood in his veins, will dispute the right of a people, or of any portion of a people to rise against oppression, to demand redress of grievances, and in case of denial of justice to take up arms to vindicate the sacred principle of liberty. Few Englishmen or Americans will deny that the source of government is the consent of the governed, or that every nation has the right to govern itself according to its will. When the silent consent is changed to *fierce* remonstrance, the revolution is impending. The right of revolution is indisputable. It is written on the whole record of our race. British and American history is made up of rebellion and revolution. Many of the crowned kings were rebels or usurpers; Hampden, Pym, and Oliver Cromwell ; Washington, Adams, and Jefferson, all were rebels. It is no word of reproach ; but these men all knew the work they had set themselves to do. They never called their rebellion " peaceable secession." They were sustained by the consciousness of right when they overthrew established authority, but they meant to overthrow it. They meant rebellion, civil war, bloodshed, infinite suffering for themselves and their whole generation, for they accounted them welcome substitutes for insulted liberty and violated right. There can be nothing plainer, then, than the American right of revolution. But then it should be called revolution. "Secession, as a revolutionary right," said Daniel Webster in the Senate nearly 30 years ago, in words that now sound prophetic,—

"Is intelligible. As a right to be proclaimed in *the midst of civil commotions, and asserted at the head of armies*, I can understand it. But as a practical right, existing under the Constitution, and in conformity with its provisions, it seems to be nothing but an absurdity, for it supposes resistance to Government under authority of Government itself; it supposes dismemberment without violating the principles of Union; it supposes opposition to law without crime; it supposes the violation of oaths without responsibility; it supposes the total overthrow of Government without revolution."

The men who had conducted the American people through a long and fearful revolution, were the founders of the new commonwealth which permanently superseded the subverted authority of the Crown. They placed the foundations on the unbiassed, untrammelled consent of the people. They were sick of leagues, of petty sovereignties, of Governments which could not govern a single individual. The framers of the Constitution, which has now endured three-quarters of a century, and under which the nation has made a material and intellectual progress never surpassed in history, were not such triflers as to be ignorant of the consequences of their own acts. The Constitution which they offered and which the people adopted as its own, talked not of Sovereign States—spoke not the word confederacy. In the very preamble to the instrument are inserted the vital words which show its character: "We, *the people* of the United States, to ensure a more perfect union, and to secure the blessings of liberty for ourselves and our posterity, *do ordain and establish this Constitution.*" *Sic volo, sic jubeo.* It is the language of a Sovereign solemnly speaking to the world. It is the promulgation of a great law, the *norma agendi* of a new commonwealth. It is no compact.

"A compact (says Blackstone) is a promise proceeding from us. Law is a command directed to us. The language of a compact is, "We will or will not do this; that of a law is, Thou shalt or shalt not do it."—(1 B. 38, 44, 45.)

And this is throughout the language of the Constitution. Congress shall do this; the President shall do that; the States shall not exercise this or that power. Witness, for example, the important clauses by which the "Sovereign"

States are shorn of all the great attributes of sovereignty:—no State shall coin money, nor emit bills of credit, nor pass *ex post facto* laws, nor laws impairing the obligations of contracts, nor maintain armies and navies, nor grant letters of marque, nor make compacts with other States, nor hold intercourse with foreign Powers, nor grant titles of nobility; and that most significant phrase, "this Contitution, and the laws made in pursuance thereof, *shall be the supreme law of the land.*"

Could language be more Imperial? Could the claim to State "sovereignty" be more completely disposed of at a word? How can that be sovereign, acknowledging no superior, supreme, which has voluntarily accepted a supreme law from something which it acknowledges as superior?

The Constitution is perpetual, not provisional or temporary. It is made for all time—"for ourselves and our posterity." It is absolute within its sphere. "This Constitution shall be the supreme law of the land, any thing in the Constitution or laws of a State to the contrary notwithstanding." Of what value, then, is a law of a State declaring its connection with the Union dissolved? The Constitution remains supreme, and is bound to assert its supremacy till overpowered by force. The use of force—of armies and navies of whatever strength—in order to compel obedience to the civil and constitutional authority, is not "wicked war," is not civil war, is not war at all. So long as it exists, the Government is obliged to put forth its strength when assailed. The President, who has taken an oath before God and man to maintain the Constitution and laws, is perjured if he yields the Constitution and laws to armed rebellion without a struggle. He knows nothing of States. Within the sphere of the United States Government he deals with individuals only, citizens of the great Republic in whatever portion of it they may happen to live. He has no choice but to enforce the laws of the Republic wherever they may be resisted. When he is overpowered the Government ceases to exist. The Union is gone, and Massachusetts, Rhode Island, and Ohio are as much separated from each other as they are from Georgia or Louisiana. Anarchy has returned upon us. The dismemberment of the Commonwealth is complete. We are again in the chaos of 1785.

But it is sometimes asked why the Constitution did not make a special provision against the right of secession. How could it do so? The people created a Constitution over the whole land, with certain defined, accurately enumerated powers, and among these were all the chief attributes of sovereignty. It was forbidden to a State to coin money, to keep armies and navies, to make compacts with other States, to hold intercourse with foreign nations, to oppose the authority of Government. To do any one of these things is to secede, for it would be physically impossible to do any one of them without secession. It would have been puerile for the Constitution to say formally to each State, "Thou shalt not secede." The Constitution, being the supreme law, being perpetual, and having expressly forbidden to the States those acts without which secession is an impossibility, would have been wanting in dignity had it used such superfluous phraseology. This Constitution is supreme, *whatever laws a State may enact*, says the organic law. Was it necessary to add, " and no State shall enact a law of secession?" To add to a great statute, in which the sovereign authority of the land declares its will, a phrase such as " and be it further enacted that the said law shall not be violated," would scarcely seem to strengthen the statute.

It was accordingly enacted that new States might be admitted; but no permission was given for a State to secede.

Provisions were made for the amendment of the Constitution from time to time, and it was intended that those provisions should be stringent. A two-thirds vote in both Houses of Congress, and a ratification in three-quarters of the whole number of States, are conditions only to be complied with in grave emergencies. But the Constitution made no provision for its own dissolution, and, if it had done so, it would have been a proceeding quite without example in history. A Constitution can only be subverted by revolution, or by foreign conquest of the land. The revolution may be the result of a successful rebellion. A peaceful revolution is also conceivable in the case of the United States. The same power which established the Constitution, may justly destroy it. The people of the whole land may meet, by delegates, in a great national convention, as they did in 1787, and declare that the Constitution no longer answers the purpose for which it was ordained; that it no longer can secure the blessings of liberty for the people in present and future generations, and that it is therefore forever abolished. When that project has been submitted again to the people voting in their primary assemblies, not influenced by fraud or force, the revolution is lawfully accomplished, and the Union is no more.

Such a proceeding is conceivable, although attended with innumerable difficulties and dangers. But these are not so great as those of the civil war into which the action of the seceding States has plunged the country. The division of the national domain and other property, the navigation and police of the great rivers, the arrangement and fortification of frontiers, the transit of the Isthmus, the mouth of the Mississippi, the control of the Gulf of Mexico, these are significant phrases which have an appalling sound; for there is not one of them that does not contain the seeds of war. In any separation, however accomplished, these difficulties must be dealt with, but there would seem less hope of arriving at a peaceful settlement of them now that the action of the seceding States has been so precipitate and lawless. For a single State, one after another, to resume those functions of sovereignty which it had unconditionally abdicated when its people ratified the Constitution of 1787, to seize forts, arsenals, custom-houses, post-offices, mints, and other valuable property of the Union, paid for by the treasure of the Union, was not the exercise of a legal function, but it was rebellion, treason, and plunder.

It is strange that Englishmen should find difficulty in understanding that the United States Government is a nation among the nations of the earth; a constituted authority, which may be overthrown by violence, as may be the fate of any state whether kingdom or republic, but which is false to the people if it does not its best to preserve them from the horrors of anarchy, even at the cost of blood. The "United States" happens to be a plural title, but the commonwealth thus designated is a unit,—"*e pluribus unum.*" The Union alone is clothed with imperial attributes; the Union alone is known and recognized in the family of nations; the Union alone holds the purse and the sword, regulates foreign intercourse, imposes taxes on foreign commerce, makes war and concludes peace. The armies, the navies, the militia, belong to the Union alone, and the President is Commander-in-Chief of all. No State can keep troops or fleets. What man in the civilized world has not heard of the United States? What man in England can tell the names of all the individual States? And yet, with hardly a superficial examination of our history and our Constitution, men talk glibly about a confederacy, a compact, a co-partnership, and the right of a State to secede at pleasure, not knowing that, by admitting such loose phraseology and such imaginary rights, we should violate the first principles of our political organization, should fly in the face of our history, should trample under foot the teachings of Jay, Hamilton, Washington, Marshall, Madison, Dane, Kent, Story, and Webster, and, accepting only the dogmas of Mr. Calhoun as infallible, surrender forever our national laws and our national existence.

Englishmen themselves live in a united empire; but if the kingdom of Scotland should secede, should seize all the national property, forts, arsenals, and public treasure on its soil, organize an army, send forth foreign Ministers to Louis Napoleon, the Emperor of Austria, and other Powers, issue invitations to all the pirates of the world to prey upon English commerce, screening their piracy from punishment by the banner of Scotland, and should announce its intention of planting that flag upon Buckingham Palace, it is probable that a blow or two would be struck to defend the national honor and the national existence, without fear that the civil war would be denounced as wicked and fratricidal. Yet it would be difficult to show that the State of Florida, for example, a Spanish province, purchased for national purposes some forty years ago by the United States Government for several millions, and fortified and furnished with navy yards for national uses, at a national expense of many more millions, and numbering at this moment a population of only 80,000 white men, should be more entitled to resume its original sovereignty than the ancient kingdom of William the Lion and Robert Bruce.

The terms of the treaty between England and Scotland were perpetual, and so is the Constitution of the United States. The United Empire may be destroyed by revolution and war, and so may the United States; but a peaceful and legal dismemberment without the consent of a majority of the whole people, is an impossibility.

But it is sometimes said that the American Republic originated in secession from the mother country, and that it is unreasonable of the Union to resist the seceding movement on the part of the new confederacy. But it so happens that the one case suggests the other only by the association of contrast. The thirteen colonies did not intend to secede from the British empire. They were forced into secession by a course of policy on the part of the mother country such as no English administration at the present day can be imagined capable of adopting. Those Englishmen in America were loyal to the Crown; but they exercised the right which cis-Atlantic or transatlantic Englishmen have always exercised, of resistance to arbitrary government. Taxed without being represented, and insulted by measures taken to enforce the odious, but not exorbitant imposts, they did not secede, nor declare their independence. On the contrary they made every effort to avert such a conclusion. In the words of the "forest-born Demosthenes"—as Lord Byron called the great Virginian, Patrick Henry—the Americans "petitioned, remonstrated, cast themselves at the foot of the throne, and implored its interposition to arrest the tyrannical hands of the Ministers and Parliament. But their petitions were slighted, their remonstrances procured only additional violence and insult, and they were spurned with contempt from the foot of the throne."

The "Boston massacre," the Boston port-bill, the Boston "tea-party," the battle of Lexington, the battle of Bunker's Hill, were events which long preceded the famous Declaration of Independence. It was not till the colonists felt that redress for grievances was impossible that they took the irrevocable step, and renounced their allegiance to the crown. The revolution had come at last, they had been forced into it, but they knew that it was revolution, and that they were acting at the peril of their lives. "We must be unanimous in this business," said Hancock; "we must all hang together." "Yes," replied Franklin, "or else we shall all hang separately."

The risk incurred by the colonists was enormous, but the injury to the mother country was comparatively slight. They went out into darkness and danger themselves, but the British empire was not thrown into anarchy and chaos by their secession.

Thus their course was the reverse of that adopted by the South. The prompt secession of seven States because of the constitutional election of a President over the candidates voted for by their people, was the redress in advance of grievances which they may, reasonably or unreasonably, have expected, but which had not yet occurred. There is the high authority of the Vice-President of the Southern "Confederacy," who declared a week after the election of Mr. Lincoln that the election was not a cause for secession, and that there was no certainty that he would have either the power or the inclination to invade the constitutional rights of the South.* In the Free States it was held that the resolutions of the convention by which Mr. Lincoln was nominated were scrupulously and conscientiously framed to protect all those constitutional rights. The question of slavery in the Territories, of the future extension of slavery, was one which had always been an open question and on which issue was now joined. But it was no question at all that slavery within a State was sacred from all interference by the General Government, or by the free States, or by individuals in those States; and the Chicago Convention strenuously asserted that doctrine.

The question of free trade, which is thrust before the English public by many journals, had no immediate connection with the secession, although doubtless the desire of *direct* trade with Europe has long been a prominent motive at the South. The Gulf States seceded under the moderate tariff of 1857, for which South Carolina voted side by side with Massachusetts. The latter State, although for political not economical reasons, it thought itself obliged since the secession to sustain the Pennsylvania interest by voting for the absurd Morrill Bill, is not in favor of protection. On the contrary, the great manufactories on the Merrimac River have long been independent of protection, and export many million dollars' worth of cotton and other fabrics to foreign countries, underselling or competing with all the world in open market. It would be impossible for any European nation to drive the American manufacturer from the markets of the American continent in the principal articles of *cheap clothing* for *the masses*, tariff or no tariff. This is a statistical fact which cannot be impugned.

The secession of the colonies, after years of oppression and grievances for which redress had been sought in vain, left the British empire, 3,000 miles off, in security, with constitution and laws unimpaired, even if its colonial territory were seriously diminished. The secession of the southern States, in contempt of any other remedy for expected grievances, is fol-

* See Stephens' Speech, page 219, *seq.*

lowed by the destruction of the whole body politic of which they were vital parts.

Not only is the United Republic destroyed if the revolution prove successful; but, even if the people of the Free States have the enthusiasm and sagacity to reconstruct their Union, and by a new national convention to re-ordain and re-establish the time-honored Constitution, still an immense territory is lost. But the extent of that territory is not the principal element in the disaster. The world is wide enough for all. It is the loss of the southern marine frontier which is fatal to the Republic. Florida and the vast Louisiana territory purchased by the Union from foreign countries, and garnished with fortresses at the expense of the Union, are fallen with all these improvements into the hands of a foreign and unfriendly Power. Should the dire misfortune of a war with a great maritime nation, with England or France for example, befall the Union, its territory, hitherto almost impregnable, might now be open to fleets and armies acting in alliance with a hostile " Confederacy," which has become possessed of an important part of the Union's maritime line of defence. Moreover, the Union has 12,000 ships, numbering more than 5,000,000 tons, the far greater part of which belongs to the Free States, and the vast commerce of the Mississippi and the Gulf of Mexico requires and must receive protection at every hazard.

Is it strange that the Union should make a vigorous, just, and lawful effort to save itself from the chaos from which the Constitution of 1787 rescued the country ? Who that has read and pondered the history of that dark period does not shudder at the prospect of its return ? But yesterday we were a State—the Great Republic—prosperous and powerful, with a flag known and honored all over the world. Seventy years ago we were a helpless league of bankrupt and lawless petty sovereignties. We had a currency so degraded that a leg of mutton was cheap at $1,000. The national debt, incurred in the War of Independence, had hardly a nominal value, and was considered worthless. The absence of law, order, and security for life and property was as absolute as could be well conceived in a civilized land. Debts could not be collected, courts could enforce no decrees, insurrections could not be suppressed. The army of the Confederacy numbered *eighty men.* From this condition the Constitution rescued us.

That great law, reported by the general Convention of 1787, was ratified by the people of all the land voting in each State for a ratifying convention chosen expressly for that purpose. It was promulgated in the name of the people : " We, the people of the United States, in order to form a more perfect Union, and to secure the blessings of liberty for ourselves and our posterity, do ordain and establish this Constitution." It was ratified by the people—*not by the States* acting through their governments,

legislative and executive, but by the people electing especial delegates within each State; and it is important to remember that in none of these ratifying conventions was any reserve made of a State's right to repeal the Union, or to secede.

Many criticisms were offered in the various ratifying ordinances, many amendments suggested, but the acceptance of the Constitution, the submission to the perpetual law, was in all cases absolute. The language of Virginia was most explicit on this point. " The powers granted under the Constitution, *being derived from the people of the United States,* may be *resumed by them* whenever the same shall be perverted to their injury or oppression." That the people of the United States, expressing their will solemnly in national convention, are competent to undo the work of their ancestors, and are fully justified in so doing when the Constitution shall be perverted to their injury and oppression, there is no man in the land that doubts. This course has been already indicated as the only peaceful revolution possible ; but such a proceeding is very different from the secession ordinance of a single State resuming its sovereignty of its own free will, and without consultation with the rest of the inhabitants of the country.

" There was no reservation (says Justice Story) of any right on the part of any State to dissolve its connection, or to abrogate its dissent, or to suspend the operation of the Constitution as to itself."

And thus, when the ratifications had been made, a new commonwealth took its place among the nations of the earth. The effects of the new Constitution were almost magical. Order sprang out of chaos. Law resumed its reign ; debts were collected ; life and property became secure ; the national debt was funded and ultimately paid, principal and interest, to the uttermost farthing ; the articles of the treaty of peace in 1783 were fulfilled, and Great Britain, having an organized and united State to deal with, entered into a treaty of commerce and amity with us—the first and the best ever negotiated between the two nations. Not the least noble of its articles (the 21st) provided that the acceptance by the citizens or subjects of either country of foreign letters of marque should be treated and *punished as piracy.* Unfortunately, that article and several others were limited to 12 years, and were not subsequently renewed. The debts due to British subjects were collected, and the British Government at last surrendered the forts on our soil.

At last we were a nation, with a flag respected abroad and almost idolized at home as the symbol of union and coming greatness; and we entered upon a career of prosperity and progress never surpassed in history. The autonomy of each State, according to which its domestic and interior affairs are subject to the domestic legislature and executive, was secured by the reservation to each State of powers not expressly granted to the Union by the Constitution. Supreme within its own orbit, which is traced from the same centre of popular power whence the wider circumference of the General Government is described, the individual State is surrounded on all sides by that all-embracing circle. The reserved and unnamed powers are many and important, but the State is closely circumscribed. Thus, a State is forbidden to alter its form of government. "Thou shalt forever remain a republic," says the United States Constitution to each individual State. A State is forbidden, above all, to pass any law conflicting with the United States Constitution or laws. Moreover, every member of Congress, every member of a State legislature, every executive or judicial officer in the service of the Union or of a separate State, is bound by solemn oath to maintain the United States Constitution. This alone would seem to settle the question of secession ordinances. So long as the Constitution endures, such an ordinance is merely the act of conspiring and combining individuals, with whom the General Government may deal. When it falls in the struggle, and becomes powerless to cope with them, the Constitution has been destroyed by violence. Peaceful acquiescence in such combinations is perjury and treason on the part of the chief magistrate of the country, for which he may be impeached and executed. Yet men speak of Mr. Lincoln as having plunged into wicked war. They censure him for not negotiating with envoys who came, not to settle grievances, but to demand recognition of the dismemberment of the Republic which he has just sworn to maintain.

It is true that the ordinary daily and petty affairs of men come more immediately than larger matters under the cognizance of the State governments, tending thus to foster local patriotism and local allegiance. At the same time, as all controversies between citizens of different States come within the sphere of the Federal courts, and as the manifold and conflicting currents of so rapid a national life as the American can rarely be confined within narrow geographical boundaries, it follows that the Federal courts, even for domestic purposes as well as foreign, are parts of the daily, visible functions of the body politic. The Union is omnipresent. The custom-house, the court-house, the arsenal, the village post-office, the muskets of the militia make the authority of the General Government a constant fact. Moreover, the restless, migratory character of the population, which rarely permits all the members of one family to remain denizens of any one State, has interlaced the States with each other and all with the Union to such an extent that a painless excision of a portion of the whole nation is an impossibility. To cut away the pound of flesh and draw no drop of blood surpasses human ingenuity.

Neither the opponents nor friends of the new Government in the first generation after its establishment held the doctrine of secession. The States' right party and the Federal party disliked or cherished the Government because of the general conviction that it was a constituted and centralized authority, permanent and indivisible, like that of any other organized nation. Each party continued to favor or to oppose a strict construction of the instrument; but the doctrine of nullification and secession was a plant of later growth. It was an accepted fact that the United States was not a confederacy. That word was never used in the Constitution except once by *way of prohibition*. We were a nation, not a copartnership, except indeed in the larger sense in which every nation may be considered a copartnership—a copartnership of the present with the past and with the future. To borrow the lofty language of Burke:—

"A State ought not to be considered as nothing better than a partnership agreement in a trade of pepper and coffee, calico or tobacco, or some other such low concern, to be taken up for a little temporary interest, and to be dissolved by the fancy of the parties. It is to be looked upon with other reverence, because it is not a partnership in things subservient only to gross animal existence, of a temporary and perishable nature. It is a partnership in all science, a partnership in all art, a partnership in every virtue and in all perfection, a partnership not only between those who are living, but between those who are living, those who are dead, and those who are to be born."

And the simple phrase of the preamble to our Constitution is almost as pregnant:—" To secure the blessings of liberty to us and our *posterity*."

But as the innumerable woes of disunion out of which we had been rescued by the Constitution began to fade into the past, the allegiance to the Union, in certain regions of the country, seemed rapidly to diminish. It was reserved to the subtle genius of Mr. Calhoun, one of the most logical, brilliant, and persuasive orators that ever lived, to embody once more, in a set of sounding sophisms, the main arguments which had been unsuccessfully used in a former generation to prevent the adoption of the Constitution, and to exhibit them now as legitimate deductions from the Constitution. The memorable tariff controversy was the occasion in which the argument of State sovereignty was put forth in all its strength. In regard to the dispute itself there can be no doubt that the South was in the right and the North in the wrong. The production by an exaggerated tariff of a revenue so much over and above the wants of Government, that it was at last divided among the separate States, and foolishly squandered, was the most triumphant *reductio ad absurdum* that the South could have desired. But it is none the less true that the nullification by a State legislature of a Federal law was a greater injury to the whole nation than a foolish tariff, long since repealed, had inflicted. It was a stab to the Union in its vital part. The blow was partially parried, but it may be doubted whether the wound has ever healed.

Tariffs, the protective system, free trade,—although the merits of these questions must be considered as settled by sound thinkers in all civilized lands, must nevertheless still remain in some countries the subjects of honest argument and legitimate controversy. When all parts of a country are represented—and especially in the case of the United States, where the Southern portion has three-fifths of a certain kind of "property" represented, while the North has no property represented—reason should contend with error for victory, trusting to its innate strength. And until after the secession of the Gulf States the moderate tariff of 1857 was in operation, with no probability of its repeal. Moreover, the advocates of the enlightened system of free trade should reflect that should the fourteen Slave States become permanently united in a separate confederacy, the state of their internal affairs will soon show a remarkable revolution. The absence of the Fugitive law will necessarily drive all the slaves from what are called the border States; and he must be a shallow politician who dreams here in England that free trade with all the world, and direct taxation for revenue, will be the policy of the new and expensive military empire which will arise. Manufactures of cotton and woollen will spring up on every river and mountain stream in the Northern Slave States, the vast mineral wealth of their territories will require development, and the cry for protection to native industry in one quarter will be as surely heeded as will be that other cry from the Gulf of Mexico, now partially suppressed for obvious reasons, for the African slave trade. To establish a great Gulf empire, including Mexico, Central America, Cuba, and other islands, with unlimited cotton fields and unlimited negroes, this is the golden vision in pursuit of which the great Republic has been sacrificed, the beneficent Constitution subverted. And already the vision has fled, but the work of destruction remains.

The mischief caused by a tariff, however selfish or however absurd, may be temporary. In the last nineteen years there have been four separate tariffs passed by the American Congress, and nothing is more probable than that the suicidal Morrill tariff will receive essential modifications even in the special session of July; but the woes caused by secession and civil war are infinite; and whatever be the result of the contest, this generation is not likely to forget the injuries already inflicted.

The great Secession, therefore, of 1860-61, is a rebellion, like any other insurrection, against established authority, and has been followed by civil war, as its immediate and inevitable consequence. If successful, it is revolution; and whether successful or not, it will be judged before the tribunal of mankind and posterity according to the eternal laws of reason and justice.

Time and history will decide whether it was a good and sagacious deed to destroy a fabric of so long duration, because of the election of Mr. Lincoln; whether it were wise and noble to substitute over a large portion of the American soil a Confederacy of which slavery, in the words of its Vice-President, is the corner-stone, for the old Republic, of which Washington, with his own hand, laid the corner-stone.

It is conceded by the North that it has received from the Union innumerable blessings. But it would seem that the Union has also conferred benefit on the South. It has carried its mails at a large expense. It has recaptured its fugitive slaves. It has purchased vast tracts of foreign territory, out of which a whole tier of slave States has been constructed. It has annexed Texas. It has made war with Mexico. It has made an offer—not likely to be repeated, however—to purchase Cuba, with its multitude of slaves, at a price according to report as large as the sum paid by England for the emancipation of her slaves. Individuals in the free States have expressed themselves freely on slavery, as upon every topic of human thought, and this must ever be the case where there is freedom of the press and of speech. The number of professed abolitionists has hitherto been very small, while the great body of the two principal political parties in the free States have been strongly opposed to them. The Republican party was determined to set bounds to the extension of slavery while the Democratic party favored that system, but neither had designs secret or avowed against slavery within the States. They knew that the question could only be legally and rationally dealt with by the States themselves. But both the parties, as present events are so signally demonstrating, were imbued with a passionate attachment to the Constitution—to the established authority of Government by which alone our laws and our liberty are secured. All parties in the free States are now united as one man inspired by a noble and generous emotion to vindicate the sullied honor of their flag, and to save their country from the abyss of perdition into which it seemed descending.

Of the ultimate result we have no intention of speaking. Only the presumptuous will venture to lift the veil and affect to read with accuracy coming events, the most momentous perhaps of our times. One result is, however, secured. The Montgomery Constitution with slavery for its corner-stone, is not likely to be accepted, as but lately seemed possible, not only by all the slave States, but even by the border free States; nor to be proclaimed from Washington as the new national law, in the name of the United States. Compromises will no longer be offered by peace conventions, in which slavery is to be made national, negroes declared property over all the land, and slavery extended over all Territories now possessed or hereafter to be acquired. Nor is the United States Government yet driven from Washington.

Events are rapidly unrolling themselves, and it will be proved, in course of time, whether the North will remain united in its inflexible purpose, whether the South is as firmly united, or whether a counter revolution will be effected in either section, which must necessarily give the victory to its opponents. We know nothing of the schemes or plans of either Government.

The original design of the Republican party was to put an end to the perpetual policy of slavery extension, and acquisition of foreign territory for that purpose, and at the same time to maintain the Constitution and the integrity of the Republic. This at the South seemed an outrage which justified civil war; for events have amply proved what sagacious statesmen prophesied thirty years ago—that secession is civil war.

If all is to end in negotiation and separation, notwithstanding the almost interminable disputes concerning frontiers, the strongholds in the Gulf, and the unshackled navigation of the great rivers throughout their whole length, which, it is probable, will never be abandoned by the North, except as the result of total defeat in the field, it is at any rate certain that both parties will negotiate more equitably with arms in their hands than if the unarmed of either section were to deal with the armed. If it comes to permanent separation, too, it is certain that in the Commonwealth which will still glory in the name of the United States, and whose people will doubtless re-establish the old Constitution, with some important amendments, the word secession will be a sound of woe not to be lightly uttered. It will have been proved to designate, not a peaceful and natural function of political life, but to be only another expression for revolution, bloodshed, and all the horrors of civil war.

It is probable that a long course of years will be run, and many inconveniences and grievances endured, before any one of the free States secede from the reconstructed Union. J. L. M.

Doc. 147.
SECESSION MILITARY ACT.
AN ACT TO RAISE AN ADDITIONAL MILITARY FORCE TO SERVE DURING THE WAR.

The Congress of the Confederate States of America do enact, That in addition to the Volunteer force authorized to be raised under existing laws, the President be and he is hereby authorized to accept the services of volunteers who may offer their services without regard to the place of enlistment, either as cavalry, mounted riflemen, artillery or infantry, in such proportion of these several arms as he may deem expedient, to serve for and during the existing war, unless sooner discharged.

SEC. 2. That the volunteers so offering their services may be accepted by the President in companies, to be organized by him into squadrons, battalions, or regiments. The President shall appoint all field and staff officers, but the company officers shall be elected by the men composing the company, and if accepted, the officers so elected shall be commissioned by the President.

SEC. 3. *Be it further enacted,* That any vacancies occurring in the ranks of the several companies mustered into service under the provisions of this act, may be filled by volunteers accepted under the rules of such companies, and any vacancies occurring shall be filled by elections in accordance with the same rules.

SEC. 4. Except as herein differently provided, the volunteer forces hereby authorized to be raised shall in all regards be subject to and organized in accordance with the provisions of "an act to provide for the public defence," and all other acts for the government of the armies of the Confederate States.

Doc. 147½.
SPEECH OF A. H. STEPHENS,
DELIVERED IN THE HALL OF THE HOUSE OF REPRESENTATIVES OF GEORGIA, NOV. 14, 1860.

MR. STEPHENS entered the Hall at the hour of 7 P. M., and was greeted with long and rapturous applause. He rose and said:

FELLOW-CITIZENS: I appear before you tonight at the request of members of the Legislature and others to speak of matters of the deepest interest that can possibly concern us all of an earthly character. There is nothing—no question or subject connected with this life—that concerns a free people so intimately as that of the Government under which they live. We are now, indeed, surrounded by evils. Never since I entered upon the public stage has the country been so environed with difficulties and dangers that threatened the public peace and the very existence of society as now. I do not now appear before you at my own instance. It is not to gratify desire of my own that I am here. Had I consulted my own ease and pleasure I should not be before you; but, believing that it is the duty of every good citizen to give his counsels and views whenever the country is in danger, as to the best policy to be pursued, I am here. For these reasons, and these only, do I bespeak a calm, patient, and attentive hearing.

My object is not to stir up strife, but to allay it; not to appeal to your passions, but to your reason. Good governments can never be built up or sustained by the impulse of passion. I wish to address myself to your good sense, to your good judgment, and if after hearing you disagree, let us agree to disagree, and part as we met, friends. We all have the same object, the same interest. That people should disagree in republican governments, upon questions of public policy, is natural. That men should disagree upon all matters connected with human investigation, whether relating to science or human conduct, is natural. Hence, in free governments parties will arise. But a free people should express their different opinions with liberality and charity, with no acrimony toward those of their fellows, when honestly and sincerely given. These are my feelings to-night.

Let us, therefore, reason together. It is not my purpose to say aught to wound the feelings of any individual who may be present; and if in the ardency with which I shall express my opinions, I shall say any thing which may be deemed too strong, let it be set down to the zeal with which I advocate my own convictions. There is with me no intention to irritate or offend.

The first question that presents itself is, shall the people of the South secede from the Union in consequence of the election of Mr. Lincoln to the presidency of the United States? My countrymen, *I tell you frankly, candidly, and earnestly, that I do not think that they ought.* In my judgment, the election of no man, constitutionally chosen to that high office, is sufficient cause for any State to separate from the Union. It ought to stand by and aid still in maintaining the constitution of the country. To make a point of resistance to the Government, to withdraw from it because a man has been constitutionally elected, puts us in the wrong. We are pledged to maintain the Constitution. Many of us have sworn to support it. Can we, therefore, for the mere election of a man to the Presidency, and that too in accordance with the prescribed forms of the Constitution, make a point of resistance to the Government without becoming the breakers of that sacred instrument ourselves, withdraw ourselves from it? Would we not be in the wrong? Whatever fate is to befall this country, let it never be laid to the charge of the people of the South, and especially to the people of Georgia, that we were untrue to our national engagements. Let the fault and the wrong rest upon others. If all our hopes are to be blasted, if the Republic is to go down, let us be found to the last moment standing on the deck, with the Constitution of the United States waving over our heads. (Applause.) Let the fanatics of the North break the Constitution, if such is their fell purpose. Let the responsibility be upon them. I shall speak presently more of their acts; but let not the South, let us not be the ones to commit the aggression. We went into the election with this people. The result was different from what we wished; but the election has been constitutionally held. Were we to make a point of resistance to the Government and go out of the Union on that account, the record would be made up hereafter against us.

But it is said Mr. Lincoln's policy and principles are against the Constitution, and that if he carries them out it will be destructive of our rights. Let us not anticipate a threatened evil. If he violates the Constitution then will come

our time to act. Do not let us break it because, forsooth, he may. If he does, that is the time for us to strike. (Applause.) I think it would be injudicious and unwise to do this sooner. I do not anticipate that Mr. Lincoln will do any thing to jeopard our safety or security, whatever may be his spirit to do it; for he is bound by the constitutional checks which are thrown around him, which at this time renders him powerless to do any great mischief. This shows the wisdom of our system. The President of the United States is no emperor, no dictator—he is clothed with no absolute power. He can do nothing unless he is backed by power in Congress. The House of Representatives is largely in the majority against him.

In the Senate he will also be powerless. There will be a majority of four against him. This, after the loss of Bigler, Fitch, and others, by the unfortunate dissensions of the National Democratic party in their States. Mr. Lincoln cannot appoint an officer without the consent of the Senate—he cannot form a Cabinet without the same consent. He will be in the condition of George III., (the embodiment of Toryism,) who had to ask the Whigs to appoint his ministers, and was compelled to receive a cabinet utterly opposed to his views; and so Mr. Lincoln will be compelled to ask of the Senate to choose for him a cabinet, if the Democracy of that body choose to put him on such terms. He will be compelled to do this or let the Government stop, if the National Democratic men —for that is their name at the North—the conservative men in the Senate, should so determine. Then, how can Mr. Lincoln obtain a cabinet which would aid him, or allow him to violate the Constitution?

Why then, I say, should we disrupt the ties of this Union when his hands are tied, when he can do nothing against us? I have heard it mooted that no man in the State of Georgia, who is true to her interests, could hold office under Mr. Lincoln. But, I ask, who appoints to office? Not the President alone; the Senate has to concur. No man can be appointed without the consent of the Senate. Should any man then refuse to hold office that was given to him by a Democratic Senate? [Mr. Toombs interrupted and said if the Senate was democratic it was for Mr. Breckinridge.] Well, then, continued Mr. S., I apprehend no man could be justly considered untrue to the interests of Georgia, or incur any disgrace, if the interests of Georgia required it, to hold an office which a Breckinridge Senate had given him, even though Mr. Lincoln should be President. (Prolonged applause, mingled with interruptions.)

I trust, my countrymen, you will be still and silent. I am addressing your good sense. I am giving you my views in a calm and dispassionate manner, and if any of you differ with me, you can, on any other occasion, give your views as I am doing now, and let reason and true patriotism decide between us. In my judgment, I say under such circumstances, there would be no possible disgrace for a Southern man to hold office. No man will be suffered to be appointed, I have no doubt, who is not true to the Constitution, if Southern Senators are true to their trusts, as I cannot permit myself to doubt that they will be.

My honorable friend who addressed you last night, (Mr. Toombs,) and to whom I listened with the profoundest attention, asks if we would submit to Black Republican rule? I say to you and to him, as a Georgian, I never would submit to any Black Republican *aggression* upon our constitutional rights. I will never consent myself, as much as I admire this Union for the glories of the past, or the blessings of the present, as much as it has done for the people of all these States, as much as it has done for civilization, as much as the hopes of the world hang upon it, I would never submit to aggression upon my rights to maintain it longer; and if they cannot be maintained in the Union, standing on the Georgia platform, where I have stood from the time of its adoption, I would be in favor of disrupting every tie which binds the States together.

I will have equality for Georgia and for the citizens of Georgia in this Union, or I will look for new safeguards elsewhere. This is my position. The only question now is, can they be secured in the Union? That is what I am counselling with you to-night about. Can it be secured? In my judgment it may be, but it may not be; but let us do all we can, so that in the future, if the worst come, it may never be said we were negligent in doing our duty to the last.

My countrymen, I am not of those who believe this Union has been a curse up to this time. True men, men of integrity, entertain different views from me on this subject. I do not question their right to do so; I would not impugn their motives in so doing. Nor will I undertake to say that this Government of our fathers is perfect. There is nothing perfect in this world of a human origin. Nothing connected with human nature, from man himself to any of his works. You may select the wisest and best men for your judges, and yet how many defects are there in the administration of justice? You may select the wisest and best men for your legislators, and yet how many defects are apparent in your laws? And it is so in our Government.

But that this Government of our fathers, with all its defects, comes nearer the objects of all good Governments than any other on the face of the earth is my settled conviction. Contrast it now with any on the face of the earth. [England, said Mr. Toombs.] —England, my friend says. Well, that is the next best, I grant; but I think we have improved upon England. Statesmen tried their apprentice hand on the Government of England, and then ours was made. Ours sprung

from that, avoiding many of its defects, taking most of the good and leaving out many of its errors, and from the whole constructing and building up this model Republic—the best which the history of the world gives any account of.

Compare, my friends, this Government with that of Spain, Mexico, the South American Republics, Germany, Ireland—are there any sons of that down-trodden nation here to-night?— Prussia, or if you travel further East, to Turkey or China. Where will you go, following the sun in its circuit round our globe, to find a Government that better protects the liberties of its people, and secures to them the blessings we enjoy? (Applause.) I think that one of the evils that beset us is a surfeit of liberty, an exuberance of the priceless blessings for which we are ungrateful. We listened to my honorable friend who addressed you last night, (Mr. Toombs,) as he recounted the evils of this Government.

The first was the fishing bounties, paid mostly to the sailors of New England. Our friend stated that forty-eight years of our Government was under the administration of Southern Presidents. Well, these fishing bounties began under the rule of a Southern President, I believe. No one of them during the whole forty-eight years ever set his Administration against the principle or policy of them. It is not for me to say whether it was a wise policy in the beginning; it probably was not, and I have nothing to say in its defence. But the reason given for it was to encourage our young men to go to sea and learn to manage ships. We had at the time but a small navy. It was thought best to encourage a class of our people to become acquainted with seafaring life; to become sailors; to man our naval ships. It requires practice to walk the deck of a ship, to pull the ropes, to furl the sails, to go aloft, to climb the mast; and it was thought, by offering this bounty, a nursery might be formed in which young men would become perfected in these arts, and it applied to one section of the country as well as to any other.

The result of this was, that in the war of 1812 our sailors, many of whom came from this nursery, were equal to any that England brought against us. At any rate, no small part of the glories of that war were gained by the veteran tars of America, and the object of these bounties was to foster that branch of the national defence. My opinion is, that whatever may have been the reason at first, this bounty ought to be discontinued—the reason for it at first no longer exists. A bill for this object did pass the Senate the last Congress I was in, to which my honorable friend contributed greatly, but it was not reached in the House of Representatives. I trust that he will yet see that he may with honor continue his connection with the Government, and that his eloquence, unrivalled in the Senate, may hereafter, as heretofore, be displayed in having this bounty, so obnoxious to him, repealed and wiped off from the statute-book.

The next evil that my friend complained of was the Tariff. Well, let us look at that for a moment. About the time I commenced noticing public matters, this question was agitating the country almost as fearfully as the slave question now is. In 1832, when I was in college, South Carolina was ready to nullify or secede from the Union on this account. And what have we seen? The Tariff no longer distracts the public councils. Reason has triumphed! The present Tariff was voted for by Massachusetts and South Carolina. The lion and the lamb lay down together—every man in the Senate and House from Massachusetts and South Carolina, I think, voted for it, as did my honorable friend himself. And if it be true, to use the figure of speech of my honorable friend, that every man in the North that works in iron and brass and wood has his muscle strengthened by the protection of the Government, that stimulant was given by his vote, and I believe every other Southern man. So we ought not to complain of that.

Mr. Toombs—The tariff assessed the duties.

Mr. Stephens—Yes, and Massachusetts with unanimity voted with the South to lessen them, and they were made just as low as Southern men asked them to be, and that is the rates they are now at. If reason and argument, with experience, produced such changes in the sentiments of Massachusetts from 1832 to 1857, on the subject of the Tariff, may not like changes be effected there by the same means—reason and argument, and appeals to patriotism on the present vexed question; and who can say that by 1875 or 1890 Massachusetts may not vote with South Carolina and Georgia upon all those questions that now distract the country, and threaten its peace and existence. I believe in the power and efficiency of truth, in the omnipotence of truth, and its ultimate triumph when properly wielded. (Applause.)

Another matter of grievance alluded to by my honorable friend was the navigation laws. This policy was also commenced under the Administration of one of these Southern Presidents who ruled so well, and has been continued through all of them since. The gentleman's views of the policy of these laws and my own do not disagree. We occupied the same ground in relation to them in Congress. It is not my purpose to defend them now. But it is proper to state some matters connected with their origin.

One of the objects was to build up a commercial American marine by giving American bottoms the exclusive carrying trade between our own ports. This is a great arm of national power. This object was accomplished. We have now an amount of shipping, not only coastwise, but to foreign countries, which puts us in the front rank of the nations of the world. England can no longer be styled the Mistress of the Seas. What American is not proud of the result? Whether those laws should be continued is another question. But one thing is certain: no President, Northern or Southern, has ever yet recommended their repeal. And my friend's efforts to get them repealed were met with but little favor, North or South.

These, then, were the true main grievances or grounds of complaint against the general system of our Government and its workings—I mean the administration of the Federal Government. As to the acts of the Federal States, I shall speak presently, but these three were the main ones used against the common head. Now, suppose it be admitted that all of these are evils in the system, do they overbalance and outweigh the advantages and great good which this same Government affords in a thousand innumerable ways that cannot be estimated? Have we not at the South, as well as the North, grown great, prosperous, and happy under its operation? Has any part of the world ever shown such rapid progress in the development of wealth, and all the material resources of national power and greatness, as the Southern States have under the General Government, notwithstanding all its defects?

Mr. Toombs—In spite of it.

Mr. Stephens—My honorable friend says we have, in spite of the General Government; that without it I suppose he thinks we might have done as well, or perhaps better, than we have done this in spite of it. That may be, and it may not be; but the great fact that we have grown great and powerful under the Government as it exists, there is no conjecture or speculation about that; it stands out bold, high, and prominent like your Stone Mountain, to which the gentleman alluded in illustrating home facts in his record—this great fact of our unrivalled prosperity in the Union as it is admitted; whether all this is in spite of the Government—whether we of the South would have been better off without the Government—is, to say the least, problematical. On the one side we can only put the fact against speculation and conjecture on the other. But even as a question of speculation I differ with my distinguished friend.

What we would have lost in border wars without the Union, or what we have gained simply by the peace it has secured, no estimate can be made of. Our foreign trade, which is the foundation of all our prosperity, has the protection of the navy, which drove the pirates from the waters near our coast, where they had been buccaneering for centuries before, and might have been still had it not been for the American Navy under the command of such spirits as Commodore Porter. Now that the coast is clear, that our commerce flows freely outwardly, we cannot well estimate how it would have been under other circumstances. The influence of the Government on us is like that of the atmosphere around us. Its benefits are so silent and unseen that they are seldom thought of or appreciated.

We seldom think of the single element of oxygen in the air we breathe, and yet let this simple, unseen, and unfelt agent be withdrawn, this life-giving element be taken away from this all-pervading fluid around us, and what instant and appalling changes would take place in all organic creation.

It may be that we are all that we are in "spite of the General Government," but it may be that without it we should have been far different from what we are now. It is true there is no equal part of the earth with natural resources superior perhaps to ours. That portion of this country known as the Southern States, stretching from the Chesapeake to the Rio Grande, is fully equal to the picture drawn by the honorable and eloquent Senator last night, in all natural capacities. But how many ages and centuries passed before these capacities were developed to reach this advanced age of civilization? There these same hills, rich in ore, same rivers, same valleys and plains, are as they have been since they came from the hand of the Creator; uneducated and uncivilized man roamed over them for how long no history informs us.

It was only under our institutions that they could be developed. Their development is the result of the enterprise of our people under operations of the Government and institutions under which we have lived. Even our people without these never would have done it. The organization of society has much to do with the development of the natural resources of any country or any land. The institutions of a people, political and moral, are the matrix in which the germ of their organic structure quickens into life—takes root and develops in form, nature, and character. Our institutions constitute the basis, the matrix, from which spring all our characteristics of development and greatness. Look at Greece. There is the same fertile soil, the same blue sky, the same inlets and harbors, the same Ægean, the same Olympus; there is the same land where Homer sung, where Pericles spoke; it is in nature the same old Greece—but it is living Greece no more. (Applause.)

Descendants of the same people inhabit the country; yet what is the reason of this mighty difference? In the midst of present degradation we see the glorious fragments of ancient works of art—temples with ornaments and inscriptions that excite wonder and admiration—the remains of a once high order of civilization which have outlived the language they spoke—upon them all Ichabod is written—their glory has departed. Why is this so? I answer, their institutions have been destroyed. These were but the fruits of their forms of government, the matrix from which their grand development sprung, and when once the institutions of a people have been destroyed, there is no earthly power that can bring back the Promethean spark to kindle them here again, any more than in that ancient land of eloquence, poetry, and song. (Applause.)

The same may be said of Italy. Where is Rome, once the mistress of the world? There are the same seven hills now, the same soil, the same natural resources; nature is the same, but what a ruin of human greatness meets the eye of the traveller throughout the length and breadth of that most down-trodden land! Why have not the people of that Heaven-favored clime the spirit that animated their fathers? Why this sad difference?

It is the destruction of her institutions that has caused it; and, my countrymen, if we shall in an evil hour rashly pull down and destroy those institutions which the patriotic band of our fathers labored so long and so hard to build up, and which have done so much for us and the world, who can venture the prediction that similar results will not ensue? Let us avoid it if we can. I trust the spirit is amongst us that will enable us to do it. Let us not rashly try the experiment, for if it fails as it did in Greece and Italy, and in the South American Republics, and in every other place, wherever liberty is once destroyed, it may never be restored to us again. (Applause.)

There are defects in our Government, errors in administration, and shortcomings of many kinds, but in spite of these defects and errors, Georgia has grown to be a great State. Let us pause here a moment. In 1850 there was a great crisis, but not so fearful as this, for of all I have ever passed through, this is the most perilous, and requires to be met with the greatest calmness and deliberation.

There were many amongst us in 1850 zealous to go at once out of the Union, to disrupt every tie that binds us together. Now do you believe, had that policy been carried out at that time, we would have been the same great people that we are to-day? It may be that we would, but have you any assurance of that fact? Would you have made the same advancement, improvement, and progress in all that constitutes material wealth and prosperity that we have?

I notice in the Comptroller-General's report, that the taxable property of Georgia is $670,-000,000 and upwards, an amount not far from double that it was in 1850. I think I may venture to say that for the last ten years the material wealth of the people of Georgia has been nearly if not quite doubled. The same may be said of our advance in education, and every thing that marks our civilization. Have we any assurance that had we regarded the earnest but misguided patriotic advice, as I think, of some of that day, and disrupted the ties which bind us to the Union, we would have advanced as we have? I think not. Well, then, let us be careful now before we attempt any rash experiment of this sort. I know that there are friends whose patriotism I do not intend to question, who think this Union a curse, and that we would be better off without it. I do not so think; if we can bring about a correction of these evils which threaten—and I am not without hope that this may yet be done—this appeal to go out, with all the provisions for good that accompany it, I look upon as a great and I fear a fatal temptation.

When I look around and see our prosperity in every thing, agriculture, commerce, art, science, and every department of education, physical and mental, as well as moral advancement, and our colleges, I think, in the face of such an exhibition, if we can without the loss of power, or any essential right or interest, remain in the Union, it is our duty to ourselves and to posterity to—let us not too readily yield to this temptation—do so. Our first parents, the great progenitors of the human race, were not without a like temptation when in the garden of Eden. They were led to believe that their condition would be bettered—that their eyes would be opened—and that they would become as gods. They in an evil hour yielded—instead of becoming gods they only saw their own nakedness.

I look upon this country with our institutions as the Eden of the world, the paradise of the universe. It may be that out of it we may become greater and more prosperous, but I am candid and sincere in telling you that I fear if we rashly evince passion and without sufficient cause shall take that step, that instead of becoming greater or more peaceful, prosperous, and happy—instead of becoming gods, we will become demons, and at no distant day commence cutting one another's throats. This is my apprehension. Let us, therefore, whatever we do, meet these difficulties, great as they are, like wise and sensible men, and consider them in the light of all the consequences which may attend our action. Let us see first clearly where the path of duty leads, and then we may not fear to tread therein.

I come now to the main question put to me, and on which my counsel has been asked. That is, what the present Legislature should do in view of the dangers that threaten us, and the wrongs that have been done us by several of our Confederate States in the Union, by the acts of their legislatures nullifying the fugitive slave law, and in direct disregard of their constitutional obligations. What I shall say will not be in the spirit of dictation. It will be simply my own judgment for what it is worth. It proceeds from a strong conviction that according to it our rights, interests, and honor—our present safety and future security can be maintained without yet looking to the last resort, the "*ultima ratio regum.*" That should not be looked to until all else fails. That may come. On this point I am hopeful, but not sanguine. But let us use every patriotic effort to prevent it while there is ground for hope,

If any view that I may present, in your judgment, be inconsistent with the best interests of Georgia, I ask you, as patriots, not to regard it.

After hearing me and others whom you have advised with, act in the premises according to your own conviction of duty as patriots. I speak now particularly to the members of the Legislature present. There are, as I have said, great dangers ahead. Great dangers may come from the election I have spoken of. If the policy of Mr. Lincoln and his Republican associates shall be carried out, or attempted to be carried out, no man in Georgia will be more willing or ready than myself to defend our rights, interest, and honor at every hazard, and to the last extremity. (Applause.)

What is this policy? It is in the first place to exclude us by an act of Congress from the Territories with our slave property. He is for using the power of the General Government against the extension of our institutions. Our position on this point is and ought to be, at all hazards, for perfect equality between all the States, and the citizens of all the States, in the Territories, under the Constitution of the United States. If Congress should exercise its power against this, then I am for standing where Georgia planted herself in 1850. These were plain propositions which were then laid down in her celebrated platform as sufficient for the disruption of the Union if the occasion should ever come; on these Georgia has declared that she will go out of the Union; and for these she would be justified by the nations of the earth in so doing.

I say the same; I said it then; I say it now, if Mr. Lincoln's policy should be carried out. I have told you that I do not think his bare election sufficient cause: but if his policy should be carried out in violation of any of the principles set forth in the Georgia Platform, that would be such an act of aggression which ought to be met as therein provided for. If his policy shall be carried out in repealing or modifying the Fugitive Slave law so as to weaken its efficacy, Georgia has declared that she will in the last resort disrupt the ties of the Union, and I say so too. I stand upon the Georgia Platform, and upon every plank, and say if those aggressions therein provided for take place, I say to you and to the people of Georgia, keep your powder dry, and let your assailants then have lead, if need be. (Applause.) I would wait for an act of aggression. This is my position.

Now, upon another point, and that the most difficult and deserving your most serious consideration, I will speak. That is the course which this State should pursue towards these Northern States, which by their legislative acts have attempted to nullify the Fugitive Slave law. I know that in some of these States their acts pretend to be based upon the principles set forth in the case of PRIGG against Pennsylvania; that decision did proclaim the doctrine that the State officers are not bound to carry out the provisions of a law of Congress—that the Federal Government cannot impose duties upon State officials; that they must execute their own laws by their own officers. And this may be true. But still it is the duty of the States to deliver fugitive slaves, as well as the duty of the General Government to see that it is done.

Northern States, on entering into the Federal compact, pledged themselves to surrender such fugitives; and it is in disregard of their obligations that they have passed laws which even tend to hinder or obstruct the fulfilment of that obligation. They have violated their plighted faith; what ought we to do in view of this? That is the question. What is to be done? By the law of nations you would have a right to demand the carrying out of this article of agreement, and I do not see that it should be otherwise with respect to the States of this Union; and in case it be not done, we would, by these principles, have the right to commit acts of reprisal on these faithless Governments, and seize upon their property, or that of their citizens wherever found. The States of this Union stand upon the same footing with foreign nations in this respect. But by the law of nations we are equally bound, before proceeding to violent measures, to set forth our grievances before the offending Government, to give them an opportunity to redress the wrong. Has our State yet done this? I think not.

Suppose it were Great Britain that had violated some compact of agreement with the General Government, what would be first done? In that case our Minister would be directed in the first instance to bring the matter to the attention of that Government, or a Commissioner be sent to that country to open negotiations with her, ask for redress, and it would only be when argument and reason had been exhausted that we should take the last resort of nations. That would be the course towards a foreign Government, and towards a member of this Confederacy I would recommend the same course.

Let us, therefore, not act hastily in this matter. Let your Committee on the State of the Republic make out a bill of grievances; let it be sent by the Governor to those faithless States, and if reason and argument shall be tried in vain—all shall fail to induce them to return to their constitutional obligations, I would be for retaliatory measures, such as the Governor has suggested to you. This mode of resistance in the Union is in our power. It might be effectual, and if in the last resort, we would be justified in the eyes of nations, not only in separating from them, but by using force.

[Some one said the argument was already exhausted.]

Mr. Stephens continued—Some friend says that the argument is already exhausted. No, my friend, it is not. You have never called the attention of the Legislatures of those States to this subject, that I am aware of. Nothing has ever been done before this year. The attention of our own people has been called to this subject lately.

Now, then, my recommendation to you would be this: In view of all these questions of difficulty, let a convention of the people of Georgia be called, to which they may be all referred. Let the sovereignty of the people speak. Some think that the election of Mr. Lincoln is cause sufficient to dissolve the Union. Some think those other grievances are sufficient to dissolve the same, and that the Legislature has the power thus to act, and ought thus to act. I have no hesitancy in saying that the Legislature is not the proper body to sever our Federal relations, if that necessity should arise. An honorable and distinguished gentleman, the other night, (Mr. T. R. R. Cobb,) advised you to take this course—not to wait to hear from the cross-roads and groceries. I say to you, you have no power so to act. You must refer this question to the people and you must wait to hear from the men at the cross-roads and even the groceries; for the people in this country, whether at the cross-roads or the groceries, whether in cottages or palaces, are all equal, and they are the sovereigns in this country. Sovereignty is not in the Legislature. We, the people, are the sovereigns. I am one of them and have a right to be heard, and so has any other citizen of the State. You legislators, I speak it respectfully, are but our servants. You are the servants of the people, and not their masters. Power resides with the people in this country.

The great difference between our country and all others, such as France and England and Ireland, is, that here there is popular sovereignty, while there sovereignty is exercised by kings and favored classes. This principle of popular sovereignty, however much derided lately, is the foundation of our institutions. Constitutions are but the channels through which the popular will may be expressed. Our Constitution came from the people. They made it, and they alone can rightfully unmake it.

Mr. Toombs—I am afraid of conventions.

Mr. Stephens—I am not afraid of any convention legally chosen by the people. I know no way to decide great questions affecting fundamental laws except by representatives of the people. The Constitution of the United States was made by the representatives of the people. The Constitution of the State of Georgia was made by representatives of the people chosen at the ballot-box. But do not let the question which comes before the people be put to them in the language of my honorable friend who addressed you last night. Will you submit to abolition rule or resist?

Mr. Toombs—I do not wish the people to be cheated.

Mr. Stephens—Now, my friends, how are we going to cheat the people by calling on them to elect delegates to a convention to decide all these questions without any dictation or direction? Who proposes to cheat the people by letting them speak their own untrammelled views in the choice of their ablest and best men, to determine upon all these matters, involving their peace.

I think the proposition of my honorable friend had a considerable smack of unfairness, not to say cheat. He wished to have no convention, but for the Legislature to submit their vote to the people—submission to abolition rule or resistance? Now, who in Georgia would vote "submission to abolition rule"? (Laughter.)

Is putting such a question to the people to vote on, a fair way of getting an expression of the popular will on all these questions? I think not. Now, who in Georgia is going to submit to abolition rule?

Mr. Toombs—The convention will.

Mr. Stephens—No, my friend, Georgia will never do it. The convention will never secede from the Georgia Platform. Under that there can be no abolition rule in the General Government. I am not afraid to trust the people in convention upon this and all questions. Besides, the Legislature were not elected for such a purpose. They came here to do their duty as legislators. They have sworn to support the Constitution of the United States. They did not come here to disrupt this Government. I am therefore for submitting all these questions to a convention of the people. Submit the question to the people, whether they would submit to abolition rule or resist, and then let the Legislature act upon that vote? Such a course would be an insult to the people. They would have to eat their platform, ignore their past history, blot out their records, and take steps backwards, if they should do this. I have never eaten my record or words, and never will.

But how will it be under this arrangement if they should vote to resist, and the Legislature should reassemble with this vote as their instruction? Can any man tell what sort of resistance will be meant? One man would say secede; another pass retaliatory measures; these are measures of resistance against wrong —legitimate and right—and there would be as many different ideas as there are members on this floor. Resistance don't mean secession— that in no proper sense of the term is resistance. Believing that the times require action, I am for presenting the question fairly to the people, for calling together an untrammelled convention, and presenting all the questions to them whether they will go out of the Union, or what course of resistance in the Union they may think best, and then let the Legislature act, when the people in their majesty are heard, and I tell you now, whatever that convention does, I hope and trust our people will abide by. I advise the calling of a convention with the earnest desire to preserve the peace and harmony of the State. I should dislike above all things to see violent measures adopted, or a disposition to take the sword in hand, by individuals, without the authority of law.

My honorable friend said last night, "I ask you to give me the sword, for if you do not give it to me, as God lives, I will take it myself."

Mr. Toombs—I will. (Applause on the other side.)

Mr. Stephens—I have no doubt that my honorable friend feels as he says. It is only his excessive ardor that makes him use such an expression; but this will pass off with the excitement of the hour. When the people in their majesty shall speak, I have no doubt that he will bow to their will, whatever it may be, upon the "sober second thought." (Applause.)

Should Georgia determine to go out of the Union, I speak for one, though my views might not agree with them, whatever the result may be, I shall bow to the will of her people. Their cause is my cause, and their destiny is my destiny; and I trust this will be the ultimate course of all. The greatest curse that can befall a free people is civil war.

But, as I said, let us call a convention of the people; let all these matters be submitted to it, and when the will of a majority of the people has thus been expressed, the whole State will present one unanimous voice in favor of whatever may be demanded; for I believe in the power of the people to govern themselves when wisdom prevails and passion is silent.

Look at what has already been done by them for their advancement in all that ennobles man. There is nothing like it in the history of the world. Look abroad from one extent of the country to the other, contemplate our greatness. We are now among the first nations of the earth. Shall it be said, then, that our institutions, founded upon principles of self-government, are a failure?

Thus far it is a noble example, worthy of imitation. The gentleman, Mr. Cobb, the other night said it had proven a failure. A failure in what? In growth? Look at our expanse in national power. Look at our population and increase in all that makes a people great. A failure? Why we are the admiration of the civilized world, and present the brightest hopes of mankind.

Some of our public men have failed in their aspirations; that is true, and from that comes a great part of our troubles. (Prolonged applause.)

No, there is no failure of this Government yet. We have made great advancement under the Constitution, and I cannot but hope that we shall advance higher still. Let us be true to our cause.

Now, when this convention assembles, if it shall be called, as I hope it may, I would say in my judgment, without dictation, for I am conferring with you freely and frankly, and it is thus that I give my views, I should take into consideration all those questions which distract the public mind; should view all the grounds of secession so far as the election of Mr. Lincoln is concerned, and I have no doubt they would say that the constitutional election of no man is a sufficient cause to break up the Union, but that the State should wait until he at least does some unconstitutional act.

Mr. Toombs—Commit some overt act.

Mr. Stephens—No, I did not say that. The word overt is a sort of technical term connected with treason, which has come to us from the mother country, and it means an open act of rebellion. I do not see how Mr. Lincoln can do this unless he should levy war upon us. I do not therefore use the word overt. I do not intend to wait for that. But I use the word unconstitutional act, which our people understand much better, and which expresses just what I mean. But as long as he conforms to the Constitution he should be left to exercise the duties of his office.

In giving this advice I am but sustaining the Constitution of my country, and I do not thereby become a Lincoln aid man either, (applause,) but a Constitutional aid man. But this matter the convention can determine.

As to the other matter, I think we have a right to pass retaliatory measures, provided they be in accordance with the Constitution of the United States, and I think they can be made such. But whether it would be wise for this Legislature to do this now is the question. To the convention, in my judgment, this matter ought to be referred. Before we commit reprisals on New England we should exhaust every means of bringing about a peaceful solution of the question.

Thus did Gen. Jackson in the case of the French. He did not recommend reprisals until he had treated with France, and got her to promise to make indemnification, and it was only on her refusal to pay the money which she had promised that he recommended reprisals. It was after negotiation had failed. I do think, therefore, that it would be best, before going to extreme measures with our confederate States, to make presentation of our demands, to appeal to their reason and judgment to give us our rights. Then, if reason should not triumph, it will be time enough to commit reprisals, and we should be justified in the eyes of a civilized world. At least let the States know what your grievances are, and if they refuse, as I said, to give us our rights under the Constitution of our country, I should be willing as a last resort to sever the ties of this Union. (Applause.)

My own opinion is, that if this course be pursued, and they are informed of the consequences of refusal, these States will secede; but if they should not, then let the consequences be with them, and let the responsibility of the consequences rest upon them. Another thing I would have that convention to do. Reaffirm the Georgia Platform with an additional plank in it. Let that plank be the fulfilment of the obligation on the part of those States to repeal these obnoxious laws as a condition of our remaining in the Union. Give them time to con-

sider it, and I would ask all States south to do the same thing.

I am for exhausting all that patriotism can demand before taking the last step. I would invite, therefore, South Carolina to a conference. I would ask the same of all the other Southern States, so that if the evil has got beyond our control, which God, in his mercy, grant may not be the case, let us not be divided among ourselves—(cheers,)—but, if possible, secure the united coöperation of all the Southern States; and then, in the face of the civilized world, we may justify our action; and, with the wrong all on the other side, we can appeal to the God of battles to aid us in our cause. (Loud applause.) But let us not do any thing in which any portion of our people may charge us with rash or hasty action. It is certainly a matter of great importance to tear this Government asunder. You were not sent here for that purpose. I would wish the whole South to be united if this is to be done; and I believe if we pursue the policy which I have indicated, this can be effected.

In this way our sister Southern States can be induced to act with us, and I have but little doubt that the States of New York and Pennsylvania and Ohio, and the other Western States, will compel their Legislatures to recede from their hostile attitudes if the others do not. Then with these we would go on without New England if she chose to stay out.

A voice in the assembly—We will kick them out.

Mr. Stephens—I would not kick them out. But if they chose to stay out they might. I think moreover that these Northern States being principally engaged in manufactures, would find that they had as much interest in the Union under the Constitution as we, and that they would return to their constitutional duty —this would be my hope. If they should not, and if the Middle States and Western States do not join us, we should at least have an undivided South. I am, as you clearly perceive, for maintaining the Union as it is, if possible. I will exhaust every means thus to maintain it with an equality in it. My principles are these:

First, the maintenance of the honor, the rights, the equality, the security, and the glory of my native State in the Union; but if these cannot be maintained in the Union, then I am for their maintenance, at all hazards, out of it. Next to the honor and glory of Georgia, the land of my birth, I hold the honor and glory of our common country. In Savannah I was made to say by the reporters, who very often make me say things which I never did, that I was first for the glory of the whole country, and next for that of Georgia.

I said the exact reverse of this. I am proud of her history, of her present standing. I am proud even of her motto, which I would have duly respected at the present time by all her sons—Wisdom, Justice, and Moderation. I would have her rights and that of the Southern

States maintained now upon these principles. Her position now is just what it was in 1850, with respect to the Southern States. Her platform then has been adopted by most, if not all, the other Southern States. Now I would add but one additional plank to that platform, which I have stated, and one which time has shown to be necessary.

If all this fails, we shall at least have the satisfaction of knowing that we have done our duty and all that patriotism could require.

Mr. Stephens continued for some time on other matters, which are omitted, and then took his seat amidst great applause.

N. Y. Times, November 22, 1860.

Doc. 148.

THE ENGLISH PRESS ON THE FALL OF FORT SUMTER.

NATURE, or something that stands in its stead, is still strong in the Americans. They fight " willing, but with unwilling minds." They lift the hand to strike, they wing the instrument of death, but a mysterious power averts the stroke, or blunts the edge, or deadens the blow. Are they in earnest, or are they playing at war, or dreaming that they strike, and still strike not? It sounds more like a dangerous game than a sad reality. Seven batteries breached and bombarded Fort Sumter for forty hours, burnt down its barracks, blew up several magazines, threw shells into it innumerable, and did a vast show of destruction. The fort replied with like spirit. At length it surrendered, the garrison marched out prisoners of war, and it was then found that not a man was killed or an officer wounded on either side. Many a " difficulty " at a bar has cost more bloodshed. Was this a preconcerted feat of conjuring? Were the rival Presidents saluting one another in harmless fireworks to amuse the groundlings? The whole affair is utterly inexplicable. It sounds like the battles when the coat of mail had come to its perfection, and when the only casualty, after a day's hard fighting, was a case of suffocation and a few bruises. Odin's heroes, as they renew their daily warfare, are really wounded, though their wounds are quickly healed. This is sparring with boxing-gloves—not the loaded cæstus of modern warfare. It is a mere spectacle. The population and even the ladies of Charleston poured forth to see the sight. Ten thousand soldiers lined the works, watching the sport and contributing their share. Our own Cockneys have seen as much, and done as much, at Cremorne, or the Surrey Gardens, not more unscathed, and, let us hope, in not more pacific mood. But, perhaps, this is only the interchange of courtesies which in olden times preceded real war. The result is utterly different from all we are accustomed to hear of the Americans. There, " a word or a blow " has been the rule. In this case, the blow, when it does at last come, falls like snow and lights as gently as thistle-down. Surely it cannot be a " cross "? If it be, half the old Union is in the conspiracy, for all are arming and rushing to war, as if they expected serious work.

What next? An attempt to recapture Fort Sumter? A contest for Fort Pickens? A struggle for the Capital? A diversion in Texas? A renewal of negotiations? No one knows, and, what is worse, no one credits President Lincoln for any plan. We can only compare the two sides, and strike a balance. In the North there is an army and a navy, and money, and a more numerous white population, without, too, the incubus of Slavery. There is also the tradition of the Union, the Capitol, and the successor of Washington. Modern warfare cannot go on without money, and the Northern States can more easily raise and spend a hundred millions of dollars a year than the Southern can raise ten millions. All that is outside, and material, is in favor of the North. It has the preponderance of every thing that can be counted, measured, and weighed, that can be bought and sold; that can be entered in legers and put on a balance-sheet. It has the manufactories, the building yards, the dock-yards,—the whole apparatus of national wealth and strength. It has the money market, and it borrows more easily than the South, where, however, political zeal sustains a fictitious credit. So, in the North we read of numerous gatherings of State forces—of many steamers chartered, stripped of their finery, filled with soldiers' food and ammunition, and steaming southward. So much for the North. In the South, on the contrary, there is little or nothing but that which often becomes the counterbalance to every thing else. There are the men of action, who can combine, conspire, keep the secret, have a plan, and carry it out without wavering or flinching. The politicians at Washington have been vacillating between peace and war, between compromise and resistance. In the South there has been one steady, uninterrupted progress toward secession and war. To the very last, President Lincoln has been behindhand. His ships, sent to relieve Fort Sumter, only arrived in time to be distant spectators of the scene; they came, in fact, but to contribute to the glory of the captors, and to bring shame and distrust on themselves and their cause. If this is to be an omen of the result, the rich and unready North will be no match for the fiery forwardness of the South.

But long shots are very different from close quarters. A fight of batteries across a river, watched with telescopes, and quietly witnessed by a large population, affords little clue for the result of a battle, hand to hand, step by step, with revolvers, knives, and what not, round the very building of the Capitol. That appears to be the thing next apprehended, and President Lincoln has summoned to his aid all the miscellaneous local corps of the several Northern States that may choose to hear him. Strange that the spot once held so sacred and so carefully insulated from local or partial associations, should become the object of the first civil war! That is, indeed, what we have come to. Many of us remember, not without a tingle of shame for our own country, the wanton attack of the British army on the Capitol, and the foolish injuries done there, destined to be more than avenged. This was but a *souvenir* of the old War of Independence. No British officer would have dared to insult the shrine of American union and liberty, had it not been felt that, besides the question then at issue, there was an account still to settle for the former war. Since the year 1812, there has been a generation of mutual respect—of even affection. That is all gone by. Other combatants gather round Washington. The War Minister of the Southern Confederacy publicly promises that the Secession flag shall float over the Capitol by the 1st of May. Any day it is expected that Virginia, whether by choice or necessity, will join the Secession, and then the sacred district of Columbia, which was to have been the common ground of the world's great brotherhood, will be the debateable border of a divided allegiance and a bloody quarrel. Meanwhile time brings round anniversaries, which are celebrated as of yore, but with the feeling that they are now a solemn mockery. What are the Declaration of Independence, the Battle of Lexington, the Birthday of Clay, and the other red-letter days in the American Calendar, now that the glorious fabric is itself in the dust, and the mountain made with hands shattered to pieces? It was but the other day, that all eyes were fixed on the Capital of the Old World as the single object of interest, and the expected scene of the great events that were to mark the latter years of this century. Rome occupied the attention of all men. A hundred questions were asked, but all were of Rome. Will Rome be still a Capital? Will it be the head of a Confederation, or the throne of a King, or the seat of a foreign Viceroy, or the See of a Universal Bishop, or the Senate of a National Republic? Before these questions could be answered, and while they are still asked, the Capital of the New World comes to the foreground, and is the object of much the same inquiries. The two cities of Rome and Washington are not so differently situated at this moment, nor are their prospects so different as might be. For the present, indeed, we shall all think more of Washington than of Rome.

—*London Times*, April 27.

We have at last the intelligence that hostilities have broken out between the Federal Government and the Southern States. Fort Sumter has fallen, after what is described as a gallant resistance on the part of Major Anderson and his force, of forty hours' duration. But, singular enough—and fortunate as it is singular—during this protracted cannonade, in the course of which some 1,700 rounds of shot and shell were fired by both parties, not one single man was killed on either side, and it is doubtful whether any one has been wounded. This bloodless conclusion of the first encounter, taken in connection with the circumstances which preceded and followed it, seems to indicate that there is no very bitter or rancorous feeling on either side, and favors the hope that a good deal of the pent-up irritation of the Southerners has found vent in the first and comparatively harmless passage of arms. From the correspondence between General Beauregard and Major Anderson immediately before the forts opened fire, *it was quite obvious that bloodshed was not intended, and that the commander of Fort Sumter, in resisting the demand to evacuate, stood simply on a point of honor, and, in returning the fire of the Secessionists, only desired to justify himself to his Government, and remove the impression which his passive conduct appears to have created at Washington.* We say all this is to be gathered from the correspondence in question, and derives confirmation from the fact that, immediately after Major Anderson hauled down his flag, he proceeded to Charleston, where he became the guest of General Beauregard. It is further observable that, although there were ships of war under the orders of the Federal Government, in the offing, no attempt was made to relieve Fort Sumter, nor when the commander commenced to reply to the Secessionists' fire. The excitement both at Charleston and at Washington is described as intense; but it would seem the feeling has not reached the occupants of the White House, who, and more especially the President, are said to be calm and composed. Neither has the news from the South, notwithstanding its gravity, produced any thing like a panic at New York. The stocks generally receded, it is true, but the Government Securities are reported to have been firmly held—*a fact in itself of sufficient significance, as indicating confidence in the proceedings of the Administration.* The suspension of business in Wall street was the natural consequence of the report of the actual outbreak of hostilities, but the absence of any thing approaching to a panic could not fail to be regarded as a proof that the mercantile community, at least, do not regard civil war with all its horrors, as inevitable, or that the general interruption of trade is the necessary consequence of the existing state of things. Nevertheless, *notwithstanding the reluctance of the Federal Government to resort to hostilities, it is obvious that they are prepared to take a determined stand against the Secessionists, wherever the rights or property of the Union are attacked. It rests, therefore, with the Southern Convention to say whether they are disposed to listen to terms, or whether they are prepared to persevere in the course they have adopted, regardless of the consequences.* —*London Shipping Gazette*, April 26.

The fall of Fort Sumter must soon, we fear, if we may rely at all on the drift of the recent news, issue in civil war. The rumor that the Southern Confederation intends to anticipate an attack by moving upon Washington, is scarcely likely to be true, for President Davis is too sagacious a man to take a step which would so enrage the North as to induce it to enter heart and soul into an internecine contest with the South. If he were wise, indeed, he would not have ventured any active collision at all, such as has taken place at Charleston. It would have been better to trust exclusively to blockade for the reduction of the Federal garrisons in the revolted States. The moral shock of any collision is most dangerous, as the accounts of the frantic excitement in Washington, on the arrival of the news of the collision at Fort Sumter and the surrender of Major Anderson, sufficiently prove. It is true that American rage even at its highest pitch usually manages to stop short where policy would direct, and that we in England are exceedingly liable to be deceived by its effervescent symptoms. Still there is now the gravest reason to apprehend a serious civil war; indeed all the Free States seem already to have intimated to the President, through the telegraph, their readiness to support a war policy; and, if it is prevented at all, it will only be by the unwillingness of the northern statesmen to risk the adhesion of the border States by an actual invasion. But if the Southern States should, as is rumored, be so foolish as to take the initiative by invading Washington, they would play directly into the hands of the extreme party in the North. All compunction would immediately be at an end, and in all probability the border States would themselves be induced by such a step to fight with the North. The situation is very similar to the attitude of Austria and Sardinia. The neutrals will inevitably throw their influence into the scale of the party attacked. Mr. Lincoln, as far as his own popularity and political position are concerned, can wish for nothing better than to be relieved by his antagonist of the responsibility of a decision. His difficulty has hitherto been, that the great power and wealth of the North have been passive and reluctant to foment a fratricidal strife. But let once the slave States take the guilt upon themselves, as in some degree they have already done, and Mr. Lincoln would find his hands strengthened and his cause enthusiastically supported by a power such as does not exist in the Southern States at all. We do not believe, then, in the reported invasion of Washington. A course so blind and insane is utterly inconsistent with the general ability shown by the Southern Government. But we do fear that the strife and defeat at Charleston will render it very difficult for Mr. Lincoln, in the attitude in which he now stands, to evade some attempt at reprisal, and that thus a regular war may soon break out.

Under these grave circumstances it is that Mr. Gregory proposes to ask the House of Commons on Tuesday next to affirm the expediency of an *immediate recognition of the Southern Confederation.* We can imagine no course more disgraceful to England, or less likely to command the assent of the popular body appealed to. Not that we desire to see a civil war in America, even though the North should be completely triumphant. We have often said that, unless there were a Union party in the Southern States considerable enough to make some head even without external assistance, the defeat of the newly-confederated States by the North could scarcely lead to any good result. It would be mere military conquest; and a power like the American Union cannot hope to hold together its territory by military force. And seeing that there is, unhappily, but little trace of a powerful Unionist minority among the seceded States, we cannot wish to see a fratricidal strife which would multiply indefinitely the mutual hatreds of North and South without solving the ultimate difficulty. But this is not the question for us to consider. It has been England's universal rule to acknowledge a *de facto* revolutionary government whenever it has established its practical independence by incontrovertible proofs—then and not sooner. Whatever be the wisdom or folly of the war, which there is but too much reason to believe is now declared between the Federal Government at Washington and the revolted States—it is not yet begun, or is only just beginning—there can be no question whatever of the constitutional right of President Lincoln to treat the hostile confederation as a treasonable rebellion, which, so far as it trenches on Federal property and laws, he may resist by force. This is his present attitude. He hopes, however little we may hope, to suppress the rebellion. He thinks, however little we may think, that he shall be able to enforce the laws enacted at Washington, and to redeem the United States property from the hands of the seceders. This may be sanguine; nay, it may even be a mere hallucination. With that we have nothing to do. We profess always to abstain from judging the rights of a quarrel between a people and its rulers, and to guide our conduct by the plain results of political fact. We are now on the eve of seeing what these results will be. Either war or compromise seems now inevitable. If it be compromise, we shall know how to act. *If it be war, we are bound to await the results of that war. A premature recognition of the Southern Confederation would be a departure from the recognized course of England,* and could not but therefore express a political *bias* in favor of the seceders.

— *London Economist.*

Doc. 149.

A PRAYER FOR THE TIMES.

At the opening of the Tennessee Legislature, on the 25th ult., Rev. James Bardwell offered up the following prayer:

Almighty and most merciful God, our heavenly Father, we adore Thee as the king eternal, immortal and invisible, the only living and true God,—the creator and governor of all worlds—ruling in the armies of Heaven and among the inhabitants of the earth. Thy favor is life and thy frown is death—with reverence and profound humility would we present ourselves before Thee, to confess our sins and implore Thy mercy, through Jesus Christ our Redeemer. In his name do we present our petitions, and for his sake we humbly invoke Thy favor. We have sinned against Thee, O Lord, as individuals, and we have sinned against Thee, as a people.

We have been unthankful for our blessings; we have abused mercies; we have misimproved our privileges; we have too often disregarded Thy authority and rejected Thy counsel. In the pride and vanity of our hearts we have forgotten Thee, the God of our fathers, and arrogated to ourselves the glory which is due to Thee alone. Lord, we confess our sins, we acknowledge our transgressions, and we humbly implore Thy pardoning mercy. Be merciful unto us, O God, be merciful unto us. For the sake of Thy dear Son, our Redeemer, in the midst of divine wrath, make known and remember mercy. Doubtless Thou art our God, though Abraham be ignorant of us, and Israel acknowledge us not. Thou hast been the God of our fathers, their refuge in every trouble. And we now look to Thee as our God and Redeemer. In this the time of our calamity and trouble, we invoke Thy guidance and protection.

Bless, we beseech Thee, the Governor of this Commonwealth, encircle him with Thy mercy, and grant unto him that wisdom and strength that may be necessary to direct and sustain him in the discharge of all the responsible duties now devolving upon him. And bless, we humbly pray Thee, the Legislature of this State, now convened under circumstances of peculiar solemnity and responsibility. Preside over and direct, in wisdom and great mercy, both houses of this general assembly. Give unto our senators wisdom—a spirit of knowledge and sound understanding. Place Thy fear before their eyes, and write Thy laws upon their hearts. May they all realize the solemn responsibilities devolving upon them at this critical juncture. Deliver them from strife and division in sentiment and action, unite them in fear and in firm maintenance of the cause of justice and truth.

Deliver us as a people from dissension and conflict at home; save us from passion, from violence, and from wickedness of all kinds. But grant unto us wisdom, prudence, firmness, and efficiency in all our deliberations and actions. O Lord, our help is in Thee, and we humbly invoke Thy protection. Wilt Thou not defend the right, and bring to nought the wickedness of the wicked?—Restrain, we beseech Thee, the wrath of man. Put Thy hook in the nose of him who deviseth mischief against us, and turn him back by the way he came. Circumvent and frustrate all his wicked devices; and may it yet please Thee to save us from the horrors

of civil war and bloodshed. Graciously pardon all our sins, remove us from Thy judgment, arrest and bring to repentance our enemies, and protect and defend us in the maintenance of all our rights, and once more give us peace and prosperity; and to Thy great name shall be all the praise, through Christ Jesus, our Lord. Amen.

—*Charleston News*, May 10.

Doc. 150.

THE FIRST REGIMENT VERMONT VOLUNTEERS.

THE following is a full list of the officers of this regiment:

FIELD AND STAFF OFFICERS.

Colonel, J. Wolcott Phelps; Lieutenant-Col., P. T. Washburn; Major, H. N. Worthen; Adjutant, Hiram Stephens; Quartermaster, E. A. Morse; Surgeon, E. K. Sanborn; Assistant Surgeon, Willard Childe; Sergeant Major, C. G. Chandler; Drum Major, Thos. R. Clark; Fife Major, Martin J. McManus; Chaplain, Rev. Levi H. Stone.

COMPANY OFFICERS.

Co. A, *Brandon, First Regiment*—Captain, Joseph Bush; First Lieutenant, William Cronan; Ensign, and 64 privates.

Co. B, *Middlebury, First Regiment*—E. S. Hayward, Captain; Charles W. Rose, First Lieutenant; and 64 privates.

Co. D, *Rutland, First Regiment*—W. Y. W. Ripley, Captain; Geo. T. Roberts, First Lieutenant; L. G. Kingsley, Ensign; and 65 privates.

Co. E, *Northfield, First Regiment*—Wm. H. Boynton, Captain; C. A. Webb, First Lieutenant; and 64 privates.

Co. C, *Swanton, Fourth Regiment*—L. D. Clark, Captain; A. B. Jewett, First Lieutenant; and 71 privates.

Co. A, *Woodstock, Second Regiment*—Wm. W. Pelton, Captain; Andrew J. Dike, First Lieutenant; and 64 privates.

Co. E, *Cavendish, Second Regiment*—O. S. Tuttle, Captain; A. Clark, First Lieutenant; S. Dutton, Ensign; and 65 privates.

Co. B, *St. Albans, Fourth Regiment*—Geo. G. Hunt, Captain; Hiram F. Perkins, First Lieutenant; F. E. Bell, Ensign; and 67 privates.

Co. A, *Burlington, Fourth Regiment*—D. Brainard Peck, Captain; O. G. Mower, First Lieutenant; G. J. Hagar, Ensign; and 67 privates.

Co. B, *Bradford, Second Regiment*—Dudley K. Andross, Captain; John B. Picket, jr., First Lieutenant; Boswell Farnum, Second Lieutenant; and 70 privates.

—*N. Y. Herald*, May 11.

Colonel Phelps, who commands the regiment, is a graduate of West Point, and has served twenty years in the army. He resigned two years ago, and has been living quietly at Brattleboro till the opening of the campaign, when he at once offered his services to the State, and was placed in command of this regiment.

Lieutenant-Colonel Washburn, of Woodstock, is one of the most prominent lawyers in the State. At the same time he is a military man, and a disciplinarian of the highest order.

Major Worthen, of Bradford, is also a lawyer, and a graduate of the Norwich University. Adjutant Stevens, also, has formerly followed the profession of the law.

The regiment numbers seven hundred and eighty men. Among them are several giants, taller by some inches than the President of the United States, and nearly all are accustomed to hard out-door work. One of the officers states that he selected ten of his tallest, and had them lie down on the ground for measurement, when it was found that the ten formed a line *sixty-seven feet and ten inches in length.*

—*N. Y. Evening Post*, May 11.

Doc. 151.
A PROCLAMATION
By the President of the United States of America.

Whereas, An insurrection exists in the State of Florida, by which the lives, liberty, and property of loyal citizens of the United States are endangered;

And *whereas,* It is deemed proper that all needful measures should be taken for the protection of such citizens and all officers of the United States in the discharge of their public duties in the State aforesaid;

Now, therefore, be it known that I, ABRAHAM LINCOLN, President of the United States, do hereby direct the Commander of the forces of the United States on the Florida coast to permit no person to exercise any office or authority upon the Islands of Key West, the Tortugas, and Santa Rosa which may be inconsistent with the laws and Constitution of the United States, authorizing him at the same time, if he shall find it necessary, to suspend there the writ of *habeas corpus*, and to remove from the vicinity of the United States fortresses all dangerous or suspected persons.

In witness whereof, I have hereunto set my hand and caused the seal of the United States to be affixed.

Done at the City of Washington, this tenth day of May, in the year of our Lord one thousand eight hundred and sixty-one, and of the Independence of the United States the eighty-fifth.   ABRAHAM LINCOLN.

By the President:
  WILLIAM H. SEWARD, Secretary of State.

Doc. 152.
AN ENGLISH VIEW OF THE CIVIL WAR IN AMERICA.

THE effect of the civil war in America upon European commerce is certainly one of the most important questions which ever engaged public attention. The commercial relations between this country and America are so multifarious, that any disturbance of them must necessarily cause infinite perplexity and great pecuniary loss; but those perplexities and losses will be seriously aggravated if the policy, which the British Government intends to pursue, is not defined with as much accuracy as possible. The British Government, as the greatest power at sea, has the deepest interest in adopting a principle of action which, while it secures every advantage to commerce, will not limit the action of the British Navy in the event of a war. Lord Palmerston, therefore, is acting with statesmanlike prudence in declining to bind himself to any course of action without the maturest deliberation. And Mr. Walpole deserves well of his country in lending the weight of his authority and influence to support Ministers in their cautious policy. In the meantime it may be useful to endeavor to indicate the position which the States under President Davis now occupy with relation to those under President Lincoln, and the position which both of these Confederacies now occupy with relation to Great Britain and the rest of the world.

In the first place, it is clear that, in the case of a rebellion in the territories of any government, other governments may adopt either of two lines of action: They may take no notice of the disturbance which is going on; or they may recognize the state of insurrection, and treat each of the contending parties as at war with each other. This latter course has been adopted in the present instance by the Foreign Minister, and in this respect he has acted with perfect prudence and in complete accordance with international law. Whether a province in a state of rebellion is to be treated as a provisionally independent power has always been considered a matter of discretion. It may be said that where, as in the case of America, half a continent has risen in arms against the other half, and has inaugurated an independent government—more especially when the peculiar Constitution of the United States is considered—according to all precedent the Southern Confederation must be treated as an independent power, and as entitled to belligerent rights. But the recognition of those rights is a step not to be taken without the gravest consideration of its consequences. No power was ever more free to act according to the clear dictates of justice and humanity than Great Britain in relation to this conflict. It is apprehended that in strict law, President Lincoln is still entitled to treat all those American subjects who adhere to the cause of President Davis as traitors, and to punish the South American cruisers as pirates. As this principle, however, if strictly followed, would certainly lead to terrible bloodshed and intolerable atrocities, it is obvious that the Northern and Southern combatants will treat each other as regular enemies, and observe, as far as possible, all the usages of war

This, however, will take place without any recognition of the only ground on which such a claim could legally be based, the independence of the Southern Confederacy. It is a political question worth considering, whether such a *de facto* concession might not be made to the Southern authorities by England; an exemption from the liabilities of pirates, without acknowledging in them the belligerent rights, which would give them unnecessarily a title to interfere with our commerce, and raise a league of slaveholders to a place among the nations of the world. The recognition of belligerent rights in the South would render the relations of this country to either of the American combatants precisely similar to the relations which subsisted during the Crimean War between Prussia on the one hand, and Russia, England, or France, on the other hand. If, indeed, the Declaration of Paris had been signed by America, the case might have been different; but as that Declaration only bound those Governments which signed it, and as America declined to do so, the law of Neutrals during war remains precisely as it was before the year 1854. The result is that both President Lincoln and President Davis may issue letters of marque to those who respectively acknowledge their authority. The lawfully commissioned vessels of war of either power are entitled to all the privileges usually accorded to the public vessels of war of an independent state, always on the supposition that the belligerent rights of the South are acknowledged. The right of search, which, notwithstanding the strange ideas of some journalists who ought to know better, has always been allowed to exist in time of war, will become capable of being exercised by the cruisers both of the North and of the South. The doctrine of the English Admiralty, according to Chancellor Kent, on the right of visitation and search, and on the limitation of the right, has been recognized in its fullest extent by courts of justice in America. And although that right does not entitle a belligerent to search for his subjects or seamen, it does entitle him to search for enemy's property, contraband of war, or for men in the land and naval services of the enemy. The English and French merchant ships and those of all neutrals must, therefore, expect to be searched by the armed vessels commissioned by either of the two rival Presidents. If in the course of searching a neutral friend's ship the goods of an enemy are discovered, it is the established law of England that such goods are liable to confiscation. If, therefore, a cargo of Manchester goods belonging to a New York merchant were found on board an English ship by a Southern cruiser, a British court would hold that they ought to be confiscated. But in American courts the result is more doubtful. According to American jurists, the rule of public law, that the property of an enemy is liable to capture on the vessel of a friend, is now declared on the part of the American Government

to have no foundation in natural right; and that the usage which undoubtedly exists, rests entirely on force. These doctrines were propounded when it was the object of Americans to enlarge the rights of neutrals. It remains to be seen whether they will be upheld in the present crisis. If they are, the neutral powers may insist that the American cruisers shall not seize the goods of an enemy when found on board a neutral friend's ship. On the other hand, if, in the course of searching an enemy's ship, the goods of a neutral friend are found, it is the admitted law of nations that such goods are not liable to be seized. But the Americans have carried this principle a step further; for it seems that the Supreme Court of the United States has twice carried the principle of the immunity of neutral property on board an enemy's ship to the extent of allowing it to be laden on board an armed belligerent cruiser, and the Court seems to have held moreover that the goods did not lose their neutral character even in consequence of resistance made by the armed vessel—provided the neutral did not aid in such armament or resistance—and this rule prevails notwithstanding the neutral had chartered the whole vessel, and was on board at the time of resistance. A contrary decision has no doubt been given by the English Judges. But if the Americans adhere to their opinion, it will be competent for any Englishman or Frenchman, or other neutral, to hire a fleet in the South, which may be armed by the captains, to load the ship with corn or cotton, or any other merchandise; and even although the American captains of these vessels resist the cruisers of the North, the merchandise belonging to the neutrals will be quite safe and will be directed to be restored.

It is difficult to imagine any state of law more favorable to neutral nations than that which must prevail if the American Judges adhere to the principles of those decisions which have been pronounced by the Supreme Court at Washington. It is hardly necessary to remark that the only way by which neutral ships can be excluded from the ports either of the North or of the South is by an effective blockade. With regard to the North, such a blockade is at present obviously out of the power of President Davis. With regard to the South, it remains to be seen what number of ships President Lincoln may be able to muster.

In the midst of the complications which must arise by the events of either Confederacy adopting principles of law different from those which have hitherto been proclaimed at Washington, it might, perhaps, be advisable to settle the moot points by a temporary convention. This is especially necessary in the case of the Confederate States of the South, because they may decline to be bound by the decisions which have already been pronounced by the Supreme Court of the United States.

—*London Daily News*, May 9.

Doc. 153.
MARYLAND RESOLUTION,
PASSED IN THE LEGISLATURE, MAY 10.

Whereas, The war against the Confederate States is unconstitutional and repugnant to civilization, and will result in a bloody and shameful overthrow of our institutions; and whilst recognizing the obligations of Maryland to the Union, we sympathize with the South in the struggle for their rights—for the sake of humanity we are for peace and reconciliation, and solemnly protest against this war, and will take no part in it;

Resolved, That Maryland implores the President, in the name of God, to cease this unholy war, at least until Congress assembles; that Maryland desires and consents to the recognition of the independence of the Confederate States. The military occupation of Maryland is unconstitutional, and she protests against it, though the violent interference with the transit of Federal troops is discountenanced; that the vindication of her rights be left to time and reason, and that a Convention, under existing circumstances, is inexpedient.

—*N. Y. Times,* May 11.

Doc. 154.
THE RIOT AT ST. LOUIS, MO., MAY 10, 1861.

THE camp of Gen. Frost, at Lindell's Grove, was a camp of instruction, intended to be continued for the term of six days, and which was formed in pursuance of orders from the governor of the State, who had directed the other militia districts also to go into encampments, with the view of acquiring a greater degree of proficiency in military drill. The encampment was commenced on the 4th instant.

ST. LOUIS, May 10.

Unusual, and to some extent alarming, activity prevailed early yesterday morning at each rendezvous of the "Home Guard," and in the vicinity of the Arsenal. The men recently provided with arms from the Arsenal, to the number of several thousands, were ordered, we understand, to be at their different posts at 12 o'clock, in readiness to march as they might be commanded. A report gained some currency that Gen. Harney was expected on the afternoon train, and that the troops were to cross the river to receive him, and escort him to the city. Very little reliance, however, was placed in this explanation of the military movements, and at about 2 o'clock P. M., the whole town became greatly agitated upon the circulation of the intelligence that some five or six thousand men were marching up Market street, under arms, in the direction of Camp Jackson. The news proved to be correct, except as to the numbers, and in this case the report rather under-estimated the extent of the force. According to our best information, there were probably not less than seven thousand men under

Capt. Lyon, (commanding the United States troops at this post,) with about twenty pieces of artillery.

The troops, as stated before, marched at quick time up Market street, and on arriving near Camp Jackson, rapidly surrounded it, planting batteries upon all the heights overlooking the camp. Long files of men were stationed in platoons at various points on every side, and a picket guard established covering an area of say two hundred yards. The guards, with fixed bayonets, and muskets at half cock, were instructed to allow none to pass or repass within the limits thus taken up.

By this time an immense crowd of people had assembled in the vicinity, having gone thither in carriages, buggies, rail-cars, baggage-wagons, on horseback, and on foot. Numbers of men seized rifles, shot-guns, or whatever other weapons they could lay hands upon, and rushed pell-mell to the assistance of the State troops, but were, of course, obstructed in their design. The hills, of which there are a number in the neighborhood, were literally black with people —hundreds of ladies and children stationing themselves with the throng, but as they thought out of harm's way.

Gen. Frost, commanding Camp Jackson, received the intelligence of the advance of the Arsenal troops with equanimity, but with some astonishment. He had heard reports that it was the design of Capt. Lyon to attack his camp, but was not at first disposed to place credence in them. So rapidly did these rumors come to him, however, that yesterday morning he addressed Capt. L. a note of which the following is a copy:

HEAD-QUARTERS, CAMP JACKSON, }
Missouri Militia, May 10, 1861. }

Captain N. LYON, Commanding United States Troops in and about St. Louis Arsenal.

SIR: I am constantly in receipt of information that you contemplate an attack upon my camp, whilst I understand that you are impressed with the idea that an attack upon the Arsenal and United States troops is intended on the part of the militia of Missouri. I am greatly at a loss to know what could justify you in attacking citizens of the United States who are in the lawful performance of duties devolving upon them under the Constitution, in organizing and instructing the militia of the State in obedience to her laws, and therefore have been disposed to doubt the correctness of the information I have received. I would be glad to know from you personally whether there is any truth in the statements that are constantly poured into my ears. So far as regards any hostility being intended towards the United States, or its property or representatives, by any portion of my command, or, as far as I can learn, (and I think I am fully informed,) of any other part of the State forces, I can say positively that the idea has never been entertained. On the contrary, prior to your taking command of the Arsenal, I proffered to Major Bell, then in command of the very few troops constituting its guard, the service of myself and all my command, and, if necessary, the whole power of the State to protect the United States in the full possession of all her property. Upon Gen. Harney's taking command of this department, I made the same proffer of services to him, and authorized his Adjutant-General, Capt. Williams, to communicate the fact that such had been done to the War Department. I have had no occasion since to change any of the views I entertained at that time, neither of my own volition nor through orders of my constitutional commander. I trust that after this explicit statement we may be able, by fully understanding each other, to keep far from our borders the misfortunes which so unhappily afflict our common country.

This communication will be handed to you by Col. Bowen, my Chief of Staff, who will be able to explain any thing not fully set forth in the foregoing.

I am, sir, very respectfully, your obedient servant, Brig. Gen. D. M. FROST,
Commanding Camp Jackson, M. V. M.

Capt. L. refused to receive the above communication. He forwarded Gen. Frost the following about the time, if we are not mistaken, of the surrounding of his camp:

HEAD-QUARTERS, UNITED STATES TROOPS, St. Louis, (Mo.,) May 10, 1861.

Gen. D. M. FROST, Commanding Camp Jackson:
SIR: Your command is regarded as evidently hostile towards the Government of the United States.

It is, for the most part, made up of those secessionists who have openly avowed their hostility to the General Government, and have been plotting at the seizure of its property and the overthrow of its authority. You are openly in communication with the so-called Southern Confederacy, which is now at war with the United States, and you are receiving at your camp, from the said Confederacy and under its flag, large supplies of the material of war, most of which is known to be the property of the United States. These extraordinary preparations plainly indicate none other than the well-known purpose of the Governor of this State, under whose orders you are acting, and whose purpose recently communicated to the Legislature, has just been responded to by that body in the most unparalleled legislation, having in direct view hostilities to the General Government and co-operation with its enemies.

In view of these considerations, and of your failure to disperse in obedience to the proclamation of the President, and of the eminent necessities of State policy and welfare, and the obligations imposed upon me by instructions from Washington, it is my duty to demand, and I do hereby demand of you an immediate surrender of your command, with no other conditions than that all persons surrendering under this demand shall be humanely and kindly treated. Believing myself prepared to enforce

this demand, one-half hour's time, before doing so, will be allowed for your compliance therewith.

Very respectfully, your obedient servant,
N. LYON, Captain,
2d Infantry, Commanding Troops.

Immediately on the receipt of the foregoing, Gen. Frost called a hasty consultation of the officers of his staff. The conclusion arrived at was that the brigade was in no condition to make resistance to a force so numerically superior, and that only one course could be pursued —a surrender.

The demand of Capt. Lyon was accordingly agreed to. The State troops were therefore made prisoners of war, but an offer was made to release them on condition that they would take an oath to support the Constitution of the United States and would swear not to take up arms against the Government. These terms were made known to the several commands, and the opportunity given to all who might feel disposed to accede to them to do so. Some eight or ten men signified their willingness; but the remainder, about eight hundred, preferred, under the circumstances, to become prisoners. (A number of the troops were absent from the camp in the city on leave.) Those who declined to take the prescribed oath said that they had already sworn allegiance to the United States and to defend the Government, and to repeat it now would be to admit that they had been in rebellion, which they would not concede.

The preparations for the surrender and for marching, as prisoners, under the escort of the Arsenal troops, occupied an hour or two. About half-past five the prisoners left the grove and entered the road, the United States soldiers enclosing them by a single file stretched along each side of the line. A halt was ordered and the troops remained standing in the position they had deployed into the road. The head of the column at the time rested opposite a small hill on the left as you approach the city, and the rear was on a line with the entrance to the grove. Vast crowds of people covered the surrounding grounds and every fence and housetop in the vicinity. Suddenly the sharp reports of several firearms were heard from the front of the column, and the spectators that lined the adjacent hill were seen fleeing in the greatest dismay and terror. It appeared that several members of one of the German companies, on being pressed by the crowd and receiving some blows from them, turned and discharged their pieces. Fortunately no one was injured, and the soldiers who had done the act were at once placed under arrest. Hardly, however, had tranquillity been restored when volley after volley of rifle reports were suddenly heard from the extreme rear ranks, and men, women, and children were beheld running wildly and frantically away from the scene. Many, while running, were suddenly struck to the sod, and the

Doc.—26

wounded and dying made the late beautiful field look like a battle-ground. The wounded, who were unable to be moved, were suitably cared for on the grounds. The total number killed and injured was about twenty-five. It was reported that the Arsenal troops were attacked with stones, and a couple of shots discharged at them by the crowd before they fired. The most of the people exposed to the fire of the soldiers were citizens with their wives and children, who were merely spectators, and took no part in any demonstration whatever. The firing was said to have been done by Boernstein's company, and at the command of an officer. The United States troops are now in possession of Camp Jackson, with all the equipage, tents, provisions, &c. The prisoners of war are, we believe, at the Arsenal.

It is almost impossible to describe the intense exhibition of feeling which was manifested in the city. All the most frequented streets and avenues were thronged with citizens in the highest state of excitement, and loud huzzas and occasional shots were heard in various localities. Thousands upon thousands of restless human beings could be seen from almost every point on Fourth street, all in search of the latest news. Imprecations, loud and long, were hurled into the darkening air, and the most unanimous resentment was expressed on all sides at the manner of firing into the harmless crowds near Camp Jackson. Hon. J. R. Barret, Major Uriel Wright, and other speakers addressed a large and intensely excited crowd in front of the Planters' House, and other well-known citizens were similarly engaged at various other points in the city. All the drinking saloons, restaurants, and other public resorts of similar character were closed by their proprietors, almost simultaneously, at dark; and the windows of private dwellings were fastened in fear of a general riot. Theatres and other public places of amusement were entirely out of the question, and nobody went near them. Matters of graver import were occupying the minds of the citizens, and every thing but the present excitement was banished from their thoughts. Crowds of men rushed through the principal thoroughfares, bearing banners and devices suitable to their several fancies, and by turns cheering and groaning. Some were armed and others were not armed, and all seemed anxious to be at work. A charge was made on the gun-store of H. E. Dimick, on Main street, the door was broken open, and the crowd secured fifteen or twenty guns before a sufficient number of police could be collected to arrest the proceedings. Chief McDonough marched down with about twenty policemen, armed with muskets, and succeeded in dispersing the mob and protecting the premises from further molestations. Squads of armed policemen were stationed at several of the most public corners, and the offices of the Missouri Democrat and Anzeiger des Westens were placed under guard for protection. —*St. Louis Republican*, May 11.

Doc. 155.

BLOCKADE OF CHARLESTON.

THE steam frigate Niagara, which, it was stated some days since, was coming off this port to blockade the harbor, was first noticed off here at an early hour on Saturday by pilot boat No. 4, then outside the bar, and also from the steeple of the Custom House. The pilot boat had observed in the offing on Friday evening what appeared to be a merchant ship bound into this harbor, and which not being in sight on Saturday, was no doubt ordered off by the Niagara. Towards midday the frigate disappeared, but returned off the port in the afternoon.

On Saturday, Capt. Robert Lockwood, pilot, in boat No. 2, (the W. Y. Leitch,) took to sea the schooner Minnehaha, for Baltimore, and soon after leaving the schooner outside, he went on board his boat, when he made in the offing, standing in, a square rigged vessel. Night coming on, and the Niagara being in sight, he thought it best to send his pilot boat into port, and to take his skiff and one hand and proceed to the bark. He reached her about seven P. M., and found her to be the bark Hilja, from Liverpool in ballast, consigned to Messrs. R. Mure & Co., of this city.

The tide being too late to get her into port, he remained on board during Saturday night, his skiff being taken on deck and carefully placed away. On Sunday morning, it being calm, the pilot was unable to get her under way, and about half-past eight A. M. she was boarded by a boat from the Niagara, commanded by Lieutenant R. L. May, who informed the captain of the Hilja that the port was blockaded, the rebels inside having fired on Fort Sumter with a garrison of less than 100 men, gave him a Yankee paper, containing the latest news, and mentioned that an army of 100,000 men had been landed on the coast of Louisiana. The captain of the Hilja informed the Lieutenant that he was short of water, and requested to know if the Niagara could supply him; but he was informed that the frigate had a shorter supply of that than any other necessary article. The following is a copy of the endorsement of Lieutenant R. L. May, on the papers of the Hilja:

Boarded May 12th, and ordered off the whole Southern coast of the United States of America, it being blockaded.

R. L. MAY,
Lieutenant United States steamship Niagara.

The officer remained by the Hilja for about twenty minutes, when he left. The boat's crew had a revolver each in a belt attached to the waist. Mr. Lockwood left the Hilja about 10 o'clock, and reached the city in his skiff, accompanied by a valuable boat hand, who remained faithful, although appearances indicated that the boy had only to open his mouth, when he might have had a passage to some other place than "Dixie's Land." The Hilja went off during the day, and will proceed to the British Provinces.

The British ship Monmouth, from Liverpool and the ship General Parkhill, from the same place, were seen off the bar yesterday and were ordered off, and we understand that the Niagara had previously sent off three other square-rigged vessels. During Sunday the Niagara went well off shore, accompanied by two of the above vessels, and while she was absent the British ship A. and A., Captain Hutchinson, from Belfast, stood in from the eastward, when the Niagara made after her; but the ship, having much the start, was run into shoal water, where the frigate could not well approach her, when the Niagara put about and proceeded south. Should the boats of the Niagara omit to board the A. and A. before morning, she may be got into port with the aid of steam. The race was anxiously watched from the wharves, and also by a party of gentlemen who were out in the pilot boat Rover, Captain Evans. They went alongside and spoke the ship.

—*Charleston Mercury*, May 13.

Doc. 156.

GENERAL HARNEY'S PROCLAMATION.

To the People of the State of Missouri and the city of St. Louis.

MILITARY DEPARTMENT OF THE WEST, ST. LOUIS, MAY 11, 1861.

I HAVE just returned to this post, and have assumed the military command of this department. No one can more deeply regret the deplorable state of things existing here than myself. The past cannot be recalled. I can only deal with the present and the future.

I most anxiously desire to discharge the delicate and onerous duties devolved upon me, so as to preserve the public peace. I shall carefully abstain from the exercise of any unnecessary powers, and from all interference with the proper functions of the public officers of the State and city. I therefore call upon the public authorities and the people to aid me in preserving the public peace.

The military force stationed in this department by the authority of the Government, and now under my command, will only be used in the last resort to preserve the peace. I trust I may be spared the necessity of resorting to martial law, but the public peace *must be preserved*, and the lives and property of the people protected. Upon a careful review of my instructions, I find I have no authority to change the location of the "Home Guards."

To avoid all cause of irritation and excitement, if called upon to aid the local authorities in preserving the public peace, I shall in preference make use of the regular army.

I ask the people to pursue their peaceful avocations, and to observe the laws and orders of their local authorities, and to abstain from the excitements of public meetings and heated discussions. My appeal, I trust, may not be in vain, and I pledge the faith of a soldier to the earnest discharge of my duty.

WILLIAM S. HARNEY,
Brigadier-General U. S. A., Commanding Dept.
—*National Intelligencer*, May 17.

Doc. 157.

THE FIRST CONNECTICUT REGIMENT.

LIST OF OFFICERS.

STAFF.—Colonel, Alfred H. Terry, of New Haven; Lieut. Colonel, David Young, of Norwich; Major, Robert O. Tyler, of Hartford; Surgeon, Archibald T. Douglass, M. D., of New London; Surgeon's Mate, Francis Bacon, of New Haven.

Infantry Company A, Hartford, Capt., John C. Comstock, 80 men; Infantry Company B, Hartford, Capt., Ira Wright, 77 men; Infantry Company C, Windsor Locks, Capt., Levi L. Hilman, 77 men; Infantry Company D, Waterbury, Capt., John L. Chatfield, 84 men; Infantry Company E, Danbury, Capt., E. E. Wildman, 77 men; Infantry Company F, West Meriden, Capt., Byxbee, 77 men; Infantry Company G, New Britain, Capt., Frederick W. Hart, 89 men; Infantry Company H, Bridgeport, Capt., Richard Fitzgibbons, 77 men; Rifle Company A, Hartford, Capt., Joseph R. Hawley, 84 men; Rifle Company B, Bridgeport, Capt., John Spiedal, 77 men.

—*National Intelligencer*, May 15.

Doc. 158.

APPORTIONMENT OF TROOPS.

THE following is the number of infantry regiments to be received from each State for a total increase of seventy-five regiments of three years' volunteers, under the recent determination of the Government, viz:

Virginia	2	New York	11
Maine	1	Pennsylvania	10
Maryland	1	Ohio	9
Connecticut	1	Illinois	6
New Hampshire	1	Indiana	4
Vermont	1	Massachusetts	5
Rhode Island	1	Missouri	4
Minnesota	1	Kentucky	2
Delaware	1	Wisconsin	2
Kansas	1	Michigan	3
Nebraska	1	Iowa	2
District of Columbia	1	New Jersey	3

The other regiment, namely, of cavalry, is not assigned.

—*N. Y. Herald*, May 13.

Doc. 159.

REPORT OF THE SOUTHERN BAPTIST CONVENTION, MAY 13, 1861.

THE following report from the Committee on the state of the country, was unanimously adopted by the Southern Baptist Convention in session at Savannah, Ga. It was drawn up by Rev. Dr. Fuller, of Baltimore, who had until recently had the reputation of being a firm friend of the Constitution and the Union:—

We hold this truth to be self-evident, that governments are established for the security, prosperity, and happiness of the people. When, therefore, any government is perverted from its proper designs, becomes oppressive, and abuses its power, the people have a right to change it.

As to the States once combined upon this continent, it is now manifest that they can no longer live together as one confederacy.

The Union constituted by our forefathers was one of coequal sovereign States. The fanatical spirit of the North has long been seeking to deprive us of rights and franchises guaranteed by the Constitution; and after years of persistent aggression, they have at last accomplished their purpose.

In vindication of their sacred rights and honor, in self-defence, and for the protection of all which is dear to man, the Southern States have practically asserted the right of seceding from a Union so degenerated from that established by the Constitution, and they have formed for themselves a Government based upon the principles of the original compact—adopting a charter which secures to each State its sovereign rights and privileges. This new Government, in thus dissolving former political connections, seeks to cultivate relations of amity and good will, with its late confederates and with all the world; and they have thrice sent special Commissioners to Washington with overtures for peace, and for a fair, amicable adjustment of all difficulties. The Government at Washington has insultingly repelled these proposals, and now insists *upon letting loose hordes of armed soldiers to pillage and desolate the entire South, for the purpose of forcing the seceded States back into unnatural Union, or of subjugating them, and holding them as conquered provinces.*

While the two sections of the land are thus arrayed against each other, it might naturally have been hoped that at least the churches of the North would interpose and protest against this appeal to the sword, this invoking of civil war, this deluging the country in fratricidal blood; but with astonishment and grief we find churches and pastors of the North breathing out slaughter, and clamoring for sanguinary hostilities with a fierceness which we would have supposed impossible among the disciples of the Prince of Peace. In view of such premises, this Convention cannot keep silence. Recognizing the necessity that the whole moral influence of the people, in whatever capacity or organization, should be enlisted in aid of the rulers who, by their suffrages, have been called to defend the endangered interests of person and property, of honor and liberty, it is bound to utter its voice distinctly, decidedly, emphatically; and your Committee recommend, therefore, the subjoined resolutions:

Resolved, That impartial history cannot charge upon the South the dissolution of the Union. She was foremost in advocating and cementing that Union. To that Union she clung through long years of calumny, injury, and insult. She has never ceased to raise her warning appeals against the fanaticism which has obstinately and incessantly warred against that Union.

Resolved, That we most cordially approve of the formation of the Government of the Confederate States of America, and admire and applaud the noble course of that Government up to this present time.

Resolved, That we shall assiduously invoke the Divine direction and favor in behalf of those who bear rule among us, that they may still exercise the same wise, prompt, elevated statesmanship which has hitherto characterized their measures; that their enterprises may be attended with success; and that they may attain a great reward, not only in seeing these Confederate States prosper under their administration, but in contributing to the progress of the transcendant kingdom of our Lord Jesus Christ.

Resolved, That we most cordially tender to the President of the Confederate States, to his Cabinet, and to the members of the Congress now convened at Montgomery, the assurances of our sympathy and entire confidence. With them are our hearts and our hearty coöperation.

Resolved, That the lawless reign of terror at the North, the violence committed upon unoffending citizens, above all, the threats to wage upon the South a warfare of savage barbarity, to devastate our homes and hearths with hosts of ruffians and felons burning with lust and rapine, ought to excite the horror of all civilized people. God forbid that we should so far forget the spirit of Jesus as to suffer malice and vindictiveness to insinuate themselves into our hearts; but every principle of religion, of patriotism, and of humanity, calls upon us to pledge our fortunes and lives in the good work of repelling an *invasion designed to destroy whatever is dear in our heroic traditions; whatever is sweet in our domestic hopes and enjoyments; whatever is essential to our institutions and our very manhood; whatever is worth living or dying for.*

Resolved, That we do now engage in prayer for our friends, brothers, fathers, sons, and citizen soldiers, who have left their homes to go forth for the defence of their families and friends and all which is dearest to the human heart; and we recommend to the churches represented in this body, that they constantly invoke a holy and merciful God to guard them from the temptations to which they are exposed, to cover their head in the day of battle, and to give victory to their arms.

Resolved, That we will pray for our enemies in the spirit of that Divine Master, who "when he was reviled, he reviled not again," trusting that their pitiless purposes may be frastrated, that God will grant to them a more politic, a more considerate, and a more Christian mind; that the fratricidal strife which they have decided upon, notwithstanding all our commissions and pleas for peace, may be arrested by that Supreme Power, who maketh the wrath of man to praise him; and that thus, through a divine blessing, the prosperity of these sovereign and once allied States, may be restored under the two Governments to which they now and henceforth respectively belong.

Resolved, We do recommend to the churches of the Baptist denomination in the Southern States, to observe the first and second days of June, as days of humiliation, fasting, and prayer to Almighty God, that he may avert any calamities due to our sins as a people, and may look with mercy and favor upon us.

Resolved, That whatever calamities may come upon us, our firm trust and hope are in God, through the atonement of his Son, and we earnestly beseech the churches represented in this body, (a constituency of six or seven hundred thousand Christians,) that they be fervent and importunate in prayer, not only for the country, but for the enterprises of the Gospel which have been committed to our care. In the war of the Revolution, and in the war of 1812, the Baptist bated no jot of heart or hope for the Redeemer's cause. Their zeal and liberality abounded in their deepest afflictions. We beseech the churches to cherish the spirit and imitate the example of this noble army of saints and heroes; to be followers of them, who, through faith and patience, inherit the promises; to be steadfast, unmoveable, always abounding in the work of the Lord, for as much as they know that their labor is not in vain in the Lord.

Resolved, That these resolutions be communicated to the Congress of the "Confederate States" at Montgomery, with the signatures of the President and Secretaries of the Convention.

P. H. MELL, Ga.
JAS. E. BROOME, Fla.
G. H. MARTIN, Miss.
W. CAREY CRANE, La.
R. FULLER, Md.
JAS. B. TAYLOR, Va. } Committee.
R. B. C. HOWELL, Tenn.
L. W. ALLEN, Ky.
J. L. PRICHARD, N. C.
E. T. WINKLER, S. C.
B. MANLY, SR., Ala.

The vote being taken, the report was unanimously adopted.

True extract from the minutes.

R. FULLER, President.

W. CAREY CRANE, } Secretaries.
GEO. B. TAYLOR. }

—*N. Y. Times,* May 21.

Doc. 160.

MAJOR MORRIS'S LETTER,

TO JUDGE GILES, AT BALTIMORE.

AT the date of issuing your writ, and for two weeks previous, the city in which you live and where your Court has been held, was entirely under the control of revolutionary authorities. Within that period United States soldiers, while committing no offence, had been perfidiously attacked and inhumanly murdered in your streets; no punishment had been awarded, and I believe no arrests had been made for these atrocious crimes; supplies of provisions intended for this garrison had been stopped; the intention to capture this fort had been boldly proclaimed; your most public thoroughfares were daily patrolled by large numbers of troops armed and clothed, at least in part, with articles stolen from the United States; and the Federal flag, while waving over the Federal offices, was cut down by some person wearing the uniform of a Maryland soldier. To add to the foregoing, an assemblage elected in defiance of law, but claiming to be the legislative body of your State, and so recognized by the Executive of Maryland, was debating the federal compact. If all this be not rebellion, I know not what to call it. I certainly regard it as sufficient legal cause for suspending the writ of *habeas corpus.* Besides, there were certain grounds of expediency on which I declined obeying your mandate.

1st. The writ of *habeas corpus* in the hands of an unfriendly power might depopulate this fortification and place it at the mercy of "a Baltimore mob," in much less time than it could be done by all the appliances of modern warfare.

2d. The ferocious spirit exhibited by your community toward the United States army would render me very averse from appearing publicly and unprotected in the city of Baltimore to defend the interests of the body to which I belong. A few days since a soldier of this command, while outside the walls, was attacked by a fiend or fiends in human shape, almost deprived of life, and left unprotected about half a mile from garrison. He was found in this situation and brought in, covered with blood. One of your evening prints was quite jocose over this laughable occurrence.

And now, sir, permit me to say, in conclusion, that no one can regret more than I this conflict between the civil and military authorities. If, in an experience of thirty-three years, you have never before known the writ of *habeas corpus* to be disobeyed, it is only because such a contingency in political affairs as the present has never before arisen. I claim to be a loyal citizen, and I hope my former conduct, both official and private, will justify this pretension. In any condition of affairs, except that of civil war, I would cheerfully obey your order, and as soon as the present excitement shall pass away I will hold myself ready, not only to

produce the soldier, but also to appear in person to answer for my conduct; but, in the existing state of sentiment in the city of Baltimore, I think it your duty to sustain the federal military and to strengthen their hands, instead of endeavoring to strike them down. I have the honor to be, very respectfully, your obedient servant, W. W. MORRIS,
Major, Fourth United States Artillery,
May 14. Commanding Fort McHenry.

Doc. 161.

SENATOR BAYARD ON SECESSION.

To the People of the State of Delaware:

FELLOW-CITIZENS:—Though, like all men who have mingled actively in political contests, I have often been subjected to misrepresentations and calumnies, under no past circumstances have I ever felt it necessary to reply to merely personal attacks, but have been content to let my general character and course of action be the answer to my assailants. From occurrences, however, within the last ten days, and the excited state of popular feeling, which seems to accept the falsest and most absurd charges as truths, it is due to myself to make to you the following statement, which, though it will not satisfy the bitterness of partisan hostility or the malignity of personal hatred, will, I trust, vindicate, in the opinion of the mass of my fellow-citizens, both my motives and my acts, though I may differ from many of them in my political opinions.

In the speech which I made in the Senate in March last, you have my views and opinions expressed frankly and without reserve on the present unhappy and distracted condition of our country, and the course which I believed the happiness and welfare of the people of the United States required should be adopted by the General Administration. The views and opinions then expressed were the result of grave consideration and positive conviction, and subsequent events have not changed but confirmed that conviction. I preferred peaceful separation of a part of the States from the Union, leaving that Union unbroken as to the far greater number, and the Federal Government as the Government of a powerful and great nation, to the alternative of civil war. Time and the progress of events will, I confidently believe, vindicate the wisdom of my counsel. If the arguments and views presented in that speech and my past course cannot convince you of my attachment to the Union, it would be hopeless to urge others now.

On the 8th of April last, I left home on a short visit to New Orleans, solely for social and business purposes—a visit I had contemplated and promised to make more than a year before, but which my professional and public duties had compelled me to postpone. I had no political purpose or object in view in making that visit, nor did I, during my absence, engage in any political arrangement or consultation intended or calculated to affect the action of the people of Delaware in relation to their allegiance and fidelity to the Union. I trust you have known me long enough, and I am sure you ought to have known me well enough, to be certain that, whatever political action I contemplated, I would openly and boldly avow and advocate before you. If I err in this, then it will be a vain hope for any public man to expect, however candid and open may have been his past course, that his fellow-men will justly estimate his character. When I left home, though the political horizon was clouded, no excitement existed beyond the ordinary conflict of party warfare, and I neither did nor could anticipate the events which occurred after my departure, or my visit certainly would not have been made. I took the Southern route, and reached Montgomery on Friday afternoon, the 12th of April, remained there till Sunday following, and left that day on the steamer for New Orleans. I saw many persons in Montgomery whom I had known well and intimately in Washington, but I had no political arrangements to make with them, nor were any proposed to me. After reaching New Orleans, in consequence of the rapid progress of events, I remained but three days, cut short my visit, and returned home as speedily as practicable up the river, though I had originally intended to return by sea to New York.

I make this statement, because I have been told that many fair-minded and well-intentioned men have attributed my visit to the South to political objects, and it is only to such it is intended to be addressed.

I reached home on Saturday, the 4th of May, and was met by a telegram, purporting to be from Middletown to Philadelphia, in which it was stated that I had been two weeks at Montgomery, in consultation with the leaders of the Confederate States. My answer is, that the telegram is utterly and unqualifiedly false, and whether it came from Middletown or elsewhere, it was the mere coinage of a reckless political partisan or a personal enemy. This was followed by an announcement placarded in Wilmington, and published in the papers, that a Prince of the Golden Circle had returned home, or some such absurd stuff. On principle, I never had the slightest connection with any secret association in my life; and, in my connection with the Democratic party, I have never been even a member of a club. I was told, also, that rumors had been spread in my absence, such as that I had gone to Montgomery to sell my State, and others of like kind. I paid little attention to these things, as I believed I could live them down, for I was not aware of the extent of passionate excitement to which the public mind had been strung, and still less did I dream that there was a deliberate intention by such means, to induce personal violence against me here, in my native town, or in Philadelphia.

I was mistaken in this, and have become satisfied that there was a deliberate conspiracy to make me the victim of a mob on the first occasion on which I went to Philadelphia. I have no knowledge of the parties engaged in this conspiracy either here or in Philadelphia, nor do I fear the ruffians who would instigate such action here, because I have confidence that in the people of Delaware, however decided may be their dissent from my political views, the love of order and law is too deeply implanted to tolerate lawless violence.

Without the slightest anticipation of any intended violence, I left home in the morning train for Philadelphia, on Tuesday last, and arrived at the Prime station about half-past 8 A. M. There was no mob or assemblage at the station and I took my seat in the second passenger railway car, which, after it had turned into Catherine street, was stopped by a police officer, and the inquiry made, "Is Senator Bayard here?" I answered affirmatively, and the reply was, "Come here if you please, we want you." I left the car at once, and it went on, and the officer said immediately, "There is a mob ahead waiting for you, and you had better go with us," alluding to another officer who had joined him.

Having no desire to encounter or be the victim of a mob, I assented, and walked on with them down Catherine street for three or four squares. One of the officers then turned off, and I went with the other to the Mayor's office. During our walk I had some conversation with the officer, and expressed my utter surprise at the existence of the mob, and my then belief that it had been instigated by the false statements in the telegrams and newspapers as to the object of my recent visit to the South. The officer also told me he had arrested me for my own protection. I remained at the Mayor's office till the arrival of Mr. Henry, with whom I had a short conversation, and then left with a friend.

I must add that the conduct of the police officers was both courteous and judicious, and not having a sufficient force at the station to disperse or control a mob, they protected me from its violence by wisely evading it.

I did not see this mob, but from the statement of others, it was between two and five hundred in number. That it was prearranged in consequence of a communication from Wilmington, cannot be doubted, for it had organized for the sole purpose of assaulting me, and selected its position on Fifteenth street, about three squares from the station, where I should, in a passenger car, have been entirely defenceless. It was utterly impracticable that such a mob could have been so collected and arranged between the time of the arrival of the train, and the few minutes afterward when I was called by the officer out of the passenger car, without previous information that I was coming in the train.

The car was stopped for a moment, about two squares from the place I left it, and I was inquired for, and, being told that I was at the station, it was permitted to proceed without further interruption. I have no knowledge as to the further action of my intended assailants.

I am well aware that in cities and large towns, there will always be men ready to instigate and embark in lawless action, but it can scarcely be considered evidence of strong attachment to the Union, when a mob can be collected in the city of one State to assault a citizen and representative of another, on the false statements of unknown persons by telegraphic or other communications in the newspapers. That I escaped a danger greater than I then realized, I cannot doubt, but I do not hold the deluded men who composed this mob in Philadelphia, as morally culpable as I do the Press of Philadelphia, for the mode in which it sought in its reports of this affair to slur over, palliate and encourage, and in some papers even to justify such mob action.

It is true that, in a single paper, such action is condemned in an editorial, but in the same paper to its report of this lawless attempt, is appended a statement relating to my political action on two previous occasions, utterly false, and intended as justification of the action of the mob in the particular case.

Perhaps, when one of their own citizens has become the victim of an outrage similar to that intended to be perpetrated upon me, the people of Philadelphia will begin to realize the dangers attendant upon these reckless and mendacious slanders upon individuals, which are now so common in the papers of that city, induced generally by partisan bitterness, but not unfrequently by personal enmity.

At a time when there is so much excitement in the community, I do not expect to escape personal defamation either here or there; but Wilmington is my residence, and though I may avoid personal violence in Philadelphia, I shall meet it, if attempted here, as best I may. I know my duties, both as a citizen of Delaware and of the United States, and am conscious of no violation of them; but I know also my rights, and shall not shrink from maintaining them.

The object of this address, fellow-citizens, has been to give a general refutation to groundless calumnies accumulated during my absence in part springing from political motives, with a view merely to political effect, and in part from the malevolence of personal enemies. Having done this, I shall rest hereafter, as hitherto, on my character, my past course, and my future actions as the surest safeguards against either class of assailants.

My standard of duty and of action has always been conscious rectitude of purpose, and, though many may misjudge me now, I shall leave to time and the progress of events, the correction of present errors of opinion.

I am one of your representatives in the Senate of the United States, and my term of office does not expire until March, 1863. I view, however, the relation of constituent and representative as one of confidence, and when I am satisfied that civil war cannot be averted, and find that the public sentiment of my State prefers such a result to the peaceful separation of those States which have withdrawn from the Union, I shall cheerfully and gladly resign into your hands an office which I obtained without solicitation, and which neither my sense of duty nor my self-respect would permit me to hold, when I ascertain that I differ in opinion with you on so momentous and vital a question as peace or war. It can require but few days after Congress has assembled to determine whether the last hope of peace has fled, if, indeed, the hope can linger until then; and before that time I shall become fully satisfied as to your will. Do not fear that I will betray the confidence you have reposed in me, or be capable of misrepresenting that will. If I cannot conscientiously obey your mandate, I will not use the position I occupy as your representative, to prevent its performance by another agent. But the right of private opinion and its expression, is a personal right, beyond public control. It is secured to every freeman under a government of laws, and a Republic must be a government of laws alone, or it will end in anarchy or despotism. I have no faith either in the government of the sword or the mob, and shall resist the establishment of either.

JAMES A. BAYARD.

WILMINGTON, May 13, 1861.

—*N. Y. Tribune*, May 20.

Doc. 162.

GEN. HARNEY'S PROCLAMATION.

"MILITARY DEPARTMENT OF THE WEST,
ST. LOUIS, May 14, 1861.

" *To the People of the State of Missouri:*

" ON my return to the duties of the command of this department I find, greatly to my astonishment and mortification, a most extraordinary state of things existing in this State, deeply affecting the stability of the Government of the United States, as well as the governmental and other interests of Missouri itself.

" As a citizen of Missouri, owing allegiance to the United States, and having interests in common with you, I feel it my duty as well as privilege to extend a warning voice to my fellow-citizens against the common dangers that threaten us, and to appeal to your patriotism and sense of justice to exert all your moral power to avert them.

" It is with regret that I feel it my duty to call your attention to the recent act of the General Assembly of Missouri, known as the Military bill, which is the result, no doubt, of the temporary excitement that now pervades the public mind. This bill cannot be regarded in any other light than *an indirect secession ordinance, ignoring even the forms resorted to*

by other States. Manifestly its most material provisions are in conflict with the Constitution and *laws* of the United States. *To this extent it is a nullity, and cannot and ought not to be upheld or regarded by the good citizens of Missouri.* There are obligations and duties resting upon the people of Missouri under the Constitution and laws of the United States which are paramount, and which I trust you will carefully consider and weigh well before you will allow yourselves to be carried out of the Union, under the form of yielding obedience to this Military bill, which is clearly in violation of your duties as citizens of the United States.

" It must be apparent to every one who has taken a proper and unbiased view of the subject, that, whatever may be the termination of the unfortunate condition of things in respect to the so-called ' cotton States,' *Missouri must share the destiny of the Union.* Her geographical position—her soil, productions, and in short all her material interests, point to this result. We cannot shut our eyes against this controlling fact. It is seen, and its force is felt throughout the nation. So important is this regarded to the great interests of the country, that I venture to express the opinion that *the whole power of the Government of the United States, if necessary, will be exerted to maintain Missouri in her present position in the Union.* I express to you in all frankness and sincerity my own deliberate convictions, without assuming to speak for the Government of the United States, whose authority, here and elsewhere, I shall at all times and under all circumstances endeavor faithfully to uphold.

" I desire, above all things, most earnestly to invite my fellow-citizens dispassionately to consider their true interests as well as their true relation to the Government under which we live, and to which we owe so much.

" In this connection I desire to direct attention to one subject, which no doubt will be made the pretext for more or less popular excitement. I allude to the recent transactions at Camp Jackson, near St. Louis. It is not proper for me to comment upon the official conduct of my predecessor in command of this Department, but it is right and proper for the people of Missouri to know that the main avenue of Camp Jackson, recently under command of General Frost, had the name of Davis, and a principal street of the same camp that of Beauregard; and that a body of men had been received into that camp by its commander, which had been notoriously organized in the interests of the secessionists, the men openly wearing the dress and badge distinguishing the army of the so-called Southern Confederacy. It is also a notorious fact that a quantity of arms had been received into the camp, which were unlawfully taken from the United States arsenal at Baton Rouge, and surreptitiously passed up the river in boxes marked marble.

" Upon facts like these, and having in view what occurred at Liberty, the people can draw their own inferences, and it cannot be difficult for any one to arrive at a correct conclusion as to the character and ultimate purpose of that encampment. No government in the world would be entitled to respect, that would tolerate for a moment such openly treasonable preparations.

"It is but simple justice, however, that I should state the fact that there were many good and loyal men in the camp, who were in no manner responsible for its treasonable character.

"Disclaiming, as I do, all desire or intention to interfere in any way with the prerogatives of the State of Missouri or with the functions of its executive or other authorities, yet I regard it as my plain path of duty to express to the people in respectful, but at the same time decided language, that, within the field and scope of my command and authority, the '*supreme law*' of the land must and shall be maintained, and no subterfuges, whether in the forms of legislative acts or otherwise, can be permitted to harass or oppress the good and law-abiding people of Missouri. I shall exert my authority to protect their persons and property from violations of every kind, and I shall deem it my duty to suppress all unlawful combinations of men, whether formed under pretext of military organizations or otherwise.

"WM. S. HARNEY, Brigadier-General
"United States Army, Commanding."
—*St. Louis Republican*, May 14.

Doc. 163.
THE CONFEDERATE FAST.

IN the open session of the Confederate Congress, May 14, several resolutions of interest were offered and adopted. The first of these is a resolution presented by Mr. T. R. R. Cobb, of Georgia, in reference to a general day of Fasting and Prayer.

As the sentiments and intent of the resolutions are good, I shall give them to your readers entire, as follows:

"The dependence of nations, as of individuals, upon an overruling Providence, at all times, we fully recognize; but when perils surround, and national existence is threatened, it peculiarly becomes a people to manifest their submission to the will and guidance of the Omnipotent Ruler of the universe. If the cause be righteous and the quarrel just, we may confidently rely on Him who reigneth alike over the armies of earth and the hosts of heaven. At the same time, we recognize our duty to appeal humbly to Him who hath said: 'I will be inquired of my people.' To the end, therefore, that the whole people of these Confederate States may, in union and with one accord, approach the Throne of the Most High, to invoke his blessing upon us in our defensive struggle for the right of self-government, and the enjoyment of the liberty He vouchsafed to

our fathers, and to protect us from those who threaten our homes with fire and sword, our domestic circles with ruthless lust, our fathers' graves with the invaders' feet, and our altars with infidel desecration:

"*Resolved by the Congress of the Confederate States,* That the President be requested to issue his Proclamation, appointing a day of fasting and prayer, in the observance of which all shall be invited to join, who recognize our dependence upon God, and who desire the happiness and security of that people 'whose God is the Lord.'"

It is hardly necessary to say that the preamble and resolution were unanimously adopted.
—*Charleston Courier*, May 18.

Doc. 164.
EAST BALTIMORE RESOLUTIONS,
MAY 14, 1861.

Resolved, That we will still cling to the Union with fidelity and faith, believing that our rights can be better maintained and protected in the Union than out of it, and in pursuance of the above sentiment we do hereby solemnly pledge our lives, our fortunes, and our sacred honors in defence of the same.

Resolved, That the State of Maryland is part and parcel of the Federal Government, and that the said Federal Government has a right to all roads leading through our State; and it is furthermore our duty to protect and assist them in their transit to the National Capital, (in obedience to the call of the President,) which is now threatened by domestic traitors.

Resolved, That the chairman appoint a committee of five, whose duty it shall be to enroll the Union men of East Baltimore, and to make such other arrangements as they may deem necessary for the preservation of our State, honor, and our duty as loyal citizens of the Union.
—*National Intelligencer*, May 17.

Doc. 165.
GEN. BUTLER'S PROCLAMATION.
DEPARTMENT OF ANNAPOLIS, }
FEDERAL HILL, BALTIMORE, May 14, 1861. }

A DETACHMENT of the forces of the Federal Government under my command have occupied the city of Baltimore for the purpose, among other things, of enforcing respect and obedience to the laws, as well of the State—if requested thereto by the civil authorities—as of the United States laws, which are being violated within its limits by some malignant and traitorous men, and in order to testify the acceptance by the Federal Government of the fact that the city and all the well-intentioned portion of its inhabitants are loyal to the Union and the Constitution, and are to be so regarded and treated by all. To the end, therefore, that all misunderstanding of the purpose of the Government may be prevented, and to set at rest all unfounded, false, and seditious rumors; to relieve all apprehensions, if any are felt, by the well-disposed portion of the community, and to make it thoroughly understood by all traitors, their aiders and abettors, that rebellious acts must cease; I hereby, by the authority vested in me as commander of the department of Annapolis, of which Baltimore forms a part, do now command and make known that no loyal and well-disposed citizen will be disturbed in his lawful occupation or business, that private property will not be interfered with by the men under my command, or allowed to be interfered with by others, except in so far as it may be used to afford aid and comfort to those in rebellion against the Government, whether here or elsewhere; all of which property, munitions of war, and that fitted to aid and support the rebellion, will be seized and held subject to confiscation, and, therefore, all manufacturers of arms and munitions of war are hereby requested to report to me forthwith, so that the lawfulness of their occupation may be known and understood, and all misconstruction of their doings be avoided. No transportation from the city to the rebels of articles fitted to aid and support troops in the field will be permitted, and the fact of such transportation, after the publication of this proclamation, will be taken and received as proof of illegal intention on the part of the consignors, and will render the goods liable to seizure and confiscation.

The Government being ready to receive all such stores and supplies, arrangements will be made to contract for them immediately, and the owners and manufacturers of such articles of equipment and clothing, and munitions of war and provisions, are desired to keep themselves in communication with the Commissary-General, in order that their workshops may be employed for loyal purposes, and the artisans of the city resume and carry on their profitable occupations.

The acting Assistant-Quartermaster and Commissary of Subsistence of the United States here stationed, has been instructed to proceed and furnish, at fair prices, 40,000 rations for the use of the army of the United States, and further supplies will be drawn from the city to the full extent of its capacity, if the patriotic and loyal men choose so to furnish supplies.

All assemblages, except the ordinary police, of armed bodies of men, other than those regularly organized and commissioned by the State of Maryland, and acting under the orders of the Governor thereof, for drill and other purposes, are forbidden within the department.

All officers of the militia of Maryland, having command within the limits of the department, are requested to report through their officers forthwith to the General in command, so that he may be able to know and distinguish the regularly commissioned and loyal troops of Maryland from armed bodies who may claim to be such.

The ordinary operations of the corporate government of the city of Baltimore and of the civil authorities will not be interfered with, but, on the contrary, will be aided by all the power at the command of the General, upon proper call being made, and all such authorities are cordially invited to coöperate with the General in command to carry out the purposes set forth in the proclamation, so that the city of Baltimore may be shown to the country to be, what she is in fact, patriotic and loyal to the Union, the Constitution, and the laws.

No flag, banner, ensign, or device of the so-called Confederate States or any of them will be permitted to be raised or shown in this department, and the exhibition of either of them by evil-disposed persons will be deemed, and taken to be evidence of a design to afford aid and comfort to the enemies of the country. To make it the more apparent that the Government of the United States by far more relies upon the loyalty, patriotism, and zeal of the good citizens of Baltimore and vicinity than upon any exhibition of force calculated to intimidate them into that obedience to the laws which the Government doubts not will be paid from inherent respect and love of order, the commanding General has brought to the city with him, of the many thousand troops in the immediate neighborhood, which might be at once concentrated here, scarcely more than an ordinary guard, and until it fails him, he will continue to rely upon that loyalty and patriotism of the citizens of Maryland, which have never yet been found wanting to the Government in time of need. The General in command desires to greet and treat in this part of his department all the citizens thereof as friends and brothers, having a common purpose, a common loyalty, and a common country. Any infractions of the laws by the troops under his command, or any disorderly, unsoldierlike conduct, or any interference with private property, he desires to have immediately reported to him, and pledges himself that if any soldier so far forgets himself as to break those laws that he has sworn to defend and enforce, he shall be most rigorously punished.

The General believes that if the suggestions and requests contained in this proclamation are faithfully carried out by the coöperation of all good and Union-loving citizens, and peace and quiet, and certainty of future peace and quiet are thus restored, business will resume its accustomed channels, trade take the place of dulness and inactivity, efficient labor displace idleness, and Baltimore will be in fact what she is entitled to be, in the front rank of the commercial cities of the nation.

Given at Baltimore, the day and year herein first above written.		BENJ. F. BUTLER,
Brig.-General Com. Department of Annapolis.
E. G. PARKER, Lieut.-Col., Aide-de-Camp.

Gen. Butler's proclamation was scattered in extras by the thousands. Everybody on the streets and in the hotels seemed to have it. The assurance contained in it that the troops were not in their midst to interrupt the business of the city, but to protect the people, preserve the peace, and sustain the laws, gave general satisfaction.

—*N. Y. Commercial Advertiser*, May 15.

Doc. 166.
GOV. HICKS' PROCLAMATION.

Whereas, The President of the United States, by his proclamation of 15th April, 1861, has called upon me, the Governor of Maryland, for four regiments of infantry or riflemen to serve for a period of three months, the said requisition being made in the spirit and in pursuance of the law, and

Whereas, To the said requisition has been added the written assurance of the Secretary of War, that said four regiments shall be detailed to serve within the limits of the State of Maryland, or for the defence of the Capital of the United States and not to serve beyond the limits aforesaid;

Now, therefore, I, Thomas Holliday Hicks, Governor of Maryland, do, by this my proclamation, call upon loyal citizens of Maryland to volunteer their services to the extent of four regiments, as aforesaid, to serve during a period of three months within the limits of Maryland, or for the defence of the capital of the United States, to be subject under the conditions aforesaid, to the orders of the Commander-in-chief of the army of the United States.

Given under my hand and the great seal of the State of Maryland, at the city Frederick, this fourteenth day of May, eighteen hundred and sixty-one.   THOS. H. HICKS.

—*N. Y. Times*, May 16.

Doc. 167.
SECOND CONNECTICUT REGIMENT.
LIST OF OFFICERS.

Colonel, Daniel Tyler, Norwich; Lieut.-Colonel, George S. Burnham, Hartford; Major, John L. Chatfield, Waterbury; Adjutant, Theodore C. Bacon, New Haven; Quartermaster, Justin Hodge, Harkhamsted; Surgeon, C. P. Stearns, Hartford; Surgeon's Mate, Frederick Dibble, New Haven; Sergeant-Major, J. L. Spalding, Norwich; Quartermaster Sergeant, J. V. B. Williams, Preston.

—*National Intelligencer*, May 17.

Doc. 168.
BY THE QUEEN—A PROCLAMATION.

VICTORIA R.

Whereas, We are happily at peace with all Sovereigns, Powers, and States;

And whereas hostilities have unhappily commenced between the Government of the United States of America and certain States styling themselves "the Confederate States of America;"

And whereas we, being at peace with the Government of the United States, have declared our Royal determination to maintain a strict and impartial neutrality in the contest between the said contending parties;

"We, therefore, have thought fit, by and with the advice of our Privy Council, to issue this our Royal Proclamation:

And we do hereby strictly charge and command all our loving subjects to observe a strict neutrality in and during the aforesaid hostilities, and to abstain from violating or contravening either the laws or statutes of the realm in this behalf, or the law of nations in relation thereto, as they will answer to the contrary at their peril.

And *whereas*, in and by a certain statute made and passed in the fifty-ninth year of His Majesty King George III., entitled "an act to prevent the enlisting or engagement of His Majesty's subjects to serve in a foreign service, and the fitting out or equipping, in His Majesty's dominions, vessels for warlike purposes, without His Majesty's license," it is, among other things, declared and enacted as follows:

"That if any natural born subject of His Majesty, his heirs and successors, without the leave or license of His Majesty, his heirs or successors, for that purpose first had and obtained, under the sign manual of His Majesty, his heirs or successors, or signified by Order in Council, or by proclamation of His Majesty, his heirs or successors, shall take or accept, or shall agree to take or accept, any military commission, or shall otherwise enter into the military service as a commissioned or non-commissioned officer, or shall enlist or enter himself to enlist, or shall agree to enlist or to enter himself to serve as a soldier, or to be employed, or shall serve in any warlike or military operation in the service of, or for, or under, or in aid of any foreign Prince, State, Potentate, Colony, Province, or part of any Province or people, or of any person or persons, exercising or assuming to exercise the powers of government in or over any foreign country, colony, province, or part of any province or people, either as an officer or soldier, or in any other military capacity; or if any natural born subject of His Majesty shall, without such leave or license as aforesaid, accept, or agree to take or accept, any commission, warrant or appointment, as an officer, or shall enlist or enter himself, or shall agree to enlist or enter himself, to serve as a sailor or marine, or to be employed or engaged, or shall serve in and on board any ship or vessel of war, or in and on board any ship or vessel used or fitted out, or equipped, or intended to be used for any warlike purpose, in the service of, or for, or under, or in aid of any foreign power, prince, State, potentate, colony, province, or part of any province or people, or of any person or persons exercising or assuming to exercise the powers of government in or over any foreign country, colony, province, or part of any province or people; or, if any natural born subject of His Majesty shall, without such leave and license as aforesaid, engage, contract, or agree to go, or shall go, to any foreign State, country, colony, province, or part of any province, or to any place beyond the seas, with an intent or in order to enlist or enter himself to serve, or with intent to serve, in any warlike or military operation whatever, whether by land or by sea, in the service of, or for, or under, or in aid of any foreign prince, State, potentate, colony, province, or part of any province or people, or in the service of, or for, or under, or in aid of any person or persons exercising or assuming to exercise the powers of government in or over any foreign country, colony, province, or part of any province, or people, either as an officer or a soldier, or in any other military capacity, or an officer or sailor, or marine in any such ship or vessel as aforesaid, although no enlisting money, or pay, or reward shall have been or shall be in any or either of the cases aforesaid actually paid to or received by him, or by any person to or for his use or benefit; or if any person whatever, within the United Kingdom of Great Britain and Ireland, or any part of His Majesty's dominions elsewhere, or in any country, colony, settlement, island or place belonging to or subject to His Majesty, shall hire, retain, engage, or procure, or shall attempt or endeavor to hire, retain, engage, or procure any person or persons whatever to enlist, or enter, or engage to enlist, or to serve or to be employed in any such service or employment as aforesaid, as an officer, soldier, sailor or marine, either in land or sea service, for or under or in aid of any foreign prince, State, potentate, colony, province, or part of any province or people, or for, or under, or in aid of any person or persons exercising or assuming to exercise any powers of government as aforesaid, or to go or to agree to go or embark from any part of His Majesty's dominions, for the purpose or with intent to be enlisted, entered, engaged or employed as aforesaid, whether any enlisting money, pay or reward shall have been or shall be actually given or received, or not; in any or either of such cases every person so offending shall be deemed guilty of a misdemeanor, and upon being convicted thereof, upon any information or indictment, shall be punishable by fine and imprisonment, or either of them, at the discretion of the Court before which such offender shall be convicted."

And it is in and by the said act further enacted:

"That if any person, within any part of the United Kingdom or in any part of His Majesty's dominions beyond the seas, shall without the leave and license of His Majesty, for that purpose first had and obtained as aforesaid, equip, furnish, fit out, or arm, or attempt or endeavor to equip, furnish, fit out, or arm, or procure to be equipped, furnished, fitted out, or armed, or shall knowingly aid, assist, or be concerned in the equipping, furnishing, fitting out, or arming of any ship or vessel, with intent or in order that such ship or vessel shall be employed in the service of any foreign prince, State, or potentate, or of any foreign colony, province, or part of any province or people, or of any person or persons, exercising or assuming to exercise any powers of government in or over any foreign State, colony, province, or part of any province or people, as a transport or store ship, or with intent to cruise or commit hostilities against any prince, State, or potentate, or against the subjects or citizens of any prince, State, or potentate, or against the persons exercising or assuming to exercise the powers of government in any colony, province, or part of any province or country, or against the inhabitants of any foreign colony, province, or part of any province or country, with whom His Majesty shall not then be at war; or shall, within the United Kingdom, or any of His Majesty's dominions, or in any settlement, colony, territory, island, or place belonging or subject to His Majesty, issue or deliver any commission for any ship or vessel to the intent that such ship or vessel shall be employed as aforesaid, every such person so offending shall be deemed guilty of a misdemeanor, and shall upon conviction thereof, upon any information or indictment, be punished by fine and imprisonment, or either of them, at the discretion of the Court in which such offender shall be convicted; and every such ship or vessel, with the tackle, apparel, and furniture, together with all the materials, arms, ammunition and stores which may belong to or be on board of any such ship or vessel, shall be forfeited; and it shall be lawful for any officer of His Majesty's Customs or Excise, or any officer of His Majesty's navy, who is by law empowered to make seizures, for any forfeiture incurred under any of the laws of Customs or Excise, or the laws of trade and navigation, to seize such ships and vessels aforesaid, and in such places and in such manner in which the officers of His Majesty's Customs or Excise and the officers of His Majesty's navy are empowered respectively to make seizures under the laws of Customs and Excise, or under the laws of trade and navigation; and that every ship and vessel, with the tackle, apparel, and furniture, together with all the materials, arms, ammunition, and stores which may belong to or be on board of such ship or vessel, may be prosecuted and condemned in the like manner, and in such courts as ships or vessels may be prosecuted and condemned for any breach of the laws made for the protection of the revenues of Customs and Excise, or of the laws of trade and navigation."

And it is in and by the said act further enacted:

"That if any person in any part of the United Kingdom of Great Britain and Ireland, or in any part of His Majesty's dominions beyond the seas, without leave and license of His Majesty, for that purpose first had and obtained as aforesaid, shall, by adding to the number of the guns of such vessel, or by changing those on board for other guns, or by the addition of any equipment for war, increase or augment, or procure to be increased or augmented, or shall be knowingly concerned in increasing or augmenting the warlike force of any ship or vessel of war or cruiser, or other armed vessel, which at the time of her arrival in any part of the United Kingdom, or any of His Majesty's dominions, was a ship of war, cruiser, or armed vessel in the service of any foreign prince, State, or potentate, or of any person or persons exercising or assuming to exercise any powers of government in or over any colony, province, or part of any province or people belonging to the subjects of any such prince, State, or potentate, or to the inhabitants of any colony, province, or part of any province or country under the control of any person or persons so exercising or assuming to exercise the powers of government, every such person so offending shall be deemed guilty of a misdemeanor, and shall, upon being convicted thereof, upon any information or indictment, be punished by fine and imprisonment, or either of them, at the discretion of the Court before which such offender shall be convicted."

Now, in order that none of our subjects may unwarily render themselves liable to the penalties imposed by the said statute, we do hereby strictly command, that no person or persons whatsoever do commit any act, matter or thing whatsoever, contrary to the provisions of the said statute, upon pain of the several penalties by the said statute imposed, and of our high displeasure.

And we do hereby further warn all our loving subjects, and all persons whatsoever entitled to our protection, that if any of them shall presume, in contempt of this Royal Proclamation, and of our high displeasure, to do any acts in derogation of their duty as subjects of a neutral sovereign, in the said contest, or in violation or contravention of the law of nations in that behalf—as, for example and more especially, by entering into the military service of either of the said contending parties as commissioned or non-commissioned officers or soldiers; or by serving as officers, sailors, or marines on board any ship or vessel of war or transport of or in the service of either of the said contending parties; or by serving as officers, sailors, or marines on board any privateer bearing letters of marque of or from either of the said contending parties; or by engaging to go or going to any place beyond the seas with intent to enlist or engage in any such service, or by procuring or attempting to procure within Her Majesty's dominions, at home or abroad, others to do so; or by fitting out, arming or equipping any ship or vessel to be employed as a ship-of-war, or privateer, or transport, by either of the said contending parties; or by breaking, or endeavoring to break, any blockade lawfully and actually established by or on behalf of either of the said contending parties; or by carrying officers, soldiers, despatches, arms, military stores or materials, or any article or articles considered and deemed to be contraband of war according to the law of modern usage of nations, for the use or service of either of the said contending parties, all persons so offending will incur and be liable to the several penalties and penal consequences by the said statute, or by the law of nations, in that behalf imposed or denounced.

And we do hereby declare that all our subjects and persons entitled to our protection who may misconduct themselves in the premises will do so at their peril and of their own wrong, and that they will in nowise obtain any protection from us against any liability or penal consequences, but will, on the contrary, incur our high displeasure by such misconduct.

Given at our Court at the White Lodge, Richmond Park, this 13th day of May, in the year of our Lord 1861, and in the 24th year of our reign.

GOD save the QUEEN.
—*London Gazette,* May 14.

DISCUSSION IN THE HOUSE OF LORDS.

In the House of Lords, on the 16th ult., the Earl of Ellenborough said he wished to put a question to his noble friend the Lord President, on the subject of Her Majesty's recent proclamation. It seemed to him to be of essential importance that the proclamation which instructed Her Majesty's subjects how they were to conduct themselves with regard to the unfortunate war which now existed in America, should be so clear and unambiguous, that it should not be necessary for a man to consult his lawyer how it should be interpreted, or if he did consult his lawyer, that the lawyer should have the means of giving a clear answer, which as things now stood, he did not think he had. As to the law of England, the proclamation was clear enough, but it was different with regard to that part which treated of the law of nations. A great deal of doubt existed as to the meaning of the proclamation on that point. Her Majesty's subjects were "warned not to break or endeavor to break any blockade lawfully and actually established by either of the belligerent parties." Now, he wanted to know in what sense they were to understand the expression, lawfully and actually established. They were at present under an obligation to adhere to the Maritime law agreed to by the Plenipotentiaries at the Congress of Paris, which declared that, "in order to be binding, a blockade must be an effectual blockade"—that was to say, that it should be maintained by a force sufficient to prevent access to the enemy's coasts. If these words were to be understood in their strict literal signification, a blockade was a thing almost physically impossible, because no nation in the world possessed a fleet large enough for this purpose. It must, therefore, be capable of receiving some explanation. Blockades were carried on by ships at sea, and by ships under sail, because no ships could carry coal enough to keep up a constant blockade by steam. During the war of the Revolution, he recollected, when their ships were blockading Toulon, they were on one occasion driven by storm across the Mediterranean to the coasts of Africa. Such an event might occur again, and, according to the strict literal meaning of the words, if it did, it would not be an effective blockade. Therefore, the words must be susceptible of some explanation, and he thought they must be understood with that qualification which commanded all the operations of man at sea—namely, wind and weather. If the words were to be taken with that qualification, then he thought it was to be regretted that Her Majesty's Government, instead of adopting words totally new, had not adopted the usual form, namely, "lawfully established and effectually maintained," because a blockade was not lawful unless it was effectual. He wished to know in what sense they were to understand the words used in the proclamation. Did they intend to convey the exact meaning of the words used in the Treaty of Paris, or, on the other hand, did they intend to qualify it? As to the second question, he could not help regretting that there was so much vagueness in the expression, "contraband of war according to the law and modern usage of nations." How were plain men to find out what was considered contraband of war by the law and modern usage of nations? They must look to all the recent decisions of the Courts of Admiralty, not only in this, but in foreign countries, and it was probable that those decisions would be found conflicting. He wished to know what were the further articles not mentioned, to which the proclamation applied, and which Her Majesty's subjects were cautioned not to convey. He apprehended that the articles contraband of war were constantly changing, and followed all the alterations made in the mode of conducting war. The time was when the armor alone would have been considered contraband of war. But he thought he had read in books of law that all these changes were controlled by one principle, which was *that contraband of war was that which, in the possession of an enemy, would enable him the better to carry on the war.* That was clear, reasonable, and intelligible to every one. He regretted that Her Majesty's Government did not go back to that principle which all could understand, instead of using new words; he therefore wished to know what were the articles not mentioned to which the proclamation referred.

Earl Granville said the questions put by the noble Earl were very important and very difficult to answer. At the same time it was his duty to give the noble Earl all the information in his power. If, however, he fell into any mistake on the subject, he should feel grateful to any noble and learned lord on either side of the house to correct him. With regard to the first question as to the meaning of the words

"lawful and actual blockade," he thought the noble Earl somewhat embarrassed the question by referring to the Declaration of the Congress of Paris. He apprehended that no change had been made by that Declaration as regarded those countries who were not parties to that agreement. The question of international law remained the same as previously, except with regard to paper blockades, which were formerly held to be good. *There was no doubt that blockade was lawfully and actually established, if maintained in a proper form and manner, and by such a force as to make it, not impossible, but difficult, for vessels to enter or come out.* It was more difficult to give an answer to the second question put by the noble Earl. But the Government pursued the same course on the present occasion as had formerly been pursued. The noble Earl had partially answered his own question, because he had admitted that the meaning of contraband of war must vary with the changes in the mode of conducting war. Certain articles were clearly contraband of war, and the character of others could only be determined by the decision of the prize courts. Her Majesty's Government, therefore, had pursued a wise course, in his opinion, in not specifying what was contraband of war. [Hear, hear.]

The Earl of Derby said the answer of the noble Earl was entirely satisfactory. He did not feel inclined to complain of the terms of the proclamation as being vague and uncertain. It was impossible to introduce such a definition of a blockade, or of contraband of war, as his noble friend seemed to wish should be laid down. Nor did he complain of the proclamation as going beyond the necessity of the case—he meant as to the warning given to all British subjects with regard to their taking part in privateering expeditions. The proclamation wisely and properly informed the subjects of Her Majesty that whatever might be the result, if they engaged in these expeditions they would have no right to claim the protection of this country in case of any penal consequences arising from their own act. He did not complain of that extensive and solemn warning being given. But there were two points upon which it was absolutely necessary that Her Majesty's Government should lose no time in coming to a thorough understanding with the Government of the United States. First, with regard to this blockade, the Northern States have given notice of their intention to blockade the whole of the Southern ports. Now they knew that even if the fleet of the United States was three times as numerous as it was, it was not in their power to effectually blockade the whole coast of the Southern States; and though, no doubt, they might effectually blockade a port here and there, it was important that Her Majesty's Government should not commit themselves to the doctrine that the United States were to lay down the principle of a universal blockade, or that that universal blockade would be recognized by Her Majesty, or that all Her Majesty's subjects would be liable to penalties. Her Majesty's Government should make it clearly understood that a mere paper blockade, alleged to extend over a wide extent of coast which it was impossible to blockade, would not be recognized as valid by the British Government. But there was another more important point. Words had been used by his noble and learned friend on a previous occasion, which, coming from such high authority, might give rise to serious consequences if misconstructed. His noble and learned friend said that by the law of nations privateering was piracy, and if that were so, the Northern States would be justified in carrying out the theory and treating privateering as piracy. *He apprehended that if any thing was clearer than another, it was that privateering was not piracy, and that no law could make that piracy, as regarded the subjects of one nation, which was not piracy by the law of nations.* (Hear, hear.) *Consequently the United States must not be allowed to entertain this doctrine, and to call upon Her Majesty's Government not to interfere.* They must not strain the law so as to visit with penalty of death, as for piracy, persons entitled to Her Majesty's protection. That was a question which could not be viewed with indifference, but must be seriously considered by the Government. It is quite right that the people of this country should be warned of the peril; but, on the other hand, it was essential that the United States should not be induced to deny the general interpretation of international law, and to inflict a punishment on privateering which was never inflicted by that law. He knew it was said that the United States treated the Confederate States of the South as mere rebels, and that as rebels these expeditions were liable to all the penalties of high treason. That was not the doctrine of this country, because we have declared that they are entitled to all the rights of belligerents. The Northern States could not claim the rights of belligerents for themselves, and, on the other hand, deal with other parties not as belligerents, but as rebels. These were the two points on which it was most desirable that no misunderstanding should exist between the Government of Her Majesty and the United States—that we would not recognize any thing but a clear and effectual blockade actually enforced, and that we would not recognize the doctrine that any declaration or law of the United States against the Southern States should have the power, as regarded others, of constituting privateering piracy, and visiting it with all the penalties attached to piracy. (Hear, hear.)

Lord Brougham said it was clear that privateering was not piracy by the law of nations, however much it might be lamented that it was not so. But if any person or subject of this country entered into an expedition against another country, with which we were at peace, that was of itself a piratical act, and they had

themselves to blame who, after full warning, chose to take that course, and could not expect their Government to interpose to save them from the extreme penalties attached to that course. As had been said in the previous discussion upon this subject, their blood would be upon their own heads. With regard to articles contraband of war, it would have been much better if the Government could have introduced some invariable, certain, and definite descriptions, but with the progress in naval science things become contraband of war which were not so before, and it was impossible, therefore, to lay down any fixed or invariable terms. He entirely agreed with his noble friend in holding that it was not necessary to constitute a blockade that every port of the coast should be so blockaded as to make entrance impossible, but it was enough that it should be made such as to afford a reasonable chance that no entrance could be effected.

Lord Chelmsford thought it might be as well to bring his noble and learned friend's opinion to a test. The Southern Confederation was admitted by the Government of this country to be a belligerent Power. Now, he wanted to know whether his noble and learned friend meant to say that if an Englishman was commissioned by the Southern Confederation—it being recognized as a belligerent Power—to fit out a privateer against the Federal Government, that that person, under those circumstances, would be guilty of piracy. *That he ought to be, was the opinion of many judges.* [The Lord Chancellor: *"No, No."*] *Well, it was the opinion of many.* Now, undoubtedly those persons would be answerable to their own Government for an infraction of the Foreign Enlistment Act; but it was clear, upon the question of international law, that they would not be liable to be treated as pirates. The warning given by the proclamation was very useful and most necessary; and if persons would engage in expeditions of this kind after the notice that the Government would not interfere, they must take the consequences they had drawn upon themselves. If the Southern Confederacy had not been recognized as a belligerent Power, he agreed with his noble and learned friend, that, under those circumstances, if any Englishman were to fit out a privateer for the purpose of assisting the Southern States against the Northern States, he would be guilty of piracy. (Hear, hear.) And the question arose, after the abdication of James II., when he commissioned persons to fit out enterprises against the commerce of this country. The question arose after James II. had been expelled from Ireland, and when he had not a foot of territory there, and when, therefore, he was merely claiming the right *de jure.* Now the question came before the Lords of the Privy Council, and they desired to have the opinions of learned civilians, and a report was given in a very grave and curious way by Dr. Tindal, who was one of the counsel. Sir

Thomas Pinfold had asserted that those persons were not pirates, and for a very strange reason—he said he argued against this being piracy, as it was impossible they could be pirates, for a pirate was *hostis humani generis*—but they were not enemies to all mankind, and therefore they were not pirates. (Laughter.) Whereupon, the report said, "all smiled." (Renewed laughter.) And he was asked if there was any such thing as piracy, if to be a pirate a man must be at war with all mankind? To which, as was natural, Sir Thomas made no reply, but only repeated what he had laid down before. (Laughter) Upon which one of the Lords of the Privy Council pressed the learned civilian with another question. He said: "Supposing any of His Majesty's subjects, by virtue of a commission of the late King, should by force seize the goods of their fellow-subjects by land—whether that would excuse them from being guilty at least of robbery; and if it would not of robbery, why should it more excuse them of piracy?" To which he made no reply. Now it was perfectly clear, under these circumstances, that those parties would be guilty of piracy, but he thought it was equally clear that in the case assumed by his noble and learned friend they would not be guilty of piracy. That was a matter that ought to be clearly understood, and as his noble and learned friend had, he thought, left it in some uncertainty, he had taken the liberty of trespassing upon their lordships' attention—(hear.)

The Lord Chancellor said his noble friend, the President of the Council, had laid down the law upon this subject in a perfectly correct manner. There was no doubt that if an Englishman engaged in the service of the Southern States, he violated the laws of the country and rendered himself liable to punishment, and that he had no right to trust to the protection of his native country to shield him from the consequences of his act. *But though that individual would be guilty of a breach of the law of his own country, he could not be treated as a pirate, and those who treated him as a pirate would be guilty of murder.* (Hear, hear.)

Lord Kingsdown said, *as to the state of the law there could be no doubt a privateer acting under a Government was not a pirate.* No doubt the United States did not put the extravagant proclamation they had issued upon the ground that privateers were pirates, because they themselves insisted upon the right of privateering. But they put it upon this ground, that they were dealing with rebels, and that they would hang them not, properly speaking, as pirates, but as persons who were guilty of high treason against the State to which they were subject. (Hear, hear.) Of course it was a matter for their own consideration what was to be the operation of that proclamation. He believed that the enforcement of that doctrine would be an act of barbarity which would produce an outcry throughout the civilized world, but he hoped that it was a mere *brutum ful-*

men, and not intended to be carried out. But that being the case with regard to their own country, the case with regard to England was quite different. We had recognized the Southern Confederacy, not as an independent State, but as a belligerent Power; and therefore, *if the Federal Government should act upon the principle they had laid down as against British subjects, he apprehended that this Government might with perfect justice interfere, and under some circumstances they might, by the influence of public opinion, be compelled to interfere.* (Hear, hear.). Yet, at the same time, the offender could not as a right, having acted in violation of the feeling of his own country, and therefore of his own Government, call upon his Government to interfere. That, he apprehended, was the state of the case, and he must say he thought it impossible that the Government could have framed the proclamation more prudently than they had done with respect to articles contraband of war. For instance, provisions might become contraband of war, if sent to a port where there was an army of a State at war, and that army was in great want of provisions. Again, coals sent to a country at war, if sent for manufacturing purposes, were not contraband of war; but they would become so if sent where there were war steamers, and for the purpose of supplying those war steamers. It was, therefore, quite impossible to frame a proclamation under which there would be no difficulty of definition. With respect to the matter of blockade, the practice had been very much modified and altered by the introduction of steam, as one steamship would take the ground of a number of sailing vessels; but it had been held that a blockade could not be constituted by drawing a line which would prevent vessels from going to particular ports to which they had a right to go.

Lord Brougham hoped and trusted that all persons would take notice of the warning given in the proclamation that British subjects serving in the American war must run the risk of whatever penalty they might be liable to, whether they served on the one side or the other, at sea or on land. *A case had occurred about thirty years ago, where two British subjects were tried and hanged for piratical interference on land, and no step was taken to save their lives or avenge their death.*

The Earl of Ellenborough said the object of the proclamation was certainly to deter Englishmen from engaging on either side in war in America, and they were told that if they acted in this respect against the law of their country and against the law of nations, they must not expect any protection from the British Government. But he very much feared that a great deal that had passed that night would tend much to diminish the effect of the proclamation. He only hoped that it would not do so, because he was quite sure that long before diplomacy could interfere in the matter, the offender would be hanged.

THE PRESS ON THE DEBATE.

The answer that can be given to Lord Ellenborough is, that a blockade must be, on the one hand, a great deal more than a mere paper prohibition. A hen may be induced to believe that a broad chalk line forms a barrier which she cannot pass, but mankind have a right to require that before their natural liberty be taken from them, something more substantial shall be interposed between them and the port they desire to enter. On the other hand, *it would be absurd to say that a blockade shall not be respected unless it be completely effective.* Such a rule would be to invite a perpetual breaking of blockades, since the very fact of a successful evasion would prove conclusively, according to the definition, that it was no blockade at all, on the same principle that treason never prospers, because rebellion, when triumphant, ceases to be treason.

Still less reasonable was the complaint of Lord Ellenborough, that the proclamation did not enable plain men to find out what articles are contraband of war. Until some means can be devised of defining, not only all that has been, but all that will be invented by the perverse ingenuity of man, acting upon a very rapidly increasing development of physical science, for the systematic destruction of his fellow-creatures, it will be utterly impossible to point out beforehand what is to be considered contraband of war. The most harmless materials, when taken alone—the ingredients of gunpowder, for instance—when associated together, may produce the most deleterious compounds ; and things apparently quite unconnected with war—such as food and fuel, for instance—may, with reference to the purpose with which they were shipped, assume a highly contraband character. War is a great exploder of fiction ; its conduct and its rules are based upon the very sternest of all stern and practical realities. It eludes the attempt to circumscribe it by metaphysical definitions, and bases itself instead upon the laws of nature and the possibilities open to us by the discoveries of physical science. A topic far more worthy of mature consideration than the questions proposed by Lord Ellenborough, was the doctrine with regard to "privateering" enunciated by Lord Derby. The argument of Lord Derby seems to be that the North, by declaring a blockade of the Southern ports, claims from neutral nations the respect due to its rights as a belligerent Power ; and, therefore, that, whatever the North may choose to do with the citizens of the Southern States captured on board the privateers fitted out under letters of marque from Mr. Jefferson Davis, the North has no right to treat the belligerent rights of the South as a nullity with regard to the subjects of countries from whom it claims respect for its own belligerent rights. The result would be that the North, by declaring a blockade of the Southern ports, has bound itself not to execute as pirates the subjects of

Doc.—27

neutral States serving on board such privateers. The argument is one of great subtlety and refinement, and seemed to receive confirmation from the arguments of subsequent speakers. It is clear that English subjects serving on board an American "privateer" are not pirates, though, if they choose so to act, the English Government, by the Proclamation, seems to avow its intention of leaving them to a pirate's fate. It may possibly deserve consideration whether this decision can be strictly adhered to. At any rate, we cannot doubt that the authoritative declaration of the law by so many judges of eminent authority, will go very far to prevent the danger apprehended, and may possibly be the means of introducing into the very commencement of a dreadful civil war those principles of humanity and moderation, the operation of which might otherwise be suspended until enforced and demonstrated by the barbarous logic of reprisals.

—London Times.

The uniform tenor of intelligence from the United States cannot be expected to please the secret sympathizers with the Secessionists, or the still more numerous class among us who, dwelling rather upon differences between the forms of administrative Government in England and America than upon their common possession of Anglican liberty, have disqualified themselves for fairly judging the acts of the Federal Administration. It is now seen how false and shallow were the estimates of the Washington Government, which, until lately, obtained currency here. Simply because people did not know what Mr. Lincoln was doing, they were quite sure they knew he was doing nothing. The favorite argument from ignorance has never been carried further. All who had paid any attention to American affairs knew well enough what the President must be about. The slight and flimsy work for doing which Jefferson Davis got unmeasured praise, was nothing to that which had to be done. At Montgomery they had simply to make a government. Mr. Lincoln had also to do that ; but he also had to unmake one. He had to destroy the coils which Southern traitors had taken care to wind about the new President, to dispossess a whole army of disaffected officers before it was safe to venture a single step. The instant that was effected the whole scene changed. The North then displayed a military energy which has astonished the South, and which has already changed the tone of the Secessionists. Instead of the cheap boast of a march to Washington, the braggarts at Montgomery are whining about their rights, and thinking how best to defend themselves from the justice which is shortly to call them to account. The force at the disposal of the Federal Government is overwhelming. So obvious has this fact become, that a new difficulty is started, and those who were lately chiding Mr. Lincoln for not exerting himself, now insist that it is all in vain, and ask incredulously what he is going to do. And here, again, as Governments do not usually publish the plans of their campaigns, the argument from ignorance appears to great advantage. For our parts, we prefer to notice from day to day the success which attends Mr. Lincoln's action. The progress of disintegration has been stopped with a strong hand, and in States which, like Maryland and Virginia, were falling under the tyranny of the lawless and violent, enlightened and peaceable citizens are recovering their due influence. From the Ohio to the Gulf of Mexico men talk more reasonably, and if the voice of patriotism gains a hearing there, it will be because Mr. Lincoln has so ordered it. If the destinies of the Union are to be submitted to the arbitrament of war, he has acted wisely. If a peaceful separation, with all the difficulties attendant upon such questions as tariffs, extradition treaties, division of territories, and the like, is to be attempted, we say again he has taken the only prudent course, for no settlement could be lasting if made under the menace of a Slave Power.

All the facts that come to hand only place in a stronger light the duty which lies upon neutral Powers, and above all upon England, of leaving the people of the United and Confederate States to settle this quarrel in their own way. The English Government has done its duty in issuing the Proclamation which lately appeared in our columns, and which was the subject of an important discussion on Thursday evening in the House of Lords. The manifold relations between this country and the American States, the probability that one of the parties now engaged in civil war will apply to British subjects for aid, and importance to the North of being able to close up the Southern ports, made it desirable that the law upon the various legal questions which may arise should be clearly defined. After perusing the speeches of the various eminent lawyers who delivered their opinions upon the points mooted by Lord Ellenborough, it must be confessed that the unanimity of opinion is not so striking as might be desired. It is necessary to bear in mind continually that ministers have determined to grant to both parties in America—the North and the South—belligerent rights. The meaning of this is, that England is prepared to treat the United States and the Confederate States as two Powers, not, indeed, independent, but at war with each other, and entitled to belligerent rights. England, therefore, occupies towards each of them the position of a neutral, and is bound to conduct herself with perfect impartiality to both parties. The fact, however, that to us these parties occupy such a position as entitles them to belligerent rights, does not alter the relations of the North and South to each other. President Lincoln may still regard himself as President of the thirty-three United States and may treat Jefferson Davis and his followers as traitors and rebels. *In strict law it must be admitted that the South cannot claim to be at war with the North, for in the eyes of the Northern constitutionalists the South has no independent existence.* As Lord Kingsdown said, whether President Lincoln chooses to treat the Southern seceders literally as rebels must be matter for his own consideration, but he could not help thinking that to act upon such a view would be to have recourse to a piece of barbarity which would raise an outcry throughout the whole civilized world. If, then, President Lincoln and his Cabinet adopt the opinion of Lord Kingsdown, there can be no doubt that any citizen of a Southern State—although a rebel—will be entitled, if taken by the North, to all the rights of an enemy.

—*London News.*

Doc. 169.

BISHOP WHITTINGHAM'S CIRCULAR.

REVEREND AND DEAR BROTHER: I have learned, with extreme regret, that in several instances, the "Prayer for the President of the United States, and all in Civil authority," has been omitted, of late, in the performance of divine service in the diocese.

Such omission, in every case, makes the clergyman liable for presentment for wilful violation of his ordination vow, by mutilation of the worship of the Church, and I shall hold myself bound to act on any evidence of such offence laid before me, after the issue of this circular.

I beseech my brethren to remember that current events have settled any question that might have been started concerning citizenship and allegiance. Maryland is admitted and declared by the Legislature and Governor of the State, to be at this time one of the United States of America. As resident in Maryland, the clergy of this diocese are citizens of the United States, and bound to the recognition and discharge of all duties appertaining to that condition. It is clearly such a duty by the express word of God, to make supplication and prayer for the Chief Magistrate of the Union, and for all that are in authority, that we may lead a quiet and peaceable life, in all godliness and honesty ; and it is clearly my duty, by the same direction, to put those whom God has committed to my charge in mind to be subject to principalities and powers, to obey magistrates, to speak evil of no man, to be no brawlers.

To my deep distress and disgust I have too much reason to fear that in at least one instance a minister of Christ may have so far forgot himself, his place and his duty, as actually to commit the canonical offence known as "brawling in Church," while venturing to do what an archangel durst not do, and to defend transgression of an injunction of the Word of God.

We of the clergy have no right to intrude our private views of the questions which are so terribly dividing those among whom we minister, into the place assigned us that we may speak for God, and minister in His worship. Still less claim have we to assume to frame and fashion the devotions of our brethren by our private notions, and to that end mutilate or interpolate the service of the Church. In such times as these we are more strictly than ever bound to adhere to the precise letter of prescribed form, and to deserve the praise of non-interference with others' rights by the closest seclusion within the limits of our own plain duty.

It is not merely my advice, dear brother, but it is the solemn injunction and caution of the Word of God, to be reverenced and regarded accordingly as you believe it to be His: " My son, fear thou the Lord and the King, and meddle not with them that are given to change; for their calamity shall rise suddenly; and who knoweth of them both? These things belong to the wise."

Your loving friend and brother,
WM. R. WHITTINGHAM,
Bishop of Maryland.

BALTIMORE, May 15, 1861.

—*N. Y. Times*, May 21.

Doc. 169½.

THE TAKING OF POTOSI, MO.

THE Union men of Washington county having been threatened with extermination, and some of them having been driven from Potosi, the county seat, complaint was made to Gen. Lyon, of the St. Louis Arsenal, and that brave and gallant officer determined to give the Union men in that section of the country protection. Accordingly an expedition was planned and put under the command of Capt. Coles, of company A, Fifth Regiment of U. S. Volunteers. At 10 o'clock, P. M., Tuesday, May 14th, Capt. Cole's command, consisting of some 150 men, left the Arsenal on a special train for their destination. They arrived at Potosi at 3 o'clock, A. M., on Wednesday, and immediately threw a chain of sentinels around the entire town. Guards were then stationed around the dwellings of the most prominent secessionists, and, shortly after daylight, some 150 men found themselves prisoners, and were marched off to the Court House. Here the prisoners were formed in line, and by the assistance of a gentleman who had been driven out of Potosi, who knew all the inhabitants of the place, the Union men were recognized and released, amounting to over half of those taken prisoners. Some fifty of the secessionists were also released, on parole of honor, after subscribing to the usual oath, *not to take up arms against the United States*, and nine of the leaders were marched off to the cars. The guard then made a descent on a secession lead manufactory, and captured near four hundred pigs of that very useful article in time of war, which belonged to a man who had been furnishing lead

to the Southern rebels. The man's name is John Dean, and he is now a prisoner at the Arsenal. It appears he was not satisfied to simply sell the lead to the enemy, in defiance of the authority of the Government, but was engaged with his own team in hauling it to near the Arkansas line, where the traitors could get possession of it without danger. The guard captured several pistols, rifles, shot guns, and a quantity of secession uniforms, most of them unfinished, and some uniform cloth.

After being furnished with breakfast and dinner, and very handsomely treated by the Union men of Potosi, and invited to stay a month in that place, at their expense, the command started for home. On their way back, the train made a halt at De Soto, in Jefferson county, where there was to be a grand secession " love feast" and flag-raising. Here they found a company of secession cavalry drilling for the occasion, which took to their heels as soon as they got a sight of the United States troop. In their flight, the cavalry left some 30 of their horses, which were captured by the troops and placed under guard. The pole, one hundred feet high, on which the rebels were going to fly the secession flag, was soon graced with the Stars and Stripes, amid the wildest enthusiasm of the Union men and Government troops. The next move was to capture the rebel flag, which was known to be in town, and for this agreeable duty, Captain Cole detailed a guard of six men, under command of Sergeant Walker, accompanied by Dr. Franklin, Surgeon of the Fifth Regiment. The guard surrounded the house supposed to contain the flag, and Dr. Franklin and Sergeant Walker entered. After searching in vain for some time, the Doctor thought he observed the lady of the house sitting in rather an uneasy position, and he very politely asked her to rise. At first the lady hesitated, but finding the Doctor's persuasive sauvity irresistible, she rose slowly, and lo! the blood red stripe of the rebel ensign appeared below the lady's hoops. The Doctor, bowing a graceful " beg pardon, madam," stooped and quietly catching hold of the gaudy color, carefully delivered the lady of a secession flag, thirty feet long and nine feet wide. The Doctor bore off his prize in triumph to the camp, where the troops greeted him with wild shouts, and characterized his feat as the crowning glory of the occasion. Here the troops captured another rebel leader, and after placing thirty men under Lieutenant Murphy, to guard the Union flag, and the thirty horses, Capt. Cole's command started on their way. At Victoria, the train stopped a moment, when another secessionist came up hurrahing for Jeff. Davis, and quick as thought the ardent rebel was surrounded by a half dozen bayonets, and marched into the cars a prisoner of war, and the train moved on. They arrived at the Arsenal about 6 1-2 o'clock, P. M, where a crowd of soldiers and visitors awaited them. The spoils were unloaded, and the prisoners marched to safe and comfortable quarters.—Gen. Lyon received them in the spirit of a true soldier, and the troops gave three cheers for Gen. Lyon, three for Col. Blair and three for the Stars and Stripes, and then caught the Secession flag and tore it into shreds in a twinkling.

—*St. Louis Democrat*, May 17.

Doc. 170.

LETTER OF SENATOR MASON

ON THE VIRGINIA ELECTION.

To the Editor of the Winchester Virginian:—

The question has been frequently put to me, What position will Virginia occupy, should the ordinance of secession be rejected by the people at the approaching election? And the frequency of the question may be an excuse for giving publicity to the answer.

The ordinance of secession withdrew the State of Virginia from the Union, with all the consequences resulting from the separation. It annulled the Constitution and the laws of the United States within the limits of this State, and absolved the citizens of Virginia from all obligations and obedience to them.

Hence it follows, if this ordinance be rejected by the people, the State of Virginia will remain in the Union, and the people of the State will remain bound by the Constitution of the United States, and obedience to the Government and the laws of the United States will be fully and rightfully enforced against them.

It follows, of course, that in this war now carried on by the Government of the United States against the seceding States, Virginia must immediately *change sides*, and, under the orders of that Government, *turn her arms against her Southern sisters.*

From this there can be no escape. As a member of the Union, all her resources of men and money will be at once at the command of the Government of the Union:

Again: For mutual defence, immediately after the Ordinance of Secession passed, a treaty, or "military league" was formed by the Convention, in the name of the people of Virginia, with the Confederate States of the South, by which the latter were bound to march to the aid of our State, against the invasion of the Federal Government. And we have now in Virginia, at Harper's Ferry, and at Norfolk, in face of the common foe, several thousand of the gallant sons of South Carolina, of Alabama, of Louisiana, Georgia, and Mississippi, who hastened to fulfil the covenant they made, and are ready and eager to lay down their lives, side by side, with our sons in defence of the soil of Virginia.

If the Ordinance of Secession is rejected, not only will this "military league" be annulled, but it will have been made a trap to inveigle our generous defenders into the hands of their enemies.

Virginia remaining in the Union, duty and loyalty to her obligations to the Union will require that those Southern forces shall not be permitted to leave the State, but shall be delivered up to the Government of the Union; and those who refuse to do so, will be guilty of treason, and be justly dealt with as traitors.

Treason against the United States consists, as well "in adhering to its enemies and giving them aid," as in levying war.

If it be asked, what are those to do who in their consciences cannot vote to separate Virginia from the United States—the answer is simple and plain: honor and duty alike require that they should not vote on the question; if they retain such opinions, they must leave the State.

None can doubt or question the truth of what I have written, and none can vote against the ordinance of secession, who do not thereby (whether ignorantly or otherwise) vote to place himself and his State in the position I have indicated.   J. M. MASON.

WINCHESTER, VA., May 16, 1861.

—*Winchester Virginian*, May 22.

Doc. 171.

GENERAL BUTLER'S SPEECH,

AT WASHINGTON, MAY 16, 1861.

FELLOW-CITIZENS:—Your cheers for the old Commonwealth of Massachusetts are rightly bestowed. Foremost in the rank of those who fought for the liberty of the country in the Revolution were the men of Massachusetts. It is a historical fact, to which I take pride in now referring, that in the Revolution, Massachusetts sent more men south of Mason and Dixon's Line to fight for the cause of the country, than all the Southern Colonies put together; and in this second war, if war must come, to proclaim the Declaration of Independence anew, and, as a necessary consequence, establish the Union and the Constitution, Massachusetts will give, if necessary, every man in her borders—aye, and woman! (Cheers.) I trust I may be excused for speaking thus of Massachusetts; but I am confident there are many within the sound of my voice, whose hearts beat with proud memories of the old Commonwealth. There is this difference, I will say, between our Southern brothers and ourselves, that while we love our State with the true love of a son, we love the Union and the Country with an equal devotion. (Loud and prolonged applause.) We place no "States' rights" before, above, or beyond the Union. (Cheers.) To us our country is first, because it is our country, (three cheers,) and our State is next and second, because she is a part of our country and our State. (Renewed applause.) Our oath of allegiance to our country, and our oath of allegiance to our State, are interwreathed harmoniously, and never come in conflict or clash. He who does his duty to the Union does his duty to the State; and he who does his duty to the State, does his duty to the Union—"one and inseparable, now and forever." (Renewed applause.) As I look upon this demonstration of yours, I believe it to be prompted by a love of the common cause, and our common country—a country so great and good, a Government so kind, so beneficent, that the hand from which we have only felt kindness is now for the first time raised in chastisement. (Applause.) Many things in a man's life may be worse than death. So, to a Government there may be many things, such as dishonor and disintegration, worse than the shedding of blood. (Cheers.) Our fathers purchased our liberty and country for us at an immense cost of treasure and blood, and by the bright heavens above us, we will not part with them without first paying the original debt, and the interest to this date! (Loud cheers.) We have in our veins the same blood as they shed ; we have the same power of endurance, the same love of liberty and law. We will hold as a brother him who stands by the Union ; we will hold as an enemy him who would strike from its constellation a single star. (Applause.) But, I hear some one say, "Shall we carry on this fratricidal war ? Shall we shed our brothers' blood, and meet in arms our brothers in the South ? " I would say, "As our fathers did not hesitate to strike the mother country in the defence of our rights, so we should not hesitate to meet the brother as they did the mother." (Sensation.) If this unholy, this fratricidal war is forced upon us, I say, " Woe, woe to them who have made the necessity. Our hands are clean, our hearts are pure ; but the Union must be preserved, (Gen. Butler was interrupted here by an intense cheering. When silence was restored, he continued :) at all hazard of money, and, if need be, of every life this side the Arctic Regions." (Cheers.) If the 25,000 Northern soldiers who are here are cut off, in six weeks 50,000 will take your place ; and if they die by fever, pestilence, or the sword, a quarter of a million will take their place, till our army of the reserve will be women with their broomsticks, to drive every enemy in the Gulf. (Cheers and laughter.) I have neither fear nor doubt of the issue. I feel only horror and dismay for those who have made the war. God help them! we are here for our rights, for our country, for our flag. Our faces are set South, and there shall be no footstep backward. (Immense applause.) He is mistaken who supposes we can be intimidated by threats or cajoled by compromise. The day of compromises is past.

The Government must be sustained, (cheers ;) and when it is sustained, we shall give every one in the Union his rights under the Constitution, as we always have, and every one outside of the Union the steel of the Union, till he shall come under the Union. (Cheers, and cries of " Good, go on.") It is impossible for me to go on speech-making ; but if you will go home to your beds, and the Government will let me, I will go South fighting for the Union, and you will follow me. —N. Y. Times, May 17.

Doc. 172.

JUDGE SPRAGUE'S CHARGE, May 16.

AFTER citing provisions from the laws of 1790, 1820, 1825, 1846, and 1847, as to what constitutes the general crime, with the different degrees of penalty, the judge remarks that these enactments were founded upon the clause in the Constitution which gives Congress the power to define and punish piracy. But the constitutional power to regulate commerce also affords a basis for additional penal enactments, covering all possible aggressions and depredations upon our commerce. The judge then lays down the following important principles, the bearing of which will be sufficiently evident in the present crisis :—

The statutes, being enacted pursuant to the Constitution, are of paramount authority, and cannot be invalidated or impaired by the action of any State or States ; and every law, ordinance, and constitution made by them for that purpose, whatever its name or form, is wholly nugatory and can afford no legal protection to those who act under it. But suppose that a number of States undertake, by Revolution, to throw off the Government of the United States, and erect themselves into an independent nation, and assume in that character to issue commissions authorizing the capture of vessels of the United States, will such commissions afford protection to those acting under them against the penal laws of the United States? Cases have heretofore arisen where a portion of a foreign empire —a colony—has undertaken to throw off the dominion of the mother country, and assumed the attitude and claimed the rights of an independent nation, and in such cases it has been held that the relation which the United States should hold to those who thus attempt and claim to institute a new government, is a political rather than a legal question ; that, if those departments of our Government which have a right to give the law, and which regulate our foreign intercourse and determine the relation in which we shall stand to other nations, recognize such new and self-constituted government as having the rights of a belligerent in a war between them and their former rulers, and the United States hold a neutral position in such war, then the judiciary, following the other departments, will, to the same extent, recognize the new nation. But if the legislative and executive departments of the Government utterly refuse to recognize such new government, or to acknowledge it as having any belligerent or national rights, and, instead of taking a neutral attitude, endeavor by force to suppress depredations on commerce by such assumed government, as violating the rights and infringing the laws of the United States, then the judiciary will hold that such depredations are not to be considered as belligerent, and entitled to the immunities of lawful war, but as robbery or other lawless depredations, subject to the penalties denounced by our law against such offences. The judiciary certainly cannot adopt a more indulgent rule towards those who are in open rebellion against the authority of the United States, or towards aliens co-operating with, and acting under, the assumed authority of such rebels. While the other departments of the Government and the nation refuse to regard any State or association of States as having the rights of a belligerent, or as carrying on legitimate war, and are exerting not only moral but physical force against them as rebels and lawless aggressors upon the United States and its citizens, the courts also must so regard them, and cannot admit that any legislation or assumption of power by such State or States can authorize acts in violation of the laws of the United States, or change the character of offences under them. There is another view. Mere rebellion absolves no man from his allegiance. Citizens of the United States, therefore, may not only be subject to the penalties of treason, but if they commit hostilities upon the commerce of the United States, under a commission from any foreign nation, even the oldest and best established, such as England or France for example, they may be dealt with as pirates by the express enactments in the ninth section of the statute of 1790, which has already been referred to. And aliens who are subjects or citizens of any foreign State with whom we have a treaty, such as is described in the statute of 1847, chapter 51, which has already been quoted; if, in violation of such treaty, they make war upon the United States, or cruise against our vessels or property under a commission from any foreign government, however long acknowledged, may, by the clear provisions of that statute, be dealt with as pirates. If aliens, subjects of a nation with whom we have no such treaty, commit acts of hostility upon our commerce, under the alleged authority or commission of a new and self-created government claiming to be independent, it may be material to inquire whether such government is to be regarded as having the immunities of a belligerent, or whether such aliens may be treated as robbers on the seas, and this inquiry will be governed by the principles which I have already stated.

—*Boston Journal*, May 17.

Doc. 173.
THE SECOND REGIMENT MAINE S. V.

THE following are the officers of this regiment: Colonel, Chas. D. Jameson; Lieut.-Colonel, C. W. Roberts; Major, George Varney; Adjutant, John E. Reynolds; Quartermaster, C. Vesey Lord; Assistant Quartermaster, L. H. Pierce; Sergeant-Major, E. L. Appleton, all of Bangor; Surgeon, W. H. Allen, Orono; Assistant Surgeon, A. C. Hamlin, Bangor, nephew of the Vice-President; Hospital Steward, A. D. Palmer, Orono; Chaplain, A. F. Mines, Bath.

First company, Bangor Light Infantry, Capt. Bartletts. Second company, of Bangor, Capt.

Chaplin. Third company, Milo Artillery, Capt. Sampson. Fourth company, Grattan Guards, Capt. Carroll. Fifth company, Brewer Artillery, Capt. Jones. Sixth company, Bangor Chasseurs, Capt. Meincke. Seventh company, of Bangor, Capt. Emerson. Eighth company, of Oldtown, Capt. Foss. Ninth company, of Bangor, Capt. Sargeant. Tenth company, Castline Light Infantry, Capt. Devereux. Each company contains 78 men and officers.

—*N. Y. Evening Post*, May 17.

Doc. 174.
CORRESPONDENCE BETWEEN GOV. ANDREW AND GEN. BUTLER.

COMMONWEALTH OF MASSACHUSETTS,
EXECUTIVE DEPARTMENT,
COUNCIL CHAMBER, BOSTON, April 25, 1861.

GENERAL :—I have received through Major Ames a despatch transmitted from Perryville, detailing the proceedings at Annapolis from the time of your arrival off that port until the hour when Major Ames left you to return to Philadelphia. I wish to repeat the assurance of my entire satisfaction with the action you have taken, with a single exception. If I rightly understood the telegraphic despatch, I think that your action in tendering to Governor Hicks the assistance of our Massachusetts troops to suppress a threatened servile insurrection among the hostile people of Maryland was unnecessary. I hope that the fuller despatches, which are on their way from you, may show reasons why I should modify my opinion concerning that particular instance; but in general I think that the matter of servile insurrection among a community in arms against the Federal Union, is no longer to be regarded by our troops in a political, but solely in a military point of view, and is to be contemplated as one of the inherent weaknesses of the enemy, from the disastrous operations of which we are under no obligation of a military character to guard them, in order that they may be enabled to improve the security which our arms would afford, so as to prosecute with more energy their traitorous attacks upon the Federal Government and Capital. The mode in which such outbreaks are to be considered should depend entirely upon the loyalty or disloyalty of the community in which they occur; and, in the vicinity of Annapolis, I can on this occasion perceive no reason of military policy why a force summoned to the defence of the Federal Government, at this moment of all others, should be offered to be diverted from its immediate duty, to help rebels who stand with arms in their hands, obstructing its progress toward the city of Washington. I entertain no doubt that whenever we shall have an opportunity to interchange our views personally on this subject, we shall arrive at entire concordance of opinion. Yours faithfully,

JOHN A. ANDREW.

To Brigadier-General BUTLER.

DEPARTMENT OF ANNAPOLIS,
HEAD-QUARTERS, ANNAPOLIS, May 9, 1861.

*To His Excellency, John A. Andrew, Governor
and Commander-in-Chief.*

SIR: I have delayed replying to your Excellency's despatch of the 25th April, in my other despatches, because as it involved disapprobation of an act done, couched in the kindest language, I supposed the interest of the country could not suffer in the delay; and incessant labor up to the present moment, has prevented me giving full consideration to the topic. Temporary illness, which forbids bodily activity, gives me now a moment's pause.

The telegraph, with more than usual accuracy, had rightly informed your Excellency that I had offered the services of the Massachusetts troops under my command to aid the authorities of Maryland in suppressing a threatened slave insurrection. Fortunately for us all, the rumor of such an outbreak was without substantial foundation. Assuming, as your Excellency does in your despatch, that I was carrying on military operations in an enemy's country, when a war *à l'entrance* was to be waged, my act might be a matter of discussion. And in that view, acting in the light of the Baltimore murders, and the apparent hostile position of Maryland, your Excellency might, without mature reflection, have come to the conclusion of disapprobation expressed in your despatch. But the facts, especially as now aided by their results, will entirely justify my act, and reinstate me in your Excellency's good opinion.

True, I landed on the soil of Maryland against the formal protest of its Governor and of the corporate authorities of Annapolis, but without any armed opposition on their part, and expecting opposition only from insurgents assembled in riotous contempt of the laws of the State. Before, by letter, and at the time of landing, by personal interview, I had informed Gov. Hicks that soldiers of the Union, under my command, were armed only against the insurgents and disturbers of the peace of Maryland and of the United States. I received from Gov. Hicks assurances of the loyalty of the State to the Union—assurances which subsequent events have fully justified. The Mayor of Annapolis also informed me that the city authorities would in nowise oppose me, but that I was in great danger from the excited and riotous mobs of Baltimore pouring down upon me, and in numbers beyond the control of the police. I assured both the Governor and the Mayor that I had no fear of a Baltimore or other mob, and that, supported by the authorities of the State and City, I should repress all hostile demonstrations against the laws of Maryland and the United States, and that I would protect both myself and the City of Annapolis from any disorderly persons whatsoever. On the morning following my landing I was informed that the City of Annapolis and environs were in danger from an insurrection of the slave population, in defiance of the laws of the State. What was I to

do? I had promised to put down a white mob and to preserve and enforce the laws against that. Ought I to allow a black one any preference in a breach of the laws? I understood that I was armed against all infractions of the laws, whether by white or black, and upon that understanding I acted, certainly with promptness and efficiency. And your Excellency's shadow of disapprobation, arising from a misunderstanding of the facts, has caused all the regret I have for that action. The question seemed to me to be neither military nor political, and was not to be so treated. It was simply a question of good faith and honesty of purpose. The benign effect of my course was instantly seen. The good but timid people of Annapolis who had fled from their houses at our approach, immediately returned; business resumed its accustomed channels; quiet and order prevailed in the city; confidence took the place of distrust, friendship of enmity, brotherly kindness of sectional hate, and I believe to-day there is no city in the Union more loyal than the City of Annapolis. I think, therefore, I may safely point to the results for my justification. The vote of the neighboring County of Washington, a few days since, for its delegate to the Legislature, wherein 4,000 out of 5,000 votes were thrown for a delegate favorable to the Union, is among the many happy fruits of firmness of purpose, efficiency of action, and integrity of mission. I believe, indeed, that it will not require a personal interchange of views, as suggested in your despatch, to bring our minds in accordance; a simple statement of the facts will suffice.

But I am to act hereafter, it may be, in an enemy's country, among a servile population, when the question may arise, as it has not yet arisen, as well in a moral and Christian, as in a political and military point of view. What shall I do? Will your Excellency bear with me a moment while this question is discussed?

I appreciate fully your Excellency's suggestion as to the inherent weakness of the rebels, arising from the preponderance of their servile population. The question, then, is—In what manner shall we take advantage of that weakness? By allowing, and of course arming, that population to rise upon the defenceless women and children of the country, carrying rapine, arson, and murder—all the horrors of San Domingo, a million times magnified, among those whom we hope to reunite with us as brethren, many of whom are already so, and all who are worth preserving will be, when this horrible madness shall have passed away or be threshed out of them? Would your Excellency advise the troops under my command to make war in person upon the defenceless women and children of any part of the Union, accompanied with brutalities too horrible to be named? You will say, "God forbid!" If we may not do so in person, shall we arm others so to do over whom we can have no restraint, exercise no control, and who, when once they have tasted blood, may turn the very arms we put in their hands against ourselves, as a part of the oppressing white race? The reading of history so familiar to your Excellency, will tell you the bitterest cause of complaint which our fathers had against Great Britain in the war of the Revolution, was the arming by the British Ministry of the red man with the tomahawk and the scalping-knife against the women and children of the colonies, so that the phrase, "May we not use all the means which God and nature have put in our power to subjugate the colonies?" has passed into a legend of infamy against the leader of that Ministry who used it in Parliament. Shall history teach us in vain? Could we justify ourselves? Although with arms in our hands amid the savage wildness of camp and field, we may have blunted many of the finer moral sensibilities in letting loose four millions of worse than savages upon the homes and hearths of the South. Can we be justified to the Christian community of Massachusetts? Would such a course be consonant with the teachings of our holy religion? I have a very decided opinion upon the subject, and if any one desires, as I know your Excellency does not, this unhappy contest to be prosecuted in that manner, some instrument other than myself must be found to carry it on. I may not discuss the political bearings of this topic. When I went from under the shadow of my roof free, I left all politics behind me, to be resumed only when every part of the Union is loyal to the flag, and the potency of the Government through the ballot box is established.

Passing the moral and Christian view, let us examine the subject as a military question. Is not that State already subjugated which requires the bayonets of those armed in opposition to its rulers, to preserve it from the horrors of a servile war? As the least experienced of military men, I would have no doubt of the entire subjugation of a State brought to that condition. When, therefore—unless I am better advised—any community in the United States, who have met me in honorable warfare, or even in the prosecution of a rebellious war in an honorable manner, shall call upon me for protection against the nameless horrors of a servile insurrection, they shall have it, and from the moment that call is obeyed, I have no doubt we shall be friends and not enemies.

The possibilities that dishonorable means of defence are to be taken by the rebels against the Government, I do not now contemplate. If, as has been done in a single instance, my men are to be attacked by poison, or as in another, stricken down by the assassin's knife, and thus murdered, the community using such weapons may be required to be taught that it holds within its own border a more potent means for deadly purposes and indiscriminate slaughter than any which it can administer to us.

Trusting that these views may meet your Ex-

cellency's approval, I have the honor to be, very respectfully, your obedient servant,
BENJ. F. BUTLER.
—N. Y. Times, May 16.

Doc. 174½.

MR. SEWARD'S LETTER ON TREASON.

The following important letter was written by the Secretary of State:

DEPARTMENT OF STATE, }
WASHINGTON, May 16, 1861. }

SIR: I have received your letter of yesterday's date, asking me to give you, in writing, my reasons for considering an acceptance on your part of Governor Letcher's proposition to purchase the steamships Yorktown and Jamestown, recently seized by his orders and now in his possession, an act of treason. With this request I readily comply. An insurrection has broken out in several of the States of this Union, including Virginia, designed to overthrow the Government of the United States. The executive authorities of the State are parties to that insurrection, and so are public enemies. Their action in seizing or buying vessels to be employed in executing that design is not merely without authority of law, but is treason. It is treason for any person to give aid and comfort to public enemies. To sell vessels to them, which it is their purpose to use as ships-of-war, is to give them aid and comfort. To receive money from them in payment for vessels which they have seized for these purposes would be to convert the unlawful seizure into a sale, and would subject the party so offending to the pains and penalties of treason, and the Government would not hesitate to bring the offender to punishment. I am, sir, your obedient servant,
WM. H. SEWARD.

To G. HEINEKEN, Esq., agent New York and Virginia Steamship Company, Washington.
—N. Y. Herald, May 18.

Doc. 175.

SUBMARINE BOAT AT PHILADELPHIA.

MAY 17, 1861.

NEVER, since the first flush of the news of the bombardment of Fort Sumter, has there been an excitement in the city equal to that which was caused in the upper wards this morning, by the capture of a mysterious vessel which was said to be an infernal machine, which was to be used for all sorts of treasonable purposes, including the trifling pastime of scuttling and blowing up Government men-of-war.

For a few days past the police have had their attention directed to the movements, not of a "long, low, black schooner;" but of an iron submarine boat, to which very extraordinary abilities and infernal propensities were attributed. The Harbor Police, under the direction of Lieutenant Benjamin Edgar, were directed to be especially spry, and they kept their optics wide open for the mysterious stranger. Yesterday afternoon they stumbled upon a queer contrivance which lay at the lower end of Smith's Island, and proved to be the submarine monster of which they were in search.

Externally it had the appearance of a section of boiler about twenty feet long, with tapered ends, presenting the shape and appearance of an enormous cigar with a boiler iron wrapper, and for all the world like Winans' celebrated steamer in respect to shape. The after end was furnished with a propeller, which had a contrivance for protecting it from damage from coming in contact with external objects. The forward end was sharkish in appearance, and the shark idea was carried out in other respects, as only the ridge of the back was above water, while the tail and snout were submerged. Near the forward end was the hatchway or "man-hole," through which egress and ingress were obtained. This hole was covered with a heavy iron flap, which was made air tight, and which was secured in its place by numerous powerful screws and hooks. Two tiers of glass bull's eyes along each side of the submarine monster, completed its external features, afforded light to the inside, and gave it a particularly wide awake appearance.

But its Argus eyes did not avail to save it from capture. About twelve o'clock last night the harbor policemen saw a skiff loaded with pig lead move off from South street wharf, in charge of two young men, and they paid a visit to the submarine ship, in which a portion of the same description of lead had already been placed. The submariners with their skiff and lead were seized and brought to the city, and at about two o'clock this morning their iron pet was towed to town and moored at Noble street wharf.

The news of the capture soon flew around, and by little after daylight, the rush of people to the spot commenced. All sorts of stories were afloat, and thousands upon thousands gathered at the wharves, scaled the neighboring board piles, and importuned the amphibious policemen, who had the monster in charge, for permission to board her and see how she looked inside. But "no admission" was the rule, and the interior remained invisible to the million.

The harbor men very courteously offered us a peep inside. After dropping from a high wharf into a skiff and then jumping a few feet, we found ourselves upon the back of the iron mystery. After much unscrewing and unhooking, the top of the man-hole was lifted off, and divesting ourselves of coat and hat, we squeezed into the machine, under the gaze of a curious and admiring multitude of about five thousand people.

We suddenly found ourselves squatting inside of a cigar-shaped iron vessel, about four feet in diameter. There was a crank for the purpose of operating upon the propeller already described, apparatus for steering, rods, connecting with fins outside, which could be moved at pleasure, and which had something to do with steadying and sinking the craft. There was a large reel of wire which might be intended for galvanic purposes, pumps, brass faucets, pigs of ballast lead, and numerous other things, which might be intended for either infernal or humane purposes for aught we know. The interior was abundantly lighted by means of the double tier of bull's eyes we have described.

By making inquiry in proper quarters, we learned the history of the machine. It seems that it is the invention of a Frenchman named De Villeroi. The cash for building it is said to have been furnished by a relative of the late Stephen Girard. It was constructed in this city about two years ago, and since that time it has been lying at New Castle, Marcus Hook, and Rancocas. It has been tried frequently at those points, and marvellous stories are told of the facility with which it can be sunk beneath the water, again raised to the surface, and propelled and steered either beneath the surface or upon it.

After visiting the submarine affair, we had an interview with the submariners at the Central Station. They gave their names as Alexander Rhodes, a Frenchman, aged 30, and Henry Kriner, an American, aged 19. In reply to our questions, they told us that the vessel was intended for all submarine purposes. It had been under water for three hours at a time, and could be moved about at pleasure. The persons in it could leave it while under water, as though it was a diving bell. They manufacture, while under water, they said, the supply of air needed for respiration.

They informed us that the vessel had been lying at Rancocas for five months past, and that they brought it away from there on Tuesday last, their object being to test it at the Navy Yard here, for the purpose of obtaining a patent for it. They stated that M. de Villeroi had got permission from the officers of the yard to make the trial. Upon the other hand, we hear from the police, that the authorities at the yard know nothing of the machine, and that no such arrangement has been made. The business will be properly investigated, and if the submarine craft is bound upon any errand that is not friendly to the Union, it will not be likely to reach its destination very speedily. Under any circumstances, its appearance in the river at this time, and its capture, have created an extraordinary excitement.

—*Philadelphia Evening Bulletin*, May 17.

Doc. 175½.

ARKANSAS SECESSION ORDINANCE.

AN ORDINANCE to dissolve the Union now existing between the State of Arkansas and the other States united with her under the compact entitled "The Constitution of the United States of America."

Whereas, In addition to the well-founded cause of complaint set forth by this Convention in resolutions adopted on the 11th March, A. D. 1861, against the sectional party now in power at Washington City, headed by Abraham Lincoln, he has, in the face of the resolutions passed by this Convention, pledging the State of Arkansas to resist to the last extremity any attempt on the part of such power to coerce any State that seceded from the old Union, proclaimed to the world that war should be waged against such States, until they should be compelled to submit to their rule, and large forces to accomplish this have by this same power been called out, and are now being marshalled to carry out this inhuman design, and longer to submit to such rule or remain in the old Union of the United States would be disgraceful and ruinous to the State of Arkansas:

Therefore, we, the people of the State of Arkansas, in Convention assembled, do hereby declare and ordain, and it is hereby declared and ordained, that the "ordinance and acceptance of compact," passed and approved by the General Assembly of the State of Arkansas on the 18th day of October, A. D. 1836, whereby it was by said General Assembly ordained that, by virtue of the authority vested in said General Assembly, by the provisions of the ordinance adopted by the Convention of delegates assembled at Little Rock, for the purpose of forming a Constitution and system of Government for said State, the propositions set forth in " an act supplementary to an act entitled an act for the admission of the State of Arkansas into the Union, and to provide for the due execution of the laws of the United States within the same, and for other purposes, were freely accepted, ratified, and irrevocably confirmed articles of compact and union between the State of Arkansas and the United States," and all other laws, and every other law and ordinance, whereby the State of Arkansas became a member of the Federal Union, be, and the same are hereby in all respects, and for every purpose herewith consistent, repealed, abrogated, and fully set aside; and the union now subsisting between the State of Arkansas and the other States under the name of the United States of America, is hereby forever dissolved.

And we do further hereby declare and ordain that the State of Arkansas hereby resumes to herself all rights and powers heretofore delegated to the Government of the United States of America—that her citizens are absolved from all allegiance to said Government of the United States, and that she is in full possession and exercise of all the rights and sovereignty which appertain to a free and independent State.

We do further ordain and declare that all rights acquired and vested under the Constitution of the United States of America, or of any act or acts of Congress, or treaty, or under any law of this State, and not incompatible with this ordinance, shall remain in full force and effect, in no wise altered or impaired, and have the same effect as if this ordinance had not been passed.

Adopted and passed in open Convention on the 6th day of May, Anno Domini 1861.

ELIAS C. BOUDINOT,
Secretary of the Arkansas State Convention.
—*N. Y. Tribune,* June 5.

Doc. 176.

FOURTEENTH NEW YORK REGIMENT.

The following is a list of the officers of the regiment:—

FIELD.—Colonel, A. M. Wood; Lieutenant-Colonel, E. B. Fowler; Major, James Jourdan.

STAFF.—Adjutant, A. W. H. Gill; Engineer, Captain R. Butt; Chaplain, Captain J. S. Inskip; Surgeon, Captain J. M. Homeston; First Assistant Surgeon, Lieutenant J. L. Farley; Second Assistant Surgeon, F. Swalm; Paymaster, Lieutenant A. G. Gaston; Quartermaster, Lieutenant A. S. Cassiday; Commissary, Lieutenant H. L. Cranford.

NON-COMMISSIONED STAFF.—Sergeant Major, T. Head; Sergeant Standard Bearer, F. Head; Quartermaster Sergeant, J. Howard; Right General Guide, J. Miller; Left General Guide, W. A. Burnett.

LINE.—Company A.—Captain R. B. Jordan; First Lieutenant, J. D. McClaskey; Second Lieutenant, John H. Styles.

Company B.—Captain, George Mallery; First Lieutenant, J. Uffendell; Second Lieutenant, E. E. Pearce.

Company C.—Captain, William M. Burnett; First Lieutenant, David Myers; Second Lieutenant, Wm. H. Burnett.

Company D.—Captain, C. F. Baldwin; First Lieutenant, J. Thornton; Second Lieutenant, J. Jones.

Company E.—Captain, Wm. L. B. Steers; First Lieutenant, W. H. Middleton; Second Lieutenant, George S. Elcock.

Company F.—Captain, A. G. A. Harnikell; First Lieutenant, T. Salters; Second Lieutenant, James Jordan.

Company G.—Captain, G. Plass; First Lieutenant, L. L. Laidlaw; Second Lieutenant, R. A. Goodenough, Jr.

Company H.—Captain, Wm. H. DeBevoice; First Lieutenant, George Davey; Second Lieutenant, Charles H. Morris.

Sappers and Miners, organized as a howitzer company.—First Lieutenant, John McLeer; Second Lieutenant, H. Kalt; First Sergeant, Phil. H. Grogan.

Leader of the Band.—J. H. Fielding. Sergeant of the Drum Corps.—J. Flint.

—*N. Y. Herald,* May 19.

Doc. 177.
ATTACK ON SEWELL'S POINT,
MAY 19, 1861.

THE following is the official report of the action between the United States war-steamer Star and the Sewell's Point battery, on the 19th inst.

UNITED STATES STEAMER STAR, May 19, 1861.

FLAG OFFICER S. H. STRINGHAM, Commander of the Home Squadron:—

From the time I reported to you yesterday I kept a strict watch on the movements of the enemy in and about the Sewell's Point battery. Several noises were heard during the night, but not distinct enough for me to trace them. At half-past five, P. M., I heard distinct blows, as if from an axe securing timber platforms for gun-carriages inside of the embrasures, and immediately I ordered a shot to be fired over them. The rebels immediately hoisted a white flag, with some design on it, and fired a shot that cut the fore spencer guys near the gaff. I immediately went to quarters, and returned their fire, which was continued by them. I expended fifteen round of grape, twelve ten-inch shot, thirty-two ten-inch shell, ten shell for thirty-two pounders, and forty-five thirty-two pound shot; making a total of one hundred and fourteen shots, which I think did some execution among the rebels. I only desisted for want of ammunition, having only five eight-pound charges remaining for the pivot gun. I regret that want of ammunition compelled me to retire, as I am satisfied I could have silenced the battery in a short time.

I cannot too highly praise the courage and patriotism of the officers and men under my command. They acted nobly, and with great coolness, as the repeated firings as above will show. The action continued from 5·30 to 6·45, P. M., a duration of one hour and fifteen minutes.

The battery is masked, thirteen embrasures having been erected behind a sand bank. The rebels had three rifled cannons, and fired several volleys of Minié balls, which struck the ship. The ship was struck five times by the rifled cannot shot in the hull and upper works. The damage can be repaired by ourselves.

I herewith enclose the report of the medical officer of this ship, by which you will perceive that two men were slightly wounded during the action.

I cannot close this communication without calling the attention of the Flag Officer to the valuable services of Lieutenant Daniel L. Braine, who had charge of our pivot gun, and who during the whole action displayed great coolness and skill in the management.

HENRY EAGLE, Commander.

—*National Intelligencer*, May 27.

NORFOLK, May 20, 1861.

The ball has been opened in this neighborhood, and now it may be, the war will commence in earnest.

Last Saturday the steamtug Kahokee took down a number of negro laborers, to complete a fortification that had been commenced on Sewell's Point, which is situated immediately at the mouth of Elizabeth River, and from which the entrance into James River may be commanded. The enemy had an *improvised* war steamer, the Monticello, stationed off the point. The Kahokee perceiving from certain demonstrations on the part of the Monticello that it would be unsafe to proceed to her destination, landed her men at Boush's bluff, a point some two miles this side of Sewell's, where a small battery had been erected. This had hardly been accomplished, before the Monticello steamed up and fired two shots, both of which passed over the tug without inflicting any damage. The fire was responded to by the battery at Boush's bluff, which had the effect of causing the Monticello to relinquish the chase of the Kahokee and dropping to her former position. She opened her guns on the incomplete battery at Sewell's Point, with the intention of destroying the work. She fired in all about thirty shots, only two of which took effect, but no serious damage was done.— Two companies of soldiers were at the point, with about a hundred negro laborers. The soldiers stood their ground bravely when the shells fell about them, but there was scampering among the darkies.

During the night several heavy pieces of artillery and an additional force of laborers were sent down by land from this place, a distance of nine miles. By 4 o'clock yesterday (Sunday) afternoon, three short 32-pounders and two rifle 6-pounders had been placed in position and were ready for action. They had not long to wait. Some brushwood by which the operations had been masked, was removed, and no sooner was the battery exposed to view, than at once the Monticello opened on it. She mounts six guns of the heaviest calibre, and for about two hours threw shot and shell about the work with fearful rapidity, and oftentimes with great precision. Our men returned the fire with spirit, but, wanting experience, the guns were served with no great skill. Still several shots from the rifle cannon took effect, and, about nightfall, the steamer was obliged to draw off, evidently in a disabled state.

The second shot from the battery struck near the water line, which she instantly signalized to the war vessels in the Roads by sending up a rocket. Later in the conflict she sent up another rocket, when two steamtugs, the Yankee and the Young America, came to her assistance. The Yankee took part in the engagement, but receiving a shot in the stern, which raked her deck and carried away her flag-staff, she prudently withdrew to a safer distance. Her example was quickly followed by the other two steamers, the Monticello making headway very slowly, and rolling heavily, as if partially filled with water.

Thus in this first encounter in our waters, victory remains with us. The troops that achieved it were a company from Columbus, Ga., Capt. Colquitt, and the Woodis Rifles, from this place, Capt. Lamb. A detachment of the Junior Rifles of this place were also in the work. The men, all accounts agree, exhibited the coolness and courage of veterans. No troops could have behaved better.

When the affair was ended, Captains Colquitt and Lamb both made speeches to the command, and complimented them on their gallant and soldierly bearing. Gen. Gwynn, who was present during a part of the engagement, also spoke in high terms of the bravery that the troops exhibited.

As usual, in the battles that have thus far occurred during the present singular war, "nobody was hurt." That is, nobody on our side, except one man who got a bruised shin from a spent fragment of a shell, and Col. Collier, aid to Gen. Gwynn, who, I learn, was rapped so severely over the knuckles by a flying splinter, as to damage his hand somewhat. These, I believe, are the only casualties, great or small, that occurred on our side.

On the part of the enemy, the list, it is to be hoped, presents a bloodier appearance.

Last night, four of the heaviest guns, and a force of nearly a thousand men, were moved down to the point. It was expected that warm work would occur there this morning, but up to the present writing (10 A. M.) every thing is quiet.

Among the troops moved last night, were the five Petersburg companies heretofore stationed at Ferry Point, and the Richmond Grays, all under command of Col. Weisiger. Let these boys have a chance, and they will surely give a good account of themselves. They marched with the greatest alacrity, and shouted when the order was given. They all have the proper mettle.

NORFOLK, May 20, 9 P. M.

All is quiet here to-night.

Between 1,500 and 2,000 Confederate troops were concentrated at Sewell's Point last night, but the Yankee mercenaries did not return, as apprehended, and our men, who were actually eager for the fray, had nothing to do.

The steamer West Point, Captain Rowe, belonging to the York River Railroad line, left the railroad wharf at Portsmouth, to-day, under a flag of truce, to visit the Federal fleet off Old Point Comfort, for the purpose of carrying to that destination all the women and children who desire to join their Northern friends. The steamer was accompanied by Capt. Thos. T. Hunter, commander of the Virginia Navy.

The families of the following, among other persons, left in the steamer :

James Hepenstall, L. T. Barnard, J. Lucas, Geo. Richard Boush, John Harbonner, Jos. D. Knapp, Thomas Nelson, Robert Gill, John Butler, W. H. Lewis, and James H. Hardwick.

The West Point having accomplished its mission, has returned.

Captain Hunter reports the Monticello as having fared very badly in her engagement with our battery at Sewell's Point, yesterday. The boat is seriously damaged in both hull and machinery, and it is thought that it will be some time before she can indulge in another bombardment.

Six men were killed on board, and several badly wounded.

We have been unable to learn the names of the killed, or the extent of the injuries of the maimed.

—*Richmond Examiner*, May 22.

Doc. 178.

MEETING OF THE N. Y. BIBLE SOCIETY, MAY 19, 1861.

WM. ALLEN BUTLER, Esq., presided at the meeting. After the reading of selections of the Scripture, and prayer by the Rev. Mr. Hastings, followed by the singing of a hymn by the congregation, Mr. Butler said that in this Christian land, where the recruit was sworn into service upon the Bible, there needed no special plea to justify an effort to place the Gospel in the hands of every soldier, as his best companion for the war. It might have been said that there were other things with which our troops should be supplied rather than Bibles; they needed muskets instead of Bibles. He agreed that muskets were the first thing needed. The Society he represented was not a society for the suppression of muskets or any weapons of war that would make our troops victorious. When liberty was first imperilled in Massachusetts, her men seized the firelock, and did not turn back even for their Bibles. He believed that men who loved their Bibles most, and who wore upon their heart of hearts its most sacred truths the most deeply graven, would be the first to employ those Bibles to press home those bullets which were to be fired in the defence of rights, such as were imperilled to-day. (Cheers.) But no such necessity existed. We were able to equip our army as became a Christian people. Mistakes in this direction consequent upon haste were to be corrected. When the foundations of truth and justice were to be re-established for a thousand generations, there would be time allowed for preparation. They meant to place the New Testament in the hand of every soldier as the very best manual of duty.

Mr. Pierson then made a statement of the operations of the Society, from which it appeared that there had been 29 city regiments fully supplied, and 5 in the course of supply. To these, 23,000 Testaments had been furnished. It was proposed to distribute 7,000 Testaments among the 16 regiments now forming in the city, which will bring up the total issues of the

Society to volunteers, by the second week in June, to 30,000 copies. Many of Ellsworth's Fire Zouaves said, on receiving the Testaments, "We will fight for the book, sir; we will defend it, sir."

Mr. Smythe also gave an account of his experience as a Bible distributor. He referred to the action of Miss Brown, and said how delightful it was to think that at the moment her father was preparing to meet the enemy at Fort Pickens, she was going about at Fort Hamilton, like an angel of light, offering the gospel to the soldiers.

The Rev. Dr. Hitchcock, in commencing his address, related an incident of one of the Massachusetts troops, who, on unbuttoning his coat, drew from one pocket a Bible, and from the other a revolver. The State militant should furnish the revolver, and the church militant should furnish the Bible; that was a union of Church and State which he thought all would agree was legitimate and necessary. (Cheers.) The grand peril of our armies was the moral peril they were to encounter. But it should be understood that they believed in war, in such a war as the present, vindicating the rights of man. (Cheers.) The Bible enforced righteous war. The question had become a very simple one: Should we suffer our nationality to be assassinated, or should we strike down the assassin? There were also two questions before the American people: the first was, Should a State or States be allowed to secede violently! The people were answering in indignant thunder tones, No! (Cheers.) The other question looming in the horizon was, Should States be suffered to secede by peaceful means? Until recently many had held that if States were determined to go out, and adopted peaceful measures to accomplish their purpose, they must be allowed to go. But a Providence had guided us more wisely than we could ourselves, and the people throughout the length and breadth of the land, were coming to say that there should never be a disruption of this Union either in peace or by war. (Cheers.) If a division were allowed, how long could parties live beside the imaginary line without quarrelling? War in such case would come; and we might as well meet it at the threshold. (Cheers.) Suppose Rhode Island should want to go. We could afford to keep that State for a clam bed, but we could never allow another flag to wave over it than the Stars and Stripes. (Cheers.) So we could afford to keep Louisiana for alligators, but no other flag but ours should wave over it. (Cheers.) If the blood of thousands upon thousands were needed to seal the issue, with bowed heads we could only say, Thy will, O God, be done.

George Douglas, Esq., (who gave $1,000 to the Society,) said he believed Providence had appointed General Scott to be the leader of our forces in this second war for liberty, as He had General Washington in the first.

Dr. S. H. Tyng next addressed the meeting:

Never were a people brought together to maintain dearer rights or more imperilled and important interests than those involved in the present contest. He could not take a pirate's hand, who was going to secure a prize of twenty dollars a head for every man he murdered, and put a Bible in his hands, as a sanction for his course. What kind of a Union would that be where the chains of the slave should sound from one end of the land to the other, and the infernal boast be realized that a man should count the roll of his slaves on Bunker Hill? This was not a war of sections; it was not a civil war. He would dignify it by no such name. There were hundreds and thousands in the Southern land praying for the power which should give them help. In Virginia, the scene of eighteen years of his ministry, there were tens of thousands, he believed, who were anxiously waiting for that which is called the army of the North to deliver them from the tyranny that had been usurped over them. He would not descend to call it civil warfare. He would not meet pirates upon the deck, and call it warfare. He would hang them as quick as he would shoot a mad dog. (Cheers.)

There was one road to peace, and that was absolute and entire subjection. (Cheers.) He did not mean the subjection of the South, but of the riotous mob which there had control of affairs. The sword of justice was the only pen that could write the final treaty. Referring to the troops that had been raised, the speaker asked who ever saw such an army as has been gathered in our land? He would not except the rare birds of Billy Wilson's regiment. He might venture to say of them that their salvation might lie in the very consecration they have made of themselves to their country. (Cheers.) Twenty-three thousand Bibles had been given to the troops who go to fight for their country; did anybody believe there were five hundred copies in the army of renegades who are meeting them in the contest? It would scald and singe their polluted hands. We had every cause to be proud of our army. They are worthy of the Bible. How their names will glisten in glory! One of the noblest results he looked for was a land without a slave upon it. (Cheers.) A nation in which no more shall God's image be sold upon the block by the auctioneer. Said a gentleman, "The Bible authorizes human slavery; you must acknowledge that slavery is a Divine institution." The old minister to whom the remark was addressed, gathered himself up and replied, "Yes, sir; in the same sense in which hell is." (Cheers.)

—*N. Y. Tribune*, May 20.

Doc. 179.

NORTH CAROLINA ORDINANCE OF SECESSION.

We, the people of the State of North Carolina, in Convention assembled, do declare and ordain, and it is hereby declared and ordained, that the ordinance adopted by the State of North Carolina, in the convention of 1789, whereby the Constitution of the United States was ratified and adopted, and also all acts and parts of acts of the General Assembly, ratifying and adopting amendments to the said Constitution, are hereby repealed, rescinded, and abrogated.

"We do further declare and ordain that the Union now subsisting between the State of North Carolina and the other States, under the title of the United States of America, is hereby dissolved, and that the State of North Carolina is in the full possession and exercise of all those rights of sovereignty which belong and appertain to a free and independent State.

"Done at Raleigh, 20th day of May, in the year of our Lord 1861."

The following ordinance was also passed:

"We, the people of North Carolina, in Convention assembled, do declare and ordain, and it is hereby declared and ordained, that the State of North Carolina does hereby assent to and ratify the 'Constitution for the Provisional Government of the Confederate States of America, adopted at Montgomery, in the State of Alabama, on the 8th of February, 1861, by the Convention of Delegates from the States of South Carolina, Georgia, Florida, Alabama, Mississippi, and Louisiana, and that North Carolina will enter into the federal association of States upon the terms therein proposed, when admitted by the Congress or any competent authority of the Confederate States.

"Done at Raleigh, 20th day of May, in the year of our Lord 1861."

—*N. Y. Times*, May 26.

Doc. 180.
SECOND REGIMENT N. Y. S. M.

The following are the officers:—

Col., S. W. B. Tompkins; Lieut.-Col., John H. Wilcox; Major, J. J. Dimock; Adjutant, A. V. Rea; Special Aid, Capt. Joseph Byrne; Quartermaster, H. R. Foote; Assistant Quartermaster, Clinton Berry; Surgeon, Alfred Powell; Assistant Surgeon, George Ferguson; Commissary, —— Coffin; Ordnance officer, John Armour; Paymaster, W. H. Newman; Captain of Engineers, E. H. Sage; Chaplain, W. H. Reynolds; Acting Chaplain, Alfred Stevens.

The Company officers are:—

Company A—Captain Graham; 1st Lieut., Henry A. Maxwell; 2d Lieut., Julius Hart.

Company B—Captain Reed; 1st Lieut., Thomas W. Baird; 2d Lieut., Richard Campbell.

Company C—Captain Sted; 1st Lieut., John Bookhout; 2d Lieut., —— Robinson.

Company D—Captain Kennedy; 1st Lieut., John Vaughan; 2d Lieut., not appointed.

Company E—Captain Houston; 1st Lieut., Robert Burns; 2d Lieut., John Murray.

Company F—Captain Brady; 1st Lieut., J. Hughes; 2d Lieut., Jas. Mullvehill.

Company G—Captain Dowling; 1st Lieut., S. Meinbeir; 2d Lieut., Oscar Hoefar.

Company H—Captain De Courcey; 1st Lieut., J. W. Dempsey; 2d Lieut., not appointed.

Company I—Captain Delany; 1st Lieut., Thomas W. Davis; 2d Lieut., Frank Mott, (son of Dr. Mott of this city.)

Company K—Captain Darrow; 1st Lieut., M. Vaughan; 2d Lieut., Wm. Demock.

Howitzer corps—Capt. Thaddeus Mott; 1st Lieut., —— Downey.

Engineer corps—Captain Sage; 1st Lieut., J. Vanderpoel.   —*N. Y. World*.

Doc. 181.
GOV. MAGOFFIN'S PROCLAMATION.

FRANKFORT, KY., Monday, May 20.

Proclamation appended to a preamble declaring:

Whereas, Many good citizens requested him to forbid the march of any forces over Kentucky to attack Cairo, or otherwise disturb the peaceful attitude of Kentucky with reference to the deplorable war now waging between the United and Confederate States; also, stating that the same citizens requested him to forbid the march of any United States force over Kentucky soil for the occupation of any post or place within Kentucky; and whereas, every indication of public sentiment shows a determined purpose of the people to maintain a fixed position of self-defence, proposing and intending no invasion or aggression towards any other State or States, forbidding the quartering of troops upon her soil by either hostile section, but simply standing aloof from an unnatural, horrid, and lamentable strife, for the existence whereof Kentucky, neither by thought, word, nor act, is in anywise responsible; and whereas, this policy is, in judgment, wise, peaceful, safe, and honorable, and most likely to preserve the peace and amity between the neighboring border States on both shores of the Ohio, and protect Kentucky from deplorable civil war; and whereas, the arms distributed to the Home Guard are not to be used against the Federal or Confederate States, but to resist and prevent encroachment on her soil, rights, honor, and sovereignty, by either of the belligerent parties, and hoping Kentucky may become a successful mediator between them, and in order to remove a founded distrust and suspicion of purposes to force Kentucky out of the Union at the point of the bayonet, which may have been strongly and wickedly engendered in the public mind in regard to my own position and that of the State Guard;

Now, therefore, I hereby notify and warn all other States, separated or united, especially the United and Confederate States, that I solemnly forbid any movement upon Kentucky soil, or occupation of any post or place therein for any purpose whatever, until authorized by invitation or permission of the legislative and executive authorities. I especially forbid all citizens of Kentucky, whether incorporated in the State Guard or otherwise, making any hostile demonstrations against any of the aforesaid sovereignties, to be obedient to the orders of lawful authorities, to remain quietly and peaceably at home, when off military duty, and refrain from all words and acts likely to provoke a collision, and so otherwise conduct that the deplorable calamity of invasion may be averted; but meanwhile to make prompt and efficient preparation to assume the paramount and supreme law of self-defence, and strictly of self-defence alone.

—N. Y. Times, May 21.

Doc. 182.
SECOND TENNESSEE REGIMENT.

THE following are the commanding officers: Colonel, Wm. B. Bate; Lieut.-Col., Goodall, Major, Doak; Quartermaster, M. W. Cluskey; Surgeon, Dr. Kennedy; Assistant Surgeon, Dr. Erskine.

The following are the company officers: A, Capt. Stephen White; B, Capt. Anderson; C, Capt. Chaney; D, Capt. Henry Rutherford; E, Capt. Hunt; F, Capt. T. D. White; G, Capt. Erthman; H, Capt. Dennison; I, Capt. Tyre; J, Capt. Humphrey Bate. The Carolina Grays (Capt. Hunt) is the flag company of the regiment.

The regiment is called the "Walker Legion," in compliment to the Secretary of State of the Southern Confederacy. The Colonel is from Gallatin county, is a distinguished lawyer, and a man of undoubted ability; besides, he has acquired fame on the bloody fields of Mexico. The Lieutenant-Colonel (of Sumner county) was one of the first to scale the walls of Monterey at the siege of that place by the Americans. Major Doak is also an old Mexican volunteer, and a member of the Tennessee Legislature. M. W. Cluskey, the Quartermaster, (of the Memphis *Avalanche,*) is well known to the whole country as the author of the "Political Text Book," and former Postmaster of the United States House of Representatives; while the surgeons of the regiment are both members of the Legislature, and leading members of their profession. The regiment is made up of citizens of Davidson, Rutherford, Maury, and Shelby counties, and is composed of the very best material. They came here for the purpose of going to Washington. They are more than willing to have a hand in driving the Vandals from that place.

—Richmond Examiner, May 22.

Doc. 183.
DEBTORS TO U. S. CREDITORS.

THE following is the text of the act on this subject, passed at the last session of the Confederate Congress:

An Act to authorize certain Debtors to pay the Amounts due by them into the Treasury of the Confederate States:

SECTION 1. The Congress of the Confederate States of America do enact, that all persons in any manner indebted to individuals, or corporations, in the United States of America, (except the States of Delaware, Maryland, Kentucky, and Missouri, and the District of Columbia,) be, and are hereby, prohibited from paying the same to their respective creditors, or their agents or assignees, pending the existing war waged by that Government against the Confederate States, or any of the slaveholding States before named.

SEC. 2. Any person indebted as aforesaid shall be, and is hereby, authorized to pay the amount of his indebtedness into the Treasury of the Confederate States, in specie or treasury notes, and shall receive from the Treasurer a certificate, countersigned by the Register, showing the amount paid, and on what account, and the rate of interest which the same was bearing.

SEC. 3. Such certificate shall bear like interest with the original contract, and shall be redeemable at the close of the war and the restoration of peace, in specie or its equivalent, on presentation of the original certificate.

SEC. 4. All laws and parts of laws militating against this act, be, and the same are hereby, repealed.

HOWELL COBB,
President of the Congress.

Approved May 21, 1861.   JEFFERSON DAVIS.

—N. Y. Tribune, June 30.

Doc. 184.
AMERICAN AFFAIRS IN GERMANY.

IT is not to be denied, that, from a military point of view, the rebels in the United States have just now several great advantages over the Government. They have an ably organized army, which has been trained for several months, and which must needs fight and plunder in order to be kept together; while the Government can oppose to their attacks only raw and undisciplined troops. Moreover, as the war is to be carried on in the border slave States and in the southern ports, the Government troops will suffer from the summer heats, which do not so affect the secessionists. It is, therefore, quite possible that the first results will be in favor of the rebels.

We have, however, no doubt that intelligence and enduring strength are on the side of the Government, and that victory cannot but remain with the loyal side. We judge from the recent news that the people of the North have at last learned to recognize and value justly the objects and power of the rebels, who threaten their national existence; and we believe that the North is now determined never to lay down its arms till the authority of the law is once more restored in all the seceded Sates, and the political power of slavery, which has grown to so mischievous a strength, is destroyed. Twenty-three millions of people, strengthened by all the arts of peace, and possessed of inexhaustible resources, are opposed to three hundred and fifty thousand slaveholders, four millions of slaves, and three millions of poor whites, who, with the exception of a few cities, are thinly scattered over a broad space of country, and are accustomed to the most primitive and unsocial conditions of life.

The whole civilized world has an interest in this war. It is a war which the people of the Northern States, conservative by the nature of their industrial and political habits, could not longer put off; and it is a war which under perhaps other names many a nation of Europe will have to take up in its turn. It is with them (the United States) as with us: the feudalism of the middle ages is arrayed in arms against the citizenship of the nineteenth century; an exploded theory of society is lifting up its head against the triumphs of our thinking industrial and progressive century; *the poverty-struck Don Quixotes of the Southern plantations gave battle to the roaring windmills and smoking chimneys of the wealthy North.* It is the supercilious noble in arms against the spirit of the century, in which the *citizen* is supreme. In such an issue we can wish success only to the constitutional Government.

—*Cologne Gazette*, May 5.

Doc. 185.

SAM HOUSTON'S SPEECH

At Independence, Texas, May 10.

The troubles which have come upon the community are neither unexpected to me, nor do I fail to realize all the terrible consequences yet to ensue. Since the passage of the Nebraska and Kansas bill, I have had but little hope of the stability of our institutions. The advantages gained to the North by that measure, through the incentive to Anti-Slavery agitation and the opening of a vast territory to Free-Soil settlement, were such that I saw that the South would soon be overslaughed, and deprived of equality in the Government—a state of things which a chivalrous people like ours would not submit to. Yet I fostered the longing hope that when the North saw the dangers of disunion, and beheld the resolute spirit with which our people met the issue, they would abandon their aggressive policy, and allow the Government to be preserved and administered in the same spirit with which our forefathers created it. For this reason I was conservative. So long as there was a hope of obtaining our rights, and maintaining our institutions, through an appeal to the sense of justice and the brotherhood of the Northern people, I was for preserving the Union. The voice of hope was weeks since drowned by the guns of Fort Sumter. It is not now heard above the tramp of invading armies. The mission of the Union has ceased to be one of peace and equality, and now the dire alternative of yielding tamely before hostile armies, or meeting the shock like freemen, is presented to the South. Sectional prejudices, sectional hate, sectional aggrandizement, and sectional pride, cloaked in the name of the Government and Union, stimulate the North in prosecuting this war. Thousands are duped into its support by zeal for the Union, and reverence for its past associations; but the motives of the Administration are too plain to be misunderstood.

The time has come when a man's section is his country. I stand by mine. All my hopes, my fortunes, are centred in the South. When I see the land for whose defence my blood has been spilt, and the people whose fortunes have been mine through a quarter of a century of toil, threatened with invasion, I can but cast my lot with theirs and await the issue.

For years I have been denounced on account of my efforts to save the South from the consequences of the unhappy measures which have brought destruction upon the whole country. When, in the face of almost my entire section, and a powerful Northern strength, I opposed the Kansas and Nebraska bill, the bitterness of language was exhausted to decry and vilify me. When I pictured the consequences of that measure, and foretold its effects, I was unheeded. Now, when every Northern man who supported that measure is demanding the subjugation of the South, our people can see the real feelings which actuate them in supporting it. Devoted as I was to peace and to the Union, I have struggled against the realization even of my own prophecies. Every result I foresaw has already occurred. It was to bring peace and strength to the South. It has brought war, and spread free soil almost to the northern border of Texas. All we can now do is to stand firm by what we have, and be more wise in the future.

The trouble is upon us; and no matter how it came, or who brought it on, we have to meet it. Whether we have opposed this Secession movement or favored it, we must alike meet the consequences. I sought calm and prudent action. I desired a united and prepared South, if we must leave the Union. Entire coöperation may not now be possible, but we have ample strength for the struggle if we husband it aright. We must fight now whether we are prepared or not.

My position was taken months since. Though I opposed secession, for the reasons mentioned, I saw that the policy of coercion could not be permitted. The attempt to stigmatize and crush out this revolution, comprehending States and millions of people, as a rebellion, would show that the Administration at Washington did not comprehend the vast issues involved, or refused to listen to the dictates of reason, justice, and humanity. A stubborn resort to force when moderation was necessary, would destroy every hope of peace and the reconstruction of the Union. That my views on this point might not be misunderstood, I sent to the Legislature, prior to the passage of the Secession Ordinance by the Convention, a message, in which I said:

"Having called you together to provide for an expression of the sovereign will of the people at the ballot-box, I also deem it my duty to declare that, while the people of the State of Texas are deliberating upon this question, no impending threats of coercion from the people of another State should be permitted to hang over them, without at least the condemnation of their representatives. Whatever that sovereign will may be when fairly expressed, it must be maintained. Texas, as a man, will defend it. While the Executive would not counsel foolish bravado, he deems it a duty we owe to the people, to declare that, even though their action shall bring upon us the consequences which now seem impending, we shall all (be our views in the past and present what they may) be united."

Now that not only coercion, but a vindictive war is about to be inaugurated, I stand ready to redeem my pledge to the people. Whether the Convention acted right or wrong is not now the question. Whether I was treated justly or unjustly is not now to be considered. I put all that under my feet, and there it shall stay. Let those who have stood by me do the same, and let us show that at a time when peril environs our beloved land, we know how to be patriots and Texans.

Let us have no past, except the glorious past, whose heroic deeds shall stimulate us to resistance to oppression and wrong, and burying in the grave of oblivion all our past difficulties, let us go forward, determined not to yield from the position which the people have assumed until our independence is acknowledged, or if not acknowledged, wrung from our enemies by the force of our valor. It is no time to turn back now—the people have put their hands to the plough; they must go forward. To recede would be worse than ignominy. Better meet war in its deadliest shape than cringe before an enemy whose wrath we have invoked. I make no pretensions as to myself. I have yielded up office and sought retirement to preserve peace among our people. My services, perhaps, are not important enough to be desired. Others are perhaps more competent to lead the people through this revolution. I have been with them through the fiery ordeal once, and I know that with prudence and discipline their courage will surmount all obstacles. Should the tocsin of war, calling forth the people to resist the invader, reach the retirement to which I shall go, I will heed neither the denunciations of my enemies, nor the charms of my own fireside, but will join the ranks of my countrymen to defend Texas once again. Then I will ask those who have pursued me with

malignity, and who have denounced me as a traitor to Texas and the South, to prove themselves more true, when the battle shock shall come. Old and worn as I am, I shall not be laggard. Though others may lead, I shall not scorn to follow; and though I may end life in the ranks, where I commenced it, I shall feel that the post of duty is the post of honor.

We have entered upon a conflict which will demand all the energies of the people. Not only must they be united, but all of the heroic virtues which characterize a free people must be brought into requisition. There must be that sacrificing spirit of patriotism which will yield the private desires for the public good. There must be that fortitude which will anticipate occasional reverses as the natural consequences of war, and meet them with becoming pride and resignation; but, above all, there must be discipline and subordination to law and order. Without this, armies will be raised in vain, and carnage will be wasted in hopeless enterprises. The South, chivalric, brave, and impetuous as it is, must add to these attributes of success thorough discipline, or disaster will come upon the country. The Northern people by their nature and occupation are subordinate to orders. They are capable of great endurance and a high state of discipline. A good motto for a soldier is, Never underrate the strength of your enemy. The South claims superiority over them in point of fearless courage. Equal them in point of discipline, and there will be no danger. Organize your forces; yield obedience to orders from head-quarters. Do not waste your energies in unauthorized expeditions; but in all things conform to law and order, and it will be ten times better than running hither and thither, spending money and time, without accomplishing any of the plans of a campaign which your leaders have marked out. Once organized, stay organized.

Do not be making companies to-day and unmaking them to-morrow. If you are dissatisfied with your captain, wait until the battle-day comes, and he gets killed off, then you can get another. It is better to fight up to him and get rid of him in that way than to split off, and make a new company to be spilt up in the same way. I give this advice as an old soldier. I know the value of subordination and discipline. A good citizen, who has been obedient to law and civil authority, always makes a good soldier. I have ever been conservative, was conservative as long as the Union lasted—am a conservative citizen of the Southern Confederacy, and giving to the constituted authorities of the country, civil and military, and the Government which a majority of the people have approved and acquiesced in, an honest obedience, I feel that I should do less than my duty did I not press upon others the importance of regarding this the first duty of a good citizen.   —*N. Y. Tribune*, May 31.

Doc.—23

Doc. 186.

SPEECH OF HOWELL COBB,

AT ATLANTA, GEORGIA, MAY 22.

FELLOW-CITIZENS:—I feel that I cannot compensate you for the trouble you have taken to call me out. You, as citizens of Atlanta, know that there has been no instance of my being called upon by you, in which I failed to respond, unless for the very good reason that I had *nothing to say;* and this evening I must offer this excuse for failing to address you at length. I presume that a curiosity to know what we have been doing in the Congress recently assembled at Montgomery, has induced you to make this call upon me.

We have made all the necessary arrangements to meet the present crisis. Last night we adjourned to meet in Richmond on the 20th of July. I will tell you why we did this. The "Old Dominion," as you know, has at last shaken off the bonds of Lincoln, and joined her noble Southern sisters. Her soil is to be the battle-ground, and her streams are to be dyed with Southern blood. We felt that her cause was our cause, and that if she fell we wanted to die by her. (Cheers.) We have sent our soldiers on to the posts of danger, and we wanted to be there to aid and counsel our brave "boys." In the progress of the war further legislation may be necessary, and we will be there, that when the hour of danger comes, we may lay aside the robes of legislation, buckle on the armor of the soldier, and do battle beside the brave ones who have volunteered for the defence of our beloved South. (Loud cheers.)

The people are coming up gallantly to the work. When the call was made for twelve months' volunteers, thousands were offered; but when it was changed to the full term of the war, *the numbers increased!* The anxiety among our citizens is not as to who shall *go* to the wars, but *who shall stay at home?* No man in the whole Confederate States—the gray-haired sire down to the beardless youth—in whose veins was one drop of Southern blood, feared to plant his foot upon Virginia's soil, and die fighting for our rights.

In Congress, the other day, I told them that if no other arm was raised to defend Virginia, noble old Georgia—proud in her love of independence—would rise up to a man, and crossing to the southernmost bound of Abolitionism, would say to Lincoln and his myrmidons, "Thus far, *traitor!* shalt thou come; but *no farther!*" (Tremendous applause.) This good old Commonwealth—solitary and alone, if need be—will fight until she sees the last foul invader in his grave! And I know, fellow-citizens, that there is no loyal son of Georgia before me, whose heart does not beat a warm response to this pledge. (Cries of, "We will! we will!")

But we not only need soldiers, we must have treasure to carry on this war. Private contributions have been offered to a vast amount. I will mention an instance which occurred on the Mississippi a few days ago. An aged man—whose gray hairs and tottering limbs forbade his entering the ranks, and whose children of the first and second generations were in the ranks of his country's defenders—was asked how much he would give to carry on the war. The spirit of the old man rose up in him—"Tell them," he said, "that my yearly crop of 1,000 bales of cotton they may have. Only give me enough to sustain me, and let the balance go to my country!" Offers of this sort come pouring in upon the Government from all parts of the country.

But the Government does not require contributions from individuals; she has the means within herself of sustaining this war. No donations are necessary, except for the equipment of your own volunteers, and those you can and will provide for. But I tell you what you may do. Those of you who raise large crops of cotton, when your cotton is ready for market, give it to your Government at its market value, receive in return its bonds, and let it sell your produce to Europe for the specie to sustain our brave "boys" in Virginia. This was agreed on at Montgomery, and we promised to throw out the suggestion, that the people might think about it.

I raise some cotton, and every thing above my necessary expenses my Government shall have. When this was proposed in Congress, a gentleman from Mississippi rose up and said that he did not raise cotton; it was his misfortune not to be able to help his country in that manner. "But," said he, "I will go home and canvass my section, and every man that I meet, who raises cotton, sugar, and rice, I will persuade him to sell it to his Government."

But this patriotism is not confined to the men; the women, with warm hearts and busy fingers, are helping the soldiers. I will give you an instance that happened at Montgomery. A message was received on Friday evening that a thousand sand-bags were wanted, with which to build batteries to protect our men at Pensacola. What could be done? Some one suggested that the ladies be made acquainted with our wants. It was done on Saturday morning. Monday evening I received notice to attend a meeting to be held at 5 o'clock in the Methodist church. Between the reception of the message and 5 o'clock that evening, the money had been raised, the cloth purchased, and the lovely women of that city, with their own delicate hands, at their homes and in the sanctuary of the living God, were making bags; and on Tuesday I saw the sand-bags start for Pensacola, to protect our brave soldiers! (Cheers.) Talk about *subjugating* us! Why, we might lay aside the men, and all Abolitiondom *couldn't run down the women even!* (Prolonged applause.)

They say at the North that we are alarmed. What cause have we to be so? When the Congress assembled at Montgomery there were only six States represented. Now there are nine, and every breeze that comes from Tennessee bears us news that her people are rising up unanimously against the usurpations of Lincoln. North Carolina—the State of my parentage, and I love her with a love next to my native State—she, too, is aroused, and her Convention has unanimously adopted the ordinance of secession; and these States will soon shine as bright stars in our galaxy. With such aids as these, and with so many brave hearts in our land, we can *never be conquered!*

I have spoken enthusiastically, but pardon me. I can say nothing more. (Cries of, "Go on!") You will excuse me, as I have been speaking at every town on the road, and am quite hoarse.

—Ohio Statesman, May 29.

Doc. 187.

SECRETARY CAMERON'S LETTER.

WAR DEPARTMENT, WASHINGTON, May 22, 1861.

DEAR SIR:—By reference to General Orders, No. 15, of the War Department, appended, a copy of which I herewith forward you, giving the plan of the organization of the volunteer forces called into the service of the United States by the President, you will perceive that all regimental officers of those volunteers, from Colonels down to Second Lieutenants, inclusive, are appointed by the Governors of States.

Having thus confided to you the appointment of all these officers for the regiments furnished by your State, you will, I trust, excuse this Department for impressing upon you in advance the necessity of absolute adherence in your appointments, to the following suggestions, which are deemed of the highest importance by the General-in-Chief, under whose advice they are submitted to you:

First.—To commission no one of doubtful morals or patriotism, and not of sound health.

Second.—To appoint no one to a Lieutenancy, Second or First, who has passed the age of 22 years; or to a Captaincy over 30 years; and to appoint no Field-officers, Major, Lieutenant, or Colonel, unless a graduate of the United States Military Academy, or is known to possess military knowledge and experience, who has passed the respective ages of 35, 40, and 45 years.

This Department feels assured it will not be deemed offensive to your Excellency to add this general counsel, that the higher the moral character and general intelligence of the officers so appointed, the greater the efficiency of the troops and the resulting glory to their respective States.

I am, sir, respectfully,

SIMON CAMERON,
Secretary of War.

—National Intelligencer, May 24.

Doc. 188.

SECOND REGIMENT N. Y. S. V.

THE following is a list of the officers: Colonel, Joseph B. Carr; Lieutenant-Colonel, R. Wells Kenyon; Major, Richard D. Bloss; Adjutant, Timothy Quinn; Surgeon, Reed B. Bontecou; Surgeon's Mate, Leroy McLean; Quartermaster, C. L. McArthur; Chaplain, V. B. Lewis; Sergeant-Major, L. G. Benedict; Quartermaster-Sergeant, J. P. Donnelly; Drum-Major, Thomas E. Bulger.

Company A, Captain, J. W. Armitage; First Lieutenant, Calvin W. Link; Second Lieutenant, George W. Hitchcock. Company B, Captain, Wm. A. Olmsted; First Lieutenant, T. C. Haddock; Second Lieutenant, Lee Churchill. Company C, Captain, Geo. H. Otis; First Lieutenant, Lee Perkins; Second Lieutenant, W. H. Pitt. Company D, Captain, Michael Cassidy; First Lieutenant, John Maguire; Second Lieutenant, John McCaffrey. Company E, Captain, Geo. W. Wilson; First Lieutenant, John H. Quackenbush; Second Lieutenant, C. Wilson. Company F, Captain, S. W. Park; First Lieutenant, James Cross; Second Lieutenant, Wm. H. Harrison. Company G, Captain, W. B. Tibbits; First Lieutenant, James Savage; Second Lieutenant, Wm. Sullivan. Company H, Captain, J. G. McNutt; First Lieutenant, Wm. O'Brien; Second Lieutenant, W. H. McFeeters. Company I, Captain, —— McConihe; First Lieutenant, Jos. Lafuira; Second Lieutenant, George Taft. Company K, Captain, John Arts; First Lieutenant, Henry Jansen; Second Lieutenant, Auguste Kalbe.

—N. Y. Herald, May 20.

Doc. 188½.

SPEECH OF DR. McCLINTOCK,

AT EXETER HALL, LONDON.

(From the Methodist.)

"EXETER HALL was probably never the scene of greater enthusiasm than on the occasion of the address of our corresponding editor. Formally the speech was in behalf of the cause of missions, but in point of fact, it became an appeal for the American people and the American Government grappling with a formidable rebellion. Dr. McClintock said:

* * * "I don't know whether any of you read the *Times* or not, but I do sometimes; and the *Times* has been trying to persuade the British people recently that there is no American republic any more; that it has all sunk fathoms deep. I do not know but that this man 'from the country' has got hold of an old copy of the *Times* with that in. (Loud laughter.) The *Times* said, the day before yesterday, just in the words that I will now quote: 'The great republic is no more;' and Gervase Smith left us out of his speech! Shall I go home and tell my friends that I don't know whether you believe with the *Times* or not? I am inclined to think you do not, but if you have the slight-

est disposition to believe any such doctrine as that let me tell you, 'lay not the flattering unction to your soul.' No, I don't believe that Britons will rejoice to see the day when the 'Great Republic' shall be no more. (Tremendous cheering.) But, if they shall, let me tell you the day of their rejoicing is very far away. (Cheers.) What sort of a prophet would that have been who, just at the beginning of the conflict of the American Revolution, when Great Britain was going to fight her rebellious colonies, should have said Great Britain was no more.

"What would have been thought of the man who would have said, after you had given up the American colonies—a far bigger territory than any you had left at that time—what would have been thought of the newspaper that should have said, at that moment, 'The great power of the British Crown is no more, the British empire is defunct?' He would have been a splendid prophet, would he not? Suppose, too, that we in New York, editing papers (and I have tried my hand at that business myself, in a religious sort of way) at the time of your rebellion in the East Indies, should have made use of such an expression as that—I am not afraid of talking about the *Times*, because I am not an Englishman—and if we had printed for two or three days that Great Britain was no more, and the diadem was about to fall from the head of Victoria, because there was a rebellion in India, it would have been quite a parallel case.

* * * "Now, whatever the *Times* tells you, don't you say that the republic is drowned. (Hear, hear.) Now, I just want to cut another point out of the countryman's speech; and that is the hit about the slave. I do not think there was a single thing in that great speech of Mr. Smith's that took with this audience more than the part about the slave. Now, let me say to you, Mr. President, and this vast audience of Wesleyan ministers, and good, sensible, intelligent people, do not let your political newspapers, or your politicians, debauch your intellects or morals upon the present exciting American question. For the first time in the whole history of the human race, a people to the extent of twenty millions have risen up to say: 'We will forfeit our *prestige* before the world; we will jeopard our name even as a great republic; we will run the risk even of a terrible civil war, such as the world has never seen; we will do all this sooner than we will suffer that human slavery shall be extended one inch.' (Tremendous cheering.) I am in earnest about that point, and I do not want you to forget it, and if you read the *Times* you will need to remember it.

"When I took up the *Times* at breakfast this morning, and read the first fifteen or twenty lines, it stopped my appetite for breakfast—I could not get on—I had to vent myself in a few angry words to my wife before I could get my appetite back again. (Laughter.) I had a pa-

per put into my hands called the *Telegraph*, which they tell me has a larger circulation than the *Times* now; it seemed a capitally written paper, though I did not like the doctrines of it. What did I read in that one article on American affairs? This sentence: 'Are the Americans going to cut each other's throats about a miserable question of the liberty of blackamoors?' That in the city of London—not in any pro-slavery paper in New York or Charleston, but in the city of London, in a newspaper that is said to be read by more people than the *Times*. Now, if you read either of these papers, I hope you will read between the lines hereafter. (Laughter.)

"So far at least as this congregation is concerned, I hope you will not be debauched. We used to think, years ago, we heard voices coming across the great Atlantic, such voices as this man, Gervase Smith's, telling us to be brave for the slaves; and three or four years ago, when I was here, I was abused in newspapers printed in the city of London because I was a pro-slavery man; it was said—not enough of an abolitionist; and we thought that Britain was in earnest in this. And yet, if we were to believe these newspapers, all these professions have been a sham and a humbug, and all your anti-slavery feeling has been simply fanaticism! God preserve us, for I am sure the newspapers never will. (Loud cheers.)"

—*N. Y. Evening Post*, May 23.

Doc. 189.

SPEECH OF A. H. STEPHENS,

At Atlanta, Georgia, May 23.

My Fellow-Citizens:—The time for speech-making has passed. The people have heard all that can be said. The time for prompt, vigorous, decisive action is upon us, and we must do our duty. Upon the surface, affairs appear to be quiet, and I can give you no satisfaction as to their real condition. It is true that threats of an attack on Pensacola have been made, but it is uncertain whether any attack will be made. As you know, an attack was made on Sewell's Point, near Norfolk, but the vessel making it was repulsed and disabled. But the general opinion and indications are that the first demonstration will be at Harper's Ferry, and that there, where John Brown inaugurated his work of slaughter, will be fought a fierce and bloody battle. As for myself, I believe that there the war will begin; and that the first boom of cannon that breaks upon our ears will come from that point. But let it begin where it will, and be as bloody and prolonged as it may, *we are prepared for the issue!*

Some think there will be no war; as to that I know not. But whatever others wanted, the object of the Confederate Government is *peace*. Come peace or war, however, it is determined to maintain our position at every hazard and at every cost, and to drive back the myrmidons of

Abolitionism. It is to be hoped that Lincoln will perceive his error and cease his warlike preparations. The war is against all the principles on which the Government of the United States is based. The arrest of Ross Winans, by the order of President Lincoln, is an act of despotism which the autocrat of Russia, with all his absolute power, never thought of exceeding. It is an assumption of power on the part of the Executive which even Congress had never dared to usurp; for the Constitution of the United States expressly provides that no citizen thereof shall be deprived of his life, liberty, or property, except as a punishment for crimes, and after a fair trial by his peers.

The proclamation declaring our ports in a state of blockade, is in violation of the oath taken by Lincoln when he was inaugurated President of the United States; for he swore to maintain the Constitution of the United States, which declares that "no preference shall be given by any regulation of commerce or revenue to the ports of one State over those of another State;" and he considers us a part of the United States; yet the ports of Boston and New York were open to the world, while Charleston and other Southern ports were declared to be in a state of blockade. How dare he issue such an ukase? How *dare* he, with the oath upon his lips to support the Constitution, trample that instrument in the dust? But he declared, shortly after his inauguration, that he had an "oath registered in high Heaven." By this he means that he has sworn the subjugation of the South to the legions of Abolitiondom. Well, let them come. *We are prepared for them.*

The acts of Lincoln exhibit the spirit of anarchy which is abroad in the North, and total disregard of all constitutional obligations and limits by the Abolition despot now in power. The North is fast drifting to anarchy and an established despotism. On you, therefore, as citizens of the Confederate States, depend the success and perpetuation of constitutional liberty; for the day is not far off when freedom will exist only south of Mason & Dixon's line, and your stout arms and brave hearts her only support on all this continent.

We prefer and desire peace if we can have it; but if we cannot, we must meet the issue forced upon us. We must meet Lincoln and his myrmidons on their own ground, and on their own terms—on constitutional principles. So far, our progress has been all that we could expect. A Government has been organized, Executive Departments and offices supplied, all needful laws passed, and all necessary arrangements made to meet any contingency. At the head of our Government is President Davis—who led the Mississippi Rifles at Buena Vista—and whose flag never yet trailed in the dust. This noble and true son of the South goes to Richmond, to take command in person of our soldiers there, and to lead them upon the battle field against all the military power and talent they can summon—even to their veteran chieftain, General Scott himself.

Whether brought to a bloody conflict or not, we are prepared. Our people everywhere are full of enthusiasm, and strong in their determination never to submit to the rule of Lincoln. Fathers, and mothers, and sisters are all ready, and doing all they can in aid of the cause. We are in the right; and justice is upon our side. We must succeed. The same God who guided our fathers in the bloody Revolution, and who made the glory of the late United States, is yet upon the side of right and justice. Relying upon Him who holds the destinies of all nations in His hands, we will go forth to battle, resolved to conquer or die!

—*Ohio Statesman*, May 30.

Doc. 190.

FIFTH REGIMENT N. Y. VOLUNTEERS.

THE following is a list of the officers of the 5th Volunteers: Colonel, A. Duryea; Lieut-Colonel, E. K. Warren; Major, —— Davies; Adjutant, Joseph Hamlin; Surgeon, Dr. R. H. Gilbert; Assistant Surgeon, Dr. B. E. Martin; Chaplain, the Rev. G. Winslow.

Company A, Capt., H. D. Hull; Lieut., W. T. Partridge; Ensign, J. W. Patten.

Company B, Capt., R. S. Dumont; Lieut., Gouv. Carr; Ensign, T. S. Demart.

Company C, Capt., Hy. E. Davis; Lieut., G. D. Florence; Ensign, Chas. H. Seymour.

Company D, Capt., J. L. Wall; Lieut., —— Lewis; Ensign, —— Corcoran.

Company E, Capt., H. Duryea; Lieut., G. Duryea; Ensign, H. H. Burnett.

Company F, Capt., H. A. Swartout; Lieut., A. Wetmore; Ensign, Carlisle Boyd.

Company G, Capt., A. Teneyek; Lieut., Jacob Duryea; Ensign, Jos. H. Bradley.

Company H, Capt., G. Gilpatrick; Lieut., S. S. Cambreling; Ensign, Jas. Miller.

Company J, Capt., Chas. C. Bartlett; Lieut., Jas. S. York; Ensign, S. Hayward Whitmore.

Company K, Capt., Cleaveland Winslow; Lieut., W. H. White; Ensign, —— Ferguson.

—*N. Y. Tribune*, May 24.

Doc. 190½.

FIRST AND SECOND OHIO REGIMENTS.

THE officers of the First regiment are: A. D. McCook, Colonel; E. S. Parrott, Lieutenant-Colonel; J. Hughes, Major; J. S. Parrott, Adjutant; J. McKinsey, Sergeant Major; Jas. Hill, Quartermaster; M. Steele, Quartermaster Sergeant; C. G. Smyth, Color Sergeant.

COMPANIES.—Co. A, Lancaster Guard, Capt. Stafford; Co. B, Dayton Lafayette Yagers, Capt. Deisher; Co. C, Dayton Light Guard, Capt. Pease; Co. D, Dayton Montgomery Guard, Capt. Crowe; Co. E, Cleveland Grays,

Capt. Paddock; Co. F, Franklin Blues, Capt. Kell; Co. G, Light Guard, Capt. Bayley; Co. H, Zanesville Guard, Capt. Hazlett; Co. I, Mansfield Guard, Capt. McLaughlin; Co. K, Jackson Guard, Capt. Brook. This Regiment is accompanied by the Cleveland Brass Band.

The officers of the Second Regiment are Col. Wilson, Lieut.-Col. Mason, and Major Perry.

COMPANIES.—Co. A, Rover Guard, Capt. Finch; Co. B, Columbus Videttes, Capt. Sprall; Co. C, State Fencibles, Capt Mitchell; Co. D, Cincinnati Zouaves, Capt. Baldwin; Co. E, Lafayette Guard, Capt. Haldenhoff; Co. F, Springfield Zouaves, Capt. Mason; Co. G, Pickaway Guard, Capt. Black; Co. H, Steubenville Guard, Capt. Cook; Co. I, Harris Guard of Cincinnati, Capt. Harrold; Co. K, Baldwin Rifles of Urbana, Capt. Baldwin. The Hillsboro Band is with this Regiment.

—*National Intelligencer*, May 24–27.

Doc. 191.

THE THIRD CONNECTICUT REGIMENT.

THE following is a list of the officers: Colonel, J. Arnold; Lieutenant-Colonel, A. P. Brady; Major, A. Warner; Adjutant, T. J. Peck; Quartermaster, R. Halcomb; Surgeon, J. McGregor; Assistant Surgeon, M. T. Newton; Sergeant Major, W. E. Brady; Assistant Quartermaster, J. H. Alexander; Drum Major, L. B. Fannin; Fife Major, W. R. Miller; Infantry company A, Captain D. Famber; Rifle company B, Captain J. R. Cook; Infantry company C, Captain S. J. Roat; Infantry company D, Captain F. Frye; Rifle company E, Captain J. A. Nelson; Rifle company F, Captain A. Stevens; Rifle company A, Captain G. N. Lewis; Rifle company D, Captain E. Harland.

—*Washington National Republican*, May 27.

Doc. 192.

INSTRUCTIONS TO PRIVATEERS.

1. THE tenor of your commission, under the act of Congress entitled " An act recognizing the existence of war between the United States and the Confederate States, and concerning letters of marque, prizes, and prize goods," a copy of which is hereto annexed, will be kept constantly in your view. The high seas referred to in your commission, you will understand generally to refer to the low-water mark, but with the exception of the space within one league, or three miles, from the shore of countries at peace with the United States and the Confederate States. You nevertheless execute your commission within the distance of the shore of the nation at war with the United States, and even on the waters within the jurisdiction of such nation, if permitted to do so.

2. You are to pay the strictest regard to the rights of neutral Powers and the usages of civilized nations, and in all your proceedings towards neutral vessels you are to give them as little molestation or interruption as will consist with the right of ascertaining their neutral character, and of detaining and bringing them in for regular adjudication in the proper cases. You are particularly to avoid even the appearance of using force or seduction with the view to deprive such vessels of their crews or the passengers, other than persons in the military service of the enemy.

3. Towards enemy vessels and their crews you are to proceed, in exercising the rights of war, with all the justice and humanity which characterize this Government and its citizens.

4. The master, and one or more of the principal persons belonging to the captured vessels, are to be sent, as soon after the capture as may be, to the Judge or Judges of the proper court in the Confederate States, to be examined upon oath touching the interest or property of the captured vessel and her lading, and at the same time are to be delivered to the Judge or Judges all papers, charter parties, bills of lading, letters, and other documents and writings found on board; and the said papers to be proved by the affidavit of the commander of the captured vessel, or some other person present at the capture, to be produced as they were received, without fraud, addition, subtraction, or embezzlement.

5. Property, even of the enemy, is exempt from seizure on neutral vessels, unless it be contraband of war. If goods contraband of war are found on any neutral vessel, and the commander thereof shall offer to deliver them up, the offer shall be accepted, and the vessel left at liberty to pursue its voyage, unless the quantity of contraband goods shall be greater than can be conveniently received on board your vessel, in which case the neutral vessel may be carried into port, for the delivery of the contraband goods.

The following articles are declared by this Government contraband of war, as well as all others that are so declared by the laws of nations, viz.: All arms and implements serving for the purpose of war by land or sea, such as cannons, mortars, guns, muskets, rifles, pistols, petards, bombs, grenades, balls, shot, shell, pikes, swords, bayonets, javelins, lances, horse furniture, holsters, belts, and generally all other implements of war. Also, timber for shipbuilding, pitch, tar, rosin, copper in sheets, sails, hemp, cordage, and generally whatever may serve directly to the equipment of vessels, wrought-iron and planks only excepted.

Neutral vessels conveying enemies' despatches or military persons in the service of the enemy forfeit their neutral character, and are liable to capture and condemnation. But this rule does not apply to neutral vessels bearing despatches from the public ministers or ambassadors of the enemy residing in neutral countries.

By the command of the President of the Confederate States.   ROBERT TOOMBS,
                                           Secretary of State.

National Intelligencer, May 27.

Doc. 193.

SEVENTH N. Y. VOLUNTEER REGIMENT.

THE following are the officers of the regiment:

Colonel, John E. Bendix; Lieut.-Colonel, Ed. Kapf; Major, C. Reller; Adjutant, Schaffner; Sergeant Major, Emil Bodicker; Surgeon, Eisenlard; Assistant Surgeon, Jaeckel; Chaplain, Rev. Dr. Foersch. Company A, 77 men: Capt., F. A. Gaebel; 1st Lieut., Ed. Becker; 2d Lieut., Thibault. Company B, 77 men: Capt., H. Baecht; 1st Lieut., Ch. Karbaum; 2d Lieut., H. Rothe. Company C, 77 men: Capt., Charles Brestel; 1st Lieut., Victor Traxmarer; 2d Lieut., Chas. Hensler. Company D, 77 men: Capt., E. Pfeiffer; 1st Lieut., Anton Herman; 2d Lieut., William Krager. Company E, 77 men: Capt., Rud Anselm; 1st Lieut., Oscar Van Herringen; 2d Lieut., Fred. Mosebach. Company F, 77 men: Capt., Louis Hochheim; 1st. Lieut., Gustav Von Branssen; 2d Lieut., C. Von Hohenhausen. Company G, 77 men: Capt., Sixtus Kapp; 1st Lieut., Wm. Dietz; 2d Lieut., Emil Edler. Company H, 77 men: Capt., Jacob Schoenleber; 1st Lieut., Augustus Feilon; 2d Lieut., Theo. Glaubensklee. Company I, 77 men: Capt., Charles Bethon; 1st Lieut., Theo. Schaedle; 2d Lieut., Joseph Allen. Company K., 77 men: Capt., Edward Wratislaw; 1st Lieut., Louis Wiederhold; 2d Lieut., Julius de Boeshe.

This regiment is composed of German riflemen. Previous to their departure they were presented with a stand of colors by Judge Daly of New York, who, at the presentation, delivered the following speech:

"Colonel Bendix: The flags which I have the honor to offer for the acceptance of your regiment are the gifts of women, members of some of our oldest families, whose ancestors came from Germany and settled in this country before the Revolution. Though separated by several generations from those of German birth, the German blood still running in their veins recognizes the promptitude with which the countrymen of their ancestors have taken up arms when the unity of these States is threatened.

"The principle of national unity is a deeply-implanted German sentiment. Gibbon tells us that when the ancestors of the present Germans first appeared upon the banks of the Maine, they were made up of distinct tribes, who gradually coalesced into a great and permanent nation, calling themselves by the name of Allemanni, or all kinds of men, to denote their various lineage and common bravery. From that united condition they became broken into small nationalities; and to bring them back again, to unite all speaking the German tongue in one confederated Germany, is an object for which German patriots have struggled for three hundred years, and struggled in vain.

"The American people have presented a similar spectacle on this side of the water—a new Allemanni—a people composed of many races confederated together in one nationality, and having hitherto a common destiny. By the establishment of the Constitution and Government of the United States we made ourselves a nation, and those who raise the flag of secession would make us what Germany now is—a body of contiguous but several States, with no other tie than a common language. The present condition of Germany is the work of her aristocracy, and those who would accomplish a similar work here proclaim to the world that they are the aristocracy of the country.

"You are not the first of the German race who have taken up arms in defence of this country. On that balcony before you, arrayed in the old Continental uniform of a Major-General, is the portrait of that noble German soldier whose honored name you bear. The aide-de-camp of Frederick the Great, and profoundly skilled in the art of war, acquired under the leadership of his great commander, Baron Steuben quitted a life of luxurious ease, and came to this country at a critical period to offer his services as a volunteer. He was the tactician of our Revolution. As Inspector-General of the American armies he revised our imperfectly disciplined troops, and taught them the art of war. His name is, and ever will be, associated with Monmouth and Valley Forge, and with the heights of Yorktown; and when the Revolution was over he selected our country as his home, and his body lies buried in its soil. At this time, when officers of the United States army hold so lightly to the obligation of their honor and their oath, it may be well to remember how Steuben regarded this class of traitors. When acting as Inspector-General in Virginia, he heard among the roll of recruits the name of Arnold. He ordered the young man to the front, and said: 'I cannot, sir, enlist you by the name of a traitor.' 'It is not my fault,' said the recruit, 'what other name can I take?' 'Take mine,' was the reply, and the soldier enlisted by the name of Steuben. This detestation of traitors is an old intrinsic German feeling. Tacitus tells us that the German tribes regarded as among the highest of crimes, and as a disgrace which could never be wiped out, the voluntary abandonment by a soldier of his shield.

"What was true then is true now; for no soldiers have surpassed the Germans in fidelity. Steuben was preëminently distinguished for this German virtue, and as a mark of especial merit received the cross of the Order of Fidelity. It was the only one of his decorations that he ever valued. It was the one he always wore, and by his request it was buried with him.

"The ladies whom I represent thought that you could carry no worthier symbol than Steuben's Cross of Fidelity. They have accordingly had it copied from the portrait in the City Hall, and emblazoned on this small flag, which I now present you.

"I commit also to your charge this flag of the United States, with its clustered stars and its many memories. It now depends upon you, and all arrayed like you in defence of the Union, whether a star shall be effaced or not from its blue field. You are American citizens; you are soldiers; you are Germans; you require no exhortation from me to stand faithfully by your colors. The history of your country for seventeen hundred years answers for you."

—*N. Y. Evening Post*, May 25.

Doc. 194.

JEFFERSON DAVIS' PROCLAMATION

TO THE PEOPLE OF THE CONFEDERATE STATES.

WHEN a people who recognize their dependence upon God, feel themselves surrounded by peril and difficulty, it becomes them to humble themselves under the dispensation of Divine Providence, to recognize His righteous government, to acknowledge His goodness in times past, and supplicate His merciful protection for the future.

The manifest proofs of the Divine blessing hitherto extended to the efforts of the people of the Confederate States of America, to maintain and perpetuate public liberty, individual rights, and national independence, demand their devout and heartfelt gratitude. It becomes them to give public manifestation of this gratitude, and of their dependence upon the Judge of all the earth, and to invoke the continuance of His favor. Knowing that none but a just and righteous cause can gain the Divine favor, we would implore the Lord of Hosts to guide and direct our policy in the paths of right, duty, justice, and mercy, to unite our hearts and our efforts for the defence of our dearest rights; to strengthen our weakness, crown our arms with success, and enable us to secure a speedy, just, and honorable peace.

To these ends, and in conformity with the request of Congress, I invite the people of the Confederate States to the observance of a day of fasting and prayer by such religious services as may be suitable for the occasion, and I recommend Thursday, the 13th day of June next, for that purpose, and that we may all, on that day, with one accord, join in humble and reverential approach to Him in whose hands we are, invoking Him to inspire us with a proper spirit and temper of heart and mind to bear our evils, to bless us with His favor and protection, and to bestow His gracious benediction upon our Government and country.

JEFFERSON DAVIS.

By the President:

R. TOOMBS, Secretary of State.

—*N. O. Picayune*, May 28.

Doc. 195.

THE MARCH INTO VIRGINIA.

FRIDAY, May 24.

THURSDAY night was a stirring one. Through the day and evening the reports of contemplated military movements kept the people on the *qui vive*, to which excitement fresh fuel was added on its being whispered that various regiments had been ordered to prepare for immediate service; the words dropped also by Gen. Thomas at the Seventh Regiment camp, to the effect that the storm was about to burst, indicated that a decisive move was to be taken. The general idea among the troops was that an advance was to be made into Virginia, but nobody seemed to be advised as to the exact purposes entertained at head-quarters.

At 11 o'clock we pushed off for the Long Bridge to see what was developing thereabouts. We found the vigilant sentries of the Washington Light Infantry (company A) posted some distance up Maryland avenue, and a portion of the same company somewhat lower down. A squad of the Infantry had also been detailed to a point near the monument, to keep an eye on any boats going out of the canal. Near the bridge and on the bridge were the Infantry, a company of Rhode Islanders, a Massachusetts company, a United States cavalry company, a company of United States artillery, (two pieces,) the Putnam Rifles, the Turner Rifles, National Rifles, Metropolitan Rifles, and company F, Union Volunteers; while company E, Washington Light Infantry, (Capt. Powell's Zouaves,) and the Constitutional Guards, occupied the Virginia end of the bridge.

A full moon looked peacefully down, and perfect quiet reigned on all the neighboring shores. But this was to give place very speedily to more stirring movements. Somewhat after midnight Capt. Smead's company, the National Rifles, and Capt. Powell's company were advanced across the bridge to the neighborhood of Roach's Spring. Scouts were sent out in all directions, who managed to get past the line of the Virginia pickets. Somewhat later the Virginia pickets, getting the alarm, set spurs to their horses and made off down the road towards Alexandria in hot haste.

The Constitutional Guards, Capt. Digges, about eighty strong, were on duty over the bridge. Col. Stone, of the District of Columbia volunteers, asked them if they had any objections to go beyond the District, as they were very close to Alexandria. The men answered unanimously in favor of going anywhere; and they were accordingly advanced along the road and through the country down as far as the Four-mile Run. The Virginia picket guard stationed near Roach's Spring ran, and about an hour after the alarm bells were rung in Alexandria.

This (Friday) morning, at two o'clock, in pursuance of orders previously given, a large body of United States troops crossed the Potomac from Washington and its neighborhood into Virginia. Ellsworth's Zouaves, in two steamers, with the steamer James Guy as accompanying tender, left their camp on the Eastern Branch and made directly for Alexandria by water. The Michigan Regiment, under Col. Wilcox, accompanied by a detachment of United States cavalry, and two pieces of Sherman's battery, under command of Lieut. Ransom, proceeded by way of the Long Bridge directly for Alexandria.

The Seventh New York Regiment halted under orders at Hughes' tavern, at the Virginia end of the Long Bridge; the Second New Jersey Regiment is at Roach's Spring, half a mile from the end of the bridge; the New York Twenty-fifth, and one cavalry company, and the New York Twelfth, and the Third and Fourth New Jersey Regiments proceeded to the right, after crossing the bridge, for the occupation of the Heights of Arlington. They were joined by other troops which crossed at the Georgetown Aqueduct.

At four o'clock, A. M., at about the same moment, the Zouaves landed at Alexandria from the steamers, and the troops before named, who proceeded by the bridge, reached that town. As the steamers drew up near the wharf, armed boats left the Pawnee, whose crews leaped upon the wharves just before the Zouaves reached the shore. The crews of the Pawnee's boats were fired upon by the few Virginia sentries as the boats left the steamship, by way of giving the alarm, when these sentries instantly fled into the town. Their fire was answered by impromptu shots from some of the Zouaves on the decks of the steamers bearing them. Immediately on landing Col. Ellsworth marched the Zouaves up into the centre of the town, no resistance whatever to their progress being offered.

Thus quiet possession was taken of that part of Alexandria in the name of the United States, by the portion of the troops immediately commanded by Col. Ellsworth.

Those commanded by Col. Wilcox, at about the same moment, as explained above, marched into the town by the extension of the Washington turnpike, the cavalry and artillery marching in two or three streets below. The destination of both these detachments was the depot of the Orange and Alexandria Railroad, which they instantly seized. They also found near by a disunion company of cavalry, commanded by Capt. Ball, (thirty-five men and as many horses,) who were made prisoners, not having heard the alarm made by the firing of the sentries below.

Every thing found in the depot, in the way of rolling stock, etc., is, of course, in the hands of the Government troops holding it.

A number of secession officers were captured in the Marshall House. They are held as prisoners.

At four o'clock in the morning, a number of Government wagons went across the Long Bridge loaded with picks, shovels, and all manner of tools of that description, and accompanied by a full corps of carpenters and workmen. The United States forces are now busily engaged in throwing up fortifications on the heights of the Virginia bank of the Potomac.

The whole of Sherman's battery (six pieces) crossed the Long Bridge in the advance during the night, two pieces going to Alexandria, and four pieces turning off to the right, Arlington way. At noon to-day Rickett's Light Artillery (six pieces) also went over the river from here.

Col. Wilcox, of the Michigan Regiment, is now in command at Alexandria.

The citizens of Alexandria appeared terrified. Many of the Union men shouted for joy at the success of the military demonstration, declaring that free speech and free institutions were again established there.

—*Washington Star*, May 24.

THE MOVEMENT UPON VIRGINIA.

The Government, at last, has moved in force upon Virginia. On the night of Thursday, ten thousand men crossed the Potomac at Washington, captured Alexandria without resistance, while a detachment pushed forward to seize the point of junction of the Manasses Gap, with the Orange and Alexandria Railroad, to cut off all communication between Richmond and the Northern portion of the State. This movement, if successful, completely breaks the lines of the rebels, isolates Harper's Ferry from the base of their operations, and involves either the dispersion or capture of the forces at that point. We also learn that a body of Ohio troops is moving from Wheeling by way of the Baltimore and Ohio Railroad upon the same point. We had no intelligence yesterday from Fort Monroe, but it is probable that the troops concentrated at that fortress under Gen. Butler, have moved in the direction of Richmond, so that every important point on the enemy's lines will, at the same instant, be either threatened or attacked.

We could not wish for a more favorable opening of the campaign. We desire to see all the secession forces upon the soil of Virginia. The rebellion is brought within reach of the most effective blows we can deal. We can move our forces into that State in one-fourth of the time, and at one-fourth of the expense at which the secessionists can place their own there. We could not well follow them to Georgia, Alabama, or Mississippi. The inhospitable climates of those States would prove more fatal than the arms of the rebels. But in Virginia we have an acceptable and healthy battle-field, where we can concentrate and put forth our whole power.

There is another reason why Virginia should be the battle-field of all the seceding States. She has been the greatest offender. She, more than any other State, is responsible for the great rebellion. Her spirit is the most vindictive and intolerant of all. A just retribution is already upon her. In a few days more than a hundred thousand fighting men will be on her soil which will be devastated by the terrible storm of war, her people driven from their homes, their fields blasted, their property destroyed, and their great institution at the mercy of their foes. Virginia should never have been a slave State. For the first time in her history, it is in our power to make it a *free* one.

In support of the advance upon the State, there must now be nearly 40,000 troops in or near Washington. Of these 30,000 could be made available for offensive operations. The number is daily and rapidly augmented by the constant arrival of regiments from every portion of the Northern States. This is a very formidable force, much larger we believe than can be opposed to it, should Harper's Ferry and Norfolk be attacked or threatened by competent forces at the same time. We possess great advantages, not only in the superiority of numbers, but in our means of concentration against any menaced points. In a very few days our active forces could be accumulated either at Washington or Fort Monroe. It would take as many weeks for the rebels to make a similar movement. Our position controls the entire field, with unlimited means for transportation, while the enemy must move upon its exterior, which, for a portion of the distance, is without either railroad or water-line. Such an advantage ought to be conclusive of the issue—as it fulfils the grand condition of success in military affairs—superior forces at point of contact.

We trust the present movement is the signal for efficient offensive operations. If the positions already taken are held, an important advantage has been gained. Our capital has been freed from the possibility of an attack. Up to yesterday the enemy, from Arlington Heights, might have shelled every part of the city. Northern Virginia has been completely cut off from the Southern portion of it. Such advantages should be instantly followed up. We need, if we can achieve it, an early success. The rebellion takes its character from the future fortune it meets. If successful, it is elevated to the dignity of a national contest. If unsuccessful it is only a conspiracy of a faction. We must expect foreign Governments to shape their policy by the same tests. If England sees us masters of the occasion, she will either maintain neutrality or side with us. If we are defeated, we must expect her hostility. It is, therefore, of the utmost importance that we make an early and decided demonstration. We cannot in the end fail to triumph, and we should instantly put forth every effort to such a result. The rebels will never give in so long as there is the shadow of hope of foreign interference in their favor. By destroying this hope, we put an end to the contest.

—*N. Y. Times.*

THE SOUTHERN PRESS ON THE OCCUPATION OF ALEXANDRIA.

The Rubicon has been passed. Yesterday a column of five thousand Federal troops crossed the Potomac, and took formal military possession of the unprotected town of Alexandria.

This is the first response of the Lincoln despotism to the shouts for freedom and independence which went up on Thursday from every portion of Virginia.

Alexandria has been declared by the Washington tyrants a portion of the District of Columbia, and as she gave, in the very face of the Federal army, an overwhelming majority for Secession, Lincoln has sent his troops there to develop and protect a Union sentiment.

Do these besotted fanatics flatter themselves that Alexandria is to be kept in chains like those which bind poor Baltimore to the car of the Federal despotism?

We congratulate the people of Virginia that the last flimsy pretext of the Rump Government at Washington, of regard for constitutional laws, has been thrown aside. The sovreign State of Virginia has been invaded by the Federal hirelings, without authority of Congress, which alone has the war-making power. Heretofore, the pretence that it was the duty of the Federal Government to repossess itself of the forts and arsenals in the seceded States, has been put forward to justify the aggressive movements of Federal troops. But in the present case there is no such pretence; no forts, or arsenals, or other Federal property have been seized at Alexandria. The "bloody and brutal" purposes of the Abolitionists, to subjugate and exterminate the Southern people, stands confessed by this flagrant outrage upon Virginia soil.

Virginians, arise in your strength and welcome the invader with "bloody hands to hospitable graves." The sacred soil of Virginia, in which repose the ashes of so many of the illustrious patriots who gave independence to their country, has been desecrated by the hostile tread of an armed enemy, who proclaims his malignant hatred of Virginia because she will not bow her proud neck to the humiliating yoke of Yankee rule. Meet the invader at the threshold. Welcome him with bayonet and bullet. Swear eternal hatred of a treacherous foe, whose only hope of safety is in your defeat and subjection.

It is not in the occupation of Alexandria that any cause for mortification exists—that has been for some time expected by those who were careful observers of events. It is in the continuance of the enemy upon our soil that we shall have cause for mortification. It is the fault of the enemy that he has invaded Virginia; it will be our fault if he does not pay the penalty of his rashness. An army full of strength and power went from France to Moscow; a broken remnant of starving and miserable men returned to France to tell the sad tale of disaster and defeat. Virginia will be the Moscow of the Abolitionists—our armies are gathering to the prey, and so surely as the patriot freemen of the Southern army come in conflict with the mercenary hordes of the North, so surely will they give the world another example of the invincibility of a free people fighting on their own soil for all that is dear to man. —*Richmond Enquirer.*

Virginia is invaded. That horde of thieves, robbers, and assassins in the pay of Abraham Lincoln, commonly known as the army of the United States, have rushed into the peaceful streets of a quiet city of the State, and stained the hearth of Virginia homes with the blood of her sons. Alexandria had been captured without resistance, for none had been prepared. The city was left (perhaps with strategic reason) without a picket guard, and no attempt has ever been made to blow up or batter down the bridge across the Potomac River, over which the troops of Lincoln marched to it.

One trait of true heroism has signalized this unhappy affair. A citizen of Alexandria, named Jackson, lacked the prudence to haul down the flag of his country, which streamed over his dwelling. That band of execrable cut-throats and jail-birds, known as the "Zouaves of New York," under the chief of all scoundrels, called Col. Ellsworth, surrounded the house of this Virginian, and broke open the door to tear down the flag of the South. The courageous owner of that house neither fled nor submitted. He met the favorite hero of every Yankee there in his hall, he alone, against thousands, and shot him through the heart! As a matter of course, the magnanimous soldiery surrounded him, and hacked him to pieces with sword bayonets, on the spot, in his own violated home. But he died a death which Emperors might envy, and his memory will live in history, and in the hearts of his countrymen, through endless generations. Here, indeed, was courage! He stood by his flag, he fell alone in defence of his hearth, and taught the invader what soil he trod on.

Apart from the sufferings of our devoted countrymen in Alexandria, the capture of the city in itself is not important.
—*Richmond Examiner.*

The intelligence of yesterday, that the myrmidons of Federal power had advanced upon the soil of Virginia, produced an electrifying effect in our community, and among the soldiery. Every eye brightened, and every heart beat with stern delight that the hour of vengeance is at hand. If Virginia can be overrun by a host of Northern militiamen, if one man in defence of his fireside is not equal to two invaders, then this onward movement of our detestable enemy is founded in wisdom. But when that day comes, it will be a new day in the history of nations, and one which will prove that we deserved to be conquered. It has been given out repeatedly of late by the

Lincoln press, that Gen. Scott desired to delay an advance till cool weather, and till his army was fully organized. But they could not brook the whole delay recommended by the only General in their ranks that deserves the name, and the Republican papers at Washington pronounced Scott behind the times. They will discover before long that it would have been well for them to take his counsel. They disregarded his advice once before in their attempt to reinforce Fort Sumter, and they will find a worse result from their present contempt of his military experience and judgment. This ferocious and vile attempt to subjugate Virginia will be crushed at very point where it is made, and there is not a man in the Commonwealth who does not rejoice that it is made now, when the season and other advantages which it is unnecessary to mention will unite to consign it to a speedy disaster and annihilation.
—*Richmond Dispatch.*

ASSASSINATION OF ELLSWORTH.

The special correspondent of the N. Y. Tribune, writing from Washington, gives the following account of this occurrence:—" I have already given by telegraph a brief account of the successful movement of to-day, and of our sorrowful calamity, and I hasten to send such details as my own observation enables me to supply. The part of the expedition with which I moved was that under command of the late Col. Ellsworth. His regiment of Zouaves was certainly the most actively employed, and was the earliest upon the hostile ground; and with him were associated the most startling events of the day. Of the general forces which are now assembled in Alexandria, others can speak better than I, for their operations were wholly distinct, until the time of the junction, when they were combined under one command. The exact nature of the inroad, as well as the means by which it was to be effected, were of course withheld from the public up to the latest hour, and the only sure method of gaining accurate knowledge of the result was by joining what seemed likely to be the leading body in the movement.

It was generally understood in Washington, on Thursday evening, that an advance of some sort was contemplated, though the rumors fixed no exact time or point of assault. But as the night advanced, the slight fever of excitement which the half-authorized intelligence created, wore away, and the city fell into its usual tranquillity. The contrast between its extreme quiet and the bustle which pervaded some of the expectant camps, was very remarkable. I crossed the Potomac, from Seventh street, in a little boat, and before I had half reached the Zouave camp, unusual indications of busy preparation came echoing over the water. The night was peculiarly still and clear, and the moon so full and lustrous, that the camp was almost visible from the opposite shore. Above the slight murmur caused by the rustle of arms and the marching, a song would occasionally be heard, and once the whole regiment burst out into 'Columbia, the Gem of the Ocean,' with all the fervor they could bring to it. It was not early when I reached the camp, but the exercise was still progressing under the vigilance of the Colonel, who threw in now and then clear and energetic counsels for the guidance of his men in the morning's work. Before midnight every thing needful had been done, and the troops were scattered to their tents for two hours of rest. The Colonel did not sleep until much later. He sat at his table completing the official arrangements which remained to him, and setting carefully before his subordinates the precise character of the duties they were to be charged with. After this he was alone, and I thought, as I entered his tent a little before he turned to his straw and blankets, that his pen was fulfilling a tenderer task than the rough planning of a dangerous exploit. He was so much a stranger to fear, this brave little Colonel, that his friends sometimes wondered at him; but it seemed, then, that he was not insensible to the awful hazards of his station. I hope that those who were nearest to him will find a touch of consolation in the assurance that the last moments he passed alone were given to them.

For more than an hour the encampment was silent. Then it began to stir again, and presently was all alive with action. At 2 o'clock, steamboats appeared off the shore, from one of which Capt. Dahlgren, the commander of the Navy Yard, came to announce that all was ready for the transportation. The men marched forward in line, and were drawn up by companies to the beach. At this time, the scene was animated in the highest degree. The vivid costumes of the men—some being wrapt from head to foot in their great red blankets, but most of them clad in their gray jackets and trowsers and embroidered caps; the peaks of the tents, regularly distributed, all glowing like huge lanterns from the fires within them; the glittering rows of rifles and sabres; the woods and hills, and the placid river, which here meet in exquisite proportion, enfolding all—and all these suffused with the broad moonlight, were blended in such novel picturesqueness that no man among the throng could fail to be moved by it. The embarkation was rapidly conducted, and, although the spot chosen was not apparently the most advantageous, was completed in less than two hours. The entire regiment, excepting the small guard necessarily left behind, nearly one thousand men, were safely bestowed and on their way down the river by 4 o'clock, just as the dawn began to shine over the hills and through the trees.

The night had passed without any noteworthy incident. It had been thought possible that the rebels, who could by some means undoubtedly have gained premonition of the movement, might fire the bridge by which other regiments were to advance upon them, and thus diminish the attacking force for a time. Nothing of this kind, however, had been attempted, and as we steamed down the river, (very slowly, for the boats were heavily laden,) there was no sign that we were expected, or that any inroad was provided against. This seemed at first suspicious, especially as on nearing Alexandria we found it sharing the same appearance of repose. It could hardly be credited that at least a rumor of warning should not have reached them. But if it had, it would appear that their enormous self-confidence was not to be even thus disturbed, for it afterward was found that no preparations either for resistance or for evacuation had been made until early in the morning, when, if I am rightly informed, the sloop-of-war Pawnee had sent ashore a summons to surrender the town, which I believe the garrison were considering, or had partially assented to, when we arrived. It was not until our boats were about to draw up to the wharf that our approach was noticed in any way; but at the latest minute a few sentinels, whom we had long before discerned, fired their muskets in the air as a warning, and, running rapidly into the town, disappeared. Two or three of the Zouaves, fancying that the shots were directed toward them, (which they certainly were not,) discharged their rifles after the retreating forms, but no injury to any body followed. The town was thus put on its guard, but yet so early was the hour, and so apparently unlooked-for our arrival, that when we landed, about half-past 5 o'clock, the streets were as deserted as if it had been midnight.

Before our troops disembarked, a boat, filled with armed marines, and carrying a flag of truce, put off from the Pawnee, and landed ahead of us. From the officer in charge we learned that the Pawnee had already proposed terms of submission to the town, and that the Rebels had consented to vacate within a specified time. This seemed to settle the question of a contest in the negative; but in the confusion of mustering and forming the men, the intelligence was not well understood, and received but little attention. Indeed, I am quite sure that the Pawnee's officer did not seek Col. Ellsworth, to communicate with him, and that the Colonel only obtained a meagre share of information by seeking it directly from the bearer of the flag of truce himself. No doubt this omission arose from the confused condition in which affairs then stood. But it would have caused no difference in the Colonel's military plans. No attack was meditated, except in case of a forcible resistance to his progress. On the other hand, the idea of the place being under a truce seemed to banish every suspicion of a resistance either from multitudes or individuals. It was just possibly this consideration that led Col. Ellsworth to forego the requisite personal precautions, which, if taken, would have prevented his unhappy death. But I am sure none of us at that time estimated the probability of the danger which afterward menaced us. Perhaps the thought of actual bloodshed and death in war was too foreign to our experiences to be rightly weighed. But it certainly did not enter our minds then, as poor Ellsworth's fate has since taught us it should have done, that a town half waked, half terrified, and under truce, could harbor any peril for us. So the Colonel gave some rapid directions for the interruption of the railway course, by displacing a few rails near the depot, and then turned toward the centre of the town, to destroy the means of communication southward by the telegraph; a measure which he appeared to regard as very seriously important. He was accompanied by Mr. H. J. Winser, Military Secretary to the Regiment, the Chaplain, the Rev. E. W. Dodge, and myself. At first he summoned no guard to follow him, but he afterward turned and called forward a single squad, with a sergeant from the first company. We passed quickly through the streets, meeting a few bewildered travellers issuing from the principal hotel, which seemed to be slowly coming to its daily senses, and were about to turn toward the telegraph office, when the Colonel, first of all, caught sight of the secession flag, which has so long swung insolently in full view of the President's House. He immediately sent back the sergeant, with an order for the advance of the entire first company, and, leaving the matter of the telegraph office for a while, pushed on to the hotel, which proved to be the Marshall House, a second-class inn. On entering the open door the Colonel met a man in his shirt and trowsers, of whom he demanded what sort of flag it was that hung above the roof. The stranger, who seemed greatly alarmed, declared he knew nothing of it, and that he was only a boarder there. Without questioning him further the Colonel sprang up stairs, and we all followed to the topmost story, whence, by means of a ladder, he clambered to the roof, cut down the flag with Winser's knife, and brought it from its staff. There were two men in bed in the garret whom we had not observed at all when we entered, their position being somewhat concealed, but who now rose in great apparent amazement, although I observed that they were more than half dressed. We at once turned to descend, Private Brownell leading the way, and Colonel Ellsworth immediately following him with the flag. As Brownell reached the first landing-place, or entry, after a descent of some dozen steps, a man jumped from a dark passage, and hardly noticing the private, levelled a double-barrelled gun square at the Colonel's breast. Brownell made a quick pass to turn the weapon aside, but the fellow's hand was firm, and he discharged one barrel straight to its aim, the slugs or buckshot with which it was loaded entering the Colonel's heart, and killing him at the instant. I think my arm was resting on poor Ellsworth's shoulder at the moment. At any rate, he seemed to fall almost from my own grasp. He was on the second or third step from the landing, and he dropped forward with that heavy, horrible, headlong weight which

always comes of sudden death inflicted in this manner. His assailant had turned like a flash to give the contents of the other barrel to Brownell, but either he could not command his aim or the Zouave was too quick with him, for the slugs went over his head, and passed through the panels and wainscot of a door which sheltered some sleeping lodgers. Simultaneously with this second shot, and sounding like the echo of the first, Brownell's rifle was heard and the assassin staggered backward. He was hit exactly in the middle of the face, and the wound, as I afterward saw it, was the most frightful I ever witnessed. Of course Brownell did not know how fatal his shot had been, and so before the man dropped, he thrust his sabre bayonet through and through the body, the force of the blow sending the dead man violently down the upper section of the second flight of stairs, at the foot of which he lay with his face to the floor. Winser ran from above crying, "Who is hit?" but as he glanced downward by our feet, he needed no answer.

Bewildered for an instant by the suddenness of this attack, and not knowing what more might be in store, we forbore to proceed, and gathered together defensively. There were but seven of us altogether, and one was without a weapon of any kind. Brownell instantly reloaded, and while doing so perceived the door through which the assailant's shot had passed, beginning to open. He brought his rifle to the shoulder, and menaced the occupants, two travellers, with immediate death if they stirred. The three other privates guarded the passages, of which there were quite a number converging to the point where we stood, while the Chaplain and Winser looked to the staircase by which we had descended, and the adjoining chambers. I ran down stairs to see if any thing was threatened from the story below, but it soon appeared there was no danger from that quarter. However, we were not at all disposed to move from our position. From the opening doors, and through the passages, we discerned a sufficient number of forms to assure us that we were dreadfully in the minority. I think now that there was no danger, and that the single assailant acted without concert with anybody; but it is impossible to know accurately, and it was certainly a doubtful question then. The first thing to be done was to look to our dead friend and leader. He had fallen on his face, and the streams of blood that flowed from his wound had literally flooded the way. The Chaplain turned him gently over, and I stooped and called his name aloud, at which I thought then he murmured inarticulately. I presume I was mistaken, and I am not sure that he spoke a word after being struck, although in my despatch I repeated a single exclamation which I had believed he uttered. It might have been Brownell, or the Chaplain, who was close behind me. Winser and I lifted the body with all the care we could apply, and laid it upon a bed in a room near by. The rebel flag, stained with his blood, and purified by this contact from the baseness of its former meaning, we laid about his feet. It was at first difficult to discover the precise locality of his wound, for all parts of his coat were equally saturated with blood. By cautiously loosening his belt and unbuttoning his coat we found where the shot had penetrated. None of us had any medical knowledge, but we saw that all hope must be resigned. Nevertheless, it seemed proper to summon the surgeon as speedily as possible. This could not easily be done; for, secluded as we were in that part of the town, and uncertain whether an ambush might not be awaiting us also, no man could volunteer to venture forth alone; and to go together, and leave the Colonel's body behind, was out of the question. We wondered at the long delay of the first company, for the advance of which the Colonel had sent back before approaching the hotel; but we subsequently learned that they had mistaken a street, and gone a little out of their way. Before they arrived we had removed some of the unsightly stains from the Colonel's features, and composed his limbs. His expression in death was beautifully natural. The Colonel was a singularly handsome man, and, excepting the pallor, there was nothing different in his countenance now from what all his friends had so lately been accustomed to gladly recognize. The detachment was heard approaching at last, a reënforcement was easily called up, and the surgeon was sent for. His arrival, not long after, of course sealed our own unhappy belief. A sufficient guard was presently distributed over the house, but meanwhile I had remembered the Colonel's earnestness about the telegraph seizure, and obtained permission to guide a squad of Zouaves to the office, which was found to be entirely open, with all the doors ajar, yet apparently deserted. It looked like another chance of a surprise. The men remained in charge. I presume it was not wholly in order for me, a civilian, to start upon this mission; but I was the only person who knew the whereabouts of the office, and the Colonel had been very positive about the matter. When I returned to the hotel, there was a terrible scene enacting. A woman had run from a lower room to the stairway where the body of the defender of the secession flag lay, and recognizing it, cried aloud with an agony so heart-rending that no person could witness it without emotion. She flung her arms in the air, struck her brow madly, and seemed in every way utterly abandoned to desolation and frenzy. She offered no reproaches—appeared indeed almost regardless of our presence, and yielded only to her own frantic despair. It was her husband that had been shot. He was the proprietor of the hotel. His name was James T. Jackson. Winser was confident it was the same man who met us at the door when we entered, and told us he was a boarder. His wife, as I said, was wild almost to insanity. Yet she listened

when spoken to, and although no consolation could be offered her by us for what she had lost, she seemed sensible to the assurance that the safety of her children, for whom she expressed fears, could not possibly be endangered.

It is not from any wish to fasten obloquy upon the slayer of Col. Ellsworth, but simply because it struck me as a frightful fact, that I say the face of the dead man wore the most revolting expression of rage and hatred that I ever saw. Perhaps the nature of his wound added to this effect, and the wound was something so appalling that I shall not attempt to describe it, as it impressed me. It is probable that such a result from a bullet-wound could not ensue once in a thousand times. Either of Brownell's onslaughts would have been instantaneously fatal. The saber-wound was not less effective than that of the ball. The gun which Jackson had fired lay beneath him, clasped in his arms, and as we did not at first all know that both barrels had been discharged, it was thought necessary to remove it, lest it should be suddenly seized and made use of from below. In doing this, his countenance was revealed.

As the morning advanced, the townspeople began to gather in the vicinity, and a guard was fixed, preventing ingress and egress. This was done to keep all parties from knowing what had occurred, for the Zouaves were so devoted to their Colonel that it was feared if they all were made acquainted with the real fact, they would sack the house. On the other hand, it was not thought wise to let the Alexandrians know thus early the fate of their townsman. The Zouaves were the only regiment that had arrived, and their head and soul was gone. Besides, the duties which the Colonel had hurriedly assigned before leaving them had scattered some companies in various quarters of the town. Several persons sought admission to the Marshall House, among them a sister of the dead man, who had heard the rumor, but who was not allowed to know the true state of the case. It was painful to hear her remark, as she went away, that "of course they wouldn't shoot a man dead in his own house about a bit of old bunting." Many of the lodgers were anxious to go forth, but they were detained until after I had left. All sorts of arguments and persuasions were employed, but the Zouave guards were inexorable.

At about 7 o'clock, a mounted officer rode up, and informed us that the Michigan 1st had arrived, and had captured a troop of rebels, who had at first demanded time for reflection, but who afterward concluded to yield at discretion. Not long after this, the surgeon made arrangements for the conveyance of Col. Ellsworth's body to Washington. It was properly veiled from sight, and, with great tenderness, taken by a detachment of the Zouaves and the 71st New York Regiment (a small number of whom, I neglected to state, embarked in the morning at the Navy Yard, and came down with us) to the steamboat, by which it was brought to the Navy Yard. It now remains in the care of Capt. Dahlgren.

Washington is greatly excited over the strange news, and there seems to be much doubt among the citizens as to what has really been accomplished. I am as yet ignorant of the movements of other troops sent to occupy the place, but there can be no question but that an ample force, for all the purposes we need to carry out, is now there. I only attempt to furnish a record of that part of the expedition which I witnessed, and to supply the particulars, which would surely be sought after, of the bereavement which has caused our grievous sorrow. I am sure that no young officer in our Northern land could be more sincerely and universally mourned than Col. Ellsworth will be. Perhaps none so much so, for his name was a familiar token for all that was brave, and loyal, and true. There is not a town that did not know him, and could not speak of him to his honor. His friends, while lamenting his early fall, may assure themselves that he perished in performing a daring and courageous action—in resenting a shameful and long-unredressed insult to his Government and the Chief Magistrate of his country. It may be said that his deed was rash, but I should not like to hear this reproach too hardly urged against him. He was young, and ardent, and full of ambition, and perhaps knew not that sense of caution which a colder nature would possess. But it would be well for many of us if we were as free from faults, and as rich in manly virtues, as was this gallant, noble, and devoted soldier.

I find that I have been free in speaking of my own very slight connection with the events of this morning. It certainly was not from any anxiety on my part to do so; but because I could not, in making a rapid and yet particular narration of a matter in which so few persons acted, avoid alluding to each incident precisely as it occurred, without pausing to consider at this time the question of personality.

—*N. Y. Tribune*, May 26.

COL. ELLSWORTH TO HIS PARENTS.

HEAD-QUARTERS FIRST ZOUAVES, }
Camp Lincoln, Washington, May 23, 1861. }

MY DEAR FATHER AND MOTHER :—The regiment is ordered to move across the river to-night. We have no means of knowing what reception we are to meet with. I am inclined to the opinion that our entrance to the city of Alexandria will be hotly contested, as I am just informed that a large force have arrived there to-day. Should this happen, my dear parents, it may be my lot to be injured in some manner. Whatever may happen, cherish the consolation that I was engaged in the performance of a sacred duty, and to-night, thinking over the probabilities of the morrow and the occurrences of the past, I am perfectly content to accept whatever my fortune may be, confident that He who noteth even the fall of a sparrow will have some purpose even in the fate of one like me. My darling and ever-loved parents, good-bye. God bless, protect, and care for you.

ELMER.

—*National Intelligencer*, May 29.

Doc. 196.

FIRST REGIMENT OF N. Y. VOLUNTEERS.

AT half-past four o'clock, the regiment embarked on the Staten Island boat for New York. On the passage, the soldiers sang numerous stirring songs, suited to the occasion, and the full-voiced music rolled over the heaving billows like a refrain from some far distant isle, inhabited by the genius of song and the spirit of patriotism. Arriving at the Battery, they found a large and enthusiastic congregation of people waiting for their coming; and as they stepped from the boat, they were received with three uproarious cheers. But the enthusiasm had just commenced. Marching up Broadway preceded by a band of music, they were received with a continual ovation of cheers and shouts. Every tongue gave a welcome; and hats waved in enthusiastic greeting. It was enough. The gallant boys knew that they were departing upon a mission in which the heart of New York went with them; and the proud step and mantling cheek showed that they appreciated the eminent position.

On arriving at the Astor House, the regiment formed in line, and Major-General Dix, accompanied by Dr. A. B. Mott, passed along the entire length, for review, with heads uncovered. The officers were called to the front, and the following letter was read to them:

" Col. Allen, First Regiment N. Y. Volunteers : In the conviction that the regiment in your command, will prove worthy of the great cause to which they have sworn fidelity, knowing that the requisites of so large a body of men generally exceed the outfit allowed by the Government, we desire to offer our services in preparing any garments you may need, either at the present time or a later period of the war. A note stating your necessities, addressed to any of the undersigned, will meet with prompt attention.

"ARABELLA P. MOTT, 209 Tenth street.
GEORGIANA S. PETERS, 19 E. 15th street.
ELEANOR F. STRONG 38 E. 22d street.
ELLA COLES, 298 Fifth avenue.
MARY BENKARD, 96 Fifth avenue."

Colonel Allen replied with some difficulty, as he was suffering from a severe cold. The officers then entered a room in the Astor House, where the ladies were, and Dr. Mott said:

" Col. Allen and officers of the First Regiment :—The ladies present, are those who have attached their names to the letter read to you, offering their services to contribute whatever is necessary for the use of the regiment. It would take too long a time to introduce them to you personally, but the occasion calls for a fervent expression of feeling, which I am physically unable to express, and will therefore let Major Turner, to-day, say for me what I wish. He will be kind enough to express our kind feelings and intentions.

Major Turner then spoke as follows:

"In obedience, ladies, to the request made by the colonel, and equally for myself, I can utter but one sentiment expressing that entertained by my associate officers. It is indeed a source of consolation for us to know, that in leaving our homes, there are those behind coming forward, as you have, representing a large and formidable body of strong hearts, that have produced soldiers, and can cheer them in action —sustain them in the trials of life, and in the last and best, make them to know that you will assist those whom they leave behind them.

"For myself—and it is the sentiment entertained by the officers of this regiment—I can say that they are more than grateful. We can promise you, that inasmuch as we have the honor to be the First Regiment of New York Volunteers, we will pledge ourselves to sustain the high position that we hold; and permit me to assure you, ladies, that in our absence, you at home, when you hear of us, shall have no occasion to regret having proffered the valuable services you have tendered.

"We should not be indifferent to the fact that, on going to the field, we are not going to meet a foreign foe, but we are going to quell a rebellion at home. We are going to put down treason against the best interests of our country. We are going to preserve the liberties that we were born in possession of, and we will do more than that; we will prove to the world that we are not only the First Regiment numbered in the position of our army, but that we are the first nation on this earth. I thank you, ladies, in behalf of my associates. Let me assure you, ladies, there are many hearts throbbing in unison with those that are here.

"We will endeavor to discharge our duty, conscious that those who set us in the field had confidence in us. Again, ladies, let me, in the names of the officers of the First Regiment, return our sincere and most grateful thanks."

The following impromptu lines, by E. T. P. Beach, were presented to Col. Allen:

HAIL TO OUR BANNER!

Hail to the Banner that waveth in glory!
  Hail to the Flag of our dear cherished land!
Hail to the standard long honored in story!
  Boldly defend it, my brave, gallant band.
    Hail to the donors fair,
    Who in their country's share
    Ever stand ready in peril or need;
    Hail to each tender heart,
    Break though it may part,
    Bravely will own their dearest "God speed."

Guard well the Banner we give to your keeping,
  It shieldeth your honor, your fair, and your land;
Let the bright eyes that in farewells are weeping,
  Behold it in glory return with your band!
    Hail to the Banner bold!
    Guard well each precious fold!
    Cherish our starry-gemmed red, white, and blue;
    God will uphold the right!
    Bravely, then, to the fight—
    God speed the noble First, brave hearts and true!

The officers then returned to the regiment, and soon after it proceeded up Broadway, receiving again a great amount of cheering. Windows were beautified by the faces of the fair, who waved their handkerchiefs to the passing regiment. At length it turned down Canal street, and embarked on board the State of Georgia.

The following is a list of the officers of the regiment:

STAFF.—Wm. H. Allen, Colonel; Garrett Dyckman, Lieutenant-Colonel; James M. Turner, Major; Walter Scott, Adjutant; J. Lawrence Hicks, M. D., Surgeon; John Howe, M. D., Surgeon's mate; Robt. S. Wormsley, Quartermaster.

NON-COMMISSIONED STAFF.—Benjamin Page, Sergeant-Major; James C. Briscoe, Color-Sergeant; Robert B. Montgomery, Quartermaster-Sergeant; James Murray, Officers' Mess-Steward; John S. Brush, Right General Guide; Richard J. Perry, Drum-Major; Richard Willis, Fife-Major.

Co. A, Captain, Leon Barnard; First Lieutenant, John C. Campbell; Second Lieutenant, N. S. Marcemus. Co. B, Captain, James Clancy; First Lieutenant, George W. Duncan; Second Lieutenant, Wm. T. Allen. Co. C, Captain, Wm. L. Coles; First Lieutenant, James C. Shaw; Second Lieutenant, David E. Carpenter. Co. D, Captain, Henry M. Burleigh; First Lieutenant, Chas. Ingersoll; Second Lieutenant, John C. Horton. Co. E, Captain, Timothy Waters; First Lieutenant, Jos. Yeomans; Second Lieutenant, Henry E. Ayers. Co. F, Captain, David Tuomey; First Lieutenant, Jas. F. Hyde; Second Lieutenant, Jas. Dolan. Co. G, Captain, Wm. H. Underhill; First Lieutenant, Geo. S. Melville; Second Lieutenant, Henry S. Hetheringer. Co. H, Captain, Jas. H. Brennan; First Lieutenant, N. C. Hamilton; Second Lieutenant, C. M. Martin. Co. J, Captain, Ole P. Balling; First Lieutenant, Christian T. Christiansen; Second Lieutenant, Alfred Furberg. Co. K, Captain, Winer Bjing; First Lieutenant, Nicholas Grosbeck; Second Lieutenant, John Allen.

—N. Y. Times, May 27.

Doc. 197.

MAJOR SPRAGUE'S LETTER.

SAN ANTONIO, TEXAS, April 24, 1861.

DEAR SIR:—Since my last letter events have culminated here so rapidly it is impossible for me to narrate them in detail. To myself, the most important event is my arrest as a prisoner of war. The decided measures adopted in Washington towards the Confederate States alarmed the authorities at Montgomery, when orders were transmitted to arrest and disarm the United States troops en route out of Texas, under the agreement made by Gen. Twiggs, and to arrest the United States officers on duty in San Antonio, "as prisoners of war." The sacred engagement made by Texas that the entire command serving in that State should pass out unmolested has been disregarded, and Texas, through her recently acknowledged government, has participated in this most graceless act. Fifteen officers have been arrested and marched through the streets of San Antonia, surrounded by a guard of Texas volunteers. Most of these officers have served from five to ten years protecting the frontier. When coming into the seceding States, in February last, on my way to New Mexico, I had serious apprehensions of the present result, and endeavored by timely application to the proper authorities to avoid it, but was unsuccessful, and here I am, " a prisoner of war." If taken in conflict, or in any honorable mode of warfare, I would not grumble; but to be crushed in this manner, a victim to the treachery of others, is more than man can bear. I have served for twenty-two years under our flag, and seen it go up and down with the rising and setting sun, and have witnessed its blessings, with a proud heart, in all parts of our country. To this Union I am devoted, and though for a time my sword may rest in its scabbard, yet my tongue, heart, intellect, and pen shall be devoted to an eternal warfare against those who, with vindictive spleen and pretended wrongs, would destroy this Government, under which we have lived and prospered so many years.

Political parties and questions are now at an end; the negro has gone under, neck and heels, and it becomes every man who cherishes his home to stand by the Union. We have paroles offered obligating us not to bear arms during what they, the enemy, call the war, unless exchanged, or to remain close prisoners of war. All communication with the States, by mail or otherwise, is cut off, and the entire country is under the control of ranging volunteers. The officers and men, though removed from all connection with the Government, and entreated by the agents of the Confederate States to join their cause, with the prospect of increased rank and pay, have remained true to their colors, in the firm conviction in the ability and patriotism of the people to redress our wrongs. Shall we remain here as prisoners, or take a parole and trust to luck? That is the question.

I give you a few of the heavy items received by the last mail from New Orleans, which are certainly not encouraging to prisoners of war in a foreign land, viz.: President Lincoln fled from Washington; Gen. Scott resigned and joined the Confederate States; Tennessee, Kentucky, Maryland, and Virginia out of the Union; the Seventh New York Regiment cut up *en route* through Baltimore for Washington; fifty thousand men from the South surrounding Washington, and the women and children notified to leave; Gosport navy-yard taken by Virginia after a sharp conflict—forty Union men killed. How true the foregoing is we are yet to learn, doubtful if we ever know the truth if depending upon the newspapers received here. It is thus that the citizens of this section are

Doc.—29

taught to believe that the Government of the United States is at an end. I send this by a friend, who will put it in the first reliable post-office—probably St. Louis.

Another item has just come to hand through the stage way-bill from Indianola, on the coast, one hundred and fifty miles distant. The Star of the West, awaiting the arrival of the United States troops to embark to New York, has been stolen by the Secessionists, and the troops under Major Sibley, while on board lighters off the bar, have been surrounded by two armed steamers from New Orleans containing six hundred men, with artillery, and made prisoners of war. The officers and men, it is said, have taken paroles. Here again the attempt was made to seduce them from their colors by rank and pay, but without success. It is thus events accumulate around us, sad and disastrous indeed, but our faith is firm. We may be discouraged, treated with indignity, our Government derided, even our allegiance, under these disasters, ridiculed; still there is an unwavering fidelity to our Union among the officers and soldiers of the army in this quarter which cannot be questioned nor surpassed. It looks rather dark at present, but daylight is breaking, even in this remote and foreign land. I never thought the time would come when I should be a stranger among my own countrymen. I fear there is a worm planted within our bosoms that will never die.

As ever, truly yours,
J. T. SPRAGUE.

—*National Intelligencer*, May 27.

Doc. 197½.

JOSEPH HOLT'S LETTER

ON THE PENDING REVOLUTION.*

WASHINGTON, May 31, 1861.

J. F. SPEED, ESQ.:

My Dear Sir:—The recent overwhelming vote in favor of the Union in Kentucky has afforded unspeakable gratification to all true men throughout the country. That vote indicates that the people of that gallant State have been neither seduced by the arts nor terrified by the menaces of the revolutionists in their midst, and that it is their fixed purpose to remain faithful to a Government which, for nearly seventy years, has remained faithful to them. Still it cannot be denied that there is in the bosom of that State a band of agitators, who, though few in number, are yet powerful from the public confidence they have enjoyed, and who have been, and doubtless will continue to be, unceasing in their endeavors to force Kentucky to unite her fortunes with those of the rebel Confederacy of the South. In view of this and of the well-known fact that several of the seceded States have by fraud and violence been driven to occupy their present false and

* Printed from the Louisville edition.

fatal position, I cannot, even with the encouragement of her late vote before me, look upon the political future of our native State without a painful solicitude. Never have the safety and honor of her people required the exercise of so much vigilance and of so much courage on their part. If true to themselves, the Stars and Stripes, which like angels' wings, have so long guarded their homes from every oppression, will still be theirs; but if, chasing the dreams of men's ambition, they shall prove false, the blackness of darkness can but faintly predict the gloom that awaits them. The Legislature, it seems, has determined by resolution that the State, pending the present unhappy war, shall occupy neutral ground. I must say, in all frankness and without designing to reflect upon the course or sentiments of any, that in this struggle for the existence of our Government, I can neither practise, nor profess, nor feel neutrality. I would as soon think of being neutral in a contest between an officer of justice and an incendiary arrested in an attempt to fire the dwelling over my head; for the Government whose overthrow is sought, is for me the shelter not only of home, kindred, and friends, but of every earthly blessing which I can hope to enjoy on this side of the grave. If, however, from a natural horror of fratricidal strife, or from her intimate social and business relations with the South, Kentucky shall determine to maintain the neutral attitude assumed for her by her Legislature, her position will still be an honorable one, though falling far short of that full measure of loyalty which her history has so constantly illustrated. Her Executive, ignoring, as I am happy to believe, alike the popular and legislative sentiment of the State, has, by proclamation, forbidden the Government of the United States from marching troops across her territory. This is, in no sense, a neutral step, but one of aggressive hostility. The troops of the Federal Government have as clear a constitutional right to pass over the soil of Kentucky as they have to march along the streets of Washington, and could this prohibition be effective it would not only be a violation of the fundamental law, but would, in all its tendencies, be directly in advancement of the revolution, and might, in an emergency easily imagined, compromise the highest national interests. I was rejoiced that the Legislature so promptly refused to endorse this proclamation as expressive of the true policy of the State. But I turn away from even this to the ballot-box, and find an abounding consolation in the conviction it inspires, that the popular heart of Kentucky, in its devotion to the Union, is far in advance alike of legislative resolve and of Executive proclamation.

But as it is well understood that the late popular demonstration has rather scotched than killed rebellion in Kentucky, I propose inquiring, as briefly as practicable, whether, in the recent action or present declared policy of the Administration, or in the history of the pending revolution, or in the objects it seeks to accomplish, or in the results which must follow from it if successful, there can be discovered any reasons why that State should sever the ties that unite her with a Confederacy in whose councils and upon whose battle-fields she has won so much fame, and under whose protection she has enjoyed so much prosperity.

For more than a month after the inauguration of President Lincoln the manifestation seemed unequivocal that his Administration would seek a peaceful solution of our unhappy political troubles, and would look to time and amendments to the Federal Constitution, adopted in accordance with its provisions, to bring back the revolted States to their allegiance. So marked was the effect of these manifestations in tranquillizing the Border States and reassuring their loyalty, that the conspirators who had set this revolution on foot took the alarm. While affecting to despise these States as not sufficiently intensified in their devotion to African servitude, they knew they could never succeed in their treasonable enterprise without their support. Hence it was resolved to precipitate a collision of arms with the Federal authorities, in the hope that, under the panic and exasperation incident to the commencement of civil war, the Border States, following the natural bent of their sympathies, would array themselves against the Government. Fort Sumter, occupied by a feeble garrison, and girdled by powerful if not impregnable batteries, afforded convenient means for accomplishing their purpose, and for testing also their favorite theory that blood was needed to cement the new Confederacy. Its provisions were exhausted, and the request made by the President in the interests of peace and humanity, for the privilege of replenishing its stores, had been refused. The Confederate authorities were aware—for so the gallant commander of the fort had declared to them—that in two days a capitulation from starvation must take place. A peaceful surrender, however, would not have subserved their aims. They sought the clash of arms and the effusion of blood as an instrumentality for impressing the Border States, and they sought the humiliation of the Government and the dishonor of its flag as a means of giving prestige to their own cause. The result is known. Without the slightest provocation a heavy cannonade was opened upon the fort, and borne by its helpless garrison for hours without reply, and when, in the progress of the bombardment, the fortification become wrapped in flames, the besieging batteries in violation of the usages of civilized warfare, instead of relaxing or suspending, redoubled their fires. A more wanton or wicked war was never commenced on any Government whose history has been written. Contemporary with and following the fall of Sumter, the siege of Fort Pickens was and still is actively pressed; the property of the United States Government continued to be seized wherever found, and its troops, by fraud or force, captured in the State of Texas in violation of a solemn compact with its authorities that they should be permitted to embark without molestation. This was the requital which the lone star State made to brave men who, through long years of peril and privation, had guarded its frontiers against the incursions of the savages. In the midst of the most active and extended warlike preparations in the South, the announcement was made by the Secretary of War of the seceded States, and echoed with taunts and insolent bravadoes by the Southern press, that Washington City was to be invaded and captured, and that the flag of the Confederate States would soon float over the dome of its Capitol. Soon thereafter there followed an invitation to all the world—embracing necessarily the outcasts and desperadoes of every sea—to accept letters of marque and reprisal, to prey upon the rich and unprotected commerce of the United States.

In view of these events and threatenings, what was the duty of the Chief Magistrate of the Republic? He might have taken counsel of the revolutionists and trembled under the menaces; he might, upon the fall of Sumter, have directed that Fort Pickens should be surrendered without firing a gun in its defence, and proceeding yet further, and meeting fully the requirements of the "let-us-alone" policy insisted on in the South, he might have ordered that the Stars and Stripes should be laid in the dust in the presence of every bit of rebel bunting that might appear. But he did none of these things, or could he have done them without forgetting his oath and betraying the most sublime trust that has ever been confided to the hands of man. With a heroic fidelity to his constitutional obligations, feeling justly that these obligations charged him with the protection of the Republic and its Capital against the assaults alike of foreign and domestic enemies, he threw himself on the loyalty of the country for support in the struggle upon which he was about to enter, and nobly has that appeal been responded to. States containing an aggregate population of nineteen millions have answered to the appeal as with the voice of one man, offering soldiers without number, and treasure without limitation, for the service of the Government. In these States fifteen hundred thousand freemen cast their votes in favor of candidates supporting the rights of the South, at the last Presidential election, and yet everywhere, alike in popular assemblies and upon the tented field, this million and a half of voters are found yielding to none in the zeal with which they rally to their country's flag. They are not less the friends of the South than before; but they realize that the question now presented is not one of administrative policy, or of the claims of the North, the South, the East, or the West; but is, simply, whether nineteen millions of people shall tamely or ignobly permit five or six millions to overthrow and destroy institutions which are the common property, and have been the common blessings and glory of all. The great thoroughfares of the North, the East, and the West, are luminous with the banners and glistening with the bayonets of citizen soldiers marching to the Capital, or to other points of rendezvous; but they come in no hostile spirit to the South. If called to press her soil, they will not ruffle a flower of her gardens, nor a blade of grass of her field in unkindness. No excesses will mark the footsteps of the armies of the Republic; no institution of the States will be invaded or tampered with, no rights of persons or of property will be violated. The known purposes of the Administration, and the high character of the troops employed, alike guarantee the truthfulness of this statement. When an insurrection was apprehended a few weeks since in Maryland, the Massachusetts regiment at once offered their services to suppress it. These volunteers have been denounced by the press of the South as "knaves and vagrants," "the dregs and offscourings of the populace," who would "rather filch a handkerchief than fight an enemy in manly combat;" yet we know here, that their discipline and bearing are most admirable, and, I presume, it may be safely affirmed, that a larger amount of social position, culture, fortune, and elevation of character, has never been found in so large an army in any age or country. If they go to the South, it will be as friends and protectors, to relieve the Union sentiment of the seceded States from the cruel domination by which it is oppressed and silenced, to unfurl the Stars and Stripes in the midst of those who long to look upon them, and to restore the flag that bears them to the forts and arsenals from which disloyal hands have torn it. Their mission will be one of peace, unless wicked and blood-thirsty men shall unsheath the sword across their pathway.

It is in vain for the revolutionists to exclaim that this is "subjugation." It is so, precisely, in the sense in which you and I and all the law-abiding citizens are subjugated. The people of the South are our brethren, and while we obey the laws enacted by our joint authority, and keep a compact to which we are all parties, we only ask that they shall be required to do the same. We believe that their safety demands this: we know that ours does. We impose no burden which we ourselves do not bear; we claim no privilege or blessing which our brethren of the South shall not equally share. Their country is our country, and ours is theirs; and that unity both of country and Government which the providence of God and the compacts of men have created, we could not ourselves, without self-immolation, destroy, nor can we permit it to be destroyed by others.

Equally vain is it for them to declare that they only wish "to be let alone," and that, in establishing the independence of the seceded States, they do those which remain in the old Confederacy no harm. The free States, if allowed the opportunity of doing so, will undoubtedly concede every guarantee needed to afford complete protection to the institutions of the South, and to furnish assurances of her perfect equality in the Union; but all such guarantees and assurances are now openly spurned, and the only Southern right now insisted on is that of dismembering the republic. It is perfectly certain that in the attempted exercise of this right neither States nor statesmen will be "let alone." Should a ruffian meet me in the streets, and seek with his axe to hew an arm or a leg from my body, I would not the less resist him because, as a dishonored and helpless trunk, I might perchance survive the mutilation. It is easy to perceive what fatal results to the old Confederacy would follow should the blow now struck at its integrity ultimately triumph. We can well understand what degradation it would bring to it abroad and what weakness at home; what exhaustion from incessant war and standing armies, and from the erection of fortifications along the thousands of miles of new frontier; what embarrassments to commerce from having its natural channels encumbered or cut off; what elements of disintegration and revolution would be introduced from the pernicious example; and, above all, what humiliation would cover the whole American people for having failed in their great mission to demonstrate before the world the capacity of our race for self-government.

While a far more fearful responsibility has fallen upon President Lincoln than upon any of his predecessors, it must be admitted that he has met it with promptitude and fearlessness. Cicero, in one of his orations against Catiline, speaking of the credit due to himself for having suppressed the conspiracy of that arch-traitor, said, "if the glory of him who founded Rome was great, how much greater should be that of him who had saved it from overthrow after it had grown to be the mistress of the world?" So it may be said of the glory of that statesman or chieftain who shall snatch from the vortex of revolution this republic, now that it has expanded from ocean to ocean, has become the admiration of the world, and has rendered the fountains of the lives of thirty millions of people fountains of happiness.

The vigorous measures adopted for the safety of Washington and the Government itself may seem open to criticism, in some of their details, to those who have yet to learn that not only has war like peace its laws, but that it has also its privileges and its duties. Whatever of severity, or even of irregularity, may have arisen, will find its justification in the pressure of the terrible necessity under which the Administration has been called to act. When a man feels the poignard of the destroyer at his bosom, he is not likely to consult the law books as to the mode or measure of his right of self-defence. What is true of individuals is in this respect equally true of governments. The man who thinks he has become disloyal because of what the Administration has done, will probably discover, after a close self-examination, that he was disloyal before. But for what has been done, Washington might ere this have been a smouldering heap of ruins.

They have noted the course of public affairs to little advantage who suppose that the election of Mr. Lincoln was the real ground of the revolutionary outbreak that has occurred. The roots of the revolution may be traced back for more than a quarter of a century, and an unholy lust for power is the soil out of which it sprang. A prominent member of the band of agitators declared in one of his speeches at Charleston, last November or December, that they had been occupied for thirty years in the work of severing South Carolina from the Union. When General Jackson crushed nullification, he said it would revive again under the form of the slavery agitation: and we have lived to see his prediction verified. Indeed, that agitation, during the last fifteen or twenty years, has been almost the entire stock in trade of Southern politicians. The Southern people, known to be as generous in their impulses as they are chivalric, were not wrought into a frenzy of passion by the intemperate words of a few fanatical abolitionists; for these words, if left to themselves, would have fallen to the ground as pebbles into the sea, and would have been heard of no more. But it was the echo of those words, repeated with exaggerations for the thousandth time by Southern politicians, in the halls of Congress, and in the deliberative and popular assemblies, and through the press of the South, that produced the exasperation that has proved so potent a lever in the hands of the conspirators. The cloud was fully charged, and the juggling revolutionists who held the wires and could at will direct its lightnings, appeared at Charleston, broke up the Democratic Convention assembled to nominate a candidate for the Presidency, and thus secured the election of Mr. Lincoln. Having thus rendered this certain, they at once set to work to bring the popular mind of the South to the point of determining in advance, that the election of a Republican President would be, per se, cause for a dissolution of the Union. They were but too successful, and to this result the inaction and indecision of the Border States deplorably contributed. When the election of Mr. Lincoln was announced, there was rejoicing in the streets of Charleston, and doubtless at other points in the South; for it was believed by the conspirators that this had brought a tide in the current of their machinations which would bear them on to victory. The drama of secession was now open, and State after State rapidly rushed out of the Union, and their members withdrew from Congress. The revolution was pressed on with this hot haste in order that no time should be allowed for reaction in the Northern mind, or for any adjustment of the slavery issues by the action of Congress or of the State Legislatures. Had the Southern members continued in their seats, a satisfactory compromise would, no doubt, have been arranged and passed before the adjournment of Congress. As it was, after their retirement, and after Congress had become Republican, an amendment to the Constitution was adopted by a two-thirds vote, declaring that Congress should never interfere with slavery in the States, and declaring, further, that this amendment should be irrevocable. Thus was falsified the clamor so long and so insidiously rung in the ears of the Southern people, that the abolition of slavery in the States was the ultimate aim of the Republican party. But even this amendment, and all others which may be needed to furnish the guarantees demanded, are now defeated by the secession of eleven States, which, claiming to be out of the Union, will refuse to vote upon, and in effect will vote against, any proposal to modify the Federal Constitution. There are now thirty-four States in the Confederacy, three-fourths of which, being twenty-six, must concur in the adoption of any amendment before it can become a part of the Constitution; but the secession of eleven States leaves but twenty-three whose vote can possibly be secured, which is less than the constitutional number.

Thus we have the extraordinary and discreditable spectacle of a revolution made by certain States professedly on the ground that guarantees for the safety of their institutions are denied them; and, at the same time, instead of coöperating with their sister States in obtaining these guarantees, they designedly assume a hostile attitude, and thereby render it constitutionally impossible to secure them. This profound dissimulation shows that it was not the safety of the South, but its severance from the Confederacy, which was sought from the beginning. Contemporary with, and in some instances preceding these acts of secession, the greatest outrages were committed upon the Government of the United States by the States engaged in them. Its forts, arsenals, arms, barracks, custom-houses, post-offices, moneys, and, indeed, every species of property within the limits of these States, were seized and appropriated, down to the very hospital stores for the sick soldiers. More than half a million of dollars was plundered from the mint at New Orleans. United States vessels were received from the defiled hands of their officers in command; and, as if in the hope of consecrating official treachery as one of the public virtues of the age, the surrender of an entire military department by a General, to the keeping of whose honor it had been confided, was deemed worthy of the commendation and thanks of the conventions of several States. All these lawless proceedings were well understood to have been prompted and directed by men occupying seats in the Capitol, some of whom were frank enough to declare that they could not and would not, though in a minority,

live under a Government which they could not control. In this declaration is found the key which unlocks the whole of the complicated machinery of this revolution. The profligate ambition of public men, in all ages and lands, has been the rock on which republics have been split. Such men have arisen in our midst —men who, because unable permanently to grasp the helm of the ship, are willing to destroy it in the hope to command some one of the rafts that may float away from the wreck. The effect is to degrade us to a level with the military bandits of Mexico and South America, who, when beaten at an election, fly to arms, and seek to master by the sword what they have been unable to control by the ballot-box.

The atrocious acts enumerated were acts of war, and might all have been treated as such by the late Administration; but the President patriotically cultivated peace, how anxiously, and how patiently, the country well knows. While, however, the revolutionary leaders greeted him with all hails to his face, they did not the less diligently continue to whet their swords behind his back. Immense military preparations were made, so that when the moment for striking at the Government of the United States arrived, the revolutionary States leaped into the contest clad in full armor.

As if nothing should be wanting to darken this page of history, the seceded States have already entered upon the work of confiscating the debts due from their citizens to the North and North-west. The millions thus gained will doubtless prove a pleasant substitute for those guarantees now so scornfully rejected. To these confiscations will probably succeed soon those of lands and negroes owned by the citizens of loyal States; and, indeed, the apprehension of this step is already sadly disturbing the fidelity of non-resident proprietors. Fortunately, however, infirmity of faith springing from such a cause, is not likely to be contagious. The war begun is being prosecuted by the Confederate States in a temper as fierce and unsparing as that which characterizes conflicts between the most hostile nations. Letters of marque and reprisal are being granted to all who seek them, so that our coasts will soon swarm with these piratical cruisers, as the President has properly denounced them. Every buccaneer who desires to rob American commerce upon the ocean, can, for the asking, obtain a warrant to do so, in the name of the new republic. To crown all, large bodies of Indians have been mustered into the service of the revolutionary States, and are now conspicuous in the ranks of the Southern army. A leading North Carolina journal, noting their stalwart frames and unerring marksmanship, observes, with an exultation positively fiendish, that they are armed, not only with the rifle, but also with *scalping knife and tomahawk*.

Is Kentucky willing to link her name in history with the excesses and crimes which have sullied this revolution at every step of its progress? Can she soil her pure hands with its booty? She possesses the noblest heritage that God has granted to his children; is she prepared to barter it away for that miserable mess of pottage, which the gratification of the unholy ambition of her public men would bring to her lips? Can she, without laying her face in the dust for very shame, become a participant in the spoliation of the commerce of her neighbors and friends, by contributing her star, hitherto so stainless in its glory, to light the corsair on his way? Has the war-whoop, which used to startle the sleep of our frontiers, so died away in her ears that she is willing to take the red-handed savage to her bosom as the champion of her rights and the representative of her spirit? Must she not first forget her own heroic sons who perished, butchered and scalped, upon the disastrous field of Raisin?

The object of the revolution, as avowed by all who are pressing it forward, is the permanent dismemberment of the Confederacy. The dream of reconstruction—used during the last winter as a lure to draw the hesitating or the hopeful into the movement—has been formally abandoned. If Kentucky separates herself from the Union, it must be upon the basis that the separation is to be final and eternal. Is there aught in the organization or administration of the Government of the United States to justify, on our part, an act so solemn and so perilous? Could the wisest of her lawyers, if called upon, find material for an indictment in any or in all the pages of the history of the Republic? Could the most leprous-lipped of its calumniators point to a single State or Territory, or community, or citizen, that it has wronged or oppressed? It would be impossible. So far as the Slave States are concerned, their protection has been complete, and if it has not been, it has been the fault of their statesmen, who have had the control of the Government since its foundation.

The census returns show that during the year 1860 the Fugitive Slave Law was executed more faithfully and successfully than it had been during the preceding ten years. Since the installation of President Lincoln not a case has arisen in which the fugitive has not been returned, and that, too, without any opposition from the people. Indeed, the fidelity with which it was understood to be the policy of the present Administration to enforce the provisions of this law, has caused a perfect panic among the runaway slaves in the free States, and they have been escaping in multitudes into Canada, unpursued and unreclaimed by their masters. Is there found in this reason for a dissolution of the Union?

That the slave States are not recognized as equals in the Confederacy has, for several years, been the cry of demagogues and conspirators. But what is the truth? Not only according to the theory, but the actual practice of the Government, the slave States have ever been, and still are, in all respects, the peers of the free. Of the fourteen Presidents who have been elected, seven were citizens of slave States, and of the seven remaining, three represented Southern principles, and received the votes of the Southern people; so that, in our whole history, but four Presidents have been chosen who can be claimed as the special champions of the policy and principles of the free States, and even these so only in a modified sense. Does this look as if the South had ever been deprived of her equal share of the honors and powers of the Government? The Supreme Court has decided that the citizens of the slave States can, at will, take their slaves into all the Territories of the United States; and this decision, which has never been resisted or interfered with in a single case, is the law of the land, and the whole power of the Government is pledged to enforce it. That it will be loyally enforced by the present Administration, I entertain no doubt. A Republican Congress, at the late session, organized three new Territories, and in the organic law of neither was there introduced, or attempted to be introduced, the slightest restriction upon the right of the Southern emigrant to bring his slaves with him. At this moment, therefore,—and I state it without qualification—there is not a Territory belonging to the United States into which the Southern people may not introduce their slaves at pleasure, and enjoy their complete protection. Kentucky should consider this great and undeniable fact, before which all the frothy rant of demagogues and disunionists must disappear as a bank of fog before the wind. But were it otherwise, and did a defect exist in our organic law, or in the practical administration of the Government, in reference to the rights of Southern slaveholders in the Territories, still the question would be a mere abstraction, since the laws of climate forbid the establishment of slavery in such latitudes; and to destroy such institutions as ours for such a cause, instead of patiently trying to remove it, would be little short of national insanity. It would be to burn the house down over our heads merely because there is a leak in the roof; to scuttle the ship in mid-ocean merely because there is a difference of opinion among the crew as to the point of the compass to which the vessel should be steered; it would be, in fact, to apply the knife to the throat, instead of to the cancer of the patient.

But what remains? Though, say the disunionists, the Fugitive Slave Law is honestly enforced, and though, under the shelter of the Supreme Court, we can take our slaves into the Territories, yet the Northern people will persist in discussing the institution of slavery, and therefore we will break up the Government. It is true that slavery has been very intemperately discussed in the North, and it is equally true that until we have an Asiatic despotism, crushing out all freedom of speech and of the press, this discussion will probably continue. In this age and country all institutions, human and divine, are discussed, and so they ought to be; and all that cannot bear discussion must go to the wall, where they ought to go. It is not pretended, however, that the discussion of slavery, which has been continued in our country for more than forty years, has in any manner disturbed or weakened the foundation of the institution. On the contrary, we learn from the press of the seceded States that their slaves were never more tranquil or obedient. There are zealots—happily few in number—both North and South, whose language upon this question is alike extravagant and alike deserving our condemnation. Those who assert that slavery should be extirpated by the sword and those who maintain that the great mission of the white man upon earth is to enslave the black, are not far apart in the folly and atrocity of their sentiments.

Before proceeding further, Kentucky should measure well the depth of the gulf she is approaching, and look well to the feet of her guides. Before forsaking a Union in which her people have enjoyed such uninterrupted and such boundless prosperity, she should ask herself, not once, but many times, WHY do I go, and WHERE am I going? In view of what has been said, it would be difficult to answer the first branch of the inquiry, but to answer the second part is patent to all, as are the consequences which would follow the movement. In giving her great material and moral resources to the support of the Southern Confederacy, Kentucky might prolong the desolating struggle that rebellious States are making to overthrow a Government which they have known only in its blessings; but the triumph of the Government would nevertheless be certain in the end. She would abandon a Government strong and able to protect her, for one that is weak, and that contains, in the very elements of its life, the seeds of destruction and early dissolution. She would adopt, as the law of her existence, the right of secession—a right which has no foundation in jurisprudence, or logic, or in our political history; which Madison, the father of the Federal Constitution, denounced; which has been denounced by most of the States and prominent statesmen now insisting upon its exercise; which, in introducing a principle of indefinite disintegration, cuts up all confederate governments by the root, and gives them over a prey to the caprices, and passions, and transient interests of their members, as autumnal leaves are given to the winds which blow upon them. In 1814, the Richmond Enquirer, then, as now, the organ of public opinion in the South, pronounced secession to be treason, and nothing else, and such was then the doctrine of Southern statesmen. What was true then is equally true now. The prevalence of this pernicious heresy is mainly the fruit of that farce called "State rights," which demagogues have been so long playing under tragic mask, and which has done more

than all things else to unsettle the foundations of the republic, by estranging the people from the Federal Government, as one to be distrusted and resisted, instead of being, what it is, emphatically their own creation, at all times obedient to their will, and in its ministrations the grandest reflex of the greatness and beneficence of popular power that has ever ennobled the history of our race. Said Mr. Clay: "I owe a supreme allegiance to the General Government, and to my State a subordinate one." And this terse language disposes of the whole controversy which has arisen out of the secession movement in regard to the allegiance of the citizen. As the power of the State and Federal Governments are in perfect harmony with each other, so there can be no conflict with the allegiance due to them; each, while acting within the sphere of its constitutional authority, is entitled to be obeyed; but when a State, throwing off all constitutional restraints, seeks to destroy the General Government, to say that its citizens are bound to follow in this career of crime, and discard the supreme allegiance they owe to the government assailed, is one of the shallowest and most dangerous fallacies that has ever gained credence among men.

Kentucky, occupying a central position in the Union, is now protected from the scourge of foreign war, however much its ravages may waste the towns and cities upon our coasts or the commerce upon our seas: but, as a member of the Southern Confederacy, she would be a frontier State, and necessarily the victim of those border feuds and conflicts which have become proverbial in history alike for their fierceness and frequency. The people of the South now sleep quietly in their beds, while there is not a home in infatuated and misguided Virginia that is not filled with the alarms and oppressed by the terrors of war. In the fate of this ancient Commonwealth, dragged to the altar of sacrifice by those who should have stood between her bosom and every foe, Kentucky may read her own. No wonder, therefore, that she has been so coaxingly besought to unite her fortune with those of the South, and to lay down the bodies of her chivalric sons as a breast-work, behind which the Southern people may be sheltered. Even as attached to the Southern Confederacy she would be weak for all the purposes of self-protection as compared with her present position. But amid the mutations incident to such a helpless and self-disintegrating league, Kentucky would probably soon find herself adhering to a mere fragment of the Confederacy, or it may be standing entirely alone, in the presence of tiers of free States with populations exceeding by many millions her own. Feeble States, thus separated from powerful and warlike neighbors by ideal boundaries, or by rivers as easily traversed as rivulets, are as insects that feed upon the lion's lip—liable at every moment to be crushed. The recorded doom of multitudes of such has left us a warning too solemn and impressive to be disregarded.

Kentucky now scarcely feels the contribution she makes to support the Government of the United States; but as a member of the Southern Confederacy, of whose policy free-trade will be a cardinal principle, she will be burdened with direct taxation to the amount of double, or it may be triple, or quadruple that which she now pays into her own treasury. Superadded to this will be required from her her share of those vast outlays necessary for the creation of a navy, the erection of forts and custom-houses along a frontier of several thousand miles, and for the maintenance of that large standing army which will be indispensable at once for her safety, and for imparting to the new government that strong military character which, it has been openly avowed, the peculiar institutions of the South will inexorably demand.

Kentucky now enjoys for her peculiar institutions the protection of the Fugitive Slave Law, loyally enforced by the Government; and it is this law, effective in its power of recapture, but infinitely more potent in its moral agency in preventing the escape of slaves, that alone saves that institution in the Border States from utter extinction. She cannot carry this law with her into the new Confederacy. She will virtually have Canada brought to her doors in the form of Free States, whose population, relieved of all moral and constitutional obligations to deliver up fugitive slaves, will stand with open arms inviting and welcoming them, and defending them, if need be, at the point of the bayonet. Under such influences, slavery will perish rapidly away in Kentucky, as a ball of snow melts in a summer's sun.

Kentucky in her soul abhors the African slave trade, and turns away with unspeakable horror and loathing from the red altars of Dahomey. But although the traffic has been temporarily interdicted by the seceded States, it is well understood that this step has been taken as a mere measure of policy for the purpose of impressing the Border States, and of conciliating the European powers. The ultimate legalization of this trade, by a Republic professing to be based upon African servitude, must follow as certainly as does the conclusion from the premises of a mathematical proposition. Is Kentucky prepared to see the hand upon the dial-plate of her civilization rudely thrust back a century, and to stand before the world the confessed champion of the African slave-hunter? Is she, with her unsullied fame, ready to become a pander to the rapacity of the African slave-trader, who burdens the very winds of the sea with the moans of the wretched captives whose limbs he has loaded with chains, and whose hearts he has broken. I do not, I cannot, believe it.

For this catalogue of what Kentucky must suffer in abandoning her present honored and secure position, and becoming a member of the Southern Confederacy, what will be her indemnity? Nothing, absolutely nothing. The ill-woven ambition of some of her sons may possibly reach the Presidency of the new Republic; that is all. Alas! alas! for that dream of the Presidency of a Southern Republic, which has disturbed so many pillows in the South, and perhaps some in the West also, and whose lurid light, like a demon's torch, is leading a nation to perdition.

The clamor, that in insisting upon the South to obey the Laws, the great principle that all popular Governments rest upon, the consent of the governed, is violated, should not receive a moment's consideration. Popular government does, indeed, rest upon the consent of the governed, but it is upon the consent, *not of all*, *but of a majority of the governed*. Criminals are every day punished and made to obey the laws, certainly against their will, and no man supposes that the principle referred to is thereby invaded. A bill passed by a Legislature, by the majority of a single vote only, though the constituents of all who voted against it should be in fact, as they are held to be in theory, opposed to its provisions, still is not the less operative as a law, and no right of self-government is thereby trampled upon. The clamor alluded to assumes that the States are separate and independent governments, and that laws enacted under the authority of all may be resisted and repealed at the pleasure of each. The people of the United States, so far as the powers of the General Government are concerned, are a unit, and laws passed by a majority of all are binding upon all. The laws and Constitution, however, which the South now resists, have been adopted by her sanction, and the right she now claims is that of a feeble minority to repeal what a majority has adopted. Nothing could be more fallacious.

Civil war, under all circumstances, is a terrible calamity, and yet, from the selfish ambition and wickedness of men, the best governments have not been able to escape it. In regarding that which has been forced upon the Government of the United States, Kentucky should not look so much at the means which may be necessarily employed in its prosecution, as at the machinations by which this national tragedy has been brought upon us. When I look upon this bright land, a few months since so prosperous, so tranquil, and so free, and now behold it desolated by war, and the firesides of its thirty millions of people darkened, and their bosoms wrung with anguish, and know, as I do, that all this is the work of a score or two of men, who, over all this national ruin and despair, are preparing to carve with the sword their way to seats of permanent power, I cannot but feel that they are accumulating upon their souls an amount of guilt hardly equalled in all the atrocities of treason and of homicide, that have degraded the annals of our race from the foundations of the world. Kentucky may rest well assured that this conflict, which is one of self-defence, will be pursued on the part of the Government in the paternal spirit in which a father seeks to reclaim his erring offspring. No conquest, no effusion of blood is sought. In sorrow, not in anger, the prayer of all is, that the end may be reached without loss of life or waste of property. Among the most powerful instrumentalities, relied on for re-establishing the authority of the Government, is that of the Union sentiment of the South, sustained by a liberated press. It is now trodden to the earth under a reign of terrorism which has no parallel but in the worst days of the French Revolution. The presence of the Government will enable it to rebound and look its oppressors in the face. At present we are assured that, in the seceded States, no man expresses an opinion opposed to the revolution but at the hazard of his life and property. The only light which is admitted into political discussion is that which flashes from the sword or gleams from glistening bayonets. A few days since, one of the United States Senators from Virginia published a manifesto, in which he announces, with oracular solemnity and severity, that all citizens who would not vote for secession, but were in favor of the Union—not should or ought to—but "MUST leave the State." These words have in them decidedly the crack of the overseer's whip. The Senator evidently treats Virginia as a great negro quarter, in which the lash is the appropriate emblem of authority, and the only argument he will condescend to use. However the freemen of other parts of the State may abase themselves under the exercise of this insolent and proscriptive tyranny, should the Senator, with this scourge of slaves, endeavor to drive the people of Western Virginia from their homes, I will only say, in the language of the narrative of Gilpin's ride:

"May I be there to see."

It would certainly prove a deeply interesting spectacle.

It is true that before this deliverance of the popular mind of the South from the threatenings and alarm which have subdued it can be accomplished, the remorseless agitators who have made this revolution, and now hold its reins, must be discarded alike from the public confidence and the public service. The country in its agony is feeling their power, and we well understand how difficult will be the task of overthrowing the ascendency they have secured. But the Union men of the South—believed to be in the majority of every seceded State, except, perhaps, South Carolina—aided by the presence of the Government, will be fully equal to the emergency. Let these agitators perish, politically, if need be, by scores;

"A breath can unmake them, as a breath has made."

but destroy this Republic and—

"Where is that Promethean heat,
That can its light relume?"

Once entombed, when will the Angel of the Resurrection descend to the portals of its sepulchre? There is not a voice which comes to us from the cemetery of nations that does not answer: "Never, never!" Amid the torments of perturbed existence, we may have glimpses of rest and of freedom as the maniac has glimpses of reason between the paroxysms of his madness, but we shall attain to neither national dignity nor national repose. We shall be a mass of jarring, warring, fragmentary States, enfeebled and demoralized, without power at home, or respectability abroad, and, like the republics of Mexico and South America, we will drift away on a shoreless and ensanguined sea of civil commotion, from which, if the teachings of history are to be trusted, we shall be finally rescued by the iron hand of some military wrecker, who will coin the shattered elements of our greatness and of our strength into a diadem and a throne. Said M. Fould, the great French statesman to an American citizen, a few weeks since: "Your Republic is dead, and it is probably the last the world will ever see. You will have a reign of terrorism, and after that two or three monarchies." All this may be verified, should this revolution succeed.

Let us then twine each thread of the glorious tissue of our country's flag about our heartstrings, and looking upon our homes and catching the spirit that breathes upon us from the battle-fields of our fathers, let us resolve that, come weal or woe, we will in life and in death, now and forever, stand by the Stars and Stripes. They have floated over our cradles, let it be our prayer and our struggle that they shall float over our graves. They have been unfurled from the snows of Canada to the plains of New Orleans, and to the halls of the Montezumas, and amid the solitudes of every sea; and everywhere, as the luminous symbol of resistless and beneficent power, they have led the brave and the free to victory and to glory. It has been my fortune to look upon this flag in foreign lands and amid the gloom of an oriental despotism, and right well do I know, by contrast, how bright are its stars, and how sublime are its inspirations! If this banner, the emblem for us of all that is grand in human history, and of all that is transporting in human hope, is to be sacrificed on the altars of a Satanic ambition, and thus disappear forever amid the night and tempest of revolution, then will I feel —and who shall estimate the desolation of that feeling?—that the sun has indeed been stricken from the sky of our lives, and that henceforth we shall be wanderers and outcasts, with nought but the bread of sorrow and of penury for our lips, and with hands ever outstretched in feebleness and supplication, on which, in any hour, a military tyrant may rivet the fetters of a despairing bondage. May God in his infinite mercy save you and me, and the land we so much love, from the doom of such a degradation. No contest so momentous as this has arisen in human history, for, amid all the conflicts of men and of nations, the life of no such government as ours has ever been at stake. Our fathers won our independence by the blood and sacrifice of a seven years' war, and we have maintained it against the assaults of the greatest power upon the earth; and the question now is, whether we are to perish by our own hands, and have the epitaph of suicide written upon our tomb. The ordeal through which we are passing must involve immense suffering and losses for us all, but the expenditure of not merely hundreds of millions but of billions of treasure will be well made, if the result shall be the preservation of our institutions.

Could my voice reach every dwelling in Kentucky, I would implore its inmates—if they would not have the rivers of their prosperity shrink away, as do unfed streams beneath the summer heats—to rouse themselves from their lethargy, and fly to the rescue of their country before it is everlastingly too late. Man should appeal to man, and neighborhood to neighborhood, until the electric fires of patriotism shall flash from heart to heart in one unbroken current throughout the land. It is a time in which the workshop, the office, the counting-house, and the field may well be abandoned for the solemn duty that is upon us, for all these toils will but bring treasure, not for ourselves, but for the spoiler, if this revolution is not arrested. We are all, with our every earthly interest, embarked in mid ocean on the same common deck. The howl of the storm is in our ears, and "the lightning's red glare is painting hell on the sky," and while the noble ship pitches and rolls under the lashings of the waves, the cry is heard that she has sprung a leak at many points, and that the rushing waters are mounting rapidly in the hold. The man who, in such an hour, will not work at the pumps, is either a maniac or a monster.

Sincerely yours,

J. HOLT.

Doc. 198.

EXPORTATION OF COTTON.

AN ACT TO PROHIBIT THE EXPORTATION OF COT-
TON FROM THE CONFEDERATE STATES, EXCEPT
THROUGH THE SEAPORTS OF SAID STATES, AND
TO PUNISH PERSONS OFFENDING THEREIN.

SECTION 1. The Congress of the Confederate States of America do enact, that, from and after the 1st day of June next, and during the existence of the blockade of any of the ports of the Confederate States of America by the Government of the United States, it shall not be lawful for any person to export any raw cotton or cotton yarn from the Confederate States of America, except through the seaports of the said Confederate States; and it shall be the duty of all the marshals and revenue officers of the said Confederate States to prevent all violations of this act.

SEC. 2. If any person shall violate, or attempt to violate or evade the provisions of the foregoing sections, he shall forfeit all the cotton or cotton yarn thus attempted to be illegally exported, for the use of the Confederate States; and in addition thereto, he shall be guilty of a misdemeanor, and on conviction thereof shall be fined in a sum not exceeding five thousand dollars, or else imprisoned in some public jail or penitentiary for a period not exceeding six months, at the discretion of the court, after a conviction upon trial by a court of competent jurisdiction.

SEC. 3. Any person informing as to a violation or attempt to violate the provisions of this act, shall be entitled to one-half the proceeds of the article forfeited, by reason of his information.

SEC. 4. Any justice of the peace on information under oath from any person, of a violation or attempt to violate this act, may issue his warrant, and cause the cotton or cotton yarn specified in the affidavit, to be seized and retained until an investigation can be had before the court of the Confederate States.

SEC. 5. Every steamboat or railroad car which shall be used with the consent of the owner or person having the same in charge for the purpose of violating this act, shall be forfeited in like manner to the use of the Confederate States. But nothing in this act shall be so construed as to prohibit the exportation to Mexico, through its coterminous frontier.

CONGRESS C. S. A., May 21, 1861.

I, J. J. Hooper, Secretary of the Congress of the Confederate States of America, do hereby certify that the foregoing is a true and correct copy of an act "To prohibit the exportation of cotton from the Confederate States, except through the seaports of said States, and to punish persons offending therein," which passed Congress, and was approved on the 21st day of May, 1861.

J. J. HOOPER, Secretary.

—Mobile Register.

Doc. 198½.

BISHOP POTTER'S LETTER

TO A SECESSIONIST.

PHILADELPHIA, May 13, 1861.

MY DEAR SIR:—You "beg me to explain how it is possible that (I) could, under the circumstances, give so much sanction and encouragement to those engaged in this *unholy, unprovoked, wanton attempt to destroy us and all that is dear to us.*"

Your misconception is so radical that I almost despair of correcting it. What you regard as an "attempt to destroy you, and all that is dear to you," is considered by us as simply an attempt to defend ourselves and the capital of our country from threatened invasion, our Constitution from destruction, and even our Southern brethren from that which is the surest destruction of themselves and their peculiar institutions. From the secession of South Carolina to the storming of Fort Sumter, the General Government remained all but passive. It then became indispensable that we should know whether it was a Government, whether it could retain its hold of Washington, and whether the whole system that Washington and his compeers inaugurated in 1789 was not a delusion and imposture. This, my dear sir, is the whole story. Your theory not only disregards your own obligations under the Constitution, but it leaves to us no Government except in name—opening the door for perpetual discord and for secession without end. I do not believe that at the North one man in fifty desires an invasion of your soil or the destruction of your social system. They simply desire that you should not break up the Union by your method of leaving it, but refer all subjects of complaint to a Convention of all the States which will be either competent to redress all grievances, or to provide a way in which you can retire from the Union without dissolving the whole fabric of our General Government.

Under the present exasperated state of the sections, it is impossible to say to what lengths this conflict may go. But I assure you that in the few lines above, you have the whole *animus* of the loyal States, and of the Union men everywhere. Only the smallest number of fanatics think or talk of slavery. The whole question is one of self-defence, and of *Government or no Government*. Yours sincerely,

ALONZO POTTER.

—*Louisville Journal*, June 12.

Doc. 199.

GEN. McCLELLAN'S PROCLAMATION

TO THE PEOPLE OF WESTERN VIRGINIA.

HEAD-QUARTERS, DEP'T OF THE OHIO, }
CINCINNATI, May 26, 1861. }

To the Union Men of Western Virginia:

VIRGINIANS:—The General Government has long endured the machinations of a few factious rebels in your midst. Armed traitors have in vain endeavored to deter you from expressing your loyalty at the polls; having failed in this infamous attempt to deprive you of the exercise of your dearest rights, they now seek to inaugurate a reign of terror, and thus force you to yield to their schemes, and submit to the yoke of the traitorous conspiracy, dignified by the name of Southern Confederacy. They are destroying the property of citizens of your State, and ruining your magnificent railways. The General Government has heretofore carefully abstained from sending troops across the Ohio, or even from posting them along its banks, although frequently urged by many of your prominent citizens to do so. It determined to await the result of the late election, desirous that no one might be able to say that the slightest effort had been made from this side to influence the free expression of

your opinion, although the many agencies brought to bear upon you by the rebels were well known. You have now shown, under the most adverse circumstances, that the great mass of the people of Western Virginia are true and loyal to that beneficent Government under which we and our fathers have lived so long. As soon as the result of the election was known, the traitors commenced their work of destruction. The General Government cannot close its ears to the demands you have made for assistance. I have ordered troops to cross the river. They come as your friends and your brothers—as enemies only to the armed rebels who are preying upon you. Your homes, your families, and your property are safe under our protection. All your rights shall be religiously respected.

Notwithstanding all that has been said by the traitors to induce you to believe that our advent among you will be signalized by interference with your slaves, understand one thing clearly—not only will we abstain from all such interference, but we will, on the contrary, with an iron hand, crush any attempt at insurrection on their part. Now, that we are in your midst, I call upon you to fly to arms and support the General Government. Sever the connection that binds you to traitors—proclaim to the world that the faith and loyalty so long boasted by the Old Dominion, are still preserved in Western Virginia, and that you remain true to the Stars and Stripes.

G. B. McCLELLAN,
Major-General Commanding.

ADDRESS TO THE VOLUNTEER ARMY.

HEAD-QUARTERS, DEPARTMENT OF THE OHIO, }
CINCINNATI, May 26, 1861. }

SOLDIERS:—You are ordered to cross the frontier and enter upon the soil of Virginia. Your mission is to restore peace and confidence, to protect the majesty of the law, and to rescue our brethren from the grasp of armed traitors. You are to act in concert with the Virginia troops and to support their advance.

I place under the safeguard of your honor the persons and property of the Virginians. I know that you will respect their feelings and all their rights. Preserve the strictest discipline; remember that each one of you holds in his keeping the honor of Ohio and of the Union.

If you are called upon to overcome armed opposition, I know that your courage is equal to the task; but remember that your only foes are the armed traitors,—and show mercy even to them when they are in your power, for many of them are misguided. When, under your protection, the loyal men of Western Virginia have been enabled to organize and arm, they can protect themselves, and you can then return to your homes, with the proud satisfaction of having preserved a gallant people from destruction.

G. B. McCLELLAN,
Major-General Commanding.

—*Ohio Statesman*, May 30.

Doc. 200.

FIRST NEW HAMPSHIRE REGIMENT.

This regiment, which for the past month has been encamped in Camp Union, at Concord, N. H., struck their tents on Saturday morning, and at 8 A. M. started by special train to Norwich, Connecticut, where they embarked on the steamers Commodore and Connecticut for New York. Their progress through Massachusetts and Connecticut was an ovation, crowds assembling at all the stations to greet them. The Connecticut arrived at Pier No. 39 North River, at 10 A. M. on Sunday, May 26, with the first detachment, and the Commodore with the second detachment on board arrived at the Pier at 11 A. M. The disembarkation took place in an orderly and expeditious manner, when the regiment headed by the Regimental Board and a Committee of the sons of New Hampshire in New York, marched through Vestry street and Canal street to the Brandreth House, where an American flag was presented by the Committee. On presenting the banner, Judge Bonney made an eloquent address, in which he reviewed the history of the support which the State of New Hampshire has always given the Constitution, at its adoption, as well as whenever it has been menaced since.

Col. Tappan responded in a short and patriotic speech in which he pledged himself and his regiment to maintain the Constitution and to avenge the insults which have been heaped upon that glorious flag, (pointing to the banner presented.) The regiment then resumed the line of march to the Division Arsenal, corner of Elm and White streets, where the Committee had made arrangements for temporarily quartering the men, and where they partook of a dinner, the army rations being served to the men.

The officers then proceeded to the Astor House with the Committee, where they dined and spent several hours in company with their friends, who flocked there eagerly to see them. When the funeral *cortege* of the late Col. Ellsworth approached the Astor House, on its way to Courtlandt street, Col. Tappan and staff mounted their horses and joined the escort. The 1st Regiment is more completely equipped than any regiment that has left our city or passed through it. The men are fully armed and equipped, and in addition to the United States musket and bayonet, nearly all the soldiers were presented with revolvers by their friends on their departure. Beside the full supply of rations for the journey to Washington, they have a baggage train of seventeen wagons, with four horses to each wagon. The wagons are loaded with provisions, ammunition, engineers' and sappers' and miners' tools, tents and camp equipage; and one is loaded with extra uniforms for the soldiers. Each company in the regiment is accompanied by four female nurses, who have volunteered for the war. The Regimental Band is composed of Baldwin's Band of Manchester, and consists of 25 performers, who have volunteered for the war.

The uniform is plain dark gray, with red cord facings, and the regulation gray cap, with a red band. The men are not above the ordinary height, but are all young, hardy, and active. They execute all their movements with great activity. They are composed principally of mechanics, who are not afraid of work, and accustomed to exposure. They are, in fact, the bone and sinew of New Hampshire.

The following is a list of the staff and line officers, and the localities from which they hail:

STAFF.—Colonel, M. W. Tappan, of Bradford; Lieutenant-Colonel, Thos. J. Whipple, of Laconia; Major, A. F. Stevens, of Nashua; Adjutant, E. Q. Fellows, of Sandwich; Quartermaster, R. A. Batchelder, of Manchester; Staff-Secretary, Chas. L. Brown, of Manchester; Surgeon, A. B. Crosby, of Hanover; Assistant-Surgeon, H. C. Shaw, of Hanover; Chaplain, L. G. Abbot, of Bradford.

NON-COMMISSIONED STAFF.—Sergeant Major, Geo. Y. Lawyer, of Nashua; Quartermaster Sergeant, A. Lull, of Nashua; Fife Major, Frs. H. Pike, of Manchester; Drum Major, Wm. Carr; Paymaster, Moses K. Hagleton.

LINE-OFFICERS.—Company A, of Dover—Captain, L. Bell of Farmington; Lieut., Geo. W. Colliath, of Dover; Ensign, O. M. Clark, of Dover.

Company B, of Dover—Captain, D. R. Kenny, of Laconia; Lieut., Chas. W. Sawyer, of Dover; Ensign, J. G. Wallace, of Dover.

Company C, of Manchester—Captain, J. L. Kelly; Lieut., M. V. B. Richardson; Ensign, Chas. O. Jennison.

Company D, of Newport— Captain, J. McL. Barton; Lieut., E. Nettleton; Ensign, Dexter Reed.

Company E, of Nashua—Captain, O. F. Greenleaf; Lieut., W. L. Greeley; Ensign, J. W. Thompson.

Company F, of Nashua—Captain, A. S. Edgerly; Lieut., G. W. Hanley; Ensign, C. H. Drummer.

Company G, of Keene—Captain, A. J. Sargent; Lieut., H. T. H. Pierce; Ensign, ——.

Company H, of Salem—Captain, J. D. Drew; Lieut., J. M. Clough; Ensign, J. Drew.

Company I, of Concord—Captain, E. E. Sturtevant; Lieut., H. W. Fuller; Ensign, E. W. Goss.

Company K, of Manchester—Captain, G. E. Sleeper; Lieut., E. Q. Fellows; Ensign, H. O. Dudley.

Ten companies, 77 men each, which, with staff officers and band, make nearly 850 men.

About six o'clock in the afternoon the men were ordered under arms, and proceeded to the Jersey Ferry, and at 8 o'clock departed on a special train of twenty cars, beside a long train of freight cars for the wagons and horses, for Washington, *through* Baltimore.

In consequence of the impossibility of at

once supplying rations for all the men, the Messrs. Leland entertained a company at the Metropolitan, free of charge. Mr. Wm. B. Dinsmore, at his own expense, provided for another company at the St. Nicholas.

—*N. Y. Tribune,* May 27.

Doc. 201.

JUDGE THOMPSON'S PROCLAMATION

AT WHEELING, VA., MAY 28.

I, GEORGE W. THOMPSON, one of the Judges of the Circuit Court, acting under the Constitution and the laws of Virginia, and under the Constitution of the United States, and by my oath of office, imposed on me by the State of Virginia, in virtue of the obligation voluntarily and solemnly assumed by the State in her ratification of the Constitution of the Union, to declare the Constitution of the United States, and the laws made in pursuance thereof, the supreme law of the land, " any thing in the Constitution or laws of any State to the contrary notwithstanding;" (Art. VI., sections 2 and 3;) and being by the laws of the State, a conservator of the peace, and desirous and intending to maintain both Constitutions and the laws made in pursuance thereof, by the faithful discharge of my duties, I hereby, in the names of those Constitutions and the laws made in pursuance thereof, in times of peace and prosperity, and with the consent of all the good people of the Commonwealth, as necessary for the protection of life, liberty, property, and the lawful pursuit of happiness, do call on all the good citizens to obey these wise and salutary laws, and to aid me in their firm and salutary enforcement by obedience themselves, and for the punishment of the lawless.

It is only in obedience to Constitutions that families are safe in life, liberty, or property; and no majorities, cabals, mobs, however numerous they may be, or by whatever motive they may be actuated, are above these exalted safeguards of human welfare and prosperity; and under these, individuals and minorities are entitled to protection. If majorities, acting lawlessly, are above them, then majorities in States, regardless of the Constitutions, will rule; but this may not be until the reign of lawlessness and violence is inaugurated. And I call upon all citizens, in virtue of these supreme laws of the land, to stand by the faithful and impartial administration of the laws. To those citizens of West Virginia whose large majority against Secession show a firm determination to maintain and defend their constitutional obligations, I appeal to maintain the law and order which both of these instruments guarantee and enforce. If one is a matter of conscience and of law, so is the other; and, in maintaining all these obligations to the utmost extent possible, in times like the present, we show ourselves worthy of peace, and the order and the protection of those laws whose sov-

ereignty we have vindicated by our recent vote, or become obnoxious to their just punishment.

To those citizens in Western Virginia, who claim the right of secession, in like manner I appeal to lay down their arms against their brethren and fathers, and submit to the judgment and wish of their own people, in so large a portion of the State as West Virginia. If it is right for one portion of the people in mass to violate or set aside the Constitution, so as to free themselves from political intercourse with other portions of the people of the United States, surely it should be permitted to so large a body of people as West Virginia, exercising their sovereignty in a lawful manner under the Constitution and in support of the Constitution, to choose their destinies. This, at the late election, they have done in no equivocal manner. They should be permitted, and especially by you, their brethren, exercising with such unanimity this sovereign and constitutional right, to stand by the Constitution and the laws in peace; to maintain the solemn integrity of the institutions under which they have grown and prospered. By this vote they have solemnly said they have no cause of revolution; they are satisfied; let them remain in peace. If you are dissatisfied, go in peace; go where you will have the support and sympathy of those whose cause you espouse; and in God's name, in the name of our ancient friendships and fireside relations; in the name of that peace, the skirts of whose robe will be dabbled in blood, if you remain in arms; in virtue of the holy ties of relationship, and for the preservation of whatever of constitutions and the laws are left, while yet the ruin has not reached you and us; while the vengeance of civil war has not broken up all domestic ties, and the sword of private revenge has not crossed your own thresholds and sprinkled them with blood, and left your homes and your households in ruin; by all the solemn memories of the past and the obligations of the present to recognize the wishes of the people of West Virginia, to seek their own happiness and welfare in a lawful and peaceful manner; in the solemn majesty of those laws, and in a higher appeal of justice and the cry, depart, depart in peace, and give not up West Virginia, which otherwise will remain in safety, if not repose, to the horrors of a terrible war. With such a large majority, neither Eastern Virginia nor the South will be disposed to coerce us to their own local and peculiar policy. With such a position as West Virginia occupies, separated by vast mountain ranges from old Virginia, accessible to the whole West, and the whole North, the whole will be a unit in our defence. West Virginia never can be coerced or conquered. Her streams may run blood, and her households may be desolated, and if this shall be so, it will be the work of those in West Virginia, who remain in arms to oppose and resist the wishes of the majority of her people. Retire, disband, and let us alone in peace, under the Constitution and the laws, and do not require those laws and Constitution to be maintained here at this mighty sacrifice.

—Wheeling (Va.) Intelligencer, May 28.

Doc. 202.

COL. DURYEA'S PROCLAMATION.

FORT MONROE, Va., May 27th, 1861.

SPECIAL ORDERS No. 5.—Col. A. Duryea, Fifth Regiment Volunteers, will at once assume command of the camp of the two New York regiments, Mr. Segar's farm, and issue such orders and make such regulations, consistent with the Articles of War, as will insure good order and a thorough system of instruction and discipline; he will see that a proper guard is posted each night over the well and on and near the bridge leading toward the fort, in such manner that there can be no danger of harm to them. Any depredations committed upon the property of citizens, or any unnecessary inconvenience imposed upon them by any number of the command, must be promptly noticed and reported in writing to the Major-General commanding the Department.

By command of Major-General Butler.

GRIER TALMADGE,
Acting Assistant Adjutant-General.

To the Inhabitants of Hampton and vicinity:

Having been placed by order of Major-Gen. Butler, in command of the troops in this vicinity, outside of the walls of Fort Monroe: hereby notify all, that their rights of person and property will be entirely respected; that their co-operation in maintaining law and order is expected, both by reporting every violation of them, when committed by any one attached to the camp, and by preserving local order and restraining such of their fellow-citizens as may entertain perverted intentions.

You can rely that all offences against you will be severely punished; that no effort will be spared to detect the guilty, and that you, as a community, will also be held responsible for every act committed by any one of your numbers, where the particular offender is not surrendered.

Be assured that we are here in no war, against you, your liberty, your property, or even your local customs; but to keep on high that flag of which your own great son was the bearer; to sustain those institutions and those laws made by our ancestors and defended by their common blood.

Remember all these things, and if there be those among you who, maddened by party feeling, misled by wilful falsehoods or a mistaken sense of duty, have thought to obliterate the national existence, let them at least pause till they learn the true value of what they have imperilled, and the nature of that into which they are asked to plunge. We have all confidence that, in Virginians in arms against us, we have honorable foes, whom we hope yet to make our friends.

COL. A. DURYEA, Acting Brigadier-General.

N. Y. Times, May 31.

Doc. 203.

EIGHTH REGIMENT N. Y. S. V.

THE officers of the Eighth are as follows: —Colonel, Louis Blenker; Lieutenant-Colonel, Julius Stahel; Major, Andrew Lutz; Quartermaster, D. Shultze; Adjutant, Drschack. Company A, Captain, Hammerstein; First Lieutenant, Matzann; Second Lieutenant, G. Struve. Company B, Captain, Bocorni; First Lieutenant, Mengersen; Second Lieutenant, Henkel. Company C, Captain, Stumpf; First Lieutenant, Herzberg; Second Lieutenant, Claus. Company D, Captain, Rust; First Lieutenant, Koerner; Second Lieutenant, Thenerkauf. Company E, Captain, Forstner; First Lieutenant, Kuchenbacker; Second Lieutenant, Schultz. Company F, Captain, Gellman; First Lieutenant, Coburger, Second Lieutenant, Baum. Company G, Captain, Thum; First Lieutenant, Geiger; Second Lieutenant, Bossart. Company H, Captain, Kron; First Lieutenant, Engels; Second Lieutenant, Pauls. Company I, Captain, Hedferich; First Lieutenant, Moller; Second Lieutenant, Brandt. Company K, Captain, Wutschell; First Lieutenant, Schuhmacker; Second Lieutenant, Weil.

There are 1,046 men in the regiment, all told, but those that did not go wait to be equipped, and will probably be sent off on Saturday. The officers all equipped themselves at their own individual expense.

Company K is the artillery corps, and its captain (Wutschell) has had considerable experience in the Austrian army. Col. Blenker has had a thorough military education, and has served in Greece, seeing there a great deal of active service. He also fought with distinction throughout the German Revolution of 1848. Lieutenant-Colonel Stahel is a Hungarian, and was in the Austrian army, which he left to fight the battles of his native land under Kossuth and Görgey. He bears the scars of many a hard-contested field upon his person. Several of the captains and subalterns have likewise borne the brunt of actual war, and many of the men are European veterans.

—N. Y. Tribune.

Doc. 204.

WESTERN VIRGINIA.

THE ADVANCE OF FEDERAL TROOPS.

THE passage of the troops who left for Western Virginia has been one continued ovation, as far as they have gone. We went down on the train carrying the troops from Camp Carlisle, the Ohio Regiment coming soon after. Those who witnessed the parting scenes at the depot will not soon forget them. Some of them were very touching. At Benwood, one mother, who had come out to exchange the parting word with her son, said, with tears standing in her eyes, as the train rolled away, "Go; you leave sore hearts behind you, but all will be well when you return." And a gray-haired sire, at the same place, hobbling on a cane, shouted after the train as it moved away: "I have three sons with you now, and I wish I could go myself." Such was the spirit manifested everywhere, and a corresponding feeling pervaded the hearts of the men.

All the way out through Marshall the utmost enthusiasm was awakened by the appearance of the soldiers. They had not known them to be coming, but they divined at once their mission, and the most joyful excitement was everywhere exhibited. Owing to the alarming reports of the night before, rumors that Southern troops were approaching, we found crowds at every stopping place, who cheered the trains as they passed, with wild vehemence. At Glen Easton we found a company of twenty-five or thirty-eight riflemen, and further on passed another company of them numbering perhaps forty, all marching towards Cameron, which they heard was to be attacked and burnt by State troops. At Cameron we found a crowd assembled of some three hundred, perhaps, who insisted in standing out in a pelting rain and cheering the soldiers nearly all the time they were there. The report of the advance of Southern troops had been received the night before, and a hundred riflemen had been under arms, guarding the town all night; and at this time men with rifles on their shoulders were coming in from all directions, word having been sent out the night before. It really looks just like what we read of as having taken place in the days of '78, when men left the plough standing in the furrow, dropped the uplifted hammer, and rushed to the defence of their country. At every station and every house people greeted the soldiers with cheering and the waving of hats and handkerchiefs, and the women and girls, when they had no handkerchiefs, waved their bonnets and aprons. The men returned all the salutations, and enjoyed the demonstration immensely. At one house by the roadside an old lady, who seemed excited to the highest pitch, waved her hand till the trains were entirely past, and then gave vent to her over-wrought feelings by yielding to a flood of tears. Such was the exuberant joy with which the people, alarmed but the hour before by undefined apprehension, welcomed the appearance of their defenders.

Our trains reached Mannington a little after noon, and the appearance of the troops there, as everywhere else, took the people completely by surprise. They had heard, however, that a train was coming from the West, and, as this was unusual since the burning of the bridges, a considerable crowd was at the depot waiting. As the trains rolled in, they displayed the American flag, and with that, and the gleaming of a

thousand bayonets, the people almost went wild with enthusiasm. In a very few minutes the whole town was there, and the gladdest set of people a man ever laid eyes on. Their joy scarcely knew bounds. Hardly had the soldiers been there five minutes, till they had arrested and under guard as many secessionists, viz.: a tavern-keeper named Wells; Mr. Knotts, a merchant; Charles Mathews, superintendent on that section of the Baltimore and Ohio Railroad; Dr. Grant, defeated secession candidate for the Legislature, and one Zeke Snodgrass, a constable, who tried to give leg bail, but didn't succeed quite sufficiently to save his bacon. They were arraigned before Col. Kelly, who released Wells, Knotts, and Grant, on their taking the oath of fidelity, but retained Mathews and Snodgrass.

The train soon after moved on down to the first burned bridge, where the men disembarked and paraded in a meadow. Col. Kelly then detailed six companies and started for Farmington, a notorious secession nest, some three miles below, from which it was said the men who burnt the bridges had come, and where it was stated some fifty armed secession troops were stationed. Meanwhile, the remainder of the troops stacked arms, after throwing out pickets and scouts on the neighboring hills, with orders to bring in any persons they might find. In less than ten minutes after their arrival, they brought in six, some of whom, it was positively asserted by some Union men from the country around, were accessory to the destruction of the bridges. Squads of men continued to go out in different directions, and to bring in prisoners, until they must have had at least a dozen under guard at once. Several of them were released after an examination by the officers, but at least six or eight were retained until the return of Col. Kelly. It was rather exciting to see the scouts, or "Snake Hunters," as they style themselves, on a trail. As certainly as they would spy a man anywhere in sight, a squad of them would seize their guns, and start after him on a run, and before very long, would bring him in; for they were sure of their game if they got eyes on it. The prisoners were all treated with the utmost courtesy, but nevertheless some of them looked terribly frightened.

In the evening the companies returned from Farmington, bringing with them several prisoners, and reporting that their scouts had killed one secessionist and wounded another. When they reached Farmington they found it almost entirely deserted, the secessionists having got wind of their approach through the offices of one Jolliffe, who, when the trains entered Mannington, mounted a horse and galloped off in hot haste to Farmington, to warn the secessionists of their danger.

Finding the town deserted, Col. Kelly ordered his men to scour the woods surrounding it, and it was not long till they had unearthed several of the fugitives, most of whom they captured. The men who were shot were running from their pursuers, who called out to them to surrender. Not heeding this, they were told that they would be shot unless they did. No attention was paid to the command, and several shots were fired, killing one instantly, and wounding another.

The bridges burned were over Buffalo Creek, and were common open railroad pier bridges, all iron except the sills and the cross-ties of the track, both of which were consumed. The upper one is about four miles below Mannington, and the other some quarter of a mile below it. It is feared that others are destroyed between there and Grafton. The anxiety about the splendid iron bridge over the Monongahela is especially very great.

Sunday night several bridges between Mannington and Glover's Gap were guarded by the citizens of the former place. At the same time they had need of guarding their town, for the gang at Farmington had threatened to burn it to the ground, and there were various rumors afloat about accessions to their number.

Glover's Gap is a way station several miles above Mannington, inhabited by but one or two families, but surrounded by a secession country, which polled some sixty or seventy secession votes. These men live around among the hills and are almost inaccessible. That part of the road will bear watching. As the train came west this morning, the telegraph was found cut not half a mile from this place.

The Ohio Regiment reached Mannington Monday evening, just at dark, having felt their way over the road, examining all the bridges to see that they had not been injured. The whole town assembled to receive them. They paraded in the street, while their band, a superior one, played the "Star Spangled Banner" and other airs. At the conclusion, the crowd gave three cheers for Ohio, which compliment was returned by the Ohio men, who gave three for the citizens of Mannington. The citizens then proffered their houses for quarters for the soldiers. Some were put in the church, some in the Odd Fellows' Hall, others at the hotel, others in private houses, until they were all provided for, the people all manifesting the most cordial feeling for them.

And well they merited such treatment; for, besides that they came here to protect us, they are a splendid set of fellows—tall, handsome, and soldier-like in appearance, and dignified and gentlemanly in demeanor. They were immensely pleased with their reception all along the road, and particularly with the substantial compliments of the good people of Cameron and Belton. The citizens of Cameron were taken by surprise by the train that conveyed the Wheeling Regiment, but learning that more were on the way, they went to work and got together all the provisions in the place, bread, pies, cakes, a barrel of crackers, meat, butter, and eggs, and had them all boxed up and ready for them. By the time the Ohio men reached Cameron there had collected from the surrounding country some eight hundred or a thousand people, who received them with enthusiastic demonstrations.

—*Wheeling (Va.) Intelligencer*, May 29.

Doc. 204½.

SPEECH OF SENATOR DOUGLAS.

HIS LAST WORDS FOR THE UNION.

Senator Douglas and wife reached Chicago, Ill., on their return from Washington, on the evening of the 1st day of May, and were met at the depot by an immense assemblage of citizens of all parties, who insisted on escorting Mr. Douglas in procession to the great Wigwam, which was already packed with ten thousand persons. Room having been made for the admission of Mr. Douglas, he was addressed by Thomas B. Bryan, in behalf of Chicago. Mr. Douglas replied:

Mr. Chairman:—I thank you for the kind terms in which you have been pleased to welcome me. I thank the Committee and citizens of Chicago for this grand and imposing reception. I beg you to believe that I will not do you nor myself the injustice to believe this magnificent ovation is personal homage to myself. I rejoice to know that it expresses your devotion to the Constitution, the Union, and the flag of our country. (Cheers.)

I will not conceal gratification at the uncontrovertible test this vast audience presents—that what political differences or party questions may have divided us, yet you all had a conviction that when the country should be in danger, my loyalty could be relied on. That the present danger is imminent, no man can conceal. If war must come—if the bayonet must be used to maintain the Constitution—I can say before God my conscience is clean. I have struggled long for a peaceful solution of the difficulty. I have not only tendered those States what was theirs of right, but I have gone to the very extreme of magnanimity.

The return we receive is war, armies marched upon our capital, obstructions and dangers to our navigation, letters of marque to invite pirates to prey upon our commerce, a concerted movement to blot out the United States of America from the map of the globe. The question is, Are we to maintain the country of our fathers, or allow it to be stricken down by those who, when they can no longer govern, threaten to destroy?

What cause, what excuse do disunionists give us for breaking up the best Government on which the sun of heaven ever shed its rays? They are dissatisfied with the result of a Presidential election. Did they never get beaten before? Are we to resort to the sword when we get defeated at the ballot-box. I understand it that the voice of the people expressed in the mode appointed by the Constitution must command the obedience of every citizen. They assume, on the election of a particular candidate, that their rights are not safe in the Union. What evidence do they present of this? I defy any man to show any act on which it is based. What act has been omitted to be done? I appeal to these assembled thousands that so far as the constitutional rights of the Southern States, I will say the constitutional rights of slaveholders, are concerned, nothing has been done, and nothing omitted, of which they can complain.

There has never been a time from the day that Washington was inaugurated first President of these United States, when the rights of the Southern States stood firmer under the laws of the land than they do now; there never was a time when they had not as good a cause for disunion as they have to-day. What good cause have they now that has not existed under every Administration?

If they say the Territorial question—now, for the first time, there is no act of Congress prohibiting slavery anywhere. If it be the non-enforcement of the laws, the only complaints that I have heard have been of the too vigorous and faithful fulfilment of the Fugitive Slave Law. Then what reason have they?

The slavery question is a mere excuse. The election of Lincoln is a mere pretext. The present secession movement is the result of an enormous conspiracy formed more than a year since, formed by leaders in the Southern Confederacy more than twelve months ago.

They use the Slavery question as a means to aid the accomplishment of their ends. They desired the election of a Northern candidate, by a sectional vote, in order to show that the two sections cannot live together. When the history of the two years from the Lecompton charter down to the Presidential election shall be written, it will be shown that the scheme was deliberately made to break up this Union.

They desired a Northern Republican to be elected by a purely Northern vote, and then assign this fact as a reason why the sections may not longer live together. If the disunion candidate in the late Presidential contest had carried the united South, their scheme was, the Northern candidate successful, to seize the Capitol last spring, and by a united South and divided North hold it. That scheme was defeated in the defeat of the disunion candidate in several of the Southern States.

But this is no time for a detail of causes. The conspiracy is now known. Armies have been raised, war is levied to accomplish it. There are only two sides to the question. Every man must be for the United States or against it. There can be no neutrals in this war; *only patriots—or traitors.*

Thank God Illinois is not divided on this question. (Cheers.) I know they expected to present a united South against a divided North. They hoped in the Northern States, party questions would bring civil war between Democrats and Republicans, when the South would step in

Doc.—30

with her cohorts, aid one party to conquer the other, and then make easy prey of the victors. Their scheme was carnage and civil war in the North.

There is but one way to defeat this. In Illinois it is being so defeated by closing up the ranks. War will thus be prevented on our own soil. While there was a hope of peace I was ready for any reasonable sacrifice or compromise to maintain it. But when the question comes of war in the cotton-fields of the South or the corn-fields of Illinois, I say the farther off the better.

We cannot close our eyes to the sad and solemn fact that war does exist. The Government must be maintained, its enemies overthrown, and the more stupendous our preparations the less the bloodshed, and the shorter the struggle. But we must remember certain restraints on our action even in time of war. We are a Christian people, and the war must be prosecuted in a manner recognized by Christian nations.

We must not invade Constitutional rights. The innocent must not suffer, nor women and children be the victims. Savages must not be let loose. But while I sanction no war on the rights of others, I will implore my countrymen not to lay down their arms until our own rights are recognized. (Cheers.)

The Constitution and its guarantees are our birthright, and I am ready to enforce that inalienable right to the last extent. We cannot recognize secession. Recognize it once, and you have not only dissolved government, but you have destroyed social order, upturned the foundations of society. You have inaugurated anarchy in its worst form, and will shortly experience all the horrors of the French Revolution.

Then we have a solemn duty—to maintain the Government. The greater our unanimity the speedier the day of peace. We have prejudices to overcome from the few short months since of a fierce party contest. Yet these must be allayed. Let us lay aside all criminations and recriminations as to the origin of these difficulties. When we shall have again a country with the United States flag floating over it, and respected on every inch of American soil, it will then be time enough to ask who and what brought all this upon us.

I have said more than I intended to say. (Cries of "Go on.") It is a sad task to discuss questions so fearful as civil war; but sad as it is, bloody and disastrous as I expect it will be, I express it as my conviction before God, that it is the duty of every American citizen to rally round the flag of his country.

I thank you again for this magnificent demonstration. By it you show you have laid aside party strife. Illinois has a proud position—United, firm, determined never to permit the Government to be destroyed. (Prolonged cheering.)

—*N. Y. Tribune,* June 13.

Doc. 205.

THE WASHINGTON ARTILLERY.

The following is a list of the officers:

Staff—Major J. B. Walton; Adjutant, Lieut. W. M. Owen; Surgeon, Dr. E. S. Drew; Quartermaster, Lieut. C. H. Slocomb.

Non-Commissioned Staff.—Sergeant-Major, C. L. C. Dupuy; Color Sergeant, Louis M. Montgomery; Quartermaster Sergeant, S. Kennedy.

Color Guard.—Corporals George W. Wood, E. J. Jewell, A. H. Peale, and J. H Dearie.

First Company.—Capt. M. M. Isaacson; First Lieutenant, J. B. Richardson, Jr.; Second Lieutenant, H. G. Geiger.

Second Company.—First Lieutenant, C. C. Lewis, commanding; First Lieutenant, Samuel J. McPherson; Second Lieut., C. H. Slocomb.

Third Company.—Captain M. B. Miller; 1st Lieutenant, J. B. Whittington; 2d Lieutenant, L. A. Adam; 1st Sergeant, Frank McElroy; 2d do., A. V. Hero; 3d do., L. Prados; 4th do., J. T. Handy; 1st Corporal, E. J. Jewell; 2d do., A. H. Peale; 3d do., W. H. Ellis; 4th do., Collins.

Fourth Company.—Captain, B. F. Eshleman; 1st Lieutenant, Jos. Norcom; 2d Lieutenant, Harry A. Battles; 2d Sergeant, W. J. Behan; 3d do., G. E. Apps; 4th do., J. D. Reynolds; 1st Corporal, George Wood; 2d do., J. W. Dearn.

DR. PALMER'S SERMON TO THE WASHINGTON ARTILLERY.

The following is a report of the eloquent and patriotic exhortation of Dr. Palmer to the Washington Artillery, delivered from the portico of the City Hall to the troops just before marching to the depot, on their departure for the scene of war in Virginia. Besides the military, there were not less than five thousand citizens present on this interesting occasion:

Gentlemen of the Washington Artillery:

At the sound of the bugle you are here, within one short hour to bid adieu to cherished homes, and soon to encounter the perils of battle on a distant field. It is fitting that here, in the heart of this great city—here, beneath the shadow of this Hall, over which floats the flag of Louisiana's sovereignty and independence, you should receive a public and a tender farewell. It is fitting that religion herself should with gentle voice whisper her benediction upon your flag and your cause. Soldiers, history reads to us of wars which have been baptized as holy; but she enters upon her records none that is holier than this in which you have embarked. It is a war of defence against wicked and cruel aggression—a war of civilization against a ruthless barbarism which would dishonor the dark ages—a war of religion against a blind and bloody fanaticism. It is a war for your homes and firesides—for your wives and children—for the land which the Lord has given us for a heritage. It is a war for the maintenance of the broadest principle for which a free people can contend—the right of self-government.

Eighty-five years ago our fathers fought in defence of the chartered right of Englishmen, that taxation and representation are correlative. We, their sons, contend to-day for the great American principle that all just government derives its powers from the will of the governed. It is the corner-stone of the great temple which, on this continent, has been reared to civil freedom; and its denial leads, as the events of the past two months have clearly shown, to despotism, the most absolute and intolerable, a despotism more grinding than that of the Turk or Russian, because it is the despotism of the mob, unregulated by principle or precedent, drifting at the will of an unscrupulous and irresponsible majority. The alternative which the North has laid before her people is the subjugation of the South, or what they are pleased to call absolute anarchy. The alternative before us is, the independence of the South or a despotism which will put its iron heel upon all that the human heart can hold dear. This mighty issue is to be submitted to the ordeal of battle, with the nations of the earth as spectators, and with the God of Heaven as umpire. The theatre appointed for the struggle is the soil of Virginia, beneath the shadow of her own Alleghanies. Comprehending the import of this great controversy from the first, Virginia sought to stand between the combatants, and pleaded for such an adjustment as both the civilization and the religion of the age demanded. When this became hopeless, obeying the instincts of that nature which has ever made her the Mother of Statesmen and of States, she has opened her broad bosom to the blows of a tyrant's hand. Upon such a theatre, with such an issue pending before such a tribunal, we have no doubt of the part which will be assigned you to play; and when we hear the thunders of your cannon echoing from the mountain passes of Virginia, will understand that you mean, in the language of Cromwell at the castle of Drogheda, "to cut this war to the heart."

It only remains, soldiers, to invoke the blessing of Almighty God upon your honored flag. It waves in brave hands over the gallant defenders of a holy cause. It will be found in the thickest of the fight, and the principles which it represents you will defend to "the last of your breath and of your blood." May victory perch upon its staff in the hour of battle, and peace —an honorable peace—be wrapped within its folds when you shall return.

It is little to say to you that you will be remembered. And should the frequent fate of the soldier befall you in a soldier's death, you shall find your graves in thousands of hearts, and the pen of history shall write the story of your martyrdom. Soldiers, farewell! and may the Lord of Hosts be round about you as a wall of fire, and shield your heads in the day of battle!

—*N. O. Picayune*, May 28.
—*N. O. Delta*, May 29.

Doc. 206.

NINTH REGIMENT N. Y. S. M.

THE following is a list of the officers of this regiment:

Colonel, J. W. Stiles; Lieutenant-Colonel, W. H. Hallock; Major, E. L. Stone; Adjutant, J. B. Coppinger; Surgeon, J. W. Fisher; Quartermaster, Alex. Henriques; Chaplain, Rev. Mr. Phillips; Commissary, H. L. Stephens; Assistant Quartermaster, A. L. Squires. Company A—Captain, J. J. Morrison; First Lieutenant, John Dalrymple; Second Lieutenant, E. H. Andrews. Company B—Captain, John Deppeler; First Lieutenant, Louis Bellows; Second Lieutenant, Frederick Guyer. Company C—Lieutenant Provost, Commanding; Second Lieutenant, E. H. Miller. Company D—Captain, J. W. Davis; First Lieutenant, F. Van Buren; Second Lieutenant, J. W. Field. Company E—Captain, Henry C. Smith; First Lieutenant, Henry Brooks; Second Lieutenant, T. Galbraith. Company F—Captain, Allen Rutherford; First Lieutenant, G. W. Braind; Second Lieutenant, vacant. Company G—Captain, Wm. Atterbury; First Lieutenant, W. Hendrickson; Second Lieutenant, Joseph Wickham. Company H—Captain, F. E. Tuthill; First Lieutenant, —— Dockman; Second Lieutenant, J. Tuthill.

The artillery corps attached to this regiment did not leave yesterday, owing to the fact of their battery not being in readiness. Next Monday they expect to be *en route* to join their comrades. The corps is officered as follows: First Lieutenant, H. V. Cramer; Second Lieutenant, Eugene Durnin; Third Lieutenant, John Dolan.

—*N. Y. Times*, May 28.

Doc. 207.

CASE OF GEN. CADWALLADER.

GENERAL CADWALLADER having declined acceding to the demand for the body of Merriman, until he could hear from Washington, a writ of attachment was issued against him, for contempt of court. The Marshal reported that, on going to Fort McHenry to serve the writ, he was refused admittance.

Chief-Justice Taney then read the following statement:

"I ordered the attachment, yesterday, because upon the face of the return the detention of the prisoner was unlawful, upon two grounds:

"*First.*—The President, under the Constitution and laws of the United States, cannot suspend the privilege of the writ of *habeas corpus*, nor authorize any military officer to do so.

"*Second.*—A military officer has no right to arrest and detain a person, nor subject him to the Rules and Articles of War for an offence against the laws of the United States, except in aid of the judicial authority, and subject to its control; and if the party is arrested by the military, it is the duty of the officer to deliver him over immediately to the civil authority, to be dealt with according to law.

"I forbore yesterday to state orally the provisions of the Constitution of the United States which make these principles the fundamental law of the Union, because an oral statement might be misunderstood in some portions of it, and I shall therefore put my opinion in writing, and file it in the office of the Clerk of the Circuit Court in the course of this week."

The Judge added that the military authority was always subordinate to civil. That, under ordinary circumstances, it would be the duty of the Marshal to proceed with *posse comitatus* and bring the party named in the writ into Court; but from the notoriously superior force that he would encounter, this would be impossible. He said the Marshal had done all in his power to discharge his duty.

During the week he should prepare his opinion in the premises, and forward it to the President, calling upon him to perform his constitutional duty, and see that the laws be faithfully executed, and enforce the decrees of this Court.

—*N. Y. Times*, May 29.

Doc. 207½.

BRITISH RELATIONS WITH AMERICA.

HOUSE OF COMMONS, Tuesday, May 28.

LORD J. RUSSELL brought up copies of a correspondence with the Government of the United States of America. The noble lord said: In moving that this correspondence should lie upon the table, it may be convenient to the House, and especially so to the commercial interests in his country, that I should state the substance of the correspondence which has lately taken place with the Government of the United States of America with regard to the blockade. On the 19th of April, the President of the United States issued a notification that it was intended to institute a blockade of the ports of the seven States which had seceded; and on the 27th of April another notification was issued, announcing that it was intended to blockade the ports of North Carolina and Virginia. When Lord Lyons applied for an official notification of the establishment and commencement of the blockade, he was told by the Secretary of State that it was not usual to make such a notification, but that it would be made by the different naval commanders at the several ports when the blockade was instituted. It results from the correspondence that the blockade is to be notified in that manner, and that one blockade has already been so notified—viz., that of the ports of Virginia and North Carolina by the flag officer Prendergast, who has declared that he is in a situation to make an efficient blockade of those ports. There has been no notification of a similar kind with regard to the ports of the other States which it was declared were also to be blockaded. The rules, so far as

Lord Lyons has been able to ascertain them, and of which he has given an account to Admiral Milne, commanding the squadron in those waters, are, first, that the notification is in each place to be made by the naval officer commanding the squadron or the ships which institute the blockade; and, in the next place, that fifteen days are to be allowed, after the establishment of the blockade, for vessels to come out of the ports. It appears that whether they were loaded or not at the time the blockade was established, provided they come out within fifteen days, their passage is to be allowed. On the other hand, it is not permitted by the United States Government that vessels should be sent to ports which are blockaded for the purpose of bringing away the property of British subjects, or the vessels or property of other nations. An application for such permission was made, to which the Secretary of State replied that if such a facility were granted it would be used by American citizens wishing to bring away property. Lord Lyons ends his communication to Admiral Milne very properly. He says that if the blockade is carried into effect according to the rules established by the law of nations, we must of course conform to it; and that we can only see that the blockade is sufficient and regular. (Hear, hear.)

Mr. T. Duncombe.—I think that the noble lord ought to inform the House what means he has taken to give protection to British subjects and British property in the Slave States of America. I understand that the greatest outrages are being committed upon British subjects in these States. The noble lord may have no information upon the subject, but I this morning received letters from persons upon whom I can depend, and who have requested me to ask what the Government are doing or intend to do in this matter. There is not the least complaint made against the Government of the free States. But in the Confederate States neither life nor property is safe, and British subjects who went there with wholly different objects, and under very different circumstances, are compelled to take up arms and fight in the Pro-Slavery ranks. The noble lord took great credit to himself for having issued a proclamation, and for declaring that the Foreign Enlistment act will be put in force. But if that be so, all persons engaged in this war under such circumstances will be treated as pirates. The mercantile marine of America, particularly of the Southern States, is chiefly manned by Irishmen and Englishmen, and others from our own colonies, who will now be compelled to remain and to enter the ranks of the belligerents, and if taken, though they may be loyal subjects of the Queen who wanted to get away, but had not the means of doing so, under the noble lord's proclamation they will be treated as pirates. We talk of our neutrality; we boast of it. A letter which I have received from a gentleman asks: "Is it nothing that a British officer," the captain of a merchant vessel, "has been tarred and feathered?" (Laughter.) It is all very well for honorable gentlemen to laugh, but I foresee that these are questions which will involve us in difficulty before long. (Hear, hear.) "Is it nothing," this gentleman asks, "that a British subject has been tarred and feathered; nothing that free men of color, British subjects, are imprisoned; nothing that men of colonial birth are forced to sea in an open boat; others held as prisoners, and that Englishmen should be compelled to fight in Pro-Slavery ranks? At this moment there is an advertisement in the newspapers of the Slave States, offering, on the part of the Confederate States, $20 for every person killed aboard an American vessel. What a set of savages they must be! Who would care for going to war with such a people? Do you suppose the people of Canada will submit to have their fellow-subjects dragged away, and compelled to fight for Slavery? They will stand no nonsense, and after a time your very neutrality will lead you into war. The question which I have been requested to ask is, whether it is not intended immediately to increase the British squadron on the Southern coast, and to have every vessel examined, so that Englishmen, Irishmen, and subjects of our colonial empire, who may be serving compulsorily on board American vessels, shall have an opportunity of getting away in case they wish to do so. I have received letters from men on whom I can depend, and they all state that occurrences such as I have adverted to have already taken place, and more will undoubtedly follow, unless England adopts a more decided tone. We have no right to sit down and occupy ourselves exclusively in quarrelling about the paper duties, (laughter,) while our fellow-subjects are suffering by hundreds and thousands in the hands of these savages.

Mr. B. Osborne.—I must, at this early stage, protest against the language made use of and the sentiments expressed by my honorable friend the member for Finsbury, (hear, hear,) who has altogether prejudged this question. He talks of reliable information which he has received from certain friends of his; but I am also in possession of reliable information which gives the direct lie to the statements made by the hon. gentleman. (Laughter.) I am not only in a position to deny that any of those outrages have been committed in the Southern States; but, if this were the proper time, I could point to outrages committed by the militia of New York in one of the Southern States occupied by them, where the general commanding, on the pretext that one of his men had been poisoned by strychnine, issued an order of the day threatening to put a slave into every man's house to incite the slaves to murder their masters. Such was the general order issued by Gen. Butler. Therefore, don't let us be led away by old wives' tales into appeals to that very powerful and very dangerous element in this House—I mean the Exeter Hall feeling. (Hear, hear.) I do hope the feeling of the House will be strongly expressed against any thing like a debate upon this subject at the present moment, (general cries of "Hear, hear;") and the hon. gentleman will not be tempted to follow my hon. friend, but will rather imitate the judicious silence which the noble lord has always maintained on this point. ("Hear," and a laugh.)

Mr. BRIGHT.—I think nothing could be more injudicious or more unfortunate than to read from private letters accounts of particular outrages said to be committed in America. We know, before war is terminated, there or anywhere else, there will be outrages enough; but of this I think we may be quite assured, that in the North as well as in the South, and in the South quite as much as in the North, there will be the greatest possible disposition to avoid any thing which can bring about a quarrel with this country. (Hear, hear.) Nothing could be more unfortunate for the South, nothing could be more unfortunate for the North, whatever quarrels there may be between the two sections of the American Republic, than that the quarrel should extend to this country. I feel confident that we are not more anxious to remain at peace with both the sections than they are to continue on good terms with us. In the policy which the noble lord has announced—that of strict neutrality— I agree as cordially as any other member of this House; and I think it would be well if that policy were not confined merely to the Government, but if individual members of the House were as far as possible to adopt the same line of action. (Hear, hear.) It is an unhappy thing that these dissensions should have arisen; but let us hope, and I hope still, that among a population more extensively educated, probably, than the population of any other country in the world, it may yet be possible to surmount the vast difficulties which have arisen in that country without those extensive cruelties which always accompany a civil war. With that expression of opinion I wish to make a request—and the House, I am sure, will feel that I am only asking what is reasonable and prudent—that we should avoid, as much as possible, discussions on matters which I believe we cannot influence for good, (hear, hear,) but with regard to which we may create a state of feeling, either in the North or South, that will add to the difficulties of the Government in preserving the line of action which they have laid down. (Hear, hear.)

Mr. GREGORY said—I really must warn the House not to be led away by stories and by letters which one gentleman has received from another gentleman, on whom he places the most implicit reliance, but who very probably knows nothing more of the matter than the gentleman who reads the communication with such perfect faith in the accuracy of its contents. As to the nonsensical trash of $20 being offered by the Confederate States for

every man put to death on board an American ship, the House knows perfectly well that neither letters, newspapers, nor accredited information of any kind can at present be received from the South, but is stopped on the borders. Any thing which does see the light is cut into slips and published in the New York papers. Very few communications of the kind have reached this country, and they are principally the State documents which have been put forward by the South. I cannot better evidence the spirit by which they are animated, than by referring to the late address of President Davis; and I will ask the House whether it breathes a single one of those bloodthirsty, wicked, terrible opinions, (hear, hear,) which my hon. friend is anxious to impress on the House as being the doctrine of the Southern States. I beg to take this opportunity of saying that I shall certainly bring forward my motion on the subject of the recognition of the Southern Confederacy on the 7th of June, when I trust the matter will be fairly discussed, and in the mean time that we shall not throw imputations on one party or the other. (Hear, hear.)

Mr. BOUVERIE.—In the question of notification of blockade, to which reference has been made, a matter which is very important for the commercial interests of the country is involved. The rule, I believe, is this: Public notification must be given to the State of which a neutral who seeks to violate a blockade is a member, before he can be held to have subjected himself to forfeiture of his vessel and goods; or actual notice must have been given to the neutral himself. The House will see that this is a most important question, because the intent to sail to a blockaded port, as to which a neutral merchant has received a notice of blockade, is considered as a violation of neutrality, and the ship will be accordingly condemned in the prize court of the capturing Power. He wished the noble lord would state distinctly whether or not the mercantile interests of this country were to understand that a public notification of blockade of the ports to which he had referred would be given; or that merely an intimation of the blockade to neutral ships arriving off those ports would be given to them when they got there.

Lord JOHN RUSSELL, who was very indistinctly heard, was understood to say: I cannot give any further information to my right honorable friend with regard to the blockade; but the papers on the subject will shortly be laid on the table, and when they are submitted, the House will be in possession of the exact state of the case. But my right honorable friend will understand that, whatever the form of notification of the blockade may be, there is no former precedent that applies fully to the present proceedings. Mr. Seward has not given a general notification of a blockade, but has left it to the naval officers commanding on each station to declare the several ports blockaded, and when that blockade has been instituted it is to be considered regular. I will not now go into questions that may have to be argued and decided hereafter in the Prize Courts with regard to the regularity of the blockade. No doubt the Government of the United States has fully considered existing precedents before it took the course it has done. With respect to the question of the honorable member for Finsbury, I must say it is founded on rather a vague statement. The particular case to which he referred is one on which no proceedings can be taken. He alluded to the case of the master of a merchant ship who was tarred and feathered. It occurred some months ago, and some weeks before any state of civil war existed, when the whole country was at peace. I am not sure there was not then some intention of seceding; but no secession had then taken place, though there were rumors of it. The master of the merchant ship was, in fact, ill-treated by a mob; but the authorities endeavored to arrest the rioters, and our consul stated that the authorities had done every thing it was possible to effect. As to the steps Her Majesty's Government have taken in consequence of the blockade, orders have been given by the Admiralty to send out some ships of war to strengthen the squadron under the command of Admiral Milne. With regard to the law of the United States and of the Southern Confederacy as to persons serving in the militia, such laws vary in the different States of Europe, and they vary also in the different States of America. No doubt the powers of these laws will be exercised at the discretion of the several Governments, according to the law of nations. I still hope that this conflict will be of short duration, and while a great and free State like America is exposed to all the evils of a civil war, I hope no language will be used with regard to it, that will tend to create exasperation either on one side or the other.

—*New York Tribune*, June 11.

Doc. 208.

LETTERS OF EDWARD BATES

TO JOHN MINOR BOTTS.

WASHINGTON CITY, April 29, 1861.

Hon. John Minor Botts, Richmond, Va.:—

DEAR SIR: * * * You and I, Mr. Botts, know each other's characters very well. Heretofore yours has been marked by bold, frank, and manly traits, which won for you many friends and admirers all over the country, and hence my astonishment on receiving from you such a note with such an enclosure. I do not impute the blame to you, for I cannot avoid the conclusion that you are acting under duress—that you have become the victim of a set of desperadoes, who, having wantonly plunged into the guilt of treason and the danger of ruin, would gladly sacrifice you and me, and ten thousand such men, if thereby they can make a way of escape for themselves from the least of the dangers which they have so wickedly incurred.

Here at Washington, perhaps, we know a little more about the machinations of the conspirators at Richmond than they are aware of. But besides that, the documents (your note to Colonel Russell, your note to me, and the printed slip) bear internal evidence of a concerted plan, a scheme invented (not by the bold and patriotic Botts, but) by those same conspirators, who, failing to intimidate the Government by bullying violence, have changed their tactics, and still hope to win the victory and destroy the nation by a less hazardous but more cunning process.

1. Your note to Colonel Russell (which he showed me) imports that you are safe and comfortable at Richmond, while we have melancholy testimony that such men as you are neither safe nor comfortable there.

2. Your note to me of April 23d (covering the printed letter, but not mentioning it) contains several phrases which I am persuaded you would not have used if left to your own free action. The note begins by stating its main object thus—" I write hurriedly to say that I have consented to the publication of my letter to you, with the hope, &c." Which letter to me? I have received several letters from you, but none of the 19th of April. " Consented to the publication "—at whose instance? The phrase and the context invite the inference that the publication was made at my instance and that inference was, I believe, generally drawn in this city, and will probably be drawn all over the country; whereas, you do know that I had nothing to do with the publication.

The note concludes with this very suggestive line:—" I am not at liberty to speak of what is going on here." I can easily comprehend that humiliating fact; and I do painfully sympathize with you and with all good and faithful men in my native State, when I behold the capital of the once free and proud Virginia *subjected to the tyranny of a lawless mob.*

3. The printed letter. Alas! that I should live to see such a letter under the hand of the gallant and gifted John M. Botts! I shall not go into any minute criticism of the letter—to show how it contradicts all the main facts in your high and honorable political history, and countermarched the whole line of your active and useful career, onward and upward for the last thirty years. My personal regard and my great respect for your character forbid me to do that. But I cannot forbear to say that the whole scope and tendency of the letter, if not its design, is an argument in favor of dissolving the Union, and blotting from the map of the world the nation of the United States. It is a silent approval, by failing to condemn, of the violent and revolutionary proceedings of the people of the Southern States, in several of them before the idle form of secession was gone through with, in plundering the money and

arms, and other property of the United States; in seizing upon our ungarrisoned forts; in making open war upon such as refused to surrender; in firing upon, and in some instances actually degrading, the flag of our country; and in schemes and projects boastfully announced in the public press, and partially acted out in military preparations, to seize this capital by violence, and break up the Government.

Your letter does not in terms assert, but by necessary implication assumes, that this Administration can, if it will, restore the peace of the country, by the cheap and easy experiment of issuing a proclamation "proposing a truce of hostilities and the immediate assembling of a national convention!" It seems to me, my dear sir, that there are some serious objections to this cheap plan of peace; and first, the President has no power to call a national convention. Second, if he did call it, there is not the remotest probability that the insurgent States would obey the call. Third, if they did obey it, there is little hope that they would agree to come in equal terms with the other States, by recanting their recent assumptions of separate and absolute sovereignty, and by restoring all that they have taken by violence from the United States. In short, after all that is past, it seems to me that there are but two alternatives left to this Administration: first, to submit implicitly to all the claims of the insurgent States, and quietly consent to a dismemberment of the nation; or second, to do its best to restore peace, law, and order, by supporting "the Constitution and the Union, and the enforcement of the laws." Let the nation judge which horn of the dilemma the Administration ought to take, in view of all its obligations in regard to the permanent interests of the country, and to its own patriotism and constitutional duty.

I am amazed at the course of things in Virginia. Your convention was not called to dissolve the Union, nor trusted with the power of secession. By the act of its creation that sovereign power was reserved to the people of Virginia. Yet as soon as the convention had secretly acted upon the subject, without any promulgation of the ordinance, and while the people were yet ignorant of its existence, the executive officers of Virginia rushed, incontinently, into open war against the United States. They endeavored to obstruct the harbor of Norfolk, in order to secure the plunder of the Navy Yard at Gosport, and sent a military power to complete the work of its spoliation. The enterprise failed indeed to clutch the spoil, but it caused the destruction of millions of dollars' worth of public property. The same thing was, substantially, done at Harper's Ferry. Virginia troops were marched upon the place to seize the arsenal. They did not get possession, as John Brown did, only because the vigilant little garrison, knowing its inability to resist such superior numbers, destroyed the property and made good its retreat. They menaced this

capital by open threats of military force, by obstructing the roads leading to it, and by active endeavors to command the navigation of the Potomac. And all this was done while the State, according to the letter of its own law, remained a member of the Union. Think you, my dear sir, that men who do these things in open day, and in contempt of the rights and powers of the people of Virginia, have such a reverence for "reason, order, law, liberty, morality, and religion," as to give much heed to the President's "proclamation proposing a truce?" I lack the faith to believe it.

In conclusion, I assure you in all sincerity that I do deeply sympathize in your present distress. I love the people of my native State, and mourn over the guilt and wretchedness into which they thoughtlessly allow themselves to be plunged by their reckless misleaders.

With long cherished respect and regard,
I remain your obedient servant,
EDWARD BATES.

SECOND LETTER.

WASHINGTON, May 5, 1861.

Hon. John M. Botts, Richmond, Va.:

My DEAR SIR:—In answer to your letter of May 2d I have not and ought not to have much to say. This much, however, both my inclination and my duty require me to say, my personal respect for you remains undiminished. My friendly feelings toward you are not only not diminished, but are made more deep and tender by the distressing circumstances which surround you. And these facts make me regret very much that I should have been compelled by circumstances to write you such a letter as to inflict any pain or mortification, and especially to the degree indicated by your answer, and explained more at large by the friend who bore it. I disclaim all intention to wound your feelings, or to offer you the slightest indignity, and if there be any thing in my letter from which an intention to insult you can possibly be inferred, I retract it.

This much I say with the intention and hope of preventing any breach, or even weakening, of the personal relations between us. Let us be friends still.

But it seems now that we differ so widely in opinion upon matters of fact that it is impossible for us to reason upon the same line of argument. You think that the Union is already dissolved—the nation already destroyed. On the contrary, I believe no such thing. You believe that a peaceful dissolution of the Union, in the manner and by the means already employed, is possible. I believe it impossible. I believe that the insane effort at national destruction persisted in, *will involve a war more terrible than any the world has witnessed since the thirty years' war in Germany.* You think that a great nation like this can consent to die, and may hope to die an easy death. I think that nations, like individuals, are under God's great law of self-defence, and when pressed down by superior force will die in convulsive agonies. You seem to think that Virginia can go out of the Union, and still preserve her integral Statehood. I think that when she dismembers the nation she will herself be dismembered. But I will not continue the contrast. My heart is sorrowful when I contemplate the present degradation of Virginia. "How are the mighty fallen?" With the loss of her power she has lost all prestige also, and can no longer lead the people and direct the counsels of other States. She remembers her patriots and sages of former times only to boast of them—not to imitate their talents and virtues—but (by implicit faith) to impute to the present generation the posthumous reputation of the glorious dead. Formerly she proudly marched in the van of all the States; now she creeps in the rear of South Carolina, and consents to be detailed as a picket guard, to man an outpost of the "Cotton States." Poor old Virginia! In my heart I pity her. Already they boast in the South that they have transferred the seat of war from their homes to yours. And soon their devouring legions will be upon you to eat up your substance and do your voting at the disunion election. Now mark my prophecy. Unless Virginia by a rapid revolution redeems herself from the gulf that lies open just before her, she will be degraded, impoverished, and dismembered. For her I hope almost against hope.

And for you, I remain, as heretofore,

Your friend,
EDWARD BATES.

— *Wheeling (Va.) Intelligencer*, May 28.

Doc. 209.

NEW YORK AND GEORGIA.

INTERESTING CORRESPONDENCE.

NEW YORK, May 13, 1861.

To His Excellency, E. D. Morgan, Governor of the State of New York:

SIR:—By proclamation dated 26th day of April last, Joseph E. Brown, Governor of the State of Georgia, sets forth and declares that property of the citizens of Georgia, whenever found within the limits of the anti-slavery States, in which the said Governor includes the State of New York, is seized, and forcibly taken from its owners.

And Gov. Brown further forbids and refuses to allow the citizens of Georgia to pay their indebtedness of whatever kinds or nature, to any citizens of this State, but invites them to pay the same into the Treasury of the State of Georgia, in any funds bankable in Augusta or Savannah, and to receive therefor a certificate of sums so deposited.

We now, as officers of banks in the City of New York, doing business with banks, bankers, and merchants of Georgia and other States, known as the Confederate States of America, now in revolt against the Government of the United States, deem it proper to apprise your Excellency that we do distinctly deny the truth of the statements so made by the said Governor of the State of Georgia.

The Banks of this City have paid, and continue to pay, in every case, all drafts against funds deposited, whether by Southern, Western, or Northern banks, bankers, or other dealers, and any statement or allegation to the contrary is wholly unfounded.

JNO. A. STEVENS,
President of Bank of Commerce, New York.
GEO. S. COE,
President of the American Exchange Bank.
JAS. GALLATIN,
President of National Bank.
JNO. J. CRANE,
President of Bank of Republic.
G. D. ANGELIS,
Cashier of Mechanics' Bank, New York.
JAS. M. MORRISON,
President of Manhattan Bank.
J. E. WILLIAMS,
President of Metropolitan Bank.

REPLY OF GOVERNOR MORGAN.

STATE OF NEW YORK, EXECUTIVE DEPARTMENT, }
ALBANY, May 18, 1861. }

GENTLEMEN: I have received your communication of the 13th inst., formally denying the truth of the statements made by Gov. Brown, of Georgia, in his proclamation of the 26th ult.

You affirm that "the banks of the City of New York have paid, and continue to pay, in every case, all drafts against funds deposited, whether by Southern, Western, or Northern banks, bankers, and dealers, and that any statement or allegation to the contrary is wholly unfounded." This course I believe to be emphatically in consonance with the sentiment of the commercial and business classes throughout this State.

The sterling uprightness of the bankers of the City of New York is widely known. Their sensitiveness is, therefore, natural under the circumstances, and it is but proper that they should meet, with a prompt and broad denial, the loose and ill-founded assertions of his Excellency, the Governor of Georgia, so far as they affect them.

The position taken by you, that business obligations must be respected as well now as in ordinary times, should command the respect of rebel as well as of loyal States. Rebellion affords neither at the North nor South an excuse for repudiation by individuals or corporations; and when the excitements which now disturb the country shall have been allayed, no one will have the courage to plead it as a reason for disregarding his obligations.

I have the honor to be,

Very respectfully yours,
E. D. MORGAN.

To John A. Stevens, Esq., President Bank of Commerce, George S. Coe, President of the American Exchange Bank, and others.

—*N. Y. Times*, May 28.

Doc. 210.

THE GARIBALDI GUARD.

THE following is a list of the officers:

Staff.—Fred. George D'Utassy, Colonel; Alexander Repetti, Lieut.-Colonel; George E. Waring, Major in the Field; L. W. Tinelli, Major Commanding Depot; John M. Sickel, Adjutant; James C. Rice, Lieut. Adjutant; Adolf Majer, M. D., Surgeon.

Non-Commissioned Staff.—Chas. B. Norton, Paymaster; W. P. Molo, Commissary; E. D. Lazell, Quartermaster; Standard Bearers, John Lindner, Chas. Schwickardy, T. Hoffman; Sergeants, A. P. Zyla, A. E. D. Hughes. Company A, Captain, C. Osnaghi; Lieutenant, Antonio del Molin; Ensign, —— Alegretti. Company B, Captain, J. Schmidt; Lieutenant, G. Ceatain; Ensign, A. Miller. Company C, Captain, C. Schwartz; Lieutenant, A. Vakey; Ensign, Joseph Aigner. Company D, Captain, J. Lorrens; Lieutenant, J. Romero; Ensign, C. A. de la Messe. Company E, Captain, John N. Siegl; Lieutenant, W. Robitseck; Ensign, Fritz Bauer. Company F, Captain, Chas. Wiegand; Lieutenant, C. Schondorf; Ensign, E. Hollinde. Company G, Captain, F. Takats; Lieutenant, J. Junger; Ensign, N. Tenner. Company H, Captain, O. Bernstein; Lieutenant, B. Baer; Ensign, T. Kaufman. Company I, Captain, —— Umverth; Lieutenant, J. C. Rice; Ensign, Geo. Bray. Company K, Captain, L. Lassillier; Lieutenant, V. Channoni; Ensign, Ant. Dunrazer.

The regiment contains 830 men and officers, of whom 205 are married. The nationalities are: one company French, one Italian, three Hungarian, three German, one Swiss, and one Spanish. —*N. Y. Tribune*, May 29.

Doc. 211.

MEETING OF THE BAPTISTS,

AT BROOKLYN, N. Y., MAY 29, 1861.

A. B. CAPWELL, Esq., presided, and the following officers were appointed:

Vice-Presidents—Hon. George N. Briggs, Rev. G. S. Webb, D. D., Thomas Watson, Esq., A. Hubbell, Esq.

Secretaries—Rev. W. H. Shailer, D. D., Rev. J. B. Simmons.

Rev. George C. Baldwin, D. D., opened the proceedings with prayer, after which

The Committee, appointed at a preliminary meeting—Rev. Dr. Wm. R. Williams, N. Y.; Rev. Dr. Rufus Babcock, N. J.; Rev. Dr. E. E. Cummings, New Hampshire; Rev. Dr. S. Baker; Rev. J. H. Smith, of Penn.; Rev. Dr. W. H. Shailer, Me.; Rev. Dr. S. B. Swain, Mass.,—presented, through the Chairman, Rev. Dr. Williams, the following report:

The Assembly of Baptists gathered from the various Northern States of the Union would, in the present solemn crisis of our National history, put on record some expression of their judgment as Christians, loving their country, and seeking, in the fear and from the grace of God, its best interests. We are threatened to be rent as a people into two hostile camps; several States of the Union have claimed to release themselves by their own act, from the National Constitution and Union, having formed what they designate as a Confederacy. They have seized the National forts, armaments, and ships. Such proceedings on the part of a neighboring community would be held actual war. Yet there has been no precedent such as in modern contests inaugurates ordinary hostilities. They have bombarded a National garrison. The General Government at Washington have refused to recognize the right of secession, and have proclaimed alike their own right and their own purpose to occupy the national property and defences now usurped. One of the foremost statesmen in the new movement, and himself the Executive officer of the new assumed Confederacy, had declared African slavery the immediate cause of the revolution thus attempted. He has alleged that the old—and, as the North deems it, the only existing Constitution—regarded such slavery as wrong in principle, and that the founders of this Constitution expected the bondage, in some way, and at some time, to vanish. He declares of the new Confederate States that they assume, as their basis, the fundamental erroneousness of such original estimate and expectation on the part of the fathers of our land. Accepting not only the propriety, but the perpetuity of such servitude, he places the new government on the alleged inferiority of the negro race, as its corner stone. He claims for the new Confederacy that it is the first government in all history thus inaugurated on this new truth, as he would call it. He invites the North-Western States to enter the Confederacy. But he anticipated the disintegration of the older States, and he declares, that in case of these last, admission to the new Confederacy must not be merely by reconstruction, but reorganization and assimilation. In other words, African bondage seems required as the mortar that is to agglutinate, and the rock that is to sustain the recombined and rebuilt sovereignty that shall include even these last. Men high in position in the new organization of the South, have proclaimed the intent of seizing the National Capitol, and planting their flag on the seats of Northern State Government. The President of the United States has summoned a large, formidable force to the metropolis of the Union, rallying to the defence of the General Government. Remembering their own character, as the servants of the Prince of Peace, this assembly would speak fraternally, not heedlessly, exasperating strife, but also with a frankness and decision, as not endorsing injustice. The Church is a kingdom not of the world. But the men of the Church are not the less bound to recognize and loyally to uphold all rightful secular government. The powers that be are ordained of God, and the magistracy is by His will to bear the sword not in vain. Christ, in His Messiahship, would not be made a judge or a divider as to the statutes and estates of this earth; but He did not, therefore, abrogate the tribunals of earthly judgment. To Cæsar He bade us render Cæsar's dues. He cherished and exemplified patriotism when answering to the appeal made to Him in the behalf of that Gentile ruler as far as one who loved "our" Jewish nation. He showed it when weeping, as He predicted the coming woes of His own people, and of their chief city. The Gospel of Christ, then, sanctions and consecrates true patriotism. Shall the Christians of the North accept the revolution thus to be precipitated upon them as warranted and necessary? or shall they acquiesce in it as inevitably dismissing the question of its origin in the irrevocable past? Shall they wait hopefully the verdict of the nations and the sentence of Providence upon the new basis of this extemporized Confederacy? Meanwhile shall they submit passively to the predicted disintegration of their own North, pondering wistfully upon the possibilities of their own reorganization to qualify them for admission on the novel platform, and for their initiation into the new principles of this most summary revolution? The memories of the past and the hopes of the future; history and scripture; the fear of God, and regard to the well-being of man; the best interest of their own estranged brethren at the South, and their own rights and duties, not to themselves and their children only, but as the stewards of constitutional liberty in behalf of all other nations, encouraged by our success, as such remotest nations are baffled and misled, as by our failure such nations would necessarily be—all considerations unite in shutting up the Christians of the North to one course. The following resolutions present correspondingly what, in our judgment, is the due course of our churches and people:

Resolved, That the doctrine of secession is foreign to our constitution, revolutionary, suicidal—setting out in anarchy, and finding its ultimate issue in despotism.

Resolved, That the National Government deserves our loyal adhesion and unstinted support, in its wise forbearing, and yet firm maintenance of the national unity and life; and that sore, long, and costly as the war may be, the North has not sought it, and the North does not shun it, if Southern aggressions press it; and that a surrender of the National Union, and our ancestral principles, would involve sorer evils, and longer continuance, and vaster costliness.

Resolved, That the wondrous uprising, in strongest harmony and largest self-sacrifice, of the whole North, to assert and vindicate the national unity, is the cause of grateful amazement and devoutest acknowledgment to the God who sways all hearts and orders all events; and that this resurgent patriotism, wisely cherished and directed, may, in God's blessed discipline, correct evils that seemed growing chronic and irremediable in the national character.

Resolved, That fearful as is the scourge of war, even in the justest cause, we need as a nation to humble ourselves before God for the vain glory, self-confidence, greed, venality, and corruption of manners, too manifest in our land; that in its waste of property and life, its invasion of the Sabbath, its demoralization and its barbarism, we see the evils to which it strongly tends; but that waged in a good cause, and in the fear of God, it may be to a people, as it often in past times has been, a stern but salutary lesson for enduring good. In this struggle, the churches of the North should, by prayer for them, the distribution of Scripture and tract, and the encouragement of devout chaplains, seek the religious culture of their brave soldiers and mariners.

Resolved, That the North seek not, in any sense, the subjugation of the South, or the horrors of a servile war, or the devastation of their homes by reckless and embruted mercenaries; but believe most firmly the rejection, were it feasible, of the Constitution and Union, would annihilate the best safeguard of Southern peace.

Resolved, That the churches of our denomination be urged to set apart the last Friday in June as a day of solemn humiliation and prayer for the interposition of God's gracious care to hinder or to limit the conflict, to stay the wrath and to sanctify the trial; and that one hour also in the Friday evening of each week be observed as a season of intercession, privately, for our country during this period of her gloom and peril.

Resolved, That, brought nearer as eternity and judgment are in such times of sharp trial and sudden change, it is the duty of all to redeem the fleeting hour; the duty of all Christ's people to see that the walls of Zion be built in troublous times, and to hope only and ever in that wonder-working God, who made British missions to India and the South Seas to grow amid the Napoleon wars, who trained, in Serampore Missions, Havelock, the Christian warrior, as two centuries before He had prepared, in the wars of the Commonwealth, the warrior Baxter, who wrote, as army chaplain, the Saint's Everlasting Rest, and the Bunyan who described for all after time, the Pilgrim's Progress and the Holy War.

Resolved, That what was bought at Bunker Hill, Valley Forge, and Yorktown, was not, with our consent, sold at Montgomery; that we dispute the legality of the bargain, and, in the strength of the Lord God of our fathers, shall hope to contest, through this generation if need be, the feasibility of the transfer.

WILLIAM R. WILLIAMS, N. Y.
RUFUS BABCOCK, JR., N. J.
E. E. CUMMINGS, N. H.
J. HYATT SMITH, PA.
SAMUEL BAKER, N. Y.
S. B. SWAIN, MASS.

Rev. Dr. Welch supposed it was intended to adopt the report without debate. He would, however, ask the privilege of speaking a few words on the question before the meeting. With all his heart he subscribed to the sentiment expressed in the preamble and resolutions; but under the present trying, solemn circumstances of the country, they were too tame, far too weak in their expression. There was truth that could not be gainsayed, and that history would present beyond the reach of controversy. It was true that a great nation had been arrested in a career of peace and prosperity. It was true that their nation had been ruthlessly pulled down from its proud eminence, and humbled before the world. The banner of their glorious Union, which led their forefathers on to victory, was riddled with shot, and the destruction of their Republic threatened. He descended himself from a race of sailors and soldiers, and although his profession differed from theirs—he being a minister of the Gospel of Jesus Christ—he inherited their patriotic devotion to the flag of their country. His paternal grandfather was with Paul Jones in his adventures in the frigate Alliance. He thought the resolutions did not come up to the expression which they should, as a Church, publish to the world in the present state of the country, and he could not submit to the adoption of the short beautiful rhetoric in terms of appeal, which had been read as representing fully the views of the Denomination. They had appealed to the honor and magnanimity of the South. The South did not know the meaning of the term. (Applause.) They never knew it. The barbarism of Slavery had crushed it out. (Applause.) He was ready then to look on the struggle from Mount Zion, to view it from the point where the Saviour had led captivity captive. When he contemplated the question in that light, there was another class of feelings which took possession of him, which he would wrong them and himself to suppress. He had been in favor of excluding the vexed question of slavery from the associations and conventions with which he was connected, on the ground that the institution belonged to the kingdom of Cæsar, and not to the kingdom of Christ. But the time had come when the religious aspect of slavery could not be ignored by them as a people. The clergy at the North had been misrepresented at the South, and even God's Holy Word was said to contain the Divine sanction of slavery. Ministers were made to be the chief and especial patrons of the sin. He would not give the sanction of his voice to uphold slavery, nor would he entertain Christian fellowship for its supporters till he should meet them among the redeemed. He thought that the report would be much improved by being stronger in language and purposes, and would thus be adapted to the crisis which they had been convened as Baptists to consider.

Ex-Governor Briggs said he had listened with increasing interest to every word of the report, as it fell from the feeble but silvery voice of his esteemed brother, (Dr. Williams,) and his heart, his head, and his whole soul and nature, were moved, and responded Amen to the report. The brother who had preceded him had said it was too tame, but he would say that it was just tame enough for him. (Applause.) It was couched in decorous, significant, respectful but forcible language, and was eminently appropriate to proceed from a Christian body. There was nothing in it calculated to exasperate, while it was firm and patriotic in sentiment, and he did not believe that it could be improved. The great truth had been proclaimed thousands of years since, that a soft answer turneth away wrath, and the force and meaning of the sentence remained unchanged since it was written. (Applause.) The public wanted no inflammatory material at the present time. The rights of the country and the trying circumstances surrounding it, were expressed in the resolution, in the spirit which should animate the heart of the Christian. Their Divine Master had set an example, when He wept over Jerusalem. He knew what the people whom He had served would do to Him. Did He address them in words calculated to exasperate them, or embitter their hearts? No; from his peaceful lips went forth the plaintive words, "Oh, Jerusalem, Jerusalem, thou that killest the prophets, and stonest them that are sent unto thee, how often would I have gathered thee, even as a hen doth gather her chickens, and ye would not. Behold your house is left unto you desolate." That was the spirit which should actuate the followers of Christ. He hoped the report would be adopted without a dissenting voice.

Rev. Mr. Malcom moved an amendment in favor of taking out the clause recommending one hour on each Friday to be spent by the members in private prayer for the country. He for one would not spend an hour in prayer. The time had come for them to act and pray while in action. That course would be too much like that of the Pharisees, who commanded their people to carry heavy burdens, which they would not so much as move with their own fingers. It was simply like a red tape proceeding, and he hoped it would be omitted.

Rev. Dr. Hague supported the amendment, remarking that the time had arrived when they should stand by their guns. He considered the document too long, and thought it would not be sufficiently effective on those who were battling for the country. England was wavering as to whom she should recognize, and the Baptists of England, through Spurgeon and other preachers, should be apprized in the report of the position of their brethren.

Rev. Dr. Gillette suggested that the words "social meetings" should be inserted, instead of private prayer meetings, which was accepted by the Committee, when the amendment was withdrawn.

Hon. Wm. D. Murphy moved the recommittal of the report. Lost.

Rev. Dr. Welch—I protest with my whole soul against the adoption of the report. It will put our denomination in a position of shameful absurdity before the world.

On motion, it was resolved that a copy of the resolutions be presented to the President of the United States, and a collection was taken up to print it in circular form.

The meeting then adjourned.

—N. Y. Express, May 29.

Doc. 212.

MILITARY DEPARTMENTS.

Department of the East.—This department has been subdivided into three parts, as follows:

Department of Washington.—The District of Columbia, according to its original boundary; Fort Washington and the country adjacent; and the State of Maryland, including Bladensburg and Baltimore. Head-quarters at the National Capital.

Department of the South.—Eastern Virginia, North Carolina, and Tennessee. Head-quarters Fort Monroe, Virginia.

Department of Annapolis.—The country for twenty miles on each side of the railroad from Annapolis to the city of Washington, as far as Bladensburg, Maryland. Head-quarters at Annapolis.

Department of Pennsylvania.—The State of Pennsylvania; the State of Delaware; all of Maryland not embraced in the foregoing department. Head-quarters at Philadelphia.

Department of the West.—The country west of the Mississippi River and east of the Rocky Mountains, except those portions of it included within the limits of New Mexico. Head-quarters at St. Louis, Missouri.

Department of Texas.—The Government not having issued any new orders relative to this department, and the forts having been evacuated, it may be said to remain in *statu quo.*

Department of New Mexico.—The Territory of New Mexico. Head-quarters at Santa Fe.

Department of the Pacific.—The country west of the Rocky Mountains. Head-quarters at San Francisco.

Department of Utah.—The Territory of Utah, except the portion of it lying west of the 117th degree of west longitude. Head-quarters at Camp Floyd.

There will probably be three or more subdivisions of the late Department of the East, to meet the requirements of the service.

—National Intelligencer, May 29.

Doc. 213.

TO VOLUNTEER NURSES.

WAR DEPARTMENT, MILITARY HOSPITAL.

BE it known to all whom it may concern that the free services of Miss D. L. Dix are ac-cepted by the War Department, and that she will give at all times all necessary aid in organizing military hospitals for the care of all sick or wounded soldiers, aiding the chief surgeons by supplying nurses and substantial means for the comfort and relief of the suffering; also, that she is fully authorized to receive, control, and disburse special supplies bestowed by individuals or associations for the comfort of their friends or the citizen soldiers from all parts of the United States.

Given under the seal of the War Department this twenty-third day of April, in the year of our Lord one thousand eight hundred and sixty-one, and of the independence of the United States the eighty-fifth.

SIMON CAMERON, Secretary of War.

Army Hospital Service.

SURGEON GENERAL'S OFFICE, MAY 1, 1861.

This Department, cheerfully and thankfully recognizing the ability and energy of Miss D. L. Dix in her arrangements for the comfort and welfare of the sick soldier in the present exigency, requests that each of the ladies who have offered their services as nurses would put themselves in communication with her before entering upon their duties, as efficient and well-directed service can only be rendered through a systematic arrangement. It is further suggested that the ladies exert themselves to their fullest extent in preparing or supplying hospital shirts for the sick, also articles of diet, which may be preserved, as delicacies may be needed for individual cases, and such as cannot be supplied at an hour's notice.

Miss Dix's residence is at No. 505 Twelfth street, between E and F.   Respectfully,

R. C. WOOD, Act. Surgeon General.

WASHINGTON, MAY 4, 1861.

The great number of humane persons impelled by self-sacrificing benevolence to offer their services as nurses, in the event of necessity, in the military hospitals, makes it proper to communicate a few facts briefly through the medium of the press:

1. It is the wish of the acting Surgeon General that qualified persons communicate their names and residence to the writer; and, as no serious sickness exists at present, they are respectfully requested not to proceed to head-quarters at Washington or elsewhere till such time as their valuable aid may be needed, when immediate notice will be given.

2. It is believed that all who offer as nurses do so with the understanding that this is a *free* service—looking for no pecuniary recompense; and the writer respectfully and earnestly suggests that all who enter upon this work be provided with the means of sustaining all their personal expenses—especially as, by the army regulation, no provision is made for such service.

The matrons allowed each regiment are laundresses for special work, and in the hospitals have charge of the linen, bandages, etc., which they wash and prepare for use.

With respectful consideration, D. L. Dix.

NOTICE.—Benevolent ladies desiring to furnish means for increasing the comforts and benefit of hastily established military hospitals, will insure success by consulting surgeons of practical knowledge and experience in their vicinity.

Pillows of various sizes and of various material for various purposes will be of much use.

At present the stock of flannel body garments and of warm socks is quite deficient and already in request. Very respectfully,

D. L. Dix,
505 Twelfth street, Washington.

Rev. Dr. Bellows, Drs. Van Buren, Harris, and Harson, representing three associations of New York for sanitary reform in the army, have been busily engaged the last three or four days urging several measures upon the Administration. They ask the appointment of a mixed commission, with a general supervision of all matters connected with the sanitary condition of the army. Special attention will be given to four points, namely: The inspection of the troops, with a view to the exclusion of unsuitable persons; enlistment of a skilful cook in each company; employment of nurses educated by the Women's Association, and of volunteer dressers, composed of young medical men.

The committee have been much pleased with their reception by the President and the heads of Departments, all of whom manifest a disposition to profit by their friendly criticism and adopt salutary reforms. It is not fully decided whether all the measures recommended by the committee will be adopted, but they will be fully considered, as all who have been consulted take a great interest in the matter.

—*National Intelligencer*, May 29.

Doc. 214.

COL. MANN'S REGIMENT OF PENN.

LIST of the officers of the regiment:

REGIMENTAL OFFICERS.— Colonel, Wm. B. Mann; Lieut.-Col., Albert Magilton; Major, Wm. McCandless; Adjutant, James L. Hall; Quartermaster, Chas. F. Hoyt.

COMPANY OFFICERS.—Company A—Capt., Richard Ellis; 1st. Lieut, John Corley; 2d Lieut., George Young; Orderly Sergeant, S. L. McKinny. Company B—Capt., Timothy Meely; 1st Lieut., Peter Summers; 2d Lieut., Robt. H. Porter; Orderly Sergeant, James Johnson. Company C—Capt., Robt. M. McClure; 1st Lieut., Edwin W. Cox; 2d Lieut., Fred. A. Conrad; Orderly Sergeant, John St. John. Company D—Capt., Patrick McDonough; 1st Lieut., John D. Shoch; 2d Lieut., John Gill; Orderly Sergeant, Wm. Crow. Company E— Capt., —— Bringhurzt; 1st Lieut., George Keit, 2d Lieut., Wm. J. D. Eward; Orderly

Sergeant, Christ. P. Rass. Company F—Capt., William Knox; 1st Lieut., Thomas Weir; 2d Lieut., Thomas Jack; Orderly Sergeant, David Chitester. Company G—Capt., James Brynes; 1st Lieut., John P. Robinson; 2d Lieut., Francis Knox; Orderly Sergeant, Jas. R. Nightengale. —*Easton (Pa.) Express*, May 30.

Doc. 214½.

THE WAR IN AMERICA.

IT is a very proper prudence which restrains speakers and writers on both sides the Atlantic from answering the question, "What next?" in regard to the war and its prospects. We are glad to see that the disinclination to prophesy is on the increase; and that the Northern newspapers and letter-writers seem to be on their guard against the folly of disparaging their enemy. They have a warning, by what they read in Southern reports, of the mischief and danger of brag of their own prowess, and ignorant contempt of an untried antagonist. We, at this distance, can only wait to see what happens. But there is no reason why we should not, and every reason why we should, gather together such facts as are within our knowledge, bearing upon the present conditions of the struggle, in order to obtain some idea of how matters are likely to go. While awaiting news of the first clash of arms, or other kind of exploit, we may review the leading considerations of the case.

The main considerations seem to us to be four. The first in importance is the question of the strength of the Union party in the Slave States. The Washington Cabinet declares, from its special sources of information, that the Union party is strong in every region of the South. The Montgomery leaders insist that the whole South is united as one man in favor of Secession. Newspapers tell us, on the one hand, that the whole South is a chaos of factions, and on the other, that it is a scene of perfect fraternity. We can learn nothing by authority or hearsay, it is clear. But there are now facts to judge by. Thus far, in every State in which opinion could express itself, the Union party has proved so strong as to neutralize the action of the Secessionist authorities. In Texas, in Missouri, in Kentucky, in Virginia, and in Maryland, and now in Louisiana, there is enough loyalty to the Washington Government to cause a virtual split in each State, resembling that of the Republic itself. If, in every case in which opinion can declare itself, there is a strong opposition to Secession, it is reasonable to suppose that the same thing will appear in the other States, as soon as they can get leave to speak; and at all events we perceive that it is not true that the desire for Secession is universal. All the gentry who have effected their escape from the plantations bear testimony to the forcible repression of opinion by the dominant "faction," as they call it, in their respective neighborhoods; and in fact no doubt remains of there being a strong antagonism of parties in the Slave States—a circumstance important in the highest degree to the prospects of the war. If Virginia, Kentucky, and Missouri are divided between allegiance and Secession, the probability is that other Slave States are also divided. At all events, while opinion is not free, the Montgomery Government cannot be entitled to affirm that they are not.

In the second place, it is known with clearness and certainty, that there is a serious deficiency of food in the Slave States. For many years it has ceased to be true that the South excelled the North in agricultural production—even including cotton and tobacco in the estimate; and of late the cereal growth of the Western Free States has increased prodigiously, while, in the South, great expanses of corn land have been given over to cotton growing, though food was brought down from the Northwest. Northern food products have for some years been on sale in every Southern city. At present there is severe scarcity——amounting in some places to famine—in Mississippi; and we have seen before what efforts have been made to obtain grain and other food on credit since the winter. The Federal forces and the loyalists of Illinois now hold the passage of the Mississippi, aided by Missouri loyalists, and no cargoes can pass Cairo. The blockade by sea being by this time complete, it is difficult to see how the war can be supported while the Southern corn crop is growing. Strong appeals, we observe, are made to the planters to grow corn instead of cotton this year; but, beside that the crops have to grow, there is no getting any work done on the plantations. The owners are summoned to the war, with all sons above sixteen; and even their overseers are not often allowed to remain, however strong are the remonstrances of the proprietors. Thus, left to the management of old gentlemen, boys, or ladies, and taking advantage of the general excitement, the negroes are beginning to make holiday; and if the community depends on them for its food, it is likely to suffer hunger. Whatever may be the fact about the existing supply in particular places, the fact of dearth in any one State, while all access to food markets is cut off, points to a short duration of the war.

In the third place, there is the question of the negroes, free and bond. In the South the free negroes are anxiously and peremptorily summoned to the war. Their money is invested in Southern loans, and they are put under drill as soldiers, or set to work on fortifications. Their zeal is extolled in the newspapers, but their Northern kindred well understand that they are thus to be kept out of mischief. There is little expectation of seeing them on any battle-field; but if they appear, it will not be, their kindred say, to fight with their best friends. In the free States the people of color are eager to help on the loyal side. They have

for many weeks past formed themselves into companies, and got themselves drilled and armed—refused at present a place in the loyal forces, but resolved to be ready for the call, which they believe will come. The authorities of Pennsylvania have refused a passage through their State to companies of free negroes from New England and New York; but the black volunteers extend their organization week by week. They are not a very large element in the population; but they avow their determination to offer themselves to a man, leaving only the infirm and children out of their training system. They certainly believe that the question is that of the abolition of Slavery; and their preparation has the religious fervor and solemnity which befit such an occasion as the redemption of their race. Under such circumstances, the mood of the slaves becomes a very interesting inquiry. Thus far, the most certain fact is, that wherever any Federal force has appeared, slaves have deserted to them at every opportunity. Hitherto, they have been all returned. It was so in Maryland, and it was so in Florida; and we hear the same story from every station of the United States troops. After the first collision in the field there will be an end of returning deserters; and the fugitives will be too useful as guides and aids to be slighted. The despatch of Governor Andrew, of Massachusetts, shows the changing feeling of the North on this point of policy. It is asserted with so much detail as to have every appearance of truth, that mounted bands are trained in various States, and especially in the North-west, for the purpose of running off slaves, and, if necessary, of raising them in insurrection. We hear of an insurrection in Kentucky; and whether it is true or not we shall hear of more, both because the owners are always fancying plots, and because the slaves seize every occasion of relaxed supervision to help themselves to what it pleases them to take and to do. At present the known facts are that the free blacks are prepared to take a part in the war, and that there is a purpose on the part of these blacks and their friends to use the opportunity for putting an end to the captivity of their race. There are incidents connected with this which lead us to the fourth consideration.

The fourth consideration is of the quality of the Southern army. What sort of soldiers the Northern men will make we can hardly judge by facts. It is the boast of the South that the force for the Mexican war was furnished chiefly by that section; and the assertion is ratified by the Northern boast that the free States supplied a very small force to that atrocious war, and that that contingent consisted mainly of the adventurer class, who are always sent away to a distance with great alacrity. Except in the Seminole war in Florida, the Northern men have hardly appeared in the field at all, and there they contrasted most favorably with the Southern troops. They little knew what they went for. They were unaware that the object of the so-called war was the capture of escaped slaves, together with the children of negro women who had mated with Indians, on the Southern plea that the children follow the fortunes of the mother. When the truth came out, the heart-burning in the North was sore enough to account, with other like provocations, for the present conflict. Parents and all society mourned the young men slaughtered by Indians in the swamps in such a cause. But the troops made themselves a reputation for spirit and discipline which has never been rivalled by Southern soldiery.

When we hear of the military genius of the South, we naturally turn to what we know. We know something of the Mexican war, of which they make their boast. We know what a miserable enemy they had there; and we know what a miserable hand they made of several of the enterprises of the campaign. There is testimony enough to prevent its being ever forgotten that the commanders were at their wits' ends to get their troops out and home again, and what to do with them while abroad. In the absence of discipline on the one hand, and of due legal authority on the other, offences were constantly occurring which there were no proper means of dealing with; and punishments were inflicted which disgusted every foreigner in the force, (and there were many immigrants from Europe.) Soldiers were tied neck and knees together, and set down by the roadside, to be mocked by the troops marching past. Whatever could break a man's spirit or torture his passions was invented to supply the deficiency of authority; and the troops grew wilder every day. When ordered to pursue the enemy they piled their arms and went to play. When appointed to any service, as part of a scheme, they announced that they were going home; and the commanders cursed the very name of volunteers. The practical question now is whether that boasted Southern army and the present are at all of the same quality. All that we can know is that that army must be composed of certain elements. The slaveholders are a mere handful of men; and of them we know that very few are likely to fight their Northern kindred and customers with any relish. The non-slaveholders are the largest element; and they showed their quality in Mexico and in Kansas. The better part, in the Kansas case, went over to Northern views as soon as they learned what they were; and the worse portion were a mere banditti. The free blacks will hardly be sent North. It is announced that the Indians of three tribes have offered their services to the Confederacy; but they will be employed near home, no doubt, if at all. It is impossible to foresee what the campaign will be like, in circumstances so singular; but we may remember, while awaiting news, that the military reputation of the South, such as it is, has been gained in fields where there was no honor to win; and that the

Southern vaunt is of the bravery, and not of the discipline, of the so-called chivalry.

On the whole, these four considerations seem to point to a not distant conclusion, and to a desultory kind of conflict meantime. Tidings may be on the way to contradict or to confirm this view; but the facts on which it is founded seem to be as clear in their substance as they are serious in their significance.

—*London News,* May 29.

Doc. 215.

"CONTRABAND NEGROES."

GEN. BUTLER TO GEN. SCOTT

THE following is the material part of Gen. Butler's letter to Gen. Scott, asking for advice as to the course he should pursue:

Since I wrote my last, says Gen. Butler, the question in regard to slave property is becoming one of very serious magnitude. The inhabitants of Virginia are using their negroes in the batteries, and are preparing to send their women and children South. The escapes from them are very numerous, and a squad has come in this morning, (May 27,) and my pickets are bringing their women and children. Of course, these cannot be dealt with upon the theory on which I designed to treat the services of able-bodied men and women who might come within my lines, and of which I gave you a detailed account in my last despatch.

I am in the utmost doubt what to do with this species of property. Up to this time I have had come within my lines men and women, with their children—entire families—each family belonging to the same owner. I have, therefore, determined to employ, as I can do very profitably, the able-bodied persons in the party, issuing proper food for the support of all, and charging against their services the expense of care and sustenance of the non-laborers, keeping a strict and accurate account as well of the services as of the expenditures, having the worth of the services and the cost of the expenditure determined by a board of survey hereafter to be detailed. I know of no other manner in which to dispose of this subject, and the questions connected therewith. As a matter of property, to the insurgents it will be of very great moment—the number that I now have amounting, as I am informed, to what in good times would be of the value of $60,000.

Twelve of these negroes, I am informed, have escaped from the erection of the batteries on Sewall's Point, which fired upon my expedition as it passed by out of range. As a means of offence, therefore, in the enemy's hands, these negroes, when able-bodied, are of great importance. Without them the batteries could not have been erected, at least for many weeks. As a military question it would seem to be a measure of necessity, and deprives their masters of their services.

How can this be done? As a political question and a question of humanity, can I receive the services of a father and a mother and not take the children? Of the humanitarian aspect I have no doubt; of the political one I have no right to judge. I therefore submit all this to your better judgment; and, as these questions have a political aspect, I have ventured—and I trust I am not wrong in so doing—to duplicate the parts of my despatch relating to this subject, and forward them to the Secretary of War.

Your obedient servant,
BENJ. F. BUTLER.

Lieutenant-General Scott.

—*N. Y. Times*, June 2.

SECRETARY OF WAR TO GENERAL BUTLER.

WASHINGTON, May 30, 1861.

SIR: Your action in respect to the negroes who came within your lines, from the service of the rebels, is approved. The Department is sensible of the embarrassments, which must surround officers conducting military operations in a State, by the laws of which slavery is sanctioned. The Government cannot recognize the rejection by any State of its Federal obligation, resting upon itself, among these Federal obligations. However, no one can be more important than that of suppressing and dispersing any combination of the former for the purpose of overthrowing its whole constitutional authority. While, therefore, you will permit no interference, by persons under your command, with the relations of persons held to service under the laws of any State, you will, on the other hand, so long as any State within which your military operations are conducted, remain under the control of such armed combinations, refrain from surrendering to alleged masters any persons who come within your lines. You will employ such persons in the services to which they will be best adapted, keeping an account of the labor by them performed, of the value of it, and the expenses of their maintenance. The question of their final disposition will be reserved for future determination.

SIMON CAMERON, Secretary of War.

To Major-General Butler.

—*N. Y. Tribune,* May 31.

Doc. 216.

SECOND REG'T MAINE VOLUNTEERS.

THE following is a correct list of the officers: Colonel, Charles Jameson; Lieutenant-Colonel, C. W. Roberts; Major, George Varacy; Adjutant, John E. Reynolds; Quartermaster, C. V. Lord; Assistant Quartermaster, L. H. Pierce; Surgeon, W. H. Allen; Assistant Surgeon, A. C. Hamlin; (nephew of Vice-President Hamlin;) Chaplain, J. F. Mines; Sergeant-Major, E. L. Appleton.

Company A—Captain, H. Bartlett; First Lieutenant, R. Wiggins; Second Lieut., Dean. Company B—First Lieut., Tilden, commanding; Second Lieut., Wardwell. Company C—Capt., Jones; First Lieut., Skinner; Second Lieut., Merill. Company D—Capt., Sampson; First Lieut., Sturdevant; Second Lieut., Kittridge. Company E—Capt., Emmerson; First Lieut., Adams; Second Lieut., Richardson. Company F—Capt., Chaplin; First Lieut., Wilson; Second Lieut., Boynton. Company G—Capt., Sargent; First Lieut., Gettiell; Second Lieut., Morse. Company H—Capt., Meinicke; First Lieut., Farnham; Second Lieut., Garnsay. Company I—Capt., Carroll; First Lieut., Casey; Second Lieut., Sweeney. Company K—Capt., Foss; First Lieut., Fellows; Second Lieut., Cowan.

—*National Intelligencer,* June 3.

Doc. 217.

MR. W. H. RUSSELL'S LETTERS,

OF APRIL 30 AND MAY 1.

THE STATE OF SOUTH CAROLINA, April 30.

NOTHING I could say can be worth one fact which has forced itself upon my mind in reference to the sentiments which prevail among the gentlemen of this State. I have been among them for several days. I have visited their plantations, I have conversed with them freely and fully, and I have enjoyed that frank, courteous, and graceful intercourse which constitutes an irresistible charm of their society. From all quarters have come to my ears the echoes of the same voice; it may be feigned, but there is no discord in the note, and it sounds in wonderful strength and monotony all over the country. Shades of George III., of North, of Johnson, of all who contended against the great rebellion which tore these colonies from England, can you hear the chorus which rings through the State of Marion, Sumter, and Pinckney, and not clap your ghostly hands in triumph? That voice says, "If we could only get one of the royal race of England to rule over us, we should be content." Let there be no misconception on this point. That sentiment, varied in a hundred ways, has been repeated to me over and over again. There is a general admission that the means to such an end are wanting, and that the desire cannot be gratified. But the admiration for monarchical institutions on the English model, for privileged classes, and for a landed aristocracy and gentry, is undisguised and apparently genuine. With the pride of having achieved their independence is mingled in the South Carolinians' hearts a strange regret at the result and consequences, and many are they who "would go back to-morrow if we could." An intense affection for the British connection, a love of British habits and customs, a respect for British sentiment, law, authority, order, civilization, and literature, preëminently distinguish the inhabitants of this State, who, glorying in their descent from ancient families on the three islands, whose fortunes they still follow, and with whose members they maintain not unfrequently familiar relations, regard with an aversion of which it is impossible to give an idea to one who has not seen its manifestations, the people of New England and the populations of the Northern States, whom they regard as tainted beyond cure by the venom of "Puritanism." Whatever may be the cause, this is the fact and the effect. "The State of South Carolina was," I am told, "founded by gentlemen." It was not established by witch-burning Puritans, by cruel persecuting fanatics, who implanted in the North the standard of Torquemada, and breathed into the nostrils of their newly-born colonies all the ferocity, bloodthirstiness, and rabid intolerance of the Inquisition. It is absolutely astounding to a stranger who aims at the preservation of a decent neutrality to mark the violence of these opinions. "If that confounded ship had sunk with those —— Pilgrim Fathers on board," says one, "we never should have been driven to these extremities!" "We could have got on with these fanatics if they had been either Christians or gentlemen," says another; "for in the first case they would have acted with common charity, and in the second they would have fought when they insulted us; but there are neither Christians nor gentlemen among them!" "Any thing on earth!" exclaims a third, "any form of government, any tyranny or despotism you will; but"—and here is an appeal more terrible than the adjuration of all the Gods— "nothing on earth shall ever induce us to submit to any union with the brutal, bigoted blackguards of the New England States, who neither comprehend nor regard the feelings of gentlemen! Man, woman and child, we'll die first." Imagine these and an infinite variety of similar sentiments uttered by courtly, well-educated men, who set great store on a nice observance of the usages of society, and who are only moved to extreme bitterness and anger when they speak of the North, and you will fail to conceive the intensity of the dislike of the South Carolinians for the free States. There are national antipathies on our side of the Atlantic which are tolerably strong, and have been unfortunately pertinacious and long-lived. The hatred of the Italian for the Tedesco, of the Greek for the Turk, of the Turk for the Russ, is warm and fierce enough to satisfy the prince of darkness, not to speak of a few little pet aversions among allied powers and the atoms of composite empires; but they are all mere indifference and neutrality of feeling compared to the animosity evinced by the "gentry" of South Carolina for the "rabble of the North."

The contests of Cavalier and Roundhead, of Vendean and Republican, even of Orangeman and Croppy, have been elegant joustings, regulated by the finest rules of chivalry, compared with those which North and South will carry

Doc.—31

on if their deeds support their words. "Immortal hate, the study of revenge" will actuate every blow, and never in the history of the world, perhaps, will go forth such a dreadful *væ victis* as that which may be heard before the fight has begun. There is nothing in all the dark caves of human passion so cruel and deadly as the hatred the South Carolinians profess for the Yankees. That hatred has been swelling for years, till it is the very life-blood of the state. It has set South Carolina to work steadily to organize her resources for the struggle which she intended to provoke if it did not come in the course of time. "Incompatibility of temper" would have been sufficient ground for the divorce, and I am satisfied that there has been a deep-rooted design, conceived in some men's minds thirty years ago, and extended gradually year after year to others', to break away from the Union at the very first opportunity. The North is to South Carolina a corrupt and evil thing, to which for long years she has been bound by burning chains, while monopolists and manufacturers fed on her tender limbs. She has been bound in a Maxentian union to the object she loathes. New England is to her the incarnation of moral and political wickedness and social corruption. It is the source of every thing which South Carolina hates, and of the torrents of free thought and taxed manufactures, of abolitionism and of filibustering, which have flooded the land. Believe a southern man as he believes himself, and you must regard New England and the kindred States as the birthplace of impurity of mind among men and of unchastity in women—the home of free love, of Fourrierism, of infidelity, of abolitionism, of false teachings in political economy and in social life; a land saturated with the drippings of rotten philosophy, with the poisonous infections of a fanatic press; without honor or modesty; whose wisdom is paltry cunning, whose valor and manhood have been swallowed up in a corrupt, howling demagogy, and in the marts of a dishonest commerce. It is the merchants of New York who fit out ships for the slave trade, and carry it on in Yankee ships. It is the capital of the North which supports, and it is the northern men who concoct and execute the filibustering expeditions which have brought discredit on the slaveholding States. In the large cities people are corrupted by itinerant and ignorant lecturers—in the towns and in the country by an unprincipled press. The populations, indeed, know how to read and write, but they don't know how to think, and they are the easy victims of the wretched impostors on all the 'ologies and 'isms who swarm over the region, and subsist by lecturing on subjects which the innate vices of mankind induce them to accept with eagerness, while they assume the garb of philosophical abstractions to cover their nastiness in deference to a contemptible and universal hypocrisy.

"Who fills the butchers' shops with large blue flies?"

Assuredly the New England demon, who has been persecuting the South till its intolerable cruelty and insolence forced her, in a spasm of agony, to rend her chains asunder. The New Englander must have something to persecute, and as he has hunted down all his Indians, burnt all his witches, and persecuted all his opponents to the death, he invented abolitionism as the sole resource left to him for the gratification of his favorite passion. Next to this motive principle is his desire to make money dishonestly, trickily, meanly, and shabbily. He has acted on it in all his relations with the South, and has cheated and plundered her in all his dealings by villanous tariffs. If one objects that the South must have been a party to this, because her boast is that her statesmen have ruled the Government of the country, you are told that the South yielded out of pure good-nature. Now, however, she will have free trade, and will open the coasting trade to foreign nations, and shut out from it the hated Yankees, who so long monopolized and made their fortunes by it. Under all the varied burdens and miseries to which she was subjected, the South held fast to her sheet anchor. South Carolina was the mooring ground in which it found the surest hold. The doctrine of State rights was her salvation, and the fiercer the storm raged against her—the more stoutly demagogy, immigrant preponderance, and the blasts of universal suffrage bore down on her, threatening to sweep away the vested interests of the South in her right to govern the States—the greater was her confidence, and the more resolutely she held on her cable. The North attracted "hordes of ignorant Germans and Irish," and the scum of Europe, while the South repelled them. The industry, the capital of the North increased with enormous rapidity, under the influence of cheap labor and manufacturing ingenuity and enterprise, in the villages which swelled into towns, and the towns which became cities under the unenvious eye of the South. She, on the contrary, toiled on slowly, clearing forests and draining swamps to find new cotton grounds and rice-fields, for the employment of her own industry and for the development of her only capital—"involuntary labor." The tide of immigration waxed stronger, and by degrees she saw the districts into which she claimed the right to introduce this capital closed against her, and occupied by free labor. The doctrine of "squatter sovereignty," and the force of hostile tariffs, which placed a heavy duty on the very articles which the South most required, completed the measure of injuries to which she was subjected, and the spirit of discontent found vent in fiery debate, in personal insults, and in acrimonious speaking and writing, which increased in intensity in proportion as the abolition movement, and the contest between the federal principle and State rights, became more vehement. I am desirous of showing in a few words, for the information of English readers, how it is that the confederacy which Europe knew simply as a political entity has succeeded in dividing itself. The slave States held the doctrine, or say they did, that each State was independent as France or as England, but that for certain purposes they chose a common agent to deal with foreign nations, and to impose taxes for the purpose of paying the expenses of the agency. We, it appears, talked of American citizens when there were no such beings at all. There were, indeed, citizens of the sovereign State of South Carolina, or of Georgia or Florida, who permitted themselves to pass under that designation, but it was merely a matter of personal convenience. It will be difficult for Europeans to understand this doctrine, as nothing like it has been heard before, and no such confederation of sovereign States has ever existed in any country in the world. The northern men deny that it existed here, and claim for the Federal Government powers not compatible with such assumptions. *They* have lived for the Union, they served it, they labored for and made money by it. A man as a New York man was nothing—as an American citizen he was a great deal. A South Carolinian objected to lose his identity in any description which included him and a "Yankee clockmaker" in the same category. The Union was against him; he remembered that he came from a race of English gentlemen who had been persecuted by the representatives—for he will not call them the ancestors—of the Puritans of New England, and he thought that they were animated by the same hostility to himself. He was proud of old names, and he felt pleasure in tracing his connection with old families in the old country. His plantations were held by old charters, or had been in the hands of his fathers for several generations; and he delighted to remember that, when the Stuarts were banished from their throne and their country, the burgesses of South Carolina had solemnly elected the wandering Charles king of their state, and had offered him an asylum and a kingdom. The philosophical historian may exercise his ingenuity in conjecturing what would have been the result if the fugitive had carried his fortunes to Charleston.

South Carolina contains 34,000 square miles and a population of 720,000 inhabitants, of whom 385,000 are black slaves. In the old rebellion it was distracted between revolutionary principles and the loyalist predilections, and at least one-half of the planters were faithful to George III., nor did they yield till Washington sent an army to support their antagonists and drove them from the colony.

In my next letter I shall give a brief account of a visit to some of the planters, as far as it can be made consistent with the obligations which the rites of hospitality impose on the guest as well as upon the host. These gentlemen are well-bred, courteous, and hospitable. A genuine aristocracy, they have time to cultivate their minds, to apply themselves to politics and the guidance of public affairs. They travel and read, love field sports, racing, shooting, hunting, and fishing, are bold horsemen, and good shots. But, after all, their state is a modern Sparta—an aristocracy resting on a helotry, and with nothing else to rest upon. Although they profess (and I believe, indeed, sincerely) to hold opinions in opposition to the opening of the slave trade, it is nevertheless true that the clause in the Constitution of the Confederate States which prohibited the importation of negroes, was especially and energetically resisted by them, because, as they say, it seemed to be an admission that slavery was in itself an evil and a wrong. Their whole system rests on slavery, and as such they defend it. They entertain very exaggerated ideas of the military strength of their little community, although one may do full justice to its military spirit. Out of their whole population they cannot reckon more than 60,000 adult men by any arithmetic, and as there are nearly 30,000 plantations, which must be, according to law, superintended by white men, a considerable number of these adults cannot be spared from the state for service in the open field. The planters boast that they can raise their corps without any inconvenience by the labor of their negroes, and they seem confident that the negroes will work without superintendence. But the experiment is rather dangerous, and it will only be tried in the last extremity.

SAVANNAH, Ga., May 1.

It is said that "fools build houses for wise men to live in." Be that true or not, it is certain that "Uncle Sam" has built strong places for his enemies to occupy. To-day I visited Fort Pulaski, which defends the mouth of the Savannah River and the approaches to the city. It was left to take care of itself, and the Georgians quietly stepped into it, and have been busied in completing its defences, so that it is now capable of stopping a fleet very effectually. Pulaski was a Pole who fell in the defence of Savannah against the British, and whose memory is perpetuated in the name of the fort, which is now under the Confederate flag, and garrisoned by bitter foes of the United States.

Among our party were Commodore Tatnall, whose name will be familiar to English ears in connection with the attack on the Peiho Forts, where the gallant American showed the world that "blood was thicker than water;" Brigadier-General Lawton, in command of the forces of Georgia, and a number of naval and military officers, of whom many had belonged to the United States regular service. It was strange to look at such a man as the Commodore, who for forty-nine long years had served under the Stars and Stripes, quietly preparing to meet his old comrades and friends, if needs be, in the battle-field—his allegiance to the country and to the flag renounced, his long service flung away, his old ties and connections severed—and all this in defence of the sacred right of rebellion on the part of "his State." He is not now, nor has he been for years, a slave-owner; all his family and familiar associations connect him with the North. There are no naval stations on the Southern coasts, except one at Pensacola, and he knows almost no one in the South. He has no fortune whatever, his fleet consists of two small river or coasting steamers, without guns, and as he said, in talking over the resources of the South, " My bones will be bleached many a long year before the Confederate States can hope to have a navy." "State Rights!" To us the question is simply inexplicable or absurd. And yet thousands of Americans sacrifice all for it. The river at Savannah is broad as the Thames at Gravesend, and resembles that stream very much in the color of its waters and the level nature of its shores. Ricefields bound it on either side, as far down as the influence of the fresh water extends, and the eye wanders over a flat expanse of mud and water, and green osiers and rushes, till its search is arrested on the horizon by the unfailing line of forest. In the fields here and there are the white-washed square wooden huts in which the slaves dwell, looking very like the beginnings of the camp in the Crimea. At one point a small fort, covering a creek by which gun-boats could get up behind Savannah, displayed its "garrison" on the walls, and lowered its flag to salute the small blue ensign at the fore which proclaimed the presence of the Commodore of the Naval Forces of Georgia on board our steamer. The guns on the parapet were mostly field-pieces mounted on frameworks of wood instead of regular carriages. There is no mistake about the spirit of these people. They seize upon every spot of vantage ground and prepare it for defence. There were very few ships in the river; the yacht Camilla, better known as the America, the property of Captain Deasy, and several others of those few sailing under British colors, for most of the cotton ships are gone.

After steaming down the river about twelve miles, the sea opened out to the sight, and on a long, marshy, narrow island near the bar, which was marked by the yellowish surf, Fort Pulaski threw out the Confederate flag to the air of the Georgian 1st of May. The water was too shallow to permit the steamer to go up to the jetty, and the party landed at the wharf in boats. A guard was on duty at the landing—tall, stout young fellows, in various uniforms, or in rude mufti, in which the Garibaldian red shirt and felt slouched hats predominated. They were armed with smooth-bore muskets (date 1851), quite new, and their bayonets, barrels, and locks were bright and clean. The officer on duty was dressed in the blue frock-coat dear to the British linesman in days gone by, with brass buttons, emblazoned with the arms of the State, a red silk sash, and glazed kepi, and straw-colored gauntlets.

Several wooden huts, with flower gardens in

front, were occupied by the officers of the garrison; others were used as hospitals, and were full of men suffering from measles of a mild type. A few minutes' walk led us to the fort, which is an irregular pentagon, with the base line or curtain face inlands, and the other faces casemated and bearing on the approaches. The curtain, which is simply crenellated, is covered by a Redan surrounded by a deep ditch, inside the parapet of which are granite platforms ready for the reception of guns. The parapet is thick, and the scarp and counterscarp are faced with solid masonry. A drawbridge affords access to the interior of the Redan, whence the gate of the fort is approached across a deep and broad moat, which is crossed by another drawbridge.

As the Commodore entered the Redan, the guns of the fort broke out into a long salute, and the band at the gate struck up almost as lively a welcome. Inside the parade presented a scene of life and animation very unlike the silence of the city we had left. Men were busy clearing out the casemates, rolling away stores and casks of ammunition and provisions, others were at work at the gin and shears, others building sand-bag traverses to guard the magazine doors, as though expecting an immediate attack. Many officers were strolling under the shade of the open gallery at the side of the curtain which contained their quarters in the lofty bomb-proof casemates.

Some of them had seen service in Mexican or border warfare; some had travelled over Italian and Crimean battle-fields; others were West Point graduates of the regular army; others young planters, clerks, or civilians who had rushed with ardor into the first Georgian Regiment. The garrison of the fort is 650 men, and fully that number were in and about the work, their tents being pitched inside the Redan or on the terreplein of the parapets. The walls are exceedingly solid and well built of hard gray brick, strong as iron, upwards of six feet in thickness, the casemates and bomb-proofs being lofty, airy, and capacious as any I have ever seen, though there is not quite depth enough between the walls at the salient and the gun-carriages. The work is intended for 128 guns, of which about one-fourth are mounted on the casemates. They are long 32's with a few 42's and columbiads. The armaments will be exceedingly heavy when all the guns are mounted, and they are fast getting the 10-inch columbiads into position en barbette. Every thing which could be required, except mortars, was in abundance—the platforms and gun-carriages are solid and well made, the embrasures of the casemates are admirably constructed, and the ventilation of the bomb-proof carefully provided for. There are three furnaces for heating red-hot shot.

Nor is discipline neglected, and the officers with whom I went round the works were as sharp in tone and manner to their men as Volunteers well could be, though the latter are enlisted for only three years by the State of Georgia. An excellent lunch was spread in the casemated bomb-proof, which served as the Colonel's quarter, and before sunset the party were steaming towards Savannah through a tideway full of leaping sturgeon and porpoises, leaving the garrison intent on the approach of a large ship, which had her sails aback off the bar and hoisted the Stars and Stripes, but which turned out to be nothing more formidable than a Liverpool cotton ship.

It will take some hard blows before Georgia is driven to let go her grip of Fort Pulaski. The channel is very narrow and passes close to the guns of the fort. The means of completing the armament have been furnished by the stores of Norfolk Navy Yard, where between 700 and 800 guns have fallen into the hands of the Confederates; and, if there are no columbiads among them, the Merrimac and other ships, which have been raised, as we hear, with guns uninjured, will yield up their Dahlgrens to turn their muzzles against their old masters.

May 2.—May day was so well kept yesterday that the exhausted editors cannot "bring out" their papers, and consequently there is no news; but there is, nevertheless, much to be said concerning "Our President's" Message, and *there is a suddenness of admiration for pacific tendencies which can with difficulty be accounted for,* unless the news from the North these last few days has something to do with it. *Not a word now about an instant march on Washington! no more threats to seize on Faneuil Hall!*

The Georgians are by no means so keen as the Carolinians on their border—nay, they are not so belligerent to-day as they were a week ago. Mr. Jefferson Davis's Message is praised for its "moderation," and for other qualities which were by no means in such favor while the Sumter fever was at its height. Men look grave, and talk about the interference of England and France, which "cannot allow this thing to go on." But the change which has come over them is unmistakable, AND THE BEST MEN BEGIN TO LOOK GRAVE. As for me, I must prepare to open my lines of retreat—my communications are in danger.

—London Times.

Doc. 218.

N. Y. SEVENTH REGIMENT PAPERS.

HEAD-QUARTERS DEPARTMENT, }
WASHINGTON, MAY 26th, 1861. }

COLONEL LEFFERTS,

Commanding N. Y. Seventh Regiment:

Sir: Your regiment has accomplished all that was intended by it in crossing over to Arlington to take possession of the heights, and have labored on the intrenchments manfully, also. The security of this city renders it imperative you should resume your encampment on this side; and you will this afternoon march over accordingly, and hold your regiment here ready to turn out when called upon.

Very respectfully,
J. H. K. MANSFIELD,
Brig.-Gen., and Commanding.

WASHINGTON, D. C., April 29, 1861,
HEAD-QUARTERS, COMMANDERS OF COMPANIES,
8TH REGIMENT, MASSACHUSETTS VOL. MILITIA.

To COL. LEFFERTS, officers, and members, New York Seventh Regiment:

At a meeting of this regiment, held this morning, the following preamble and resolutions were unanimously adopted:

Whereas, The trials and fortunes of war have brought us into close intimacy and companionship with the New York Seventh Regiment, (National Guard,) therefore

Resolved, That we feel it a duty, owing not only to them, but to our own hearts, to express so far as it may be in our power, our grateful obligations to them for their many favors.

Resolved, That we deeply appreciate the hearty welcome extended to us on landing at Annapolis, and their kind attention after the fatigues of transportation, and hazardous though successful service.

Resolved, That they have done all in their power to lessen the just feelings of dissatisfaction which have prevailed throughout the regiment, by sharing with us their rations and their little conveniences, and by ever being the first to offer assistance.

Resolved, That especially are our thanks due to the noble 7th for the generous entertainment, so spontaneous, so bounteous, so heartily appreciative of our condition, furnished on the afternoon of Saturday, April 27th, that no words can do it justice, or do justice to our gratitude.

Resolved, That in one other and *very* especial particular does their generosity and benevolence touch our hearts; we refer to the voluntary subscription raised among them, for the benefit of one of our officers accidentally wounded.

Resolved, That the term so often used in connection with the volunteer militia, "holiday soldiery," has, in all the conduct of the regiment to which we are so much indebted, been triumphantly refuted; and that it will hereafter be worthy of the highest fame—fame that will now attach to the name of the "*generous, gallant, glorious Seventh.*"

Resolved, That wherever the Seventh may go we would go; where they lodge we would lodge; if ever their colors go down before the hosts of the enemy, the *Eighth of Massachusetts* would be first to avenge their fall with the *heart's blood of every man.*

KNOTT V. MARTIN, Chairman.
GEO. T. NEWHALL, Secretary.

WAR DEPARTMENT, ADJUTANT-GENERAL'S OFFICE,
WASHINGTON, May 30, 1861.

Special Order No. 146.

The commanding officer of the Seventh Regiment of New York Volunteers, will proceed with his regiment to the city of New York, where it will be mustered out of the service of the United States, by Lieut. M. Cogswell, Eighth Regiment.

It is the desire of the War Department, in relinquishing the services of this gallant regiment, to make known the satisfaction that is felt at the prompt and patriotic manner in which it responded to the call for men to defend the capital when it was believed to be in peril, and to acknowledge the important service which it rendered by appearing here in an hour of dark and trying necessity. The time for which it had engaged has now expired. The service which it was expected to perform has been handsomely accomplished, and its members may return to their native city with the assurance that its services are gratefully appreciated by all good and loyal citizens, whilst the Government is equally confident that when the country again calls upon them, the appeal will not be made in vain to the young men of New York. By order,
L. THOMAS, Adjutant-General.

COL. LEFFERTS, Commanding Seventh Regiment, Camp Cameron.

HEAD-QUARTERS, SEVENTH REGIMENT, N. Y. S. M.,
CAMP CAMERON, May 30, 1861.

GENERAL ORDER No. 21.—Special Order No. 146, Head-quarters United States Army, is hereby promulgated, and in compliance therewith this Regiment will parade fully uniformed, in overcoats, armed and equipped for the march, at 3½ o'clock P. M., 31st inst.—blankets rolled and strapped upon the knapsack. Each soldier must carry his canteen and haversack. Pistols, unloaded, must be packed in the knapsacks. The Commissary will provide two days' rations for each man. By order of
Col. MARSHALL LEFFERTS,
J. H. LIEBENAR, Adjutant.

UNION DEFENCE COMMITTEE
OF THE CITIZENS OF NEW YORK,
OFFICE, No. 30 PINE STREET.
NEW YORK, May 31, 1861.

In Executive Committee,

Resolved, That this committee desire to express their cordial recognition of the efficient service rendered to the cause of the country at a critical emergency of its public affairs by the Seventh Regiment of the New York State Militia, commanded by Col. Marshall Lefferts, and sharing so fully in the general feeling of gratification which pervades this community at learning that the commanding general of the U. S. Army, under the sanction of the President of the United States, has acknowledged, in special general orders, "the important service rendered by that regiment in an hour of dark and trying necessity;" the committee desire to unite their congratulations with those of their fellow-citizens, in extending a welcome hand to cheer the return of a body of soldiers who conferred such high honor on the city of New York.

Resolved, That this committee will take

pleasure in attending the reception to be given to the Seventh Regiment, on its arrival in this city to-morrow.

Resolved, That these proceedings be published, and a copy furnished to Col. Lefferts.

Extract from the minutes.

J. J. ASTOR, JR., Chairman *pro tem.*
Executive Committee.

PROSPER M. WETMORE,
Secretary Executive Committee.

Doc. 219.

FIRST MAINE REGIMENT.

THE regiment numbers seven hundred and eighty men, and is officered as follows:

FIELD AND STAFF OFFICERS.—Colonel, Nathaniel J. Jackson; Lieutenant-Colonel, Albion Witham; Major, Geo. G. Bailey; Adjutant, J. L. Fillibrown; Quartermaster, Wm. S. Dodge; Surgeon, Dr. W. R. Richardson; Chaplain, Rev. Geo. Knox; Assistant Surgeon, A. A. C. Williams; Quartermaster's Sergeant, S. H. Manning; Sergeant-Major, Foster Randall; Drum Major, David Jones; Fife Major, Cyrus Freeman.

Co. A, Portland Light Infantry—Captain, G. W. Tukay; First Lieutenant, Geo. H. Chadwell; Second Lieutenant, Chas. L. McAllister. Co. B, Portland Mechanic Blues—Captain, Charles Walker; First Lieutenant, Charles G. Pennell; Second Lieutenant, James M. Black. Co. C, Portland Light Guard—Captain, M. R. Fessenden; First Lieutenant, Wm. B. Jordan; Second Lieutenant, Benj. M. Redlon. Co. D, Portland Rifle Corps—Captain, Charles H. Meserve; First Lieutenant, Wm. A. Pierce; Second Lieutenant, Geo. H. Bailey. Co. E, Portland Rifle Guard—Captain, Wm. M. Shaw; First Lieutenant, A. H. Estes; Second Lieutenant, John M. Marston. Co. F, Lewiston Light Infantry—Captain, J. T. Stevens; First Lieutenant, Wm. D. Knowlton; Second Lieutenant, E. M. Shaw. Co. G, Norway Light Infantry—Captain, Geo. L. Beal; First Lieutenant, Henry Rust, Jr.; Second Lieutenant, Jonathan Blake. Co. H, Auburn Artillery—Captain, Chas. S. Emerson; First Lieutenant, J. F. C. Folsom; Second Lieutenant, Phineas W. Udell. Co. I, New Rifle Guard, Portland—Captain, William Quimby; First Lieutenant, N. T. Furbish; Second Lieutenant, Hebron Mayhew. Co. K, Lewiston Guard—Captain, Silas B. Osgood; First Lieutenant Elijah D. Johnston; Second Lieutenant, George H. Neve. —*N. Y. Herald*, June 3.

Doc. 220.

FIGHT AT ACQUIA CREEK.

THE following is the official report of the action at Acquia Creek:—

U. S. STEAMER THOS. FREEBORN,
OFF ACQUIA CREEK, Potomac River, May 31.

My immediate commanding officer, Flag Officer Stringham, not being present to receive it,

I communicate directly to the department, the report of a serious cannonade made by this vessel, supported by the Anacosta and Resolute steamers, upon the batteries of Acquia Creek this morning. After an incessant discharge kept up for two hours by both our 32-pounders, and the expenditure of all the ammunition suitable for distant firing, and silencing completely the three batteries at the railroad terminus, the firing from shore having been rapidly kept up by them until so silenced, and having been recommenced from the new batteries on the heights back, which reached us in volleys, dropped the shot on board and about us like hail for nearly an hour, fortunately wounding but one man, I hauled the vessel off, as the heights proved wholly above the reach of our elevation. Judging from the explosion of our 10-second shells in the sand batteries, two of which were thrown by the Anacosta, it is hardly possible the enemy can have escaped considerable loss. Several other of the Anacosta's shells dropped in the vicinity of the battery. I cannot speak in too high terms of the officers and men, whose coolness and activity under great exposure are beyond praise. As the former are all acting, having volunteered from civil life, none but myself being of the regular Navy, I beg leave to ask for them a favorable consideration by the Government. The long thirty-two pounder in use is of the old pattern, cast in 1819, and cannot be excelled in precision. Both of the guns are on carriages of the new construction devised by myself, and answered admirably, working with such ease, that the crews came out of the action wholly unfatigued. To the extreme sweep of 140 degrees which these carriages have, together with their ease and rapidity of movement, enabling the vessel to constantly change position, yet keep up accurate fire, which impaired the enemy's range and direction, he firing always with rifled cannon, is to be materially attributed our escape without loss of life or damage to the vessel or machinery. The men say they are as fresh from fatigue, as when they entered action. We cannonaded for an hour before the same batteries the day before yesterday; but, the tide being out, neither party reached with any considerable certainty. I doubt if it is possible to reduce the batteries now established on the heights, from ships, nor is it at all important, considering they are remote from the ship channel of the river, and command only the railroad terminus. Yesterday I landed in person, with Acting Master Budd, and Master's Mate Lee, and a small party of seamen, and made a most minute exploration, extending over the whole of Matthias Point. I am, therefore, able to speak with ocular certainty, and to say that not a sign of a movement, the cutting of a sapling, driving a stake, or carting a shovel-full of earth towards the erection of a battery exists. The jungle is very thick, but we penetrated a belt of it three hundred yards wide from the shore and three miles in length.

Assuring ourselves of the facts as stated in this report, I have especially to ask for the steamers Reliance and Resolute of this flotilla, each a small rifled cannon in addition to the smooth-bored gun with which they are provided. For the want of a rifled gun in them, I was obliged to forbid their coming closely under a fire to which they could not reply with even an approximate effect. Lieutenant commanding, N. Collins, of the Anacosta, will make his own report.

I have the honor to be, sir, your obedient servant, J. H. WARD.
Commander U. S. Navy commanding Flotilla.
To the Hon. GIDEON WELLES, Secretary of the Navy, Washington, D. C.
—*National Intelligencer*, June 3.

Doc. 221.
SKIRMISH AT FAIRFAX COURT-HOUSE.

THE following is the official report of General McDowell to General Scott, of the fight at Fairfax Court-House. Lieutenant Tompkins, who commanded the company, was severely wounded, so much so that he was unable to make his report :—

HEAD-QUARTERS, DEPARTMENT EASTERN VIRGINIA, ARLINGTON, June 1, 1861.

Colonel E. D. TOWNSEND, Assistant Adjutant-General,
Head-quarters of the Army, Washington :—

SIR: The following facts have just been reported to me by the Orderly Sergeant of Company B, of the Second cavalry, commanded by Lieutenant Tompkins, the commanding officer being too unwell to report in person.

It appears that a company of the Second cavalry, commanded by Lieutenant Tompkins, aggregate number seventy-five, left their camp at half-past ten o'clock last night on a scouting expedition. They reached Fairfax Court-House about three in the morning, where they found several hundred men stationed—Captain Ewell, late of the United States Dragoons, said to be in command. A skirmish then took place, in which a number of the enemy were killed, how many the Sergeant does not know. Many bodies were seen on the ground, and several were taken into the Court-House, and seen there by one of our cavalry, who was a prisoner in the Court-House for a short time, and afterwards made his escape.

The following is the report by the Sergeant of our loss :—

KILLED.
Private Saintilair 1

WOUNDED.
Corporal Max, ball through the hip . . 1
Corporal Turner, ball in the ankle . . 1
Private Lynch, ball in the hand . . 1
Private Baggs, ball in the foot . . . 1

MISSING.
Private Sullivan 1
—
Total casualties 6

Five prisoners were captured by our troops, their names being as follows :—John W. Ryan, private of the Old Guard; H. F. Lynn, Prince William Cavalry ; John A. Dunnington, Prince William Cavalry ; F. W. Worders, Prince William Cavalry ; W. F. Washington, son of the late Col. Washington, of the United States Army. Having no good means of keeping prisoners here, they are sent to head-quarters for further disposition.

As soon as Lieut. Tompkins recovers, a less hurried report than this will be submitted by Col. Hunter commanding the brigade.
IRWIN McDOWELL,
Brigadier-General Commanding.

A file of soldiers who captured the prisoners brought them to Gen. Mansfield's quarters, who immediately remanded four of them to the Navy Yard, to be placed with those heretofore captured. Young Washington was still in custody of Gen. Mansfield. I have not heard what disposition is to be made of him. He is a fine-looking fellow, well dressed, and exceedingly intelligent. The other four are not very prepossessing in their appearance. One of them informed me that there were only about three hundred soldiers at Fairfax—three companies of cavalry, and one of infantry.
—*National Intelligencer*, June 3.

LIEUT. TOMPKINS' REPORT.

The following is the report of Lieutenant Tompkins to Colonel Hunter, his superior officer :

"Sir : I have the honor to report that, pursuant to verbal instructions from the colonel, commanding, I left on the evening of the 31st, in command of Co. B Cavalry, to reconnoitre the vicinity of Fairfax Court-House. Approaching the town, the enemy's picket was surprised and captured. Several documents were found upon them, which I enclose. On entering the town of Fairfax, my command was fired upon by rebel troops from windows and housetops. I charged and drove the mounted rifles from the town. Immediately two or three companies came to their relief and fired upon us, which I returned. Perceiving I was outnumbered, I deemed it advisable to retreat, which I did in good order, with five prisoners fully armed and equipped, and two horses.

"My loss is three men missing, three slightly wounded, and twelve horses lost. The loss of the rebels is from twenty to twenty-five in killed and wounded. From observations I should judge that the rebels at that point numbered fully 1,500 men. Captains Carey, Fearing, and Adjutant Frank of the New York 5th regiment accompanied me, and I regret to state that Captain Carey was wounded in the foot. Lieut. Gordon of the 2d Dragoons rendered valuable services. The prisoners, horses, and equipments have been sent to General Mansfield.
"Yours respectfully,
"CHAS. H. TOMPKINS."

REBEL ACCOUNT OF THE FAIRFAX FIGHT.

The following account of the attack at Fairfax Court-House, is from *The Richmond Enquirer* of the 3d inst. It carefully refrains from mentioning the Virginia cavalry, who occupied the place; but the reason of this neglect is discovered in a private letter from the brother of Capt. Marr, (the secession officer killed by our troops,) which states that "the Virginia cavalry who first encountered the enemy, ingloriously fled:"

The enemy, on Friday morning, about 3 o'clock, in numbers about 80 strong, entered the town of Fairfax Court-House, under command of Lieut. Tompkins. The company was the United States regulars from Texas. The enemy dashed into town so unexpectedly that the Warrenton Rifles, Capt. John Q. Marr, had only some ten minutes to prepare for them. The enemy fired at the quarters of the troops, killing Capt. Marr instantly, and though near to his command, his death was not known until after 9 o'clock, when his body was found. The enemy pushed on through the town. The Warrenton Rifles then formed, under Col. Ewell and Gov. Smith, into two platoons, and proceeded down the road after the enemy, and taking position on the side of the road, waited the return of the enemy. Very soon the enemy returned in disorder, when a volley from the rifles scattered them, and caused a retreat up the road. They reformed into "fours," and came up in good order, when another fire from the rifles again scattered them, and they returned by a cross road to Alexandria. Our troops took four horses, branded "U. S." "B," and killed three horses. The retreating detachment were seen near Anandals, with fifteen led horses and a wagon containing wounded men. Four prisoners were taken during the fight, and nine others are reported as having been found in the neighborhood during the next day, (Saturday.) Five United States soldiers were killed. Several carbines, dragoon swords, officers' swords, a double-barrel shot-gun, and eight dragoon revolvers, were picked up by our troops. Our loss was Capt. Marr, killed—a brave and efficient officer, the support of a widowed mother, and a most useful citizen. He was a member of the Virginia Convention, and had filled many responsible positions. Col. Ewell was slightly wounded in the shoulder. A member of the Rappahannock company was also severely wounded. Capt. Marr's company were badly armed, having only rifles *without bayonets*, and had to encounter United States regulars, armed with sabres, carbines, and revolvers. They nobly performed their duty, notwithstanding there was no officer of the company to command them. Captain Marr was killed before the company was formed, and Lieutenant Shackelford was absent. Captain Marr's death was caused by a random shot, while selecting ground upon which to form his company. The darkness prevented any one seeing him fall, and his death was not known until late the next morning.

The Nashville Union has the following notice of Capt. Marr:

The telegraphic wires bring us the sad intelligence that Capt. John Marr, brother to our respected friend and associate, Mr. Thomas S. Marr of *The Union and American* office, has been the first soldier of the South to baptize the soil of the Old Dominion with his patriotic blood, in an engagement with the enemy. Earnest and sincere as is our sympathy with the friends and relatives of this noble martyr to Southern independence, deeply as we condole with them in the decree of Providence which has singled him out as the only victim to Black Republican vengeance at Fairfax, yet we cannot but console them with the inspiring and manly thought that his name now stands side by side, on the roll, with the great and good of earth, who have died for their country and its sacred altars. He has found the grave a pathway to glory, and the libation which he has offered up to the independence of the South will moisten a plant that will bloom in eternal beauty, and give forth immortal fragrance. The heart-stricken grief that must needs follow the announcement of his death, will be assuaged by the glorious sentiment of a Latin poet, *Dulce et decorum est pro patria mori.* The sweetest flowers of Spring will bloom in their brightest hues, and the most enchanting minstrels of the forests of Virginia will warble forth their most thrilling notes over the grave of that young soldier, who gave up his young and promising life to shield his proud old Commonwealth from sacrilege and disgrace, her fields and homes from desolation, her smiling plains from the ravages of a ruthless foe, her men from slavery, and her fair daughters from pollution. He had but one life to lose. That he has given to the nursing mother that gave it to him, to the good old Commonwealth, who has drawn her sword to defend her stainless escutcheon, and who will never drop it from her grasp until the tyrants are beneath her feet. Surely a soldier and a soldier's friends can never repine at death when it comes in such a form. Capt. Marr was a member of the late Convention which dissolved the relations of Virginia to the old Federal Union. He was a gentleman of the highest position, social and political, in his native State, and rushed with the first summons to the field to drive back its invaders. We are not sufficiently posted as to his history, to enter minutely into details. Suffice that he has lived a life of honor and usefulness, and died a glorious death. Peace to his ashes; glory to his name! —*N. Y. Tribune.*

Doc. 222.

SPEECH OF PRESIDENT DAVIS,

AT RICHMOND, JUNE 1.

FRIENDS AND FELLOW-CITIZENS:—I thank you for the compliment your presence conveys. It is an indication of regard, not for the person, but for the position which he holds. The cause in which we are engaged is the cause of the advocacy of rights to which we were born, those for which our fathers of the Revolution bled—the richest inheritance that ever fell to man, and which it is our sacred duty to transmit to our children.

Upon us is devolved the high and holy responsibility of preserving the constitutional liberty of a free government. Those with whom we have lately associated have shown themselves so incapable of appreciating the blessings of the glorious institutions they inherited, that they are to-day stripped of the liberty to which they were born. They have allowed an ignorant usurper to trample upon all the prerogatives of citizenship, and to exercise powers never delegated to him; and it has been reserved to your own State, so lately one of the original thirteen, but now, thank God, fully separated from them, to become the theatre of a great central camp, from which will pour forth thousands of brave hearts to roll back the tide of this despotism.

Apart from that gratification we may well feel at being separated from such a connection, is the pride that upon you devolves the task of maintaining and defending our new Government. I believe that we shall be able to achieve this noble work, and that the institutions of our fathers will go to our children as safely as they have descended to us.

In these Confederate States we observe those relations which have been poetically ascribed to the United States, but which never there had the same reality—States so distinct that each existed as a Sovereign, yet so united that each was wound with the other to constitute a whole; or, as more beautifully expressed, " Distinct as the billows, yet one as the sea."

Upon every hill which now overlooks Richmond you have had, and will continue to have, camps containing soldiers from every State in the Confederacy; and to its remotest limits every proud heart beats high with indignation at the thought that the foot of the invader has been set upon the soil of old Virginia. There is not one true son of the South who is not ready to shoulder his musket, to bleed, to die, or to conquer in the cause of liberty here.

Beginning under many embarrassments, the result of seventy years of taxation being in the hands of our enemies, we must at first move cautiously. It may be that we shall have to encounter sacrifices; but, my friends, under the smiles of the God of the Just, and filled with the same spirit that animated our fathers, success shall perch on our banners. I am sure you do not expect me to go into any argument upon those questions which, for 25 years, have agitated the country. We have now reached the points where, arguments being exhausted, it only remains for us to stand by our weapons. When the time and occasion serve, we shall smite the smiter with manly arms, as did our

fathers before us, and as becomes their sons. To the enemy we leave the base acts of the assassin and incendiary, to them we leave it to insult helpless women; to us belongs vengeance upon man.

Now, my friends, I thank you again for this gratifying manifestation. (A voice. " Tell us something of Buena Vista.")

Well, my friends, I can only say we will make the battle-fields in Virginia another Buena Vista, and drench with blood more precious than that which flowed there. We will make a history for ourselves. We do not ask that the past shall shed our lustre upon us, bright as our past has been, for we can achieve our own destiny.

We may point to many a field, over which has floated the flag of our country when we were of the United States—upon which Southern soldiers and Southern officers reflected their brave spirits in their deeds of daring; and without intending to cast a shadow upon the courage of any portion of the United States, let me call it to your remembrance, that no man who went from these Confederate States has ever yet, as a general officer, surrendered to an enemy.

Pardon me if I do not go into matters of history, and permit me, again, to thank you for this kind manifestation of your regard, to express to you my hearty wishes for the individual prosperity of you all, with the hope that you will all pray to God to crown our cause and our country with success.

He then retired from the windows amid prolonged cheers.

Calls were then made for ex-Governor Wise, to which, after a short delay, he responded as follows:

SPEECH OF EX-GOV. HENRY A. WISE.

MY FRIENDS:—You all know that I am a civil soldier only, and that in that capacity I was nearly worn down in the siege of the Virginia Convention. Thank God, however, that with a little rest, some help, and some damage from the doctors, I have been enabled to recruit my exhausted energies.

The time of deliberation has given place to the time of action, and I have taken up my bed as an individual, in common with others, to march to Richmond to meet the President of our now separate and independent republic. I am ready to obey his orders, not only with pride, pleasure, and devotion to the cause, and respect to the office he fills, but with respect to the man himself as one who has our fullest confidence.

You have to meet a foe with whom you could not live in peace. Your political powers and rights, which were enthroned in that Capitol when you were united with them under the old constitutional bond of the Confederacy, have been annihilated. They have undertaken to annul laws within your own limits that would render your property unsafe within those limits. They have abolitionized your border, as the disgraced North-west will show. They have invaded your moral strongholds and the rights of your religion, and have undertaken to teach you what should be the moral duties of men.

They have invaded the sanctity of your homes and firesides, and endeavored to play master, father, and husband for you in your households; in a word, they have set themselves up as a petty Providence by which you are in all things to be guided and controlled. But you have always declared that you would not be subject to this invasion of your rights.

Though war was demanded, it was not for you to declare war. But now that the armies of the invader are hovering around the tomb of Washington, where is the Virginian heart that does not beat with a quicker pulsation at this last and boldest desecration of his beloved State? Their hordes are already approaching our metropolis, and extending their folds around our State as does the anaconda around his victim. The call is for action.

I rejoice in this war. Who is there that now dares to put on sanctity to depreciate war, or the "horrid glories of war." None. Why? Because it is a war of purification. You want war, fire, blood, to purify you; and the Lord of Hosts has demanded that you should walk through fire and blood. You are called to the fiery baptism, and I call upon you to come up to the altar. Though your pathway be through fire, or through a river of blood, turn not aside. Be in no hurry—no hurry and flurry.

Collect yourselves, summon yourselves, elevate yourselves to the high and sacred duty of patriotism. The man who dares to pray, the man who dares to wait until some magic arm is put into his hand; the man who will not go unless he have a Minié, or percussion musket, who will not be content with flint and steel, or even a gun without a lock, is worse than a coward—he is a renegade. If he can do no better, go to a blacksmith, take a gun along as a sample, and get him to make you one like it. Get a spear—a lance. Take a lesson from John Brown. Manufacture your blades from old iron, even though it be the tires of your cart-wheels. Get a bit of carriage spring, and grind and burnish it in the shape of a bowie knife, and put it to any sort of a handle, so that it be strong—ash, hickory, oak. But, if possible, get a double-barrelled gun and a dozen rounds of buckshot, and go upon the battle-field with these.

If their guns reach further than yours, reduce the distance; meet them foot to foot, eye to eye, body to body, and when you strike a blow, strike home. Your true-blooded Yankee will never stand still in the face of cold steel. Let your aim, therefore, be to get into close quarters, and with a few decided, vigorous movements, always pushing forward, never back, my word for it, the soil of Virginia will

be swept of the Vandals who are now polluting its atmosphere.

The band then struck up "Dixie," which was followed by "We may be Happy yet."

—*N. Y. Express, June 13.*

Doc. 222½.

PROCLAMATION OF COL. PORTERFIELD.

THE following proclamation was issued prior to the attack on Phillippa:

HEAD-QUARTERS VIRGINIA FORCES,
PHILLIPPA, VA., May 30, 1861.

To the People of North-western Virginia:

FELLOW-CITIZENS:—I am in your section of Virginia, in obedience to the legally constituted authorities thereof, with the view of protecting this section of the State from invasion by foreign forces and to protect the people in the full enjoyment of their rights—civil, religious, and political. In the performance of my duties, I shall endeavor to exercise every charitable forbearance, as I have hitherto done. I shall not inquire whether any citizens of Virginia voted for or against the Ordinance of Secession. My only inquiry shall and will be as to who are the enemies of our mother—the Commonwealth of Virginia. My duty impels me now to say to all that the citizens of the Commonwealth will at all times be protected by me and those under my command. Those who array themselves against the State will be treated as her enemies, according to the laws thereof.

Virginians! allow me to appeal to you, in the name of our common mother, to stand by the voice of your State, and to defend her against all enemies, and especially to repel invasion from any and every quarter. Those who reside within the State, who invite invasion, or who in any manner assist, aid or abet invaders, will be treated as enemies to Virginia. I trust that no Virginian, whether native-born or adopted, will refuse to defend his State and his brothers against invasion and injury. Virginians! be true, and in due time your common mother will come to your relief.

Already many of you have rallied to the support of the honor of your State and the maintenance of your liberties. Will you continue to be freemen, or will you submit to be slaves? Are you capable of governing yourselves? Will you allow the people of other States to govern you? Have you forgotten the precepts of Madison and Jefferson? Remember that the price of liberty is "eternal vigilance." Virginia has not made war! War has been made upon her and the time-honored principles. Shall she be vindicated in her efforts to maintain the liberties of her people, or shall she bow her head in submission to tyranny and oppression? It seems to me that the true friend of national liberty cannot hesitate. Strike for your State! Strike for your liberties! Rally! rally at once in defence of your mother!

G. A. PORTERFIELD,
Colonel of Volunteers, Commanding.
—*N. Y. Times*, May 30.

Doc. 223.

THE CONFEDERATE POST-OFFICE.

CIRCULAR No. 4, Confederate States of America, Post-Office Department, Montgomery, May 20th, 1861:—

SIR—You are hereby instructed, as the postal service of the Government of the United States within the Confederate States will be suspended, under the authority of the Confederate States, on and after the 1st day of June next, to retain in your possession, subject to the further orders of this department, for the benefit of the Confederate States, all mail bags, locks and keys, marking and other stamps, blanks for quarterly returns of postmasters, and all other property belonging to or connected with the postal service, and to return forthwith to the chief of the appointment bureau of this department a full inventory of the same. You will also report to the chief of the finance bureau of this department, on the 1st day of June proximo, your journal or ledger account with the United States for the service of the Post-Office Department, up to and including the 31st day of the present month of May, in accordance with the general regulations embraced in Chapter 24 of the edition of Laws and Regulations of the Post-Office Department, issued May 15, 1859, page 106, exhibiting the final balance in your possession. I am very respectfully,

Your obedient servant,
JOHN H. REAGAN,
Postmaster General.

To ——, Esq., Postmaster at ——.
—*N. Y. Herald*, June 7.

Doc. 224.

L. W. BLISS' PROCLAMATION.

WHEREAS existing exigencies demand immediate and adequate measures for the protection of the financial condition of this Territory, on account of the insurrectionary combinations existing in the States, I, L. W. Bliss, Acting Governor of Jefferson Territory, do hereby forbid the transmission by the people of this Territory, under any pretext whatever, to the Government of the United States, or to any of the States thereof, any money, bills, drafts, gold dust, or other things of value, either in payment of any debt now due, or hereafter to become due, or for or on account of any other cause whatever, until the termination of hostilities. In the mean time, however, the citizens of Jefferson Territory are invited to pay the amount of their indebtedness to the citizens of the United States, so fast as it becomes due, into the Treasury of the Territory, where it will remain on deposit till the close of hostilities. These deposits will be charged ten per cent. per annum, and the faith, credit, and public property of the whole Territory are pledged for their security. As we have thus far maintained a neutral position with regard to the difficulties now pending, I would counsel a moderate course. Let our action be on the defensive only; and for the better defence of the Territory, I would advise the arming of the Arrapahoes and other tribes of friendly Indians. In the mean time I earnestly invoke the coöperation of all good citizens in the measures hereby adopted for the successful retention of valuables in this Territory, and to secure happiness and prosperity throughout our country.

Done at Denver, this 21st day of May, A. D. 1861.

L. W. BLISS,
Acting Governor, Jefferson Territory.
—*National Intelligencer*, June 18.

Doc. 225.

THE CENTRAL COMMITTEE'S ADDRESS
TO THE PEOPLE OF NORTHWESTERN VIRGINIA.

HAVING submitted to you the resolutions of the Convention held at Wheeling, on the 13th instant, with a brief address, we now crave your earnest attention whilst we discuss, yet further, the very grave and important questions submitted for your consideration and action. We are yet freemen, Virginia freemen, in the full possession and enjoyment of the sacred and inalienable rights guaranteed to us by the Bill of Rights and Constitution of our State, and the Constitution of the United States. In that character and under those sanctions we now address you, and it will remain for us in our future action to determine whether we shall retain them or not.

As shown in the resolutions of the Convention already submitted to you, we have been called to pass upon the acts of one of the highest and most solemn assemblages known to our system of Government—the representatives of the people of Virginia in Convention assembled. We must here correct an error of fatal effect and consequence, which meets us at the threshold of our discussion The Convention of Virginia, which was elected on the 4th of February last, and assembled at Richmond on the 13th of the same month, was not the embodiment of the sovereignty of the people of Virginia. They were not clothed with the powers they have assumed to exercise; else could they have undone the work of our fathers, abolished our republican form of Government, and re-established the Crown of Great Britain as our supreme governing power. The act of our Legislature, convening this Convention, expressly provided that the distinct question should be submitted to the people of Virginia, whether any ordinance in any manner affecting or changing our relations to the Government of the United States, or the Constitution of our own

State, should be referred to the people, or not. By an unusual, unprecedented majority, the people decided, substantially, that no change should be made, either in our allegiance to the Constitution of the United States or in our State Constitution, without having first received the sanction and approval of our people. The second article of our Bill of Rights declares "that all power is vested in, and consequently derived from, the people; that magistrates are their trustees and servants, and at all times amenable to them." Therefore no act or ordinance of the Convention changing our Government, either State or Federal, can be of any force or effect until the people have, by a free, deliberate, and unconstrained vote, passed upon it; and then only subject to the Constitution of the United States.

This leads us to the next, and yet more important question, as to the power, effect, and obligation of the Constitution of the United States. In this address we intend to speak with perfect frankness and candor. Claiming to understand our rights, we know that we are addressing those of equal intelligence, and who, whilst understanding their rights, have the courage and manhood to vindicate and maintain them. The Hon. Jefferson Davis, President of the so-called Confederate States, on the 29th of the last month, sent a message to the Congress at Montgomery, convened in extra session. He has availed himself of this occasion, as the head and chief of the States who have attempted to withdraw themselves from our Federal Union, to "declare the causes which impel them to the separation." He says to the Congress: "The occasion is indeed an extraordinary one. It justifies me in a brief review of the relations heretofore existing between us and the States which now unite in warfare against us, and a succinct statement of the events which have resulted in this warfare; to the end that mankind may pass intelligent and impartial judgment on its motives and objects." When our fathers declared their country's independence, it was not the act of one man; but the instrument bore the signatures of men the story of whose lives is the history of the times in which they lived. This message of Mr. Davis is the authoritative declaration of the Seceding States, and we receive it in the character he has assumed for it.

The single, naked proposition upon which rests the whole claim of the right of secession is distinctly stated in the second of the "Articles of Confederation" adopted by the original Thirteen States during the War of the Revolution, as framed by the Delegates of the United States of America in Congress assembled, on the 9th of July, 1778. This article is in these words:

"Each State retains its sovereignty, freedom, and independence, and every power, jurisdiction, and right which is not by this Confederation expressly delegated to the United States in Congress assembled."

This was the vital defect in the articles of Confederation, and on the 21st of February, 1787, the Congress, after declaring the inefficiency of the Federal Union, and the necessity of devising such further provisions as should render the same adequate to the exigencies of the Union, and being satisfied that a Convention was—

"The most probable means of establishing in these States a firm National Government, resolved that it was expedient that a Convention of Delegates appointed by the several States should be held on the second Monday in May then next, at Philadelphia, for the sole and express purpose of revising the Articles of Confederation, and reporting to Congress and the several Legislatures such alterations and provisions therein as shall, when agreed to in Congress and confirmed by the States, render the Federal Constitution adequate to the exigencies of Government and the preservation of the Union."

The Congress and the patriotic men of that day had become satisfied, from the experience and trials of the Revolutionary War, and the few years which had elapsed subsequent to its close, that the so-called "sovereignty and independence," reserved to the States under the Articles of Confederation, were the fruitful source of all the manifold troubles and difficulties they encountered. They found that their Government was so imperfect as to be inadequate to the great ends of all Governments, as laid down in their Declaration of the 4th of July, 1776, and that it had therefore become their duty "to alter or abolish it, and to institute a new Government, laying its foundation on such principles and organizing its powers in such form as to them *should* seem most likely to effect their safety and happiness."

The Convention which assembled in May, 1787, at Philadelphia, and which immortalized itself in the Constitution of the United States, thoroughly reflected the will of those whom they represented. They framed that Constitution in the name and on behalf of the people of the United States, and not of the several States, as separate and distinct sovereignties. In the debates had in that Convention, on the formation of the Constitution, the following language was used by that distinguished son of Virginia, James Madison:

"Some contend that States are sovereign, when in fact they are only political societies. There is a gradation of power in all societies from the lowest corporation to the highest sovereign. The States never possessed the essential rights of sovereignty. These were always vested in Congress. Their voting as States in Congress is no evidence of sovereignty. The State of Maryland voted by counties, did this make the counties sovereign? The States at present are only great corporations, having the power of making by-laws, and these are effectual only if they are not contradictory to the General Confederation."

In the memorable preamble to that Constitution they declare as follows:

"We the people of the United States, in order to form a more perfect Union, establish justice, insure domestic tranquillity, provide for the common defence, promote the general welfare, and secure the blessings of liberty to ourselves and our posterity, do ordain and establish this Constitution for the United States of America."

It was the act of the people and not of the States. George Washington, the President of the Convention, in communicating to the Congress the Constitution which had been thus framed, in his letter of the 17th of September, 1787, uses this most remarkable and significant language:

"It is obviously impracticable, in the Federal Government of these States, to secure all rights of independent sovereignty to each and yet provide for the interest and safety of all."

This Constitution was not submitted to the States for ratification, but to the people of the several States in Conventions assembled. On the 25th of June, 1788, the Convention of Virginia, by their ordinance assenting to and ratifying that Constitution, declared and made known:

"That the powers granted under the Constitution, being derived from the people of the United States, may be resumed by them whensoever the same shall be perverted to their injury or oppression, and that every power not granted thereby remains with them and at their will."

We still hold to the great political truths our fathers have taught us. Our National Government is not a mere league between sovereign States, which each may revoke at its pleasure, but the solemn act of the people of the several States, which they alone can revoke.

We do not deny the right of revolution; on the contrary, we maintain and vindicate it. Whenever a Government, in its administration, is destructive of the legitimate ends of all Governments, "it is the right of the people to alter or abolish it;" but in so doing the people must be consulted, and they will ever take care that the Government they have established shall not be changed for light and transient causes. Nothing has occurred to warrant or justify the change in our Government proposed by the ordinances of our Convention. Adopting the language of our fellow-citizens of the county of Berkeley, at their late mass meeting, we can truthfully declare:

"That we have never yet agreed to break our allegiance to that Constitution which was signed by George Washington, framed by James Madison, administered by Jefferson, judicially expounded by John Marshall, protected by Jackson, defended by Webster, and lived for by Clay."

"That we have never known Virginia save as a State in the United States; and all our feelings of State pride are indelibly associated with her, as a bright star in the constellation of a glorious and united country."

"That we have lived happily under the great Government of the United States, and if that Government has oppressed us by any of its acts, legislative, executive, or judicial, during its existence, we do not know it."

Such, we are well persuaded, must be the declaration of every calm, deliberate, and conscientious citizen. How, then, can we approve and ratify the ordinance of secession? As if nothing should be wanting to arouse and excite our most determined opposition, the manner of its adoption, the circumstances which preceded it, the unjustifiable acts of aggression and warfare against the Government of the United States, committed prior even to the attempted disruption of the Union, and the still more flagrant outrage upon our rights and liberties, in the passage of the ordinance annexing our State to the Confederate States, and the introduction of the armed soldiers of that Confederacy for the avowed purpose of making war upon the United States, all combine to strengthen and confirm our solemn determination not to submit to such violation of our rights secured to us by the Constitutions of both Virginia and the United States. We will maintain inviolate our fealty and allegiance to both. There is and can be no conflict in this double allegiance. The ordinances of the Convention intended to withdraw our State from the United States and annex her to the Confederate States, are unconstitutional, null, and void; and the acts of the Governor and his subordinates, so far as they are intended to execute those ordinances, are mere usurpations of power, unwarranted by the Constitution and laws of our State.

To show conclusively how far the existing authorities of our State Government have compromised her honor and dignity and abused the trust and confidence of her people, we make the following extract from the message of the Hon. Jefferson Davis, to which we have before referred:

"Having been officially notified by the public authorities of the State of Virginia that she had withdrawn from the Union, and desired to maintain the closest political relations with us which it was possible at this time to establish, I commissioned the Hon. Alex. H. Stephens, Vice-President of the Confederate States, to represent its Government at Richmond. I am happy to inform you that he has concluded a convention with the State of Virginia by which that honored Commonwealth, so long and justly distinguished among her sister States, and so dear to the hearts of thousands of her children in the Confederate States, has united her power and her fortunes with ours, and become one of us."

The fourteenth article of the Bill of Rights of our State is in these words:

"That the people have a right to uniform government; and therefore that no government separate from or independent of the government of Virginia ought to be erected or established within the limits thereof."

But in direct violation of this fundamental law of our State, without the authority, aye, without the knowledge of our people, a government separate from and independent of the government of Virginia has been erected and established within her limits. The new government, called the Confederate States of America, has, by the usurpation of our Convention, been placed over a large portion of our State, put in possession of the Governor and his subordinate executive officers, our whole military force and military operations, offensive and defensive; and, to complete our degradation as a free people, by the introduction of large bodies of Confederate troops, and the alteration of our Constitution and laws relating to elections, that foreign government has obtained the control of the ballot-box. We are very sure that no man, whose faith has not been shaken in the great political axiom of our fathers, that *man is capable of self-government*, can calmly and dispassionately consider the acts of the Convention and Executive of our State without feeling aroused within him the same spirit of indignant resistance which led our fathers into and through the war of the Revolution.

Questions of the grave import as are those submitted to you are not to be decided under the sudden and rash impulse of passion, prejudice, or the promptings of misled State pride. We have loved and honored our State for her past history—a history made glorious by her loyalty to the great Union which she more than any other State contributed to create, establish, and perpetuate. No mere vituperation or sneering can or ought to move us from our honest convictions of duty. We are not the followers of any man or set of men, but the conscientious supporters of the Government, both National and State, which our fathers created, and which for nearly three-quarters of a century has covered our country with blessings.

Admitting, as we do, the right of revolution, but denying, as we must, that there is any case, sufficient or otherwise, to demand or justify it, to what description of Government has our Convention attempted to annex us? We cannot better answer this question than in the language of one of Maryland's most patriotic and gifted sons:

"On one side of us is a united nation of nineteen millions of people; on the other, a divided population of nine millions. We stand between them. If we remain true to the Union, we shall have protection and peace, and hereafter an easy settlement of all our complaints. If we desert the Union, we shall be driven into a Confederacy which has but little sympathy with our interests, and less power to protect us against the ravages of the frequent wars which must inevitably arise between the two sections."

"The Southern Confederacy is essentially weak in the basis of its construction. It is founded on a principle which must lead to the ever-recurring danger of new secessions, and the exhibition of a worse than Mexican anarchy. It may witness *pronunciamientos* upon every discontent, and the strife of the parties ending in further disintegration. If the Border States go into that Confederacy, the opposition of material interests will soon develop the utter want of capacity in the new Government to secure its cohesion."

Wisely, therefore, did our late Convention, looking to the geographical, social, commercial, an industrial interests of Northwestern Virginia, resolve "that the Virginia Convention, in assuming to change the relations of the State of Virginia to the Federal Government, have not only acted unwisely and unconstitutionally, but have adopted a policy utterly ruinous to all the material interests of our section, severing all our social ties, and drying up all the channels of our trade and prosperity." We are very confident that every reflecting and candid man must concur in this resolution; and that, therefore, if our reasoning upon the constitutional question be sound, both our duty as true and loyal citizens of Virginia and the United States, and our interests of every kind, are in perfect harmony the one with the other.

It is neither our right nor our duty to anticipate the action of the Convention which will assemble on the 11th of June. Ere this address reaches you, your will, at least in parts of our State, will have been expressed through the ballot-box. How far that will may sustain the positions we have here assumed, we know not, but they are nevertheless submitted to you with the confident assurance that they cannot be successfully assailed. We are equally confident that it will be your determination to maintain and vindicate the loyalty of our State in the Union, in such manner and by such constitutional and lawful means as future consultation and deliberation shall determine to be the best and wisest. We have sought to strengthen and confirm your attachment to our Government as it existed prior to the usurpations of the Convention and Executive of our State; to satisfy you that your love for the Union of our fathers was not a *mere* sentiment, but was firmly based upon truth and duty; that your fealty to the State of Virginia demanded and compelled your fealty to the Union; and that, however our brethren in other parts of the State might decide for themselves in this solemn crisis of our country's history, we of Northwestern Virginia, having an equal right with them so to decide, will abide by and maintain the Constitution and laws of the United States and of Virginia.

Whilst we have a Constitution and code of laws for our State Government, and local officers to administer them, the Executive and his immediate subordinates have submitted themselves to the Government of the Confederate States. They have thrown off their allegiance to the United States, and are now diligently and laboriously preparing themselves to wage war against the Government of the Union. We need not characterize, in terms, such conduct, but as true and loyal citizens of Virginia we can and must declare that, in our calm and deliberate judgment, it will be the duty of the people of Northwestern Virginia to provide, in the lawful and constitutional mode, for the exercise of those executive and legislative functions of our State Government which have been intrusted to those who are faithless and disloyal, and thus save ourselves from that anarchy which so imminently threatens us. In submitting this grave subject for your consideration, we do so in the earnest faith and hope that you will send to the Convention of the 11th of June your best and truest men, that such action may be secured as will best subserve the interests of our State and secure the perpetuity of its union with the United States.

JOHN S. CARLILE,	G. R. LATHAM,
JAMES S. WHEAT,	ANDREW WILSON,
C. D. HUBBARD,	S. H. WOODWARD,
F. H. PIERPOINT,	JAMES W. PAXTON,
CAMPBELL TARR,	

Central Committee.

WHEELING, (VA.,) May 22, 1861.

—*National Intelligencer,* June 1.

Doc. 226.

SEVENTY-NINTH REGIMENT N. Y. S. M.

THE regiment was escorted to the cars by the Caledonian club, nearly half of whose members are in the ranks of the 79th. The regiment numbers 800 men, exclusive of the band and drum corps. The Regimental band is Robinson's first city band, of 14 musicians, under the leadership of Mr. Robinson. The band has also volunteered for the war. The following is a list of the officers of the 79th :—

STAFF :—Lieut.-Col. commanding, S. McK. Elliott; Major, D. W. McLellan; Adjutant, D. Ireland; Quartermaster, P. Hause; Engineer, John Shaw; Surgeon, Dr. Norval; Chaplain, Charles Doty.

NON-COMMISSIONED STAFF :—Sergeant Major, John Windsor; Quartermaster Sergeant, A. W. Elliott; Paymaster, J. R. Watson; Color Sergeant, James Cummings; Right Gen. Guide, D. McFadgyen; Left Gen. Guide, J. Y. Ireland; Bugler, Charles Landerson; Drum Major, David Renanycink.

FIELD :—Company A—Captain, William Manson; 1st Lieut., William Morrison; 2d Lieut., John McPherson. Company B—Captain, James Farish; 1st Lieut., John Whyte; 2d Lieut., D. Falconer. Company C—Captain, F. Barclay; 1st Lieut., Kenneth Mathison; 2d Lieut., W. A. L. Ostrander. Company D (Fourth Company)—Captain, D. Brown; 1st Lieut., John Moore; 2d Lieut., —— Faulkner. Company E—Captain, D. Morrison; 1st Lieut., J. B. Ayres; 2d Lieut., J. B. Sinclair. Company F —Captain, James Christie; 1st Lieut., R. Mc-

Nie; 2d Lieut., vacant. Company G—Captain, James Laing; 1st Lieut., J. L. Dick; 2d Lieut., W. B. Ives. Company H—Captain, James Colter; 1st Lieut., Robert Campbell; 2d Lieut., Wm. B. Drake. Company I—Captain, R. T. Shillinglaw; 1st Lieut., W. B. Elliott; 2d Lieut., George Pier. Company K—Captain, H. A. Ellis; 1st Lieut., S. R. Elliott; 2d Lieut, vacant.

Lieut.-Col. Elliott has three sons in the regiment. The arms of the regiment consist of about 100 Enfield rifles, and 700 altered muskets, and the ordinary bayonet.

Sixty members of the 71st go out with the 79th to join their comrades in Washington. They are under the command of Capt. Ellis, and will form a part of the engineer corps of that regiment. Twenty-five members of the 9th Regiment, N. Y. S. M., also go to Washington with the 79th. They are in charge of Sergeant Strong.　　—*N. Y. Tribune,* June 3.

Doc. 227.

SENATOR ROUSSEAU'S SPEECH

IN THE KENTUCKY SENATE, MAY 21, 1861.

[The question before the Senate was on discharging the Committee on Military Affairs from the further consideration of a petition of sundry citizens of Paducah, praying for an appropriation for the purpose of establishing a fort at that place. Senator Johnson made a very able speech against the discharge of said Committee.]

SENATOR ROUSSEAU said :—I shall vote for the discharge of the Committee. The petition comes from the respectable constituents of the Senator from McCracken—Dr. Johnson. They ask for an appropriation to fortify Paducah. Their request has been duly and respectfully considered by the Committee on Military Affairs, and said Committee desires to be discharged from the further consideration of the subject. The Senator from McCracken says he has but little hope of obtaining the appropriation, or that his people will be heard by the Legislature, that they are defenceless, and provision should be made for their defence. I asked that Senator against whom they would defend themselves? He was then on the floor of the Senate, but declined to answer. There could have been but one reply to the question, and that he would not give. I will give him the answer. The assumed preparation for defence was, in fact, a preparation to fight our own Government. Of this I have no doubt, and hence no reply to my question. Can it be that defensive measures are desired to oppose Jeff. Davis? Manifestly not. He would be sustained by that Senator, and those that act with him. But who threatens Paducah? Who offers to assail her? Who will assail her? Will our own Government assail her? Surely not. Then why fortify Paducah more than Covington, Newport, Louisville, Maysville, and other exposed points on the Ohio River? There is no reason for it. But the Senator tells us that Louisville, too, might be fortified. I am much obliged to him. Louisville is in no danger. She is already fortified by the strong arms of her brave and patriotic citizens. They are loyal and true to the Union. She has no fears of our own Government. She knows that the United States Government is *hers*, and she loves it for its blessings, and relies upon it for her protection. If assailed by the seceded States, and hard pushed, she knows where. to find defenders, and she will have them. Her people will not tolerate the enormous expense necessary to her fortification, nor will she, in any event, fortify against her own Government. As her representative here, I'll lend myself to no such atrocious purpose. I will not fight, nor prepare to fight, against my own Government, nor countenance the schemes of those who do. Never! No, sir, let those who would fight the United States, and like the work, go at it. I will not aid them in their treasonable projects, but will resist them to the last.

But I wish to sum up, Mr. Speaker. Permit me to tell you, sir, what I think of this whole atrocious scheme of secession. I speak for myself only, and am alone responsible for what I say; and I thank God that I may still speak what I think on Kentucky soil. Yes, sir, good, brave old Kentucky, my mother, "my own native land," is still free. There is no reign of terror here. We still have free speech, a free press, and, as yet, we are free men. Kentucky is true and loyal to the Government. She still rests her head in peace and security upon the fond breast of her mother the Union; and there may she rest forever. She has called upon her gallant sons to rally around her, and beat off the Vandals who would tear her away from her earliest and holiest associations, and bear her to certain destruction.

But Kentucky is in a false position. I felt it from the first. Yet, she having assumed a neutral attitude, I felt it to be my duty to stand by her, and I have faithfully done so. I am willing still to stand by the position of Kentucky, if we can do so in peace and security. But the position is an awkward one, and may be more awkward yet before our difficulties are ended. The Union is threatened; the Government is threatened by those who have not one well-grounded complaint to make against it —by those who have controlled its destinies for years. I denounce the effort, and those who make it. I say it is wrong—infamous; and if successful it must entail ruin upon us and ours. We see the work of mischief going on, and quietly sit by with folded arms while it is done.

Kentucky has as much interest in the Union as any other State. She loves it as devotedly and shares its benefits and blessings in common with her sister States. She owes it her allegiance and her aid. Her people work for the Union they talk for it; they pray for its preservation; yet they stand idly by, and let others, who have no more interest in it than themselves, defend it, and save it if they can. It is in a death struggle for existence, yet we have not a hand to raise in its defence. You say that it is the best government that ever existed on earth—it has ever protected and never oppressed you. But we are told that this is a fratricidal war—a *wicked* war! Well, who began it? Who caused it? Who attempted to break up the Government? Who set the will of the people at defiance, and overturned the "best government on earth"? Let recently passed events, and those which are daily being enacted, answer.

I say the laws should be enforced if we have any. If we have a government let it be maintained and obeyed. And if a wicked, factious minority, without cause, undertakes to override the will of the majority, and rob us of our constitutional and vested rights, let that factious and wicked minority be put down—peaceably if we can, but forcibly if we must. If you don't, they will put you down as certain as fate. Make your election. Don't stand passively by and see your own laws violated; your own Government destroyed, and your liberties swallowed up in tyranny, for fear of a "fratricidal war." If your fellow-citizen turns out to rob and murder you and yours, *stop* him. If you have to hang him why stop him in *that* way. But when he commits a murder and you would execute the law on him, he says, "O, none of that—no coercion; I am your brother; you must not hurt me;" and for fear of hurting your "brother," as he calls himself, you would permit him to go on in his work of crime. Let the will of the sovereign people be respected and obeyed. Let the laws of the land be enforced on all alike. If they are obeyed peaceably, so much the better; but, *let them be obeyed*. Then you will have peace and security at home, and power and respectability abroad. Unless you do this, you will have neither.

But the position of Kentucky will soon be more awkward than it is now. Secessionists will not allow you to maintain your armed neutrality one moment longer than they can help it. You will see it. They will destroy it when they can, and in any way they can. They have constantly denounced it, and have only *submitted* to it till they could do better. They will soon get up another programme of disunion, and make, or *try* to make, you play your part. The old game, in a new form of bloodshed and sensations, will be reënacted for your destruction. You know not what may come; you may be overpowered by these men at home, or from abroad, and that is threatened now. What would you do then? Yield up your liberties into the hands of these broken-down, disappointed, and disgraced politicians? Will *you* submit to the sway of anarchy and the reign of terror now existing in all the seceded States? If not, what will you do? Why, you will call on your Government to do its duty and take care of you. That is what you will do, and you will not call in vain. And will it not be a little embarrassing to call on a

Government to aid you in your extremity which you would not help when it was assailed by treasonable foes? I think it would. But you would get the help; no doubt of that. The Constitution of the United States pledges every State, and all the people of the United States, to put down insurrections and rebellion, and secure to all within its limits a republican form of government. And, unless the State shall disregard—as some would have us do ours —its constitutional pledges and obligations, it will receive the protection of the General Government. I hope we shall never need it. It would be the last resort, but when the Union men of Kentucky are driven to that necessity, the appeal will be made. *Mark that.*

The truth is, our duty at first was to stand by our Government, and protect and defend it. If fit to live under, it was entitled to our respect and confidence and allegiance. If unfit, it should have been abandoned at once, and another formed more perfect. But while we owe our allegiance to it, let us acknowledge it like true men, and not turn our backs upon its greatest peril. We should not do this if we desire its preservation. We should stand by it like men, or pull it down at once. But we should not stand by and see others pull it down over our heads against our will, to the destruction of our liberties, and say:

"We oppose you. We love the Government. It is the Government of our fathers; bought with their blood, and bequeathed to us. It is the best Government on earth, and in its destruction we see ruin to us and ours; but as you and we live in slave States, go on and do as you please. We will not resist you. Ruin us if you will."

And so never lift a hand to save us and our children the blessings of liberty. In my heart I do not approve of this course, and what I do not approve, no power on earth shall make me say. I am for the old Constitution of Washington and his compeers. For the old flag, the Stars and Stripes. God bless them; and I am against all factions that would take them from me. It matters not who they are or whence they come. Whether they come from England, France, Massachusetts, or South Carolina. If they would destroy the Government of our fathers, I am against them. No matter what may be the pretext. No, sir, I am for the Union, and I am willing to defend it by any and all proper means. Our Government is the best in the world. It has answered well all the ends for which governments are made. We all know this. It has oppressed no man, nor has it burdened us a feather's weight. It has brought us nothing but blessings. Under it we have been happy, prosperous, and free. What more can we ask. All that Government can do, our Government has done for us. We have been free, as no nation was ever free before; we have prospered as no nation ever prospered before, and we have rested in peace and security. Yet all this would not do. Mr. Lincoln was

Doc.—32

elected, and corrupt politicians lost their places. They had controlled the Government in their own way for years. When they lost their power, they declared that the Government was corrupt and oppressive, and that they would destroy it. They robbed it of its arms and munitions of war, sending them South; they involved the Government in a debt of nearly a hundred millions of dollars; robbed the treasury; and thus leaving the Government impoverished and distracted they commenced the atrocious business of secession. They had lost the offices, and they thought it necessary to create new ones for the benefit of the defunct politicians, and they did it.

This is the grand secret of the whole affair. Had they retained their grip upon the offices, you had never heard of secession. All our losses, all our troubles and suffering, are the legitimate results of secession. We must bear all, we must submit to all this in silence, that those disappointed politicians may be presidents, ministers, and high officials. Their day was ended by the election of Lincoln. They knew this, and seceded—made new offices and filled them.

Now behold the result of secession. Distress and ruin stare men in the face; strong men, honest and industrious men, cannot get bread for their wives and children; the widow and the orphan, helpless and destitute, are starving; in all the large cities the suffering is intense; work is not to be obtained, and those who live by their labor get no money; property of every description has depreciated until it is almost worthless; in the seceded States, Union men are driven penniless from their homes, or hanged; and all this, Mr. Senator from McCracken, that peaceable secession may go on, and that politicians may fill offices. And after you gentlemen bring all these calamities upon us, you falsely say that "Lincoln did it," and that we Union men are abolitionists and aid him. But I tell you that Lincoln has not done it. He was elected President by your help. You ran a candidate for the Presidency that the Democratic party might be divided, and Lincoln elected. That was your purpose, and you accomplished it; and now you have elected Lincoln thus, you must break up the Government because he is elected. Nothing can satisfy you but secession. You will accept no compromise. To talk of compromise irritates secession gentlemen—it irritates them to talk of the rights of anybody but themselves —they are indeed a very irritable set of people. If you speak of enforcing the laws of the land, why it's coercion, and at this word they forthwith go into spasms. They can't stand it at all. It is subjugation of the South by the North. If they threaten to hang you when they get the power—because you are true to the old Constitution and the old flag of Washington—and you get arms to defend yourself, why, it irritates them, and they won't stand it.

The Union men of Kentucky, seeing the condition of Union men in the seceded States, and seeing that they had to be hanged or be silent, and still wishing to be free as of yore, have lately purchased arms with which to defend themselves. This act is pronounced as a crime —a great crime. And how it irritates them. Garrett Davis received 1,200 stand of arms the other day, and a young gentleman of the secession persuasion became so irritated that he could not stand it at all; that the "States' Rights" men would not submit to it—no, never. Well, said I, I would not put up with it if I were in your place. I tell you what I would do, I would go and take Garrett's guns away from him. But—he didn't.

South Carolina was irritated at the presence of Major Anderson and fifty-five men at Fort Sumter, so irritated that she could not bear it. She tried to starve him to death; she tried to knock his head off, and burn him up. She bombarded the people's fort; shot into the flag of our Government, and drove our soldiers from the place. It was not Mr. Lincoln's fort; not his flag nor his soldiers, but ours. Yet after all these outrages and atrocities, South Carolina comes with embraces for us, saying: "Well, we tried; we intended to kill that brother Kentuckian of yours; tried to storm him, knock his brains out, and burn him up. Dont you love us for it? Won't you fight with us, and for us, and help us to overthrow your Government?"

Was ever a request so outrageously unnatural; so degrading to our patriotism? And yet, Mr. Speaker, there were those among us who rejoiced at the result, and termed the assault upon their own fort and the capture of their own flag and their own soldiers a *heroic victory!*

Mr. Speaker, I am sick and tired of all this gabble about irritation over the exercise by others of their undoubted right, and I say once for all to you secession gentlemen, that we Union men know our rights, and intend to maintain them; and if you get irritated about it, why—get irritated. Snuff and snort yourselves into a rage; go into spasms if you will; die if you want to, and can't stand it—who cares? What right have you to get irritated because we claim equal rights and equality with you? We are for peace; we desire no war, and deprecate collision. All we ask is peace. We don't intend you any harm. We don't want to hurt you, and don't intend you shall injure us if we can help it. We beg of you to let us live in peace under the good old Government of our fathers. We only ask that. Why keep us ever on the alert watching you, to prevent you from enslaving us by a destruction of that Government?

Senator JOHNSON—It is already destroyed.

Mr. ROUSSEAU—Not a bit of it. The Union will never be dissolved. I know you say it is; but, believe me, it will *never* be dissolved. We may have much suffering; we may endure many calamities. War, pestilence and famine may befall us; our own good old Kentucky may be overrun and trodden under foot, and her soil may be drenched in blood, but the Union will never, *never* be dissolved. I have never had a doubt on this subject, never. I know we must suffer, but we must preserve the Union.

You, Mr. Senator from McCracken, are a sanguine man. You think the Union is destroyed. Well, you sometimes err. I believe you had a correspondence with "Uncle Abe," in which you committed a glaring error. But that was only a semi-official correspondence, and perhaps should not be alluded to here.

Senator JOHNSON (good-humoredly)—Oh! yes; tell.

Mr. ROUSSEAU—I thank you. Well, as one of the Senators of Kentucky, you made your most solemn protest against the stationing of troops at Cairo, Ill. The protest was very elegant, as is generally what comes from you—a little highfalutin, it is true. You forwarded your protest to "Uncle Abe," and, in due time, received a reply, which was too good a joke for a good-natured gentleman like yourself to keep all to yourself, and so you disclosed it. Uncle Abe replied to you that your letter had been received, duly considered, and in reply, he had to say to you, (one of the Senators of Kentucky,) that if he had known that Cairo, Ill., was in your Senatorial District, he would not have sent any soldiers within a hundred miles of that point.

Mr. Speaker, I have but a word to say. Kentucky is an armed neutral, it is said. I submit, with others, to that position. I hope that circumstances may not drive us from it. I hope that our secession friends will be, in fact, neutral. If we remain so, it is said we shall have peace. I hope so; but the neutrality that fights all on one side I do not understand. Troops leave Kentucky in broad daylight, and our Governor sees them going to fight against our own Government, yet nothing is said or done to prevent them. Is this to be our neutrality? If it is, I am utterly opposed to it. If we assume a neutral position, let us be neutral in fact. It is as little as we can do.

Our Government, constitutionally administered, is entitled to our support, no matter who administers it. If we will not support it, and yet enjoy its blessings, in Heaven's name let us not war against it, nor allow our people to do so. Let us be true to our position, whatever it may be. We are nullifying at any rate. Our Government has not objected to it. But who can look an honest man in the face, while professing neutrality, refusing to help his Government to preserve its existence, yet secretly and traitorously warring against it? For one, sir, I'll none of it. Away with it. Let us be men, honest men, or pretend to be nothing but vagabonds.

I hear it said that Kentucky will go out of the Union; that if she goes anywhere she will go South, &c., &c.

Mr. Speaker, let me tell you, sir, Kentucky will not "go out." She will not stampede.

That has been tried. Secessionists must invent something new in the way of secession appliances before they can either frighten or "drag" Kentucky out of the Union. I tell you, sensation gentlemen, that your exciting events have ceased to affect us. Try something else. Get up a fight at Cairo, that you may get us to side with you: That is your game, and you will play it whenever you think you can succeed at it. You tried to scare us, but you failed in your purpose. And if you illegally and against right assault Cairo, I hope every man of you will get his head knocked, or be taken prisoner, and that the Cairo folks will never permit you to come to Kentucky again. That's what I wish, and what I believe would happen in such an event.

But we won't "go out"—have not the least notion of it in the world. You must take us out according to law and right, or take us dead. Believe this, and act accordingly. It would be better for all of us. We shall be but too happy to keep peace, but we cannot leave the Union of our fathers. When Kentucky goes down it will be in blood. Let that be understood. She will not go as other States have gone. Let the responsibility rest on you, where it belongs. It is all your work, and whatever happens will be your work. We have more right to defend our Government than you have to overturn it. Many of us are sworn to support it.

Let our good Union brethren of the South stand their ground. I know that many patriotic hearts in the seceded States still beat warmly for the old Union—the old flag. The time will come when we shall all be together again. The politicians are having their day. The *people* will yet have theirs. I have an abiding confidence in the *right*, and I know that this secession movement is all wrong. There is, in fact, not a single substantial reason for it. If there is, I should be glad to hear it; our Government has never oppressed us with a feather's weight. The direst oppression alone could justify what has brought all our present suffering upon us.

May God, in his mercy, save our glorious Republic.

—*N. Y. Tribune*, June 3.

Doc. 227½.
GEN. McDOWELL'S PROCLAMATION,

IN REFERENCE TO DAMAGES CAUSED BY THE WAR.

THE following is an important order from Gen. McDowell:

HEAD-QUARTERS DEPARTMENT OF N. E. VIRGINIA,
ARLINGTON, June 2, 1861.

GENERAL ORDER No. 4.—Statements of the amount, kind, and value of all private property taken and used for Government purposes, and of the damage done in any way to private property, by reason of the occupation of this section of the country by the United States troops, will, as soon as practicable, be made out and transmitted to department head-quarters of brigades by the commanders of brigades and officers in charge of the several fortifications. These statements will exhibit:

First.—The quantity of land taken possession of for the several field works, and the kind and value of the crops growing thereon, if any.

Second.—The quantity of land used for the several encampments, and the kind and value of the growing crops, if any.

Third.—The number, size, and character of the buildings appropriated to public purposes.

Fourth.—The quantity and value of trees cut down.

Fifth.—The kind and extent of fencing, &c., destroyed.

These statements will, as far as possible, give the value of the property taken, or of the damage sustained, and the name or names of the owners thereof. Citizens who have sustained any damage or loss as above will make their claims upon the commanding officers of the troops by whom it was done, or in cases where these troops have moved away upon the commander nearest them.

These claims will accompany the statement above called for. The commanders of brigades will require the assistance of the commanders of regiments or detached companies, and will make this order known to the inhabitants in their vicinity, to the end that all loss or damage may as nearly as possible be ascertained while the troops are now here, and by whom or on whose account it has been occasioned, that justice may be done alike to the citizen and the Government. The name of the officer, or officers, in case the brigade commanders shall institute a board to fix the amount of loss or damage, shall be given in each case.

By order of Brig.-Gen. McDowell.

JAMES B. FRY, Assistant Adjutant-General.

—*N. Y. Tribune*, June 16.

Doc. 228.
THE BATTLE AT PHILIPPI.

OFFICIAL REPORT OF THE COMMANDER OF THE TROOPS.

PHILIPPI, Va., June 4, 1861.

BRIGADIER-GENERAL THOMAS A. MORRIS:—I herewith submit to you a report of the operations of my command on the morning of the 3d day of June, 1861, at this place. On the 2d day of June you directed me, with eight companies of the Seventh Regiment of Indiana volunteers, to proceed to Webster, that I might be there reinforced with four companies of the Ohio volunteers, under the command of Colonel Steedman, the artillery of his command being under the immediate command of Lieutenant-Colonel Sturgis, and with four companies of the Sixth Indiana volunteers, under the command of Colonel Crittenden. At eight o'clock on the night of the 2d day of June, I took up my line of march from Grafton, and at Webster was reinforced, as stated above, and proceeded towards this place to meet the enemy. The night was very dark, and before the troops left the cars a terrible storm was raging, which continued without abatement until just before the attack was made. It was so exceedingly dark that it was with the utmost difficulty that I could form the command in the order which I desired to move it forward, and after it was so formed I found it almost impossible to pass from front to rear to direct the command. The order of march was as follows: —First, a small detachment of twenty men of Captain Morgan's company, Seventh Regiment Indiana volunteers, under the immediate command of Lieutenant Benjamin Ricketts, followed at the distance of four hundred yards by Company A of said regiment, under the command of Captain Burgess. In order of that company, and at the distance of four hundred paces, followed the remaining companies of the Seventh Indiana Regiment. The artillery was led by Lieutenant-Colonel Sturgis and seven companies of the Fourteenth Ohio Regiment, commanded by Colonel Steedman, and the four companies of the Sixth Indiana Regiment, commanded by Colonel Crittenden, followed in the order named. Darkness, rain, and mud impeded the march and rendered it impossible to arrive before Philippi at four o'clock, the time indicated in your order. At five o'clock the advance took such a position by a file movement, under the direction of Colonel Lander, as to allow the artillery to advance to the front; then advanced immediately in the rear of the artillery. Scarce had the disposition been made when the picket of the enemy opened a brisk fire upon us from the heights immediately above the town, and from the woods and bushes on both sides of the road. Lieut.-Col. Sturges, with great promptness, got the guns in position to command the town, and, under the direction of Col. Lander, (I think,) opened the fire. A moment's delay to the infantry was occasioned by want of knowledge on my part as to which of the two roads led to the bridge leading into the town across the river. At the forks of the road I halted my command, and, riding rapidly to the guns, got the desired information from Col. Lander. So informed, I proceeded on the double quick down the declivity of the hill, and here had a full view of the enemy, and I must confess that I never saw a flight determined on with greater promptness, or executed with more despatch. The enemy was under the command of Col. G. A. Porterfield. What his strength was, is variously estimated. On my own judgment I would say from 1,500 to 2,000, of which I would think 500 were cavalry.

They had no artillery but a swivel. I have conversed with many of the citizens of the town as to the strength of Col. Porterfield's command. Some say the Colonel himself professed to have 2,500 troops. It is my opinion

that he had but magnified his own strength, with a view to intimidate the people and crush out the Union sentiment.

When I first saw the enemy, it seemed to me he was pushing for the bridge, which I was rapidly approaching; but it turned out that it was necessary to converge towards the bridge to gain the street leading out of the town on the opposite side from that entered by my command. The bridge is a narrow structure, some three or four hundred feet in length, spanning the Valley River, a branch of the Monongahela. A small body of determined troops could have impeded our progress, and crippled us at the bridge, and I apprehended resistance at this point.

Toward it my men poured down the hill, in good order, and with an energy and determination that assured me in advance that victory was certain. In a moment I was at the mouth of the bridge; one of the passages was barricaded, the other clear; through it (Company B, commanded by Captain Morgan, in advance,) my men pushed; the Seventh Indiana first, then Colonel Steedman's command, not including the artillery, then Colonel Crittenden's, and opened upon the enemy, then retreating in wild disorder. Both parties being upon the full run, and the distance between them being quite considerable, but little execution could be done. I pursued the enemy from the bridge through the town and for several miles beyond. At one time I thought I should be able to capture his entire baggage train; but the horses, to prevent this, were cut from many of the wagons and mounted, and the wagons and contents left as our booty. The wagons were filled with munitions of war, blankets, knapsacks, clothing, baggage of officers and men, and with a considerable amount of flour and forage. Having pursued the assault and pursuit of the enemy, I speak particularly of these officers, because being of my immediate command, their conduct was under my personal observation; and because thrown suddenly in command of different detachments of troops, to the officers of which I am a stranger, I am unable to mention the names of many whose bearing and courage are worthy of praise. The detachment of the Fourteenth Regiment of Ohio volunteers, commanded by Colonel Steedman, crossed the bridge immediately after the Seventh Indiana, and was followed quickly by the Sixth Indiana, under Colonel Crittenden. Colonel Steedman captured a large amount of tents, a number of muskets and rifles, and other munitions of war, and I believe some prisoners; we were separated during the engagement, but his conduct, as well as that of his officers and men, is spoken of with much praise by those who witnessed it. Lieutenant-Colonel Sturges, of the same regiment, in charge of the artillery, managed his guns with great celerity. I understand that he was assisted and directed by Colonel Lander, by special delegation from the commanding general. So informed, I did not myself give any directions in regard to the guns. Colonel Crittenden was necessarily placed in the rear, for he left the cars at Webster, after a tedious journey, but to take up his march on Philippi, his men marching in the rear, in the darkness of midnight, and in the raging storm, would necessarily be vastly more fatigued than those in front. . Still, they and their gallant commander held up with unfaltering spirit, and did as great service in the fight and chase as it was possible for good officers and good men to do. While descending the hill towards the bridge a body of troops made their appearance on the heights to the left. A friendly cheer assured us it was the command of the gallant Colonel Milroy, and the First Virginia regiment, commanded by Colonel Kelly, and a detachment from Colonel Irvine's Ohio regiment. A rapid descent down the declivity enabled them to strike the retreating enemy, but not with so much effect as if the descent could have been made a few minutes sooner. Colonel Milroy assaulted that part of the enemy who had left the main road and betook themselves to the hills to enjoy the protection of the trees, while Cols. Kelly and Irvine's command pursued the enemy up the road leading towards Beverly. They succeeded in overtaking, killing, and wounding a number, but, unfortunately, Col. Kelly himself fell severely wounded by a pistol shot in the breast; my men carried him into the town, when surgical assistance was immediately rendered by Dr. Geo. W. New, of my regiment, who had proved himself as gallant and courageous in the field, as he is skilful in his profession. Just before we had approached the town, he volunteered to make a reconnoissance of the bridge, and bore my message along the line repeatedly, seemingly unmindful of his own personal safety.

Captain G. W. Robinson, of Col. Kelly's command, reports to me that he captured Capt. J. W. Willey, of the rebel army, and upon his person found his commission from Adjutant-General Garnett, of the rebel forces, and other papers of importance which he reports he holds subject to my order. I enclose his report. It perhaps is not my province to speak much of that part of the expedition which marched by way of Evansville, under the command of Colonel Kelly, consisting of Kelly, Milroy, and Irvine and their commands. I know nothing personally of their march prior to arriving before Philippi, and only speak of what I myself saw. The two commands or bodies of troops arrived almost simultaneously upon different hills overhanging the town, and did all that could be done to arrest the flight and punish the enemy.

I only undertake to report the particulars of that part of the expedition under my immediate command, and which marched upon Philippi by way of Webster and the bridge. I speak of the part of the expedition commanded by Colonels Kelly, Milroy and Irvine, only because Colonel Kelly's condition is such as to render a report from him impossible. In doing so, I may have made some mistakes, but not intentionally. I herewith hand to you the reports made to me by Colonels Crittenden, Milroy, and Steedman. Our loss was two wounded and two missing; what the enemy's loss was is not certainly known, as he succeeded in carrying off many of his dead. It was inconsiderable, perhaps not to exceed forty. I have heard the conduct of Jonathan W. Gordon of Col. Milroy's command, spoken of in terms of decided approbation by the officers of the same command. Since we have been here he had a small mounted scouting party on a hazardous expedition, and performed it in a very satisfactory manner. David W. Cheek, Commissary and Quartermaster's Clerk, at my instance, mounted a horse, and rode at my side, bore messages and rendered me very valuable services, and proved himself brave and courageous. The colors presented by the ladies of Aurora to the Seventh Indiana regiment, were the Stars and Stripes which first floated over the town.

The disunion flag was captured by Captain Ferry's command, of my regiment, and the Stars and Stripes were run up and given to the breeze in its place.

Captain William C. Moreau, of Colonel Crittenden's command, has rendered me very valuable assistance in a business point of view, since I took command of this post; and I hear his conduct in the recent engagement spoken of in terms of praise both by his officers and men. I recommend Corporal Charles Bryant and Sergeant John Griffin of Company G, Seventh Indiana, for good conduct.

I have the honor to be, your obedient servant,

E. Dumont,
Commanding troops at Philippi.
—*N. Y. Herald*, June 16.

THE VICTORY AT PHILIPPI.

Grafton, Monday Night, June 3.

Yesterday morning, at ten o'clock, four regiments left here in two divisions—one consisting of the 1st Virginia regiment, part of the Ohio 16th, and the Indiana 7th, under command of Col. Kelly; the other the Indiana 9th and the Ohio 14th, commanded by Col. Lander, of Indian fighting, wagon-road, and Potter and Prior duel notoriety. Col. Kelly's division moved east by railroad to Thornton, a small way station, five miles distant from here. Thence they marched to Philippi, a distance of twenty-two miles. The Indiana Regiment moved out the N. W. Virginia Railroad to Webster, where they were joined by the Ohio 14th, from which place they pushed forward on foot to Philippi, twelve miles distant.

The march of the two divisions was performed last night, through darkness, rain, and mud. It was a terrible undertaking, but they all went bravely through it, unshrinkingly and without complaint. All night they toiled on through the darkness and storm, the soft earth yielding beneath their feet, till the gray dawn found them in the presence of the enemy.

Col. Lander reports that as they neared Philippi they were discovered by a woman, who fired at him twice, and who sent her little boy across the hills (as he afterward found) to apprise the enemy of their approach. He arrived on the hill across the river from, and below Philippi, and commanding the town and encampment, (just below the town,) a little before daylight this morning. They at once planted two pieces of artillery on the brow of the hill, just above the camp, and prepared to open on them when the time arrived—four o'clock was the hour at which the attack was to be made simultaneously by both divisions.

Colonel Kelly was to attack them in the rear and cut off their retreat, while Col. Lander was to attack them in front. But Col. Kelly's division was behind the appointed hour, owing to the terrible fatigue of their forced march of twenty-two miles, and, in addition to this, they missed the point, and instead of coming in on the Beverly road, above Philippi, and effectually cutting of all retreat, they came, when they did come, just below the town.

When the day began to dawn upon the impatient forces of Colonel Lander, it discovered to them the camp below in a state of commotion, evidently in great alarm and preparing for fight. The hour appointed for the attack came and passed, but still Colonel Kelly's division had not arrived. Impatient to begin the attack, and fearful that the rascals, almost within his grasp, should escape without smelling powder, Colonel Lander ordered the artillery to begin the attack; and at a quarter past four the guns were unlimbered and dropped the first messengers of terror into the rebel camp less than a quarter of a mile away. Simultaneously with the roar of the first gun, Colonel Kelly, at the head of his command, came in sight across the river below the camp, and, comprehending the position of affairs, they rushed forward at once in the direction of the camp.

Meanwhile, the battery having, after the first shot or two, got an accurate range, played upon the camp with marked effect, tearing through tents and houses at a fearful rate. This the chivalry couldn't stand, and they scattered like rats from a burning barn. They had no time to retreat in order. They didn't even retreat at all—they ran, fled most ingloriously—ran like sheep in every direction that promised safety, after firing a random and scattering volley which did no damage whatever. Col. Kelly's command was close after, the Virginia troops in advance, the Henry Clay Guards in front, and Col. Kelly and Capt. Fordyce leading. At the same time Col. Lander's force came rushing down the hill to the bridge, and they all put out after the fugitives, yelling like Indians.

But the legs of the fugitive chivalry knew them too well, and they could not be overtaken by our already exhausted men, who, after chasing them a couple of miles, returned to the evacuated camp, to learn the painful fact that their victory, though complete, was dearly, too dearly bought. Col. Kelly, who, with a bravery amounting to rashness, was foremost from first to last, was rallying his men in the upper part of the town, the enemy having all apparently fled, when he fell by a shot from a foe concealed either behind a fence or in a house; some say the assailant fired from behind a wagon; others that Col. Kelly was pressing him hard with a view of capturing him, when he wheeled and fired. This is not substantiated. At any rate, the shot was fired after the engagement was over, and was just such a piece of assassination as that by which fell the loved and lamented Ellsworth. The assassin was an assistant quartermaster in the Confederate force. His name is Simms, and he hails from Chesterfield, across the river from Richmond. He was immediately seized, and it is a great wonder that they did not make mincemeat of him instanter. The pistol with which he shot Kelly is an old-fashioned, old Virginia horse-pistol, carrying a very large ball and inflicting a most dangerous wound. The ball entered the left breast, and passing clear through lodged beneath the skin, just underneath the shoulder blade. It has been extracted, and every attention of the highest medical and surgical skill is lavished upon the wounded officer. If human skill can save him he will be saved; but if he is beyond the reach of human aid, he will die, as he said to-day to a friend who bent over his couch, in a just and glorious cause. "I expect I shall have to die," said the wounded Colonel; "I would be glad to live, if it might be, that I might do something for my country; but if it cannot be, I shall have at least the consolation of knowing that I fell in a just cause."

Several hats, apparently belonging to officers, were picked up, and a horse and buggy, belonging to B. F. Martin, at Pruntytown, a lawyer and defeated secession candidate for the Legislature, were part of the spoils. Thos. Surghnor, "the inimitable Tom," as Bill Cooper used to style him, "Captain of the Barbour forces," as he styles himself, and late editor of the Barbour Jeffersonian, at the first approach of danger, made tracks; he ran with all the speed the shortness of his legs would permit, and as fear lent him wings, he managed to get out of harm's way.

The American flag has taken the place of the secession emblem in all the houses of Philippi. Several of these piratical flags were captured. The people are coming in from the country, and expressing their gladness at the change of colors.

—*Wheeling (Va.) Intelligencer*, June 6.

Doc. 229.

LETTER FROM LORD JOHN RUSSELL

TO THE COMMISSIONERS OF THE ADMIRALTY.

THE following is a copy of the letter laid before the House of Commons by Lord John Russell:

FOREIGN OFFICE, June 1, 1861.

" *To the Lords Commissioners of the Admiralty* :

" My Lords:—Her Majesty's Government are, as you are aware, desirous of observing the strictest neutrality in the contest which appears to be imminent between the United States and the so-styled Confederate States of North America; and with the view more effectually to carry out this principle, they propose to interdict the armed vessels, and also the privateers of both parties, from carrying prizes made by them into ports, harbors, roadsteads, or waters of the United Kingdom, or any of Her Majesty's colonies or possessions abroad.

" I have accordingly to acquaint your lordships that the Queen has been pleased to direct that orders, in conformity to the principle above stated, should forthwith be addressed to all proper authorities in the United Kingdom, and to Her Majesty's naval and other authorities in all quarters beyond the United Kingdom, for their guidance in the circumstances.

" I have, &c.,   J. RUSSELL."

Similar letters have been addressed to the Secretaries of State for India, War, and the Colonies.

—*Baltimore American*, June 18.

Doc. 230.

GEN. PATTERSON'S PROCLAMATION.

HEAD-QUARTERS, DEPARTMENT OF PENN., }
CHAMBERSBURG, (Pa.,) June 3, 1861. }

To the United States Troops of this Department.

THE restraint which has necessarily been imposed upon you, impatient to overcome those who have raised their parricidal hands against our country, is about to be removed. You will soon meet the insurgents.

You are not the aggressors. A turbulent faction, misled by ambitious rulers, in times of profound peace and national prosperity, have occupied your forts and turned the guns against you; have seized your arsenals and armories, and appropriated to themselves Government supplies; have arrested and held prisoners your companions marching to their homes under State pledge of security, and have captured vessels and provisions voluntarily assured by State legislation from molestation, and now seek to perpetuate a reign of terror over loyal citizens.

They have invaded a loyal State, and intrenched themselves within its boundaries in defiance of its constituted authorities.

You are going on American soil to sustain the civil power, to relieve the oppressed, and to retake that which is unlawfully held.

You must bear in mind you are going for the good of the whole country, and that, while it is your duty to punish sedition, you must protect the loyal, and, should the occasion offer, at once suppress servile insurrection.

Success will crown your efforts; a grateful country and a happy people will reward you.

By order of Major-General Patterson.

F. J. PORTER, Ass't Adj. General.

—*National Intelligencer*, June 6.

Doc. 231.

THE FIRST SCOTT LIFE GUARD.

THE following is a list of the officers of the Fourth Regiment New York Volunteers, or First Scott Life Guard:

Col., Alfred W. Taylor; Lieut.-Col., John D. McGregor; Major, Wm. Jameson; Adjt., Wm. Henriques; Quartermaster, James M. Bayles. Company A—Capt., Joseph Henriques; First Lieut., I. Lenoske; Second Lieut., James Walker. Company B—Capt., John S. Downs; First Lieut., Fogarty; Second Lieut., Thornton. Company C—Capt., James Mooney; First Lieut., Henry Rasco; Second Lieut., T. C. Shiblee. Company D—Capt., Cruger; First Lieut., Smith; Second Lieut., Schafer. Company E—Capt., Wm. B. Pariesen; First Lieut., Moulton; Second Lieut., Wynne. Company F—Capt., J. H. H. Camp; First Lieut., McDonald; Second Lieut., Bosworth. Company G—Capt., John B. Brahams; First Lieut., Seaton; Second Lieut., Parker. Company H—Capt., John Quinn; First Lieut., Metcalfe; Second Lieut., Bowers. Company J—Capt., Houstani; First Lieut., Wm. Walsh; Second Lieut., Godfrey. Company K—Capt., Constantine; First Lieut., Rodman; Second Lieut., Hepburn.

THIRD REGIMENT N. Y. VOLUNTEERS.

The following is a list of the officers:

Frederick Townsend, Colonel, Albany; S. M. Alford, Lieut.-Col., Albany; George D. Bayard, Major, West Point; J. Owen Moore, Adjutant, Albany; J. H. Chase, Quartermaster, Albany; A. H. Haff, M. D., Surgeon, Albany; J. J. Van Rensselaer, Assistant-Surgeon, Albany; A. G. White, Quartermaster Sergeant, Albany; Aug. Limburger, Sergeant Major, Brooklyn; Francis Schoppelrei, Drum Major, Albany; Charles Gates, Fife Major, Albany.

Company 1 (Brooklyn)—Capt., A. Smith; Lieut., J. J. Fay; Ensign, M. A. Stearns.

Company 2 (Albany)—Capt., H. S. Hurlbert; Lieut., W. N. S. Saunders; Ensign, T. E. Lord.

Company 3 (Syracuse)—Capt., J. G. Butler; Lieut., Chas. Burdick; Ensign, Jay Wicks.

Company 4 (Oneida)—Capt., E. S. Jenny; Lieut., Wm. E. Blake; Ensign, Leon H. Ballard.

Company 5 (Albany)—Capt., E. G. Floyd;

Lieut., George Van Vechten; Ensign, G. E. Mink.

Company 6 (Oswego)—Capt., J. S. Catlin; Lieut., Wm. S. Couch; Ensign, T. M. Stone.

Company 7 (Albany)—Capt., J. W. Blanchard; Lieut., B. B. Walen; Ensign, R. M. Goodwait.

Company 8 (Havana)—Capt., J. E. Mulford; Lieut., W. N. Babcock; Ensign, E. S. Tuthill.

Company 9 (Albany)—Capt., J. H. Teneyck, jr.; Lieut., Henry Cooper; Ensign, R. H. Chapin.

Company 10 (Newburgh)—Capt., S. W. Fullerton, jr.; Lieut., E. J. Jones; Ensign, Alexander Mann.

—*N. Y. Tribune*, June 4.

Doc. 232.

RECTOR'S PROCLAMATION.

HEAD-QUARTERS THIRD BRIGADE, FIRST DIVISION,
FORT SMITH, May 4, 1861.

1. THE authority of the United States has ceased upon this frontier.

2. All persons claiming to interpose in public in the name and by the authority of the United States on this frontier, will be arrested and placed in the guard-house for examination.

3. Captain Perkins will take possession of the records and other property of the late United States Court at Van Buren, Arkansas, and place the keys in the custody of the Circuit Court Clerk of Crawford county, Arkansas.

4. Stationery and twenty minutes' time will be allowed the attachés of said court, should they desire, to write their resignations.

5. All persons in possession of public property, taken without proper authority, are required to report the same immediately to the Assistant Adjutant-General at head-quarters of this command, and all arms or other property belonging to the United States will be seized.

By order of Gen. N. B. Burrow, Commanding.
W. F. RECTOR, Assistant Adjutant-General.
—*N. Y. Herald*, June 6.

Doc. 233.

GEN. PRICE'S PROCLAMATION.

HEAD-QUARTERS MISSOURI GUARDS,
JEFFERSON CITY, June 4.

To the Brigadier-Generals commanding the several military districts in Missouri:

To correct misrepresentation and prevent all misunderstanding of my opinions and intentions in reference to the military trust confided to me by the Government of Missouri, I desire to state to you and to the people generally that my past and present position as a private citizen, as a member of our State convention, and as a military commander, and my influence, have been exerted to prevent the transfer of the seat of war from the Atlantic States to our own State. Having taken no steps towards dissolving our connection with the Federal Government there was no reason whatever for disturbing the peace and tranquillity of Missouri. I have, therefore, desired, and such I am authorized to say has been, and still is, the desire of the Chief Executive, under whose orders I acted, that the people of Missouri should exercise the right to choose their own position in any contest which might be forced upon them, unaided by any military force whatever. Their right to bear arms in defence of themselves and of their State cannot be questioned, secured, as it is, both by the Constitution of the United States and of this State. For the purpose, therefore, of securing to the people of Missouri a free exercise of their undoubted rights, and with a view to preserve peace and order throughout the State, an agreement has been entered into between General Harney and myself, which I consider alike honorable to both parties and Governments represented. The Federal Government, however, has thought proper to remove Gen. Harney from the command of the Department of the West, but as the successor of Gen. Harney will certainly consider himself and his Government in honor bound to carry out this agreement in good faith, I feel assured that his removal should give no cause of uneasiness to our citizens for the security of their liberties and property. I intend, on my part, to adhere both in its spirit and to the letter. The rumor in circulation, that it is the intention of the officers now in command of this Department to disarm those of our citizens who do not agree in opinion with the Administration at Washington, and put arms in the hands of those who in some localities of this State are supposed to sympathize with the views of the Federal Government, are, I trust, unfounded. The purpose of such a movement could not be misunderstood, and it would not only be a violation of the agreement referred to, and an equally plain violation of our constitutional right, but a gross indignity to the citizens of the State, which would be resisted to the last extremity.

My wish and hope is, that the people of the State of Missouri be permitted in peace and security to decide upon their future course, and so far as my abilities can effect this object, it shall be accomplished.

The people of Missouri cannot be forced, under the terrors of a military invasion, into a position not of their free choice.

A million of such people as the citizens of Missouri were never yet subjugated, and, if attempted, let no apprehensions be entertained of the result. I enjoin upon you, gentlemen, to see that all citizens, of whatever opinions in politics or religion, be protected in their persons and property.

STERLING PRICE,
Major-General Commanding.
—*N. Y. World*, June 5.

Doc. 234.

BEAUREGARD'S PROCLAMATION.

HEAD-QUARTERS, DEP'T OF ALEXANDRIA, }
Camp Pickens, June 5, 1861. }

A PROCLAMATION.—*To the People of the Counties of Loudon, Fairfax, and Prince William.*

A RECKLESS and unprincipled tyrant has invaded your soil. Abraham Lincoln, regardless of all moral, legal, and constitutional restraints, has thrown his Abolition hosts among you, who are murdering and imprisoning your citizens, confiscating and destroying your property, and committing other acts of violence and outrage, too shocking and revolting to humanity to be enumerated.

All rules of civilized warfare are abandoned, and they proclaim by their acts, if not on their banners, that their war-cry is "BEAUTY AND BOOTY." All that is dear to man—your honor and that of your wives and daughters—your fortunes and your lives, are involved in this momentous contest.

In the name, therefore, of the constituted authorities of the Confederate States—in the sacred cause of constitutional liberty and self-government, for which we are contending—in behalf of civilization itself, I, G. T. Beauregard, Brigadier-General of the Confederate States, commanding at Camp Pickens, Manassas Junction, do make this my Proclamation, and invite and enjoin you by every consideration dear to the hearts of freemen and patriots, by the name and memory of your Revolutionary fathers, and by the purity and sanctity of your domestic firesides, to rally to the standard of your State and country; and, by every means in your power, compatible with honorable warfare, to drive back and expel the invaders from your land.

I conjure you to be true and loyal to your country and her legal and constitutional authorities, and especially to be vigilant of the movements and acts of the enemy, so as to enable you to give the earliest authentic information at these head-quarters, or to the officers under my command.

I desire to assure you that the utmost protection in my power will be given to you all.

G. T. BEAUREGARD,
Brigadier-General Commanding.

Official—THOMAS JORDAN,
Acting Assistant Adj't-General.
—*Richmond Enquirer.*

The most objectionable of all the pronunciamientos of the Secessionists that has come under our notice, since the beginning of the contest, is the Proclamation of Gen. Beauregard to certain "good people" in Virginia. How any man of his standing could put his name to such a production we are at a loss to conceive. We would fain hope that it is not genuine. We would fain believe that so gross and unwarranted a misrepresentation of the purposes of the United States Government must have been foisted upon the public by some enemy of Gen. Beauregard. The publication is credited, however, to the Richmond *Enquirer*, and therefore leaves no doubt of its being official. Without venturing any lengthy comments upon it, we beg leave to suggest that if the prominent leaders of that side are driven to such methods of widening the breach between the sections, the cause must be low down which requires such disreputable and untruthful means to "breath into it the breath of life."

The particular passage to which we would call the especial attention of our readers is a tolerably fair parallel to a paragraph we gave the other day from a speech made by ex-Gov. Wise, in which he invites the people of Virginia to "wade through a path of blood." Gen. Beauregard says:

"A reckless and unprincipled tyrant has invaded your soil. Abraham Lincoln, regardless of all moral, legal, and constitutional restraints, has thrown his Abolition hosts among you, who are murdering and imprisoning your citizens, confiscating and destroying your property, and committing other acts of violence and outrage, too shocking and revolting to humanity to be enumerated. All rules of civilized warfare are abandoned, and they proclaim by their acts, if not on their banners, that their war-cry is 'Beauty and Booty.' All that is dear to man—your honor and that of your wives and daughters—your fortunes and your lives, are involved in this momentous contest."

We cannot avoid contrasting with the above the offer of General Butler to put down "servile insurrections" in his first landing at Annapolis, and the subsequent address of General Patterson to the Pennsylvania troops, that it might be their duty to "suppress servile insurrections."

Can the people of Virginia be imposed upon by such productions as this of General Beauregard's? Can *any* intelligent community in the South be thus cheated into madness? Surely if they can be, they are to be pitied, and we have only to say that so poor a compliment paid by any high functionary to the intelligence of the people of Maryland, would receive their scorn and reprobation.
—*Baltimore American*, June 18.

Doc. 235.

NINTH REGIMENT N. Y. VOLUNTEERS.

COLONEL, Rush C. Hawkins; Lieutenant-Colonel, George F. Betts; Major, Edwin A. Kimball; Adjutant, James W. Evans; Quartermaster, Henry H. Elliott, Jr.; Paymaster, Thomson P. McElrath; Chaplain, —— Conway; Surgeon, James H. Humphreys; Assistant Surgeon,

——.

Company A—Captain, Andrew Graham; First Lieutenant, Charles Child; Ensign, J. Klingsoehr. Company B—Captain, William

Barnett; First Lieutenant, George A. C. Barnett; Ensign, Thomas Bartholomew. Company C—Captain, Otto W. Parisen; First Lieutenant, John W. Ennis; Ensign, John Mitchell. Company D—Captain, Harry Wright; First Lieutenant, J. S. Harrison; Ensign, H. C. Perley. Company E—Captain, Adolph L. Baire; First Lieutenant, John Bartlett; Ensign, William Bartlett. Company F—Captain, William W. Hammill; First Lieutenant, J. K. Perley; Ensign, W. H. Prescott. Company G—Captain, Edward Jardine; First Lieutenant, Almar P. Webster; Ensign, Thomson P. McElrath. Company H—Captain, Joseph C. Roderigues; First Lieutenant, Lawrence Leaby; Ensign, R. H. Morris. Company I—Captain, H. W. Copcutt; First Lieutenant, —— Roessel; Ensign, John H. Fleming. Company K—Captain, —— Steiner; Lieutenants, —— Silva and —— Doughty.

—*N. Y. World*, June 6.

Doc. 236.

LETTER OF CASSIUS M. CLAY

TO THE LONDON TIMES.

To the Editor of the Times:—

SIR: Allow me your journal to make a few remarks upon the complications of the United States of America, which, I am surprised to find, are so little understood this side of the Atlantic.

1. "*What are we fighting for?*" "We, the people of the United States of America," (to use the language of our Constitution,) are fighting to maintain our *nationality* and the *principles of liberty* upon which it was founded; that nationality which Great Britain has pledged herself, both by past comity and the sacred obligations of treaty, to respect; those great principles of liberty, that all power is derived from the consent of the governed; trial by jury, freedom of speech, and the press; that "without *law* there is no liberty"—which we inherited from Great Britain herself, and which, having been found to lie at the base of all progress and civilization, we desire to perpetuate for ourselves and the future of all nations. The so-called "Confederate States of America" *rebel* against *us*—against our nationality, and against all the principles of its structure. Citizens of the United States—of the one Government (not of Confederated States, as they would have the world believe—but of "us, the people,") they propose, not by common legal consent, but by arms, to sever our nation into separate independencies. Claiming to "be let alone," they conspire against us; seize by force our forts, stores, and arms; appropriate to themselves our mints, moneys, and vessels at sea; capture our armies, and threaten even the capital at Washington!

The word "secession" is used to cover up treason and delude the nations. They stand to us in the relation of one "people:" the idea of "State sovereignty" is utterly delusive. We gave up the old "confederation" to avoid just such complications as have now occurred. The States are by our Constitution deprived of all the rights of independent sovereigns, and the National Government acts not through State organizations, but directly upon the citizens of the States themselves—to that highest of power, the right of *life* and *death*. The States cannot keep an army, or navy, or even repel invasion, except when necessity will not allow time for national action; can make no treaty, nor coin money, nor exercise any of the first great essential powers of "sovereignty." In a word, they can no more "secede" from the Union than Scotland or Ireland can secede from England.

The professed friends of the independence of nations and popular rights, they have not only overthrown the Constitution of the United States, but the constitution of the "Confederate States," themselves, refusing *in every case* to refer their new usurpations to the votes of the people, thus making themselves doubly traitors to both the States and the nation. The despotic rulers over four millions of enslaved Africans, they presume to extend over us, the white races of all nations, the same despotism, by ignoring the political rights of all but their own class, by restrictions upon the popular franchise, by the suppression of the freedom of speech and of the press, by the terrorism of "Lynch-law," or tyrannical enactments, backed by standing armies, to crush out the independence of thought, the ineradicable instincts of our world-wide humanity—with the atrocious dogma that negro slavery is the only basis of conservatism and progressive civilization; and that the true solution of the contest of all time between labor and capital is that *capital* should *own* the *labor*, whether *white* or *black*.

The success of such demands would send the tide of barbarism not only over the millions of the New World and the isles of the western oceans, but roll it back over England and emancipated Europe, and blot out from history this the greatest glory of our times.

2. "*But can you subdue the revolted States?*" Of couse we can. The whole of the revolted States (2,173,000) have not as much white population as the single State of New York (3,851,563) by 1,500,000 people. If all the slave States were to make common cause, they have only 8,907,894 whites, with 4,000,000 slaves, while the Union has about 20,000,000 of homogeneous people, as powerful in peace and war as the world has seen. Intelligent, hardy, and "many-sided," their late apparent lethargy and weakness was the self-possession of conscious strength. When they had made up their minds that *force* was necessary, they moved upon Washington with such speed, numbers, and steadiness as is not surpassed in history. We have the money, (at a lower rate of interest than ever before,) the men, and the command

of the seas, and the internal waters. We can blockade them by sea, and invade them by land, and close up the rebellion in a single year, if we are " *let alone !* " For the population of the slave States is divided, perhaps equally, for and against the Union—the loyal citizens being for the time overawed by the organized conspiracy of the traitors, while the North is united to a man, the late allies of the South—the democratic party—being now more earnest for the subjugation of the rebels than the republicans.

3. " *But can you govern a 'subjugated' people and reconstruct the Union ?* " We do not propose to " subjugate " the revolted States— we propose to put down simply the *rebel* citizens. We go to the rescue of the loyal Unionists of all the States. We carry safety, and peace, and liberty to the Union-loving people of the South, who will of themselves (the tyranny overthrown) send back their representatives to Congress, and the Union will be " *reconstructed* " without a change of a letter in the Constitution of the United States. Did England subjugate Ireland and Scotland ? Are the united kingdoms less homogeneous than of old, before the wars against rebellion ? So will the United States rise from the smoke of battle with renewed stability and power. In turn, now let us ask the British public some questions.

1. " *Where should British honor place her in this contest ?* " We overthrow that political element in America which has all through our history been the studied denouncer and real hater of the British nation, while we have been always from the beginning the friends of England. Because, though under different *forms of government*, we had common sympathies, and a common cause, and, therefore, a common interest. England was the conservator of liberty in Europe—the old world ; we in the new. If the " Confederate States " are right, then is England wrong. If slavery must be extended in America, then must England restore it in the West Indies, blot out the most glorious page of her history, and call back her freedmen into chains ! Let her say to the martyrs of freedom from all the nations who have sought refuge and a magnanimous defence on her shores, return to your scaffold and your prison-house ; England is no more England. Let the *Times* cease to appeal longer to the enlightened opinion of the world : nay, let the statues of the great dead, through which I passed in reverence yesterday, to the Houses of her political intelligence, be thrown from their pedestals, when England shall forget the utterances of her Chathams, her Wilberforces, and her Broughams—that natural justice is the only safe diplomacy and lasting foundation of the independence of nations.

2. " *What is the interest of England now ?* " If we may descend to such inferior appeals, it is clearly the interest of England to stand by the Union of the States. We are her best consumer ; no tariff will materially affect that fact.

We are the best customer of England ; not because we are cotton-growers or cotton-spinners, agriculturists or manufacturers, but because we are *producers and manufacturers*, and have *money to spend*. It is not the South, as it is urged, but the North who are the best consumers of English commerce. The free white laborer and capitalist does now, and always will, consume more than the white master and the slave. The Union and the expansion of the States and the republican policy make us the best market for England and Europe. What has the world to gain—England, France, or any of the powers to gain—by reducing the United States to a Mexican civilization ?

3. " *Can England afford to offend the great nation which will still be ' The United States of America,' even should we lose part of the South ?* " Twenty millions of people to-day, with or without the slave States, in twenty years we will be 40,000,000 ! In another half century we will be *one hundred millions.* We will rest upon the Potomac, and on the west banks of the Mississippi River, upon the Gulf of Mexico. Our railroads will run four thousand miles upon a single parallel, binding our empire, which must master the Atlantic and the Pacific oceans. Is England so secure in the future against home revolt or foreign ambition as to venture now in our need to plant the seeds of revenge in all our future ?

If Ireland, or Scotland, or Wales shall attempt to secede from that beneficent government of the United Kingdom which now lightens their taxation and gives them security and respect at home and abroad, shall we enter into a piratical war with our race and ally, and capture and sell in our ports the property, and endanger the lives of peaceable citizens of the British empire all over the world ? I enter not into the discussion of details. England, then, is our *natural ally.* Will she ignore our aspirations ? If she is just, she ought not. If she is honorable and magnanimous, she cannot. *If she is wise, she will not.*

Your obedient servant, C. M. CLAY,
United States Minister Plenipotentiary, &c., to St. Petersburg.
Mortley's, London, May 17.

THE REPLY OF THE TIMES.

We call attention to the letter of Mr. Clay, Minister from the United States to St. Petersburg. This lively letter-writer proposes six questions—three relating to his own country, three relating to England. The first question he is more successful in asking than answering —" What are we fighting for ? " " We are fighting," says Mr. Clay, " for nationality and liberty." We can understand a fight for nationality between different races, but a fight for nationality between men of the same nationality is to us, we candidly confess it, an inexplicable enigma ; nor can we better understand how a people, fighting to put down rebellion, to force their fellow-citizens to remain in a Confederacy which they detest, and to submit to institutions which they repudiate, can be called the champions of liberty. If the South seriously threatened to conquer the North, to put down trial by jury, freedom of the press, and representative government, the contest must be for liberty; but, as this is not so, the introduction of such topics is mere rhetorical amplification. "Can you subdue the revolted States?" "Of course we can," says Mr. Clay. So on that point there is no more to be said. "Can you reconstruct the Union when one-half of it has conquered the other?" "Nothing easier," says Mr. Clay. The victim of to-day will become the confederate of to-morrow: the traitor will be cast out, and the Union firmer than ever—witness the happy results of the conquest of Ireland by England, repeated over and over again, and always repeated in vain.

Having answered the questions which he supposes to be addressed to him by England, Mr. Clay becomes the questioner, and asks us where our honor would place us in this contest. Clearly by the side of the Union, because, he says, if slavery be extended in America, it must be restored in the West Indies. If any one doubts the force of this demonstration we are sorry for it, for Mr. Clay has no other to offer. Our examiner next asks us to consider our interest. Clearly, he says, it is to stand by the Union, because they are our best customers, and because, though they have done all they can, since the separation of the South gave them the power, to ruin their trade with us, they will, in spite of their own hostile tariff, remain our best customers.

Lastly comes the momentous question, "Can England afford to offend the United States?" "Certainly not," says Mr. Clay, "for in half a century they will amount to a hundred millions of people, and will have railways four thousand miles long." But is Mr. Clay quite sure that, if we should offend them now, the people of America will bear malice for half a century; and, if they do, is he quite certain that his hundred millions must all be members of one Confederacy, and that we may not then, as we might now, secure either half of the Union as our ally in a war against the other? Mr. Clay must really allow us to give our own version of the honor and interest of England. Our honor and interest is to stand aloof from contests which in no way concern us, to be content with our own laws and liberties, without seeking to impose them upon others, "to seek peace and insure it," and to leave those who take to the sword to fall by the sword. In war we will be strictly neutral; in peace we will be the friends of whatever Power may emerge out of the frightful chaos through which Mr. Clay sees his way so clearly. And that neutrality which is recommended alike by our interest and our honor, we will not violate through fear—no, not of a hundred millions of unborn men. Let Mr. Clay and his countrymen look well to the present, and they will find enough to occupy their attention without troubling themselves with long visions of humiliation and retribution, which no man now alive will ever see accomplished.

—*London Times*, May 20.

MINISTER CLAY'S LETTER.

In order to estimate the character and quality of the letter of the American Ambassador to St. Petersburg, which appeared in *The Times* of last Monday, and which naturally attracts a good deal of attention, it is necessary to consider who the writer is, what position he holds in public affairs, and why he wrote that letter.

Mr. Cassius M. Clay is a Kentucky man, and a relative of the late Henry Clay; but he has never followed the political track of his eminent relative. Henry Clay used to boast that it was by his doing that Kentucky was a slave State. At the time of its organization as a State, a majority of the inhabitants desired to emancipate their negroes, and encourage the immigration of free labor; but Mr. Clay discountenanced the notion, and used his influence with success, to induce his neighbors to follow the Southern practice in regard to the tenure of labor. To do this in such a country as Kentucky was to incur a very grave responsibility. The inhabitants have never taken heartily to Slavery with one accord; their soil and climate are favorable to the employment of white as well as free negro labor; they have seen, across the river, Ohio rising into high prosperity, while Kentucky made little or no progress; and there have been not a few citizens in Mr. Clay's State who have always felt that he was answerable for its inferiority in numbers, wealth, and intelligence, to the States on the opposite bank of the Ohio. Among those who have asserted the higher principles on which the State ought to have been organized, and on which it must have flourished beyond perhaps any other region in the Union, Mr. Cassius M. Clay has been the most prominent. For a long course of years he has testified against the false policy of his State, at the risk of his life, and to the great injury of his fortunes. He has been hunted out of the State: he has been imprisoned, prosecuted, threatened, and brought within an inch of his life by Lynch law: and his property has been thrown into the Ohio, burnt, or broken up: but nothing could daunt his spirit, or silence his protests. His Southern habits of self-defence, and his Northern habits of political reasoning, have, on the whole, made him too strong for his enemies. He was an accursed Abolitionist; yet he has lived to come to Europe as an Ambassador. He never belonged to the small body of Abolitionists proper; but, though he carried pistols, and walked about in the style of the Kentucky giants, he was so far an Abolitionist that he early emancipated his own slaves, and has ever since fought a stout battle, by his own printing-press, public speaking, and whole course of life, on behalf of the liberties of whites and blacks, all over the Union.

Such is the man who now, having just landed in England on his way to Russia, is evidently struck with surprise at the ignorance he meets with, or is led to infer from the tone of some of the newspapers on the great American question. The impulse was to write to *The Times*, to set the case clearly before us, and rectify some current mistakes. He has met with rather hard measure in return; but a few more days in England would have shown him that a somewhat closer and clearer statement of his case would have answered better with an audiance which he addresses on the very ground that it is critical instead of sympathetic.

It is certain, however, that *The Times* misapprehends Mr. Clay when it dismisses as mere rhetorical amplification his notice of trial by jury, liberty of the press, and representative government as objects of conflict between North and South. Mr. C. M. Clay has but too much reason to know what the systematic perversion of justice is, under the influence of the Southern oligarchy; and we ourselves need look no further than the condition of the Supreme Court, under Southern management, to be aware what the North has to do in upholding justice. Fair jury trial is not to be had in half the States: the coercion of the press is as bad as any thing Mr. C. M. Clay will find in Russia: and as for representative government, we need only point to the three-fifths suffrage of the slave States, and the virtual exclusion from the polls there of all "mean whites" whose opinions might be supposed likely to be inconvenient. Mr. Clay is certainly justified in saying that the free States are fighting for liberty under these and other forms, as the liberty and the forms have always and everywhere been crushed by Southern rule. But he must allow for Englishmen being unable to imagine, without due explanation, that such fundamental liberties as these are really to be fought for now in the great Republic. The successive Southern Governments of recent years have encroached more and more on these common rights, so that they are now actually in question; but Mr. Clay must remember that, while he has been contending for them at the risk of his life, and to the loss of his fortune, most of us have been supposing them the birthright of every white American, as of ourselves.

The paragraph of Mr. Clay's letter which cites the demands of the Southern Confederacy is certainly accurate. Every point of it may be proved by facts within the memory of most of us; and the one truth, that in every instance the Confederate authorities "have refused to refer their new usurpations to the votes of the people," should be well considered by any Englishman whose mind is open to evidence in the case. The demands are essentially barbaric in such a country at such a date; and Mr. Clay is indisputably justified in saying that the great question of the war is whether this barbarism is or is not to be allowed to swamp the whole Republic. To smile at such a statement as a rhetorical feat is to manifest the ignorance which Mr. Clay proposes to rebuke and correct.

As for whether the North can repress the rebellion, everybody can judge whether Mr. Clay's confidence is rational or not. This may be decided by the facts of population and the comparative resources of food, stores, money, &c. We are not aware that anybody pretends that there is an approach to equality in the resources of the two sections—even if the Border States joined the South, and notwithstanding the enormous embezzlements by which the Federal treasury has been emptied. Mr. Clay's letter, however, confirms the largest estimates yet made of the strength of the loyal Federal element throughout the country. Perhaps the most valuable part of his letter is that which he occupies with a statement, not new to our readers, but too much needed generally, of the relation which the people individually bear to the Government, and with which the States have nothing to do. The real question is, who and how many the rebels are. A little time will show whether there are most Union men or Secessionists in the States over which Mr. Jefferson Davis professes to bear sway. If Mr. Clay is right in believing that any thing like half the citizens are loyal to the Union, they will soon have the means of declaring themselves, and the contest will be at an end. It is certainly true, as Mr. Clay points out, that the political party at the North which is answerable for the long domination of the Pro-Slavery faction at Washington, has become the most loyal of all parties since its Southern comrades took to rebellion.

Another valuable statement of Mr. Clay's is that there is no question of the "subjugation" of any State. Our contemporaries have been raising the difficulty, one after another, of what is to be done with a subjugated territory; and Mr. Davis, the leader of the aggressive party, who met with long-suffering to the last moment, now invites his followers to declare against "subjugation." It is no question of territory or conquest at all. Rebels must return to their allegiance, or obtain terms which do not involve trouble to their loyal neighbors. They will probably have the choice of going away or living in peace and order under the laws. We believe Mr. Clay to be mistaken if he thinks the Constitution may remain precisely what it is. There must be amendments, by which the free States will be released from all implication with Slavery; and there are other points which will not be again sanctioned. But his general statement that the Constitution exists still for the whole country, and that there is no political adversary to subjugate, will be of great use to those who wish to understand the case.

The ignorant complaints of Mr. Lincoln's supposed indecision or apathy must come to an end, now that people are beginning to remember that he proclaimed a term of grace, during which the Secessionists might return to their allegiance. He had enough to do in the interval; and now the time for action has come. Meantime, a schism has taken place in each of the Border States, and in some others, which goes to confirm Mr. Clay's account of the strength of the loyalists wherever they have the means of asserting themselves. Considering this, and the command which the Union forces have, not only of the coasts, but of the Mississippi, it seems probable that the war will be a short one.

Mr. Clay may rely on England wishing and doing no injury to his country and Government; but, if his letter means that he expects us to take an active part, he will, of course, soon learn better. Our sympathies will, we trust, be found on the side of right, freedom, and civilization, but we shall not interfere in any way. Mr. Clay probably refers to privateering invitations to our countrymen, and by this time, he must have heard of the Queen's Proclamation. If he means more, he had better have waited a few days to learn our policy. We do not "ignore" good "aspirations" on any hand; but aspirants must work out their own welfare, and there is every possible evidence before the world's eyes that the American people are abundantly able to do it.

—London News, May 23.

Doc. 237.

GOVERNOR LETCHER'S ORDERS

FOR DESTROYING ROADS AND BRIDGES.

RICHMOND, VA., May 25, 1861.

DEAR SIR:—When you get matters in proper condition at Grafton, take the train some night, run up to Wheeling and seize and carry away the arms recently sent to that place by Cameron, the United States Secretary of War, and use them in arming such men as may rally to your camp. Recover the State arms also recently seized by the malcontents at Kingwood.

It is advisable to cut off telegraphic communication between Wheeling and Washington, so that the disaffected at the former place cannot communicate with their allies at Headquarters. Establish a perfect control over the telegraph, (if kept up,) so that no despatch can pass without your knowledge and inspection before it is sent.

If troops from Ohio and Pennsylvania shall be attempted to be passed on the railroad, *do not hesitate to obstruct their passage by all means in your power, even to the destruction of the road and bridges.*

Having confidence in your discretion, I am sure you will manage all things wisely and well. Yours truly, JOHN LETCHER.

Col. PORTERFIELD, Grafton, Va.

The following is a letter written by Porterfield, in pursuance of the above instructions, to Col. W. J. Willey, whom the Federal troops now have a prisoner at Phillippi:

GRAFTON, May 25, 1861.

DEAR COLONEL: From information just received, it is essential to the safety of my command that the bridges be destroyed as far west as possible. You will please proceed on the next train, and have it carried into effect without delay. Yours, G. A. PORTERFIELD.

To Col. WILLEY.

—Wheeling (Va.) Intelligencer, June 6.

Doc. 238.

THE THIRD MAINE REGIMENT.

THE Third Maine Regiment numbers 1,010 men. They are fully armed and equipped, bringing with them their tents and baggage, and forty horses furnished by the State. They are men accustomed to muscular pursuits, and are of fine size for hard service. The following is the list of the officers:

Colonel, Oliver O. Howard; Lieutenant-Colonel, I. M. Tucker; Major, H. G. Staples; Adjutant, Edward Burt; Assistant Surgeon, Dr. J. Palmer; Chaplain, Rev. Dr. Church; Quartermaster, W. D. Haley; Quartermaster-Sergeant John S. Smith; Hospital Steward, F. H. Getchell; Sergeant-Major, James H. Plasted. Co. A—Captain, Reuben Sawyer; First Lieutenant, John Wiggin. Co. B—Captain, E. A. Batcheldor; First Lieutenant, Albert B. Hall; Second Lieutenant, Edward Bird. Co. C—Captain, William Jarvis; First Lieutenant, James Colson; Second Lieutenant, George Andrew. Co. D—Captain, Charles L. Sampson; First Lieutenant, William H. Watson; Second Lieutenant, Warran H. Madison. Co. E—Captain, David Nash; First Lieutenant, John W. Sanborn; Second Lieutenant, Gorham Johnson. Co. F—Captain, Eldridge G. Savage; First Lieutenant, Royal B. Stearns; Second Lieutenant, Henry A. Boyce. Co. G—Captain, F. S. Hazeltine; First Lieutenant, N. Hanscomb; Second Lieutenant, W. A. Hatch. Co. H—Captain, Wm. S. Heath; First Lieutenant, Frank E. Heath; Second Lieutenant, John R. Day. Co. I—Captain, Moses B. Lakeman; First Lieutenant, Albert R. Quimby; Second Lieutenant, Henry M. Rines. Co. K—Captain, Newell Strout; First Lieutenant, B. S. Kelley; Second Lieutenant, Wm. Elder.

—National Intelligencer, June 9.

This regiment arrived in New York on the 6th of June, by the steamer Bay State, of the Fall River line. It left Augusta, at 5:30 A. M., on Wednesday. In Boston they met with a generous reception, which took the form of a hearty supper. On their arrival at Pier No. 4 North River, they were met by the Committee of the Sons of Maine, who escorted them through Battery Place and Broadway to the White street Arsenal, where the men piled arms, unslung their knapsacks, and made themselves as comfortable as the circumstances would permit. The ceremony of the presentation of a handsome United States flag, here took place. The flag is the gift of the Sons of Maine, residing in New York. Before the ceremony of presentation took place, Col. Howard requested that, if any clergyman was present, the ceremonial should open with a prayer, when the Rev. I. K. Kalloch, formerly of Boston, and now of the Laight street Baptist Church, made an appropriate prayer. The presentation was then made by Stewart L. Woodford, Esq., Assistant United States District Attorney, who spoke as follows:

MEN OF MAINE, CITIZENS OF THE UNION :—I had expected to present this standard to you in the Park. I am somewhat surprised that soldiers of Maine should not have faced the storm, for as soldiers you should have learned to keep your powder dry, and as citizens of a State that has given the temperance law, you ought not to be afraid of God's cold water. After your tiresome journey I shall be very brief. Indeed, words, except those of God-speed and loving and prayerful eulogy in behalf of the dead, are idle now. The time for discussion is past. Open rebellion has trampled upon our Constitution. We have the issue, and in this State men's minds are one. We have laid aside our partisan wranglings and we have sworn as the Lord liveth that treason shall be crushed, (great cheering,) if the Carolinas be a forest of gibbets. My friends, the men of Maine resident in this city have desired to bid you welcome, and almost in the same breath, farewell. They wish to give you as they part a token that shall speak of their brotherhood. Each mother has given to her boy in your ranks that fittest pledge of a mother's love, her Bible. Each dear one has given some pledge that speaks of softer and sweeter hours. Your brethren in this hour of battle would give you a strong man's gift—your country's flag. That flag shall be your guardian. Its starry eyes shall look upon you in watchful love—its blended stripes shall stream above you with protection. It is the flag of history. Those thirteen stripes tell the story of our colonial struggle, of the days of '76. They speak of the wilderness savage, of old Independence Hall, of Valley Forge, and Yorktown. Those stars tell the story of our nation's growth, how it has come from weakness to strength, from thirteen States to thirty-four, until the gleam that shines in the sunrise over the forests of Maine crimsons the sunset's dying beams on the golden sands of California. Let not the story of the flag be folded now, and lost forever. Wherever your axe has rung, the school-house has been reared alongside the hut of the fisherman and the pioneer. Maine is the child of Massachusetts, and in your hearts flows the blood of the Old Bay State. Soldiers! I know that every heart gives an eager response to those which the Massachusetts man uttered as he fell stricken by a Maryland mob, " All hail! to the Stars and Stripes." (Tremendous cheering.) We give this flag to you, and with it we give you our prayers, and not ours alone, but as the loved home circle gathers far in the Pine Tree State, gray-haired fathers and loving mothers will speak in prayer the name of their boy. Sir, in behalf of the Sons of Maine in this city, I give you this flag. Guard it as a woman guards her honor, as children keep the ashes of their father. That flag shall float in triumph, on your avenging march, as those steel fingers point the way through Baltimore to Sumter. That flag shall hover with more than mother's love over your dead. We hear to-day, above the sound of conflict, the voice of the Archangel crying, " Victory is on the side of Liberty, Victory is on the side of Law." With unbroken ranks may your command march beneath its folds. God bless you. Farewell.

Col. Howard responded as follows :—Brethren, sons of Maine, brethren of New York, brethren of the Union, and all present before me, especially those who have been engaged in the presentation of this beautiful emblem of Liberty and Law, through me receive the warmest thanks of the body of brave men that I have the honor to command. I was born in the East, but I was educated by my country. I know no section ; I know no party, and I never did. I know only my country to love it, and my God that is over my country. We go forth to battle, and we go in defence of righteousness and liberty, civil and religious. We go strong in muscle, strong in heart, strong in soul, because we are right. (Cheers.) I have endeavored to live in all good conscience before God, and I go forth to battle without flinching, because the same God that has given his spirit to direct me, has shown me that our cause is righteous, and I could not be better placed than I am now, because he has given me the warm hearts of as noble a regiment as the United States have produced. (Cheers.)

Col. Howard then asked for three for New York, the Union, the Constitution, and for the President of the United States, which were given with tremendous effect, every man springing to his feet the instant the call was made by the Colonel.

A few remarks were then made by the Rev. Dr. Hitchcock, when Mr. Hawkins, in the name of the Committee, invited Col. Howard and the officers of the regiment to dine at the Astor House.

Col. Howard then placed the regiment in charge of Sergeant Fish of Co. F, directing the men to their knapsacks for their dinner.

The Regimental Band of 23 performers, under the leadership of Mr. Fen. G. Barker of Augusta, accompanies the regiment. A full drum corps is also attached.

Col. Howard is a graduate of West Point, and until recently was Professor of Mathematics in the West Point Academy. He says he was fifteen or twenty minutes behind time at Augusta and at Boston, but that he should endeavor to be more punctual in his departure from New York. Such prompt action will astonish the laggards in New York, who are usually three or four hours behind. Major Sowell of Portland accompanies the regiment, by the instructions of the Governor of the State of Maine. The regiment is fully armed and equipped, and have tents and camp equipage. The uniform is Canada gray throughout. The march through Broadway was enthusiastically cheered by those who had courage enough to brave the storm. At 5 o'clock the regiment left for Philadelphia *via* Camden and Amboy. For the purpose of going through Baltimore respectably, the Colonel ordered the men to be supplied with ten rounds each of ball cartridge, which was done on board the Bay State. The Rev. L. C. Lockwood, on behalf of the Y. M. C. A. of New York, presented to the regiment, before their departure, 250 Soldiers' Text Books, donated by a lady of the city, and 200 of Horace Waters' Patriotic Song Books.

—*N. Y. Tribune,* June 7.

Doc. 239.

SPEECH OF J. M. MASON,

AT RICHMOND, VA., JUNE 8.

SOLDIERS OF THE MARYLAND LINE :—I am deputed to do a most grateful duty ; first, in the name of Virginia, to give you an earnest and cordial welcome to the "Old Dominion ;" and next, to present to you, in behalf of the ladies of Maryland, this flag. I see, soldiers of Maryland, that you are "rough and ready"—the highest honor of a soldier in revolutionary times. We all know who you are. We all know what brought you here, and we are all ready, as I trust you have experienced, to extend to you a soldier's welcome—the only welcome, indeed, that can be extended in times like these. Your own honored State is with us heart and soul in this great controversy. By your enterprise, your bravery, and your determined will, you have escaped from the thraldom of tyranny which envelopes that State ; and you know, I know—for I have been among its people—we all know, that the same spirit which brought you here, actuates thousands who remain at home. (Applause.) I welcome you, soldiers of Maryland, upon the threshold of the second great war of independence—a war that will be transmitted by history to the future as the greatest of two wars of independence ; a war that is waged against the South with less provocation, less reason, less regard to humanity and to honor, than was that waged by the mother country in 1776.

Your presence here is proof that you participate in this sentiment. And I tell you further, my countrymen, in view of these circumstances, there is not a man among you who will dare to return to Maryland with that flag dishonored. Not one. I tell you further, there is not a man among you who will dare to return to Maryland except as a soldier in victory. Do you ask me why ? Because we are engaged in a great and holy war of self-defence. In after ages, when history records the transactions of this epoch—when the passions of men

shall have subsided, and the historian can take a calm and philosophical view of the events which have led to the present collision between the two sections, he will write that the people of the Southern States understood and protected civil liberty, and that the misguided North either did not comprehend, or abandoned it ? For what have we witnessed ? The spectacle of the Chief Justice of the United States, the man who stands at the head of the principal department of the Federal Government—the man who has illustrated in his life, for more than four generations, all that adorns honor, virtue, and patriotism—a native-born citizen of your own State of Maryland—Roger B. Taney—that man has put the judicial fiat of condemnation upon the Government of the United States for its shameless abandonment of the very cornerstone of our liberties. A native Marylander, he remains at home to defend the last refuge of civil liberty against the atrocious aggressions of a remorseless tyranny. I honor him for it ; the world will honor him, posterity will honor him ; and there will be inscribed on his monument the highest tribute ever paid to a man. He has stood bravely in the breach, and interposed the unspotted arm of justice between the rights of the South and the malignant usurpation of power by the North. There he still remains, " a cloud by day and a pillar of fire by night," to direct the welfare of our nation in this atrocious aggression upon our liberty.

Now, my countrymen, why are you here ? What has brought you across the border ? What is your mission to Virginia ? You tell your own tale. You have arms in your hands ; you are under a gallant leader, and you are to march under a flag honored by the ladies of your own State, worked by their own fair hands. You are here not merely to fight our battles. No, I am not so selfish as to presume that ; but to fight the battles of civil liberty in behalf of the entire South. You are on a high mission.

You are not the first Marylanders who have crossed the border. We had, in the days of the first Revolution, a Maryland line, whose name has passed into history without one blot upon its fair escutcheon—a Maryland line who illustrated upon every field in the South their devotion to the civil liberty of that day—a Maryland line, who, in the remote savannahs of the Carolinas, spilled their blood like water at Camden, at Guilford Court-House, at the Cowpens, and at Eutaw, where the last battle was fought, and the enemy finally surrendered. They were your ancestry. They travelled barefooted, unclothed, without blankets or tents, and but few muskets, and you came after them. But you have this peculiar distinction : You are volunteers in a double sense—you are volunteers for the war, and you are volunteers for the great cause of the South against the aggressions of the North. You are no strangers ; you are our neighbors. My own home is upon the confines of your State. I went there, four weeks ago, immediately after Virginia had denounced the unholy movements in the North, to learn the spirit of your people. I went to Frederickstown, where the Legislature were assembled, anxious to ascertain whether Virginia could rely upon you in the hour of trial. I knew the political incubus by which your people were crushed to the earth; but such were the indications I perceived on every side, that when I returned to Virginia I unhesitatingly reported that Maryland is with the South. I staked my word upon it as a man of principle and a man of truth. The giant arm of the oppressor has been too strong for the time being, but the spirit is still alive, unsubdued and unrepressed. You are here to confirm this fact by your presence.

You are in Richmond. What is Richmond? It is a large city—a city of gallant men and refined women; a city whose inhabitants are engaged in all the useful and honorable pursuits of life tending to the advance of civilization and prosperity. At the present moment, however, Richmond is a huge camp, where but one mind, one heart, and one determination animates every occupant, man, woman, and child. (Applause.) Our wives, mothers—and I appeal to the ladies, if I may not also say our sweethearts—have entered into it with a zest, which shows that their hearts and affections are fully in the work. You will have no child's play. There is no time now for vain boasting. I confide as much as I can in the prowess of the men of this section, and you will be false to the fame of your fathers if you are not victors; but your enemy relies upon mere brute force. There are doubtless brave soldiers among them whom it will be hard to conquer, but you will remember that you are fighting for your fathers, mothers, and firesides. They are mercenaries fighting for pay, you are men fighting for your homes and rights. All you require is subsistence. "Give us," you say, "the means of living, the arms to fight with, and show us the enemy." (Applause.) It may be, that in the providences of war, not one among all those who are before me will return. You have come here, if necessary, to lay your lives upon the altar of your country, and I feel assured that every man will do his duty.

I will tell you an incident connected with the Alabama troops. They were attended by a minister of the Gospel, who was a guest at my house. He told me that he had with him a purse of gold, which had been given to him by the parents of two young men in the ranks, with the injunction that it should be sacredly preserved during the war, unless his sons should fall upon the field of battle. Then, said the father, "Give them a Christian burial." There was a patriot father, who had devoted his sons to the service of his country, and that man does not stand alone.

Such is the object with which you have engaged in this war. The true duty of the soldier is not merely to fight a battle or kill an enemy. He has also to endure the trials of the camp; the weariness of the forced march; the vigilance of day and night; the restraints of discipline, and the patience to bear with discomforts and disappointments. This is the real test of courage, and he who comes out of the war with the reputation of having thus done his duty through the sunshine and through storm, is the true man, and the thorough soldier.

But I will not detain you longer, except to discharge the grateful duty which remains, of presenting to you in behalf of the ladies of Baltimore this beautiful banner. There it is unfurled before you for the first time. There are emblazoned the fifteen stars of the Southern States, looking prospectively to the day when they will all be with us! The star of Maryland is among them, and the women of your State have put it there, confiding it to your safe keeping. Look upon it as a sacred trust. In passing through the storm of battle, it may be tattered and soiled, but I believe I can say that you will bring it back without a spot of dishonor upon it. But you are not only to return that flag here—you are to take it back to Baltimore. (Cheers, and cries of "We will.") It came here in the hands of the fair lady who stands by my side, who brought it through the camp of the enemy, with a woman's fortitude, courage, and devotion to our cause; and you are to take it back to Baltimore, unfurl it in your streets, and challenge the applause of your citizens. (Applause.)

—*Richmond Dispatch*, June 10.

Doc. 240.

PROCLAMATION BY GOV. HICKS.

State of Maryland, Executive Chamber, }
Frederick, June 7, 1861. }

Whereas, Some of the arms and accoutrements belonging to the State have been placed beyond the control of the constituted authorities, as is believed for disloyal purposes, by persons connected with some of the military companies of the city of Baltimore, in violation of their duties as soldiers and as citizens; and whereas, a very large number of the arms and accoutrements of the State still remain in the hands of the various military companies of said city, some of whom are known to be disloyal to their country; and whereas, there are just grounds for apprehending that a portion of said arms and accoutrements are about to be carried beyond the limits of this State for hostile purposes, and others are about to be destroyed or concealed—

Now, therefore, I, Thomas Holliday Hicks, Governor of Maryland, by virtue of the power vested in me by the law of the State, do hereby, by this my proclamation, warn and enjoin upon all citizens of Baltimore, the loyal as well as the disloyal, having in their hands and possession any arms and accoutrements belonging to the State, to surrender and deliver up the same to Colonel E. R. Petherbridge, who is

Doc.—33

fully authorized to reclaim and take possession of such arms and accoutrements, and to take all necessary steps, on behalf of the State, to secure from those to whom said arms and accoutrements have been confided, a strict compliance with the condition of their bonds for the preservation of such arms and accoutrements, and for their re-delivery to the State whenever thereto required by my order.

Given under my hand.

THOMAS H. HICKS.

—*N. Y. Express*, June 10.

Doc. 241.

GEN. MORRIS'S PROCLAMATION.

GENERAL MORRIS has issued the following proclamation, in connection with that of General McClellan:

HEAD-QUARTERS OF UNITED STATES VOLUNTEERS,
WESTERN VIRGINIA, GRAFTON, June 8, 1861.

VIRGINIANS:—In issuing the above proclamation of the commanding General, Department of Ohio, I have now the pleasure of announcing that we have routed and completely discomfited the secessionists in arms at Philippi. Their forces are demoralized, desertions are numerous, and the panic-stricken remnant has taken refuge in the passes of the mountains. Western Virginia is free from enemies to her freedom and peace. In full confidence of your ability and desire to protect yourselves, I now call upon you to come to the support of your constitutional Government. I am empowered to muster you into the service of the United States, to serve only in defence of your own soil. Arms and munitions will be furnished you. Assemble at once at your various county seats, and report to me for instructions. Cavalry and infantry will be received at once.

T. A. MORRIS,
Brig.-Gen. Commanding U. S. Troops at Philippi.

—*Baltimore (Md.) American*, June 12.

Doc. 242.

THE VERMONT REGIMENT.

HEAD-QUARTERS 1ST REGIMENT, V. V. M.,
NEWPORT NEWS, VA., June 1, 1861.

WHEN I wrote you last, our regiment was located in the Hygeia Hotel, a house that is capable of accommodating 1,000 instead of 6,000 guests, and in which eleven of us were packed in a room 12 × 16, instead of the whole company; but we have changed our position twice since then, the particulars of which I will endeavor to relate to you.

I see by the papers that our regiment captured Hampton, taking 300 prisoners, and have performed sundry other exploits, which would almost render us immortal. May be I had better say nothing of our doings, fearing the truth would lower us in the eyes of our friends; yet I think I will proceed, for the truth will out eventually.

May 23.—Five companies of our regiment marched over to Hampton, a village of about 1,000 inhabitants, containing a female seminary —it is three miles N. W. of the fort. On coming near the village, a secession officer rode up to Col. Phelps, asking him the object of his visit? The reply was, that we intended to destroy any hostile battery that might be erected there, and disperse any armed force. He was requested to remain where he was while the said officer might return and consult with his superior, but the Col. told him he thought he should continue on. The secession officer rode quickly back, and soon was seen a thick black smoke arising. The Col. taking the first platoon of the Swanton company, pushed forward double quick and soon discovered that the bridge had been set on fire in the centre. Three barrels of tar were set on fire and were burning briskly, but our boys soon extinguished the fire by tearing up the planks and throwing them into the water. Soon the bridge was mended and we all marched across, but no enemy appeared against us. The officer, I know not his name, said they had nothing but a home guard, formed to protect their homes, and did not wish to quarrel with us. Upon that our Col. gave the order "right about face, march," and we were on our way back to the fort. Thus ended the battle of Hampton. A negro told us they had a small field-piece on the bridge, which they thought at first they would fire at us three or four times and then run, but upon seeing so many of us they threw their cannon into the water and ran away without firing a shot.

All the white inhabitants fled at our approach, leaving none but the darkies to receive us; they flocked around us in large numbers. They do not fear us, notwithstanding their masters telling them that the Yankees would kill every one of them, or else take them and set them hard at work. They say they never have had so many holidays before in their lives as they have had since we came here; their masters have run away, leaving them to shift for themselves. Every day numbers of them come into camp from places twenty miles distant, asking protection. They all unite in berating their masters, not wishing to see them again. One negro came into camp the other day, who had been shot not long since by his master for attempting to escape. He says he would kill him if he could get a chance. Judging from what I have seen and heard, it would not be a very difficult matter to free every negro in the State. They call us Mr. Lincoln's men. They like them they say. They bring in eggs, strawberries, &c., to camp, and give us all the information they possess of the movements of the rebels. They will be a great aid to us in the great struggle which is commencing.

May 25.—We were ordered to leave the hotel, as Gen. Butler desired it for a general hospital. We marched across the bridge on the north side of the fort, and encamped on

Seager's farm. Just west of us are encamped the Troy Regiment, and north of *them* are Col. Duryea's Regiment of N. Y. Zouaves. They are a rough set of fellows, aching for a fight. Not finding any other enemy, they have pitched into the rebels' cattle, hogs, and any thing else eatable wherever they could find them. The country near them will suffer wherever they go. You little know in Vermont the evils of war. Could you but see, as I have seen, houses for miles around, stripped of every thing, windows broken, every thing left desolate, you might have an idea of the state of things here.

Sunday, May 26.—We had divine service, conducted by our chaplain, Rev. Mr. Stone. It was very solemn to us, I assure you. He spoke very feelingly, having a good occasion for it; for, on the morrow, it was expected by every man in the regiment that we should have a severe conflict with the enemy, and not a few of us might fall. He exhorted us to be true to our country, and do battle in its cause manfully, praying that the God of Battles might watch over us, bringing us safely and victoriously through the fight, and that every man might be prepared to meet whatever fate awaited him.

May 27.—We were aroused at 5½ o'clock A. M.; ate our breakfast; filled our haversacks with two days' rations, consisting of four hard crackers and two pieces of fat pork; struck our tents, and were on the march at 6 o'clock A. M. We knew not where our destination was to be, but expected to go to Sewell's Point, to take those batteries that our ships have been engaging with so many times. We expected to have a hard fight, for we supposed the enemy had a large force to receive us; but not a man in the regiment hung back; all were ready and eager for the fray. Some that had been sick, and, in fact, were unfit for duty, refused to stay behind, but shouldered their muskets and went with us. We embarked on board the steamer Cataline, and were soon steaming up the river. An hour's sail brought us to this point, where we landed unmolested. The Harriet Lane was here to protect us, should the enemy appear. The Rutland and Middlebury companies had gone on ahead. They were drawn up in line along the shore, and had nothing to do but to wait patiently our coming. After marching to the place intended for our camp—a wheat field—and having our guns, knapsacks, &c., all went at work hauling up cannon, bringing stores, &c. After this, "the boys" went to work fixing places to sleep in, by putting up rails and covering them with brush, under which I enjoyed as good a night's rest as I ever had on a feather bed in Old Vermont. I was tired. Our tents, camp utensils, &c., were left behind. The Fourth Massachusetts Regiment followed us, and were stationed on our left.

May 28.—Our camp equipage arrived this morning, and soon our "houses" were up again, ready for their old occupants. The Seventh Regiment, N. Y. V. M., was landed here this morning. They lay off the landing all day yesterday, unable to land; the boat being of too heavy draught to land at the wharf, and the wind blew too hard for them to land in small boats. They are placed on our right. All of them are Germans, with two or three exceptions; many of them are unable to talk or even understand English. We may have some trouble with them, especially when they are on guard. It would please you to see them when they are relieving guard, or when some one attempts to pass them—they cannot go through with the formality of receiving the countersign and passing a man. Some of *our* boys make some ludicrous mistakes occasionally. As soon as our tents were pitched, we were set at work fortifying our camp, (a plan of which I will endeavor to make and send you.) Since Tuesday we have been hard at work, not even ceasing on this, the Sabbath day; for we wish to be prepared for the enemy. We sleep on our arms every night, expecting an attack from 8,000 men that are preparing to march upon us from Yorktown. Our Colonel has command of the post, which does not please the Massachusetts boys. There are about 2,500 men here, including a few regulars who are to work the cannon; of which we have four fine brass field-pieces: one 6-pounder, placed on the extreme right; one 12-pounder, on the right of our regiment; one 6-pounder, on its left; and one 12-pounder, on the extreme left. A battery of heavy guns is being erected on the shore, to command the river. I do not know how many guns are to be placed there, as they have not arrived here yet.

Look upon the map of this State, and you will see that the James River, near its mouth, runs a few miles directly south, and then turns to the east; in this bend, on the south side, is our camp. The name of it is Camp Butler, and the name of the place is Newport News. There is no village here; though there are two wharves and one store. The merchant continues his trade, and says he is glad we came, as now he has customers, while before he had none. This point is nine miles west of Fortress Monroe. A boat runs up here every afternoon. The Harriet Lane remains here to come to our aid. She is a small vessel, carrying eight or nine guns;) but is a tough customer to deal with, as the rebels will find. No rations were dealt out to us till the second night after our arrival; consequently, some of our boys became quite hungry, having had nothing but those four crackers, and some of them took the liberty of stepping out and helping themselves to some eatables that the rebels had left behind in their sudden flight. Where a man remained at home and attended to his business, he was not meddled with; but when they found a house deserted, and the owner a soldier in the rebel army, *his* eatables were not allowed to spoil. I do not think there are ten white men within five miles of us, among the farmers. I know of but two, and those boys who have been out, saw none in their travels. But there are plenty of negroes; and they bring forth their masters' stores plentifully. The boys of our regiment generally remained in camp, and attended to building the embankments. But the Massachusetts boys and the " Dutchmen" went into it quite extensively. The latter have filled their camp with horses, mules, carts, wagons, and often furniture; but Gen. Butler has put a stop to such proceedings. He has given strict orders against any one's plundering the enemy, and the consequence was, that the day his order was received, over fifty men were put under guard. They were out when the order was received, and when they returned, laden with spoil, *both* were taken care of, much to their chagrin. But four or five of our regiment were caught in such disgraceful acts.

Night before last, those long looked-for provisions came, and if you ever wished to see a set of fellows highly delighted, you ought to have seen the B. L. G. When box after box and package after package were opened, containing the choicest delicacies of " home," many a blessing was showered upon the generous donors, as we ate the cakes. and cheese, butter, and other dainties too numerous to mention—delicacies that we have been strangers to for four weeks—I was going to say four months, for that *seems* to be the length of time that I have been absent. But when you come to be deprived of the best of living, and feed upon the hardest of crackers, salt pork, beef and coffee, you will then be able to appreciate food that you now call quite plain.

If we could but have more vegetables we could get along very well. We do not expect pies or cakes, nor nice wheat or brown bread, but we *do* think we ought to have something better in that line, than these crackers, (shingles the boys call them,) called pilot-bread. If any more provisions are sent, put in a good supply of Boston or soda crackers, and some vegetables.

Those Havelocks were received before we came here, and right glad were we to get them. Our faces and necks have become badly sunburnt, so that some of them were quite sore. All are black enough, I assure you.

The good people of Burlington will be long remembered by the Light Guard. We shall endeavor to merit the kindness bestowed upon us, and not betray the trust reposed in us by turning from the enemy as long as there is hope of success.

A few of our company are sick, but none are dangerous. All are doing well.

The embankment we have been building, is 110 rods long, 6½ feet high, and 5 feet wide at the top, and 10 at the bottom, sloping outwards to the bottom of the ditch, but so steep that you could not climb up to the top. The inside of the wall is perpendicular, large timbers being set in the ground, (most of which were brought from the woods by hand,) and

the dirt pounded down hard. The ditch is 7 feet deep and 8 feet wide at the top; the bottom is to be set full of wooden pickets, sharpened at the top. It would not be very pleasant to fall into it. One part is built, and we are at work on the bastion on the right, and shall have to help the others, as I fear these never will be completed.

I find the Vermonters are a little better to work than most other men that I have seen.

Our tents have little piazzas built out in front covered with boughs, which makes them quite pleasant in this hot climate, the thermometer standing at from 70 to 80 degrees.

I am thus particular about our fortification, thinking that any thing we fellows do would be interesting to you.   A. S. H.

Doc. 243.

ADDRESSES OF THE CONVENTION OF THE BORDER STATES.

To the people of the United States—

FELLOW-CITIZENS: The delegates to a convention of the Border Slave States, assembled in the city of Frankfort, desire to address you in relation to the present condition of the country.

None of us have ever expected to live to see the spectacle now exhibited in our distracted land. The cry to arms resounds throughout our borders, and in a few short weeks we have seen all over the land the marshalling of troops ready for the conflict. The pursuits of peace are neglected and abandoned, and the fell spirit of war has seized almost every heart, until even gentle and tender woman yields to the fierce impulse, and encourages the strife, and the maternal eye scarce gathers a tear as the son seizes his arms, and rushes toward the field of carnage and of death.

If this warlike spirit—this terrible energy—were displayed in preparing to meet the legions of an invading enemy, our hearts would exult in the exhibition of the martial spirit of our countrymen; but alas! the combatants are descendants of sires who stood side by side in the day of battle, to maintain the independence of our country, and in the approaching conflict brother is to fall by the hand of brother.

Can we hope in this day of fierce passion that our voice, crying for peace, will be heard? Will any portraiture of the horrors of civil war, that we can give, have any influence with those who are rushing madly on to destroy each other? We fear not. States which should have been with us, and whose voice would have increased the potency of our demands for peace, have been seized with the prevailing madness, and have rushed to arms. Still we feel bound to make our voice to be heard, with the hope that our words will have their influence at some day, when men shall behold the wasting and desolation that their madness has produced.

All the slave States except four are arrayed in hostility to the General Government, and are demanding that the confederation which they have formed shall be recognized as a separate sovereign nation. The process by which they have attempted to form themselves into a distinct nation has been, for each State by itself to declare all connection with the General Government terminated, and then unite in forming a confederation among themselves.

Our present purpose does not require us to discuss the propriety of the acts of these States, yet it may be proper for us to say, that they find no warrant in any known principle of our Government, and no justification in the facts existing when they seceded.

While these States claim that their sovereignty as a nation shall be recognized, and have collected armies to make good their claim, the Government of the United States insists that the ordinances of secession are utterly void, and that the Constitution and laws of the United States are still in force within the seceded States, just as they are within any of the other States, and to maintain this position armies are rapidly gathering on the borders of the seceded States.

If there could be any intervention by which the shedding of blood and the desolation of civil war could be avoided, the practical good sense of the American people might discover some mode of adjusting the difficulties which would be alike honorable and beneficial to both the contending parties. But while one side demands the recognition of its sovereignty, and the other insists that such a recognition is a constitutional impossibility, it is manifest that there can be no arbiter but the sword, unless the people themselves, acting upon and through their representatives, State and national, shall interpose, arrest the strife, and enforce a settlement without bloodshed. If any terms or adjustment would be satisfactory to both parties, which would fall short of the recognition of the sovereignty of the seceded States, and still satisfy them, and short of the obedience of the seceded States to the Constitution and laws of the United States, and still satisfy the people of the United States, it is the duty of each party to notify the other of such terms as would be satisfactory, so that an attempt at adjustment might be made.

But we repeat, if the recognition of the sovereignty of the seceded States continue a *sine qua non*, and if the Government continue to disclaim the constitutional power to make such recognition, there is no peaceful solution of the difficulty possible, other than such as the people themselves may, by their action, produce.

It is proper for us to say that in our opinion the Constitution delegates to no one department of the Government, nor to all of them combined, the power to destroy the Government itself, as would be done by the division of the country into separate confederacies, and that the obligation exists to maintain the Con-stitution of the United States, and to preserve the Union unimpaired.

It has been suggested, in quarters entitled to the highest respect, that the independence of the States which have seceded might be acknowledged by a National Convention, adopting an amendment to the Constitution for that purpose, as such an amendment would have the support and acquiescence of the seceded States. But we leave that for the decision of the people and their representatives, when they shall feel the imperative necessity of such a settlement.

We now turn to the consideration of what ought to be done for the purpose of quieting apprehension within the few slave States which still adhere to the Union established by their fathers.

We ask no concession of new or additional rights. We do not fear any immediate encroachment upon our rights as slave States. The amendment to the Constitution proposed by the last Congress gives assurance that at present there is no danger that our rights will be assailed. But we are few in number, and the preponderance of the free States is continually increasing. The security to our rights now afforded by the sense of justice in the minds of the free States may be lost by a change of popular feeling in the future. One great object in constitutions is to protect the rights of minorities.

In the Constitution there are general grants of power to the Congress of the United States, which might be perverted to our injury, contrary to the spirit of the instrument, and still the letter of the grant be claimed to authorize the injurious legislation. Such are the power "to regulate commerce between the States," and the power of "exclusive legislation over the District of Columbia," and over "forts, dock-yards, and arsenals in the several States." It would not now be claimed by Congress that these grants authorized an interference in the sale of slaves between the people of different States, nor would it be claimed that they authorized the abolition of slavery in the District of Columbia, while Maryland and Virginia remained slave States, nor the like abolition in forts and other places within slave States. But what will be claimed in the future we cannot know. So also, in relation to the territories belonging to the United States. While we are aware that all the territories, then unorganized, were organized by acts of the last Congress which contain no prohibition of slavery, and while we know that this was the action of a Congress in which the free States had the control at the time the acts were passed, still these are but acts of Congress, subject to repeal or alteration as public feeling may change under temporary excitement.

It is but just that the rights of the slave States, now in a small minority of the whole States, should be guarded in the particulars mentioned by such constitutional guarantees as shall render them secure against future legislation in times of excitement. Our distinguished fellow-citizen, the Hon. John J. Crittenden, for the purpose of securing by constitutional guarantees rights already possessed, presented to Congress certain propositions to amend the Constitution, which met with general approval, and were satisfactory to us and to our people, and those propositions, as originally offered, or any that are equivalent, would be now satisfactory and would quiet apprehensions that exist to some extent in the minds of real friends of the Union, and which are industriously excited by those who are enemies of the Union and of the people. Whether any such constitutional guarantees would have the effect of reconciling any of the seceded States to the Government from which they have torn themselves away we cannot say, but we allow ourselves to hope that the masses in those States will, in time, learn that the dangers they were made to fear were greatly exaggerated, and that they will then be disposed to listen to the calls of interest and of patriotism, and return to the family from which they have gone out. One effect of giving such guarantees, certainly will be to prove to the world, by the frank recognition of the rights of the few slave States adhering to the Union, that the States which have seceded have abandoned the best Government in the world, without any good or sufficient cause.

It may be urged that there are not now a sufficient number of States acting in the Union to ratify any such constitutional amendments as will furnish the guarantees we require. But it is to be remembered that there is no time fixed by the Constitution for such ratification, and if they should be ratified by the free States, then at the end of the present civil war, terminate as it may, either in the restoration of the seceded States to the Union, or in the establishment of their separate national existence, there will be the number of States required for the ratification.

Fellow-citizens of the United States, you are about to be engaged in a war in which the horrors that ordinarily attend that state are likely to be aggravated by the fact that you are of the same family, and have long lived together in intimate intercourse and in friendly relations. The kind feelings that once existed have been changed to bitterness, soon to degenerate, it may be, into deadly animosity. We desire to remind you that you are contending about a question of principle upon which we would fain believe that you are on each side convinced that you are right. It is no longer a question of party politics, no longer a question about the right to hold slaves in territories, or to retake them when they escape; the question now to be settled is, Whether we shall live in the same Union as formerly, or whether our fathers formed a government upon such principles that any one State may, at her own pleas-

ure, without the consent of the others, and without responsibility to any human power, withdraw from her connection with the Government and claim to be sovereign as a separate nation. It will be readily seen that this, as a question of principle, is not affected by the number of States that have withdrawn. It would have been well if this question could have been solved in some other mode than by a resort to war; but it may be that nothing but a divine interposition now can determine it by other means. A war upon such a question ought not to produce any higher exasperation or excite any greater degree of animosity than is incident to all wars. In the mean time let the spirit of humanity and of the high civilization of the age, strip this war of the horrors that generally attend such civil strife.

Our States desire, and have indicated a purpose to take no part in this war, and we believe, that in this course we will ultimately best serve the interests of our common country. It is impossible that we should be indifferent spectators; we consider that our interests would be irretrievably ruined by taking part in the conflict on the side where the strongest sympathies of our people are, and that our sense of honor and of duty requires that we should not allow ourselves to be drawn or driven into a war in which other States, without consulting us, have deliberately chosen to involve themselves. Our safety and our dignity as among the most powerful of the slave States demand of us that we take this position. If the time shall come when our friendly mediation may arrest the further progress of the strife, our most earnest and strenuous efforts shall not be wanting to bring about peace, and it is by such efforts that we hope to serve the interests of our country.

And now, in conclusion, we make our solemn appeal to the people of the United States. This is your Government—its preservation is your preservation—its overthrow is your ruin, and you are the rightful arbiters of its fate.

We hope you will take the subject of this address to your own consideration. Act with the energy and decision of a free people. In you and you alone we have confidence. You have the intelligence and the power to rule this fearful crisis. Make known your will in some emphatic form, that shall give it authority with your representatives everywhere.

May we not earnestly hope that you, the people, the whole people, without regard to parties or sections, will be able to command a settlement of the national difficulties, and will see the propriety and necessity of having a cessation of present hostilities, so that the measures of pacification which your wisdom may devise, can be calmly considered by your constitutional authorities.

We venture to suggest for your consideration and action, two specific propositions as most likely to lead to pacification:

1st. That Congress shall at once propose

such constitutional amendments as will secure to slaveholders their legal rights, and allay their apprehensions in regard to possible encroachments in the future.

2d. If this should fail to bring about the results so desirable to us and so essential to the best hopes of our country, then let a voluntary convention be called, composed of delegates from the people of all the States, in which measures of peaceable adjustment may be devised and adopted, and the nation rescued from the continued horrors and calamities of civil war.

To our fellow-citizens of the North we desire to say: Discard that sectional and unfriendly spirit, manifested by teaching and action, which has contributed so much to inflame the feelings of the Southern people, and justly create apprehension on their part of injury to them.

To our fellow-citizens of the South we desire to say: Though we have been greatly injured by your precipitate action, we would not now reproach you as the cause of that injury, but we entreat you to re-examine the question of the necessity for such action, and that if you find it has been taken without due consideration, as we verily believe, and that the evils you apprehended from a continuance in the Union were neither so great nor so unavoidable as you supposed, or that Congress is willing to grant adequate securities, then we pray you to return promptly to your connection with us, that we may be, in the future, as we have been in the past, one great, powerful, and prosperous nation.

Indications have already been afforded that a Divine power is ready to interpose and prevent brethren from slaughtering each other. While the bombardment of Fort Sumter continued, no life was lost. When a Providential interposition was no longer needed to prevent the effusion of blood in civil strife, several lives were lost in the performance of a mere ceremony. We would invoke the presence and aid of that Power to preserve our fellow-citizens, on both sides, from slaughter, and we would commit the interests of our distracted country to His hands who can bring forth peace and order out of strife and confusion when man's wisdom utterly fails.

J. J. CRITTENDEN, *President.*
JAS. GUTHRIE,
H. R. GAMBLE,
WM. A. HALL,
J. B. HENDERSON,
WM. G. POMEROY,
     } Of Missouri.
R. K. WILLIAMS,
ARCH'D DIXON,
F. M. BRISTOW,
JOSHUA F. BELL,
C. A. WICKLIFFE,
G. W. DUNLAP,
J. F. ROBINSON,
JNO. B. HUSTON,
ROB'T RICHARDSON,
JOHN CALDWELL, of Tennessee,

TO THE PEOPLE OF KENTUCKY.

Having been elected by you as your delegates to "A Convention of the Border Slave States and such other slave States as have not passed ordinances of secession," with power to meet with delegates from other States in convention, "to consult on the critical condition of the country, and agree upon some plan of adjustment;" and having met, at Frankfort, on the 27th of May, in pursuance of the act; we deem it proper to inform you, briefly, of what was done by us in the Convention.

It was a matter of regret to us that while the call for this Convention originated in Virginia and had, apparently, the concurrence of all the Border Slave States, yet there were delegates in attendance from Kentucky and Missouri only. One representative chosen by the counties of McMinn and Sevier, in Tennessee, appeared, and, although not coming with such credentials as were necessary to constitute him a delegate, he was invited to participate in our deliberations.

After a continuous session from day to day, during which the condition of the country, and the various causes that led to it were maturely considered, it was resolved that the Convention should address an appeal to the people of the United States, and the delegates from Kentucky determined to present to you a separate address, in which views of your members should be embodied. In the discharge of this duty we now attempt to address you.

Your State, on a deliberate consideration of her responsibilities—moral, political, and social—has determined that the proper course for her to pursue is to take no part in the controversy between the Government and the seceded States but that of *mediator* and *intercessor*. She is unwilling to take up arms against her brethren residing either North or South of the geographical line by which they are unhappily divided into warring sections. This course was commended to her by every consideration of patriotism, and by a proper regard for her own security. It does not result from timidity; on the contrary, it could only have been adopted by a brave people—so brave that the least imputation on their courage would be branded as false by their written and traditional history.

Kentucky was right in taking this position—because, from the commencement of this deplorable controversy, her voice was for reconciliation, compromise, and peace. She had no cause of complaint against the General Government, and made none. The injuries she sustained in her property from a failure to execute laws passed for its protection, in consequence of illegal interference by wicked and deluded citizens in the free States, she considered as wholly insufficient to justify a dismemberment of the Union. That, she regarded as no remedy for existing evils, but an aggravation of them all. She witnessed, it is true, with deep concern, the growth of a wild and frenzied fanaticism in one section, and a reckless and defiant spirit in another, both equally threatening destruction to the country; and tried earnestly to arrest them, but in vain. We will not stop to trace the causes of the unhappy condition in which we are now placed, or to criminate either of the sections to the dishonor of the other, but can say that we believed both to have been wrong, and, in their madness and folly, to have inaugurated a war that the Christian world looks upon with amazement and sorrow; and that Liberty, Christianity, and Civilization stand appalled at the horrors to which it will give rise.

It is a proud and grand thing for Kentucky to stand up and say, as she can, truthfully, in the face of the world, " We had no hand in this thing; our skirts are clear." And, in looking at the *terrorism* that prevails elsewhere—beholding freedom of speech denied to American citizens, their homesteads subjected to lawless visitation, their property confiscated, and their persons liable to incarceration and search—how grandly does she not loom up, as she proclaims to the oppressed and miserable, We offer you a refuge! Here, constitutional law, and respect for individual rights, still exist! Here is an asylum where loyalty to the name, nation, and Flag of the Union predominates; and here is the only place, in this lately great Republic, where true freedom remains—that freedom for which our fathers fought—the citizen being free to speak, write, or publish any thing he may wish, responsible only to the laws, and not controlled by the violence of the mob.

Is not this an attitude worthy of a great people, and do not her position and safety require her to maintain it? If she deviates from it; if she suffers herself in a moment of excitement to be led off by sympathy with either side or the other—to ally herself with either section—inevitable and speedy ruin must fall upon her. What reason can be urged to incline her to such a fatal step? She is still, thank God, a member of the Union, owing constitutional allegiance to it—an allegiance voluntarily given, long maintained, and from which she has derived countless benefits. Can she, by her own act, forfeit this allegiance, and by the exercise of any constitutional power sever herself from that Government? In our opinion the statement of the proposition insures its rejection. It is of no more rational force than the argument of the suicide to commit self-slaughter. Secession is not a right. That the right of revolution exists, is as true in States as the right of self-defence is true of individuals. It does not exist by virtue of legal enactment or constitutional provision, but is founded in the nature of things—is inalienable and indestructible, and ought to be resorted to only when all peaceable remedies fail. Revolution is an extreme remedy, finds its justification alone in an escape from intolerable oppression, and hazarding the consequences of failure, as success or defeat makes the movement one of rightful

resistance or rebellion, it becomes the stern duty of Kentucky to look not only to the motives that might impel her to revolt, but to the probable results. She must contemplate her condition in a complex character—National and State—and see what must be her fate in the event of a separation.

Under the National Government, she has a right to the protection of thirty-three great States, and with them, thus protected, can defy the world in arms. Under it, she becomes prosperous and happy. Deprived of it, she finds herself exposed to imminent danger. She has a border front on the Ohio River of near seven hundred miles, with three powerful States on that border. She has four hundred miles on the South by which she is separated from Tennessee by a merely conventional line. Her eastern front is on Virginia, and part of her western on Missouri—thus making her antagonistic, in the event of collision, to Virginia, which is our mother, and to Missouri, which is our daughter. Hemmed in thus on every side by powers—each one of which is equal to her own—her situation, and her sense of loyalty to the Union, imperatively demand of her to insist on the integrity of the Union, its Constitution, and Government. Peace is of vital consequence to her, and can only be secured to her by preserving the Union inviolate. Kentucky has no cause of quarrel with the Constitution, and no wish to quarrel with her neighbors; but abundant reason to love both. Of the great West she was the pioneer, and became the starting point of emigration to all around her. There is not a western or a south-western State in which Kentucky families are not settled, and she is bound to all by ties of interest and brotherhood. She has ever been loyal to the Government, answering to its requisitions, and sharing its burthens. At the command of that Government, when war was declared to protect the rights of sailors, although she had no vessels to float on the ocean, yet she offered up her blood freely in the common defence from the Lakes to the Gulf of Mexico. Again, when war, growing out of a territorial controversy, far from her own borders, was proclaimed, she was amongst the foremost in the fight, and Monterey and Buena Vista were made famous in history by the valor of Kentuckians. Never has she faltered in her duty to the Union.

In declining to respond to a call made by the present Administration of the Government, and one that we have reason to believe would not have been made if the Administration had been fully advised of the circumstances by which we were surrounded, Kentucky did not put herself in factious opposition to her legitimate obligations; she did not choose to throw herself in hostile collision with the slave States of Missouri, Maryland, and Delaware, which have not seceded on the one hand, nor the slave States which have and are in process of secession on the other, and shed the blood of brethren and kindred at the very moment when she was striving to be an apostle of peace. Nature herself revolted at the thought, and her conduct in this matter had so much of love to God, and love to man, in it, that it will meet the sanction of an approving world. So far from being denounced for this action, it is everywhere looked upon as an act of purest patriotism, resulting from imperious necessity, and the highest instincts of self-preservation—respected by the very Administration that alone could have complained of it, and will, we doubt not, be ratified by it; if not in terms, at least by its future action. That act did not take her out of the Union.

Kentucky, in so grave a matter as this, passes by mere legal technicalities and a discussion of theoretical difficulties of Government, poises herself upon her right to do what the necessities of her condition imperatively demanded of her, and relies upon the good sense and magnanimity of her sister States, seeing that there is no parallel in her condition and theirs to do her justice.

In all things she is as loyal as ever to the constitutional administration of the Government. She will follow the Stars and Stripes to the utmost regions of the earth, and defend them from foreign insult. She refuses allegiance with any who would destroy the Union. All she asks is permission to keep out of this unnatural strife. When called to take part in it, she believes there is more honor in the breach than in the observance of any supposed duty to perform it.

Feeling that she is clearly right in this, and has announced her intention to refrain from aggression upon others, she must protest against her soil being made the theatre of military operations by any belligerent. The war must not be transferred, by the warring sections, from their own to her borders. Such unfriendly action cannot be viewed with indifference by Kentucky.

Having thus referred to this subject in its general aspects, we would invite your individual attention to its direct bearings upon yourselves.

It is not now a question of party politics, although it may be the interest of some to make it so. The day of mere party platforms has, we trust, gone forever. It has passed from being a mere struggle for place that may gratify personal ambition, to one for the present and future welfare of a whole people, for the safety of homes and firesides. Whatever divisions have heretofore existed should now cease. In times past, in our elections, the questions which divided men related to mere party differences, and the members of all the parties rivalled each other in their expression of devotion to the Union, and were equally clamorous for their rights, in the Union and not out of it. Now these party differences are passed away and forgotten. The direct question is Union or no Union—Government or no Government—

Neutrality or no Neutrality. Before this grand and commanding question every thing else gives way.

All can see that such a state of things cannot continue without war, and that such a war was unnecessary. It resulted from the ambition of men, rather than from the wrongs done the people. There was a remedy for every thing, already provided by the Constitution, which, with wise foresight, provided against the trials to which it might be subjected. There were countervailing powers to check encroachments, whether by a President or by Congress; and it so happened that at this dangerous crisis, when a sectional President had been elected, there was a majority in opposition to him in both houses of Congress, by which he could have been controlled, and the people protected. It was the duty of the opposition to have stood to their posts till the danger of encroachment had passed away. But Senators and Representatives, following the example of their States, vacated their seats and placed a President who would have been in a minority at the head of a triumphant majority. It was a great wrong for which they must answer to posterity. Kentucky remained true to herself, contending with all her might for what were considered to be the rights of the people, and although one after another of the States that should have been by her side ungenerously deserted her, leaving her almost alone in the field, yet she did not surrender her rights under the Constitution, and never will surrender them. She will appear again in the Congress of the United States, not having conceded the least item of power to the Government that had not heretofore been granted, and retaining every power she had reserved. She will insist upon her constitutional rights in the Union, and not out of it.

Kentucky is grieved to think that any thing should have been done by her sister States that has made it necessary for her to assume the position she now occupies. It is not one of submission as it has been insultingly called—it is one of the most exalted patriotism. But if she had no higher or holier motive; if she were not earnestly for peace among her brethren; the great law of self-protection points out her course and she has no alternative. Already one section declares that there will be no war at home, but that it shall be in Kentucky and Virginia. Already the cannon and bayonets of another section are visible on our most exposed border. Let these hostile armies meet on our soil and it will matter but little to us which may succeed, for destruction to us will be the inevitable result. Our fields will be laid waste, our houses and cities will be burned, our people will be slain, and this goodly land be re-baptized "the land of blood." And even the institution, to preserve or control which this wretched war was undertaken, will be exterminated in the general ruin. Such is the evil that others will bring upon us, no matter which side we take, if this is to be the battle-field. But there is danger at home more appalling than any that comes from beyond. People of Kentucky look well to it that you do not get to fighting among yourselves, for then, indeed, you will find that it is an ill fight where he that wins has the worst of it. Endeavor to be of one mind, and strive to keep the State steady in her present position. Hold fast to that sheet-anchor of republican liberty, that the will of the majority constitutionally and legally expressed must govern. You have, in the election by which this Convention was chosen, displayed a unanimity unparalleled in your history. May you be as unanimous in the future; may your majorities be so decided that a refusal to obey may be justly called factious. Trust and love one another. Avoid angry strife. Frown upon the petty ambition of demagogues who would stir up bad passions among you. Consider, as wise men, what is necessary for your own best interest, and in humble submission trust and look to that Almighty Being, who has heretofore so signally blessed us as a nation for His guidance through the gloom and darkness of this hour.

J. J. CRITTENDEN, Pres't.
JAMES GUTHRIE,
R. K. WILLIAMS,
ARCH'D DIXON,
F. M. BRISTOW,
JOSHUA F. BELL,

C. A. WICKLIFFE,
G. W. DUNLAP,
C. S. MOREHEAD,*
J. F. ROBINSON,
JOHN B. HUSTON,
ROBT. RICHARDSON.

—*Louisville Courier*, June 8.

Doc. 244.

THE FIGHT AT GREAT BETHEL.

GENERAL BUTLER'S OFFICIAL REPORT.

HEAD-QUARTERS, DEPARTMENT OF VIRGINIA,
FORTRESS MONROE, June 10, 1861.

To Lieutenant-General Scott:

GENERAL:—Having learned that the enemy had established an outpost of some strength at a place called Little Bethel, a small church about eight miles from Newport News, and the same distance from Hampton, from whence they were accustomed nightly to advance both on Newport News and the picket guards of Hampton to annoy them, and from whence also they had come down in small squads of cavalry and taken a number of Union men, some of whom had the safeguard and protection of the troops of the United States, and forced them into the rebel ranks, and that they were also gathering up the slaves of citizens who had moved away and left their farms in charge of their negroes, carrying them to work in intrenchments at Williamsburg and Yorktown, I had determined to send up a force to drive them back and destroy their camp, the head-quarters of which was this small church. I had also learned that

---

* I have signed the foregoing address, because I approve of the policy therein indicated, of refusing to furnish troops to the General Government to prosecute the civil war now going on, and the policy of neutrality, without considering myself committed to all that is said upon other matters.   C. S. MOREHEAD.

at a place a short distance further on, on the road to Yorktown, was an outwork of the rebels, on the Hampton side of a place called Big Bethel, a large church, near the head of the north branch of Back River, and that there was a very considerable rendezvous, with works of more or less strength in process of erection, and from this point the whole country was laid under contribution.

Accordingly, I ordered General Pierce, who is in command of Camp Hamilton, at Hampton, to send Duryea's regiment of Zouaves to be ferried over Hampton Creek at one o'clock this morning, and to march by the road up to Newmarket Bridge, then crossing the bridge, to go by a by-road and thus put the regiment in the rear of the enemy, and between Big Bethel and Little Bethel, in part for the purpose of cutting him off, and then to make an attack upon Little Bethel. I directed General Pierce to support him from Hampton with Colonel Townsend's regiment, with two mounted howitzers, and to march about an hour later. At the same time I directed Col. Phelps, commanding at Newport News, to send out a battalion, composed of such companies of the regiments under his command as he thought best, under command of Lieutenant-Colonel Washburn, in time to make a demonstration upon Little Bethel in front, and to have him supported by Colonel Bendix's regiment, with two field-pieces.

Bendix's and Townsend's regiments should effect a junction at a fork of the road leading from Hampton to Newport News, something like a mile and a half from Little Bethel. I directed the march to be so timed that the attack should be made just at daybreak, and that after the attack was made upon Little Bethel, Duryea's regiment and a regiment from Newport News should follow immediately upon the heels of the fugitives, if they were enabled to cut them off, and attack the battery on the road to Big Bethel, while covered by the fugitives; or, if it was thought expedient by General Pierce, failing to surprise the camp at Little Bethel, they should attempt to take the work near Big Bethel.

To prevent the possibility of mistake in the darkness, I directed that no attack should be made until the watchword should be shouted by the attacking regiment, and, in case that by any mistake in the march the regiments that were to make the junction should unexpectedly meet and be unknown to each other, also directed that the members of Colonel Townsend's regiment should be known, if in daylight, by something white worn on the arm. The troops were accordingly put in action as ordered, and the march was so timed that Colonel Duryea had got in the position noted upon the accompanying sketch, and Lieutenant-Colonel Washburn, in command of the regiment from Newport News, had got into the position indicated upon the sketch, and Colonel Bendix's regiment had been posted and ordered to hold the fork of the road, with two pieces of artillery, and Colonel Townsend's regiment had got to the place indicated just behind, and were about to form a junction as the day dawned.

Up to this point the plan had been vigorously, accurately, and successfully carried out; but here, by some strange fatuity, and as yet unexplained blunder, without any word of notice, while Colonel Townsend was in column *en route*, and when the head of the column was within one hundred yards, Col. Bendix's regiment opened fire with both artillery and musketry upon Col. Townsend's column, which, in the hurry and confusion, was irregularly returned by some of Col. Townsend's men, who feared that they had fallen into an ambuscade. Col. Townsend's column immediately retreated to the eminence near by, and were not pursued by Col. Bendix's men. By this almost criminal blunder two men of Col. Townsend's regiment were killed, and eight more or less wounded.

Hearing this cannonading and firing in his rear, Lieutenant-Colonel Washburn, not knowing but that his communication might be cut off, immediately reversed his march, as did Col. Duryea, and marched back to form a junction with his reserves.

General Pierce, who was with Colonel Townsend's regiment, fearing that the enemy had got notice of our approach, and had posted himself in force on the line of march, and not getting any communication from Col. Duryea, sent back to me for reinforcements, and I immediately ordered Col. Allen's regiment to be put in motion, and they reached Hampton about seven o'clock. In the mean time the true state of facts having been ascertained by General Pierce, the regiments effected a junction, and resumed the line of march. At the moment of the firing of Colonel Bendix, Colonel Duryea had surprised a part of an outlaying guard of the enemy, consisting of thirty persons, who have been brought into me.

Of course by this firing all hope of a surprise above the camp at Little Bethel was lost, and, upon marching upon it, it was found to have been vacated, and the cavalry had pressed on toward Big Bethel. Col. Duryea, however, destroyed the camp at Little Bethel, and advanced. General Pierce, then, as he informs me, with the advice of his colonels, thought best to attempt to carry the works of the enemy at Big Bethel, and made dispositions to that effect. The attack commenced, as I am informed—for I have not yet received any official reports—about half-past nine o'clock.

At about ten o'clock General Pierce sent a note to me saying that there was a sharp engagement with the enemy, and that he thought he should be able to maintain his position until reinforcements could come up. Acting upon this information, Colonel Carr's regiment, which had been ordered in the morning to proceed as far as Newmarket Bridge, was allowed to go forward. I received this information, for which

I had sent a special messenger, about twelve o'clock. I immediately made disposition from Newport News to have Colonel Phelps, from the four regiments there, forward aid if necessary. As soon as these orders could be sent forward I repaired to Hampton, for the purpose of having proper ambulances and wagons for the sick and wounded, intending to go forward and join the command. While the wagons were going forward a messenger came, announcing that the engagement had terminated, and that the troops were retiring in good order to camp.

I remained upon the ground at Hampton, personally seeing the wounded put in boats and towed round to the hospital, and ordering forward Lieutenant Morris, with two boat howitzers, to cover the rear of the returning column in case it should be attacked. Having been informed that the ammunition of the artillery had been expended, and seeing the head of the column approach Hampton in good order, I waited for General Pierce to come up. I am informed by him that the dead and wounded had all been brought off, and that the return had been conducted in good order, and without haste. I learned from him that the men behaved with great steadiness, with the exception of some few instances, and that the attack was made with propriety, vigor, and courage; but that the enemy were found to be supported by a battery, variously estimated as of from fifteen to twenty pieces, some of which were rifled cannon, which were very well served, and protected from being readily turned by a creek in front.

Our loss is very considerable, amounting perhaps to forty or fifty, a quarter part of which you will see was from the unfortunate mistake —to call it by no worse name—of Colonel Bendix.

I will, as soon as official returns can be got, give a fuller detail of the affair, and will only add now that we have to regret especially the death of Lieut. Greble, of the Second Artillery, who went out with Colonel Washburn from Newport News, and who very efficiently and gallantly fought his piece until he was struck by a cannon shot. I will endeavor to get accurate statements to forward by the next mail.

I think, in the unfortunate combination of circumstances, and the result which we experienced, we have gained more than we have lost. Our troops have learned to have confidence in themselves under fire, the enemy have shown that they will not meet us in the open field, and our officers have learned wherein their organization and drill are inefficient.

While waiting for the official reports, I have the honor to submit thus far the information of which I am possessed.

I have the honor to be, most respectfully,
Your obedient servant,
BENJ F. BUTLER,
Major-General Commanding.

BRIGADIER-GENERAL PIERCE'S ORDERS.

HEAD-QUARTERS, CAMP HAMILTON, ?
June 9, 1861. ¿

GENERAL ORDERS, No. 12.—A plan of attack to-night is herewith enclosed and forwarded to Col. Duryea, commanding 5th regiment N. Y. State troops, who will act accordingly. Col. Townsend, commanding 3d regiment N. Y. State troops, will march his command in support of Col. Duryea. Col. Carr, commanding 2d regiment New York volunteers, will detach the artillery company of his regiment, with their field-pieces, caissons, and a suitable supply of ammunition, and take their position at the burnt bridge, near Hampton. Cols. Allen, Carr, and McChesney will hold their entire command in readiness, fully prepared to march at a moment's notice. All the troops will be supplied with one day's rations, and each man with twenty rounds of ball cartridge.

That no mistake may be made, all the troops, as they charge the enemy, will shout— "Boston."

Cols. Allen, Carr, Townsend, Duryea, and McChesney will take notice and act accordingly.

By command of

E. W. PIERCE, Brigadier-General.

R. A. PIERCE, Brig.-Major.

COL. DURYEA'S REPORT.

HEAD-QUARTERS, CAMP HAMILTON, NEAR ?
FORTRESS MONROE, Tuesday, June 11, 1861. ¿

SIR :—In accordance with your instructions previously received, I proceeded, on the night of the 9th of June, at half-past eleven o'clock P. M., on the march to Bethel.

The first two miles to Hampton Bridge, we proceeded leisurely along, waiting for the howitzer, which should be placed at the head of the advancing column. Arriving at Hampton Creek, much delay was occasioned by the non-arrival of the surf-boats, which were to convey the regiment across the river, and it was ten o'clock before the column was formed, ready to push forward upon the other side.

We now advanced rapidly, and soon came up with our two companies of skirmishers, under Captains Bartlett and Kilpatrick, who had been despatched ahead an hour and a half previous. Proceeding steadily on without resting a moment, we came. about four o'clock in the morning, to Little Bethel, a distance of about thirteen miles. At this point we discovered and surprised the picket guard of the enemy, and a mounted officer, with four or five foot, were taken prisoners. While pushing forward towards Big Bethel we suddenly heard a heavy fire of musketry and cannon in our rear, bespeaking a severe engagement. Supposing it to be an attempt of the enemy to cut off our reserve, we immediately countermarched in quick and double-quick time, when, having proceeded about five miles, we came upon two of our regiments, and learned that in the darkness of the night they had mistaken each other for enemies, and that an unfortunate engagement, accompanied with some loss, had taken place. We then by your command returned, and advanced upon Great Bethel, being supported by the Seventh Regiment, under Colonel Bendix, and the Third, under Col. Townsend.

Proceeding to within a mile of County Bridge, the column halted, Capts. Kilpatrick and Bartlett having discovered that the enemy were holding a strong position in the battery at the head of the road. We now drew up in line of battle on the right, at the skirts of the woods, and the artillery, two howitzers, and a brass six-pounder, were pushed some thirty rods up the road. At this point Lieut.-Col. Warren rode into the field and assumed his position in the regiment, and, from his previous knowledge of the ground, proved of invaluable assistance.

Capts. Winslow, Bartlett, and Kilpatrick having been ordered to advance, under Lieut.-Col. Warren, as skirmishers, the regiment was formed on the left, from whence I led the column in person up the road toward the enemy's battery ; but the fire proving very destructive, we marched in good order till we were covered by the woods on the right, where we halted for some time for rest, and in order to complete the preparations for charging the batteries in flank. In the mean time, Lieut.-Col. Warren made a reconnoissance and reported a plan of attack.

I then led off the troops to the left, in the open field, and also to the right, supported on the right by the German Rifles. After several attempts to charge the batteries, being prevented by the creek, we withdrew, by your command, to the rear, and having collected our killed and wounded, such as we could find, proceeded down the main road. Lieut.-Col. Warren, however, with a small detachment, remained and brought away the body of Lieut. Greble, with the field-piece he was serving with such effect at the time of his death. Our chaplain also remained to care for the wounded, but being cut off by a company of cavalry, he only escaped by taking to the woods, and escaping under cover of the night. We continued our march toward Hampton, and reached the bridge, having only four killed, twelve wounded, and two missing.

The following names deserve an honorable mention :—Lieut.-Col. Warren, for his aid in forming the plan of attack, and remaining among the last to bring away a brother officer ; also Chaplain Winslow, for his many kind attentions to the wounded ; also Captains Bartlett, Kilpatrick and Winslow for the effective manner in which they skirmished before the enemy's heavy fire ; also, Lieut. J. Duryea, who led the charge up to the left flank of the batteries ; also, Lieuts. York and Cambreling ; Surgeon Gilbert for performing upon the field of battle successful amputations and for his continued attention to the suffering and wounded, not only on the field, but afterward at the hospital, when almost exhausted ; also, Lieut.

Gouv. Carr, who was commanding Company B, his captain being ill, and Lieut. Geo. Duryea; also, Sergeants Agnes, Onderdonk, Allison, and Corporal Brunner.

Yet there was no flinching on the part of any officer or private, and I might mention many more with honor. In closing I cannot but speak of Col. Townsend, of the Third, who, with his whole command, stood up nobly in my support, until compelled to retreat by the terrible fire.

Per order,   Col. A. DURYEA.
Lieut. MALLORY, Aide-de-Camp.

To Brigadier-Gen. PIERCE.

CAPTAIN KILPATRICK'S REPORT.

HEAD-QUARTERS, CAMP HAMILTON, }
June 11, 1861. }

SIR:—In accordance with your orders, I have the honor to submit the following report of my command, acting as the Advance Guard, on the evening of the 9th, and a brief account of my command during the engagement on the following day, at the New County Bridge. I left camp with my command at 10 P. M., consisting of fifty men of Company H, one lieutenant, (Cambreling,) four sergeants, and four corporals; Company I, Capt. Bartlett, one lieutenant, (York,) four sergeants, and two corporals crossed the river at Hampton 10½ P. M.; reached Newmarket Bridge at 1 A. M., threw out scouts in all directions and waited for the main body, which arrived at 3 A. M. According to your orders, I advanced on the road to New County Bridge, the point where the enemy was reported to have made a stand. A little before daylight, when within a mile and a quarter of the bridge, we discovered the outlying picket guard of the enemy, and were challenged, "Who comes there?" I replied, "Who stands there?" A horseman attempted to leave. Corporal Ellerson, of Company H, sprang in advance, directing him to halt. I, supposing the enemy to be in force, gave the command to fire and charge. In a moment the affair was over, twenty or thirty shots had been given and exchanged; the officer of the guard was captured and disarmed. At this time, hearing firing in the rear, and supposing that our rear guard was attacked, I returned to follow the main body under Col. Duryea, who was advancing by forced march in the direction of the firing, only to discover that by mistake our own forces coming in different directions, and supposing each to be the enemy, had fired several shots before the mistake was discovered. I again advanced, and at 8 A. M. met with and drove in the picket guards of the enemy. I then detached a portion of my command, made an armed reconnoissance, and found the enemy with about from 3,000 to 5,000 men posted in a strong position on the opposite side of the bridge—three earthworks and a masked battery on the right and left; in advance of the stream thirty pieces of artillery and a large force of cavalry, all of which infor-

mation I reported to you at once. I was ordered to advance and engage the enemy in throwing out skirmishers on the right and left of the road leading to the bridge. We rapidly advanced, supported by the Advance Guard of Col. Duryea and three pieces of artillery under Lieut. Greble, of the First Regiment United States Artillery. The enemy soon opened fire on us from the rifled cannon in front. We answered his discharges by a cheer, and continued to advance, clearing all before us, till we reached a point just on the edge of the woods, where the fire was so hot and heavy that we were compelled to halt, and there we remained as directed by Lieut.-Col. Warren, till that gallant officer had made dispositions to turn their flanks. The enemy's fire at this time began to tell upon us with great effect. My men were falling one after another, as was the case of the rest of the command.

After remaining in this position about two hours, and our object having been accomplished, numbers of our men being killed and wounded, having received a grape shot through my thigh, which tore off a portion of the rectangle on Col. Duryea's left shoulder, passed through my leg and killed a soldier in the rear, I withdrew my men to the skirts of the wood. We managed to reach Lieut. Greble's battery and bring to his aid several of my men. The charge was then sounded, Lieut. Greble opened fire with grape and canister within two hundred yards of the enemy's lines. Capts. Winslow, Bartlett, and myself charged with our commands in front; Capt. Denike and Lieut. Duryea, (son of Col. Duryea,) and about two hundred of the Troy Rifles upon the right; Col. Townsend with his men to the left. The enemy were forced out of the first battery, all the forces were rapidly advancing, and every thing promised a speedy victory, when we were ordered to fall back. Where this order came from I do not know. We maintained our position till Col. Townsend began to retire with his whole command. Being left thus alone and no prospects of receiving aid, we ordered the men to fall back, which they did, and in good order, forming their line of battle about one hundred and fifty yards in the rear. A few minutes afterwards orders came from Gen. Pierce to cease firing and retire. It gives me great pleasure to mention the gallant conduct of Capt. Bartlett, who came up with the reserve, reinforcing my line, and who was ever at the point of danger, encouraging his men. Lieut. York, in command of my left, and Lieut. Cambreling, in command of my right, displayed the greatest bravery. Lieut. York's sword was broken by a grape shot, and he was slightly wounded in the leg.

I shall ever be grateful to Capt. Winslow, who rescued me after our forces had left. He came to my aid, assisted by Sergeants Onderdonk and Agnes, at the last moment, but in time to rescue me from the enemy.

I would also favorably mention private Wood,

who brought me valuable information, and who fired the first shot; private John Dunn, whose arm was shattered by a cannon ball, and who bore himself with the greatest bravery, and who said to Surgeon Gilbert, while amputating his arm, that he could not have lost it in a nobler cause. The whole command, men and officers, did themselves the greatest credit, and I am satisfied can conquer any thing except impossibilities. Respectfully submitted,

JUDSON KILPATRICK,
Captain, Company H.
To Colonel A. DURYEA.

COL. ALLEN'S REPORT.

CAMP HAMILTON, VIRGINIA, June 11, 1861.

MAJOR-GENERAL B. F. BUTLER:

SIR:—I have the honor to report that, in accordance with orders received from General Pierce on the night of the 9th inst., my command was ordered under arms at eleven P. M., and marched to Hampton Creek to support Colonels Townsend and Duryea. I returned to this camp at four A. M., of the 10th inst., and was again ordered out at six A. M. to proceed forward to Big Bethel, where the enemy was reported to be stationed in force. After a rapid march of twelve miles I reached the ground and found the action going on. Upon reporting to General Pierce, he directed me to proceed to the front and deploy my regiment in front of the battery, which I did, and so remained for one hour and forty minutes under a heavy fire of at least twenty guns, some of them rifled and about four shell guns—the enemy deploying in my front with about 1,200 men and two guns, but made no advance. They, however, threw out two heavy flanking parties on my right and left, the former with two guns, and completely outflanked the entire brigade, at which time General Pierce deemed it proper to retire. From the most reliable information I am certain there were at least four thousand of the enemy on the ground, with constant reinforcements from Yorktown.

Very respectfully,		WM. H. ALLEN,
Colonel First regiment.

LETTER FROM BRIGADIER-GENERAL PIERCE.

CAMP HAMILTON, June 12, 1861.

To the Editor of the Boston Journal:

Please correct the erroneous report set afloat by my enemies. There were but seven killed of the forces that went from this camp, in the expedition to Little and Great Bethel, on the 10th of this month, and Col. Townsend, of the Third Regiment New York Volunteers, who was formerly Adjutant-General of the State of New York, offers to certify that I gave my orders properly, and that under the circumstances the battle could not have been managed better.

This I write that the public may not judge me before I have time to be heard.

Capt. Haggerty and Major Winthrop, of Gen. Butler's Staff, were with me and advising me to do as I did. Gen. Butler has not intimated to me as yet that he blames me at all.

In haste, yours, &c.,		E. W. PIERCE.

A CONFEDERATE ACCOUNT.

THE following account of the battle of Big Bethel, is given by one who participated in the defence:

YORKTOWN, June 11, 1861.

An engagement lasting four hours took place yesterday (Monday) between five regiments of the troops from Old Point, and 1,100 Confederate troops, consisting of Virginians and North Carolinians under Gen. Magruder, at Bethel Church, York County. Before telling you of the battle, I will give you some circumstances preceding it. About two weeks ago a party of 300 Yankees came up from Hampton and occupied Bethel Church, which position they held a day or two and then retired, leaving written on the walls of the church, several inscriptions, such as "Death to the Traitors," "Down with the Rebels," &c. To nearly all these the names of the writers were defiantly signed, and all of the penmen signed themselves as from New York, except one, who was from Boston, Mass., U. S. To these excursions into the interior, of which this was the boldest, Gen. Magruder determined to put a stop, and accordingly filled the place after the Yankees left with a few companies of his own troops. In addition to this, he determined to carry the war into the enemy's country, and on Wednesday last Stanard's battery of the Howitzer Battalion was ordered down to the church, where it was soon joined by a portion of Brown's battery of the same corps. The North Carolina Regiment, under Col. Hill, was also there, making in all about 1,100 men and seven howitzer guns. On Saturday last the first excursion of considerable importance was made. A detachment of 200 infantry and a howitzer gun under Major Randolph, and one of 70 infantry and another howitzer under Major Lane, of the North Carolina Regiment, started different routes to cut off a party which had left Hampton. The party was seen and fired at by Major Randolph's detachment, but made such fast time that they escaped. The troops under Major Lane passed within sight of Hampton, and as they turned up the road to return to Bethel, encountered the Yankees, numbering about 90, who were intrenched behind a fence in the field, protected by a high bank. Our advance guard fired on them, and in another moment the North Carolinians were dashing over the fence in regular French (not New York) Zouave style, firing at them in real squirrel-hunting style. The Yankees fled for their lives after firing for about three minutes without effect, leaving behind them three dead and a prisoner. The fellow was a stout, ugly fellow from Troy, N. Y. He said he had nothing against the South, but somebody must be soldiers, and he thought he had as well enlist. None of our men were hurt. This bold excursion, under the very guns of the enemy, determined the authorities at Old Point to put a stop to it, and clear us out from Bethel. This determination was conveyed to us from persons who came from the neighborhood of the enemy. On Monday morning 600 infantry and two guns, under General Magruder, left the camp and proceeded towards Hampton, but after advancing a mile or two, received information that the Yankees were coming in large force. We then retired, and after reaching camp the guns were placed in battery and the infantry took their places behind their breastwork. Everybody was cool, and all were anxious to give the invaders a good reception. About 9 o'clock the glittering bayonets of the enemy appeared on the hill opposite, and above them waved the Star-Spangled Banner. The moment the head of the column advanced far enough to show one or two companies, the Parrott gun of the Howitzer Battery opened on them, throwing a shell right into their midst. Their ranks broke in confusion, and the column, or as much of it as we could see, retreated behind two small farm-houses. From their position a fire was opened on us, which was replied to by our battery, which commanded the route of their approach. Our firing was excellent, and the shells scattered in all directions when they burst. They could hardly approach the guns which they were firing for the shells which came from our battery. Within our encampment fell a perfect hail-storm of canister-shot, bullets, and balls. Remarkable to say, not one of our men was killed inside of our encampment. Several horses were slain by the shells and bullets. Finding that bombardment would not answer, the enemy, about 11 o'clock, tried to carry the position by assault, but met a terrible repulse at the hands of the infantry as he tried to scale the breastworks. The men disregarded sometimes the defences erected for them, and, leaping on the embankment, stood and fired at the Yankees, cutting them down as they came up. One company of the New York 7th Regiment, under Capt. Winthrop, attempted to take the redoubt on the left. The marsh they crossed was strewn with their bodies. Their captain, a fine-looking man, reached the fence, and, leaping on a log, waved his sword, crying, "Come on, boys; one charge, and the day is ours." The words were his last, for a Carolina rifle ended his life the next moment, and his men fled in terror back. At the redoubt on the right, a company of about three hundred New York Zouaves charged one of our guns, but could not stand the fire of the infantry, and retreated precipitately. During these charges the main body of the enemy on the hill were attempting to concentrate for a general assault, but the shells from the Howitzer Battery prevented them. As one regiment would give up the effort, another would be marched to the position, but with no better success, for a shell would scatter them like chaff. The men did not seem able to stand fire at all. About one o'clock their guns were silenced, and a few moments

after, their infantry retreated precipitately down the road to Hampton. Our cavalry, numbering three companies, went in pursuit, and harassed them down to the edge of Hampton. As they retreated many of the wounded fell along the road and died, and the whole road to Hampton was strewn with haversacks, overcoats, canteens, muskets, &c., which the men had thrown off in their retreat. After the battle, I visited the position they held. The houses behind which they had been hid had been burnt by our troops. Around the yard were the dead bodies of the men who had been killed by our cannon, mangled in the most frightful manner by the shells. The uniforms on the bodies were very different, and many of them are like those of the Virginia soldiery. A little further on we came to the point to which they had carried some of their wounded, who had since died. The gay-looking uniforms of the New York Zouaves contrasted greatly with the paled, fixed faces of their dead owners. Going to the swamp through which they attempted to pass to assault our lines, presented another bloody scene. Bodies dotted the black morass from one end to the other. I saw one boyish, delicate-looking fellow lying on the mud, with a bullet-hole through his breast. His hand was pressed on the wound from which his life blood had poured, and the other was clenched in the grass that grew near him. Lying on the ground was a Testament which had fallen from his pocket, dabbed with blood. On opening the cover I found the printed inscription: "Presented to the Defenders of their Country, by the New York Bible Society." A United States flag was also stamped on the title-page. Among the haversacks picked up along the route were many letters from the Northern States, asking if they liked the Southern farms, and if the Southern barbarians had been whipped out yet. The force of the enemy brought against us was 4,000, according to the statement of the six prisoners we took. Ours was 1,100. Their loss in killed and wounded must be nearly 200. Our loss is one killed and three wounded. The fatal case was that of a North Carolinian who volunteered to fire one of the houses behind which they were stationed. He started from the breastwork to accomplish it, but was shot in the head. He died this morning in the hospital. The wounded are Harry Shook, of Richmond, of Brown's battery, shot in the wrist; John Werth, of Richmond, of the same battery, shot in the leg, and Lieut. Hudnall, of the same battery, shot in the foot. None of the wounds are serious. The Louisiana Regiment arrived about one hour after the fight was over. They are a fine-looking set of fellows. As there was force enough at Old Point to send up to Bethel and surround us, we took up the line of march, and came up to Yorktown, where we now are. I hear to-day that troops from Old Point are now marching up to attack us, but cannot say whether it is so or not.

—*Richmond Despatch*, (*Extra*,) June 12.

Doc. 245.

FOURTH CONNECTICUT REGIMENT.

The following are the officers of the regiment: Colonel, Levi Woodhouse, Hartford; Lieutenant-Colonel, N. L. White, Hamburg; Major, H. W. Berge, Norwich; Adjutant, T. S. Trumbull, Hartford; Quartermaster, G. A. Washburn, Hartford; Surgeon, S. W. Skinner, Windsor Locks; Assistant Surgeon, Edward Bently, Norwich; Chaplain, E. Walker, New Haven; Sergeant Major, E. A. Gillette, Hartford; Quartermaster Sergeant, F. A. Pratt, Hartford; Commissary Sergeant, E. P. Allen, Hartford.

Company A, from Hartford—Captain L. G. Hemmingway; 1st Lieutenant, Wm. G. Fitch; 2d Lieutenant, Charles M. Robbins. Company B, from Derby—Captain, E. S. Kellogg; 1st Lieutenant, T. S. Gilbert; 2d Lieutenant, Geo. Ager. Company C, from Suffield—Captain, R. S. Burbank; 1st Lieutenant, W. S. Pomeroy; 2d Lieutenant, Wm. Soby. Company D, from New London—Captain, J. C. Dunford; 1st Lieutenant, G. B. Cook; 2d Lieutenant, T. J. Mills. Company E, from New Haven—Captain, Oscar Dennis; 1st Lieutenant, T. H. Rockwood; 2d Lieutenant, E. F. Hendricks. Company F, from New Haven—Captain, N. S. Hallenbeck; 1st Lieutenant, E. C. Dow; 2d Lieutenant, G. M. Harmon. Company G, from Middletown—Captain, R. G. Williams; 1st Lieutenant, E. W. Gibbons; 2d Lieutenant, E. C. Beman. Company H, from Middletown—Captain, C. C. Clark; 1st Lieutenant, John A. Turner; 2d Lieutenant, D. R. Hubbard. Company I, from Wolcottville—Captain, S. H. Perkins; 1st Lieutenant, A. F. Brooker; 2d Lieutenant, E. H. Mix. Company K, from Hartford—Captain, D. W. Siprell; 1st Lieutenant, Oliver Burke; 2d Lieutenant, A. S. Dickinson.

—N. Y. Tribune, June 12.

Doc. 246.

JEFFERSON DAVIS' LETTER

TO THE MARYLAND COMMISSIONERS.

MONTGOMERY, Ala., Saturday, May 25.

GENTLEMEN: I receive with pleasure the assurance that the State of Maryland sympathizes with the people of the Confederate States in their determined vindication of the right of self-government, and that the people of Maryland are enlisted with their whole hearts on the side of reconciliation and peace.

The people of these Confederate States, notwithstanding their separation from their late sister, have not ceased to feel deep solicitude in her welfare, and to hope that at no distant day that State, whose people, habits, and institutions are so closely related and assimilated with theirs, will seek to unite her fate and fortunes with those of this Confederacy.

The government of the Confederate States receives with respect the suggestion of the State of Maryland, that there should be a cessation of the hostilities now impending until the meeting of Congress in July next, in order that said body may, if possible, arrange for an adjustment of the existing troubles by means of negotiations rather than the sword.

But it is at a loss how to reply without a repetition of the language it has used on every possible occasion that has presented itself since the establishment of its independence.

In deference to the State of Maryland, however, it again asserts, in the most emphatic terms, that its sincere and earnest desire is for peace, and that while the government would readily entertain any proposition from the government of the United States, tending to a peaceful solution of the present difficulties, the recent attempts of this government to enter into negotiations with that of the United States were attended with results which forbid any renewal of proposals from it to that government.

If any further assurance of the desire of this government for peace were necessary, it would be sufficient to observe that being formed of a confederation of sovereign States, each acting and deciding for itself, the right of every other sovereign State to assume self action and self government is necessarily acknowledged.

Hence conquests of other States are wholly inconsistent with the fundamental principles and subversive of the very organization of this government. Its policy cannot but be peace—peace with all nations and people.

Very respectfully,
JEFFERSON DAVIS.

To Messrs. McKaig, Yellott, and Harding, committee of the Maryland Legislature.

—Rochester (N. Y.) Daily Union, June 14.

Doc. 246½.

THE HOME GUARD OF NEW YORK CITY.

At a meeting of the committee of the Home Guard, held April 26—Present, A. M. Bininger, in the chair. Judge Edmonds, Col. Wakeman, Col. Tappan, Gen. Tallmadge, Messrs. H. Ketchum, C. Tracy, and F. Hotaling, Committee. Gen. J. A. Dix, Cols. A. Warner, and O. D. F. Grant. The following general order of the Home Guard was passed:

JNO. NEWHOUSE, SEC.

HOME GUARD,
PALACE GARDEN, April 26.

GENERAL ORDERS.

The commandant promulgates the following order, for the organization of the corps:

1. The corps shall be known as the HOME GUARD.

2. It shall be divided into companies of fifty men each, to be selected, as far as practicable, from the same vicinity.

3. To each company there shall be a captain, two lieutenants, and four sergeants.

4. The corps shall be armed as follows: The commandant, his staff and the captains, and

lieutenants with swords, the residue with muskets, with waist belts of black leather.

5. The uniform shall be: Black frock coat, dark gray pantaloons, and black felt hat, with the Union cockade.

6. Each man will furnish his own arms, equipments, and uniform.

7. Until further orders, the companies will meet at least three times a week for drill, at such places as the captains shall appoint, and the whole corps shall meet at Palace Garden every Tuesday evening, at 7½ o'clock.

8. The captains of companies will have perfect rolls of their respective commands, with the residence and place of business of each man; will have a permanent place of meeting in their vicinity, and concerted signals by which the members may know when to assemble on extra occasions.

9. Col. Andrew Warner and Col. O. De Forest Grant are appointed aids to the commandants, with power in his absence, in the order here named, to exercise all his authority in the corps; and Lieutenant-Colonel Maximilian Rader is appointed adjutant.

JOHN A. DIX, Commandant.
—*N. Y. World.*

Doc. 247.
GOV. JACKSON'S PROCLAMATION.
JUNE 12, 1861.

To the People of Missouri:

A series of unprovoked and unparalleled outrages have been inflicted on the peace and dignity of this Commonwealth, and upon the rights and liberties of its people, by wicked and unprincipled men, who profess to act under the authority of the United States Government; the solemn enactments of your Legislature have been nullified, your volunteer soldiers have been taken prisoners, your commerce with your sister States has been suspended, your trade with your fellow-citizens has been and is subjected to increasing control of an armed soldiery; peaceable citizens have been imprisoned without warrant of law; unoffending and defenceless men, women, and children have been ruthlessly shot down and murdered, and other unbearable indignities have been heaped on your State and yourselves. To all these outrages and indignities you have submitted with patriotic forbearance, which has only encouraged the perpetrators of these previous usages to attempt still bolder and more daring usurpations. It has been my earnest endeavor under all these embarrassing circumstances to maintain the peace of the State, and avert, if possible, from our borders, the desolating effects of civil war. With that object in view I authorized Major-General Price several weeks ago to arrange with Gen. Harney, commanding Federal forces in this State, the terms of an agreement by which the State might be preserved. They came on May 21st to an understanding,

Doc.—34

which was made public. The State authorities have labored faithfully to carry out the terms of that agreement. The Federal Government, on the other hand, not only manifested its strong disapprobation of it by the instant dismissal of that distinguished officer, who on his part entered into it, but it at once began and has unintermittingly carried out, a system of hostile operations in utter contempt of this agreement, and in reckless disregard of its pledged faith. The acts have latterly portended revolution and civil war so unmistakably that I resolved to make one further effort to avert these dangers from you. I therefore solicited an interview with Brigadier-General Lyon, commanding the Federal army in Missouri. It was granted on the 11th, and waiving all questions of personal and official dignity, I went to St. Louis accompanied by Brigadier-General Price. We had an interview on the 11th inst., with General Lyon and F. P. Blair, Jr., at which I submitted to them these propositions:

That I would disband the State Guard, and break up its organization.

That I would disarm all the companies that had been ordered out by the State.

That I would pledge myself not to attempt to organize the militia under the military bill.

That no arms or munitions of war should be brought into the State.

That I would protect all citizens equally in all their rights, regardless of their political opinions.

That I would repress all insurrectionary movements in the State.

That I would repel all attempts to invade it from any quarter, and by whomsoever made.

That I would thus maintain a strict neutrality in this unhappy contest, and preserve the peace of this unhappy State; and I further proposed that I would, if necessary, invoke the assistance of the United States troops to carry out these pledges.

All this I proposed to do upon condition that the Federal Government would undertake to disband the Home Guard which it has illegally organized and armed throughout the State, and pledge itself not to occupy with its troops any localities in the State not occupied by them at this time. Nothing but the most earnest desire to avert the horrors of civil war from our beloved State could have tempted me to propose those humiliating terms. They were rejected by the Federal officers. They demanded not only disorganization and disbanding of the State militia and the nullification of the military bill, but they refused to disband their own Home Guard, and insisted that the Federal Government should enjoy the unrestricted right to move and station its troops throughout the State whenever and wherever it might, in the opinion of its officers, be necessary either for the protection of the loyal subjects of the Federal Government or for repelling invasion, and they plainly announced that it was the intention of the Administration to take military possession under these pretexts of the whole State, and to reduce it, as avowed by Gen. Lyon himself, to the exact condition of Maryland. The acceptance by me of these degrading terms would not only have sullied the honor of Missouri, but would have roused the indignation of every citizen, and have precipitated the very conflict it has been my desire to prevent. We refused to accede to them, and the conference was broken up.

Fellow-citizens, all our efforts towards conciliation have failed; we can hope nothing from the justice or moderation of the Federal agents in this State. They are energetically hastening the execution of their bloody and revolutionary schemes for the inauguration of civil war in your midst, and for the military occupation of your State by armed bands of lawless invaders, —for the overthrow of your State Government, and for the subversion of those liberties which the Government has a right to protect, and they intend to bring their whole power to subjugate you if possible to the military despotism which has assumed the powers of the Federal Government. Now, therefore, I, C. F. Jackson, Governor of Missouri, do, in view of the foregoing facts and by virtue of the power vested in me by the Constitution and laws of this commonwealth, issue this, my proclamation, calling the militia of the State, to the number of 50,000, into service of the State for the purpose of repelling such invasion, and for the protection of the lives, liberty, and property of the citizens of this State, and I earnestly exhort all good citizens of Missouri to rally to the flag of their State for the protection of their endangered homes and firesides, and the defence of their most sacred rights and dearest liberties. In issuing this proclamation, I hold it to be my most solemn duty to remind you that Missouri is still one of the United States, and that the executive department of the State Government does not arrogate to itself the power to disturb that relation. That power has been wisely vested in the convention which will, at the proper time, express your sovereign will, and that meanwhile it is your duty to obey all constitutional requirements of the Federal Government; but it is equally my duty to advise you—first, allegiance due to your own State, and that you are under no obligations whatever to obey the unconstitutional edicts of the military despotism which has introduced itself at Washington, nor submit to the infamous and degrading sway of its wicked minions in this State. No brave hearted Missourian will obey the one or submit to the other. Arise, then, and drive out ignominiously the invaders who have dared to desecrate the soil which your labors have made fruitful, and which is consecrated by your homes.

CLAIBORNE F. JACKSON.

—*Rochester (N. Y.) Union, June 14.*

Doc. 248.

THE TWENTIETH REGIMENT, N. Y. S. V.

"UNITED TURNER RIFLES."

DEPARTURE FROM NEW YORK, JUNE 13.

THE Turners constitute a great social, educational, musical, gymnastic, and semi-military popular society, to which every German, of whatever rank, so he be of good moral character, is expected to belong. The brotherhood affords so many cheap advantages that it is almost universal among the Germans; and in virtue of this fact, the 20th Regiment leaves with as many warm wishes for fortune and success from as numerous a circle of devoted friends as the Firemen's Regiment itself, and owing to the nature and manner of its organization, will live in the hearts of the brothers and sisters of the Bund, and be watched in its future movements, perhaps, more closely than any other of our volunteers.

The regiment is not only thoroughly equipped and sworn for the war, but every man is perfectly and completely drilled in the manual and manœuvres of the soldier, as well as ready and anxious to be of service to his country. Gymnastic training, in most cases the work of years, has made the men tough and muscular, and capable of great endurance. As they marched from Forty-third street, down Second avenue, through Twentieth street, down Broadway, and thence by way of Pearl and Chatham streets to Canal street, many thousand people greeted them from the sidewalks and windows, bestowing high and unqualified praise upon them. There were many, hitherto knowing nothing of their existence, who awarded them the palm for stout soldierly bearing, among all the regiments that have yet left New York.

The procession, including the escort, was quite imposing, as every German society in the city resolved to be out, and was represented on the parade, to which add a battalion of the Turner Schützen corps, five companies of Von Gilsa's De Kalb Regiment, a fire company from Union Hill, the noble "Duysing Zouaves," numerous citizens, four-horse baggage wagons, and an emblematical warlike tableau, drawn by six fine horses, and consisting of a tent, with soldiers on guard, and specimens of the colors, the arms, and the various equipments of our now *Grand Army.*

Among the societies represented were the following: New-Yorker Sangerbund, Social Reform Gesang Verein, Fidelia, Mozart Mannerchor, Arion, Helvetia Mannerchor, Dramatic Club, New-Yorker Rifle Corps, the associations of Turners from Bloomingdale, Williamsburgh, Brooklyn, and the old Turners, who were the original founders of the Verein, all in their uniforms of white. At a seasonable hour the societies formed in line opposite Turn Halle, in Orchard street, and marched to Grand street, where they were joined by a body of the Social Reformers, thence through Hester street to

Metropolitan Hall, and soon swelled in numbers as they approached Union Square, where they met the regiment at 4 o'clock.

The display of society banners, badges, and mottoes was numerically fine, the most common being those of Turner Societies exhibiting an ogling night owl with a torch in one claw and a sword in the other, superscribed by the word " Bahnfrei," (Clear the track.)

In front of the City Hall, a review by the Common Council, and presentations by private citizens, took place. The Hon. Samuel B. Ruggles presented a flag, and said :

Colonel Weber and the Officers and Soldiers under your command :—

In behalf of Mrs. Charles Edward Strong, and other patriotic ladies of the City of New York, I present you this National Flag for your Regiment, which they commit, with undoubting faith, to your brave and loyal keeping. To whom could they more properly entrust it than to you, the lineal descendants of the Germans of those early ages who, amid the verdant forests and sparkling waters of the Fatherland, bravely battled for liberty and freedom against the cruel domination of imperious, slaveholding, and all-enslaving Rome ?

Gallant Germans! Friends and brethren! we hail you as fellow-countrymen and co-equal heirs of our nation's destiny. The land of poetry, of song, of science; the birthplace of Schiller, and Mozart, and Kepler, has given you to us, to share our fortunes and our fate. This goodly Western continent is not less yours than ours; upon its broad and teeming bosom we stand or fall together. Side by side, we now battle for our nation's life.

For this very purpose it was that you sought this western world. You came here that you of the present generation might enjoy that long-deferred but dearly-cherished object of every German heart, a comprehensive and united nationality. You left your native land, dismembered and disintegrated by long centuries of strife, that you might here breathe in freedom the invigorating air of a great, united, indivisible Republic. You left without regret the rival and contending Hapsburghs and Hohenzollerns, that you and your descendants, through coming ages, might inhabit and enjoy the land of Washington; that you might lawfully inherit and peacefully occupy the one great continental nation of the globe, stretching in unbroken expanse from ocean to ocean.

Noble Germans! Will you now permit this goodly heritage to be rudely torn from you? Will you abandon, without a struggle, this your magnificent domain, your own chosen land of refuge, to dismemberment and ruin? With the example fresh in memory of the fatherland, frittered by internal strife into dozens of petty principalities, can you now consent to dash down and demolish this majestic Republic, a dominant power among the nations of the earth, to set up in its place four and thirty rebel " sovereignties," falsely so-called, " all in a row "?

Thanks to the excellence of your German schools, you are men of education. Have you not been taught, and do you not instinctively know, that men in these modern days must live in nations and can no longer live in tribes? But what is the present treasonable attempt, alike wicked and weak, to throw down the united, organic sovereignty of our nation, but an attempt to restore the ancient rule of chieftains and tribes; to substitute the rattlesnake for the eagle; to hold aloft, not the immortal ensign of the Republic, radiant with its united stars, but local emblems, suited only for Chickasaws and Choctaws, the aboriginal and veritable inventors of " State sovereignty "?

Intelligent and patriotic Germans! You now go bravely forth to arrest this suicidal work of madness and ruin. Trebly armed with the justice of the cause, you march to battle to uphold the priceless boon of national existence, vital not alone to us, the natives of the soil, but to the hundreds of thousands of loyal German hearts thickly congregated in all our cities, and already counted by millions between our two great oceans. You go to prevent dismemberment, not alone from the misguided South, but from all your brethren of the German race clustered around our widespread western waters; to preserve the national unity, not only of this great Republic, but of your race itself.

In this flag as a symbol, you carry with you the affectionate regards, the fervent prayers, of the men and women of New York, invoking in your behalf the gracious protection of that All-Wise Being, the Great Architect of Nations, to uphold and reward your bravery, your patriotism, your public virtue.

At the conclusion of Mr. Ruggles' remarks, Mrs. Rupp, on behalf of a committee of ladies, presented, with a brief speech, a regimental standard, with mottoes of the society of Turners.

Miss Sophie L. Beisel presented (also in behalf of a committee of ladies) the German colors of black, red, and gold, and made a neat speech, reminding the soldiers that the present was given to remind them of the donors and those left behind, their brothers and weeping sisters, hoping, too, that they would be gallant, and return with the prestige of many victories.

Mrs. Stapps, a tall, masculine, but finely-spoken and intelligent lady of forty-five, who served as a private, disguised, under Hecker, in the revolution of 1848, delivered a stirring speech, calling upon the soldiers to be courageous, to fight nobly for their second fatherland; as they loved their sisters and wives, to promise to contend fitly for universal freedom, so that cannons and church bells might welcome them back with honor, pride, and general joy.

Col. Weber made a brief reply, thanking the

donors, on behalf of the regiment, for their regard, their presents, and their encouraging words; pledging that not only would the United Turner Rifles do honor to their original fatherland, but their adopted fatherland, whose flag they would seek to vindicate, and whose honor to raise above rebellion.

The following is a list of the officers of the 20th Regt. :

FIELD AND STAFF OFFICERS:—Colonel, Max Weber ; Lieutenant-Colonel Francis Weiss ; Major, Engelberth Schnepf; Adjutant, Rudolph Kluckhuhn ; Quartermaster, George Minch ; Surgeon, Julius Hausen ; Assistant Surgeon, Charles Heiland ; Sergeant Major, Henry R. Walter ; Assistant Quartermaster, Charles Lorch ; Drum Major, William Kaufman ; Bugle Major, Paul Gruchlin.

Company A—Captain, Lorenz Meyer ; 1st Lieut., William Knecht ; Ensign, Herman Stoeckel. Company B—Captain, Anthony Brecklin ; 1st Lieut., Franz Munich ; Ensign, Fritz Letzeiser. Company C—Captain, Charles Hochleitner ; 1st Lieut., Otto Hoym ; Ensign, Gustav Lorens. Company D—Captain, J. W. Einbigler ; 1st Lieut., William Drackers ; Ensign, Conturier Charles. Company E—Captain, Ernst Otto Bernet ; 1st Lieut., Henry Clober ; Ensign, Chares Voelker. Company F—Captain, Charles Semsey ; 1st Lieut., Herman Benecke ; Ensign, Rudolph Beutler. Company G—Captain, William Schoen ; 1st Lieut., William Syring ; Ensign, Jacob Pabst. Company H—Captain, William Von Doehr ; 1st Lieut., William Schul ; Ensign, Robert Merkle. Company I—Captain, Henry Stumpf ; 1st Lieut., Adolph Wilson ; Ensign, George Koenig. Company K—Captain, Joseph Hoeffling ; 1st Lieut., Wm. Hafner ; Ensign, Louis Kroeck.

—N. Y. Tribune, June 14.

Doc. 249.

SIXTH REGIMENT N. Y. VOLUNTEERS.

DEPARTURE FROM NEW YORK, JUNE 13.

THE regiment arrived from Staten Island, at the foot of Fourteenth street, and proceeded without delay through Fourteenth street and Fifth avenue to No. 63 Clinton place, where a magnificent silk banner was to be presented to them by the ladies of the Relief Committee. On arriving at the house the men were disposed in lines, the officers in front, and a large concourse of people surrounding the place.

Rev. S. H. Weston, chaplain of the Seventh regiment, accompanied by Mrs. George Strong, who held the banner, proceeded to present it in the following speech :—

FELLOW-SOLDIERS—I say fellow-soldiers, for we are all comrades in this holy war—I have been requested by the fair donors to address to you a few words on the presentation of this flag. I trust you appreciate this beautiful flag as thoroughly as I do being allowed the honor of participating in this interesting ceremony. Fellow-

soldiers, this standard of our beloved country is confided to your care. It is a precious charge, for it is an emblem of your country's integrity and renown. See to it, then, that these stars ever float over your heads as bright and pure as those above. Preserve its stripes stainless as the virtuous hearts that tender you this magnificent gift. As it sways to the breeze of Heaven, let it marshal you to an honorable career. Under its folds you may win imperishable glory, and write your names in the pages of history, to be proudly read by your children and a grateful posterity. Tread with alacrity, then, the path it points out to you. If it lead perchance to a bloody grave, it is "sweet to die for your country," and all coming time will hallow your resting place as the bed of glory. You have seen what a burial has been already accorded to the first martyrs in this war. If you come back victorious—which God grant—a grateful people will know how to honor the brave, and hail your return with thunders of applause. Douglass and the heart of Bruce ; Henry of Navarre, on the eve of a tremendous conflict, bade his soldiers look for the crisis of battle where streamed the white plume on his helmet. So let this flag wave wherever ebbs and flows the fiercest tide of war. I need not bid you bring it back with you, for I am sure if you return you will bear this standard in your midst. The Greeks slain in battle were borne home on their shields—it was a dishonor to return without them. Remember, then, the counsel of the Spartan mother to her son, when she presented him with his buckler : "With this, or on this." Bring back, then, this starry flag, without a stain, or let it be your winding sheet. You have the highest incentive that can rouse the energies of man. You are engaged in a righteous quarrel ; never was there a juster, a holier cause. "Thrice armed is he who hath his quarrel just." You will contend under this banner for constitutional liberty ; you will help to solve the mighty problem of self-government. The eyes of the whole world will be on you. The lovers of freedom in all lands will watch the strife with tearful eyes and beating hearts. This flag is the exponent of liberty ; the hope of humanity.

You will march under no bastard ensign, with half the stars blotted out, and the remainder travelling in dark eclipse. No palmetto abomination will flaunt treason over your heads, but above you will stream the banner triumphant on a hundred battle-fields, and under which your dauntless sires rushed to victory and renown. As fellow-soldiers, around these Stars and Stripes cluster dear memories and hallowed associations. Every thread in that dear flag has a tongue eloquent of human liberty, and reminds you of the priceless legacy bequeathed to you by your fathers. Every stitch is eloquent of canonized Lexington, Bunker Hill, Saratoga, and Yorktown. They adjure you by the memory of your heroic sires—by their suffering, toil, and blood—not to suffer it to be dishonored. Thank God, we have such a rallying point in this struggle. Its very presence in the fight hallows the cause and is an earnest of success. Every star that blazes in those azure folds is worth a hundred thousand men. The ring of your battle cry will be louder and clearer—your hearts firmer—your arms stronger—where it leads you on. Its very sight must palsy the hands of the traitors, and, blaspheme it as they may, they hesitate to strike it down. It is like an unnatural son striking at the heart of the mother that bore him; for beneath its honored folds were they born, and under its fostering care have they lived and won all they possess of prosperity and renown. This proud ensign then represents not only the hopes of the future, but the glories of the past. Every friend of human progress alive bids it God speed, and if the spirits of the illustrious departed are permitted to visit the scenes of their early triumphs, then are the shadows of the mighty dead leaving the skies to witness this conflict—all the martyrs of liberty down the track of time, from Marathon and Thermopylæ to Lexington and Concord. You will fight under a cloud of witnesses—both the living and the dead. But I adjure you, comrades, in the soldier do not forget the Christian and the man. War too often appeals to the worst passions of our nature, and tends to deaden the sensibilities, brutalize the heart, and make even the compassionate cruel. In the heat, then, of victorious fight ever remember mercy. Be a magnanimous enemy in the hours of triumph. You may disdain to ask quarter for yourselves, but never refuse it to a suppliant or prostrate foe. Let no wanton cruelty stain the laurels you may win. War, at best, is a tremendous calamity. Add not to its horrors the devilish spirit of hatred and revenge. It was said of Washington—Liberty unsheathed his sword, Necessity stained it, Victory returned it. In this unnatural strife, let the pleading voice of humanity be heard even over the roar of battle. Smite with the sword of the Lord and Gideon when duty commands; but in the flush of conquest, remember the Divine promise—"Blessed is the merciful man, for he shall obtain mercy." Above all, remember Him who giveth the victory. The race is not always to the swift, nor the battle to the strong. Implore the protection of the God of Battles. You may feel indifferent now. You will be serious, thoughtful, in the presence of the enemy. You will not regret then your daily prayers. If your duties are exciting you may make them brief. That was a short prayer of the publican—"God, be merciful to me, a sinner." It was accepted. Imitate the great captain when about to rush into a desperate conflict. You can remember it—"Oh, my God, if I forget Thee this day, do not Thou forget me." Pray, then, yourselves, and dear ones at home will pray for you. And now God be with you, and bear your shield and buckler against all your foes, temporal or spiritual, and return you to your homes—conquerors for humanity's sake, your country's sake,—conquerors for Christ's sake. Amen.

REPLY OF COLONEL WILSON.

Colonel Wilson received the banner from the hands of Mrs. George Strong, and, carrying it into the ranks, gave it into the hands of the color-sergeant. Colonel Wilson and the color-sergeant then returned to the foot of the steps, both grasping the banner of liberty. The Colonel seemed deeply affected, and his utterance was choked for some time. His wife stood on the stoop, regarding him with tearful emotion. At length he summoned courage and spoke as follows:—

I can hardly speak; utterance has been taken from me. When I see my wife, when I see the ladies of New York city, who have done so much, I have to say of that flag that I love it better than my wife or child; better than I love her, my wife, do I love the honor of that flag. For my God first, for my country next, and for my family next. (Cheers.) I have sacrificed every thing except my God for that flag—(cheers)—and I do believe as enthusiastically as the men who went to Palestine to fight, that the man who fights for that flag, although he dies, he dies holy, and fighting for the Almighty. (Enthusiastic cheering.) I feel this in my heart; I can hardly speak, for I know not what I had to say. What I do say I say from my heart, and it is as God directs me—that this is a religious war. It is a war for the intelligence—for the freedom of the world—not for this country. (Cheers.) It is a war to protect men, women, and children; that the liberties of the people may be protected in spite of aristocrats or would-be traitors. (Cheers.) It is not for the glory of fighting or being the colonel of any regiment that I go forth to fight. It is because I devote my life to this cause. (Cheers.) I love my wife and child second to my flag, which I am ready to defend and die for. (Cheers.) The ladies of New York, God bless them, for they are Heaven-born angels—they have proved Heaven-born angels to me—to bless and protect the poor traveller as he passes through the world. They have looked on me as one who was disgraced in the world—and some of my men bore hard names once. But they are honest and true. They are nature's noblemen. (Cheers.) They are such men as those who guarded the liberty of this country—such as those who guarded the liberties of England, made the King sign Magna Charta—(cheers); they are such men as made Rome a republic, and fought for liberty in France. (Cheers.) They are as the sons of Abraham, who went forth to fight the Philistines. I love that flag, (pointing to the banner,) and though I go upon the torrid, sandy beach of Pensacola, and die there; though I go on the plains of Texas, it matters not. If I go on the plains of Virginia and gain renown, it is well; but wherever we are told to go. we go there, as long as it is for the honor and perpetuity of the flag, the freedom of the world, and the protection of the beautiful city of New York. (Tremendous cheering.) That man (pointing to the standard-bearer) will carry that flag, and when he goes another will carry it who will not be afraid of ten thousand traitors—(cheers) —and when he dies every man will jump to grasp the flag. (Cheers.) It will take, however, a good many to kill him, and I don't think the ball is moulded, or will be moulded this year, to kill either him or me. (Cheers and laughter.) Ladies, I thank you from the inmost recesses of my heart. I again express every feeling in full on behalf of my gallant officers and my devoted and patriotic men. (Loud applause.)

OFFICERS OF THE SIXTH REGIMENT.

The following is a list of the field, staff, and line officers :

FIELD OFFICERS :—Colonel, William Wilson ; Lieut.-Col., John Creighton ; Major, William B. Newby.

STAFF OFFICERS :—Adjutant, J. J. Heary ; Quartermaster, M. E. Bradley ; Surgeon, P. B. Peace ; Assistant Surgeon, Edward Lynch.

Company A—Captain, Burgess ; 1st Lieut., Latham ; Ensign, Cox. Company B—Captain, A. T. Whiting ; Ensign, Vangieson. Company C—Captain, R. H. Hazeltine ; 1st Lieut., R. Baily ; Ensign, M. Hanham. Company D—Captain, Patrick Duffy ; 1st Lieut., Haggerty ; Ensign, Enwhistle. Company E—Captain, Dufraine ; 1st Lieut., Roddy ; Ensign, Matthews. Company F—Captain, Norman ; 1st Lieut., Heary ; Ensign, Barker. Company G—Captain, Dobie ; 1st Lieut., D'Orville ; Ensign, Black. Company H—Captain, Peter Duffy ; 1st Lieut., Clapp ; Ensign, Evarts. Company I—Captain, McCormick ; 1st Lieut., Kauffman ; Ensign, Spence. Company K—Captain, Hoelzle ; 1st Lieut., Silloway ; Ensign, Kraehl. —N. Y. Herald, June 14.

Doc. 249½.

AN APPEAL TO MARYLAND.

BY JOHN P. KENNEDY.

IT is the most deplorable misfortune of our unhappy country, at this moment, that it has no authentic voice to speak its honest, sober judgment on the public affairs. Here we are in Maryland, involved in a dreadful revolution which has already convulsed society to the centre, torn up its prosperity by the roots, sown discord in families, alienated old and familiar friends, and spread consternation through the whole community. It has visited peaceful and thriving households with want, stricken down fortunes acquired by long and patient industry, scattered the small accumulations of humble thrift, and reduced to absolute beggary thousands and thousands of the best and most useful of our working population. These are the ravages of the first act in the Great Drama.

The second act is about to open upon us. The pride and flower of our youth are in arms. Hostile camps are gathering their forces. Wild, ungovernable, and savage men are openly and stealthily armed with terrible weapons. Hatreds are cast abroad and sown in fierce hearts. Denunciation and proscription are uttered in under tones and with ominous threats of mischief. Soon we shall hear the clash of arms. What then ? Read the wars of the Roses ; read the marches and the raids of Cromwell ; the ravages of the Palatinate ; the fusilades of Lyons. Read, at random, any page that records the rage, the demonism, the hellish passion of civil war, and fancy the sack of cities, the brutal and indiscriminate murder of old and young of either sex, the rape and rapine, the conflagration, the shriek of surprised families, the midnight flight of mothers and children tracking their way with bleeding feet—the mourning, the desolation, the despair which are all painted in such horrid colors in that history—fancy all these pictures converted into the realities of our own experience, and we shall then come to the perception of the second act of this portentous drama.

How does it come to pass that this, our prosperous State of Maryland—this, our beautiful City of Baltimore, is suddenly hurled into the bosom of this commotion ? Why is it that Maryland, so remote from the first theatre of revolution, so little concerned in its issues, so reluctant to take sides in this miserable quarrel—Maryland, happy and peaceful—why is it that she is doomed to stand forward, the first to encounter the sweep of this storm, to bear its continuous brunt, and to give up her substance, her children, and her homes, to the alternate ravage of contending factions, until war, wearied with slaughter and exhausted by its own destruction, shall no longer find a victim or a country to punish ?

We answer this terrible question truly when we say that Maryland, like her sisters of the Confederacy, is allowed no free and honest expression of her thoughts. It is too painfully obvious that Maryland opinion is surrendered to the control of influences that repress all wise and earnest consideration of the momentous topics that belong to the public welfare. Its key note is derived from the heated utterances of passionate and thoughtless youth, of impressible women and girls, of infuriated politicians, of all that multitude of excitable, rash, unreasoning persons who fly to conclusions under the impulse of prejudice, desire, or interest ; and lastly and more significantly, of wily, unscrupulous partisan leaders who are moved by premeditated design to accomplish a selfish party triumph. In the domineering ascendency of these agencies over the public mind, the quiet, reflective good sense of the community is repressed ; the orderly and industrious are kept in the background ; the timid are overawed ; the weak are silenced, and the credulous are misled.

The whole movement towards secession, even in the States most favorable to it, has been artfully promoted by the fabrications of a false opinion. It has been borne along by a whirlwind of contrived excitement. The passions of the people have been inflamed by exaggerated representations of impending dangers; by skilful exhibition of the idle ravings of mad and wicked fanatics as the settled views of the Government; by startling conjunctures preconcerted by the managers to madden the temper and overwhelm the discretion of the populace, and by provoking outbreak and violence as the topics for frantic appeal to the manhood and patriotism of the State. The unnecessary bombardment of the starving garrison of Sumter was intended to stimulate the reluctant mind of Virginia to secession. The simultaneous seizures of Gosport Navy Yard and of Harper's Ferry were the arranged stimulants to confirm the wavering resolution of that State. The futile and calamitous attempt to resist the passage of the troops through Maryland was but another spur to quicken the speed of secession, by driving the State against its better judgment into rebellion. The secession enterprise, everywhere, has been remarkably characterized by the signs of a conspiracy to give the minority a command over the majority. It avoids reference to the popular consent, screens its plans from public criticism by secret sessions, and plies the machinery of passion to rush the people into the abyss of revolution, with the renunciation of all thought and forecast of its consequences.

There is something ungenerous, and even worse, in the advantage which the Seceding States have taken of the wise and patriotic sentiment of the Border States against coercion. When these latter States pledged themselves, in the beginning of the rupture, that they would not sanction any attempt of the Government to coerce the Seceders into submission, it was a pledge that the experiment of secession should be allowed to take its allotted course in peace, with the hope that peace would bring calm judgment into action, and, through its influence, an early return to harmony in the Union. Such a pledge implied a counter-pledge of moderation of counsel and honest confidence in the unbiassed judgment of the people, by the Seceding States. It implied that the good sense of the country should be left free to act, with perfect immunity from artificial excitement, on the whole subject wherever it might be brought into debate. Instead of granting this freedom from agitation to the Border States, the secession party of the South, taking advantage of the promise against coercion, has busily employed itself in provoking collision by assault and spreading panic by alarm, and thus stirring the population of the Border into sudden revolt against the Government. They contrive a necessity for coercion, and then call on the Border States to resist it, in fulfilment of a promise really made to secure peace.

Such are the conditions in which Maryland is now invoked to imbrue her hands in the blood of civil war. It cannot escape observation, that, notwithstanding the large majority of the people of Maryland are now, and ever have been, true and faithful to the Union, and averse to every design to drag them into this ruinous career of revolution, there is an active, intelligent, and ardent minority in the State, who are bent upon forcing her into the Southern Confederacy; and that although this secession party, now accidentally in possession of the legislative power, finds itself compelled to succumb to the force gathering around it, and to temporize with the difficulties it cannot surmount, it still cherishes the purpose of future control, and only lies at lurch, waiting the events of the day to make a new effort to array the State against the Government.

In this condition of things, it is of the profoundest moment that we should invoke the good sense of every patriotic citizen in our Commonwealth to look the danger around us in the face, and before it is too late to make a united effort to recall our excited brothers to an honest and sober consideration of our destiny. The men of Maryland, of all parties, are too earnest, too faithful to their duty to themselves and the community in which they live, too honorable, frank, and just, knowingly to perpetrate a wrong against the prosperity and happiness of their own homes and kindred—their children and their friends. We accord the fullest honesty of intention even to the rashest and most thoughtless of those who are endeavoring to cast our lot upon the path of disunion. We believe them sincere in thinking that the honor and the welfare of the State demand that we should follow the lead of the bold spirits of the South who have plunged the country into this commotion. Our ingenuous and excitable youth have yielded to what we regard as but a natural impulse, when they bravely rushed to arms to resent what they were taught to think an invasion of our rights. In doing this, they have only demonstrated a noble and mistaken ardor proper to their age and temper, and which now but wants a good cause to win all the applause to which they aspire. They prove to us how much we may depend upon their manhood when the country really requires their arm. But they, like many of their elders, are acting under a delusion.

Maryland has no cause to desert our honored Stars and Stripes. Out of this Union, there is nothing but ruin for her. In the Union, dark as may be the present day, the stout resolve of Maryland to maintain her fealty to the faith of her fathers, will secure to her yet a glorious future.

Let us not fall into the fatal error of thinking that the great interests of the Union are irretrievably lost by the election of an Administration we do not like. At the worst the present predominance of a sectional party in the National Government is but a transient evil. We shall never have another but through the ignoble surrender of the loyal men of the South. Even indeed now, the perpetuation of such a party is an impossibility in the North. The excitement and storm of this day—if it has, for a season, unseated the prosperity of the nation —is worth all its privations, in the good it has already accomplished. It has forever put an end to that pestilent agitation of slavery which, for thirty years, has disturbed the repose of the country; it has forever put an end to sectional Presidents and parties; it has revealed a great truth to this nation—that the Union is above all party, and that peaceful brotherhood is the most beneficent of all our blessings.

Let us bring our minds to a calm estimate of our own duty in this great crisis. There is but one issue before us, Union or Disunion. Every man in Maryland must meet that issue.

Union, on the one side, is loyalty, faith in the traditions of our ancestors, devotion to our historical renown, brave support of our country in its adversity.

Disunion—let us not evade the conclusion— is rebellion, desertion of our duty, dishonor to our flag; voluntary disgrace cast upon the names of the heroes and sages who have made our country illustrious in human annals. It is prompted by the assertion of a principle of anarchy, which makes all government impossible; a false dogma which affirms a right of disintegration that may pervade every division of society.

This assumed right of secession is scouted by the judgment of the world. No jurist, no statesman, no man of honest judgment ever affirmed it until, in these later days, it was found to be the convenient pretext for a party design. Every President who has heard it uttered, every Cabinet, every State, every party, at one period or another of our progress, has disowned it. If Washington or Jackson were alive they would account it only as rank rebellion, and would so treat it.

We may not shelter ourselves under the plea of revolution. Maryland has no cause for revolution. No man in Maryland can lay his hand upon his heart and say that this Government of ours has ever done him wrong; has ever stinted its bounty to him in the full enjoyment of his life, liberty, and pursuit of happiness. We cannot answer to God or man, therefore, for plunging into the great crime of rebellion and treason. Our honor, our faith, our religion will rise up in judgment against us, to convict us of the greatest wickedness man can commit, if, on such a pretence, we lifted a bloody hand against the blessed parent of our political life. Is loyalty nothing? Submission to law nothing? Fidelity to duty nothing? Gentlemen of Maryland, do these things no longer touch your honor? Will you listen to the sordid arguments of gain, to the mean persuasions of interest, to the fear of danger, to the wretched slanders of fanatics, to the dread of that vulgar obloquy which brands you with the name of "Submissionists," to seduce you from your allegiance to the Government you have inherited from brave ancestors? Has the cavalier blood become so diluted in your veins that you can for such motives abandon your country in her distress? We mistake you, and have long misunderstood you, if that be the spirit in which you meet this crisis. No, no. Stand by your ancient flag. Be true to Maryland, and keep her where your fathers placed her, and when the time comes redeem your country.

For what does Secession now rear a mutilated banner?

For what cause does it invite us to take up arms?

We hear different answers to these questions.

Some, who think a sectional patriotism to be their greatest duty, answer, "For Southern rights."

Others, who think worldly profit a higher motive, say, "For Southern trade."

Others again, who seem to be swayed by a kind of fatalism, say, "We have no choice— we must go as Virginia goes."

We have not yet heard the first man on that side say any thing about Maryland rights, Maryland honor, or Maryland independence.

Is it not strange that they forget Maryland has any duty to perform to herself and for herself?

Let us weigh these answers.

What are Southern rights? Everybody speaks of them, nobody defines them. So vague, so misty, so variable, they escape every attempt to grasp them.

Do they comprise, as a chief demand—as many say they do—the right to maintain the institution of slavery unmolested and unimpaired in the States that possess it?

If so, no one now disputes that right. It is affirmed and offered to be made perpetual, even by the late Republican Congress, by the enactment of an irrepealable amendment to the Constitution, which guarantees it forever.

Do they assert the right to take slaves into all the territory of the United States south of the Missouri line, as proposed by the Crittenden resolutions?

If that be the demand, that right now exists to its fullest extent, and slavery is at this day by law protected in every foot of territory south of 36° 30'; and even the three new territories north of that line are open to the admission of slaves without restriction.

Do they mean the right to recover fugitive slaves from the Free States?

If so, all impediment to that right is virtually withdrawn. The Administration affirms a purpose to execute the law, and, in point of fact, the law is now executed with more efficiency and less obstruction than it has been for thirty years past.

Are these the Southern rights for which we are invited to get up revolution and war, and will war be likely to secure them in more full enjoyment than we have them now?

Are there any other Southern rights in dispute? We hear sometimes of a right to free trade and direct taxation; a right to traffic in African slaves; a right to Cuba, to Mexico, to Central America. Is Maryland willing to fight for these?

Then as to "Southern trade," which has captivated the imagination of some who have fallen into the secession ranks.

There are many variant and contradictory notions on this point. Carolina hopes to make a New York of Charleston, Georgia claims this bounty for Savannah, Virginia demands it for Norfolk, Louisiana pleases her fancy with the miraculous growth of New Orleans. The visionaries of Maryland quietly smile at all these delusions, perfectly confident that the cornucopia is to be emptied upon Baltimore.

We say nothing of the heart-burnings and jealousies which these various hopes must engender if any one of these dreams are realized to the disappointment of the others. We are only concerned to look at the probable result upon Maryland.

This supposed commercial advantage is founded upon the idea, much commended in the South, of free trade with all the foreign world, and heavy restrictions upon the trade with the United States; a system of commerce built upon complacency on one side and revenge on the other. The Southern Confederacy, it is presumed, will, in the future permanent arrangement of its policy, encumber one-half of its trade—and that its most indispensable and necessary supply—with heavy duties, and leave the other half, which chiefly concerns its luxuries, free. Does any experienced merchant believe this? What will the South gain by laying duties upon the thousand productions of the North that now enter so largely into their common household and agricultural wants? Will they get their farming implements, their machinery, their wooden ware, their fish, their beef, their hay, their ice, their carriages, shoes, hats, and clothing—any part of their whole inventory of family requisitions—more cheaply for that? No other country can supply them so well, and the experiment will soon prove that every cent of tax so levied is but a charge upon themselves. When that is proved, and the passion of the day subsides, it is reasoning against all the motives of human conduct to suppose that a merely vindictive restriction will be allowed to exist. The North would soon grow to be in the same category to the South with all the rest of the world—in war, enemies, in peace, friends; and the free trade system, if practicable at all, will be extended equally to all within the range of Southern commerce.

There are some who think these discriminations will be made with a view to the establishment of large manufacturing interests in the South. But to this there is the obvious reply, that no manufacturing system ever was built up in companionship with free trade; and the Southern Constitution has already put a veto upon the attempt by a specific prohibition of all power to protect any domestic industry.

The Northern manufactures are sufficiently established and prosperous to compete with the world in free trade, and they will always continue to find a Southern market from their exact adaptation to Southern wants. But the manufactures of Maryland, in great part, are precisely those which would wither and perish under the free trade policy. We could supply no iron from our mines, no iron fabrics from our workshops. Our great steam enginery, our railroad apparatus, our heavy works of the foundry, our cast and rolled metal, could never hold their own in the presence of free importations from England. It will occur to any one conversant with our workshops, that much of our most important industry here in Baltimore, and throughout the State, would be compelled to yield under the pressure of European rivalry.

Again, free trade implies direct taxation to raise revenue for the support of government. A glance at this will supply another element for the consideration of those who fancy that Maryland is to prosper in a Southern Confederacy.

The expenses of the new Government are inevitably to be cast upon a higher estimate than we have ever witnessed in our heretofore harmonious Union. Large armies and navies are to be provided as the necessary apparatus of government. Fifty millions a year will not be an unfamiliar experience to the Southern financier. If that amount is to be levied upon some nine millions of free population, which about represent the present number of the whole of the Southern States, it affords a ratio of more than five dollars a head. If but thirty millions be the expenditure, it will be over three dollars a head. Maryland contains near six hundred and fifty thousand free persons, and thus we estimate her annual share of the tax at over three millions per annum, on a fifty million expenditure, and on the supposition of thirty millions, something near two millions per annum. Our present State tax is about two hundred and fifty thousand dollars. The addition to this, for the support of the Confederate Government, will, on the first supposed rate of expenditure, be twelve, on the other, eight times the present tax. I give these figures as a formula of calculation which any one may apply to his own estimate of the probable expenditure of the new Government, if its revenues are to be supplied by direct taxation.

How the trade and industry of Maryland may reconcile themselves to such a system, I leave those to judge who are best acquainted with the tax bills our present necessities impose upon us.

If it should be discovered, as I have no doubt it will be, after some sore and short experience, that this free trade fancy is but an expensive delusion, and that the old, long-tried, universal and inevitable system of duties, known to and practised by all nations, as the most commendable system of national support, must be substituted by the Confederate States, what then will be the condition of their commerce? It will then be found that the revolution has been a vain work The bubble will have burst, and the experimenters, after having turned the whole nation back a quarter of a century in its career—having ruined a generation, subverted more capital than would suffice to purchase every slave in the nation, accumulated a debt impossible to be paid, and spread repudiation and bankruptcy over a whole circle of States—happy, if to these evils it has not added the clothing of every household in mourning—the experimenters will then find themselves vainly endeavoring to restore trade to the same relations and arrangement in which it was at the fatal moment when they initiated their new career. All that will then have been achieved will be the creation of a double set of political dignitaries, and the distribution of a double supply of loaves and fishes to the patriots of the ferment.

A tariff of duties for revenue once adopted, it then becomes the plain policy of the United States of the old Confederacy to enact the same rates, and commerce will immediately oscillate back to the track and custom of its old career.

Even if it should not be drawn again into that current, what has Baltimore to hope for? Will she import for the South, from the head of the Chesapeake, whilst Norfolk lies on the margin of the sea at its mouth, with an admirable harbor, and with all the means of Western and Southern distribution by railroads that penetrate to the Mississippi and Ohio? Do old and sagacious merchants of Baltimore allow this delusion to seize their minds? Boys may prate about such things, but surely men of sense will repeat no such absurdity. But, we have heard it said, if Maryland be not a member of the Southern Confederacy, Virginia, in time of war, may close all access to the Chesapeake against us. That is true. But if Maryland should be a member of that Confederacy, then the North, in time of war, may also shut up the Chesapeake against us; and not only that, but may also shut up our Western and Northern railroads. It may deny us the Ohio River; it may deny us access to Philadelphia, to New York—utterly obliterate not only our trade, but cut off our provisions. In the other case, Virginia could not do that, nor even impede our transit on the Baltimore and Ohio Railroad, as long as Western Virginia shall stand our friend, as assuredly it will if we are true to ourselves.

The last argument popularly used in favor of the secession of Maryland, is that which asserts a necessity that compels us "to go as Virginia goes."

It is supposed that the recent attempted secession of Virginia leaves us no choice. It is declared that our sympathies as well as our interests are with Virginia; in fact, that our fate is in her hands. If this were true, it would have been but a becoming decorum in Virginia to have invited us into her counsels, or, at least, to have warned us of the complications she was preparing for us. As it is, she has led us blindfold to the edge of the precipice, and those of our own fellow-citizens who renounce for us all freedom of opinion on our own destiny, tell us we have no choice but to take the leap.

We deny that Maryland is so bound up in the fortunes of Virginia. We regard the interest of that State to be quite as dependent upon the favor of Maryland as Maryland is upon her. In all that denotes vigor, growth of power, and capacity for great enterprise, Maryland is ahead of Virginia. Whilst our population in the last decade has increased twenty-five per cent., that of Virginia has not advanced over twelve. What we have accomplished in public works and in the extension of commercial activity, bears a still more favorable comparison in the estimate of the resources of the two States. Let us not so derogate from the influence and capability of our own State as to surrender our independence to the control of politicians who have as yet shown so little capacity in governing their own. In truth, we might, with good reason, reverse the affirmation of the argument we are considering, and say that Virginia should look to Maryland, and should adapt her policy, on this question of separation, to ours. She should at least consult the other Border States, Kentucky, Tennessee, Missouri, as well as Maryland, and shape her course in conformity with their common views.

When we speak of Virginia, there is another most significant question to be considered. To what portion of Virginia are we to attach our fortunes? Is it to that waning Eastern section which at present holds the political power over the State—that section whose population, scattered over the region visited by the tide, is gradually declining in numbers and losing its ascendency in the public affairs, and whose power at this day is founded rather upon the traditions of the past than upon any inherent capacity to govern? or is it to that vigorous and healthful Western Virginia, upon whom nature has lavished her bounty in the provision of all the elements of a prosperous and powerful community?

Virginia is divided into two distinct sections, altogether different in physical quality and in moral character. The one teems with a redundant slave population, of which the excess is kept down by a continual drain of emigration to the South. Its habits are Southern, its affinities are for the South. These are not less nourished by the character of its labor than by the temper of its leading men—talented and impulsive and educated in strong sympathy with the Secession States.

The other division includes the land of the mountaineer—a land of mineral wealth, of rapid streams, of fertile pastures, of bracing atmosphere, where the people have little dependence on slave labor, and who see in the resources of the soil and climate an invitation to all the varied industry of populous and thriving States.

We of Maryland are solicited to associate ourselves with the first of these divisions. It is said our natural relationship is with them.

We certainly have had abundant reason, in the past, to know that the governing power of Virginia does not reciprocate the favor of this relationship. Maryland has no more persistent and steady antagonism to her policy to contend against than she has ever found in the domination of this low country influence. Let those who have had the management of our public works, our railroad and canal, say what difficulties they have had to encounter in the hostility of Virginia to the grant of the smallest privilege or aid from that State; and let them describe how all solicitations have been refused until the friendly intercession of the Western counties, often baffled, has at last by peremptory demand secured us the grace of being permitted to expend millions of Maryland capital upon Virginia soil.

The true friends and allies of our policy are in the West. At this moment that region is making its protest against secession. It is a matter of the deepest moment that we should wisely appreciate this fact. It is not for us now to discuss the probable contingencies of the future, which may spring out of the state of opinion in the Western counties; but we shall not blindly adopt a policy in the present juncture, which may forever alienate them from the interest which makes them the guardians and protectors of our road and the ministers to our trade.

The singular change of opinion which has recently brought Virginia into secession is one of the inexplicable things of the day. Time may perhaps prove it to be a forced assent obtained by the arts which have, everywhere in the seceding States, more or less subdued and coerced public opinion. At present the world can only perceive that "the Mother of States," in spite of her protestations of independence, in spite of the contumely and insult heaped upon her, has succumbed to the dictation of Carolina—has been "dragged" into revolution, and compelled to an act of submission, by which she has surrendered her lofty position as a mediator in the national quarrel, and sunk into a secondary power in the new Confederacy. She is the first of the Border States that has given way. Let Maryland be the last to follow her example.

We cannot forget that the Southern Confederacy has hitherto repudiated all connection with the Border States; that they were contemptuously repelled as unworthy of consultation. It is only now, when a severe experience has demonstrated the necessity of friends able both to pay and to fight, that these States are approached with flattering appeals to take a stand in the very front of war and bear the brunt of its worst assaults. We who never

felt or professed any respect for their cause, who, indeed, accuse them of having produced all the difficulties and disgraces which have resulted from the recent Presidential Election, are now counselled to patient submission to this coercion, and even to embrace it with thankful avidity as an honorable duty. Virginia has placed herself at the head of the Submissionists, and men whom we have esteemed, here in Maryland, for their manhood, tell us we have no choice but to follow her example!

I draw this view of our condition to a close by repeating my clear conviction that the interest and safety of Maryland coincide with her loyalty to the Union, that disunion is ruin to her.

Let us not be moved by the taunt that we are aiding the Republican cause and vidicating the Administration of Mr. Lincoln. That is but the party vituperation of those who seek to frighten us by false clamor into an abandonment of our opposition to their own party schemes. We deplore the unfortunate ascendency of the Republican party; we censure the policy of the Administration. We may claim much more respect for our sincerity in this than our opponents are entitled to ask, since it is only by their machinations that the Republican party has won its ascendency, and by their desertion of their posts and their duty in Congress, that Mr. Lincoln's Administration has obtained any power to involve the country in the present commotion. In the stage at which the public embarrassments have now arrived, all the questions of the late canvass have disappeared. The country is aroused to the protection of the Union, to the defence of our system of government. The men who were most earnest in opposing the election of Mr. Lincoln, throughout the whole North and West, are united into a compact body, in a unanimous determination to vindicate the right of the people to the Union bequeathed to them by their fathers. Large numbers in the South, whose voices are suppressed by the despotism of party rule, have the same sentiment deeply impressed upon their hearts. The conservative Northern men who have come so sternly and with such alacrity to this duty of defence—a majority of the Northern people—will visit with indignant disgust the fanatical agitators of the slavery question, whose wicked pertinacity has raised this storm in the nation, and we shall hear no more of the wretched cant of the sin of slavery in the South. That abuse of the peace of the nation will be purged away by this commotion, if no other good result from it.

On one side of us is a united nation of nineteen millions of people. On the other, a divided population of nine millions. We stand between them. If we remain true to the Union, we shall have protection and peace, and hereafter an easy settlement of all our complaints. If we desert the Union, we shall be driven into a Confederacy which has but little sympathy with our interests, and less power to protect us against the ravage of the frequent wars which must inevitably arise between the two sections.

The Southern Confederacy is essentially weak in the basis of its construction. It is founded on a principle which must lead to the ever-recurring dangers of new secessions, and the exhibition of a worse than Mexican anarchy. It may witness *pronunciamientoes* upon every discontent, and the strife of parties ending in further disintegration. If the Border States go into that Confederacy, the opposition of material interests will soon develop the utter want of capacity in the new Government to secure its cohesion.

Maryland, under any circumstances of peace or war, must soon become a free State, and she will then be found to be wholly ungenial to the principle upon which the Southern Confederacy is established. It would, therefore, not be long before she would be compelled to retire from the alliance, and become a suppliant for shelter under the wing of that old Union which in a rash moment she had abandoned.

If she remain where she is, her example may influence the course of the other Border States which now are drawn to the verge of secession, and with them may happily bring about a restoration of the whole Union. Four years hence, this Administration will give place to another. A popular, conservative President then elected will restore confidence to the whole country. The Union sentiment of the South will make itself heard in the remotest sections of the secession, and disenthralled from the domination that now forbids it to speak, it will once more assert its attachment to the Stars and Stripes.

Let the true voice of our State now be heard on these questions. The Legislature now in session has one solemn duty to perform. It is to give the State an opportunity to declare its wish. Much has been said about the desire of Maryland to fall into the ranks of the Seceding States. There has been a great clamor for a Convention by those who have been anxious for secession. Let the Legislature now put the question to the people—Do you want a Convention, with power to declare Maryland out of the Union?

Put that question, and we shall then know what part Maryland will take in the Great Drama.

BALTIMORE, *May* 9, 1861.

Doc. 250.

SPEECH OF JOHN S. CARLILE,

IN THE WHEELING CONVENTION, JUNE 14, 1861.

I THINK, sir, that a moment's consideration will satisfy this Convention that upon this question there is at least no difference of opinion between the advocates of a separation of this State. If I may be allowed, I can claim some credit for my sincerity, when I say that it has

been an object for which I have labored at least since the year 1850. The Convention that met in Richmond in that year and adopted our present State Constitution, clearly disclosed, to my mind, the utter incompatibility consistent with the interests of the people of North-western Virginia of remaining in a connection with the Eastern portion of the State. And, sir, the first favorable opportunity that discovered itself to me for affecting that separation was in the Convention that met in this city in May last. And I appeal to members who are present, and who were members of that Convention, to say if I did not zealously press that measure. Why did I do it? For the reason which I then stated—for the reason that now prevents me doing it. I then stated that we were still citizens of the United States, according to even the theory of the Disunionists; that a separation could be effected then by the provision of the U. S. Constitution providing for it; but when the 23d of May came and went, and the sun had set behind the hills in the evening of that day, we would be transferred, according to the theory of the Secessionists, to another and different Confederacy, and would be deprived of the Constitution of the United States, and the mode and manner in which a separation could thereafter be effected under the authority of these Secessionists by virtue of that transfer, could only be by treaty and recognition; that although all Virginia should agree to the separation, yet she would have to obtain the consent of the Southern Confederacy, expressed in accordance with the Constitution which she has adopted for its government, before we could be allowed to transfer ourselves to what they would then call another, a different, and a hostile Government. I saw difficulties innumerable and insurmountable if we did not act then. But the wisdom of that body thought otherwise, and I gracefully, as I should, bowed to its decision.

Now, sir, where are we? I call the attention of my friend from Monongalia, and I tell him if he beats me in this race of separation, he will have to be swifter than I think he is. We have no Legislature now; and mark you, it is only by the assent of the Legislature a separation can be effected. The people themselves, through their representatives assembled, cannot assent to a separation. It can only be done as is provided in the Constitution of the United States, by the assent of the Legislature of the State. Now, sir, have we a Legislature? Gov. Letcher would say that we have; and its members will be sworn to support the Constitution of the Southern Confederacy. Then you see we can never effect a separation in the manner in which we would have accomplished it.

Now, sir, let us pursue the policy laid down in the declaration, and let us repudiate Letcher and his transfer; let us assemble a Legislature here of our own, sworn to support, not the Southern Confederacy Constitution, but that which Washington and Madison formed, the

Constitution of our fathers, under which we have grown and prospered, as never people grew and prospered before. Let us maintain our position under that tree of Liberty, watered by the blood and tears of the patriots of the Revolution—planted by them, its roots having taken deep and firm hold in the hearts of a great people, and having, from a little spot on earth, spread from the Atlantic to the Pacific, embracing, I might say, a continent, and spreading its branches of protection over the whole unbounded land.

Let us organize a Legislature, swearing allegiance to that Government, and let that Legislature be recognized by the United States Government, as *the* Legislature of Virginia.

Then we have still a direct recognition of the protecting care of our ancient Government, and then we will effect this separation. But now, with no Legislature recognized as owing allegiance to the Constitution of the United States, we could not do it. But with the Legislature recognized as still the Legislature of the State; with Virginia in the Union; with a Legislature recognized by the Government of the United States, and with its assent to our separation, our way is clear. And if the Southern Confederacy dares to interpose, we have the strong arm of that same old Government to be thrown around us, and to shelter us from harm.

Let us then go on as we propose. Let us be recognized as the true and lawful authorities, speaking for and on behalf of the loyal people of the whole State of Virginia. Give us that recognition, and then the separation will come. And I here say that one of the first acts I shall perform, if no one else does it—and I believe it a duty I owe to the people who have honored me with a seat in Congress, will be to obtain from that body a legislative declaration recognizing this Legislature you will assemble here, as the Legislature of the State; and then let my friends, the representatives, assent to it, and my word for it, we will be the State of New Virginia.

It is a mere question now whether we shall wait until we are solemnly recognized as the true, legal, constitutional representatives of the people of Virginia, or whether we shall now attempt an impossibility; for every man who will reflect a moment will know that, until rebellion is crushed, no assent will be attained for our separation from the rebellious portion of this State.

But, sir, there is another object which I have at heart. Two great objects influence and govern my actions. The first, I am free to say the dearest, the highest, and the nearest my heart, is the perpetuity of the Union.

Keeping forever undimmed the thirty-four stars that now deck the constellation of our national ensign, adding to them, as we have done, star after star—when that is done—when safety and perpetuity are again secured to that flag—then we can consider our own State interests; then we can consider the interests of our own immediate section of this State; but until then, we owe it to our loyal brothers throughout the length and breadth of this great land, to stand by them and aid them in resisting a crime, the greatest that has ever been attempted to be perpetrated on humanity. Let us do this, succeed in this, and we will succeed in all we desire in a very short time. Let us bring peace again to our Loudon, Alexandria, and Hampshire friends. Let our brothers over the mountains, through our aid and assistance, and that of this great and good Government of ours, again see harmony throughout the land; again sit around their hearthstones with their families, and again instil, in the quiet hours of peace, the lessons the Father of his Country has bequeathed to us in his Farewell Address. Then we may say to them: "We love you still as brothers, but your interests and ways and ours are diverse. Let this line be drawn between us. We will have two separate and distinct sovereign States; but, brethren, we will be American citizens!"

—*N. Y. Tribune,* June 20.

Doc. 251.

THE FIRST PRIVATEER.

A REAL, but not very formidable specimen of a privateer, sailing under the pirate flag of the Southern Confederacy, with a letter-of-marque duly signed by Jeff. Davis, arrived at New York in charge of Midshipman McCook, and a prize crew from the U. S. frigate Minnesota, on the 15th of June. She is a "low black" schooner, but not "long," being only some fifty tons' measurement, with raking masts like a pilot-boat, and, for an old-fashioned vessel, is quite sharp, and is said to be a first-rate sailer. She has no name on the stern, but the word Savannah, in raised letters, on the front part of her trunk cabin, is no doubt the name of the vessel. She has been a Charleston pilot-boat, and for two years past was laid up in that port, condemned.

She carries a formidable 18-pounder gun, mounted on a swivel amidships, and on each side of the mainmast are small open lockers for holding the ammunition for immediate use. In these lockers there were observed a quantity of hollow pointed shot, with grape, canister, and other missiles. The gun is of old English make, having a crown on the top, with figures denoting its rate, &c. There is a magazine in the after part, under the cockpit, containing a large quantity of ammunition of every description. She had on board, when she left Charleston, nominally provisions and water enough for a two weeks' cruise, but really sufficient for a much longer time. Her cabin is well supplied with small arms, such as cutlasses, of a rather antique pattern, hanging across each other on hooks driven up for the purpose, holsters and revolving pistols, old style, dirks, muskets, handcuffs, &c., such as might have furnished a respectable outfit for a pirate in the time of Robert Kidd. The after part, or cabin, was occupied by the commander and his associate pirates who ranked as officers, while the forward part of the hold was set apart for the pirates of second grade, and also answered as a cooking galley. There could scarcely be room for more than one-half of her crew below decks at a time.

As soon as she came to anchor, Mr. McCook proceeded to the United States marshal's office, to surrender the prize to his custody. Among the officers in charge of the prize is Mr. Isaac Seeds, of New Jersey. Mr. Seeds states that he arrived at Charleston on the 12th of May, as mate of the schooner H. & J. Neil, of Baltimore, from Cardenas, with a cargo of molasses. This vessel was stopped by the secessionists, and in order to escape from the place, he went on board of an English schooner bound to Nassau. This vessel was stopped by the Minnesota as she was going to sea, and compelled to return, and discharge her cargo of rice. Mr. Seeds accordingly took refuge on board of the frigate Minnesota. He states that he saw the Savannah in the harbor of Charleston on the 30th of May, and heard the people of Charleston speaking of her as a privateer fitting out to cruise for merchant vessels. It was the intention to send her across the Gulf to Great Abaco, where she was to intercept vessels near the "Hole in the Wall," which might pass that way on the voyage to Cuba. Cargoes of provisions were to be particularly looked after. The little craft was observed lying at anchor under Fort Sumter, having the Confederate flag flying, and evidently in sea trim. Twelve to fifteen men were noticed on board.

On the Sunday following, viz.: the 2d of May, the Minnesota, which is blockading off Charleston, had occasion to proceed to the southward in pursuit of a suspicious vessel, when the piratical craft seized the opportunity to emerge from the harbor by the north channel and sailed northward, in order to elude observation. Her movements were noticed on board the frigate, but as there were many little craft continually plying about the entrance to the port, she did not attract particular attention.

On Monday, the 3d of May, the pirate fell in with the brig Joseph, of Rockland, Me, with a cargo of sugar, from Cardenas, Cuba, bound to Philadelphia, and consigned to Welch & Co. On seeing the Joseph, she set an American ensign in her main rigging, which is understood to be a signal to speak, for latitude and longitude, or any other purpose. When the Joseph had come within speaking distance, the commander of the pirate ordered the captain to lower his boat and come on board of the schooner. As soon as the captain had come on board, he was told that his vessel was a prize under authority of the Confederate States of America, his vessel being fitted out by authority of the

Confederate States to seize all American vessels. He found on the pirate schooner twenty-two men, including officers. Resistance was useless, and they submitted as prisoners, the captain being detained on board of the schooner, while the crew of the Joseph was allowed to remain on their own vessel. A prize crew of eight armed men, with muskets, cutlasses, bowie-knives, and revolvers, were put on board. The brig was sent into Georgetown, S. C.

About 5 P. M. of the same day, the brig Perry hove in sight, the schooner running for the Perry, under the belief that they had another merchant prize ahead. Their surprise can be imagined when they discovered that the vessel was one of Uncle Sam's men-of-war, and that they were already in her power. The pirate immediately hauled on a wind, and endeavored to escape by sharp sailing, believing that they could thus run away from the Perry. This was at 5 o'clock P. M. The Perry set all sail and took chase after the little pirate, firing her guns to bring her to. The Savannah returned four shots, which passed over the Perry, one shot going through the rigging, but without doing her any damage. At 1 o'clock A. M., the Perry had hauled close on to the pirate, and ordered her to heave to, when the schooner lowered down all her sails, and the officers ran below. The Perry lowered away her two quarter boats, and in a few minutes more, men were alongside and sprang upon the pirate's deck. The men came forward and surrendered their side-arms, and in a moment more the leaders also came out of the cabin and gave themselves up. They were ordered into the Perry's boats, and in a short time were transferred to that vessel. The men were ironed and the officers put under guard.

A prize crew was put in charge, and the captured vessel followed the Perry to Charleston Bar, where they met the Minnesota on Thursday, at 4 P. M. Here the prisoners were transferred to the Minnesota, and the schooner was handed over to her commander. On Friday night, Midshipman McCook, with a crew from the same vessel, was ordered to carry the schooner to New York. One of the parties on board the Savannah is a young man hailing from New York, who represents that he was impressed on board of the privateer while unconscious. He had been two months in the hospital in Charleston, and from appearances he is very much broken down in health, and the last man who would adopt privateering as a profession. He states that the name of the captain of the schooner was Baker, and that he had been in the Chilian navy. The other officers were a Commissary, Lieutenant, Prize-Master, and Navigator, whose names he did not know. He refuses to give his own name, but says he is a Northern man with Northern sentiments.

—N. Y. Times, June 16.

Doc. 252.

FIRST REGIMENT MASS. VOLUNTEERS.

THE following is a list of the officers:

Colonel, Robert Cowdin; Lieutenant-Colonel, George D. Wells; Major, Charles P. Chandler; Adjutant, William H. Lawrence, Quartermaster, John B. Lee, of Salem; Assistant-Surgeon, Dr. Samuel A. Green; Sergeant-Major. James W. Hall; Quartermaster-Sergeant, Wm. P. Cowie; Commissary-Sergeant, John B. Gibbs; Hospital Steward, Edward R. Hutchins.

Company A—Captain, Edward A. Wilde, vice Chandler, promoted to major; First Lieutenant, Wm. L. Chandler; Second Lieutenant, Chas. L. Chandler. Company B (Union Guards) —Captain, Edward Pearl; First Lieutenant, George H. Smith; Second Lieutenant, Chas. S. Kendall. Company C (True Blues)—Captain, Gardner Walker; First Lieutenant, Joseph Hibbert; Second Lieutenant, D. G. E. Dickinson. Company D (Roxbury City Guard)— Captain, Ebenezer W. Stone, Jr.; First Lieutenant, Chas. M. Jordan; Second Lieutenant, Oliver Walton. Company E (Pulaski Guards) —Captain, C. B. Baldwin; First Lieutenant, John H. Johnson; Second Lieutenant, Miles Farwell. Company F (National Guards)—Captain, Albert W. Adams; First Lieutenant, John L. Ruggles; Second Lieutenant. George E. Henry. Company G (Independent Boston Fusiliers)—Captain, Henry A. Snow; First Lieutenant, —— Smith; Second Lieutenant, Francis H. Ward. Company H (Chelsea Light Infantry)—Captain, Sumner Carruth; First Lieutenant, Albert S. Austin; Second Lieutenant, Robert S. Saunders. Company I (Schouler Volunteers)—Captain, Chas. F. Rand; First Lieutenant, Chas. E. Mudge; Second Lieutenant, Elijah B. Gill, Jr. Company K (Chadwick Light Infantry)—Captain, A. G. Chamberlain; First Lieutenant, Wm. H. Sutherland; Second Lieutenant, F. W. Carruth.

—*N. Y. World*, June 17.

Doc. 253.

TO THE GERMANS OF KENTUCKY.

THE following address to the Germans of Kentucky, from the pen of one of the best of their countrymen, well deserves attention:

FRANKFORT, Ky., June 11, 1861.

You and I are Germans by birth, but we are all American citizens from choice, and as such we are now called upon to aid either in sustaining or overthrowing the Government of our adoption. Let the enemies of the country disguise and falsify facts as they may, there is but really one question submitted to the brave and free people of Kentucky, and that is this: Shall we any longer have a free Government or not? I warn you, my German brethren and fellow-citizens of Kentucky, not to be deceived by those who are trying to overthrow the Government,

and reduce you and me to bondage again. We all left our fatherland because we desire to rid our necks of the heel of the tyrant that trampled upon our rights. We have learned to hate tyrants—the proud spirit of our race will never submit to the yoke of bondage which Jeff. Davis and his followers are striving to fasten upon us.

My countrymen, beware of all the tricks and treachery of Disunionists, for they are traitors to their Government. They will approach you pretending to be your best friends, and under the sacred guise of friendship seek to seduce you from your allegiance and your duty. Tell the rebel who may thus approach you that you have left the sacred graves of your ancestors and the homes of your fathers to enjoy the blessings of this free Government—that you have crossed the ocean to enjoy its benefits; and tell him also that you have taken a solemn oath to support in good faith its Constitution and laws, and that you intend to make good your obligations and your oath; and should he still ask you to violate your oath, and assist him in destroying the Government which you have sworn to support, reply to the insult as becomes your patriotism and your unquestioned manhood. In all your deportment show yourselves worthy of the freedom which this glorious country has hitherto bestowed upon you, which you can only do by yielding to it your earnest and unreserved support—follow its fortunes and its flag wherever they go, and proudly share their fate.

Having once tasted of the sweets of liberty, let us surrender it only with our lives. If this Government is destroyed, liberty will be again banished from the face of the earth. The Southern States will soon become so many little monarchies and despotisms, continually at war with each other, subduing and subdued in turn, until they become a hiss and a by-word among the nations of the earth. They will be far less desirable for us than the oppressed lands from which we have all fled.

The plain duty of the United States Government is to protect us, to guard our rights as its adopted citizens wherever and by whomsoever they may be invaded, and this duty has been performed to the letter. No adopted citizen ever claimed the protection of this Government upon any land or sea where its flag waved, where his rights were not immediately guaranteed and his wrongs redressed. In return for all this our plain duty is to support the Government that protects us in good faith—to stand by it in this hour of peril, and sustain it, if need be, with our fortunes and our lives.

Then stand firmly by the Union which you have sworn to support—vote for the Union men and Union measures alone—respect and obey the laws of your adopted State and nation, and labor unceasingly for their peace and prosperity.

Again, I say, take an immovable stand for the Union, which is alone able to protect you from the despotism with which we are all threatened. Very respectfully,

LEONARD STREIFF.

—*Louisville Journal.*

Doc. 254.

THE GREAT CONSPIRACY.

AN ADDRESS DELIVERED AT MOUNT KISCO, WESTCHESTER COUNTY, NEW YORK, ON THE 4TH OF JULY, 1861, BY JOHN JAY.

MY FELLOW-COUNTRYMEN:—We have assembled to celebrate the eighty-sixth birthday of American independence, and we come together under circumstances that seem to make us contemporaries, and co-actors as it were, with our fathers of the Revolution. The crisis which they met, and which their heroism decided after a seven years' war with Great Britain, again meets us face to face. The early scenes of their struggle for constitutional liberty have found in our recent experience an historic parallel of even chronological exactness.

The blood of Massachusetts, shed at Lexington on the 19th of April, 1775, was not shed more gloriously than that of the sons of the same old commonwealth, who, marching by our national highway to the defence of our common capital, were slain at Baltimore on the 19th of April, 1861. The midnight ride of Paul Revere, famed in history and song, rousing the sleepers as he passed to hasten to defend their country, created no deeper emotion among the colonists of that day, than did our electric wires flashing far and wide the news of the assault on Sumter and the massacre at Baltimore, and thrilling with a simultaneous burst of sympathy the loyal heart of the American people.

On the 4th of July, 1776, the Congress that met in the State House at Philadelphia approved the solemn instrument that declared the independence of the American colonies, and announced to the world the birth of a nation. Eighty-five years have rolled by: the actors in that eventful scene have long since gone to their graves; their names belong to history; their sons have grown to manhood and age, and have followed them to the unseen world; and we of the third and fourth generations occupy the stage they trod, and represent the nationality which then was born. Eighty-five years of almost uninterrupted prosperity and unexampled growth! eighty-five years of culture and experience in a century of progress such as the world has never seen before! eighty-five years of thoughtful reflection on the character of the men who laid the foundation of our national glory and of the broad principles of right on which they based the edifice of American freedom!

Those years have passed; their results are written on the map of America, on the page of history, and to-day, the 4th of July, 1861, the American Congress convenes again at the call of the President, at the capital bearing the name of Washington, to meet the question, whether the republic is to be maintained in its integrity, with the Constitution proclaimed by Washington, based on the will of the majority, or whether it is to be sundered and shattered by a defeated faction, that sets at defiance the will of the people and would trample the Constitution in the dust?

If ever the spirits of the departed are permitted to revisit the scenes they loved, and hover like angels around the steps of their successors, we may suppose that Hancock and the Adamses, Sherman and Wolcott, Carroll and Livingston, Jefferson and Franklin, Robert and Lewis Morris, Wilson and Rush and all their noble compeers look down from heaven in this hour upon the Congress at Washington; and God grant that the sturdy spirit which inspired the first Congress may equally inspire the last!

"Whatever may be our fate," said John Adams, with prophetic vision, after the adoption of the Declaration—" be assured that this Declaration will stand. It may cost treasure and it may cost blood, but it will richly compensate for both. Through the thick gloom of the present I see the brightness of the future as the sun in heaven. We shall make this a glorious and immortal day. When we are in our graves our children will honor it. They will celebrate it with thanksgiving, with festivities, with bonfires, with illuminations. On its annual return they will shed tears, not of subjection and slavery, not of agony and distress, but of exultation, of gratitude, and of joy. Sir, before God, I believe the hour is come; all that I have, all that I am, all that I hope for in this life, I am now ready here to stake upon it, and I leave off as I began, that live or die, sink or swim, survive or perish, I am for the Declaration. It is my living sentiment, and by the blessing of God it shall be my dying sentiment—Independence now, and independence forever!"

The integrity and independence of our country are again in peril, and to-day the issue is with us. We come together now, not as in past years, to rejoice over a national domain boundless in extent, peopled by countrymen differing, it may be, in their views and institutions, but united in loyalty and affection, at peace in their own borders, and with the great arm of the Union protecting its citizens alike on sea or land, at home or in foreign climes. But we meet in sadness to overlook a divided nation, and to listen to the tramp of martial forces larger than ever before trod the soil of America: the one army bearing proudly aloft the Stars and Stripes, and keeping step to the music of the Union; the other grasping the banner of rebellion and the black flag of piracy, proclaiming death to the Constitution and the Union, and ruin to the commerce of the Republic.

Several States, about one-fourth of our whole number, profess to have resumed their sovereignty and *seceded*, as they term it, from the Federal Union; and certain persons, professing to act in their name, have extemporized what they call the Southern Confederacy, elected a president, Jefferson Davis, and a vice-president, Alexander H. Stephens, organized an army, issued letters of marque, and declared war on the people and the Government of the United States; and they have publicly announced, through Walker, the secretary of Davis, their intention of speedily seizing our capital at Washington, with its national archives and muniments of title.

To meet the rebel force arrayed against the capital, President Lincoln has called upon the loyal States, and at the word, fresh from the plough, the loom, and the workshop, fresh from college seats and the professor's chair, from the bar, the pulpit, and the counting-house, fresh from every department of American industry, the army of the Union is in the field, and the world awaits the impending crisis. Europe looks on with undisguised and wondering interest, and while France and Germany seem instinctively to appreciate our situation, the British cabinet and the British press have strangely blundered, and have muttered something we do not understand, about "rights of belligerents," "a wicked war," and the "bursting of the bubble of democracy."

Such in brief is our position at home and abroad, and this day is destined to be memorable—perhaps as memorable in history as that which we have met to celebrate. The action of the Congress now assembled will decide whether the national independence, established against the united strength of the British empire in '76, is to fall ignominiously before the attacks of a rebel minority of our own countrymen in '61.

It is to decide the question, whether in the next century our descendants shall refer to the Fourth of July as the forgotten birthday of an extinct republic, or whether, when we shall sleep with our fathers, and our children shall slumber by our side, their grandsons shall meet as we do this day to bless our memories as we bless those of our revolutionary sires; to spread to the breeze from the Atlantic to the Pacific, on every hill-side and in every valley, the flag of our Union, the Stars and Stripes that we so proudly love, and join their voices in swelling the cry of Adams—"Independence now, and independence forever!"

While the great issue, the success or failure of the American experiment, the continuance of our Union or its disintegration, rests immediately with the President and with Congress, it rests in an almost equal degree upon each one of us. The American people are at once citizens and sovereigns—the fountain and source of the supreme authority of the land, and to us, the people, will our servants in Congress naturally and properly look for guidance in this extremity. Already have you seen how fairly an honest Executive represents the sentiments of the majority of his countrymen, availing himself of their counsels, gathering strength from their energy and determination, and so directing the Government that its action keeps time to the beating of the national pulse. Already in response to the nation's call has the national Government arisen in gigantic strength from the depths of imbecility to which it had fallen, to a position of grandeur, dignity and power, which has silenced the half-uttered sarcasms of European declaimers about the internal weakness of popular institutions.

Most of you, perhaps all of you, have made up your minds deliberately, intelligently, and dispassionately, in regard to your duty; and it is a general and proper sentiment among us that this is a time for energetic action, not for discussion. But still as I am here, honored by your appointment, to say something befitting the occasion, I think you will permit me, if indeed you do not regard it as my especial province, to speak frankly of our present duty; to say something of the great theme which engrosses the nation; of which we think when we rise in the morning and when we retire at night, as we go to our work and return to our meals, when we open the morning paper for news and close it for reflection, when we kneel at the family altar and by our own bedsides—the one great overwhelming subject, the issue of this rebellion, the destiny of our country.

I can speak to you about it more familiarly perhaps than I should speak to strangers; for you are familiar with the whole matter, you know by heart the history of the revolutionary war in which the county of Westchester bore from the beginning so prominent a part, and from boyhood our thoughts and associations have been intimately connected with the facts of our colonial dependence and the incidents that marked the struggle by which that dependence was at length terminated. Let me refer for an instant to some of the local memories which linger all around us. On the angle of Connecticut, which juts into the State of New York close by this town of Newcastle, stands the boundary rock still bearing the initials "G. R.," brief memento of King George III., whose sovereignty over our fathers, loyal subjects though they were, and backed as was the crown by the armies of Great Britain, faded before the steadfastness of their resistance to unconstitutional usurpation.

New York in '76 being selected by the British as the centre of their operations, commanding, as they did, the Hudson River, and acting in connection with a force from Canada, their march into Westchester was designed to control the two principal routes to New England, by the way of Rye and Bedford, and so cut off the American army from its Eastern supplies. Washington, penetrating their designs, skilfully conducted his forces northwardly from King's Bridge, moving in a line parallel with the British, keeping a little in advance, facing them constantly with the Bronx in his front, the banks of the stream being fortified in convenient places.

I need not remind you of the battle of White Plains on the 28th October, 1776, where Alexander Hamilton distinguished himself as a captain of artillery, nor of the heights of Newcastle to which Washington repaired after the battle. At Bedford, where we hold our farms under Indian titles, bearing the mark of Katonah, sagamore, that were confirmed by patent of Queen Anne, some houses were burned in '79 by Lieut.-Colonel Tarleton heading a detachment of the Queen's Rangers, as related in his despatch to Sir Guy Carleton. At Poundridge and Hitching's corner occurred bloody skirmishes. Then, there are near by us Mile-square, where the Americans kept a strong guard; Pine's Bridge, which served as the principal communication between the hostile lines, and where Enoch Crosby, the Westchester spy—known to all readers of our great novelist as Harvey Birch, commenced his career of secret service; King's Bridge, the barrier of the British lines on the Harlem River, commanded in New York by Lord Cathcart, where the Cow-boys made their rendezvous when they had plundered the surrounding hills, and where a battle was fought between the Continentals and the Hessians. Indeed the whole of the "neutral ground," as portrayed by Fenimore Cooper, extending to the Croton, the banks of the Hudson, Northcastle, and Salem, connected with the sad drama of André, and the, till recently, unsurpassed treason of Arnold, all abound with revolutionary incidents; not forgetting Valentine's Hill, at Mile-square, where Washington was encamped in '76, Sir William Erskine in '78, and where in '82, as Mr. Bolton tells us, a grand foray was made with some 6,000 men by Sir Guy Carleton in person, attended, among other officers of note, by the young Duke of Clarence, afterwards William the Fourth.

Dwelling as you do amid scenes so suggestive, there should be no traitors in Westchester, unless, indeed, they are the descendants of the Cow-boys and Skinners, those pests of the Revolution, who were at once selfish, treacherous, cowardly, and cruel; and if any traitors should again be found in our borders—men ready, for their own selfish interests, to betray either the national principles or the national integrity, that our fathers bought for us at so great a price, do not forget to remind them that the "Cow-boy oak" yet stands near Yonkers, on which their traitorous ancestors were suspended with "a short shrift and a sure cord;" and that equally patriotic oaks in every part of Westchester send forth their broad arms ready to perform for our country, should its safety at any time unhappily demand it, the same excellent service.

You are familiar also with the history of our Constitution and with those marked lines of distinction between the authority of the States and that of the Federal Government, which to some of the statesmen and authors of England seem so difficult of comprehension; and in regard to which, perhaps naturally enough, they occasionally fall into blunders, which unfortunately are not always as harmless as the droll liberties they are accustomed to take with our history, our geography, and our nomenclature.

If ever the constitutional history of America shall receive in the education of English gentlemen a tithe of the attention bestowed on the constitutions of Greece and Rome, or a share of that devoted to the fabulous heroes, the gods and goddesses of classic mythology, the British Senate may occasionally find a familiarity with our institutions of no slight value, especially if it shall save them from rashly interrupting the cordial friendship of a kindred people.

The universality of such knowledge here, makes us perhaps more ready to remark the want of it in foreign critics. Dr. Franklin said during the last century, and the progress of education and improvements in our newspapers have made the remark more true of the present than of the past,—"We are more thoroughly an enlightened people with regard to our political interests than perhaps any other under heaven."

You remember that in 1774 the members of the first Congress at Philadelphia, on behalf of the colonies which they represented, entered into certain articles of association "under the sacred ties of virtue, honor, and love of country." That in 1778 the States united in a confederacy, or what they called "a firm league of friendship with each other," under the title of the United States, and that under this league made by the States they continued until 1789, when, "in order to form a more perfect union," —not the States—but "We, the people of the United States," ordained and established the present Federal Constitution. You remember that from the date of the peace in '83, when we were a mere league of petty sovereignties, we sank rapidly, in the words of Mr. Motley, whose conclusive essay in the London *Times* has enlightened Europe, "into a condition of utter impotence, imbecility, and anarchy," which continued until we were rescued from it by "The Constitution of the United States," which made us, in every sense, one nation— with one supreme Government, although for convenience we retained the plural title under which we had achieved our independence, of "The United States."

Any argument, therefore, addressed to you upon the constitutional right alleged by the rebels, of a State to secede from the Union would be quite superfluous. Men have been allowed to talk of State sovereignty as it liked them, because ours is a free country, and in ordinary times the utmost liberty of speech is permissible, but the doctrine has not even a respectable foothold. Washington, as if foreseeing the evil it has assisted to bring forth, denounced it as "that monster, state sovereignty." Webster and Jackson successively demolished it, and the argument now insolently advanced by leaders of the rebel States, that in seceding from the Union and seizing its property, they are only exercising their reserved rights under the Constitution, is one which to every intelligent and loyal American carries with it its own refutation. The man who attaches to it the weight of a feather, is either singularly ignorant of American history, or his reasoning powers are hopelessly perverted.

The rebels, despite their pretended plea of constitutional right, virtually admit its groundlessness, and fall back on the right of revolution. That is a right which no American can deny, when the causes of justification are sufficient. The simple cry of rebel and revolutionist has no terror for us who remember that Washington and our ancestors occupied the position of both the one and the other.

All then depends upon the reality and sufficiency of the assigned causes of this attempt at revolution. Are they such as to justify the effort to break in pieces the American Union? to destroy this last experiment of popular government?

The arguments offered by the insurrectionists and their friends, to show that the Federal Government and the loyal States should quietly allow them to depart and form a separate confederacy, are these:

That the rebellion or revolution is the act of the people of those States, exercising their sovereign will.

That they have been compelled to this step in self-defence by the election of Mr. Lincoln, and the refusal of certain Northern States to fulfil the constitutional obligation of returning fugitive slaves.

That the present position of the rebels, and the fact of their having ousted the Federal Government from its forts and other property, exhibit their strength, make the revolution an accomplished fact, and render the attempt to subjugate the Southern people utterly hopeless.

That even if they were subjugated, harmonious feeling could never be restored; and that for these reasons, and especially the last, a war to maintain the integrity of the Union would be alike wicked and foolish.

These, I believe, are their strong points fairly stated, and I will briefly state some of the grounds on which we believe them to be, one and all, erroneous and delusive.

In the first place, the fact is clear that the rebellion at the South was not in its inception like the rebellion of the American colonies—a calm, deliberate, determined movement of the people; but that it was a conspiracy originating with a few ambitious politicians, and was by them suddenly precipitated upon the people, whose right to pass upon their acts of secession has been purposely, systematically, and practically denied. "There is," said Webster —and his words were never before so fearfully illustrated—"no usurpation so dangerous as that which comes in the borrowed name of the people; which, calling itself their servant, ex-

ercises their power without legal right or constitutional sanction."

You all remember the stern rebukes uttered by the Southern press, of the rash precipitancy of South Carolina, and the efforts made by their prominent statesmen, among whom Mr. Stephens was one, to stay the efforts of the rebel leaders to plunge the South into rebellion. Even after several States had by their conventions—and the convention of Louisiana was elected by a minority of the people—been declared out of the Union; and after delegates from those conventions had met in congress at Montgomery, and extemporized their new confederacy, the bolder part of the Southern press did not hesitate to denounce the usurpation.

The "*Augusta Chronicle and Sentinel*"—a leading paper of Georgia—openly declared that the result had been produced by "wheedling, coaxing, and bullying, and all the arts of deception." It said:

"We know as well as any one living that the whole movement for secession and the formation of a new government, so far at least as Georgia is concerned, proceeded only on a *quasi* consent of the people, and was pushed through under circumstances of great excitement and frenzy by a fictitious majority." And then, passing to the Montgomery congress, it added:

"The Georgia convention and the confederate congress have gone forward in their work, as none can deny, without explicit and direct authority from the people." * * * "It is time that this assumption of power should cease, and that the people should be heard. Sooner or later they must be heard." * * * "Before the convention assumes to ratify the permanent constitution let them submit it to a vote of the people—or else, let us have an election for a new convention. For union—for harmony—for strength—we ask this simple act of justice."

Simple justice was not the aim of Jefferson Davis and his co-conspirators. To this day the people of the South have been allowed no opportunity of passing upon the profoundest question that can affect a nation—the preservation or overthrow of its institutions; and the rebel government is an usurpation of the grossest kind, not only against the people of the United States in their sovereign capacity, but against the people of the States in whose name it assumes to act, and by whose will it pretends to have been established.

The declaration, so solemnly made by the seceding conventions, appealing to the world for the justice of their cause, that Mr. Lincoln's election, the non-execution of the fugitive slave law, and the personal liberty laws of Northern States, compelled them to separate from a Government that threatened their dearest rights, is equally disproven out of their own mouths. Listen to the following utterances from the very leaders of the rebellion:

Mr. Rhett said:—"The secession of South

Carolina is not the event of a day. It is not any thing produced by Mr. Lincoln or by the non-execution of the fugitive slave law. It is a matter which has been gathering head for years."

Mr. Parker:—"It is no spasmodic effort that has come suddenly upon us, but it has been gradually culminating for a long series of years."

Mr. Keitt:—"I have been engaged in this movement ever since I entered political life."

Mr. Inglis:—"Most of us have had this matter under consideration for the last twenty years."

That these declarations had a broad basis of truth, and that a plot to destroy the Union has been hatching for a long period, and has been deferred only until a convenient opportunity, is no longer a matter of speculation. The election of Mr. Lincoln was not the cause, but only the occasion. Mr. Everett, in a recent letter, said, that he was "well aware, partly from facts within his personal knowledge, that leading Southern politicians had for thirty years been resolved to break up the Union as soon as they ceased to control the United States Government, and that the slavery question was but a pretext for keeping up agitation and rallying the South"

The *Richmond Enquirer* in 1856 declared, "If Fremont is elected the Union will not last an hour after Mr. Pierce's term expires," and a careful examination will show that, from the attempt at nullification by South Carolina in 1832, which was defeated by the stern determination of General Jackson that the "Union must and shall be preserved," a sentiment that was enthusiastically responded to by the country at large, the design has been secretly cherished, by a knot of conspirators at the South, of destroying the Union whenever the men entertaining this design should no longer be able to control its Government. So long as they could enjoy its honors and emoluments, and use its prestige, its treasury, its army, and its navy, for their own purposes, they were content that it should stand; but the moment these were wrested from their grasp by the will of the people, that moment the Union was to be destroyed.

So long ago as the year 1799, Judge Marshall, in a letter to Washington, dated at Richmond, remarked:

"To me it seems that there are men who will hold power by any means rather than not hold it, and who would prefer a dissolution of the Union to the continuance of an Administration not of their own party." And Mr. Stephens declared, in regard to the present conspiracy, that the ambition of disappointed office-seekers constituted "a great part of the trouble."

General Jackson, after the South Carolina rebellion of 1832 was suppressed, foretold its attempted revival at no distant period, remarking that "the first time the pretence was the

tariff, and that next it would be the negro question."

In 1836, twenty-five years ago, a political novel, called the "Partizan Leader," was published by Professor Beverly Tucker, of William and Mary College, in Virginia. It excited no sensation then, but it possesses a singular interest now. It proceeds upon the theory that the events it describes as then happening would happen twenty years after, that is, in 1856, when Fremont would have probably been elected but for the frauds in Pennsylvania; and it gives, with singular accuracy, the programme of the conspiracy which is now in progress. The author describes the Southern States as seceding "by a movement nearly simultaneous," and immediately forming a Southern Confederacy. Let me quote a single paragraph:

"The suddenness of these measures was less remarkable than the prudence with which they had been conducted. The two together left little doubt that there had been a preconcert among the leading men of the several States, arranging previously what should be done. * * Nor was it confined to the seceding States alone. In Virginia also there were men who entered into the same views. * * Not only had they sketched provisionally the plan of a Southern Confederacy, but they had taken measures to regulate their relations with foreign powers."

What a flood of light is thrown upon the conspiracy by these few words from one of the earliest of the conspirators, who seems to have anticipated in part the rôle to be played by his own State of Virginia. There being indications of her ultimate accession to the confederacy, the author says:

"The leading men" referred to "had determined to wait for her no longer, but to proceed to the execution of their plans, leaving her to follow."

Could the acute novelist have anticipated the proceedings of the pseudo-peace convention, and the conduct of Virginia traitors, headed by an ex-President Tyler and an ex-Governor Wise, he might have eulogized the leaders of the Ancient Dominion for their treacherous skill in deluding the country with schemes of compromise while the preparations of the rebels were advancing to completion.

Mr. Everett, who was a warm advocate for the peace convention, has told us that "those conciliatory demonstrations had no effect in staying the progress of secession, because the leaders of that revolution were determined not to be satisfied."

In reference to the measures referred to by Professor Tucker, looking towards the relations of the new confederacy with foreign powers, it may be worth while to allude to a recent statement that in the days of Mr. Calhoun a plan for the dissolution of the Union and the formation of a great slaveholding power, was presented by his friends to Lord Aberdeen, and that some words attributed to that statesman, are supposed to have given rise to the hopes of British sympathy, in which Southern politicians have so frequently indulged. It is said on high authority that at different times, and especially in 1851, these projects have been broached to members of the British ministry, and that on that occasion they were disclosed by Lord Palmerston to our minister, Mr Abbott Lawrence, and that the Southern commissioners, disheartened by the coolness with which their overtures were received, and also by the fate of the Lopez expedition, returned discomfited to the United States.

In 1857 Mr. Mason, of Virginia, announced as a fact on the floor of the Senate that the British Government had changed its opinion on the slavery question; but an early occasion was taken by that government to contradict the assertion of Mr. Mason, the Duke of Argyll declaring that he was instructed by her Majesty's ministers to do so.*

Blind as we have all been to the catastrophe that awaited us, unconscious as were the people, both at the North and at the South, of this preconcert among a few leaders in the different States, we can now trace step by step the progress of the conspiracy, and read the history of the last thirty years without an interpreter; we can understand the motive of the Texan rebellion, the war with Mexico, the persistent efforts to secure Cuba, the filibustering expeditions to Central America, and the determination to re-open the African slave trade. We can appreciate, too, the caution with which the plan of the rebellion was concealed, and especially the adroitness with which the people were allowed no time for reflection, no opportunity for action, their consent assumed on the plea of necessary haste, and the acts of secession pushed through the conventions, as charged by the Georgian editor, with no regard to popular rights, and under circumstances of excitement and frenzy by fictitious majorities.

The doctrine of secession, earnestly as it had been advocated, failed to convince the capitalists, the planters, and the common-sense statesmen of the South—even in South Carolina.

A few years since Mr. Boyce, of that State, late a member of the House of Representatives, in an address to the people, after showing that by secession they would lose the vitality of a State, that they would exist only by tolerance, a painful and humiliating spectacle, that it would involve a sacrifice of the present without in anywise gaining in the future, emphatically declared, " such is the intensity of my conviction on the subject, that if secession should take place, of which I have no idea, for I cannot believe in such stupendous madness, I shall consider the institution of slavery as doomed, and that the great God in our blindness has made us the instrument of its destruction."

Even so late as the autumn of 1860, and after the Presidential election that announced the defeat of the slave power which had so long ruled the country, the leading men of the South who had not been in the plot, battled manfully against it. On the 14th of November last, Mr. Stephens, of Georgia, now the vice-president of the rebel confederacy, delivered a long and able speech in the Georgia house of representatives, in which, in answer to the question whether the Southern States should secede in consequence of Mr. Lincoln's election, he said:

"My countrymen, I tell you frankly, candidly, and earnestly, that I do not think that they ought."

Reminding them of the sacred obligation resting on them to be true to their national engagements, he exclaimed:

"If the Republic is to go down, let us be found to the last moment standing on the deck, with the Constitution of the United States waving over our heads." And this sentiment was greeted with applause.

He expressed his belief that Mr. Lincoln would do nothing to jeopard their safety or security, and showed them the wisdom of our system with its checks and guards. He reminded them that the President was powerless unless backed by Congress—that the House of Representatives was largely against him, and that there would be a majority of four against him in the Senate, and referring to a remark that no Georgian, who was true to his State, could consistently hold office under Mr. Lincoln, reminded them that such office could be honorably held, for it would be conferred by the approval of a Democratic Senate—and this exposition was received with "prolonged applause."

Mr. Stephens frankly avowed that he would never submit to any Republican aggression on their constitutional rights to preserve the Union; but insisted that all their rights could be secured in the Union, and emphatically declared, "That this Government of our fathers with all its defects, comes nearer the objects of all good governments than any other on the face of the earth, is my settled conviction." * * "Have we not at the South, as well as at the North, grown great, prosperous, and happy under its operation? Has any part of the world ever shown such rapid progress in the development of wealth, and all the material resources of national power and greatness as the Southern States have under the General Government, notwithstanding all its defects?"

Mr. Stephens then, with philosophic skill, showed that the institutions of a people constitute the matrix from which spring all their characteristics of development and greatness. "Look," he said, "at Greece. There is the same fertile soil, the same blue sky, the same inlets and harbors, the same Ægean, the same Olympus; there is the same land where Homer sung, where Pericles spoke; it is the same old Greece—but it is living Greece no more." He pictured its ruin of art and civilization, and traced that ruin to the downfall of their insti-

* See a letter dated London, December 10, 1858, published and endorsed by the *Commercial Advertiser*, January 30, 1861.

tutions. He drew the same lesson from Italy and Rome, once mistress of the world, and solemnly warned them that where liberty is once destroyed it may never return again.

Coming back to the State of Georgia he referred to the anxiety of many there in 1850 to secede from the Union—and showed that since 1850 the material wealth of Georgia, as a member of the Union, had nearly if not quite doubled.

He spoke of the prosperity in agriculture, commerce, art, science, and every department of education, physical and mental, and warned them against listening to the like temptation as that offered to our progenitors in the Garden of Eden—when they were led to believe that they would become as gods, and yielding in an evil hour saw only their own nakedness.

"I look," he said, "upon this country, with its institutions, as the Eden of the world, the paradise of the universe. It may be that out of it we may become greater and more prosperous; but I am candid and sincere in telling you, that I fear if we rashly evince passion, and without sufficient cause shall take that step, that instead of becoming greater or more peaceful, prosperous, and happy—instead of becoming gods, we will become demons, and at no distant day commence cutting one another's throats."

There, my countrymen, we have the testimony of the vice-president of the rebel confederacy, and the fact that Mr. Stephens, like our progenitors of whom he spoke, yielded to temptation and became a chief abettor of the scheme of ruin which he so strongly deprecated, detracts nothing from the value of this remarkable speech. His treachery proves only his own weakness, it impeaches neither the truth of his facts, the aptness of his illustrations, nor the conclusions to which he was led by his historic experience and irresistible logic.

Already in South Carolina, first and chiefest of the seceding States, have men professing to be respectable, men whose names connect them in past generations with Englishmen of gentle blood and Huguenots of heroic fame, men who for years have borne in foreign climes the proud title of American citizens, and who know the simple dignity of the American Republic among the nations of the earth—already are these men, since they discarded the protection of the Federal Government, so lost to self-respect that they are not only ready to submit to a foreign yoke, but, according to their eulogist, Mr. Russell, in a paragraph I will presently quote, they actually whimper like children for the privilege of becoming the vassals of an European princelet.

We have glanced at the secret history of the conspiracy. Now, let me ask, on what ground does this usurping confederacy ask to be recognized as independent, and admitted to the family of nations?

In the convention of South Carolina, in reply to an objection that the declaration reported by the committee dwelt too much on the fugitive slave law and the personal liberty bills, as giving it the appearance of special pleading, Mr. Memminger said: "Allow me to say to the honorable gentleman, that when you take position that you have a right to break your faith, to destroy an agreement that you have made, to tear off your seal from the document to which it is affixed, you are bound to justify yourself fully to all the nations of the world, for there is nothing that casts such a stain upon the escutcheon of a nation as a breach of faith."

In this Mr. Memminger was clearly right, and the alleged breach of faith by the North, touching the execution of the fugitive slave law, was resorted to as affording a plausible pretext for seceding from the Union. But the debates show that this pretext was a sham, and Mr. Rhett frankly declared that he regarded the fugitive slave law as unconstitutional, and that Mr. Webster and Mr. Keitt had expressed the same opinion.

You have seen, too, from Mr. Stephens, that all the constitutional rights of the South were protected within the Union—and that the South was indebted to the Union for her safety, prosperity, and happiness.

What then is the real ground on which the breach of faith committed by the seceding States is to be justified, if it can be justified at all; on what ground is it recommended to the prejudices of the South and to the impartial judgment of the world?

After secession was an accomplished fact, so far as their conventions could manage it by usurped authority and fictitious majorities, and Mr. Stephens had become not only a member but a prominent leader of the conspiracy, he said at Atlanta:

"The foundations of our new government are laid, its corner-stone rests upon the great truth that the negro is not equal to the white man; that slavery, subordination to the superior race, is his natural and moral condition. This, our new government, is the first in the history of the world based upon this great physical, philosophical, and moral truth."

Mr. Stephens enlarged upon this distinguishing characteristic of the government, to establish which the Union was to be dissolved, sneered at the principle that all men are equal, enunciated by our fathers in the Declaration of Independence, "as the pestilent heresy of fancy politicians"—declared that "African inequality and the equality of white men were the chief corner-stone of the Southern republic!" and claimed that with a government so founded, the world would recognize in theirs the model nation of history."

Here we have their only apology for this rebellion, stripped of all shams and disguises, and thus at length, in the latter half of the nineteenth century, stand face to face in deadly conflict the antagonist systems of the new world.

"All men," said the founders of the American Republic, "are created free and equal, and endowed with certain inalienable rights, among which are life, liberty, and the pursuit of happiness." "Let it ever be remembered," said the Continental Congress, "that the rights for which we have contended were the rights of human nature," and on that foundation arose the fair fabric of our liberties.

The dark shadow arises of another confederacy which Davis, and Keitt, and Floyd, and Toombs, are striving to establish on the ruins of the republic erected by Washington and Franklin, and Hamilton and Jefferson, and the one great plea with which this new power seeks to recommend itself to the Christian world is, the assumption that the white man was born to be the master and the black man was created to be his slave.

The attempt of the slavery insurrectionists to bring into contempt the great principle of the Declaration of Independence, and their characterizing the men who uttered it and the men who believe in it as "fancy politicians," shows how absolutely antagonist in their principles were those who rebelled in '76 against unconstitutional acts of parliament, and those who in '61 are rebelling against the Constitution of the United States. Even in the august year which we are met to celebrate, the principles and reasonings of our fathers commanded the admiration of Europe, and called forth in the House of Lords that magnificent eulogy of Chatham, when he said that for himself he must declare that he had studied and admired the free states of antiquity, the master states of the world; but that for solidity of reasoning, force of sagacity, and wisdom of conclusion, no body of men could stand in preference to the Congress of Philadelphia.

Whatever may be the future of America the past is safe.

The confederates of the slave republic, unrivalled as may be their skill in robbing us of material wealth and power, cannot rob the founders of our Union of their glory—cannot filch from us the treasures we possess in their great principles, cannot lessen by the tithe of a hair, the truth and force of their example.

On the contrary, the formation of the Southern Confederacy adds new proof to their farsighted and prophetic sagacity. Look at the rebel States, plunged into anarchy and war by Jefferson Davis, with a fettered press, free speech silenced, forced loans, and an army enlarged by conscription, and then listen to a single passage from William Pinkney, the great orator of Maryland, which occurs in a speech made in the Maryland House of Delegates, in 1789: and remember as you listen to it the proof I have already given you that the so-called Southern confederacy is a military despotism, extemporized and precipitated on the people of the South, who have never been allowed to express their will in regard to the substitution of the Montgomery constitution, for the ancient Constitution and Government which the confederates are striving to destroy.

Said Mr. Pinkney:

"That the dangerous consequences of the system of bondage have not as yet been felt does not prove that they never will be. * * * To me, sir, nothing for which I have not the evidence of my senses is more clear than that it will one day destroy that reverence for liberty which is the vital principle of a republic.

"While a majority of your citizens are accustomed to rule with the authority of despots within particular limits, while your youth are reared in the habit of thinking that the great rights of human nature are not so sacred but they may with innocence be trampled on, can it be expected that the public mind should glow with that generous ardor in the cause of freedom which alone can save a government like ours from *the lurking demon of usurpation?* Do you not dread contamination of principle? Have you no alarms for the continuance of that spirit which once conducted us to victory and independence when the talons of power were unclasped for our destruction? Have you no apprehension that when the votaries of freedom sacrifice also at the gloomy altars of slavery, they will at length become apostates from the former? For my own part, I have no hope that the stream of general liberty will flow forever unpolluted through the foul mire of partial bondage, or that they who have been habituated to lord it over others, will not in time be base enough to let others lord it over them. If they resist, it will be the struggle of *pride and selfishness*, not of *principle.*"

The hour so philosophically predicted seventy-two years ago has come. The usurping hand is lifted against the most benignant government the world has ever seen. The usurpation is unresisted, the country is precipitated into war, and popular government overthrown, and a military rule established: the people, it would seem, have cast to the world the historic memories we this day meet to celebrate. Mr. Russell, the correspondent of the London *Times*, now travelling at the South, treated with every attention, charmed with their courtesy, and evidently inclined to regard their rebel movement with a favorable eye, writes from South Carolina on the 30th April, and makes this sad disclosure: "From all quarters have come to my ears the echoes of the same voice; it may be feigned, but there is no discord in the note, and it sounds in wonderful strength and monotony all over the country. Shades of George III., of North, of Johnson, of all who contended against the great rebellion which tore these colonies from England, can you hear the chorus which rings through the State of Marion, Sumter, and Pinckney, and not clash your ghostly hands in triumph? that voice says, 'If we could only get one of the royal race of England to rule over us we should be content.'"

Let me say next a word of the means by which a conspiracy so contemptible in its origin, so destitute of moral weight and of popular support, has attained to its present dimensions, ousting the Federal Government of its jurisdiction in more than half of our national territory to the east of the Rocky Mountains, and obtaining possession of arsenals and navy-yards and fortresses, seventeen in number, which had cost the American people more than seven millions of dollars.

On the 29th October, 1860, before the Presidential election, Lieut.-General Scott wrote a letter to President Buchanan, in which he referred to the secession excitement which the leaders of the conspiracy were actively fanning at the South, and remarked that if this glorious Union were broken by whatever line political madness might contrive, there would be no hope of reuniting the fragments except by the laceration and despotism of the sword; pointing out the danger, he proceeded to point out the prevention.

"From a knowledge of our Southern population," he said, "it is my solemn conviction that there is some danger of an early act of rashness preliminary to secession, viz., the seizure of some or all of the following posts: Forts Jackson and Philip in the Mississippi, below New Orleans, both without garrisons; Fort Morgan below Mobile, without a garrison; Forts Pickens and McRae, Pensacola harbor, with an insufficient garrison for one; Fort Pulaski below Savannah, without a garrison; Forts Moultrie and Sumter, Charleston harbor, the former with an insufficient garrison, and the latter without any; and Fort Monroe, Hampton Roads, without a sufficient garrison. In my opinion all these works should immediately be so garrisoned as to make any attempt to take any one of them, by surprise or *coup de main*, ridiculous.

"With an army faithful to its allegiance, and the navy probably equally so, and with a Federal Executive for the next twelve months of firmness and moderation, which the country has a right to expect—moderation being an element of power, not less than firmness—there is good reason to hope that the danger of secession may be made to pass away without one conflict of arms, one execution, or one arrest for treason."

Gentlemen, Lieut.-General Scott knew well, we all know, that what he recommended Mr. Buchanan to do, an honest Executive might have done. Again and again in the history of our country have attempts been made to resist the execution of the laws, and again and again has the Federal Government triumphantly vindicated its supremacy.

The first armed rebellion was that headed by Shay, in Massachusetts, in the winter of 1787. The rebels attempted to seize the arsenal, and were met with cannon that killed three and wounded another of their number, and the State militia, under the command of Gen. Lincoln, routed their forces, taking many prisoners,

and peace was restored, not by any compromise, but by the enforcement of the laws.

As a Lincoln suppressed the first rebellion, so will a Lincoln suppress the last.

You will readily call to mind other similar occasions, where the Federal Government, by prompt action, maintained its supremacy unimpaired.

First came the whiskey rebellion in Pennsylvania, during the administration of Washington, to suppress which the President called out fifteen thousand men from three different States, led by their Governors and General Morgan, whom Washington at first proposed himself to accompany across the Alleghanies.

Next President Jefferson crushed in the bud the opening conspiracy of Aaron Burr.

President Madison, during the war of 1812, when doubts were entertained of the loyalty of the Hartford conventionists, who were falsely reported to be in correspondence with the enemy, stationed Major Jessup, of Kentucky, at Hartford, with a regiment, to suppress any sudden outbreak. Gen. Jackson, about the same time, in New Orleans, proclaimed martial law in consequence of attempts by the civil authorities to embarrass the necessary measures of defence.

President Jackson, in 1832, repressed by the arm of General Scott, and amid the hearty applause of the nation, the defiant nullification of South Carolina, and President Tyler, in 1843, with the approval of his Secretary, Mr. John C. Calhoun, sent United States troops to Rhode Island to suppress the State revolution, organized by a majority of the people of the State, but in violation of the existing State constitution, under the leadership of Governor Thomas W. Dorr.

When in 1860 General Scott, in advance of any outbreak, recommended President Buchanan to reinforce the forts, instead of recommending active measures of interference, such as his predecessors whom I have named did not hesitate to take, he simply asked of the President to do what any intelligent school-boy could see was absolutely proper and essential, and what he could accomplish by a single word. Mr. Buchanan, guided by his Secretary of War, the traitor and thief, John B. Floyd, refused to order the reinforcement of the fortresses; all the forts named by General Scott, excepting Fort Pickens, were seized by the confederates; and on the fact of their quiet possession and the aid and comfort thus given to the rebels by the Federal cabinet, was based the secession of the traitorous States and the formation of the new confederacy.

The fact thus becomes clear as day, that not simply all the strength the rebel confederacy originally possessed, but its very organization and existence, were due not to the people of the South on whom without their sanction it was precipitated, nor to the leaders, skilful as they have been, who had neither arms nor armies to overpower the Government, but they were due to the Federal Executive and his advisers of the cabinet. This fact is so interesting as a matter of history, it is so important to a right understanding of the whole subject, and bears so clearly upon the question, what is our duty as citizens and what the policy of our Government, as regards the tolerance or suppression of this rebellion, that you will allow me to quote one authority upon the point from among the rebels themselves.

The Richmond *Examiner* in an elaborate eulogy of Floyd, who in the extent and infamy of his treachery certainly excelled his fellow-traitors in the cabinet, makes this plain avowal: "All who have attended to the developments of the last three months and knew aught of the movements of the Buchanan Administration up to the time of Floyd's resignation, will justify the assertion that the Southern Confederacy would not and could not be in existence at this hour but for the action of the late Secretary of War.

"The plan invented by General Scott to stop secession was, like all campaigns devised by him, very able in its details and nearly certain of general success. The Southern States are full of arsenals and forts commanding their rivers and strategic points; General Scott desired to transfer the army of the United States to these forts as speedily and as quietly as possible. The Southern States could not cut off communication between the Government and the fortresses without a great fleet, which they cannot build for years; or take them by land without one hundred thousand men, many hundred millions of dollars, several campaigns, and many a bloody siege. Had Scott been able to have got these forts in the condition he desired them to be, the Southern Confederacy would not now exist."

Such is the truth fairly stated by the Richmond *Examiner*, in the interest of the rebels. The Union has been severed, not by violence from without, but by treachery within. It has been convulsed from its centre to its circumference, not from any internal weakness in our Federal system, but by the infernal villany of our Federal rulers.

Traitors have betrayed the Union, traitors have betrayed our forts; and the betrayal no more proves moral weakness in the one case than it does material weakness in the other. There is no fortification so impregnable but that a traitorous governor may yield it without a blow—neither is there any government on God's earth that secret treachery may not enfeeble or temporarily overthrow.

"If," said Webster, "those appointed to defend the castle shall betray it, woe betide those within. Let us hope," he added, and how vain the hope as regards ourselves! "that we shall never see the time when the Government shall be found in opposition to the Constitution, and when the guardians of the Union shall become its betrayers."

I do not mean to say, gentlemen, that President Buchanan, who at the close of his Administration, partially redeemed his character, by calling to his counsels those brave men and true patriots, Mr. Holt and General Dix, was personally privy to the designs of the false secretaries whom they replaced; but it is nevertheless true that he is the man who, under the Constitution, is directly responsible to the American people for the acts of his Administration.

In his position timidity was treason and inaction was crime. He alone could execute the laws, he had the power to execute them, and he did not execute them; and for the simple want of their non-execution the country drifted rapidly towards destruction. This was a case which the founders of our Republic had not anticipated. As Mr. Sherman, of Ohio, aptly said, "the Constitution provided against every probable vacancy in the office of President, but did not provide for utter imbecility."

I am aware that Mr. Buchanan's friends attribute his conduct in the whole matter to an amiable credulity and a humane desire to avoid the shedding of a drop of blood. I am sure that none of us would wish to deprive him of whatever benefit he may derive from the plea of virtuous motives, but allowing them all the force they are entitled to, we must still exclaim: "Curse on his virtues, they've undone his country!"

For no other of the confederates in this great villany will the candid historian venture with success, the apology of mental imbecility or moral cowardice. They are men who make the boast that for long years it has been the aim of their existence to overthrow, not by open and honorable opposition, but secretly, traitorously, and by subornation of treason, the most benignant Government in the world, and one to which they were bound by solemn oaths and by sacred honor. They are men who, pretending to be gentlemen, have made conspiracy a trade, and perjury a habit. They have blended professions of patriotism with the practice of treason, linked the duties of a senator with the position of a spy, and made a seat in the cabinet the office of a thief. With a refinement of meanness that could belong to no chivalry but that of slaveholding, and would be practised by no knights save those of "the golden circle," they have to the last moment drawn their official salaries from the nation they were betraying; they have perfected their schemes of plunder in the very capital which they were seeking to cripple, and beneath the folds of the flag that they were swearing to support and plotting to humble. They are men, in brief—for the subject is a revolting one—who, imitating Judas and rivalling Arnold, have made their daily life simply and purely a daily lie.

Did time permit me I would like briefly to refer to the national events that, following in quick succession, have interrupted what Mr. Seward happily calls "the majestic march of our national progress: " the successive seizure of Southern forts in obedience to telegrams from the Senate chamber, the spread of Southern treason like the wild fire of the prairies; the consternation of the people, the apathy of the Executive, the plot to seize the capitol, intended to be executed in January and repeatedly postponed till the attempt involved too serious danger, the systematic efforts in the departments of the Treasury, of the Interior, of War, and, I fear, also of the Navy, to cripple the United States, to strengthen the rebels, and to close the term of the Administration by a coup d'etat, that should give to the new confederacy the power and the prestige of the old Government, and the preparations made by Northern confederates, who, the rebels had been taught to believe, represented the great Northern Democracy, for assisting the plot and joining at the right moment in a general revolution.

Lost themselves to a sense of honor, they ceased to believe in its existence at the North. They seem to have been unable to distinguish between a defence of the constitutional rights of slaveholders within the Union and under the Constitution, and a war in behalf of slavery for the severance of the Union, the overthrow of the Constitution, the desecration of our flag, and the humiliation of our country. Then came the interruption of their plans by the premature discovery of the theft of the Indian bonds and other villanies, compelling the retirement of the traitorous secretaries Cobb, Thompson, and Floyd; the advent of Holt and Dix, reviving the hopes of the nation, and the immortal order of the latter, which rung like a trumpet through the land, "If any man shall attempt to pull down the National Flag, shoot him on the spot."

Then came the official announcement to the country, by the counting of the electoral votes, of the people's choice, next the safe arrival of Mr. Lincoln in Washington, unharmed by the assassins who had sworn to take his life; then the inauguration, simple and imposing, the oath administered by the Chief Justice of the United States, and the quiet transfer of such remnants of the Federal property as had not been stolen from the people under the retiring Administration.

A month of apparent inaction on the part of the new Administration, engaged in disentangling the web of treachery, and learning how much of treason lingered in the departments— a month of active preparation by the rebel confederates, and we began to hear the bitter taunts of England at the spiritless people of the great North, who were being driven to dissolution and infamy without an effort at resistance, and relinquishing their nationality to a rebellion without striking a blow in its defence.

We had a brief foretaste of the ignominy that awaits a nation which basely surrenders its integrity and its independence, and we heard the prelude of the shout that would greet the downfall of the Union, and the epitaph that should record—

> * * * " But yesterday it might
> Have stood against the world ; now lies it there
> And none so poor to do it reverence."

Assured of the integrity and patriotism of the President, and the wisdom of his cabinet, the North waited as only a brave people, conscious of their strength and of the justice of their cause, could afford to wait. The strength of the Government was gradually developed, the war and navy departments began to exhibit signs of life—and the great statesman of the West, who, sacrificing political ambition and personal preferences, had consented to preside over a depleted treasury, renewed the miracle attributed by Webster to Alexander Hamilton: " He smote the rock of the national resources, and abundant streams of revenue gushed forth. He touched the dead body of the public credit, and it sprang upon its feet."

Desperate as our situation seemed, capitalists demanded no other security than the name of Chase; and when he asked for a loan of eight millions, more than thirty millions were instantly offered.

Gentlemen, I have not time to dwell on the attack on Sumter, the attack of ten thousand men on one hundred men, and the ill-judged boast of Governor Pickens that they had humbled the star spangled banner for the first time in seventy years. They themselves by that act and that boast initiated an irresistible conflict that will hardly cease till the Stars and Stripes again float in their beauty from every fortress in our land.

That bombardment, as was remarked by one of the Judges of the Supreme Court, " blew all the plots of the traitors into the air, and inaugurated a change in the sentiment of the country that seemed all but miraculous." It awoke the deep love of country which had slumbered beneath the platforms of party and commercial interest. It ended at once the absurd cry of " no coercion," as applicable to a Government in enforcing its laws and protecting its existence. The rebels by that act closed the door of compromise and reconciliation which had thus far been kept open. They rejected the appeal to a convention of the American people, to which the President in his inaugural had assented— they selected instead the arbitrament of force, the great trial by battle. They struck at the very heart of the nation when they sought to humble the flag of our Union, that had protected them from infancy, and which from childhood we have loved. They themselves inaugurated war. They imposed upon us the most sacred duty that can devolve upon a people, of protecting their nationality, and the world that had wondered at a forbearance which they could not understand, now wondered again at the spontaneous uprising of a mighty nation.

The threatened attack on Washington, the disloyalty of Baltimore, the cutting off of all communication by railroad and telegraph between the national capital and the great North, completed the work begun at Sumter.

Party lines grew faint and vanished as though they had never existed. Washington has been described as leaning in the darkest hour of the revolution, with one arm resting on Massachusetts, and the other on South Carolina. The faithlessness of the latter to her historic memories, prevents the parallel being now complete; but we may say of Lincoln what can be said of no other President since Washington, that in this dark hour he rests with one great arm upon his political friends, and the other on his political opponents, and that, as he looks abroad over the country whose destinies are in his keeping, he sees neither republicans nor democrats—neither nativists nor aliens, he sees but two classes, loyal citizens on the one side, and traitors on the other.

The feeling exhibited throughout the loyal States is not, as some Europeans have supposed, an ebullition of enthusiasm, based upon sudden and evanescent passion, but the expression of a profound conviction gradually forced upon them by a long train of facts that culminated at Sumter, that both duty and honor imperatively demand that they shall crush this gigantic conspiracy against the integrity of the country.

It was this that, within six weeks, called forth, as if by magic, any army of 200,000, converting our cities into camps, and making the repression of this rebellion the one great business of the American people.

The scene has been one which, day by day, has thrilled us with emotion, one upon which the Bancroft and the Motley of the next century will linger with admiration.

Massachusetts first in the field, as in the olden days of trial, shedding the first blood at Baltimore, first to occupy and protect the capital, where her great senator was stricken down, against the traitors, whose hatred to him foreshadowed their hatred towards the American Constitution, of which he had been the faithful and eloquent expounder.

New York, "herself the noblest eulogium on the Union," following close behind with her gallant Seventh, reaching Washington by a march already famous, and insuring by their presence the safety of Washington. The New England States, Pennsylvania and the Great West, pouring in their quotas with generous rivalry, and our foreign population rising instantly to the grandeur of the occasion, and hastening to the defence of their adopted country, present features of strength in the American Republic of which the most ardent of its eulogists had hardly dreamed.

If any man has regarded our large foreign element as one that threatened danger to the perpetuity of popular institutions, let him glance at the regiments now gathering to battle in their behalf. He will find among them men who have fought for freedom in other lands, and who have pined for their love of it in continental dungeons. He will find scholars from far-famed universities, and graduates of the military schools of Europe who have emerged from positions in which they were gaining an independency to proffer to their country their dear-bought experience, and guide and instruct the military ardor that sweeps like a whirlwind over the land. Call the roll of nationalities and you will have responses from England and Ireland, Scotland and Wales, from natives of Catholic France and Protestant Germany—you will have replies from Poles who yet dream of an independent Poland, from Hungarians in whose ears still lingers the eloquence of Kossuth, from Italians rejoicing in a regenerated Italy, and who are fresh from executing the policy of the lamented Cavour and from fighting by the side of Garibaldi. Every people of Christendom has its representatives in the army of the Union that has gone forth to fight for national unity, national independence, and the rights of human nature, against the confederated forces of slavery and treason.

In this crisis of our national history it is natural that we should regard with interest the view taken of our course by the great powers of Europe, and especially by that country with which as colonies we were so long connected, and which, despite the two wars that have been waged between us, we are accustomed to remember as our mother-land. Mingled with our Dutch and Huguenot ancestry, a very large proportion of the older families of America trace their descent from England, and many who do not are yet connected with her by no common ties. For myself, I may say that I have always entertained for her people an hereditary feeling of attachment, from the fact that my Huguenot ancestors, when they fled from Rochelle, after the revocation by Louis XIV. of the edict of Nantes, found upon her soil a welcome and a home; and that one of them, volunteering for King William against James II., shed his blood for English freedom at the battle of the Boyne, that great era in English history, ending, as we hope, forever her civil wars, from which dates the establishment on a firm basis, of the unity, the strength, and the world-wide dominion of the British empire. Such memories, and doubtless, my countrymen, you have many such, descend from father to son undimmed by national revolutions. They inspire sentiments of affection and kinship, that like family heir-looms gather new value from the lapse of time, and instead of fading as years and centuries roll by, seem the more sacred and imperishable from the thought of the generations by whom they have been cherished, and who have each in turn added a link to the chain of association.

The recent visit of the Prince of Wales, coming to us as the representative of the British nation, characterized as it was by the most graceful courtesy and cordiality on his part, and by the heartiest welcome upon ours, with the single exception of the rude treatment he met at Richmond—now the head-quarters of the rebels—had accomplished what no diplomacy could have effected. It seemed to have blotted out the last lingering remnant of ill-feeling, and left, on this side the Atlantic at least, the belief that henceforth there was a firm alliance between England and America, not based on treaty stipulations, but upon that heartfelt cordiality which springs from mutual regard, and from a common devotion to the great principles of right which belong to the institutions of both countries, and which their example is recommending to the world; nor should we overlook the belief cherished by many thoughtful men, that if in the distant future England should be set upon by the despotisms of Europe, and should require the aid of her American daughter to save her from annihilation, that aid would be promptly, effectively, and cordially given.

It is with profound regret that we have seen that friendly feeling suddenly converted into one of intense and bitter disappointment by the conduct and tone of the English government and the ill-judged comments of the English press.

The election of Mr. Lincoln for the first time entitled to the control of the Federal Government a party with whose political principles the English people were supposed to sympathize. By a scheme of treachery unparalleled in baseness, a few of the defeated faction holding office in the cabinet, in Congress, in the army, and in the navy, conspired together to betray the forts, arsenals, and other property of the Government into the hands of their confederates, with the view of destroying the Union, and erecting upon its ruins a Southern confederacy, of which slavery is to be the grand, permanent, and distinguishing characteristic. They accomplish the seizure of the public property without difficulty, for they themselves were intrusted with its guardianship, and they proceed to develop the great conspiracy and organize the rebel government, while the loyal citizens of the United States are helplessly compelled to await the inauguration of the new President. The 4th of March arrives at last, Mr. Lincoln takes the oath to maintain the Constitution and the laws, and when in obedience to that oath he orders the rebels to disperse, and calls upon the country for assistance, the loyal States, as one man, prepare to crush the conspiracy and restore the integrity and the honor of the nation. Neither from England nor from any foreign power have we asked or would we accept assistance in regulating our own household; but from England, of all the states of the world, we thought we had a right to expect a ready sympathy, and that moral support which is given by the countenance of a great nation.

The Southern rebels also counted upon the support of England, on the simple ground that her interest in cotton would incline her to their side; but we, although well aware of the demoralizing effect of interest upon national principles, still believed it impossible that the British government could consent from pecuniary motives to look with complacency on the progress of a rebellion whose only strength was gained by treachery, and which was avowedly prosecuted for the maintenance of a system which England herself had taught the world to regard with abhorrence. In thus believing, we were confirmed by the tone of the English press when the insurrection first began, one of the ablest representatives of which indignantly declared in substance that Manchester and Birmingham would be the first to reject as an insult the idea that they were to be moved from their position by pecuniary appeals, and that if any British cabinet should sacrifice the anti-slavery principles of the nation to the question of cotton, England would lose, and deservedly lose, her place at the council table of Europe.

The exclamation of Lord John Russell, in reply to a question as to the position of England, "For God's sake let us keep out of it," was followed by what is termed a proclamation of neutrality, in which British subjects are forbidden to render assistance to either the United States on the one hand, or the States calling themselves the Confederate States on the other, both of which parties are recognized by the proclamation as "belligerents."

The British government is accustomed to preserve an attitude of neutrality towards contending nations; but it would seem that neutrality does not so far interfere with the sympathies and freedom of its subjects as to compel it to issue proclamations against Irishmen enlisting with Francis Joseph, or Englishmen fighting for Victor Emanuel and Garibaldi.

The proclamation in this case is so warmly eulogized by the British press as precisely the proclamation demanded by the crisis, they profess such profound astonishment that the American people are not satisfied with it, and rate so severely Mr. Cassius M. Clay for expressing with Western bluntness his frank surprise, that I will dwell for a moment on what seems to be its meaning and effect.

What has the proclamation effected? How did we stand before it was issued, and how do we stand now?

In the case of the United States, the laws of England and its treaty stipulations with our Government already forbade its subjects from engaging in a conspiracy to overthrow our institutions. The proclamation, therefore, in forbidding English subjects to fight in the service of the rebels against the United States, simply declared the law as it was already understood; while in forbidding Englishmen to fight for the United States against the rebels, it intervened to change the existing practice, to revive the almost obsolete act of Geo. III. forbidding English subjects from engaging in foreign service without the royal consent, which had slumbered in regard to Austria and Italy, for the purpose of forbidding Englishmen from assisting to maintain in the United States constitutional order against conspiracy and rebellion, and the cause of freedom against chattel slavery.

The first effect of the proclamation, therefore, was to change the position in which England and Englishmen stood to the United States, 'to the disadvantage of the latter. Before the proclamation, for an Englishman to serve the United States Government in maintaining its integrity was regarded honorable; after the proclamation such service became a crime. The proclamation makes it an offence now for an Englishman to fight for the Government at Washington as great as it was for Englishmen before the proclamation to fight for the rebels of Montgomery. It thus, in a moral view, lowered the American Government to the level of the rebel confederacy, and in the next place, it proceeded, in an international view, to place the rebel confederacy on a par with the American Government, by recognizing them, not as rebels and insurgents to be dealt with by our Government as our Constitution and laws should determine, but as a *belligerent* power, to be classed with the United States, (of which they were but a rebellious fraction,) and equally entitled with the United States to the rights of belligerents under the law of nations.

No ingenuity can blind us to these facts :— Before the proclamation, to support our Government was an honorable office for the subjects of Great Britain, and the rebels were insurgents, with no rights save under the American Constitution. After the proclamation, for an Englishman to serve the United States is a crime, and the rebels are elevated into a belligerent power—and this intervention of England, depriving us of a support which her practice permitted, and giving the rebels a status and right they did not possess, we are coolly told is neutrality. Dr. Johnson in his famous letter gave us a sketch of a Chesterfieldian patron seeing a man struggling for life in the water, and when he reached ground encumbering him with help. Lord John has taught us the meaning of British neutrality towards a nation supposed to be in like condition. Let us trust that the English people will not endorse the definition.

What would England have said to such a proclamation of *neutrality* from us in her domestic troubles in Canada, in Ireland, or in India? What would the English people have thought of a state paper from Washington, declaring it the sovereign will of the people of the United States to remain perfectly neutral in the contest being waged in Hindostan between the British government on the one side and the Mogul dynasty on the other, and forbidding American citizens to enter the service of either of the said belligerents? What would they have thought of the American President intimating with cold etiquette that it was a matter of profound indifference to this Government which of the belligerents should be vic-

torious, the King of Oude and Nana Sahib, or Lord Canning and the immortal Havelock? Or is it that the British have become so enamored of rebellion, aye and of treachery too among their sepoys, that they thus court our great mogul and his fellow-traitors of Montgomery?

This Queen's proclamation strikes not simply at the moral position of our Government, but according to the English press it strikes also at our right to execute our own laws against piracy ; and we are told by the London *Times* that if we venture to hang, under these laws, a pirate who is licensed to plunder and murder by Jefferson Davis's letters of marque, now endorsed by the sovereigns of England and France, it will be regarded as an outrage by the civilized world ; and this gentle intimation comes to us from a nation who are hardly recovered from the effects of a rebellion, to end which, without staying to ask the opinion of the world, they blew their rebels from the guns.

It was intimated that the British cabinet were puzzled how to act in regard to the United States on the one hand, and her rebel conspirators on the other, and that after a careful search for precedents, one was found in the royal proclamation touching the war between Greece and Turkey, and that on that was based the proclamation which has so displeased and wounded the American people.

It could not have escaped the cabinet in their search for precedents, for we know with what thoroughness such searches are made, that a very similar state of things existed but a few years since between Great Britain and the United States, when the integrity and honor of the British empire were assailed by her Canadian colonists, and she had occasion to learn what in the opinion of the United States constitutes the duties of neutrality towards a friendly nation. Unsuccessful rebellions are soon forgotten, and perhaps many Englishmen may be surprised on being told that the Canadian rebellion was so deeply seated and so widely spread, as seriously to threaten the crown with the loss of the Canadas. Mr. Leader declared in Parliament that all the English government could do would be to subjugate and hold the principal cities, leaving the country occupied by rebels. The number of British troops under Sir John Colbourne was only 20,000, while the rebels are said to have had 14,000 at Montreal, 4,000 at Napiersville, and thousands more in arms in different parts of the Canadas, fierce with indignation at the murder of a party of patriots by Indians in the employ of the British government.

In November '37 two battles were fought between the British and the rebels, the one at St. Dennis, and the other at St. Charles, which was taken from a force of 3,000 Canadians, of whom 200 were killed, and 30 wounded.

In December, Mackenzie, the head rebel, who seems to have been the prototype of Davis, organized a provisional government and assuming the right to dispose of " ten millions of acres of land fair and fertile," took possession of *Montgomery* House, near Toronto, with a band of insurgents, and sent a demand to Sir Francis B. Head to dissolve the provincial parliament and to leave Toronto within fifteen days.

Then came Lord Gosford's proclamation at Quebec, declaring martial law, and denouncing the conspiracy and rebellion, and on the 8th of January, 1838, came the first proclamation from President Van Buren. After reciting the efforts made by him and by the Governors of New York and Vermont to prevent any *unlawful interference* on the part of our citizens in the contest unfortunately commenced in the British provinces, and notwithstanding the presence of the civil officers of the United States, who, by his direction, had visited the scenes of commotion, arms and ammunition have been procured by *the insurgents* in the United States, the proclamation proceeded :

" Now, therefore, to the end that the authority of the laws may be maintained, and the faith of treaties observed, I, Martin Van Buren, do most earnestly exhort all citizens of the United States who have violated their duties, to return peaceably to their respective homes, and I hereby warn them that any persons *who shall compromise the neutrality of this Government by interfering in an unlawful manner* with the affairs of the neighboring British provinces, will render themselves liable to arrest and punishment under the laws of the United States," &c., &c.

At the request of Lord Durham, Mr. Van Buren had directed our commanding officer on Lake Ontario to coöperate in any measures which might be suggested by Lord Durham for rooting out the band of pirates who had their quarters among " the thousand isles," without the slightest regard to the official proclamation of their chief, Mr. William Johnson, holding a commission from the patriot government, that the patriots would carefully respect neutral waters and the rights of all citizens of the United States.

On the 21st November, 1838, President Van Buren issued a second proclamation, calling upon the misguided and deluded persons to abandon projects dangerous to their own country, fatal to those whom they profess a desire to relieve, impracticable of execution without foreign aid, which they cannot rationally expect to obtain, and giving rise to imputations, however unfounded, against the honor and good faith of their own government.

The proclamation further called upon " every officer, civil and military, and upon every citizen, by the veneration due by all freemen to the laws which they have assisted to enact for their own government, by his regard for the honor and good faith of his country, by his love of honor and respect for that sacred code of laws by which national intercourse is regulated, to use every power to arrest for trial and punishment every offender against the laws providing for the performance of our obligations to the other powers of the world."

On the 4th of December, 1838, the President, in his message to Congress, declared, " If an insurrection existed in Canada the amicable disposition of the United States, as well as their duty to themselves, would lead them to maintain a strict neutrality, and to restrain its citizens from all violation of the laws which have been passed for its enforcement. But the Government recognizes a still higher obligation to repress all attempts on the part of its citizens to disturb the peace of a country where order prevails or has been reëstablished."

Such was the neutrality on the part of the United States towards Great Britain. It recognized the rebels of Canada not as *belligerents*, but as *insurgents*, and it enforced its neutrality not by forbidding its citizens to assist Great Britain to maintain its authority against the insurgents, but by forbidding them to interfere *in an unlawful manner* with the affairs of the provinces.

It needs no intimate knowledge of international law, no study of Grotius, or Puffendorf, or Vattel, or Wheaton, no definitions of the rights of belligerents and privateers from the *Consolato del Mare*, from Lampredi, Galiani, Moser, or Hübner, to enable us to appreciate the wide difference between the neutrality we practised towards England and her rebels, and that which England has inaugurated against us ; and no refinement of reasoning, nor subtle glosses indulged in by the English press, have at all blinded the American people to the unfriendly character of this royal proclamation.

The recognition of the independence of the Southern Confederacy is a matter in the discretion of England, and of all foreign nations. When this independence is established as a matter of fact we expect it to be recognized ; but England does not so recognize it. She recognizes the confederacy as simply struggling for independence, as were the insurgents in Canada, and pending the struggle she volunteers, under professions of neutrality, to ignore our constitutional right to subdue them, and to recognize their rebellion as lawful war. Bound to us by treaty stipulations, she elevates them to an equality of position as regards belligerent rights under the law of nations. She places their usurped government, based on treachery and slavery, on a par with that founded by Washington and his associates on the broad consent of the American people. She introduces Jefferson Davis and his confederates to a limited extent into the family of nations, endorses the licenses given by them to pirates whose brutal cupidity is stimulated by bribes of blood-money—twenty dollars for every murdered American! and transforms them into letters of marque which the ships of all nations are bound to recognize, respect, and obey.

Had she treated them as *insurgents* they would have had no other rights on the sea than had Bill Johnson, the pirate of the St. Lawrence. Having proclaimed them belligerents she has given them a commission not simply to capture American property in American vessels, but to capture on the high seas American property on board of whatever vessel it may be found, and to carry the neutral vessel and cargo into a belligerent port for further examination. She recognizes the right of the men who have robbed our treasury, betrayed our forts, and filched our navy-yards and arsenals, to establish prize courts to decide upon the lawfulness of captures made by their commissioned cruisers, and brought into court for adjudication, and the title to be given by Davis's courts is to be held valid by the law of nations.

This is what the proclamation of neutrality really means. This is the neutrality which England has inaugurated and which France has adopted; and those two great powers, who recently declared in the Congress at Paris that privateering is and shall remain abolished—by royal and imperial proclamation have countersigned letters of marque for the destruction of American ships, and which threaten with spoliation the commerce of the world. The aim and effect of the British proclamation seem to us so clearly unfriendly and injurious, that it is hardly worth while to note the discourtesy of adopting such a policy and giving it a definite and irreversible shape in advance of the arrival of Mr. Adams, without allowing us the opportunity to offer a word of explanation or remonstrance. Mr. Adams reached Liverpool the 13th of May. The next day the proclamation was printed in London.

The United States by their neutrality broke the back of the Canadian rebellion, dashed the hopes cherished by the rebels of effective American sympathy, in good faith assisted the British government in maintaining its authority, and restoring order, and thus materially diminished the cost of treasure and of life at which alone their subjection could have been accomplished.

The British government by their neutrality have made our task far more difficult, apart from the injury we may anticipate from the fleet of privateers whose letters are so respectably countersigned. But we learn from this proclamation one lesson, that will be perhaps worth all that it shall cost us, we learn the treatment we may expect if we fail to maintain our national integrity and the honor of our flag.

If a mere supposition that the rebels of Montgomery are likely to be successful, can in a moment dash from the memory of the English government all recollection of past friendship, and induce her in our moment of trial to condescend to a course so different from that we had pursued towards her, what treatment may we not expect from her, and from every other European cabinet, if we ourselves by our conduct admit that we are powerless at home? How will we be treated abroad, if we yield to

the threats of a fraction of our own population? What will be our standing among nations if, consenting to separation, we lose nearly half of our territory, and two-thirds of our Atlantic seaboard, and descend to the position of a third-rate power? Or what respect will be paid us, if to maintain our territory we compromise with rebellion? If we yield at the cannon's mouth what the people have deliberately refused at the polls, if we teach the world by such an example that we may be bullied with success, and that when we resist on principle unreasonable demands, it is only necessary to humble our flag, and to threaten Washington, to induce us ignominiously to submit?

Let us discard all reliance upon other help than that of God, a right cause, and a strong arm, and let us recognize the stubborn fact that "the government or nation that fails to protect itself against foes, whether foreign or domestic, deserves to perish ingloriously." *

Before leaving the question of England's neutrality, I think we should distinguish between the hasty action of the British cabinet and the deliberate conviction of the British people.

That the heart of that great nation is sound, and that as soon as they understand the motives and manner of this rebellion as you understand them, they will appreciate our position, approve our resolution, and wish us God speed in our great work of restoring the Federal Union to its integrity and its great original principles of freedom, I cannot, I will not doubt.

Already their cabinet has partially atoned for the first proclamation by an order that will prevent the privateers of Davis from entering British ports, and both the government and the people must soon recognize the fact that we have the ability and the will to crush this rebellion and maintain our integrity, however long the struggle, however great the cost; and that we no more recognize the right of England nor of Europe to dictate to us in this matter, than England would have recognized our right to interfere between her and Nana Sahib. The material interests based on cotton must yield to the national and moral duties that to-day devolve upon the American people, in determining, perhaps for untold ages, the destiny of the American continent.

The English people will see that our resolve to crush the conspiracy for the establishment of a slave empire, is not based on any evanescent burst of enthusiasm, but on the most sober calculations of honor, duty, safety, and economy; and that it is the true interest of England, her pecuniary, her political, and her moral interest, that the war should be as brief as possible, that the rebels may no longer be deluded into the belief that any true Englishman who understands the history and the object of their rebellion, can regard it with other feelings than

* Guetano Filangieri.

those naturally aroused by a policy of fraud, treachery, and oppression.

That the restoration of the integrity of our Union is to be accomplished without a vast expenditure of treasure, and perhaps of blood, no one anticipates. We all know something of the cost of European wars, but we know also our own resources, and the immense stake for which we will be fighting. Our fathers fought for seven years for our national freedom, and the spirit abroad throughout our land indicates that their sons, if necessary, will fight seven years more to save it from destruction and disgrace. Whether the debt incurred for its preservation shall be hundreds or thousands of millions, it will be a sacred legacy to future generations. A debt of five hundred millions, as remarked by an English journalist, would leave this nation less severely taxed than any nation of Europe.

If any man supposes that this Republic can be advantageously sundered into two, let him cast his eye upon the map and endeavor to find a natural line to separate the two confederacies. The geographical formation of our country indicates that it is one; nature has provided no boundary line between the North and the South; no river like the Mississippi, no mountain chain like the Alleghanies, or the Rocky Mountains, running from the West to the Atlantic, and forming an Alpine boundary to divide the sections. On the contrary, the Father of waters stretches out his great arms to the East and to the West, bearing on his bosom to the Gulf the generous products of the valleys which they fertilize, and carrying back in their place the cotton, rice, and sugar of our Southern borders, and imports from foreign climes.

The Mississippi, source and channel of prosperity to North and South alike in every mile of its progress; on the West to Minnesota, Iowa, Missouri, Arkansas, and Louisiana; on the East to Wisconsin, Illinois, Kentucky, Tennessee, and Mississippi, proclaims to the citizens of the immense region which it waters through thousands of miles in extent, from North to South, and East to West, that our country is one and indivisible.

Our duty to the South forbids our acquiescence in this rebellion, for it would reverse the American policy for the last half century, and reconsign to foreign invasion, to anarchy and ruin, the immense territories which we have rescued from European sway, and united as parts of our great nation.

Look back to the olden time and see what the Southern country would again become. Trace the history of Florida from the days of Charles V., from the adventures of De Leon and De Soto, the persecution of Protestants from France, and the retaliation on the murderous Spaniards; the capture of St. Augustine by Sir Francis Drake, the buccaneering inroads of the English, the transfer of Florida to the British crown; its partial settlement from Italy and Greece, the privateering exploits in our revolution, the capture of Baton Rouge and Pensacola, until its purchase by our Government in 1819.

Remember that the Spaniards navigated the Gulf of Mexico for two centuries, without discovering that it was the outlet of the great river of the North; a fact which, perhaps, induces the Southern confederates to imagine that we also may be persuaded to forget its existence. Look at Louisiana from the days of Law and the Mississippi bubble to its cession to Spain in 1762, and its retrocession to France in 1800, when we hastened to buy it from the First Consul, and you will find nothing in Florida, in Louisiana, nor indeed in Texas, to indicate even the first beginning of the prosperity which has been so rapidly developed under the fostering protection of the Federal Government.

Let the American Union be dismembered, and what is to prevent foreign powers from reentering upon our national domain from which at such great cost and labor they have been ousted?

An old officer of the French empire writing to the *Courrier des Etats-Unis*, has predicted that in the first place France would retake Louisiana, according to ancient treaties, that Spain would reclaim Florida, that England perhaps would seek to appropriate Oregon, and that Mexico, under foreign protection, would retake New Mexico, Texas, and California; or supposing that we should consent to the establishment of the so-called Southern Confederacy, which we know to be a mere military despotism, what possible guarantee can we have for peace in the future, when each State reserves the right to secede at pleasure and enter at will into foreign alliances, inaugurating universal chaos and chronic dissolution? Even now, while the struggle is being waged, the leading men of South Carolina, already sick of their independence before it is accomplished, repudiate republican institutions, and sigh for a British prince to lend the odor of royalty to the aristocracy which they boast—an aristocracy based not upon historic deeds and noble heroism, but simply upon the color of their skins, and their despotic dominion over helpless slaves —an aristocracy whose wealth is invested in human flesh, and whose revenues are collected in the field by the lash, and on the auction block by the hammer!

Let our Union be divided with the view of accomplishing present peace, and not only would the United States fall from her position of a first-class power to that of a minor republic, with a contracted seaboard and a defenceless border—but the act of separation would inaugurate an exposure to hostilities; first, from our new and unfriendly neighbor, and then from every foreign power with which one or all of the Southern States might choose to form an alliance. Either contingency would necessarily change our national policy, require the maintenance of a standing army, and complicate endlessly our commercial relations. Now, we stand aloof from the quarrels of the rest of the world, and can devote our energies to the development of our marvellous resources and the extension of civilization and freedom over the American continent; then we should be compelled to an attitude of perpetual self-defence to save us from constant entanglement in the web of European politics. Already have we had a foretaste of the sort of treatment which Europe will accord to the severed fragments of the American Republic.

To maintain the respect of the world we must maintain first the integrity of our national territory, and next the integrity of our fundamental principles. As for the argument that if the rebellion is crushed harmony can never be restored, Canada furnishes the refutation. The bloody feuds of 1838 have hardly left a trace to mar the tranquil prosperity which marks the progress of that great province. There is reason to believe that the Union men of the South await but the coming of the Federal forces in sufficient strength, to show themselves again the cordial supporters of the Federal Government. But even if this were not so, and there was reason to fear a long period of distrust and disaffection, the fact remains that the interests of the American people imperatively demand that the integrity of the Union shall be preserved, whether the slavery propagandists of the South like it or like it not.

This is one of those decisive epochs that occur in the history of all great nations. One came to our fathers in 1776. Submission to usurped authority, or national independence, was the issue; and on the day we commemorate they chose the latter; and the force of their example on the world is yet to be determined. To-day the imperious demand comes from slavery, "Submit or be destroyed!" Already has a blow been struck by slavery at our Republic, the force of which reverberates through the world. Two hundred millions of debts due from rebels to loyal citizens are repudiated, the business of the country is arrested, bankruptcy stares us in the face; worse than all, our flag has been insulted, our prestige impaired, and from foreign courts we have received treatment that our American pride can illy brook. Honor, interest, self-respect, and the highest duty, call upon us to crush, and crush speedily, the insolent traitors whose secret and atrocious perfidy has temporarily crippled us; and while we recall the motives that combine to compel us to resistance, let us not forget the duty which this nation owes to the oppressed race who are the innocent cause of all our troubles, and who have no friends to look to but ourselves, to prevent the spreading of slavery over every foot of American territory, and the waving of the flag of the slave trader over the fearful horrors of the middle passage.

Gentlemen, as in our revolutionary struggle our fathers had to contend with the timid and

Doc.—36

the avaricious, who feared the evils of war and continually cried peace! peace! where there was no peace, so may we expect to be constantly hampered by declaimers in favor of compromise. I do not stop to consider the fitness of our lending an ear to such a cry until the insult to our flag has been atoned for, and until our supremacy is acknowledged, for the great mass of the people of the country will be unanimous on this point; they will regard the bare suggestion of treating with the rebels whose hands are stained with the blood of the sons of Massachusetts, of Ellsworth and of Winthrop, of Greble and of Ward, as a personal insult, and will reply to it as did Patrick Henry—"We must fight! I repeat it, sir, we *must* fight!" The sword is now the only pen with which we can write "peace" in enduring characters on the map of America.

The day of compromise is gone; "that sort of thing," as the Secretary said, "ended with the Fourth of March." We have had devices enough for saving the Union, devices suggested by the men who are now striving to destroy it.

There is one good old plan provided by the Constitution that was successfully practised by Washington and Jackson; we are about to try *that*; let us try it thoroughly; it is simply the due execution of the laws by whatever degree of force the exigency may require. If our army of 300,000 men is insufficient, a million stand ready to follow them to the field.

It would be difficult, my countrymen, to exaggerate the solemn importance of our national position. A struggle for life and death has commenced between freedom and slavery, and on the event of the struggle depends our national existence. Let us falter, let us compromise, let us yield, and the work of our fathers and the inheritance of our children, our own honor, and the hopes of the oppressed nationalities of the world, will be buried in a common grave! Let us be demoralized by defeat in the field, or what is infinitely worse, by submission to rebellion, and in foreign lands a man will blush and hang his head to declare himself an American citizen. A whipped hound should be the emblem of the Northern man who whimpers for a peace that can only be gained by dishonor.

But let us remember our fathers who, eighty-five years ago, this day, made universal freedom and equal right, the corner-stone of this republic; let us exhibit, as we have begun to do, their stern resolve and high devotion in behalf of constitutional freedom, and we shall secure for our children and our children's children, a gigantic and glorious nationality, based upon principles of Christian civilization, such as the world has never seen before.

There is nothing impossible, nothing improbable, in our speedy realization of a glorious future.

The seeds of this rebellion have long lurked in our system; for years it has been coming to a head, and simply from want of proper treatment, it has now burst with angry violence; but the pulse of the nation beats coolly and calmly, the partial local inflammation but serves to exhibit the lusty health of the body politic, and when this rebellion is extinguished, and its cause removed, we may hope that we are safe from an organized rebellion for at least a century to come.

With what speed this rebellion shall be crushed depends solely upon yourselves. Let public feeling lag throughout the land, and the War Department will lag in Washington. Let us become careless and indifferent about the matter, and contractors will cheat our soldiers, incompetent officers will expose them to defeat, official indifference will produce general demoralization. But let us keep ever in mind the lesson we have so dearly learned—that eternal vigilance is the price of liberty. Let the administration and the army feel that their every act is canvassed by an intelligent people, and, when approved, greeted by a hearty appreciation; that every branch of industry awaits the ending of the war, and that from every part of the land comes the cry of "forward," and the arm of the Union at Washington will obey the heart of the nation, whenever a prayer rises in its behalf, or its flag kisses the breeze of heaven.

Let us with this sleepless vigilance on our part, repose a generous confidence in our President, who has won the generous applause of his Democratic opponents, nor scan too impatiently the warlike policy of Scott.

Like all true-hearted and brave veterans, he wishes to spare as far as possible the blood alike of loyal soldiers and deluded rebels, and to carry with the flag of our Union not simply the power to make it respected, but the more glorious attributes that cause it to be loved. "Not," to adopt the words of Gov. Andrew, of Massachusetts, "to inaugurate a war of sections, not to avenge former wrongs, not to perpetuate ancient griefs, or memories of conflict," will that flag move onwards until it floats again in its pride and beauty over Richmond, and Sumter, and Montgomery, and New Orleans; but to indicate the majesty of the people, to retain and re-invigorate the institutions of our fathers, to rescue from the despotism of traitors the loyal citizens of the South, and place all, loyal or rebel, under the protection of a Union that is essential to the welfare of the whole.

The eyes of the whole world are this day fixed upon you. To Europeans themselves, European questions sink to insignificance compared with the American question now to be decided. Rise, my countrymen, as did our fathers on the day we celebrate, to the majestic grandeur of this question in its twofold aspect, as regards America, and as regards the world. Remember that with the failure of the American Republic will fall the wisest system of republican government which the wisdom of man has yet invented, and the hopes of popular freedom cherished throughout the globe.

Let us, standing by our fathers' graves,

swear anew, and teach the oath to our children, that with God's help the American Republic, clasping this continent in its embrace, shall stand unmoved, though all the powers of slavery, piracy, and European jealousy should combine to overthrow it; that we shall have in the future, as we have had in the past, one country, one Constitution, and one destiny; and that when we shall have passed from earth, and the acts of to-day shall be matter of history, and the dark power now seeking our overthrow shall have been itself overthrown, our sons may gather strength from our example in every contest with despotism that time may have in store to try their virtue, and that they may rally under the Stars and Stripes to battle for freedom and the rights of man, with our olden war cry, "Liberty and Union, now and forever, one and inseparable."

Doc. 254½.

SOVEREIGNTY OF SOUTH CAROLINA.

THE ADDRESS OF THE PEOPLE OF SOUTH CAROLINA, ASSEMBLED IN CONVENTION, DECEMBER, 1860, TO THE PEOPLE OF THE SLAVEHOLDING STATES OF THE UNITED STATES.[*]

It is now seventy-three years since the Union between the United States was made by the Constitution of the United States. During this period their advance in wealth, prosperity, and power, has been with scarcely a parallel in the history of the world. The great object of their Union was external defence from the aggressions of more powerful nations; now complete, from their mere progress in power, thirty-one millions of people, with a commerce and navigation which explores every sea, and of agricultural productions which are necessary to every civilized people, command the friendship of the world. But, unfortunately, our internal peace has not grown with our external prosperity. Discontent and contention have moved in the bosom of the Confederacy for the last thirty-five years. During this time South Carolina has twice called her people together in solemn convention, to take into consideration the aggressions and unconstitutional wrongs perpetrated by the people of the North on the people of the South. These wrongs were submitted to by the people of the South, under the hope and expectation that they would be final. But these hopes and expectations have proved to be void. Instead of being incentives to forbearance, our submission has only instigated to new forms of aggression and outrage, and South Carolina, again assembling her people in convention, has this day dissolved her connection with the States constituting the United States.

The one great evil, from which all other evils have flowed, is the overthrow of the Constitution of the United States. The Govern-

* See Document, page 3.

ment of the United States is no longer a government of a confederated republic, but of a consolidated democracy. It is no longer a free government, but a despotism. It is, in fact, such a government as Great Britain attempted to set over our fathers, and which was resisted and defeated by a seven years' struggle for independence.

The Revolution of 1776 turned upon one great principle, self-government and self-taxation, the criterion of self-government. Where the interests of two people united together under one government are different, each must have the power to protect its interests by the organization of the government or they cannot be free. The interests of Great Britain and of the colonies were different and antagonistic. Great Britain was desirous of carrying out the policy of all nations toward their colonies, of making them tributary to their wealth and power. She had vast and complicated relations with the whole world. Her policy towards her North American colonies was to identify them with her in all these complicated relations, and to make them bear, in common with the rest of the empire, the full burden of her obligations and necessities. She had a vast public debt; she had a European policy and Asiatic policy, which had occasioned the accumulation of her public debt, and which kept her in continual wars. The North American colonies saw their interests, political and commercial, sacrificed by such a policy. Their interests required that they should not be identified with the burdens and wars of the mother country. They had been settled under charters which gave them self-government, at least so far as their property was concerned. They had taxed themselves, and had never been taxed by the government of Great Britain. To make them a part of a consolidated empire, the Parliament of Great Britain determined to assume the power of legislating for the colonies in all cases whatsoever. Our ancestors resisted the pretension. They refused to be a part of the consolidated government of Great Britain.

The Southern States now stand exactly in the same position towards the Northern States that our ancestors in the colonies did towards Great Britain. The Northern States, having the majority in Congress, claim the same power of omnipotence in legislation as the British Parliament. "The general welfare," is the only limit to the legislation of either; and the majority in Congress, as in the British Parliament, are the sole judges of the expediency of the legislation this "general welfare" requires. Thus the Government of the United States has become a consolidated Government, and the people of the Southern States are compelled to meet the very despotism their fathers threw off in the Revolution of 1776.

The consolidation of the Government of Great Britain over the colonies was attempted to be carried out by the taxes. The British Parliament undertook to tax the colonies to promote British interests. Our fathers resisted this pretension. They claimed the right of self-taxation through their colonial legislatures. They were not represented in the British Parliament, and therefore could not rightly be taxed by its legislature. The British Government, however, offered them a representative in the British Parliament; but it was not sufficient to enable them to protect themselves from the majority, and they refused it. Between taxation without any representation, and taxation without a representation adequate to protection, there was no difference. By neither would the colonies tax themselves. Hence they refused to pay the taxes laid by the British Parliament.

The Southern States now stand in the same relation towards the Northern States, in the vital matter of taxation, that our ancestors stood towards the people of Great Britain. They are in a minority in Congress. Their representation in Congress is useless to protect them against unjust taxation; and they are taxed by the people of the North for their benefit, exactly as the people of Great Britain taxed our ancestors in the British Parliament for their benefit. For the last forty years the taxes laid by the Congress of the United States have been laid with a view of subserving the interests of the North. The people of the South have been taxed by duties on imports, not for revenue, but for an object inconsistent with revenue—to promote, by prohibitions, Northern interests in the productions of their mines and manufactures.

There is another evil in the condition of the Southern towards the Northern States, which our ancestors refused to bear towards Great Britain. Our ancestors not only taxed themselves, but all the taxes collected from them were expended amongst them. Had they submitted to the pretensions of the British Government, the taxes collected from them would have been expended on other parts of the British empire. They were fully aware of the effect of such a policy in impoverishing the people from whom taxes are collected, and in enriching those who receive the benefit of their expenditure. To prevent the evils of such a policy was one of the motives which drove them on to revolution. Yet this British policy has been fully realized towards the Southern States by the Northern States. The people of the Southern States are not only taxed for the benefit of the Northern States, but after the taxes are collected three-fourths of them are expended at the North. This cause, with others connected with the operation of the General Government, has provincialized the cities of the South. Their growth is paralyzed, whilst they are mere suburbs of Northern cities. The basis of the foreign commerce of the United States are the agricultural productions of the South; yet Southern cities do not carry it on. Our foreign trade is almost annihilated. In 1740 there were five ship yards in

South Carolina to build ships to carry on our direct trade with Europe. Between 1740 and 1779 there were built in these yards twenty-five square-rigged vessels, besides a great number of sloops and schooners, to carry on our coast and West India trade. In the half century immediately preceding the Revolution, from 1725 to 1775, the population of South Carolina increased seven-fold.

No man can for a moment believe that our ancestors intended to establish over their posterity exactly the same sort of government they had overthrown. The great object of the Constitution of the United States, in its internal operation, was, doubtless, to secure the great end of the Revolution—a limited free government—a government limited to those matters only which were general and common to all portions of the United States. All sectional or local interests were to be left to the States. By no other arrangement would they obtain free government by a constitution common to so vast a confederacy. Yet by gradual and steady encroachments on the part of the people of the North, and submission on the part of the South, the limitations in the Constitution have been swept away, and the Government of the United States has become consolidated, with a claim of limitless powers in its operations.

It is not at all surprising, whilst such is the character of the Government of the United States, that it should assume to possess power over all the institutions of the country. The agitations on the subject of slavery in the South are the natural results of the consolidation of the Government. Responsibility follows power; and if the people of the North have the power by Congress "to promote the general welfare of the United States" by any means they deem expedient, why should they not assail and overthrow the institution of slavery in the South? They are responsible for its continuance or existence, in proportion to their power. A majority in Congress, according to their interested and perverted views, is omnipotent. The inducements to act upon the subject of slavery, under such circumstances, were so imperious as to amount almost to a moral necessity. To make, however, their numerical power available to rule the Union, the North must consolidate their power. It would not be united, on any matter common to the whole Union—in other words, on any Constitutional subject—for on such subjects divisions are as likely to exist in the North as in the South. Slavery was strictly a sectional interest; if this could be made the criterion of parties at the North, the North could be united in its power, and thus carry out its measures of sectional ambition, encroachment, and aggrandizement. To build up their sectional predominance in the Union, the Constitution must be first abolished by constructions; but, that being done, the consolidation of the North to rule South by the tariff and slavery issues, was in the obvious course of things.

The Constitution of the United States was an experiment. The experiment consisted in uniting under one government different peoples, living in different climates, and having different pursuits of industry and institutions. It matters not how carefully the limitations of such a government be laid down in the Constitution, its success must at least depend upon the good faith of the parties to the constitutional compact in enforcing them. It is not in the power of human language to exclude false inferences, constructions, and perversions in any constitution; and when vast sectional interests are to be subserved, involving the appropriation of countless millions of money, it has not been the usual experience of mankind that words on parchment can arrest power. The Constitution of the United States, irrespective of the interposition of the States, rested on the assumption that power would yield to faith—that integrity would be stronger than interest; and that thus the limitations of the Constitution would be observed. The experiment has been fairly made. The Southern States, from the commencement of the Government, have striven to keep it within the orbit prescribed by the Constitution. The experiment has failed. The whole Constitution, by the constructions of the Northern people, has been swallowed up by a few words in its preamble. In their reckless lust for power, they seem unable to comprehend that seeming paradox, that the more power is given to the General Government the weaker it becomes. Its strength consists in its generality and limitations.

To extend the scope of its power over sectional or local interests, is to raise up against it opposition and resistance. In all such matters the General Government must necessarily be a despotism, because all sectional or local interests must ever be represented by a minority in the councils of the General Government—having no power to protect itself against the rule of the majority. The majority, constituted from those who do not represent these sectional or local interests, will control and govern them. A free people cannot submit to such a Government. And the more it enlarges the sphere of its power, the greater must be the dissatisfaction it must produce, and the weaker it must become. On the contrary, the more it abstains from usurped powers, and the more faithfully it adheres to the limitations of the Constitution, the stronger it is made. The Northern people have had neither the wisdom nor the faith to perceive, that to observe the limitation of the Constitution was the only way to its perpetuity.

Under such a Government there must, of course, be many and endless "irrepressible conflicts" between the two great sections of the Union. The same faithlessness which has abolished the Constitution of the United States, will not fail to carry out the sectional purposes for which it has been abolished. There must be conflict; and the weaker section of the Union can only find peace and liberty in an independence of the North. The repeated efforts made by South Carolina, in a wise conservatism, to arrest the progress of the General Government in its fatal progress to consolidation, have been unsupported, and denounced as faithless to the obligations of the Constitution by the very men and States who were destroying it by their usurpations. It is now too late to reform or restore the Government of the United States. All confidence in the North is lost in the South. The faithlessness of half a century has opened a gulf of separation between them, which no promises or engagements can fill.

It cannot be believed that our ancestors would have assented to any union whatever with the people of the North if the feelings and opinions now existing among them had existed when the Constitution was framed. There was then no tariff—no negro fanaticism. It was the delegates from New England who proposed, in the Convention which framed the Constitution, to the delegates from South Carolina and Georgia, that if they would agree to give Congress the power of regulating commerce by a majority, they would support the extension of the African slave trade for twenty years. African slavery existed in all the States but one. The idea that they would be made to pay that tribute to their Northern confederates, which they had refused to pay to Great Britain; or that the institution of African slavery would be made the grand basis of a sectional organization of the North to rule the South, never crossed their imaginations. The union of the Constitution was a union of slaveholding States. It rests on slavery, by prescribing a representation in Congress for three-fifths of our slaves. There is nothing in the proceedings of the convention which framed the Constitution, to show that the Southern States would have formed any other Union; and still less that they would have formed a Union with more powerful non-slaveholding States, having a majority in both branches of the Legislature of the Government. They were guilty of no such folly. Time and the progress of things have totally altered the relations between the Northern and Southern States since the Union was established. That identity of feelings, interests, and institutions which once existed, is gone. They are now divided between agricultural, and manufacturing, and commercial States—between slaveholding and non-slaveholding States. Their institutions and industrial pursuits have made them totally different people. That equality in the Government between the two sections of the Union which once existed, no longer exists. We but imitate the policy of our fathers in dissolving a Union with non-slaveholding confederates, and seeking a confederation with slaveholding States.

Experience has proved that slaveholding States cannot be safe in subjection to non-slaveholding States. Indeed, no people ever expect to preserve their rights and liberties unless they are in their own custody. To plunder and oppress where plunder and oppression can be practised with impunity, seems to be the natural order of things. The fairest portions of the world have been turned into wildernesses, and the most civilized and prosperous communities have been impoverished and ruined by anti-slavery fanaticism. The people of the North have not left us in doubt as to their designs and policy. United as a section in the late Presidential election, they have elected as the exponent of their policy one who has openly declared that all the States of the United States must be made free States or slave States. It is true that amongst those who aided in his election, there are various shades of anti-slavery hostility. But if African slavery in the Southern States be the evil their political combinations affirm it to be, the requisitions of an inexorable logic must lead them to emancipation. If it is right to preclude or abolish slavery in a Territory, why should it be allowed to remain in the States? The one is not at all more unconstitutional than the other, according to the decisions of the Supreme Court of the United States. And when it is considered that the Northern States will soon have the power to make that Court what they please, and that the Constitution never has been any barrier whatever to their exercise of power, what check can there be in the unrestrained counsels of the North to emancipation? There is sympathy in association, which carries men along without principle; but when there is principle, and that principle is fortified by long-existing prejudices and feelings, association is omnipotent in party influences.

In spite of all disclaimers and professions, there can be but one end by the submission of the South to the rule of a sectional anti-slavery Government at Washington; and that end, directly or indirectly, must be the emancipation of the slaves of the South. The hypocrisy of thirty years—the faithlessness of their whole course from the commencement of our union with them—show that the people of the non-slaveholding North are not and cannot be safe associates of the slaveholding South under a common government. Not only their fanaticism, but their erroneous views of the principles of free government, render it doubtful whether, separated from the South, they can maintain a free government among themselves. Brute numbers with them is the great element of free government. A majority is infallible and omnipotent. "The right divine to rule in kings" is only transferred to their majority. The very object of all constitutions, in free popular governments, is, to restrain the majority. Constitutions, therefore, according to their theory, must be most unrighteous inventions, restricting liberty. None ought to exist, but the body politic ought simply to have a political organization, to bring out and enforce the will of a majority. This theory may be harmless in a small community having an identity of interests and pursuits, but over a vast State—still more over a vast Confederacy, having various and conflicting interests and pursuits—it is a remorseless despotism. In resisting it, as applicable to ourselves, we are vindicating the great cause of free government, more important perhaps to the world than the existence of all the United States. Nor, in resisting it, do we intend to depart from the safe instrumentality the system of government we have established with them requires. In separating from them we invade no rights—no interest of theirs. We violate no obligation or duty to them.

As separate, independent States in convention, we made the Constitution of the United States with them; and, as separate independent States, each State acting for itself, we adopted it. South Carolina, acting in her sovereign capacity, now thinks proper to secede from the Union. She did not part with her sovereignty in adopting the Constitution. The last thing a State can be presumed to have surrendered is her sovereignty. Her sovereignty is her life. Nothing but a clear, express grant can alienate it. Inference should be dumb. Yet it is not at all surprising that those who have construed away all the limitations of the Constitution, should also by construction claim the annihilation of the sovereignty of the States. Having abolished all barriers to their omnipotence by their faithless constructions in the operations of the General Government, it is most natural that they should endeavor to do the same towards us in the States. The truth is, they having violated the express provisions of the Constitution, it is at an end as a compact. It is morally obligatory only on those who choose to accept its perverted terms. South Carolina, deeming the compact not only violated in particular features, but virtually abolished by her Northern confederates, withdraws herself as a party from its obligations. The right to do so is denied by her Northern confederates. They desire to establish a despotism, not only omnipotent in Congress, but omnipotent over the States; and as if to manifest the imperious necessity of our secession, they threaten us with the sword, to coerce submission to their rule.

Citizens of the slaveholding States of the United States, circumstances beyond our control have placed us in the van of the great controversy between the Northern and Southern States. We would have preferred that other States should have assumed the position we now occupy. Independent ourselves, we disclaim any design or desire to lead the counsels of the other Southern States. Providence has cast our lot together, by extending over us an identity of pursuits, interests, and institutions. South Carolina desires no destiny separated from yours. To be one of a great slaveholding confederacy, stretching its arms over a territory larger than any power in Europe possesses—with a population four times greater than that of the whole United States, when they achieved their independence of the British empire—with productions which make our existence more important to the world than that of any other people inhabiting it—with common institutions to defend, and common dangers to encounter—we ask your sympathy and confederation. Whilst constituting a portion of the United States, it has been your statesmanship which has guided it in its mighty strides to power and expansion. In the field, as in the cabinet, you have led the way to its renown and grandeur. You have loved the Union, in whose service your great statesmen have labored, and your great soldiers have fought and conquered—not for the material benefits it conferred, but with the faith of a generous and devoted chivalry. You have long lingered and hoped over the shattered remains of a broken Constitution. Compromise after compromise, formed by your concessions, has been trampled under foot by your Northern confederates. All fraternity of feeling between the North and the South is lost, or has been converted into hate, and we of the South are at last driven together by the stern destiny which controls the existence of nations.

Your bitter experience of the faithlessness and rapacity of your Northern confederates may have been necessary to evolve those great principles of free government, upon which the liberties of the world depend, and to prepare you for the grand mission of vindicating and re-establishing them. We rejoice that other nations should be satisfied with their institutions. Self-complacency is a great element of happiness with nations as with individuals. We are satisfied with ours. If they prefer a system of industry, in which capital and labor are in perpetual conflict—and chronic starvation keeps down the natural increase of population—and a man is worked out in eight years—and the law ordains that children shall be worked only ten hours a day—and the sabre and bayonet are the instruments of order—be it so. It is their affair, not ours. We prefer, however, our system of industry, by which labor and capital are identified in interest, and capital, therefore, protects labor, by which our population doubles every twenty years; by which starvation is unknown, and abundance crowns the land; by which order is preserved by an unpaid police, and the most fertile regions of the world where the Caucasian cannot labor are brought into usefulness by the labor of the African, and the whole world is blessed by our own productions. All we demand of other peoples is to be let alone to work out our own high destinies. United together, and we must be the most independent, as we are the most important amongst the nations of the world. United together, and we require no other instrument to conquer peace than our beneficen productions. United together, and we must be a great, free and prosperous people, whose renown must spread throughout the civilized world, and pass down, we trust, to the remotest ages. We ask you to join us in forming a confederacy of slaveholding States.

—*Missouri Republican*, Dec. 29, 1860.

Doc. 255.
SLAVES AND SLAVERY.

Mr. Jefferson Davis, in his Message to those whom he calls "Gentlemen of the Congress" of the "Confederate States," of April 29, 1861, sets forth certain alleged reasons why Southern men ought to refuse to live under the same General Government with Northern men, should engage in battle with them on land, and attack their commerce at sea. The Message is a carefully prepared document, devised and intended to excite Southern men to this dreadful work, and to justify it in the view of the civilized world. For this purpose, it was necessary to impute to Northern men a character and conduct worthy to be blamed, and to be punished with all the inflictions of war. He accordingly inserted in his Message the two following paragraphs:

"When the several States delegated certain powers to the United States Congress, a large portion of the laboring population consisted of African slaves imported into the country by the mother country. In twelve out of the thirteen States negro slavery existed, and the right of property in slaves was protected by law. This property was recognized in the Constitution, and provision was made against its loss by the escape of the slave. The increase in the number of slaves by further importation from Africa was also secured by a clause forbidding Congress to prohibit the slave trade anterior to a certain date; and in no clause can there be found any delegation of power to Congress, authorizing it in any manner to legislate to the prejudice, detriment, or discouragement of the owners of that species of property, or excluding it from the protection of the Government.

"The climate and soil of the Northern States soon proved unpropitious to the continuance of slave labor, whilst the converse was the case at the South. Under the unrestricted free intercourse between the two sections, the Northern States consulted their own interest by selling their slaves to the South, and prohibiting slavery within their limits. The South were willing purchasers of a property suitable to their wants, and paid the price of the acquisition, without harboring a suspicion that their quiet possession was to be disturbed by those who were inhibited, not only by want of constitutional authority, but by good faith as vendors, from disquieting a title emanating from themselves."

In a communication published in the *Courier*

of May 8, this accusation against the North was called "an old lie." On reflection, we doubt whether it is many years old. It was indeed full-grown when Mr. Davis found it and adopted it, and we presume, believed it, as he is evidently "given up to strong delusions;" but it is probably not much older than secession, having been invented for the purpose of making Northern men appear so hateful that Southern men would be willing to "secede" from them, and kill them. If so, it was skilfully invented; and as a device for exciting the passions which produce and sustain civil war, it is deserving of serious attention.

Mr. Everett, in his late oration at New York, treats this calumny as worthy of a brief notice, He says:

"The theory of a change in the Northern mind, growing out of a discovery made *soon after* 1789, that our soil and climate were unpropitious to slavery, (as if the soil and climate then were different from what they always had been,) and a consequent sale to the South of the slaves of the North, is purely mythical; as groundless in fact as it is absurd in statement. I have often asked for evidence of this last allegation, and I have never found an individual who attempted even to prove it."

A disparaging assertion, put forth for a purpose evidently depreciatory, and which no one even attempts to prove, may commonly be left to die of itself; but when, as is now the case, it is efficient in producing rebellion, devastation, and slaughter, it is fortunate that we can show its true character by unquestionable documentary proof.

The first census of the United States was taken in 1790, which was "soon after 1789," the time spoken of by Mr. Davis. According to that census, there were then the following numbers of slaves in what are now the "Free States":

New Hampshire	158
Vermont	17
Rhode Island	952
Connecticut	2,759
New York	21,324
New Jersey	11,423
Pennsylvania	3,737
Total	40,370

In Massachusetts, including Maine, there were no slaves, and had been none for some ten years.

These 40,370 slaves, Mr. Davis says, "the North," finding them unprofitable, sold to "the South," and "the South" bought and paid for. Let us see:

NEW HAMPSHIRE.

The whole colored population was, in—

	Free.	Slave.	Total.
1790	630	158	788
1800	856	8	864
1810	970	none.	970

From 1790 to 1800, the slaves had diminished 150, and the free blacks had increased 226. From 1800 to 1810, the 8 remaining slaves disappeared, and the free blacks increased 114. Evidently, there had been no extensive sale of slaves to the South.

VERMONT.

	Free.	Slave.	Total.
1790	255	17	272
1800	557	none.	557

The 17 slaves disappeared, and the free increased 302. Here, too, there could have been no sale of slaves to the South. In fact, no slaves were ever held by the people of Vermont, under the laws of that State. The 17, in 1790, if not a mistake, must have been there temporarily, for some peculiar reason.

RHODE ISLAND.

	Free.	Slave.	Total.
1790	3,469	952	4,421
1800	3,304	381	3,685
1810	3,609	108	3,717
1820	3,598	48	3,646
1830	3,561	17	3,578
1840	3,238	5	3,243
1850	3,544	none.	3,544

From 1790 to 1800, the number of slaves diminished 571, and the number of the free, 165; and of the total, 736. This may look, at first sight, as if about one-eightieth part of the slaves at the North had been virtually sold to the South; but, fortunately, we are able to explain it. The diminution of the free, 165, indicates an emigration; and we know, from the census of Massachusetts, that the increase of free blacks in that State, during those ten years, was about 715 above the average rate of increase. In New Bedford, they increased from 38 to 160; in Nantucket, from 110 to 228; in Duke's County, from 33 to 202; in Suffolk County the increase was 407. There was a great flocking to the whaling ports and to Boston, to engage as seamen. These 715 must have come from somewhere, and there is no indication in the census of any other State of a corresponding loss. On the contrary, as we shall see, there was a similar migration into Connecticut. If, of the 3,469 who were free in 1790, 715 migrated to Massachusetts, the number remaining would be only 2,754, instead of 3,304, leaving 550 places of free men to be supplied by emancipation. And such, nearly, was doubtless the fact. For the next ten years, the increase of the free is greater than the decrease of slaves.

CONNECTICUT.

	Free.	Slave.	Total.
1790	2,801	2,759	5,560
1800	5,330	951	6,281
1810	6,453	310	6,753
1820	7,944	97	8,041
1830	8,047	25	8,072
1840	8,104	17	8,121
1850	7,486	none	7,486

The decrease of slaves from 1790 to 1800 was 1,808; and the increase of the free was 2,529; that is, 721 more than the decrease of slaves. There had evidently been an immigration into Connecticut, as well as Massachusetts; but much of it probably came from New York, though not improbably some of it was from Rhode Island. So, in the succeeding decades, the increase of the free is greater than the decrease of slaves.

NEW YORK.

	Free.	Slave.	Total.
1790	4,654	21,324	25,978
1800	10,374	20,343	30,717
1810	25,333	15,017	40,360
1820	31,980	10,088	42,068
1830	44,870	775	44,915
1840	50,027	4	50,031
1850	47,914	none	47,914

In every decade while slaves remained, the increase of the free was greater than the decrease of slaves. There could have been no sale of the slaves to the South. All that became free, and more, were added to the number of the free.

NEW JERSEY.

	Free.	Slave.	Total.
1790	2,762	11,423	14,185
1800	4,402	12,422	16,824
1810	7,843	18,851	18,694
1820	12,609	7,557	20,166
1830	18,103	2,254	20,357
1840	21,044	674	21,718
1850	23,093	222	23,815

Here, too, every decrease of slaves was attended by an increase, more than equivalent, of the free. There was no sale to the South.

PENNSYLVANIA.

	Free.	Slave.	Total.
1790	6,537	3,737	10.274
1800	14,561	1,706	16,267
1810	22,492	795	23,287
1820	32,153	211	32,364
1830	37,930	403	38,333
1840	47,854	64	47,918
1850	53,323	none	53,323

Here, too, the increase of the free always exceeds the decrease of the slaves. There has been no diminution of the total, such as must have been caused by a general sale of slaves to the South.

It stands out plainly, on the face of these tables, that emancipation, in most of the Northern States, has been a gradual work, spread out over about half a century. So far as effected by legislation, it has been conducted on what is called "the *post nati* principle," that those born after a certain date shall be free at a certain age. This plan was adopted, in part, for the sake of obliging those who had profited by the labor of slaves while able to labor, to support them in their old age and decrepitude. Such an operation is very different from that which Mr. Davis charges upon "the North."

It is obvious, too, from the number of free blacks in the several States in 1790, that the work of emancipation, without sale to "the South," was already far advanced. In every State except New York and New Jersey, it was more than half done; for the free were more numerous than the slaves. This, too, utterly disproves the assertion of Mr. Davis, that the Northern movement began "soon after" 1789. Even in 1787, when the Constitution of the United States was formed, it had been going on for years. This will be still more evident, when we look at the case of

MASSACHUSETTS.

Slavery was never abolished in Massachusetts by legislative action. A State Constitution was adopted in 1780, with a Bill of Rights prefixed, declaring that "all men were born free and equal, and have certain natural, essential, and unalienable rights," among which is liberty. The Courts decided that under this Constitution slavery could not and did not exist. This was a very different process from that described by Mr. Davis.

But were the slaves thus made free "sold to the South"? Happily, that question may be answered. According to the census of the Province of Massachusetts Bay, taken in 1765, the colored population in 182 towns was 4,978. Dr. Jesse Chickering, in his "Statistical View of the Population of Massachusetts," a work of the very highest authority, estimates that a number not exceeding 147 ought to be added for 16 towns from which there were no returns, and 74 for two towns where the returns did not specify color, making 5,199 in all. The next census was that of 1790. The table for Massachusetts reads thus:

	Total Colored Population.
1765	5,199
1790	5,463
1800	6,452
1810	6,737

From 1765, fifteen years before slavery ceased, to 1790, ten years after its cessation, the colored population, instead of being diminished by a sale of slaves to the South, increased 264. In the next ten years, "soon after" 1789, it increased 989. In the next, the increase was only 285. The great increase of 989, from 1790 to 1810, was at the very time of the decrease of colored people in Rhode Island, as stated above. The increase for the next ten years, 285, represents very nearly the usual increase in subsequent decades. Even that small increase has been due mostly, and perhaps wholly, to immigration; for their natural increase, in our climate, is about nothing.

So far is this statement, which Mr. Davis has put forth with all the solemnity of an official document, from being true; so unsupported are some of the grounds on which Southern men are officially exhorted to separate themselves utterly from their fellow-citizens of the North; and so easily detected and conclusively proved is a misrepresentation, which would be so discreditable to us, as a fact. May we not hope that men who, whether deliberately or carelessly, indulge in such statements, will soon lose their present control over Southern minds?

—*Boston Courier, July 9.*

Doc. 256.

DECLARATION OF THE PEOPLE OF VA.,

REPRESENTED IN CONVENTION IN WHEELING, JUNE 17, 1861.

THE true purpose of all government is to promote the welfare and provide for the protection and security of the governed, and when any form of organization of government proves inadequate for, or subversive of this purpose, it is the right, it is the duty of the latter to alter or abolish it. The Bill of Rights of Virginia, framed in 1776, reaffirmed in 1830, and again in 1851, expressly reserves this right to the majority of her people, and the existing Constitution does not confer upon the General Assembly the power to call a Convention to alter its provisions, or to change the relations of the Commonwealth, without the previously expressed consent of such a majority. The act of the General Assembly, calling the Convention which assembled at Richmond in February last, was therefore a usurpation; and the Convention thus called has not only abused the powers nominally intrusted to it, but, with the connivance and active aid of the Executive, has usurped and exercised other powers, to the manifest injury of the people, which, if permitted, will inevitably subject them to a military despotism.

The Convention, by its pretended ordinances, has required the people of Virginia to separate from and wage war against the Government of the United States, and against the citizens of neighboring States, with whom they have heretofore maintained friendly, social, and business relations:

It has attempted to subvert the Union founded by Washington and his co-patriots in the purer days of the Republic, which has conferred unexampled prosperity upon every class of citizens and upon every section of the country:

It has attempted to transfer the allegiance of the people to an illegal confederacy of rebellious States, and required their submission to its pretended edicts and decrees:

It has attempted to place the whole military force and military operations of the Commonwealth under the control and direction of such Confederacy, for offensive as well as defensive purposes:

It has, in conjunction with the State Executive, instituted wherever their usurped power extends, a reign of terror, intended to suppress the free expression of the will of the people, making elections a mockery and a fraud:

The same combination, even before the passage of the pretended Ordinance of Secession, instituted war by the seizure and appropriation of the property of the Federal Government, and by organizing and mobilizing armies, with the avowed purpose of capturing or destroying the Capital of the Union:

They have attempted to bring the allegiance of the people of the United States into direct conflict with their subordinate allegiance to the State, thereby making obedience to their pretended Ordinance treason against the former.

We, therefore, the delegates here assembled in Convention to devise such measures and take such action as the safety and welfare of the loyal citizens of Virginia may demand, having mutually considered the premises, and viewing with great concern the deplorable condition to which this once happy Commonwealth must be reduced, unless some regular adequate remedy is speedily adopted, and appealing to the Supreme Ruler of the Universe for the rectitude of our intentions, do hereby in the name and on the behalf of the good people of Virginia, solemnly declare, that the preservation of their dearest rights and liberties, and their security in person and property, imperatively demand the reorganization of the Government of the Commonwealth, and that all acts of said Convention and Executive, tending to separate this Commonwealth from the United States, or to levy and carry on war against them, are without authority and void; and the offices of all who adhere to the said Convention and Executive, whether legislative, executive, or judicial, are vacated.

Doc. 257.
GENERAL LYON'S PROCLAMATION.

St. Louis, Mo., June 17.

To the Citizens of Missouri:

PRIOR to the proclamation issued by Gov. Jackson, of date of June 12, it is well known to you that the Governor and Legislature sympathized with the rebellion movements now in progress in the country, and had adopted every means in their power to effect a separation of this State from the General Government. For this purpose, parties of avowed secessionists have been organized into military companies throughout the State, with the full knowledge and approval of the Governor. The establishment of encampments in the State at an unusual period of the year, and authorized for an indefinite period, could have had no other object than the concentration of a large military force, to be subjected to the provisions of the military law then in contemplation, and subsequently passed—a bill so offensive to all peaceable inhabitants, and so palpably unconstitutional, that it could be accepted by those only who were to conform to its extraordinary provisions for the purpose of effecting their cherished object —the disruption of the Federal Government. That bill provides for an obligation to the State on the part of all persons enrolled under its provisions irrespective of any obligation to the United States, when the Constitution requires all State officers to take an oath of allegiance to the United States. This of itself is a repudiation of all authority of the Federal Government, whose Constitution is the supreme law, on the part of the State Government, its officers, and such citizens as might choose to adopt the provisions of the bill, and, coupled as it was, on the part of the Legislature and the Governor, with declarations hostile to its authority and in sympathy with those who were arrayed in a condition of actual hostility against it, could leave no doubt of its object to carry out the provisions of this extraordinary bill, having in direct view hostilities to the Federal Government. It was so denounced by Gen. Harney, who characterized it as a secession ordinance in his proclamation of 14th May last. That proclamation, doubtless, gave rise to an interview between Gen. Harney and Gen. Price, that resulted in an agreement which it was hoped would lead to a restoration of tranquillity and good order in your State. That a repudiation of the military bill, and all efforts of the militia of the State under its provisions was the basis of the agreement, was shown as well by this proclamation of Gen. Harney immediately preceding it, as by a paper submitted to Gen. Price, containing the preliminary conditions to an interview with him.

This agreement failed to define specifically the terms of the peace, or how far a suspension of the provisions of the military bill should form a part of it, though from the express declaration of General Harney at the time of the conference, as well as from the foregoing paper, a suspension of any action under the bill until there could be a judicial termination of its character by some competent tribunal, must in good faith be regarded as a fundamental basis of the negotiation.

Nevertheless, immediately after this arrangement, and up to the time of Gov. Jackson's proclamation inaugurating complaints of attempts to execute the provisions of this bill, by which most exasperating hardships have been imposed upon peaceful loyal citizens, coupled with persecutions and proscriptions of those opposed to its provisions, have been made to me as commander of the United States forces here, and have been carried to the authorities at Washington, with appeals for relief, from the Union men of all parties of the State who have been abused, insulted, and, in some instances, driven from their homes.

That relief I conceive it to be the duty of a just government to use every exertion in its power to give. Upon this point the policy of the Government is set forth in the following communication from the department at Washington:

ADJUTANT-GENERAL'S OFFICE, }
WASHINGTON, May 27, 1861. }

Brig.-Gen. W. S. HARNEY, *Commanding Department West St. Louis:*

SIR: The President observes with concern that, notwithstanding the pledge of the State authorities to co-operate in preserving the peace of Missouri, loyal citizens in great numbers continue to be driven from their homes. It is immaterial whether these outrages continue from inactivity or indisposition on the part of the State authorities to prevent them. It is enough that they continue, and it will devolve on you the duty of putting a stop to them summarily by the force under your command, to be aided by such troops as you may require from Kansas, Iowa, and Illinois. The professions of loyalty to the Union by the State authorities of Missouri are not to be relied upon. They have already falsified their professions too often, and

are too far committed to secession to be admitted to your confidence, and you can only be sure of their desisting from their wicked purposes when it is not in their power to prosecute them. You will, therefore, be unceasingly watchful of their movements, and not permit the clamors of the partisans and opponents of the measures already taken to prevent you from checking every movement against the Government, however disguised, under the pretended State authority. The authority of the United States is paramount, and whenever it is apparent that a movement, whether by order of State authority or not, is hostile, you will not hesitate to put it down.
L. THOMAS, Adjutant-General.

It is my design to carry out these instructions in their letter and spirit. Their justice and propriety will be appreciated by whoever takes an enlightened view of the relations of the citizens of Missouri to the General Government. Nor can such policy be construed as at all disparaging to the rights or dignity of the State of Missouri, or as infringing in any sense upon the individual liberty of its citizens. The recent proclamation of Gov. Jackson, by which he has set at defiance the authorities of the United States, and urged you to make war upon them, is but a consummation of his treasonable purposes, long indicated by his acts and expressed opinions, and now made manifest. If, in suppressing these treasonable projects, carrying out the policy of the Government and maintaining its dignity as above indicated, hostilities should unfortunately occur, and unhappy consequences should follow, I would hope that all aggravation of those events may be avoided, and that they may be diverted from the innocent, and may fall only on the heads of those by whom they have been provoked.

In the discharge of these plain but onerous duties, I shall look for the countenance and active co-operation of all good citizens, and I shall expect them to discountenance all illegal combinations or organizations, and support and uphold, by every lawful means, the Federal Government, upon the maintenance of which depend their liberties and the perfect enjoyment of all their rights.
N. LYON,
Brig.-General United States Vols., Commanding.

Doc. 258.

AFFAIR AT VIENNA, VA.

REPORT OF GEN. SCHENCK.

To Lieut.-Gen. Scott:

I LEFT camp with six hundred and sixty-eight rank and file and twenty-nine field and company officers, in pursuance of General McDowell's orders to go upon this expedition with the available force of one of my regiments. The regiment selected was the First Ohio Volunteers.

I left two companies, Company I and Company K, in the aggregate one hundred and thirty-five men, at the crossing of the road. I sent Lieutenant-Colonel Parrott with two companies of one hundred and seventeen men to Fall's Church and to patrol the roads in that direction.

I stationed two companies, Company D and Company F, one hundred and thirty men, to guard the railroad and the bridge between the crossing and Vienna. I then proceeded slowly to Vienna with four companies, Company E, Captain Paddock; Company C, Lieutenant Woodward, (afterwards joined by Captain Pease;) Company G, Captain Bailey, and Company H, Captain Hazlett. Total, two hundred and seventy-five men.

On turning the curve slowly, within one quarter of a mile of Vienna, *we were fired upon by raking masked batteries* of, I think, three guns, with shells, round shot and grape, killing and wounding the men on the platform and in the cars before the train could be stopped. When the train stopped the engine could not, on account of damage to some part of the running machinery, draw the train out of the fire. The engine being in the rear, we left the cars, and retired to the right and left of the train through the woods.

Finding that the enemy's batteries were sustained by what appeared about a regiment of infantry and by cavalry, which force we have since understood to have been some fifteen hundred South Carolinians, we fell back along the railroad, throwing out skirmishers on both flanks, and this was about 7 P. M. Thus we retired slowly, bearing off our wounded five miles to this point, which we reached at 10 o'clock.

The following is a list of the casualties: Captain Hazlett's Company H—two known to be killed, three wounded, five missing. Captain Bailey's Company G—three killed, two wounded, two missing. Capt. Paddock's Company E—one officer slightly wounded. Company C—Captain Pease and two men missing.

The engineer, when the men left the cars, instead of retiring slowly, as I ordered, detached his engine with one passenger car from the rest of the disabled train and abandoned us, running to Alexandria, and we have heard nothing from him since. Thus we were deprived of a rallying point, and of all means of conveying the wounded, who had to be carried on litters and in blankets. We wait here, holding the road for reinforcements. The enemy did not pursue.

I have ascertained that the enemy's force at Fairfax Court House, four miles from Vienna, is now about four thousand.

When all the enemy's batteries opened upon us, Major Hughey was at his station in the foremost car. Colonel McCook was with me in one of the passenger cars. Both these officers with others of the commissioned officers and many of the men, behaved most coolly under this galling fire, which we could not return, and from batteries which we could not flank or turn from the nature of the ground.

The approach to Vienna is through a deep cut in the railway. In leaving the cars, and before they could rally, many of my men lost their haversacks or blankets, but brought off all the muskets, except it may be a few that were destroyed by the enemy's first fire or lost with the killed.

ROBERT C. SCHENCK, Brigadier-General.

THE AMBUSCADE AT VIENNA.

A correspondent of the N. Y. *Tribune*, writing from the federal camp near Vienna, the day after the surprise, says: In the case of our surprise near Vienna, yesterday afternoon, there is another reason why a minute narrative should be received with interest. The general plan and intention of the rebels, for the present, seem to have been indicated here, and it will be our own fault if, understanding thus early their indisposition to meet us in an open way—until they shall have united their forces in some desperate stronghold—and their fondness for lurking slaughter and precipitate retreat, we do not take thorough precautions against such fatal consequences in future as those which yesterday unhappily befell us.

It is probably known that no important movement in advance was intended by the Ohio regiment. The railway from Alexandria to Vienna had just been restored, and the day before a number of troops had passed over the line, and returned, though not without molestation. The shot which wounded the Connecticut soldier should have served us as a warning that treachery flourished in all this region. It was evident that the road would not remain safe without a proper protection, and the duty upon which the First Ohio regiment started was that of stationing efficient guards at all the bridges and other dangerous positions. The Ohio camp was situated about three miles outside of Alexandria, in the direction of Vienna, which is some thirteen miles distant. The expedition—if an affair with so comparatively peaceful a purpose requires to be called so— was under the direction of Brigadier-General Schenck, who, I believe, arranged the details. The immediate command of the regiment was in the hands of Col. McCook. The troops were embarked, and on their way early in the afternoon. They proceeded leisurely, pausing at intervals, and detailing guards. By this process, the regiment naturally grew thinner at every mile, until, when at the outskirts of Vienna, only four companies were left. However wise or necessary this plan of dropping squads behind might be in an ordinary advance, it certainly was of doubtful expediency in this case. There were no villages or groups of houses along the route, among which the enemy's men could have established themselves in force, and the only point from which an attack could be seriously apprehended was Vienna itself. Had the entire regiment—and a larger body would have been better—been pushed rapidly down to Vienna, we should have been more fully prepared to encounter and act against an ambush; and, had all proved quiet, nothing would have been lost, since we had the advantage of railroad speed, by stationing the guards on the return, instead of the advance. It is true that the entire course of the road is through a valley, and that the hills on either side, and the heavy thickets which screen them, appear to offer excellent situations for ambuscade; but the roads in the neighborhood are few, and those which exist are quite impracticable for the ready transportation of troops, not to speak of artillery. Decidedly the suspicious spot was Vienna and its vicinity. A certain disposition to tardy caution was frustrated by the carelessness of the engine-driver. He had been directed to stop at the distance of a mile from the town, whence skirmishers were to be thrown out, and proper reconnoissances to be made. Instead of doing so, he shot ahead until within half a mile or less, so that this single chance of averting the impending danger was wasted. The train was rounding a gentle curve, and the men were laughing, quite unconscious of peril, when the first round of shot fell among them, tearing five of them to pieces, and wounding many others. The rebels' guns had been carefully planted in the curve, and were hidden until the worst part of their work was accomplished. The first discharge was the most fatal. The four companies were disposed upon open platform cars, and were first of all exposed to the enemy's fire. The engine was at the rear of the train. It was fortunate that most of the men were sitting, for the shot flew high, and only those who stood erect were struck. Major Hughey was among the foremost, but was unharmed. Gen. Schenck and Col. McCook were in a covered car behind the troops. The Col. instantly sprang out, and gathered the best part of his men together. The enemy's field-pieces had been stationed to command the line of the railroad and nothing else. They were at the termination of the curve, to the left of the track, and elevated a few feet above the grade. With the exception of that company which was the most exposed, and which suffered the most, the men promptly assembled near Col. McCook, who proceeded to form them in line of battle, and to lead them into the protection of a little wood, or thicket, at the right of the track, apart from the range of the battery. Meanwhile shot and shell continued to assail the train, and those who lingered near it. The engine-driver, in a panic, detached his locomotive and a single car, and dashed off at full speed. The rebel artillerists then directed their range, so as to menace Col. McCook's three companies, upon which the Col. quietly marched them over to the left of the track, into another clump of trees, where he collected all his little force, and arrayed them boldly in line. The shot from the rebels now flew very wild, cutting the trees overhead and around, and, in their hurry, they made the frequent blunder of discharging their shell without opening the fuze. But, notwithstanding this, Col. McCook's position was far from comfortable. He saw that he was prodigiously outnumbered, and that if the enemy could only keep their wits for a few minutes, he must inevitably be captured, or venture a struggle at fearful odds. He had only about 180 men, while the rebel force exceeded 2,000. Their field-pieces alone, decently managed, would have destroyed the little Ohio band in a twinkling. But the Ohio men never flinched, and this was the reward of their bravery: The rebels observing such a mere handful bearing themselves undaunted before their superior host, were at first amazed, and then startled into the conviction that powerful reinforcements must be close at hand. How else, it seemed to them, could this sprinkling of troops hold their ground. It could be nothing but the confidence of overwhelming strength that sustained them. And this is not conjecture. The information since received from Vienna proves it to have been their real belief. Disheartened by this belief, they became irresolute, their fire slackened, they wavered, and, in a few minutes, broke up their lines and slowly retired. At the same time Col. McCook, having secured his wounded, also withdrew, his two thousand assailants making no attempt or motion to oppose his retreat.

Thus, by a manly defiance, our Ohio men preserved themselves. The first indication of weakness or trepidation would have undone them. But now they can proudly and truly say that they stood before ten times their number of opponents, and saw those opponents, all men of South Carolina, glide away from their sight, while they never for an instant swerved. Their own retreat was in perfect order, and they would have carried away their dead, as well as wounded, had any been visible at the moment of their departure. But the poor fellows were all lying out of sight upon the platform cars, and were for a short time overlooked. When they were missed, their bodies were sought, and brought in. In most of the cases, death must have been instantaneous. They were frightfully mangled. One man's arm was torn or wrenched away by a round shot, and hung to the socket by a half-severed muscle. The rush of blood through the ruptured arteries must have put him beyond all suffering at once. Another's head was shot almost from the neck, and with another, the missile passed straight through his chest, beneath the shoulder. Still another was literally cut into shreds, below the waist, and his musket was bent into a curve. It was evident that all had been killed by heavy shot, and that the shell and smaller projectiles had inflicted only serious wounds, at the worst. The bodies, folded in blankets, were all brought to the 1st Ohio regiment's camp this morning. They were tenderly taken in charge by their former comrades, and in the afternoon, among the shadows of the woodland, the last offices were fulfilled, and they were buried together in the soil which their sacrifice makes truly sacred.

The rebels deserted Vienna, but their brief opposition transformed our movement into a regular and important advance. Many regiments have since changed places. The 69th New York regiment moved on to Vienna. The two Ohio regiments are encamped upon the way. The Connecticut men are near at hand. Cavalry and artillery support the 69th, so that, if an attack is made upon them, (which is not immediately apprehended,) they will be able to show the rebels, in whatever force they come, that retreating is a game of which we do not seek to share the glory. The Ohio men are fixed in their new position. Last night they slept upon the grass, without shelter, in the rain. But no one thought of the exposure. They were looking forward, and you may feel sure that when these men and the men of South Carolina meet, the reckoning will be no light one.

A REBEL ACCOUNT.

A gentleman who arrived in Richmond, direct from the scene of action, furnishes the following account of the Vienna fight:

On Sunday morning, Col. Gregg received orders to go out on a reconnoitring expedition. He took with him 600 South Carolinians, a company of Kemper's artillery, and two companies of cavalry, including 45 of Capt. Ball's Chester company and Capt. Terry's company, of Bedford. He started at 8 o'clock A. M. They remained Sunday night at a place called Dranesville. On Monday morning, Col. Gregg, with a detachment of cavalry, went forty-five miles down to the Potomac River to make observations. They remained in the vicinity about an hour, and distinctly saw tents and men on the Maryland side. They judged they were about 300 men encamped at that point.

Col. Gregg afterwards returned to Dranesville, formed his command into column and marched down the road to a place called Vienna. Here they remained only long enough to tear up the track of the Alexandria, Loudon and Hampshire railroad, and destroy a water tank—probably about an hour—after which they started to return to Dranesville. The troops had proceeded about half a mile when the whistle of the locomotive was heard in the distance, whereupon Col. Gregg ordered a halt, wheeled his column, and marched rapidly back to Vienna. They had scarcely time to place two cannon in position, when a train of cars, consisting of six flats and a baggage car, came slowly around the curve, pushed by a locomotive. Each flat was crowded with armed men, whose bayonets glistened in the evening sun, and gave our men an impression that a severe contest was at hand. This, however, was not realized, as the result will show.

Just as the train was about to stop, the artillery fired a well-directed shot from one of their guns, which raked the Hessians fore and aft. Consternation and dismay were distinctly visible, and, after another fire, the enemy were seen hastily leaving the cars and taking to the woods. The engineer of the train was smart enough to uncouple the locomotive and take the back track for Alexandria, leaving the entire train to be captured by our troops. Col. Gregg's infantry and the cavalry pursued the fugitives a short distance through the woods, but were unable to overtake them. A few of the party exhibited some bravery, and endeavored by shouts to rally their flying comrades, but it was impossible. They then turned and discharged their pieces at our men without effect. Six of the enemy were left dead upon the ground.

It is believed that this invading party consisted of regulars and Michigan volunteers. Col. Gregg has received information that a detachment of Federalists came to Vienna on Sunday evening, and brought timber to repair the bridge ; and that they stated, while there, that they would come on Monday with men enough to whip and hang every d—d secessionist in the neighborhood. They made a slight mistake in their calculations.

About twelve rounds were fired by our artillery, but the enemy scattered after the second. Neither the infantry nor cavalry fired a shot.

Our troops burnt the cars and captured a considerable quantity of carpenters' tools, blankets, and other baggage, together with about twenty muskets and a number of pistols. Mr. Hancock brings with him as trophies a U. S. soldier's cap, a havelock thoroughly saturated with blood, and a bayonet.

The fire of our artillerists was most effective. One man was found with his hand shot completely off, another with his arm shot off at the shoulder, and other ghastly objects proved the destructive effect of the shots. It is thought by some that one of the balls broke the couplings of the locomotive ; at all events, the engine was taken away from the scene of action with all possible speed.

After the engagement, Colonel Gregg retired with his command to Fairfax Court House.

—*Louisville Courier*, June 29.

Doc. 258½.

THE BATTLE OF BOONEVILLE.

HEAD-QUARTERS DEP'T OF THE WEST, }
BOONEVILLE, Mo., June 17, 1861. }

THE steamers A. McDowell, Iatan, and City of Louisiana, left Jefferson City yesterday afternoon at two o'clock, and reached a point a mile below Providence last night, where it was thought best to lie up a few hours. Three companies of Boernstein's regiment under his command were left to protect the capital. We were cheered enthusiastically by the little town of Marion, as we passed there yesterday evening. This morning we took an early start, and reached Rocheport before six o'clock, where we made a short stop, but found the people mostly surly and not disposed to be communicative. We learned, however, that the enemy were in considerable force a few miles below this place, and preparing to make a vigorous defence. Leaving there, and taking the steam ferry-boat Paul Wilcox with us, we ran up steadily till we had passed the foot of the island eight miles below here, and seeing a battery on the bluffs, and scouts hastening to report our arrival, we fell back to a point opposite to the foot of the island, and at 7 o'clock A. M. disembarked on the south shore, where the bottom land between the river and bluffs is some mile and a half wide. No traitors were visible there, and the troops at once took the river road for this city. Following this road somewhat over a mile and a half to where it ascends the bluffs, several shots from our scouts announced the driving in of the enemy's pickets.

We continued to ascend a gently undulating slope for nearly half a mile, when the enemy were reported in full force near the summit of the next swell of ground, about three hundred yards from our front. The enemy were exceedingly well posted, having every advantage in the selection of their ground, but as you will see, it has been clearly demonstrated that one secessionist is hardly superior to many more than his equal number.

Arriving at the brow of the ascent, Capt. Totten opened the engagement by throwing a few 9-pounder explosives into their ranks, while the infantry filed oblique right and left and commenced a terrible volley of musketry, which was for a short time well replied to, the balls flying thick and fast about our ears, and occasionally wounding a man on our side. The enemy were posted in a lane running towards the river from the road along which the grand army of the United States were advancing, and in a brick house on the north-east corner of the junction of the two roads. A couple of bombs were thrown through the east wall of that house, scattering the enemy in all directions. The well-directed fire of the German Infantry, Lieut.-Col. Schaeffer on the right, and Gen. Lyon's company of regulars and part of Col. Blair's regiment on the left of the road, soon compelled the enemy to present an inglorious aspect. They clambered over the fence into a field of wheat, and again formed in line just on the brow of the hill. They then advanced some twenty steps to meet us, and for a short time the cannons were worked with great rapidity and effect. Just at this time the enemy opened a galling fire from a grove just on the left of our centre, and from a shed beyond and still further to the left.

The skirmish now assumed the magnitude of a battle. The commander, Gen. Lyon, exhibited the most remarkable coolness, and preserved throughout that undisturbed presence of mind shown by him alike in the camp, in private life, and on the field of battle. "Forward on the extreme right;" "Give them another shot, Capt. Totten," echoed above the roar of musketry clear and distinct, from the lips of the general, who led the advancing column. Our force was 2,000 in all, but not over 500 participated at any one time in the battle. The enemy, as we have since been reliably informed, were over 4,000 strong, and yet, twenty minutes from the time when the first gun was fired, the rebels were in full retreat, and our troops occupying the ground on which they first stood in line. The consummate cowardice displayed by the "seceshers" will be more fully understood when I add that the spurs or successive elevations now became more abrupt, steep, and rugged, the enemy being fully acquainted with their ground, and strong positions behind natural defences, orchards, and clumps of trees offering themselves every few yards. Nothing more, however, was seen of the flying fugitives until about one mile west of the house of William M. Adams, where they were first posted. Just there was Camp Vest, and a considerable force seemed prepared to defend the approaches to it. Meanwhile, a shot from the iron howitzer on the McDowell announced to us that Capt. Voester, with his artillery men, and Capt. Richardson's company of infantry, who were left in charge of the boats, were commencing operations on the battery over a mile below Camp Vest. This but increased the panic among the invincible (?) traitors, and Capt. Totten had but to give them a few rounds before their heels were again in requisition, and Captain Cole and Miller, at the head of their companies, entered and took possession of the enemy's deserted breakfast tables.

About twenty horses had by this time arrived within our lines with vacant saddles, and the corps reportorial were successfully mounted on chosen steeds. The amount of plunder secured in Camp Vest, or Bacon, as the citizens here call it, from the name of the gentleman owning a fine house close by, was very large. One thousand two hundred shoes, twenty or thirty tents, quantities of ammunition, some fifty guns of various patterns, blankets, coats, carpet sacks, and two secession flags were included in the sum total.

Leaving Captain Cole in command of the camp, we pushed on towards Booneville, chasing the cowardly wretches who outmanned us two to one. The McDowell now came along up in the rear and off to the right from our troops, and having a more distinct view of the enemy from the river, and observing their intention to make another stand at the Fair Grounds, one mile east of here, where the State has an armory extemporized, Captain Voester again sent them his compliments from the old howitzer's mouth, which, with a couple of shots from Captain Totten, and a volley from Lo-

throp's detachment of rifles, scattered the now thoroughly alarmed enemy in all directions. Their flight through the village commenced soon after 8 o'clock, and continued till after 11 o'clock. Some three hundred crossed the river, many went south, but the bulk kept on westwardly. A good many persons were taken at the different points of battle, but it is believed the enemy secured none of ours.

Capt. Richardson had landed below, and, with the support of the howitzer from the steamer McDowell, captured their battery, consisting of two 6-pounders, (with which they intended to sink our fleet,) twenty prisoners, one caisson, and eight horses with military saddles. The enemy did not fire a shot from their cannon. Speaking of prizes, the brilliant achievement in that line was by our reverend friend, W. A. Pill, chaplain of the First regiment. He had charge of a party of four men, two mounted and two on foot, with which to take charge of the wounded. Ascending the brow of a hill, he suddenly came upon a company of twenty-four rebels, armed with revolvers, and fully bent upon securing a place of safety for their carcasses. Their intentions, however, were considerably modified, when the parson ordered them to halt, which they did, surrendering their arms. Surrounded by the squad of five men, they were then marched on board the Louisiana, prisoners of war. The parson also captured two other secessionists during the day, and at one time, needing a wagon and horses for the wounded, and finding friendly suggestions wasted on a stubborn old rebel, placed a revolver at his head, and the desired articles were forthcoming. In time of peace the preacher had prepared for war.

After passing the Fair Grounds, our troops came slowly towards town. They were met on the east side of the creek by Judge Miller of the District Court, and other prominent citizens, bearing a flag of truce, in order to assure our troops of friendly feelings sustained by three-fourths of the inhabitants, and if possible prevent the shedding of innocent blood. They were met cordially by Gen. Lyon and Col. Blair, who promised, if no resistance was made to their entrance, that no harm need be feared. Major O'Brien soon joined the party from the city, and formally surrendered it to the Federal forces. The troops then advanced, headed by the Major and Gen. Lyon, and were met at the principal corner of the street by a party bearing and waving that beautiful emblem under which our armies gather and march forth conquering and to conquer. The flag party cheered the troops, who lustily returned the compliment. American flags are now quite thick on the street, and secessionists are nowhere.

As usual, the traitors had destroyed the telegraphic communication with the East, and I have therefore been unable to transmit the news of our victory. The gallant bearing of our men is the subject of constant remark and praise from the officers, while Colonel Blair,

Lieutenant-Colonel Andrews, Adjutant Hascock, Major Conant, and many others, won golden opinions from the soldiers for their fearless and determined behavior. There were two men killed on our side—Jacob Kiburz, commissary of Company B, Second regiment, who kept a segar manufactory on Second street, St. Louis, between Plum and Poplar, and M. N. Coolidge, of Company H, First regiment. Nine of our men were wounded, but few of them severely. One man is also missing, who was known to have been badly shot. Thos. McCord, of Lothrop's regulars, was one of the most seriously hurt. The loss of the enemy will, probably, never be fully ascertained. It did not fall short of fifty, and probably will run nearly as high as a hundred. Among their dead are Dr. William Quarles, Isaac Hodges, and thirteen others of the Cooper County Company; Francis A. Hulin, of the Pettis County Rifles, and many others more or less prominent, some of whom have not yet been recognized.

The enemy had two regiments of 1,800 men, under command of Col. J. S. Marmaduke of Arrow Rock, and nine hundred cavalry, besides other companies whose muster-rolls have not been captured. Horace H. Brand was Lieutenant-Colonel of Marmaduke's regiment. It was reported, and for some time generally believed, that he was among the dead, but he has since been heard from, taking a meal several miles away. Gov. Jackson was also seen at 3 o'clock this afternoon, at a blacksmith's shop, about fifteen miles from here. Gen. Price left Sunday morning, on the steamer H. D. Bacon, for Arrow Rock. His *health* was *very poor* when he left.

One can hardly imagine the joy expressed and felt by the loyal citizens when the Federal troops entered the city. Stores which had been closed all day, began to open, the national flag was quickly run up on a secession pole, cheers for the Union, Lyon, Blair, and Lincoln were frequently heard, and every thing betokened the restoration of peace, law, and order. True men say had the troops delayed ten days longer, it would have been impossible for them to remain in safety. Irresponsible vagabonds had been taking guns wherever they could find them, and notifying the most substantial and prosperous citizens to leave. As a specimen of the feeling here, Mr. McPherson, proprietor of the City Hotel, denounces the whole secession movement as the greatest crime committed since the crucifixion of Our Saviour.

At one time, when bullets were flying thick and Gen. Lyon was at the head of the column mounted, he undertook to dismount, that his position might be a trifle less conspicuous, when his horse suddenly jumped with fright, throwing the general to the ground, but without injuring him seriously. The rumor suddenly spread through the ranks that General Lyon had been shot from his horse, and the indignation and cries of vengeance were terrific. At the Fair Grounds several hundred muskets were seized at the armory, where flint locks were being altered. Capt. Totten says he fired about 100 rounds of ball, shell, and canister.

The following companies of Col. Blair's regiment, though actively engaged in the skirmishing, had none of their men killed or wounded: Companies A, Capt. Fusch; C, Capt. Stone; D, Capt. Richardson; E, Capt. Cole; F, Capt. Gratz; G, Capt. Cavender; K, Capt. Burke. Company B, Capt. Maurice, has one wounded and one missing; Company H, Capt. Yates, has one killed and four wounded; Company I, Capt. Miller, one wounded.

The following interesting documents were found among others equally interesting and more decidedly treasonable:

HEAD-QUARTERS FIRST REG'T RIFLES, M. S. G., }
BOONEVILLE, MO., June 14, 1861. }

GENERAL ORDERS No. 3.—The commanders of companies of the regiment and of the troops attached will bring their companies to Booneville with the greatest despatch. They will proceed to move the instant this order is received, bringing with them all arms and ammunition it is possible to procure. The expenses of said movements will be paid by the State. All orders of a prior date conflicting with this from any head-quarters whatever will be disobeyed. By order of

COLONEL J. S. MARMADUKE.
JOHN W. WOOD, Adjutant.

CAPTAIN—Hurry on day and night. Everybody, citizens and soldiers, must come, bringing their arms and ammunition. Time is every thing. In great haste,

J. S. MARMADUKE.
—*St. Louis Democrat.*

A SECESSION ACCOUNT.

An eye-witness of the fight at Booneville, on Monday last, at 8 A. M., about six miles below that town, gives the subjoined facts:

Major-General Price was ill on Sunday, and issued an order for the retirement of the State troops towards Arkansas. He, himself, left for his home, at Brunswick. The forces under General Lyon landed near Rocheport, on the south side of the Missouri River, and marched thence toward Booneville. A few companies of State troops met them about six miles below Booneville, and attacked Lyon's forces, Company B, Blair's regiment, being the party receiving the fire. About ten of said company were killed and wounded, as the result of that fire. The company firing then retreated. Several other State companies, at this point of time, kept firing from different directions on Lyon's forces. Gen. Lyon then planted his cannon, and fired about twenty rounds on the State troops, using grape and ball. None of the State troops were killed by this cannonading, so far as is known. But those who were seeking the State troops, to join in the fight, were made prisoners to the number of fifteen or twenty, and three are known to be killed. These prisoners were taken, and the men killed after a retreat was ordered by the officers commanding the State troops.

The State troops retired in good order, not more than three hundred having engaged in the skirmish. Some *ten* of the Federal troops were killed, and as many as from twenty to thirty wounded, some mortally.

Col. Marmaduke commanded the State troops; and Gov. Jackson was in person on the ground. No cannon were captured by the Federal troops; all having been saved, except some pieces which were thrown into the river, these having been placed in position on the river, four miles south of Booneville.

Gen. Parsons, with some fifteen pieces of ordnance, was advancing to meet the State troops, at the time they were retreating. All these were saved. No word of disbanding the State troops was ever heard of; nor of the flight of Governor Jackson, who, on the contrary, coolly remained two hours after the retreat of the State troops. Gov. Jackson is now with his men; the order to retreat was given on Sunday, purely as a strategic movement; while some of the boys determined to have the fun of making the invaders smell burning gunpowder anyhow; and the attack was made with the distinct purpose of retreating immediately afterward. It was currently reported at Booneville that Gen. Lyon remarked, if the fire of the State troops had been continued, he must have ordered a retreat. The Federal forces stood their ground and returned the fire; but the State troops were covered by a woodland, and fired from different directions on Lyon's forces. Lyon has now possession of Booneville, and has issued a proclamation. The State troops are concentrating at a point fifteen or twenty miles west of Booneville, and are organizing, and preparing fully for the conflict.

Ben. McCulloch, it is stated, is now advancing between Springfield and Tipton with 10,000 men and 20,000 extra stand of arms. Gov. Jackson intends to deal kindly and humanly, not only with any prisoners who may be taken in battle, but with all those citizens of Missouri, whether native or adopted, who have been misled and deceived by the wicked teachings of the enemies of the State and its institutions. Those men who have been forced by want of bread to enter the Federal service, have nothing to fear, either in war or peace, from the civil government of the State, or from the State troops, who may be made prisoners of war.

—*Louisville (Ky.) Courier*, June 26.

Doc. 259.

COL. BOERNSTEIN'S PROCLAMATION.

HEAD-QUARTERS CAPITAL, }
JEFFERSON CITY, June 17. }

To the Citizens of Cole County and the adjoining counties of Missouri:

CITIZENS: I have been appointed by the commanding general commander of this place, with the view to extend my authority over Cole and the adjacent counties, in order to preserve the peace and tranquillity of all citizens, and assist the authorities in the maintenance of the Government and of the Union, the enforcement of the constitutional laws of the country.

By the precipitate flight of Gov. C. F. Jackson and others, you have been left without State authority and without a government. This state of things would have produced lawlessness and anarchy and all their consequent evils. It has therefore been deemed necessary to supply this lack by appointing a commander of this place, having surveillance over the city and its vicinity. I therefore call upon the city authorities, as well as the authorities of this county, to continue the legal exercise of their official duties, and I will be always ready to lend them my assistance for the enforcement of the constitutional laws of the country. I do not wish to interfere with their official business, neither do I intend to meddle with the private business of the citizens. Your personal safety will be protected and your property will be respected. Slave property will not be interfered with by any part of my command, nor will slaves be allowed to enter my lines without written authority from their masters; and notwithstanding we are in times of war, I shall endeavor to execute my instructions with moderation and forbearance, and at the same time shall not suffer the least attempt to destroy the Union and its Government by the performance of any unlawful act. I shall prosecute and deliver up to the proper authorities all traitors and their accomplices, aiders, and abettors.

I call upon all friends of the Union, and upon all good citizens, to form themselves into companies of Home Guards for the protection of the Union; to arm themselves and to drill. I will be very glad to have them, as far as possible, instructed by my officers, and to contribute with all my power to their military education. Every citizen who has business with the commander of the place, or intends to bring some complaint before him, will have free access to my head-quarters from 10 to 12 o'clock.

All my soldiers will observe the strictest discipline, and I hope that the support of all good citizens will enable me to keep this city and vicinity in perfect peace and order, and to keep far from them the terror and devastation of the war.

HENRY BOERNSTEIN,
Col. Commanding 2d Reg't Mo. Volunteers.

Doc. 260.

GENERAL LYON'S PROCLAMATION.

BOONEVILLE, June 18, 1861.

To the People of Missouri :

UPON leaving St. Louis, in consequence of war made by the Governor of this State against the Government of the United States, because I would not assume on its behalf to relinquish its duties, and abdicate its rights of protecting loyal citizens from the oppression and cruelty of the secessionists in this State, I published an address to the people, in which I declared my intention to use the force under my command for no other purpose than the maintenance of the authority of the General Government, and the protection of the rights and property of all law-abiding citizens.

The State authorities, in violation of an agreement with Gen. Harney on the 2d of May last, had drawn together and organized upon a large scale the means of warfare, and, having made a declaration of war, they abandoned the Capital, issued orders for the destruction of the railroad and telegraph lines, and proceeded to this point to put into execution their hostile purposes toward the General Government. This devolved upon me the necessity of meeting this issue to the best of my ability, and accordingly I moved to this point with a portion of the force under my command, attacked and dispersed the hostile forces gathered here by the Governor, and took possession of the camp-equipage left, and a considerable number of prisoners, most of them young and of immature age, and who represent that they have been misled by frauds, ingeniously devised and industriously inculcated by designing leaders, who seek to devolve upon unreflecting and deluded followers the task of securing the object of their own false ambition.

Out of compassion for these misguided youths, and to correct the impressions created by unscrupulous calumniators, I liberated them upon the condition that they will not serve in the impending hostilities against the United States Government.

I have done this in spite of the well-known facts that the leaders in the present rebellion, having long experienced the mildness of the General Government, still feel confident that this mildness cannot be overtaxed even by factious hostilities, having in view its overthrow ; but lest, as in the case of the late Camp Jackson affair, this c emency shall still be misconstrued, it is proper to give warning that the Government cannot always be expected to indulge in it to the compromise of its evident welfare.

Hearing that those plotting against the Government have falsely represented that the Government troops intended a forcible and violent invasion of Missouri for purposes of military despotism and tyranny, I hereby give notice to the people of this State that I shall scrupu-

lously avoid all interference with the business, right, and property of every description recognized by the laws of the State, and belonging to law-abiding citizens. But it is equally my duty to maintain the paramount authority of the United States with such force as I have at my command, which will be retained only so long as opposition makes it necessary, and that it is my wish, and shall be my purpose, to visit any unavoidable rigor arising in this issue upon those only who provoke it.

All persons, who, under the misapprehensions above mentioned have taken up arms, or who are preparing to do so, are invited to return to their homes and relinquish their hostilities towards the Federal Government, and are assured that they may do so without being molested for past occurrences.

N. LYON,
Brigadier U. S. Army, Commanding.

Doc. 261.

TWENTY-SECOND PENN. REGIMENT.

THE following are the names of the commanding officers :

Colonel, Max Einstein ; Lieutenant-Colonel, Chas. Angeroth ; Major, William Schœnleber ; Adjutant, Shreve Ackley ; Aide-de-camp, Chas. A. Deron, M.D. ; Quartermaster, Frederick Breitinger ; Surgeon, H. Heller ; Assistant-Surgeon, M. Heller, Jr. ; Sergeant-Major, Wash. Cromlin ; Quartermaster-Sergeant, B. Reiter ; Commissary-Sergeant, A. Gallen ; Regimental Ensign, Herman Hayman ; Drum-Major, Chr. Baker.

Company A—Capt., Solomon Rodelsheimer ; First Lieutenant, Charles Auer ; Second Lieutenant, Henry Florsheim. Company B—Capt., W. Jatho ; First Lieutenant, John Ehrenberg ; Second Lieutenant, Samuel Wool. Company C—Capt., Charles Angeroth ; First Lieutenant, Augustus Riedt ; Second Lieutenant, Gustavus H. Bopp. Company D—Capt., Jacob Keifer ; First Lieutenant, Hermann A. Vogelbach. Company E—Capt., Albert N. Kidney ; First Lieutenant, Charles Friele ; Second Lieutenant, Francis Bierwith. Company F—Capt., Chauncey Spering ; First Lieutenant, C. S. Harrington ; Second Lieutenant, John M. Carson. Company G—Capt., James Harvey ; First Lieutenant, Martin C. Frost ; Second Lieutenant, Lawrence Kelley. Company H—Capt., Raphael Vogel ; First Lieutenant, Albert Heubel ; Second Lieutenant, Lewis F. Resay. Company I—Capt., John M. Lang ; First Lieutenant, Walter F. Evans ; Second Lieutenant, John H. Steiner. Company K—Capt., Duplat Hagemeister ; First Lieutenant, Henry Memminger ; Second Lieutenant, Peter A. McKoon. The men are armed with percussion-cap smoothedbore muskets, and their uniforms are of dark blue cloth. The band numbers about twentysix instruments, and as they marched along performed admirably. Upon their arrival at the depot and at the request of several gentlemen, they played the Star-Spangled Banner, Washington's March, Hail Columbia, and Yankee Doodle, and were greatly cheered.

This regiment carry with them a magnificent horse, said to be one of the best-blooded animals in the country, and which will be presented to Lieutenant-General Winfield Scott as a testimonial of the regard of his friends. The animal attracted considerable attention, and was purchased for the sum of $2,300.

—*Baltimore American,* June 18.

Doc. 262.

DUKE OF NEWCASTLE'S ORDER

IN REFERENCE TO PRIVATEERS.

DOWNING STREET, 1st June, 1861.

SIR: You are already aware that the Queen is desirous of observing the strictest neutrality in the contest which appears to be imminent between the United States and the so-styled Confederate States of North America. I have now to inform you that, in order to give full effect to this principle, Her Majesty has been pleased to interdict the armed ships, and also the privateers of both parties from carrying prizes made by them into the ports, harbors, roadsteads, or waters of the United Kingdom, or of any of Her Majesty's colonies or possessions abroad.

It is Her Majesty's desire that this prohibition should be forthwith notified to all proper authorities within her dominions, and I am to desire that you take measures to secure its effectual observance within the limits of your Government. I have, &c.,

NEWCASTLE.

Governor—The Right Honorable Sir E. W. HEAD, Bart, &c. —*Boston Transcript,* June 20.

Doc. 263.

FOURTEENTH REGIMENT, N. Y. S. V.,

ARRIVED AT NEW YORK, JUNE 18.

THE regiment landed at the foot of West Fourteenth street. The Oneidas of the Metropolis, to the number of two hundred or upwards, decorated with an appropriate badge, and under the direction of William W. Backus, the marshal of the occasion, assisted by John A. Bryan, Morris S. Brown, James M. Tower, A. D. Barber, Robert J. Hubbard, J. O. Candee, and Albert T. Battel, assistant-marshals, formed a line and received the volunteers with the usual honors; and, preceded by a city band of music, escorted them through Fourteenth street and Fifth Avenue to Washington Parade Ground, where the flag presentation took place. A large concourse of ladies and gentlemen, many of them natives of Oneida County, witnessed the ceremony. The welcoming speech was made by Charles P. Kirkland. He said:—

Col. McQuade and the Officers and Men of the Fourteenth Regiment:

In the name and on behalf of the "Sons of Oneida," residents of New York and Brooklyn, I most cordially welcome you to this city on your way to the defence of that blessed Constitution and Union, which are now attempted to be overthrown by parricidal hands— by those who owe to them all the blessings they have ever enjoyed. The contest in which you are about to be engaged, is the most interesting and important that ever occupied the attention of men; for this war is emphatically a war to sustain the only truly free government on earth. Its only object is to maintain and to transmit to future generations the great boon of civil and religious liberty purchased for them by the blood of our fathers. It is, indeed, a glorious cause; and the lovers of liberty everywhere are watching the contest with the deepest interest. On its result may well be said to depend the momentous question of man's capacity for self-government.

We, your old friends and neighbors, welcome you with the most earnest heartiness; and we, at the same time, congratulate you on the fact that the result can by no possibility be doubtful. You go to certain victory, you march to certain triumph; for who so mad as to believe that seven millions of people, resting on a volcano of four millions of slaves, can resist twenty millions led on by the holiest patriotism, and with no such dreadful element in their midst? You come, my friends, from a county distinguished in the history of our great Revolution; and as long as the battle of Oriskany and the siege of Fort Stanwix are remembered, so long will the men of Oneida remember the brave deeds of their fathers, and be eager to imitate their example. This war is not second in importance to that of the Revolution. That made us a nation; this is to preserve and perpetuate that nation, now among the first of the world. I may be allowed to say that my greatest honor at the present moment is that my two sons are in the ranks of the 71st New York regiment, at Washington, engaged in the same holy work of duty and of patriotism on which you are about entering. They are both native sons of Oneida. Thrice welcome, my friends! Your watchwords are " our Constitution—our Union—our Country." You and your brave compatriots, from more than twenty States, will march hand in hand to victory, as certainly as a just and beneficent God rules on earth and in Heaven. Your cause is the cause of truth, of right, of civil and religious liberty, and human history records no defeat in such a cause. I will add one word: if, in the course of events, it be your good fortune to fall in with any one or more of five men named Cobb, Floyd, Thompson, Twiggs, or Davis, do not, I pray, permit them to escape you. They are wanted to satisfy the stern demands which humanity makes on traitors more infamous than any whose names have yet been mentioned among men.

Our best wishes attend you. Again I say—welcome, thrice welcome, ye gallant men of the Fourteenth!

The regimental color was now brought forward, and Charles Tracy addressed the regiment as follows:

Col. McQuade and Officers and Members of the Regiment:

The Sons of Oneida County residing in New York and Brooklyn present to you this regimental color. The Oneidas here, not forgetting the land of their nativity and the associations of their boyhood, were unwilling that the third regiment from that county—the first which passes by our present home—should go to the field without some token of our fraternity. This is the most we can do, except to assure you of our sympathy in the glorious cause you have adopted. The memory of Oneida County, to a man who has passed his boyhood among its green hills, its rich valleys, and its noble woods, never dies out, but deepens with growing years. But beyond the charms of its external beauty and the thrift of its people, the county is full of inspiring associations. It was there that the Baron Steuben, celebrated for his gallant part in the war of the Revolution, passed the closing years of his life, and found his grave. It was there, in 1777, that the patriot forces in Fort Schuyler, a hundred miles from any relief, endured a siege of twenty days, and repelled their besiegers. It was there that the farmers of the Valley of the Mohawk, under General Herkimer, met the enemy in the forest of Oriskany, resisted two attacks in the same day, and drove away both British and Indians. During that battle, the general, dismounted, and bleeding from a mortal wound, sat upon his saddle on a log, continued the direction of the fight, and smoked his pipe with his usual calmness. Any one familiar with those old battle-fields, who has traced the hacks of the tomahawk, and clambered over the ruins of the ancient forts, and now witnesses the uprising at the same place, may truly exclaim:

> "Again there breathe that haunted air
> The sons of sires who conquered there;
> With arm to strike, and soul to dare,
> As quick, as far, as they."

Upon the flag you see emblazoned, in a single shield, the arms of the Union and the arms of the State of New York—the Stars and Stripes quartered with the rising sun—the morning rays bright with promise, the motto always EXCELSIOR—HIGHER. Well joined! What State is more identified with the American Union? The very first Congress of the colonies, long before the revolution, was held in Albany. The first Congress under the Constitution was held in this city, in 1789. The first President of the United States, George Washington, was inaugurated in Wall street, and was sworn into office by the Chancellor of

this State. In the war of 1812, New York furnished vastly beyond its quota both of militia and volunteers; and now, to this sacred war of liberty, she sends forty thousand men. These united arms will fly together upon the flags of our volunteers, until secession and treason shall be crushed out of the whole land.

Ours is a war of defence. The whole area of the Union is our country. Upon every acre of this soil we are at home, until our feet step into the Gulf of Mexico. We paid for Florida, and our army will see to it that our national flag again waves over its entire territory. It is a holy war—a war for principles, a war for our kind. This country, for three-quarters of a century, has stretched out its hands to the oppressed of all nations. The victims of tyranny and of want have fled hither, and found a place of refuge and an abode of prosperity. What a spectacle is now presented to the world, when traitors rise among us to crush this beneficent Government, and dishearten all men who struggle for liberty! What crime can surpass secession! If it could prevail, the heart of every man sighing for liberty in Europe must sink, and every dungeon of tyranny must deepen its gloom. The time has come, in the affairs of men, when liberty and justice in this country must be maintained. To wage war against such treason is to wage it against the enemies of humanity.

War is now a necessity. Alas! politics, theories, philosophy, arts and the like, do much to ameliorate the condition of man; but in the matter of civil government, there never was, there never can be, any great deliverance secured to man, except by the sword. Some may shrink from this proposition; but it is inevitable truth; and it makes the profession of arms a sacred calling.

It is no pastime, no mere parade, no Fourth of July celebration to which you are going. Yours are the actual and mortal risks of war. Lamartine has eloquently said:—"Every revolution must have its birth; every birth its throes; every throe its pang; every pang its groan." The hazards of camp and battle are before you. Great is the sacrifice. Yet deem yourselves fortunate that you can thus devote your lives to such a cause. Many who are kept at home, by various but controlling causes, are ready to envy your lot so full of honor. Whatever your fate may be, the people of this day and of the future will not forget you. If, in the perilous duties which are before you, any shall receive the last summons, then, though the call of death come by a singing bullet, yet shall

> "Its voice sound like a prophet's word,
> And in its hollow notes be heard
> The thanks of millions yet to be."

Go forth, gallant men. Go with no doubt of your perfect success. Go, assured that you are remembered by us in every thing that can serve you, and not forgotten in our prayers. May the Almighty Upholder of the Right, THE

God that judgeth in the earth, guard your heads in the day of battle, and bring you back with the triumphs of victory.

Mr Tracy thereupon placed the banner in the hands of Col. McQuade, who responded as follows:

Mr. Tracy and Gentlemen:—I regret that an unfortunate detention on the river will not give me time to make a fitting response to the very eloquent address which has been delivered to us. I can say, sir, we shall ever cherish this color on account of the donors. We shall defend it in the great and holy cause in which we are embarked. I assure you, sir, that those of us who may live to return it shall return it without blemish, except it may be the blood of traitors shed in the struggle.

He then turned to his regiment, and said:—"If there is any man in the ranks who is not determined to defend the flag to the last drop of his blood, let him now leave."

Not a soldier moved; and, after a moment's silence, a deafening shout of hurrah arose along the ranks and from the spectators, testifying that all were true.

The citizens of Oneida were again formed in column by their marshal, and marched in front of the regiment through Broadway (both flags flying) to the Park barracks, where the regiment took up its quarters for the night. On the following day the Volunteers were escorted in like manner to the New Jersey Railroad Station, and took the cars for Washington.

The regiment contains the full quota of 780 men, enlisted for three years. The officers are as follows:

Field.—Colonel, James McQuade; Lieutenant-Colonel, Chas. H. Skillen; Major, Chas. B. Young.

Commissioned Staff.—Surgeon, A. Churchill; Quartermaster, Thomas H. Bates; Adjutant, John F. McQuade; Surgeon's Mate, J. E. West; Chaplain, Rev. George M. Hewes.

Non-Commissioned Staff.—Quartermaster-Sergeant, James P. Ballou; Sergeant-Major, Cassius B. Mervine; Drum-Major, Thomas J. Hines; Fife-Major, Samuel E. Catlin.

Line.—Company A—Thomas M. Davies, Captain; George H. Cone, Lieutenant; R. D. Crocker, Ensign. Company B—Wm. P. Brazee, Captain; Rufus Dugget, Lieutenant; Geo. T. Hallingworth, Ensign. Company C—Fred. Harrer, Captain; Joseph Smith, Lieutenant; Wm. Rantenberg, Ensign. Company D—Wm. L. Cowan, Captain; Robert H. Foote, Lieutenant; George E. Lee, Ensign. Company E—Lewis Michael, Captain; Alfred Sears, Lieutenant; William War, Ensign. Company F—Chas. A. Muller, Captain; Wm. A. Rowan, Lieutenant; Dilos Craymer, Ensign. Company G—J. Babcock, Captain; Seth L. Wadworth, Lieutenant; John Stryker, Jr., Ensign. Company H—Samuel E. Thompson, Captain; Henry Goss, Lieutenant; Geo. Morgan, Ensign. Company I—Horace B. Lake, Captain; Geo. W. Bartlett, Lieutenant; Sterling W. Hazen, Ensign. Company K—Wm. H. Seymour, Captain; Leman Bradley, Lieutenant; Fayette Butler, Ensign.

Among the officers and soldiers there are several naturalized Welshmen.

Doc. 264.

HARPER'S FERRY.

REASON OF THE EVACUATION.

The Richmond *Enquirer* says:

We are now at liberty, on the best authority, to make public the true motives actuating General Johnston in what the Northern and some of the Southern papers have called the "Evacuation of Harper's Ferry." The general, like other military men of education, had long known that Harper's Ferry, *in itself*, is faulty and untenable, from the facility with which it can be turned. It lies, as it were, in the small end of a "funnel," the broader end of which could with great ease be occupied by the enemy. The heads directing the operations of the Yankee forces were well aware of this fact, but forgot that there were fully as astute heads on our side. The minute and able investigations of Major Whiting, chief engineer to General Johnston, had satisfied our leaders of the justness of these views. General Scott's plan was to turn Harper's Ferry by a column from Pennsylvania under General Patterson, effect a junction near Winchester or Strasburg with another column of McClellan's army, passing through Romney, and cut off Beauregard's and Johnston's armies from each other. This plan was completely foiled, and the enemy checkmated at their own game, as we shall explain.

On or about Thursday, the 16th instant, General Johnston having waited at Harper's Ferry long enough to make the enemy believe that he intended to contest that position to the last, and learning that they were advancing on Williamsport and Romney, sent a portion of his force to Winchester by rail. On Friday he continued this movement, sent back his tent equipage and other heavy baggage, his sick, &c., set fire to and burned the railroad bridge, and such of the public buildings as could be burned without endangering private property, spiked such of the heavy guns at Harper's Ferry as could not be removed, and on Saturday moved, with his whole army, marching on foot, in the direction of Winchester, encamping about three and a half miles southwest of Charlestown. The enemy, taking this movement as it was intended they should take it, as a retreat, crossed a brigade of their advance division, commanded by General Cadwalader, (who joined their forces on Saturday or Sunday morning,) which was moved forward towards Martinsburg.

On Sunday morning, however, General Johnston changed his line of march at right angles, and moved square towards Martinsburg, encamping at Bunker's Hill, on the Winchester and Martinsburg turnpike, twelve miles from Martinsburg, to offer battle there, or advance an attack if necessary. This movement placed the enemy in a predicament. He had not crossed his whole force, and if the opposing forces had closed he must have been beaten in detail. He therefore "acknowledged the corn," turned tail and retreated, recrossed the river, and evacuated the valley, retiring beyond Hagerstown. A lieutenant-colonel and another (member of the Eighth Pennsylvania Volunteers) were taken prisoners during this retreat.

A day or two after this, Col. Hill, Thirteenth Virginia regiment, in command of a part of the forces who had "retreated" from Harper's Ferry, and who had been pushed forward towards Romney, as our readers have learned from our Saturday's edition, sent forward towards New Creek, on the Potomac River, eighteen miles west of Cumberland, four companies of Tennessee and Virginia troops, under Col. Vaughan, of Tennessee, who found the Yankees posted on the Maryland side of the Potomac. Our brave fellows, in the face of the enemy, forded the stream, waist-deep, drove them off in the utmost confusion, captured two pieces of *loaded* artillery and a stand of colors, destroyed the railroad bridge at that point, and returned to Romney, making the march of thirty-six miles and gaining a brilliant victory within twenty hours.

Our readers will thus see what General Johnston's " retreat from Harper's Ferry," has done. It has thoroughly broken up General Scott's paper programme, destroyed his whole Western combination, and compelled him to remodel his whole plan. If our " retreats" do thus much, we wait with confidence to see what our advance will do.

Doc. 265.
LETTER OF GOV. CALL OF FLORIDA,

TO J. S. LITTELL, OF PENNSYLVANIA.

LAKE JACKSON, Feb. 12th, 1861.*

MY DEAR SIR:—We live in an age of miracles and wonders. Great events are in progress, and I look with amazement and mortification at the developments of every day and hour. We are in the midst of the most extraordinary revolution, and the most stupendous ruin is now in rapid progress that the world has ever known.

A great nation has been dismembered. The bonds of the American Union, the work of Washington, of Franklin, of Madison, and other great sages and statesmen of a glorious age, have been rent and snapped like cobwebs; and the greatest fabric of human government, *without complaint of wrong* or *injustice*, has been

* This letter is out of its place in the order of time, not having been received until August. As it contains some remarkable and perhaps important suggestions, we give the letter in this place.—(*Ed. R. R.*)

destroyed in a few months—*madly* and *rashly destroyed*, without reflection, and without loss of life or stain of blood.

Star after star from the once glorious, but now drooping, banner has fallen, others are waning in their light, and the whole heavens are covered with the gloomy portent of universal destruction. When shall this ruin end? Where is the rock which will stand and throw back the mad destructive waves of revolution, and arrest the fearful, fatal, desolating progress of secession! Through the mist of the tempest, I think I see *that rock* rising in *moral* power and sublimity along the whole southern line of North Carolina, Tennessee, and Arkansas, supported by Missouri, Kentucky, Virginia, Maryland, and Delaware, and above the mad, riotous, and exulting shout of successful secession and triumphant revolution. From that rock I hear a voice, like the voice of God, saying to the raging sea, "Thus far shalt thou go and no further, and here shall thy proud waves be stayed." Here I trust, is the rock of safety, standing in the centre of the American Union. The extremities may become cold, and lose their sensibilities, their love for our gallant flag, their pride for our prestige and national glory, won on so many battle-fields, and consummated by so many civic achievements; they may retire to the idolatrous worship of their local and sectional divinities, but the American heart will love and worship the God of our fathers; it will continue to beat in the American bosom, in the centre of the American Union; its warm blood will continue to circulate on both sides of the line of slavery, binding together, in national bonds, the kindred affections of one race in different communities.

Here, I trust in God and in the wisdom and virtue of my countrymen, that there is and that there ever will be an American Union, bearing as the emblem of its power and glory, the broad stripes and bright stars, the banner of freedom at home, and the sign and hope of liberty to the world. Here, at least, I hope, a glorious Union of sovereign States may stand forever, to vindicate the success of the representative Republican system, to vindicate the success of the great experiment of popular government, to rebuke despotic power, to disrobe tyranny of its pomp and pride, to rebuke anarchy and riot in the sanctuary of secession; to sustain the cause of law and government, the holy cause of civil and religious liberty; to bless the living, honor the dead, justify the blood of our glorious Revolution, and vindicate the cause in which Hampden, Elliot, and Moore suffered and died; to vindicate the cause in which the hundreds and thousands of victims, through ages and generations, have been sacrificed on the altar of human liberty! May God bless and preserve this remnant of the great American Republic for all these high purposes, and permit it to stand forever as a perpetual monument to the memory and glory of the patriotic men who shall have the wisdom, virtue, and courage to resist local sectional feelings, to resist the progress of a mad, desolating revolution!

Disunion, under certain contingencies, may be justified; it may become an imperative necessity, but it should be the last resort; like the *rite of extreme unction*, it should be reserved for the last, and administered only in the dying hour of the only remaining hope within the Union. Disunion must be fatal!—fatal to the peace, safety, and happiness of both divisions of the country—fatal to the progress of liberty and civilization—fatal to the pride and glory of the American name.

Every enlightened statesman may see, even through the mist of prejudice, that there is not room between the lakes of Canada and the Gulf of Mexico for two great nations of the same race and lineage, the same language and religion, the same pride, ambition, energy, and high courage, to live in peace and good fellowship together. Every one may see, from the map of our country, that there is no desert waste, no mountain bar, dividing the Northern from the Southern States. Every one may see the great rivers, with their outstretched arms, rising in the Northern States, flowing down the rich valleys through the Southern States, to the Gulf of Mexico, proclaiming the unity of a great empire, and indicating the design of the Creator, that this beautiful land should be forever one country, for one great, united, prosperous people. And why should this unity be destroyed? Why should this beautiful land be divided? Why should this one kindred people become two hostile nations, to exhaust in ruinous wars and battles between themselves, those vast resources, those great energies heretofore so successfully united for the unequalled progress of one country, one great and happy people?

There is one disturbing, one dangerous cause, —the angry controversy arising on the institution of African slavery, and unless this controversy can be amicably adjusted *there must be a perpetual end of the Union, an everlasting separation of the North from the South.*

The institution of slavery, then, demands the earnest attention and the unprejudiced consideration of every American citizen. It should be viewed as it is, and not as we might wish that it should be. Not as an abstract question of right or wrong, not as a blessing or a curse, but as an existing reality, for good or evil, thrown upon us by inheritance from a past generation and another Government, and for which no man of the present day is in any manner the least responsible. It should be considered as it is, an institution interwoven and inseparably connected with our social and *political system*, as a domestic institution of the States, and *a national institution, created by the American people and protected by the Constitution of the United States.* It should be considered as an institution which *cannot be disturbed in its present political* relation to some of the States of the Confederacy, *without*

great detriment to all, and without, perhaps, *destruction to some one of the parties to this relation.* It should be considered as an institution which *could not now be abolished, even with the consent of all, without fatal consequences to some of the parties holding relations to it.*

The history of African slavery in this country proves all the relations I claim for it, and it is as wonderful as any other portion of our wonderful history. The discovery of America, with its boundless resources, started all the maritime nations of Europe on the great enterprises of conquest and dominion in the New World. To dig the golden treasure from the mountains, to open the springs of vegetable life on the plains and in the valleys, to quarry the rocks, to fell and clear the forest, and make America the home of civilization, *human labor was indispensably necessary.* The climate within the tropics, where the experiment was first made, proved unfriendly to the success of European labor, and fatal to European laborers. Recourse was first had, as a substitute, to the labor of the natives. Many of them were subdued by conquest, and became slaves to the conquerers. But the brave warrior spurned the fetters of the slave, and when his bow and arrow could not defend his liberty, his proud heart broke, and he died under the degradation, and in the humility of bondage. Whole tribes became extinct,—perished and disappeared. And it was in the fatal progress of this destruction of human life, and the ill success of slavery among the native tribes, that Portugal, in 1503, sent from her possessions on the coast of Africa the first African slaves to America. The experiment of African labor proved eminently successful. Here was an animal, in the form of man, possessing the greatest physical power, and the greatest capacity for labor and endurance, without one principle of his nature, one faculty of mind or feeling of heart, without spirit or pride of character, to enable him to regard slavery as a degradation. A wild barbarian, to be tamed and civilized by the discipline of slavery. Here was the discovery of an animal power almost as essential as the discovery of the new continent, to bring forth the vegetable, animal, and mineral productions of America, to supply the wants and relieve the necessities of Europe. And without this discovery, and the application of this great element of laboring power, the discovery of America, with all its boundless, uncultivated resources of wealth, would have been of little value to the civilized world. This fact, so far as it relates to the South, is fully illustrated in the great prosperity of the Spanish, French, and English provinces, during the whole time of the existence of slavery in them, and the sudden and continuous decline of every agricultural and other interest in each and every one of those provinces, from the day on which African slavery was abolished. Every colonial nation availed itself of this great element of laboring power. Spain, under Charles the Fifth, France, under Louis Thirteenth, and England, under Elizabeth, all granted to favorite subjects a monopoly of the slave trade, and each derived revenue from the traffic ; and African slavery and the slave trade became a part of the *political system* of each of these great European powers. England was the last to approve and encourage this traffic. At first its advantages were rejected by her continental provinces, but at length they engaged in it with great activity and success; and the profit to the colonist, as well as to the crown, induced England to demand from Spain, by the treaty of 1763, a monopoly in the African slave trade. It continued until suspended by our Revolution. And in 1788, when Mr. Pitt presented a petition to Parliament for its prohibition, it was estimated to amount annually to 30,000 slaves, with an export of English goods to the amount of £800,000 sterling, bringing a return value of £1,400,000 and a revenue to the country by the tax on slaves of £256,000 sterling. And it is now little more than two centuries, since a few of these wild barbarians, naked, savage idolaters, black from the burning sun of their native clime, with knotted and combined locks, more like the wool of the beast than the hair of the human head, savage in taste, manner, and disposition, were brought as slaves from the wilderness of Africa, to clear the forest and open the way for civilization in the British colonies of North America. Nobly has this race done the great work required, and in doing it they have become civilized, and they have multiplied in numbers with a rapidity far exceeding the increase of the Israelites during their bondage in Egypt, until now they number nearly 4,000,000 of people. And their improvement in personal appearance, in feeling and sympathies, in civilization and religion, is not less wonderful than their increase of population. And while they have been elevated in the scale of human beings, while they have been lifted up from the condition of the untamed, naked barbarian, from a condition of superiority only to the brute in the form of man, to a comparatively high social position, to a capacity for receiving and enjoying the blessings of the Christian faith, while they have made comfortable homes and supplied themselves abundantly with food and raiment, the surplus productions of their labor has done more for commerce, navigation, manufactories, and the general prosperity of our own country, has done more to give employment, has done more to feed the hungry and clothe the naked of other nations, than any other institution on earth. Under the cultivation and care of African slaves, an exotic plant, known for ages in the tropical regions of Asia, Africa, and America, but there comparatively of little value to commerce and the civilized world, a stranger to our soil and climate, it has been by their strong hands brought to a perfection before unknown. The fibre of this plant, filling an important place between flax and wool, next to bread has become one of the most important productions of human labor. Besides the clothing of nations, besides the employment of labor and capital, with the great profits in our own country, besides a medium of exchange between Europe and America to the annual value of near 200,000,000 of dollars, besides giving employment to more tonnage and navigation than any other article of commerce, and besides the profit and employment which it gives to people of other foreign nations, it gives employment and subsistence to nearly six millions of people in the British empire. All this is a part of the great work and results of African slavery. And though England, ever foremost in every great enterprise, has searched the globe for soil and climate, and has tried, by rigorous compulsion, with many other races, under a far worse system of bondage, she has found no other country, and she has found no other labor, to supply her great and increasing demand for cotton ; and she feels and knows her dependence on us, and on our African slave labor, to supply a material constituting one of the greatest sources of her wealth, and essential to sustain her vast national power. A failure of our cotton crop for three years would be a far greater calamity to England than three years war with the greatest power on earth. And, next to the failure of the grain crops of Europe and America, she would suffer most from a failure of our cotton crop.

This race, so distinctly marked by nature with inferiority, physical, moral, and mental, as forever to forbid amalgamation, and keep it distinct from our own, has become a great class of laboring, civilized people, domesticated with the white race, and dependent on the discipline of that race for the preservation of the civilization it has acquired. It has now become a *nation considerable* in *numbers*, and *justly considerable*, for its usefulness to the whole civilized world. Members of this race form a part of the domestic association of almost every family in the South ; and although the relation of master and slave is that of authority on one hand and obedience on the other, there is a mutual dependence, which produces mutual sympathies, mutual kindness, and mutual attachments. The African seems designed by the Creator for a slave ; docile and humble, with a heart full of the kindest sensibilities, generally grateful and affectionate, and with a mind incapable of a higher elevation than that which is required to direct the machinery of his limbs to useful action. He is naturally social, cheerful, and contented ; and when he has a good master, which is generally the case, he is much the happiest man. The rapid increase of numbers proves his comforts of life. All his wants are abundantly supplied, and he has no care for to-morrow, either for himself or his posterity. His spirit and pride of character wants the elevation, and his mind wants the capacity, to contemplate slavery as a degradation ; and no liberty, **no** freedom from the control of his master, can exalt him to a higher moral and intellectual condition. You may give him physical liberty, but it will be only the liberty of indulgence in sloth and indolence—the liberty of gratification in animal passions and propensities. No human power can ever liberate his mind. It is enslaved in the despotism of superstition and ignorance, of natural imbecility and inertness. It can never be elevated to the comprehension of the dignity and sublimity of that human liberty which, with all its imperfections and inferiority, approaches nearest to the liberty and power of God. He never can be exalted to that society and regulation of liberty which gives man his high place, his proud dominion on earth. Whether physically bond or free, *mentally* he must ever remain in bondage. He has animal courage as high and as fierce as the energy of the beast, when driven to desperation ; but he is docile and submissive, with a moral timidity arising from his instinctive knowledge of natural inferiority, which makes him ever yield passive obedience to every reasonable will of his master. He looks on his master as a superior being, depends on him for instruction and direction in all things, and looks to him for support and protection. Though naturally indolent and improvident, he works cheerfully for his master (*even without compulsion*) much better than *he does for himself*. He feels himself identified with his master ; he is interested in all that belongs to his master. He participates in his master's pride of reputation, fortune, and success. He prides himself on his master's position in society, rejoices with him in prosperity and happiness, and mourns with him, deeply and feelingly, in all his sorrows and afflictions. His heart is filled with the kindest affections, and there are few friendships among men more true and faithful than those of the African slave for a kind master. Those who have seen the unfeigned sorrow of the African nurse, watching over the dying child of her mistress, with anguish little less than the heart-rending affliction of the mother, those who have heard the lamentations, and seen the tears, of the slaves around the grave of the master, can want no higher proof of their fidelity and attachment. And under the civilizing and humane influence of the Christian religion, there are few communities of people of any race or color who would be more shocked and distressed, or who would shudder and shrink with greater horror and dismay from scenes of bloodshed and human suffering, than the African slaves of this country.

I am describing African slavery, not as fiction —not from fancy—but as *I see* and *know it to exist*—at least in some places. I have marked its condition and progress for many years, while living a plantation life, and I have seen with delight the continued progress of improvement in the condition of all slaves within my knowledge. And I have seen a development of ca-

pacity as it has advanced, for a yet higher improvement, which it must and will attain, with the progress of improvement in other institutions. In the description I have here given of African slavery and the African race, may be found the true reason why this black man is a slave in Africa, Asia, Europe, and America— the reason why he has ever been a slave, and the reason why he will *ever remain a slave, so long as there is a superior race, willing to be his master*. This is the reason why I sleep soundly with my doors unlocked, unbarred, unbolted, when my person is accessible to the midnight approach of more than two hundred African slaves. This is the reason why I feel security in knowing that if there should be danger, every slave would be a voluntary, faithful, and vigilant sentinel over my slumbers. And this is the reason why every slaveholder may sleep in the same manner, and with equal security, if the white man will not corrupt the virtue, or seduce the fidelity, of the faithful African slave. This general security from assault and violence is fully proven by the history of the slave in this country. There have, indeed, been some few individual cases of shocking murders of masters and overseers by slaves ; but they are by no means so frequent, nor have they been marked by greater treachery and ferocity, than the murders committed by white men on both races within the same time. There should be no better evidence required of the fidelity and attachment of the slaves to their masters than the results developed in the mission of John Brown. For six months, without suspicion of his fiendlike treachery, he was domesticated among the slaves, and hospitable masters of Virginia, on the very border from which, in a few hours, they might have made successful escape. And when his bloody and horrible plans were all matured ; when he thought it only necessary for him to strike, and all must fall ; when he thought it only necessary for him to light the torch for the slaves to rise and burn alive their masters and mistresses, men, women, and children, while they slept, to his amazement, no slave rose against his master ; and when he called John at midnight, (the faithful servant of Col. Washington,) when he told him he must fight, putting a *murderous pike into his hands to butcher* his master, the faithful African, in the virtues of humanity, civilization, and Christian charity, far above the devil who tempted his fidelity with the promise of freedom, reproved his hell-born tempter by the earnest inquiry, " *On which side will Mass John fight? I want to be with him.*" Never did treachery and depravity receive a more withering rebuke ; never was fidelity better vindicated ; never was human virtue more triumphant over damning, insidious temptation. But besides the security arising from the fidelity and attachment of the slave to the master, there is one which will ever be found in the total incapacity of the African mind to conceive the plan, and combine the elements, necessary to the success of a general revolt over any considerable district of country. The success of the murderous insurrection in St. Domingo arose from its limited territory, its isolated situation, the peculiar character of both races of the islanders, one cruel, the other savage, the vastly superior number of the slaves, and the unfriendly relations existing between the Spanish and French divisions of the island. The extent of slave territory in this country has ever constituted a great element of strength to the institution; and so long as there shall be a just correspondence between the area of slavery and the number of slaves, this security will remain. In every attempt of insurrection in the United States, the plot has been confined to very few persons; and most generally in that small number some one, shocked at the proposition of murdering a kind master, mistress, or tender nursling, has disclosed the horrible design before its maturity, and thus averted the terrible calamity. Thus it has generally been, and so it will be, so long as the slaves have room enough to work, and to live comfortably and happily with their masters.

With this brief historical sketch of the institution of slavery, and the description I have given of the slave, the relation subsisting between the master and slave, we are prepared to examine the angry controversy which has arisen on this institution, which has already caused seven States to withdraw from the Confederacy, and if not soon amicably adjusted, may cause every Southern State to retire with indignant scorn from a Union prostituted of every virtue, and proposed to be continued only for the advantage of one section, the ruin of another, and the violation of the rights of humanity.

The first point arising in this dangerous controversy is from the disregard and violation, by certain Northern States, of the law and the Constitution requiring the rendition of fugitive slaves to their masters. This alone, if continued, must be fatal to the Union. But there is another point, involving still more dangerous consequences. It has been proposed by statesmen of great ability, and a sectional party has come triumphantly into power on the proposition, to *confine slavery forever within its present limits.* This proposition is not the result of hasty and thoughtless determination. It has been long discussed, maturely considered, and deliberately made. And yet I could hope, for the sake of law and justice, for the sake of humanity, and the civilization of the age, I could hope that the far-sighted statesman by whom this proposition has been made, and that few of the Christian men by whom it has been successfully maintained, have yet fully contemplated, and measured, the stupendous and terrible consequences which must inevitably follow the execution of this fearful design. It is admitted by those sagacious statesmen, and by all other intelligent men, that the Government of the United States has no power to abolish slavery in any State of the Confederacy; and yet here is a proposition distinctly made, and a President of the United States has been elected on an implied pledge to carry that proposition into execution, *which must destroy slavery in all the States, and may destroy* 4,000,000 *of slaves and their increase,* or drive the white population beyond those limits. The present population of the slaveholding States is now estimated at 12,000,000 of people; of this number, near 4,000,000 are slaves. When we look back fifty years, and see the number of slaves of that time, and consider the present number, it may not be an extravagant calculation to estimate the slave population within its present limits, at the end of the next half century, at 20,000,000 of people. The natural increase of this prolific race far exceeds the increase of the white race. But its proportion to the white race, within this area, will be augmented by another process. The black race *must remain forever where it is.* The white man, following the native instinct of the Anglo-Saxon, as well as obeying the impulse of necessity, must emigrate as the population becomes more dense, and the means of subsistence more limited, leaving the slaves behind. Thus producing annually a greater increase of one, and a decrease of the other. And this disproportion must continue to augment year after year, in a ratio not now to be calculated, until the black race must so far preponderate, unless destroyed by want and famine, war or pestilence, as to compel their masters to abandon their homes, and leave them to the possession of their famished slaves; who, when relieved from the authority and discipline of their masters, to which alone they are indebted for their elevation as a civilized and Christian people—when the white man shall have retired, and left them to themselves—will follow their native instincts of indolence and sloth—they will fall back to the vices and barbarism from which they have been but partially redeemed, through a succession of generations and the progress of centuries. Here another Africa, with all its loathsome depravity, would be established in the heart of America. The confinement of African slavery to its present limits must either produce this result, or it must be followed by the *destruction of one of the races; they never can live together in social equality,* even if there should be room enough. This is the proposition of a Christian people, in the nineteenth century of the Christian religion. There is no crime or barbarity of the present day which may not claim some precedence on the records of past ages. Thus this revolting proposition, though unequalled in the number of victims it would sacrifice, and the extent of human suffering it would inflict, may find something approximating to a parallel in the history of heathen nations. The Egyptians murdered the children of the Hebrew women to prevent the increase of numbers, and the heathen people of India smothered their Christian prisoners in the loathsome dungeon of Calcutta; but here is a proposition, deliberately made by a Christian people, under the immediate influence of the Gospel of God, teaching charity and humanity, " peace on earth, good will to men "— a proposition *to confine forever* 4,000,000 *of unoffending people within a boundary, where, from the natural increase of numbers in a few years, they must perish from famine, pestilence, and war, or drive* 8,000,000 *of white men into exile to avoid the same calamities.* Can the philanthropist, the Christian, the civilized man, find a place in his heart, or a precept in his religion, for a sentiment which contemplates the misery or destruction of so many millions of the human race? Can the statesman find a place in his mind, or a principle in his philosophy of government, to justify a policy, which must produce ruin to so many of his countrymen, and bring desolation to so large a portion of the country? Is the design merciful? Is the intent charitable? Is the institution of slavery so shocking to humanity, so repugnant to the principles of Christianity and civilization, as to justify the *destruction of the slave,* and the ruin of the master, in its abolition? If so, in what new school of humanity has this sublimated refinement of the Christian charities been matured to this heaven-born perfection? In the New England school of morals, religion, and benevolence. In the same New England whose men, ships, and money, were foremost in catching the wild barbarian on the coast of Africa, and bringing the " *merchandise of human flesh, and human souls and bodies,*" to the colonies of Britain. The same New England that peopled America with the African race, would now commit greater barbarity by destroying millions of civilized people. The same New England whose present commercial and manufacturing wealth is founded on the rich inheritance derived from the profit of the African slave trade, and the profitable productions of African slave labor.

But if the confinement of slavery within its present limits should produce consequences less terrible and fatal, if it should be followed only by the *abolition of slavery;* while it would be a *palpable violation of the Constitution of the United States,* would it *elevate the slave? would it make him more comfortable, more happy, than he is in his present condition?* Would it *provide him with a better home?* would it give him a more elevated social position? would it make him more the equal of the white man than he now is? Let these questions be answered by New England men, with a third and fourth generation of liberated Africans among them, where the number is not so great as to crowd the humble place they fill in New England life and society. Let them say what they, with all their charitable sympathy for the African— with all their religious benevolence and humane generosity, have been able to accom-

plish by an experiment of half a century, in giving elevation, dignity, and social equality to the free African. Let men of Old England answer and say, what liberty has done for the African in Jamaica; let Frenchmen answer for the liberated African in Hayti. Search through the history of all time, and you will search in vain to find *any portion of the African race, from its first appearance on record until the present day, in the aggregate, so elevated, intelligent, enlightened, civilized, comfortable, and happy, as that portion of this degraded race* found as slaves in our country. You will not find it among the barbarian hordes of Africa. You will not find it under the Crescent, in Europe or Asia. You will not find it under the sign of the Cross, of South America. You will not find it in Hayti, Jamaica, or New England. In every country where there is an approach to equality between the races, it is in the degradation of the one, and not the elevation of the other. If then the condition of the African slave would be rendered worse by liberation, why this *mad crusade against African slavery?* The theory of universal human freedom is the mad offspring of delusion and passion, and not the result of enlightened reason. Liberty is the refinement of blessing to enlightened people, capable of its rational enjoyments, while it is the greatest curse which can befall a race incapable of estimating the value of freedom. History is full of proofs to illustrate this truth. History proves that the votaries of freedom of a great nation, in an enlightened age, once in their madness placed the Goddess of Liberty in their adoration above the God of nature, and the night of atheism closed upon these deluded worshippers of a false divinity, until they saw no other light, and they impiously denied the existence of a living God. New England will not go so far in her madness. There is a conservative power of wisdom and virtue among her great and enlightened people, and a moral energy, which, although it has long slumbered, is not yet dead, and it will come forth in dignified authority to rebuke fanaticism, and, with the sceptre of reason, expel the idolatrous worshippers of *negro freedom* from their altars, as Napoleon drove the mad votaries from the worship of their heathen divinity, and restored the worship of the true and living God. But the time has arrived when she must awake and come to the judgment—when she must aid, by her counsel, in deciding the most vital question, and one involving more stupendous considerations than any other that can arise in the relations of mankind. It is time that New England—Old England—Europe—America—and the whole civilized world, should come to the judgment bar, to consider the mission, the relations, the value of the institution of African slavery. It has too long been considered as a mere question of right in the master to property in slaves. It has so been regarded for ages, and the universal judgment of all civilized nations has confirmed and approved the right of the master. That right is now denied. Great and unquestionable as I regard this right, it would sink in my estimation far below its present position, if it did not involve the *high considerations of humanity*, the great *consideration of political and domestic economy*. The race is now too numerous, and it is increasing too rapidly to be confined within its present limits. Though divided into families, and domesticated with white families, it is a *distinct nation of near 4,000,000 of people, and constitutes a part of the American* people. The institution of African slavery forms *part of our political system of government*. It is entitled, then, to a higher consideration than the mere right of the master to property in the slave. The institution of slavery must now be considered in its relation to the American people, in its relation to our constitutional government, and in relation to the American Union, whose safety it has placed in jeopardy, and whose ruin it may yet accomplish. Slaves must be considered in their personal relation; they must be considered as both *persons and property*. Slavery never can be confined within its present limits. It is freed from that confinement by the granted freedom of the Constitution of the United States. If it were otherwise, the bonds of the Constitution *are not strong enough*, with all their *reverenced power*, to resist the *energies of the imperative necessity which demands its expansion*. It must expand with the extension of the white race, into every region congenial to its nature and possible for its labor Each has its sphere of action—each its place of usefulness in accomplishing the great design of Providence. The African, in the humble inferiority of his nature, must ever, as he has done, give place to the European race. They commenced their labors together in the wilderness of Massachusetts; and from time to time, as the white man, from the increase of population, has required the place, the labor, and the head of the African, it has been yielded. The African has gone with the pioneer of the forest, over rivers, mountains, hills, and valleys, from State to State, until his arrival at the present boundary. But his destiny is not yet fulfilled, his career of usefulness not yet completed. A vast unmeasured wilderness lies yet before him. He must go into that wilderness, to make room again, as he has done before, for the white man, who will want his present place in a few years in many, and in time in most of the present slaveholding States. He must go into new territories, open new cotton, sugar, and tobacco-fields. He must drain other swamps, to form new rice-fields, to supply the increasing demands of commerce, and relieve the increasing necessities of nations. The productions of slave labor are carrying commerce into every land, navigation over every sea: civilization and Christianity are going hand in hand with commerce and navigation into every barbarous country. The insti-

tution of slavery is doing more in the agency of the world's great progress, more for the improvement and comfort of human life, more for the preaching of the Gospel to heathen nations, more for the fulfilment of prophecy, than any other institution on earth.

This institution cannot be stopped in its career of usefulness to the whole world. *It cannot be confined to its present limits. Dire and uncontrollable necessity will impel the master and the slave to cut their way through every barrier which may be thrown around it, or perish together in the attempt. The consequences of confinement are too terrible to be borne. The attempt to confine the explosion of gunpowder, or stop the eruption of the burning volcano*, would not be more perilous and unavailing. If the institution of African slavery was not already in existence, with its immediate connection with the interests and necessities of all nations, *it could not now be established. I would not bring one other African to this continent.* The principles and prejudices of the whole world are against it. But the entire world has helped to build up the institution, through the progress of centuries. The whole world is deriving advantages from its continuance, and the whole world has not the right to abolish it, if, by doing so, they should destroy (as I have endeavored to prove that they would) 4,000,000 of people, or render their condition far worse than it is, and destruction or ruin to the master. If the institution is beneficial to mankind; if it has elevated a part of the African race to a position in civilization, intelligence, morality, religion, and the comforts of human life, which have never been attained by any other portion of that degraded race; and if the discipline of slavery is essentially necessary to sustain this improved position, and prevent a recession to its original condition of indolence, ignorance, superstition, and depravity—the whole world should unite in sustaining it, and give every encouragement in raising it to a still higher degree of civilization, intelligence, and respectability, and a still higher degree of usefulness to mankind. It may be in the Providence of God that the American Union, which has cheered the whole world with its promises, like the star which stood for a while over the cradle of Bethlehem, may fall and lose its light forever. It may be in his dispensation of human events, that the great American family shall be divided into many nations. But divided or united, the path of destiny must lead the Anglo-Saxon race to the mastery of this whole continent. And if the whole column should not advance, the division of this race will, with the institution of African slavery, *advance from the banks of the Rio Grande to the line under the sun*, establishing in their march the waymarks of progress, the altars of the reformed religion, the temples of a higher civilization, a purer liberty, and a better system of human government. And when this great work shall be done, as all the institutions of man must perish like man's mortality, here the institution of slavery may end. Here the day of African bondage on this continent may close. Here the slave may be free. And here, under the same burning sun which yet beams on the birthplace of his ancestors, released from the discipline of the master, (if the earth shall endure so long,) a few succeeding generations of his posterity will find the African on America the same naked, wild barbarian that his forefathers were when landed on the shores of Massachusetts, or the coast of Virginia, vindicating the truth of Scripture, and verifying the eternal curse on the children of Ham. But until this great consummation of destiny, the African slave is entitled to a comfortable home with his master. He is entitled to pure air to breathe, land to work and to live on, with the enjoyment of abundance. Although the government of the United States has no right to liberate the slave by any measure, direct or indirect, no right to interpose between the master and the slave; though the authority of the master must remain despotic, mitigated and softened in its administration by State laws, the progress of civilization, and the charities of the Christian religion, the government is bound by every principle of justice to accord to the slave every right of humanity; thus it can never confine him within limits where he must suffer and perish for the want of bread without the violation of all these sacred obligations. If the extension of slavery into yet unexplored and unpeopled regions, where the climate and soil are congenial to the nature of the slave, and the productions profitable to his labor, be, as every one must know it must be, necessary for his abundant and comfortable subsistence, his life and happiness, I challenge the application of any principle of the Constitution of the United States to prohibit that extension; and I maintain that the denial of the government to the master the right to emigrate with his slave to such region would be as wrongful, arbitrary, unjust, and despotic, as the denial of the master's right himself to emigrate without the slave. African slaves, under the Constitution of the United States, are regarded both as *persons* and *property*. As property, the master has unquestionably the moral and legal right to carry his slave to any territory within the jurisdiction of the United States, and there is no expressed or implied constitutional power to interpose a prohibition. *As persons*, in what letter, of principle, of our free and beneficent Constitution, can the arbitrary and despotic power be found to prohibit the emigration of the slave with his master, more than to prohibit the emigration of the master with his apprentice, the ward with the guardian, or the child with the parent? The Constitution of the United States, in all its provisions for those persons and relations, places the apprentice and the slave in the same personal and proprietary condition. It regards the apprentice, during the term of ser-

vice for which he is bound, on the same footing as the slave for life. The master of the absconding apprentice, and the master of the runaway slave, have the same *right to the rendition of their property*, when found in any State into which the apprentice or slave may escape. If the right of the master to carry his apprentice into any territory of the United States has never been questioned, can any sufficient reason be assigned why the master should not carry his slave into the same territory? The public domain is the property of the nation. The institution of slavery *is a national institution*. History proves that for more than a century the young and vigorous energies of our whole nation under the colonial government of Britain were directed to the building up of this institution. History proves that Britain during the past century demanded and received from Spain, as the price of peace and friendship, the exclusive right and monopoly of the African slave-trade. History proves that the New England States were the great reapers of this rich harvest of commerce in African slaves,—in "human flesh," if you prefer. History proves that the foundation of the present wealth and prosperity of Massachusetts, Rhode Island, and Connecticut, was laid in the profitable traffic and in the labor of slaves. History proves that every one of the original thirteen States of this nation were once slave States, and that New York and New England had much more to do in building up the institution of slavery in this country than all the Southern States of the Confederacy. And history proves that, for twenty years after the date of the Constitution, the whole people of the United States, and every State of the Union, either by active participation or by tacit acquiescence, gave encouragement and aid in building up the institution of African slavery. It is, therefore, essentially and emphatically, a national institution, though now only existing in the South. It is as truly national as the custom-house on the import on commerce in the city of Boston. It was created by the nation; the nation has derived wealth and power from its creation; the nation is responsible for it. The Constitution protects it, and the nation is bound to find a comfortable home for these 4,000,000 of the African race, with their masters.

The African is a foreign and inferior race, domesticated with and attached to the American people, doing a great work—a work which must be done—a work not degrading to the proud white man—but a work he cannot do. It is exalting to the natural degradation of the black man. These laborers are numbered in the ratio and represented in the popular branch of the American government. The nation is bound by the charities of the Christian faith, by the principles of benevolence, and the rights of civilization, to administer to the African race born on its soil, cherished in its bosom, enriched by its labor, all the rights of humanity. I do

424

REBELLION RECORD, 1860–61.

not pretend that African slavery is without its evils and its objections. It has many, very many. But it has not so many, nor are they so great, as the evils which must inevitably fall on both races from the liberation of the slaves by the process of confinement to present limits. By turning loose an inferior race—amounting to one out of three in a whole population—a nation of near 4,000,000 of people—without a country, without homes, to wander as vagabonds, without social position in the land of their masters, without the care of these to make them labor for their daily bread and necessities, and without restraint of their vices, can any one imagine a greater calamity to befall master and slave? And in what way have either master or man deserved such a visitation of calamity at the hands of Northern men, who brought the African to our common country, and who sold their slaves to the South as soon as they could procure white labor cheaper than that of the black man? Every State has a right to exclude slavery, or abolish slavery, within the limits of its own jurisdiction. But no State has a right to disregard its nationality; no State has a right to *secede* from the moral and legal *national* obligations to sustain the institution of African slavery where it is, or where it may be lawfully established. I have opposed secession persistently, vehemently. I have thrown myself in the breach to oppose it. In resisting it I have stood almost alone, while, others gave way to its angry surges which dashed around. I dared to oppose it, because I thought secession, whether in the majority or the minority, whether supported by one man, or by millions of men, wrong, eminently wrong, and that the approval of multitudes can never make it right. If it has a principle in the philosophy of human government, it is a *principle of destruction.* The secession of a Southern State from the Union is not more disloyal to the government, not more revolutionary than the treachery, insubordination, and hostile resistance, of a Northern State to the obligations of the Constitution. They are both violations of the public law—both defiant of the public authority—with this difference in favor of the Southern State, that she is not the aggressor, that she has not stricken the first blow. She is resenting an insult, avenging a wrong. True, not where resentment is merited, not where revenge is due. She strikes not the offender, but in her madness she strikes her country, and wounds herself. At a single dash she breaks the bonds of the Union, she braves all dangers, defies all power, denies herself all advantages, and proudly disdains all protection from the Union. A proud spirit, wounded by wrongs, excited by passion, led by bold, ambitious leaders, and hurried on with the *pittiful taunt of "submissionist,"* indiscriminately thrown upon all who have the courage and firmness to resist the *mad impulse* of secession, however determined they may be to resist every aggression.

The offending Northern States act with no passionate precipitation. She deliberately meditates and coolly consummates a violation of the Constitution. While she withdraws her allegiance to the government, by denying the authority of its judicial and legislative power in special cases, while she withholds her allegiance to some of the bonds of the Constitution, she sings anthems of praise and glory to the Union she has violated, and claims all the blessings and advantages of the government to which she renders only a partial fealty, a selfish allegiance. It is thus that the two extremities are madly rending the vitals of our once great and glorious country. It is thus the American Union, once the pride of every American heart, once the admiration and wonder of the whole civilized world, has been disrupted and destroyed. It is thus the public peace has been broken, and we stand on the verge of calamitous, desolating, ruinous, civil war. But may we not hope, sir, that some propitiating power may interpose to save us, and avert this dire and fearful calamity? May we not hope that the doomsday of the great American Union has not yet dawned? I cannot believe that our nation is yet so mad as to spurn, and impiously reject, the blessings which a beneficent Providence has sown broadcast over a whole land, and given indiscriminately to a whole people. I have ever regarded our Constitutional Union as the greatest structure of human government, and I have cherished for it and for our whole country the deepest devotion. I have considered the union of the North and the South indispensable to the peace and happiness of both sections—almost as essential to each other as hands and feet to the human body. While I have shed bitter tears over the present ruin, I have been cheered with the hope that the North, reanimated with love and duty to our whole country, would return with renewed allegiance to the Constitution, that she would award cheerfully every legitimate right and privilege to the South, and that our once glorious Union might be reconstructed more permanently, and more happily, than before. But we are now approaching the culminating point in our national fortunes. The "Ides of March" is at hand; then, for the first time, a sectional party will take possession of our government. The fate of the nation may be decided by the policy that party may inaugurate. The application of any coercive measure to drive back a seceded State, *will be fatal to the last remaining hope of the Union.* Although I deny the right of secession, I acknowledge the right of revolution, and hold to the principles enunciated in our Declaration of Independence. And if it be the will of the majority of the people of the seceded States to form an independent government, they *have the right, and it can be only a question of power. No coercive measures can reunite them with the North.* It is forbidden by the genius of our free institutions, and any attempt at coercion must unite every Southern

State and every Southern man in the most determined and energetic resistance. I was opposed to the seizure of the fortifications, and other property, of the government in the South, but *they can never be restored to the government until every constitutional right of the South shall have been fully acknowledged by the North.* If it should be the determination of Mr. Lincoln and the party which has brought him into power, *to confine slavery to its present limits, the day of battle need not be deferred,* and, when it comes, I trust in God that every Southern man will be ready and willing to die rather than yield to a proposition so unjust, so abhorrent, and so dishonorable.

I rejoice at the noble and patriotic stand taken by the conservative Southern States, in resisting the impulse of secession, not because I am disposed to submit to wrong and injustice, not because I am willing to preserve the Union longer than it continues to be the Union of the Constitution, but because I hope they will do, what I had hoped the whole South would have done; because I hope they *will with one voice demand of the North a full and perfect recognition of every constitutional right and privilege of the South, and if this just demand should not be complied with,* then with my long-cherished devotion to the Union of our fathers, I shall be reconciled *to see it end forever!* The North and South can never live in peace together except on terms of perfect social and political equality, therefore a separation, with war, and all its attendant calamities, will be far better than a discontented unity, *with the confinement of slavery to its present limits.* This I shall regard not only as the greatest indignity and insult to the South, but the greatest calamity which could be inflicted, and rather than bear this insult, and endure this calamity, I prefer that the last Southern man should fall, on the last battle-field of the terrible war, in which we may soon be engaged.

But I trust that Mr. Lincoln may not be unmindful of his official oath, that he will not disregard the obligations of the Constitution, that he will feel the high responsibilities of his position,—a responsibility more sublime than that of the Roman senate in the last days of the republic, higher and more stupendous than the responsibility of the Roman general, on the fatal battle-field of Pharsalia. The American destiny is, under a directing Providence, in his hands! The peace, the safety, the life of a great nation, the happiness of 30,000,000 people—the hope, anxiety, and expectation of the world—depend on his wisdom, virtue, firmness, and patriotism, for a wise and peaceable adjustment of our national differences. He may save, or he may consummate the ruin of this country! If he should adhere to the false theory of government on which he has advanced to power, if he should attempt to put that theory into practice, if he should attempt the recapture of the fortifications, before the just demands of the South shall have been conceded,

ALL IS LOST FOREVER! If he, and the sectional party he leads, should recede from the hostile position they have assumed to the Constitution, and the people of the South, all may yet be well. I trust, in that event, that there would be conservative men enough, both North and South, men who remember the past happiness and prosperity of the people, the past fame and glory of our country, to reconstruct our glorious Union, with greater stability, and restore peace and tranquillity to our now divided and unhappy nation! Oh! that I had the genius to lead, the power to reach, and win the hearts of my countrymen, in every latitude, in every place, how earnestly I would plead the cause of my unhappy country! In the name of the living and the dead, in the name of unborn millions of our posterity, how fervently I would invoke the union of all hearts and minds—to reconstruct and preserve for all time the Union of our fathers! How gladly would I hail the returning sign of peace, the gallant flag—no missing star—no rent in the stripes of the banner, which has waved so proudly over the destinies of our once united, great, and glorious country! And if the death of *one man* could atone for the improprieties of a whole nation, if the blood of one man could redeem the lost American glory, how freely mine should flow, how cheerfully would I hail the death that should bring regenerated life, peace, and safety to our once again united, happy country!

I have written you a very long letter, and have discussed the great issues of the day, and placed them, in some respects, in a different light from any in which they have ever yet appeared before the public.

I beg you to be assured that I am prompted by no desire to gratify either pride or ambition. My only wish is, if I can, to be serviceable to our unhappy country, and aid in restoring it once more to Union, peace, and happiness.

I expect to visit the North during the next season, even though it should be a foreign country; foreign it never can be to me; and then I shall see you again at your own hospitable home.

We are all very quiet here at present. The excitement is passing away, and I think every thing depends on the policy of Mr. Lincoln. As I have already said, *any attempt at coercion must be fatal to all hopes of reunion.*

Accept, dear sir, the assurance of my friendship, and high regard.

R. K. CALL.

JOHN S. LITTELL, Esq., Germantown, Penn., Chairman of the Pennsylvania Delegation to the late Baltimore National Union Convention.

GERMANTOWN, 4th March, 1861.

MY DEAR GENERAL :—In the exercise of the discretion accorded by your accompanying note, I did not hesitate, after reading your letter of the 12th ultimo, as to the proper disposition of it. I cannot doubt that an appeal conceived in so catholic a spirit will arrest the attention of the thoughtful; and I was unwilling, moreover, to suppress what is so honorable to yourself in this characteristic plea for "Unity, Peace, and Concord." The manly devotion to the Union which you have always manifested, both in the field and in executive office, entitles you to deferential hearing; and no intelligent reader will fail to acknowledge your special claim to confidence and affection, when he shall recall the distinguished services which your name will suggest, through your intimate connection, in early manhood, with the celebrated chief who proclaimed, in the evil days of his own energetic administration, that that "Union must and shall be preserved."

Your letter is in the hands of a careful printer, who will do justice to this noble, affectionate, and touchingly patriotic appeal to the people of the North, for recognition and enforcement of Constitutional obligations, and the preservation of what is left of our once glorious Union.

I thank you for the association of my name with an appeal so able, so full of manly thought and earnest eloquence. The letter is a fresh laurel added to those which you earned in other years—for "peace hath her victories no less than war"—and which you have so long and so gracefully worn. They will not wither in "time's ungentle tide."

With great respect and regard,
Your faithful friend,
GENERAL CALL. JOHN S. LITTELL.

Doc. 266.
EIGHTEENTH REGIMENT, N. Y. S. V.

The following is a list of officers:

FIELD AND STAFF.—Col., Wm. A. Jackson; Lieut.-Col., Wm. H. Young; Major, Geo. R. Meyers; Adjutant, John H. Russell; Quartermaster, Wm. V. Horsfall; Surgeon, Dr. James L. Van Ingen; Asst.-Surgeon, Dr. Al. A. Edmestor; Chaplain, A. A. Farr.

LINE OFFICERS.—Co. A—Capt., W. P. Gridley; Lieut., Daly; Ensign, E. W. Groote. Co. B—Capt., John Hastings; Lieut., Vands; Ensign, L. M. Norton. Co. C—Capt., A. Wiltsie; Lieut., A. B. Mitchell; Ensign, Sam. Leith. Co. D—Capt., J. C. McGuinniss; Lieut., Barry; Ensign, R. M. Sayres. Co. E—Capt., S. Truax; Lieut., W. Horsfall; Ensign, John Vedder. Co. F—Capt., M. H. Donovan; Lieut., Ed. Fisher; Ensign, John Mooney. Co. G—Capt., Stephen Farriot; Lieut., J. H. Morgan; Ensign, W. H. Ellis. Co. H—Capt., Peter Hogan; Lieut., T. C. Rogers; Ensign, J. M. Carmichael. Co. I—Capt., Thomas Radcliff; Lieut., Fisher; Ensign, C. W. Heald. Co. K—Capt., D. L. Bartlett; Lieut., A. Seeley; Ensign, H. G. Goodnow.

NON-COMMISSIONED STAFF.—Sergeant-Major, T. M. Holden; Quartermaster-Sergeant, Vance; Color-Sergeant, H. Roger; Drum-Major, Griffin; Fife-Major, T. S. Green.

—*N. Y. Express*, June 19.

Doc. 267.
MESSAGE OF JEFFERSON DAVIS,

ACCOMPANYING THE CORRESPONDENCE BETWEEN JUDGE JOHN A. CAMPBELL AND SECRETARY SEWARD, MAY 8.

GENTLEMEN OF THE CONGRESS:—In the Message addressed to you on the 29th inst., I referred to the course of conduct of the Government of the United States towards the Commissioners of this Government sent to Washington for the purpose of effecting, if possible, a peaceful adjustment of the pending difficulties between the two Governments. I also made allusion to "an intermediary, whose high position and character inspired the hope of success;" but I was not then at liberty to make my communication on this subject as specific as was desirable for a full comprehension of the whole subject. It is now, however, in my power to place before you other papers which I herewith address to you from them. You will perceive that the intermediary referred to was Hon. John A. Campbell, a Judge of the Supreme Court of the United States, who made earnest efforts to promote the successful issue of the mission intrusted to our Commissioners, and by whom I was kept advised, in confidential communication, of the measures taken by him to secure so desirable a result. It is due to you, to him, and to history, that a narration of the occurrences with which he was connected should be made known, the more especially as it will be seen by the letters hereto appended, that the correctness and accuracy of the recital have not been questioned by the Secretary of State of the United States, to whom it was addressed.

I avail myself of this opportunity to correct an error in one of the statements made in my Message of the 29th of April. It is there recited that I was prompted to call you together in extraordinary session by reason of the declarations contained in the Proclamation of President Lincoln of the 15th of April. My Proclamation, convoking you, was issued on the 12th April, and was prompted by the declaration of hostile purposes contained in the Message sent by the President to the Governor of South Carolina, on the 8th April. As the proclamation of President Lincoln of the 15th April repeated the same hostile intention in more specific terms, and on a much more extensive scale, it created a stronger impression on my mind, and led to the error above alluded to, and which, however unimportant, I desire to correct. JEFFERSON DAVIS.

MONTGOMERY, Wednesday, May 8, 1861.

Following is the correspondence alluded to in the Message:—

WASHINGTON CITY, Saturday, April 13, 1861.

SIR:—On the 15th March, ult., I left with Judge Crawford, one of the Commissioners of the Confederate States, a note in writing to the effect following:—

"I feel entire confidence that Fort Sumter will be evacuated in the next ten days. And this measure is felt as imposing great responsibility on the administration.

"I feel entire confidence that no measure changing the existing status, prejudiciously to the Southern Confederate States, is at present contemplated.

"I feel an entire confidence that an immediate demand for an answer to the communication of the Commissioners will be productive of evil, and not of good. I do not believe that it ought at this time to be pressed."

The substance of this statement I communicated to you the same evening by letter. Five days elapsed, and I called with a telegram from Gen. Beauregard, to the effect that Sumter was not evacuated, but that Major Anderson was at work making repairs.

The next day, after conversing with you, I communicated to Judge Crawford, in writing, that the failure to evacuate Sumter was not the result of bad faith, but was attributable to causes consistent with the intention to fulfil the engagement; and that as regarded Pickens, I should have notice of any design to alter the existing status there. Mr. Justice Nelson was present at these conversations, three in number, and I submitted to him each of my written communications to Judge Crawford, and informed Judge C. that they had his (Judge Nelson's) sanction. I gave you, on the 22d March, a substantial copy of the statement I had made on the 15th.

The 30th of March arrived, and at that time a telegram came from Gov. Pickens inquiring concerning Col. Lamon, whose visit to Charleston he supposed had a connection with the proposed evacuation of Fort Sumter.

I left that with you, and was to have an answer the following Monday, (1st April.) On the 1st of April I received from you the statement in writing, "I am satisfied the Government will not undertake to supply Fort Sumter without giving notice to Gov. Pickens." The words "I am satisfied" were for me to use as expressive of confidence in the remainder of the declaration.

The proposition, as originally prepared, was, "The President *may desire* to supply Sumter, but will not do so," &c., and your verbal explanation was that you did not believe any such attempt would be made, and that there was no design to reinforce Sumter.

There was a departure here from the pledges of the previous month, but with the verbal explanation I did not consider it a matter then to complain of—I simply stated to you that I had that assurance previously.

On the 7th April, I addressed you a letter on the subject of the alarm that the preparations by the Government had created, and asked you if the assurances I had given were well or ill founded. In respect to Sumter, your reply was, "Faith as to Sumter, fully kept—wait and

Doc.—38

see." In the morning's paper I read, "An authorized messenger from President Lincoln informed Gov. Pickens and Gen. Beauregard, that provisions will be sent to Fort Sumter peaceably, or *otherwise by force.*"

This was the 8th of April, at Charleston, the day following your last assurance, and is the evidence of the full faith I was invited to wait *for* and *see*. In the same paper I read that intercepted despatches disclose the fact that Mr. Fox, who had been allowed to visit Major Anderson, on the pledge that his purpose was pacific, employed his opportunity to devise a plan for supplying the fort by force, and that this plan had been adopted by the Washington Government, and was in process of execution.

My recollection of the date of Mr. Fox's visit carries it to a day in March. I learn he is a near connection of a member of the Cabinet.

My connection with the Commissioners and yourself was superinduced by a conversation with Justice Wilson. He informed me of your strong disposition in favor of peace, and that you were oppressed with a demand of the Commissioners of the Confederate States for a reply to their first letter, and that you desired to avoid, if possible, at that time. I told him I might, perhaps, be of some service in arranging the difficulty. I came to your office entirely at his request, and without the knowledge of the Commissioners. Your depression was obvious to both Judge Nelson and myself. I was gratified at the character of the counsels you were desirous of pursuing, and much impressed with your observation that a civil war might be prevented by the success of my mediation. You read a letter of Mr. Weed, to show how irksome and responsible the withdrawal of troops from Fort Sumter was. A portion of my communication to Judge Crawford on the 15th of March, was founded upon these remarks, and the pledge to evacuate Sumter is less forcible than the words you employed. Those words were, "Before this letter reaches you, (a proposed letter by me to President Davis), Sumter will have been evacuated."

The Commissioners who received those communications conclude they have been abused and overreached. The Montgomery Government hold the same opinion. The Commissioners have supposed that my communications were with you, and upon the hypothesis prepared to arraign you before the country in connection with the President. I placed a peremptory prohibition upon this as being contrary to the terms of my communications with them. I pledged myself to them to communicate information upon what I considered as the best authority, and they were to confide in the ability of myself, aided by Judge Nelson, to determine upon the credibility of my informant.

I think no candid man who will read over what I have written, and consider for a moment what is going on at Sumter, will agree that the equivocating conduct of the Administration, as measured and interpreted in connection with these promises, is the proximate cause of the great calamity.

I have a profound conviction that the telegrams of the 8th of April, of Gen. Beauregard, and of the 10th of April, of Gen. Walker, the Secretary of War, can be referred to nothing else than their belief that there has been systematic duplicity practiced upon them throughout. It is under an oppressive sense of the weight of this responsibility, that I submit to you these things for your explanation.

Very respectfully,
JOHN A. CAMPBELL,
Associate Justice of the Supreme Court.

Hon. WM. H. SEWARD, Secretary of State.

DESPATCHES.

To L. P. WALKER, Secretary of War:—

An authorized messenger from President Lincoln just informed Gov. Pickens and myself that provisions will be sent to Fort Sumter peaceably, or otherwise by force.

Gen. P. G. T. BEAUREGARD:—

If you have no doubt of the authorized character of the agent who communicated to you the intention of the Washington Government to supply Fort Sumter by force, you will at once demand its evacuation; and if this is refused, proceed in such manner as you may determine to reduce it.

WASHINGTON CITY, Saturday, April 20, 1861.

SIR:—I enclose you a letter corresponding very nearly with one I addressed to you one week ago, (13th April,) to which I have not had any reply. The letter is simply one of inquiry in reference to facts concerning which I think I am entitled to an explanation. I have not adopted any opinion in reference to them which may not be modified by explanation, nor have I affirmed in that letter, nor do I in this, any conclusion of my own unfavorable to your integrity in the whole transaction.

All that I have said, and mean to say, is, that an explanation is due from you to myself. I will not say what I shall do in case this request is not complied with; but I am justified in saying, that I shall feel at liberty to place these letters before any person who is entitled to ask an explanation of myself.

Very respectfully,
JOHN A. CAMPBELL,
Associate Justice of the Supreme Court of the U. S.

Hon. W. H. SEWARD, Secretary of State.

No reply has been made to this letter.
April 24, 1861.

MONTGOMERY, Ala., May 7.

SIR:—I submit to you two letters that were addressed by me to Hon. Wm. H. Seward, Secretary of State of the United States, that contain an explanation of the nature and result of an intervention by me in the intercourse of the Commissioners of the Confederate States with that officer. I considered that I could perform no duty in which the entire American people, whether of the Federal Union or of the Confederate States, were more interested than that of promoting the counsels and the policy that had for their object the preservation of peace. This motive dictated my intervention. Beside the interview referred to in these letters I informed the Assistant Secretary of State of the United States, (not being able to see the Secretary,) on the 11th April, ultimo, of the existence of a telegram of that date from Gen. Beauregard to the Commissioners, in which he informed the Commissioners that he had demanded the evacuation of Sumter, and, if refused, he would proceed to reduce it. On the same day, I had been told that President Lincoln had said that none of the vessels sent to Charleston were war vessels, and that force was not to be used in the attempt to supply the fort. I had no means of testing the accuracy of this information, but offered that, if the information was accurate, I would send a telegram to the authorities at Charleston, and that it might prevent the disastrous consequences of a collision at that fort between the opposing forces. It was the last effort that I would make to avert the calamity of war. The Assistant Secretary promised to give the matter attention, but I had no other intercourse with him or any other person on the subject, nor have I had any reply to the letters submitted to you.

Very respectfully,
JOHN A. CAMPBELL.

GEN. DAVIS,
President of the Confederate States.

POETRY AND INCIDENTS.

SHOP AND FREEDOM.

Though with the North we sympathize,
  It must not be forgotten
That with the South we've stronger ties,
  Which are composed of cotton.
Whereof our imports mount unto
  A sum of many figures;
And where would be our calico
  Without the toil of niggers?

The South enslaves those fellow-men,
  Whom we love all so dearly;
The North keeps Commerce bound again,
  Which touches us more nearly.
Thus a divided duty we
  Perceive in this hard matter—
Free trade or sable brothers free?
  Oh, won't we choose the latter!

          —*London Punch.*

THE FIGHT AT SUMTER.

I.

'Twas a wonderful brave fight!
Through the day and all night,
March! Halt! Left! Right!
  So they formed:
And one thousand to ten,
The bold Palmetto men
  Sumter stormed.

II.

The smoke in a cloud
Closed her in like a shroud,
While the cannon roared aloud
  From the Port;
And the red cannon-balls
Ploughed the gray granite walls
  Of the Fort.

III.

Sumter's gunners at their places,
With their gunpowdered faces,
Shook their shoulders from their braces,
  And stripped
Stark and white to the waist,
Just to give the foe a taste,
  And be whipped.

IV.

In the town—through every street,
Tramp, tramp, went the feet,
For they said the Federal fleet
  Hove in sight;
And down the wharves they ran,
Every woman, child, and man,
  To the fight.

V.

On the fort the old flag waved,
And the barking batteries braved,
While the bold seven thousand raved
  As they fought;
For each blinding sheet of flame
From her cannon, thundered shame!—
  So they thought.

VI.

And strange enough to tell,
Though the gunners fired well,
And the balls ploughed red as hell
  Through the dirt;
Though the shells burst and scattered,
And the fortress walls were shattered—
  None were hurt.

VII.

But the fort—so hot she grew,
As the cannon-balls flew,
That each man began to stew
  At his gun;
They were not afraid to die,
But this making Patriot pie
  Was not fun.

VIII.

So, to make the story short,
The traitors got the fort
After thirty hours' sport
  With the balls;
But the victory is not theirs,
Though their brazen banner flares
  From the walls.

IX.

It were better they should dare
The lion in his lair,
Or defy the grizzly bear
  In his den,
Than to wake the fearful cry
That is raising up on high
  From our men.

X.

To our banner we are clinging,
And a song we are singing
Whose chorus is ringing
  From each mouth;
'Tis "The old Constitution
And a stern retribution
  To the South."

      —*Vanity Fair.* April 27.

TO MASSACHUSETTS SOLDIERS.

Soldiers, go! Your country calls!
See, from Sumter's blackened walls,
Floats no more our nation's flag,
But the traitors' odious rag.

Long the patient North has borne
All their treachery, taunts, and scorn;
Now let slavery's despots learn
How our Northern blood can burn.
Swift their hour of triumph's past,
For their first must be their last!

By the memory of your sires,
By the children round your fires,
By your wives' and mothers' love,
By the God who reigns above—
By all holy things—depart!
Strong in hand and brave in heart.

Nobly strike for truth and right;
We will pray while you shall fight.
Mothers, daughters, wives, are true
To our country and to you.
To the breeze our banner show:
Traitors meet you where you go.
In the name of God on high,
Win—or in the conflict die!

BROOKLINE, MASS.   H. W.
                              Boston Transcript, April 17.

THE FLAG OF FORT SUMTER.

" We have humbled the Flag of the United States."
                                    [*Gov. Pickens.*

Our banner humbled!—when it flew
    Above the band that fought so well,
And not, till hope's last ray withdrew,
    Before the traitors' cannon fell!

No, Anderson! with loud acclaim
    We hail thee hero of the hour
When circling batteries poured their flame
    Against thy solitary tower.

Stood Lacedæmon then less proud,
    When her three hundred heroes, slain,
No road but o'er their breasts allowed
    To Xerxes and his servile train?

Or does New England blush to show
    Yon hill, though victory crowned it not—
Though Warren fell before the foe,
    And Putnam left the bloody spot?

The voices of earth's noblest fields
    With the deep voice within unite—
'Tis not success true honor yields,
    But faithful courage for the right.

Keep, then, proud foe, the crumbled tower,
    From those brave few by thousands torn,
But keep in silence, lest the hour
    Should come for vengeance on your scorn.

Yet I could weep; for where ye stand,
    In friendly converse have I stood,
And clasped, perchance, full many a hand,
    Now armed to shed a brother's blood.

O, God of Justice! Smile once more
    Upon our flag's victorious path;
And when a stern, short strife is o'er,
    Bid mercy triumph over wrath!
DORCHESTER, *April 20th*, 1861.

—Rev. S. G. BULFINCH, in the Boston *Transcript*,
April 24th.

THE BATTLE OF MORRIS' ISLAND,

A CHEERFUL TRAGEDY.

(AIR:—"*King of the Cannibal Islands.*")

I.

The morn was cloudy and dark and gray,
When the first Columbiad blazed away,
Showing that there was the d—l to pay
    With the braves on Morris' Island;
They fired their cannon again and again,
Hoping that Major Anderson's men
Would answer back, but 'twas all in vain
    At first, on Morris' Island:
Hokee pokee, winkee wum,
Shattering shot and thundering bomb,
Fiddle and fife and rattling drum,
    At the battle of Morris' Island!

II.

At length, as rose the morning sun,
Fort Sumter fired a single gun,
Which made the chivalry want to run
    Away from Morris' Island;
But they had made so much of a boast
Of their fancy batteries on the coast,
That each felt bound to stick to his post
    Down there on Morris' Island.
Hokee pokee, winkee wum, etc.

III.

Then there was firing in hot haste;
The chivalry stripped them to the waist,
And, brave as lions, they sternly faced
    —Their grog, on Morris' Island!
The spirit of Seventy-six raged high,
The cannons roared and the men grew dry—
'Twas marvellous like the Fourth of July,
    That fight on Morris' Island!
Hokee pokee, winkee wum, etc.

IV.

All day they fought, till the night came down;
It rained; the fellows were tired and blown,
And they wished they were safely back to town,
    Away from Morris' Island.
One can't expect the bravest men
To shoot their cannons off in the rain,
So all grew peaceful and still again,
    At the works on Morris' Island.
Hokee pokee, winkee wum, etc.

V.

But after the heroes all had slept,
To his gun each warrior swiftly leaped,
Brisk, as the numerous fleas that crept
    In the sand on Morris' Island;
And all that day they fired their shot,
Heated in furnaces, piping hot,
Hoping to send Fort Sumter to pot
    And glory to Morris' Island.
Hokee pokee, winkee wum, etc.

VI.

Finally, wearying of the joke,
Starved with hunger and blind with smoke
From blazing barracks of pine and oak
    Set fire from Morris' Island,
The gallant Anderson struck his flag
And packed his things in a carpet-bag,
While cheers from bobtail, rag, and tag,
    Arose on Morris' Island.
Hokee pokee, winkee wum, etc.

VII.

Then came the comforting piece of fun
Of counting the noses one by one,
To see if anything had been done
    On glorious Morris' Island:
"Nobody hurt!" the cry arose;
There was not missing a single nose,
And this was the sadly ludicrous close
Of the battle of Morris' Island:
Hokee pokee, winkee wum, etc.

VIII.

But, gentle gunners, just wait and see
What sort of a battle there yet will be;
You'll hardly escape so easily,
    Next time on Morris' Island!
There's a man in Washington with a will,
Who won't mind shooting a little "to kill,"
If it proves that We Have a Government still,
    Even on Morris' Island!
Hokee pokee, winkee wum,
Shattering shot and thundering bomb,
Look out for the battle that's yet to come
    Down there on Morris' Island!
            —*Vanity Fair*, April 27.

MY COUNTRY.

BY AUGUSTA COOPER KIMBALL.

I TREMBLE, O, my country! for thy long exalted
    name;
For the purity and glory that has gathered round
    thy fame;
For the ancient blood-bought altars, where the fires
    of Freedom burn,
Enkindled from the ashes of each Pilgrim Father's
    urn:
I tremble, O my country! lest the lamp that flamed
    of yore,
And lit thy crown of radiance, shall burn for thee
    no more.

Are there not spirits brave, among the sons of
    patriot sires,
To stand beside these menaced shrines and guard
    the sacred fires?
Shall Justice no true champions find? shall Tyranny
    take down
From Freedom's light-encircled brow her star-en-
    ameled crown?
It cannot be—I'll not believe that Truth has fought
    in vain,
And left thee, O my country! with a deeper, viler
    stain.

And yet I live so anxiously! as mothers watch and
    fear,
When Death seems almost hovering around the
    loved and dear;

Or, as a maiden on the beach, stands with a shud-
    dering form,
And knows the one light of her life, is perilled in the
    storm;
As fearfully and tenderly, my country, tempest tost,
I watch in pained suspense to learn if thou art saved
    or lost.

Yet, what may Woman do for thee! her voice may
    not be heard,
To rouse the apathetic mind with soul-impassioned
    word;
Her small hand was not formed to aid the fearful
    battle throng,
Howe'er her heart may burn and bleed for all her
    country's wrong;
Yet, there's a power, all these above—she may in
    meekness wear,
And wield in humble majesty—the matchless power
    of Prayer.

Deem it not weak, my country! this aid we bring to
    thee,
For thy tried and worthy rulers, for their firm in-
    tegrity;
By the fervent prayers of Woman, by the glory that
    is shed
Around the memory of those who for thy honor
    bled,
I charge thee, O my Country! by thy pilgrim-hal-
    lowed sod
Be thou true, and be thou faithful, to Freedom and
    to God!
            —*New York Tribune*, April 28th.

THE STRIPES AND THE STARS.

BY EDNA DEAN PROCTOR.

(AIR:—"*The Star-spangled Banner.*")

O STAR SPANGLED BANNER! the Flag of our pride!
Though trampled by traitors and basely defied,
Fling out to the glad winds your Red, White, and
    Blue,
For the heart of the North-land is beating for you!
And her strong arm is nerving to strike with a will
Till the foe and his boastings are humbled and still!
Here's welcome to wounding and combat and scars
And the glory of death—for the Stripes and the
    Stars!

From prairie, O ploughman! speed boldly away—
There's seed to be sown in God's furrows to-day—
Row landward, lone fisher! stout woodman, come
    home!
Let smith leave his anvil and weaver his loom,
And hamlet and city ring loud with the cry,
"For God and our country we'll fight till we die!
Here's welcome to wounding and combat and scars
And the glory of death—for the Stripes and the
    Stars!"

Invincible Banner! the Flag of the Free!
O where treads the foot that would falter for thee?
Or the hands to be folded, till triumph is won
And the Eagle looks proud, as of old, to the sun?
Give tears for the parting—a murmur of prayer—
Then Forward! the fame of our standard to share!
With welcome to wounding and combat and scars
And the glory of death—for the Stripes and the
    Stars.

O God of our Fathers! this Banner must shine
Where battle is hottest, in warfare divine!
The cannon has thundered, the bugle has blown,—
We fear not the summons—we fight not alone!
O lead us, till wide from the Gulf to the Sea
The land shall be sacred to Freedom and Thee!
With love, for oppression; with blessing, for scars—
One Country—one Banner—the Stripes and the
    Stars!

                       —*Independent.*

A SUGGESTION, TO MAJOR ANDERSON.

Although without question
All credit is due
To your courage and skill,
Dear Anderson; still,
One little suggestion
V. F. makes to you.
Why didn't you throw,
When the first bullet fell
Round your fort, a few shell
Ten inches or so
Towards the town
Where they say,
All the people came down
To see, through their glasses
(The pitiful asses!)
How soon stout Fort Sumter would crumble away?
Suppose that a bomb—
Or a dozen—had come
Majestically sailing
Right over the railing,
That runs round the green,
(Which a delicate flattery
Has christened "The Battery,")
How many brave Southerners there had been seen?
And each beautiful lady
Of the "Five Thousand" fair,
Who "held themselves ready"
Would they have staid there?
'Twas a thing to have done,
If only for fun,
Just to show how the gallant spectators could run!
                  — *Vanity Fair*, April 27.

TO THE MEN OF THE NORTH AND WEST.

Men of the North and West,
    Wake in your might,
Prepare, as the Rebels have done,
        For the fight;
You cannot shrink from the test,
Rise! Men of the North and West!

They have torn down your banner of stars;
    They have trampled the laws;
They have stifled the freedom they hate,
        For no cause!
Do you love it, or slavery best?
Speak! Men of the North and West.

They strike at the life of the State—
    Shall the murder be done?
They cry, "We are two!" And you?
      " *We are one!*"
You must meet them, then, breast to breast,
On! Men of the North and West!

Not with words; they laugh them to scorn,
    And tears they despise;
But with swords in your hands, and death
        In your eyes!
Strike home! leave to God all the rest,
Strike! Men of the North and West!
                  R. H. STODDARD.
New York, *April* 17, 1861.
                —*Evening Post*, April 18.

VIRGINIA TO THE NORTH.

Thus speaks the sovereign Old Dominion
To Northern States her frank opinion:

FIRST.

Move not a finger : 'tis coercion,
The signal for our prompt dispersion.

SECOND.

Wait, till I make my full decision,
Be it for union or division.

THIRD.

If I declare my ultimatum,
Accept my terms, as I shall state 'em.

FOURTH.

Then—I'll remain, while I'm inclined to,
Seceding when I have a mind to.
            —*Commercial Advertiser*, March 21.

STARS IN MY COUNTRY'S SKY.

Are ye all there? Are ye all there,
    Stars of my country's sky?
Are ye *all* there? *Are ye all there*,
    In your shining homes on high?
"Count us! Count us," was their answer,
    As they dazzled on my view,
In glorious perihelion,
    Amid their field of blue.

I cannot count ye rightly;
    There's a cloud with sable rim;
I cannot make your number out,
    For my eyes with tears are dim.
Oh! bright and blessed Angel,
    On white wing floating by,
Help me to count, and not to miss
    One star in my country's sky!

Then the Angel touched mine eyelids,
    And touched the frowning cloud;
And its sable rim departed,
    And it fled with murky shroud.
There was no missing Pleiad,
    'Mid all that sister race;
The Southern Cross gleamed radiant forth,
    And the Pole-Star kept its place.

Then I knew it was the Angel
    Who woke the hymning strain
That at our dear Redeemer's birth
    Pealed out o'er Bethlehem's plain;
And still its heavenly key-tone
    My listening country held,
For all her constellated stars
    The diapason swelled.
Hartford, Conn.   L. H. S.
            —*Boston Transcript*, January 10.

NORTHMEN, COME OUT!

DEDICATED TO THE MASSACHUSETTS REGIMENTS.

BY CHARLES GODFREY LELAND.

(AIR—*Burschen heraus!*)

Northmen, come out!
Forth unto battle with storm and shout!
Freedom calls you once again,
To flag and fort and tented plain;
Then come with drum and trump and song,
And raise the war-cry wild and strong:
Northmen, come out!

Northmen, come out!
The foe is waiting round about,
With paixhan, mortar, and petard,
To tender us their Beau-regard;
With shot and shrapnell, grape and shell
We'll give them back the fire of hell;
Northmen, come out!

Northmen, come out!
Give the pirates a roaring rout;
Out in your strength and let them know
How Working Men to Work can go.
Out in your might and let them feel
How Mudsills strike when edged with steel;
Northmen, come out!

Northmen, come out!
Come like your grandsires stern and stout;
Though Cotton be of Kingly stock,
Yet royal heads may reach the block,
The Puritan taught it once in pain,
His sons shall teach it once again;
Northmen, come out!

Northmen, come out!
Forth into battle with storm and shout!
He who lives with victory's blest,
He who dies gains peaceful rest.
Living or dying, let us be
Still vowed to God and liberty!
Northmen, come out!

OUR STAR-GEMMED BANNER.

A GATHERING SONG FOR THE NORTH.

God bless our star-gemmed banner, shake its folds
out to the breeze,
From church, from fort, from house-top, o'er the
city, on the seas;
The die is cast, the storm at last has broken in its
might;
Unfurl the starry banner, and may God defend the
right.

Too long our flag has sheltered rebel heart, and
stormy will;
Too long has nursed the traitor who has worked to
do it ill;
That time is past—the thrilling blast of war is heard
at length,
And the North pours forth her legions that have
slumbered in their strength.

They have roused them to the danger, armed and
ready forth they stand,
A hundred thousand volunteers, each with weapon
in his hand;
They rally round that banner, they obey their country's call,
The spirit of the North is up, and thrilling one and
all.

'Tis the flag our sires and grandsires honored to
their latest breath,
To us 'tis given to hold unstained, to guard in life
and death;
Time-honored, from its stately folds who has dared
to strike a star
That glittered on its field of blue?—who but traitors
as they are?

Would to God it waved above us with a foreign foe
to quell,
Not o'er brother faced to brother, urging steel, and
shot and shell!
But no more the choice is left us, for our friendly
hand they spurn,
We can only meet as foemen—sad, but resolute
and stern.

Father—dash aside the tear-drop, let thy proud boy
go his way—
Mother—twine thine arms about him, and bless thy
son this day—
Sister—weep, but yet look proudly, 'tis a time to do
or die—
Maiden—clasp thy lover tenderly, as he whispers
thee good-bye!

Onward, onward to the battle! who can doubt
which side shall win?
Right and might both guide our squadrons, and
the steadfast hearts within!
Shall the men who never quailed before, now falter
in the field;
Or the men who fought at Bunker Hill be ever made
to yield?

Then bless our banner, God of hosts! watch o'er
each starry fold;
'Tis Freedom's standard, tried and proved on many
a field of old;
And Thou, who long hast blessed us, now bless us
yet again,
And crown our cause with Victory, and keep our
flag from stain!

H. E. T.

DECEMBER 26TH, 1910.

A BALLAD OF MAJOR ANDERSON.

BY MRS. J. C. R. DORR.

Come, children, leave your playing this dark and
stormy night;
Shut fast the rattling window blinds, and make the
fire burn bright;
And hear an old man's story, while loud the fierce
winds blow,
Of gallant Major Anderson and fifty years ago.

I was a young man then, boys, but twenty-eight
    years old,
And all my comrades knew me for a soldier brave
    and bold;
My eye was bright, my step was firm, I measured
    six feet two,
And I knew not what it was to shirk when there
    was work to do.

We were stationed at Fort Moultrie, in Charleston
    harbor, then,
A brave band, though a small one, of scarcely sixty
    men;
And day and night we waited for the coming of the
    foe,
With noble Major Anderson, just fifty years ago.

Were they French or English, ask you? Oh,
    neither, neither, child!
We were at peace with other lands, and all the na-
    tion smiled
On the stars and stripes, wherever they floated, far
    and free,
And all the foes we had to meet we found this side
    the sea.

But even between brothers bitter feuds will some-
    times rise,
And 'twas the cloud of civil war that darkened in
    the skies;
I have not time to tell you how the quarrel first began,
Or how it grew, till o'er our land the strife like
    wildfire ran.

I will not use hard words, my boys, for I am old
    and gray,
And I've learned it is an easy thing for the best to
    go astray;
Some wrong there was on either part, I do not
    doubt at all;
There are two sides to a quarrel—be it great, or be
    it small!

But yet, when South Carolina laid her sacrilegious
    hand
On the altar of a Union that belonged to *all* the
    land;
When she tore our glorious banner down, and trailed
    it in the dust,
Every patriot's heart and conscience bade him
    guard the sacred trust.

You scarce believe me, children. Grief and doubt
    are in your eyes,
Fixed steadily upon me in wonder and surprise;
Don't forget to thank our Father, when to-night
    you kneel to pray,
That an undivided people rule America to-day.

We were stationed at Fort Moultrie, but about a
    mile away
The battlements of Sumter stood proudly in the
    bay;
'Twas by far the best position, as he could not help
    but know,
Our gallant Major Anderson, just fifty years ago.

Yes, 'twas just after Christmas, fifty years ago to-
    night;
The sky was calm and cloudless, the moon was
    large and bright;

At six o'clock the drum beat to call us to parade,
And not a man suspected the plan that had been
    laid.

But the first thing a soldier learns *is* that he must
    obey,
And that when an order 's given he has not a word
    to say;
So when told to man the boats, not a question did
    we ask,
But silently, yet eagerly, began our hurried task.

We did a deal of work that night, though our num-
    bers were but few;
We had all our stores to carry, and our ammunition
    too;
And the guard-ship—'twas the Nina—set to watch
    us in the bay,
Never dreamed what we were doing, though 'twas
    almost light as day.

We spiked the guns we left behind, and cut the
    flag-staff down—
From its top should float no color if it might not
    hold our own—
Then we sailed away for Sumter as fast as we could go
With our good Major Anderson, just fifty years ago.

I never can forget, my boys, how the next day, at
    noon,
The drums beat and the bands played a stirring
    martial tune,
And silently we gathered round the flag-staff strong
    and high,
For ever pointing upward to God's temple in the
    sky.

Our noble Major Anderson was good as he was
    brave,
And he knew without His blessing no banner long
    could wave;
So he knelt, with head uncovered, while the chap-
    lain read the prayer,
And as the last Amen was said, the flag rose high
    in air.

Then our loud huzzas rang out, far and widely o'er
    the sea!
We shouted for the stars and stripes, the standard
    of the free!
Every eye was fixed upon it, every heart beat warm
    and fast,
As with eager lips we promised to defend it to the
    last!

'Twas a sight to be remembered, boys—the chap-
    lain with his book,
Our leader humbly kneeling, with his calm, un-
    daunted look;
And the officers and men, crushing tears they would
    not shed—
And the blue sea all around us, and the blue sky
    over head!

Now go to bed, my children, the old man's story 's
    told—
Stir up the fire before you go, 'tis bitter, bitter cold;
And I'll tell you more to-morrow night, when loud
    the fierce winds blow,
Of gallant Major Anderson and fifty years ago.

                                    —*Evening Post, April* 13.

RUMORS AND INCIDENTS.

The following singular narrative is given by the *Evening Post*. It was originally told nearly thirty years ago, by an eye-witness:

THE SPOTTED HAND.

THE other morning, at the breakfast table, when I, an unobserved spectator, happened to be present, Calhoun was observed to gaze frequently at his right hand and brush it with his left in a hurried and nervous manner. He did this so often that it excited attention. At length one of the persons comprising the breakfast party—his name, I think, is Toombs, and he is a member of Congress from Georgia—took upon himself to ask the occasion of Mr. Calhoun's disquietude. "Does your hand pain you?" he asked of Mr. Calhoun. To this Mr. Calhoun replied, in rather a hurried manner, "Pshaw! it is nothing but a dream I had last night, and which makes me see perpetually a large black spot, like an ink blotch, upon the back of my right hand; an optical illusion, I suppose." Of course these words excited the curiosity of the company, but no one ventured to beg the details of this singular dream, until Toombs asked quietly, "What was your dream like? I am not very superstitious about dreams; but sometimes they have a great deal of truth in them." "But this was such a peculiarly absurd dream," said Mr. Calhoun, again brushing the back of his right hand; "however, if it does not intrude too much on the time of our friends, I will relate it to you." Of course the company were profuse in their expressions of anxiety to know all about the dream, and Mr. Calhoun related it. "At a late hour last night, as I was sitting in my room, engaged in writing, I was astonished by the entrance of a visitor who, without a word, took a seat opposite me at my table. This surprised me, as I had given particular orders to the servant that I should on no account be disturbed. The manner in which the intruder entered, so perfectly self-possessed, taking his seat opposite me without a word, as though my room and all within it belonged to him, excited in me as much surprise as indignation. As I raised my head to look into his features, over the top of my shaded lamp, I discovered that he was wrapped in a thin cloak, which effectually concealed his face and features from my view; and as I raised my head, he spoke: 'What are you writing, senator from South Carolina?' I did not think of his impertinence at first, but answered him voluntarily, 'I am writing a plan for the dissolution of the American Union.' (You know, gentlemen, that I am expected to produce a plan of dissolution in the event of certain contingencies.) To this the intruder replied, in the coolest manner possible, 'Senator from South Carolina, will you allow me to look at your hand, your right hand?' He rose, the cloak fell, and I beheld his face. Gentlemen, the sight of that face struck me like a thunder-clap. It was the face of a dead man, whom extraordinary events had called back to life. The features were those of General George Washington. He was dressed in the Revolutionary costume, such as you see in the Patent Office." Here Mr. Calhoun paused, apparently agitated. His agitation, I need not tell you, was shared by the company. Toombs at length broke the embarrassing pause. "Well, what was the issue of this scene?" Mr. Calhoun re-

sumed. "The intruder, as I have said, rose and asked to look at my right hand, as though I had not the power to refuse. I extended it. The truth is, I felt a strange thrill pervade me at his touch; he grasped it and held it near the light, thus affording full time to examine every feature. It was the face of Washington. After holding my hand for a moment, he looked at me steadily, and said in a quiet way, 'And with this right hand, senator from South Carolina, you would sign your name to a paper declaring the Union dissolved?' I answered in the affirmative. 'Yes,' I said, 'if a certain contingency arises, I will sign my name to the Declaration of Dissolution.' But at that moment a black blotch appeared on the back of my hand, which I seem to see now. 'What is that?' said I, alarmed, I know not why, at the blotch on my hand. 'That,' said he, dropping my hand, 'is the mark by which Benedict Arnold is known in the next world.' He said no more, gentlemen, but drew from beneath his cloak an object which he laid upon the table—laid upon the very paper on which I was writing. This object, gentlemen, was a skeleton. 'There,' said he, 'there are the bones of Isaac Hayne, who was hung at Charleston by the British. He gave his life in order to establish the Union. When you put your name to a Declaration of Dissolution, why, you may as well have the bones of Isaac Hayne before you—he was a South Carolinian and so are you. But there was no blotch on his right hand.' With these words the intruder left the room. I started back from the contact with the dead man's bones and—awoke. Overcome by labor, I had fallen asleep, and had been dreaming. Was it not a singular dream?" All the company answered in the affirmative, and Toombs muttered, "Singular, very singular," and at the same time looking curiously at the back of his right hand, while Mr. Calhoun placed his head between his hands and seemed buried in thought.

A GENTLEMAN at Baltimore, Md., lately returned from Fort Sumter, details an impressive incident that took place there on Major Anderson taking possession. It is known that the American flag brought away from Fort Moultrie was raised at Sumter precisely at noon on the 27th ultimo, but the incidents of that "flag-raising" have not been related. It was a scene that will be a memorable reminiscence in the lives of those who witnessed it. A short time before noon Major Anderson assembled the whole of his little force, with the workmen employed on the fort, around the foot of the flag-staff. The national ensign was attached to the cord, and Major Anderson, holding the end of the lines in his hand, knelt reverently down. The officers, soldiers, and men clustered around, many of them on their knees, all deeply impressed with the solemnity of the scene. The chaplain made an earnest prayer—such an appeal for support, encouragement and mercy as one would make who felt that "man's extremity is God's opportunity." As the earnest, solemn words of the speaker ceased, and the men responded Amen with a fervency that perhaps they had never before experienced, Major Anderson drew the "Star-spangled Banner" up to the top of the staff, the band broke out with the national air of "Hail, Columbia!" and loud and exultant cheers, repeated again and again, were given by the officers, soldiers, and workmen. "If," said the narrator, "South Carolina had at that moment attacked the fort, there would have been no hesitation upon the part of any man within it about defending the flag." —*Baltimore American, Jan. 9.*

Dec. 27.—A correspondent in Charleston says, "Fight crops out everywhere, especially in the speech of youthful South Carolina; like New York " Mose," he is literally "spiling " for lack of one. You might deservedly apostrophize him as John Willett did his son, "With his hat cocked, with a fire-eating, bilin' water-drinking, swaggering, military air, too, are you going to kill the wintner, sir?" substituting for the last-named person the name of our sorely-tried parent, Uncle Sam. For information, I take up to-day's *Courier*, the oldest and most respectable of Charleston dailies, at random. I find in it a communication, over the expressive signature of " Rifle," suggesting that one of "the crack regiments " of the North " should charter a couple of steamboats and come on to Charleston, to the rescue" of the forts; that the first shedding of fraternal blood may be precipitated in a manner congenial to the aspirations of youthful South Carolina! The same paper chronicles an application for five hundred of Colt's pistols, received from Alabama, under the title of *Short arguments!* Here, as a nineteenth century anniversary of the divine annunciation of "Peace on earth and good will towards man," (the *Courier*, by-the-by, has a very pretty and decidedly pious editorial on the subject), we have the border ruffian spirit endorsed and approved of as the *ultimatum* of human reason!—*Evening Post, Dec. 31.*

Dec. 29.—On Christmas Day Major Anderson dined formally with the secession authorities— chiefs—in Charleston, and was duly carried back to Fort Moultrie by early moonlight, *apparently very much overcome* by the good things drinkable set before him. Those in charge of the steamer posted in the channel to watch his movements in the fort therefore *thought it would be safe for them to relax their vigilance, and themselves take a Christmas night frolic,* and in the midst of which Anderson and his force spiked Moultrie's guns and landed safely in Fort Sumter. The apparent intoxication of Anderson was but a feint to have the very effect it did have.—*Washington Star, Dec. 29.*

THE venerable J. S. Pettigru, one of South Carolina's noblest names, continues to bear witness to the Union against the traitors who surround him. He has no faith in the practicability of their measures, and is prepared for the worst results to the State and the country. Lately, while attending the church, where, by his presence, he for so many years showed that the character of the statesman was complete only when religion gave it grace and solidity—the services were purged (by nullification) of the usual prayer for the President of the United States—the stern-hearted old patriot rose from his seat and left the church, thus giving a silent but pointed, rebuke to treason, where last it should be found, but where now, in South Carolina. it is most rampant.—*Washington Star, Dec. 28.*

WASHINGTON, *Dec.* 20.—Orders have been issued to Major Anderson to surrender Fort Moultrie if attacked. Major Anderson telegraphs here that he had surrendered a large number of arms which had been removed from the arsenal to Fort Moultrie, to the authorities of Charleston, on a demand being made for them. This was done in obedience, as he says, to the spirit of orders he had received from Washington. The South Carolina ordinance of secession was received this afternoon by President Buchanan. A number of Southern men were with him at the time. He exhibited much agitation on hearing the news. The news of the passage of the ordinance produced intense excitement in Congress. The South Carolina members were congratulated by the Southern men.—*N. Y. Times, Dec. 20.*

Dec. 22.—It is reported in Charleston, to day, that Major Anderson has been ordered to surrender the forts to the constituted authorities of South Carolina, in case the forts are attacked; but not to surrender to irresponsible parties.

Dec. 26.—Bigler, of Pennsylvania, meeting John Cochrane, casually, in Willard's Hotel, in the hall at Washington, said, "What about this Bailey fraud, Cochrane; do you hear any thing in addition?" "Oh," replied Cochrane, "there is nothing in Addition, it's all in Subtraction."—*Evening Post, Dec. 26.*

IT is rumored that an address has been prepared, to be submitted to members of Congress from the border States, recommending a conference at Baltimore on the 13th of February. The object to be attained is a union of the border slave States in favor of the secession of all the cotton States. It is also proposed to devise a programme of action for the border States in case of such an emergency. —*N. Y. Evening Post, Dec. 27.*

WASHINGTON, *Dec.* 26.—"I saw a letter from one of the soldiers at Fort Sumter to his mother to-day. He says the fort is in excellent condition for defence, full of ammunition and arms, and with a few more men, could defy any enemy that could approach it. He says, all hands expect a conflict, and feel greatly alarmed at the prospect, because their numbers are so small. They hope the Government will do something to aid them,—if not, they will defend the fort to the best of their ability. The closing words are quite touching and solemn."— *Letter from Washington, Times, N. Y.*

THE Democratic office holders in New York threaten to hold over. Attorney-General Black has written to the Collector, that if South Carolina secedes it is a virtual dissolution of the Union, and that the Collector of the port of New York and his federal assistants are relieved from all further accountability, and have a right to collect and retain the revenues accruing here, and keep them until the legislature of New York or the city authorities attach the same. If a single State goes out of the Union, Mr. Schell regards it as broken up, and says, "Lincoln is not President;" and neither he nor any of the federal officials will resign or surrender their power and the public money to any except to the city treasury. Mr. John J. Cisco, the Subtreasurer, takes the same view. He has several millions at his disposal. A large portion is in bars of gold, valued at $1,000 each. These are being painted white, so as not to attract attention in case of being removed from the sub-treasury vaults in case of a riot or of Lincoln claiming to be the President.—*N. Y. Correspondent of Mobile Register.*

IT is asserted in Charleston, that President Buchanan had pledged his honor to South Carolinians that the forts should not be reinforced, that they should be given up to the State authorities when demanded, and also that General Cass's resignation originated in his condemning this promise of treason.—*Cor. Evening Post, Dec.* 31.

"MACON, Ga., *Dec.* 27.—"Rumors of a rising among the slaves in the southwestern part of the State prevail here. It is impossible to say with certainty whether an insurrection has really taken place, or is only threatened. The planters are hastily getting all things ready to send their wives and young children to the North."—*N. Y. Tribune.*

GOVERNOR BROWN, of Georgia, has solicited from the Secretary of War, and obtained, a year's leave of absence for Colonel Hardee, late Commandant at West Point, to go to Europe to purchase guns and munitions of war for the State of Georgia.—*N Y. Times, Dec.* 27.

Dec. 28.—The South Carolina Commissioners have had a conference with President Buchanan and his Cabinet, and demand that the troops be withdrawn immediately, or this shall be their last interview, and they will return to South Carolina and prepare for the worst.—*Evening Post, Dec.* 29.

IT is said that Mr. Buchanan is doing all he can to favor the schemes of the revolutionists. The conduct of Major Anderson, in evacuating Fort Moultrie and taking up a stronger position at Fort Sumter, is understood to meet the decided disapprobation of the Administration. It seems he acted without orders. Government arms have been sold to the State of Georgia by the Secretary of War, and there is reason to believe that the President will take no measures to suppress any revolutionary efforts which may be made by Southerns.—*Idem.*

GENERAL SCOTT threatens to resign, if President Buchanan recalls Major Anderson, and will offer his services to his country.—*Idem.*

IT is said that merchants and other men of property in South Carolina, are compelled by threats of personal violence, to become subscribers to the State loan. It is also reported, and there is no reason to doubt the truth of the report, that a tax has been privately levied on slaveholders, of $16 per head for each slave owned by them—a tax so onerous that, in some cases, the slaves will be confiscated and sold in order to meet it. This is a *forced* loan as thoroughly as was ever any loan during the French Revolution, or during the chronic revolutions of Mexico. The secession movement is in the hands of the *mob;* and the planters, merchants, and other men of substance, are powerless against them.—*Cor. Albany Evening Journal, Dec.* 28.

Dec. 31.—PHILADELPHIA.—There is a report in circulation that "Wheatland," the residence of Mr. Buchanan, has been burned.

IN addition to Bates of Missouri, Cabinet places have been offered by Mr. Lincoln to Alexander H. Stephens of Georgia, and Robert T. Scott of Virginia.—*N. Y. Evening Post, Dec.* 31.

THE *Raleigh Standard* says : North Carolina still commands us to obey the Federal laws and to respect the Federal authorities. Up to this moment these laws and these authorities have breathed nothing but respect for our State, and have offered nothing but protection to our citizens. It will be time enough to talk about levying war and capturing forts when the State shall have dissolved her relations with the Union. She has not done so yet, and we trust that no such step will be required. She is too brave to run out of the Union under temporary panics, and she is too wise to commit herself to revolution for the purpose merely of imitating the examples of other States.

"THE Northern people have an enemy at their own doors *who will do our work for us,* if we are not insane enough to take their myrmidons off their hands. 'The winter of their discontent' is but beginning to dawn. They have a long, dark winter, of cold and hunger, impending over their heads; *before it is over, they will have millions of operatives without work, and without bread.*

"In all human probability, before another summer melts their ice-bound hills, *blood—human blood—will have flowed in their streets.* When cold and hunger begin their work, *this deluded rabble will ask alms at the doors of the rich, with pike and firebrand in their hands.* Our Northern enemies will then find that they have business enough to attend to at their own doors, without troubling themselves about keeping forts on Southern soil. 'They have got the wolf by the ears,' and they have a fair prospect of being bit, unless we are charitable enough to take the beast off their hands. *If the North can furnish bread for its paupers for the next five months, well.* If not, their rulers will answer for it in blood. It was simply the want of bread that brought Louis XVI. to the guillotine; and New York, as well as Paris, can furnish her Theroign de Maricourt, who may sing her *carmagnole* up Broadway with Seward's head upon a pike.

"Our Northern enemies are locked up with their million of operatives for the winter, and *how they are to be kept quiet no man can tell.*"—*Charleston Courier.*

WASHINGTON, *Jan.* 2, 1861.—"Scarce a man here from the Free States, and few from the border Slave States, (I refer to men in society,) hesitates now to declare in the most emphatic language, that the Union must and shall be preserved. Even Gen. B. F. Butler, of Massachusetts, one of the most ultra of Breckinridge's supporters, and the bitterest of Anti-Republicans, does not hesitate to assure Southern men that the Free States are forgetting all political parties and uniting as one man for the Union. Talking with a South Carolina Commissioner, the latter is reported to have told him that if Massachusetts should send 10,000 men to 'preserve the Union' against Southern secession, she would have to fight twice the number of her own citizens at home, who would oppose the policy. 'By no means,' Mr. Butler replied ; 'when we come from Massachusetts we will leave not a single traitor behind, unless he is hanging upon a tree.' Private accounts from Charleston state that a thousand negroes are engaged in the erection of fortifications in the harbor, and that the channels leading to Fort Sumter have been obstructed by sunken vessels, and the buoys removed. Also that Governor Pickens has received the offer of 10,000 volunteers from without the State, who hold themselves in readiness to march at a minute's warning."—*Times, Jan.* 3.

Jan. 4.—"A resident of Chicago, Ill., who has been travelling through the Southern States for the last two months, in a quiet and observant manner, says: that the greatest alarm and fear exist among the slave owners, in consequence of certain evidences which they have discovered, of an expectation on the part of the slaves of events soon happening which will result in their universal liberation. Every one who has been much in the South, knows the manner in which intelligence is disseminated among the slaves. The hotel waiters, the barbers, the private servants of gentlemen and families in cities, are the first ones to hear what is going on. Constantly present with their masters, and the travelling population, they hear all the conversation, and if it bears upon their own interests, they treasure it up with a very retentive memory. The constant theme in the South for the last two months, has been the election of the ' Abolitionist Lincoln, and the free negro Hamlin,' to the Presidential chair, and the consequences that were to result from these events. The slaves have heard all this, and they have told it to their companions, and the news has spread to the plantations with that celerity which is so remarkable a feature of slave life. The news has not lost any by travelling, and there exists now a very general belief among the slaves that an army from the North is soon to march down to the South and liberate all the slaves. They think their liberation will be accelerated if they make a rising themselves; and some such struggles have been made. They have been put down with great severity, and hushed up as much as possible. Some slaves have been burned at the stake, others hung, others sold to go further South; and every one says as little about the insurrection as possible. But so fearful are the planters of a rising, that the slaves have all been deprived of their usual Christmas indulgences and visits, and have been confined closely to their own plantations. The police regulations are made still more strict, and every precaution possible is taken to prevent an eruption of the smouldering volcano, which sooner or later must take place. The large planters, as a general thing, are not earnest secessionists, and they fear the effect of secession upon the value of their property. The chief secessionists are the politicians of the towns and cities, and they have produced such a state of feeling that no one dares openly to express anti-secession opinions."—*Chicago Democrat.*

A WRITER in Washington says: "In conversation, this evening, with several of the North Carolina delegation, they inform me that they had been aware, for some time past, that the small squad of secessionists in that State had been for weeks past concocting schemes to seize the Federal property, which, perhaps, might have been consummated without the knowledge of the Union men of the State, whereby the latter might possibly have been drawn into it; but having been advised of that fact, the members of Congress immediately telegraphed to their friends, to suppress all such revolutionary schemes, which advice was at once taken, and this movement thus interrupted. Having implicit confidence in the honesty and ability of Gov. Ellis, they also sent a dispatch to him to quell all such

insurrections, and it is believed he will use all his power to prevent an outbreak. They also state that there need be no alarm as to North Carolina taking any such precipitate action. It is recommended by these members that a convention be immediately called to discuss this question, and to present some plan for the adjustment of all these difficulties, and thus save their State from being drawn into this vortex of certain ruin. It is not unlikely that such a convention will be called in the course of a few days."—*N. Y. Times, Jan.* 5.

Jan. 5.—The Southern senators at Washington say, that the United States frigate Brooklyn, if sent to Charleston, will be sunk in the harbor; that the light-houses will be darkened, the buoys removed, and the battery opened upon the steamer from Morris Island.—*Boston Transcript, Jan.* 6.

IT is rumored that when South Carolina is brought to submission, that State is to be occupied as a black republic, by the slaves liberated from the border States.—*Athenæum.*

Jan. 7.—A gentleman from Charleston says that every thing there betokens active preparations for fight. Last Sunday, he says, not a lady was at the church he attended. They were all at home making cartridges and cylinders, and scraping lint. The thousand negroes busy in building batteries, so far from inclining to insurrection, were grinning from ear to ear at the prospect of shooting the Yankees. Extravagant reports were current as to the hostile designs of the Federal Government, such as that the Macedonian was on her way with five hundred troops.—*Evening Post, Jan.* 7.

WASHINGTON, *Jan.* 7.—The Cabinet have entertained the idea of causing the arrest of Senator Toombs for treason, the treasonable act being that of sending the alleged despatch urging the immediate seizure of the Georgia forts, which was done.—*Washington Star, Jan.* 7.

Jan. 8.—It is stated that a movement had, last week, obtained the sanction and support of several wealthy merchants of New York, for sending relief to the gallant Anderson, and that a large amount of money and materials were contributed, and a steamer selected for the purpose. On Saturday the parties who were at the head of the movement were informed that the United States Government had undertaken to send supplies and men to that post, and that consequently their patriotic services would not be required. It is understood that South Carolina has agents in New York, and at other important points, who promptly notify the Governor of every movement of troops intended for reinforcing the military posts at the South. We have good reason to know that it is now understood on Governor's Island that an order has been received in this city from the War Department, in obedience to which all the available troops at this station will be mustered and critically inspected at Governor's Island on Thursday next. Lest any man should be absent at roll-call the utmost strictness is exercised in making out the daily liberty lists; and no soldier can leave the island except by special permission. The order is supposed to have authorized the complete equipment and preparation for the road of all the troops in garrison.—*N. Y. Times, Jan.* 8.

Jan. 9.—Reports of the suffering at Charleston continue. A dispatch from Washington confirms the previous accounts. It says;

"A gentleman arrived this evening from Charleston, in company with Com. Shubrick. Both say the panic which prevails there is unparalleled. There is a great lack of food, business is prostrated; the people are idle, and patrols are wandering up and down to preserve order. On the day Com. Shubrick left there was unusual excitement, and upon inquiry he found that news had been received that the steamer Macedonian was on her way with eight hundred troops to bombard the city and reinforce Major Anderson. He could not convince them to the contrary, and expresses the opinion that they cannot hold out in their present condition long, unless Georgia comes to their relief. No vessel entered or left the harbor while they were there."

THE *Tribune* has the following editorial paragraph:

"We learn, through a private letter, from a perfectly responsible source in Charleston, that the other day a body of twenty minute-men from the country entered a large private house in that city and demanded dinner. A dinner was given them, and then they demanded ten dollars each, saying that they had not come to Charleston for nothing; and the money was furnished also. Another fact of still greater significance has come to our knowledge. Governor Pickens has written to an officer of high rank in the United States army, a native of South Carolina, who is loyal to the stars and stripes, requesting him to come to Charleston and protect them from the mob. The officer has declined, saying that he can serve his country elsewhere, and that he does not wish to have any part in the proceedings now going forward in that State."

THE Baltimore *Clipper* has information of a similar character. It says:

"We learn, by the fresh arrival of a stone-cutter from Columbia, South Carolina, at his home in Washington city, that a sad and sorrowful state of things prevails there. Business and work of all kinds are in a paralyzed condition, owing to the excitement existing among the people about the approaching inauguration of what they term a hostile Government. The talk of war has caused every thing else to be suspended. He represents the people as excited almost to derangement, and relates a case where a fellow-mechanic of his had been completely crazed and made an inmate of a lunatic asylum, by the warlike demonstrations around him. Nearly every mechanic employed on the Capitol of the State has left, and those remaining behind will follow in a few days. Other mechanics employed elsewhere will soon take their departure, and unless times shall soon improve, many of the native mechanics and laboring force of the State will seek employment in other States."

THE *Journal of Commerce*, a few days ago, contained this specious apology for one of the numerous acts of treason to the Union by which Secretary Floyd endeavored to efface from the public mind all recollection of his more despicable, if less noteworthy crimes:

"Arms for the South:—The *Evening Post*, under the head of 'A Suspicious Proceeding,'

publishes a rumor that 'five hundred cases of muskets, from the Watervliet arsenal, opposite Troy, have been shipped to this city and put on board the steamer Florida, for Savannah.' As the *Post's* paragraph will be copied, with amplifications, into Republican papers throughout the country, it may be well to state the real facts upon which the above ridiculous report is probably based. Several weeks ago, five hundred cases of muskets were shipped to Savannah, to supply, it is said, the legal demand of Georgia for her quota of guns from the United States. There was no mystery about the transaction. The arms came down the Hudson River on a barge, and were taken on board the Savannah steamer like any other cargo. If this shipment had occurred at any other time, it would have caused no remark. Its occurrence now is explained by the fact, that *Georgia had previously neglected to draw out the quota of arms to which she was entitled, and which the General Government could not legally or equitably deny to her.* Within a week or two, the Adjutant-general of this State has drawn all the arms to which New York was entitled, and no good reason can be given why every other State, as long as it remains in the Union, should not exercise the same right." It is a little singular that the State of Georgia should be entitled to a quota of ten thousand stand of arms, that being the number contained in five hundred cases, (as I learn from a highly intelligent officer of the service,) when the annual appropriation for arming the militia is only $200,000 per annum. The muskets are worth about $11 50 each, so that the ten thousand would cost $115,000. Now, if we reflect that the State of Georgia constituted, in 1850, only one-thirtieth part of the Union, and that, at the present time, it bears a still smaller proportion to the whole, we shall see how absurd is the pretence that she has only received her proper share of arms. Divide $200,000 by thirty, and we have for her distributive share $6,666; so that the 10,000 muskets would be her quota for *seventeen years* and more. Perhaps the *Journal of Commerce* can reconcile these facts with its smooth and plausible statement. It is well known, that besides the arms thus given to the States, Secretary Floyd has been putting others in the Southern arsenals during the summer, in order that the secessionists may arm themselves whenever they see fit to rebel against the Government. There were not more than twenty thousand stand of arms in the Charleston arsenal a year ago; there are now seventy thousand, if the Charleston papers can be relied upon. These arms were sent there to be seized by the State authorities, and no one can feel surprised that the present has been accepted. The mob in Savannah has imitated the Government of South Carolina, and among the latest items of news, we learn that the United States Government has been dispossessed of its armory at that place. Floyd was industriously engaged up to the date of his resignation, in sending arms and munitions of war to all the seceding States. This seems to have been the only public measure in which he took an interest. When not employed in arming the rebel States by disarming the Government which he had sworn to support, his attention seems to have been entirely occupied with various and complicated schemes for depleting the treasury; and I know of no man who will have stronger claims to the gratitude of the rebellious States than he who did so much to bring dishonor and bankruptcy upon the Government of the Union, while he supplied its enemies with the sinews of war.—*Times.*

AMONG the items of news from Charleston floating around in secession circles, is a story that the Hon. Wm. Aiken has been made to "disgorge, in aid of the cause, much against his will," as follows: He was notified that he was expected to advance $40,000 to that end; and plead his right to advance or not, as he might please, adding that he did not have the money. He was then promptly notified that he had been assessed that amount and must promptly pay it, under penalty of having it raised by the immediate confiscation and sale of his property in Charleston, worth many times as much. To save that from utter destruction, he did raise the amount demanded, and in paying it remarked, that his lot would be better if he was a journeyman carpenter at the North, shoving a jack-plane at $2 per day wages, than the South Carolina millionaire he was before it was essayed to reduce the South under a military despotism. He is now "one of the suspected," his course in refusing to seem to be pleased with paying the forced loan having earned him the dangerous reputation of being disaffected to the cause.— *Washington Star.*

DURING the approach of the Star of the West, and the firing upon her from Morris Island, Maj. Anderson ordered the ports fronting Fort Moultrie and Morris Island to be opened, and the guns were unlimbered. As the firing continued, one of the lieutenants who commanded a heavy gun, entreated Maj. Anderson to let him "give 'em just one shot." "Be patient," was the only reply from the commander, who remained in the look-out, with glass in hand, intently watching the approaching steamer. How long Maj. Anderson had determined in his own mind to "be patient," he alone can tell; but just at what appeared the critical juncture, when every instant the order to "fire" was expected, the Star of the West was observed to suddenly port her helm, and swinging with her head seaward, doubled upon her track and proceeded out over the bar. [Account of a laborer then in the fort.]—*N. Y. Times, Jan.* 19.

Jan. 10.—A recent number of *Once a Week* contains the following amusingly exaggerated personal sketch of our next President:

"Abraham Lincoln is a gaunt giant more than six feet high, strong and long-limbed. He walks slow, and, like many thoughtful men (Wordsworth and Napoleon, for example), keeps his head inclined forward and downward. His hair is wiry black, his eyes are dark gray; his smile is frank, sincere and winning. Like most American gentlemen, he is loose and careless in dress, turns down his flapping white collars, and wears habitually what we consider evening dress. His head is massive, his brow full and wide, his nose large and fleshy, his mouth coarse and full; his eyes are sunken, his bronzed face is thin, and drawn down into strong corded lines, that disclose the machinery that moves the broad jaw. This great leader of the 'Republican' party—this Abolitionist—this terror of the 'Democrats'—this honest old lawyer, with face half Roman, half Indian, so wasted by climate, so scarred by a life's struggle, was born in 1809, in Kentucky.

His grandfather, who came from Virginia, was killed by the Indians. His father died young, leaving a widow and several children. They removed to Indiana, Abe being at that time only six years old. Poor and struggling, his mother could only afford him some eight months' rough schooling; and in the clearings of that new, unsettled country, the healthy stripling went to work to hew hickory and gum-trees, to grapple with remonstrating bears, and to look out for the too frequent rattle-snake. Tall, strong, lithe and smiling, Abe toiled on as farm-laborer, mule-driver, sheep-feeder, deer-killer, wood-cutter, and, lastly, as boatman on the waters of the Wabash and the Mississippi."

A LETTER from Hayneville, in Alabama, says the people are greatly excited on two subjects: the certain withdrawal of Alabama from the Union, and negro insurrections. About twenty miles from that place, they have discovered a plot among the negroes, headed by a white man, or perhaps more than one, to rise and murder all the white folks they could find. The plot was providentially discovered, the white man arrested, and, after establishing their guilt beyond a doubt, he was hung up, together with five or six negroes. Another plot has been discovered in another direction. Three white men have been arrested and about thirty negroes—report says they will hang. The white men are northern men.

Another letter from Greensboro, Alabama, says: "There was a servile insurrection about sixty miles north of this place, last week, when four whites were killed and sixteen negroes were hung. In Montgomery, for the same thing, two white men (abolitionists) and four negroes were hung. We hope all this will soon pass off, but there is great fear that insurrections will rise all over the South. —*Evening Post, Jan.* 10.

NEWS was received, at Washington, last night from Major Anderson, to the effect that he had notified the commander of Fort Moultrie that he expected a ship with reinforcements, and that if it was fired upon, or her passage through the channel interfered with in any way, he would fire upon Fort Moultrie. The commander replied that he 'might fire and be d——d.' This is regarded as an indication that the secessionists intended to attack the vessel, and intense anxiety for her safety, and in regard to the probable issue of affairs in Charleston harbor, therefore prevails.—*Phila. Press, Jan.* 10.

A COMMITTEE of the Louisiana State Convention, appointed to prepare a flag and seal for that State, thus express their opinion of that Pelican which has so long been the cherished emblem of Louisiana: "On consultation, and especially with those descended from the ancient colonists of the country, the Committee found, that what has been considered the symbol of Louisiana, commands neither their favor nor their affection. The pelican is in form unsightly, in habits filthy, in nature cowardly." The Committee also learned from Audubon, to their amazement, that the story of the pelican's feeding its young with its own blood is, in expressive phrase, "gammon." Therefore they do not commend this water-fowl as a fit subject for their flag, but rather as one of loathing and contumely.—*N. Y. Times.*

LAISSER ALLER.

BY FRANKLIN LUSHINGTON.

No more words ;
    Try it with your swords!
Try it with the arms of your bravest and your best !
You are proud of your manhood, now put it to the
        test ;
    Not another word ;
    Try it by the sword.

No more *notes ;*
    Try it by the throats
Of the cannon that will roar till the earth and air
        be shaken :
For they speak what they mean, and they cannot be
        mistaken ;
    No more doubt ;
    Come—fight it out.

No child's play !
    Waste not a day ;
Serve out the deadliest weapons that you know ;
Let them pitilessly hail on the faces of the foe ;
    No blind strife ;
    Waste not one life.

You that in the front
    Bear the battle's brunt—
When the sun gleams at dawn on the bayonets
        abreast,
Remember 'tis for government and country you
        contest ;
    For love of all you guard,
    Stand and strike hard.

You at home that stay
    From danger far away,
Leave not a jot to chance, while you rest in quiet
        ease ;
Quick ! forge the bolts of death ; quick ! ship them
        o'er the seas ;
    If war's feet are lame,
    Yours will be the blame.

You, my lads, abroad,
    "Steady ! " be your word :
You, at home, be the anchor of your soldiers young
        and brave ;
Spare no cost, none is lost, that may strengthen or
        may save ;
    Sloth were sin and shame ;
    Now play out the game.
                    —*Transcript*, April 17.

A VOLUNTEER SONG.

THE choir of the Broadway Tabernacle church,
wishing to sing the *Marseillaise,* called upon the
pastor to prepare a patriotic hymn. The following
attempt to adjust inflexible English syllables to the
tortuous notes of the French Air of Liberty, was the
response. The hymn, such as it is, was sung with
good effect at the Tabernacle last Sabbath evening—
the vast audience joining with great enthusiasm in
the chorus. By request of many, it is given to the
public :

Arise ! Arise ! ye sons of patriot sires !
    A Nation calls ! and Heaven speed your way.
Now Freedom lights anew her waning fires,
    And spreads her banner to the day,
    And spreads her banner to the day.
While to His Throne our hearts are swelling,
    Freedom, and Law, and Truth, and Right,
    May God defend by his own might,
By his right arm the treason quelling !
    Ye loyal sons, and true,
        Sons of the brave and free,
    Join hearts, join hands, to strike anew
        For God and Liberty.

With faith your all to Him confiding
    Who crowned with victory our fathers' hand,
With courage in his strength abiding,
    Go forth in Freedom's sacred band,
    Go forth to save our native land.
Defend from faction's wild commotion,
    Our homes, our laws, our schools and spires,
    The names and graves of patriot sires,
Till Freedom reigns to farthest ocean.
    Ye loyal sons and true,
        Sons of the brave and free,
    Join hearts, join hands, to strike anew
        For God and Liberty.
                        —*Independent.*

TO THE BRITISH RIFLE COMPANY.

BY GEORGE W. MORGAN.

Air, "Yankee Doodle."

Old England sends a Rifle Corps
    To dear New England greeting ;
And will, if wanted, send still more,
    At every future meeting ;
For, though this ain't our native land,
    It still is very handy,
As riflemen, to lend a hand,
    To Yankee Doodle Dandy.
Chorus—Brother Britons, keep it up,
        Keep the ball in motion,
    And show this love of liberty
        Is a *British*-Yankee notion.

" Down South" they seem to think we are
    Divided in opinion,
And that they'll have an easy task
    To conquer a dominion.
They'll find out, though, p'raps to their cost,
    In forming such conclusions,
They've reckoned there without their host,—
    Their facts were but delusions.
Chorus—Brother Britons, keep it up, &c.

They say there's black sheep in our fold,
    And traitors in the city ;
We don't believe it, though we're told ;—
    If 'tis so, more's the pity.
We'll hold ourselves in readiness
    To paint their black skins white, sirs,
Or else make good large apertures
    That will let in the light, sirs.
Chorus—Brother Britons, keep it up, &c.

And if to Bunker Hill they come,
    To call their rolls of slaves, sirs,
They'll make it their perpetual home
    In mighty pleasant graves, sirs.

Old England and New England's sons
Are bound as loving brothers ;
Both hearts and hands, their swords and guns,
Alike are one another's.
Chorus—Brother Britons, keep it up, &c.
BOSTON, *April* 24, 1861.
—*Boston Transcript.*

THE STARS AND STRIPES.

BY FRANCIS DE HAES JANVIER.

The Stars and Stripes ! What hand shall dare
To desecrate the flag we bear?
The flag of stars, whose cheering light
Brightened oppression's gloomy night !
The flag of stripes, whose heavenly dyes
Flashed Freedom's day-spring through the skies !
Our flag ! The standard of the free !
Symbol of hope and liberty !

The Stars and Stripes ! What memories rise,
Whene'er that banner greets our eyes !
By patriots borne, o'er land and sea,
It led the way to victory !
When slaughter swept the surging main—
When carnage strewed the crimson plain—
It marked the spot where heroes stood,
It was baptized in heroes' blood !

The Stars and Stripes ! What power shall stay
Immortal Freedom's onward way !
The heavens are the triumphal arch
Through which she takes her mighty march !
Her mighty march ! Nor shall she halt
Till, like the spangled azure vault,
O'er every land around the world
The Stars and Stripes shall be unfurled !
WASHINGTON, *March* 19, 1861.
—*N. Y. Evening Post*, March 22.

A VISION OF JANUARY 4TH.

Lying on my couch a night or two ago,
I had a solemn vision of penitential woe ;
Of that great time of fasting and of humiliation
Proposed by pious James unto our sinful nation.

All the stores were closed, the whole length of
Broadway,
As on that great occasion, the Prince's procession
day,
And the solemn chimes of Trinity through the air
began to swim,
Tolling the grand Old Hundred and Luther's Judg-
ment Hymn.

Ah, soon the great procession moved slowly from the
Park ;
'Twas headed by the Mayor, and brought up by men
of mark,
Barefooted marched through mingled mud and snow ;
Girdled with rope, and ashes-strewn, and clad in
weeds of woe.

There were some Republican leaders, feeling very
blue indeed,
That their party, after hard fighting, had the ill luck
to succeed ;

They were all for " conciliation," " concession," and
" compromises ;"
Hungry to eat their own words and back out of their
own devices.

Houses in Southern trade, although their skirts were
clear,
Had, for the sake of example, come in from far and
near ;
They bore a sable banner, all lettered in golden foil,
"After eating *so much dirt*, are we asked to swallow
free soil ? "

Merchants with " woolly " clerks, or those who, in
sinful way,
Had thought their own thoughts sometimes on the
questions of the day,
Marched with sorrowful tread, in garments as dark
as death,
Beating their breasts, and crying "*Mea culpa*" with
every breath.

There was the British Consul, walking subdued and
meekly ;
He had read that statesmanlike paper of Morse in the
recent *Weekly*,
Unmasking the foul designs of the island across the
ocean,
And he hastened to add his mite of penitence and
devotion.

Many were the devices the mournful band upbore,
In token of heartfelt sorrow that would go and sin
no more ;
Loyal—repentant—humble—and all that sort of
thing—
There was one in the style of Blondel—"O Cotton !
O our King ! "

It was a gloomy progress—no shouts or waving of
palms—
They chanted *De Profundis* and the Penitential
Psalms,
Or a verse of *Dies Iræ* by way of a little variety,
Tears and groans and ejaculations thrown in to pre-
vent satiety.

Whenever the song was still the bands took up the
wail—
(The drums and bugles wore crape as deep as a
widow's veil)—
And the players moved along, solemn and slowly all,
To the music of Roslin Castle and the Dead March in
Saul.

The route of the procession was up Broadway to
Grace,
Where prayers were to be offered befitting the des-
perate case ;
But a breakfast-bell rang near me, and roused by its
thrilling stroke,
Just on the corner of Tenth street, I lost the vision
and woke.   CATHARINE LEDYARD.
—*Evening Post.*

A NORTHERN RALLY.

BY JOHN CLANCY.

We've borne too long this Southern wrong,
That ever sought to shame us ;
The threat and boast, the braggart toast,
" That Southern men would tame us."

We've bent the knee to chivalry,
  Have borne the lie and scorning,
But now, thank God, our Northern blood
  Has roused itself from fawning.

The issue's made, our flag's displayed,
  Let he who dare retard it;
No cowards here grow pale with fear,
  For Northern swords now guard it.
The men that won at Lexington
  A name and fame in story,
Were patriot sires, who lit the fires
  To lead their sons to glory.

Like rushing tide down mountain side,
  The Northern hosts are sweeping;
Each freeman's breast to meet the test
  With patriot blood is leaping.
Now Southern sneer and bullies' leer,
  Will find swift vengeance meted;
For never yet, since foemen met,
  Have Northern men retreated.

United now, no more we'll bow,
  Or supplicate, or reason:
'Twill be our shame and lasting blame
  If we consent to treason.
Then in the fight our hearts unite,
  One purpose move us ever;
No traitor hand divide our land,
  No power our country sever.
            —*N. Y. Leader*, April 20.

OUT AND FIGHT.

Out and fight! The clouds are breaking,
  Far and wide the red light streams,
North and west see millions waking,
  From their night-mare, doubting dreams,
War is coming. As the thunder
  Mid the mountain caverns rolls,
Driving rains in torrents under,
  So the wild roar wakes our souls.

Out and fight! The time is over
  For all truce and compromise,
Words of calm are words of folly,
  Peaceful dreams are painted lies;
Sumter's flames in Southern waters,
  Are the first wild beacon light,
And on Northern hills reflected
  Give the signal for the fight.

Out and fight! Endure no longer,
  Goading insult, brazen guilt;
Be the battle to the knife blade,
  And the knife blade to the hilt,
Till the sacred zone of Freedom
  Girds the whole Atlantic strand,
And the braggart and the Gascon
  Be extinguished in the land.
      CHAS. G. LELAND, in *Vanity Fair*, April 27.

THE MASSACHUSETTS REGIMENTS.

BY ALMIRA SEYMOUR.

They were reared on the soil whence the Adamses
    sprung,
  That to Hancock and Warren gave birth;

Descendants of sires whose proud names have been
    sung
  In the noblest hosannas of earth.
They were trained in our shops, they were trained in
    our schools,
  They've been taught on our free waves to sail;
They have learned of *Progression* the practice and
    rules,
  But they know not the meaning of FAIL.

They marched 'neath that Banner whose glorious
    light
  Has been the world's Hope-star in heaven;
They march in defence of the True and the Right,
  And God's power to each strong arm is given.
That flag will still wave o'er the Land of the Free,
  Though Treason by millions assail;
The sons of the Bay State have sworn it shall be,
  And they know not the meaning of FAIL.

Go, join them, brave brothers! still rallying, go!
  Wives and sisters are calling the rolls—
On their cheeks fall sad tears, but they're quenched
    in the glow
  That rays out from their Patriot souls.
They were reared in the Bay State, they're tender
    and true,
  But at Duty's stern glance never quail;
The Future is calling to them and to you—
  And no word of the answer is FAIL.
            —*Boston Transcript.*

THE SECESSION FLAG.

[Upon the proposition of the secessionists to adopt
the stars and stripes for the flag of the Southern
Confederacy, adding the crescent as the only change.]

    Unfurl not to the Southern breeze
      Our flag of glorious name,
    Nor mar with heathenish device
      The symbol of our fame!

    Our stars and stripes o'er Freedom's grave—
      Dissevered brotherhood—
    Would bear the deep-dyed mark of Cain
      Daguerreotyped in blood.

    It ne'er again would thrill the heart
      That quails before a foe,
    Nor kindle in the patriot's breast
      A warmer, brighter glow.

    It ne'er would shield beneath its folds
      Th' expatriate on the sea,
    Nor call from Heaven, by mute appeal,
      A blessing on the free.

    But, as the prostrate soldier, slain
      Upon the battle-field,
    Clasps with convulsive grasp the hilt,
      Despoil'd the power to wield—

    In lifeless folds, Columbia's flag
      Would tell no nation's story;
    Awake no harmonies divine,
      Of a *whole* nation's glory.

    Thus, as the ark of God of old,
      Let forth by traitor hands,
    Stay'd not the curse of dire defeat
      To Israel's chosen bands—

Its hovering cloud—Jehovah's pledge—
  Had rolled itself away;
The empty symbol failed to prove
  A wicked people's stay.

So would that constellation strange
  Those wand'ring stars unite,
Themselves in magic form arrange,
  And "Ichabod" would write.
                    JOSEPHINE MORSS.
February 22, 1861.
                    —*Evening Post.*

UP, BROTHERS, ALL.

Up, brothers, all! this is no time
  To idle on your oars;
Look! how the waves are madly tost;
The winds wail, like a spirit lost;
  The distant thunder roars.

Up, brothers, all! for mother, sire,
  For hearthstone, child, and wife,
Ere on the fatal rocks we go,
And hearts sink with the fearful blow—
  Pause not for word of strife.

Ho! brothers of the North and South!
  Ho! brothers East and West!
Pull all together, would you save
The "Union" which your fathers gave,
  Unwrecked the billows breast.

God help us! may we haste to land
  In port of peaceful weather;
The ties of friendship strong and bright,
(Pull all together with your might!)
  For dangers passed together.
                    FANNY FALES.
                    —*Boston Transcript.*

YANKEE DOODLE'S SUGGESTIONS.

BY G. W. WESTBROOK.

Yankee Doodle's come again
  Among the sons of Gotham—
Not to see the gods and shows,
  But to see the facts, and quote 'em.

He heard of South Carolina's boast
  That Jonathan was craven—
That Cotton was the king of earth,
  And nothing else could save 'em.

But Yankee Doodle says, "Dear sirs,
  You know not what's the matter—
You see through glasses darkly smoked
  With error and tobacker!

"Your darkies plough, and hoe, and dig,
  To raise your rice and cotton,
And sugar, too, and cornstalks big,
  And many things forgotten.

"You orter know that Yankees make
  Your cotton into muslin,
And thread, and tape, and hosiery,
  And ladies' wear quite puzzlin'.

"Besides, they make the canvas sheets
  That forms the wings of commerce,
That takes your schooners and your fleets
  To every harbor on earth.

"They also make the canvas bags,
  And send them to the prairies
Of Indiana, Illinois,
  As the soil and climate varies,

"To hold potatoes, corn, and oats,
  And wheat, and rye, and barley,
And sometimes coal and ice in boats,
  And coverings for the darkey.

"They also take your rice in ships
  Built by the Yankee nation—
From Charleston's docks and New York slips
  All over the creation.

"Your sugar, too, the Yankees take—
  Although they tap the maple,
That produces matter saccharine,
  And forms a Yankee staple.

"Tobacker, too, the Yankees chew,
  And smoke and snuff in plenty—
The ladies, too, if you only knew,
  Send to you by the twenty—

"For early fruits and early flowers,
  Before the North can raise 'em,
To decorate their lovely bowers,
  Their sweethearts to amaze 'em.

"Then why this strife? like man and wife
  In a domestic quarrel—
That after all must end with life,
  With no unfading laurel?

"Jonathan's advice, therefore,
  Is, peacefully be living,
And kind and true to every one,
  Forbearing and forgiving.

"If you refuse to take this hint
  Intended for your favor,
We'll show you how the cap and flint
  Will cause you much more labor."
                    —*N. Y. Atlas.*

THE STARS AND STRIPES.

Rally round the flag, boys—
  Give it to the breeze!
That's the banner *we* love,
  On the land and seas.

Brave hearts are under it;
  Let the *Traitors* brag;
Gallant lads, fire away!
  And fight for the flag.

Their flag is but a rag—
  Ours is the *true* one;
Up with the Stars and Stripes!
  Down with the new one!

Let our colors fly, boys—
  Guard them day and night;
For Victory is Liberty,
  And God will bless the Right.
                    —*Boston Transcript.*

GOD SAVE OUR NATIVE LAND.

BY JAMES WALDEN.

AIR—"*America.*"

God save our native land
From the invader's hand—
Home of the free!
Though ruthless traitors aim
To crush our nation's fame,
Yet still, in Freedom's name,
We cling to thee!

O Lord! we humbly pray,
Far distant be the day
Ere that shall be;
Though lawless bands combine
To shatter Freedom's shrine,
With faith and hope divine
We cling to thee!

O Lord! when, hand to hand,
Brothers as foes shall stand,
Shield thou the right!
Stay these unhappy wars,
Join us in one great cause—
To guard our nation's laws
With freemen's might!

Lord! may this strife soon cease;
Grant us a lasting peace—
Parted we fall!
Long may our banner wave
Over the free and brave—
O Lord! our country save—
God save us all!

—*Sunday Times.*

OUR FATHERLAND.

God save our Fatherland! from shore to shore;
God save our Fatherland, one evermore.
No hand shall peril it,
No strife shall sever it,
East, West, and North and South!
One evermore!
Chorus—God save our Fatherland! true home of
Freedom!
God save our Fatherland, one evermore;
One in her hills and streams,
One in her glorious dreams,
One in Love's noblest themes—
One evermore!

Strong in the hearts of men, love is thy throne;
Union and Liberty crown thee alone;
Nations have sighed for thee;
Our sires have died for thee;
We'll all be true to thee—
All are thine own.
Chorus—God save our Fatherland, &c.

Ride on, proud Ship of State, though tempests lower;
Ride on in majesty, glorious in power;
Though fierce the blast may be,
No wreck shall shatter thee—
Storms shall but bring to thee
Sunshine once more.
Chorus—God save our Fatherland, &c.

—*Evening Post*, Feb. 23.

THE NEW YEAR AND THE UNION.

BY GEORGE D. PRENTICE.

God has made
A wilderness of worlds; His will, and strong
Creative spirit shook ten thousand worlds,
Like golden dewdrops, from his waving wing,
To roll in beauty through abysmal space,
And chant the chorus of his love divine.
He made the milky-way to span the sky,
A pearly bow of promise, every drop
That sparkles there a singing, shining world!
He woke the music of the Northern Harp,
The wild weird chiming of the Pleiades—
And bade the arches of a Southern sphere
Reverberate their hallelujahs high.

The mighty One
Who sweeps the lyre of Ages, and commands
The praises of ten thousand singing worlds,
Creates the stars of Union, and attunes
The lofty heart of liberty! . . . shall we,
Proud children of the brave, the free,
Behold our banner, blazoned by the breath
Of glory, sullied by a slave?—our stars,
Of Union tossing wildly to and fro
Upon the wave of faction, as they were
But shining shadows, not eternal orbs,
For ever circling through the boundless heaven
Of everlasting purpose?—or shall we
Hear *Dissolution* sounded, and forbear
To brand the traitor hearts that dare forget
The bond for which our fathers fought and bled?
Cursed be the traitors—doubly, trebly doomed—
The pit of Discord for her victims yawns,
Then, back recoiling, shudders to receive
Their hearts,—a fouler and a fiercer hell!

God save the Union!—Give the dawning year
This proud baptismal anthem—let its last
Dissolving sigh be—Union undissolved!
New States, with starry emblems, one by one,
Come stealing through the Future's twilight dim,
Like orbs of evening from its dusky sky,
To take their place at last with those that tread
Their high, unwearied and unwearying round
Before the golden gates and battlements
Of Paradise. The harp of Liberty
Shall sound amain, till Death himself expire;
Till God has made us free, immortally,
And Time is dust upon his broken Lyre!
Thrice raptured moment!—if all blessed like thee
Are Heaven's bright centuries, how brief will be
Its countless ages of Eternity!

THE SEVENTH.

BY FITZJAMES O'BRIEN.

AIR—"*Gilla Machree.*"

I.
Och! we're the boys
That hearts desthroys
Wid making love and fighting;
We take a fort,
The girls we court,
But most the last delight in.
To fire a gun,
Or raise some fun,
To us is no endeavor;

So let us hear
One hearty cheer—
The Seventh's lads for ever!

Chorus—For we're the boys
That hearts desthroys,
Wid making love and fighting;
We take a fort,
The girls we court,
But most the last delight in.

II.

There's handsome Joe,
Whose constant flow
Of merriment unfailing,
Upon the tramp,
Or in the camp,
Will keep our hearts from ailing.
And B—— and Chat
Who might have sat
For Pythias and Damon,
Och! whin they get
Their heavy wet,
They get as high as Haman.

Chorus—For we're the boys
That hearts desthroys, &c.

III.

Like Jove above,
We're fond of love,
But fonder still of victuals;
Wid turtle steaks
An' codfish cakes
We always fills our kittles.
To dhrown aich dish,
We dhrinks like fish,
And Mumm's the word we utther;
An' thin we swill
Our Léoville,
That oils our throats like butther.

Chorus—For we're the boys
That hearts desthroys, &c.

IV.

We make from hay
A splindid tay,
From beans a gorgeous coffee;
Our crame is prime,
Wid chalk and lime—
In fact, 'tis quite a throphy.
Our chickens roast,
Wid butthered toast,
I'm sure would timpt St. Pether.
Now you'll declare
Our bill of fare
It couldn't be complether.

Chorus—For we're the boys
That hearts desthroys, &c.

V.

Now silence all,
While I recall
A memory sweet and tender;
The maids and wives
That light our lives
With deep, enduring splendor—
We'll give no cheer
For those so dear,
But in our hearts we'll bless them,

And pray to-night,
That angels bright
May watch them and caress them.

Chorus—For we're the boys
That hearts desthroys,
Wid making love and fighting;
We take a fort,
The girls we court,
But most the last delight in.

—*N. Y. Times.*

THE UNITED STATES FLAG—1861.

INSCRIBED TO S. P. RUSSELL, ESQ.

(*As read by* John Keynton, Esq., *at the great
Union Meeting at Yorkville, N. Y.*

BY WILLIAM ROSS WALLACE.

Flag of the valiant and the tried,
Where Marion fought and Warren died!
Flag of the mountain and the lake!
Of rivers rolling to the sea
In that broad grandeur fit to make
The symbols of Eternity!
O fairest Flag! O dearest Land!
Who shall your banded children sever?
God of our fathers! here we stand,
A true, a free, a fearless band,
Heart pressed to heart, hand linked in hand,
And swear that Flag shall float forever!

Still glorious Banner of the Free!
The nations turn with hope to thee:
And when thy mighty shadow falls
Along the armory's trophied walls,
The ancient trumpets long for breath;
The dinted sabres fiercely start
To vengeance from each clanging sheath,
As if they sought some traitor's heart!

O sacred Banner of the Brave!
O standard of ten thousand ships!
O guardian of Mount Vernon's grave!
Come, let us press thee to our lips!—
There is a heaving of the rocks—
New England feels the patriot-shocks;
There is a heaving of the lakes—
New York, with all the West, awakes;
And, lo! on high the glorious shade
Of Washington lights all the gloom,
And points unto these words, arrayed
In fire around his tomb—

"*Americans!* your fathers *shed*
their blood *to rear the Union's* * *fame;*
For this that fearless Banner spread
On many a gory plain!
Americans! let no one dare,
On mountain, valley, prairie, flood,
By hurling down that Temple there,
To desecrate that blood!
The Right shall live, while Faction dies!
All traitors draw a fleeting breath!
But Patriots drink, from God's own eyes,
Truth's light that conquers Death!"

* *How pure the spirit in that form enshrined.*—Gov. Chase.

Then, dearest Flag, and dearest Land!
  Who shall your banded children sever?
God of our fathers! here we stand,
A true, a free, a fearless band,
Heart pressed to heart, hand linked in hand,
  AND SWEAR THAT FLAG SHALL FLOAT FOREVER!
        —*N. Y. Dispatch.*

NATIONAL GUARD MARCHING SONG.

BY A. J. H. DUGANNE.

AIR—"*Lutzow's Wild Chase.*"

A sound through the nation is rolling amain,
  With the power and the grandeur of thunder;
It beats in the bosom and throbs in the brain
  Of a people awaking in wonder;
Oh! if you ask why the thunders rolled—
'Tis to rouse for Union, the free and the bold—
Rouse for Union the hearts of the free and the bold!

"An army with banners" moves mightily on;
  Every heart to its country is plighted;
The stars of those banners outdazzle the sun,
  With the blaze of their glories united!
Oh! if you ask what is here foretold—
'Tis to range in Union the free and the bold—
Range in Union the hearts of the free and the bold!

They are marching, all marching, in Liberty's cause,
  With the flag of their love floating o'er them;
And on its bright folds they have graven the laws
  Of the beautiful mother who bore them;
And if you ask why the flag's unrolled—
'Tis to lead in Union the free and the bold—
Lead in Union the hearts of the free and the bold!

Not a whisper of doubt or a shadow of dread
  In their gallant and noble communion;
For they tread in the paths of the patriot dead,
  And they step to the music of Union!
And if their purpose you would be told—
'Tis to band in Union the free and the bold—
Band in Union the hearts of the free and the bold!
        —*Boston Saturday Express.*

SONGS OF THE REBELS.

WAR SONG.

AIR—"*March, march, Ettrick and Teviotdale.*"

[The writer has a husband, three sons, two nephews,
other relatives, and friends, in the companies mentioned, to whom these lines are most respectfully
inscribed.]

March, march on, brave "PALMETTO" boys,
  "SUMTER" and "LAFAYETTES," forward in order;
March, march, "CALHOUN" and "RIFLE" boys,
  All the base Yankees are crossing the *border.*
    Banners are round ye spread,
    Floating above your head,
Soon shall the *Lone Star* be famous in story.
    On, on, my gallant men,
    Vict'ry be thine again,
Fight for your *rights,* till the green sod is gory.
      March, march, &c.

Young wives and sisters have buckled your armor on,
  Maidens ye love bid ye *go* to the battle-field;
Strong arms and stout hearts have many a vict'ry won,
  Courage shall strengthen the weapons ye wield.
    Wild passions are storming,
    Dark schemes are forming,
Deep snares are laid, but they *shall not* enthral
    ye;
    Justice your cause shall greet,
    Laurels lay at your feet,
If each brave band be but watchful and wary.
      March, march, &c.

Let fear and unmanliness vanish before ye;
  Trust in the Rock who will shelter the righteous;
Plant *firmly* each step on the soil of the *free*—
  A heritage left by the sires who bled for us.
    May each heart be bounding,
    When trumpets are sounding,
And the dark traitors shall strive to surround ye;
    The great God of Battle
    Can *still* the war-rattle,
And brighten the land with a sunset of glory.
      March, march, &c.
      —*Charleston Mercury.*

ON FORT SUMTER.

It was a noble Roman,
  In Rome's imperial day,
Who heard a coward croaker
  Before the battle say—
"They're safe in such a fortress;
  There is no way to shake it"—
"On! on!" exclaimed the hero,
  "I'LL FIND A WAY, OR MAKE IT!"

Is FAME your aspiration?
  Her path is steep and high;
In vain he seeks the temple,
  Content to gaze and sigh;
The crowded town is waiting,
  But he *alone* can take it,
Who says, with "SOUTHERN FIRMNESS,"
  "I'LL FIND A WAY, OR MAKE IT!"

Is *Glory* your ambition?
  There is no royal road;
Alike we all must labor,
  Must climb to her abode;
Who feels the thirst for *glory,*
  In Helicon may slake it,
If he has but the "SOUTHERN WILL,"
  "To find a way, OR MAKE IT!"

Is SUMTER worth the getting?
  It must be bravely sought;
With wishing and with fretting,
  The boon cannot be bought;
To *all* the prize is open,
  But only he can take it,
Who says, with "*Southern courage,*"
  "I'LL FIND A WAY, OR MAKE IT!"

In all impassioned warfare,
  The tale has ever been,
That victory crowns the valiant,
  The brave are they who win.
Though strong in "*Sumter Fortress,*"
  A HERO still may take it,
Who says, with "SOUTHERN DARING,"
  "I'LL FIND A WAY, OR MAKE IT!"
      —*Charleston Mercury.*

RUMORS AND INCIDENTS.

It was feared that Major Anderson might be short of fuel, but it is found that there are extensive old buildings at the fort, and sheds and timbers used during the construction of the works, which need to be removed, and which will afford abundant fuel for six months to come.—*N. Y. Times, Jan.* 11.

Hon. Owen Lovejoy was asked what he thought of Senator Seward's speech, noted somewhat for its conciliatory tone. "We want," said Lovejoy, "no Melancthons now; we want Martin Luthers. We want no one to write essays upon the Union and the sin and disasters of secession, but some one to throw the inkstand right at the Devil's head."—*N. Y. Times, Jan.* 16.

The following query appeared in the *New Haven Journal:* "Editor Journal: In the autumn of 1828, or previous, Rev. Dyer Bull occupied the first front chamber in the old Roger Sherman House, near South College, New Haven. Mr. Bull then had with him as private pupil, a short black-eyed young man, whom he introduced to the writer as Mr. Benjamin. Benjamin soon went out, and the writer asked Mr. Bull if that man was a member of college? 'No,' said he; 'he has been, but has left the college. He steals so that it seems almost impossible to break him of it—steals from his classmates, and any thing that he happens to fancy, that he can put his hands upon. Whether this same young man has not since risen to offices of high financial trust, has not been a senator in Congress, and has not directly or indirectly been cognizant of the late wholesale mint robbery at New Orleans, may be well a subject of inquiry.—Veritas.

"He is the same man. He left college under a discovery of theft.—[Ed. Journal.]"

"There was one of the class of 1829 whose name cannot be found on the list of graduates, or any annual catalogue after 1827. He was and still is a handsome little fellow, looking very small in his class, who, with a few exceptions, were of full manly growth. This youth hailed from a great State of 'the chivalrous sunny South,' bright-eyed, dark complexion, and 'ardent as a southern sun could make him.' In the early part of 1828 there was a mysterious trouble in that class. Watches, breastpins, seals, pencil-cases, penknives, two-bladed knives, four-bladed knives, &c., &c., &c., and lastly, sundry sums of money, 'lying around loose' in students' rooms, disappeared unaccountably. The losers looked gloomy at each other, and suspiciously at others. Something must be done, and they finally constituted themselves a volunteer 'detective force,' set their trap, baited with thirty-five dollars in good bank-notes, and soon caught the thief. He confessed. On opening his trunk, in his presence, they found it nearly full of missing valuables—jewelry, pocket cutlery and horology enough to stock a Chatham-street store. He begged pitifully not to be exposed; they looked piteously into his handsome young face, and relented at the thought of blasting his opening life. He had been a universal favorite, the pet of his class; so they agreed not to inform either the city magistrates or the Faculty of the University, but ordered him to 'clear out' at once and forever. He went instantly to good President Day, obtained a certificate of honorable dismission,

and vanished. That little thief is now a senator in Congress, advocating and justifying and threatening the robbery of forts and the stealing of the military cutlery, and hardware generally, of the Federal Government, without any more color or shadow of pretext than he had for his like operations on his fellow-students just thirty-three years ago. A third of a century has not made, and can never make, any change in such an originally born rascal. Had these early filchings been a mere thoughtless, boyish *escapade*, a momentary yielding to temptation while in great want, they would not deserve mention now; but they were systematized theft—long-continued, accumulated and hoarded pilferings, from trustful bosom friends. Had the fellow not at length reproduced his private morality in public life, I would have allowed the secret of his early crimes to remain in the hearts of the few who then knew and now remember it."—*N. Y. Independent.*

Written after reading General Wool's recent letter.[*]

Such soldier talk assures the land
   It isn't wholly bursted;
Our *Wool* against their *cotton*, and
   Secession schemes are *worsted.*
          —*Boston Atlas.*

A friend of Lincoln writes: Lincoln goes for no compromise with Southern leaders of secession —not at all. I speak advisedly. Again and again he has said to me, "Compromise is not the remedy —not the cure. The South, *i. e.* the leaders, don't want it—won't have it—no good can come of it. The system of compromise has no end. Slavery is the evil out of which all our other national evils and dangers have come. It has deceived us, led us to the brink of ruin, and it must be stopped. It must be kept where it now is." Such are his views, and calmly he awaits the forty-seven days longer, when, if his life is spared, he will fearlessly tell the millions of the land the line of policy he intends to pursue. He received a letter from General Wool a few days ago, saying to him, that he (General Wool) was commander of the eastern division of the United States army, and as the times were threatening, he desired Mr. Lincoln to say what forces he desired at the capital on the 4th of March, and they should be on hand. Mr. Lincoln said to me, "I never saw General Wool; but it was a most comforting letter, and I wrote to him in reply—' As you and General Scott are as well and better acquainted with the nature and extent of the dangers, and the necessary means to meet them, I take pleasure in committing all that to your discretion,' and so the matter rests."—*Newark Daily Mercury.*

Jan. 20.—There is no doubt that the command of the Southern Army has been offered to Jefferson Davis, and it is equally well understood that he is in a state of mind bordering on despair. He seems to be the only rational man among the secessionists, and clearly comprehends the terrible fate which must befall the South in the event of a conflict with the General Government. He does

---

[*] See Document II.

not disguise his gloomy apprehensions from his friends; and his only remaining hope is that war may be prevented, and the Union reconstructed. Mr. Davis was a fiery Secessionist ten years ago, but gradually the fires have died out, until his intelligent mind is left free to comprehend the perilous position to which the South, with its institution of Slavery, has been brought by the madness of her sons.—*Times, Jan. 23.*

SHERRARD CLEMENS, in his speech, on the 22d of January, treated the Republicans to a Democrat's opinion of that party, and paid his respects to the Abolitionists in strong terms of denunciation. When he attacked secession and showed his own section the disasters to them, and the loss consequent upon dissolution and the formation of two separate Confederacies, there was an intense excitement on the Democratic side. In the midst of this, his hour expired, and upon an attempt to extend his time, a boisterous scene ensued, which at one time threatened a row. Martin of Virginia, and Rust of Arkansas, attacked Clemens bitterly, in violation of the rules and orders of the House. Martin said: "Let him go on with his treason; we will teach the traitor when he gets to Virginia." Logan, of Illinois, replied: "If his speech is treason, there is no man in Virginia who can answer it." Foulk, of Illinois, insisted upon Clemens going on. Rust and Hindman, of Arkansas, declared he should not, and upon an attempt being made to give him leave, first the Southern men very discourteously refused it. Their excited behavior showed that he had told the truth, and touched them to the quick.—*Times, Jan. 23.*

HOW THE RUMOR OF AN ATTACK ON THE BROOKLYN NAVY YARD GREW.

AN Irishman named Patrick Meed wished to obtain work in the Navy Yard, and fancying that Jas. E. Kerrigan might have some influence in that quarter, he solicited it; and the two went over the river together to see what could be done. When there, the first application was made to the "boss laborer," who informed them that his department was full at present. From thence they went to the machine shop; but met with no better success. Kerrigan said to his companion, "Let us take a stroll down to the dock," the object being to see if work might not be found in that direction. As they went along the Irishman said, "This damned place ought to be burned up." The expression uttered by the companion of Kerrigan was enough, in the opinion of a few laborers who overheard it, to fix the idea in their minds that "something was afloat;" and as they talked one with the other, the molehill began soon to assume the dimensions of a mountain. When the laborers left the yard a rumor spread around the city—doubtless by a word or two dropped in such and such a store, then amended, added to and reorganized, until the whole city was alarmed—and the "authenticated" fact that James E. Kerrigan was at the head of a large and secret army, and intended to take and burn down the navy yard, was universally believed. The police were augmented and the militia ordered out, because a man in the heat of his temper, caused by disappointment and chagrin, uttered one simple hasty expression. But during the silent midnight hours, at which the attack was to be made, where

was Kerrigan? The worthy "leader of ten thousand rebels" was quietly enjoying himself at the Brennan coterie, held in Irving Hall, completely unconscious of his great and elevated position. He was seen by many persons to be in the building from an early hour in the evening till four o'clock next morning, and certainly did not seem to have on his mind so mighty a plan as the seizure of the federal property of this State. In fact, the next morning he could scarcely believe his own eyes, as he read the startling news in the city papers, and expressed surprise how his name could have got mixed up in the affair. But as J. E. K. is a boy full of deviltry and nonsense, he fancied that he might have joked upon the subject, until the above facts came to his remembrance, when he soon discovered the "nigger in the woodpile."—*Herald, Jan. 26.*

Jan. 24.—Advices from Charleston are, that the British Consul at Charleston has been instructed, and that the British Consul at New Orleans will be instructed, to certify to all clearances that may be issued from those ports. Also that the British and French Governments will recognize a Southern Confederacy.—*Charleston Mercury.*

Jan. 27.—Mr. Winthrop, one of the Boston Union Committee, called on Senator Mason, and, referring to his former visit to Massachusetts, remarked in the blandest tones, "I hope, Mr. Mason, we shall see you again at Bunker Hill." To which the Senator stiffly jerked out the response—"Not unless I come as an ambassador, sir."—*Times.*

Jan. 29.—The Cincinnati *Commercial* states that George N. Sanders, is at Louisville assuming to be the mouth-piece of Judge Douglas, and, as such, advising the immediate secession of the border States, with a view to "reconstruction."

Feb. 1.—Lieut. James E. Jouett reported himself at Washington, to Secretary Toucey. Lieut. Jouett is attached to the steamer Crusader, now in the Gulf, but was temporarily employed on the Wyandotte. He went ashore at Pensacola, and was immediately seized as a prisoner, but released on parol of honor, not to bear arms against the State of Florida, and a passport was furnished him. Having proceeded to New Orleans, with the hope of being able to join his vessel from that point, he was again threatened by Collector Hatch with arrest, unless he departed speedily. The next train found him *en route* for Washington. After hearing the statement, Secretary Toucey requested the statement to be committed to writing, as the position of Jouett is a novel one. This statement has been made, and, with the passport, laid before the Government. Jouett does not consider his parole binding, should the Department order him back to the Gulf. He silently received his passport, but gave no promise whatever.—*N. Y. Times, Feb. 2.*

A MONKEY over an open powder magazine would represent, with tolerable exactness, the late conduct and present position of the President of the once United States. No great confederacy, or family of states, was ever before cursed with a President so utterly ignorant of the real character of the people and principles he was called on to rule or direct.—*Charleston Mercury, Feb. 2.*

"ETHAN SPIKE" writes, that Hornby has "seceded," and that he consequently resigns his seat in the Maine Legislature. The following resolutions were passed at a public meeting of the new "sovereignty":

Resolved, That we are opposed to koertion, except when exercised by ourselves.

Resolved, That the okepation of the Baldwin lightus, by a State keeper, is a irritatin' circumstance, an' onless he is withdrawn, aour army be instructed to take possession of the same in the name of the taoun.

Resolved, That ef aour reasonable demands is not complied to, that we will take possession of, an' hold *for aour own use*, the State's prison, and the insane assylum.

Resolved, That the haybius korpus act, taxes, an' the Main law be an' is suspended. Also an ordnance relating to weights and measures as used in the likker trade. Be it enacted, That henceforth and for ever, in this ere realm, *every quart pot shall hold a gallon*.

Ordered that the foregoin' articles shall be the constitution of this suvrinty.—*Portland Transcript.*

THERE is good reason to believe that Maj. Anderson has received a very considerable accession to the forces under his command. A correspondent states that he has reliable authority for asserting that ten or twelve officers and about three hundred men have been introduced into the fort, within the last fortnight. They are supposed to have been taken down by the *Brooklyn*, and to have been landed at night in small boats with muffled oars. This, if true, will account for the reports which, from time to time, have emanated from Charleston, of small boats having been seen at night rowing in the neighborhood of the fort. We may mention, as corroborative of this report, the fact, that letters have been received in this city from a gentleman who left here four weeks since, and is *now within Fort Sumter*. They are very guarded in their language, as if the writer did not repose unbounded confidence in the inviolability of letters intrusted to the Charleston Post-office. But of the fact that he has recently obtained access to the fort, and is now serving there under Maj. Anderson, there is no doubt whatever.—*N. Y. Times, Feb. 4.*

Feb. 12.—The Charleston *Courier* observes that, "The seceding States have pursued a brave, direct, decided course. They regard the United States as a foreign power. They are prepared to maintain a separate and independent nationality. If they are let alone they will never give Mr. Lincoln any trouble, and if the spirit of fanaticism is layed, and the North returns to its senses, they will establish intercourse with the Southern confederacy, and a better feeling will prevail between the two sections than has existed during the long period of their forced Union. But the patriotic and short-sighted compromisers propose to remain where they are and fight."

It continues: "The South *might*, after uniting, under a new confederacy, treat the disorganized and demoralized Northern States as *insurgents*, and deny them recognition. But if peaceful division ensues, the South, after taking the federal capital and archives, and being recognized by all foreign powers as the government *de facto*, can, if they see proper, recognize the Northern confederacy, or confederacies, and enter into treaty stipulations with them. Were this not done, it would be difficult for the Northern States to take a place among nations, and their flag would not be respected or recognized."

The Spartans, as the fierce people of the State of Laconia were generally called from their capital city, were this proverbially hard and undaunted people, small in number, but each man a host. Their narrow territory was peopled by two classes proper—laborers and fighters. The laborers were slaves and the freemen fighters. The South could detach one-half its whole male population to wage war, with as much ease as the North could one-fifth, and in case of need the proportionate array of fighters which we could marshal would astonish the world, and it would be still more astonished by the solvent prosperity of our condition when we came out of a contest requiring such effort. When they talk about coercing, conquering the South, let the valiant Northmen consider that every Southern State is several modern Laconias, and all the States a grand aggregate of Laconias, which we verily believe could defy the invading armies of the whole world.—*Mobile Advertiser.*

Feb. 14.—Some time ago it was gravely proposed in South Carolina to abolish the Fourth of July, and to select some other day for the annual occasion of blowing off the surplus patriotism of the Palmettoes. In the course of the popular revolt several favorite national airs were pronounced against, struck from the music books, and replaced by sundry French revolutionary melodies, with variations to suit the peculiar phases of South Carolina Jacobinism. More temperate counsels prevailed in Georgia, and the Savannah Republican, after commending the action of the Southern Confederacy in "reviving the government and constitution of the fathers," calls upon the Congress to re-erect "the stars and stripes" as their national flag, and resume upon the Southern lyre "those glorious old tunes, 'Hail Columbia,' and 'The Star-spangled Banner.'" Yesterday this question came up in the Congress. Mr. Brooke, of Mississippi, protested that the "stars and stripes" were the "idol of his heart," when Mr. Miles of South Carolina, who has been drawing his salary pretty regularly for several years from the federal government, said that he had always, even from the cradle, looked upon that flag as "the emblem of tyranny and oppression." We sincerely trust that these fugitive States, after having stolen our constitution, will not claim also our flag.—*Commercial Advertiser, Feb. 14.*

A NEW PHASE OF THE GEORGIA SEIZURES.

ACCORDING to the Savannah *Republican*, Governor Brown of Georgia acted hastily in seizing the New York vessels. Governor Morgan did *not* refuse to accede to the demand for the surrender of the arms seized by the police of this city. On receiving the telegraphic message from Governor Brown he wrote to inquire as to its authenticity; "and (says the *Republican*) so far as appears, he gave no intimation of his intention to refuse the demand for the arms." The same paper adds this significant paragraph, from which it is to be inferred that Governor Brown hoped to accomplish a master-stroke by an act of "devotion to the South," so as to strengthen his claims for a prominent place in the new Confederation:

"Under these circumstances it were impossible to beat it out of the brains of some uncharitable persons that our Governor, in his hasty proceedings, was *quite as intent on bringing something from Montgomery* as he was from New York. For ourselves, we pretend to no opinion on the subject."— *Evening Post, Feb. 15.*

A NEW SONG OF SIXPENCE.

Sing a song of Sumter,
 A Fort in Charleston bay;
Eight-and-sixty brave men
 Watch there night and day.

Those brave men to succor,
 Still no aid is sent;
Isn't James Buchanan
 A pretty President!

James is in his Cabinet
 Doubting and debating;
Anderson's in Sumter,
 Very tired of waiting.

Pickens is in Charleston,
 Blustering of blows;
Thank goodness March the Fourth is near,
 To nip Secession's nose.— *Vanity Fair.*

The following is one of Mr. Lincoln's stories. These he tells often in private conversation, rarely in his speeches:

"I once knew a good, sound churchman, whom we'll call Brown, who was on a committee to erect a bridge over a very dangerous and rapid river. Architect after architect failed, and at last Brown said he had a friend named Jones who had built several bridges and could build this. 'Let's have him in,' said the committee. In came Jones. 'Can you build this bridge, sir?' 'Yes,' replied Jones; 'I could build a bridge to the infernal regions, if necessary.' The sober committee were horrified; but when Jones retired, Brown thought it but fair to defend his friend. 'I know Jones so well,' said he, 'and he is so honest a man, and so good an architect, that, if he states soberly and positively that he can build a bridge to Hades—why, I believe it. But I have my doubts about the abutment on the infernal side.' 'So,' Lincoln added, 'when politicians said they could harmonize the Northern and Southern wings of the democracy, why, I believed them. But I had my doubts about the abutment on the Southern side.'"— *Commercial Advertiser.*

Feb. 25.—It is said that Jefferson Davis is at Charleston. Shortly after his arrival it was quietly arranged for him to pay a visit to Fort Sumter, which was accomplished privately. The interview is represented to have been an earnest and prolonged one, but all not immediately in the secret were left wholly to conjecture as to what took place between him and Major Anderson. It has, however, been knowingly given out at Charleston that there will be no fight at Fort Sumter—great stress evidently being placed upon the fact that these two old acquaintances in the army cannot be brought into bloody conflict with each other. On the other hand, it is believed that if the alleged visit had elicited any particular comfort for the great leader of the secession movement, such good news would not have been kept for private consumption merely. — *New York Times.*

A TRAVELLER passing through one of the counties of Tennessee, on horseback, stopped at a modest cottage on the roadside, and asked for shelter, as it was quite dark and raining. The "head of the family" came to the door, and accosted the traveller with, "What do you want?" "I want to stay all night," was the reply. "What are yer?" This interrogatory was not fully understood by the traveller, and he asked an explanation, "I mean what's yer politics?" rejoined the former. "Air yer fur this Union or agin it?" This was a poser, as the traveller was not certain whether the "man of the house" was a Union man or a secessionist, and he was anxious to "tie up" for the night; so he made up his mind and said, "My friend, I am for the Union." "Stranger, you kin kum in."— *N. Y. Herald.*

"The writer of an elaborate four-column article in the *Charleston Mercury* contends that the prohibition of the slave-trade by the provisional government at Montgomery is intolerable—that it must be rebelled against. He says that it sets a stain, a stigma, upon slavery itself, and is little if any better than abolition. The secession party has swallowed the apple of discord, and the seeds are vigorously sprouting in its stomach."

"Jeff. Davis, in his Montgomery speech, said: 'Fellow-citizens and brethren of the Confederate States of America—for now we are brethren not in name merely, but in fact—men of one flesh, one bone,' &c. The confederationists may be of one *bone* with their new President and Vice-President, but if they are of one *flesh* with them, they are the lankest nation of bipeds ever known to natural history."

"Save the Union, and make kindling wood of all your partisan platforms."

"The *Nashville Union*, having despaired of being able to sustain secession in Tennessee by any other means, has taken itself to *prayer.* Has it made a sufficient trial of cursing?"

"The *Memphis Appeal* says, that the four years of Mr. Lincoln's administration will be 'the reign of steel.' The four years of Mr. Buchanan's have been the reign of stealing."

"We don't think that South Carolina has any warrant for her conduct, but she evidently has a good deal of war-rant."

"A new national flag proposed for the Southern Confederacy bears in its centre the figure of a Phœnix in the act of rising from a bed of flame and ashes, with the motto, 'We rise again.' The Phœnix and the flame is thought to be beautifully typical of the death of the old and the resurrection of the new Union. We don't like the Phœnix as well as the snake, for if you cut off the tail of the latter it will wriggle a little after the separation, while the proposed bird of fable lives alone without a mate, and goes out like a pipe in its own ashes. But the confederated South should remember the history of another Phœnix, son to a king of Argos, who ingratiated himself into the favors of his father's mistress, and was deprived of his eyesight by divine vengeance."— *Louisville Journal.*

JEFFERSON DAVIS is a prim, smooth-looking man, with a precise manner, a stiff, soldierly carriage, and an austerity that is at first forbidding. He has naturally, however, a genial temper, companionable qualities, and a disposition that endears him to all by whom he may be surrounded. As a speaker he is clear, forcible and argumentative; his voice is clear and firm, without tremor.

ALEXANDER H. STEPHENS from childhood has been afflicted with four abscesses and a continued derangement of the liver, which gives him a consumptive appearance though his lungs are sound. He has never weighed over ninety-six pounds, and to see his attenuated figure bent over his desk, the shoulders contracted, and the shape of his slender limbs visible through his garments, a stranger would ever select him as the "John Randolph" of our time, more dreaded as an adversary and more prized as an ally in a debate than any other member of the House of Representatives. He is a careful student, but so very careful that no trace of study is perceptible as he dashes along in a flow of facts, arguments and language that to common minds is almost bewildering. He has the appearance of having undergone great bodily anguish, and his advanced age and gray hairs contribute to give to his eye a restless nervous movement. His size is medium, and figure remarkably slim. His forehead is much wrinkled, and his locks flow over the shoulders, which stoop very much. A habit of wearing the hat advanced to the left gives to his whole contour an appearance at once remarkable and prepossessing.—*Herald, March 4.*

"SUMTER is to be ours without a fight," says the *Charleston Mercury.* "All will be rejoiced that the blood of our people is not to be shed in our harbor, in either small or great degree. To those who have troubled themselves with vague fears of war on a large scale, and the horrors of war extensively, the relief will be as great as the apprehension has been grievous. For ourselves, notwithstanding all the Northern thunder, we have never been able to bring ourselves seriously to believe in the probability of any more than a few collisions, sufficient to show that we are in earnest, and competent to make good our position of independence against our would-be masters. These gentry 'hold our valor light,' as also the honesty of the determination of the Southern peoples to be quit of them and their impertinent and detrimental interference through a government in common. It may, perhaps, yet be necessary to instruct them a little in these particulars. But it appears that for the present, under the circumstances in this case, they are inclined sensibly to dispense with experiment and its teachings. How far this discretion will revivify the hopes and stimulate the efforts of Reconstructionists throughout the South, is a matter to be discovered by observation. The temper and intention of the Northern people has now been so thoroughly developed and exposed to the eyes of all those at the South who will see, that we trust Union-menders are too late in their attempts upon the virtue and integrity of our people. Crushed eggshells and friendship abused can never be mended. We have no doubt, however, that herculean efforts will be made in that direction, and must only take good care of these weaker brethren at the South, whose sentiments are stronger than their reason, or who live in the past rather than the future. The strait-jacket was a valuable invention.

But, in the mean time, the prospect of having Sumter is very pleasant."

THE editor of the Norwich (Ct.) *Bulletin,* sent Jefferson Davis, the President of the "Six Nations," a pen-holder made from a rafter of the house in which Benedict Arnold was born. In closing his letter of presentation the editor says: "I have taken occasion to present you this pen-holder, as a relic whose associations are linked most closely to the movement of which you are the head. Let it lie upon your desk for use in your official duties. In the 'eternal fitness of things,' let that be its appropriate place. It links 1780 with 1861. Through it, West Point speaks to Montgomery. And if we may believe that spirits do ever return and haunt this mundane sphere, we may reckon with what delight Benedict Arnold's immortal part will follow this fragment of his paternal roof-tree to the hands in which is being consummated the work which he began."

NEARLY all the favorites of Mr. Buchanan are engaged in the secession conspiracy. The monstrous transaction of Twiggs, in Texas, which bears the double character of unmitigated treason and individual dishonesty, has been long in process, and the celebrated Ben McCullough, one of Mr. Buchanan's most intimate friends, has been engaged in it. His household editor, William M. Browne, is at Montgomery, assisting disunion with all his ability, while his late Secretary of the Treasury, his late Secretary of War, his late Secretary of the Interior, and most of those who advocated his policy in Congress, either hold position under the Southern Confederacy, or occupy prominent places in the organization which sustains it."—*Phila. Press.*

THE city of New York has to employ fourteen hundred extra mounted policemen constantly, to keep the enormous crowds of starving people in that city from committing acts of violence.—*Charleston Courier.*

CONFEDERATES AND UNITED STATESMEN.—The southern secessionists must be admitted to be blest with at least the philosophical virtue of self-knowledge. They term their new league the "Confederate States of America." Thus they call themselves by what they doubtless feel to be their right name. They are confederates in the crime of upholding slavery. A correct estimate of their moral position is manifest in that distinctive denomination of theirs—"Confederate States." This title is a beautiful antithesis to that of the United States of America. The more doggedly confederate slave-mongers combine, the more firmly good republicans should unite.—*London Punch.*

LETTER FROM UNITED STATES SENATOR LANE.—We have great pleasure in publishing the following letter from that brilliant statesman, the Hon. Joseph Lane, of Oregon. It may seem somewhat paradoxical that a Pacific statesman should be ferociously warlike, but that is evidently none of our business. We cannot comply with Mr. Lane's request in regard to hoisting the Palmetto flag, but we will say that we admire his (we allude to Mr. Lane, and not the flag, of course) boldness, candor, and eloquence:

SENIT CHAMBIR, Washington, {
March the thurd, 18 & 60 *onct.* }

Eds. Vannurty Faire—if god spairs my live I shall seeseed with in 20 dase. jonson of tennysea is fernenst me, but he haint got no intellect into him. Sivil war is sertin & I wants to here the Kannin Rore. Hist the Palmettoe banner from on top your offiis & let it waive to the Brees. Don't mucillate this mannerscript and be particular not to maike no Misstaiks in the spellin and punktooate it proper, amerykan Staitsmen suffers from scrofulus papers which tries to bring them into ridicool by mucillatin there mannerscripts.

On to the frey! the god of Bottles smiles upon the palmettoe flag.

yours respectaply,   GOSEF LANE.
—*Vanity Fair.*

AN INCIDENT AT THE FORTS.—At an early hour yesterday morning, while the gunners were firing blank cartridges from the guns of the Iron Battery at Cumming's Point, one of the guns, loaded with ball, the men not being aware of the fact, was discharged. The ball struck the wharf of Fort Sumter, close to the gate. This, it appears, caused some excitement in the garrison of Sumter, for three or four of the ports fronting Cumming's Point were soon after thrown open. No warlike reply to the unintentional shot was given, however; and about two hours afterwards a boat was sent over to explain the occurrence to Major Anderson. The Major received the messenger in good part, and thus the matter ended, after having caused no little talk at the harbor forts and in the city.—*Charleston Mercury,* 19th *March.*

WASHINGTON, *March* 10.—The question of reinforcing Fort Sumter has been under consideration in the Cabinet, and it is understood that the question whether or no it is not desirable to withdraw all the troops, except two or three men, rather than incur the bloodshed which will probably occur before troops and supplies are put into it, is now to be decided.

The immediate necessity of settling this question, grows out of the fact, that there is only a limited supply of bread at Fort Sumter, but plenty of salt meat, and that it must either be re-supplied or abandoned very soon. The question has been under discussion in high military circles for several days.

Gen. Scott advises that reinforcements cannot now be put in, without an enormous sacrifice of life. Of course his views on the subject, cannot be known officially to the public; but he is understood to say that we have neither military nor naval force at hand, sufficient to supply the fort against the threatened opposition, which it would require twenty thousand men to overcome. Besides, if it should initiate civil war, in addition to uniting the South and overwhelming the Union sentiment there in the waves of passion, it would require two hundred and fifty thousand Government soldiers to carry on the struggle, and a hundred millions of money to begin with. In such an event, twenty thousand men would be needed to preserve Washington and the Government archives.

The general impression here on the streets is that the Administration has determined on withdrawing the troops from Fort Sumter, leaving only one Corporal, two men, and the Stars and Stripes, compell

ing the chivalry to capture the fort after all. They have been threatening to do it for three months, and failed when there were only about seventy men in it. They may have an opportunity to accomplish it against only three.—*Times, March* 11.

IN New York city a bill was found posted on the sheriff's bulletin, this morning, for recruits for the army of Georgia. Its appearance in the absence of any local excitement, created considerable amusement. The bill had the appearance of having been folded in a letter, and its recipient doubtless stuck it up among the sheriff's auction notices for a "sell."—*Commercial Advertiser, March* 7.

THE authority of the Government of the United States has been called in question, to a greater or less extent, on eleven different occasions, viz. :—

The first was in 1782, and was a conspiracy of several officers of the Federal army to consolidate the thirteen States into one, and confer the supreme power on Washington.

The second was in 1787, called "Shay's Insurrection," in Massachusetts.

The third was in 1794, popularly called "The Whisky Insurrection of Pennsylvania."

The fourth was in 1814, by the Hartford Convention Federalists.

The fifth—on which occasion the different sections of the Union came into collision—was in 1820, under the administration of President Monroe, and occurred on the question of the admission of Missouri into the Union.

The sixth was a collision between the Legislature of Georgia and the Federal Government, in regard to certain lands, given by the latter to the Creek Indians.

The seventh was in 1820, with the Cherokees, in Georgia.

The eighth was the memorable nullifying ordinance of South Carolina, in 1832.

The ninth was in 1842, and occurred in Rhode Island, between the "Suffrage Association" and the State authorities.

The tenth was in 1856, on the part of the Mormons, who resisted Federal authority.

The eleventh, the present (1861) rebellion in the Southern States.

COLONEL DONALD, of Leake county, Mississippi, recently gave a novel party to the young people of his neighborhood. The ticket sent to each young lady, required that she should come dressed in Mississippi manufactured apparel, in the manufacture of which she must in some way assist. The young gentlemen were also required to dress in the manufacture of Mississippi, made in Leake and Attala. There were nearly one hundred persons of both sexes in attendance, all attired as directed. The scene was not brilliant, but the papers say it was patriotic.—*Evening Post, March* 29.

THE *Charleston Courier* is credibly informed that Gov. BROWN of Georgia, has attached the Northern stock in the Macon and Western Railroad, amounting to about one million of dollars.—*Times Telegram, March* 10.

March 21.—Old Abe's administration is just now in a most woeful fix. If coercion is attempted towards the seceded States, the Border Slave States will go out of the Union, and the country will be lost. If a pacific policy is adopted, the Chicago platform will go to pieces, and the Black Republican party will be broken into fragments. The President's position may now be likened to an intoxicated individual, who was one very cold night holding on to a spile on the edge of the dock, and who thus moralized: "If I hold on here," said he, "I shall certainly freeze to death, and if I let go I shall fall in the water and be drowned."—*Charleston Mercury.*

WHAT is martial law? Few there are who understand the full significance of this term. At this time, a correct understanding of its meaning is unusually important.

Martial law is defined by Bouvier, as "a code established for the government of the army and navy of the United States," whose principal rules are to be found in the articles of war, prescribed by act of Congress. But Chancellor Kent says, this definition applies only to *military* law, while martial law is quite a distinct thing, and is founded on paramount necessity, and produced by a military chief.

Martial law is generally and vaguely held to be, a suspension of all ordinary civil rights and process— and, as such, approximates closely to a military despotism.

It is an arbitrary law, originating in emergencies. In times of extreme peril to the State, either from without or from within, the public welfare demands extraordinary measures. And martial law being proclaimed, signifies that the operation of the ordinary legal delays of justice are suspended by the military power, which has for the time become supreme.

It suspends the operation of the writ of *habeas corpus;* enables persons charged with treason to be summarily tried by court-martial, instead of grand jury; justifies searches and seizures of private property, and the taking possession of public high-ways and other means of communication. Involving the highest exercise of sovereignty, it is of course, capable of great abuse; and it is only to be justified in emergencies of the most imperative and perilous nature, such as now appear to exist in Baltimore and Washington.

WASHINGTON, *March* 26.—Capt. Fox, who visited Fort Sumter on the requisition of the War Department, has returned here and reported the result of his mission. It is very well understood that he had a plan for introducing reinforcements, which had been submitted to members of the Cabinet, and was regarded as measurably practicable, but attended with the probability if not certainty of collision, which constituted the chief objection to its adoption. He is perfectly familiar with all the approaches to the harbor of Charleston, having been long connected with the Coast Survey, and had practical experience as the commander of one of Aspinwall's steamers. His scheme did not contemplate any serious danger in running the gauntlet of the batteries on the islands which guard the channels, but only in landing the men and provisions at Sumter, after it had been reached. If a fire was opened upon his transports from Fort Moultrie or the other batteries, it would be necessary for Sumter to silence them in order to discharge the reinforcements. Any attempt, therefore, looking to that object would almost inevitably lead to bloodshed, and be-

fore resorting to it, the Administration would be constrained to expect that alternative. Even if successful without great loss of life, nothing would be gained but the retention of a fortress which has only a local value in protecting Charleston, and is of no national moment whatever.

Capt. Fox is fully impressed with the courage, integrity and sincerity of Major Anderson, with whom, however, his communication was necessarily limited, as Gov. Pickens sent Capt. Hartstein, late of our Navy, as an escort with him to the fort, who kept within earshot during most of the interview, or at least, near enough to prevent any free communication. He considers that the fort can be reinforced either by a military operation, which, of course, would require a force not at the disposal of the President, or by the strategy already referred to, with its attendant hazards of a desperate conflict. The supply of provisions now in the garrison, will probably enable Major Anderson to sustain his command reasonably well until the 15th of April. From all the facts disclosed by this investigation, it is manifest that Fort Sumter must be abandoned, or civil war inaugurated. Capt. Fox is cautious, intelligent and well-informed, and was brought to the notice of the government by Mr. Aspinwall and some of the principal ship-owners of New York and Boston.—*N. Y. Tribune.*

THE HEIGHT OF IMPUDENCE.—Parson Brownlow thus felicitously describes "the height of impudence."

"An Alabama secession paper inquires if the border States know what is 'The Height of Impudence?' We answer for the border States, that it is to see and hear a man swaggering and swearing in every crowd he enters, that he will go out of the Union because he can't get his rights, by having the privilege guaranteed to take slaves in the Territories, when in fact, he does not own a negro in the world, never did, and never will; and withal can't get credit in any store in the country where he lives, for a wool hat or a pair of brogans!"

NEW YORK, *April* 3.—It is reported from New-Orleans that the Mexican General Ampudia was marching to invade Texas with 3,000 men, and that he had declared the State to belong to Mexico by right, and as it was no longer defended by the Union, a good opportunity was offered to Mexico to reassert her authority.—*N. Y. Tribune.*

March 31.—Mr. George N. Sanders telegraphed to-day from Montgomery, a special despatch to the N. Y. Tribune, that "Newport is again to become the commercial rival of New York. If Sprague is elected Governor of Rhode Island, that plucky little State will at once abandon the old hulk of the Union, offering at once a commercial depot and a summer residence for Southerners. The estimated value of the traffic thus diverted from New York, may be set down at $50,000,000 annually, so long as the latter remains in the Union.

"Fort Pickens will soon be reduced to the same condition as Fort Sumter. Glorious accounts come from all parts of the New Confederation."—*New York Tribune, April* 1.

AN interesting incident is told, concerning the independent and successful stand taken by a woman in New Orleans, on behalf of the Union. She and her husband—a Mississippi steamboat captain —occupied the middle front room of the lowest range of sleeping apartments in the St. Charles Hotel, at the time when the city was to be illuminated in honor of secession. She refused to allow the illuminating candles to be fixed in the windows of her room, and the proprietors remonstrated in vain—she finally ordering them to leave the room, of which she claimed, while its occupant, to have entire control. The rest of the story is thus told:—

"Determined not to be outdone in a matter of such grave importance, the captain, who was not in the room during the above proceedings, was next found and appealed to. He heard their case; said his wife had reported him correctly on the Union question, nevertheless, he would go with them to the room and see if the matter could be amicably arranged. The captain's disposition to yield was not to be seconded by his better half. The proprietors next proposed to vacate the best chamber in her favor, in some other part of the house, if that would be satisfactory; but the lady's 'No!' was still as peremptory as ever. Her point was gained, and the St. Charles was doomed to have a dark front chamber. Pleased with this triumph, Mrs. —— devised the following manoeuvre to make the most of her victory.—Summoning a servant, she sent him out to procure for her an American flag, which, at dusk, she suspended from her window. When evening came the streets, animated by a merry throng, were illuminated, but, alas! the St. Charles was disfigured by its sombre chamber, when suddenly a succession of lamps, suspended on both sides of the flag, revealing the stars and stripes, were lit up, and the ensign of *the Union* waved from the centre of a hotel illuminated in honor of its overthrow! The effect was, to give the impression that the whole house was thus paying homage to the American flag; and what is more significant, is the fact that the latter was greeted by the passing crowd with vociferous applause. So much for the firmness of a true Union woman."—*Phila. Press.*

The Missouri *Democrat* has a letter from a soldier at Fort Smith, Ark., bearing the date of March 5, in which the following passage occurs:

"Yesterday the citizens of Fort Smith raised a Palmetto flag in town, and one of the soldiers, private Bates, company E, First cavalry, went out and climbed up the tree upon which the flag was suspended, took it down and brought it into the garrison. Captain Sturgiss ordered him to take it and put it back where he got it. He said he never would. The captain ordered him to the guard house, and in going he tore the flag in pieces. He was then ordered to be put in irons, and was sent to the blacksmith shop for that purpose; but the smith (a citizen) refused to put them on, and he was discharged in consequence. D company, First cavalry, farrier was then ordered to put them on, and *he* refused, and was sent to the guard-house. E company, First cavalry, farrier then put them on. The soldiery then gave three shouts for Bates, and the blacksmith who refused to put the irons on."—*The World, April 1.*

"My son," said a New York merchant, to his heir and namesake, on Thursday, "I would rather give $1,000 than have you go to Washington soldiering." "Father," was the kindly but decisive response, "if you could make it $100,000 it would be of no use; for where the Seventh Regiment goes, I go."—*Tribune, April 20.*

It is not an insignificant sign of the feeling at New York, in regard to the course of affairs, that not only do Government Six per cents stand firm on the Stock Exchange in the face of the cannonade of Fort Sumter, but when Kentucky Sixes were called to-day, the whole Board sprang to their feet, and gave three long cheers for the gallant Major Anderson.

It is also a noticeable feature that when one of the members of the Board offered to sell Government Stock "short" on time, he was instantly hissed down.—*Evening Post, April 12.*

A CHARLESTON despatch states that "the first shot from Stevens's battery was fired by the venerable Edmund Ruffin of Virginia." A piece of the first hemp that is stretched in South Carolina should be kept for the neck of this venerable and bloodthirsty Ruffian.—*Idem, April 13.*

BALTIMORE, *April* 13.—A man made his appearance on the streets in this city this morning, wearing a large secession cockade on his hat. He was pursued by a crowd, and had to be protected by the police.—*Idem.*

April 13.—Among the ridiculous rumors to day, are the following: that the South Carolinians "have made a breach in Fort Sumter;" that Senator Chesnut fired a shot, "as an experiment," and made a hole in the wall of the Fort; that Major Anderson is the guest of General Beauregard, and that Senator Wigfall received the sword and returned it to Maj. Anderson.—*Tribune, April 16.*

April 11.—The President received a letter from St. Louis directed to "Old ABE or any other man." On one side was the Confederacy flag, on the other the seal and flag of the United States, with the words "played out." Inside was a five-dollar note on the Union Bank of South Carolina, "to help pay the expenses of reinforcing Fort Sumter.—*Times, April 12.*

An incident occurred during the cannonading, of Fort Sumter, which, for its peculiarity, deserves particular mention. Roger A. Pryor, of Virginia, ex-Member of Congress, was one of the second deputation that waited upon Major Anderson. He was the very embodiment of Southern chivalry. Literally dressed to kill, bristling with bowie-knives and revolvers, like a walking arsenal, he appeared to think himself individually capable of capturing the fort, without any extraneous assistance. Inside of the fort he seemed to think himself master of every thing—monarch of all he surveyed—and, in keeping with this pretension, seeing upon the table what appeared to be a glass of brandy, drank it without ceremony. Surgeon Crawford, who had witnessed the feat, approached him and said: "Sir, what you have drank is poison—*you are a dead man.*" The representative of chivalry instantly collapsed, bowie-knives, revolvers and all, and passed into the hands of Surgeon Crawford, who, by purgings, pumpings, and pukings, defeated his own prophecy in regard to his fate. Mr. Pryor left Fort Sumter "a wiser, if not a better man."—*N. Y. Tribune, April* 19.

" WHEN the State of Maine arrived at Fort Monroe with the Massachusetts troops, the Virginian residents around the fort, who were all Secessionists, were very much surprised, enraged and mortified. They collected around the captain of the steamer, who is as cool and intrepid a specimen of a Yankee as New England contains, and told him significantly, that the troops would never go back to Massachusetts. He replied that that was the last thing they thought of; that the country was so fine they intended to settle, and send for their friends, and he was going to New York to get another load. Another set, belonging to an armed schooner, engaged in enforcing the local laws of Virginia, insolently claimed the right of searching the State of Maine for negroes. The captain told them they should not go aboard to take out anybody, black or white. They replied that, by the laws of Virginia they had the right of search. He retorted that they knew nothing about the laws of Virginia, but sailed by the laws and under the flag of the United States. He also assured them, if there were any negroes there who were desirous of a voyage to New York, he should be very happy to accommodate them, and closed the conversation by saying—'You have been preaching all your lives that the Yankees are a pack of misers and cowards, who won't fight; now you'll have a favorable opportunity to test the accuracy of your opinions on that point.' "—*Boston Transcript.*

THE people of the North have had good reason to complain of the hoaxing done by the telegraph; but the way in which the people of the South have been humbugged is positively shocking. All over the South, they had, on the morning of the 20th, the resignation of Gen. Scott; his joining Virginia; the defeat of the New York 7th Regiment with an immense loss; capture of Norfolk Navy Yard, and Harper's Ferry Arsenal; the probable resignation of President Lincoln—in fact, the utter discomfiture of the North. The *Natchez Free Trader* says: "Forthwith our citizens thronged the streets, the bells of all the churches and public buildings rang out a long-continued, merry peal, sky rockets and other fireworks lit up the night, guns were fired, the cannon roared and the people shouted most lustily and harmoniously. A grand mass meeting, gathered in ten minutes' notice, was held at the Court House, which with its surrounding grounds and the adjoining streets, was thronged. Speeches were made by sundry citizens, interrupted by frequent applause and cheering. Natchez never was so grand, nor her people so jubilant. The pen fails to make the record a just one. We are hoarse with shouting and exalted with jubilancy."—*N. Y. Tribune, April* 23.

MR. GEORGE N. SANDERS, who is now in Montgomery, telegraphs from there yesterday, that " in order to prevent anarchy and war *the Democrats at the north should at once rebel* and accept the constitution of the Confederate States." How the rebellion of a political minority against the lawful government can prevent anarchy and war is somewhat difficult to conceive. But what means this well known Democrat by the term " should at *once* rebel "? Is it only a matter of time? Is the Democratic party pledged to rebellion, and only waits the occasion? Who will explain.—*Commercial Advertiser, April* 11.

WHEN the Massachusetts agent sent to Mr. Stetson for his bill against that State, he received the following reply:

ASTOR HOUSE, NEW YORK, April 27, 1861.

GOV. ANDREW, *Massachusetts.*

DEAR SIR:—The Astor House has no charge for feeding Massachusetts troops.

Yours, respectfully,

STETSON & CO.

—*Tribune.*

THE Mobile *Mercury* says that the South Carolinians "will have to learn to be a little more conforming to the opinions of others, before they can expect to associate comfortably with even the cotton States, under a federative government." It is pleasing to see that Alabama is so rapidly getting acquainted with her Palmetto sister.—*Prov. Jour.*

J. C. WRIGHT of Oswego, from Washington, says that General Scott remarked to a group of gentlemen, who pointed to him the report about his resignation:—" He could more easily believe that they would trample the American flag in the dust than he be suspected of resignation at this hour of trial. No, sirs! please God, I will fight for many years yet for this Union, and that, too, under the protecting folds of the star spangled banner."—*Exeter News Letter, May* 6.

THE Skowhegan (Me.) *Clarion* says, that some ladies of that village " got out the field-piece and fired a salute of thirty-four guns." Can you find ladies elsewhere, that have their courage?

COL. PRENTIS, the commanding officer at Cairo received the following despatch from three of the most prominent citizens of Cincinnati:

" General Pillow has several steamers ready at Memphis. He meditates an immediate attack on Cairo, Illinois."

Col. Prentiss replied:

" Let him come. He will learn to dig his ditch on the right side. I am ready."—*Portsmouth (N. H.) Ballot.*

EVEN the Quakers are aroused, as appears by the following:

A Quaker merchant in New York said to one of his clerks:

" Well, friend ——, is thee willing to enlist?"

" I have thought of it," replied the clerk, " but hesitated because I feared to lose my situation."

" If thee will enlist," replied the Quaker, " not only shall thee have thy situation, but thy salary shall go on while thee is absent. But if thee will not serve thy country, thee cannot stay in this store."

This is but a fair sample of the spirit now being displayed all over the free States. Can freedom be crushed out among such a people? Not all the Yanceys, Wigfalls and Jeff. Davises in creation could do it!—*Evening Post.*

IF the secessionists succeed in taking Fort Pickens, they *will* be acknowledged—a confederacy of Pickens *and stealings.*—*Punch.*

THE GREAT BELL ROLAND.

SUGGESTED BY THE PRESIDENT'S CALL FOR VOLUNTEERS.

[Motley relates that the famous bell Roland of Ghent was an object of great affection to the people, because it always rang to arm them when liberty was in danger.]

BY THEODORE TILTON.

I.

Toll! Roland, toll!
—High in St. Bavon's tower,
At midnight hour,
The great bell Roland spoke,
And all who slept in Ghent awoke.
—What meant its iron stroke?
Why caught each man his blade?
Why the hot haste he made?
Why echoed every street
With tramp of thronging feet—
All flying to the city's wall?
It was the call
Known well to all,
That Freedom stood in peril of some foe:
And even timid hearts grew bold
Whenever Roland tolled,
And every hand a sword could hold;—
For men
Were patriots then,
Three hundred years ago!

II.

Toll! Roland, toll!
Bell never yet was hung,
Between whose lips there swung
So true and brave a tongue!
—If men be patriots still,
At thy first sound
True hearts will bound,
Great souls will thrill—
Then toll! and wake the test
In each man's breast,
And let him stand confess'd!

III.

Toll! Roland, toll!
—Not in St. Bavon's tower
At midnight hour—
Nor by the Scheldt, nor far-off Zuyder Zee;
But here—this side the sea!—
And here in broad, bright day!
Toll! Roland, toll!
For not by night awaits
A brave foe at the gates,
But Treason stalks abroad—inside!—at noon!
Toll! Thy alarm is not too soon!
To Arms! Ring out the Leader's call!
Re-echo it from East to West,
Till every dauntless breast
Swell beneath plume and crest!
Toll! Roland, toll!
Till swords from scabbards leap!
Toll! Roland, toll!
—What tears can widows weep
Less bitter than when brave men fall?
Toll! Roland, toll!

Till cottager from cottage-wall
Snatch pouch and powder-horn and gun—
The heritage of sire to son,
Ere half of Freedom's work was done!
Toll! Roland, toll!
Till son, in memory of his sire,
Once more shall load and fire!
Toll! Roland, toll!
Till volunteers find out the art
Of aiming at a traitor's heart!

IV.

Toll! Roland, toll!
—St. Bavon's stately tower
Stands to this hour,—
And by its side stands Freedom yet in Ghent;
For when the bells now ring,
Men shout, "God save the King!"
Until the air is rent!
—Amen!—So let it be;
For a true king is he
Who keeps his people free.
Toll! Roland, toll!
This side the sea!
No longer they, but we,
Have now such need of thee!
Toll! Roland, toll!
And let thy iron throat
Ring out its warning note,
Till Freedom's perils be outbraved,
And Freedom's flag, wherever waved,
Shall overshadow none enslaved!
Toll! till from either ocean's strand,
Brave men shall clasp each other's hand,
And shout, "God save our native land!"
—And love the land which God hath saved!
Toll! Roland, toll!

—*The Independent*, April 18.

THE SENTINEL OF THE SEVENTY-FIRST.

BY J. B. BACON.

In the midnight zenith gleam the stars.
Swift as their rays my soul speeds on,
Leaping the streams and the forest bars,
On to the heights of Washington.
There on the star-lit camp-guard's round,
Footfalls I hear of a sentinel,
Steps that I love, and the welcome sound
Of a voice I know—it cries, "All's well!"

"Well!" for our land and our starry flag;
"Well!" for the rights and the hopes of man,
Echoes from plain and from mountain crag,
"Well! all's well!" from the army's van.
Sons of our homes! while the smiles ye love
Prayerfully float round your banners of war,
Look, 'mid the gleam of your bayonets, above!
God holds the guerdon of Victory's star!

—*N. Y. Tribune*, May 3.

WORK TO DO.

BY R. H. STODDARD.

From the North and the West,
That are joined, heart and hand,
For the flag of their sires,
And the laws of the land,

Come forth, ye free men,
    That are loyal thereto,
For Freedom has work
    For her children to do!

Not the work that ye know,
    That is best for the free,
Sowing towns in new lands,
    Ploughing ships through the sea;
Ye are perfect in this—
    It is old; but the new—
'Tis a grim work your sires
    Left their children to do!

Could they speak from their graves,
    They would shout to their sons:
"Leave your ploughs, drop your tools,
    Run, and shoulder your guns!
Ye must march to the South,
    Ye must cut your way through,
Or—leave the stern work
    For your children to do!"

We hear the alarm,
    Like the lightning it runs,
And thousands of freemen
    Have shouldered their guns;
They will fall on the South,
    They will crush and subdue,
Nor leave the sad work
    For their children to do!

For the North and the West,
    They have taken their stand
For the flag that they love,
    And the laws of the land!
They'll maintain them till death,
    Ay, and after it, too;
For they'll still leave the work
    Which their children will do!

May 6, 1861.   —*The World.*

"ALL WE ASK IS TO BE LET ALONE."

As vonce I valked by a dismal swamp,
There sot an old Cove in the dark and damp,
And at everybody as passed that road
A stick or a stone this Old Cove throwed.
And venever he flung his stick or his stone,
He'd set up a song of "Let me alone."

"Let me alone, for I loves to shy
These bits of things at the passers-by;
Let me alone, for I've got your tin,
And lots of other traps snugly in;
Let me alone—I am rigging a boat
To grab votever you've got afloat;
In a veek or so I expects to come
And turn you out of your ouse and ome;
I'm a quiet Old Cove," says he, with a groan;
"All I axes, is, Let me alone."

Just then came along, on the self-same vay,
Another Old Cove, and began for to say—
"Let you alone! That's comin' it strong!
You've *ben* let alone—a darned sight too long!
Of all the sarce that ever I heerd!
Put down that stick! (You may well look skeered.)
Let go that stone! If you once show fight,
I'll knock you higher than ary kite.

You must have a lesson to stop your tricks,
And cure you of shying them stones and sticks;
And I'll have my hardware back, and my cash,
And knock your scow into tarnal smash;
And if ever I catches you round my ranch,
I'll string you up to the nearest branch.
The best you can do is to go to bed,
And keep a decent tongue in your head;
For I reckon, before you and I are done,
You'll wish you had let honest folks alone."

The Old Cove stopped, and the t'other Old Cove,
He sot quite still in his cypress grove,
And he looked at his stick, revolvin' slow,
Vether 'twere safe to shy it, or no;
And he grumbled on, in an injured tone,
"All that I axed vos, *Let me alone.*"

                    —*Hartford Courant.*

ORIGINAL ODE,

*Sung at the Union and State Rights Celebration, at
    Charleston, S. C., July 4th,* 1831.

Hail, our country's natal morn!
Hail, our spreading kindred born!
Hail, thou banner, not yet torn,
    Waving o'er the free!
While this day in festal throng,
Millions swell the patriot song,
Shall not we thy notes prolong,
    Hallowed jubilee?

Who would sever freedoms shrine?
Who would draw the invidious line?
Though by birth one spot be mine,
    Dear is all the rest;—
Dear to me the South's fair land,
Dear the central mountain-band,
Dear New England's rocky strand,
    Dear the prairied West.

By our altars, pure and free,
By our Law's deep-rooted tree,
By the past's dread memory,
    By our WASHINGTON!
By our common parent tongue,
By our hopes, bright, buoyant, young,
By the tie of country strong,
    We will still be ONE.

Fathers! have ye bled in vain?
Ages! must ye droop again?
MAKER! must we rashly stain
    Blessings sent by THEE?
No! receive our solemn vow,
While before Thy throne we bow,
Ever to maintain as now,
    "UNION—LIBERTY."

                    —*Commercial Advertiser.*

THE NEW BIRTH,

APRIL 15TH, A. D. 1861.

Ring out the tidings round the earth,
To all the families of men;
A nation hath been born again,
Regenerate by a second birth!

Rent are the bonds of gain and greed,
Once coiled around our common life:
Hushed are the hate of party strife,
And jealousies of race and creed.

We see the light the prophets saw,
In eyes of age and eyes of youth—
The sacred flame of trust and truth,
Of justice, liberty, and law.

In furrowed fields, in city walls,
Forgot are lust, and sloth and fear;
One voice alone—one voice we hear—
Our Country to her children calls.

Lord God of Hosts, to whom we pray
In all times, favored or forlorn,
We thank thy name that thus is born
A nation in a single day!

In faith to Thee our fathers fought;
In faith to Thee we arm to-day,
And hopeful guard, with stern array,
The commonweal Thy hand hath wrought.

"O, brothers! blest by partial fate
With power to match the will and deed,"
This is the hour of sorest need;
Go forward ere it be too late!

W. W. HOWE.
—*N. Y. Tribune.*

AN APPEAL FOR THE COUNTRY.

BY MRS. ELLEN KEY BLUNT.

[The following patriotic and impressive lines were
written by Mrs. BLUNT, in London, on the 4th of
January, after she had complied with the President's recommendation to observe it as a day of
humiliation and prayer. The time, the circumstances under which they were written, and the character and associations of the writer, all combine to
give a solemn interest to the appeal.]

"Glory to God in the highest, and on earth peace, good
will towards man."

From lake to gulf, from sea to sea
We have knelt in one solemn Fast,
That God may heal our country's strife,
Forgiving us all the past.
Hear we no voice as we listening stand?
Comes there no touch on the angry hand?
Thrills not one heart-throb through the land?
Peace, brothers, peace!

Oh, by our homes so bright and fair,
Where the Christmas garlands wave!
Oh, by our loved ones nestling there
By each cradle, by each grave!
By the church bells ringing in the air,
By the praying of our common prayer;
By the Bible on which our people swear!
Peace, brothers, peace!

Would you rend our country's breast in twain?
It lies bare to the mortal blow,
But the sword that could drink her holy vein
Should be that of a foreign foe.
Not of her children, cradled free,
Not of her home-born; never be
Such written page of History!
Peace, brothers, peace!

Would ye part the river which north and south
Rolls grandly its career?
Sounds not a tone from its mighty mouth
Teaching us, far and near,
That the North and the South, like it, must be
One power, one home, one unity;
One time and one eternity?
Peace, brothers, peace!

Brothers, beware; the storm is high—
Our ship of state strains heavily—
And her flag, whose spangles have lit the sky,
Is fluttering—tattered and torn to be.
God of our Father Washington,
Our trust is in Thy arm alone;
Count Thou her stars, keep every one!
Peace, brothers, peace!

LONDON, *January* 4, 1861.

—*National Intelligencer,* Feb. 6.

"LIBERTY AND UNION, ONE AND INSEPARABLE."

There floats our glorious ensign,
There still our eagles fly!
And lives the coward heart or hand
Dare pluck them from the sky?

Dare raise the parricidal arm
With impious grasp to seize,
And tear from out the firmament
The glory of the breeze?

The curse of Cain on him who wields
The brand of civil war,
Or blots from that proud galaxy,
One single gleaming star.

Still floats our glorious ensign,
And still our eagles soar,
Yet weeping eyes now fear to gaze
And see them fly no more.

Oh! brethren in the Union strong,
Bethink ye of the day
When our sires, beneath that banner,
Rushed eager to the fray;

When first its glories were unfurled
O'er Freedom's sacred ground,
And thirteen States confederate stood,
In loyal union bound.

Its stripes were dyed at Monmouth;
In Brandywine's red strea;
On Saratoga's trampled plain;
By Lexington's sad green.

Its stars shone out o'er Bunker's height;
Fort Moultrie saw them gleam;
And high o'er Yorktown's humble camp
They flashed in dazzling sheen.

Rise! souls of martyred heroes,
　Rise from your troubled grave,
And guard once more our Union,
　Our broken country save!

Rise, Stark, from old New Hampshire,
　Rise, Lincoln, from the Bay,
Rise Sumter from the rice fields,
　As on that glorious day.

Again o'er broad savannahs
　Rise Marion's swart brigade,
Whose fiery tramp, like whirlwind rush,
　Swept down the everglade.

Why now sleeps Henry's patriot heart;
　Why Otis' tongue of flame;
Hancock and Adams, live they yet,
　Or live they but in name?

They cannot die! immortal truth
　Outlasts the shock of time,
And fires the faithful human heart
　With energy sublime.

They live! on every hill and plain,
　By every gleaming river,
Where'er their glowing feet have trod,
　They live and live for ever.

The mem'ry of the past shall raise
　Fresh altars to their name;
And coming years, with reverent hand,
　Protect the sacred flame.

We know no North, nor South, nor West;
　One Union binds us all;
Its stars and stripes are o'er us flung—
　'Neath them we'll stand or fall.

Then stay your hands, ye traitor host,
　And cease your vain endeavor;
God guards our Union good and strong,
　For ever and for ever.

He sleepeth not like heroes dead,
　And mouldering in the grave;
His outstretched arm is quick to smite,
　Omnipotent to save.

Lo! he shall break the coward hand,
　And brand the traitor knave,
With more than Arnold's deathless shame—
　With his accursed grave.　　F. A. H.
　　　　　　　　　　—Evening Post.

THE NINETEENTH OF APRIL, 1861.

This year, till late in April, the snow fell thick and
　light;
Thy flag of peace, dear Nature, in clinging drifts of
　white
Hung over field and city:—now everywhere is
　seen,
In place of that white quietness, a sudden glow of
　green.

The verdure climbs the Common, beneath the an-
　cient trees,
To where the glorious Stars and Stripes are floating
　on the breeze,

There, suddenly as Spring awoke from Winter's
　snow-draped gloom,
The Passion Flower of Seventy-six is bursting into
　bloom.

Dear is the time of roses, when earth to joy is wed,
And garden-plat and meadow wear one generous
　flush of red;
But now in dearer beauty, to Freedom's colors
　true,
Blooms the old town of Boston in red and white
　and blue.

Along the whole awakening North are those true
　colors spread;
A summer noon of patriotism is burning overhead.
No party badges flaunting now,—no word of clique
　or clan:
But "Up for God and Union!" is the shout of
　every man.

Oh, peace is dear to Northern hearts; our hard-
　earned homes more dear;
But Freedom is beyond the price of any earthly
　cheer;
And Freedom's flag is sacred;—he who would work
　it harm,
Let him, although a brother, beware our strong
　right arm!

A brother! ah, the sorrow, the anguish of that
　word!
The fratricidal strife begun, when shall its end be
　heard?
Not this the boon that patriot hearts have prayed
　and waited for;—
We loved them, and we longed for peace: but they
　would have it war.

Yes; war! on this memorial day, the day of Lex-
　ington,
A lightning-thrill along the wires from heart to
　heart has run.
Brave men we gazed on yesterday, to-day for us
　have bled:
Again is Massachusetts blood the first for freedom
　shed.

To war—and with our brethren, then,—if only this
　can be!
Life hangs as nothing in the scale against dear
　Liberty!
Though hearts be torn asunder, we for Mother-
　Land will fight;
Our blood may seal the victory, but God will shield
　the Right!

　　Lucy Larcom, in the Boston Transcript, April 25.

THROUGH BALTIMORE!

THE VOICE OF THE PENNSYLVANIA VOLUN-
TEERS.

I.

'Twas Friday morn, the train drew near
　The city and the shore:
Far through the sunshine, soft and clear,
We saw the dear old flag appear,
And in our hearts arose a cheer
　　For Baltimore.

II.

Across the broad Patapsco's wave,
    Old Fort McHenry bore
The starry banner of the brave,
As when our fathers went to save,
Or in the trenches find a grave,
                At Baltimore.

III.

Before us, pillared in the sky,
    We saw the statue soar
Of Washington, serene and high—
Could traitors view that form, nor fly?
Could patriots see, nor gladly die
                For Baltimore?

IV.

" Oh, city of our country's song,
    By that swift aid we bore
When sorely pressed, receive the throng,
Who go to shield our flag from wrong,
And give us welcome, warm and strong,
                In Baltimore ! "

V.

We had no arms; as friends we came,
    As brothers evermore,
To rally round one sacred name,
The charter of our power and fame:
We never dreamed of guilt and shame
                In Baltimore.

VI.

The coward mob upon us fell:
    McHenry's flag they tore:
Surprised, borne backward by the swell,
Beat down with mad, inhuman yell,
Before us yawned a traitorous hell
                In Baltimore!

VII.

The streets our soldier-fathers trod
    Blushed with their children's gore;
We saw the craven rulers nod,
And dip in blood the civic rod—
Shall such things be, O righteous God,
                In Baltimore?

VIII.

No, never! By that outrage black,
    A solemn oath we swore,
To bring the Keystone's thousands back,
Strike down the dastards who attack,
And leave a red and fiery track
                Through Baltimore!

IX.

Bow down, in haste, thy guilty head!
    God's wrath is swift and sore:
The sky with gathering bolts is red—
Cleanse from thy skirts the slaughter shed,
Or make thyself an ashen bed—
                Oh Baltimore!
    BAYARD TAYLOR, in the *N. Y. Tribune.*

UNDER THE WASHINGTON ELM,

CAMBRIDGE, APRIL 27, 1861.

BY OLIVER WENDELL HOLMES.

I.

Eighty years have passed, and more,
    Since under the brave old tree
Our fathers gathered in arms, and swore
They would follow the sign their banners bore,
    And fight till the land was free.

II.

Half of their work was done,
    Half is left to do—
Cambridge, and Concord, and Lexington!
When the battle is fought and won,
    What shall be told of you?

III.

Hark! 'tis the south wind moans—
    Who are the martyrs down?—
Ah, the marrow was true in your children's bones,
That sprinkled with blood the cursed stones
    Of the murder-haunted town!

IV.

What if the storm-clouds blow?
    What if the green leaves fall?
Better the crashing tempest's throe,
Than the army of worms that gnawed below;
    Trample them one and all!

V.

Then, when the battle is won,
    And the land from traitors free,
Our children shall tell of the strife begun
When Liberty's second April sun
    Was bright on our brave old tree!

SUMTER.

I thought of Sumter all the night;
    Of those beleaguered few
Who stood up nobly in the fight
For loyalty and freedom's right,
    Against that recreant crew.

I saw that chain of rebel bands
    Surround the sacred fort;
I saw five thousand traitors' hands,
Red with hot hate, their foul demands
    With blustering arms support.

I saw five thousand on the shore,
    Less than one hundred fight!
I heard the coward cannons roar,
And shot and shell relentless pour
    Destruction through the night.

I saw might vanquish right, and then
    I heard the miscreants brag
Of " victory," when those starving men,
Shut up within a fortressed pen,
    Were forced to lower their flag!

O State, which patriots once did claim,
  How is it with thee now?
False to thy country and thy name ;
Henceforward, let the curse of shame
  Be branded on thy brow!

AN AMERICAN.
—*Evening Post.*

THE TWO ERAS.

APRIL 19TH, 1775, AND APRIL 19TH, 1861.

The Bay State bled at Lexington,
  But every drop that ran,
By transmutation strange and strong,
  Sprung up an armèd man :—

Sprung up, indomitably firm,
  And multiplied and spread,
Till Freedom's amaranthine crown
  Enwreath'd our country's head.

Yet, when the born of Lexington,
  Who kept their natal day,
Were writing fourscore years and six
  Upon their annals gray,

The Bay State bled at Baltimore,—
  Wherefore, I may not speak ;
For sad and tender memories rush
  From heart to moisten'd cheek.

And sighs of buried fathers break
  The cold, sepulchral bed,
And hideous harpies clap their wings
  When brothers' blood is shed :

And stars that in their courses sang,
  Their constellations shroud,
And wind-borne echoes cry *forbear !*
  From yonder cloven cloud :

While contrite souls from holy church
  And shaded hearth-stone pray,
That He who rules above the skies,
  Would turn his wrath away,

And rule the spirit that of old
  The Shepherd Abel slew,
And link the hands in loving clasp,
  Now red with battle dew ;

Yes, all our Nation's sins remit,
  And bid His judgments cease,
And in His own good time restore
  The blessed balm of peace.

L. H. S.

HARTFORD, Conn., April 19th.

THE SIXTH AT BALTIMORE.

BY B. P. SHILLABER.

Our country called on her sons for aid,
And we shouldered the gun and drew the blade,
Leaving the anvil, the plough, and the saw,
To fight for the Union and for law—
To fight for the flag our Fathers bore—
And our pathway led through Baltimore.

There was no moment for doubts or fears,
There was no time for sighs or tears ;
We said " good bye " with hurried breath,
Then marched to the field of life or death,
And fealty to our land we swore
Ere we marched to its aid through Baltimore.

And godly hands in blessing were spread,
And smiles from beauty were on us shed,
And the starry flag that we bore in pride,
Was cheered and lauded on every side,
With devotion never known before,
As we took up our march for Baltimore.

'Twas April nineteenth, and the sun
That had seen the carnage at Lexington,
Shone on us as we took our way
Through lanes of traitors in hate's array,
And a scowling look each stern face wore,
That we saw as we marched through Baltimore.

Then hateful glances took sterner form,
And rained upon us a fearful storm ;
Fierce terrible missiles around us fell,
'Mid oaths 'twould shame the sons of hell,
But we quailed not 'mid the angry roar
That swept through the streets of Baltimore.

Not a shout or cry in our ranks was heard,
But our rifles spoke the voiceless word,
And our leaden sentences went deep
To put seditious hearts to sleep ;
But sadly, though sternly, we deplore
Our own brave, fallen at Baltimore.

But the guerdon of glory 's for those who fall ;
For the nation's flag is their funeral pall,
And the nation's tears the turf bedew
That covers their hearts so bold and true ;
Deathless are they who life gave o'er
On the bloody pavements of Baltimore.

The dead return—the arms to nerve
And hearts to strengthen that else might swerve ;
They speak again from the silent sod
In a voice that stirs like the voice of God,
And heroes vow from their hearts' deep core
To follow the Sixth through Baltimore.

—*Boston Evening Gazette.*

COL. CORCORAN'S BRIGADE.

I.

Prompt to the gathering summons,
  True as the lifted steel,
Into the foremost phalanx,
  See where their columns wheel !

II.

Souls of the careless daring !
  Souls of the trustful love !
Hear you the voices swelling
  Ever your march above ?

III.

Tones of your mournful mother,
  Reft of her queenly dower,
Pale at the gate of nations,
  Waiting her destined hour !

IV.

Strains from the hills where Summer
  Empties her lap of flowers!
Strains from the woods that glisten
  Wet with the noonday showers!

V.

See you the graceful shadows
  Gliding around you there!
Shapes with the gleaming helmet
  Over their flowing hair!

VI.

Forms of a softer beauty!
  Heads with the Eastern veil!
Eyes of a dewy splendor!
  Shades of the buried Gael!

VII.

Oh! for their clouded glory,
  "Sons of the ancient race!"
Still, in the rushing battle,
  Yours be the victor's place!

VIII.

Spells from the past be with you,
  To charm the shields you bear!
Might from the secret voices
  Lifted in woman's prayer!   ENUL.
          —*New York Leader.*

APRIL 19TH, 1775–1861.

Once more, (our dear old Massachusetts!)
  How the thought comes over us—and well it
    may!
Of the drops wherewith that ancient green was
  reddened—
It is six and eighty years this very day.

Six and eighty years—and it seemed but a
  memory—
Little left of all that glory—so we thought—
Only the old fire-locks hung on farm-house chimneys,
And rude blades the village blacksmith wrought.

Only here and there a white head that remembers
  How the Frocks of Homespun stood against King
    George—
How the hard hands stretched them o'er the scanty
  embers
When the sleet and snow came down at Valley
  Forge.

Ah me, how long we lay, in quiet and in error,
  Till the Snake shot from the coil he had folded on
    our hearth—
Till the Dragon-Fangs had sprouted, o'erhatched of
  hate and terror,
And hell, in armèd legions, seemed bursting from
  the earth.

Once more, dear Brother-State! thy pure, brave
  blood baptizes
  Our last and noblest struggle for freedom and
    for right—
It fell on the cruel stones!—but an awful Nation
  rises
In the glory of its conscience, and the splendor
  of its might.   H. H. B.
        —*Hartford (Conn.) Press.*

"ALL HAIL TO THE STARS AND STRIPES."

BY GEORGE T. BOURNE.

"After the soldiers from the Old 'Bay State' had been brutally shot down, one young man, scarcely twenty years old, lay upon the ground mortally wounded. With his eyes fast growing dim, he raised himself erect, and tossing his arms wildly about, exclaimed, 'All hail to the Stars and Stripes,' and fell back dead."   [*Extract from a Letter.*]

When home returning from the fight
  They wend their way, with noble scars,
They'll point to wounds by traitorous hands
  Which fought against the Stripes and Stars.
But noble wounds will be forgot
  As each his blood-stained sabre wipes,
And thinks how rose that dying voice,
  "All hail the glorious Stars and Stripes."

"All hail the Stars and Stripes!" The words
  Are graven now, on every heart,
A Nation's watchword—Freedom's song!—
  Of every future act a part.
"All hail the glorious Stars and Stripes!"
  The echo leaps from hill to hill!
We first drew breath beneath its folds,
  We'll live and die beneath it still!

"All hail the Stars and Stripes," the cry,
  From forest home to ocean shore!
Ten thousand times ten thousand hands
  Are raised to *free* that flag once more.
To each proud heart new hope is sent,
  To each strong arm new strength is given,
And raised aloft from every home,
  The Stars and Stripes float nearer heaven!
NEW YORK, April 18, 1861.   —*N. Y. Tribune.*

SONGS OF THE REBELS.

THE WAR STORM.

Often by a treacherous seaside
  I have heard the ocean's roar,
Often, at its ebb or flood tide,
  Listened to its mystic lore.

Sometimes it would whisper to me
  Words of smooth and liquid tone,
And its pictures, memory drew me,
  Sweet as breath from tropic zone;

Ever to me sang its story,
  Ever to me talked the sea;
Evening sun would paint its glory,
  Bringing sober thoughts to me.

I would think how like the passions
  Is the smooth or stormy sea;
Breath of heat or cold may fashion
  Rage, or hope, or gloom, or glee.

I, to-day, have seen the flood tide
  Of our country's strength and youth,
Plain as waves upon the seaside,
  And as mighty as is truth.

No faint breath has caused this motion,
  No faint ripple raised this storm;
But like tempest o'er the ocean—
  In the summer, calm and warm—

We have listened to the muttering
  Of the thunder in the sky,
Till at length its mighty uttering
  Is the battle's wildest cry.

Stormy clouds, of blackest error,
  Drove along this battle-car,
Freighted it with bloody terror,
  And plunged us in this fearful war.

Rain of lead we know will rattle,
  Steel will flash, and blood will flow,
Cannon thunder through the battle,
  And its ending none can know.

Yes! there is a glorious lightness
  In the soldier's scarlet shroud;
History touches it with brightness;
  Fame will sound his requiem loud,

Lasting as the long forever,
  Reaching ages as they come,
Telling round the fireside, ever,
  How he died defending home.
                              —N. O. Picayune.

THE ILLUMINATION OF THE CITY OF RICHMOND,

In honor of the Victory of the Battle of Fort Sumter, gained by the Confederate States, April 12th, 1861.

BY MARY COPLAND.

Honor to General Beauregard, and to the noble
        South,
Who have proclaimed their freedom through the
        thundering cannon's mouth;
But be the glory given, as to Carolina due,
The bravest, and the noblest, and truest of the true.

Then Richmond gleamed with a thousand lights,
And bonfires blazed on a thousand heights;
While the light of the stars was paled by
The glow, that flashed 'gainst the clear blue sky;
And over all streamed, full and free,
The flag of twice-won liberty;
And all Virginia's capital
Rejoiced o'er the conquered citadel.

Honor to noble Davis, brave soldier and true man,
Who dares to be, and dares to do, all that a great
        man can;
But be the glory given, as to Carolina due,
The noblest, and the bravest, the truest of the true.

And an hundred cannon thundered forth
Their message to the impatient earth,
And a nation rose, in its power and might,
To prove that Virginia's heart was right;
And every breast in that human tide,
Throbs with a fuller, freer pride;
Then a thousand voices they upraise,
To shout forth Carolina's praise.

Honor to Brave old Ruffin, to that true and faith-
        ful heart,
The four-score years old patriot, who took the fore-
        most part;
But be the glory given, as to Carolina due,
The bravest of the brave, and truest of the true.

Oh, favored land, that boasts a son,
Davis, the second Washington,
Know that Virginia, now by thee,
Will battle for her liberty;
Her sons, beneath thy flag unfurled,
Will hurl defiance to the world;
And, fighting hand in hand with thee,
Will conquer, to be doubly free.

Honor to glorious Wise, the fearless and the bold,
Who dared to tell a nation the truth, that should
        be told;
But unto Carolina be the glory evermore,
For she hath done a bolder deed than e'er was done
        before.

Aye, clothe her name with glory bright—
Around it throw a radiant light;
For, oh! it is a glorious sight,
This nation rising in the right;
And Carolina well may claim
The greatest, most unsullied name—
Brave, and magnanimous, and pure,
Her fame will e'er remain, her power endure.

Honor to them all—to each brave and gallant
        heart
That manfully and earnestly will strive to do his
        part;
But be the glory given, as to Carolina due,
The noblest, and the bravest, the truest of the true.

RICHMOND April 17, 1861.
                              —Charleston Mercur

SUMTER—A BALLAD OF 1861.

'Twas on the twelfth of April,
  Before the break of day,
We heard the guns of Moultrie
  Give signal for the fray.

Anon across the waters
  There boomed the answering gun,
From north and south came flash on flash,
  The battle had begun.

The mortars belched their deadly food
  And spiteful whizz'd the balls,
A fearful storm of iron hailed
  On Sumter's doomèd walls.

We watched the meteor flight of shell,
  And saw the lightning flash—
Saw where each fiery missile fell,
  And heard the sullen crash.

The morn was dark and cloudy,
  Yet till the sun arose,
No answer to our gallant boys
  Came booming from our foes.

Then through the dark and murky clouds
  The morning sunlight came,
And forth from Sumter's frowning walls
  Burst sudden sheets of flame.

Then shot and shell flew thick and fast,
  The war-dogs howling spoke,
And thundering came their angry roar,
  Through wreathing clouds of smoke.

Again to fight for liberty,
  Our gallant sons had come,
They smiled when came the bugle call,
  And laughed when tapped the drum.

From cotton and from corn field,
  From desk and forum, too,
From work bench and from anvil, came
  Our gallant boys and true!

A hireling band had come to awe,
  Our chains to rivet fast;
Yon lofty pile scowls on our homes,
  Seaward the hostile mast.

But gallant freemen man our guns—
  No mercenary host,
Who barter for their honor's price,
  And of their baseness boast.

Now came our stately matrons,
  And maidens, too, by scores;
Oh! Carolina's beauty shone
  Like love-lights on her shores.

See yonder, anxious gazing,
  Alone a matron stands,
The tear drop glistening on each lid,
  And tightly clasped her hands.

For there, exposed to deadly fire,
  Her husband and her son—
"Father," she spoke, and heavenward look'd,
  "Father, thy will be done."

See yonder group of maidens,
  No joyous laughter now,
For cares lie heavy on each heart,
  And cloud each anxious brow;

For brothers dear and lovers fond,
  Are there amid the strife;
Tearful the sister's anxious gaze—
  Pallid the promised wife.

Yet breathed no heart one thought of fear,
  Prompt at their country's call,
They yielded forth their dearest hopes,
  And gave to honor all!

Now comes a message from below—
  Oh! quick the tidings tell—
"At Moultrie and Fort Johnson, too,
  And Morris', all are well!"

Then mark the joyous bright'ning;
  See how each bosom swells;
That friends and loved ones all are safe,
  Each to the other tells.

All day the shot flew thick and fast,
  All night the cannon roared,
While wreathed in smoke stern Sumter stood,
  And vengeful answer poured.

Again the sun rose, bright and clear,
  'Twas on the thirteenth day,
While, lo! at prudent distance moored,
  Five hostile vessels lay.

With choicest Abolition crews—
  The bravest of *their* brave—
They'd come to pull our Crescent down
  And dig Secession's grave.

"See, see, how Sumter's banner trails,
  They're signalling for aid.
See you no boats of armèd men?
  Is yet no movement made?"

Now densest smoke and lurid flames
  Burst out o'er Sumter's walls;
"The fort's on fire," is the cry,
  Again for aid he calls.

See you no boats or vessels yet?
  Dare they not risk *one* shot,
To make report grandiloquent
  Of aid they rendered not?

Nor boat, nor vessel, leaves the fleet,
  "Let the old Major burn,"
We'll boast of what we would have done,
  If but—on our return.

Go back, go back, ye cravens;
  Go back the way ye came;
Ye gallant, *would-be* men-of-war,
  Go! to your country's shame.

'Mid fiery storm of shot and shell,
  'Mid smoke and roaring flame,
See how Kentucky's gallant son
  Does honor to her name!

See how he answers gun for gun—
  Hurrah! his flag is down!
The white! the white! Oh see it wave!
  Is echoed all around.

God save the gallant Anderson,
  All honor to his name,
A soldier's duty nobly done,
  He's earned a hero's fame.

Now ring the bells a joyous peal,
  And rend with shouts the air,
We've torn the hated banner down,
  And placed the Crescent there.

All honor to our gallant boys,
  Bring forth the roll of fame,
And there in glowing lines inscribe
  Each patriot hero's name.

Spread, spread, the tidings far and wide,
  Ye winds take up the cry,
"Our soil's redeemed from hateful yoke,
  We'll keep it pure or die."
                E. O. M.
        —*Columbia (S. C.) Banner.*

RUMORS AND INCIDENTS.

The Philadelphia *Press* contains the following:

" *Mr. Editor :* In your paper of the 1st instant is inserted a copy of a letter to a mercantile house in our city, from A. C. & A. B. Beech, of Nashville, promising to make an effort to pay their Eastern indebtedness when the *war is over and the smoke of battle clears away ; until then, nothing can be done !*"

As an offset to the above, do us the favor to publish, side by side, the following patriotic letter of Morgan & Co., Nashville:

" NASHVILLE, April 23, 1861.

" *Gentlemen :* Enclosed find check of the Union Bank, on Manhattan Co., New York, for *three thousand dollars.* We would have remitted more to-day, but could not procure the exchange. We intend to meet all our engagements promptly, *war or no war !* Repudiation is not the weapon we fight with, if fight we must, which God, in His infinite mercy, forbid.   Your friends,
                                        " MORGAN & Co."

A SPY HUNG.—Captain William Jones, of the sloop *Isabel*, has terminated his brief but notorious career at the end of a rope. The account we hear is, that on the arrival of the cars at Scooba, a passenger on the train pointed out Jones, as boasting to him of being the person who " provisioned Slemmer," and that he was then on the way to Washington, with despatches to Lincoln's Government. He was arrested, the proofs of his treason found upon him, and he was executed upon the spot by the enraged citizens.—*Mobile Advertiser.*

THE OTHER "ABOU BEN-ADHEM."—The following ingenious and witty parody of a poem universally known, is from a feminine pen. The tart and somewhat malicious allusions to " Rye " refer, we suppose, to President Buchanan's letter to some Western friends, acknowledging, with thanks, the receipt of some excellent rye whiskey:

James *B*–Uchanan, may his tribe *decrease,*
Awoke one night from a strange dream of peace,
And saw, within the curtains of his bed,
Making his t'other eye to squint with dread—
Old *Jackson,* writing in a book of gold.
Exceeding Rye had made Buchanan bold,
And to the stern Ex-President he said:
" Wha—what writ'st thou ? " The spirit shook his head,
The while he answered, with the voice of old :
" The names of those who ne'er their country sold !"
And is *mine* one ? asked J. B. " *Nary !* " cried
The General, with a frown. Buchanan sighed,
And groaned, and turned himself upon his bed,
And took another " nip " of " rye," then said :
" Well, ere thou lay thy record on the shelf,
Write me at least as one who *sold himself !*
' Democs ' and ' Rye ' so long my spirits were,
That when the ' Crisis ' came—I wasn't there !"
The General wrote, and vanished; the next night
He came again, in more appalling plight,
And showed those names that all *true men detest,*
And lo ! Buchanan's name *led all* the rest !

THE Secessionists ask, " where will Kentucky go ? " When the countryman was asked " where does this railroad go ? " he answered " the road doesn't go at all." Kentucky won't " go," she'll stay.—*Louisville Journal.*

A HEROINE IN BALTIMORE.

The band of the 6th Regiment, that left Boston consisted of twenty-four persons, who, together with their musical instruments, occupied a car by themselves from Philadelphia to Baltimore. By some accident the musicians' car got switched off at the Canton Depot, so that, instead of being the first, it was left in the rear of all the others, and after the attack had been made by the mob upon the soldiers, they came upon the car in which the band was still sitting, wholly unarmed and incapable of making any defence. The infuriated demons approached them howling and yelling, and poured in upon them a shower of stones, broken iron, and other missiles; wounding some severely, and demolishing their instruments. Some of the miscreants jumped upon the roof of the car, and with a bar of iron beat a hole through it, while others were calling for powder to blow them all up in a heap. Finding that it would be sure destruction to remain longer in the car, the poor fellows jumped out to meet their fiendish assailants hand to hand. They were saluted with a shower of stones, but took to their heels, fighting their way through the crowd, and running at random, without knowing in what direction to go for assistance or shelter. As they were hurrying along, a rough-looking man suddenly jumped in front of their leader, and exclaimed : " This way, boys ! this way !" It was the first friendly voice they had heard since entering Baltimore, and they stopped to ask no questions, but followed their guide, who took them up a narrow court, where they found an open door, into which they rushed, being met inside by a powerful-looking woman, who grasped each one by the hand and directed them upstairs. The last of their band was knocked senseless just as he was entering the door, by a stone, which struck him on the head; but the woman who had welcomed them immediately caught up their fallen comrade and carried him in her arms up the stairs.

" You are perfectly safe here, boys," said the Amazon, who directly proceeded to wash and bind up their wounds.

After having done this, she procured them food, and then told them to strip off their uniforms and put on the clothes she had brought them, a motley assortment of baize jackets, ragged coats and old trowsers. Thus equipped, they were enabled to go out in search of their companions, without danger of attack from the Plug-Uglies and Blood-Tubs, who had given them so rough a reception.

They then learned the particulars of the attack upon the soldiers and of their escape, and saw lying at the station the two men who had been killed, and the others who had been wounded. One of their own band was missing, and he has not yet been found, and it is uncertain whether he was killed or not On going back to the house where they were so humanely treated, they found that their clothes had been carefully tied up, and with their battered instruments, had been sent to the depot of the Philadelphia Railroad, where they were advised to go themselves They did not long hesitate, but started in the next train, and arrived at Philadelphia just in time to meet the 8th Regiment of Massachusetts Volunteers, under the command of Gen. Butler, who told them to hurry back to the Old Bay State to show their battered faces and broken limbs, and that they should yet come back and play Hail Columbia in the streets of Baltimore, where they had been so inhumanly assaulted.

The noble-hearted woman who rescued these men is a well-known character in Baltimore, and, according to all the usages of Christian society, is an outcast and a polluted being; but she is a true heroine, nevertheless, and entitled to the grateful consideration of the country. When Gov. Hicks had put himself at the head of the rabble rout of miscreants, and Winter Davis had fled in dismay, and the men of wealth and official dignity had hid themselves in their terror, and the police were powerless to protect the handful of unarmed strangers who were struggling with the infuriated mob, this degraded woman took them under her protection, dressed their wounds, fed them at her own cost, and sent them back in safety to their homes. As she is too notorious in Baltimore not to be perfectly well-known by what we have already told of her, it will not be exposing her to any persecution to mention her name. Ann Manley is the name by which she is known in the city of Blood-Tubs, and the loyal men of the North, when they march again through its streets, should remember her for her humanity to their countrymen.—*Boston Sat. Evening Courier.*

CASSIUS M. CLAY, Minister to Russia, offered his services to Secretary Cameron, either as an officer to raise a regiment, or as a private in the ranks. Mr. Cameron said : " Sir, this is the first instance I ever heard of where a foreign Minister volunteered in the ranks." " Then," said Clay, " let's make a little history." He has been surrounded by friends, shaking hands and congratulating him. He will not leave the country just yet. —*Times, April* 19.

THE TRAITOR'S PLOT.

A CORRESPONDENT of the *Evening Post* tells the following anecdote :—Three months ago I was returning from Washington, when Colonel Taylor, (brother of the late President Taylor,) who is now in the federal army, being on a visit to Newark, N. J., joined our party. Colonel Jeff. Davis, as is well known, ran away with General Taylor's daughter, and the families were intimate. Colonel Taylor had but a short time before held an after-dinner's conversation with Jefferson Davis, and while lamenting the approaching troubles, gave us an account of that conversation. The words of Colonel Taylor were nearly as follows :

" After a free talk about our country's troubles, we sat still smoking for some time, when I said, ' Colonel, what a bad way we are in.' ' Oh ! yes, yes,' replied Davis, with comparative indifference. Thinking to touch his pride a little, I said, ' Colonel, what a fine chance for a southern man to distinguish himself by uniting the North and South ! ' ' We shall see, we shall see,' was Davis's answer, and he went on smoking. By-and-by, wishing more to draw him out, I said, ' Well, you are a southerner, and an ambitious, talented, reckless fellow ; why don't you bring this about, and make the North and South shake hands ? You will immortalize yourself by doing that, as Washington did by founding his country.' Davis replied, taking the cigar from his mouth, ' You are at one end of the rope, colonel, and we are at the other ; let us see which of us can pull the longest and the strongest.' "

April 25.—Among the officers of the frigate Niagara who resigned at Boston, was first Lieutenant I. N. Brown, a Kentuckian. After resigning he took rooms at the Tremont House in Boston, and immediately got into hot water. The story is told as follows :

"Some excitement was created by two rumors—one of which was to the effect that he had purchased tickets over the Boston and Worcester Railroad for two slaves accompanying him, and the other, that the lieutenant had uttered treasonable sentiments in State-street. The first was unfounded, but it caused considerable excitement in the streets, and an excited mob rushed to the Worcester dépôt to prevent the slaves from being carried away. Others rushed to the State House to ask Governor Andrew to have Lieutenant Brown arrested, but they were unable to obtain an interview with his Excellency. While in State-street, Lieutenant Brown is charged with having stated that he was going to his plantation, and should fight for the flag he found flying over it, and for his native State. His remarks caused some angry feelings, but he was not molested. Application was made to District Attorney Woodbury for a warrant for the arrest of Brown, but after hearing the statements of witnesses, he said he had no authority to issue a warrant under the proclamation of the President, as rebels by that proclamation were allowed thirty days to lay down their arms. He advised Mr. W. L. Burt, who was acting in the case, to apply to Governor Andrew, who at once commanded his arrest, and by the following note from the Mayor it appears that Lieutenant Brown was placed under arrest :

" ' MAYOR'S OFFICE, City Hall, ?
Boston, April 25, 1861. ?

" ' MR. W. C. DUNHAM—Sir : Lieutenant I. N. Brown, late of the Niagara, is in the custody of the police of this city, and will so remain until released by the Governor, or other competent authority.

" ' J. M. WIGHTMAN, Mayor.'

" Before his arrest, Lieutenant Brown removed his baggage from the Tremont House, and was taken in a coach to unknown quarters. In the meantime, a crowd visited the Worcester dépôt, where a portion of Lieutenant Brown's baggage was, and broke it open, but finding no materials of war, disturbed it no farther."—*Boston Post.*

MR. LINCOLN keeps his own counsels so carefully, that Virginia sent a Committee to him to ask him to speak. Mr. Buchanan always blabbed so much, that the whole country felt disposed to send a Committee to him, to ask him to keep his mouth shut.

Married, on Saturday last, Mr. McCraw, in the 81st year of his age, to Miss Patty Haverston, aged 71 ; both of the poor-house.—*Toledo Blade.*

We are afraid, that, if the Southern Confederacy and the Northern Confederacy, after separating and living apart several years, and exhausting all their substance in war, shall conclude to be reunited, their marriage, like that of the old couple at Toledo, will have to be in the poor-house.—*Louisville Journal.*

The *Mobile Advertiser* speaks of the Northern volunteers as, " men who prefer enlisting to starvation ; scurvy fellows from the back slums of cities, whom Falstaff would not have marched through

Coventry with; but these recruits are not soldiers —least of all the soldiers to meet the hot-blooded, thoroughbred, impetuous men of the South. Trencher soldiers, who enlisted to war upon their rations, not on men; they are such as marched through Baltimore, squalid, wretched, ragged, and half-naked, as the newspapers of that city report them. Fellows who do not know the breech of a musket from its muzzle, and had rather filch a handkerchief than fight an enemy in manly combat. White-slaves, peddling wretches, small-change knaves, and vagrants, the dregs and offscourings of the populace; these are the levied 'forces' whom Lincoln suddenly arrays as candidates for the honor of being slaughtered by gentlemen—such as Mobile sent to battle. Let them come South, and we will put our negroes to the dirty work of killing them. But they will not come South. Not a wretch of them will live on this side of the border, longer than it will take us to reach the ground and drive them off."

THE TRUE SOLDIER'S SPIRIT.—The following extract is from a letter written by one of the Salem Light Infantry, (Zouaves.)

" *We have got to push our way through Baltimore in the morning at the point of the bayonet.* But our boys are determined and in for it. Our bayonet exercise has got to put the whole regiment through fire and brimstone. To tell you the truth, our boys expect to be split to pieces. But we have all made up our minds to *die at our post.* We have one great consolation before us: the famous Seventh Regiment of New York will join us to-night in Philadelphia, and at three o'clock in the morning we expect to take up our line of march. There is an unheard-of hot time before us; we are furnished with no ammunition as yet, and we are to rely on our bayonets and revolvers solely. Our Lieutenant is collecting our letters, and I must leave you. Perhaps before you receive this I may be lying on the field among those recorded with the dead. But what is more glorious than to die for one's country? I am in as good spirits as our dubious position will admit, and I will die like a soldier—and a true one if I must."—*Boston Express,* April 27.

An examination of the records at the Washington Observatory discloses the fact that Lieut. Maury has impressed upon the minds of scientific bodies abroad that the United States were destined to disruption, and that the Government would not last three weeks after the inauguration of Mr. Lincoln. —*The World.*

WHILE one of the Massachusetts regiments was in New York on its way to Washington, a gentleman residing there met one of its members on the street.

"Is there any thing I can do for you, sir?" said the New Yorker, his heart warming toward the representative of the brave Massachusetts militia who had so promptly answered the call of their country.

The soldier hesitated a moment, and finally raising one of his feet exhibited a boot with a hole in the toe, and generally worse for wear.

"How came you here with such boots as that, my friend?" asked the patriotic citizen.

"When the order came for me to join my company, sir," replied the soldier, "I was ploughing in the same field at Concord where my grandfather was ploughing when the British fired on the Massachusetts men at Lexington. He did not wait a moment; and I did not, sir."

It is unnecessary to add that the soldier was immediately supplied with an excellent pair of boots. —*Evening Post.*

A PATRIOTIC MOTHER.—Henry B. Stanton, of Seneca Falls, now in New York, received a letter from his wife, Mrs. Elizabeth Cady Stanton, Seneca Falls, stating that their two older sons had joined the army, and that she regretted that the next three were too young for service. Mrs. Stanton is daughter of Judge Daniel Cady, and grand-daughter of Colonel Livingston, who figured in the war of the Revolution, and it will be perceived that the old fire has been transmitted by inheritance.—*Idem.*

IN the Virginia Convention, when it was proposed to send a committee to ask Mr. Lincoln what was the object of his military movements, Mr. Carlisle suggested that a similar committee should be sent to Montgomery to ascertain from Jeff. Davis what he intended to do with all the troops he is raising. Henry A. Wise enquired whether Mr. Carlisle would be named as one of the committee to be sent to Montgomery, for, "if so, that would be the last they would ever see of him." That remark was in the true spirit of the Secessionists; they have taken their States out of the Union without consulting the Border States; they are trying to complicate us in difficulties and place us in false positions in the hope to compel us to join them; and, if we have the temerity to ask why large armies are raised and extraordinary expenses incurred, the threat of murder is made at once. Lynch law is the only law proffered to the friends of the Union in the Confederate States.—*Louisville Journal, April 23.*

A MAN named Steele hoisted a Secession flag at East Fairhaven, Massachusetts. He was warned day after day, but refused to take it down. A party from Mattapoisett paid him a visit and demanded the flag to be taken down. He refused to comply with the request, and threatened to shoot whoever attempted to take it down. After parleying awhile, he was taken and marched three miles to Mattapoisett, where a coat of tar and feathers was applied to a part of his person, giving him a handsome set of *tail feathers,* and then he was compelled to give three cheers for the Stars and Stripes, take an oath to support the Constitution, and never again raise other than the American flag.—*Boston Transcript, April 29.*

THE Cincinnati *Times* says: "A friend, who is just from the Military Institute, located near Frankfort, Ky., tells a good one. He says the institution employs a fifer who served in the Northwest in the second war with Great Britain, and took part in the battle of the Thames and other fights. During the late Secession tornado over Kentucky, the cadets, affected with the fever, talked pretty severely against those devoted to the Stars and Stripes. The old veteran listened, but said nothing. One evening he went into the room of our informant, and seemed to be in something of a passion. He paced backward and forward, saying nothing, and refusing to answer all questions. At last he pulled out his fife, and, sitting down, sent forth 'Yankee Doodle' with its shrillest strains. Then he played 'Hail Columbia,' and then 'The Star-spangled Banner,' while the tears rolled down his aged and weather-beaten cheeks. Concluding that, he jumped to his feet, and exclaimed: '*Now, d—n 'em, I guess they know which side I'm on!*' He and our informant instantly gave three cheers for the Union; and they will both stand by it until death. Kentucky has plenty of such men.

April 21.—A rumor having reached Virginia to the effect that Lieut.-Gen. Scott was about to resign his commission as General-in-Chief of the United States Army, Judge Robinson, an old personal friend and classmate of his, came to Washington, from Richmond, to offer him a commission as Commander-in-Chief of the forces of the "Confederate States." On learning the purport of Judge R.'s errand, Gen. Scott interrupted him with a declaration that *if he went any further in making such a proposition to him, he* (*Judge R.*) *would not be permitted to get back to Richmond; adding, that having sworn to support the Constitution of the United States, he realized all the honorable obligations of that oath, and should of course observe them.*—*N. Y. Times, April 25.*

While they were hoisting the Stars and Stripes over the officers' head-quarters at Camp Curtin, near Harrisburgh, Pa., and just as the men had seized the halliards, a large eagle, who came from no one knew where, *hovered over the flag, and sailed majestically over the encampment while the flag was run up!* Thousands of eyes were upturned in a moment, and as the noble bird looked down, the cheers of three thousand men rent the air! Never was such ovation paid the "Imperial Bird of Jove." It lingered for a few moments, apparently not a particle frightened at the terrific noise, then cleaving the air with its pinions, he disappeared in the horizon.—*Independent, May 9.*

The Savannah *Republican* says:

We were shown yesterday by Collector Boston, a number of the new Treasury Notes, of various denominations, just issued by the government of the Confederate States. They are handsomely executed, with appropriate vignettes in green, and bear an interest of one-cent per diem on the hundred dollars. We annex the inscription of the $500 note:

A   500
Twelve months after date the
Confederate States of America
Will pay the bearer
FIVE HUNDRED DOLLARS,
With interest at five cents per day.
Montgomery, April 8, 1861.
Alex. B. Clitherall, Register.   (500.)
    E. C. Elmore, Treasurer.
(Lower margin.) Receivable in payment of all Dues except Export Duties.

—*N. Y. Evening Post, April 16.*

The young man shot in the leg in the Baltimore riot, and taken to the Infirmary, and attended by Dr. Morris, appeared quite grateful for the humane attentions shown him. When asked why he came, the simple reply of the youth, was, "Oh, the flag—the stars and stripes."—*Phila. Press, May 1.*

"If we recognize the right of secession in one case, we give our assent to it in all cases; and if the few States upon the Gulf now are to separate themselves from us, and erect a barrier across the mouth of that great river of which the Ohio is a tributary, how long will it be before New York may come to the conclusion that she may set up for herself, and levy taxes upon every dollar's worth of goods imported and consumed in the Northwest, and taxes upon every bushel of wheat, and every pound of pork, or beef, or other productions that may be sent from the Northwest to the Atlantic in search of a market. * * * The proposition now, is, to separate these United States into little petty confederacies. First, divide them into two; and then, when either party gets beaten in the next election, sub-divide again; (laughter, and never;) then, whenever one gets beaten again, another sub-division; and then, when you beat on Governor's election, the discomfited will rebel again, and so it will go on. And if this new system of resistance by the sword and bayonet, to the results of the ballot box, shall prevail here in this country of ours, the history of the United States is already written in the history of Mexico. It is a curious fact, a startling fact, and one that no American citizen should ever misapprehend—that from the day that Mexico separated from Spain, down to this hour, no President of hers elected by the people has ever been inaugurated and served his term of office. In every single case, from 1820 down to 1861, either the defeated candidate has seized possession of the office by military force, or has turned out the successful man before his term expired. What is more significant? Mexico is now a bye-word for every man to scoff at. No man would deem himself treated as a gentleman, who was represented as a Mexican. Why? Because he cannot maintain his government founded upon the great principles of self-government and constitutional liberty—because he won't abide by the ballot-box—because he is not willing to redress grievances inside of the constitution, and in obedience to its provisions, instead of seizing the bayonet and the sword to resist the constituted authorities. It is not a question of union or disunion. *It is a question of order; of the stability of the government; of the peace of communities.*"—*Stephen A. Douglas, at Wheeling, April 20.*

Mrs. Major Anderson being desirous to visit her husband in Fort Sumter, Peter Hart, an officer of the Twentieth Ward, N. Y. City, was deputed to escort her to Charleston. Once inside the fort, Mr. Hart who had served under Major Anderson through the Mexican war, resolved to remain by his old commander, and aid in defending the fort. This he did, and in doing so, proved himself to be a gallant and intrepid soldier. After the stars and stripes had been shot down by the guns of the rebel forces, Hart seized the national colors, which he had so heroically defended in Mexico, and nailing the flag to a pole, raised it to its former position with his own hand, amid the cheers of Major Anderson and his soldiers.—*N. Y. Tribune, April 20.*

The horses of the Providence Marine Artillery were quartered in the stables of Jesse Wandel, in Jersey City, and well supplied with provender.

When the Quartermaster-Sergeant asked for his bill to pay for their keeping, Wandel refused to accept any thing, saying that he would feed a thousand of them if he could, at the same price.—*Idem.*

Weston & Williams, co-partners who sell Northern shoes in Richmond, in the United States Territory of Virginia—two men who came to Haverhill, Mass., probably about four months ago—swindled the shoemakers of that town out of valuable property, giving therefor something like the following lying promissory note:

HAVERHILL, Mass., ——— —, 1860.

$——
For value received, we promise to pay to the order of ——— & Co.——dollars in four months from date.
WESTON & WILLIAMS.

The notes maturing, do Messrs. Weston & Williams pay up? Yes; they coolly cancel their liabilities by sending their unfortunate creditors the following charming letter:

RICHMOND, Va., April 13, 1861.
Messrs. ———, HAVERHILL, Mass.:

Owing to the declaration of *war* against our beloved South, and the necessity of our arming and fighting, instead of pursuing the peaceful avocations of commerce, we have given up ourselves fully and freely to the work before us, and our resources are to be held at the disposal of the State until the issue is finally determined, when, if we have sufficient availabilities for assets left to meet our liabilities, it shall be done.

But until this fratricidal war *is closed*, we shall decline paying any of our own debts due to parties in the North, where they have drawn the sword against us. Hence the protest of our note in your favor this day, *which we have the funds in bank to meet.*

Very truly yours,
WESTON & WILLIAMS.
—*N. Y. Tribune.*

THE CAPTURE OF WASHINGTON.

The capture of Washington City is perfectly within the power of Virginia and Maryland, if Virginia will only make the effort by her constituted authorities; nor is there a single moment to lose. The entire population pant for the onset; there never was half the unanimity among the people before, nor a tithe of the zeal, upon any subject, that is now manifested to take Washington, and drive from it every Black Republican who is a dweller there.

From the mountain tops and valleys to the shores of the sea, there is one wild shout of fierce resolve to capture Washington City at all and every human hazard. The filthy cage of unclean birds must and will assuredly be purified by fire. The people are determined upon it, and are clamorous for a leader to conduct them to the onslaught. That leader will assuredly arise, aye, and that right speedily.

It is not to be endured that this flight of Abolition harpies shall come down from the black North for their roosts in the heart of the South, to defile and brutalize the land. They come as our enemies—they act as our most deadly foes—they promise us bloodshed and fire, and this is the only promise they have ever redeemed. The fanatical yell for the immediate subjugation of the whole South is going up hourly from the united voices of all the North; and for the purpose of making their work sure, they have determined to hold Washington City as the point from whence to carry on their brutal warfare.

Our people can take it—they will take it—and Scott the arch-traitor, and Lincoln the Beast, combined, cannot prevent it. The just indignation of an outraged and deeply injured people will teach the Illinois Ape to repeat his race and retrace his journey across the borders of the Free negro States still more rapidly than he came; and Scott, the traitor, will be given an opportunity at the same time to try the difference between "Scott's tactics" and the Shanghae drill for quick movements.

Great cleansing and purification are needed and will be given to that festering sink of iniquity, that wallow of Lincoln and Scott—the desecrated City of Washington; and many indeed will be the carcasses of dogs and caitiffs that will blacken the air upon the gallows, before the great work is accomplished. So let it be.—*Richmond Examiner, April 23.*

THE three commissioners who went abroad to endeavor to obtain the recognition of Jeff. Davis's Government, got a pretty essential snub at Havana, where they went to take ship for Europe. It seems that a day was fixed when Messrs. Commissioners should be presented to Gen. Serano, the Captain-General. The ceremony of presentation was performed by Mr. Helm, the American Consul at Havana, who introduced the trio as "Commissioners from the Confederate States of America." The reply of the Captain-General was as follows:

"Gentlemen, I receive you as citizens of the United States; but I do not acknowledge any such Power as the Confederate States of America."—*Phil. Bulletin, May 1.*

THE following advertisement appears in *The Mobile Advertiser:*

75,000 COFFINS WANTED.—Proposals will be received to supply the Confederacy with 75,000 BLACK COFFINS. No proposals will be entertained coming North of Mason and Dixon's line. Direct to JEFF. DAVIS, Montgomery, Ala.—*N. Y. Tribune.*

AT the court-house in Milledgeville, Georgia, Martin V. Brantley, confined in the penitentiary of Georgia for robbing the United States mail, was brought before Judge HARRIS on a writ of habeas corpus, sued out by his counsel. It was contended that under the new relations subsisting between the State of Georgia and the United States, the prisoner was entitled to a discharge. The Judge, however, took a different view of the case. He decided that the ordinance by which Georgia had declared her secession from the Union, does not extend beyond a separation from the other States and a withdrawal of the powers she delegated to the General Government; that upon the past exercise of those powers by the latter Government the ordinance does not assume to act, and was not designed to act; and that it does not annul any of its acts. The prisoner was therefore remanded.—*National Intelligencer, Feb. 5.*

THE following despatch was sent, a few days ago, to JAMES BUCHANAN, late President of the United States:

Resolved, By a few of the women of New York that we have read with feelings of great indignation the despatch sent to Mr. LINCOLN by JAMES BUCHANAN, late President of the United States, saying that he will "sustain the Administration;" and are determined, though abhorring this type of Southern civilization, unless said JAMES BUCHANAN keeps quiet and silent, henceforth in his cupboard at Wheatland, to provide the necessary weight of feathers and other accompaniments for the single ladies of Wheatland, who, we hear, have threatened to make a "coat" for the man who has, by his imbecility, involved us in one of the most dreadful wars the world has ever seen—the man who now offers to "sustain," yet sustained *nothing* but the designs of the rebels when he could have sustained the majesty of LAW—who said, that if States wished to secede, no one could prevent it, while knowing that the Constitution distinctly says, "The Union of these States is PERPETUAL"—the man who permitted the laws to be defied and the flag of his country to be disgraced without raising a hand to rebuke or prevent either outrage.—*N. Y. Times, April 24.*

A PATRIOTIC LADY.—Mrs. Sanford, wife of Capt. Edward H. Sanford, of Boston, drove to the door of the Boston Volunteers' Headquarters, and sent her little son up to the officer's quarters with a handsome little box, decorated outside with red, white, and blue ribbons, and inside with a hundred dollars in gold. The gift was accompanied by a pretty note, of which we give the following extract: "Please accept, with a mother's offering, a mother's fervent prayers. Our hopes are all with you. God bless and keep our darling boys—old Massachusetts' sons, our hearts' dear treasures, the defenders of our flag. Again and again, God bless you!" The money will aid to maintain the large body of men now in the quarters, and the casket will follow the fortunes of the regiment, as a pleasant souvenir from a patriotic lady.

Captain Sanford, husband of the lady above alluded to, has tendered to Governor Andrew the use of the steamer Menemon Sanford, to transport troops or munitions from this city to any of the forts in our harbor. He has also offered the services of his steam tugboat, day or night, to tow vessels carrying troops or supplies to or from any of the forts.—*Boston Saturday Express, April 27.*

A PATRIOTIC CHRISTIAN MOTHER.

The following touching letter was written by a lady of New York temporarily absent in an adjoining State, on hearing that her five sons had volunteered, and gone South.

"MY DEAR HUSBAND: Your letter came to hand last evening. I must confess I was startled by the news referring to our boys, and for the moment I felt as though a ball had pierced my own heart. For the first time I was obliged to look things full in the face. But although I have always loved my children with a love that none but a mother can know, yet, when I look at the state of my country, I cannot withhold them; and in the name of their God, and their mother's God, and their country's God, I bid them go. If I had ten sons, instead of five, I would give them all sooner that have our country rent in fragments. The Constitution must be sustained at any cost. We have a part to act and a duty to perform, and may God, our father, strengthen us, and nerve us to the task, and enable us to say, Whatever Thou requirest that will I cheerfully give and do! May He bless and protect our dear children, and bring them home to us in safety! I hope you will provide them each with a Bible, and give them their mother's love and blessing, and tell them our prayers will accompany them, and ascend on their behalf night and day."—*N. Y. Tribune, April 28.*

PENSACOLA, *April 26.*—Soldiers still arrive by every train. Three companies from Louisiana arrived to-day, also a hundred water soldiers (marines) from New Orleans. Gen. Bragg has now under his command about 8,000 troops—a larger number, I believe, than Gen. Scott commanded in the valley of Mexico. They are all in fine health, and anxious for the hour that decides the destiny of self and country. The crisis approaches nearer and nearer. Another day of soldier toil has added to the great preparation.

The commander of Fort Pickens is unceasing in his military labors. Like Bragg's, his men work day and night. They have thrown up a battery outside, but near the walls, of heavy guns, obtained from their ships, while on the ramparts they are piling bag upon bag of sand to protect their guns and men. And all this visible to the naked eye—even their muskets, stacked on the beach.

The Governor has accepted the tender of the two military companies of Pensacola, as well as that of the gallant Capt. Miller, of Santa Rosa county. Little Florida is none behind her sister States in military ardor and enthusiasm.

A shark was caught yesterday morning with a pair of red breeches and a whole parcel of bowie knives in his belly—supposed to be the remains of a Zouave. I didn't see the shark. It will be remembered I reported the drowning of a Zouave the other day.—*Cor. N. O. Picayune, April 30.*

A CURIOUS STORY.—It will be remembered that the Charleston rebels fired into the schooner *G. D. & R. F. Shannon,* of Philadelphia. The adventure befell the *Shannon* at the time when the relief fleet was off the harbor, and it appears, according to Capt. Bowen's statement, that the United States vessels all remained outside the bar because they could not get over, and pass through the tortuous channel of six or seven miles requisite to reach Fort Moultrie on the south side. But Capt. Bowen paid a visit to the *Pawnee,* and while there the commander of that vessel asked him the draft of his schooner, and on finding it but six feet, and that it could be bought for $12,000, bought it at once, and struck a bargain with the captain to load it with provisions and stores for Fort Sumter. Every arrangement was made to carry this plan into effect on Saturday night; and had Major Anderson been able to hold out, he would have got the requisite aid then. But unfortunately he surrendered on Saturday, and the enterprise had to be given up as abortive. Of course, Capt. Bowen did not tell this little incident to the Secessionists, who, after his arrival at Charleston, boarded his ship, and compelled him to make the statement which appeared in the *Courier.* He kept it to himself, and cleared for Georgetown, for which port he had a freight; but once out at sea, he thought he had seen enough of Southern trade, and made a straight course for home. When on board the *Pawnee,* the captain voluntarily tendered to the commander of that vessel any aid that he or his schooner could render to the country; and it was in consequence of this offer that the schooner was purchased.—*N. Y. Times, April 29.*

ANDY JOHNSON'S NOSE PULLED, AND HE NEAR BEING HUNG.—We once heard of a wag that seized hold of an elephant's snout on every occasion, and he always excused himself upon the pretext that he could not resist the temptation to pull a nose that he could get hold of with both hands. It seems that Andy Johnson is such a miserable traitor, that an editor at Lynchburg could not resist the temptation to pull his proboscis. Our citizens heard yesterday, with every demonstration of delight, the indignity offered Gov. Johnson on his way from Washington to Greenville. His presence in Virginia was regarded as exceedingly offensive to Virginians. He was insulted at almost every depot. At Lynchburg his nose was most handsomely pulled, while he was hooted and groaned at by the large crowd. The traitor is meeting his reward. We have heard since, from good authority, that at Liberty, in Bedford county, Va., Johnson was taken from the cars, and a rope placed around his neck preliminary to a proposed hanging. Some old citizens of the county begged for him, saying that Tennessee would do for him what they proposed to do, and he was let off.— *Memphis Avalanche, April 25.*

THE *Charleston Mercury* enumerates the following telegraphic lies which appeared in the Northern papers at the time of the attack on Fort Sumter. The second, about the South Carolinians firing on the men who were endeavoring to extinguish the fire, is being used with great effect by the Northern press:

First. That cannonading "is going on fiercely from vessels outside and along our coast."

Second. That "Major Anderson has thrown out a raft loaded with men, who are passing up buckets of water to extinguish the fire; that balls are to be seen skipping over the water and striking the unprotected raft, creating great havoc among the poor fellows."

Third. That "eleven shots penetrated the floating battery below the water line."

Fourth. That "Fort Sumter had unconditionally surrendered."

Fifth. That "Major Anderson and his men, under guard, were conveyed to Morris Island."

Sixth. That "Major Anderson had reached the city, and was the guest of Gen. Beauregard."—*N. O. Delta, April 28.*

NEW YORK, *April 24.*—The folds of a superb star-spangled banner were flung to the breeze in front of the store of A. Morton, 25 Maiden Lane, having been subscribed for by the occupants of the building. The "Star-Spangled Banner" was beautifully sung, thousands swelling the chorus and cheering the national emblem.

The banner, 20 by 30 feet, was made entirely by the family of a former Senator of this State and city, (Hon. O. Newcomb,) who generously volunteered their services, as the unprecedented demand for flags rendered it impossible for the manufacturers to get one up in less than ten or twelve days.

No less than four generations assisted in its construction. One of the ladies (having passed her sixty-seventh winter) is a great-great-grandmother, and was personally acquainted with General Washington. As the needle was plied by her not infirm hand, the big tears would fall copiously on the bunting, as she recounted her many reminiscences of Washington, and her vivid recollections of the war of 1812. "When her eyes shall behold for the last time the sun in heaven, may she still see him shining on this gorgeous ensign of a United Republic; not a stripe erased or polluted, nor a single star obscured!"

The crowd dispersed with nine cheers for the Stars and Stripes, and nine cheers for the patriotic ladies who made it.—*Commercial Advertiser, April 25.*

ACCORDING to a Memphis paper, the following is reported to be the answer of the Governor of Arkansas, to Lincoln's requisition for volunteers:

"Yours received calling for a regiment of volunteers from Arkansas. *Nary one*—see you d——d first!"—*Charleston Mercury, April 25.*

BOSTON, *April 25.*—Touching incidents of the times are hourly becoming history. Humorous ones occasionally find a niche in which they are seen, and afford amusement, but none that are "decidedly good" should be overlooked. One good one that has reached our ears, we will give. One of the Justices of the Police Court, who has seen much service in our Volunteer Militia, was holding court a few days since, when a company of volunteers passed the Court House, marching to the immortal tune of the "Star-Spangled Banner." The spectators sprang to their feet, responsive to the understood order of "Forward, to the door!" Running feet shuffled in the entry. Boom! boom! sounded the band. "O, long may it wave!" screamed a patriotic urchin outside the window. "*First Regiment, take the witness stand!*" thundered the Court, which must have imagined itself on the *green field* at the head of its command. The outburst of laughter—unconsciously provoked—which succeeded, is yet going through the bar of the county.—*Boston Traveller, April 25.*

CHARLESTON, *April 25.*—We are requested by Brig.-Gen. Simons, commanding Morris Island, to state that some firing for exercise, and to discharge guns, will be done at Morris Island to-day, and he gives notice to prevent any uneasiness in the city.— *Charleston Mercury.*

A HOME SCENE.—A member of one of the Charleston companies, on leave of absence in the city, received a summons to appear at his post on Sullivan's Island on one of the nights when the air was rife with the most startling rumors of the coming of an overwhelming fleet. With cheerful promptitude the brave soldier prepared to obey the imperative call. He is a husband, and the father of a blue-eyed little girl, who has just begun to put words together. After the preparation for the camp had been made, the soldier nerved himself for the good-bye. Those present thought that the wife felt the parting less than the husband. Lively words flowed fast, and her fair face was as bright and calm as a morning in May. Her heart seemed to be full of gladness.

She cheered him with pleasant earnestness to show himself a man, and running on in a gleeful strain, admonished him *not* to come back if he were shot in the back. With incredible fortitude she bade her child tell papa good-bye, and to say to him that she would not own him her father if he proved to be a coward. The echo of the soldier's footfall through the corridor had hardly died away, when a ghastly pallor was seen spreading over the lady's face. In a voice weak and husky she begged a friend to take her child, and before she could be supported she fell from her chair prostrate on the floor.

By a tremendous effort the noble woman had controlled her feelings; but nature could bear no longer, and she fainted. The swoon was deep, and it was some time before consciousness returned. At length she opened her eyes languidly, and looked around upon the sympathizing group, and in a tremulous tone inquired "*if she had fainted before her husband left the room.*"—*Charleston Courier, April 16.*

ON! BROTHERS, ON!

BY SARAH WARNER BROOKS.

Air—*"Hail to the Chief."*

On! brothers, on! for the Flag that is peerless!
Striped from the rainbow, and starred from the
   sky.
On, with a sturdy step! dauntless and fearless!
   On, to unfurl it in triumph, or die!
     Honored in all the lands,
     Now shall unholy hands
Trail it, defiled and despised, in the dust?
     Down with the "traitor's rag"!
     Up with the starry Flag!
Death for our Banner! and God for the just!

Fiercely at Sumter have thundered their cannon—
   Bravely the guns of our hero replied!—
On! for the ashes that slumber at Vernon!
   On! for the city whose name is our pride!
     Now let our country's guns
     Sweep down the bastard sons!
Woe for her chivalry's flower in the dust!
     Down with the "traitor's rag"!
     Up with the starry Flag!
Death for our Banner! and God for the just!

On, with a prayer! there is peril before us!
   On, in the face of death, fearless and proud!
Life! with the Flag that our fathers waved over us!
   Death! with its crimson-stained folds for a shroud!
     Now for our "fatherland,"
     Strike with true heart and hand!
Loyal our venture—and Heavenward our trust!
     Down with the "traitor's rag"!
     Up with the starry Flag!
Death for our Banner! and God for the just!
           —*Providence Journal.*

GOD FOR OUR NATIVE LAND!

BY REV. DR. BETHUNE.*

God's blessing be upon
   Our own, our native land!
The land our fathers won
   By the strong heart and hand,
   The keen axe and the brand,
When they felled the forest's pride,
And the tyrant foe defied,
The free, the rich, the wide;
   GOD FOR OUR NATIVE LAND!

Up with the starry sign,
   The red stripes and the white!
Where'er its glories shine,
   In peace, or in the fight,
   We own its high command;
For the Flag our fathers gave,
O'er our children's heads shall wave,
And their children's children's grave!
   GOD FOR OUR NATIVE LAND!

Who doth that Flag defy,
   We challenge as our foe;
Who will not for it die,
   Out from us he must go!

* Sung at his church, 21st Street, New York city, May 5,
1861.
POETRY—41

So let them understand.
Who that dear Flag disclaim,
Which won their fathers' fame,
We brand with endless shame!
   GOD FOR OUR NATIVE LAND!

Our native land! to thee,
   In one united vow,
To keep thee strong and free,
   And glorious as now—
     We pledge each heart and hand;
By the blood our fathers shed,
By the ashes of our dead,
By the sacred soil we tread,
   GOD FOR OUR NATIVE LAND!

A POEM.

BY C. F.

The morning sun shone brightly o'er a brave and
   noble band,
Who gathered there to bleed and die for their be-
   loved land;
They fought against a foreign power who strove, but
   strove in vain,
To bring America's free soil beneath Oppression's
   chain.
Then bravely rose her gallant sons,—they felt their
   cause was right,—
And the Stars and Stripes waved over them through-
   out the deadly fight;
And foremost in the fearful strife there rode a mighty
   one,
Whose name we reverence and love—our own George
   Washington.

'Tis over, and our freedom won—while glorious and
   fair,
Above us the bright Stars and Stripes are floating
   high in air;
No more we bow and tremble 'neath Old England's
   haughty sway;
America stands nobly forth, a nation from that day.
And God hath ever smiled upon our own, our blood-
   bought land,
And blessings and prosperity we meet at every hand;
Our Washington hath laid him down, and quietly
   doth rest,
But he liveth in his people's hearts, in the broad
   lands of the West.

But lo! a darker cloud appears! the sound of war
   once more
Is ringing through the land we love—is heard upon
   our shore;
It is not now a foreign power that biddeth us to
   strife—
A brother seeks a brother's blood—would take a
   brother's life;
A brother seeks to break the bonds of mutual love
   and trust;
And lo! the Banner we revere, lies trampled in the
   dust!
The sunny South is up in arms, and wishes to divide
The Union we have owned so long—for which our
   fathers died.

And shall we quietly submit, and see our country's
   laws
Lie trampled 'neath a traitor's foot—shall we forsake
   our cause?

Shall we allow our Banner, revered through all the
    world,
From its proud height of glory, by traitors to be
    hurled?
No, never—though our blood be shed! our eagle
    stoops not so;
His haughty mien is still untamed, his head not yet
    brought low;
He still is soaring proudly above the Northern land;
He finds no fitting resting-place upon the Southern
    strand.

Then let us rally round our Flag, nor rest until again
The dove of peace unfolds her wings o'er forest and
    o'er plain;
Until again we meet in love a noble brother-band,
And sheathe the sword which now is drawn in terror
    o'er our land;
Until the glorious Stars and Stripes triumphantly
    once more
Shall wave o'er a united land, the country we adore!
Oh, may we yet, Americans, in freedom take our
    stand,
And battle bravely for the right!—God for our na-
    tive land!

ARMING FOR BATTLE.

[INSCRIBED TO GOVERNOR SPRAGUE.]

Oh men! who gird yourselves with speed,
No common call is that ye heed;
Your country bids you go, and bleed

Perchance; and who shall say what more,
What less than death, there is in store
For you, ere this fell strife is o'er?—

This strife, that needs some unbreathed name
To speak its woe—its ruthless fame;
That sets a continent aflame!

Oh, reckless stroke! oh, impious hand!
That cleft the bonds which held our land
In happy league our fathers planned.

On History's page, no fouler thing
Has left its stain; and Time shall bring
No veil for it, with pitying wing.

Treason's fierce breath fanned the red fire,
In whose wild flame may yet expire
Sweet Liberty, the world's desire.

Oh, men, who haste at duty's call,
To quench that fire, or in it fall,
God speed you, arm you, keep you all!

We will not say, "Be true! be brave!"
But through our tears a boon we crave—
"Heart of your heart, oh, let us have!"

We are cast down, to see you go,
With patriot souls, and eyes aglow
With valor's light, to meet the foe—

A foe we called, but yesterday,
Brother and friend; and now we say,
"Alas, for love he spurned away!"

We know you brave—ye will not quail;
We do not fear your swords will fail;
Yet for all this, our lips grow pale

With parting words, that say, "Come back,
By God's dear grace, on Victory's track!"
But then, our brothers fall, alack!

Yet go! ye bear no wanton brand;
Honor's bright hilt in every hand;
Go! for our Flag undaunted stand.

That dear old Flag, spangled with stars—
Go, keep it full; 'tis worth some wars,
To save its crest from Treason's scars.

No upstart flag the land shall own,
Where the old stars have proudly shone,
Till Hope, Truth, Valor, all are gone.

Brave hearts, farewell! bright eyes will weep
To night, quick tears that hinder sleep—
Weeping for you, whom angels keep!
    April 19, 1861.   W. C. R.
                         —Providence Evening Press.

A SONG FOR THE UNION.*

England's heavy chains oppressed us,
    And her foot had held us down,
Till the people, full of fury,
    Raised the shout, "Resist the crown!"
All the nation heard the watchword,—
    Every town sent up the cry,
Answering, like a solemn echo,
    "We will conquer or will die!"
        Then were seen
        The brave Thirteen,
    Fighting for our liberty.

All New England's heroes wakened,
    With the courage wrongs inspire,—
Nerved themselves to stand the struggle,
    Dare and brave Old England's ire;
While from every hill and valley
    Thronging came an answering band,
Poorly clad, half-armed, but heroes,
    And for Freedom took their stand;
        Then were seen
        The brave Thirteen,
    Winning us a free-born land.

Victory crowned their gallant struggle,—
    God alone they owned as king,
And they stood a free-born people,
    Sheltered by the Almighty's wing;
While their statesmen and their heroes
    To a compact set their hand,—
"All our strength lies in our Union;
    To the world as one we'll stand."
        The Old Thirteen
        Since then have been
    Honored and blest in every land.

Oh! the contrast time now shows us!
    Scarce a hundred years have passed,
And the smothered mutterings warn us,
    This will be the Union's last.
Last! VIRGINIA, you who gave us
    Our dear Father, Statesman, Chief,

* Read at a Union meeting at Detroit, Michigan, held
Jan. 28, 1861. A full report of the meeting is given in the
Detroit Free Press, Jan. 29.

Can you let the life he fought for—
  A great nation's—be so brief?
    Strife between
      The Old Thirteen!
  Never let that sight be seen.

GEORGIA! whose chivalric soldiers
  Proved the worth of gentle blood,
When the enemy struck so boldly,
  And o'erswept you like a flood,
Will you turn your steel against those
  Who, when in your direst need,
Came to strengthen those proud spirits?
  Georgians, *dare* you say, "Secede"?
    Blood between
      That Old Thirteen—
  Brothers both in word and deed!

Thy records, CAROLINA, point where
  The first blood for Freedom fell;
By the mother who thus bore you,
  Will *you* bid us all farewell?
Wild and wilful, proud, impatient,
  Haughty sister, have you known
Through your turbulent life we loved you
  For a beauty of your own,—
    Loved you truly,
      Even unduly,
  And could never have you gone?

By the memories of the KEYSTONE,—
  By the JERSEYS' blood-stained snow,—
By old EMPIRE's glorious battles,—
  By the record of our foes,—
By Schuyler, Knox, old Putnam, Greene,—
  By Marion's men, and Harry Lee,
Let us forget all party strife,
  And only know that we are *free*.
    The world has seen
      What we *have* been.
  Oh! still preserve the Old Thirteen.

With what blindness are we smitten,
  Brother thus opposing brother!
In the nation's past 'tis written,
  Freedom is our glorious mother.
You can count her pangs of travail
  In the banner waving o'er us;
History tells the wreck and carnage
  That o'erspread her when she bore us.
    Shall love languish
      When her anguish,
  Beacon-like, still floats before us?

Palsied be the lips that frame it,—
  Helpless fall that foeman's arm,—
Turn his fiercest strength to weakness,
  Who would do a brother harm.
And, O God! wilt Thou take vengeance
  On whoe'er, by word or deed,
Broadcast o'er our noble country
  Sowed disunion's fruitful seed?
    Curse the tongue
      Of old or young,
  Who shouts the battle-cry, "Secede"!

God, our Lord, be Thou our support,
  Thou our stay in this dark hour;
Guide us through these angry mazes,
  By Thine overseeing power;

Blast the rage of party sections;
  Cause such war and strife to cease;
Give us—greatest gift to nations—
  Give us union, love, and peace.
    The Old Thirteen
      On Thee shall lean;
  Lord, let their mutual love increase.

Cast to the breeze that banner still,
  With not one single star erased,
With not one single stripe effaced;
Shout, with a hearty, brave good-will,
  "Let nought our happy land dissever,—
  The Union, *one*, and one *forever!!*"
Wake the wide echoes with that pæan,—
  The *Union*, and the *Old Thirteen*.

THE NORTHERN VOLUNTEERS.

BY GEORGE BOWERYEM.

We arm by thousands strong,
  To battle for the Right,
And this shall be our song,
  As we march into the fight:
With our country's banner o'er us,
And traitor-ranks before us,
Let Freedom be the chorus
  Of the Northern Volunteers!
    Now hearken to the cheers
    Of the Northern Volunteers!
      [Chorus of cheering.]

When the battle rages round,
  And the rolling of the drum,
And the trembling of the ground,
  Tell usurpers that WE COME!—
Then the War's deep-mouthèd thunder
Shall our lightnings cleave asunder,
And our enemies shall wonder
  At the Northern Volunteers!
    Shall wonder at the cheers
    Of the Northern Volunteers!

True, loyal sons are we
  Of men who fought and died
To leave their children free,
  Whom dastards now deride!
Tremble, traitors! at the beaming
Of our starry banner gleaming,
When like a torrent streaming,
  Come the Northern Volunteers!
    Dealing death amid their cheers,
    Come the Northern Volunteers!

When Northern men unite,
  Heart to heart and hand to hand,
For Freedom's cause to fight,
  Shall Wrong the Right withstand?
With our country's banner o'er us,
And rebels base before us,
And Liberty the chorus
  Of the Northern Volunteers,—
    How terrible the cheers
    Of the Northern Volunteers!

Where Freedom's banner waves,
  Over land or over sea,
It shall not cover slaves!
  They shall touch it and be free!

Tremble, tyrants! at the flashing
Of our arms, when onward dashing,
You shall hear their fetters crashing,
　　Broke by Northern Volunteers!
　　And your slaves give back the cheers
　　Of the Northern Volunteers!

God of Freedom! give Thy might
　　To the spirits of Thy sons!
To their bayonets in fight!
　　To the death within their guns!
Make their deeds in battle gory,
Burn and brightly shine in glory,
When the world shall read the story
　　Of the Northern Volunteers!
　　And echo back the cheers
　　Of the Northern Volunteers!

HEADQUARTERS BRITISH VOLUNTEERS, ⎱
　　New York, May 18, 1861. ⎰

THE MARCH OF THE "SEVENTH."

What means this eager rush? whence this commo-
　　tion?
Why surge the people thus, like a lashed ocean?
See, the vast multitude, crowding and craving;
See, from each lofty staff stars and stripes waving!

Banners from balcony, banners from steeple,
Banners from house to house, draping the people;
Banners upborne by all, men, women, children,
Banners on horses' fronts, flashing, bewild'ring.

Hark! there's a trumpet-blast strikes on the hearing;
Now the quick drum-beat comes rapidly nearing;
Blue forms with clubs in hand, steadily banding,
Through the compacted crowd pathway demanding.

Drums beat, and trumpets sound, louder and louder,
Bugles and cornets mix deep tones and prouder;
Whose is that solid front? whose is that thick step?
Whose, but the "Seventh's" tread, moves to that
　　quickstep?

On comes the Regiment, like to none other;
Who has not in its ranks loved son or brother?
If he has none of these, not e'en a cousin,
He served himself in it, years by the dozen.

Know ye the city's heart in that mass mingles?
Hear, the responsive throb everywhere tingles!
Now, as they're moving past, shout, sob, and greeting,
Love's deep devotion they're constantly meeting.

See, 'midst the serried ranks, none now objecting,
Hundreds of laymen the flanks seem protecting,
Crowding between platoons, filling the spaces,
Many a manly form steadily paces!

Those are the fathers, proud eyes overflowing,
On Freedom's altar their best blood bestowing;
Gladly they give their sons, each true heart bleeding,
Offering the noblest to Liberty's needing.

Oh, 'tis a costly gift now they are bringing,
And on their country's shrine willingly flinging;
One gives his five sons, others their four, three, two—
Ye who have sons there, ah, how do I envy you!

There stands brave Anderson, watching them, breath-
　　less—
Glory's new-born son, whose name now is deathless;
Looks he not proudly on? Soon they espy him,
Loud rings their homage cheer, as they pass by him.

Why does he drop a tear? why is he weeping,
As that majestic march past him is sweeping?
Ah, he beholds in them, earnest and steady,
Hearts like his noble own, for sacrifice ready.

He knows the savage horde lately contending,
Not as our sires fought, Justice defending,
But, with the tiger's fangs, stealthily seeking
Power the weak to scourge, 'midst tears and shriek-
　　ing.

Hero of Sumter! thy name is forever
Coupled with Glory, and ne'er will we sever
"Manhood and Anderson." Freedom's libation
Pours forth from million hearts through all the
　　nation.

Vengeance is now the cry, no more betraying;
Treating with traitors is senseless delaying;
Sons of the Bay State their Sumner remember;
Wrongs to be righted now wake from their slumber.

Pass on the battle-cry! sound it forth, trumpeter!
Hand it from man to man—"*Sumner and Sumter!*"
Hark! now from Baltimore comes, madly driven,
One more foul insult that can't be forgiven.

Go forth, then, gallant hearts, bearing the casket
Holding our city's blood—seek not to mask it!
Fling it before you far, fight your way to it;
Stay them not, Maryland, or you will rue it!

Fathers are arming fast, mothers are praying,
While you are noble deeds skilfully playing;
Soon we will follow you; New York is coming!
Hark, do you hear the rush, like Niagara booming?

Onward, then, "Seventh!" delay not, nor waver!
Rush to fair Freedom's side, guard her and save
　　her!
Give the vile vulture brood—kites, buzzards, ma-
　　rauders—
The feast that they're lusting for from their own
　　borders!　　　　　　　　　　　R. S. O.

　　　　　　　　　　　—*N. Y. Tribune*, April 23.

A TALE OF 1861.

BY EDW. SPRAGUE RAND, JR.

Come, children, leave your playing; a tale I have to
　　tell—
A tale of woe and sorrow, which long ago befell;
'Twas in the great rebellion, in eighteen sixty-one;
Within the streets of Baltimore the bloody deed was
　　done.

Of gallant Major Anderson I told you yesternight,
Of Moultrie's shattered battlements, and Sumter's
　　bloodless fight;
And how the cannon's echo shook the North and East
　　and West,
And woke a flame in loyal hearts which would not be
　　repressed.

Oh, 'twas a goodly sight to see the uprising of the people;
To hear the clanging bells ring out from every tower and steeple;
To see our glorious flag flung wide all through the loyal land;
To know at last the North stood up a firm united band!

A call went forth through all the land: "On, on to Washington!"
On, for the Union that we prize! for Right and Freedom, on!
'Twas sunset ere the call was known, but ere the break of day,
Our brave militia were in arms, and ready for the fray.

They left the plough, forsook the loom, bade hasty, sad farewell,
To all they loved, with looks which spoke far more than words could tell;
And loving wives and mothers wept and blessed them on their way;
But, 'mid the throng of anxious ones, not one would bid them stay.

As on through loyal towns they went, 'twas one prolonged ovation;
Of all a patriot people did, would weary the narration.
On, on for Washington they pressed, for there the patriot band,
For the Union and for Liberty, for Right must take their stand.

'Twas the nineteenth of April;—O most auspicious day!
It ushered in at Lexington the bloody, fatal fray,
Baptized our Revolution; and 'twas again to be
For Massachusetts men to bleed for Freedom and the free.

Through Baltimore their pathway led, and boldly on they passed,
But bitter taunts and angry words fell on them thick and fast;
'Twas the low rabble of the town by whom the deed was done,
But men of wealth and rank were there, and urged and cheered them on.

O who shall tell of all that chanced, or in that fearful fray
Tell what was done, or truly write the history of that day!
How, not content with scoffs and taunts, the pavement up they tore,
And showered the stones upon our troops, around, behind, before.

"Why did they let them?" O alas! forgetful grows my mind;
The others had passed safely on, a few were left behind;
For thus Secession's chivalry its boldest deeds has done,
And often have they bravely fought, *a hundred against one.*

On, on, in close-set ranks they pressed, turned not to left or right;
They all were Massachusetts men; they never thought of flight;
But as the stones came thick and fast, the curses deep and loud,
In self-defence, at bay, they turned and fired upon the crowd.

O many a taunting traitor fell beneath their deadly fire;
But thicker flew the showers of stones, and fiercer grew their ire.
Enough—they fought their passage through, and then kept marching on,
Obedient to their country's call, to rescue Washington.

Yet not unscathed; four noble ones fell in the bloody fray,
And many carry scarring wounds in memory of that day;
And high on honor's scroll are writ the names of those who fell,
First martyrs to maintain the rights, the land we love so well.

Yes, Washington was saved, my boy: another time I'll tell
Of Freedom's armies, marshalled there, of all that there befell.
The blood then spilt at Baltimore roused all the loyal land,
And such an army sprung to birth no traitors could withstand.

I mind me when the honored dead in solemn pomp came home;
How our starry banner drooped half-mast on the high State House dome;
How minute-guns spoke sharply out, and sad the bells were tolling,
And mournfully upon the breeze the funeral dirge was rolling.

O there was that within the looks, within the eyes of men,
A stern determination, I never saw but then;
With hard-pressed lips and swimming eyes they watched the funeral train,
With bowed, uncovered heads, they stood amid the falling rain.

In vision yet I seem to see the biers with flags entwined;
The memory of that solemn dirge will never flee my mind;
And Massachusetts lifts her head more proudly at this day,
That twice in Freedom's battles her sons have led the way.

O children, guard your heritage; be to your country true;
Be proud of Massachusetts, and let her be proud of you!
Be ready in her cause to fight, and for her sake to fall!
But cherish in your heart of hearts the Union above all.

—*Boston Transcript*, May 22.

TO ARMS!

BY MARTHA PERRY LOWE.

Traitors and foes! We shall arm! We shall arm!
Brethren are ye?—but it matters us not—
Men of the South! We are calm! We are calm!
You are like madmen, misguided and hot!

Long have we patiently borne with your hate;
Shame has been rising and flushing our brow;
Oh! we've entreated you, early and late—
God only knows what has come o'er us now!

We are not angry—the fire is too deep;
We will not taunt—that's for boys, and not men;
Yet we have sworn, and our word we will keep,
Never shall you trample on us again!

You have dishonored the Stripes and the Stars!
The pale North a moment *did* hold in her breath;
Now thousands of eyes, like the red planet Mars,
Do glare on you steady defiance and death!

You love not to work, you are all gentle-men;
Arms are your pastime, and "fight" is your word;
We love the plow, and the loom, and the pen;
Nobler is Peace, to our hearts, than the Sword.

You have been plotting all over the land—
You have been training to tear down the State;
We've not been playing with weapons in hand,
But we'll tear down *your* flag, at the Capitol's gate!

Lord of the Nations! Restrain us! Restrain!
Terrible, mighty, our waking will be;
Blood, when it falls, will come down as the rain,
Flooding the earth like the surge of the sea!

Then courage, ye men of the North and the West!
A nation is springing again into birth!
In the beautiful garments of liberty drest,
Forever to stand the desire of the earth!
—*N. Y. Tribune.*

A BUGLE NOTE.

Air—*Marseillaise.*

Oh, freemen's sons, arouse to battle,
'Gainst the proud, insulting foe;
Shall their cannon 'round us rattle,
And no arm to strike a blow?—
And no arm to strike a blow?
Too long has tolerance been given,
By forbearance kind and free;
But let now the war-cry be,
Our blest land shall ne'er be riven!

To arms! to arms, ye brave!
Our trampled flag reclaim
From traitor's grasp, and nobly win
A patriot's honored name.

Hear, hear the cannon loudly roaring,
'Round our brave and valiant band;
And a nation loud deploring
The stained honor of our land—
The stained honor of our land.

And will you tamely now surrender
To a false and perjured host,
Your glorious country's boast,
Refusing to defend her?

To arms! to arms, ye brave!
Our trampled flag reclaim
From traitor's grasp, and nobly win
A patriot's honored name.

EMILY.
Phila. Inquirer, April 24

SEND THEM HOME TENDERLY.*

BY G. W. BUNGAY.

I.

In their own martial robes arrayed,
With cap, and cloak, and shining blade,
In the still coffin softly laid,
Oh, send them tenderly.
Our bleeding country's gallant corps
Of noble dead can sleep no more
Where monuments at Baltimore
Libel our Liberty.

II.

Oh, touch them tenderly, I pray,
And softly wipe the blood away
From the red lips of wounds, that say,
"How sweet it is to die
For one's dear Country, at a time
Coincidence crowns, with sublime
Associations, deeds that chime
In human history!"

III.

Deal gently with the pale, cold dead,
For Massachusetts bows her head—
But not with shame; her eyes are red
With weeping for the slain.
Like Rachel, she is sad indeed;
And long her broken heart will bleed
For children true in word and deed
She cannot meet again.

IV.

Whisper no word of treason when
Ye bear away our bravest men
From the foul traitor's hateful den,
Red with our brother's blood;
A spot that must forever be,
Like Sodom sunk beneath the sea,
It sinks in coward treachery,
Unwept beneath the flood.

V.

Lift up each gallant son of Mars,
And shroud him in the flag of stars,
Beneath whose folds he won the scars
Through which his spirit fled
From glory here, to glory where
The banner blue in fields of air
Is bright with stars forever there,
Without the stripes of red.
—*N. Y. Tribune.*

* See Gov. Andrew's despatch to the Mayor of Baltimore, p. 34, Diary of Events, Rebellion Record.

SONG OF COLUMBIA'S DAUGHTERS.

BY ELIZABETH D. WRIGHT.

Oh, go ! brothers, go !
　Hark to Freedom calling !
See her bleeding stand
　While her sons are falling !
Mothers, yield your darlings ;
　Wives, your husbands send ;
Children, spare your fathers—
　God will be your friend !
　　Rally round our standard !
　　　Hasten on to save !
　　Be our watchword ever,
　　　" Freedom, or the grave ! "

Onward !　See our Country—
　Once a peaceful home,
Where the world's oppressed ones
　Might for refuge come—
Now all torn and fainting,
　Wounded sore she lies ;
Forward to the rescue,
　Ere our Union dies !
　　Rally round our standard, &c.

Oh, fight ! brothers, fight !
　Our fathers fought before you ;
Your blows are for the right,
　And Freedom's God is o'er you.
Remember, when in battle,
　How we at home will pray,
That He, as your Commander,
　Will aid you win the day.
　　Rally round our standard !
　　　Hasten on to save !
　　Be our watchword ever,
　　　" Freedom, or the grave ! "

NEW YORK, *April 22, 1861.*
　　　　　　　　—*N. Y. Tribune.*

THE MAJOR AND HIS MEN.

In Charleston Bay Fort Sumter stood,
　Begirt by traitor guns,
Its garrison just seventy—
　Columbia's bravest sons.
" I'll have that fort," quoth Beauregard,
　" Or else may I be curst ! "
" But then," says Major Anderson,
　" You'll have to fight me first ! "

CHORUS—Cheer, boys, cheer !
　And pass the bowl again ;
Till time shall end, we'll ne'er forget
　The Major and his Men.

The traitors built their batt'ries round,
　And thousands counted they ;
But Sumter with its seventy
　Still held them all at bay !
" Surrender now," says Beauregard ;
　" I'll have you in a trap."
" Not yet," says gallant Anderson,
　" My fuss-and-feather chap ! "

CHORUS—Cheer, boys, cheer !
　The traitors in their den
Could not with all their guns appall
　The Major and his Men.

To Sumter, straight from Washington,
　A secret message came :
" Till we make sure the Capital,
　Hold Sumter all the same.
If traitors fire, return their fire,
　Until the fleet you see ;
Then leave the fort, brave Anderson,
　And bring thy men with thee."

CHORUS—Cheer, boys, cheer !
　The ball was opened then,
And traitors were outwitted by
　The Major and his Men.

One day the rebel batteries,
　That numbered near a score,
Commenced to fire at Sumter's walls
　With an infernal roar.
The Major and his seventy,
　By numbers undismayed,
The rebels' iron compliments
　With shot and shell repaid !

CHORUS—Cheer, boys, cheer !
　We shall not see again
Such pluck as that which gave to fame
　The Major and his Men.

For forty hours that gallant band
　Held Sumter from the foe,
And gaily their columbiads
　Dealt ruin high and low ;
But when the fleet from Uncle Sam
　Made signals fair in sight,
That Washington was safe enough,
　The Major stopped the fight.

CHORUS—Cheer, boys, cheer !
　And pass the glass again ;
The " trick " that time was taken by
　The Major and his Men.

The Major left the battered fort,
　A crumbling, empty pen,
And ere the rebels can repair,
　We'll have it back again !
Their harbor is blockaded now,
　And Anderson is here,
With sword still girded by his side,
　And stranger still to fear !

CHORUS—Cheer, boys, cheer !
　We'll have it back again !
And who shall be our comrades but
　The Major and his Men ?
　　　—*N. Y. Sunday Atlas,* May 12.

OUR NATIONAL FLAG.

BY EMELINE S. SMITH.

Who said that the stars on our banner were dim—
　That their glory had faded away ?
Look up, and behold ! how bright, through each fold,
　They are flashing and smiling to-day.
A few wand'ring meteors only have paled—
　They shot from their places on high ;
But the *fixed* and the *true* still illumine the blue,
　And will, while old Ages go by !

Who said the fair temple, so patiently reared
　By heroes, at Liberty's call,
Was built insecure—that it could not endure—
　And was tottering e'en now to its fall ?

False, false, every word; for that fame is upheld
  By the stoutest of hearts and of hands;
Some columns unsound may have gone to the ground,
  But proudly the temple yet stands.

Who said there were murmurs of grief in our midst,
  When loved ones departed to-day?*
Ah, no!—'twas not so—every heart hushed its woe,
  And gave them "God speed" on their way.
With their banner above, loving glances around,
  And blessings and prayers as a shield,
We trusted this band, the fair flower of the land,
  To the perilous risks of the field.

Who said the good name of our country was gone—
  That her flag would be honored no more?
Over valley and plain, over mountain and main,
  Rolls an answer like Thunder's deep roar;
A million brave spirits all shout with one voice,
  "We will die for the rights we demand!
Let traitors beware! By their dark plots we swear,
  That no shadow shall rest on our land!"

Who questions the promise? Not we who behold
  This love and this national pride
Sweeping on through the clime, in a torrent sublime,
  And bearing all hearts on its tide.
Who fears for the issue? Ah, that must be left
  To the Mightiest Leader of all;
While He holds the scale, Truth and Right will pre-
    vail,
  And Error and Treason will fall.

A stain on our banner? Oh! shame to the heart
  Or the lip that could breathe such a thought!
Every hue is as clear, every fold is as dear,
  As when first the bright symbol was bought.
With the blood of brave men it was purchased, and we
  Pledge our own lives to keep it unstained;
On the land or the sea, where'er it may be,
  Its honor shall still be maintained.

Heaven's blessings upon it! Its stars never shone
  With a lustre so pure and so warm;
Like a beacon's calm ray, pointing out the safe way,
  They gleam through this gathering storm.
Their heart-cheering light led our fathers aright,
  Through all the dark perils they knew;
The same magic glow shall lead us to the foe,
  And guide us to VICTORY too!
               —*N. Y. Times*, April 29.

WESTERN VIRGINIA ON THE SEIZURE OF SHERRARD CLEMENS.

A good sword and a trusty hand,
  A merry heart and true,—
The Richmond men shall understand
  What Wheeling lads can do.

And have they fixed the where and when?
  And must our Clemens die?
Here's twenty thousand mountain boys
  Will see the reason why!

The West shall set this matter right,
  The West shall heeded be;
Though Richmond jail had Moultrie's guns,
  We'd set our Clemens free.

* Alluding to the departure of the Seventh Regiment.

We'll cross the hills, a lively band,
  The James shall be no stay,
All side by side, and hand to hand,—
  And who shall bid us nay?

And when we come to Richmond's wall,
  Our Stars and Stripes in view,—
Come forth, come forth, ye traitors all,
  To better men than you.

Our Clemens, he's in keep and hold,
  Our Clemens, he may die:
But here's twenty thousand freemen bold
  Will see the reason why!
           —*Boston Transcript*, April 22.

THE BALLAD OF COCKEY'S FIELD.

It was on Sunday's holy day,
  There came a fearful sound;
Five thousand hostile, armed men,
  Were marching on the town.

They were as far as Cockeysville;
  Five thousand in the van,
And with ten thousand more behind—
  'Twas thus the rumor ran.

The children cried, the women screamed—
  For scream they always will;
And did you ever know a fright
  Enough to keep them still?

And good folks in the churches met,
  Arose and went away,
As if, in such a din as this,
  It was no use to pray.

And sober folks, who'd lost their wits,
  Were running up and down
To see if they could buy, or beg,
  Some arms—beside their own.

Until, at last, some wiser head
  Suggested he would go
And see how many men there were,
  Or if it could be so;

And started off in hottest haste:
  The horse had caught the fire,
And flew along the old York road
  As if he could not tire!

And there he found two thousand men,
  Unarmed, in helpless plight;
They did not have a thing to eat—
  Had slept out-doors all night.

And so he rode up brave, and said:
  "What are you doing here?
Why did you come? What do you want?
  How many in the rear?

And so the Captain he replied,
  Most courteously to him:
"We stopped because the bridge was gone;
  We had to stop—*or swim*.

"We're going on to Washington,
  Because we have been sent;
We are unarmed; we have no food,
  Nor any base intent.

"But when 'Old Abe' the war-note sounds,
    From East and West we come,
Armed and unarmed, the young, the old,
    The Vandal and the Hun.

"Hurrah for our old Stars and Stripes,
    Afloat, on ship or shore !
It never waved o'er coward heads ;
    God guard it evermore ! "

And so came back the messenger,
    As fleet as comes the wind ;
The very horse half understood
    The load he left behind.

And then they called the fathers out,
    The fathers of the town,—
Wisdom has always dwelt with them
    From pagan Romans down ;—

And they resolved, "No hostile foot
    Shall ever cross our soil ;
That all should arm themselves, and keep
    Our fields and towns from spoil.

"We'll tear our railroads up a space ;
    We'll burn our bridges down ;
That no invading foe may harm
    Our old and stately town."

And when defence was all arranged,
    All warlike plans were laid,
The softer counsels of the heart
    Stole upwards to the head.

"We'll send them something up to eat,
    Or all these famished men
Will not have strength enough to go
    Back to their homes again."

And so great loads of all good things
    Went creaking up the road ;
A sort of music in the wheels,
    A moral in the load.

Hurrah for South ! Hurrah for North !
    Hurrah for our great land !
Three cheers for this old Brotherhood—
    The Brotherhood of Man !
Baltimore Co., Md., *April* 30, 1861.
                            —*Baltimore Co. American.*

THE CALL FOR VOLUNTEERS.

BY GEORGE W. BUNGAY.

I.

The thunder of the rebel's gun,
Before the morn had seen the sun,
    Proclaimed the treason of the traitors,
Where the tide heaves its breast, and sighs,
And the free waves in tumult rise,
    And the free winds are agitators.

II.

Hot shells explode in lurid glare,
Like meteors in morning air,
    Hoarse cannon unto cannon calling.
War's tropic tempest fiercely rains,
Belching red fire in crinkling chains,
    The iron drops on Sumter falling.

III.

Shall our good swords in scabbards rust,
Our flag, dishonored, trail in dust,
    When rebels seek our subjugation ?
Perish the thought ! our blades are drawn,
Thick as the summer blades of corn,
    Swift to defend our bleeding nation.

IV.

The breach in Sumter's battered walls,
With black lips to the nation calls,
    To rise, from inland to the borders.
Our flag of stars, by traitors' slaves
Trod in the dust, in triumph waves
    With stripes for cowards and marauders.

V.

Oh, clang the old bell in the tower,
That spoke for Freedom in the hour
    "That tried the souls" of bravest mortals.
Let patriots rock old Faneuil Hall,
And mantles on our heroes fall,
    From those who climbed Fame's starry portals.

VI.

We have a chief whose battle scars
Were won beneath the Stripes and Stars,
    Whose name will live in song and story.
Green are the laurels he has won—
Our Scott stands next to Washington
    Upon the radiant scroll of glory.
                            —*N. Y. Tribune.*

THE DEPARTURE.

The gallant young men of Rhode Island
    Are marching, in haste, to the wars ;
Full-girded for strife, they are hazarding life
    In defence of our Banner of Stars.

That flag is in danger from Treason,
    Disowned and dishonored by States,
Whose blazon of stars may be turned into scars,
    If the great Northern Legion but waits.

Oh, eyes that are weary with weeping,
    For husbands, and brothers, and sons,
Who are marching away, for many a day,
    To face that which no true hero shuns :

Look up to the Star-spangled Banner ;
    Shall one ray of its glory be lost ?
Then dry every tear, change weeping to cheer,
    For the brave men whose swords have been crossed

In the patriot oath to defend it
    From Treason, and Faction's wild lust ;
Be proud they are true to their flag and to you,
    And in them, and their God, put your trust.

Look on to the day, when, returning
    With victory crowned, from the fray,
Their shouts shall burst forth—" O'er the South and
        the North
Waves the Star-spangled Banner for aye ! "
April 25, 1861.   W. C. R.
                        —*Providence Evening Press.*

NEW ORLEANS, *April* 28.—The courts being closed, and the lawyers having nothing to do, those of the Second and Third Districts have formed a military company, in the ranks of which none are received under the age of 45 years. The roll contains already 69 names, the first among the privates being that of Hon. Pierre Soulé. The Captain is Judge Louis Duvignaud; the Lieutenants, J. P. Monnier and Emile Wiltz; the Sergeants, J. Mallet, P. Caudrain, Fenelon F. Coquet; and the Corporals, A. Dreyfous, L. Rigand, Rudolph Hetch, L. N. Johan, A. Duvignaud, L. Deroche, J. P. Montagnet, and Amédée Porche.

Most of these gentlemen are already renowned for their deeds in another field. If Cicero could come up, what would he say, he who uttered once those famous words, *Cedant arma togæ* —*N. O. Picayune, April* 28.

THE *Richmond Whig* says that the last reliable intelligence represents that Old Abe had been beastly intoxicated for the previous thirty-six consecutive hours, and that eighty Border Ruffians, from Kansas, under the command of Lane, occupied the East Room to guard His Majesty's slumbers. It is broadly hinted in a Washington paper, that his guard exerts a despotic control over the Presidential inmate—that all his decrees are of its inspiration. The paper (*The States and Union*) then proceeds to shed a becoming quantity of tears over this "sad subject for contemplation."—*N. O. Sunday Delta, April* 28.

THE following has been placarded on all the dead walls in the upper part of the city of New York:

CONDITIONS OF PEACE REQUIRED OF THE SO-CALLED SECEDED STATES.

Art. 1. Unconditional submission to the Government of the United States.

Art. 2. To deliver up one hundred of the Arch Traitors to be hung.

Art. 3. To put on record the names of all others who have been traitorous to the Government, who shall be held infamous and disfranchised forever.

Art. 4. The property of all traitors to be confiscated to pay the damage.

Art. 5. The seceded States to pay the balance of the expense, and to restore all stolen property.

Art. 6. The payment of all debts due to Northerners, and indemnity for all indignities to persons, loss of time, life, and property.

Art. 7. The removal of the cause of all our difficulties, which can only be done by the immediate and unconditional abolition of slavery.

Art. 8. Until a full compliance with all the above terms, the so-called seceded States to be held and governed as United States territory.

The above is the least an indignant people will accept, outraged as they have been by the foulest and most heinous and gigantic instance of crime recorded in history.—*N. Y. Express, April* 26.

A CORRESPONDENT of the *Richmond Whig*, writing from Norfolk, gives the following account of affairs at the time of the destruction of the Gosport Navy Yard:—

The truth is, everybody was drunk, from Commodore Macaulay, the commandant, down. The Commodore was so drunk as to be incapable of any duty, and had to be borne to the ship on a litter. Nearly every officer, it was reported, was having a high old time. It seems we have a swilling set opposed to us, even those filling the highest stations. A gentleman arrived here this morning, who, with several others, was arrested while passing through Washington, for being Southerners, and taken into the presence of the august Baboon. He declares that Lincoln was so drunk that he could scarcely maintain his seat in the chair; and it was notorious in Washington that he had been in a state of intoxication for more than thirty-six hours. The man is scared nearly to death, and few people in that city are in any better condition.—*N. O. Delta, April* 29.

A GENTLEMAN from Washington reports that the following is the language of Mr. Lincoln to the Baltimore Committee:—

GENTLEMEN : You have come here to ask for peace on any terms. Such a desire, on such terms, is not like the course of Washington or Jackson. They—the rebels—attacked Fort Sumter, and you attack the troops sent to the Federal Government for the protection of the same, and for the defence of the lives and the property of the inhabitants of this city. My intention was never to attack Maryland, but to have those troops, as I said before, for the protection of Washington. Now, gentlemen, go home and tell your people, that if they will not attack us, we will not attack them; but if they do attack us, we will return it, and that severely. Those troops must come to Washington, and that through Maryland. They can neither go under it nor can they fly over it, and they shall come through it.—*Philadelphia Press April* 26.

A DEPUTATION of sixteen Virginians and eight Marylanders visited the President on the 21st of April, and demanded *a cessation of hostilities* until after the session of Congress. Mr. Lincoln of course *declined the proposition.* One of the deputation said that 75,000 Marylanders would contest the passage of troops over her soil; *to which the President replied, that he presumed there was room enough on her soil to bury* 75,000 *men.*—*N. Y. Times, April* 27.

WHEN Major Anderson and his command passed out of the harbor on their way to join the fleet of the United States, the Marion Artillery, a company which, according to high military authority, contributed very materially to the reduction of Fort Sumter, in testimony of their appreciation of his gallant defense, formed on the beach and stood with uncovered heads until the Isabel had passed their position.—*N. O. Delta, April* 25.

NEW ORLEANS, *April* 25.—In the ranks of the Louisville Blues, now at Montgomery, from Barbour County, is the Rev. Alexander McLenan, of the Methodist Episcopal Church, who, with his two sons, have enlisted with the company for the term of twelve months, in the service of the Confederate States. In a speech made by him at Clayton, on their way to Columbus, he remarked that "our cause was honored of God, and He would crown it with success." Mr. McLenan is upwards of sixty years of age, and the greater part of his manhood has been dedicated to the service of the ministry. Equality and justice to the South is a motto to which he has always been religiously devoted.—*Columbus Sun, April* 21.

FIRST CATCH THE RABBIT.—Ole Dabe threatens to burn Baltimore if the railways leading to Washington be obstructed. Hadn't he better get Baltimore before he burns it? Ole Dabe ought to consult Miss Leslie's recipe for hare soup—"first catch the hare," &c.—*N. O. Delta, April 26.*

THE conduct of the Eighth Massachusetts Regiment at Annapolis, Md., is deserving of the greatest praise. When Gen. Butler asked if any of them could sail the Constitution, *fifty-four men stepped from the ranks, one of whom was the son of the man who built her!* A similar incident occurred when the General called for mechanics to put the dislocated engine together. One stalwart Yankee stepped from the ranks, and said, "*Well, General, I rather think I can—I made that engine;*" and in two hours the engine was at work drawing trains with the troops towards Washington. The efficiency of the stalwart six-footers with which the regiment abounds, was a most fortunate thing for the vast body of troops concentrating there.—*N. Y. Times, April 27.*

THE insane fury of New York arises from purely mercenary motives. She is concerned about the golden eggs which are laid for her by the Southern goose with the sword. Let us assure her we have more fear of her smiles than of her frowns. New York will be remembered with especial hatred by the South to the end of time. Boston we have always known where to find; but this New York, which has never turned against us till the hour of trial, and is now moving heaven and earth for our destruction, shall be a marked city to the end of time.—*Richmond Dispatch, April 25.*

THE following is an extract from a private letter, dated 22d April, from a Southern lady, now in Washington City, to a lady friend and relative in New Orleans:

This place is in a terrible condition; the streets are thronged with soldiers; it is really unsafe for a lady to walk out alone. Old Lincoln sleeps with a hundred armed men in the east room to protect him from the Southern army. He is expecting them to attack the city every night; he keeps a sentinel walking in front of his bed-room all night, and often gets so frightened that he leaves the White House, and sleeps out, no one knows where. These are facts. Mrs. Lincoln, a few nights since, heard whispering in the hall in front of her room; she rose from bed, dressed, and sat up the remainder of the night watching for the Southern army to blow up the White House, as they are confidently expecting it.

Senator Gwin's son, a fine-looking, intelligent young man, about twenty years old, has thrown up a cadetship at West Point, and gone to Montgomery to seek an appointment in the Confederate Army. The Senator himself has gone to California, and his family have broken up housekeeping, and will spend the summer on his plantation in Isaquena County, Mississippi, and thus Mrs. Gwin and her daughter may grace New Orleans with her presence during the summer, if there is no epidemic in your city.—*N. O. Delta, April 28.*

AT New York, a matronly lady, accompanied by her son, a fine youth of about nineteen years, entered a gun store on Broadway, and purchased a full outfit for him. Selecting the best weapons and other articles for a soldier's use, that could be found in the store, she paid the bill, remarking, with evident emotion, "This, my son, is all that I can do. I have given you up to serve your country, and may God go with you! It is all a mother can do." The incident attracted considerable attention, and tearful eyes followed this patriotic mother and her son, as they departed from the place.—*N. Y. Times, April 29.*

AT the great demonstration at Union Square, New York, April 26th, for the defence of the Union, a committee was appointed, which was subdivided into other committees, and among them a committee to obtain subscriptions in aid of the fund to be provided. Mr. A. T. Stewart, who is one of the latter, headed his own subscription list with the sum of *Ten Thousand Dollars!*—*N. Y. Times, April 26.*

RICHMOND, Va., *April 23.*—It is reported here that a dispatch has been received by Gov. LETCHER from Mr. CAMERON, the Secretary of War at Washington, inquiring whether if he came to Richmond he would be protected, his purpose being to ask for an armistice of sixty days.

WM. B. DOBBIN, of the Fifty-third Regiment of Maryland, arrived here last night from Baltimore, and says that no report had reached here with regard to the rumored slaughter of the Seventh Regiment at Annapolis.—*N. Y. Times, April 27.*

THE CONFEDERATE FLAG IN HAVANA.

A vessel from a Florida port came in the other day with the Confederate flag flying as her nationality. The boat of the Captain-General immediately came alongside, and required that it should be at once lowered, as it represented no known nation, and the master, who had an American flag ready at hand, hoisted that in place. He then went to the Vice-Consul, Mr. Savage, acting since the departure of Major Helmn, and presented a register from the Confederate States. The Consul replied he could recognize no such papers: but on the captain representing that he was innocent in the matter, having taken command at the last moment, and the register having been taken out in the name of a previous master, the consul said that if he would make oath that the vessel was owned wholly by citizens of the United States he would give him a sea-letter, which would enable him to return to any port in the United States, but that he should retain his register and forward it to Washington.

The case was an anomalous one; the owners might be really loyal citizens, but forced in absence of regular United States officers, to take out Confederate States papers, and in the absence of any instructions from Washington, Mr. Savage hardly felt willing to take the responsibility of entirely refusing to have any thing to do with the vessel, after she had hoisted the United States flag, and thus of condemning her to lie here, unable to leave, an indefinite time. Perhaps it would have been better to have assumed the responsibility, and have declined any connection with a vessel that could not prove her right to fly the United States flag, by her papers. But for a Vice-Consul, and so near home, and so easily within reach of instructions, to assume to decide in so grave a case, is a thing that could hardly be expected. It would certainly seem, however, as if it were very desirable that immediate instructions should be given by our Government, in regard to such cases.—*N. Y. Express*, *April* 27.

When the boats from the *Baltic* landed at Fort Monroe, one of them was left at the fort under the command of Lieut. Snyder, U. S. A., who was a passenger in the *Baltic*. Soon afterwards he started from the fort, having in his boat a howitzer, with two boxes of ammunition and 16 boxes of rifle cartridges. The current was so strong that the heavy-laden boat could not make the ship, and was only brought up about five miles away from her by making an anchor of a box of rifle cartridges, and she drifted into shallow water, awaiting either a change of tide or succor from the *Baltic*. While lying there, two horsemen came down to the beach, and after surveying the boat for a few minutes, retired and reported to a company of soldiers, who were concealed in the bushes at some distance from the beach. The horsemen returned in about half an hour, and riding into the water, flourishing their swords, hailed the boat and asked who she was, and what was her business there. Lieut. Snyder replied that it was a boat from the *Baltic*, with a howitzer and ammunition for that vessel. The horsemen rode off without further question, the word howitzer probably conveying the idea of sharper work than they were prepared to encounter, and Lieut. S. was unmolested during the remainder of the night. At the change of tide he made his way to the *Baltic*, reaching her about daylight, with the loss of one box of rifle cartridges.—*N. Y. Times*, *April* 27.

The vestry of Grace Church, in New York, were desirous that an American flag should wave from the very apex of the spire of the Church, at a height of 260 feet from the ground. Several persons offered to undertake the dangerous feat, but on mounting by the interior staircase to the highest window in the steeple, thought they would scarcely have nerve enough to undertake it. At last, William O'Donnell and Charles McLaughlin, two young painters in the employ of Richard B. Fosdick of Fifth avenue, decided to make the attempt. Getting out of the little diamond-shaped window about half way up, they climbed up the lightning-rod on the east side of the spire, to the top. Here one of the men fastened the pole securely to the cross, although quite a gale was blowing at the time. The flag thus secured, the daring young man mounted the cross, and, taking off his hat, bowed to the immense crowd which were watching his movements from Broadway. As the flag floated freely in the air, they burst into loud and repeated cheers.—*N. Y. Tribune*, *April* 26.

When Gen. Benjamin F. Butler, in command of the Massachusetts regiment, landed at Annapolis, Md., some of the authorities protested against the passage of Massachusetts troops over Maryland soil; when he replied: "Sir, we came here not as citizens of Massachusetts, but as citizens of and soldiers of the United States, with no intention to invade any State, but to protect the capital of our common country from invasion. We shall give no cause of offence; but there must be no fugitive shots or stray bricks on the way."—*N. Y. Commercial Advertiser*, *April* 26.

The first official act of the representative of a foreign Government indicating a recognition of the independence of the Old Dominion, was performed April 19, by Hon. Mr. Moore, Her British Majesty's Consul at Richmond. In preparing the usual clearance papers for a British brig from Halifax, N. S., he erased the printed words "United States of America," and wrote "Commonwealth of Virginia."—*Boston Journal*, *April* 25.

REIGN OF TERROR IN NEW YORK.

A gentleman of Richmond, Va., was in New York. The scenes which he witnessed in the streets reminded him of the descriptions of the Reign of Terror in Paris. Nothing was wanting but the bloody guillotine to make the two pictures identical. The violent and diabolical temper everywhere conspicuous, showed but too clearly whither all things are tending in the commercial metropolis. A spirit is evoked, which can only be laid in blood. The desperadoes of that great city are now in the ascendant. At present, they are animated by very bloody designs against the South. They have been persuaded, or urged by hunger, to believe that by enlisting for the war they will win bread and honor and riches. By-and-by, they may come to reflect there is an abundance of meat and bread, and inexhaustible supplies of money all around them—in the banks, the palatial residences, in the fire-proof safes of the princely merchants. They may consider that all this meat and bread and money may be won with fewer risks of cracked pates and bloody noses than the meagre, unsavory food of the poor South. That they have only to demand to have it. That they have as much right, as men and Christians, to call for it and help themselves, as to be compelled to travel five or six hundred miles to plunder a poor people, who never did them any harm. It is quite natural for such thoughts as these to come into the heads of men who, having no means of subsistence, and being elated with a sudden idea of their great importance, and seeing a wealth of treasure and good things all around them —to be had for the taking. We do not know that their quick wits have yet comprehended all the advantages of their position. But they will not be very slow in finding that they are masters of the situation. They have only, in swaggering along Broadway and looking into some of the magnificent stores that grace that vaunted street, or stepping into one of the Banks, or looking over the list of the recipients of specie by the last steamer from California—or the names of the subscribers to the last Government loan —the Grinnell's-King's Sons, &c., to be convinced that a military contribution on New York would yield a hundred fold more than they could hope to realize in ten bloody and desperate campaigns in the South.—*Richmond Whig*, *April* 22.

Washington, *April* 27.—A gentleman from Richmond this morning, gives some information of the feeling prevalent there. He represents it as a perfect reign of terror, and an excitement that he never saw paralleled. The troops in the city, he thinks a fine, hardy body of men, but ignorant beyond belief. It is upon the ignorance of these men that the leaders play. Some of the statements he heard made, would hardly be credited as the assertions of sane men. He listened to one man who publicly stated that the Seventh Regiment had been cut to pieces in the streets of Annapolis, and *that he himself saw* more than 100 of their dead bodies lying in the streets of that city. Another man he heard assure the crowd that the Massachusetts vagabonds (her glorious volunteers) had been quartered in the Capitol at Washington, and had amused themselves by running their bayonets through the pictures which adorned it, and that the rich hangings of the different rooms have been pulled down and made into blankets and wrappers for the use of the troops.

Another man, who was organizing a corps of infantry, told them they had nothing to do but to march to glory and wealth. "What," said he, "could a Northern army do on our sterile hills—they would starve to death. But you," he continued, "have but to march to Washington, and lay that in ashes—then to Philadelphia, which is rich in all kinds of wealth —from that through all the North; there is a village every five miles, and every village has a bank, and every bank has a vault of specie, and you have but to help yourselves."—*Cor. N. Y. Times, May* 1.

It is rumored that LINCOLN has been *drunk for three days*, and that Capt. LEE has command at the Capitol, and also that Col. LEE, of Va., who lately resigned, is *bombarding Washington* from Arlington Heights. If so, it will account for his not having arrived here to take command, as was expected.— *Norfolk* (*Va.*) *Herald, April* 22.

NEW YORK, *April* 27.—They get some very curious telegraphic despatches down South nowadays. For instance, *The Mobile Tribune* publishes, with a great flourish of sensation headings, the following:

"NEW ORLEANS, April 20.—The details from Baltimore say the citizens have no arms except those seized from the Federal troops.

"They are fighting like heroes, with pavingstones."

"NEW ORLEANS, April 20.—The Baltimoreans captured the Seventh Pennsylvania Regiment, taking eight hundred stand of arms.

"It is reported that one hundred lives were lost. Maryland has raised her State flag.

"Rumors of fighting in St. Louis."

"LOUISVILLE, April 20.—Kentucky has declared, through her Legislature, that she will *secede*.

"Lincoln will instantly resign in obedience to Gen. Scott's example."

—The news that Kentucky has seceded and that Mr. Lincoln is about to follow Gen. Scott's example and resign, *The Mobile Tribune* declares to be specially worthy of confidence.—*N. Y. Tribune, April* 27.

GEN. SCOTT, it seems, has taken position against his native State. It is a sight to see the drivelling old fop, with his skinny hands and bony fingers, undo, at one dash, the labors of a long and active life. With the red-hot pencil of infamy he has written upon his wrinkled brow the terrible, damning word, "Traitor."—*Abingdon* (*Va.*) *Democrat, May.*

ANNAPOLIS, MD., *April* 28.—"To give you an example of the punishment traitors receive, we can see from where I am writing, about two miles from shore, on the yard-arm of the U. S. Brig Caledonia, *two men hanging*—one for smuggling provisions and powder to the rebels at Charleston, the other for piloting the Seventh Regiment on the Chesapeake bar, with the intention that the Baltimoreans might get possession of Annapolis before the Seventh could land."—*Ex. from a Letter, date Annapolis, in N. Y. Sunday Atlas, May* 5.

SUNDAY AT THE CAPITOL AT WASHINGTON.—Rev. Dr. Weston, Chaplain of the Seventh Regiment of New York, preached in the Hall of the House of Representatives on Sunday, April 28, and the Regiment improvised a choir of 20 choice singers. The services were as follows:

MORNING SERVICE.

Voluntary,..........................By the Band.
Chant,...............................Venite.
Chant,...............................Benedictus.
Psalm,......"For Thou, O God, art seated high."
Hymn 171, 3, "Guide me, O Thou great Jehovah."
Voluntary,..........................By the Band.

EVENING SERVICE.

Voluntary,..........................By the Band.
Psalm 47, L. M............."Portuguese Hymn."
MS. "My country, 'tis of thee,"........America.
Voluntary,..........................By the Band.

At 10½ A. M., the Regiment, except those on guard, was mustered for worship. The decorations of the interior—gilding, painting, enamel, oak, marble, and velvet—blended together to the eye in the dim, religious light, that falls from the ceiling. The reporters' gallery afforded a place for the band; the speaker's desk, tapestried with the country's flag, held the Bible and Prayer-Book of the chaplain; and the choir ranged themselves in the clerk's circle below. The Regiment nearly filled the floor and galleries, and the whole scene was impressive.

The opening voluntary swelled to the remotest corner of a room better adapted to proper musical effect than any ever entered before.

The words of the Collect—"Defend us, thy humble servants, in all assaults of our enemies; that we, surely trusting in Thy defence, may not fear the power of any adversaries"—had a meaning never felt before.

The chaplain selected for his text the 39th verse of the Sermon on the Mount:

"But I say unto you, That ye resist not evil: but whosoever shall smite thee on the right cheek, turn to him the other also."

—*N. Y. Express, April* 29.

A REGIMENT OF SMITHS.—We understand that it is the intention of Mr. Chas. Smith, connected with Hodge's banking establishment, to organize a regiment to be composed entirely of members of the Smith family, for the purpose of establishing a right of way through Baltimore. All persons of the name of Smith, (none other need apply,) who are capable of bearing arms, and desire to join such a regiment, are requested to call at No. 558 Broadway.—*N. Y. News, April* 29.

WHEN the Sixth Massachusetts Regiment passed through Trenton, N. J., a person residing there asked one of the soldiers "if he had any whiskey to stimulate him." The other put his hand in his pocket, and drawing out a *Bible*, said, "That is my stimulant." A noble answer, worthy of the cause in which he is engaged. History informs us of an army which carried Bibles and sang hymns, and "no enemy ever saw their backs."—*Phila. Inquirer.*

AN IRISH REGULAR.—The following dialogue really took place between Lieutenant A. C. C——d, late of the United States Texan army, and Pat Fletcher, one of the privates of the Second Cavalry, now at Carlisle, then near Fort Bliss:—

Officer—Well, Pat, ain't you going to follow the General (Twiggs)?

Pat—If Gineral Scott ordhers us to folly him, sir, begor Toby (Pat's horse) can gallop as well as the best of 'em.

Officer—I mean, won't you leave the abolition army, and join the free South?

Pat—Begor I never enlisted in th' abolition army, and never will. I agreed to sarve Uncle Sam for five year, and the divil a pin mark was made in the contract, with my consint, ever since. When my time is up, if the army isn't the same as it is now, I won't join it agin.

Officer—Pat, the "Second" (Cavalry) was eighteen months old when you and I joined. The man who raised our gallant regiment is now the Southern President; the man who so lately commanded it, is now a Southern General. Can you remain in it, when they are gone?

Pat—Well, you see, the fact of the matther is, Lieut. C., I ain't much of a scholar; I can't argue the question with you, but what would my mother say, if I desarted my colors? Oh, the divil a give-in I'll ever give in, now, and that's the ind of it. I tried to run away once, a few weeks after enlistin', but a man wouldn't be missed thin. It's quite different now, Lieutenant, and I'm going not to disgrace naither iv my countries.

Officer—Do you know that you will have to fire on green Irish colors, in the Southern ranks?

Pat—And won't you have to fire on them colors, (pointing to the flag at Fort Bliss,) that yerself and five of us licked nineteen rangers under? Sure, it isn't a greater shame for an Irishman to fire on Irish colors, than for an American to fire on American colors. An' th' oath 'll be on my side, you know, Lieutenant.

Officer—D—n the man that relies on Paddies, I say.

Pat—The same compliments to desarters, your honor.—*N. Y. Commercial*, April 29.

REMARKABLE COINCIDENCE—WAS IT ACCIDENT?— It has already been noticed, that the attack upon the Sixth Massachusetts Regiment at Baltimore, occurred on the anniversary of the battle of Lexington—the one being on April 19th, 1861, and the other on April 19th, 1775, just 86 years previous. This fact was remarkable, but not as much as another in the same connection.

It appears from a Boston letter in the New York *World*, that that Regiment was all from Middlesex County, which embraces the battle-fields of Lexington, Concord, and Bunker Hill. One or two of the companies are entirely composed of the lineal descendants of the patriots who were in the "Concord Fight." The gallant Sixth was first sent forward because it first reported itself at head-quarters with fullest ranks. Col. Jones received his orders at Lowell on Monday night at 11 o'clock, in the midst of a driving northeast storm. He mounted his horse, and rode all night through the scattered towns in which his companies were. Every company was in Boston with full ranks next Tuesday noon, and, if the equipments furnished by the State had been ready, the Regiment would have left that afternoon for Washington, instead of twenty-four hours later, which was done.

The Stoneham Company, Capt. Dike, which performed a conspicuous part in the affair at Baltimore, has a rather remarkable record for promptitude.

The town is situated about midway between Bunker Hill and Lexington. The company belonged to the Seventh Regiment, which had not been ordered out. On Tuesday night it was determined at head-quarters to attach the Stoneham Company to the Sixth. Capt. Dike, who had no warning of this intention, received his orders at 4 o'clock in the morning. At 10 o'clock, he and his company, with sixty-four muskets, and every uniform full, were at Faneuil Hall ready to march. The same (Wednesday) afternoon they left for Washington with the Sixth Regiment; on Thursday they were in New York; on Friday they were in the midst of the fight at Baltimore, where Capt. Dike and ten of his men were wounded, and one has been reported killed.

The most remarkable of all is, that the first man who fell at Baltimore was a member of the Stoneham Company, and *he a lineal descendant of the first one killed at Lexington!* Thus we have the connection in the days of the year, and the late and unexpected change of the Stoneham Company from the Seventh to the Sixth Regiment, with a seeming design to the remarkable connection in the first victims of the two wars—the one to establish freedom in this country, and the other to defend and maintain it.—*Toledo Blade*.

FIGHTING RESOURCES OF THE NORTH.—The extreme Southern editors seem to be as thoroughly ignorant of the spirit that animates the whole North, as if they had never been acquainted with the people of the United States at all. For instance, see what the *Mobile Advertiser* says of the fighting *materiel* at the disposition of our Government:—

Paradoxical as it may seem, a chief element of the strength of the North is its poverty. It is levying for its war upon us, for our subjugation, (save the mark!) a pauper soldiery. We have reports that corporations make appropriations for the support of the families of volunteers. We need not mistake this for patriotic liberality. It is any thing but that. It is the coercion of necessity. The armies that are marching against us are composed of mercenary pauper soldiery. We all know the stagnation of industrial and mechanical pursuits which has ensued at the North; how thousands of operatives and mechanics are begging bread,—are, with their families, supported by public charities. To this class, so numerous in the cities which are offering the most imposing contingents, the call for volunteers was a God-send, indeed, for it gave them a chance to get bread at the public cost which could not be earned by individual exertion, and was bitter in the eating if the dole of public or private charity.

So, on the call for volunteers, these poverty-stricken and starving creatures rush where rations may be obtained, and the men with families are encouraged to enlist by the promise that their responsibilities will be cared for. Men of the South rush to arms spurred by patriotic zeal, not compelled by the pangs of starvation, like these mongrel hordes of all nationalities of the operative class of the Northern cities. Our sons of the soil, patriots by birthright, grasp their weapons, leaving their homes of plenty, spring impetuously to arms, ask but one favor—that they may be placed face to face with the foe. Our volunteer soldiery is not the soldiery of necessity—men worth their hundreds of thousands carry the musket in the ranks. Plenty reigns in our dwellings, and is gladly abandoned for the privations of the camp. Such is the *materiel* with which we meet a mercenary pauper soldiery. Who would doubt the issue when it is man to man? The creatures of one side, sordid and indifferent, fight for so much per diem as the alternative of starvation. The men on the other side fight for rights and liberties, filled with ardor by the noblest impulses. Let these foes meet in pitched battle, and the sons of the South will triumph were the enemy five to one.—*N. Y. Express, April* 29.

The *Raleigh* (N. C.) *Banner*, urging an attack upon Washington, says:—

The army of the South will be composed of the best material that ever yet made up an army; whilst that of Lincoln will be gathered from the sewers of the cities—the degraded, beastly offscourings of all quarters of the world, who will serve for pay, and run away as soon as they can when danger threatens them.—*Idem.*

In the Concord Company which is with the Fifth Massachusetts Regiment, are four Buttricks, sons of one man, and he the descendant of Col. Buttrick who gave the word of command at Concord Bridge, on the 19th of April, 1775, "Fire! fellow-soldiers! for God's sake, Fire!"—*Boston Transcript, April* 29.

While Fernando Wood was speaking at the New York Union Meeting, there was a brief interruption to read a despatch. Just then one of the roughs, who perched himself in a tree just over the Mayor's head, leaned down and said: "Now, Fernandy, jist you look out what you say, 'cause you've got to stick to this." The Mayor heard and heeded.—*Idem.*

Baltimore, Md., *April* 23.—There is but one feeling now in Maryland, and that is for our own State, and a united South. We cannot consent that Lincoln & Co. shall take advantage of our former loyalty to the old Union, and turn it to the support of Black Republicanism under the guise of defending a broken, dissevered Government. No! to a man, without a dissenting voice, we rally under the Southern flag. We have been driven from a conservative position by the mad, stubborn folly of fanaticism, to turn our thoughts from patriotic reminiscences and memories, and soar to the azure field and broader stripes of your Confederate ensign, hoping its constellation will soon number many more glittering jewels. We implored peace; we offered the Crittenden resolutions; Virginia came as a pacific messenger; she sought a Peace Conference; Kentucky and other noble States stood by her side, but all were indignantly spurned, and now we have fallen back with one heart, one impulse, upon our reserved rights, prepared to defend and maintain them at every hazard. Endurance has ceased to be a virtue.—*Cor. N. O. Picayune, April* 30.

All the United States vessels are provided with engines for pouring volleys of hot water upon their assailants. We trust that the Southern defences will all be supplied with this efficient agent. We are naturally a hospitable people in the South, and ought to give the new-comers a reception appropriate to their merits. Scalding and skinning is the very least mark of distinction we can bestow upon these invading swine.—*Charleston Mercury, April* 19.

The *N. Y. Herald* makes up a table of voluntary contributions by cities, counties, and individuals in the North, all $1,000 or over, each, which sum up to $11,230,000, of which New York city gives $2,155,000, and the N.Y. State Legislature $3,000,000 more. And all this has been subscribed since the 15th of April.

Of sums below a thousand dollars subscribed by private individuals, and of which no mention is made in this statement, it is no exaggeration to set down the aggregate at $5,000,000. If we take the average expenditure of each volunteer of the 250,000 men who are now drilling and under arms in the free States at $10, it will give us a further amount of $2,500,000 Besides these sums, we may put down $5,000,000 more for the contributions made by families towards the more comfortable outfit and equipment of such of their members as have taken up arms in defence of the national flag. And of casual sums given on the spur of the moment to applicants needing aid, in rifles, money, or clothing, and of which no notice has been taken, the total is probably not far short of another $5,000,000. These different amounts thus figure up:—

Contributions of $1,000 and upwards,..........	$11,230,000
Contributions below $1,000,..............	5,000,000
Expenditure of volunteers, ($10 each,)..........	2,500,000
Contributions of families to outfit,..............	5,000,000
Casual contributions in money and clothing,....	5,000,000
Total,...........................	$28,730,000

Making an aggregate of nearly twenty-nine millions of dollars spontaneously donated to the Government in less than a fortnight. Could the people of the South but have foreseen this wonderful unanimity of feeling and patriotic self-devotion on the part of the North, it is safe to assume that the national flag would still have been left floating over Fort Sumter.

Thirteen banks of the city of New York contributed nearly half a million of dollars for the defence of the Government. Added to the previous subscription of $250,000 by the Broadway Bank, these contributions amount, thus far, to $715,000, divided as follows:—

Bank of Commerce, by J. A. Stevens, President,..	$100,000
New York Exchange Bank, by S. Van Duzer, President,....................	10,000
Mechanics' Bank, by S. Knapp, President,........	25,000
National Bank, by James Gallatin, President,....	25,000
Merchants' Bank, by A. E. Silliman, President,...	25,000
Manhattan Bank, by J. M. Morrison, President,...	25,000
Bank of the Republic, by R. H. Lowry, Cashier,..	60,000
Phœnix Bank, by M. P. Bryson, Cashier,.........	25,000
Bank of New York, by A. P. Halsey, President,...	50,000
Bank of North America, by J. Seymour, President,	20,000
Bank of America, by J. Punnett, President,.......	50,000
Bank of the State of New York, by R. Withers, President,.....................	25,000
Shoe and Leather Bank, by A. V. Stout, President,	25,000
Broadway Bank,.....................	250,000
Total,...........................	$715,000

—*N. Y. Herald, April* 29.

Among the men whose names should never be forgotten, until they have been duly punished for the atrocious crimes in which they have involved themselves at Baltimore, Ross Winans, Thomas Winans, Abel of the *Baltimore Sun*, Kane, the Police Marshal, S. Teakle Wallis, and some others, are already known to the country. They are all traitors of the blackest dye, and amply merit the traitor's doom. We now learn the name of another of these conspirators to destroy the Union and ruin Maryland. It is signed to the following order served upon a peaceful citizen of Baltimore on Tuesday last:

"Baltimore, April 23.

"Mr. John T. Burgess:—You are hereby notified to leave the State of Maryland within twenty-four hours after receipt of this note from date, by authority of the Regulators' Committee of the State.

"W. G. H. EHRMAN."

When the final settlement of accounts takes place at Baltimore, Mr. W. G. H. Ehrman, of the Regulators' Committee of the State, need not fear that he will be overlooked or forgotten.—*N. Y. Tribune, April 29.*

GENERAL PILLOW, being about raising a brigade of volunteers for the Southern army, sent a message to the noted Parson Brownlow, requesting him to serve as Chaplain. The "Reverend" individual replied in characteristic style, saying : "When I shall have made up my mind to go to hell, I will cut my throat, and go *direct*, and not travel round by way of the Southern Confederacy." It is not necessary that the "Reverend gentleman" should cut his throat to go to the place he mentions, as it is pretty evident he is making there direct without any such operation.—*Charleston Mercury, May 1.*

THE following incidents of the late riot in Baltimore, and the concluding statements concerning the intentions and doings of the rebels there, are derived from a letter written by a prominent officer in the rebel forces :—

"An old, gray-haired man, aged more than sixty-five years, saw one of the Massachusetts soldiers in the act of levelling his musket, when he rushed in his shirt sleeves from his shop, disarmed the man by main force, and killed him with the bayonet. Some thirty negroes engaged in unloading a vessel dropped their work and joined in the assault on the Massachusetts men, and did good work with their handspikes. Every shot-gun, rifle, or boy's pop-gun for killing tom-tits, is brought into use throughout the State, and the sentiment is universal that no more Northern troops shall cross the State without fighting their way every step, and every rock and tree on the roadside will cover a sharp-shooter. This city alone has appropriated half a million of dollars, and a million more has been given by private subscription. Winans is running 700 men night and day, in his immense establishment, casting cannon, shot, and shells, putting up grape and cannister, and preparing other munitions of war ; and every thing is moving on a grand scale."—*N. Y. Evening Post, April 29.*

ANNAPOLIS, MD., *April 25.*—The general suspension of business during the past few days, and the hopelessness of the adoption of peace measures, have caused a neglect on the part of our citizens to give proper attention to their pecuniary engagements, and the notaries have had quite a harvest in the way of protests. They have been the busiest of our population, and, what is unusual, complain of having too much to do.

The citizens of Annapolis have no occasion of complaint in reference to the conduct of the Federal troops, every proceeding being conducted in the most orderly manner. In no instance have the rights of any one been interfered with to their detriment. In cases where it was necessary to take possession of property for the use of the Government, the most ample compensation was allowed, and the owners of property were required to assess its valuation. A citizen who was the owner of four horses and carts was called upon to dispose of them for the transportation of baggage and supplies. He declined to sell them, but the officers stated that they must have them, and requested him to name his price. With the view of avoiding a sale, he asked the exorbitant price of $1,600. The property was taken, and a draft given for amount of the valuation.

The presence of the troops has had the tendency of inflating the price of every description of provisions. Flour was held at $20 per barrel.—*N. Y. Commercial, April 29.*

ON the route South, into the secession States, your baggage is examined, not directly upon your crossing the line between North Carolina and South Carolina, but at Florence, S. C., which is the inspection point. The cars ran up to a tall pole bearing the flag of the Confederate States. Then comes the revenue inspector, who calls out for passengers to hand over the keys of their baggage. Each trunk is taken out of the car, and its owner furnishes the key and aids the inspector in turning up the contents, and satisfies him that there is nothing contained in them. There is no getting off from this, and no feigned loss of keys nor bogus pretence of rusty locks can save you. No more offensive thing can be done than this to an American citizen in the United States, and it is one of the very last acts to which they will quietly submit.—*N. Y. Express, April 29.*

IT is going to be the very mischief to run the Lincolnites off Santa Rosa Island if they don't want to go. We may and will make Fort Pickens hot for them, but they have plenty of men, and can get as many more as Lincoln can send them ; when Pickens is rendered untenable, they can entrench themselves —beyond the reach of our batteries, if they like, and so keep up their camp as long as they please, or until we leave the mainland to attack them in their stronghold. We cannot starve them out without a naval force superior to that at their command. So we shall have to keep a strong force on hand to watch this nest of impudent fellows right under our noses. The knocking to pieces of Fort Pickens will not be getting rid of them if they are of a mind to stay on the island. There is plenty of sand there for batteries, and our reports show that the enemy is using it to fortify his lines.—*Mobile Adv., April 23.*

STRINGENT measures are being taken in New Orleans to rid the city of abolition agents and sympathizers. Several have been obliged to leave—with half their heads shaved.—*Galveston News, April 30.*

THE ATTACK ON WASHINGTON.—The papers in the interest of the Southern rebels have repeatedly avowed that the capture of the national capital was the ulterior object of the rebellion. The Secretary of War of the so-called Southern Confederacy publicly avowed the same purpose, in his speech at Montgomery after the evacuation of Fort Sumter. Notwithstanding this official declaration, some persons still affect to believe that no such movement was ever or is now intended. The following testimony on the subject from a gentleman whose respectability is abundantly vouched for by the *Tribune*, ought, we think, to be conclusive on the point. The gentleman was escaping from Fayetteville, North Carolina, to avoid impressment in the rebel service. He says :—

At all the stations crowds were assembled, and the secession fever ran high. At Warsaw, where our informant took the train, he found Alexander H. Stephens, who was on his way to Richmond. At nearly every station Stephens spoke. The capture of Washington was the grand idea which he enforced, and exhorted the people to join in the enterprise, to which they heartily responded. This was the only thing talked of. "It must be done!" was his constant exclamation. At Welden a man supposed to be a Northerner was whipped and tarred and feathered just before the train arrived. There was a large crowd, deeply excited, which Mr. Stephens addressed. Vigorous measures were on foot to arouse and arm the people, and they were answering to the call as one man.—*Commercial Advertiser, April 25.*

On Thursday, 11th of April, telegraphic despatches had been received, which appeared on the bulletins of the *Mercury* and *Courier*, at Charleston, S. C., stating that but three States in the North—Massachusetts, Pennsylvania, and Ohio—had responded to Old Abe's call for troops; that Old Abe had been poisoned, and that Seward held the reins of Government. Another despatch subsequently arrived, which recited that Maine and Vermont had refused to send troops out of their States. When those announcements were read by the people, who assembled round the newspaper offices, there were loud demonstrations of applause. But those remarkable flattering despatches did not stop there; they were followed by others, which declared in large capitals on bulletin boards of those journals, that the famous New York Seventh Regiment, with another corps from Boston, tendered their services to Jefferson Davis to fight against the Black Republicans of the North; and that they had chartered a vessel, and were proceeding on their way South. This was followed by the welcome announcement that Maryland, Tennessee, and North Carolina, had passed ordinances of secession. All these reports were duly credited—not a professed skeptic appearing among the tens of thousands who heard them.—*Boston Transcript, April 30.*

APRIL 15TH, 1861.

BY WILLIAM H. BURLEIGH.

Thank God! the free North is awake at last!
 When burning cannon-shot and bursting shell,
 As, from the red mouth of some volcan's hell,
Rained on devoted Sumter thick and fast,
The sleep of ages from her eyelids past.
 One bound—and lo! she stands erect and tall,
 While Freedom's hosts come trooping to her call,
Like eager warriors to the trumpet's blast!
Woe to the traitors and their robber horde!
 Woe to the spoilers that pollute the land!
 When a roused Nation, terrible and grand,
Grasps, in a holy cause, th' avenging sword,
And swears, from Treason's bloody clutch to save
The priceless heritage our fathers gave.
                    —*N. Y. Tribune, April 30.*

TO THE AMERICAN PEOPLE.

BY BAYARD TAYLOR.

I.

That late, in half-despair, I said:
"The Nation's ancient life is dead;
Her arm is weak, her blood is cold;
She hugs the peace that gives her gold—
The shameful peace, that sees expire
Each beacon-light of patriot fire,
And makes her court a traitor's den"—
Forgive me this, my Countrymen!

POETRY—42

II.

Oh, in your long forbearance grand,
Slow to suspect the treason planned,
Enduring wrong, yet hoping good
For sake of olden brotherhood,
How grander, how sublimer far,
At the roused Eagle's call ye are,
Leaping from slumber to the fight
For Freedom and for Chartered Right!

III.

Throughout the land there goes a cry:
A sudden splendor fills the sky;
From every hill the banners burst,
Like buds by April breezes nurst;
In every hamlet, home, and mart,
The fire-beat of a single heart
Keeps time to strains whose pulses mix
Our blood with that of Seventy-Six!

IV.

The shot whereby the old flag fell
From Sumter's battered citadel,
Struck down the lines of party creed,
And made ye One, in soul and deed—
One mighty people, stern and strong,
To crush the consummated wrong,
Indignant with the wrath, whose rod
Smites as the awful sword of God!

V.

The cup is full! They thought ye blind;
The props of State they undermined;
Abused your trust, your strength defied,
And stained the Nation's name of pride.
Now lift to Heaven your loyal brows;
Swear once again your fathers' vows,
And cut through traitor hearts a track
To nobler fame and freedom back!

VI.

Draw forth your million blades as one!
Complete the battle then begun!
God fights with ye, and overhead
Floats the dear banner of your dead.
They, and the glories of the Past,
The Future, dawning dim and vast,
And all the holiest hopes of man,
Are beaming triumph in your van!

VII.

Slow to resolve, be swift to do!
Teach ye the False how fight the True!
How bucklered Perfidy shall feel
In her black heart the Patriot's steel;
How sure the bolt that Justice wings;
How weak the arm a traitor brings;
How mighty they, who steadfast stand
For Freedom's Flag and Freedom's Land!

April 30, 1861.
                    —*N. Y. Independent, May 9.*

VOLUNTEERED.

I know the sun shines, and the lilacs are blowing,
 And Summer sends kisses by beautiful May;
Oh! to see all the treasures the Spring is bestowing,
 And think—my boy Willie enlisted to-day!

It seems but a day since at twilight, low humming,
  I rocked him to sleep with his cheek upon mine ;
While Robby, the four-year-old, watched for the coming
  Of father, adown the street's indistinct line.

It is many a year since my Harry departed,
  To come back no more in the twilight or dawn ;
And Robby grew weary of watching, and started
  Alone, on the journey his father had gone.

It is many a year—and this afternoon, sitting
  At Robby's old window, I heard the band play,
And suddenly ceased dreaming over my knitting,
  To recollect Willie is twenty to-day ;

And that, standing beside him this soft May-day morning,
  The sun making gold of his wreathed cigar-smoke,
I saw in his sweet eyes and lips a faint warning,
  And choked down the tears when he eagerly spoke :

"Dear mother, you know how those traitors are crowing ;
  They trample the folds of our flag in the dust ;
The boys are all fire ; and they wish I were going—"
  He stopped, but his eyes said, " Oh, say if I must ! "

I smiled on the boy, though my heart it seemed breaking ;
  My eyes filled with tears, so I turned them away,
And answered him, " Willie, 'tis well you are waking—
  Go, act as your father would bid you, to-day ! "

I sit in the window, and see the flags flying,
  And dreamily list to the roll of the drum,
And smother the pain in my heart that is lying,
  And bid all the fears in my bosom be dumb.

I shall sit in the window when Summer is lying
  Out over the fields, and the honey-bees' hum
Lulls the rose at the porch from her tremulous sighing,
  And watch for the face of my darling to come.

And if he should fall . . . . his young life he has given
  For Freedom's sweet sake . . . . and for me, I will pray
Once more with my Harry and Robby in heaven
  To meet the dear boy that enlisted to-day.

ALBION, NEW YORK.

              —*Harper's Weekly*, May 18.

WAR QUESTIONS.

TO COL. C. M. CLAY.

The battle is for the very entity of the Nation.—DR. CHAPIN.

BY WILLIAM ROSS WALLACE.

I.

O soldier ! O soldier ! why thus is your hand
With such eagerness clasped on your sharp battle-brand ?
Has your flag been insulted ? its eagle betrayed ?
For revenge flash the flames of that blood-drinking blade ?
" Not revenge, not revenge, that is arming me now,
But as white as the dove's is the plume on my brow,

Though my flag was insulted—the Star-flag that rolled
Like a storm for the Right o'er my fathers of old ! "

II.

O soldier ! O soldier ! is't glory you seek
Where the War-demon shouts, and the death-vultures shriek ?
Does your manly brow yearn for the laurels that wave
On the tree that is nursed by the blood of the brave ?
" Oh, no ! 'tis not glory that calls on my soul,
Where the black cannons roar, and the red banners roll ;
Though 'tis there that the bold, gallant hand may entwine
A green wreath for his name on a world-worshipped shrine ! "

III.

O soldier ! O soldier ! then *why* is your hand
With such eagerness clasped on that sharp battle-brand ?
While the flush on your brow, and the flush in your eye,
Show that storms of deep passion are thundering by ?
" 'Tis the Right ! 'Tis the Right ! God's own high, holy Right,
That has called me, and armed for the terrible fight !
O ye shades of my fathers ! O ye, to whose hand
We have owed the great UNION that blesses our land,
Lo, the traitors have struck ! They would rend the Star-fold
That for Freedom, and Honor, and Truth, ye unrolled !
How your grand eyes look on me ! I rush to the strife,
Not for fame or revenge, but—*the National Life !* "

              —*N. Y. Tribune*, May 2.

OH ! LET THE STARRY BANNER WAVE.

BY WM. OLAND BOURNE.

I love the flag whose radiant stars
  Within its azure field are set,
Whose crimson-flushed and stainless bars
  Are types of peace and glory met.
It floats unfurled in every clime,
  And speaks to nations yet asleep,
While million hearts await the time
  When Freedom's vow they too shall keep.

Unrivalled, as when freemen trod
  Triumphant on the battle-field,
And pledged to Freedom and to God,
  Our banner we will never yield—
It floats the standard of the Free !
  On Northern peaks and Southern plains,
On hill and vale, from sea to sea,
  On mighty streams and mountain chains.

Unfurl the Stars and Stripes to-day,
  To kindle fire in every breast !
While millions on the altar lay
  A passion that no more can rest ;
It was not dead ! It only slept,
  Self-conscious in the strength of truth,
Till traitors witness how it kept
  The vigor of its glorious youth

Unfurl the flag ! The shadows deep
 Have fallen on our brightest noon ;
And millions bow, and sadly weep
 That brother-love has failed so soon.
But shadows pass, and clouds dissolve
 In silvery mists before the sun—
And thus in Freedom's high resolve
 Shall cloudless skies once more be won.

Bright emblem of the mighty Past !
 Bedewed all through a night of tears !
Whose crimson-price our fathers cast
 With faith and prayer adown the years !
Untarnished on the page of time,
 And purer in to-morrow's beam,
Thy stars shall be a speech sublime
 Of peace, and love, and joy supreme.

Then let the starry banner wave !
 Let songs o'er all the nation ring !
To hail the flag that freemen gave—
 A costly, bright, and sacred thing !
Till stars shall crowd upon the field,
 Undimmed with aught of error's night ;
Whose bliss shall be the truth revealed,
 That Freedom is Eternal Right.
    —*N. Y. Christian Intelligencer*, May 16.

OUR COUNTRY.

BY GEORGE LUNT.

Our Country, right or wrong !
 What manly heart can doubt
That thus should swell the patriot's song,
 Thus ring the patriot's shout ?
Be but the foe arrayed,
 And war's wild trumpet blown,
Cold were his heart who has not made
 His Country's cause his own !

Where'er her flag unrolled
 Woos the saluting breeze,
Flings o'er the plain its starry fold,
 Or floats on stormy seas,
All dearest things are there,
 All that makes life divine—
Home, faith, the brave, the true, the fair,
 Cling to the flaming sign !

Oh ! is this thought a dream ?
 No ! by the gallant dead
Who sleep by hill, and plain, and stream,
 Or deep in ocean's bed ;
By every sacred name,
 By every glorious song,
By all we know and love of fame,
 Our Country, right or wrong !

THE GATHERING.

Forward ! onward ! far and forth !
An earthquake shout awakes the North.
    Forward !

Massachusetts hears that cry—
Hears, and gives the swift reply,
    Forward !

Pennsylvania draws her sword,
Echoes from her hills the word,
    Forward !

Brave New York is up and ready,
With her thirty thousand steady,—
    Forward !

Small Rhode Island flies to arms,
Shouting at the first alarms,
    Forward !

Illinois and Indiana
Shriek, as they unroll our banner,
    Forward !

Not behind the rest in zeal,
Hear Ohio's thunder-peal,
    Forward !

From Vermont, New Hampshire, Maine,
Comes the same awakening strain,
    Forward !

Old Connecticut is here,
Ready to give back the cheer,
    Forward !

Minnesota, though remote,
Swells the free, inspiring note,
    Forward !

Iowa and Michigan,
Both are ready to a man—
    Forward !

Not the last in honor's race,
See Wisconsin come apace—
    Forward !

Delaware, New Jersey, rise
And put on their martial guise.
    Forward !

Onward ! On ! a common cause
Is yours—your liberties and laws.
    Forward !

Forward, in your strength and pride !
God himself is on your side.
    Forward !
    —*Boston Transcript*, April 30.

THE YANKEE VOLUNTEERS.

*As sung by Private Ephraim Peabody, on the night after
    the march through Baltimore.*

Come, all ye true Americans that love the Stripes
    and Stars,
For which your gallant countrymen go marching to
    the wars ;
For grand old Massachusetts raise up three rousing
    cheers—
Three times three and a ti-ger for the Yankee Volun-
    teers !

The nineteenth day of April they marched unto the war,
And on that day, upon the way, they stopped at Bal-
    timore,
And trustingly expected the customary cheers
Which every loyal city gives the Yankee Volunteers.

But suddenly in fury there came a mighty crowd,
Led on by negro-drivers, with curses long and
   loud,
With frenzied imprecations, with savage threats and
   sneers,
They welcomed to the city the Yankee Volunteers.

So furious grew the multitude, they rushed at them
   amain,
And a great storm of missiles came pouring like a
   rain.
Amid a thunderous clamor, such as mortal seldom
   hears,
They tried to cross the city, did the Yankee Volunteers.

The murderous storm of missiles laid many a soldier
   low,
Yet still these gallant hearts forbore to give the answering blow,
Till all the miscreants shouted, "They're nearly dead
   with fears;
We'll hurry up and finish these Yankee Volunteers."

But, lo! the guns are levelled, and loud the volleys
   roar,
And, inch by inch, they fight their way through the
   streets of Baltimore;
Before them shrunk the traitors, above them rise the
   cheers,
As through the throng, a myriad strong, march on
   the Volunteers.

Hurrah, then, for the old Bay State that stood so well
   at bay!
Hurrah, for those who shed their blood, and gave
   their lives away!
For grand old Massachusetts, boys, let's give three
   rousing cheers!—
Three times three and a ti-ger for the Yankee Volunteers!
              —*N. Y. Tribune*, May 4.

SONGS OF THE REBELS.

SONG FOR THE TIMES.

WRITTEN FOR THE LADIES' MILITARY FAIR, NEW
ORLEANS.

Go, soldiers! arm you for the fight;
God shield the cause of Justice, Right;
May all return with victory crowned;
May every heart with joy abound;
May each deserve the laurel crown,
Nor one to meet his lady's frown.

May each deserve his lady's kiss;—
His gun ne'er find its aim amiss;
May Pickens' Fort at once be ours;
May glory bright await the hours;
May every foeman take to flight!
To arms, then, soldiers! for the fight.

To arms, ye brave! your homes are dear;
To arms! the foe is very near.

Your country calls—your cause is good;
To arms, who have fair lady woo'd!
To arms, if you would know the joy
Of her esteem, without alloy.

To arms! the Fort must now be ours;
Then fight and work with all your powers;
Let wreaths immortal crown your graves—
The surging surf and foaming waves
Your requiem sing. Oh, soldiers dear,
For you who fall we'll drop a tear.

Your cause is good—'tis honor bright,
'Tis virtue, country, home, and right;
Then should you die for love of these,
We'll waft your names upon the breeze;
The waves will sing your lullaby,
Your country mourn your latest sigh.

April 25.   L. F.
            —*N. O. Picayune*, April 23.

THE OLD RIFLEMAN.

BY FRANK TICKNOR, M.D.

Now bring me out my buckskin suit!
   My pouch and powder, too!
We'll see if seventy-six can shoot
   As sixteen used to do.

Old Bess! we've kept our barrels bright!
   Our trigger quick and true!
As far, if not as *fine* a sight,
   As, long ago, we drew!

And pick me out a trusty flint!
   A real white and blue;
Perhaps 'twill win the *other* tint,
   Before the hunt is through!

Give boys your brass percussion caps!
   Old "shut-pan" suits as well!
There's something in the *sparks;* perhaps
   There's something in the smell!

We've seen the red-coat Briton bleed!
   The red-skin Indian, too!
We never thought to draw a bead
   On Yankee-doodle-doo!

But, Bessie! bless your dear old heart!
   Those days are mostly done;
And now we must revive the art
   Of shooting on the run!

If Doodle must be meddling, why,
   There's only this to do:
Select the black spot in his eye,
   And let the daylight through!

And if he doesn't like the way
   That Bess presents the view,
He'll may-be change his mind, and stay
   Where the good Doodles do!

Where Lincoln lives;—the man, you know,
   Who kissed the Testament,
To keep the Constitution?—No!
   To keep the Government!

We'll hunt for Lincoln, Bess!—old tool—
And take him half-and-half;
We'll aim to *hit* him, if a fool,
And *miss* him, if a calf!

We'll teach these shot-gun boys the tricks
By which a war is won;
Especially how seventy-six
Took Tories on the run.

—*Richmond Dispatch*, May 23.

OUR BRAVES IN VIRGINIA.

Air—"*Dixie Land.*"

We have ridden from the brave Southwest,
On fiery steeds, with throbbing breast;
  Hurrah! hurrah! hurrah! hurrah!
With sabre flash and rifle true,—
  Hurrah! hurrah!—
The Northern ranks we will cut through,
And charge for Old Virginia, boys.
  Hurrah! hurrah!
  Then charge for Old Virginia.

We have come from the cloud-capp'd mountains,
From the land of purest fountains;
  Hurrah! hurrah! hurrah! hurrah!
Our sweethearts and wives conjure us,—
  Hurrah! hurrah!—
Not to leave a foe before us,
And strike for Old Virginia, boys, &c.

Then we'll rally to the bugle call;
For Southern rights we'll fight and fall;
  Hurrah! hurrah! hurrah! hurrah!
Our gray-haired sires sternly say,—
  Hurrah! hurrah!—
That we must die or win the day.
  Three cheers for Old Virginia, boys, &c.

Then our silken banner wave on high;
For Southern homes we'll fight and die.
  Hurrah! hurrah! hurrah! hurrah!
Our cause is right, our quarrel just,—
  Hurrah! hurrah!—
We'll in the God of battles trust,
And conquer for Virginia, boys, &c.

—*N. O. Picayune*, May 12.

SONG OF THE SOUTHERN WOMEN.

Oh, Abraham Lincoln, we call thee to hark
To the song we are singing, we Joans of Arc;
While our brothers are bleeding, we fear not to
  bleed;
We'll face the Red Horror, should there be need.
By our brothers we'll stand on the terrible field;
By our brothers we'll stand, and we'll ask for no
  shield,
By our brothers we'll stand as a torch in the dark,
To shine on thy treachery,—we Joans of Arc.

Behold our free plumes of the wild eagle dark;
Behold them, and take our white brows for thy mark;
We fear not thy cannon, we heed not thy drum;
The deeper thy thunder, the stronger we come.
Is woman a coward? No, no, she is brave!
Oh, nothing but Love ever made her a slave;
In home's happy circle she's poetry's lark,
But threaten that home, and she's Joan of Arc.

POETRY—9

Oh, Abraham Lincoln, we call thee to hark!
Thou Comet of Satan! thou Boast of the Dark!
Take off thy red shadow from Washington's land—
Back! back! for thy footstep is slavery's brand.
Future-eyed Prophecy cries to thee, DOWN!
For she sees on thy forehead the hope of a crown;
The fire that *sleeps* in our Southern eyes dark,
Would *lighten* in battle—we're Joans of Arc.

JULIA MILDRED.
—*Mobile Advertiser*, April 25.

A POEM FOR THE TIMES.

BY JOHN B. THOMPSON.

Who talks of Coercion? Who dares to deny
  A resolute people their right to be free?
Let him blot out forever one star from the sky,
  Or curb with his fetter one wave of the sea.

Who prates of Coercion? Can love be restored
  To bosoms where only resentment may dwell?—
Can peace upon earth be proclaimed by the sword,
  Or good-will among men be established by shell?

Shame! shame, that the statesman and trickster for-
  sooth
Should have for a crisis no other recourse,
Beneath the fair day-spring of Light and of Truth,
  Than the old *brutum fulmen* of tyranny—Force.

From the holes where Fraud, Falsehood, and Hate
  slink away;
  From the crypt in which Error lies buried in
  chains,
This foul apparition stalks forth to the day,
  And would ravage the land which his presence
  profanes.

Could you conquer us, men of the North—could you
  bring
  Desolation and death on our homes as a flood—
Can you hope the pure lily, Affection, will spring
  From ashes all reeking and sodden with blood?

Could you brand us as villains and serfs, know ye not
  What fierce, sullen hatred, lurks under the scar?
How loyal to Hapsburg is Venice, I wot;
  How dearly the Pole loves his father, the Czar!

But 'twere well to remember, this land of the sun
  Is a *nutrix leonum*, and suckles a race
Strong-armed, lion-hearted, and banded as one,
  Who brook not oppression, and know not dis-
  grace.

And well may the schemers in office beware
  The swift retribution that waits upon crime,
When the lion, RESISTANCE, shall leap from his lair
  With a fury that renders his vengeance sublime.

Once, men of the North, we were brothers, and still,
  Though brothers no more, we would gladly be
  friends;
Nor join in a conflict accurst, that must fill
  With ruin the country on which it descends.

But if smitten with blindness, and mad with the rage
  The gods gave to all whom they wished to destroy,
You would not act a new Iliad to darken the age
  With horrors beyond what is told as of Troy;—

If, deaf as the adder itself to the cries,
  When Wisdom, Humanity, Justice implore,
You would have our proud eagle to feed on the
    eyes
  Of those who have taught him so grandly to soar;

If there be to your malice no limit imposed,
  And you purpose hereafter to rule with the rod
The men upon whom you have already closed
  Our goodly domain, and the temples of God;—

To the breeze, then, your banner dishonored unfold,
  And at once let the tocsin be sounded afar;
We greet you, as greeted the Swiss, Charles the Bold,
  With a farewell to peace and a welcome to war!

For the courage that clings to our soil, ever bright,
  Shall catch inspirations from turf and from tide;
Our sons unappalled shall go forth to the fight,
  With the smile of the fair, the pure kiss of the
    bride;

And the bugle its echoes shall send through the
    past,
  In the trenches of Yorktown to waken the slain;
While the sods of King's Mountain shall heave at the
    blast,
  And give up its heroes to glory again.
                    —*Charleston Mercury*, May 7.

REBELS.

Gen. Beauregard, now in command of the rebel forces
in Charleston, has much fame as a tactician.—*Harper's
Weekly*, March 23.

Yes, call them rebels! 'tis the name
    Their patriot fathers bore,
And by such deeds they'll hallow it
    As they have done before.
At Lexington, and Baltimore,
    Was poured the holy chrism;
For Freedom marks her sons with blood,
    In sign of their baptism.

Rebels, in proud and bold protest,
    Against a power unreal;
A unity which every quest
    Proves false as 'tis ideal.
A brotherhood, whose ties are chains,
    Which crushes while it holds,
Like the old marble Läocoon
    Beneath its serpent folds.

Rebels, against the malice vast,
    Malice, that nought disarms,
Which fills the quiet of their homes
    With vague and dread alarms.
Against th' invader's daring feet,
    Against the tide of wrong,
Which has been borne, in silence borne,
    But borne perchance too long.

They would be cowards, did they crouch
    Beneath the lifted hand,
Whose very wave, ye seem to think,
    Will chill them where they stand.
Yes, call them rebels! 'tis a name
    Which speaks of other days,
Of gallant deeds, and gallant men,
    And wins them to their ways.

Fair was the edifice they raised,
    Uplifting to the skies;
A mighty Samson 'neath its dome
    In grand quiescence lies.
Dare not to touch his noble limb,
    With thong or chain to bind,
Lest ruin crush both you and him;—
    This Samson is not blind!

NATCHITOCHES, *May*, 1861.
            —*N. O. Picayune Supplement*, May 26.

VIRGINIA'S MESSAGE TO THE SOUTHERN STATES.

I.

You dared not think I'd *never* come;
    You could not doubt your Mother;
If traitorous chains had crushed my *form*,
    My *soul* with yours had hovered.
Yes, children, *I have come;*
We'll stand together—we'll be one;
Brave dangers, death, and wars begun!

II.

Where should this struggle work and end?
    Where should this conflict be?
Where should we all our rights defend,
    And gain our liberty?
Upon *my* soil your swords you'll wield;
Upon *my* soil your homes you'll shield;
And on *my* soil your foes *shall* yield!

III.

Where, but on *my* mountain's heights,
    And on *my* rivers' banks,—
Where, but 'neath *my* heavens' lights,
    And in *my* children's camps,
Shall all the blood be shed,
In streams of living red,
And all our foes be dead?

VI.

Upon this earth is there a spot
    So fit to give a battle-field?
In all the country, *there is not*,
    Nor one so brave to shield.
If you doubt it, scorn History's pages;
If you doubt it, *mark other ages*,
And come together for the war that rages!

V.

Then, soldiers brave, come forth!
    You sons of *noble mothers!*
They'll chide you if you're loath,
    And yield your homes to others.
Mothers! send them, then, without a tear;
Bid them go, and make all earth revere
Their country's honor and a SOLDIER'S BIER!
            —*Charleston Evening News*, May 6.

THE STARS AND BARS.

BY A. J. REQUIER.

Fling wide the dauntless banner
    To every Southern breeze,
Baptized in flame, with Sumter's name—
    A patriot and a hero's fame—
    From Moultrie to the seas!

That it may cleave the morning sun,
 And, streaming, sweep the night;
The emblem of a battle won
 With Yankee ships in sight.

Come, hucksters, from your markets;
 Come, bigots, from your caves;
Come, venal spies, with brazen lies
Bewildering your deluded eyes,
 That we may dig your graves.
Come, creatures of a sordid clown,
 And drivelling traitor's breath,
A single blast shall blow you down
 Upon the fields of Death.

The very flag you carry,
 Caught its reflected grace,
In fierce alarms, from Southern arms,
When foemen threatened all your farms,
 And never saw your face.
Ho! braggarts of New England's shore,
 Back to your hills, and delve
The soil whose craven sons forswore
 The flag in Eighteen Twelve!

We wreathed around the roses
 It wears before the world,
And made it bright with storied light
In every scene of bloody fight
 Where it has been unfurled;
And think ye, now, the dastard hands
 That never yet could hold
Its staff, shall wave it o'er our lands,
 To glut the greed of gold?

No! by the truth of Heaven,
 And its eternal Sun,
By every sire whose altar-fire
Burns on to beckon and inspire,
 It never shall be done!
Before that day, the kites shall wheel
 Hail-thick on Northern heights;
And there, our bared, aggressive steel,
 Shall counter-sign our rights!

Then, spread the flaming banner
 O'er mountain, lake, and plain!
Before its bars, degraded Mars
Has kissed the dust with all his stars,
 And will be struck again;
For could its triumph now be stayed
 By hell's prevailing gates,
A sceptered Union would be made
 The grave of sovereign States.
　　　　　　　—*N. O. Delta*, May 5.

April 23.—Massachusetts and Rhode Island have
won the praise and the blessing of all men. The
sons of Massachusetts lay dead in the streets of Baltimore on the anniversary of the battle of Lexington, before a single regiment of New York had
crossed the border between the slave and the free
States. Soldiers of Massachusetts have made their
way to Havre de Grace, seized a steamboat, reached
Annapolis, and taken a position by which they could
keep open a road to Washington, before a single
troop of New York soldiers had found a passage into
the enemy's country. Troops from Massachusetts
and Rhode Island have been sent by sea, and were
thrown into Fort Monroe, commanding Norfolk,

while the authorities at Albany were debating upon
the proper official steps to be taken in regard to the
President's Proclamation. "God save the Commonwealth of Massachusetts!"—the State that compromise was to leave out of the new Confederacy! and
blessings be upon the State of Roger Williams, so
confidently calculated on as the first of the Northern
States that would avow its allegiance to the piratical
Government of Jeff. Davis!—*The Independent.*

THAT FLAG.—The *white flag*, reported to have
been borne by the Massachusetts Regiment when it
fought its way through Baltimore, was the regular
Massachusetts standard. It is a flag of white silk,
with the arms of the Union on one side, and those
of the State on the reverse. *Massachusetts troops
ask no truce with a mob of traitors.—Boston Journal.*

SOUTHERN OPINIONS.
From the Charleston Mercury, April 30.

The bug-bear of civil war need frighten no one.
We are not engaged in civil war, and, thank Heaven!
all danger of that most dreadful of human scourges
is past. It almost reconciles us to the delay of the
Convention. That delay has made Virginia a unit—
has made the whole South a unit. The natives of
the South are leagued and confederated to repel
Northern invasion, and establish Southern independence.

Not for an hour since the first white man set his
foot on American soil have the people of the United
States been one people. From the beginning, each
colony had its separate and distinct laws and institutions, and its separate Government. We have planted
and have grown up as distinct and different peoples and
nations; and the difference and distinction between
us have been increasing and widening from the day
of our birth until the present hour. A war between
Virginia and Pennsylvania would be no civil war,
because we are separate nations; far less, then, is a
war between the North and the South. We are socially and politically as distinct a people from the
North, as from France or England. The people of
the two sections have ever hated each other, not
merely because their laws, customs, manners, and
institutions are different; but more still, because
their races, their blood, their ancestry, were different. The people of the South belong to the brave,
impulsive, hospitable, and generous Celtic race; the
people of the North to the cold, phlegmatic Teutonic
race. We include the old Greek and Roman among
the Celtic races;—and also the Anglo-Normans,
whose cleanly habits, language, laws, and personal
appearance, prove beyond a doubt that they were of
Latin origin. The South was settled by Anglo-Normans, Welshmen, Scotchmen, Irishmen, Frenchmen,
and Spaniards. These were all Celts, all belonging
to what may be classed as Mediterranean people.
Few Teutons and few Anglo-Saxons (who are of Teutonic extract) settled in the South. What Teutonic
blood did settle in the South, has been diluted and
neutralized by frequent intermarriage with our Anglo-
Norman families. Every schoolboy knows that the
Mediterranean races have almost monopolized the
chivalry of the world, and, until within the last three
hundred years, quite monopolized its civilization.
The people of the South belong to a different and
superior race from those of the North.

It suffices, however, for our present purpose to
show that we have never been one people, and that

the war between us is no civil or fratricidal war, but a very natural, orthodox, and proper war, if there can be any such war. We want to see peace established as soon as possible; and to effect that purpose we should rain down our blows as fast and furious as possible, and not permit ourselves to be unnerved and paralyzed by the raw-head-and-bloody-bone cry of civil war. The people of the two sections generally live at great distance from each other, and have intermarried very little, as well from this cause as from difference of institutions, difference of race, and mutual dislike growing out of those differences.

We wish to make peace with them as soon as possible and to keep peace with them, by having in the future nothing to do with them.—*Richmond Examiner.*

It is important that we of the South, at least, should understand the nature of this war fully. Many of us are too prone to take our enemies at their word, and look upon this war as one that must be marked with all the terrible convulsions and unnatural horrors of a civil strife. It is time to realize the fact, that we are engaged in a foreign war; that the Government at Washington represents a foreign power, which aims at our subjugation; that we have all the rights, and owe all the duties of an independent people placed in a state of belligerency; and that we have nothing to apprehend from civil war so long as we are a united people, able to maintain and worthy to enjoy our independence.

By doing this we will get rid of much morbid feeling, produced by delusive names and sophistical confusion of ideas in regard to the existing contest. Are we a homogeneous people? Are we free? Are we united? Have we a common Government to which we render cordial allegiance, and which we are ready to defend with patriotic resolution? If so, no civil war can exist within our borders. We know where the enemy is, and who he is. He is on the other side of the Potomac and the Ohio. He is the enemy of our country, of our property, of our institutions, and our homes. Let us front him manfully, and we shall come out of the conflict as safe and triumphant, as he shall come out of it discomfited and humiliated.—*New Orleans Daily Delta.*

LET THE DEVIL TAKE THE HINDMOST.—Let us see who shall get South fastest—farthest—first. Now that the word to bounce is come, let us know who can jump the biggest summersault with the most prodigious energy. Of all Secessionists that were ever seen, it is certain that the Union-shriekers make the best. Beyond other fire-eaters, are Submissionists fierce. Those who have risked every thing and dared every thing in the late struggle for Liberty and Independence—and long before it was begun, for Southern rights and Virginia's honor—are utterly confounded and struck dumb by the fiery enthusiasm of those who were lately denouncing them as rebels ripe for hemp, Southern rights as sedition, and State sovereignty a blasphemy against the Constitution. The natural congratulations of the conquerors in the fight are drowned in the shouts of triumph raised by the vanquished; and the world has lived to see that Lost Principle,—to the victors belong the spoils,—displaced by this other, that from the victors shall the spoils be taken! Long was belief, and deep was once the conviction, that the shriek of "Union" was the winning cry; and just so long as that belief endured, it was written in the Book of Judas that

Davis was a Traitor, Disunion was Treason, and the Southern Confederacy a conglomeration of every thing that was weak, wicked, and absurd. But no rapping spirits ever turned the tables like those that Lincoln's Proclamation evoked from the vasty deep of revolution. The cannon of Fort Sumter announced to all the world that the Baboon of Illinois had no more nuts for Virginia monkeys; and when once fully up to the idea that henceforth the star of empire had taken a Southern track; that there were patrons in Montgomery; that place and pay, if anywhere, must be searched for on this side of the Potomac, and earned by devotion to State Rights—there was a revival in the church politic such as no camp meeting ever saw. When McDowall Moore can sign himself "sinner saved" at the bottom of an Ordinance to unite Virginia to a rebel Confederacy of slave-owners, and Bursted Baldwin inspects the troops that are to take Washington and march on Boston—who may despair of getting to glory? No heard-of bison ever went over a precipice with precipitancy like that of our mummied Federalists and galvanized Submissionists plunging into the Southern Confederacy. It is a race to Montgomery—office is at Montgomery—and the devil take the hindmost.—*Richmond Examiner.*

CONTRABAND OF WAR, CONSTIPATION, AND COMBUSTION.—The Secretary of the Treasury at Washington has added to his list of contraband of war articles the following:—" Mercury in all its compounds, chlorate of potash, muriatic acid, chloride of potash, nitrate of soda, chloride of potassium, potash and pearlash, and nitric acids." You doubtless remember, Messrs. Editors, how a member of the Plymley family was once disturbed, when a British minister undertook thus to interfere with the bowels of mankind, and the inalienable right of people to take medicine. Old Peter Plymley, with commendable indignation, described it as an attempt "to bring the French to reason by keeping them without rhubarb," and to " exhibit to mankind the awful spectacle of a nation deprived of neutral salts." "This," said old Peter, " is not the dream of a wild apothecary, indulging in his own opinion; this is not the distempered fancy of a pounder of drugs, delirious from smallness of profit. * * * What a sublime thought, that no purge can be taken between the Weser and the Garonne; that the bustling pestle is still, the canorous mortar mute, and the bowels of mankind locked up for fourteen degrees of latitude. * * * When was this great plan of conquest and constipation fully developed? In whose mind was first engendered the idea of destroying the pride and plasters of France? Without castor oil they might, for some months, to be sure, have carried on a lingering war; but can they do without bark? Will the people live under a Government whose antimonial powders cannot be procured? Will they bear the loss of mercury? 'There's the rub.' Depend upon it, the absence of Materia Medica will soon bring them to their senses, and the cry of *Bourbon and Bolus* burst forth from the Baltic to the Mediterranean."

Now, Messrs Editors, I should like to know where our Secretary took his degrees in Chemistry and Pharmacy? Why this war upon Chlorides, Nitrates, Muriatic and Nitric Acids? What is there about the Chloride of Potassium to make it a contraband of war? Its principal use is in the manufacture of Alum; and the Confederate troops cannot have much use for that, unless the Union forces intend to set the Secessionists on fire, and prohibit the use of Alum in order to prevent the Southerners from making their clothes and bodies fire-proof. I can understand the objection to Chlorate of Potash, because that makes a terribly explosive compound, being the chief agent in the manufacture of percussion powder. But it is a dangerous article to handle, and why not let the Southerners have it, and blow themselves sky-high with it? But the prohibition in this particular amounts to nothing. The Muriatic Acid is prohibited in order to prevent the Confederate army from manufacturing Chlorine gas, by which Chlorates and Chlorides are made. Muriatic Acid is not only not essential to the manufacture of Chlorine, but it is not used at all in making that article on a large scale. It is easily made with manganese, table salt, and unconcentrated sulphuric acid. This produces Chlorine, and neither of these articles is prohibited. The manufacture of Chlorine from the Binoxide of Manganese and Muriatic Acid is so perilous, owing to the action of the acid on the lead, and the evolution of Hydrogen gas, by which a spontaneous explosive mixture of Chlorine is produced, that the attention of the Secretary is respectfully asked as to the utility of preventing the seceding States from blowing themselves up. Why prohibit them from using the dangerous articles, and allow them free access to means unattended with any peril? And why prohibit Potash, when it can easily be manufactured wherever wood can be obtained? The small quantity of Chlorine and of Potash needed for war purposes, can be obtained without the use of the Secretary's interdicted articles, and might be dispensed, as the authorities of Massachusetts sold whiskey some years since—for medicinal purposes.

The prohibition against Nitric Acid and its compounds can answer no very useful purpose. The circular explains that Nitric Acid is prohibited because it can be used in the manufacture of gun-cotton. Why should the Secretary discourage the manufacture of this article? Its use is attended with a good deal of peril to those who handle it. For war purposes it cannot be compared with gunpowder. It is much less tractable, very perilous in itself, and terrible on weapons. It has much more force than gunpowder, and does not make smoke, but it has disadvantages that counterbalance all these qualities. It may ignite from percussion, or even spontaneously, or it may be decomposed by the moisture of the atmosphere, or even spontaneously, and thus become worthless. Its explosive force is subject to great variations, and the great danger attending its manufacture has caused the almost universal abandonment of attempts at making the article. The velocity of its combustion is too great for all fire-arms, except those of unusual strength and the smallest bore. If it gives out no smoke, it gives out something more deleterious—acid fumes, which destroy health. Then, again, cotton is a fibrous body, and the physical conditions of a fibrous body are strongly opposed to its use in fire-arms.

The projectile power of gun-cotton is nearly or quite double that of gunpowder. When prepared by the American method, by treating Schönbein's gun-cotton with a saturated solution of Chlorate of Potash, it acquires a remarkable force. A pistol loaded with one grain of this cotton has driven a ball through a yellow pine board one inch thick, at the distance of twenty feet.

At the siege of Moultan, in India, gun-cotton was used for the first time for military purposes, and the brilliance and breadth of flash are said to have shown a terrific intensity. But the British Board of Ordnance have decided against the adoption of this explosive article for fire-arms, for reasons already given. It is a clear case to one of the Plymley family, that Secretary Chase, if he designs evil to the Southern Confederacy, should encourage the transit of articles for the manufacture of gun-cotton. It would be likely to injure the Confederate more than the Union armies.

Gunpowder is by far the most manageable and perfect of all explosive materials for fire-arms. It is very curious that it was invented by a priest, and greatly improved by an English Episcopal bishop. Watson, of Llandaff, and George III. once twitted the soldiers of the gospel of peace about the gunpowder direction of his mental powers. The last great improvement is due to what is called "cylinder" charcoal, made by distilling wood free of resin, in iron cylinders, thus gathering its volatile products. Gunpowder made of this charcoal is so strong, that the charges for this used in ordnance were reduced nearly one-third, as compared with gunpowder made with ordinary charcoal. Mr. Faraday, in a paper read to the Royal Institution, showed the importance of *time* in the production of the effects of gunpowder. If it exploded as instantaneously as fulminating mercury, or those terrible explosives, chloride of nitrogen or iodine, it would be useless for its present applications. It would go the wrong way. For example: Mr. Faraday placed on a plate a small particle of the iodide of nitrogen, and touched it with a long stick. The parts in immediate contact with the iodide were shattered, the end of the stick was shivered, and the spot in the plate, covered with the iodide, was drilled through as though a bullet had passed through it. Yet the stick was not *lifted* by the explosion. The merit of gunpowder is, that it lifts and projects the materials in front of it, and thus acquires its force. Instantaneous as the effects seem to be, the explosive force "does not reach its intensity until the space it occupies has been enlarged by that through which the ball has been propelled during the first moment of ignition. Its expansive force is thus brought down and kept below that which the breech of the gun can bear, whilst an accumulating, safe, and efficient momentum is communicated to the ball, producing the precise effects of gunnery." The inventor of the monster gun at Fortress Monroe has a powder made expressly for it on these principles: It is very coarse-grained, or it is made in perforated cakes, to secure the results just mentioned. But although the most perfect explosive article for war, it is wasted on a grand scale. In one day at Sebastopol the Russians fired 13,000 rounds of shot and shell, and the only result was the *wounding of three men.* At Ciudad Rodrigo, 74,987 pounds of gunpowder were consumed in thirty hours and a half; at Badajoz, 228,830 pounds in 104 hours, and this from the great guns only. I appeal to you, Messrs. Editors, should not the Secretary furnish all possible facilities to the Confederacy for manufacturing gun-cotton!

In order to prevent the manufacture of fulminating mercury for percussion powder and caps, mercury is prohibited; but why does the Secretary order an interdiction upon all the compounds of the article? Are we no longer to enjoy the privilege of being salivated? Are our teeth to remain wedged in our jaws? Are sluggish livers no longer to be spurred with the "divine remedy"? Are inflammations to go on with their deposits and effusions, and are we to

use nothing to eat them up? Must we be under the combined tyrannies of combustion and constipation? Is not gunpowder direful enough, without depriving us of the benignant offices of Mercury? Are we to be feasted on lead pills, and be debarred from mercury pills? Is daguerreotyping to come to an end from the Ohio to the Gulf, from the Atlantic to the Indian country? Are we to use buckets of water or burnished copper for mirrors? Suppose, Mr. Secretary, your liver were locked up for a week, wouldn't you want blue pill? Think of going backwards in civilized medicine, in one class of cases, to times antecedent to Paracelsus. If, Mr. Secretary, you should be stretched in fever, learn the agencies of chlorate of potash, and then let us have blue pill and chlorate of potassa. If our sufferings become intolerable, and we order blue pill and calomel from Wolverhampton, would you be gratified in seeing it convoyed from Woolwich? Are the mountains of Cinnabar in California to stand idly kissing the mountain air, because you forbid mercury to flow through the Mississippi valley? Answer us that, Master Chase. Why not forbid lancets? They shed blood as well as Minie balls. Why are we allowed quinine, if we cannot have mercury? Why is morphine regular, and chlorate of potassa contraband? Alas, Mr. Secretary, if you starve us in health, is that any reason why we should be starved in the food of sickness? Do let the mercury and chlorate of potassa come in and go through us.   JONATHAN PLYMLEY.
—*Louisville Journal, May 28.*

IN a town in Indiana, an old man of sixty-five years, with hair and flowing beard as white as snow, implored permission to join the volunteers, but being refused, he went to the barber's, had his beard cropped, and his hair and beard dyed, and again applied for admission. Not being detected, he was received, and being asked his age, replied, " Rising thirty-five."—*New Haven Palladium, May 6.*

SAVANNAH, GA., *April 30.*—On the occasion of the arrival of Mr. A. H. Stephens from Richmond a large procession was formed, which marched through the city. They carried, painted on canvas, a representation of the American flag, soiled and torn, suspended by a broken flag-staff. Underneath was the picture of a grave, with the words, " Receive me." This outrage upon the flag aroused feelings of deep disgust and indignation among the still loyal portion of the citizens; and one gentleman, a venerable pastor of the Seamen's Bethel, openly denounced the proceedings, declaring that Savannah had been the first to dishonor the glorious banner of the Union. On being threatened with violence, he told the mobocrats, that though he was an old man, he would defend himself if attacked, and some of them would bite the dust if they laid their hands on him.—*N. Y. Times, May 8.*

OF course every one can understand how Massachusetts is enabled to send so many men to the Lincolnitish army. The operative population of the State is immense. The stagnation of business and cessation of manufacturing have reduced many thousands of the operative and laboring classes to the verge of starvation. It is these paupers who are so abundantly pensioned off on the Federal Government by State and municipal authorities. The body of the Massachusetts soldiery are the merest hirelings.—*Charleston Evening News, May 7.*

THE *Richmond Dispatch* gives the following description of a company from Western Virginia, called the Grayson Dare-Devils :—
They number one hundred men, all six feet high, and unfailing rifle shots. The company consisted of one hundred and thirty-five, but it is said their commander informed them that only one hundred would be allowed to come to Richmond; and to decide which of them should enjoy that desired privilege, they fired at a mark *running,* and the hundred who struck the target nearest to or exactly in the centre, were accordingly detailed, to the chagrin of the remainder, who were as confident as their comrades that they could send a ball at every crack through the vitals of a Lincolnpoop.—*N. O. Delta, May 7.*

OLD Abe has his intermediate legs in perfect readiness to run. He has not passed a night in the White House for two weeks, but goes into the barracks to sleep with his armed hirelings all around him. He does not so much as take off his boots, that he may be ready to run at a second's warning.—*Petersburg (Va.) Express, May 4.*

EPIGRAM ON SOUTH CAROLINA.

O Carolina, sister, pray come back ;
  Scorn not our flag, nor nightly talk of wars,
Lest Uncle Sam, once fairly on your track,
  Should make you *feel* the stripes and *see* the stars.
—*N. Y. Sun, May 8.*

THE *Charleston Courier* gives the following intelligence of matters at the North :—
We learn from a passenger from Philadelphia, that one day last week at Havre de Grace, three of the Northern volunteers refused to go any further, assigning as a reason that they did not volunteer to go into a war of invasion upon the South. An officer standing by instantly cut and hacked two of the men to pieces. A third, who took the same ground, gave vent to a similar expression for the Union, and cut his own throat from ear to ear, rather than allow himself to be hacked to pieces.
Mob law (in New York city) is triumphant, and Southern men, or those known to sympathize with the South, are in constant danger of their lives. Vigilance committees visit the houses of the wealthy, and every man is heavily assessed for the support of the families of those who have volunteered their services to the Administration. Assessments of $5,000, $3,000, and $2,000, on large houses, are said to be very common. Those merchants who refuse, or make the slightest hesitation, are threatened with the cleaning out of their stores, and several already have been emptied by the mob. Three men were set upon in Florence Hotel, New York, and two killed, for expressing sympathy with the South. Merchants are packing off their clerks, and it is said that several large manufactories have been stopped, with a view of forcing the operatives into the ranks of the volunteer soldiery.
The *Mobile Advertiser* says :—
They may raise plenty of men—men who prefer enlisting to starvation, scurvy fellows from the back slums of cities, whom Falstaff would not have marched through Coventry with—but these recruits are not soldiers, least of all the soldiers to meet the hot-blooded, thoroughbred, impetuous men of the South. Trencher soldiers, who enlisted to war on their rations, not on men, they are—such as marched

through Baltimore, squalid, wretched, ragged and half-naked, as the newspapers of that city report them. Fellows who do not know the breech of a musket from its muzzle, and had rather filch a handkerchief than fight an enemy in manly combat. White-slaves, peddling wretches, small-change knaves and vagrants, the dregs and offscourings of the populace—these are the levied "forces" whom Lincoln suddenly arrays as candidates for the honor of being slaughtered by gentlemen—such as Mobile sent to battle yesterday. Let them come South, and we will put our negroes to the dirty work of killing them. But they will not come South. Not a wretch of them will live on this side of the border longer than it will take us to reach the ground and drive them over.—*N. Y. Sun, May* 8.

ONE of the Ohio regiments elected the Rev. Granville Moody, a well-known Methodist preacher of that State, their chaplain. When their choice had been declared, they sent to Brother Moody to ask him if he would go. He replied, Why, yes, he would like to be their chaplain—but with *one* condition, that they would furnish him with a musket—for, said he, "in our Methodist communion we do not believe in faith without works."—*N. Y. Evening Post, May* 8.

A COMPANY, composed of sixty-five men, bearing the name of Bedford Yankee-Catchers, was organized at Lisbon, Bedford County, Va., and the following officers were elected: Captain, John Buford; 1st Lieut., W. D. Williams; 2d Lieut., David Garrett; 3d Lieut., W. H. Hatcher; Orderly Sergeant, Robert Garrett. The Yankee-Catchers will report and be ready to enter service in a few days.—*Richmond Examiner, May* 18.

LETTER FROM MRS. PRESIDENT DAVIS.—The following letter from Mrs. Jefferson Davis was written in acknowlegment of the receipt of a beautiful workbox, manufactured and presented to her by several patriotic misses of Petersburg:—

"MONTGOMERY, ALA., *April* 29, 1861.

"MY DEAR YOUNG LADIES: Permit me, before thanking you for your kind present, and wishes for my husband's welfare, to congratulate you upon the secession of Virginia—the birthplace of my mother, as well as yours.

"The elder, and honored sister of the Southern States, is received with tearful joy among us, and many hands will fashion stars with which to mark this brilliant accession to our galaxy.

"The possession of a work-box manufactured by little Southern girls, so industrious, so enthusiastic, and so patriotic, will be much prized by me; and I will leave it to my daughter with the note which precedes it, as a precious legacy.

"Long ere you reach the responsibility of a useful womanhood, may we have united peace to independence in our Southern Confederacy.

"Wishing you, my dear young friends, a long, a happy life, I have the honor to be,

"Very gratefully and sincerely,

"Your friend, VARINA DAVIS."
—*Idem.*

MASSACHUSETTS was the first to start a regiment for Washington; Massachusetts blood was the first shed in the war; a Massachusetts regiment was the first to reinforce Fort Monroe; the first to open a pathway from Annapolis to Washington; the first to reach the capital; and is the first to invade Virginia! "God bless the Commonwealth of Massachusetts!" —*Albany Evening Journal, May* 7.

THE three greatest villains and traitors which the present war has produced, are, beyond all doubt, Hicks, Scott, and Harney. We place them in the order of their infamy. Hicks ranks his confederates by long odds. Scott and Harney have some palliation in the fact of their being mercenaries, and in their carnal weakness. But in Hicks' villainy there are no mitigating circumstances—no plea of human frailty. His treachery was deliberate, cold-blooded, cowardly, and hypocritical. Before the incensed populace of Baltimore, he quailed into submission, abjured his Unionism, and declared unqualifiedly his determination to resist the Lincoln invasion to the death. The threats for vengeance against the Yankee murderers of Baltimore citizens has hardly died away, before he slunk off to Winter Davis' den, and set to work concocting a plan to betray Maryland into Lincoln's hands. The men of the South, unfortunately, trusted his assurances, and now Baltimore and Maryland are suffering the penalty of their credulity and weakness.—*New Orleans Delta, May* 23.

A THRILLING scene is related of one of the Massachusetts men, who was mortally wounded at Baltimore by the mob on the afternoon of the fatal nineteenth of April. He soon bled to death, notwithstanding every effort was made to save him. An instant before he expired he rose, struggling with death, and, standing erect, he fixed his glassy eyes upon every person in the room, and then lifting them towards heaven, and raising his right hand, he exclaimed, with clear voice, "All hail to the Stars and Stripes!" Saying this, he fell back into the arms of his physician, and expired. This patriotic declaration of the dying man so thrilled the lookers-on, that all but his immediate attendants turned silently away, although many of them were stained with the blood of the deceased.—*N. Y. Herald, May* 5.

THE man at Bunker Hill who belonged to no regiment, and no company, and was fighting on his own hook, is well remembered. Another man of the same stamp has been found in New Hampshire. The *Littleton* (N. H.) *Journal* says, that as soon as tidings of the threatened attack on Washington reached that town, Mr. Benjamin W. Kilburn took down his rifle and started for the nation's capital, to aid in its defence. He is said to be an excellent marksman, and anxious to cover a fighting Secessionist with the sight of his gun. He bears his own expenses in the service of his country. Such promptitude equals that of John Stark of Revolutionary memory.—*New Haven Palladium, May* 6.

COL. PINCKNEY, of the Sixth Regiment of New York, on setting out from Annapolis to Washington, made a stirring address to his men:—"If any of you falter," said the Colonel, "you will be instantly shot down; and if I falter, I hope you will put a thousand bullets through my heart at once." Every officer and soldier responded with a most enthusiastic "Aye" to these remarks, which were delivered in a calm, inflexible, and determined way. Col. Pinckney evidently meant all he said, and at each telling-point every soldier's heart throbbed audibly beneath his cross-belts.—*Independent, May* 2.

KING COTTON.

[After Béranger.]

BY R. H. STODDARD.

See this new king who comes apace,
And treats us like a conquered race;
He comes from Dixey's Land by rail,
His throne a ragged cotton-bale.
   On to the White House straight
   He's marching—rather late,
   Clanking along the land,
   The shackles in his hand.
      Hats off! hats off!
Ye slaves, of curs begotten,
Hats off to great King Cotton!

"White niggers, mudsills, Northern scum,
Base hirelings, hear me, and be dumb:
What makes this country great and free?
'Tis me, I tell you—only me!
   Beware, then, of my might,
   Nor dare dispute my right,
   Or else you'll find, some day
   There'll be the devil to pay!
      Hats off! hats off!
Ye slaves, of curs begotten,
Hats off to great King Cotton!

Dare you dispraise my royal parts,
And prate of Freedom, Commerce, Arts?
What are they to my pedigree?
Why, Adam was an F. F. V.!
   My arms, (a whip, ye fools,
   Above a bloodhound, *gules!*)
   Declare my house and birth—
   The king of kings on earth!
      Hats off! hats off!
Ye slaves, of curs begotten,
Hats off to great King Cotton!

Paupers, who can resist me? None!
My wife's a pew in Washington;
My youngest son—he looks like me—
Will be in Congress soon, (S. C.)
   His brother, Colonel Fuss,
   Trained up by old U. S.,
   Tore down our dirty flag—
   A General, now, with Bragg!
      Hats off! hats off!
Ye slaves, of curs begotten,
Hats off to great King Cotton!

Let us alone, ye Federal crew,
Nor dare collect our revenue;
For gentlemen, from earliest date
Were never useful to the State.
   Thanks to my forts, and guns,
   And arsenals, (*yours*, once!)
   I can now speak my mind,
   As Ancient Abe shall find!
      Hats off! hats off!
Ye slaves, of curs begotten,
Hats off to great King Cotton!

God's ministers, we fight for you:
Aid us, ye aid the Gospel too.
For you, beast-people, (clear the track!)
Still bear our saddles on your back!
   We'll ride you all your lives;
   Your daughters, too, and wives,

   Shall serve us in our need,
   And teach our girls to read!
      Hats off! hats off!
Ye slaves, of curs begotten,
Hats off to great King Cotton!

Your musket, chaplain—(mind my toes!)
The smoke is incense in my nose!
On them, Confederates, great and small!
Down with the Union—death to all!
   From my brave ancestry,
   These rights descend to me,
   And all true Southern men,
   World without end. Amen.
      Hats off! hats off!
Ye slaves, of curs begotten,
Hats off to great King Cotton!
May 26, 1861.   —*Vanity Fair.*

THE HEAVENLY OMEN.*

BY ELIZABETH T. P. BEACH.

Oh! say, did ye see round the moon yesternight,
" Our colors " encircled in glorious light?
Our " Red, White and Blue," fair enzoning the sheen
Of the " Goddess Diana," the heavenly queen?

'Tis most wondrous, I know, but the tale is o'ertrue,
And if ye will listen, I'll tell it to you;
No vision of fancy poetic, I ween,
But an omen most blest, that by hundreds was seen!

As the brave, gallant " Seventh," were chanting last
   night,
By the calm, holy gleam of the moon's silvery light,
The songs that our fathers had sung long ago,
When our ensign they bore to the heart of the foe,

And the stars brightly smiled on the flag of our
   land,
That responsively waved to the song of the band,
The " Star-spangled Banner," in full chorus glee,
Lo! an omen soul-stirring each soldier did see!

For high in the heavens, encircling her there,
Fair Luna " our colors " did brilliantly wear!
Bright in " trinity " circlets, our " Red, White and
   Blue,"
In the pure starry skies were presented to view!

Thus she beamed, as the " Star-spangled Banner "
   they sang,
When a shout of wild gladness exultingly ran!
" To Diana the Goddess! now hail " three times
   three!"
Blest omen from Heaven of *our* victory!

" Three cheers for Diana!" loud shouted the band;
" Faint not, gallant sons of Columbia's land;
Our cause is for justice, 'gainst treason and shame,
Our rights to uphold, and our country's fair fame.

---

* A singular phenomenon appeared in the heavens as
the Seventh (New York) Regiment were floating over the
broad waters of the Chesapeake Bay, on their way to the
protection of Washington. As they were singing their
hymns and national airs beneath the clear blue evening
skies, and the notes of our " Star-spangled Banner" rang
forth over the silvery waves, the moon shone out, brightly
arrayed in " our national colors," wearing a brilliant zone
of " Red, White and Blue," which glorious sight was enthusiastically cheered by the Regiment as a blessed omen.

Sainted heroes are gazing with sad, deathless look,
On the shame that, if with us, they never would
    brook !
And the pure Queen of Night our loved colors wears,
To say that our cause e'en the "high heaven
    shares !"
—N. Y. Evening Post.

SONG OF THE IRISH LEGION.

BY JAMES DE MILLE.

E Pluribus Unum. Erin go Bragh.

Ye boys of the sod, to Columbia true,
Come up, lads, and fight for the Red, White and
    Blue !
Two countries we love, and two mottoes we'll share,
And we'll join them in one on the banner we bear :
    Erin, mavourneen ! Columbia, agra !
    E pluribus unum. Erin go bragh.

Upon them, my lads ! and the rebels shall know
How Erin can fight when she faces the foe ;
If they can't give us arms, sure, we needn't delay ;
With a sprig of shillelagh we'll open the way.
    Erin, mavourneen ! Columbia, agra !
    E pluribus unum. Erin go bragh.

"Blood Tubs" and "Plug Uglies," and others galore,
Are sick for a thrashing in sweet Baltimore ;
Be Jabers ! that same I'd be proud to inform
Of the terrible force of an Irishman's arm.
    Erin, mavourneen ! Columbia, agra !
    E pluribus unum. Erin go bragh.

Before you the tyrant assembles his band,
And threatens to conquer this glorious land ;
But it wasn't for this that we traversed the sea,
And left the Green Isle for the land of the free.
    Erin, mavourneen ! Columbia, agra !
    E pluribus unum. Erin go bragh.

Go forth to the tyrant, and give him to know
That an Irishman holds him his bitterest foe ;
And his sweetest delight is to meet him in fight,
To battle for freedom, with God for the right !
    Erin, mavourneen ! Columbia, agra !
    E pluribus unum. Erin go bragh.

GOD AND THE RIGHT.

BY DAVID J. DICKSON.

"Now, soldiers of Freedom, for love of God, rally !
Old Earth yearns to know that her children are men."
GERALD MASSEY.

Arise ! let our Banner be flung to the skies !
  See, the Northern battalions are roused to the
    fight !
The echoing mountains shall wake to our cries :
  Our Country and Liberty ! God and the Right !
The old Land comes down with the old Sword in hand ;
  She comes, as she came to the olden wars ;
Her frown shall strike death to the traitorous band
  Who would tear from her clutches the Banner of
    Stars.

Arise ! let our Banner be flung to the skies !
  See, the Northern battalions are roused to the
    fight !
The echoing mountains shall ring with our cries :
  Our Country and Liberty ! God and the Right !
POETRY—10

Then let the storm burst, and, as firm as the rock,
  We'll stand with the old Banner streaming on
    high ;
The breast of the old Land is bared for the shock ;
  Like freemen we'll live, or like freemen we'll die.
Then strike for the old Land, that never has bowed,
  And Vict'ry shall carry our Flag through the wars ;
But if we *must* fall, let our glorious shroud
  Be the Flag of our Country—the Banner of Stars.

Let the Flag of our Country be flung to the sky ;
  Our arms shall be bared for the glorious fight ;
As freemen we'll live, or like heroes we'll die !
  Our Union and Liberty ! God and the Right !
STERLING, PA., *April*, 1861.

DIXIE.

BY T. M. COOLEY.[*]

Away down South, where grows the cotton,
'Seventy-six seems quite forgotten ;
  Far away, far away, far away, Dixie land.
And men with rebel shout and thunder,
Tear our good old flag asunder,
  Far away, far away, far away, Dixie land.
Then we're bound for the land of Dixie !
    Hurrah ! hurrah !
In Dixie land we'll take our stand,
  And plant our flag in Dixie !
Away, away, away down South in Dixie !
Away, away, away down South in Dixie !

That flag—the foemen quailed before it,
When our patriot fathers bore it,
  Far away, &c.
And battle-fields are shrined in story,
Where its folds were bathed in glory,
  Far away, &c.

And now, when traitor hands assail it,
Stanch defenders ne'er shall fail it ;—
  Far away, &c.
Nor from its glorious constellation,
Stars be plucked by pirate nation ;—
  Far away, &c.

Undimmed shall float that starry banner,
Over Charleston and Savannah,
  Far away, &c.
And Bunker Hill and Pensacola
Own alike its mission holy ;—
  Far away, &c.

Then sound the march ! We pledge devotion
In our blood on land or ocean,
  Far away, &c.
Till every traitor in the nation
Gains a Haman's elevation,
  Far away, &c.

Yes, sound the march ! Our Northern freemen
Turn not back for man or demon,
  Far away, far away, far away, Dixie land.
Until once more our banner glorious
Waves o'er Dixie land victorious,
  Far away, far away, far away, Dixie land.

[*] This song has taken so well, that arrangements have
been made to send it to our regiments, that it may be the
"Michigan Patriots'" song of the campaign.—*Ann Arbor
(Mich.) News, June* 4.

Then we'll plant our flag in Dixie !
    Hurrah ! hurrah !
Whoever hauls the old flag down,
    We'll shoot him down in Dixie !
Away, away, away down South in Dixie !
Away, away, away down South in Dixie !

STAND BY THE FLAG.

I.

Stand by the Flag !—its stars, like meteors gleaming,
    Have lighted Arctic icebergs, Southern seas,
And shone responsive to the stormy beaming
    Of old Arcturus and the Pleiades.

II.

Stand by the Flag !—its stripes have streamed in
    glory,
To foes a fear, to friends a festal robe,
And spread, in rhythmic lines, the sacred story
    Of Freedom's triumph over all the globe.

III.

Stand by the Flag !—on land and ocean billow,
    By it your fathers stood, unmoved and true,
Living defended—dying, from their pillow,
    With their last blessing, passed it on to you.

IV.

Stand by the Flag !—immortal heroes bore it
    Though sulphurous smoke, deep moat, and armed
    defence,
And their imperial shades still hover o'er it—
    A guard celestial, from Omnipotence.

V.

Stand by the Flag !—it is a holy treasure ;
    Though wrong may dim some stars which should
    be light,
A steady, gentle, and persistent pressure,
    Kindly exerted, yet will make them bright.

VI.

Stand by the Flag !—though death-shots round it
    rattle,
And underneath its waving folds have met,
In all the dread array of sanguine battle,
    The quivering lance and glittering bayonet.

VII.

Stand by the Flag !—all doubt and treason scorning—
    Believe, with courage firm, and faith sublime,
That it will float until the eternal morning
    Pales, in its glories, all the lights of time !

THE ZOUAVES' BATTLE SONG.

BY J. HOWARD WAINWRIGHT.

Onward, Zouaves ! Ellsworth's spirit still leads us ;
Onward, Zouaves ! for our country still needs us ;
Onward, Zouaves ! for our banner floats o'er us ;
Onward, Zouaves ! for the foe is before us.
    CHORUS—Onward, Zouaves !
        Do nothing by halves ;
        Home to the hilt with the bay'net,
            Zouaves !

Onward, Zouaves ! for the foe hath defied us ;
Onward, Zouaves ! we have brave men to guide us ;
Let the sunlight and moonlight, from bayonets
    glancing,
Tell the foe the vanguard of the North is advancing.
    CHORUS—Onward, Zouaves !
        Do nothing by halves ;
        Home to the hilt with the bay'net,
            Zouaves !

Onward, Zouaves ! till we break down oppression ;
Onward, Zouaves ! till we crush out secession ;
We've shown them our friendship is honest and true,
We'll show them our wrath can be terrible too.
    CHORUS—Onward, Zouaves !
        Do nothing by halves ;
        Home to the hilt with the bay'net,
            Zouaves !

Onward, Zouaves ! for our bugles are clanging ;
Onward, Zouaves ! the assassins need hanging ;
No longer we'll bear with their rapine and wrong ;
Their guilt makes them weak, while our cause makes
    us strong.
    CHORUS—Onward, Zouaves !
        Do nothing by halves ;
        Home to the hilt with the bay'net,
            Zouaves !

Onward, Zouaves ! when the struggle is ended,
Homeward we'll carry the flag we've defended ;
Home, where our dear ones will greet with caress-
    ings ;
Home, where our country will greet us with blessings.
    CHORUS—Onward, Zouaves !
        Do nothing by halves ;
        Home to the hilt with the bay'net,
            Zouaves !

Onward, Zouaves ! till the traitors are punished ;
Onward, Zouaves ! till the treason hath vanished ;
Onward, Zouaves ! till once more in communion,
O'er the North and the South floats the Flag of our
    Union.
    CHORUS—Onward, Zouaves !
        Do nothing by halves ;
        Home to the hilt with the bay'net,
            Zouaves !
           —*N. Y. Evening Post.*

THE PROPHECY OF THE DEAD.

BY AMANDA T. JONES.

Is the groaning earth stabbed to its core ?
    Are the seas oozing blood in their bed ?
Have all troubles of ages before,
    Grown quick, in those homes of the dead ?
        The red plagues of yore,
    Must they to our season be wed ?

We thought the volcano of war
    Would belch out its flames in the East ;
We knew where the winds were ajar
    With the quarrel of soldier and priest :
        We shuddered—though far—
    To think how the vultures might feast.

We said, " *We* have Liberty's smile ;
    Go to ! we are safe in the West ;"

But the plague-spot was on us the while,
And the serpent was warm in our breast.
　　We can no more revile ;
　　The ox is for sacrifice dressed.

Do ye hear, O ye Dead, in your tombs—
Ye Dead, whose bold blows made us free—
Do ye hear the reveille of drums ?
Can ye say what the issue shall be ?
　　Past the midnight that comes,
　　Is the noon rising up from the sea ?

Who whispered ? Is life underneath,
Astir in the dust of the brave ?
For there steals to my ear such a breath
As can only steal out of the grave :
　　" Ye must go down to death !
　　Ye have drunk of the blood of the slave ! "

We have sinned ! we have sinned ! O ye Dead !
Our fields with the outcrying blood
Of Abel, our brother, are fed.
　　Must we therefore be drowned in the flood ?
　　Waits no Ararat's head ?
　　Is no ark guided there by our God ?

" Ye must go down to death ! Have ye heard
The tale of the writings of yore ?—
How One in the sepulchre stirred,
And cast off the grave-clothes he wore ?
　　In the flesh dwelt the Word,
　　Inheriting life evermore.

" When the foes of the nation have pressed
To its lips the sponge reeking in gall ;
When the spear has gone into its breast,
And the skies have been rent by its call ;
　　It shall rise from its rest :
　　It shall rise, and shall rule over all.
　　　　　　　　　　　—Buffalo Courier.

OUR FLAG.

" Let the Flag of our Country wave from the spire of
every church in the land, with nothing above it but the
cross of Christ."　　　　　REV. E. A. ANDERSON.

Oh, raise that glorious ensign high,
　　And let the nations see
The flag for which our fathers fought,
　　To make our country free !
Their sons beneath its ample folds,
　　With loyal hearts, and true,
May well maintain the Stars and Stripes,
　　The Red, White, and the Blue.

From every hill, in every vale,
　　Where freemen tread the sod,
And from the spires where freemen meet,
　　For prayer and praise to God ;—
Yes, on the church—no place too good—
　　Our country yet is free !
Unfurl the Flag, beneath but this—
　　The cross of Calvary !

Let Southern traitors heed their doom ;
　　The time is drawing near
When Freedom's host, with patriots' hearts,
　　Among them will appear.

The nation's pulse will leap with joy,
　　And every man that's true
Will fight while God will give him strength,
　　For Red, White, and the Blue.
SUGAR GROVE, PA.　　　　　　　　　W.

THE REPUBLIC.

" The great Republic is no more."—LONDON TIMES.

BY WM. OLAND BOURNE.

　　" No more ! "
Thus sigh the eastern winds,
　　As o'er the sea they come,
And waft their murmurs deep
　　To Freedom's radiant home ;
The sad waves die away
　　Along the ocean strand,
And whisper low, " No more !
　　No more ! O glorious land ! "

" No more ? " a voice replied ;
　　" What meaning words are these ?
A nation oft may pass
　　Through red and bloody seas !
Through fierce baptismal fires,
　　Through nights that have no ray,
God's people oft must pass,
　　To win unclouded day.
O Prophet of the world's deep woe !
　　O Prophet at the gloomy shrine !
Invoke its mystery, and show
　　The future, if thou canst divine ! "

　　A solemn tone,
That died along the New World's shore,
　　Brought back alone
The Prophet's words, " No more ! "

" No more, Columbia, shall thy banner wave
　　In lustrous azure with its peerless stars ;
Thy glory now has found a lasting grave—
　　Thy strength shall perish through the bloody Mars.

" No more the nations of the world shall sigh
　　For Freedom's vision, when they learn thy dream,
But watching where they see the mighty die,
　　Shall hopeless wait while flows the sullen stream.

" Come up, O millions ! gather round the bier,
　　Where lies the great Republic in its sleep ;
We bury nations like the loved and dear,
　　O'er whom we linger while we stand and weep

" Unlock the sepulchres of ancient Time !
　　Turn back the bolts that keep the realms of gloom !
For now we bury in an age sublime
　　A nation glorious in her early doom.

" In deep, dark caves where despots long have lain,
　　And chains have rusted with the added years,
We lay her down, no more to rise again,
　　Nor make our visions restless with our fears.

" In awful shadows and the sacred urn,
　　Her place shall be remembered, but no more
Shall Freedom's name make human hearts to burn,
　　Or swell in grandeur from the Western shore.

" The temple crumbles, and the pillars fall !
　　The altar passes, and the worship dies !
The millions gather as they bear the pall,
　　And Freedom seeks her refuge in the skies.

" In peaceful slumber let her pass away !
　　'Tis vain the ancient spirit to restore !
The sun is set, and peaceful let the day
　　Close on the mighty nation now no more ! "

　　　　　　The waves rolled on,
　　And, dying, murmured forth, " No more ! "
　　　　　The low, sad winds,
Breathed, as they lulled to rest, " No more ! "
　　　　　The ancient cliff,
　　In muttered echoes, said, " No more ! "
　　　　　And in my heart,
Where Hope was dying on the shore
　　　　　Of Doubt and Death,
The solemn pulses beat, " No more ! "

" O Prophet of the world's deep woe !
　　Is this the answer from thy shrine ?
Wait till the morrow—thou shalt know
　　That Freedom hath a life divine !
The sun shall stand in heaven to-day,
　　Nor set once more on hill or plain,
While freemen strike, and toil, and pray,
　　Till Freedom lives in bliss again ! "

　　And still the Prophet said,
　　" The nation now is dead !
The great Republic is no more ! "

　　Star after star went down ;
　　　The flag was trailed in dust ;
　　And chiefs of old renown
　　　Forsook their ancient trust ;
　　　　It seemed too true,
　　　　As the Prophet said,
　　　That the life had sped,
　　　And the soul was dead,
　　And the nation lived no more !
And e'en when Sumter fell,
The heart beat silent with its doubt,
　　A moment only—for the spell
Was broken by the freeman's shout.

　" To arms ! to arms ! " they cry ;
　" Defend that flag, or die ! "
　" To arms ! " amid their tears ;
　" To arms ! " as in the years
When heroes saw the field of battle nigh ;
　" To arms ! " replied the hills ;
　" To arms ! " the mountains grand ;
　" To arms, let him who wills ! "
　　Swept o'er the freeman's land ;
　　It leaped from hill to hill,
　　It shook the mountain crag,
　For love's electric thrill
　　Still kept the starry flag ;
　" To arms ! " replied the plains,
The hot blood throbbing through the veins,
　For millions rallied with the vow,
" We strike for Freedom surely now ;
In heaven's great name the damning wrong shall bow ! "

　　From the steep mountain side,
　　From the deep flowing tide,
　　From the green prairies wide,
　　　" Forward ! " they cry ;

　　From the far eastern hills,
　　From the pure flowing rills,
　　From the great busy mills,
　　　" Onward for aye ! "
　From the forge, old and grim,
　From the mine, dark and dim,
　Swelled the bold hero-hymn,
　　　" Onward or die ! "
And to their arms they sprung,
　Freedom on every tongue,
　True to the songs they sung,
　　Filling the sky :—

" Arm, brothers, arm ! for the foe is before us,
　Filled with deep hate to the Union we love ;
Onward we press, with the loud-swelling chorus
　Shaking the earth, and the heaven above.
　　Chorus—Arm, brothers, arm !
　　　　　For the strife be ye ready !
　　　　　With an eye ever steady !
　　　　　Arm, brothers, arm !

" On, brothers, on ! For they haste to the battle !
　The treason is theirs, whom we trusted so long ;
For Freedom we fight, and not a mere chattel ;
　The Union and Peace—the Right over Wrong.
　　Chorus—Arm, brothers, arm !

" Haste, brothers, haste ! for the moments are flying !
　An hour now lost may undo all the past !
And millions of mourners now burdened are sighing,
　And, terror-struck, bow in the force of the blast !
　　Chorus—Arm, brothers, arm !

" Come, brothers, come ! It is time for the starting !
　We pray on the field ! At the altar *they* pray
Who mourn for our loss—nor wait for the parting—
　Our children shall bless us for valor to-day !
　　Chorus—Arm, brothers, arm !

" Swear, brothers, swear ! For the Union forever !
　Resting not now till each traitor is riven !
God for our land, and of freedom the Giver,
　Onward we haste in the sunshine of Heaven."
　　Chorus—Arm, brothers, arm !

　　" She lives ! " the freeman cried ;
　　" She lives ! " my heart replied ;
　　" She lives ! " rolled o'er the plain,
　　　And thrilled the waking land,
　　That caught it back again
　　　From mountains old and grand ;
　　And starry banners waved
　　　From peak, and dome, and spire,
　　The flag of love and peace,
　　　And glory's quenchless fire.

O toiling millions on the Old World's shore !
　Look up, rejoicing, for she is not dead !
The soul is living as it lived before,
　When sainted heroes spurned the tyrant's tread ;
The strife is earnest, and the day wears on,
　And ages tremble at the mighty blow—
Beyond the conflict is a glorious dawn,
　A rapturous birth of Freedom out of woe ;
The clouds may gather, and the storm be long,
　And lightnings leap across the darkened sky,
But Freedom lives to triumph over wrong—
　It still will live, for Truth shall never die !

SHOT AND SHELL EXPENDED DURING THE BOMBARD-MENT OF FORT SUMTER.—From the statistical report of the batteries engaged during the bombardment of Fort Sumter, published in yesterday's *Mercury*, we compile the following, which will prove interesting to many readers. The number of shot and shell thrown by each battery is here given, making a grand total of 2,361 shot and 980 shell.

	SHOT.	SHELL.
Stevens' Battery, Morris Island	183	60
Trapier's Battery, Morris Island	—	170
Cumming's Point Battery, Morris Island	336	197
Rifle Cannon, Morris Island	11	19
Battery No. 1, Sullivan's Island	—	185
Battery No. 2, (Mortar,) Sullivan's Island..	—	88
Sumter Battery, Sullivan's Island	651	1
Oblique Battery, Sullivan's Island	110	5
Enfilade Battery, Sullivan's Island	600	—
Dahlgren Battery, Sullivan's Island	—	61
Floating Battery, Sullivan's Island	470	—
Mount Pleasant Battery	—	51
Lower Battery, James Island	—	90
Upper Battery, James Island	—	53
	2,361	980

—*Charleston Mercury, May 3.*

THE NEW NATION.—We have all witnessed the sudden transformation of the scene-painter's art—a whistle, a creak of a wheel, and in place of a cottage, a palace!—a sighing maiden is followed by an exultant conqueror; and seeing these delusions of the canvas, we have accustomed ourselves to look upon it as a trick of the drama, and never in our experience to be paralleled by the actual. We are to see all strange things in the 19th century, and of the very strangest is the sudden change of a Northern people from a race of quiet, patient, much-enduring, calm, "consistent members of the Peace Society," willing to compromise to the last possible interpolation of the Constitution, to a gathering of armed men, backing up courage by cash, and coming together with a union of the purse and the sword, which is to be one of the most remarkable chapters that history ever wrote.

The Macaulay of American annals will record that in one brief, earnest, intense ten of days, the chain of party melted; the organization of party shivered; the leaders of opposing opinions were as brethren; Seward, Douglas, Dix, even Caleb Cushing, wrote a full acquittance of past political strife, and declared that the life of their political doctrine was the preservation of the country's honor. Who shall ever despair of a nation after this? If from our quarrels, our pale compromises, our bondage to the Exchange and to the warehouse, from all the indolence of prosperity, such a transformation to the camp of a brave and united soldiery, a close and compact counsel—the purse inverted over the soldier's needs—the struggle who shall quickest forget his party watchword, and learn that of the line of battle—if this new life has thus sprung, the philosopher of History must learn of us new ideas of the power of a free people.

The Revolution of 1776 witnessed no such union. More families left New York and her sister colonies, because they would not show steel to King George, (and that when New York had population only of thousands where it now has hundreds of thousands,) than have now suggested doubts of our right from all the vast numbers of the Northern States. We cannot even yet realize the change these ten days have wrought. We are like those who bring all their valuables to the fire of the furnace, and recast the compound. That process is now in our midst. Does any man suppose we are to be fused in just such party shape again? Differ we shall—but the gold has been tried, and the great fact established, that those dwelling in the Northern States have that devotion to the country at whose call the mother gives her son to the battle, the capitalist his treasure to the cause, and men blend as a *Nation.* Were we ever a Nation before?

All lineages—the Mayflower man is in the front rank only to be met in line by those who look back to Delft Haven. I have found the warmest thought and act in those who but a month since were doubtful of the patriotism of those of us who could not see the merit of "compromise." The voice of Edward Everett rings out its call to arms—the men who have risked to offend the North by their ultra Southern views, have thrown all aside as the call for Union for the country's honor reached them.—*N. Y. Courier & Enquirer, May 2.*

ADVENTURE OF COMMISSARY PATTON.—On Sunday night, the 21st of April, Commissary Patton, of the New York Seventh Regiment, with important despatches from Lieut.-Gen. Scott to Brigadier-General Butler, left Washington for Annapolis in company with Major Welsh, Col. Lander, and Mr. Van Valkenburgh. They took separate seats in the cars, and held no communication with each other. They arrived safely at the Junction, but had no sooner stepped upon the platform, than some merchant, with whom Mr. Patton had done business, stepped up and said, "Hallo, Patton, what are you, a National Guard, doing here?" Mr. Patton endeavored to silence him, but not until too late, as a spy, who had followed the party, overheard the salutation. Mr. Patton walked over the fields to the Annapolis train, but, being unable to ascertain when the train would leave, he went to the hotel, in front of which a militia company was drilling. In a few moments thereafter, he saw, to his astonishment, the train start off without a passenger on board. While smoking a cigar upon the stoop, a lawyer of the place took him by the arm, and asked him what his business was, at the same time telling him that he was suspected of being a spy. Mr. Patton replied boldly, "I am no spy, sir, but a messenger from the War Department at Washington to the troops at Annapolis." The lawyer then gave a signal, upon which the militia company marched over to the House. The captain of the company also demanded to know his business, when he replied as before, and further said: "I will not be taken prisoner by any civilian. I am not aware that this State has seceded; and if you arrest me, I demand that you hold me as a prisoner of war, for I am a Government officer." He further told the captain that he had better be cautious, and set forth the responsibility of such an act. This set the doughty captain to thinking, and he went off to consult with his comrades. At the termination of the council, the captain told Mr. Patton that he must go back to Washington, and that they would send him in a wagon. To this he assented in apparent good faith, and said he would walk along the road until the wagon was ready. A short distance from the village he stopped to chat with some people at a farm-house, and was agreeably surprised to find that they were related to one of the captains of his regiment. Soon the wagon came up, and conveyed him to the outposts at Washington, where he alighted, but the vehicle was scarcely out of sight before he "faced about" and started again for Annapolis. Falling in with a countryman, he offered the man $1 for a lift, which was accepted. Being worn out with fatigue, he fell asleep in the bottom of the wagon, and thus reposed until the man arrived at his destination. Starting onward again, he overtook a boy plodding along, and after some conversation engaged him as a pilot. Thus they kept on until reaching the main road, when a drunken fellow, armed to the teeth, ordered Mr. Patton to "hold on." Mr. Patton said his name was "Moore," and that he was going to Annapolis to collect some money which was owing him; but the fellow came to the conclusion that he was a "d——d Yankee spy," and must return to the tavern near by. Here were several other rebels armed to the teeth, and very drunk. They took Mr. Patton inside, and held a "Court Martial," but were diversified in their decision as to how they should dispose of him. Some wanted to shoot him, others to hang him, and others to lock him up. Meantime drinks were called for, in which all joined. It was finally decided to hang the "God damned spy," and Mr. Patton was marched out to the yard, where he saw a rope dangling from the limb of a tree. Pending the preparations for the "execution of the spy," a gentleman on horseback came up, and, ordering the men to fall back, took Mr. Patton one side, at the same time saying, "I know you, sir; you belong to the National Guard, and I drank with you in Baltimore." Some further conversation ensued, when the gentleman, who represented himself as the commander of that district, said he would release him if he, Mr. P., would pledge his word and honor to return to Washington. This pledge he readily gave, glad to escape from the hands of a drunken rabble, and forthwith took the road for Washington. About a mile away from this scene, he met his boy, who had watched the proceedings from a distance, and paying him handsomely, discharged him. After several stoppages upon the road by the rebel patrols, he arrived in Washington, and made report to Gen. Scott. Here he found his companions, who had also been arrested, and sent back. Determining to start again for Annapolis, he disguised himself completely, and in company with a friend, who had a fast team, set out on the journey—*in search of a stolen horse.* Every person whom they met upon the road was asked about a "stray horse," but no one had seen the animal. This ruse took well, and they got along without much interruption. Reaching a tavern at night, they took supper, and apparently went to bed. Mr. Patton, however, slipped out of the back door, and started off on foot. Presently he came to a piece of woods, but had not proceeded far before he heard the tramp of horses and the voices of men. He had barely time to conceal himself in a heap of underbrush, before they came up and halted near him. From their conversation he learned that the Seventh Regiment had moved toward Washington— a fact which he was most desirous of knowing. The horsemen directly moved away after hunting about the woods, when Mr. P. left his retreat, and safely reached his hotel again, where he overheard a conversation relative to the destruction of a bridge, over which the train containing the Seventh had to pass. The nuts had been taken off the bolts in the bridge, and had the train passed over it, all on board would have been killed. Mr. P. and his companions again got under way, and, taking measures to prevent such a calamity, returned to Washington. *Mr. Patton drove eighty miles, and walked thirty miles within*

thirty hours, in order to accomplish all this.—*Cor. N. Y. Tribune, May 4.*

THE COCKADE BLACK DIAMONDS.—Quite a novel spectacle was witnessed in Petersburg, Va., as we are informed by a gentleman who arrived from that city. One hundred and twenty free negroes, uniformed with red shirts and dark pants, and bearing a flag of the Southern Confederacy, which had been presented to them by the ladies, marched through the city and embarked on the cars for Norfolk. They proceeded upon this excursion of their own free will, in response to the request made by Gen. Gwynn for the services of six hundred negroes from any portion of the State, to work upon the fortifications around Norfolk harbor. They were all in the finest spirits, and seemed anxious to "catch Old Linkum one time"— a desire which appeared to be foremost in their thoughts. They certainly deserve great credit for their disinterestedness, and will find that it is appreciated.—*Charleston Evening News, May 1.*

THE OCCUPATION OF CAIRO.—This audacious movement has had good effect in developing the purpose of our enemies to prosecute the war in earnest, and in its inspiring influence upon the Tennessee and Kentucky mind. It conveys a threat which the people of those States will join their brethren of the Confederate States in resenting with promptitude.

Geography has made Cairo a strategetical position of the utmost consequence. It is the key to the upper, as New Orleans and the Lake and the Balize are the key to the lower Mississippi. It can blockade St. Louis on the one hand, and Louisville on the other; while, if in possession of a considerable force, possessing heavy ordnance, and commanding the railroad leading south of that point, it would menace the city of Memphis, and open the way for an invading army to make that an advanced post of occupation. It is not pleasant to contemplate such a possibility. But it is good policy to face it fairly, if we would defeat it effectually.—*Jackson Mississippian, April 26.*

THE FIRST GUN in the present conflict was fired at Fort Sumter on Henry Clay's birthday. The fort surrendered on Thomas Jefferson's birthday. The contest began in the streets of Baltimore on the anniversary of the battle of Lexington and Concord.— *Charleston Mercury, May 6.*

NEW YORK, *May 6.*—A flour merchant of this city, who has just returned from Charleston, states that he was impressed into the rebel service, and was in Fort Moultrie during the whole battle. He confirms previous reports of the destructive effect of Major Anderson's fire, and adds:—

The very first shot from Fort Sumter came booming into one of the port-holes near which I was stationed, dismounted the gun, and shivered the carriage into thousands of splinters. These splinters were scattered with terrible force throughout the fort, *killing thirty-three men instantly,* and wounding many more. This was the most destructive single shot we received, but throughout the entire cannonading the havoc in Moultrie was terrible. The dead and dying lay about us in every direction, and were trampled under foot by the soldiers in their arduous labors. We had not surgeons enough to attend to them all, and the groans of the dying and their piteous cries for help were distressing in the extreme. When Sumter finally capitulated, without losing a man, thank God, the relatives of our dead and wounded hastened to Moultrie to learn their fate. Mothers came asking for their sons, sisters for brothers, sons for fathers, and all were told that all were well—that none were killed, but that confusion prevailed, and the soldiers could not be seen.

That night the bodies of the dead were boxed up and conveyed on shore, where they were buried in trenches in the negro burying-ground. *One hundred and sixty bodies were conveyed to the burial-place on a small schooner, and the others by various other conveyances.* On the following day, when relatives inquired for those who were dead, they were told that they had been sent away to other points to recruit their energies. Every possible means were resorted to, to keep the truth from being known. I myself counted *over two hundred dead bodies* in Moultrie, and know that there were others which I did not see. I have no means of knowing the extent of the slaughter at the other fortifications, but heard, incidentally, that it was serious, although not so great as at Moultrie. I was told that one shot at Stevens's Battery dismounted a cannon and killed several persons.—*N. Y. Evening Post, May 6.*

THE furore of war which absorbs the North to that degree that Yankees have ceased to calculate, will not, and cannot, be a long-lived sentiment. Invasion of the South is simply *la mode*, the fashion, the excitement of the hour. Just as they ran mad after Jenny Lind, the Japanese Tommy, Kossuth, Morus Multicaulis, Spirit Rappings, and every other new bubble, so they now unite in the great delirium of civil war, and intoxicate their brains with thoughts of blood and plunder. When all the individuals of a nation have been occupied from their birth with ledgers and cash-books, dollars and cents, the humdrum existence of trade or traffic, a "sensation" becomes a necessity to their mental constitution. No people on earth need temporary excitement like the Yankees, are more eager to get it, or will pay more for it. Their newspapers, their books, their theatres, their cities, furnish daily illustrations of their thirst after excitement. But it never lasts long. The taste is gratified, the want supplied, and Yankees become Yankees again until the next season. Once used, they never take up the cast-off fashion, and that which ran them mad with coarse and gregarious enthusiasm, becomes in a few weeks mere *caput-mortuum*, stale champagne,—old clothes. Kossuth coming, was greater than Washington ; Kossuth leaving, attracted no more attention than the dust-cart on which all the filth of the newspaper offices was emptied. The whole city of New York, men, women, and children, the upper ten and the b'hoys, assembled in one dense and shouting multitude, to see an ugly, vulgar, money-loving Swedish opera woman land from a steamboat, to sing to them to the tune of half a million of dollars ; but three months later she walked and travelled with as little notice as any other strong-minded woman and unprotected female. As with these trifles, so with mania of a character more serious. The North blazed with rage for war with England in 1812, with Mexico in 1846, and after a few weeks no more soldiers could be gotten out of it for either. The tremendous outburst of ferocity that we witness in the Northern States, is simply the repetition of one of the most common traits of their national character. It is the fashion of the day, the humbug of the hour, and it will cease as suddenly as it has commenced. Like straw on fire, the periodical sensations of the North make a great flame, but to sink to the ashes and the dust of indifference as swiftly as they sprang. It is easy, and to them amusing, to indulge their tastes of this sort in bloody talk about invading the South, in mobbing a few of them hitherto suspected of sympathy with us, in joining volunteer companies, running off to cities like Washington, by way of Annapolis, where no brickbats are on the road ; but in three or four weeks the superfluous gas will be gone, and Yankees will be Yankees again.—*Richmond Examiner, May 3.*

NEW YORK, *May 3.*—The mate of the schooner D. B. Pitts, lately arrived from Charleston, says that there is no doubt that nearly 200 men were killed in the batteries during the engagement, and that most of them were buried on the beach. He says that on the nights of the 15th, 16th, and 17th instant, the steamboat which plied between the city and the batteries took down an aggregate of about 200 coffins. He was informed also by a gentleman who had a brother and brother-in-law in the garrison of Fort Moultrie, that after writing to them repeatedly without obtaining any answer, he finally received a note from one of the officers, stating that they had both been killed, and that their bodies could be sent for, which he was about to do. He learned from various sources that the number killed in Fort Moultrie was 39, but could not ascertain the number in the other batteries. He is positive as to the shipment of a large number of coffins on board the steamboat on the nights mentioned, having seen them taken on board himself.—*N. Y. Tribune, May 3.*

WASHINGTON, *May 2.*—Some two or three months since, seven negroes, who had been slaves, effected an escape from their masters, and appeared at Fort Pickens, then commanded by Lieutenant Slemmer. That officer returned them to the rebel troops, by whom they were given up to their owners, by whom they were mercilessly punished for the attempt to gain their liberty. At the time of their surrender, Fort Pickens was greatly in need of men to defend it, and down to this moment there has been no day when these negroes would not have been of great use in the various labors about the fort. Just such laborers have since been carried thither at a great expense to the Government. Their fidelity was guaranteed by every circumstance, and was beyond question.

When General Jackson defended New Orleans, he pressed every thing that had any fighting quality about it,—Barataria pirates, free negroes, whatever came to hand, into the service.

One of the Secessionists is reported to have said, that if Lieutenant Slemmer had not returned these men, "*a nigger would not have been left in all that part of Florida.*"—*N. Y. Evening Post, May 6.*

NOVEL CHARGE.—The *Newberry Conservatist* says: "The secession of Virginia was hailed with great enthusiasm at this place on Friday, by firing off the cannon, charged with powder and *tobacco.* Hurrah for the Old Dominion State."—*Charleston Evening News, May 3.*

"REGIMENTS IN BUCKRAM."—A very funny article appears under this title in the New Orleans *Commercial Bulletin.* That paper pretends to have heard the news from Massachusetts, but it evidently is still in the dark concerning the achievements of the men of the Bay State in Maryland. We make a choice extract:—

"Massachusetts, the telegraph so reports, is all alive with the war spirit. Her regiments, according to this authority, are pouring over the North in such vast numbers, as to induce the idea that the descendants of the men who refused to go out of their own State to fight the battles of the Revolution, were really a fighting race. *But those who know these Puritan fanatics will never believe that they intend to take the field against Southern men.* They may muster into service to garrison posts comparatively free from attack, and when they can be sheltered within impregnable walls, but the hereafter will have little to tell of their deeds in the tented field, or the 'imminent deadly breach.'

"It has been wittily and very truthfully observed, in reference to Massachusetts' share in the Revolution, that she built the 'Bunker Hill Monument, and went on the Pension List.' The history of the coming struggle will not be quite so brilliant even as that, for the achievement of her arms will win no monuments—except those that commemorate her slain."—*Boston Transcript, May 2.*

A PRIVATE correspondent of *The Independent*, writing from Washington, gives the following interesting incident:—

"A member of a Worcester company was introduced to me as a man of *pluck*. He received orders at 11¼ o'clock on Monday night that his company would move for Washington at 4, A. M. At 3 o'clock he called for the young lady to whom he was engaged, in a carriage, and they immediately drove to a clergyman's and were married. At 4 o'clock he left with his company. He is a handsome young fellow, of whom his new wife may well be proud."—*Independent, May 2.*

CHARLESTON, *May* 3.—A Northern paper informs us that "there is hardly a house (in Philadelphia) from which the triune colors are not floating, and woe betide the unfortunate householder whose colors are wanting when called for."

When the Commonwealth of Rome was subverted, the people were compelled to worship the image of the despots whom the brute force of the mercenary soldiery had elevated to brief authority. So it seems the Black Republican mobs of the Northern cities compel the people to worship striped rags as evidence of their obeisance to the Abolition despots who now desecrate the seats of power in the Federal city.

It is also stated, that "every window-shutter is tied with the inevitable red, white, and blue. Canary cages are trimmed with the national colors, and dogs perambulate the streets wrapped in the star-spangled banner."

"Oh, what a fall was there, my countrymen!" The "star-spangled banner" has gone to the dogs. "Babylon the great has fallen, and is become the habitation of devils and the hold of every foul spirit, and a cage of every unclean and hateful bird."—*Charleston News, May 3.*

THIS attempt to put down the South by fire and the sword, is one of the most curious and incomprehensible things that ever occurred in the history of the world. If the case were reversed—if it were the North which had seceded from the Union, and set up a Government for itself, the South, so far from objecting, would have hailed it as an immeasurable blessing and relief. They would have said to the North, "If you want to go, go in peace, and Heaven speed you." When *we* propose to go, however, it is all different. The North wishes to keep us, unwilling and reluctant though we be, in a Union which we have repudiated, and to compel allegiance and tribute from a people known to be galled and almost maddened by the association.

There is no justice in this, no liberty, no humanity, no Christianity, no *sense*. It is the silliest and most ridiculous enterprise ever undertaken by a Government professing to be founded on the consent of the governed. It is not only senseless, but wicked, cruel, inhuman, and barbarous.—*N. O. Crescent, May 4.*

THE members of the Eighth Massachusetts Regiment were put to various useful purposes in forcing the passage through Maryland. It seems that the Annapolis Railroad was for a time entirely managed by members of the Cushing Guard. Lieutenant Hodges, a machinist, after assisting to repair the engine, was made superintendent of the road; Joseph Batchelder, son of Constable Batchelder, who was formerly an employé on the Newburyport road, and is standard-bearer of the regiment, was made engineer; and private Joseph Jewett, who will be remembered as the lecturer on music, was employed as fireman. It is believed that he is admirably adapted to firing up! The entire road was in the hands of men from that company. After the war, railroad corporations will know where to look for employés.

One exploit by members of the Newburyport company has not found its way into the papers. For two days they had nothing to eat but poor pork and a little hard bread. In their ranks are two butchers from this city—Messrs. Merrill and Cilley. They took a tramp into the pastures, and were shortly seen driving an ox to a part of the railroad where the men were at work. A sturdy blow upon the head brought the animal down; the body was strung up to a tree and flayed, and in a little while the whole gang were feasting from the best cut of beef-steak. The manner in which the men of the Eighth Regiment have turned their hands to all kinds of employment, will render them famous throughout the world, and for all time. Some of them could even keep a hotel, which every man cannot do.—*Newburyport (Mass.) Herald, May 4.*

NEW YORK, *May* 1.—A party of Congressmen who came up to-day from Annapolis to Perryville, Md., on a Government steam-tug, had an amusing adventure. While on their trip, a suspicious-looking craft was discovered in the distance. There was a good revolving howitzer on board the tug, and it was instantly got ready for action. Twenty-five marines on board were drawn up, but their services were not needed. A shot brought the craft to, when it turned out to be a schooner deeply laden with provisions. She was sailing under papers drawn up by General Trimble, of Baltimore, who is the commander of the secession troops in Baltimore. Undoubtedly the provisions were intended for the rebels in some part of the South. The name of the schooner was the Lioness. She was brought into Perryville, and her Trimble papers taken from the captain. This General Trimble will soon be taken care of by the Government. It is high time that he was tried for treason.—*N. Y. Evening Post, May* 2.

ALBANY, N. Y., *May* 3.—The Northern spirit is illustrated by the following incidents :—A few days since, a company from Ogdensburgh came without orders, the first knowledge of the existence of the company being their presence at Albany. They were inspected and mustered in. Next day, another company from the North Woods came in the same way.

Next day, Frank Palmer's company, from Plattsburgh, telegraphed that they were coming, unless forbidden. They arrived, 95 men, immediately after. Yesterday the newspapers gave notice of the Depeyster company, Capt. Curtis, coming. It arrived today, giving the first notice of its existence to the Department. This evening, Capt. Bartlett's company, from Odgensburgh, came the same way. It will be inspected and mustered here. Three hundred and eighty companies are required for the 30,000. To-day there were 415 companies entered.—*N. Y. Tribune, May* 4.

AMONG the ordinances adopted by the Virginia Convention, is the following :—

Be it ordered by the Convention of the Commonwealth of Virginia, that the flag of this Commonwealth shall hereafter be made of bunting, which shall be a deep blue field with a circle of white in the centre, upon which shall be painted, or embroidered, to show on both sides alike, the coat of arms of the State, as described by the Convention of 1776 for one side of the seal of the State, to wit :

" Virtus, the genius of the Commonwealth, dressed like an Amazon, resting on a spear with one hand, and holding a sword in the other, and treading on Tyranny, represented by a man prostrate, a crown fallen from his head, a broken chain in his left hand, and a scourge in his right. In the exergon, the word ' Virginia ' over the head of Virtus ; and underneath, the words ' *Sic Semper Tyrannis.*' "—*Boston Transcript, May* 8.

IT was, no doubt, the profound policy of Lincoln and his faction to throw the operatives of the North out of employ, to secure the recruits for the army of coercion. Starvation produces a certain sort of valor, and a hungry belly may stimulate patriotism to a kind of courage which, on a good feed, will risk the encounter with a bullet. It appears that the Lincoln recruits from Massachusetts, at Baltimore, were in large proportion cobblers. The Revolution seems to have affected their craft more than any other, according to some of the accounts ; their vocation gave them admirable facilities in the fight, especially in running ; they used their *footing* expeditiously, and took a free flight with their *soles* (souls)—not one of them apparently being anxious, under the fire of Baltimore brickbats, to see his *last.* —*Charleston Mercury, May* 8.

GENERAL LESLIE COOMBS, of Kentucky, writes to a friend in Cincinnati, under date of April 27, as follows :—

" We could not control the Governor and his co-conspirators, but we appealed to the people, and on next Saturday we expect to elect John J. Crittenden, James Guthrie, and others, to a brotherly peace conference—by a majority unparalleled heretofore in Kentucky. I shall not be surprised at fifty thousand. The destructionists, anticipating their fate,

POETRY—11

have recently resolved to abandon the contest. Then, in Heaven's name ! let us alone—keep the peace on your side of the river, and we will give treason such a rebuke in Old Kentucky that it will never again dare to raise its hideous head among us. We cannot turn our Governor out of office till his term expires, and he is the military commander-in-chief of the State ; but we can keep Kentucky in the Union —if you will let us.

" When a beardless boy, I left my father's home in Kentucky, and marched, with thousands of brave companions, to your frontiers, then invaded by hostile civilized and savage foes. I do not boast of what I did, but truthful history will tell you that I poured out my blood freely *on your soil,* and for nearly fifty years I have been incapable of manual labor. And is Kentucky to be rewarded now by having her soil invaded by the sons whose mothers we protected ? Is my house to be fired, over the heads of my children and grandchildren, by the children of those for whose sake I staked my life, and suffered innumerable hardships in 1812–'13 ? The answer is with Ohio.

" *We* have resisted official coercion in Kentucky ; let no power on earth tempt or drive *you* to bloody outrage now.

" Very truly your old friend,
" LESLIE COOMBS."
—*N. Y. Evening Post, May* 7.

THE *Boston Traveller* recites the following story, told by one of the New York Seventh Regiment :—

" While in Maryland, I wandered off one day, and came to a farm-house, where I saw a party of Rhode Island boys talking with a woman who was greatly frightened. They tried in vain to quiet her apprehensions. They asked for food, and she cried, ' Oh, take all I have, take every thing, but spare my sick husband.' ' Oh,' said one of the men, ' we ain't going to hurt you ; we want something to eat.' But the woman persisted in being frightened in spite of all efforts to reassure her, and hurried whatever food she had on the table. When, however, she saw this company stand about the table with bared heads, and a tall, gaunt man raise his hand and invoke God's blessing on the bounties spread before them, the poor woman broke down with a fit of sobbing and crying. She had no longer any fears, but bade them wait, and in a few moments had made hot coffee in abundance. She then emptied their canteens of the muddy water they contained, and filled them with coffee. Her astonishment increased when they insisted upon paying her."—*National Intelligencer, May* 9.

THE first inquiry made by the Fire Zouaves on landing at Washington, was, with grave-faced earnestness, " Can you tell us where Jeff. Davis is ? we're lookin' for him." " Yes," said another, " we're bound to hang his scalp in the White House before we go back." Another one, whose massive under-jaw and breadth of neck indicated him " some in a plug muss," remarked that they had expected to have arrived by the way of Baltimore. " We would have come through Baltimore like a dose of salts," he added, with an air of disappointment. One of them beckoned a citizen, confidentially, to his side, and inquired, " Is there any secession flags about here ? " He was assured that secession bunting was an article that did not prevail there. He nodded, and added, " I only wanted to know."

On coming down the Avenue, the Franklin Fire

Company reel passed them at a sharp run, on its way to a fire; and the familiar apparatus was saluted with such a yell of recognition along the entire line, as must have fairly astonished the staid old reel.

Somebody remarked to one of the b'hoys, that his hair was cut *rayther* short. "Oh, yes," was the reply, "we all had our heads *filed* before we left New York." They all look like fighting boys; but one company seems to have a special prestige that way. "If there's any mischief done, lay it onto Company 68," seemed to be a pet phrase amongst the b'hoys.

Some of the Zouaves, in emerging from their quarters (Columbian Market building) this morning, disdaining the tedious, common-place mode of exit by the stairway, let themselves down to the street from the third story by a rope, like so many monkeys.—*Charleston Mercury, May 8.*

WASHINGTON, *May 26.*—The Fifth Massachusetts Regiment, Col. Lawrence, having received orders to march over the Long Bridge into Virginia on Saturday night, were filed out of the Treasury Building with astonishing promptness, when it was discovered that they had only their *State* color, not having received their national ensign. Immediately, several Massachusetts gentlemen—Hon. G. W. McClelland, A. W. Fletcher, Capt. Perkins, and J. Wesley Jones—begun a search for the "Stars and Stripes" under difficulties which were happily relieved by the kindness of Mr. J. D. Hammack, who very kindly consented to sell them a beautiful new cashmere flag, of the finest quality, which the ladies had made for his hotel.

Securing a carriage, they overtook the regiment midway on the Long Bridge. Word having been passed along the line, the regiment was halted, and Col. Lawrence advanced to the carriage, doubtless expecting some change of orders. Judge of his surprise, when the committee stepped forward, and, unrolling a beautiful flag to the breezes of the Potomac, presented it to the gallant Colonel, and through him to the brave boys of the old Bay State, accompanied by a few felicitous remarks on behalf of the committee by Mr. J. W. Jones, substantially as follows:

"Soldiers of Massachusetts!—a title rendered illustrious in the early struggles for freedom on this continent, and now established by your prompt and heroic inauguration of the present *war for the Union*, is the proudest title any citizen of the world can bear.

"Soldiers of Massachusetts! with honor you have borne the beautiful ensign of your native State, even within the confines of the enemies of human freedom. Having rendered the capital of our beloved country safe, you now march towards the Gulf!—ready 'to do and to dare,' for the *true* and the *right*, which is your country's cause, and that of liberty. And we bring you now, and here, on this dividing-line between *loyalty* and *treason*, the flag of our common country—the flag of the *forever-United States*.

"Soldiers! thus far your acts are matters of history, and noble acts. But we come to give expression to the feelings of pride which we feel as Massachusetts men, at the universal praise accorded, by all the citizens of Washington, for your gentlemanly bearing and noble conduct while quartered in the capitol. Not a single complaint has been made by any citizen of Washington, friend or foe, of any uncivil conduct by any Massachusetts volunteer. Bearing this high reputation, you now advance, not as a conquering army to subjugate and enslave, but as the advance guard of the grand liberating army of deliverance, bearing the 'stars' of hope to the oppressed lovers of liberty in the South, and the 'stripes' of justice for all their *traitorous oppressors*. For bear in mind, that, though you will contend with desperate villains of the darkest hue, assassins, and poisoners, and perjured traitors, there are yet millions of the white race in the South, who, like good old Daniel, daily, with their hands outstretched towards the heavens, and their faces *eastward*, pray God for a sight of your advancing columns, as their only hope of salvation from a bondage worse than death, an oppression more terrible than Siberian convict rule. As soon as these noble men shall dare to speak, your hands will be strengthened, and your hearts cheered. Go on, then, ye heralds of civilization, establishing in your march the church, the school-house, the Bible, and the Constitution, as the only *sure* foundations of human liberty. In your veins flow the blood which ensanguined the fields of Lexington and Concord, and rendered immortal the heights of Bunker Hill, and which has rebaptized the cause of human liberty in the streets of Baltimore. With *you*, we can safely trust this glorious flag, assured that it will be borne to higher places of honor, and will never cease its triumphant march until every secession symbol shall have been trampled in the dust, and every traitorous enemy shall have been hung in mid-heaven, or be forever exiled from a land which he has cursed. Bear this flag proudly in every battle-field for liberty, guard it well and long, until triumphantly it shall forever wave 'o'er the land of the free,' *and no home of a slave!*"

The gallant Colonel, evidently much affected by this tribute of his friends, received the flag with a few felicitous remarks and with many thanks, and the column, with three cheers and many a "God-bless-you," resumed their onward march.

The night was indeed a beautiful one. A full moon, just mounting the eastern sky, cast its silvery sheen over the rippling waters of the majestic Potomac, and sparkled on the bayonets of a thousand muskets. Camp-fires and signal-lights dotted the hills on both sides, making a picture of quiet beauty never to be forgotten.—*Washington National Republican, May 27.*

OLD VIRGINIA.

Over vale and over mountain,
  Pealing forth in triumph strong,
Comes a lofty swell of music,
  Old Virginia's greeting song.
In the new-born arch of glory,
  Lo! she burns, the central star;
Never shame shall blight its grandeur,
  Never cloud its radiance mar.
    "Old Virginia! Old Virginia!"
      Listen, Southrons, to the strain;
    "Old Virginia! Old Virginia!"
      Shout the rallying cry again!

—*N. O. Picayune, May 5.*

RICHMOND, VA.—Feeling a deep interest in the coming struggle, but yet an abiding faith that Divine Providence, which has so evidently upheld us, will sustain us still; remembering, also, that God takes care of those who take proper care of themselves, we call the attention of the Government to the fact, that our noble army of volunteers have no distinguishing symbol from those at the North;—alike in uniform, language, and complexion, they will constantly fall victims to mistakes. We would suggest that, as in the wars of the Roses in England, the white or red flowers designated the different parties, so in our army the letter S, in the form of a metallic badge, about 2¼ inches in length, worn on each man's breast, would guard him in the skirmish or the battle from being slain by his own Southerners. It might have inside a secret stamp or mark, to prevent it from being pirated by the enemy.—*Charleston News, May 9.*

THE most eloquent, persuasive, and convincing speech ever delivered in America, was delivered by the rebel guns when they opened fire on Fort Sumter. That speech has compacted the loyal hearts of this broad land into a league of patriotic freemen, who, laying aside all minor issues, are now ready to defend the insulted flag of their country, or perish in the attempt. The North, long unable to believe that treason would ripen into armed rebellion, is now fully awake to the duties of the hour; and every day only adds to the firmness of the determination on the part of the free States to maintain the Government and save the Union, for themselves, their posterity, and the cause of Christian civilization throughout the world.—*N. Y. Christian Intelligencer, May 9.*

MR. LINCOLN is of a Quaker family, and it is to be remarked that a Quaker President is the first one to plunge the country into civil war, and within less than six weeks after his accession to the office. Quakers are remarkable for approaching their objects by indirect means. Thus, Lincoln, after much apparent hesitation, despatched a fleet to reinforce Fort Sumter, knowing that it would expedite the reduction of that fort, and that the flag would fire the Northern mind, while it would at the same time inaugurate war. From that initial followed incidents and episodes all tending to array the North and the South in a vexed conflict.—*N. O. Picayune, May 9.*

THE *New Orleans Crescent* thinks that one Southern man can whip two Northerners, and suggests the following mode of beginning and ending the war:—

"Let a proper battle-field, giving both armies equal chance of position, be selected. Jeff. Davis should command a Southern army, say, for the convenience of round numbers, of fifty thousand men. Abe Lincoln (or any person he may choose to designate) shall command an Abolition army of one hundred thousand men. The equipments of both armies should be equal—we mean in small arms, artillery, cavalry, etc.—only that the Northern army, outnumbering the Southern army in the proportion of two to one, shall have twice the equipments, twice the amount of small arms, twice the number of cannon, twice the regiments of cavalry, etc.—that the Southern army shall have. All around it shall be in proportion of two to one in favor of the North; and the position on the battle-field is the only one in which there shall be any equality, so far as our proposition is concerned. Topographical equality is the only quality involved.

"Then let the two armies engage, and forever settle the question between the North and the South. If Lincoln's one hundred thousand men whip Jeff. Davis's fifty thousand men, the people of the South are to bow submissively to whatever laws and regulations the Abolition Government at Washington may see fit to adopt. But if Jeff. Davis's fifty thousand men whip Lincoln's one hundred thousand men, then the Government at Washington—or wherever else it may be located, as we do not believe it will stay long there—shall agree to an amicable separation and a just division of that which was once common property."—*N. Y. Independent, May 9.*

A FRAGMENT—CABINET COUNCIL.

LINCOLN—[*solus; asleep in a rocking-chair—after a pause, springs up suddenly.*]
Give me another Scotch cap; wrap me in a military cloak!
Have mercy, Jeff. Davis! Soft—I did but dream.
    [*Loud knocking heard at the door.*]
Who knocks thus loudly?
SEWARD—[*without.*] 'Tis I, my Lord! the White House cock;
Thrice have I crowed since the day hath broke.
[*Enter Seward, Chase, Bates, Blair, Cameron, and Welles.*]
CAMERON—How doth my good Lord?
LINCOLN—Indifferently well, methinks, good Coz.
That confection of hominy and hog, which, as my wont,
Late on yester eve I ate, did most wofully affect me.
Have I no leech among my councillors chosen,
Who can minister to a body diseased? Alas, my friends!
Bred to the chicane of the law, what know ye of the leap
And bounds of rebellious blood by fitful fever stirred?
BATES—My Liege, as I glanced o'er the morning prints,
In which our glories are duly and at length set forth,
Methought much praise was given to a medicament
Yclept in foreign lore—Cephalic Pills!
LINCOLN—Away with this nostrum—I'll none of it!
For know ye, I bought a box from a harum-scarum boy,
Whom I encountered on our Western train, and who
Cried—God wot!—"Old Abe, buy some Pills?"
These I bought, and tried, and got no better fast.
BLAIR—You'd scarce expect one of my age
To speak in public on the stage. Yet I can but think
'Tis not the *confection*, but the *defection* of the Southern tier,
Which pains our Liege's ——
LINCOLN—Ass! knave! think you so?
Know you not, my babbling Coz, that this *defection*
Is all gammon?—the crisis is but artificial!
CHASE—We know it well; would we could forget it;
Yet, your Excellency, I read in some fool
Southern paper—called, I know not what—
The *Mail*, the *Mercury*, or some such absurdity—
That there is much feeling down in their unsightly swamps,
Where Afric's wrongs smell rank to heaven.
LINCOLN—What then! Let them howl!—You know full well,
That, cry as they may, there's nobody hurt!
Oh, how I do despise a peevish, complaining people—
A people who know not which side their bread is buttered.
Misguided people! who would fain tear away three stripes—
Two of red and one of white—from our Star-spangled Banner.

Seward—[aside.]   Long may it wave !
Welles—O'er the land of the free !
Bates—And the home of the brave !
Lincoln—And imagine they founded a new nation !
          And now yon fighting Colonel Davis,
With his ragged ragamuffin crew, loudly swears
He'll sit in this very chair wherein we sit—
Save the mark !—in spite of Wool or Scott.
Friends, farewell ! yet take something ere ye go ;
Leave me to myself, that I may court the drowsy
       god.
Watch well the door, that no foul traitors enter
With machines infernal, or throated revolving pistol.
Spread yourselves, and lose no opportunity to tell
Th' expectant people that all is going well ;
And while, reluctant, ye admit the Southern feeling,
Urge and declare that 'tis marvellous consoling,
That nothing is hurting anybody.   There, go !
Stand not on the order of your going, but go at
       once.
          [Seward and others bow and depart.]
New Jerusalem ! is this happiness ? When erst
I dreamt of might, majesty, and power ; when, in
       days gone by,
An humble splitter of rails, wearing but one shirt a
       week ;
Or, when in revery, I leaned in listless mood
O'er the oar (ha ! a pun) of the slow-gliding broad-
       horn,
And thought of the powerful and rich of earth,
And, envious, contrasted their gay feasts and revels
With our simple joys, our humble shuckings and
       possum hunts,
Our apple-bees and quilting frolics—alack-a-day !
As Shakespeare says in his Paradise Lost, I sadly
       feel
That " distance lends enchantment to the view."
—Nashville Patriot ; and Charleston Mercury,
May 6.

The editor of the Brookhaven (Miss.) Advertiser
offers the following argument in favor of raising
more corn than cotton :—
We have always been persistently in favor of
planting a large crop of corn, even if cotton has to
be a little neglected, particularly in times like these,
when communication with the Ohio may be cut off at
any moment.   Corn is a necessity, but cotton is only
a convenience.   A man can live very well without a
shirt, but what can he do without whiskey ?—Charleston Evening News, May 9.

As Virginia is to be the great battle-ground between the contending sections, and the first collision
of arms is likely to take place on the banks of the
Potomac, we hope that both parties will consent to
respect one spot as sacred and neutral ground.   Let
the grave of Washington be still venerated by his
countrymen of both sides, and let his ashes not be
disturbed by the clash of hostile steel or the roar of
cannon.   Let there be one spot where the descendants of the men who fought under Marion and Sumter, Putnam and Greene, can meet without shedding
each other's blood ; and if ever an amicable settlement of this unhappy civil war is to be attempted,
let us keep the holy ground of Mount Vernon dedicated to the purposes of peace, and there let the
arbitrating convention, which sooner or later must
treat on some terms for an adjustment of hostilities,
meet for the purpose.
Let the press, the only organ which can now speak

to the people, South and North, claim from the leaders on both sides, that no " military necessity " shall
excuse the defilement of the soil of Mount Vernon
with carnage, or its air by the sulphurous breath of
battle.—Augusta (Ga.) Chronicle, April 30.

The Richmond Dispatch gives the following advice to its fellow-rebels :—
" All over the State, particularly in the Tidewater
and Potomac counties, there are a great many men
who do not belong to companies, and who probably
will not for some time.   They have not regulation
weapons, but almost every man of them has a rifle,
or a shot-gun, or a flint-lock musket, and one or more
pistols of some kind.   All these men should form
neighborhood squads of from five to fifteen, according to density of population, put the weapons they
have in perfect order, make each of them a strong,
sharp sheath-knife—a large old file or rasp makes a
splendid one—keep their best and most active horse
always fresh and in good condition, and have a signal at which they shall all gather at some rendezvous.
Such squads are to act as guerillas, and if the enemy
approaches their section of the country, hang upon
his outskirts, fill the hollows, hide behind trees, in
ditches, anywhere that they can best protect themselves and cut down the enemy.   Such men, so armed
and equipped, can destroy an enemy's army more
certainly and effectively than regular troops, and any
of the weapons we have named, in the hands of a
cool, determined man, is sufficient.   Ten men, so
provided, and using proper judgment, can pick off a
hundred men in a day's march, with little risk to
themselves.   They will also prevent foraging and
marauding parties from scattering through the country, and every man they drop will be furnishing Virginia with at least another weapon.   If our men
through the country will organize thus—all of them,
boys, old men, all who are not in active service—no
army can ever reach Richmond, and our State can
never be filled with the bands of lawless stragglers
who threaten to carry so much terror and desolation
to our homes and firesides."—N. Y. Tribune, May 11.

Philadelphia, May 8.—A gentleman who has
just made his escape from Memphis, Tenn., gives the
following account of a solemn ceremony which took
place in that city a day or two before he quitted it.
He says that he was an eye-witness to the whole of
the proceedings, and as he is a man of the greatest
respectability, his statement may be relied on.   In
the one solitary square which Memphis possesses,
stands a statue of Andrew Jackson.   By the side of
this statue a large pit was dug, and on the day in
question our informant, who was standing near the
place, saw a body of about five hundred men slowly
approaching, headed by a band of music performing
the " Dead March."   After the band came eight men
bearing the dead body which was to be consigned to
the pit ; this corpse was no more nor less than a
large standard of the Stars and Stripes, which was
solemnly lowered into its final resting-place, the company assisting in respectful silence.   The earth was
then thrown upon it—" ashes to ashes, and dust to
dust "—and the pit was filled up.   The spectators
then dispersed quietly, apparently thoroughly satisfied at having paid the last respects to an old friend's
remains.   The tomb-stone has not yet been put up,
nor have we heard what sort of an epitaph is to be
inscribed on it ; but no doubt it will do credit to
Tennessee.—Philadelphia North American, May 9.

"EIN FESTE BURG IST UNSER GOTT."

(*Luther's Hymn.*)

BY JOHN G. WHITTIER.

We wait beneath the furnace blast
The pangs of transformation ;
Not painlessly doth God recast
And mould anew the nation.
Hot burns the fire
Where wrongs expire ;
Nor spares the hand
That from the land
Uproots the ancient evil.

The hand-breadth cloud the sages feared,
Its bloody rain is dropping ;
The poison plant the fathers spared,
All else is overtopping.
East, West, South, North,
It curses the earth :
All justice dies,
And fraud and lies
Live only in its shadow.

What gives the wheat field blades of steel ?
What points the rebel cannon ?
What sets the roaring rabble's heel
On the old star-spangled pennon ?
What breaks the oath
Of the men o' the South ?
What whets the knife
For the Union's life ?—
Hark to the answer :—SLAVERY !

Then waste no blows on lesser foes,
In strife unworthy freemen.
God lifts to-day the veil, and shows
The features of the demon !
O North and South,
Its victims both,
Can ye not cry,
" Let Slavery die ! "
And union find in freedom ?

What though the cast-out spirit tear
The nation in his going ?
We who have shared the guilt, must share
The pang of his o'erthrowing !
Whate'er the loss,
Whate'er the cross,
Shall they complain
Of present pain,
Who trust in God's hereafter ?

For who that leans on His right arm,
Was ever yet forsaken ?
What righteous cause can suffer harm,
If He its part has taken ?
Though wild and loud,
And dark the cloud,
Behind its folds
His hand upholds
The calm sky of to-morrow !

Above the maddening cry for blood,
Above the wild war-drumming,
Let Freedom's voice be heard, with good
The evil overcoming.
Give prayer and purse
To stay The Curse,
Whose wrong we share,
Whose shame we bear,
Whose end shall gladden Heaven !

In vain the bells of war shall ring
Of triumphs and revenges,
While still is spared the evil thing
That severs and estranges.
But, blest the ear
That yet shall hear
The jubilant bell
That rings the knell
Of Slavery forever !

Then let the selfish lip be dumb,
And hushed the breath of sighing ;
Before the joy of peace must come
The pains of purifying.
God give us grace,
Each in his place
To bear his lot,
And, murmuring not,
Endure, and wait, and labor !
—*N. Y. Independent*, June 14.

SUMTER.

BY "IKE."

Sixty men in Sumter,
Fearless hearts and true,
Stood with lighted matches :—
How the hot shots thumped her !
How the bomb-shells flew !
Twice five thousand traitors
Poured their vengeance out,
Maddened by their leaders—
And the Union-haters
Raised a mighty shout ;
For the flames were curling
Round that little band,
Who, with heads uncovered,
Sent their missiles whirling
Toward the treacherous land.
Still the fiery question
Iron lips propose—
" Will you now surrender ? "
Then, from port and bastion,
Came the thunderous " *Noes !* "
You all know the story—
How at last a band
Left that smouldering fortress,
Crowned with wreaths of glory,
Honored by the land ;
How the rebel gunners
Slept beside their guns,
Never more to waken,
Red with bloody honors,
Treason's darling sons.
—*New Haven Palladium*, May 6.

GOD PROTECT US!

BY GEORGE G. W. MORGAN.

AIR—"*God save the Queen.*"

O Lord, we humbly pray,
Thy blessing here to-day
On us may fall ;
Grant us our earnest prayer,
Shield those who need our care,
Let them Thy blessings share,—
God save us all !

O Lord, we'd lead the van,
E'er in behalf of man,
    When held in thrall;
Be with us in the fight,
Now in the cause of right;
Cursed be the Slaver's might,—
    God save us all!

O Lord, we fain would pray,
Thy grace forever may
    Direct this war;
And where our flag's unfurled,
Be Freedom's gauntlet hurled,
Bid Justice rule the world
    For evermore.*

THE YARD-ARM TREE.

I.

O! the trees on the land that grow, that grow,
    And the fruits that they produce,
Demand to be sung with vigor, I know,
    For each of them has its use.
To the oak and the beech much credit is due;
    To the birch we have all dropped a tear;
And, as for the pine, what teachings divine
    To its gum-clogged knots adhere!
But now that treason stalks the shore,
    And sails upon the main,
The tree that most is worth a toast
    From all of loyal grain,
        Is the taper Yard-Arm Tree,
        That grows on a ship in the sea.

II.

Up from the Isthmus we steam, we steam,
    With treasure in our hold;
Bars and dust that take no rust,
    And nuggets of yellow gold.
Down on our quarter sweeps a bark
    Flaunting the Cotton Flag;
A rebel bark, with a letter of marque,
    And they strive to get our swag;
But they reckoned without one skipper brave,
    And grand it was to see,
The bloated Cotton blossoms wave
    Upon our yard-arm tree.
        So here's to the Yard-Arm Tree,
        That grows on a ship in the sea!
                    —Vanity Fair.

THE UNION, RIGHT OR WRONG.

A SONG FOR THE VOLUNTEERS.

BY GEORGE P. MORRIS.

I.

In Freedom's name our blades we draw—
    She arms us for the fight!
For Country, Government and Law,
    For Liberty and Right.
The Union must—shall be preserved;
    Our flag still o'er us fly!
That cause our hearts and hands has nerved,
    And we will do, or die.

* Dedicated to England's gallant sons, THE NEW YORK
BRITISH RIFLE REGIMENT, by their admiring fellow-coun-
tryman.

CHORUS—Then come, ye hardy volunteers,
    Around our standard throng,
    And pledge man's hope of coming years—
    The Union, right or wrong!
The Union, right or wrong, inspires
    The burden of our song;
It was the glory of our sires—
    The Union, right or wrong!

II.

It is the duty of us all
    To check rebellion's sway;
To rally at the nation's call,
    And we that voice obey!
Then, like a band of brothers, go,
    A hostile league to break,
To rout a spoil-encumber'd foe,
    And what is ours, retake.

CHORUS—So come, ye hardy volunteers,
    Around our standard throng,
    And pledge man's hope of coming years—
    The Union, right or wrong!
The Union, right or wrong, inspires
    The burden of our song;
It was the glory of our sires—
    The Union, right or wrong!

WAR SONG OF THE FREE.

AIR—"Hail, Columbia."

I.

War sounds his tocsin loud and high;
Ye Freemen, hear the battle-cry:
Awake ye from your slumbers deep,
Your Country's honor still to keep!
Her hour of peril now is here!
The liberty she holds so dear,
The rebel Southrons fain would see
Consigned to blackest infamy.
Say, shall a traitor banner wave
O'er ashes of our bygone brave?
    By the names we most revere,
    By the trust we hold so dear,
    Sound abroad the wild alarm,
    Till it nerves each patriot's arm!

II.

The air ye breathe as yet is free!
The song it sings is Liberty!
That boon for which our fathers died,
That boon so long our Country's pride,
That gift to every loyal son,
From the dear hand of Washington—
Ye offspring of the honored brave,
Say, shall it find a hireling grave,
While one more drop of blood remains,
To show where Freedom's spirit reigns?
    As we bless the God we love,
    As we hope for heaven above,
    Let us all united stand,
    For the honor of our land!

III.

By traitor hands shall Freedom die?
Her sacred shrines in ruin lie?
NO! rings on every Northern breeze;
NO! comes from all our inland seas;
NO! bursts from every patriot's heart,
In country home, or city mart!

The hallowed dust we tread cries out,
" Up, Freemen, at the battle shout ;
Let not a traitor hand oppress,
While we have homes to guard and bless ! "
　By the good our fathers won,
　By immortal Washington,
　Let the cry, " WE WILL BE FREE ! "
　Echo on from sea to sea !

IV.

To arms !—and let the rebels feel
A FREEMAN'S blow, and blade of steel !
To arms ! to arms ! let all the world
See FREEDOM'S banner wide unfurled !
Let all the waiting nations know
We still have hearts to dare a foe !
That, trusting in our fathers' God,
We ne'er will heed a tyrant's rod !
That we WILL guard our LIBERTY !
That to the end we WILL be FREE !
　Then, in one united host,
　Let us stand at Duty's post,
　And let all the nations see
　How we love our LIBERTY !
　　　—Exeter (N. H.) News Letter, May 6.

ARMY HYMN.

BY OLIVER WENDELL HOLMES.

"Old Hundred."

O Lord of Hosts ! Almighty King !
Behold the sacrifice we bring !
To every arm Thy strength impart,
Thy Spirit shed through every heart !

Wake in our breasts the living fires,
The holy faith that warmed our sires ;
Thy hand hath made our Nation free ;
To die for her, is serving Thee.

Be Thou a pillared flame, to show
The midnight snare, the silent foe ;
And when the battle thunders loud,
Still guide us in its moving cloud.

God of all Nations ! Sovereign Lord !
In Thy dread name we draw the sword ;
We lift the starry flag on high,
That fills with light our stormy sky.

From treason's rent, from murder's stain,
Guard Thou its folds till Peace shall reign ;
Till fort and field, till shore and sea,
Join our loud anthem, PRAISE TO THEE !
　　　—Atlantic Monthly, June.

LITTLE RHODY.

Of all the true host that New England can boast,
From down by the sea unto highland,
No State is more true, or more willing to do,
Than dear little Yankee Rhode Island.
　Loyal and true little Rhody !
　Bully for you, little Rhody !
Governor Sprague was not very vague,
When he said, " Shoulder arms ! little Rhody ! "

Not backward at all at the President's call,
　Nor yet with the air of a toady,
The gay little State, not a moment too late,
　Sent soldiers to answer for Rhody.
　Loyal and true little Rhody !
　Bully for you, little Rhody !
Governor Sprague was not very vague,
When he said, " Shoulder arms ! little Rhody ! "

Two regiments raised, and by ev'ry one praised,
　Were soon on the march for head-quarters ;
All furnished first-rate at the cost of their State,
　And regular fighting dread-naughters !
　Loyal and true little Rhody !
　Bully for you, little Rhody !
Governor Sprague was not very vague,
When he said, " Shoulder arms ! little Rhody ! "

Let traitors look out, for there's never a doubt
　That Uncle Abe's army will trip 'em ;
And as for the loud Carolinian crowd,
　Rhode Island alone, sir, can whip 'em !
　Loyal and true little Rhody !
　Bully for you, little Rhody !
Governor Sprague is a very good egg,
And worthy to lead little Rhody !
　　　—N. Y. Sunday Mercury.

THE WILL FOR THE DEED.

BY CAROLINE A. MASON.

No sword have I, no battle-blade,
Nor shining spear ; how shall I aid
My Country in her great Crusade ?

I cannot sow with gold the sod,
Like Dragon's teeth, and from the clod
See armed men rise, battle-shod.

I may not stand in mart or hall,
And shout aloud great Freedom's call,
" Come to the rescue, one and all ! "

I am a woman, weak and slight,
No voice to plead, no arm to fight,
Yet burning to support the Right.

How shall I aid my Country's cause ?
How help avenge her trampled laws ?
Alas, my woman's heart makes pause.

With oil and wine I may not go,
Where wounded men toss to and fro,
Beneath the invader's hand laid low.

My little child looks up to me,
And lisps a stronger, mightier plea ;
God wills where he is, I should be.

Ah, well ;—I am not needed ! He
Who knows my heart, perchance, for me
Has other work than now I see.

" They also serve, who stand and wait,"—
Oh, golden words !—and not too late !
My soul accepts her humbler fate.

Content to serve in any way,
Less than the least, if so I may
But hail the dawning of that day,

When my beloved Land shall rise,
And shout as one man to the skies,
Lo ! Freedom lives, and Treason dies !
    —*Salem (Mass.) Register.*

RULE SLAVEOWNIA.

THE NATIONAL HYMN OF THE CONFEDERATE STATES.

(*Music Copyright in America.*)

When first the South, to fury fanned,
  Arose and broke the Union's chain,
This was the Charter, the Charter of the land,
  And Mr. Davis sang the strain :
Rule Slaveownia, Slaveownia rules, and raves—
  " Christians ever, ever, ever have had slaves."

The Northerns, not so blest as thee,
  At Aby Lincoln's foot may fall,
While thou shalt flourish, shalt flourish fierce and free
  The whip, that makes the Nigger bawl.
Rule Slaveownia, Slaveownia rules, and raves—
  " Christians ever, ever, ever should have slaves."

Thou, dully savage, shalt despise
  Each freeman's argument, or joke ;
Each law that Congress, that Congress thought so
    wise,
Serves but to light thy pipes for smoke.
Rule Slaveownia, Slaveownia rules, and raves—
  " Christians ever, ever, ever must have slaves."

And Trade, that knows no God but gold,
  Shall to thy pirate ports repair ;
Blest land, where flesh—where human flesh is sold,
  And manly arms may flog that *air.*
Rule Slaveownia, Slaveownia rules, and raves—
  " Christians ever, ever, ever shall have slaves."
    —*London Punch*, April 20.

TO ARMS !

BY H. A. MOORE.

Wake ! wake ! long-slumb'ring North !
Pour thy brave legions forth,
  Armed for the fight.
Hark 'tis our Country's cry—
" Brave men for Liberty
Now must not fear to *die !* "
  God speed the right !

Sons of heroic sires,
Turn from your homestead fires,
  Short farewells said ;
True sword and musket take ;
Forth from your mountains break ;
Make hill and valley shake
  'Neath your mailed tread.

Mother, give up thy son !
Wife, bind *his* armor on
  Who is thy stay !
Sister, thy brother yield !
Child, speed thy sire a-field !—
God is the patriot's shield
  In the wild fray.

Maiden, hold back the tear,
Utter no word of fear,
  Stifle thy woe.

Where could thy lover's head
Find such a glorious bed,
As with the deathless dead
  Nobly laid low ?

Arm, for the Holy War !
Arm, in behalf of Law !
  Give heart and hand,
Glad to pour loyal blood
For our dear Country's good,
Forth in a cleansing flood,
  Over the land.

Strong hearts of North and West,
Let Treason never rest,
  Even for breath.
Fair Freedom's royal name,
Traitors have brought to shame ;
Arm !   To redeem her fame—
  Fight to the death !

God leads our loyal host ;
God is our people's boast ;
  God speeds the right.
March with undaunted heart ;
Act well the soldier's part ;
Make the oppressor smart ;
  Arm for the fight !

Heaped up by shot and shell,
Hills of brave dead will swell
  Red on your sight.
Faint not ; the *end* shall be
Triumph for Liberty !
Arm ! march to victory !
  God leads the fight !

BABES IN THE WOOD.

BY " C. C."

So you've buried the flag at Memphis ?
  How many fathoms deep ?
What seal did you set on the Stars and Stripes ?
  And who that grave shall keep ?

Alas, for the dead at Memphis !
  Mere dust to dust you bear ;
No vision of Life all glorified,
  Of Love grown heavenly fair ;—

No radiant dream, with a Christly sign,
  Of the victor's living palm ;
Of the odorous golden joy that dares
  Join seraphs in their psalm !

You never read, in a rich man's cave
  The Life of a world lay, slain !
And the mourning women went to watch,
  But found—where he *had* lain.

Come, guess—Who roll'd from his cave the rock ?
  Who broke great Pilate's seal ?—
While the soldiers sleep, and the women weep,
  Base hands the Body steal.

Vain guess for knowledge ! Children dear,
  Not Death lay in that cave,
But Living Love ! While the world above
  Went wailing, " *Died to save !* "

Well—judge if Freedom's sacred sign
  Can moulder under ground,
With the march of a million men o'erhead,
  Their banners eagle-crowned?

From Plymouth Rock to the Golden Gate,
  A shout goes right and left;
The aliens' dreamful watch is done—
  The sepulchre is cleft.

Weak hands! Heap clay on the Stars of God!
  They never shone before!
They rend the shroud, and they pierce the cloud;
  All hail, then, Thirty-Four!
    —*The Independent*, June 14.

TO ELLSWORTH.

So young, so brave, so early called,
  We mourn above his laurelled bier;
His name on every heart enrolled,
  To friends, and home, and country dear.
Struck by the traitor's reckless hand,
  Falling without a chance to raise
His sinewy arm with flashing brand;
  And in the morning of his days,
Entering upon the eternal land.
He goes his waiting God to meet,
Without a sin, without a fear;
  And as he walks the golden street
Of yon fair far and wondrous sphere,
  The angels all their harps will bring,
And hymn their holy welcoming.
                    J. W. F.
  —*Wash. Sunday Morning Chronicle.*

Sons of Northern sires arising,
  "Display who gave you birth,"
And save the priceless treasure, won
  By your brave fathers' worth,—
One country, free, united,
  Called by one glorious name;
One banner floating o'er them,
  From Lakes to Gulf, the same.
Leave shop, and bench, and counter;
  Leave forge, and desk, and field;
Leave axe, and spade, and hammer,
  For weaker hands to wield

Come from Penobscot's pine-clad banks,
  Where the hardy woodman's axe
Hurls crashing down the giant tree
  Upon the bear's fresh tracks;
From the clustered hills of granite,
  Crowned with the noble name
Of him, whose home dishonored
  Has left to us his fame;
From where Ticonderoga
  Looks out on blue Champlain;
From the green shores of Erie,
  The field of Lundy's Lane;
From Bennington and Plattsburg,
  From Saratoga's plain,
From every field of battle
  Where honored dead remain.

Up, Massachusetts! seize the sword
  That won calm peace and free;*

* *Ense petit placidam sub libertate quietem.*

'Tis thine, still thine, to lead the way
  Through blood to Liberty.
On Narragansett's busy shores,
  Remember gallant Greene;
And ye, whose fathers oft he led,
  Bold Putnam's courage keen.

Through the broad Western prairies,
  The mighty river pours
Its swollen floods resistless
  On subject Southern shores.
So, freemen of the prairies,
  Pour your resistless flood;
And, as the rushing river
  Whirls down the drifting wood,
So, let your armies marching,
  O'erwhelm the traitorous band,
That dared their country's flag to touch
  With sacrilegious hand.

Kentucky! "Why in slumbers
  Lethagic dost thou lie"?
"Wake, join with" Massachusetts,
  Thy true and "old ally."
In East and West, in North and South,
  Let every patriot rise,
Till North and South, till East and West,
  Shall share the glorious prize,—
One country, undivided,
  Called by one glorious name,
One banner floating o'er us,
  From Gulf to Lakes the same.

BOSTON, *May* 18, 1861.   G. S. H.
  —*Boston Daily Advertiser*, May 25.

THE HOLY WAR.

BY MRS. HARRIET BEECHER STOWE.

"And I saw heaven opened, and beheld a white horse; and he that sat upon him was called Faithful and True, and in righteousness he doth judge and make war. His eyes were as a flame of fire, and on his head were many crowns; and he had a name written, that no man knew, but he himself. And the armies which were in heaven followed him upon white horses, clothed in fine linen, white and clean."—REV. XIX. 11, 12, 14.

To the last battle set, throughout the earth!
  Not for vile lust of plunder or of power
The hosts of justice and eternal right
  Unfurl their banner in this solemn hour.

A King rides forth, whose eyes, as burning fire,
  Wither oppression in their dazzling flame;
And he hath sworn to right all human wrong,
  By the dread power of his mysterious name.

O'er all the earth resounds his trumpet-call.
  The nations, waking from their dreary night,
Are mustering in their ranks, and thronging on
  To hail the brightness of his rising light:

And all the armies that behind him ride,
  Come in white raiment, spotless as the snow;
"Freedom and Justice" is their battle-cry,
  And all the earth rejoices as they go.

Shoulder to shoulder ride the brother bands—
  Brave hearts and tender, with undaunted eye;
With manly patience ready to endure,
  With gallant daring resolute to die.

They know not fear, for what have they to fear
  Who *all* have counted, and have *all* resigned,
And laid their lives a solemn offering down
  For laws, for truth, for freedom,—for mankind ?

No boastful words are theirs, nor murderous zeal,
  Nor courage fed with the inebriate bowl ;
But their brave hearts show in true touch and time
  The sober courage of the manly soul.

Ah ! who can say how precious and how dear
  Those noble hearts, of thousand homes the light ?
Yet wives and mothers, smiling through their tears,
  Gave them unmurmuring to the holy fight.

O brothers, banded for this sacred war !
  Keep your white garments spotless still and pure ;
Be priestly warriors, hallowing the right—
  So shall your victory be swift and sure.

So shall the spotless King with whom ye ride,
  Make vile disorder from the earth to cease ;
And Time's triumphant songs at last shall hail
  The victory of a true and righteous peace.
                                  —*The Independent.*

INK, BLOOD, AND TEARS.

THE TAKING OF FORT SUMTER.

A forty hours' bombardment ! Great guns throwing
  Their iron hail ; shells their mad mines exploding ;
Furnaces lighted ; shot at red-heat glowing ;
  Shore-batt'ries and fort-armament, firing, loading—
War's visible hell let loose for forty hours,
And all her devils free to use their powers—
And yet not one man hit, her flag when Sumter
    lowers.

"Oh, here's a theme ! " quoth *Punch*, of brag ab-
    horrent,
  "'Twixt promise and performance rare proportion !
This show-cloth, of live lions, giving warrant,
  Masking some mangy, stunted, stuffed abortion ;
These gorgeous covers hiding empty dishes,
These whale-like antics among little fishes—
Here is the very stuff to meet my dearest wishes.

" What ringing of each change on brag and bluster !
  These figures huge of speech, summed in a zero ;
This war-march, ushering in *Bombastes*' muster ;
  This entry of *Tom Thumb*, armed like a hero.
Of all great cries e'er raised o'er little wool,
Of all big bubbles by fools' breath filled full,
Sure here's the greatest yet, and emptiest, for John
    Bull !

" John always thought Jonathan, his young brother,
  A little of a bully ; said he swaggered ;
But in all change of chaff with one another,
  Nor John nor Jonathan was e'er called ' laggard.'
But now, if John mayn't Jonathan style, ' Coward,'
He *may* hint Stripes and Stars were better lowered
From that tall height to which, till now, their flag-
    staff towered."

Punch nibbed his pen, all jubilant, for galling—
  When suddenly a weight weighed down the feather,
And a red liquid, drop by drop, slow falling,
    Came from the nib ; and the drops rolled together,

And steamed, and smoked, and sung—" Not ink, but
    blood ;
Drops now, but soon to swell into a flood,
Perchance e'er Summer's leaf has burst Spring's
    guarding bud.

" Blood by a brother's hand drawn from a brother—
  And they by whom 'tis ta'en, by whom 'tis given,
Are both the children of an English mother ;
  Once with that mother, in her wrath, they've
    striven ;
Was't not enough, that parricidal jar,
But they must now meet in fraternal war ?
If such strife draw no blood, shall England scoff
    therefore ?

" If she will laugh, through thee, her chartered wit,
  Use thou no ink wherewith to pen thy scoff ;
We'll find a liquor for thy pen more fit—
  We blood-drops—see how smartly thou'lt round off
Point, pun, and paragraph in this new way ;
Till men shall read and laugh, and laughing, say,
' Well thrust !   *Punch* is in vein ; 'tis his red-letter
    day. "

The weight sat on my quill : I could not write ;
  The red drops clustered to my pen—in vain ;
I had my theme—" Brothers that meet in fight,
  Yet shed no blood ! "—my jesting mood turned
    pain.
I thought of all that civil love endears,
That civil strife breaks up, and rends, and sears,
And lo ! the blood-drops in my pen were changed to
    tears !

And for the hoarse tongues that those bloody gouts
  Had found, or seemed to find, upon my ears
Came up a gentle song in linkèd bouts,
  Of long-drawn sweetness—pity breathed through
    tears.
    And thus they sang—" 'Twas not by chance,
      Still less by fraud or fear,
    That Sumter's battle came and closed,
      Nor cost the world a tear.
    'Twas not that Northern hearts were weak,
      Or Southern courage cold,
    That shell and shot fell harming not
      A man on shore or hold.

    " It was that all their ghosts who lived
      To love the realm they made,
    Came fleeting so athwart the fire,
      That shot and shell were stayed.
    Washington with his sad still face,
      Franklin with silver hair,
    Lincoln and Putnam, Allen, Gates,
      And gallant Wayne were there.

    " With those who rose at Boston,
      At Philadelphia met ;
    Whose grave eyes saw the Union's seal
      To their first charter set.
    Adams, and Jay, and Henry,
      Rutledge and Randolph, too—
    And many a name their country's fame
      Hath sealed brave, wise, and true.

    " An awful host—above the coast,
      About the fort, they hung ;
    Sad faces pale, too proud to wail,
      But with sore anguish wrung.

And Faith and Truth, and Love and Ruth,
  Hovered the battle o'er,
Hind'ring the shot, that freight of death
  Between those brothers bore.

"And thus it happed, by God's good grace,
  And those good spirits' band,
That Death forbore the leaguer'd place,
  The battery-guarded strand.
Thanks unto Heaven on bended knee,
  Not scoff from mocking scorn,
Befits us, that to bloodless end
  A strife like this is borne!"
       —*London Punch*, May 11.

SONGS OF THE REBELS.

FORT SUMTER.

A HEROIC POEM, IN THREE CANTOS.

BY CHARLES EDWARD LEVERETT, JR.

CANTO I.

Now glory be to Uncle Abe, and Scott, his lion pet,
And Seward, the righteous pontifex, who rules the
  Cabinet;
And glory to the mighty fleet that stood off Charles-
  ton Bar,
And left the dauntless Anderson to bear the brunt of
  war!

The Patriarch in Washington had summoned to his
  side
His squad of Solons—brilliant men, the rabble's joy
  and pride,
And some were looking very black, and some were
  looking blue;
The nation was at loggerheads, and none knew what
  to do;
And little light had yet been thrown upon the States'
  affairs,
_ or Abe, though good at splitting rails, was bad at
  splitting hairs.
Then up arose that valiant man, Lieutenant-General
  Scott,
And drew his sword, like Philip's son, and cut the
  Gordian knot.
"Now, by this waxed moustache," he said, and
  looked around the group,
"And by these lips that tasted once a 'hasty plate
  of soup,'
I raise my voice for horrid war—'tis just the thing
  for me;
Too long it is since I have had a military spree.
With all our gallant peddlers, our knack at making
  clocks,
Our taste for wooden nutmegs, and glorious Plymouth
  Rocks,
Our reverence for a Higher Law, our godly pulpit
  rant,
With all the talent which in Yankee land are now
  extant,
A generalissimo, like me, would find it no great thing
To gallop through the South, and whip the Chivalry,
  by Jing!"

He said, the hero whose chief joy was hearing bullets
  whiz,
And drew a red bandana forth, and wiped his war-
  like phiz;
Around the room a stifled buzz of admiration went,
When on his trembling knees arose the doughty
  President.
"Now, by old Andrew Jackson's shade, and by the
  oaths he swore,
And by his hickory stick, and by the thunder of his
  snore,
And by the proud contempt he showed for Carolina
  gents,
And English grammar," quoth Old Abe, "them's jist
  my sentiments.
Great Seward shall gull the Southrons, like a wily
  diplomat,
With promises and flummery, with 'tother, this and
  that;
And I will launch a squadron forth, in secret, on the
  seas,
And reinforce Fort Sumter with 'old horse,' and
  bread and cheese.
Poor Doubleday, that wretched man, whose appetite
  ne'er fails,
Has been obliged, for three weeks now, to eat his
  finger nails,
While underneath his very nose, the rebels sit and
  cram
Their throats with beef, and turtle-soup, and English
  peas, and lamb.
Ho! then, for Carolina, my veterans brave and true,
'Tis high time that the Chivalry should learn a thing
  or two;
I swear my hungry soger-boys shall soon have meat
  and drink,
I, gallant spouse of Mrs. Abe, and Pa of Bobby
  Link!"

So spake the "old man eloquent," and hushed he
  there and then;
The Cabinet all looked devout, and answered him
  Amen.

CANTO II.

Oh, 'twas a fearful thing to see, just at the break of
  day,
That terrible Armada sailing up through Charleston
  Bay;
Battalions of Palmetto troops stood marshalled on
  the strand,
To greet their Yankee cousins, and to welcome them
  on land;
And banners waved, and tattoos beat, and cannon
  lined the beach,
All ready to salute, when lo! they anchored—out of
  reach!

A storm was bursting from the sky—'twas sweeping
  from the main;
Its clouds were rolling wreaths of smoke, its rain was
  iron rain;
Its lightning was the lurid bomb, its thunder was the
  roar
Of mortar and columbiad, bristling on the sandy
  shore;
A thousand guns were flashing fire, a thousand whist-
  ling balls
Were falling in hot showers upon Fort Sumter's
  blackened walls.

They fought, "the Saucy Seventy," like brave men,
    long and well,
With wondrous skill and fortitude they dodged the
    hurtling shell;
Undauntedly they blazed away, with not a single
    crumb
Of dinner to console them—not one cheering drop
    of rum;
When, seeing 'twas impossible to fast and fight much
    more,
They strike their flag, and Foster falls—perspiring at
    each pore!
Hall waves his gleaming sword, looks proud defiance
    at his foes,
Then sinks exhausted, bleeding most profusely—at
    his nose;
And Doubleday, his longing eye fixed on the distant
    ships,
Collapses, with "My stomach! oh, my stomach!"
    on his lips.

CANTO III.

A telegram is flying North, 'tis pithy, sharp and
    curt—
"Fort Sumter's taken—tell Old Abe that no-bod-y is
    hurt."

A panic strikes the Cabinet, they wriggle in their
    chairs;
Seward mutters "curses deep, not loud"—Welles
    tries to say his prayers;
Old Uncle Abe, their royal liege, grows pallid at the
    news;
Uneasy twitch the nimble feet within his nimble
    shoes;
All downward through his spindle-shanks a nervous
    tremor flows,
And fast the courage oozes from the hero's valiant
    toes;
His hair begins to stand on end, his eyes are full of
    dread;
Already in the streets he hears the Southern cohorts
    tread;
Already through the White House gates he sees the
    legions pour;
Already dreams their battle-axe is thundering at his
    door;
Already feels fierce cow-hide boots assail him in the
    rear,
And finds, alas, the seat of war uncomfortably near!
"Now if," he cries, "my councillors, ye are inclined
    to flee,
(For 'tis not every one who'd like to face the Chiv-
    alry,)
And if the prospect of a fray should fill you with
    alarm,
If ye demand a Captain who will lead you out of
    harm,
Pack up your spoils, and while the Gin'ral keeps the
    foe at bay,
Put ye your trust in Providence, and set your legs in
    play,
And follow where this soger-cloak, all streaming in
    my flight,
Is like a streak of lightning seen dissolving from the
    sight.
Ho, ho! for Illinois, my braves! hip, hip, hurrah,
    away!
Do what you choose—for me, why, *I'll be hanged*
    if I will stay!"

Now glory be to Uncle Abe, and Scott, his bully pet,
And Seward, the cook and bottle-washer of the Cabi-
    net;
And glory to the mighty fleet that stood off Charles-
    ton Bar,
And left the dauntless Anderson to bear the brunt
    of war!
                            —*Charleston Mercury.*

THE STAR OF THE WEST

I.

I wish I was in de land o' cotton,
Old times dair ain't not forgotten—
    Look away, &c.
In Dixie land whar I was born in,
Early on one frosty mornin'—
    Look away, &c.
    CHORUS—Den I wish I was in Dixie.

II.

In Dixie land dat frosty mornin',
Jis 'bout de time de day was dawnin'—
    Look away, &c.
De signal fire from de east bin roarin',
Rouse up Dixie, no more snorin'—
    Look away, &c.
    CHORUS—Den I wish I was in Dixie.

III.

Dat rocket high a blazing in de sky,
'Tis de sign dat de snobbies am comin' up nigh
    Look away, &c.
Dey bin braggin' long, if we dare to shoot a shot,
Dey comin' up strong and dey'll send us all to pot—
Fire away, fire away, lads in gray.
    CHORUS—Den I wish I was in Dixie.
                            —*Charleston Mercury.*

A NATIONAL SONG.

An appropriate national song for the Southern Confederacy appears to be one of the mooted questions of the
present exciting crisis. Plenty of patriotic poetry can be
obtained, but a purely American melody, one that will
take with the masses, is hard to be found. The popular
old ballad of "The Minstrel's Return," composed by an
American—and a Southerner, too—seems to be highly appropriate to the patriots of the South. Years ago it was
quite as popular as the negro tune of "Dixie" is at the
present day; and the composer, who is a resident professor of music of Richmond, received many compliments
for his happy conception.

A correspondent has sent us the following adaptation,
and expresses a hope that it may be taken up by the singers among our brave volunteers, and also by lady vocalists. Should the people adopt it, it will become our national anthem:—

SOUTHERN SONG OF FREEDOM.

BY J. H. H.

AIR—"*The Minstrel's Return.*"

I.

A nation has sprung into life,
    Beneath the bright cross of the South,
And now a loud call to the strife
    Rings out from the shrill bugle's mouth.
They gather from morass and mountain,
    They gather from prairie and mart,
To drink at young Liberty's fountain
    The nectar that kindles the heart.

Then, hail to the land of the pine !
   The home of the noble and free !
A palmetto wreath we'll entwine
   Round the altar of young Liberty !

II.

Our flag with its cluster of stars,
   Firm fixed in a field of pure blue,
All shining through red and white bars,
   Now gallantly flutters in view.
The stalwart and brave round it rally,
   They press to their lips every fold ;
While the hymn swells from hill and from valley :
   " Be God with our volunteers bold."
     Then, hail to the land of the pine ! &c.

III.

Th' invaders rush down from the North ;
   Our borders are black with their hordes,
Like wolves for their victims they froth,
   While whetting their knives and their swords.
Their watchword is " Booty and Beauty ;"
   Their aim is to steal as they go ;
But, Southrons, act up to your duty,
   And lay the foul miscreants low.
     Then, hail to the land of the pine ! &c.

IV.

The God of our fathers looks down,
   And blesses the cause of the just ;
His smile will the patriot crown
   Who tramples his chains in the dust.
March, march, Southrons ! shoulder to shoulder,
   One heart-throb, one shout for the cause ;
Remember, the world's a beholder,
   And your bayonets are fixed at your doors!
     Then, hail to the land of the pine ! &c.
          —Richmond Enquir

A WELCOME TO THE INVADER.

"AN ODE,"

ADDRESSED TO THE PICKED MEN OF COL. WILSON'S
NEW YORK COMMAND.

I.

What ! have ye come to spoil our fields,
   Black hearts and bloody hands !
And taste the sweets that conquest yields
   To those who win our lands?

II.

Back to your dens of crime and shame,
   Black hearts and bloody hands !
Ye but disgrace a soldier's name,
   Owning such vile commands.

III.

Your ribald chieftain is a fool,—
   Black hearts and bloody hands !
In sneaky Seward's grasp a tool—
   In Blair's—a beast he stands.

IV.

Dare ye with patriot men to strive ?—
   Black hearts and bloody hands !
And can ye hope to 'scape alive
   From their avenging brands ?
POETRY—44

V.

Thieves, ruffians, hirelings, slaves,
   Black hearts and bloody hands !
Our country will refuse its graves
   To your polluted bands.

VI.

The carrion vulture in his flight—
   Black hearts and bloody hands !
Shall scent you, as you droop in fight,
   Nor wait your ebbing sands.
          —Charleston Courier.

MARYLAND.

The despot's heel is on thy shore,
   Maryland !
His touch is at thy temple door,
   Maryland !
Avenge the patriotic gore
That flocked the streets of Baltimore,
And be the battle queen of yore,
   Maryland ! My Maryland !

Hark to the wand'ring son's appeal,
   Maryland !
My mother State, to thee I kneel,
   Maryland !
For life and death, for woe and weal,
Thy peerless chivalry reveal,
And gird thy beauteous limbs with steel,
   Maryland ! My Maryland !

Thou wilt not cower in the dust,
   Maryland !
Thy beaming sword shall never rust,
   Maryland !
Remember Carroll's sacred trust,
Remember Howard's warlike thrust—
And all thy slumberers with the just,
   Maryland ! My Maryland !

Come ! 'tis the red dawn of the day,
   Maryland !
Come ! with thy panoplied array,
   Maryland !
With Ringgold's spirit for the fray,
With Watson's blood at Monterey,
With fearless Lowe and dashing May,
   Maryland ! My Maryland !

Come ! for thy shield is bright and strong,
   Maryland !
Come ! for thy dalliance does thee wrong,
   Maryland !
Come ! to thine own heroic throng,
That stalks with Liberty along,
And give a new *Key* to thy song,
   Maryland ! My Maryland !

Dear Mother ! burst the tyrant's chain,
   Maryland !
Virginia should not call in vain,
   Maryland !
She meets her sisters on the plain—
" *Sic semper*," 'tis the proud refrain,
That baffles millions back amain,
   Maryland !
Arise, in majesty again,
   Maryland ! My Maryland !

I see the blush upon thy cheek,
> Maryland !
But thou wast ever bravely meek,
> Maryland !
But lo ! there surges forth a shriek
From hill to hill, from creek to creek—
Potomac calls to Chesapeake,
> Maryland ! My Maryland !

Thou wilt not yield the Vandal toll,
> Maryland !
Thou wilt not crook to his control,
> Maryland !
Better the fire upon thee roll,
Better the blade, the shot, the bowl,
Than crucifixion of the soul,
> Maryland ! My Maryland !

I hear the distant thunder hum,
> Maryland !
The Old Line's bugle, fife, and drum,
> Maryland !
She is not dead, nor deaf, nor dumb—
Huzza ! she spurns the Northern scum !
She breathes—she burns ! she'll come ! she'll
> come !
> Maryland ! My Maryland ! R.
> —*Charleston Mercury.*

On the list of contributors to the fund in aid of the volunteers, which is still open at the Counting-room of the *Savannah News*, are two ten-dollar subscriptions voluntarily contributed, one by a free negro, and the other by a slave of this city. They desired to the extent of their ability to prove their devotion to the cause of the South.—*Charleston Evening News, May 10.*

MONTGOMERY, ALA.—William, a slave, belonging to our townsman, Dr. W. H. Rives, has invested one hundred and fifty dollars in the Confederate States Loan Bonds. This is another rebuke to the hypocrites of the North. Intelligent slaves know that they have no friends in the world but the Southern white people.—*Montgomery Mail.*

REV. MR. BEATTIE, of the Bethel, at Cleveland, Ohio, presented a revolver to one of the soldiers of the Seventh Regiment before his departure, with the following injunction :—" If you get in a tight place and have to use it, ask God's blessing if you have time, but be sure and not let your enemy get the start of you. You can say 'Amen' after you shoot."—*N. Y. Evening Post, May 10.*

THE Newport Artillery (Company F of the Rhode Island Regiment) is one of the oldest military organizations in the country. It is an independent company, and was chartered by the British Crown in 1741. With but three exceptions since that time (during the Revolutionary war, when Newport was in possession of English and Hessian troops) the company has held annual meetings under the charter and elected officers, who consist of a Colonel and others connected with a regiment. The names of Generals Greene and Vaughan, of Revolutionary fame, Commodore Perry, and other distinguished personages, are among the enrolled members of the company, which number between two and three thousand since organization. In their armory at Newport they have an autograph letter from Gen. Geo. Washington, written in 1792, thanking them for an invitation to be with them at their annual celebration on the 22d of February of that year, which is handsomely framed. Of the fifty-two active members, forty-seven volunteered their services for the defence of the National Capital when Governor Sprague telegraphed to inquire the number of men they could furnish, and in a few hours the number was increased to one hundred and thirty-five by recruits.—*National Intelligencer, May 17.*

THE *Montgomery* (Ala.) *Weekly Post* contains the following :—

"TOO GOOD TO BE LOST.—A countryman was in the town of Lumpkin, Ga., last week, and some one asked him how he liked the war news. He replied, 'Very well.' 'Are you to go ?' he was asked. 'Yes,' he replied. 'Are you not afraid ?' 'No. If I should see a Yankee with his gun levelled and looking right at me, I would draw out my pocketbook, and ask him what he would take for his gun, and right there the fight would end.'"

Yes, the Yankee would probably sell him his *gun*, if the Lumpkiner had enough money to buy it ; but as the load would still belong to the Yankee, he would probably deliver that before he did the gun.—*Jackson (Ia.) Star.*

MOBILE, *May* 12.—Mr. W. H. Russell, the correspondent of the London *Times*, visited Forts Morgan and Gaines to-day, accompanied by several prominent citizens. *Russell made several very important suggestions* to Col. Hardee, regarding the fortifications, gathered from his experience in the Crimea ; and seemed well pleased with Col. Hardee's command. Mr. R. says Col. H. is every inch a soldier.—*Montgomery (Ala.) Mail, May* 13.

THE *Mobile* (Ala.) *Advertiser*, warm in its commendation of the declaration of war by the Congress of the seceded States, says :—

Let patriotic citizens go forth upon the trackless war paths of the ocean to fight for their country in the most effective manner. Hundreds and hundreds of millions of the property of the enemy invite them to spoil him—to "spoil these Egyptians" of the North, who would coerce us to staying when we strove peaceably to make our exodus to independence of their oppressive thrall ; to go forth from degrading fellowship with them. *The richly laden ships of the enemy swarm on every sea, and are absolutely unprotected. The harvest is ripe ; let it be gathered,* and we will strike the enemy to the heart —for we hit his pocket, his most sensitive part. His treasure ships, laden with California wealth, traverse Southern waters. Let them be the prize of the bravest and most enterprising.

His commerce is the very life of the enemy's solvency and financial vitality. Strike it, and you lay the axe to the root of his power—you rend away the sinews of war. Let the flags of privateers show themselves on the seas, and the blockade will be raised. Lincoln's fleet will scatter over the world to protect the commerce of his citizens. But they cannot protect it though they try. They are numerous enough for the blockade, *but not to guard the ocean.* The risk of the privateer will still be trifling, *and he will continue to reap the harvest,* laughing at the few scarecrows which would fright him from his profitable employment.

It is easy to put privateers afloat. There are an abundance of brave men among us ready to volunteer to fight anywhere. There are many among us ready to give money to the cause of their country, not looking for return. In this privateering the most enormous returns are promised with but trifling risk. Let the men of means fit out privateers, if they would best serve their country and advance their own interests. Let companies be formed to embark capital in privateering. If they can't get the craft here, they can get them somewhere. It is a pursuit of honor, patriotism, profit. *Let us scour the seas, and sweep their commerce from it with the besom of destruction.—N. Y. Evening Post, May* 13.

WM. C. RIVES, a delegate from Virginia to the Southern Congress, on his way to Montgomery, was called on by the people at Atlanta, Georgia, for a speech. He made the following pointless response:

"I feel highly complimented by this call from the citizens of Georgia to say a few words. I suppose you do not want to hear a speech from me, but that you do want to hear from Virginia. ["That's it," and cheers from the crowd.] She is all right, I am most happy to inform you. She is heart and hand with Georgia in this struggle, and will faithfully do her part. You have been accustomed, in political matters, in times past, to follow our lead; but now we will follow your lead in this great movement for the maintenance of the rights and independence of the South and her institutions. Our rights and liberties are assailed, and must be defended. Our cause is a just one, and brave hearts are rushing to uphold it. In the mean time you may rely upon Old Virginia. Whether she is to lead or to follow, she will be along and give a good account of herself.

"I am happy to meet with you, my fellow-citizens, for though it is the first time I ever had the pleasure of looking on your faces, I feel in Georgia like I was at home in my own State. Many of your citizens are emigrants or the children of emigrants from our State; among whom are the Gilmers, Lumpkinses, Forsyths, Earlys, Meriwethers, and many others.

"I hope you will excuse me from making any further remarks, out of respect for the day. I suppose you only wanted to hear a word about Virginia. [Here some one in the crowd asked him if there were any Federal troops in Alexandria.] No, my friend," said Mr. Rives; "there are none at that point. There are no Federal troops on any part of the soil of Virginia, except Fortress Monroe. I will not say they are afraid to come into Alexandria; but I will say that we have a trap for them into which they will fall whenever they attempt to come into that city. Thanking you for this manifestation of your feelings towards Virginia, I now bid you adieu."

While he was uttering these last words, the train was moving, and he retired amidst the applause of the crowd.—*Richmond Examiner, May* 18.

AT the session of the Wyoming (N. Y.) Conference, the following substitute was offered and passed, instead of a resolution to adopt the report of last year on slavery:—

"*Whereas*, Divine Providence has taken the work of emancipation into his own hands; therefore,

"*Resolved*, That we stand still and see the salvation of God."—*N. Y. Evening Post, May* 10.

MR. SPARROWGRASS recently joined the "Home Guard" at Yonkers, New York, and said in a speech

that "it is understood that the Home Guard is not to go to the wars, and not to leave Yonkers, *except in case of invasion.*"

This is as good as the old story of the "Bungtown Riflemen," an Ohio military company, whose by-laws consisted of two sections, namely:—

"*Article First.*—This company shall be known as the Bungtown Riflemen.

"*Article Second.*—In case of war, this company shall immediately disband."—*Idem.*

A PATRIOTIC FAMILY.—Among the many incidents connected with the present military movements, no one is more remarkable than the following:—One of the companies connected with the Ohio regiments contains sixteen brothers by the name of Finch, residents of Dayton, Ohio. They were born in Durkheim, in Germany. The family numbers in all nineteen children—sixteen boys, all of whom are with the regiment, as stated above. Their parents are living in New York, and their children obtained leave to visit them in Philadelphia. On their return, if time will permit, an entertainment will be given them by a number of Germans in Philadelphia.—*N. Y. Tribune, May* 20.

MARSHAL SAXE, a high authority in such things, was in the habit of saying, that to kill a man in battle, the man's weight in lead must be expended. A French medical and surgical gazette, published at Lyons, says this fact was verified at Solferino, even in the recent great improvements in fire-arms. The Austrians fired 8,400,000 rounds. The loss of the French and Italians was 2,000 killed and 10,000 wounded. Each man hit cost 700 rounds, and every man killed cost 4,200 rounds. The mean weight of a ball is one ounce; thus we find that it required, on an average, 272 pounds of lead to kill a man. If any one of our friends should get into a military fight, they should feel great comfort in the fact that 700 shots may be fired at them before they are hit, and 4,200 before they "shuffle off the mortal coil."—*N. Y. Commercial, May* 21.

WASHINGTON, *May* 1.—A number of the Fire Zouaves, who are encamped in the neighborhood of the Insane Asylum, took a stroll some distance into St. George's county. During their walk, they saw a farmer planting his corn, and, on entering into conversation with him, found that he was afraid that he could not get it in soon enough, for he had to do all the planting himself. The "lambs" immediately took off their jackets and went to work, and soon planted the whole field. The farmer expressed his thanks for their help in the warmest manner, and they returned to their encampment a little proud of their farming abilities.—*Wash. National Republican.*

HISTORICAL PARALLELS.—The first collision of our fathers with the British after the battle of Lexington, and the first decided military success of the war, was the capture of Forts Ticonderoga and Crown Point, and a British armed vessel on Lake Champlain, which was achieved on the 10th of May following by the Vermont hero, Col. Ethan Allen, at the head of a force of Green Mountain Boys. Massachusetts has matched the 19th of April, 1775, with the 19th of April, 1861; so Vermont now matches the 10th of May, 1775, with the 10th of May, 1861, for on that day, Capt. Lyon, a Vermonter, and U. S.

commanding officer at St. Louis, surrounds the rebel camp threatening that city, and captures 800 men in arms. Lyon's exploit, like Allen's, was done mostly on his own responsibility, and without direct orders. Allen, when asked by the British commandant at Ticonderoga his authority for demanding its surrender, could only reply, "By the authority of the Great Jehovah and the Continental Congress;" and Capt. Lyon, in his summons to Gen. Frost, demands his surrender on general grounds only. Both Allen and Lyon took the enemy by surprise, who capitulated without striking a blow.

A Boston sculptor has offered to make a statue in marble of the members of the Utica corps who will "bag" Wigfall or Jeff. Davis.—*Montgomery Weekly Post, May 14.*

A TALL, splendid-looking man, dressed in the uniform of the Allen Greys, Vermont, stood conversing with a friend on Broadway. He was entirely unconscious that his superior height was attracting universal attention, until a splendid barouche drove up to the sidewalk, and a young man sprang from it and grasped his hand, saying, "You are the most splendid specimen of humanity I ever saw. I am a Southerner, but my heart is with the Union; if it were not, such noble-looking fellows as yourself would enlist me in the cause." The subject of the remark, although surprised, was perfectly self-possessed, and answered the cordial greeting of the young Southerner with warm enthusiasm. He was several inches above six feet, and his noble, open countenance, beamed with the ancient patriotism of the Green Mountain Boys, of which he was so fine a specimen. He had walked fifteen miles from the village of Chittenden to enlist, and was the only representative of that village; but he was a host in himself. Long may he live to honor our Stars and Stripes.—*N. Y. Sun, May 14.*

A PRODUCTION called "Abe's Saturday, or Washington Sixty Days Hence," has been acted at the Mobile Theatre. It is called by the playbills a "laughable squib," and the leading ideas of the plot, as may be inferred from the title, consist in the surprise of the Capital and the capture of the President by the doughty Confederates.—*Boston Transcript, May 14.*

WE heard, says an exchange, a version of the 60th Psalm sung in one of our churches last Sunday. The following verse was sung with emphasis in every part of the house:

'Go with our armies to the fight,
Like a Confederate God;
In vain *confederate powers* unite
Against Thy lifted rod."

—*Chicago Christian Times, May 15.*

REV. DR. WORCESTER, of Salem, Mass., in addressing the City Guards of that city, previous to their departure for the war, closed his remarks amidst profound stillness, as follows:—"Soldiers, on a memorable night of ancient battle, when a few men routed many thousands, their watch-cry was, 'The sword of the Lord and of Gideon.' I give to you, soldiers, for your watch-cry, 'The sword of the Lord and of Washington.' "—*Boston Transcript, May 11.*

BEAUREGARD.

In philologic vein,
The thought came to my brain,
That *Beau Regard*, in France,
Means a "good countenance."

And then I tried, but missed,
To give the thing a twist;
Some joke to interlard
On General Beauregard.

At last, this quip I wrought,
Out of the merry thought:
How Beauregard was chosen
To lead the Union's foes on.

That Carolina's shame
For her disloyal game,
Might—in slang phrase—have "Gone it
With a good face upon it."

— *Vanity Fair, May 11.*

HOG AND HOMINY.—A "Lady of Richmond" writes to the *N. Y. Daily News* of the sensation created in the Southern churches when the chapter "Blow ye the trumpet of Zion," from the Book of Joel, was read. This chapter contains the Lord's promise to send to the people "corn, and wine, and oil." Thus the lady gives that promise :—"Then will the Lord be jealous for his land, and pity his people. Yea, the Lord will answer and say unto his people, Behold, I will send ye corn, and swine, and oil, and ye shall be satisfied therewith." Swine to the congregation! This was "addressed first to the ancient Jews," the lady says. No doubt the porky part of this must be considered as Scripture adapted to the latitude of Dixey.—*Springfield Banner, May 4.*

WASHINGTON, D. C., *May 15.*—An incident is mentioned in connection with the encampment of the First New Jersey Regiment, near Meridian Hill, which is alike honorable to all concerned. A party from this regiment called upon Mrs. Baker, an elderly lady, who has a vegetable garden near by, and attends the Northern Liberties Market, and asked her for some onions and other vegetables for a sick companion, which she freely gave them, asking no pay. The next day the party returned with a handsome Bible, which they presented her, and which she accepted as worth more than money. Those who remember how the measure of meal of the widow of Zarephath was never allowed to be empty, after her free gift to the wayfaring prophet when hungry, will readily come to the conclusion that this good old lady, animated by the same spirit, will never lack the early and the latter rain to give verdure to her fields and replenish her stores abundantly.—*National Intelligencer, May 17.*

THE WHEREABOUTS OF GEN. BEAUREGARD.
By Telegraph to Vanity Fair—After Manner of Daily Papers.

HAVRE DE GRACE, *April 26.*—Gen. Beauregard was in Richmond at 23 minutes past 6 o'clock yesterday, and will attack Washington at once.

PHILADELPHIA, *April 26.*—We learn on undoubted authority, that Gen. Beauregard was in Alexandria at 24 minutes past 6 yesterday, reconnoitring.

BALTIMORE, *April 26.*—Gen. Beauregard was in

Norfolk at 25 minutes past 6 yesterday, and took a gin cocktail with several of the first families.

HAVRE DE GRACE, *April 26.*—I learn from a gentleman just from Mobile, that Gen. Beauregard is on his way North, with 150,000 troops. Gen. Beauregard is six feet high, but will not join Blower's "Household Guards." Declines advertising the *Household Journal.*

ANNAPOLIS, *April 26.*—Gen. Beauregard was discovered in the White House rear-yard last night at 26 minutes past 6, armed with three large howitzers and a portable sledstake. He went away after reconnoitring pretty numerously.

PHILADELPHIA, *April 26.*—I learn on excellent authority that Gen. Beauregard was in Charleston at 22 minutes past 6 yesterday, and had no intention of leaving. He was repairing Fort Sumter.

The people of Bangor, Maine, and of Cape Cod, Mass., report that Gen. Beauregard has lately been seen prowling around those places.

I learn that Gen. Beauregard is within five miles of Washington.

The report in some of your contemporaries, that Gen. Beauregard is within five miles of Washington, is utterly without foundation. Sensation despatches in times like these cannot be too strongly deprecated. The public will invariably find my despatches reliable, and can always find out all about Gen. Beauregard by buying VANITY FAIR. Price 6 cents.—*Vanity Fair, May 4.*

A TENNESSEAN, who owes $7,000 in New York, has addressed the following letter to his creditors. He demands accommodations in New York for the rebel soldiers as gravely as though he were not perpetrating a waggish joke :—

"MEMPHIS, *May 8, 1861.*

" MESSRS. ——, NEW YORK :

" I have just completed my arrangement to liquidate my indebtedness at New York more completely, on account of the conservative sentiment manifested by its merchant princes towards the South ; but my native State will be involved heart and soul in the present war, and needs means to arm and equip our volunteers. I have devoted all my means to that end, am equipped and ready, and expect to be in New York in about sixty days, and hope to be welcomed by you and other friends.

" Please make arrangements to quarter our soldiers. My own regiment is already unanimously determined to occupy A. T. Stewart's dry goods house. However, arrangements equally as good have been made for the balance of the regiments. I shall take my grub at Taylor's with the general officers, but be certain to have ample arrangements. Tell Delmonico to be ready for us also. Be kind enough to meet me, and invite all the members of the following houses * * * and my particular friend —— at Taylor's. Be certain to make ample arrangements. My appetite is very good, and the camp life is said to make soldiers eat hearty.

" J. W. PROUDFIT."

—*N. Y. Evening Post, May 15.*

THE ladies of Boston, Mass., were informed that five thousand shirts, for soldiers, were required within twenty-four hours. They joined with them some of the ladies of Roxbury, secured the assistance of sewing-machines, went to work in " Liberty Hall," their head-quarters, and had the whole number completed fairly within the allotted time.—*N. Y. Tribune, May 10.*

NEW YORK, *May 10.*—A rigger from New London, Connecticut, who has found employment as such during the winter at Charleston and Wilmington, North Carolina, and in plying as a hand on board a vessel running between those places, called at the *Tribune* office yesterday morning. He said that he had just arrrived from Wilmington in the schooner which brought the garrison of the Fayetteville arsenal, and that he came to contradict the story sent from Charleston, that no one was killed in the attack on Fort Sumter. He had not seen any late Northern papers, and did not know that any thing had been printed about the hundreds killed at Morris Island and in Fort Moultrie. He was on the Battery at Charleston during the first day of the fight. The news was all the while that nobody was hurt. A number of Northern men were together, and they, doubting this story, agreed to go back and see what they could see during the night. So they went down where the boats came in.

At about 10 o'clock one of the two steamboats which plied between the town and the forts came in. Three or four long covered vehicles, with a tarpaulin curtain hanging down behind, called cabs in Charleston and covered wagons in New England, had been standing there for some time. One of them backed up on the wharf, and they began to bring dead bodies on hand-barrows from the little steamboat, and take them into the cabs, where they laid them in long boxes. There were three of these boxes in each cab, and they put two bodies in each box. He says that he and his friends saw the boxes and the bodies passed in, and when one was passed in, the tarpaulin was allowed to fall. Some of the men who were with him will soon be here on the schooner John S. Smith.

They knew of these boats running, and thought if there was any thing coming ashore they might get some news. They waited until 2 o'clock in the morning ; and during the four hours they were there, one of the boats went off and came back with another load. There were at least a dozen carts, and those which returned were not gone over three-fourths of an hour. The number of bodies carried away must have been nearly 100.

The next night also they went down to the Battery, and saw more bodies brought on shore, about half as many as on the first night. Some men who had been wounded in the hotel in Moultrieville were brought to the city in the daytime. One of this party learned from a hand on one of the boats, that the first shot at Fort Moultrie entered an embrasure and killed 30 odd men. This man was a cooper, and belonged in Bridgeport.—*N. Y. Tribune, May 10.*

IN May, 1860, at the Anniversary of the American Tract Society, Dr. Richard Fuller, now of secession notoriety, uttered the following patriotic words :—" If you Northerners dissolve this glorious Union, I'll get a large United States flag and hoist it over my house in Baltimore, and live and die under its folds." One short year must have wrought a remarkable change in the Doctor's views.—*N. Y. Examiner, May 30.*

THE following copy of a letter addressed to Gen. Winfield Scott, by one of his nearest blood relatives, has been furnished to us, with permission to publish it. We doubt whether any such appeals can ever

Influence this apostate son of Virginia. His egotism, and that callous heart, engendered by a long absence from his birthplace, amounting to almost alienage, in the possession of a vast military power, which his habits made a dictatorship, render it very certain that he will not abandon power and place from any sentiment. But there must be somewhere in his heart some spot to be touched, and wrenched by the scorn with which he is thrown off by his native State and his own kindred:—

" To WINFIELD SCOTT:

" When the future historian shall record the two great struggles on the American continent, of liberty against oppression and wrong, two names will be held up to the execration of mankind—that of Benedict Arnold and your own. The former, ere received into the pitying embraces of the tomb, lived an object of loathing to every true and loyal heart ; and it might be a profitable if not an agreeable lesson for you to ponder well on his example.

" With a sophistry unworthy the understanding of a schoolboy, you declare your determination to fight under the flag of your country, when that flag has been prostituted to the foulest and most unholy of purposes. If, haply, beneath its desecrated folds, you should pollute, with your canting myrmidons, the bosom of the honored Commonwealth, whose chiefest reproach is that she should have nurtured such a viper as yourself, there is one spot upon her soil to which I would particularly invite your presence. It is one to which now, doubtless, your recollection but rarely reverts, for *it contains the ashes of your fathers.* On that spot, deemed sacred by other men, let your war-dance be celebrated, and a crusade against freedom and religion proclaimed throughout the world.   M."
—*N. O. Picayune, May 28.*

THE BALTIMORE STEAM-GUN.—The following is a description of the Winans gun :—

It is on four wheels ; the boiler is like that of an ordinary steam fire-engine, the cylinder being upright. There is but one barrel, which is of steel, on a pivot, and otherwise is like an ordinary musket-barrel. It is fed or loaded through a hopper entering the barrel directly over the pivot. The barrel has a rotary motion, and performs the circumference, by machinery attached, at the rate of about sixteen hundred times a minute. The balls are let into the barrel through a valve at will, and every time the barrel comes round to a certain point, another valve, self-operated, lets out a ball, which is propelled solely by the velocity of the barrel in revolving. It will discharge a two-ounce ball three hundred times a minute. The range is accurate up and down, but the balls are liable to hit wide of the mark on one side or the other. The barrel revolves inside of a drum, made of boiler iron, between five and six feet in circumference, with an opening where the balls are discharged. Its range is not over one hundred yards at best, and the gun can be worked so as to discharge in any direction. The whole thing weighs 6,700 pounds, and is about the size of a steam fire-engine. It is the opinion of our informant, that the gun does not warrant the expectations of the inventor, and that it is not likely to be of much service.—*N. Y. Tribune,* (*Weekly,*) *May 4.*

A REPRESENTATIVE of one of the five Great Powers met Mr. Seward on Monday, just as he was coming out of his room on his way to dinner. Of course, the diplomat was invited to walk in. He declined, saying, " Oh, no ; I only called to tell you a good *joke.* One of our captains has just arrived, and says that when he reached Charleston and went to my Consul's office, and inquired for the Consul, he was told that he was drilling his company. ' What company ? ' inquired the captain of the ship. ' Why, one of the companies selected to march against Washington.' The captain was greatly surprised, and mentioned the fact as evidence of the universal feeling of hostility which pervades Charleston."

Mr. SEWARD—" What is the name of your Consul at Charleston ? "

DIPLOMAT—" _____ _____ _____."

Mr. SEWARD (opening the door opposite where they were standing)—" Mr. Assistant Secretary, draw up an order recalling the *exequatur* issued in favor of _____ _____, Consul at Charleston. There, that business is disposed of."

DIPLOMAT—" My God ! Seward, you are not in earnest. I only told you the story as a good joke."

Mr. SEWARD—" And I, Mr. _____, avail myself of this ' joke ' to give you practical evidence of the manner in which we intend to deal with every Foreign Power and their representatives, whenever they interfere, directly or indirectly, between us and the traitors in rebellion against our Government. The exequatur of your Consul is recalled, and the place vacant ; and I sincerely hope that no imprudence on the other side of the Atlantic will compel me as summarily to terminate the very pleasant relations now existing with all the members of the Diplomatic Corps. Your Government understands us, and is always friendly ; but it may become our duty to prove to others that we are in earnest not to permit interference in this domestic quarrel."—*N. Y. Express, May 25.*

UNIFORM OF THE CONFEDERATE STATES ARMY.— Army regulations have been issued for the uniform adopted by the War Department of the Confederate States, and are as follows :—The coat to be of cadet gray cloth, short tunic, double-breasted, two rows of buttons down the breast, two inches apart at the waist, and widening towards the shoulders. Pantaloons of sky-blue cloth, made full in the leg. The different corps of the service to be distinguished by the color of their trimmings—blue for infantry, red for artillery, and yellow for cavalry. The buttons to be of plain gilt, convex form, three-quarters of an inch in diameter. In the artillery corps, the buttons to be stamped with the letter A ; and in infantry and cavalry, the buttons will bear only the number of the regiment.

For the General and the officers of his staff, the dress will be of dark blue cloth, trimmed with gold ; for the medical department, black cloth, with gold and velvet trimming. All badges of distinction are to be marked upon the sleeves and collars. Badges of distinguished rank, on the collar only. For a Brigadier-General, three large stars ; for a Colonel, two large stars ; for a Lieutenant-Colonel, one large star ; for a Major, one small star, and a horizontal bar ; for a Captain, three small stars ; for a First Lieutenant, two small stars ; for a Second Lieutenant, one small star.

For General and Staff officers, the buttons will be of bright gilt, convex, rounded at the edge—a raised eagle at the centre, surrounded by thirteen stars. Exterior diameter of large-sized button, one inch ;

of small size, one-half inch. For officers of the corps of Engineers, the same button is to be used, except that in the place of the eagle and stars, there will be a raised E in German text. For officers of artillery, infantry, riflemen, and cavalry, the button will be a plain gilt convex, with a large raised letter in the centre—A for artillery, I for infantry, &c. The exterior diameter of large-sized button, seven-eighths of an inch; small size, one-half inch.

No cap has yet been adopted.—*N. O. Picayune*, *May* 25.

The following correspondence from the *Louisville Journal* explains itself:—

"UNIVERSITY OF VIRGINIA, *May* 17, 1861.
"PRENTICE:

"Stop my paper; I can't afford to read abbolition journals these times; the atmosphere of Old Virginia will not at all admit of such filthy sheets as yours has grown to be.

"Yours, &c., GEORGE LAKE.
"To Editors of Louisville Journal."

"LAKE!

"I think it a great pity that a young man should go to a university to graduate a traitor and a blackguard—and so ignorant as to spell abolition with two *b's*. G. D. P."
—*Vincennes (Ind.) Gazette, May* 25.

DR. JUNKIN, for more than twelve years past the efficient and popular President of Washington College, Lexington, Virginia, has resigned his position since the secession of the State from the Federal Government. We have seen some notices of this resignation which are intended to produce the impression that Dr. Junkin was *forced* to vacate his place because he was a Northern man. No one who has any knowledge of his antecedents could doubt his loyalty, heretofore, to the South and to Southern interests; but he is not, and never could be, a *Secessionist.* And when, prior to the action of the State, the students hoisted the secession flag upon the College building, and refused to permit it to be removed, the Doctor declared he would not deliver a lecture beneath its folds, and immediately resigned. This venerable College has never known greater prosperity than since Dr. Junkin's incumbency. The Trustees accepted his resignation with deep regret, and passed very flattering resolutions on the occasion.—*Banner of the Covenant, May* 25.

GREAT "POP-GUN" PRACTICE.—Toby is a high private in the First Regiment of the Mississippi army. His company is armed with the breech-loading Maynard rifle, "warranted to shoot twelve times a minute, and carry a ball effectually 1,600 yards." Men who fought at Monterey and Buena Vista call the new-fangled thing a "pop-gun." To test its efficacy, Toby's Captain told the men they must "try their guns." In obedience to command, Toby procured the necessary munitions of war, and started with his "pop-gun" for the woods. Saw a squirrel up a very high tree—took aim—fired. Effects of shot immediate and wonderful. Tree effectually stripped, and nothing of the squirrel to be found, except three broken hairs. "Pop-gun" rose in value—equal to a four-pounder. But Toby wouldn't shoot toward any more trees—afraid of being arrested for cutting down other people's timber. Walked a mile and a quarter

to get sight of a hill. By aid of a small telescope, saw hill in distance; saw large rock on hill; put in big load; shut both eyes—fired. As soon as breath returned, opened both eyes; could see, just could, but couldn't hear—at least, couldn't distinguish any sounds; thought Niagara had broke loose, or all out-doors gone to drum-beating. Determined to see if shot hit. Borrowed horse, and started toward hill. After travelling two days and nights, reached place; saw setting sun shining through hill. Knew right away that was where his shot hit. Went closer—stumbled over rocky fragments scattered for a half mile in line of bullet. Come to hole—knew the bullet hit there, because saw lead on the edges; walked in, and walked through; saw teamster on the other side, "indulging in profane language"—in fact, "cussin' considerable," because lightning had killed his team. Looked as finger directed—saw six dead oxen in line with hole through mountain; knew that was the bullet's work, but didn't say so to angry teamster. Thought best to be leaving; in consequence, didn't explore path of bullet any further; therefore, don't know where it stopped; don't know whether it stopped at all; in fact, rather think it didn't. Mounted horse; rode back through the hole made by the bullet, but never told Captain a word about it; to tell the truth, was rather afraid he'd think it a hoax.

"It's a right big story, boys," said Toby, in conclusion; "but it's true, sure as shooting. Nothing to do with Maynard rifle but load her up, turn her North, and pull trigger. If twenty of them don't clean out all Yankeedom, then I'm a liar, that's all."
—*The Intelligencer, (Oxford, Mississippi.)*

DR. WATTS TO JONATHAN.

(A Spiritual Communication.—Medium, MISS PUNCH.)

Let Dons delight to shoot and smite
Their fellers, no ways slow;
Let coons and wild-cats scratch and fight,
'Cos 'tis their natur' too;
But, Yankees, guess you shouldn't let
Sich 'tarnal dander rise;
Your hands warn't made to draw the bead
On one another's eyes.

THE venerable Gen. Samuel L. Williams, of Sterling, Ky., upon being cheered by the Union Guard of that place, thus addressed the men:—"When I was a much younger man, I followed that flag; it was in 1812; the enemy was threatening our young and rising country. Under that banner we conquered. And can I now be such a dastard as to forget it? to abandon it? No, no! If Kentucky secedes, I will not. I will be true to that Union. They may take my property—strip me of all, even take the little remnant of my life—but, as God is my witness, they can never make me recognize allegiance to any Government but the Union, with its glorious Stars and Stripes."—*N. Y. World, May* 25.

MR. JOHN LINDSAY, a prominent butcher in the First Market, at Richmond, has the honor of being the first citizen of Virginia created since the Ordinance of Secession was passed. Though for nearly 30 years a resident of Richmond, his genuine English pride had always revolted at the idea of becoming a "fellow-citizen" with the Yankees, and he withheld his allegiance to the "United States." He found, however, no compunctious visitings when taking an oath to be loyal and true to the Constitution of the Sovereign State of Virginia. If the State does not get many adopted citizens in future, they are likely to be good ones.—*Richmond Examiner, May 23.*

THE *Memphis Appeal* prints the following reply of Mr. A. T. Stewart, of New York, to a letter from Mr. J. P. Sprague, of Memphis:—

"NEW YORK, *April* 29, 1861.

"DEAR SIR:—Your letter requesting to know whether or not I had offered a million of dollars to the Government for the purposes of the war, and at the same time informing me that neither yourself nor your friends would pay their debts to the firm as they matured, has been received.

"The intention not to pay seems to be universal in the South, aggravated in your case by the assurance that it does not arise from inability; but, whatever may be your determination, or that of others at the South, it shall not change my course. All that I have of position and wealth I owe to the free institutions of the United States, under which, in common with all others North and South, protection to life, liberty, and property, have been enjoyed in the fullest manner. The Government to which these blessings are due calls on her citizens to protect the Capital of the Union from threatened assault; and, although the offer to which you refer has not in terms been made by me, I yet dedicate all that I have, and will, if need, my life, to the service of the country—for to that country I am bound by the strongest ties of affection and duty.

"I had hoped that Tennessee would be loyal to the Constitution. But, however extensive may be secession or repudiators, as long as there are any to uphold the sovereignty of the United States, I shall be with them, supporting the flag.

"Yours, &c.,   ALEXANDER T. STEWART."
—*Maine Republican Journal, May 24.*

ADVENTURES OF A MARYLANDER.—"I visited Montgomery, hoping to recover my set of mathematical and topographical instruments which were taken from me in April, or, failing in that, to obtain some remuneration. The only satisfaction obtained, was the alternative of taking service under the Jeff. Davis Government as Captain of Engineers, with the return of my instruments,—or leaving Montgomery within *ten hours,* and the 'Seceded States' within three days. I chose *the latter,* of course, and a pass, '*good for three days,*' was given me by Mr. President Davis. My trunks, containing my wardrobe and books, were at Tuskegee, but I had no leisure to go in that direction, and took the first train Northward, *unencumbered with luggage.*

"Everywhere the cars were crowded with troops hastening to Virginia. At Culpepper Custom-House I was detained all night, and threatened with a *hemp cravat.* On Tuesday morning, being *forbidden the ears,* a friend loaned me a splendid horse, and bade me 'ride him to death,' if necessary; *and I did.* He fell under me within four miles of Alexandria, having gone 46 miles in five and a half hours. During that ride I saw four men hanging to limbs of trees. I had *no leisure for inquiries,* but heard in Alexandria that several Union men had been hung for expressing their sentiments at the election polls.

"In Alexandria I was caught again by a picket guard, who were determined to detain me over night;

and, as *my* 'pass-time' would expire at midnight, they determined to indulge in a little *pastime* of their own, and hang me at daylight. I bribed the rascals, however, with all the money I had, and a gold watch; and, stealing a crazy old boat for me from a schooner, they sent me adrift, and after two hours' alternate bailing and sculling, I landed in a *swamp* on the *American side* of the Potomac. Floundering out of the mudhole, I footed it to Washington—a distance of eight miles—arriving at 9 A. M. Friday morning, and presented myself to President Lincoln, a beautiful specimen of the genus Mud-lark."—*Albany Evening Journal, May 30.*

FUN AMONG THE SOLDIERS.—A letter from Washington says:—"I am living luxuriously, at present, on the top of a very respectable fence, and fare sumptuously on three granite biscuits a day, and a glass of water, weakened with brandy. A high private in the Twenty-second Regiment has promised to let me have one of his square pocket handkerchiefs for a sheet the first rainy night; and I never go to bed on my comfortable window-brush without thinking how many poor creatures there are in this world who have to sleep on hair mattresses all their lives. Before the great rush of Fire Zouaves and the rest of the menagerie commenced, I boarded exclusively on a front stoop on Pennsylvania avenue, and used to slumber, regardless of expense, in a well-conducted ash-box; but the military monopolize all such accommodations now, and I give way for the sake of my country.

"I tell you, my boy, we're having high old times here just now, and if they get any higher, I shan't be able to afford to stay. The city is 'in danger' every other hour, and, as a veteran in the Fire Zouaves remarked, there seems to be enough danger lying around loose at Arlington Heights to make a very good blood-and-thunder fiction, in numerous pages. If the vigilant and well-educated sentinels happen to see a nigger on the upper side of the Potomac, they sing out: 'Here they come!' and the whole blessed army is snapping caps in less than a minute. Then all the reporters telegraph to their papers in New York and Philadelphia, that 'Jeff. Davis is within two minutes' walk of the Capital, with a few millions of men,' and all the free States send six more regiments apiece to crowd us a little more. I sha'n't stand much more crowding, for my fence is full now, and there were six applications yesterday to rent an improved knot-hole. My landlord says, that if more than three chaps set up housekeeping on one post, he'll be obliged to raise the rent.

"The greatest confidence in Gen. Scott is felt by all, and it would do you good to see the gay old hero take the oath. He takes it after every meal, and the first thing when he gets up in the morning.

"Those Fire Zouaves are fellows of awful suction, I tell you. Just for greens, I asked one of them, yesterday, what he came here for? 'Ha!' says he, shutting one eye, 'we came here to strike for your altars and your fires—especially your *fires!*' Gen. Scott says that if he wanted to make those chaps break through the army of the foe, he'd have a firebell rung for some district on the other side of the rebels. He says that half a million of the traitors couldn't keep the Fire Zouaves out of that district five minutes. I believe him, my boy!"—*N. Y. Express, May 31.*

THE *Memphis Avalanche* asks the Cairoites if they

are aware that the South has a company of bear-hunters awaiting their arrival at Memphis, whose special duty it will be to scalp the officers of the Sucker army. In reply, the *Springfield Journal* says :— "Scalping is not our game. Our Sucker boys are now on a grand '*whaling expedition*,' and if those Arkansas *bar*-tenders get some of Uncle Sam's harpoons in their *blubber*, they will stop *blowing*, and want *succors*."—*Cairo (Ill.) Gazette, May* 30.

ARLINGTON HOUSE, on the Potomac, opposite Washington, is now the head-quarters of Gen. McDowell. The N. Y. 8th, Col. Lyons, is quartered there, with their battery of light artillery. The mansion is in the old Revolutionary style,—solid, wide-spread, and low. Gen. Lee left many pictures and relics of the Revolution. In the entry are the paintings of Revolutionary sons, painted in his old age by George Washington Custis. The dining-room is adorned with, among other things, three deer's heads, from deer actually killed by Washington. A fine engraving of the Duke of Wellington confronts a full-length oil painting of " Light-Horse Harry," the father of Gen. Lee. A few books and letters lie about, marked with the eminent names of Lee and Custis.—*N. Y. Express, May* 30.

WHAT ONE NOBLE WOMAN CAN DO.—Mrs. Eliza Gray Fisher, a lady of Boston, Mass., past the age of threescore years, knowing from experience the necessities of the volunteer soldier, having lost a grandfather in the Revolutionary war, and a father in the war of 1812, determined, immediately upon the issue of the present call for volunteers, to provide a complete outfit of under clothing for an entire company. This, notwithstanding the severe pressure of domestic duties, with the aid of several ladies in Rev. Dr. Dewey's society, she has accomplished in the most satisfactory manner. The articles are as follows, and are of the best materials and most thorough workmanship :—130 shirts, 130 pairs of drawers, 130 towels, 130 pocket-handkerchiefs, 130 pairs of socks, 12 hospital gowns, 55 bags containing needles, pins, thread, &c., 65 Havelock caps, 500 yards bandages. Such women are of the true Revolutionary stock,—all honor to them.—*Boston Transcript, May* 27.

PREPARE FOR HARD TIMES.—We are, in all probability, upon the verge of a general and protracted war between the North and the South, in which the utmost strength of both sections will be tested. In a war, business will be utterly prostrated, money will be scarce, and times will be hard. We feel it to be our duty to warn the Southern people of this highly probable state of things in time. There should be universal preparation for it. No money should be uselessly spent. There will be no difficulty in the South on the score of courage and fighting men. But our army must be provided with subsistence ; the families of the soldiers must be maintained in their absence, if they be poor ; and the people who stay at home must live. Under such circumstances, any extravagance, or unnecessary expenditure of money, would be criminal. Every family should be put upon a war-footing, in the financial as well as military sense. And it is not too late, even now, to plant corn. Every additional acre of corn that can now be " put in," will be an additional bulwark for the support of Southern patriotism, Southern homes, and Southern honor. Now is the time for patriotic self-denial on the part of those who have hitherto

enjoyed ease and the luxuries of life. Now is the time for the patriotism of our Southern war men to manifest itself. We cannot all fight, but we can all be economical, and husband the resources of the country. While our brave boys are enduring the hardships of the camp, and are cheerfully undergoing labors to which they are not accustomed, and periling life in the trenches and in the field, and all for the defence of the homes at which we are remaining, who will complain of the necessary self-denial ? Southern ladies, wear your last year's bonnets and dresses. You will thus look much more beautiful and charming in the eyes of your patriotic husbands, fathers, brothers, and lovers. You are beautiful enough without costly outward adorning. Let us hear the conclusion of the whole matter : save money, and plant corn and potatoes, and husband every thing that will make food. Let us sacrifice our selfishness, and pride, and vanity, and consecrate all to the cause of the Church and the country—to God and Liberty. —*Natchez (Miss.) Courier, May* 29.

NEW HAVEN, CONN., *May* 26.—Mr. S. M. Brooks, a Massachusetts gentleman well known to several of our citizens as a person of unquestioned veracity, arrived in this city on Saturday night, having escaped from Fort Moultrie in an open boat, and managed to get aboard a schooner which carried him to New York. He was the guest, here, of Mr. James C. Parker, auctioneer at No. 151 Congress Avenue. He states that he and his brother were impressed into the Confederate service, and were placed in Fort Moultrie, where they assisted in working the guns during the attack on Fort Sumter.

He says that he will take a solemn oath that from six to seven hundred men were killed in that fort during the engagement !

Ten days ago he saw a schooner in the offing, and, managing to steal a skiff, put for her. After he had got some distance from the Fort he was discovered, and five or six shots were fired at him, but he escaped to the schooner, and reached New York. The above statement may be relied on.—*New Haven Palladium, May* 27.

A WRITER in the *Mobile Register* has a novel plan for capturing Fort Pickens. He says :—" It is well known that there are some chemicals so poisonous that an atmosphere impregnated with them makes it impossible to remain where they are, as they would destroy life, or interfere so much with respiration as to make fresh air indispensable. That the whole atmosphere of Fort Pickens can be so impregnated in a short time, can be shown to be by no means chimerical ; and not only chimerical, but easily effected. It will not cost so much as to be impracticable, and may cost infinitely less than a regular siege, not only in money, but life. Everybody almost knows that burning red pepper, even in small quantity, a teaspoonful, will clear the largest room of a crowd in a few moments ; that the least snuff of veratria will make one cough himself almost to death, and run great risk of coughing himself into consumption ; that some gases are so poisonous to life that the smallest quantity will kill—hydrocyanic acid and arsemurretted hydrogen, for instance. By mixing red pepper and veratria with the powder with which the shells are filled, or by filling large shells of extraordinary capacity with poisonous gases, and throwing them very rapidly into the fort, every living soul would have to leave in double quick time ; it would be impossible to breathe there. If the bombardment is effected in a dead calm, the result would be certain; and often at Fort Pickens there is not a breath of air stirring from daylight until 10 o'clock in the morning."—*National Intelligencer, May 29.*

SCOTT AND THE VETERAN.

BY BAYARD TAYLOR.

I.

An old and crippled veteran to the War Department came;
He sought the Chief who led him on many a field of fame—
The Chief who shouted " Forward ! " where'er his banner rose,
And bore its stars in triumph behind the flying foes.

II.

" Have you forgotten, General," the battered soldier cried,
" The days of Eighteen Hundred Twelve, when I was at your side?
Have you forgotten Johnson, that fought at Lundy's Lane?
'Tis true, I'm old and pensioned, but I want to fight again."

III.

" Have I forgotten ? " said the Chief; " my brave old soldier, No !
And here's the hand I gave you then, and let it tell you so;
But you have done your share, my friend; you're crippled, old, and gray,
And we have need of younger arms and fresher blood to-day."

IV.

" But, General," cried the veteran, a flush upon his brow,
" The very men who fought with us, they say, are traitors now;
They've torn the flag of Lundy's Lane—our old red, white, and blue;
And while a drop of blood is left, I'll show that drop is true.

V.

" I'm not so weak but I can strike, and I've a good old gun
To get the range of traitors' hearts, and pick them, one by one.
Your Minié rifles, and such arms, it ain't worth while to try;
I couldn't get the hang of them, but I'll keep my powder dry ! "

VI.

" God bless you, comrade ! " said the Chief; " God bless your loyal heart !
But younger men are in the field, and claim to have their part;
They'll plant our sacred banner in each rebellious town,
And woe, henceforth, to any hand that dares to pull it down ! "

VII.

" But, General,"—still persisting, the weeping veteran cried,
" I'm young enough to follow, so long as *you're* my guide;
And some, you know, must bite the dust, and that, at least, can I;
So, give the young ones place to fight, but me a place to die !

VIII.

" If they should fire on Pickens, let the Colonel in command
Put me upon the rampart, with the flag-staff in my hand;
No odds how hot the cannon-smoke, or how the shells may fly;
I'll hold the Stars and Stripes aloft, and hold them till I die !

IX.

" I'm ready, General, so you let a post to me be given,
Where Washington can see me, as he looks from highest heaven,
And say to Putnam at his side, or, may-be, General Wayne,
' There stands old Billy Johnson, that fought at Lundy's Lane ! '

X.

" And when the fight is hottest, before the traitors fly,
When shell and ball are screeching, and bursting in the sky,
If any shot should hit me, and lay me on my face,
My soul would go to Washington, and not to Arnold's place ! "

May 13, 1861.   —*The Independent.*

ELMER E. ELLSWORTH.

DIED MAY 24, 1861.

Weep, weep, Columbia ! Death, with traitorous hand,
  Has slain a Hero, quenched a manly flame;
Cast heartfelt sorrow o'er a throbbing land,
  And carved, for future years to read, a name,
  On the grand altar of our Country's fame.
    Strew roses o'er his corpse ;—a soldier's vow
  He took—a soldier's pall enwraps him now;
  At Glory's portal Death's red summons came.
Chant, O ye Land, the soldier's burial hymn
  O'er Ellsworth's bier; and as ye sadly turn,
With falt'ring voice, and eyes with teardrops dim,
  Swear ye that Retribution's torch may burn
In every breast ! A martyr's youthful blood
Cements your oath. Strike ! for your cause is good !
                                        A. A. A.
            —*N. Y. Tribune*, May 27.

ODE TO THE NORTH AND SOUTH.

O Jonathan and Jefferson,
  Come, listen to my song;
I can't decide, my word upon,
  Which of you is most wrong.
I do declare I am afraid
  To say which worse behaves,
The North, imposing bonds on Trade,
  Or South, that Man enslaves.

And here you are about to fight,
    And wage intestine war,
Not either of you in the right;
    What simpletons you are!
Too late your madness you will see,
    And when your passion cools,
"Snakes!" you will bellow; "how could we
Have been such 'tarnal fools!"

One thing is certain; that if you
    Blow out each other's brains,
'Twill be apparent what a few
    Each blockhead's skull contains.
You'll have just nothing for your cost,
    To show, when all is done.
Greatness and glory you'll have lost,
    And not a dollar won.

Oh, joined to us by blood, and by
    The bond of kindred speech,
And further, by the special tie
    Of slang, bound each to each,
All-fired gonies, soft-horn'd pair,
    Each other will you lick?
You everlastin' dolts, forbear!
    Throw down your arms right slick!

You'll chaw each other up, you two,
    Like those Kilkenny cats,
When they had better things to do,
    Improvin' off the rats.
Now come, shake hands, together jog
    On friendly yet once more;
Whip one another not; and flog
    Creation, as before!
                —*London Punch*, May 25.

"QUI TRANSTULIT SUSTINET."

(The motto upon the Coat of Arms of the State of
Connecticut.)

Dedicated to the Connecticut Volunteers.

BY L. L. WELD.

"*Qui transtulit sustinet!*" motto of light!
'Neath the folds of that banner we strike for the
    right;
Connecticut's watchword o'er hill and o'er plain,
"*The Hand that transplanted, that Hand will sus-
    tain.*"

"*Qui transtulit sustinet!*" On the broad fold
Of Connecticut's banner this motto's enrolled,
And flashed to the sunlight on morning's bright
    wings,
A promise of glory and honor it brings!
The promise of One who ne'er promised in vain,
"*The Hand that transplanted, that Hand will sus-
    tain.*"

Aye! and surely it has well sustained us thus far,
In Peace and in Plenty, in Want and in War.
When the foe has attacked us in battle array,
Then Connecticut's sons have stood first in the
    fray;
And faith in that watchword inspires us again,
For "*He who transplanted, will ever sustain.*"

And now, in the darkness of Treason's black night,
'Neath the folds of that banner we strike for the
    right!

For the RIGHT! 'tis OUR COUNTRY we're marching to
    save,—
The dear Flag of THE UNION in triumph *shall*
    wave!
Faith swells in each heart; Hope fires every vein!
"*And Thou who transplanted, oh! always sus-
    tain!*"
        —*Hartford (Conn.) Homestead*, April 18.

THE VOLUNTEER.

Hard by the porch of the village church,
    A dusty traveller halts awhile to rest;
    His head droops tired down upon his breast,
But the word of prayer wakes new life there.

"God bless the brave, who go to save
    Our country, in her dark, dread hour of danger!"
    The good man's voice was comfort to the stranger;
Duty wipes away a tear as he hurries to the war.
                —*Harvard Magazine.*

THE CAMP WAR SONG.

Raise the Banner, raise it high, boys!
    Let it float against the sky;
"God be with us!" this our cry, boys;
    Under it we'll do, or die.
1ST CHO.—Arise to glory, glory, glory!
    Our country calls—march on! march on.
2D CHO.—Co-ca-che-lunk-che-lunk-che-la-ly,
    Co-ca-che-lunk-che-lunk-che-lay,
    Co-ca-che-lunk-che-lunk-che-la-ly,
    Rig-a-ge-dig, and away we go!

Rebel miscreants, stand from under;
    Ye who bear the traitor's name!
Every star's a bolt of thunder—
    Every stripe a living flame!
    Arise, &c.

By our patriot sires in glory,
    By our sainted Washington,
We will fight, till every Tory
    Falls, that breathes beneath the sun!
    Arise, &c.

By our homes, our hearths, and altars,
    By our sweethearts, children, wives,
He who from our Union falters,
    Dies, hath he a thousand lives!
    Arise, &c.

Under Scott, our valiant leader,
    We will lay the traitors low;
Crushed to earth, each vile seceder
    Soon shall to our vengeance bow.
    Arise, &c.

Anderson! thy name shall cheer us
    'Mid the war-field's bloody strife;
Old Fort Sumter yet shall hear us
    Call her battlements to life!
    Arise, &c.

God of battles! we implore Thee,
    Nerve our souls, make strong our arms;
Bless us, as we bow before Thee,
    In the midst of war's alarms.
    Arise, &c.

Our spangled banner waving o'er us,
  We come, avengers of the free!
Shout, boys, shout! the foe's before us!
Union—God—and Liberty!

1st Cho.—Arise to glory, glory, glory!
    Our country calls—march on! march on!

2d Cho.—Co-ca-che-lunk-che-lunk-che-la-ly,
    Co-ca-che-lunk-che-lunk-che-lay,
    Co-ca-che-lunk-che-lunk-che-la-ly,
    Rig-a-ge-dig, and away we go!

THE NATION'S CALL.

BY JESSE H. BERRY.

"To arms!" the voice of Freedom calls,
  Nor calls in vain;
Up, from the fields, the shops, the halls,
The busy street, the city walls,
  Rush martial men.

Throbbing and quick, the nation's heart
  Beats rapidly;
And gathering on the nation's brow
A fearful thunder-cloud of wrath,
Illumed by lightning flashes, now
Marks in majesty and awe the path
  To victory.

Waving in grandeur o'er these hosts,
  The Stripes and Stars!
God of the bold, the brave, the free,
  Who nerved our fathers for the fight,
Grant to us *still*, our liberty,
An arm to strike for every right;—
  These are our prayers.
        Philadelphia Press, May 20.

GOD KEEP OUR ARMY PURE.

BY H. A. MOORE.

God keep our soldiers pure as brave,—
The gentle "Seventh," the "fierce Zouave,
  And all our gallant host;
Like the old warriors of Judea,
May *ours* be led by "Israel's Fear,"
  Be God their trust and boast.

May every camp amid the trees,
Where brown cheeks feel the cooling breeze,
  While firm feet press the sod,—
May every white tent on the hills,
Each round pavilion by the rills,
  Be holy unto God.

With willing hearts, but tearful eyes,
(Knowing what woe before us lies,)
  Brother and sire we send;
With ready hands, but bosoms sore,
(Knowing that some will come no more,)
  We speed each patriot friend.

We give them to the camp, the field;
The dearest things of life we yield,
  Nor grudge the sacrifice.
Take one, take *all*, O Tented Plain!
O Battle Field! But if again
  Our offerings meet our eyes;—

If from the bloody strife they come,
Once more to rest, in peace, at home,
  Return them *pure* as *brave*.
The loyal heart, the sturdy frame,
We venture; but *the clean, good name*,
  O War, thou terror, *save!*

God, save our fathers, brothers, friends,
From all the evil which attends,
  Watching for brave men's souls;
Within, without, where soldiers dwell,
In camp, and fort, and citadel,
  Too often it controls.

This war is Thine! we do not shrink;
The wine is red, but we will drink;—
  All, all we will endure.
Not *blood unto the horses' mane*,
Not *heaped-up friends, dead on the plain*,
Shall our wrung hearts of courage drain,
  So our dear host be pure!
  God, keep our soldiers pure!

REDEMPTION.

Hush quivering sighs!
  Dry streaming eyes,
Who watch the war-cloud's billowy course;
  For nations rise
  Through sacrifice;
For this, earth bears her children's loss;
For this the scourge, for this the cross.

Pray, mothers, pray!
  For those who may
'Mid warring armies sink to rest;
  But in their loss,
  Behold the cross,
And in each blood-drop from each breast,
See the red tide that Calvary pressed.

"We did not fear!"
  Year after year
The nation held its prosperous way;—
  Grew white with cant,
  And huge with rant,
And cried, "O, hear the asses bray,"
When wise men warned us of this day.

Manacled hands,
  Marred with brands,
Through weary years were reared on high,
  Pleading with tears.
  Who hears? Who hears
Their tearful pleading, woful cry,—
In Slavery's hell let us not die!

Through threatening death,
  With moaning breath,
From worse than death, they Northward fled;
  Those pleading hands,
  In Freedom's lands,
To Freedom's sons, were raised her head,
With eyes that spake their harrowing dread.

But we've stood by,
  All leashed and "spry,"
We Northern slave-hounds, giving tongue,
  Until we heard
  Our master's word—
Then off upon his track we sprung;
Fast to his bleeding form we hung.

Our manhood gone,
They gave us scorn—
Our Southern masters—for our pains ;
Hot insults hiss—
(We thought it bliss !)
Their loathsome scorns, polluting stains,
And hounded better for our shames.

They bolder grew—
(Chivalrous crew !)
And swore the people's mighty will
Should never o'er
The Southern shore
Its sovereign purposes fulfil,
Or tread the Capitoline hill.

He prayed *so* hard,
And " hem'd " and " ha'd,"
The Wheatland Sage, with feigned surprise.
And what did we ?
(Shades of the Free !)
Did we from off our knees arise ?
No ! no ! we whimpered, " Compromise ! "

It came at last—
Hell !—well, 'tis past,
That damned blow, fair in our eyes.
Our boiling blood
Flew in a flood
Through every vein. The nation cries,
War to the death ! till every traitor dies !

Hear, Freemen, hear !
Crush dastard fear !
Gird Freedom's armor on your back.
See ! see, afar,
Through gathering war,
Our banner-bird looms through the rack—
The Eagle's on the Viper's track !

It may be years,
Ere bondsmen's tears
Shall cease to flow from shore to shore.
But come it will—
(Stand still ! stand still !)
The fiery pillar goes before—
The Red Sea's crossed—They're slaves no more !

Dry streaming eyes,
Hush quivering sighs,
Who watch the war-clouds' billowy course ;
For nations rise
Through sacrifice ;
For this, earth bears her children's loss,
For this the scourge, for this the cross.

W. F. L.

IT IS GREAT FOR OUR COUNTRY TO DIE.

BY JAMES G. PERCIVAL.

Oh ! it is great for our country to die, where ranks
are contending ;
Bright is the wreath of our fame ; glory awaits us
for aye—
Glory that never is dim, shining on with light never-
ending—
Glory that never shall fade, never, O never, away !

Oh ! it is sweet for our country to die ! How softly
reposes
Warrior youth on his bier, wet by the tears of his
love,

Wet by a mother's warm tears ; they crown him with
garlands of roses,
Weep, and then joyously turn, bright where he
triumphs above.

Not to the shades shall the youth descend who for
country hath perished ;
Hebe awaits him in heaven, welcomes him there
with her smile ;
There at the banquet divine, the patriot spirit is
cherished ;
Gods love the young who ascend pure from the
funeral pile.

Not to Elysian fields, by the still, oblivious river ;
Not to the isles of the blest, over the blue, rolling
sea ;
But on Olympian heights shall dwell the devoted forever ;
There shall assemble the good, there the wise,
valiant, and free.

Oh ! then how great for our country to die—in the
front rank to perish,
Firm with our breast to the foe, Victory's shout in
our ear !
Long they our statues shall crown, in songs our
memory cherish ;
We shall look forth from our heaven, pleased the
sweet music to hear.

—*Boston Transcript*, May 28.

SONG FOR BATTLE.

AIR—*Marseillaise.*

I.

Oh, comrades going forth to battle,
Forget to doubt, forget to fear ;
And when the balls around us rattle,
Let step be firm, and eye be clear.
See how the foeman's lines are swaying ;
See how they waver left and right ;
Charge on, our Captain's voice obeying,
And put their breaking ranks to flight !

Arise ! arise, ye brave,
And take your swords in hand ;
March on, march on, resolved to save
Our Union and our land !

II.

See where our sacred flag is flying,
Each star and every stripe is there ;
Oh, swear to guard it well, relying
Upon the cause that bids us swear.
It guards us well on land and water,
And speaks a mighty Union's praise ;
Defend it now 'mid smoke and slaughter,
Where bay'nets stab and muskets blaze.

Arise, arise, ye brave,
And take your swords in hand ;
March on, march on, resolved to save
Our Union and our land.

III.

But is the strife of our beginning ?
And do we thirst for Southern blood ?
Oh, no ; when traitors cease from sinning,
We'll clasp the South in brotherhood.

Though now the battle-shouts are ringing,
And anger flames from every eye,
Yet are we safe who join our singing,
" The Union—it shall never die."

Arise, arise, ye brave,
And take your swords in hand;
March on, march on, resolved to save
Our Union and our land.   C. B.
—*N. Y. Evening Post*, May 30.

SONGS OF THE REBELS.

NORTH CAROLINA CALL TO ARMS.

AIR—"*The Old North State*."

BY MRS. WILLIS L. MILLER.

Ye sons of Carolina, awake from your dreaming !
The minions of Lincoln upon us are streaming !
Oh, wait not for argument, call, or persuasion,
To meet at the *onset* this treacherous invasion !
    Defend, defend the old North State forever ;
    Defend, defend the good old North State.

Oh, think of the maidens, the wives, and the mothers !
Fly ye to the rescue, sons, husbands, and brothers,
And sink in oblivion all party and section ;
Your hearthstones are looking to you for protection !
    Defend, defend the old North State forever, &c.

" Her name stands the foremost in Liberty's story ! "
Oh, tarnish not *now* her fame and her glory !
Your fathers to save her their swords bravely wielded,
And she never *yet* has to tyranny yielded.
    Defend, defend the old North State forever, &c.

The babe in its sweetness, the child in its beauty,
Unconsciously urge you to action and duty !
By *all* that is sacred, by ALL to you tender,
Your country adjures you, arise and defend her !
    Defend, defend the old North State forever, &c.

The national eagle above us now floating,
Will soon on the vitals of loved ones be gloating ;
His talons will tear, and his beak will devour ;
Oh, spurn ye his sway, and delay not an hour !
    Defend, defend the old North State forever, &c.

" The Star-spangled Banner," dishonored, is streaming
O'er bands of fanatics—their swords are now gleam-
    ing ;
They thirst for the life-blood of those you most
    cherish,—
With brave hearts and true, then arouse, or they
    perish !
    Defend, defend the old North State forever, &c.

Round the flag of the South, oh, in thousands now
    rally,
For the hour's departed when freemen may dally !
Your all is at stake—then go forth, and God speed
    you,
And onward to glory and victory lead you !
    " Hurrah ! hurrah ! the old North State forever !
    Hurrah ! hurrah ! the good old North State."
THOMASVILLE, N. C., *April* 15, 1861.

DIXIE.

SOUTHRONS, HEAR YOUR COUNTRY CALL YOU

BY ALBERT PIKE.

Southrons, hear your country call you !
Up, lest worse than death befall you !
    To arms ! To arms ! To arms, in Dixie !
Lo ! all the beacon-fires are lighted,—
Let all hearts be now united !
    To arms ! To arms ! To arms, in Dixie !
        Advance the flag of Dixie !
            Hurrah ! hurrah !
    For Dixie's land we take our stand,
    And live or die for Dixie !
        To arms ! To arms !
    And conquer peace for Dixie !
        To arms ! To arms !
    And conquer peace for Dixie !

Hear the Northern thunders mutter !
Northern flags in South wind flutter ;
    To arms ! &c.
        Advance the flag of Dixie ! &c.

Fear no danger ! Shun no labor !
Lift up rifle, pike, and sabre !
    To arms ! &c .
Shoulder pressing close to shoulder,
Let the odds make each heart bolder !
    To arms ! &c.
        Advance the flag of Dixie ! &c.

How the South's great heart rejoices,
At your cannons' ringing voices !
    To arms ! &c.
For faith betrayed, and pledges broken,
Wrongs inflicted, insults spoken,
    To arms ! &c.
        Advance the flag of Dixie ! &c.

Strong as lions, swift as eagles,
Back to their kennels hunt these beagles !
    To arms ! &c.
Cut the unequal words asunder !
Let them then each other plunder !
    To arms ! &c.
        Advance the flag of Dixie ! &c.

Swear upon your country's altar,
Never to submit or falter !
    To arms ! &c.
Till the spoilers are defeated,
Till the Lord's work is completed.
    To arms ! &c.
        Advance the flag of Dixie ! &c.

Halt not, till our Federation
Secures among Earth's Powers its station !
    To arms ! &c.
Then at peace, and crowned with glory,
Hear your children tell the story !
    To arms ! &c.
        Advance the flag of Dixie ! &c.

If the loved ones weep in sadness,
Victory soon shall bring them gladness.
    To arms ! &c.
Exultant pride soon banish sorrow ;
Smiles chase tears away to-morrow.
    To arms ! &c.
        Advance the flag of Dixie ! &c.
            —*Natchez* (*Miss.*) *Courier*, May 30.

FROM THE SOUTH TO THE NORTH.

BY C. L. S.

There is no union, when the hearts
  That once were bound together,
Have felt the stroke that coldly parts
  All kindly ties forever.
Then, oh ! your cruel hands draw back,
  And let us be divided
In peace, since it is proved we lack
  The grace to live united.

We cannot bear your scorn and pride,
  Your malice and your taunting,
That have for years our patience tried—
  Your hypocritic canting.
We WILL not bow our necks beneath
  The yoke that you decree us;
We WILL be free, though only death
  Should have the power to free us !

Oh, Southern sons are bold to dare,
  And Southern hearts courageous ;
Nor meekly will they longer bear
  Oppression so outrageous.
And you shall feel our honest wrath,
  If hearts so cold *can* feel ;
Shall meet us in your Southern path,
  And prove our Southern steel.

We ask no favor at your hand—
  No gifts, and no affection—
But only peace upon our land,
  And none of your protection.
We ask you now, henceforth, to know
  We are a separate nation ;
And be assured, we'll fully show
  We scorn your " proclamation."

We were not first to break the peace
  That blessed our happy land ;
We loved the quiet, calm, and ease,
  Too well to raise a hand,
Till fierce oppression stronger grew,
  And bitter were your sneers—
Then to our land we must be true,
  Or show a coward's fears !

We loved our banner while it waved
  An emblem of our Union ;
The fiercest danger we had braved
  To guard that sweet communion.
But when it proved that " stripes " alone
  Were for our sunny South,
And all the " stars " in triumph shone
  Above the chilly North ;

Then—not till then—our voices rose
  In one tumultuous wave—
We WILL the tyranny oppose,
  Or find a bloody grave !
Another flag shall lead our hosts
  To battle on the plain ;
The " rebels " will defy your boasts,
  And prove your sneering vain !

There is no danger we could fear—
  No hardship or privation,
To free the land we hold so dear,
  From tyrannous dictation.

Blockade her ports,—her seas shall swell
  Beneath your ships of war,
And every breeze in anger tell
  Your tyranny afar.

Her wealth may fail—her commerce droop
  With every foreign nation ;
But mark you, if her pride shall stoop,
  Or her determination !
The products of her fields will be
  For food and raiment too ;—
From mountain cliff to rolling sea,
  Her children will be true.

Her banner may not always wave
  On victory's fickle breath ;
The young, the chivalrous and brave,
  May feel the hand of death ;
But, when her gallant sons have died,
  Her daughters will remain—
Nor crushed will be her Southern pride,
  Till they too all are slain !

STAUNTON, VA., *May 7, 1861.*
                    —*Richmond Whig*, May 13.

REVERIES OF WAR.

BY C. J. H.

Mantle my heart with the damp, dark pall,
  Black as the midnight, and heavy as sin ;
Over my spirit let misery fall ;
  Windows of hope, let no daylight in ;
Memory sink, and close out the tone
  Of olden days ; or of treasured past,
Light the great blaze of our wrongs alone ;
  Into the scales let their weight be cast.

Mantle my heart with the garb of steel ;
  Sing her the songs of revenge and right ;
Iron of rage, through my veins may I feel
  Thy strength to flow with the crimson bright.
Energy, wake ! and courage, come !
  With stirring chant of camp and field,
Blaze on the altars of hearts and home,
  Courage, and Honor, and Right, our shield.

Mantle my heart in the soldier's attire,
  Powder-blacked, soiled, and dusty with use ;
Nerve my arm to its truest fire,
  And in its scabbard my sabre loose ;
Breathe on my spirit thy hot breath, War !
  Fire my heart with thy honest pride ;
Shine in my face like a bright golden star,
  And muster the surge of the battle's tide.

Mantle my heart with the garb of strength !
  Justice, and Honor, and Truth, awake !
Nerve on to conquest, until at length
  The dawn of our noble peace shall break.
Sons of the South ! the grass is green,
  The shadows are full, and the shade is strong ;
The graves of our manly fathers are seen,
  And their courage and honor can fill our song.

The dead of the South drops its tears on the grave
  Where Washington, Jackson, and Clay repose ;
As fresh as the dew-drop, the honest and brave
  Will carry their virtues, or scatter their foes ;

The land of their love—of our hearts—is our pride,
  And we will stand by it and cherish its sod,
Though we pour to protect it our hearts' crimson
    tide,
  And dying, will beg its protection from God.

Mantle my heart with thy stern garb, War !
  Thrill through my veins with thy clarion tone !
Like a "pillar of cloud," and a bright blazing star,
  Is the flag of our bold and our new nation thrown,
The kind breeze of heaven will kiss its bright folds,
  And float them out grandly upon the pure air ;
It emblems the pride of many brave souls,
  And carries the incense of many a prayer.
               —*N. O. Picayune.*

LAND OF THE SOUTH.

BY A. F. LEONARD.

AIR—*"Friend of My Soul."*

Land of the South ! the fairest land
  Beneath Columbia's sky !
Proudly her hills of freedom stand,
  Her plains in beauty lie.
Her dotted hills, her traversed streams,
  Their annual wealth renew.
Land of the South ! in brightest dreams,
  No dearer spot we view.

Men of the South ! a free-born race,
  They vouch a patriot line ;
Ready a foeman's van to face,
  And guard their country's shrine.
By sire and son a haloing light
  Through time is borne along ;
They "nothing ask but what is right,
  And yield to nothing wrong."

Fair of the South ! rare beauty's crown
  Ye wear with matchless grace ;
No classic fair of old renown
  Deserve a higher place.
Your vestal robes alike become
  The palace and the cot ;
Wives, mothers, daughters ! every home
  Yet make a cherished spot.

Flag of the South ! aye, fling its folds
  Upon the kindred breeze ;
Emblem of dread to tyrant holds—
  Of freedom on the seas !
Forever may its stars and stripes
  In cloudless glory wave.
Red, white, and blue—eternal types
  Of nations free and brave.

States of the South ! the patriot's boast !
  Here equal laws have sway ;
No tyrant lord, nor despot host,
  Upon the weak may prey.
Then let them rule from sea to sea,
  And crown the queenly isle ;
Union of love and liberty,
  'Neath Heaven's approving smile.

God of the South ! protect this land
  From false and open foes !
Guided by Thine all-ruling hand,
  In vain will that oppose.

So mote the Ship of State move on
  Upon the unfathomed sea ;
Gallantly o'er the surges borne,
  The bulwark of the free !

KENTUCKY.

BY "ESTELLE."

"Just send for us Kentucky boys,
  And we'll protect you, ladies."   [OLD SONG.

Then leave us not, Kentucky boys,
  Though thick upon thy border,
The vulture flaps his restless wing,
  And scowls the dark marauder.

Kentucky blood is just as proud,
  Kentucky powder ready,
Kentucky hearts are just as brave,
  Kentucky nerve as steady,

As when the flag we once revered
  Unfolded o'er her proudly,
And for the South, Kentucky's voice,
  Undaunted, echoed loudly.

The lion-hearted hero then,
  Who led that gallant number,
Must surely feel a sad unrest
  Disturb his death-cold slumber.

And one whose sire on history's page
  Is blent in proudest story,
Fell on a Southern field, and bathed
  His dying brow in glory ;

Fell overcome by savage foes,
  Yet still their rage defying,
"*These*, give my father," cried the son,
  "And tell him how I'm dying."

But now that flag is vilely stained,
  Its sacred rights invaded ;
Wrong and dishonor wield the staff,—
  Its glory's sadly shaded.

And when we would its dying spark
  Snatch from the blackening ashes,
And worship once again its light,
  As through the world it flashes,

Kentucky leans upon her arms,
  And coldly looks about her,
Till hirelings at her very door
  Dare threaten and to flout her.

Desert us now, Kentucky boys,
  And on the future dawning,
Thy faded glory scarce will streak
  The first gray light of morning.

Heed not the starveling crew who hang
  Upon the blue Ohio ;
A craven heart each traitor bears,
  And dare not venture nigher.

And should they ?—Know ye not the blood
  Within our full hearts beaming,
At once ten thousand scabbards fly,
  Ten thousand blades are gleaming.

Then waken from thy nerveless sleep,
  Gird on thy well-tried armor,
And soon the braggart North will feel
  That right has strength to harm her.

Kentucky boys and girls have we—
  From us ye may not take them ;
Sad-hearted will ye give them up,
  And for the foe forsake them ?

Oh, Tennessee, twin-sister, grieves
  To take thy hand at parting,
And feel that from its farewell grasp
  A brother's blood is starting.

It must not be !—Kentucky, come !
  Virginia loudly calls thee,
And Maryland defenceless stands
  To share what fate befalls thee.

Come, ere the tyrant's chain is forged,
  From out the war-cloud looming ;
Come, ere thy palsied knee is bent,
  To hopeless ruin dooming.
          —*Memphis Appeal.*

An incident occurred in the United States Marshal's office at San Francisco, Cal., which is too good to be lost. It is told on good authority, and is, doubtless, substantially correct.

It is well known that there are several small models of ships in the Marshal's office, which have been ornamented with little secession flags about half the size of one's hand. They are made of paper, and colored with red and blue ink. One at the masthead of the largest ship bears the name of Jeff. Davis, and the others are the ordinary three-striped rag, recently adopted as the ensigns of the Southern Slave Confederacy. On account of the display of these flags, the only public place in the city, we believe, the Marshal's office is a sort of privileged quarters for Secessionists, and nothing is more common than to hear secession talk there. This has been particularly the case since the news of the breaking out of war.

The story goes, that while several gentlemen were sitting in the Marshal's office, attending to business, a big strapping fellow, all the way from South Carolina, with a revolver peeping out from under his coat-tail, strode into the place, with the air of a Tarquin, and exclaimed :

"Well, at last, thank God ! we've got these —— d—d nutmeg-selling, mackerel-catching, cod-livered Yankee sons of —— to come to taw. That's just what I've been wanting this many a day !—the nigger-thieving, psalm-singing abolitionists ! We'll skin 'em out of their boots."

The braggart had scarcely finished his tirade, when one of the gentlemen, Captain ——, of the ship ——, who was observed to be getting nervous, suddenly jumped up, and taking his place in front of the fellow, and shaking his fists, replied :

"Now, sir, I don't know you, and don't want to know you ; but I suppose you designate me as one of those nutmeg-selling, mackerel-catching, cod-livered Yankee sons of ——. I am captain of the ship ——, and I want you to understand that I will not allow any man to use such language respecting me and my people in my presence. And if you don't recant, I'll whip you here and now. I see your pis-

tol, but I don't care for it. You have insulted me, sir, and you shall answer for it."

The boaster, seeing the captain's determined bearing, and finding that he was in downright earnest, replied by saying that his remarks were general in their nature, and not by any means intended to apply to any particular person. Nothing was further from his purpose than to insult any person present, and particularly a stranger.

To this the irate captain retorted : "The language, sir, is an insult to the American name, and I for one will not stand it from any living man. No one but a traitor and a coward can talk in that way. Retract it ! retract it !" and with this he commenced advancing upon the Secessionist, who began weakening in the knees, and finally wilted, while Tarpaulin raked the traitor's fore and aft without mercy.—*Sacramento (Cal.) Bee, April* 29.

Corporal Tyler, of the Massachusetts Sixth Regiment, when describing his experience in Baltimore, says he saw a man with three stones under his arm and one in his hand, pelting away at the troops, when he fired at him, and—to use Mr. Tyler's own language—"*The man dropped the bricks, and laid down.*"

The *Charleston Mercury* calls the Yankee troops, now threatening the South, "tin peddlers." It is true that the Yankees have, generally, in their visits South, peddled tin, but we guess they mean to peddle lead this time."—*Louisville Journal.*

Greatly Descended Men.—The son of Light-Horse Harry Lee, of Revolutionary renown, commands the forces of Virginia. His chief aid is J. A. Washington, the only living representative of Washington. The great-grandson of Thomas Jefferson commands the Howitzer Battery at Richmond. A grandson of Patrick Henry is Captain of the Virginia forces. The descendants of Chief Justice Marshall are in the ranks and in command.—*Erie (Pa.) Observer, May* 25.

The house of the celebrated, bold-hearted, and outspoken Parson Brownlow, is the only one in Knoxville, Tenn., over which the Stars and Stripes are floating. A few days ago two armed Secessionists went, at 6 o'clock in the morning, to haul down the Stars and Stripes. Miss Brownlow, a brilliant young lady of 23, saw them on the piazza, and stepped out and demanded their business. They replied they had come to "take down them d—n Stars and Stripes." She instantly drew a revolver from her side, and presenting it, said, "Go on ! I'm good for one of you, and I think for both !"

"By the looks of that girl's eye, she'll shoot," one remarked. "I think we had better not try it ; we'll go back and get more men," said the other.

"Go and get more men," said the noble lady ; "get more men, and come and take it down, if you dare ! "

They returned with a company of ninety armed men, and demanded that the flag should be hauled down. But on discovering that the house was filled with gallant men, armed to the teeth, who would rather die as dearly as possible than see their country's flag dishonored, the Secessionists retired.

When our informant left Knoxville, the Stars and Stripes still floated over Parson Brownlow's house. Long may they wave.—*Chicago Journal.*

WE find this remarkable paragraph in the editorial columns of the *Rochester Union :*—" This great and long-standing conspiracy was well known in its outlines to Mr. Buchanan himself. *We heard from his own lips,* previous to his entering upon the duties of the Presidency, that he had been reliably informed (we think he said by Gov. Wise) that the officers of the army and navy had been polled on the question whether, in case of a rupture between the two sections of the Union, *they would respectively go with the North or the South ; and that nearly every Southern man answered he would adhere to the section that gave him birth.* Here we have proof not only that this conspiracy had assumed its present determinate shape five years ago, and only waited for opportunity ; but that Mr. Buchanan was perfectly well aware of the fact at the very time when he took some of the leaders into his Cabinet ; and when he was passively aiding Cobb, Floyd, Thompson, and Toucey, in their plans to cripple the Federal Government, and assure the success of the rebellion."— *Ohio Statesman, May 25.*

A CORRESPONDENT of the *Boston Journal* gives the following reminiscence of the attack upon the Massachusetts Regiment by the Gorillas of Mobtown :—" There was one man who carried himself so bravely while in the midst of danger, that something more than a passing notice should be taken of him. Two days before that Friday, the Sixth were gathered in front of the State-House, Boston, to hear the parting words of Gov. Andrew. At the end of his remarks, the Governor presented the regiment with a standard, telling them to see to it that no foe should ever take it from them. They received it with cheers, and swore to die in its defence. Poor fellows, they little thought then how soon their mettle would be tested. Well, when they got out of the cars at Baltimore, to march across the city, the colors were given to the breeze, and borne aloft in defiance of every foe. The standard-bearer, as noble a fellow as ever wore the uniform of the Old Bay State, was Timothy Crowley. His two aids were Sergeants Derril and Marland. Unused, as, indeed, all our soldiers were, to the rough usage of actual warfare, it would not have been strange if Crowley had shown some signs of fear. Indeed, he might have rolled up the colors, which would inevitably call down upon him the hatred of the vast and murderous mob. But Crowley was not made of such stuff. He had sworn to stand by his standard, and with him it was either succeed, or die in the attempt. Pistols were freely fired, but the company saw at their head that standard proudly leading them on. No one who has never been in the service can imagine how the colors of a regiment keep up its courage. So long as they are defiant, the company have light hearts ; if they should be taken away, a strange distrust runs through the whole force. Well, the troops had lost their band ; they did not have even a fife and drum ; and so they kept their eyes fixed upon this standard. Tramp, tramp, tramp—left, left, left—the music of their own steady, measured tread—this was all they had. Crowley was the target for many a missile, for the mob knew that to disgrace the regiment, it was only necessary to down with the standard. Paving-stones flew thick and fast, some just grazing Crowley's head, and some hitting the standard itself, marks of which were shown us. And this shows the everlasting pluck of Crowley. One stone—my informant said it seemed as large as a hat—struck him just between the shoulders a terrible blow, and then rested on his knapsack. And yet Crowley did not budge. With a firm step he went on, carrying the rock on his knapsack for several yards, until one of the sergeants stepped up and knocked it off. And, said the chaplain, " Heaven only knows what our boys would have done if that standard had been taken ; they never would have recovered from such a disgrace." Such a noble act, it seems to me, is worthy of record. Crowley showed himself a man. It was not that impulsive kind of action which we call brave ; it was something better. The soldier who is only simply brave, stands only on the lowest round of the ladder of heroism. All men may be brave. Crowley was cool ; he knew beforehand what the consequences might be ; he reckoned all the chances. He showed true *courage*—an element of character which is Godlike ; it was not impulse—it was real manliness."—*N. Y. Tribune, June 8.*

THE DYING WORDS OF SENATOR DOUGLAS.—For a long time previous to his death, Senator Douglas had been in a semi-conscious condition. During the morning of his death his mind and energies rallied somewhat. Lying at apparent ease upon his bed, but with the mark of death upon his pale countenance, Mrs. Douglas, who sat, soothing him gently, by his bedside, painfully aware that the moment of final separation was approaching, asked him what message he wished to send to his sons Robert and Stephen, who were students at Georgetown. He answered not at first, and she tenderly repeated the question. " *Tell them,*" he then replied with a full voice, and an emphatic tone, " *Tell them to obey the laws and support the Constitution of the United States.*"

Let these dying words be recorded upon the tablets of undying, unfading, and undecaying history. They were the last words of a great man's advice to his beloved boys ; and let those who loved him, and have been moved by the eloquent words of his lips, take the advice to their own hearts, for their guidance in the hour when peril threatens the Republic, or disloyal influences are abroad in the land.

A short time after, he desired to be raised, and his wish was complied with, so that he might look out from his window once more, upon that city which had loved and honored him so long. One of his friends expressed a doubt as to the ease of his position, when he simply replied, " He is—comfortable." In his dying moments he faintly articulated, " Death, death, death," and his great soul passed away.— *Chicago Journal.*

CONTRABAND NEGROES.—General Ashley, member of Congress from Ohio, writes to the *Toledo* (Ohio) *Blade* the following account of the reception of the " contraband " slaves at Fortress Monroe :—

" You will have heard, by the time this reaches you, of the manner in which Gen. Butler disposed of Col. Mallory, who came into the fort under a flag of truce, to claim three of his loyal slaves who had fled from his kind and hospitable roof, and taken shelter in Fortress Monroe among strangers. Who will say that General Butler, so far as he went, was not right ? This Colonel Mallory had met General Butler in the Charleston and Baltimore Conventions, and with that impudence and assumption characteristic of the oligarchy, he came into General Butler's camp, and, though engaged in open treason against the Government, demands that he shall enforce the Fugitive Slave Law upon the soil of Virginia with United

States soldiers, and return him his happy and contented slaves.

"General Butler says, 'You hold that negro slaves are property, and that Virginia is no longer a part of the United States?'

"The Colonel answered, 'I do, sir.'

"General Butler then said, 'You are a lawyer, sir, and I want to know if you claim that the Fugitive Slave act of the United States is binding in a foreign nation; and if a foreign nation uses this kind of property to destroy the lives and property of citizens of the United States, if that species of property ought not to be regarded as contraband?'

"This was too much for the Colonel, and he knocked under and withdrew.

"This was but the beginning at Fort Monroe, and is but the beginning of a question which this Administration must meet and determine, viz., 'What shall be done with the slaves who refuse to fight against the Government of the United States, and escape from the traitors and come into our camps for protection?' If the Administration meets this question as it ought, well; if not, it will prove its overthrow. It is a question of more magnitude and importance than the rebellion itself; and woe to the public man or the party who proves false to the demands of humanity and justice.

"On Sunday, eight more stout, able-bodied men came in. General Butler said to me, 'As you went to see John Brown hung, and have some claim to control Virginia volunteers, I authorize you to see who and what those colored men are, and decide what is to be done with them.' He added, 'You had better examine them separately, and take down in writing the material part of their answers.'

WHAT THE NEGROES SAID.

"Before doing so, I went out to the fence where the slaves were standing, surrounded by about two hundred volunteers. I asked the colored men a few questions, and was about to go into the house to call them in separately, as suggested by the General, when one of the slaves said, 'Massa, what's you gwine to do wid us?'

"I told him that I did not know, but that we would not hurt them.

"'Oh, we knows dat,' quickly responded another; 'we knows you's our friends. What we wants to know is, whether you's gwine to send us back.'

"I answered that I had no authority over them, and no power to do any thing, but that my opinion was 'it would be some time before their masters would see them again.' I said this in a low, conversational tone of voice, without noticing that all the volunteers were eagerly listening; but no sooner had the words fallen from my lips, than a hundred voices shouted, 'Good! good!' and some in laughter and some in tears clapped their hands and gave three rousing cheers, which brought out the officers and General, who supposed I had been making a speech to the troops.

"This little incident tells me more plainly than ever, that what I said last winter in the House is true, when I declared that 'the logic of events told me unmistakably that slavery must die.'

"If I had time and you the space, I would give in their own words the material portion of the answers of the most intelligent slaves. There is one thing certain; every slave in the United States understands this rebellion, its causes and consequences, far better than ever I supposed. I asked one old man, who said he was a Methodist class-leader, to tell me frankly whether this matter was well understood by all the slaves, and he answered me that it was, and that he had 'prayed for it for many, many long years.'

"He said that their masters and all talked about it, and he added, 'Lor' bless you, honey—we don give it up last September dat the North's too much for us,' meaning, of course, that Mr. Lincoln's election was conceded even there by the slave masters, and was understood and hoped for by all the slaves. I asked the same man how many more would probably come into the fort. He said, 'A good many; and if we's not sent back, you'll see 'em 'fore to-morrow night.'

"I asked why so, and he said, 'Dey'll understan', if we's not sent back, dat we're 'mong our friends; for if de slaveholder sees us, we gets sent right back.' And sure enough, on Monday about forty or fifty more, of all ages, colors, and sexes, came into camp, and the guard was bound to arrest them."

THE capture of John B. Washington at Fairfax Court-House was a pleasant affair. As an infantry captain of the rebel force, he was prominent in the resistance to our cavalry, until a trooper rode up, caught him by the hair, lifted him bodily upon the pommel of his saddle, and, holding him in this position, charged twice through the town. Captain Washington complained bitterly, but, after having been lectured by Gen. Scott, he concluded to take the oath of allegiance, and was released. He is now with his family in this city.

Capt. Washington is a son of the late Col. John A. Washington, who was lost overboard from the San Francisco.—*The Independent, June 6.*

HARDEE'S TACTICS.—Hardee was Chief of a Board *to translate a system of Light Infantry Tactics* from the French. Lieut. Bennett of the Ordnance did the work, every word of it; and Hardee's name was attached to the translation! He never, in all probability, saw or read one word of it, until called upon to *study* it for the purpose of learning how to drill the cadets at West Point, when appointed to command them. He was the Commandant of Cadets, *not* the Superintendent of the Institution, for four years. As a soldier, his reputation in the army was never above mediocrity; to science he never made any pretension; and if we put him down as a tolerable cavalry officer, full justice is done him. As to "Hardee's Tactics," that is a French book, *translated* by Lieut. Bennett—Hardee being President of the Board which adopted it for our service.—*N. Y. Courier and Enquirer.*

NEW ORLEANS, *May* 1.—That the prospect is serious, we are not disposed to deny, but it contains nothing to dishearten or create alarm. The South is unconquerable on her own territory. Her armies are not composed of hired mercenaries, nor of the wretched offscourings of great cities, who are forced to choose between enrollment and starvation. They are made up for the most part of the youthful, the vigorous, the intelligent and devoted children of the soil. The cause we fight for is deemed sacred, and if its justification should demand the services of every able-bodied citizen, not one will be found to flinch from the ordeal. We may have many sacrifices to make, much suffering to endure, many precious lives to lose, much pecuniary and commercial distress to encounter, but all this and more will be cheerfully sustained, sooner than surrender our birthright to the despotic and fanatical hosts of the North. Nor must it be imagined that these losses and sacrifices will be confined to us. The North cannot live without Southern trade, and this is gone from her forever. She cannot put immense armies on a war footing and maintain them save at a fearful expense, which will tax all her resources to meet. Every blow she aims at us will recoil with terrible force upon itself. In striving to conquer us, the North is exhausting her wealth, her strength, and her productive energies, and will feel the pernicious consequences of her folly and iniquity for countless years. Her people, in the paroxysm of insanity under which they labor, fail to perceive the desperate act of suicide they are committing; but when it will have been irretrievably consummated, they will be haunted by vain regrets for the ruin and impoverishment they have brought upon themselves—and all this, too, without accomplishing the wicked object they have at heart.—*N. O. Bee, May* 4.

ANOTHER ROMAN MOTHER.—At Bangor, Me., a young man offered himself as a recruit at one of the offices in that city, who, evidently being a minor, was asked if he had his father's permission to volunteer. He replied that he had no father; but admitted that his mother was willing. "Then you must get your mother's consent," said the officer. The young man retired, and returned with the following brief but noble letter:—"*He is my all; but I freely give him to my country!*"—*Bangor Whig, and Boston Transcript, May* 4.

A PATRIOTIC BLACKSMITH.—Before the departure of the 14th N. Y. Regiment, a man who carried on a blacksmith shop in connection with two of his sons, went to the head-quarters and concluded to enlist. He said that he could leave the blacksmith business in the hands of the boys—"he couldn't stand it any longer, and go he must." He was enlisted.

Next day down comes the oldest of the boys. The blacksmith's business "wasn't very drivin'," and he guessed John could take care of it." "Well," said the old man, "Go it." And the oldest son went it. But the following day John made his appearance. He felt lonesome, and had shut up the shop. The father remonstrated, but the boy would enlist, and enlist he did. Now the old gentleman had two more sons who "worked the farm" near Flushing, Long Island. The military fever seems to have run in the family, for no sooner had the father and two older brothers enlisted, than the younger sons came in for a like purpose. The *pater-familias* was a man of few words, but he said that he "wouldn't stand this anyhow." The blacksmith business might go to—some other place, but the farm must be looked after. So the boys were sent home. Presently one of them reappeared. They had concluded that one could manage the farm, and had tossed up who should go with the Fourteenth, and he had won the chance.

This arrangement was finally agreed to. But on the day of departure the last boy of the family was on hand to join and on foot for marching. The old man was somewhat puzzled to know what arrangement could have been made which would allow all of the family to go, but the explanation of the boy solved the difficulty: "Father," said he, with a confidential chuckle in the old man's ear, "I've let the farm on shares!" The whole family, father and four sons, went with the Fourteenth Regiment.—*N. Y. Evening Post, May* 16.

FOR WHAT DOES THE SOUTH FIGHT?—For every thing worth living for. To resist aggression, to resist subjugation, to resist a military despotism, to protect our lives, and the lives of our women and children, from the brutal and infuriate passions of the mob, and to maintain the doctrine of our Revolutionary sires, that the consent of the governed is the only true and legitimate source of power! He that falters is derelict to every dictate of patriotism.—*Montgomery Mail, May* 13.

THERE were plenty of Secessionists at Cairo, Ill., but the Chicago soldiers came, and brought their artillery. A farmer of that vicinity remarked—"I tell you what it is, them brass missionaries has converted a heap of folks that was on the anxious seat."—*Providence Journal.*

NEW YORK, *May* 25.—This morning, about one o'clock, a party of ladies and gentlemen, numbering some forty in all, alighted from one of the Third Avenue cars, and drew up in line at the southwest corner of the Park Barracks. The gentlemen formed a half-circle, in the centre of which the ladies took their position—the crowd inside of the barracks clustering about the paling, wondering what was to come of the gathering. The morning was one of the very loveliest, and well calculated to bring feelings of inspiration to the bosoms of the very dullest. The queen of night shone with its clearest ray, and under the floods of splendid light which it poured down upon the camp ground, the ladies' silvery voices rang out the ever-cheering and patriotic "Star-spangled Banner."

The ladies sang unaccompanied by male voices. The effect produced by their clear, beautiful tones, was indescribable. The denizens of the Astor, who had laid themselves away for the night on couches of luxury, and the poor mendicants, who had sought repose on the forsaken door-steps, were alike charmed from their resting-places to listen to this novel concert of the early morning hour. As the last strains of the melody died away in the distance, they, too, sent up their voices with the lusty cheers of the soldiers, who complimented the ladies with three-times-three and a "tiger." It was a stirring scene, and one long to be remembered by those who witnessed it. At the conclusion of the singing, the gentlemen who accompanied the ladies stepped up to the palings, and furnished the soldiers with an abundant supply of cigars and tobacco. The company then took their departure as noiselessly as they had come, attended by the best wishes of the men they had so generously remembered.—*N. Y. Sunday Mercury, May* 26.

CHEERING SIGNS IN NEW YORK.—The *N. Y. Sun* proclaims that the rebels are already encamped in New York. "Jeff. Davis has succeeded in enlisting recruits in this city, and whoever passes through the streets, within a few blocks from our office, can hear the click of their guards and the ring of Southern steel, as they ground arms and shoulder arms. He has sentinels all the way through Long Island, from within a mile of Fort Hamilton, and through Manhattan Island, from within hail of the ferry-boats as they pass."—*Richmond Whig, May* 13.

A LETTER-WRITER in Southern Delaware says:— "It is said that Delaware lost one-fifth of her white population in cementing the Union, and will, if need be, sacrifice as many again to preserve it. The blacks here give us more trouble than any thing else. It is said they will massacre the whites. I can hardly believe it, but there are some strong indications that way. In the western part of this (' Hundred ') township, the negroes have had two or three ' buryings' within a few days of each other, and as the white population in this vicinity could not discover that any darkies were missing, they thought something must be wrong, and on opening the newly-made graves, the coffins were all right, but instead of a dead darkey, we found them filled to the brim with muskets and ammunition."—*N. Y. Times, May 12.*

JEWELS ON THE ALTAR OF HER COUNTRY.—The *Richmond Examiner* records the following worthy example of noble patriotism:—"One of the most amiable and fashionable young belles of our city placed in the hands of a friend her casket of jewels, valued at $1,200, which she instructed him to sell to the best account, and appropriate the proceeds to the benefit of such volunteer soldiers of the State as might require it. This generous gift was not all, however; she promised to put by, from her ' pin-money,' one dollar each day, as long as the revolution might continue, the aggregate to be handed over quarterly to some responsible party for the purposes the same as above. Lastly, she has patriotically determined never to wear a jewel or an ornament of any kind, until the independence of the South is recognized by the Federal Government and the world!"—*N. O. Picayune, May 12.*

A CORRESPONDENT of the *Memphis Argus*, writing from Lynchburg, Va., says:—"We have two regiments from Mississippi and one from Tennessee with us, numbering one thousand each. All are well quartered, and in fine *spirits*—and they shall not want for the latter so long as our ' mountain dew' holds out. You could not find a more cheerful set of fellows in a week's travel; they play the fiddle, banjo, dance, and sing Dixie. One fellow told me his old mammy cried the glasses clean out of her spectacles the morning he left, but on giving her *two bits* to buy another pair, she bid him go, and return to her covered all over with glory. Another said he didn't like these ' breeches' with a stripe down the leg, they pinched him; but just give him his old copperas-colored trowsers, and his own rifle, and he'd bore a hole *thru* Linkin's nose, through which to put a ring, and lead him about for a show."—*N. Y. Tribune, May 20.*

CAPTAIN LEE, of the United States Navy, in command of the Vandalia, ordered to the East Indies, learning at the Cape of Good Hope that a rebel war had broken out, promptly decided to return home with his ship, where she and her services are wanted. There are times when (as in the case of Colonel Croghan in 1811) it is the duty of an officer to disobey his orders. This was one of those occasions. The Vandalia is at the Navy Yard, ready for her work. Captain Lee's orders were "honored in the breach." He deserves the thanks of the Government and the people.—*N. Y. Commercial, May 21.*

"I WISH I WAS IN DIXIE."—"So common has become the error that this is a Southern song, and relates to Southern institutions, that I must be pardoned if I break the enchantment, and relate the facts about it. I see, also, that Mr. Albert Pike, of Arkansas, has written a song recently, in which he suggests that we

"' Advance the flag of Dixie;
        Hurrah! Hurrah!
For Dixie's land we'll take our stand,
        And live or die for Dixie!' &c.

"Now, I do not wish to spoil a pretty illusion, but the real truth is, that Dixie is an indigenous Northern negro refrain, as common to the writer hereof as the lamp-posts in New York city, seventy or seventy-five years ago. It was one of the every-day allusions of boys, at that time, in all of their out-door sports. And no one ever heard of Dixie's land being other than Manhattan Island until recently, when it has been erroneously supposed to refer to the South, from its connection with pathetic negro allegory.

"When slavery existed in New York, one ' Dixy' owned a large tract of land on Manhattan Island, and large numbers of slaves. The increase of the slaves and the increase of the abolition sentiment caused an emigration of the slaves to more thorough and secure slave sections, and the negroes who were thus sent off (many being born there) naturally looked back to their old homes, where they had lived in clover, with feelings of regret, as they could not imagine any place like Dixy's. Hence it became synonymous with an ideal locality combining ease, comfort, and material happiness of every description. In those days negro singing and minstrelsy were in their infancy, and any subject that could be wrought into a ballad was eagerly picked up; this was the case with ' Dixie.' It originated in New York, and assumed the proportions of a song there. In its travels it has been enlarged, and has ' gathered moss;' it has picked up a note here and there; a ' chorus' has been added to it, and from an indistinct ' chant' of two or three notes, it has become an elaborate melody; but the fact that it is not a Southern song ' cannot be rubbed out;' the fallacy is so popular to the contrary, that I have thus been at pains to state the real origin of it.   P."
—*Charleston Courier, June 11.*

JEFF. DAVIS boasts that "Cotton's King;"
Upon his throne's so written;
But he'll soon find, when on his swing,
    That Hemp is King of Cotton.

WASHINGTON, *June 8.*—Four soldiers of the Michigan Regiment performed a very shrewd act to-day, twelve miles out from Alexandria towards Manassas Junction. They were out "prospecting," and got away too far from camp. The sight of some rebel troopers warned them of their situation. Three of the four concealed themselves in a hedge or thicket, and left one in the highway unarmed. Two rebel troopers soon came up and arrested the Federal soldier. They dismounted, and asked the Michigan man who he was. "I belong to the Michigan Regiment of Federal troops," was his reply. "Then you are our prisoner," said the troopers. At that instant the three concealed Federal soldiers rushed from their ambush, with the exclamation—"No! you are our prisoners!" Sure enough, the Virginians were taken completely by surprise, and surrendered. The Michigan boys are in high glee over the act.—*N. Y. Evening Post, June 11.*

THE Massachusetts troops at the Relay have some amusing incidents in the daily search of the trains for contraband goods. A young lady, the other day, carried a large lunch basket by her side, covered with sponge cake and sandwiches, but upon lifting it, the basket was found to be very heavy, which was soon accounted for, the concealed contents being a large number of army buttons intended for the rebel troops.—*Idem.*

GRUMBLING AT THE SOUTH.—Grumbling at the dilatoriness of military movements is not confined to the North, where almost every editor criticizes Gen. Scott. The *Charleston Mercury* is equally aggrieved by the Fabian policy of the Confederate leaders. It says:—

We are not Generals in the field, and we do not intend to be so on paper; but there are a few plain principles and facts which any mind may understand, without having fought battles or won victories.

In the first place, delay is against us in the matter of numbers. The policy of the Confederate States, it seems to us, was and is, not to wait until vast masses are aggregated upon us, but to act promptly with such troops as we possess, and to demoralize and prevent the discipline of the troops of the United States by vanquishing them.

For, in the second place, our raw troops are far superior to the raw troops of the United States. Our people are used to arms. They are accustomed to the gun and the horse. The people of the North can neither shoot a rifle nor ride a horse, unless trained. Is it good policy to let them be trained?

And in the third place, no soldiers, especially undisciplined soldiers, as the greater part of all the soldiers now in the field must be, can stand the eternal agitations of apprehended attacks in a defensive warfare. To be called out continually to prepare for battle, and yet not to fight, will chill the hearts of the bravest troops.

And still further, instead of having one point for anxiety, attention and alarm are exacted to half a dozen. Troops, at a heavy expense, are scattered about for the protection of different points. This is the necessary incident of a defensive policy. Aggression has its object single, and carries fears before it. Both the *morale* and the economy are better.

But, more than all, the Confederate States ought not to allow one foot of Southern soil to be the battle-field between the two sections of the Union. The weak evacuation of Alexandria, and the horrors perpetrated upon its helpless women, shows the impolicy of such a warfare.

But we are not prepared to assume the aggressive. Who says so? We heard three weeks ago that there were fifteen or twenty thousand Confederate troops and sixty thousand Virginia troops in Virginia. How is it that but six hundred of these troops were in Alexandria to defend it, after weeks of information that it was to be seized, and at the last advices, there were but three regiments at Manassas Junction? Are small bodies of men to be placed unsupported in positions to either retreat without a fight or be sacrificed? Where are the ten thousand men of the regular army ordered to be raised by one of the very first acts of the Confederate Congress? If more troops are needed in Virginia, why are they not there? Have one-third of the volunteers who have been eager to go to Virginia, been accepted? Has a single regiment of horse been accepted to march to Virginia—those terrible instruments of destruction, especially to undisciplined troops

Suppose at this moment any one of our generals in Virginia had an army but of thirty thousand men and ten thousand horse under his command, can any one doubt that it would drive every Yankee across the Pennsylvania line? And is it possible that the Confederate Government, after months of legislation and preparation, with offers of hundreds of thousands of volunteers, cannot bring together this small military force to move on the enemies of the South? Is it not impossible to believe? We cannot perceive the policy, after war is declared, of allowing our country to suffer the ravages of war, and to wait on our enemies to make their attack and ravages how they please. If the six hundred troops who fled from Alexandria had imitated the brave spirit of its single defender, and had laid it in ashes rather than have surrendered it, Virginia and the South would have been in a very different position this day. Let us give over the silly idea of a war without destruction, and like the Russians of Moscow, give our enemies desolation instead of submission as the fruit of their victories.

By assuming the position of the defensive, we have lost Maryland, endangered Missouri, neutralized Kentucky, and are now making Virginia our battlefield. Is this wise statesmanship? Is it efficient generalship? Fabian tactics are out of place. We trust the war policy of the South is about to become aggressive and efficient. It is time, and we are glad to see that our gallant Commander-in-Chief, after directing the preparations of the War Bureau for two months, has made Richmond his head-quarters.—*Charleston Mercury, June 2.*

A CORRESPONDENT of the *Pittsburg Chronicle* writes of the results of the capture of Philippi by the Federal troops as follows:—" The number of arms captured is seven hundred and eighty stand, quite a number of horses, and all their camp equipage and provisions. The rebel camp flag was brought into head-quarters this afternoon. It consists of a blue field with eight stars, and two brown and one white stripe. The flag is about ten feet long and five feet wide. The field is torn by a cannon ball having passed through it, from one of Col. Kelly's six-pounders. A gentleman just from their camp informs me that the privates of Col. Kelly's command are amusing themselves by strutting around with sword and small arms, cocked hats, and other paraphernalia of the secession camp. A train has just arrived with fifteen boxes of flint muskets, furnished by the Governor of Virginia to the rebels. These arms have not been used, and are in good condition. The other arms captured are not of much account. A great number of boxes of blankets were captured, which will be of much service to our men. The amount of camp goods taken is estimated at $25,000. The officers were well dressed and equipped, and were what were denominated the flower of the chivalry; but the men, except the dragoons, were badly equipped, hastily got together, and will not fight, as there are among them many good Union men, who have been pressed into service. Colonel Willy, the secession commander, is a prisoner."

THE HOISTING OF THE REBEL FLAG IN LIVERPOOL.—A good deal of excitement was created in Liverpool on the 24th inst., by the appearance of a secession flag at the mast-head of an American barque lying at the Victoria wharf. The vessel which has acquired such an unenviable notoriety is the Annapolis, Captain Pickett, from Baltimore. We understand by private advices from our agent, that the American shippers at Liverpool were so incensed at the gratuitous insult offered to their country by the piratical skipper, that nothing but the utmost respect for law and order prevented them from hauling down his colors without leave or license.—*London American, May 20.*

NEW REFRAIN OF A SLAVE SONG.

For we're a band of niggers,
For we're a band of niggers,
A contraband of niggers,
And we can't go to the war!
—*Vanity Fair.*

ONE of the venders of Charles H. Scott's neat pamphlet edition of the Constitution of the United States was arrested at Jeffersonville for peddling without a license. When taken before the Mayor, the agent was asked what wares he was selling, and when the answer was given, the Mayor said, "The Constitution of the United States—what do you ask for a copy?" The reply was, "Only half a dime." His honor then pulled out a dime, and said, "Well, I'll take two copies, and you, sir, are discharged." The Constitution of our country is not contraband of war with our good neighbors over the river.—*Louisville Journal, June 12.*

AN INCIDENT OF FORT SUMTER.—Most of our readers are aware that we have in our office a ninety-six pound shell, which was fired from the steamer Monticello upon the Manchester Artillery, on the occasion of her attack on Sewell's Point. In connection with this incident, a gentleman who was present at the battle of Fort Sumter, states that one of these dangerous missiles entered that fortification just above the magazine, but outside of it, descended through a block of granite ten or twelve inches thick, and exploded, one of its fragments, weighing nearly twenty pounds, striking the door of the magazine, and so bending it inwards that it was afterwards found impossible to close it without the aid of a mechanic. Within a few hours of this occurrence a red-hot shot from Fort Moultrie passed through the outer wall of the magazine, penetrated the inner wall to the depth of four inches, and then fell to the ground. All this time grains of powder, spilled by the men in passing to and from the casemates and magazine, were lying loosely upon the floor, which, ignited by a spark, would have blown the structure into atoms. Throughout that entire engagement, so hotly and obstinately contested, the hand of Providence was everywhere equally visible. Death-dealing balls flew in every direction. Men heard them whistle by their ears, and had the earth torn up around their feet. Groups were spattered with the mud and dust of plunging thirty-two pounders, and splinters of wood and iron rained among the unflinching soldiers with such murderous vehemence, that nothing but a higher power could have prevented them from harm; yet "nobody was hurt." Let us hope that the God of battles, who has thus far been so gracious, may still direct our efforts, and carry us safely through the storm of war.

In this connection we may mention that Lieut. Valentine, of the Confederate Army, who commanded one of the batteries on Sullivan's Island, which did most effective work in this battle, is now

in this city, at the Exchange Hotel. On account of his labors in the fortifications around Fort Sumter for the last four months and a half, he has received a furlough of thirty days from General Beauregard; but like a true soldier, he proposes to occupy his time upon the fields of Virginia. He has no particular place to fight, but will leave in a day or two for Manassas, as the liveliest scene of operations, to take his chances of "mixing in" miscellaneously.—*Richmond Dispatch, and Charleston Courier, June 11.*

DEDICATED TO KNAVISH SPECULATORS WHO HAVE ROBBED THE STATE.

Some folks may boast their rank and birth,
    Descent and lofty station;
May claim they're made of better earth,
    And hope to rule the nation;
While others brag upon their wealth,
    And worship only Mammon;
Let honest men assert again
    Such doctrines are but " Gammon."

The world is flush of rogues and knaves,
    Who sham the patriotic,
And hope to keep the people slaves,
    By scheme and plan Quixotic;
While some are boasting what they'll do
    In " fuss and feathers " dressy,
Let honest men prepare again,
    To give the traitors " Jessie."

From top to toe, from head to foot,
    Our politics are rotten;
And those we pay are bribed to boot,
    While justice is forgotten!
For every one that gets a chance
    To serve the State, is stealing,
And honest men must pay again
    For scoundrels' double-dealing.

In court and camp it's all the same,
    From Judge to Quartermaster;
The devil takes the one that's lame,—
    He should have robbed the faster!
For pork or progress, blankets, brief,
    The roguery's defended,
And honest men are told again,
    The system can't be mended.
        —*Philadelphia Intelligencer.*

To be conquered in open and manly fight by a nation of gentlemen, and subjected to their sway, might not drive us raving distracted with rage and shame; but for Yankees—the most contemptible and detestable of God's creation—the vile wretches, whose daily sustenance consists in the refuse of all other people—for they eat nothing that anybody else will buy—for them to lord it over us—the English language must be enlarged, new words must be invented, to express the extent and depth of our feelings of mortification and shame. They have long very properly looked upon themselves as our social inferiors—as our serfs—their mean, niggardly lives—their low, vulgar, and sordid occupations, have ground this conviction into them. But of a sudden they have come to imagine that their numerical strength gives them power—and they have burst the bonds of servitude, and are running a riot with more than the brutal passions of a liberated wild beast. *Their uprising has all the characteristics of a ferocious, servile insurrection.*—*Richmond Whig.*

SECEDING VIRGINIA.

BY L. H. SIGOURNEY.

Ho! mistress of the rolling James,
　And of its mountain strand,
The oldest, noblest, proudest one,
　Of all our household band;
Thou of the stately form and step,
　The flower-encircled hair,
Prime favorite of the fruitful earth,
　And of the balmy air;
Thou who didst hold thy cresset forth
　Ere early dawn had fled,
The morning star whose lambent ray
　Our constellation led,
Yet, when a comet madly rushed
　Across the argent plain,
Why didst thou leave thy Heaven-mark'd sphere,
　And join its flaming train?

We loved thee well, Virginia!
　And gave thee deferent place,
Pleased with thine ancient dignity,
　And native, peerless grace,
And little deemed such sudden blight
　Would settle on thy bays,
And change to discord and disgust
　Our gratulating praise;
For thou hadst given thy great and good
　Our helm of State to guide;
Thy Palinurus steered our barque
　Safe through the seething tide;
And when we spake of Washington
　With grateful, reverent tone,
We called thine image forth, and blent
　Thy memory with his own.

Our mother nursed thee at her breast
　When she herself was young;
And thou shouldst still have succor'd her,
　Though fiery serpents stung;
Virginia Dare, the first-born bud
　Of the true Saxon vine,
And old Powhatan, hoary chief,
　Who led his warrior-line,
And brave John Smith, the very soul
　Of chivalry and pride,
And Pocahontas, princess pure,
　The font of Christ beside,
Dreamed *they* that thou wouldst start aside,
　When Treachery's tocsin rang?
And in her heaving bosom fix
　Thy matricidal fang?

Thou shouldst around her fourscore years
　Have bent with hovering care,
Who steadfast by thy cradle watched,
　And poured the ardent prayer.
Thou shouldst not to her banded foes
　Have lent thy ready ear,
Nor seen them desolate her joys
　Without a filial tear;
Though all beside her banner-fold
　Had trampled down and rent,
Thou shouldst have propp'd its shattered staff
　With loyalty unspent;
Though all beside had recreant proved,
　Thou shouldst have stood to aid,
Like Abdiel, dreadless seraph,
　Alone, yet undismayed.

Who sleepeth at Mount Vernon,
　In the glory of his fame?
Yet, go in silent infamy,
　Nor dare pronounce his name,
For thou hast of their sacred force,
　His farewell counsels reft,
And help'd to scatter to the winds
　The rich bequest he left;
And in the darkest trial-hour,
　Forsook the endangered side,
And, ere the cock crew thrice, thy true
　Discipleship denied.
Oh! that the pitying Prince of Peace
　On thee his glance might bend,
And from remediless remorse
　Preserve our long-loved friend.

HARTFORD, CONN., *May* 21, 1861.
　　　　—*National Intelligencer*, June 8.

AMERICA TO THE WORLD.

"You cannot be too decided or too explicit in making known to the French Government that there is not now, or has there been, nor will there be any, the least idea existing in this Government of suffering a dissolution of this Union to take place in any way whatever. There will be here only one nation and one Government, and there will be the same republic and the same constitutional Union that have already survived a dozen national changes and changes of Government in almost every other country. These will stand hereafter as they are now, objects of human wonder and human affection."—WILLIAM H. SEWARD.

I.

Tell them this Union, so great, cannot sever,
　Though it may tremble beneath the rude shock;
As it hath lived, so it shall live forever,
　Strong as the mountain oak, firm as the rock.

II.

Others have fallen—are falling around us;
　Dynasties tremble and sink to decay;
But the great heart whose strong fetters have bound us,
　Never has throbbed as it's throbbing to-day.

III.

Let them not deem in a moment of weakness,
　We can surrender our birthright and name;—
Strike the old flag, and with patience and meekness,
　Bear the foul blot on our hardly-earned fame.

IV.

Dumb be the tongue that would tell the foul story,
　Blighted the brain could conceive it in sin;
Crushed be the heart that would tarnish the glory
　And honor our country hath striven to win.

V.

Ever and ever our flag shall be streaming,
　Adding new glories of stripes and of stars;
Though the sword glancing and bayonet gleaming
　Tell us of treasons, corruptions, and wars.

VI.

Soon shall our land, to its old peace returning,
　Spring to the duties that make nations great;
And while in every heart valor is burning,
　Calmly and bravely her destiny wait.
　　　　—*Vanity Fair*, May 18.

THE VOICES OF THE HOUR.

BY S. P. D.

Hark! the rally-call of Freedom! Hark! the people's answer given,
As their thunder-toned responses echo up the vaulted heaven:
We will rally, we will gather, we will muster in our might,
For our banner must be stainless, and our God will shield the right!
Ay, though bloody may be the conquest to which we march along,
And though groans may make a dissonance in our grand victor-song,
We will rally, we will gather, we will muster in our might,
And our banner shall be stainless, for our God will shield the right!

Every hour hath prophet's utterance, and each gale from o'er the seas
Brings the crash of falling empires, and of tottering dynasties;
From Italia's classic ruins, to the ice-realm of the Czar,
Sounds the tramp of marshalled cohorts, as they muster to the war;
And from despots' shattered altars Freedom's incense-cloud is curled,
While the people's unchained voices send their *Vivas* round the world.

Then, freemen, shall we falter, as our battle surges on?
Shall we tamely yield the birthright by our fathers' valor won?
Give up this glorious heritage to Treason's foul misrule,
And serve, as willing pupils, in the anarch's villain-school?
Shall we sit in dumb despairing, or but whispered prayers repeat,
While our banner's starry splendors shall be draggled at our feet?
Shall we hug pale phantoms longer, all forgot each patriot vow,
And thus prove ourselves unequal to the stern demands of NOW?

Do we hear no warning voices from the Temple of the Past,
To whose priesthood earth's best heroes throng, and through whose arches vast
They thunder still, the sturdy chords of Freedom's natal hymn,
As they sang, by hope inspired, in the twilight cold and dim?
Do no spectres stalk before us, from their heaps of hallowed dust,
And, with finger heavenward pointing, bid us not betray our trust?
Do the winds no tidings bring us from the waves of Congaree,
As they kiss the grass-fringed battle-fields, and hurry to the sea?
Or from Bunker's storied hilltop, whence the gray stones seek the sky,
To mark the spot as holy where our fathers dared to die?

What though our sky is shrouded with the midnight robe of shame,
And the light but faintly flickers from our Freedom's altar-flame;
Darkest night precedes the dawning, and new light shall yet break through,
And a new day grandly open, bathed with heaven's unquestioned blue;
And though stars are fleeing wildly from *Night's* cloudy tournament,
The *Morning's* bow of promise we shall see above us bent;
Of promise as it glimmers from the labor-burthened hours,
When snow, to bare and bleeding feet, was warm as summer's flowers;
When days of struggle, and of toil, and nights of dark unrest,
Made the purchase of the bounties, by us, ingrates, now possessed.

Then up, and rally proudly to the foremost of the fray,
And let every patriot be a *host*, to stand and strike to-day;
While the rally-call of Freedom, and the people's answer given,
Still, in thunder-toned responses, echo up the vaulted heaven,—
We will rally, we will gather, we will muster in our might,
And bear on our stainless banner, for our God shall shield the right!

—*Boston Transcript,* June 3.

BAY STATE SONG.

" They had sent word to us from Philadelphia that we could not pass through that city, (Baltimore,) but the Colonel made up his mind that we could; and so we did. * * * * You may depend upon it, that wherever we are ordered, we shall do our duty, and not make a blot on the records of Massachusetts."—LETTER FROM A PRIVATE OF THE SIXTH REGIMENT.

" The cause of Baltimore is the cause of the whole South."—A. H. STEPHENS.

TUNE—"*There is rest for the weary,*" (with spirit.)

I.

'Tis the Old Bay State a-coming,
 With the Pine Tree waving high,
Foremost where the fight is thickest,
 Freedom still her battle-cry.
From the rocky shore of Plymouth,
 From the plains of Lexington,
From beneath the shaft of Bunker,
 Every hero sends a son.

CHORUS—To the fray comes the Bay State!
 Clear the way for the Bay State!
 Trust you may in the Bay State!
 She will do, or die.

II.

From our dear old Berkshire mountains,
 From Cape Cod's sea-beaten sand,
With one cry we rush to battle—
 Freedom, and our Native Land!
From the quiet graves of Concord,
 Still as in our fathers' day,
Where her country's need is greatest,
 Massachusetts leads the way.

CHORUS—To the fray, &c.

III.

Onward dash the Pine-Tree banner,
   Where a threatened Senate calls,
Ere a foe in Freedom's city
   Desecrate her sacred halls.
Where a son would strike a mother
   With a traitor's stealthy blow,
Forward, every loyal brother!
   Fly to crush the dastard foe.
CHORUS—To the fray, &c.

IV.

Onward, then, our stainless banner,
   Let it kiss the stripe and star,
Till in weal and woe united
   They forever wedded are.
We will plant them by the river,
   By the gulf and by the strand,
Till they float, to float forever,
   O'er a free, united land.
CHORUS—To the fray, &c.

V.

We have left the plough and anvil,
   Left the ledger and the loom;
Our shares to swords are beaten,
   And our pen's the pen of doom.
But we'll plough a deeper furrow,
   And we'll deal a heavier blow,
And upon the Nation's Ledger
   We will strike the balance now.
CHORUS—To the fray, &c.

VI.

Lay the rails and build the engines,
   O'er the stream the bridges throw;
These are little Yankee notions
   Yankees carry as they go.
To the friends we leave behind us,
   Oft we pledge a hearty health,
And one prayer to God we offer—
   Save the good old Commonwealth
CHORUS—To the fray, &c.

VII.

See an Adams and an Otis
   Look from heaven to speed us on!
Hear a Warren and a Prescott
   Bid us keep the fields they won!
See again Virginia's Patriot
   Rise to bid Disunion stand!
See the shade of Monticello
   Strike again at Treason's hand!
CHORUS—To the fray, &c.

VIII.

Forward, then, the Pine-Tree banner!
   Still as in our fathers' day,
Where her country's need is greatest,
   Massachusetts leads the way!
By our brothers' blood still crying
   From the streets of Baltimore,
Let the foe who struck behind them,
   Be struck down for evermore.
CHORUS—To the fray, &c.

IX.

Now, the Stars and Stripes forever!
   Be he cursed, each traitor son,

Who assails the starry banner
   And the flag of Washington!
For Mount Vernon's sacred ashes
   Will not rest within their bed,
With a traitor band around it,
   And a traitor flag o'erhead!
CHORUS—To the fray comes the Bay State!
   Clear the way for the Bay State!
   Trust you may in the Bay State!
   She will do, or die.
        —*N. Y. Tribune,* June 9.

COLONEL ELLSWORTH.

BY CAPT. SAM. WHITING.

[Dedicated to the New York Fire Zouaves.]

Columbia bends in sadness now,
   Above her gallant soldier's grave;
Laurel and cypress deck the brow
   Of the dead Zouave—so young, so brave.
Cut down in manhood's brightest bloom—
   Of his dear friends the hope and pride—
He sleeps within an honored tomb,
   Who for his country bravely died.

Not yet in vain such heroes fall;
   Their memory lives in every breast,
While streams of glory gild their pall,
   And beautify their place of rest.
Oh! gallant Zouave, 'twas thy proud deed
   To tear the rebel banner down;
Thy country gives thee fitting meed—
   A soldier's grave, a hero's crown.

Brave Fire Zouaves! your leader's name
   Is left you for a battle-cry;
Let Ellsworth's pure and spotless fame
   Lead you to conquer or to die.
Strike bravely when the *rebel rag*
   Shall meet your eyes on Southern plain!
Strike! till Columbia's starry flag
   O'er this whole land shall wave again.

When you shall meet the traitor band
   Which seeks our Union to o'erthrow,
Strike boldly for our glorious land,
   And call on God to nerve the blow!
Keep your dead Colonel e'er in view,
   Wherever in this war you roam,
And let this shout your zeal renew:
   "Remember Ellsworth! Zouaves, strike home!"
HEMPSTEAD, *June* 5, 1861.   —*Idem.*

WAR SONG.

BY T. P. ROSSITER.

Come, rally round our altar;
   No true heart now will falter,
When battles for our freedom are to be fought and
   won;
   Come, father, son, and brother,
   Leave sister, wife, and mother;
There's work for strong arms doing, nor peace until
   'tis done.
CHORUS—For equal right
      We only fight,
But while we breathe we will be free.
      When our dear land
      Our lives demands,
Die shouting, "God and liberty."

List how the drums are beating,
Their echoing tones repeating,
Come, rally! ho! come, rally, our hearths and
homes to save;
The blood our good sires left us,
Though all else were bereft us,
Is heritage sufficient to keep from coward's grave.

Come, flock around our standard;
Come, crowd into the vanguard;
The beacons blazing brightly upon the hillsides show
There's need of arms united,
With hearts for daring plighted,
To grapple in the death-grip which hellward hurls a foe.

On our unguarded borders
Throng hordes of fell marauders;
And our old flag base miscreants insultingly would
seize.
Still Stars and Stripes are streaming,
Thank God, in glory gleaming,
And patriot thrills are stirring as it flutters in the
breeze.

Our country now would prove us,
While floats our flag above us,
Undaunted we'll give battle, nor drop the blade or
brand,
Till all in place and station
Are loyal to the nation;
Till enemies and traitors are driven from the land.

Leave shuttle, quit the harrow,
Bring from the mines strong marrow—
Leave anvil, plane, and compass, as the tocsin sounds
alarm;
Leave mills and shops untended,
Leave books with tasks unended,
That wives and weans may nestle securely from all
harm.

Come, old, from the desk and study;
Come, youth, with brawn arms ruddy;
Come, rally! ho! come, rally, for each altar, home,
and hearth.
Our vows to each now plighting,
In life and death uniting,
For Union we inherited—God-given at our birth.
—*N. Y. Evening Post*, June 8.

BATTLE ANTHEM.

BY JOHN NEAL.

Up, Christian warrior, up! I hear
The trumpet of the North
Sounding the charge!
Fathers and sons, to horse!
Fling the old standard forth,
Blazing and large!

And now I hear the heavy tramp
Of nations on the march,
Silent as death!
A slowly-gathering host,
Like clouds o'er yonder arch,
Holding their breath!

Our great blue sky is overcast;
And stars are dropping out,
Through smoke and flame!

Hail-stones and coals of fire!
Now comes the battle-shout!
Jehovah's name!

And now the rebel pomp! To prayer!
Look to your stirrups, men!
Yonder rides death!
Now with a whirlwind-sweep!
Empty their saddles when
Hot comes their breath!

As through the midnight forest tears
With trumpeting and fire
A thunder-blast;
So, Reapers, tear your way
Through yonder camp, until you hear,
"It is enough! Put up thy sword!
Oh, Angel of the Lord!
My wrath is past!"
—*Portland (Me.) Transcript.*

NUMBER ONE.

BY H. D. SEDGWICK.

"I have flung to the Night my pirate flag;
It is black as the deeds I love.
My merry men! Ho! for beauty and swag,
For every foeman you seize and gag,
For every youth from life betrayed,
For the death-doing shame of every maid,
For each blue eye whose light you quench,
For every babe whose neck you wrench,
As the reddening sea you rove,
I'll pay you in cash by the bloody score;
I'll pay you as Rover paid never before,
For that I bid it shall be done;
In the land of slaves I am Number One!
I am Jefferson Number One!"

At the welcome sound of the Robber's cheer,
Like jackals they creep from their cave;
As the wild-cat springs at the lightsome deer,
As the viper crawls the babe to smear
With venom, and strike to its tiny grave,
They come! they come! the Corsairs brave!
Hear them scream with joy, to think
How the cups will flow, and the canakins clink;
How they'll turn men's blood to the wine they drink,
And how their pockets will chink, will chink!
And the first thief cries, "It shall be done
And I'll be Pirate Number One!
I will be Number One!"

He has filched and rigged a snake-like bark;
He has armed it with stolen guns.
Forth from the bay it swims like a shark,
Wrapped in the shrouds of its kindred dark.
All things good and strong it shuns.
How slily it steers! How slowly it steals! Hark!
What whisper they in their dreary lark?
"Stay! Are we right? Aye! Our letters of marque
Are signed and sealed. All's rightly done
They are signed by Jefferson Number One;
They are numbered Number One!"

Ho! Ho! Cheerily ho!
No longer sly! No longer slow,
The snaky bark takes wing.
No longer it creeps like a slimy rat,
But it flies like a loathsome, lickerish bat,
It flies like a venomous vampire, that

Sets his teeth and sharpens his sting,
Ere he plunge his beak in the life-blood's spring.
 "Ho! Ho! Cheerily ho!"
 The Pirates cry, " Merrily, so
 To our weltering feast of blood we go.
 How we long for its gurgling flow!
 That we dare, that shall be done;
 Hurrah for the victim Number One!
 Hurrah for Number One!"

 "What ho! What ho! A sail on the lee!
Mind you your helm, my helmsman stout;
About with the ship, sail her fast and free.
 About with the ship! About! about!
 Up to the maintop, you lubberly lout!
 Don't step as if you were cramped with gout,
Nor handle the ropes so dainty and soft;
Set every stitch alow and aloft!
 Nearer, now! nearer! the chase appears!
 Bloody boys, ready! the runaway nears!
 See her there plain on the larboard bow ,
 Sharp must she be to weather us now.
Look to your cutlasses! Look to the gun!
We'll give her a taste of Number One!
 We'll give her Number One!"

 "Ship ahoy! Ship ahoy! We'll have her this tack;
 She'll save us a lingering chase!
Ship ahoy! Yankee Dogs! Be a trifle less slack;
 Down your Black-a-moor Stripes and Stars!
 We'll up, instead, the Confederate Bars!
Down, down with the rag!—Ha! what is that crack?
What meaneth the lubber? He answereth back.
 We've a *fight* instead of a race!
Curse the impudent Yankees! For quarter and grace
They may sue and be damned. They shall have none.
 Short be their shrift from Number One!
 Short shrift from Number One!"

Ah! Sooth said the Pirate! The answer came
 From the brig like an outburst of hell!
It came in a sheet of glancing flame!
 In an iron sleet of deadly aim!
And with sheet and sleet, shot the burning shame
 To his craven breast, to learn too late
 From the Yankee's arm, and the voice of Fate,
 The truth which now he learns too well :
That plot it long, and moil in the dark,
And cover it over with letters of marque,
 Murder is still a dangerous game!
 Begin it, and two can play at the same.
 At this dark game, the rovers' luck
 Was little to score, and less their pluck.
 For the felon blows to strike they meant,
 When on their errand of greed they went,
 The Buccaneer flag instead they struck.
Those dogs of the Perry who would not run,
Have spoiled the Pirate's slaughtering fun;
The tale of their prizes they have featly begun.
It heads to-day with Number One!
 It heads with Number One!"

In the North there frowns a darksome pile—
 So darksome, men call it the Tombs.
Who are guarded there, ah! seldom they smile!
But spectred thoughts of fruitless wile,
And ghosts of schemes of deadly guile,
 Are their comrades drear in those doleful rooms,
 Where Darkness and Sin spread kindred glooms.
There's water instead of wine to drink!
And chains instead of canakins clink!

And there, with those comrades drear, they think
 Of a past that sears and a fate that dooms!
In a fitful sleep they fain would hide
From the phantoms that fill the world outside.
 But again that answering cannon booms;
 Again their souls are fevered with fear.
 By victim vanquished again, they hear
His dread summons ring in their throbbing ear.
 They start in their dream as called by Fate!
 They start and shrink! They hear the gate
 Of the cell on its rusty hinges grate!
 Through the portal whispers the voice they hate.
 'Tis the voice of the headsman; he calls, "I wait
 For the first of the pirates! The gibbet is done.
 Come forth to your reckoning, Number One!
 Come forth, doomed Number One!"
 —*N. Y. Tribune*, July 14.

A NEW VERSION OF AN OLD SONG.

[*Respectfully Dedicated to the London Times.*]

 God save Cotton, our King!
 God save our noble King!
 God save the King!
 Send him the sway he craves,
 Britons his willing slaves.
 "Rule," Cotton! "Rule the waves!"
 God save the King!

 Outweighing truth and fame,
 Cotton shall cloak our shame,
 Freedom an empty name.
 God save the King!

 Careless of good or ill,
 Cotton is sovereign still,
 While we our pockets fill.
 God save the King!

 Lowly we bend the knee
 To his autocracy;
 Cotton shall rule the free!
 God save the King!
 —*N. Y. Evening Post*, May 29.

ALL FORWARD!

WRITTEN FOR THE SECOND REGIMENT CON-
NECTICUT VOLUNTEERS, BY REQUEST

Air—"*Garibaldi's Hymn*."

 All forward! All forward!
All forward to battle! the trumpets are crying,
Forward! All forward! our old flag is flying.
When Liberty calls us we linger no longer;
 Rebels, come on! though a thousand to one!
Liberty! Liberty! deathless and glorious,
Under thy banner thy sons are victorious,
Free souls are valiant, and strong arms are stronger—
 God shall go with us and battle be won.
 Hurrah for the banner!
 Hurrah for the banner!
Hurrah for our banner, the flag of the free!

 All forward! All forward!
All forward for Freedom! In terrible splendor
She comes to the loyal who die to defend her:
 Her stars and her stripes o'er the wild wave of battle
 Shall float in the heavens to welcome us on.

All forward ! to glory, though life-blood is pouring,
Where bright swords are flashing, and cannon are
  roaring,
Welcome to death in the bullets' quick rattle—
  Fighting or falling shall Freedom be won.
    Hurrah for the banner ! &c.

    All forward !   All forward !
All forward to conquer !   Where free hearts are
  beating,
Death to the coward who dreams of retreating !
Liberty calls us from mountain and valley ;
  Waving her banner, she leads to the fight.
Forward ! all forward ! the trumpets are crying ;
The drum beats to arms, and our old flag is flying ;
Stout hearts and strong hands around it shall
  rally—
  Forward to battle for God and the Right !
    Hurrah for the banner !
    Hurrah for the banner !
    Hurrah for our banner, the flag of the free !
      —*The Independent*, June 6.

TO THE FLAG OF THE SOUTHERN AMERI-
CAN SECESSIONISTS,

FLYING IN A BRITISH PORT.

In the place of thy pride, from the mast's topmost
  height,
Thou art bathing thy folds in the sky's azure light ;
The winds are at play 'midst thy red-flowing bars,
And the sunbeams repose on thy circlet of stars.
With the sunshine around thee—the blue heaven
  above,
'Midst things that are telling of freedom and love,
But where tempests in clouds and in darkness
  career,
Where the chain and the fetter with clanging re-
  sound,
Where the slave-curse hath blasted the fruits of the
  ground,—
'Tis there, and *there* only, thy waving should be ;
How com'st thou to darken the Isles of the Free ?
Herald of ruin, and banner of doom !—
For the day of thy triumph may finish in gloom,
And thou from the place of thy pride may'st be
  reft,
And in blood and in ashes thy trail may be left.
Ensign of tyranny ! emblem of woe !
Type to the nations of honor's o'erthrow !
Standard of Mammon, and Might leagued with
  Wrong—
Down from our sight !—thou hast mocked us too
  long !
  April 18, 1861.   — *Waterford (Ireland) Mail.*

THE UPRISING OF THE NORTH.

BY J. C. HAGEN.

The Northern men are up in arms,
  To wage no servile fight ;
They've risen at their Country's call,
  To battle for the right.

The city echoes with their tread ;
  Their hosts the valleys fill ;
Their shout is borne on every stream,
  And rings from every hill.
An hundred thousand men are out ;
  A word has called them forth ;
A million more, if need there be,
  Are ready at the North !

The merchant leaves his counting-house,
  The husbandman his plough ;
All ranks, all callings rally round
  Their Country's standard now.
All minor discords are forgot ;
  All party feuds have flown ;
Each heart beats for its Country now,
  And beats for her alone.
In Freedom's, and their Country's cause,
  Thus bravely rushing forth,
Oh ! 'tis a glorious sight to see
  The uprising of the North !

Our sacred Flag, the people's boast
  And pride throughout the world,
With scoff and scorn, has, to the dust,
  By traitor hands been hurled !
But woe to those who dared to treat
  Our glorious flag with scorn—
That flag that so triumphantly
  In Freedom's cause was borne !
The nation hails with ecstasy
  Her champions rushing forth,
While Southern traitors tremble at
  The uprising of the North.

Oh ! well our hardy Northern sires
  Their sturdy sons may boast ;
And well may craven traitors quail
  Before the gathering host.
No rest they ask while despots' hands
  May freemen's homes despoil,
Or while the traitor foot remains
  To desecrate the soil.
And ne'er again, to insult our flag,
  Their hordes shall venture forth,
While memory to their vision holds
  The uprising of the North.
      —*Boston Transcript*, June 19.

THE MARRIED VOLUNTEER.

BY "SALLIE S. MCC."

A little shooting-trip, he said
  That he was going upon,
And yet my darling turned his head,
  And on his shining gun,
I saw a glistening tear ;
And in my heart of hearts I said,
God bless my darling and my pride,
  And keep my soul from fear.

For his dear sake I seeméd brave,
  And said, " Bring lots of game."
He answered, " By my soul I will,
  Or leave a noble name."
  Then back again he came,
And kissing me on lip and brow,

He said, "Remember, love, I go
    To keep our flag from shame."
It seemed so like a pleasure prank,
    "The boys" were going too;
There was Mac, and Van, and Frank,
    And almost all the crew
That went yachting long ago;
And the flag then floating from the mast,
They swear shall be their country's last,
    Or death shall lay them low.

Now Heaven be with those noble boys,
    Who, at their Country's call,
Leave stern pursuits and happy joys,
    And home, and friends, and all,
    For the banner of the free.
God speed them all who thus defend
Their country's cause, and safely send
    My husband back to me.
                    —*N. Y. Tribune*, May 4.

THE MASSACHUSETTS LINE.

BY THE AUTHOR OF "THE NEW PRIEST."

AIR—"*Yankee Doodle.*"

I.

Still first, as long and long ago,
    Let Massachusetts muster;
Give her the post right next the foe;
    Be sure that you may trust her.
She was the first to give her blood
    For freedom and for honor;
She trod her soil to crimson mud:
    God's blessing be upon her.

II.

She never faltered for the right,
    Nor ever will hereafter;
Fling up her name with all your might,
    Shake roof-tree and shake rafter.
But of old deeds she need not brag,
    How she broke sword and fetter;
Fling out again the old striped flag!
    She'll do yet more and better.

III.

In peace her sails fleck all the seas,
    Her mills shake every river;
And where are scenes so fair as these
    God and her true hands give her?
Her claim in war who seeks to rob?
    All others come in later—
Hers first it is to front the Mob,
    The Tyrant, and the Traitor.

IV.

God bless, God bless the glorious State!
    Let her have way to battle!
She'll go where batteries crash with fate,
    Or where thick rifles rattle.
Give her the Right, and let her try,
    And then, who can, may press her;
She'll go straight on, or she will die;
    God bless her! and God bless her!
DUANESBURGH, May 7, 1861.
                    —*N. Y. Evening Post*, May 20.

THE SEVENTY-NINTH.

BY THOS. FRAZER.

AIR—"*Here's to the year that's awa'.*"

Come, muster, my bonnie brave Scots,
    An' muster your clans one an' a',
Nor heed who else lags, so the free Thistle wags,
    When Treason drives Right to the wa';
For Freedom, for Union, an' Law,
    We'll do a' that true men may dare;
An' come weal or come scaithe, for these to the
        death—
    The Seventy-ninth will be there!

Come, stir, then, an' trim for the work;
    Come, Borderer, Lowlander, Celt,
An' wi' firelock in hand, our tartan-clad band
    Will soon mak the auld grit be felt.
We'll show how auld Scotland for Truth
    Has bluid in her heart yet to spare;
An' let us but ken when the Truth may want men—
    The Seventy-ninth will be there!

Then heeze out the pipes wi' a cheer,
    An' up wi' some heart-thrillin' strain,
To mind us the field is where Scots never yield,
    While ae chance to win may remain.
Syne shout, lads, the auld battle-cry—
    "Saint Andrew!"—an' let them beware
When doure Southron knaves wad mak North-folk
        their slaves—
    The Seventy-ninth will be there!

The Union, the Nation, an' Name,
    The "Stars and the Stripes," an' the Laws!
Oh! never can hand wave the death-dealing brand
    In what could be holier cause!
Then muster, my bonnie brave Scots,
    An' swear by the tartan we wear,
Where'er be the van, one in heart to a man—
    The Seventy-ninth will be there!
                    —*N. Y. Commercial Advertiser*, May 2.

LOYAL DELAWARE.

In all the range of Border States,
    To whom we've ne'er been crusty,
The staunch, unflinching Delaware's
    The only one that's trusty.

While wicked Treason rages wild
    All up and down her borders,
She still defends the Stars and Stripes,
    And waits for further orders.

Not all Virginia's treachery,
    Nor Maryland's distraction,
Can make her quit her Uncle Sam,
    For any Traitor faction.

And Delaware has had her share
    Of treason-agitators;
But then there's something in her soil
    That don't agree with Traitors!

The Union will remember her,
    When force of arms it uses,
And give to her of Maryland
    As much as e'er she chooses!

And when to future Peace we pledge
    A bumper, rare and loyal,
We'll say of gallant Delaware,
    "She's little, but she's loyal!"
                        —*N. Y. Sunday Mercury.*

JEFFERSON D.

BY H. S. CORNWELL.

You're a traitor convicted, you know very well!
    Jefferson D., Jefferson D.!
You thought it a capital thing to rebel,
    Jefferson D.!
        But there's one thing I'll say:
        You'll discover, some day,
When you see a stout cotton cord hang from a tree,
There's an accident happened you didn't foresee,
    Jefferson D.!

What shall be found upon History's page?
    Jefferson D., Jefferson D.!
When the student explores the Republican age?
    Jefferson D.!
        He will find, as is meet,
        That at Judas's feet
You sit in your shame, with the impotent plea,
That you hated the land and the law of the free,
    Jefferson D.!

What do you see in your visions at night?
    Jefferson D., Jefferson D.!
Does the spectacle furnish you any delight?
    Jefferson D.!
        Do you feel, in disgrace,
        The black cap o'er your face,
While the tremor creeps down from your heart to
        your knee,
And Freedom insulted approves the decree?
    Jefferson D.!

Oh, long have we pleaded, till pleading is vain!
    Jefferson D., Jefferson D.!
Your hands are imbued with the blood of the slain!
    Jefferson D.!
        And at last, for the Right,
        We arise in our might—
A people united, resistless, and free,
And declare that rebellion no longer shall be!
    Jefferson D.!
NEW LONDON, CONN.
                        —*N. Y. Tribune*, June 17.

THE CRISIS.

BY J. G. WHITTIER.

The crisis presses on us; face to face with us it
        stands,
With solemn lips of question, like the Sphynx in
        Egypt's sands!
This day we fashion Destiny, our web of fate we
        spin;
This day for all hereafter choose we holiness or sin;
Even now from starry Gerizim, or Ebal's cloudy
        crown,
We call the dews of blessing, or the bolts of cursing
        down!

By all for which the Martyrs bore their agony and
        shame;
By all the warning words of truth with which the
        Prophets came;
By the Future which awaits us; by all the hopes
        which cast
Their faint and trembling beams across the blackness
        of the Past,
And in the awful name of Him who for earth's free-
        dom died;
O ye people! O my brothers! let us choose the
        righteous side!

So shall the Northern pioneer go joyfully on his
        way,
To wed Penobscot's waters to San Francisco's bay;
To make the rugged places smooth, and sow the vales
        with grain,
And bear, with Liberty and Law, the Bible in his
        train;
The mighty West shall bless the East, and sea shall
        answer sea,
And mountain unto mountain call: PRAISE GOD, FOR
    WE ARE FREE!

OUR ORDERS.

Weave no more silks, ye Lyons looms,
    To deck our girls for gay delights!
The crimson flower of battle blooms,
    And solemn marches fill the nights.

Weave but the flag whose bars to-day
    Drooped heavy o'er our early dead,
And homely garments, coarse and gray,
    For orphans that must earn their bread!

Keep back your tunes, ye viols sweet,
    That pour delight from other lands!
Rouse there the dancer's restless feet,—
    The trumpet leads our warrior bands.

And ye that wage the war of words,
    With mystic fame and subtle power,
Go, chatter to the idle birds,
    Or teach the lesson of the hour!

Ye Sibyl Arts, in one stern knot
    Be all your offices combined!
Stand close, while Courage draws the lot,
    The destiny of humankind!

And if that destiny could fail,
    The sun should darken in the sky,
The eternal bloom of Nature pale,
    And God, and Truth, and Freedom die!
                        —*Atlantic Monthly*, July.

THE RISING OF THE NORTH.

Thank God! the death-like, strange repose,
    The horrid paralytic rest
Is ended, and a Nation's breast,
Fired with the old-time spirit, glows!

A people long grown servile-necked
    With bowing under Mammon's yoke,
Its bondage on a sudden broke,
To-day stands haughtily erect.

It is as when the valley heaped
   With dry bones, at the Prophet's word,
A wind miraculous had stirred ;
   Such Life from seeming Death has leaped!

No more supine, while traitorous foes
   Trample her rights, her prowess mock,
But, roused for Battle's rudest shock,
When Sumter fell, the North arose !
          —Madison (Wis.) State Journal.

A REMARKABLE LATTER-DAY PROPHECY.—The vision or prophecy of Joseph Hoag, which we publish below, is so remarkable in the accuracy of some of its details, that were its authenticity not attested by the most respectable and reliable living witnesses, we should hardly credit it. The predicted "civil war," now on the threshold of fulfilment, is not more singular than are several other features in the vision which have already been verified. As much as six months ago, a Quaker gentleman in Philadelphia, well acquainted with the history of this "vision," also with some of the children of its venerated author, expressed to us a desire to see it published in the *Press.* We have been at some pains to ascertain certain particulars respecting this remarkable man, some of which we here give as introductory to his prophecy.

Joseph Hoag was an eminent minister of the Gospel in the Society of Friends. At the date of his subjoined vision, in 1803, this Society was a unit, the division in it not having occurred until 1827. After the separation, Hoag affiliated with the Orthodox branch, in which connection he continued until his death, at the age of forty-five. His ancestors were among the early settlers of New England, and lived for several generations in the State of New Hampshire, although he was born in Duchess County, New York, but in early life removed to the home of his ancestors. In his services as a minister he travelled extensively throughout the United States, and he is well remembered by a large number of the old members of the Society of Friends in Philadelphia as a very gifted and spiritual-minded minister. Those who knew him best say that he was a man of great piety and very correct life and conversation from his youth ; also, that his spiritual perceptions were very deep and clear, so much so that he was often favored with a sense of the condition of other people without outward knowledge, and in many instances, known to persons still living, foretold circumstances which occurred long afterwards, and of which he could have had no knowledge when he predicted them. A journal of his life exists, in which the author says Hoag "was a man of good understanding, retentive memory, and a mind seasoned with grace. His conversation was truly instructive. He appeared most conspicuous in the gift of the ministry, and the spirit of prophecy." The following is

JOSEPH HOAG'S VISION,

transcribed by his daughter—who is still living—in the year 1805, since which time many duplicate MS. copies have been made and preserved by members of the Society, as a curious, interesting, and, as the sequel has shown, an amazingly premonitory document :—

"In the year 1803, in the eighth or ninth month, I was one day alone in the field, and observed that the sun shone clear, but a mist eclipsed its brightness.

"As I reflected upon the singularity of the event, my mind was struck into a silence the most solemn I ever remember to have witnessed, for all my faculties were low, and unusually brought into deep silence. I said to myself, What can all this mean ? I do not recollect ever before to have been sensible of such feelings.

"And I heard a voice from heaven, saying : 'This which thou seest is a sign of the present coming times. I took the forefathers of this country from a land of oppression ; I planted them here among the people of the forest ; I sustained them, and while they were humble I blessed them, and fed them, and they became a numerous people. But they have now become proud, and forgotten me, who nourished them, and protected them in the wilderness, and are running into every abomination and evil practice of which the old countries are guilty, and have taken quietude from the land, and suffered a dividing spirit to come among them—lift up thine eyes, and behold.' And I saw them dividing in great heat. The division began in the churches on points of doctrine. It commenced in the Presbyterian Society, and went through the various religious denominations, and in its progress and close, its effects were the same. Those who dissented went off with high heads and taunting language, and those who kept to their original sentiments appeared exercised and sorrowful. And when the dividing spirit entered the Society of Friends, it raged in as high degree as in any I had noticed or before discovered ; and as before, those who separated went off with lofty looks, and taunting, censuring language. Those who kept their ancient principles retired by themselves. It next appeared in the Lodges of the Free Masons ; it broke out in appearance like a volcano, inasmuch as it set the country in an uproar for a time.

"Then it entered politics throughout the United States, and did not stop until it produced a civil war. An abundance of blood was shed in the course of the combat ; the Southern States lost their power, and slavery was annihilated from their borders. Then a monarchical power sprang up, took the Government of the States, established a national religion, and made all societies tributary to support its expenses. I saw them take property from Friends. I was amazed at beholding all this, and I heard a voice proclaiming : 'This power shall not always stand, but with it I will chastise my Church until they return to the faithfulness of their forefathers ; thou seest what is coming upon thy native country for their iniquities and the blood of Africa, the remembrance of which has come up before me.'

"This vision is yet for many days. I had no idea of writing it for many years, until it became such a burden that, for my own relief, I have written it."— *Phila. Press, May* 19.

"LET US ALONE."—So says Jeff. Davis in his Message. So say all the Southern rebels. "We don't want any war—only let us alone, and we will not trouble you. We desire peace." Every thief and robber says the same thing. Every violator of law wants to be let alone. The expression has an appropriate origin. Certain unclean spirits first used it to Jesus of Nazareth. They had full possession, and did not want to be disturbed. The Secessionists have stolen our territory, for which we paid millions ; our forts, and navy yards, and arsenals, and ships, and custom-houses, and mints ; have cruelly treated our citizens, whipping, tarring and feathering, hanging, and murdering them; have opened their batteries upon a little handful of half-starved men, and burned them out with red-hot shot; have undertaken to break up the best Government upon earth for no other cause than that they could no longer rule it; have erected batteries around other forts, and only wait an opportunity to batter them down; have put the arms stolen from us into the hands of those who threaten our destruction, and then coolly exclaim, as soon as they see the uprising of millions of brave and patriotic hearts in the defence of the Government, "Let us alone!" They haven't let *us* alone, and they can't be let alone till the evil spirit is cast out of them, even though it be with some "rending and tearing" of the body.—*Cincinnati Gazette, May 15.*

SEIZURE OF A MAP.—Months ago Governor Letcher caused surveys to be carefully made for a military map of Virginia. The memoranda and detached plans were sent to a German employed in the Coast Survey Office, to be engraved. He recommended forwarding them to New York. A few maps were engraved, and sent with the plate and original materials toward Richmond, necessarily through Washington, where the Government took charge of them.—*N. Y. Commercial, May 21.*

BUNKER HILL DAY IN VIRGINIA.—Out a mile from the city of Alexandria, Va., on a beautiful plain, is the camp of the Massachusetts Fifth, in which are two companies from Charlestown. When at home, the 17th is kept by them as an anniversary, and they determined to remember the Battle of Bunker Hill although on Virginia soil. A half mile west from the camp there is a beautiful shady grove of oaks, and there they spread their collation. Invited guests were present—citizens of Massachusetts now in this vicinity, twenty or more. After battalion drill, the companies, under command of Capt. Boyd, proceeded to the grove. The fine band of the Michigan Regiment was engaged for the occasion, and they filled the surrounding woods with "Hail, Columbia," and "Yankee Doodle." There were long tables erected; there were cold meats, pastry, fruit, oranges, strawberries and cream, nuts, raisins, tea and punch, but no other spirituous liquors. After the feast came the patriotism—speeches and sentiments from Captains Boyd and Swan, Z. K. Pangborn, J. M. Stone, of Charlestown, Col. Lawrence, Col. Green, Hon. J. M. S. Williams, of Cambridge, and many other gentlemen; and then the boys all joined in singing an ode for Bunker Hill, written for the occasion by George H. Dow, Esq. :—

"FOR BUNKER HILL."

AIR—"*America.*"

Though many miles away
From home and friends, to-day,
   We're cheerful still;
For, brothers side by side
We stand, in manly pride,
Beneath the shadow wide
   Of Bunker Hill.

The memory of that spot,
Ne'er by one man forgot,
   Protects us here!
We feel an influence, lent
From its proud Monument—
By Freedom's angel sent,
   Our souls to cheer!

POETRY—46

If, o'er the dark'ning sky,
The piercing battle-cry
   Shall sound its call—
God of our Native Land,
Be with this little band!
Columbia's Guardian, stand
   By one and all!

By all that blesses life—
While ranked in Freedom's strife—
   With right good will
For Victory we'll try,
With hope and daring high;
Our cheers shall rend the sky,
   For Bunker Hill!

Oh, how grandly it sounded through the woods! The band took up the harmony when they had finished, and it crashed louder than before. The young Virginians, and the crowd of sable sons and daughters of the Old Dominion, listened, and were glad. The stern features of the little sons of the chivalry, who had been taught to hate the invaders, relaxed into smiles as they helped themselves to the profusion of good things left, and felt the soul-stirring strains.

It was delightful—the day, the occasion, the scene. It was the 17th of June, the anniversary of the battle of Bunker Hill. It was in Virginia. Those who celebrated it were there because they loved their country, and were true to the memory of their Revolutionary fathers, the Constitution, and their flag. They were ready to spring from that festive table up the hill that rose above them at the first alarm, and fight as their fathers fought in '75. It was a lovely scene. In the distance was the marble Capitol and the unfinished monument to the ever-blessed memory of Washington, and the winding Potomac; nearer was the city of Alexandria, the bridges, and groves, and verdant fields red with clover bloom, or waving with milk-white daisies; the tents of the encampments; the moving masses of men; the red-legged Zouaves; the dark-blue Pennsylvanians and Michiganders, their arms glistening in the sun as they wheeled and deployed, or rushed across their parade; the hurrahs of the Bunker Hill boys; the roll of distant drums, and up the plain two miles distant were the solid columns of ten thousand men in review, with their banners waving in the air. It was a scene of indescribable beauty and grandeur.

Under such auspices and amid such scenes was the ever-memorable day of victory in defeat nobly and fittingly celebrated in the Old Dominion by the ever-loyal sons whose home is beneath the shadow of Bunker Hill.—"*Carleton," in the Boston Journal.*

SUPPOSED OFFICIAL CORRESPONDENCE BETWEEN JEFF. DAVIS AND GOVERNOR MAGOFFIN.

MONTGOMERY, April 20.

DEAR BERIAH :—Doubtless ere this the glad news has reached you that another star has been added to our glorious constellation; that Old Virginia has announced herself a member of the Confederacy of States now engaged in a struggle for Southern independence. Does not your heart yearn to be among us? Will Kentucky, whose past history is so indissolubly connected with the grand achievements of the sunny South—will she prove herself an exception? Need I remind you of the promises made by her illustrious son and gallant Senator, before the Charleston Convention met? Need I tell you of his patriotic efforts, in connection with the illustrious Floyd, during the last four years, to place the South in a defensive attitude? And now, that the blow is struck, where will Kentucky be found? What is your duty in the premises? Plainly this: to call a session of the Legislature, write a message portraying vividly the nature of the contest—the two alternatives: Southern rights and peculiar institutions, or Northern fanaticism and Abolition hordes. Screw their courage up to the seceding point. Advise a secret session, and a *secession* is sure to follow. While they are arranging matters inside, you can get the State Guard ready to commence operations. Don't trust the people—precipitation is the word.

Yours, secedingly,   JEFF. DAVIS.

P. S.—Give my love to Breckinridge.

BERIAH TO JEFF.

FRANKFORT, May 6.

DEAR JEFF.:—I take my pen in hand to let you know that I am well, as this leaves me at present, hoping these few lines will find you in the same condition. I have seen Breckinridge, and he told me to tell you that Kentucky is all right—bound to secede, and go South. He told me to issue a proclamation, which I did. I have got the Legislature here, but I can't get them to shut the doors. Breck. told me to tell them to secede, and I did so. Some of them are stubborn, and say they won't do it, but Breck. says they'll be all right after a while. I have sent Blanton Duncan to you. He is a good fellow, and I hope you'll make his acquaintance. He has plenty of money, which I find is a good thing to seeesh with. Excuse haste, and believe me to remain,

Yours, till death,   B. MAGOFFIN.

P. S.—Breckinridge wishes to be remembered to you.

JEFF. TO BERIAH.

MONTGOMERY, May 12.

DEAR BERIAH:—I am glad to hear of your progress Southward. We are progressing rapidly in Montgomery. Tell Breckinridge that we will give him a place in the Cabinet as soon as he secedes. If you can only get a Secession Ordinance before the people, we'll see that it is passed. We will send up some Minute Men, who will vote every hour until the thing is done. I saw Blanton yesterday. He says Kentucky is a unit for us. He will take some of the Confederate loans, and I understand your friend, James B. Clay, will do likewise. Hoping soon to welcome Kentucky to our family altar, I am,

Yours, Confederately,   JEFF.

P. S.—Blanton sends his best respects.

BERIAH TO JEFF.

FRANKFORT, May 25.

DEAR JEFF.:—You've got me into a devil of a scrape. The Legislature won't secede. I haven't seen Breckinridge for a long time. I don't know where he is. I had to issue a neutrality proposition, because the Unionists looked as if they were going to carry things their own way. I suppose Breckinridge will be mad at it, but I can't help it. He wasn't here to tell me what to do. I think he has got scared at the Union demonstrations, and subsided. I think we'd better not be in too great a hurry with Kentucky. If we get her out, it must be by a show of fairness, otherwise it may cost us our necks. The Union men swear they'll hang us if we "precipitate" her. Neutrality is the best we can do until the turn of events gives us a favorable opening, which we shall keep a sharp look-out for. Meantime, we'll keep you frequently posted as to our progress.

Yours, undespairingly,   BERIAH MAGOFFIN.

—*Cincinnati Gazette.*

A BOLD SOLDIER BOY, belonging to the Thirteenth New York Regiment, writes from Washington to his sister:—" I have grown two feet in two days, prefer gunpowder to butter on my bread, and have made arrangements to sleep forever hereafter in a cannon."
—*Boston Transcript, May 22.*

EQUAL TO THE EMERGENCY.—Benjamin Acton, of Salem County, N. J., has planted his farm with cotton, by the advice of a practical cotton-grower.—*N. Y. Sun, May 15.*

A CONTRABAND REFRAIN,

Now much in vogue at Fortress Monroe.

Wake up, snakes, pelicans, and Sesh'ners!
  Don't yer hear 'um comin'—
    Comin' on de run?
Wake up, I tell yer! Git up, Jefferson!
  Bobolishion's comin'—
    Bob-o-lish-i-on.

IT is asked, Where shall our privateers carry their prizes while our ports are blockaded? We answer: To that neutral port which the captain shall prefer—that neutral port which may be nearest at the time of the capture—which may be reached with the least danger of re-capture—where his prize may be sold at the best price. A neutral nation violates no neutral obligation in receiving a captured prize-ship into its port. This is a matter which the laws of nations leave to the discretion of the neutral, and which it may regulate, like any other subject of internal police. It is only required that it apply the same rule to both belligerents. It is to be expected that a neutral nation not unfriendly to us will see with pleasure the arrival of prizes in its ports. Every prize will benefit the neutral city by giving employment and paying money to its inhabitants; and by selling among them valuable stocks of merchandise at the lowest prices. When admitted into the port, by the laws of nations the prize is under the protection of the neutral power; the possession by the captor is sufficient proof of his right, and his title cannot there be questioned. But the captor is responsible to his own Government; and must show, in a court of his own country, that the captured vessel was the property of the enemy; and for this purpose, the papers of the prize vessel are sufficient evidence. A district court of the Confederate States will entertain jurisdiction of the case, and render judgment, in the absence of the prize-vessel, and while it remains in safe-keeping, in the neutral port.—*Mobile Register.*

COL. W. H. THOMAS, Senator from Jackson, North Carolina, has at the service of the State one of the most remarkable bodies of men in the country. It is a company of 200 Cherokee Indians, organized for battle, and styled the "Junaluske Zouaves." It appears that Col. Thomas, who is the business agent of the Cherokees, lately called a council of the Indians, and explained to them the condition of the country. The chiefs discussed the matter, and said, after consultation, that although they did not understand the national difficulty, they did know North Carolina, and would stand by her. They were ready for any position in her defence. This is most remarkable. Out of a nation of 1,500, they muster 200 warriors for the defence of North Carolina. The Cherokees are expert riflemen. They know nothing of military tactics, but show them their work, and then they have only to be told when to cease fighting. They fight their own way, and every man for himself. The "Zouaves" are ready at a moment's notice.—*Charleston News, May 10.*

A FORMIDABLE FOE.—It will be seen by the interesting letter of our Norfolk correspondent, that among the several thousand Confederate forces now at that point, is a body of three hundred Indians. These stalwart sons of the forest are from the county of Cherokee, N. C., and under the skilful training of Gen. Jackson, a distinguished member of the North Carolina Senate from Cherokee, are now ready for immediate action. A more formidable-looking body of men, we are informed by a gentleman who has seen them, never have been congregated on this continent. Not one of them is under six feet in height, and being built in proportion, they look more like modern Samsons than any thing else to which we can compare them. The rifle has been their constant companion almost from infancy, and they are confessedly the best marksmen the world has ever seen. They shoot running or standing with the same unerring certainty, and load and fire with a rapidity which is really surprising.—*Petersburg Express.*

IT was a little boy of Portsmouth, Va., who saved the splendid dry dock there from destruction at the hands of the Federal vandals. These had placed the powder for blowing up the dock, and laid a train for exploding it. When they fled, they lighted a fuse connecting with this train. Our little hero, who had been watching them from a place of concealment, turned over a plank over which the train had in part been laid, and thus "broke the connection," and saved one of the most valuable naval works in the United States or in the world.—*Raleigh (N. C.) Register.*

May 15.—The sacred remains of Washington have been removed from Mount Vernon by Colonel Washington, who has recently joined the Confederate army. This act may appear at first sight no less than an impious outrage; but it must be borne in mind, that in the sale of Mount Vernon, Colonel Washington reserved to himself not only the tomb of Washington, but also an acre of ground around it. He also bound himself to renovate the tomb.

These details are all contained in the deed of sale now in the possession of George Riggs, Trustee of the Mount Vernon Association. It is indisputable, therefore, that Colonel Washington is the sole owner of the remains of his august ancestor, and has the legal right to remove them. But this will hardly suffice to stifle those emotions of indignation, and even horror, which will swell in every Northern heart at the shocking intelligence that the revered bones of our sainted Washington have been secretly extracted from his tomb, and hid away in some unknown and unhonored receptacle. Whatever may be the right of Colonel Washington, he has been guilty of an act of vandalism, which, for the first moment, will chill the blood of the North, and strike every one dumb with amazement. Up to this hour the North has had but one purpose—to vindicate the national flag; but never can she lay down her arms till Washington, the common property of the nation, reposes once more calmly in the tomb on the banks of the Potomac, which he so loved in life, and designated as his final resting-place. Sacrilegious is the hand that has dared to violate the last wish of the Father of his Country.—*N. Y. Herald, May* 15.

THE BONES OF WASHINGTON.

A year ago, and by the maples brown,
    O'erhanging swift Potomac's broadened wave,
Bareheaded stood the heir of England's crown,
    By the poor stone that shuts an ill-kept grave,
Giving meet reverence to the dead that lay
    Beneath the stripes and stars carved on that stone,
Which nothing of inscription doth display,
    To mar the majesty that broods upon
The ten plain letters spelling WASHINGTON.

England's crown-prince at this arch-rebel's tomb,
    First Magistrate, twice-chosen, of the States
That rose impatient for more elbow-room,
    And flung the English crown out of their gates.
The contrast of those times and these so shows,
    In this respect of Prince for President,
That e'en the trite prize-poem-maker flows
    Into some lines of grave and deep intent,
    Describing that young head in solemn reverence
    bent.

Passed there a stir from wasting bone to bone,—
    Ran there a thrill through the great chief's gray
    dust,
That the old king's great-grandson by his stone
    Should bow the head, owning him great and just?
Hovered his placid spirit near, and blest
    That latest victory of truth o'er time,
When discords, slow but sure resolved, attest
    The high and holy harmonies which chime
    Their broader music through the spheres sublime?

Or was there foresight of the woe to be
    Before the lapse of twelve months and a day?
Was that great spirit prescient to see
    The stripes and stars torn from that flag away?
To know the work that he had lived to do,
    And saw and said, was good, before he died,
Undone—his glorious Union cleft in two,
    And cleaving more and more on every side,
Till none can say how far the fragments may divide.

Saw he the day that we see with amaze,
    When those to whom his life from youth he gave,
His own Virginians, his dust should raise
    Out of the shelter of that sacred grave,
Regardless of the curse that lies on those
    Whose hands disturb even the common dead!—
Brothers, from brothers bearing, as from foes,
    His bones that oft their sires to battle led,
    Who now draw impious swords, near his dishonored bed? —*London Punch, June* 8.

THE Washington correspondent of the *Philadelphia Inquirer* writes:—"In order to determine the truth or falsity of the rumor of the removal of the remains of Washington from the tomb at Mount Vernon, General Sickles despatched three messengers thither on Saturday morning. They left on horseback at 9 o'clock A. M., and crossed the Long Bridge into Virginia. One quarter of a mile beyond the bridge they met the first picket guard. They were mounted and armed with breech-loading carbines, sabres, and revolvers. The picket did not molest the party, as they stated they were simple travellers. Every two miles they met mounted scouts, similarly armed to the picket guard. At Alexandria they saw about six hundred troops. They were all well armed and equipped, and seemed to drill well.

"The party registered their names at the Mansion House, and ordered dinner to be ready at 5 P. M. On their return they informed the landlord they were going to Mount Vernon, and that one of the party would leave for Europe on the following Wednesday, and was desirous of denying the infamous rumor of the removal of Washington's remains. On their departure they were questioned, and had their attention quietly attracted to the fact that one of the party was riding on a United States Government saddle. They pushed on, however, and were allowed to pass the scouts without being detained or suspected, until within four miles of Mount Vernon.

"Here they were overtaken by scouts, and ordered to halt. The scouts then informed them they would accompany them, which they did. In conversation, one of them stated there were seven thousand cavalry in Virginia. At 1 P. M. they arrived at Mount Vernon, went to the house, and then proceeded to examine the tomb. They found it had never been molested; cobwebs were on the bars of the gate, weeds had grown up from the ground in the interior of the vault, and the party received from Mr. Williamson, who was one of the scouts, and a member of the Loudon Cavalry, a certificate that they had visited the tomb, and telling pickets to pass them, as they were from the South, and were going to Washington to contradict the infamous libel on the State of Virginia.

"They also visited the grounds. They met a carpenter who was engaged in repairing the house, and he stated that there had been no soldiers there. The party then left, and took the outskirts of Alexandria on their way home. They were at last met by the picket near the Long Bridge, and showed the scout's pass, after being ten hours and a half in the saddle, and having ridden over forty-six miles. What will the Virginians think, when they learn that Mr. Frost, a member of the Sixth Company New York Seventh Regiment, Captain Van Nest, New York Seventy-first Regiment, and Dr. A. Rawlings, of Sickles's Brigade, were the party?—*N. Y. Evening Post*, May 22.

"THE PICAYUNE'S PEDIGREE OF GEN. BUTLER."—Under this heading, the *Boston Courier* publishes, as from the columns of this journal, the following paragraph:—

"All the Massachusetts troops now in Washington are negroes, with the exception of two or three drummer-boys. Gen. Butler, in command, is a native of Liberia. Our readers may recollect old Ben, the barber, who kept a shop in Poydras street, and emigrated to Liberia with a small competence. Gen. Butler is his son."

And the *Newburyport* (Mass.) *Herald* does the same. We can scarcely imagine that the editors of either of those journals really believe that this paragraph was ever before printed in the *Picayune*. At all events, it never was.—*N. O. Picayune*, May 22.

TORPEDOES AND SUBMARINE BATTERIES.—We are happy to be informed that, among the other defences of the Elizabeth and Nansemond rivers, are these admirable contrivances for giving an unexpected hoist to an invading fleet. In one place, we are informed, the work is of a character that would damage seriously the largest squadron that ever floated on the waters. It is also said that the same contrivances either have been or are about to be arranged at various places along the coast. The batteries around Norfolk are in tip-top condition, and any demonstration upon that point will be met in a manner that will make the eyes of the next generation of Virginians sparkle with delight when they open that illumined page of her history.—*Richmond Dispatch*, May 17.

MOLLY'S DREAM.

I had a vision t'other night,
    When all around was rain;
I dreamt I saw sweet Willie B,
    A-coming down the lane;
A cannon-ball was in his hat,
    A "Minnie" in his hand;
Says he, "We're going further South,
    To make Jeff. Davis stand.
        And now, my dearest Molly,
            Please not to weep for me;
        I'm going further South, you know,—
            Perhaps to Tennessee."

He took his hat from off his head,
    The whisky from his chin,
He laid his "Minnie" on the ground,
    And then began to grin;
He put a kiss upon my lips;
    I listened while he spake—
Says he, "We're going further South,
    Jeff. Davis for to take.
        And now, my dearest Molly,
            Please not to weep for us;
        We're going further South, you know,
            To take that Davis cuss."
                        —*Boston Post*.

FLUNKY, is a genuine Yankee word. It is only found in a Yankee dictionary, and is there defined by a periphrasis. The great Webster, who understood Yankeedom thoroughly, says: "A term of contempt for one who is mean and base-spirited; perhaps from the Scottish *flunkie*, a livery servant." Worcester, another omnipotent Yankee authority, says: "A mean-spirited person, a servile follower—used contemptuously." The word could only have had its origin in a land where the thing itself had existence. The *animal*, flunky, is an unadulterated Yankee product. Recent events go to prove that it is not merely the exclusive, but universal growth of that region.—*Charleston Mercury*.

THE SHADOW AND THE SUBSTANCE.

"MR. EDITOR:—Did the following *facts* ever occur to all of your numerous readers, in regard to the true position of the two Presidents now recognized on North American soil?

"*The First*—President Lincoln, the Shadow—with Lieut.-General Scott, and over 50,000 WELL-ARMED SOLDIERS around him, at the Capital, to protect his *dear* life!

"*The Second*—President Davis, the Substance—in a country town, amid his family associations and among his civic friends—in daily intercourse with the people, and travelling at any and all times from one portion of the Confederacy to the other !

"Truly, here is a great contrast of position ; one that should awaken Northern fanatics and insane politicians to a true sense of the unpopularity of their war against the South ; and fully picturing to them the 'shadow' and the 'substance' of North American affairs.   John."

    —*Natchez Courier, May* 21.

GEN. PILLOW, who is a clever gentleman in the private relations of life, and a very companionable man, sent us a message recently, which is explained in the following reply :—

"GEN. GIDEON PILLOW :—I have just received your message through Mr. Sale, requesting me to serve as Chaplain to your Brigade in the Southern army ; and in the spirit of kindness in which this request is made, but in all candor, I return for answer, that when I shall have made up my mind to go to hell, I will cut my throat and go *direct*, and not travel round by the Southern Confederacy.

"I am very respectfully, &c.,

        "W. G. BROWNLOW."

    —*Knoxville Whig.*

UNDER the head of "A Proposition to Major Anderson," the *New Orleans Picayune* of May 17th publishes the following, "from a well-known citizen" :—

      "NEW ORLEANS, May 16, 1861.

"MAJOR ROBT. ANDERSON, *late of Fort Sumter, S. C.* :

"SIR :—You hold my three notes for $4,500 each, with about $1,000 accumulated interest, all due in the month of March, 1862, which notes were given in part payment of twenty-nine negroes, purchased of you in March, 1860. As I consider *fair play a jewel*, I take this method to notify you that I will not pay those notes ; but, as I neither seek nor wish an advantage, I desire that you return me the notes and the money paid you, and the negroes shall be subject to your order, which you will find much improved by kind treatment since they came into my possession.

"I feel justified in giving you, and the public, this notice, as I do not consider it *fair play* that I should be held to pay for the very property you so opportunely dispossessed yourself of, and now seek to destroy both their value and usefulness to me. I ask no more than to cancel the sale, restore to you your property, and let each assume his original position ; then your present efforts may be considered less selfish, because at your expense, and not mine.

        JOHN G. COCKS."

AN INCIDENT OF CAMP LIFE AT WASHINGTON.

THE MARRIAGE AT NIGHT.—Six bold riflemen clad in blue, with scarlet doublets over the left shoulder, bearing blazing torches ; six glittering Zouaves, with brilliant trappings, sparkling in the light ; and then the hollow square, where march the bridegroom and bride ; then seven rows of six groomsmen in a row, all armed *cap-a-pie*, with burnished weapons, flashing back the lustre of the Zouave uniform ; and all around the grand regiment darkening the white tent-folds, as their ruddy faces are but half disclosed between the red and yellow glare of the fires, and the soft, silver light of the May-moon. (This is all, you will bear in mind, out on the broad, open air. The encampment occupies a conically-shaped hill-top,

flanked around the rear crescent by a wood of fan-leaved maples sprinkled with blossoming dogberries, and looking out at the cone upon the river-swards below. The plain is full of mounds and ridges, save where it bulges in the centre to a circular elevation perfectly flat, around which, like façades about a court-yard, are arrayed the spiral tents, illuminated in honor of the coming nuptials.) The bride is the daughter of the regiment ; the to-be-husband a favorite sergeant. Marching thus, preceded by two files of sixes, and followed by the glittering rows of groomsmen, the little cortege has moved out of the great tent on the edge of the circle, and comes slowly, amid the bold strains of the grand "Midsummer-Night's Dream," towards the regimental chaplain.

You have seen the colored prints of Jenny Lind on the back of the music of "*Vive la France.*" You have noted the light-flowing hair, the soft Swiss eye, the military bodice, the coquettish red skirt, and the pretty buskined feet and ankles underneath. The print is not unlike the bride. She was fair-haired, blue-eyed, rosy-cheeked, darkened in their hue by exposure to the sun, in just the dress worn by *les filles du regiment.* She was formed in that athletic mould which distinguishes the Amazon from her opposite extreme of frailty. You could not doubt her capacity to undergo the fatigues and hardships of a campaign, but your mind did not suggest to your eye those grosser and more masculine qualities which, whilst girting the woman with strength, disrobe her of the purer, more effeminate traits of body. You saw before you a young girl, apparently about eighteen years of age, with clear, courageous eye, quiverless lip, and soldierly tread—a veritable daughter of the regiment. You have seen Caroline Richings and good old Peter (St. Peter !) march over the stage as the corporal and *la fille.* Well, this girl, barring the light flaxen hair, would remind you of the latter, drilling a squad of grenadiers.

The bridegroom was of the same sanguine, Germanic temperament, as the bride. As he marched, full six feet in height, with long, light-colored beard, high cheek-bones, aquiline nose, piercing, deeply-studded blue eye, broad shoulders, long arms, sturdy legs, feet and hands of a laborious development, cocked hat with blue plume, dark blue frock, with bright scarlet blanket, tartan fashion over the shoulder, small sword, you would have taken him for a hero of Sir Walter. Faith, had Sir Walter seen him, he himself would have taken him. In default, however, of Sir Walter, I make bold to appropriate him as a hero on the present occasion. Indeed, he was a hero, and looked it, every inch of him, leading that self-sacrificing girl up to the regimental chaplain, with his robe, and surplice, and great book, amid the stare of a thousand anxious eyes, to the music of glorious old Mendelssohn, and the beating of a thousand earnest hearts !

The music ceased ; a silence as calm as the silent moon held the strange, wild place ; the fires seemed to sparkle less noisily in reverence ; and a little white cloud paused in its course across the sky to look down on the group below ; the clear voice of the preacher sounded above the suppressed breathing of the spectators, and the vague burning of the fagot heaps ; a few short words, a few heartfelt prayers, the formal legal ceremonial, and the happy "Amen." It was done. The pair were man and wife. In rain or sunshine, joy or sorrow, for weal or woe, bone of one bone and flesh of one flesh, forever and ever—amen !

The groom's people formed a hollow square around the newly-wedded couple. In one corner a gateway was left for the entrance of the men. Then came one by one the members of that troop, with a kind word each, as each touched the bride lightly on the cheek, and grasped the bridegroom heartily by the hand—of one the sworn fathers, of the other the friends and brothers, comrades in arms.—*Philadelphia Press.*

AREA OF THE CONFEDERATE STATES.—We publish the following table in a corrected form :—

	Area,	Total Population.		
States.	in sqr. miles.	Whites.	Slaves.	Total.
Virginia,	61,352	1,097,373	495,826	1,593,199
North Carolina,	50,704	679,965	328,377	1,008,342
South Carolina,	29,385	308,186	447,185	755,371
Georgia,	58,000	615,386	467,561	1,082,847
Florida,	59,268	81,885	63,809	145,694
Alabama,	50,722	520,444	435,473	955,917
Mississippi,	47,156	407,551	479,607	887,158
Louisiana,	41,255	354,245	312,186	666,431
Texas,	237,504	415,999	181,956	606,955
Arkansas,	52,198	331,710	109,065	440,775
Tennessee,	45,600	859,528	287,112	1,146,640
	733,144	5,672,272	3,607,057	9,279,320

—*N. O. Picayune, May 26.*

May 22.—In Nashville, Tenn., while secession banners wave from every other building, both public and private, one heroic lady (Mrs. McEwin) has placed the National Flag on her house, and says she will shoot whoever attempts to tear down the glorious old Stars and Stripes. Let her name be engraved on the hearts of all loyal Americans.—*Louisville Journal.*

THE REBEL COMMISSIONERS IN ENGLAND.—A gentleman who was present and heard what he reports, relates that the Commissioners from the rebel States having been formally introduced to Mr. Bates, the head of the house of Baring Brothers, the great financier told them to proceed. They commenced with a most elaborate and glowing description of the resources and wealth of the rebel States. After a pause—

Mr. BATES—"Have you finished?"

COMMISSIONERS—"Not quite." [Then a speech from Commissioner No. 2, and a pause.]

Mr. BATES—"Have you finished?"

COMMISSIONERS—"Almost." [Then a speech from Commissioner No. 3, and a pause.]

Mr. BATES—"Are you through?"

COMMISSIONERS—"Yes, sir; you have our case."

Mr. BATES—"What States did you say composed your Confederacy?"

COMMISSIONERS—"Mississippi, South Carolina, Alabama, Georgia, Florida, Texas, and Louisiana."

Mr. BATES—"And Mr. Jefferson Davis is your President?"

COMMISSIONERS—"He is. We are proud of him."

Mr. BATES—"We know Mr. Davis well by reputation. He is the same gentleman who stumped his State for two years in favor of repudiation, and justified the conduct of Mississippi in the United States Senate. We know the gentleman; and although we have no reason to be proud of him or his antecedents, I think I may safely say, that if you have brought with you to London the necessary funds to pay off, principal and interest, the repudiated millions owing to our people by your States of Alabama, Mississippi, and Florida, there is a reasonable prospect of your raising a small amount in this market! Our Mr. Sturgis will be happy to dine with you at 8 o'clock to-morrow evening." *Exeunt omnes.*

While this scene was being enacted at the Barings, Mr. Dudley Mann waited upon our countryman Peabody, who holds three hundred thousand dollars of repudiated Mississippi bonds, on which there is due more than six hundred thousand dollars of interest. Mr. Mann was very magnificent and grandiloquent, but, withal, prosy; and Peabody, suffering from gout and Mississippi repudiation, lost his temper; and, shaking his clenched fist at the rebel, emphatically said: "If I were to go on 'Change and hunt up the suffering and starved widows and orphans who have been ruined by your infamous repudiation of honest debts, and proclaim that you are here to borrow more of our gold and silver to be again paid by repudiation, (as I believe it is my duty to do,) you would inevitably be mobbed, and find it difficult to escape with your life. Good morning, sir."—*N. Y. Courier and Enquirer, May 25.*

Do the Northerners begin to recognize the inevitable decay of their system of Government, and the fact that this sudden upheaval has demonstrated, that law is at an end, and that by brute force they must keep in check their antagonistic forces? Do they see faintly, or clearly, that Government based upon the nominal equality of all, amid the ceaseless warfare of labor and capital, where labor is indiscriminately armed with that terrible scourge of the ballot, and where labor out-votes capital, is an utter failure? Have these people determined to set in motion armed men, preparatory to the grand change of their form of Government, in order to save what is worth saving, from the carnage and the devastation that must attend the anarchy which usually intervenes between a free Government, and a firmly established despotism? Have they at last learned the unwilling lesson, that they neither deserve, nor can maintain, a free Government, when deprived of the ballast, the conservatism of domestic slavery? Do they comprehend the end to which their foul licentiousness, their unbridled lusts, are fatally hurrying them, and see that the ballot cannot be taken from their laborers, till first an organized soldiery is prepared to do the behests of property, and, under the lead of some strong will, to hold their Government together in some form, till they can change it to suit them? It really seems that they are waking up to these great facts.—*Augusta (Ga.) Chronicle, May 16.*

THE Charlestonians tell a good story at their own expense, which well illustrates the want of discipline. A company was keeping guard at the arsenal. The Colonel of the regiment passing by, saw the sentinel inattentive to his duty. He took away his gun, then entered the arsenal. A subordinate officer was concocting a cocktail.

"Where is the Captain?" the Colonel asked.

"Up stairs."

"Please say to him that I want to see him."

"Well, after I take a drink," said the subaltern. After swallowing his toddy, he went up stairs to the Captain.

"The Colonel is down stairs, and wants to see you, Captain."

"Well, if he wants to see me more than I do him, just tell him to walk up," said the Captain, who was lying on a bed.

The Colonel went up stairs, and found the Captain

taking things easy. "Sir, you ought to be drilling your company. Your sentinel don't know how to do his duty, and I took his gun away from him."

"Well, I dare say he will be much obliged to you. I reckon he was tired of carrying it."

Another good story was told, which has not found its way into the Charleston papers.

The light boat which was captured, has been anchored at the mouth of the creek which leads to Stono River. Two guns have been placed on board. The one aiming down the creek is kept loaded with shot, while the one pointing toward the city is used to fire a morning and evening gun. Not long since, when the sunrise gun was fired, a twelve-pound ball ripped through a negro's shanty, and lodged in a hotel, greatly to the consternation of an old negro and several boarders. The crew of the light boat did not discover that the boat had turned with the tide during the night!—*Boston Journal, May* 18.

A PORTION of the river Indus was infested by a large old crocodile, which had carried off two or three natives. His skin was so thick that no ball would penetrate it; some young artillery officers engineered his destruction in the following way: They killed a sheep, and in its body placed a bag filled with powder and other combustible matter, to which a long wire was attached, with detonating powder at the end. The crocodile seized the prey, and carried it to his hole. Time was allowed him to swallow the sheep; the wire was pulled, there was a great explosion, and up came the crocodile with his stomach blown open. Acting upon this precedent, a Hoosier proposes to get rid of Jeff. Davis.—*Indianola Star.*

NEW ORLEANS, *May* 13.—Already a capital privateering vessel has been fitted out in this city, and is now ready, fully armed and ably officered, waiting for the letters of marque and reprisal which are daily expected from Montgomery. We have the names of the vessel and officers, which we will publish in due time. The work of fitting out another privateer is going on, something over one-fourth of the stock of $200,000 having been subscribed up to the hour of the meeting at noon yesterday in the old United States Court-room, for the purpose of furthering the enterprise. For the information of those disposed to embark in the work, we would state that the officers of the vessel are to be appointed according to the election of the stockholders. In this connection we have heard mentioned such names as Capt. Calendar Fayssoux, of this city, and Capt. Harry Maury, of Mobile, and many others suitable to command. Capt. Wilson and others taking an interest in this matter may be consulted daily, at the old United States Court-room.—*N. O. Picayune, May* 14.

A PRIVATE letter, dated Camp Defiance, Cairo, May 13, 1861, contains the following:—

"Your blood would boil if you should witness what I have witnessed. Persons are daily arriving here who have been driven away from the South—some for expressing love of the Union, and others for saying that they did not wish to fight against us. Many such have been whipped, scourged, and treated with all manner of brutalities. One man, a Philadelphian, called upon Gen. Prentiss, and invited him to his room in the hotel, where he exhibited the welts and wounds inflicted by those fiends of rebellion upon his person. The devils had not only beaten him black and blue, but had slashed his arms and body with their knives. He was the worst object I ever saw. This man was making collections in the South for a Philadelphia house, and such was the payment received from Southern creditors.

"The game of the villains is about up here. Every traitor who makes his appearance is arrested. We have one dirty dog from Columbus, Ky., under arrest, who was one of the seventy-five who took turns in lashing a man because he would not shout for Jeff. Davis's flag. Mr. Chivalry is very penitent, and he don't hear a pistol shot but he imagines it is for him. This beauty came here to see what the 'damned abolitionists' were doing, and was recognized by the victim, who reached Cairo before. Victim wanted an even show with Chivalry at any kind of a fight, and said if he did not kill him, he would submit to be hung the next minute. Chivalry did not want to fight—there were not odds enough—it was not seventy-five to one. If Gen. Prentiss had not arrested Chivalry, he would not have lived half an hour. He has been committed for future trial. Every boat brings hundreds of people flying North for safety. Such is the state of terrorism in the cities and towns below us."—*Chicago (Ill.) Post, May* 16.

GEN. TWIGGS AND PRESIDENT BUCHANAN.—Gen. Twiggs, late of the United States Army, has addressed a letter to Ex-President Buchanan, in which he says:—"Your usurped right to dismiss me from the army might be acquiesced in; but you had no right to brand me as a traitor. This was personal, and *I shall treat it as such*—not through the papers, but *in person.* I shall, most assuredly, pay a visit to Lancaster for the sole purpose of a *personal interview* with you. So, sir, prepare yourself. I am well assured that public opinion will sanction *any course* I may take with you."—*Charleston Courier, May* 18.

AMONG the gallant fellows in Meagher's Irish Zouaves, is an ex-member of the "Pope's Irish Brigade," who distinguished himself in the army of the Pontiff during the late difficulties in Italy. He goes out as Sergeant to join the Sixty-ninth Regiment. His name is John Gleeson, a six feet five Irishman, with all the bearing of a soldier. He was presented with a gold medal by Lamoriciere on the 5th of last October, for his brave services at the battle of Ancona, and was promoted from the rank of Sergeant to that of Lieutenant. This latter distinction was accorded to him for taking Monte Moratta while in charge of a company of skirmishers. He is a gallant son of Tipperary, and was wounded three times in action.—*N. Y. Herald, May* 23.

ELEVEN second cousins of Mrs. Lincoln are members of the Caroline Light Dragoons. Mrs. Lincoln was a Miss Todd, niece of the late G. T. Todd, Esq., of Caroline county. Lincoln's "foreign relations" would be glad to give him a deserved reception in the county of Caroline.—*Fredericksburg (Va.) News.*

REV. M. L. WELLER, the young, zealous, and beloved minister of the Episcopal church in Hernando, Miss., on last Tuesday morning bade adieu to all the endearments of home and the society of his attached congregation, and left for Camp Davis, near Pensacola, Florida, there to take his position as an humble private in the ranks of Capt. Tom White's company, the 9th Regiment of Mississippi Volunteers. Few more noble examples of patriotism than this are recorded even in the pages of Revolutionary heroism. Mr. Weller was anxious to have gone off with the company from Hernando when it left for Pensacola, about six weeks since, but having been located here in some sort by the Bishop of the Diocese, he disliked to leave his church without the sacred sanction of his permission. No opportunity offered for him to obtain this until a short time ago; and when he told Bishop Green that the promptings of his heart were constantly calling him by day and night to defend his country upon the battle-field, that Rev. Prelate told him to go, and God's blessing go with him—that he (the Bishop) already had two sons in the field, and that he himself would be there if occasion called for his services.

Mr. Weller goes not as a hired chaplain or salaried officer of any sort, but with his rifle in his hand and his knapsack on his back, to do the duty and the whole duty of a private in the ranks; and we will venture the assertion, that there will be no man in all that army who will do it more thoroughly, more nobly, or more fearlessly.

Mr. Weller was very dear to the hearts of his congregation before. It is needless to say that he will not be less dear in the future.

We are pleased to learn that the vestry of his church have unanimously granted him leave of absence for one year; have resolved that his position shall be kept open for him until he returns, and have continued his salary during his absence.—*People's Press, Hernando, (Miss.,) May* 16.

THE *Portland* (Me.) *Argus* publishes the following correspondence:—

" DEAR SIR :—I am requested by Secretary Mallory to indite you a few lines soliciting your acceptance of a commission, commanding in the Confederate Navy of America; your pay to go on from the date of secession of your native State, (South Carolina.) Your high capabilities and qualifications as a seaman and navigator, and knowledge in angles, &c., &c., and associations of your honorable family, proclaim you to be a man of honor, consequently adhering to the great fundamental law of nature—home first, the cause of your own hearth-side before that of strangers. But worse than all, these strangers have waged war against us, and you are abiding with them—thus endorsing their acts ; *can you wantonly abandon your country, by forming an alliance with a Northern lady?* * * * * Here you are offered rank, honor, station, and everlasting employ; whilst the cold-hearted Northerners will even refuse you, (employ.)

" Answer in haste; and if you need funds to almost any amount, fail not to let me know. I will have you supplied by Southern friends at Portland.

" In haste, yours truly,

" J. P. BENJAMIN, Atty-Gen'l, C. S. A.

" To Capt. C. LEE MOSES, Saco, Me.

" MONTGOMERY, April 9, 1861."

" OLD ORCHARD HOUSE, SACO, ME., }
                                April 17, 1861. }

" Mr. J. P. BENJAMIN :

" SIR :—Your letter of the 9th has been received, and I wish you and Mr. Mallory to distinctly understand that I hold no conference with traitors. The banner stamped upon this slip of paper is my adoration; it has real beauty; God bless it now and forever; *and curses upon him who tramples upon it in the absence of manliness to protect it.* I am and have been since last October the husband of a Saco

lady. * * * * * I was born in South Carolina, but, thank God, left it in my childhood days with all my family. I will take employ here before the mast, in preference to your highest encomiums.

" As a gentleman, I was in duty bound to reply to your letter ; *let it be your last to me.*

" The American Flag—long may she wave
    O'er the land of the free and the traitor's grave."

" C. LEE MOSES,
    " A Northern-made Sailor and Unionist."

The *Argus* states that Captain Moses is a relative of Senator Benjamin.—*N. Y. Evening Post, May* 18.

CHARLESTON, S. C., *May* 2.—It was the blasphemous saying of some great warrior—we forget now who—that God always took sides with strong regiments. We are satisfied, from all our readings of history, that God's justice prevails over all—and, whether it is the weak or the strong, that, in the end, He will support the truth, the right, the pure, the just. We are not to determine what His judgments shall be from the casualties of a single hour.

We believe that God is with us. We solemnly believe that a most Providential care has guided and strengthened us thus far against the blind rages of our enemy ; that, even in those respects in which we fancied we had lost an advantage—as in Anderson's abandonment of Moultrie and taking possession of Sumter—we were mistaken ; and that the very strategies of our enemies became the secret of their overthrow. And so of all the falsehoods of the Northern press, and so of all the mean, cunning trickery of the Government at Washington ; and so of almost every event since the beginning of our struggle for peace and independence. The strongest fortress in the country—supposed to be too strong for all the power of South Carolina, under a siege of months—is overthrown in thirty-three hours. The fortress, so impregnable, and so eagerly seized upon, becomes a rat-trap, from which the rats are smoked out. Even the military vanity, which insists upon saluting its flag at its overthrow, with one hundred guns, is rebuked by an explosion which costs the garrison more lives than were lost during the bombardment. Verily, if we needed signs and auguries, we have had them, and of the most grateful character.

Yes! we solemnly believe that a Providential interposition is about to rescue us from the cormorant tribes that have been fattening so long upon our substance. We have made them great and prosperous ! And they know not the source of their own prosperity ! They " crammed, and blasphemed their feeders." By tariffs, navigation laws, internal improvements, and infernal appropriations, they swallowed up all our revenues. In their vanity and pride of heart they mocked at God—forgot him—mocked at us—and now seek to destroy us ! Shall God suffer the guilty, the presumptuous, the vain-glorious, the usurpative, the aggressive, to thrive, and triumph over those who have been only too submissive ? No ! Their insolence nears its end ! They have reached the length of their tether ! Henceforth, the South alone shall reap the large benefits and blessings of Southern culture and industry. May the great Father of the universe keep us, while enjoying the marvellous blessings of our own section, from any undue pride of heart ! May He keep us always duly mindful of Him who is the great Source of all !—*Charleston Mercury, May* 3.

ODE, FOR 1861.

BY REV. H. HASTINGS WELD.

O God of our fathers, Thy aid we implore,
  'Mid the storm of rebellion, to shield us from
    danger;
The sunlight of union and peace to restore
  O'er the flag that defied the assault of the stranger.
To the fair open foe, our gauntlet we throw,
But the snares of sedition we scarcely can know.
Is the star-spangled banner no longer to wave
O'er the land of the free, and the home of the brave?

Thy hand we confess; Thou hast humbled our pride,
  And we trust not in chariots, or count upon
    horses,
But rest on the might and the wisdom that guide
  The sun in his path, and the stars in their courses.
From Thy people that pray, Lord, turn not away;
Let us welcome again the glad national day,
When the star-spangled banner in triumph shall wave
O'er the land of the free, and the home of the brave.

Away with all fears that our hearts might appal,
  For the gloom does but herald a happier morrow;
Heaven victory gives, if we faithfully call,
  And the garment of joy, for the spirit of sorrow.
Oh, then be the praise to the Ancient of Days,
As, for God and our Country, our voices we raise;
And the star-spangled banner in triumph shall wave
O'er the land of the free, and the home of the brave.

Religion, and virtue, and truth to maintain,
  We have brought forth our flag before Heaven's
    high altar;
The right to assert, and the laws to sustain,
  Before God we are bound, and we dare not to
    falter.
Interweave in its fold the blest symbol of old,
And let Calvary's emblem the standard uphold;
And the star-spangled banner forever shall wave
O'er the land of the free, and the home of the brave.

MOORESTOWN, N. J., July 4, 1861.

THE NATION'S VOICE.

BY REV. MARSHALL B. SMITH.

No longer shall our standard
  Ignobly trail in dust,
Or the sword within its scabbard
  Corroded be with rust;
For the Nation's heart is beating
  With quick and mighty throes,
And the Nation's hands are ready
  To subdue the Nation's foes.

From blue Penobscot's waters
  To Potomac's crystal tide,
From the great Atlantic seaboard
  To Nevada's snowy side,
One mighty voice is uttered,
  Like the thunders of the sky:
"'Neath the Stars and Stripes we'll rally,
  And for them we will die.
Though the colors of the rebels
  Float on every Southern plain,
We will tear them from the staff-head,
  And raise 'the Stripes' again.

Though the enemies of Freedom
  Come forth in all their might,
In the strength of God we'll meet them,
  And battle for the right.
We will rally for our country,
  And for human freedom, too,
And bravely meet the traitors
  'Neath the old 'Red, White, and Blue.'

"The spirit of our fathers
  Revives in us to-day,
For their valor and their courage
  Have not wholly died away;
And the ingrate and the traitor
  Shall know their power again,
Though the sands of Carolina
  Be covered with the slain.
Though the blood of Northern freemen
  In sullen torrents flow,
The valiant sons of Freedom
  Shall lay the traitors low."
For God, then, and your country—
  For freeman and for slave—
Go, brothers, to the conflict!
  God bless the true and brave!

PASSAIC, N. J.   —N. Y. Tribune.

THE SOUTHERN VOLUNTEER'S FAREWELL
TO HIS WIFE.

Fresh from snuff-dipping to his arms she went,
  And he, a quid removing from his mouth,
Pressed her in anguish to his manly breast,
  And spat twice, longingly, toward the South.

"Zara," he said, and hiccup'd as he spoke,
  "Indeed, I find it most (hic) 'stremely hard
To leave my wife, my niggers, and my debts,
  And march to glory with the 'Davis Guard;'

"But all to arms the South has called her sons,
  And while there's something Southern hands can
    steal,
You can't (hic) 'spect me to stay here at home,
  With heartless duns forever at my heel.

"To-night a hen-coop falls; and in a week
  We'll take the Yankee Capital, I think;
But should it prove (hic) 'spedient not to do't,
  Why, then, we'll take—in short, we'll take a drink.

"I reckon I may perish in the strife—
  Some bullet in the back might lay me low;
And as my business needs attendin' to,
  I'll give you some directions ere I go:

"That cotton gin I haven't paid for yet—
  The Yankee trusted for it, dear, you know;
And it's a most (hic) 'stremely doubtful thing,
  Whether it's ever used again, or no.

"If Yankee's agent calls while I am gone,
  It's my (hic) 'spress command and wish, that you
Denounce him for an abolition spy,
  And have him hung before his note is due.

"That octoroon—who made you jealous, love—
  Who sews so well, and is so pale a thing;
She keeps her husband, Sambo, from his work—
  You'd better sell her—well, for what she'll bring.

"In case your purse runs low while I'm away—
    There's Dinah's children—two (hic) 'spensive
        whelps;
They won't bring much, the way the markets are,
    But then, you know how every little helps.

"And there's that Yankee schoolmistress, you know,
    Who taught our darlings how to read and spell;
Now don't (hic) 'spend a cent to pay *her* bill;
    If she arn't tarred and feathered, she'll do well!

"And now, my dear, I go where booty calls;
    I leave my whiskey, cotton-crop, and thee;
Pray that in battle I may not (hic) 'spire,
    And when you lick the niggers, think of me.

"If on some mournful summer afternoon
    They should bring home to you your warrior dead
        (drunk?)
Inter me with a toothpick in my hand,
    And write a last (hic) *jacet* o'er my head."

KENTUCKY.

"Kentucky—she was the first State to enter the Union
after the adoption of the Constitution; she will be the last
to leave it."—[*Words inscribed on Kentucky's contribution
to the Washington Monument.*]

BY MRS. SOPHIA H. OLIVER.

"The first to join the patriot band,
    The last bright star to fade and die,"
Oh, first-born daughter of the land,
    Wilt thou thy sacred vow deny?
By all the lofty memories bright
    That crown with light thy glorious past,
Oh, speak again those words of might—
    "The first to come, to leave the last."

The land for which our fathers fought,
    The glorious heritage they gave,
The just and equal laws they wrought—
    Rise, in your might, that land to save.
No parricidal daughter thou,
    No stain be on thy fealty cast,
But faithful to thy boast and vow,
    "Be first to come, to leave the last."

Oh, list not to the siren voice
    That woos thee to a traitor cause;
But answer, "I have made my choice;
    I will support my country's laws."
Go, spurn disunion's foul cabal;
    All party ties behind thee cast;
And still at honor's, duty's call,
    "Be first to come, to leave the last."

And land of high unsullied fame,
    Hast thou no grievous wrongs to right?
Thy hero, wrapped in Sumter's flame,
    And conquered in unequal fight!
Thy banner trampled in the dust——
    Hark! shouts of freemen swell the blast,
"We will defend *our flag*—we must
    'Be first to come, to leave the last.'"

Land of my birth! how dear to me
    Has ever been thy spotless fame;
Oh, may I *never, never* see
    The brand of *traitor* on thy name.

Go, gird thee in thy armor bright;
    Be faithful to thy glorious past;
And in the battle for the *right*,
    "Be first to come, to leave the last."
                                —*Cincinnati Commercial.*

ALL OF THEM.*

BY "S. R. K."

With head erect, and lips compressed,
    He throws his hammer by;
The purpose of his manly breast
    Is now to do or die.

He seeks the camp: "Put down my name,
    (My boys will mind the shop;)
If the traitors want my heart's best blood,
    I'll sell it drop for drop.

"And here comes now my oldest boy:
    My son, what would you do?"
"Father, my brother will drive the trade;
    I've come to fight with you."

"God bless him! Well, put down his name;
    I cannot send him home.
But here's the other boy, I see:
    My son, what made you come?"

"Father, I could not work alone;
    The shop may go to—grass;
I've come to fight for the good old flag;
    Stand off here—let me pass."

"Yes, put him down—he's a noble boy;
    I've two that are younger still;
They'll drive the plough on the Flushing farm,
    And work with a right good will.

"My God! and here comes one of them!
    My son, you must not go!"
"Father, when traitors are marching on,
    I cannot plough or sow."

"Well, thank God, there is one left yet;
    He will plough and sow what he can;
But he's only a boy, and can never do
    The work of a full grown man."

With a proud, full heart, the blacksmith turned,
    And walked to the other side,
For he felt a weakness he almost scorned,
    And a tear he fain would hide.

They told him then, his youngest boy
    Was putting his name on the roll:
"It must not be," said the brave old man;
    "No, no, he's the light of my soul!"

But the lad came up with a beaming face,
    Which bore neither fears nor cares:
"Father, say nothing—my name is down;
    I have let out the farm on shares."

And now they've marched to the tented field,
    And when the wild battle shall come,
They'll strike a full blow for the Stars and Stripes,
    For God, and their Country, and Home.
                            —*N. Y. Tribune, June 1.*

* See page 112, Rumors and Incidents, *ante.*

"THE RATTLESNAKE BANNER."

BY "W. M. W."

Sung by the 7,000 "chivalry" before a small audience of Northern mudsills, at the taking of Sumter.

Oh, say, can you see by the dawn's early light,
    What so proudly we hailed at the twilight's last
        gleaming,
Whose *serpentine coilings* through the perilous fight,
    O'er the ramparts we watched, were so gallantly
        streaming :
And the rocket's red glare, the bombs bursting in air,
Gave proof through the night that our *snake* was
    still there ;
Oh, say, does the *Rattlesnake* Banner yet wave
O'er the land of the *Bond,* and the home of the
    Slave ?

On the *isle* dimly seen through the mists of the deep,
    Where the foe's *starving* host in *cowardice shud-*
        ders,
What is that which the breeze o'er the towering steep,
    As it fitfully blows, half conceals, half uncovers ?
Now it catches the gleam of the morning's first beam,
In full glory reflected, now shines on the stream :
'Tis his snakeship, our Banner—oh, long may it
    wave
O'er the land of the Bond, and the home of the
    Slave !

And where is the band who so vauntingly swore
    That the havoc of war, and the battle's confusion,
A home and a country should leave us no more ?
    The "invincible South" has dispelled their delu-
        sion ;
The mudsills are conquered—the victory's ours ;
The foe now acknowledges our chivalric powers,
And the Rattlesnake Banner in triumph doth wave
O'er the land of the Bond, and the home of the Slave.

Oh, thus be it ever, when Slavers shall stand
    Between their loved home and the war's desola-
        tion ;
Blest with cotton and niggers, may our Rattlesnake
    land
    Praise the power that hath made (?) and pre-
       served (?) us a nation.
Then conquer we must, when our cause is so just,
And this be our motto—In Davis we trust !
And the Star-spangled Banner *no longer* shall wave
O'er the land of the Bond, and the home of the Slave.
    —*Galesburg (Ill.) Free Democrat,* May 23.

THE SOUTHERN MALBROOK.

A SONG OF THE FUTURE.

BY R. H. STODDARD.

AIR—"*Malbrough s'en va-t-en guerre.*"

Jeff. Davis has gone to battle,
Tweedledum, tweedledum, tweedledee ;
Jeff. Davis has gone to battle,
Nor knows when he'll return.

He'll return on the first of April,
Tweedledum, tweedledum, tweedledee ;
He'll return on the first of April,
Or on the Fourth of July.

But the Fourth of July is over,
Tweedledum, tweedledum, tweedledee ;
But the Fourth of July is over,
And Davis does not return.

Lady Davis calls her Congress,
Tweedledum, tweedledum, tweedledee ;
Lady Davis calls her Congress,
And mounts the speaker's chair.

She there perceives her nigger,
Tweedledum, tweedledum, tweedledee ;
She there perceives her nigger,
As black as the ace of spades.

"Nigger, my high-priced nigger,
Tweedledum, tweedledum, tweedledee ;
Nigger, my high-priced nigger,
What tidings do you bring ?"

"O Gorra, missus, de tidin's,
Tweedledum, tweedledum, tweedledee ;
O Gorra, missus, de tidin's,
Dey'll make yer lily eyes weep.

"Took off yer summer muslin,
Tweedledum, tweedledum, tweedledee ;
Took off yer summer muslin,
Also yer more anteek.

"Massa Jeff. is done gone dead,
Tweedledum, tweedledum, tweedledee ;
Massa Jeff. is done gone dead,
Dead an' buried, shu-ah !

"I seed him shove in de ground,
Tweedledum, tweedledum, tweedledee ;
I seed him shove in de ground,
By de Abolitioners !

"One follored wid his message,
Tweedledum, tweedledum, tweedledee ;
One follored wid his message,
Anoder wid his letters ob Mark.

"One carried his dyin' 'fession,
Tweedledum, tweedledum, tweedledee ;
One carried his dyin' 'fession,
Anoder some 'Fed'rate bon's.

"Dey hung him on de gallus,
Tweedledum, tweedledum, tweedledee ;
Dey hung him on de gallus,
Under de Stars an' Stripes.

"Around his tomb dey planted,
Tweedledum, tweedledum, tweedledee,
Around his tomb dey planted
De cussed Palmetter tree !

"Upon de topmost branches,
Tweedledum, tweedledum, tweedledee,
Upon de topmost branches,
De Turkey buzzard sung.

"We seed his troubled spirit,
Tweedledum, tweedledum, tweedledee,
We seed his troubled spirit
Fly ober de Cotton States.

" Secesshun fell to de ground,
Tweedledum, tweedledum, tweedledee ;
Secesshun fell to de ground,
Till it got up agin,

" To sing ob de victories,
Tweedledum, tweedledum, tweedledee,
To sing ob de victories
Dat Massa Davis won.

" De sad occashun ober,
Tweedledum, tweedledum, tweedledee,
De sad occashun ober,
De folks went home to bed."
                              —*Vanity Fair.*

SONGS OF THE REBELS.

SOUTHERN WAR-CRY.

AIR—"*Scots, wha hae.*"

Countrymen of Washington !
Countrymen of Jefferson !
By Old Hick'ry oft led on
        To death or victory !

Sons of men who fought and bled,
Whose blood for you was freely shed,
Where Marion charged and Sumter led,
        For freemen's rights !

From the Cowpens glorious way,
Southron valor led the fray
To Yorktown's eventful day,
        First we were free !

At New Orleans we met the foe ;
Oppressors fell at every blow ;
There we laid the usurper low,
        For maids and wives !

Who on Palo Alto's day,
'Mid fire and hail at Monterey,
At Buena Vista led the way ?
        " Rough and Ready ! "

Southrons all, at Freedom's call,
For our homes united all,
Freemen live, or freemen fall !
        Death or liberty !
                              —*N. O. Picayune.*

THE ORDERED AWAY.

Dedicated to the Oglethorpe and Walker Light Infantries.

BY MRS. J. J. JACOBUS.

At the end of each street, a banner we meet,
    The people all march in a mass,
But quickly aside, they step back with pride,
    To let the brave companies pass.
The streets are dense filled, but the laughter is
        still'd—
    The crowd is all going one way ;
Their cheeks are blanched white, but they smile as
        they light
    Lift their hats to the—Ordered away.

They smile while the dart deeply pierces their heart,
    But each eye flashes back the war glance,
As they watch the brave file march up with a smile,
    'Neath their flag,—with their muskets and lance ;
The cannon's loud roar vibrates on the shore,
    But the people are quiet to-day,
As, startled, they see how fearless and free
    March the companies—Ordered away.

Not a quiver or gleam of fear can be seen,
    Though they go to meet death in disguise ;
For the hot air is filled with poison distilled
    'Neath the rays of fair Florida's skies.
Hark ! the drum and fife awake to new life
    The soldiers who—" can't get away ;"
Who *wish*, as they wave their hats to the brave,
    That *they* were the—Ordered away.

As *our* parting grows near, let us quell back the tear,
    Let our smiles shine as bright as of yore ;
Let us stand with the mass, salute as they pass,
    And weep, when we see them no more.
Let no tear-drop or sigh dim the light of our eye,
    Or move from our lips—as they say,
While waving our hand to a brave little band—
    Good-by to the—Ordered away.

Let them go, in God's name, in defence of their *fame*,
    Brave death at the cannon's wide mouth ;
Let them honor and save the land of the brave,
    Plant Freedom's bright flag in the *South*.
Let them go ! While we weep, and lone vigils keep,
    We will bless them, and fervently pray
To the God whom we trust, for our cause firm but just,
    And our loved ones—the Ordered away.

When fierce battles storm, we will rise up each morn,
    Teach our young sons the sabre to wield ;
Should their brave fathers die, we will arm *them* to fly
    And fill up the gap in the field.
Then, fathers and brothers, fond husbands and lovers,
    March ! march bravely on !—*we* will stay,
Alone in our sorrow, to pray on each morrow,
    For our loved ones—the Ordered away.
        AUGUSTA, GA., April 2, 1861.
                      —*Macon (Ga.) Telegraph,* **May 2.**

A SOUTHERN SONG.

BY " L. M."

If ever I consent to be married,
    (And who would refuse a good mate ?)
The man whom I give my hand to,
    Must believe in the rights of the State.

To a husband who quietly submits
    To negro equality sway,
The true Southern girl will not barter
    Her heart and affections away.

The heart I may choose to preside o'er,
    True, warm, and devoted must be,
And have true love for a Union
    Under the Southern Liberty Tree.

Should Lincoln attempt to coerce him
    To share with the negro his right,
Then, smiling, I'd gird on his armor,
    And bid him God-speed in the fight.

And if he should fall in the conflict,
  His memory with tears I will grace;
Better weep o'er a patriot fallen,
  Than blush in a Tory embrace.

We girls are all for a Union,
  Where a marked distinction is laid
Between the rights of the mistress,
  And those of the kinky-haired maid.
  —*Louisville Courier*, June 22.

TO THE WASHINGTON ARTILLERY.

BY A SOUTHERN LADY.

Ye gallant men, march on, march on,
  With strong, uplifted arm,
For angel hands shall carve the way,
  And shield ye from all harm.

Oh, Major brave, let them not shrink
  In peril or in pain;
Let memories of their Southern birth
  Gird up their hearts again.

And in the hour of battle dark,
  When foes stand man to man,
Then strike, boys, strike! for your firesides;
  Strike for your native land!

'Tis a watchword which will never fail
  To arm them with a might,
To follow their proud leader through
  The thickest of the fight.

Then onward march, ye gallant men,
  Nor let your courage pale;
While Walton holds the first command,
  There's no such word as fail!
  —*N. O. Delta*, April 30.

SECESSION SONG—DIXIE LAND.

The popular "Dixie Land" has been adopted by the
Secessionists, instead of the "Star-spangled Banner," as
their National song. The *Huntsville* (Ala.) *Examiner*
gives the version sung in that State:—

Away down South, in the Carolina,
They have guns and the ready rhino;
  Look away! look away! look away! Dixie Land!
They've the men to do the fighting—
There's no use in scratchin' and bitin';
  Hooray! hooray! hooray! Dixie Land!

CHORUS.

  Oh, I'm glad I am in Dixie! Hooray! hooray!
In Dixie Land I take my stand,
  To live and die in Dixie!
Away! away! away down South in Dixie!
Away! away! away down South in Dixie!

The sovereign State of Alabama
Will try her hand before they lam her;
  Look away! look away! look away! Dixie Land!
So will our Mississippi brother,
And Georgia, too, our mortal mother;
  Hooray! hooray! hooray! Dixie land!

And Louisiana then will come,
And Texas, too, will help us some;
  Look away! look away! look away! Dixie Land!

And Arkansaw, with her tooth-picker,
Will help us out a little quicker;
  Get away! get away! get away! Dixie Land!

And next, Old North Carolina State,
And, after that, what's good and great;
  Hooray! hooray! hooray! Dixie Land!
When Lincoln gets on a Southern brake,
We'll give him a touch of the rattlesnake;
  Get away! get away! get away! Dixie Land!

May 12.—Mr. Wigfall says in a letter to a friend
in Washington, in great confidence, that the Confederate army will capture Washington, Lincoln, and
his Cabinet, unless they leave before the middle of
June. He says they have nearly one hundred thousand well-armed troops, and in less than two weeks
will be on their way to Washington, and expect to
winter in Philadelphia.—*Charleston Mercury.*

THE TWO ARMIES.—The Southern forces consist
of two distinct armies—the Provisional and the
Regular Confederate armies. The Provisionals are
enlisted for the space of twelve months, to go
wherever they are ordered. Most of their forces
belong to this class, which is generally made up of volunteer State militia. Their uniform varies, much the
same as the volunteers of the Northern State militia.
Their pay is $11 per month. The services of all
volunteers who may offer themselves are accepted.
They are taken to Montgomery for inspection. Large
numbers of the Provisional army are there encamped, much to the annoyance of the inhabitants.
They get into town and call for what they want, but
never pay for any thing. They drink and carouse
night and day, and flourish their revolvers in the
streets, swearing vengeance on all Northern men, or
any men who dare oppose them. The citizens do
not dare to come into the streets, as they do not
know what moment they might receive a fatal shot.
Ladies are exceedingly careful how they make their
appearance in the streets.

The regulars are enlisted for three years. These
are composed of the lowest class of the white population, gathered up from the levee of New Orleans,
Mobile, and other seaports—men who resort to this
as a last means of obtaining a livelihood. Every in-
ducement is offered to them to enlist. Large placards,
announcing large bounties—money in advance—are
extensively circulated in the different cities throughout the whole Southern country. Recruiting offices
are established in Mobile, Montgomery, New Orleans,
and other smaller towns in that section, but the recruits do not come in as quickly as was anticipated.
Their uniform is indeed varied at present; but it
is to consist of red flannel shirt, black hat, and blue
pants. Their pay is only $7 per month. They are
the very hardest-looking white men that could be got
together—just like returned filibusters. They represent all nations, there being very few Americans
among them. Men are very frequently impressed
into the service.—*N. Y. Tribune, May* 28.

SOUTHERN IDEAS OF NORTHERN BRAVERY.—The
Chinese and the Yankees are exceedingly alike, and
we have always thought that they were much more
nearly related than the Japanese and the almond-
eyed people of the Flowery Kingdom.

When a Chinaman prepares for war—measuring
his enemy's courage by his own—he attempts to work
upon his fears. He puts on a hideous mask, arms

himself with a huge shield, upon which he paints some unearthly monster; and, when thus accoutred, he goes forth in cold sweat to encounter the enemy. As soon as he beholds his adversary, he utters a fearful roar, broadsides his shield, and if his opponent does not at once take to his heels, John Chinaman always does.

The wars of New England have always been conducted upon the Chinese plan. To hear their orators and read their newspapers, one would suppose that he was looking at a Chinaman clothed with all the pomp and circumstance of mask, shield, and stinkpot. The Yankee orators are only equalled by the Yankee editors in deeds of valor. Let war be breathed, and they first swear to a man that they are ready and anxious to exterminate creation, whilst the latter, not content, like Alexander, to sigh for more worlds to conquer, threaten to destroy the laws of gravity and lay violent hands upon the whole planetary system. Yet, these war mandarins are all members of the Peace Society, and would no more think of resenting a blow on the cheek, the seduction of a wife, or the dishonor of a daughter, than they would of flying. We have not forgotten how all Massachusetts collected in Boston when Anthony Burns was to be delivered to his Virginia master, and swore that it should not be done. A single file of soldiers, however, marched the fugitive from State street to the lower end of Long Wharf, through miles of streets packed with valorous fanatics, who did nothing but sing old Puritan hymns, with a most hideous and barbarous disregard to metre.—*Richmond Examiner.*

THE THREE SWORDS.—That indomitable patriot, President Jackson, had, in his day, to deal with secession. It was then called Nullification; but it was in its elements secession pure and simple. He designated it by its right name when he denounced it as treason, and he appreciated its nature when he dealt with it as such. Had he been made of different stuff; had he been less imbued with patriotism; had he lacked courage; had he been weak of purpose, or imbecile from age; had he sympathized with their objects, or for years associated with the conspirators, taken them to his counsels, or yielded to their influences; had he been content with entreaty where he had the right to command; there would have been rebellion in his time under the auspices of Calhoun and his followers, as we have it now under the guidance of Jeff. Davis and his associates. But a Jackson, and not a Buchanan, was at the head of the State, and he waited not an hour for treason to gather strength. He throttled it at once. The sword and the gallows were waiting the conspirators, and sharp justice was ready with its retribution. Treason shrunk dismayed at these preparations, and the repose of the country was secured by the man who saved it at New Orleans.

Jackson's life was full of opportunities for the display of patriotism and courage, if not always of practical wisdom and calm statesmanship. He was certainly to an unexampled degree an object of popular idolatry. Tennessee presented him with a sword; the citizens of Philadelphia gave him another; and the riflemen of New Orleans endowed him with a third. We mention only these among the hundred other testimonials that honored his active career or graced his retirement, because they have a history connected with the present as well as the past,—a history which, were the dead permitted to speak, would evoke a voice of indignant denunciation from the old hero's grave.

By his will, Gen. Jackson bequeathed the first of these three swords to his nephew and adopted son, Andrew Jackson Donelson, the second to his grandson, Andrew Jackson, and the third to his grandnephew, Andrew Jackson Coffee. The clause relative to the first runs thus:—

"*Seventh*—I bequeath to my well-beloved nephew, Andrew J. Donelson, son of Samuel Donelson, deceased, the elegant sword presented to me by the State of Tennessee, *with this injunction*, that he fail not to use it, when necessary, in support and protection of our glorious Union, and for the protection of the constitutional rights of our beloved country, should they be assailed by foreign enemies or *domestic traitors.*"

Where is Andrew J. Donelson now, and to what uses is he applying this legacy of his great kinsman, confided to his presumed patriotism, accompanied with so solemn an injunction? In the ranks of rebellion, fighting against "our glorious Union!" Among "domestic traitors," battling for the overthrow of "the constitutional rights of our country," through the destruction of the Constitution itself. Again:—

"I bequeath to my beloved grandson, Andrew Jackson, son of Andrew Jackson, Jr., and Sarah, his wife, the sword presented to me by the citizens of Philadelphia, *with this injunction, that he will always use it in defence of the Constitution and our glorious Union, and the perpetuation of our Republican system.*"

And where is this Andrew Jackson, honored by his patriotic grandfather, and where the sword intrusted to his keeping? It is rusting in its scabbard at home, while treason is hewing at the Constitution, and the cannon of rebellion thundering against the Union. The degenerate grandson is himself on the side of the traitors, aiding by his influence and his money the conspirators who are thus in arms against both, and who are battling for the overthrow of "our republican system."

And again :—

"To my grand-nephew, Andrew Jackson Coffee, I bequeath the elegant sword presented to me by the Rifle Company of New Orleans, commanded by Capt. Beal, as a memento of my regard, and to bring to his recollection the gallant services of his deceased father, Gen. John Coffee, in the late Indian and British wars, under my command, and his gallant conduct in defence of New Orleans in 1814–'15, *with this injunction, that he wield it in protection of the rights secured to the American citizen under our glorious Constitution, against all invaders, whether foreign foes or intestine traitors.*"

Where, again, is Andrew Jackson Coffee, and in what cause is he wielding the gift of his benefactor? He too is among the traitors, and the sword placed in his hands for the "protection of the rights secured to American citizens under our glorious Constitution," is pointed at the hearts of loyal men, and whetted for the destruction of that "glorious Constitution" that he was so solemnly enjoined to defend.

Such is thus far the melancholy history of these three swords, each the legacy of a great man to his kinsmen, and such the uses to which they are applied. If facts were wanting to illustrate the commonplace touching the degeneracy of the successors of great men, how abundantly are they furnished in the story of this will and its consequences?—*N. Y. Daily Times, May* 31.

APPALACHICOLA, FLORIDA.—Captain S. G. Sexton, of Savannah, pilot of the steamship Florida, and Mr. William Philips, pilot of the new steamship Mississippi, not yet completed, arrived in Macon from New York, having fled from New York for their lives. They came by the way of Cincinnati and Nashville. They report hard times with some of the Southern steamship captains. The Alabama was seized and pressed into Government service, and Captain Schenck offered the alternative of the yard-arm or to retain command of his vessel as a United States transport. He took the latter, and is now carrying troops to Annapolis. Commodore Michael Berry, of the Charleston steamship Columbia, had a narrow escape with his life. His ship was seized in like manner, and when he refused to go into service, they proceeded summarily to the work of execution; but by good luck he slipped his neck out of the rope, jumped overboard, was taken up by a steam-tug, and escaped.

A blood-thirsty spirit runs riot in New York, and no man's life is safe who does not shout for Southern invasion and massacre. Every thing which would float was being seized for the transportation of troops South, and the idea was to wipe us all out in three to six months. Mr. Sexton brought New York dates to the 24th, and important despatches to the owners of the Savannah and New York steamship lines.—*Appalachicola Times.*

THE *Bangor Whig* says that during a drill of Capt. Burton's six-footers, at Oldtown, a few days ago, while marching upon a platform toward the river, where the platform ended, no order to halt being given, they kept on until ten had jumped into the river, and commenced swimming. Had not the order been given, the whole company would have followed them, and probably kept on swimming to this day.— *Boston Transcript, May 23.*

A PRIVATE of the U. S. Dragoons engaged in the skirmish at Fairfax Court House, says :—" We were up to the Court House at 3 o'clock in the morning. On approaching it, the rebels challenged us by asking, " Who comes there ?" The answer, " Cavalry," was given. The next question was, " What cavalry ?" To this we replied, " United States cavalry," and at the same time we fired a volley into the secessionists. They then took to their heels and fled through the village like so many deer. They were all mounted, but proved themselves very inefficient dragoons. We then returned through the village, when we noticed in the twilight a company of infantry, with a field-piece, drawn up to receive us. Nothing daunted, however, we immediately charged, and cut our way through them. At this time the people were firing on us from the Court House and tavern ; but owing to the early hour—it not yet being daybreak—and to the dust which our horses raised, most of their shots were at random, and took no effect. For the same reason we cannot be positive how many men we killed, although we do not think that the number (27) set down in the public prints is exaggerated, from the fact that one of our men, who was in the hands of the enemy for a short time as a prisoner, says that he saw a great many bodies taken into the Court House. Each of us was armed with a sabre, carbine, and two revolvers. The rebels did not appear to be well equipped, although, on the whole, they ought to have made a better fight of it than they did, as they outnumbered us six to one. As

before remarked, their cavalry ran away from us in the wildest confusion.—*N. Y. Herald, June 5.*

CANADIAN OPINION.—A Quebec paper has the following singular article on the progress of events in the United States. Taking this startling statement, with some late editorial remarks of New York journals in the extreme Democratic and radical Republican interests, the reader will feel some interest in the communication :—

" We warn our readers against placing implicit reliance in the accounts of the civil war which come by telegraph. We have private letters from Charleston and New Orleans, and we have others from St. Louis and Baltimore, which put a very different face on matters from that given by the telegraphic despatches. They all represent the feeling in the South as one of the most intense hatred towards the North ; they speak of the Baltimoreans as outraged by the presence of so many detested Massachusetts soldiers; they express the utmost confidence in the ultimate victory of the South, and they make light of the blockade and of the chance of servile insurrection.

" The telegraph wires all pass through the Northern States. The press despatch published this morning shows how the Administration controls the lines. And under these circumstances there is more faith to be placed in one letter than in half a dozen telegrams. While the telegraphic despatches from New York indicate nothing but ardor for war, private advices represent the people even there as tired of the contest, which can lead to nothing but discontent and disaster. Already are the Democrats of the North beginning to argue among themselves that a strong central Government is not what they have been advocating. Already are the sympathizers with the South beginning to multiply. Already, before the first battle, are the spirits of the Northerners beginning to sink. Meanwhile, both in the North and the South, republican institutions are failing, and the advocates of a change to a dictatorship, if not to a monarchy, are gaining ground."—*N. Y. Illustrated News, July 6.*

FORTS AND FORTRESSES.—There is but one fortress in the United States—Fortress Monroe ; all the other fortified places defending our harbors are called forts. The distinction betwixt these two terms is very wide. All fortresses are forts or fortified places ; but all forts are not fortresses. A fort may be simply an advanced work to protect the extended lines or walls of a fortress. Generally fortresses are extensive *enceintes* for the reception of garrisons, and built for the protection of cities. In the United States no extensive fortified places, with large garrisons, have been constructed for the defence of cities. Fortifications in this country have had reference principally to harbor defence.

Fortress Monroe, with its capacity for a garrison, (it includes 75 acres,) was constructed for the defence of the important Navy Yard of Gosport and Norfolk, now in possession of Virginia or the Confederate States. The construction of the extensive walls of a fortress involves the highest science of engineering. Not so with the forts. The former implies polygons, bastions, curtains, glacis, covered ways, planks, scarps and counter-scarps, ravelins, redans, redoubts, and the whole vocabulary of engineering science. Add to this idea a vast *enceinte*, or circumvallation, to contain a large garrison of troops, and a fortress rises to its proportionate majesty. A full garrison for Fortress Monroe is 3,000 men.—*National Intelligencer, June 6.*

PATRIOTIC SONG.

TUNE—"*British Grenadiers.*"

Up, up, ye gallant freemen !
  Hear, hear the traitors call :
"We'll plant our flag at Washington,
  Float it o'er Faneuil Hall ! "
"NEVER !" from out a million throats
  Leaps ready answer true ;
Huzza ! huzza ! huzza ! huzza !
  For the Stripes and Starry blue !

The sun, in rising, touches
  The spire on Bunker Hill,
And on the Heights of Dorchester
  At eve lies calm and still,
And as of old, beneath their shades
  Beat loyal hearts and true ;
Huzza ! huzza ! huzza ! huzza !
  For the Stripes and Starry blue !

Green lie the plains of Lexington,
  Watered with patriot gore ;
Sires of such sons as lately fell
  In traitorous Baltimore ;
And hearts like theirs by thousands come,
  And freedom's vow renew ;
Huzza ! huzza ! huzza ! huzza !
  For the Stripes and Starry blue !

Our faith, and love, and patience,
  Have long been sorely tried ;
"Let us alone," the haughty South
  With insolence have cried ;
And while they cry, the murderous shot
  O'er gallant Sumter flew ;
Huzza ! huzza ! huzza ! huzza !
  For the Stripes and Starry blue !

From city, farm, and workshop,
  Now countless legions pour,
To stand beneath the noble flag
  Raised by their sires of yore ;
Their country calls, they onward press,
  And still the shout renew ;
Huzza ! huzza ! huzza ! huzza !
  For the Stripes and Starry blue !
     —*Boston Daily Advertiser*, June 1.

THE BATTLE-CRY.

Look there ! the beacon's crimson light
  Is blazing wide and far,
And sparkles in its towering height
  The rocket's signal-star.
Rise ! rise ! the cannon rolls at last
  Its deep and stern reply,
And heavier sleep is coming fast,
  Than seals the living eye.

And now the warning trumpet peals !
  The battle's on the way ;
The bravest heart that moment feels
  The thrilling of dismay ;
Around the loved, in shrinking fear,
  Love's straining arms are cast ;
The heart is in that single tear,
  That parting is the last.

A thousand windows flash with fires,
  To light them through the gloom,
Before the taper's flame expires,
  To glory or the tomb ;
Far down the hollow street rebounds
  The charger's rattling heel ;
And, ringing o'er the pavement, sounds
  The cannon's crushing wheel.

Then answers to the echoing drum
  The bugle's stormy blast ;
With crowded ranks the warriors come,
  And bands are gathering fast ;
Red on their arms the torch-light gleams,
  As on their footsteps spring,
To perish ere the morning beams,
  For death is on the wing.

The courier, in his arrowy flight,
  Gives out the battle-cry ;
And now march on with stern delight,—
  To fall is not to die.
Already many a gallant name
  Your country's story bears ;
Go, rival all your fathers' fame,
  Or earn a death like theirs.
     —*N. Y. Express*, June 12.

HYMN FOR A FLAG-RAISING.

BY MRS. HARRIET BEECHER STOWE.

At the raising of the Stars and Stripes over Andover Seminary, on the 5th, the following hymn, written for the occasion by Mrs. H. B. Stowe, was sung to the tune of "America" :

Here, where our fathers came,
Bearing the holy flame
  To light our days—
Here, where with faith and prayer
They reared these walls in air,
Now, to the heavens so fair,
  Their flag we raise.

Look ye, where free it waves
Over their hallowed graves,
  Blessing their sleep ;
Now pledge your heart and hand,
Sons of a noble land,
Round this bright flag to stand,
  Till death to keep.

God of our fathers ! now
To Thee we raise our vow—
  Judge and defend ;
Let Freedom's banner wave,
Till there be not a slave—
Show Thyself strong to save
  Unto the end.

THE SOLDIER'S HYMN.

TUNE—"*Old Hundred.*"

O God of our fathers, on the earth,
  Girt for the fight, Thy servants stand ;
Oh, bless us, ere the trumpet sound,
  With strength from Thy almighty hand.

The cloud of war comes from the South ;
  The battle-storm bursts o'er our heads ;
Our starry flag a rainbow bright,
  A glory round our pathway sheds.

Our fathers' spirits watch that flag,
　They left to us without a stain ;
We take their motto in our hearts—
　" To die for Liberty is gain."

And when victorious we return,
　Oh, may those folds be pure and free,
As when our father Washington
　Gave us our Flag and Liberty.

Thou God of Battles, hear our prayer !
　From Western plains to Eastern coasts,
Strong in Thy blessing forth we march,—
　Our trust is in the Lord of Hosts.
　　　　　—*Hampshire (Mass.) Gazette,* June 11.

GENERAL HARNEY.

BY " LEXINGTON."

Come, now, a cheer for Harney,
　The valiant and the true !
Faithful among the faithless,
　Give him the honor due.

Rebellion wooed and threatened ;
　Friends, kindred, claimed his aid ;
And soon the wronging whisper ran,
　" By *him,* too, we're betrayed !

" And, like the hoary traitor
　Of Pascagoula's shore,
Like Lee, and Chase, and Beauregard,
　He breaks the oath he swore ! "

But he wavered not an instant ;
　On the old flag he gazed,
With thoughts of those old battle-fields
　Where its Stars and Stripes had blazed ;

And he swore by all that touches
　A loyal soldier's heart,
To stand by that bright banner
　Till life and he should part.

So, then, a cheer for Harney !
　Long may he live to see
The flag he perils all to save,
　Wave o'er a people free !
　　　　　—*Boston Transcript.*

THE CHARGE ON THE TWELVE HUNDRED;

OR, THE

FAIRFAX STAMPEDE.

Twelve hundred " gentlemen," real F. F. V.'s,
Taking at Fairfax their elegant ease,
Early one morning, aroused by a drum,
Mustered to slay forty-five of " the scum."
　　　　　Daring Twelve Hundred !

What did those fire-eating gentlemen do,
Who were in numbers as fifty to two ?
Say, did they pitch the vile underbred foe
Straight to the place where the bad people go ?
　　　　　Furious Twelve Hundred !

Oh, not at all ; and that wasn't the worst :
Into their camp the vulgarians burst,
This way and that way like centaurs they wheeled,
While from the battle-shock helplessly reeled
　　　　　Treason's Twelve Hundred !

POETRY—47

Some of the " heroes " broke cover, and fled ;
Several who didn't, were knocked on the head ;
Others, caught up by their soap-locks, were borne
Off from the battle-ground captives forlorn.
　　　　　Hapless Twelve Hundred !

Twenty or thirty were " wiped out," and five
Sneaked from the village, much scared, but alive ;
What of the rest of those Bayards became,
Has not been breathed by the trumpet of Fame,
　　　　　Ill-used Twelve Hundred !

Brave F. F. V.'s, how your passions must boil !
Scattered like sheep on that " sacredest soil,"
Upset by " mudsills," unpedigreed loons,
Twelve hundred licked by a troop of dragoons !
　　　　　Nonplussed Twelve Hundred !

Henceforth, O " chivalry," be not so proud ;
If you *are* panic-proof, don't say it loud ;
Don't call us Northmen mere " dastardly hordes ;"
Think, how from forty-five Northerners' swords,
　　　　　Fled your Twelve Hundred !

Though we may not be all " gentlemen born,"
Don't upon that account laugh us to scorn ;
Scoffers, believe us, " elite " of the South
Oftentimes laugh on the wrong side the mouth ;
　　　　　Ask the Twelve Hundred !

Look at our muscles, all strung for the right ;
Look in our eyes, full of terrible light ;
Though we've no serfs to turn pale at our nod,
Yet we can fight for home, Freedom, and God,
　　　　　Four to One Hundred !
　　　　　　　—*Vanity Fair.*

PRO PATRIA.

INSCRIBED TO THE SECOND NEW HAMPSHIRE REGIMENT.

BY THOMAS BAILEY ALDRICH.

I.

The grand old earth shakes at the tread of the Norsemen,
　Who meet, as of old, in defence of the true ;
All hail to the stars that are set in their banner !
　All hail to the red, and the white, and the blue !
　　　　As each column wheels by,
　　　　　Hear their hearts' battle-cry,—
It was Warren's,—*'Tis sweet for our country to die !*

II.

Lancaster and Coos, Laconia and Concord,
　Old Portsmouth and Keene, send their stalwart young men ;
They come from the plough, and the loom, and the anvil,
　From the marge of the sea, from the hill-top and glen.
　　　　As each column wheels by,
　　　　　Hear their hearts' battle-cry,—
It was Warren's,—*'Tis sweet for our country to die !*

III.

The prayers of fair women, like legions of angels,
　Watch over our soldiers by day and by night ;

And the King of all Glory, the Chief of all Armies,
Shall love them and lead them who dare to be right!
    As each column wheels by,
      Hear their hearts' battle-cry,—
It was Warren's,—*'Tis sweet for our country to die!*
        —*N. Y. Tribune*, June 21.

TO THE THIRD REGIMENT OF MAINE.

BY W. C. BAKER.

When the robber and assassin
  Stealthily at midnight crept
On each dear and sacred object
  That beside us fondly slept,
How we rouse us to protect them,
  Springing on to their defence—
All unheeding our own safety,
  Till we drive the robber hence.

Thus did you, brave sons of Maine-land,
  When you heard your country's call,
Rise, and in one mighty accent,
  Answer, "We are ready, all."
Ready now, and all united,
  To repel the rebel foe,
From the wood, the field, the workshop,
  Came the glad response, "We go."

On, ye gallant sons Dirego!
  Help sustain our drooping flag;
Meet the traitor at his threshold;
  Down his rebel ensign drag.
On your arms our nation's fate hangs;
  Rally for its flag and laws;
The God of Battles will go with you,
  In this glorious, holy cause.
        —*N. Y. Herald*, June 7.

"GOOD-BYE, BOYS—I'M GOING!"

THE DYING WORDS OF A VOLUNTEER.

BY MARY A. DENISON.

The battle raged with fiercest heat;
  The guns unloosed their thunder;
Shame on the cowardly retreat!
  Shame for the cruel blunder!
Along the ground the hissing ball
  Ploughed deep—black furrows throwing,
When faintly came the dying call
  Of "Good-bye, boys—I'm going!"

Brave volunteer! Upon his brow
  Death's chilly dews were creeping;
The lagging blood ran slower now,
  And many a man was weeping;
Yet, as they knelt, 'mid bullet-rain,
  Their eyes with vengeance glowing,
Came up the sobbing cry again,
  Of "Good-bye, boys—I'm going!"

Great soul! No wish, no coward word,
  No vain regret was spoken;
And they who loved him, silent heard—
  Their very hearts were broken.
Oh, let it be their warrior-cry,
  The vilest traitor showing
How calmly brave our men can die,
  With "Good-bye, boys—I'm going!"
        —*Boston Transcript*, June 21.

THE HEMPEN CRAVAT.

BY R. H. STODDARD.

The Southern costume—have you heard of it, sirs?—
Is a single shirt-collar, and a big pair of spurs;
'Tis airy for summer, there's no doubt of that,
But not half so neat as a hempen cravat.

To begin with the collar: suppose a long march
In the hot, broiling sun, what becomes of the starch?
Why, it wilts down with sweat,—a nasty thing, that,
Which is never the case with the hempen cravat!

Their spurs may be good till a battle begins,
But won't they be likely to scratch their own shins
When they come to retreat? for they *may* come to
    that,
But they cannot retreat with the hempen cravat!

Oh, the hempen cravat is an elegant thing!
For, once on your neck, it gives you full swing;
These hot Southern gentlemen ought to like that,
For they all want to swing—in the hempen cravat!

'Tis as cheap as 'tis useful,—a blessing, to-day,
When the South, owing millions, has nothing to pay;
So, to show our good will, (they've but little of
    that,)
We'll furnish them, gratis, the hempen cravat!

We try it on Pat, when he snatches a knife,
And slithers the wind-pipe of mother, or wife;
He was crazy with whiskey,—no matter for that;
He must die like a dog in the hempen cravat!

What is Pat's little frolic, to what they have done?
'Tis the foulest conspiracy under the sun:
The treason of Arnold was nothing to that,
Yet *he* richly deserved the hempen cravat!

They plotted, like him, with no wrongs to repay;
How could they be wronged, when they had their own
    way?
They bullied the North,—we submitted to that,
And, once in a while, to the hempen cravat!

They wasted our treasure, by putting in Cobb
To shell it out freely,—in other words, rob;
When the country was bankrupt—he brought us to
    that—
He resigned, and ran off from the hempen cravat!

We had a few arsenals, so they employed
A traitor to empty them—Brigadier Floyd;
He sent our arms South, for this and for that,
And stripped us of all—but the hempen cravat!

Our gold in their pockets, our guns in their hands,
Of course we must listen to all their demands:
They will break up the Union—what say ye to that?
My answer, brave boys, is, the hempen cravat!

By the blood of our sires, that on Bunker's old hill
Was poured out like water, (it flows in us still!)
We will crush them or perish, (no danger of that!)
With sword, and with shot, and the hempen cravat!

Should we happen to meet with these bold pirateers,
They'll find a queer slip-knot tied under their ears,
And swift at the yard-arm—a gallus place, that!—
They'll dance a gay jig in the hempen cravat!

Then work all your rope-walks, and working them,
 sing,
"Oh, the hempen cravat is a wonderful thing!"
Who can mention a better, may take my old hat,
But till then I go in for the Hempen Cravat!

How the B's Stung the Chivalry.—An intelligent officer of the 28th Regiment, N. Y. S. M., writing from Arlington Heights, gives an interesting account of an interview he had with the five rebel prisoners brought into camp by Lieut. Tompkins and his dragoons, of Company B, on the morning of their capture. He says the "chivalry" behaved in a very unmanly manner, begging in the most abject style for their lives, and protesting that they only served in the rebel ranks upon compulsion. One of their officers declared, if he could only be liberated this time, he would swear fealty to the Union, and never set his foot in a slave State again.

We give an extract from the letter, from which it will be perceived that the charge of the dragoons left a lively impression upon the minds of the secessionists:—

"Their account of the fight was amusing. I will give you one, from notes written secretly twenty minutes after I heard it. It is nearly verbatim:—

"'Talk about fighting! whew, my G–d! One company of them reg'lars, or you New York fellows, can whip a thousand of our men; by G–d, that's so; I'll swar it on a Bible. You ought to have seen 'em. Look heyar, reckon I wanted to get out of the way. Sure's you're born, they're just like devils—they don't mind shots. Lord, they went down the street, where they cut, an' slashed, an' shot. Our boys run like the devil—then, J—s, you ought to have seen 'em cut up the street again—like blue devils—it makes my blood cold to think of it. They shot every way—knocked us from our hosses, took our pistols and sabres away—my G–d, how they fit. Why, sir, I'll swar on a Bible, them South and North Carolina fellows that's with us ain't no account. They won't obey nobody—no discipline—you'll lick them every time.'

"There was much more of the same sort, and I send you this specimen, profanity and all included, so you may know what the rebel prisoners think, and how they talk. I asked him what the rebels thought of our volunteers.

"'Well,' said he in reply, 'they think you New York men are just as bad as the reg'lars, but they hain't much opinion of the rest.'"—*N. Y. Tribune, June 8.*

RICHMOND THE SOUTHERN CAPITAL.

May 23.—The Capital of the Southern Confederacy is to be removed to Richmond. A more admirable location could not be found. Its beautiful and commanding position, its facilities for ready communication with all parts of the South, its healthful climate, and its obvious advantages in a military point of view, commend the soundness of the selection which has been made.

Nature seems to have designed Richmond for the central seat of a great empire. Its advantages for commercial and manufacturing greatness are unrivalled on this continent. As the Capital of the Old Dominion, it has claims which will appeal to multitudes of Southern hearts. Virginia may not have been first in the present Southern movement, but she was first in the great movement which established the liberties and independence of America, and she is behind no other in maintaining a position which she has once assumed. If a majority of Union men was at one time found in her borders, it is no less true that, when the real purposes of Lincoln were made known to Virginia, that majority, with exceptions so few and contemptible that they do not deserve to be noticed, threw themselves at once in solid mass into the front rank of resistance, where they may now be found, as every camp will testify, and this day's vote will prove, as intrepid and as loyal friends of Southern independence as gallant South Carolina ever was in the hottest days of secession.

We shall welcome with great pleasure the arrival in Richmond of that eminent body of statesmen and soldiers who compose the Montgomery Government. The President, Jefferson Davis, is a tower of strength in himself. He has the iron will of Andrew Jackson, all of Jackson's nerve, energy, and decision, and even more than his military knowledge and general education. Indeed, apart from his great qualities as a commander, he is a statesman in every way qualified to guide the helm of the ship of State in the wildest storm that ever swept the ocean. He has not only great foresight, judgment, and fertility of resources, but a wonderful composure of spirit, keeping self-poised and self-possessed in the most agitating moments; and there is about the man, evident in every line of the firm and lofty countenance, an elevation of soul which attests him a gentleman, and commands universal respect and confidence. A brilliant civic and military staff will probably accompany the President, including, perhaps, the famous Beauregard, who, we understand, will soon take command on an important line of operations in Virginia. Our city, therefore, bids fair to become, before long, a scene of stirring interest, worthy of inaugurating the magnificent history of the future Capital of the Southern Confederacy.—*Richmond (Va.) Dispatch, May 23.*

Southern Repudiation.—The Legislature of Tennessee has passed the following repudiation bill:—

"Sec. 1. Be it enacted by the General Assembly of the State of Tennessee, That no persons in any non-slaveholding State, their agents or attorneys in this State, shall have power to sue or collect any moneys owing to or any property claimed by the citizens of any such State in Tennessee during hostilities between Tennessee and the Federal Government.

"Sec. 2. Be it further enacted, That it may and shall be lawful for such debtors to pay such moneys into the Treasury of the State, which sums shall be receipted for by the Treasurer, and shall be refunded with interest upon the cessation of hostilities."

A similar bill has been passed by the Legislature of Arkansas. Georgia adopted a similar course of dishonesty a month ago.—*N. Y. Evening Post, May 27.*

June 20.—A new spy system has been discovered and broken up at Washington. It appears that letters have been, nearly every day, collected and carried down the Potomac, to a point some thirty miles from the Capital, whence they have been sent off in small ferry boats, and so forwarded to Jeff. Davis. The Government has also detected the presence of a lot of female spies at Washington, in the pay of Beauregard. This latter is certainly a most dangerous class of public enemies, and one that ought to be rigorously suppressed. "A thing of beauty" is by no means "a joy forever," when it undertakes to do the dirty work of a very dirty rebellion.

> When lovely woman stoops to folly,
>   And strives her country to betray,
> It is not a proceeding jolly,
>   However Southern rebels pay.
>
> Because, if lovely woman's taken
>   In such a base and shameful sin,
> Her chance is slim to save her bacon,
>   And very slim to get her tin.
>
> —*Boston Sat. Evening Express*, June 29.

A LESSON TO SECESSIONISTS.—A thrilling incident occurred when the secession steamer came down to Fortress Monroe with the refugees from Norfolk. There were several secessionists on board as passengers, under the flag of truce, beside the commander and officers, who were formerly in the well-paid and honorable service of the United States. Soon after she had come alongside the noble old Cumberland, Commodore Pendergrast, in full view of the Stars and Stripes on the ship and at Fortress Monroe, the State of Georgia came steaming in, with her decks, upper works, wheel-houses, and rigging covered with a fresh arrival of brave Union troops. She passed close by the Cumberland, almost jamming in the secession craft, and hiding her little flag under the shadow of the two great vessels. Then arose such cheers as patriots only can give, rolling along over the waters until they were heard far up along the ramparts of the fortress and the camps of the shore. The rigging of the Cumberland was instantly manned in reply, and such vociferous shouts as the Yankee tars gave back! It would have made your venerable senior editor's heart grow young again to have heard them. Then, to crown the whole, the splendid marine band of the Cumberland struck up with spirit the "Star-spangled Banner," and played it gloriously as the troops steamed by to the soil of the Old Dominion. It was a good work for the State of Georgia to do, and well done for the Empire State.

There stood little ex-Lieutenant Hunter, in command of his small secession craft, with his diminished and dishonored flag cast entirely into the shadow of the Stripes and Stars. He was one of the most miserable-looking men you ever saw—trotting to and fro over his Lilliputian decks, from wheel-house to wheel-house, now looking here, now there, as if he wanted to find the smallest kind of a knot-hole into which to creep.—*Baltimore American*, June 15.

THE following significant circular has been issued from Charleston, S. C. :—

"Whenever the slaves in the Gulf States are incited to servile insurrections, and the prospect bids fair for their being converted into demons incarnate, then the slave-owners in the South will be found ready to sacrifice every slave from whom danger may be apprehended. Willing hands will be found ready to execute the bloody deed. Before Southern men will suffer themselves, their wives and little ones to be butchered, and their daughters worse than butchered, by fiends in human form; before they will suffer to any considerable extent the horrors of servile insurrections, the Gulf streams will be crimson with the gore, and every Southern river choked with the festering carcasses of slaves."—*Boston Sat. Evening Express*, June 29.

THE following bit of rhyme is thought to explain "the fitness of things" in Jeff. Davis's Proclamation of a day of fasting and prayer:—

> "Jeff. Davis's last Proclamation shows *reason*—
>   A thing very rare in Jefferson's mouth—
> For the "birthday of *Scott*" he appoints as a season
>   Of fasting and prayer—*for the South*."
>
> —*Boston Sat. Evening Express*, June 29.

THE LAST AMERICAN FLAG IN NEW ORLEANS.—Mr. Richard Fairchild, lately from New Orleans, mentions the following incident :—" As late as the 22d of February last, Mr. Fairchild saw a gentleman proceed from St. Charles street, down to Front Levee street, and there raise a large American flag, on which was inscribed, under two hands clasped, the words, "United we stand, divided we fall." The announcement of this defiant act created intense excitement among the secessionists, who assembled in front of the St. Charles Hotel, and proceeded in a body to the levee with the purpose of taking down the flag. They found, however, some hundreds of determined men surrounding the flag-staff, all armed, and many with rifles, and with the avowed purpose of keeping the old flag flying on the birthday of the Father of his Country. They were undisturbed, and the bunting waved until night, when it was voluntarily taken down. This is the last instance, so far as Mr. F. is aware, of the Stars and Stripes being displayed in New Orleans."— *Banner of the Covenant*, June 15.

THE SAVER OF FORT PICKENS IN PRISON.—Silently awaiting his doom, in the prison of Montgomery, is an officer of the U. S. Navy, whose existence seems to be forgotten by his country and his friends. A sad, brief note about him was placed in my hands ten minutes since, and I cannot resist the impulse to put the statement of his case at the head of my letter. "The poor fellow," writes an Alabama secessionist, "has no money and no friends here. The little capital he had has been paid, from time to time, for food and trivial comforts to the family of his jailer." The subject of this paragraph is one of the most efficient officers in the service, and came to be imprisoned in this way :—The Government at Washington—which never mentions him in his despatches —sent Mr. Worden from the National Capital expressly to order the reinforcement of Fort Pickens. His despatches were addressed to Capt. Adams, of the Sabine.

He arrived safely at Pensacola—at Warrington—at the head-quarters of Gen. Bragg, on the very day that Gen. Bragg, Commodore Ingraham of the Confederate Navy, and Capt. Adams of the Sabine, had dined together. Worden, fearing trouble, read his orders two or three times, committed them to memory, and tore them up. He told Bragg he was a courier from the U. S. Government to the Commander-in-Chief of the United States naval forces in Florida, and wanted to go on board the Sabine. "You can go on one condition, sir," said the General. "I cannot observe any condition, General Bragg," replied the officer; "my position in the United States service forbids it." "But I have an understanding with Capt. Adams," said the General. "I cannot help it," interrupted the Lieutenant; "I merely asked to go on board that vessel, and if you can allow me, I would deem it a great favor."

After some consultation, Mr. Worden was permitted to go on board. He delivered his instructions verbally on a certain morning. At 10 o'clock that night they were obeyed. Pickens was reinforced. A miscellaneous collection of army soldiers, marines, and sailors, augmented Lieut. Slemmer's command; and Worden did his duty. But, very rashly, he thought Bragg would, on his return, let him outside the Southern line unmolested. He proposed to go on shore; Capt. Adams first objected, but finally acquiesced.

The brave Worden shoved off in his little boat, and landed. A complete change had taken place in the spirit of the chivalrous Bragg. The reinforcement enraged him. Just while a spy was narrating the circumstances of the midnight adventure—swelling out hundreds into thousands—the Lieutenant appeared. He was secured, imprisoned, sent to Montgomery, and there he is. No one has spoken or written any thing about him; and no one seems to care whether he lives or dies.—*N. Y. Tribune.*

SONGS OF THE REBELS.

PENSACOLA—TO MY SON.

BY "M. S."

Beautiful the land may be,
 Its groves of palm, its laurel trees;
And o'er the smiling, murm'ring sea,
 Soft may blow the Southern breeze—
And land, and sea, and balmy air,
May make a home of beauty there.

And bright beneath Floridian sky,
 The world to thy young fancy seems:
I see the light that fills thine eye;
 I know what spirit rules thy dreams;
But flower-gemmed shore, and rippling sea,
Are darker than the grave to me.

For storms are lowering in that sky,
 And sad may be that fair land's doom;
Full soon, perhaps, the battle-cry
 May wake the cannon's fearful boom,
And shot and shell from o'er the waves,
May plough the rose's bed for graves.

And we, whose dear ones cluster there,
 We mothers, who have let them go—
Our all, perhaps—how shall we bear
 That which another week may show?
The love which made our lives all gone,
Our hearts left desolate and lone!

Country!—what to *me* that name,
 Should I in vain demand my son?
Glory!—what a nation's fame?
 Home!—home without thee, I have none.
Ah, stay—this Southern land not *mine?*
The land that e'en in death is thine!

A country's laurel wreath for thee,
 A hero's grave—my own! my own!
And neither land nor home for *me*,
 Because a *mother's* hope is gone?
Traitor I am! God's laws command,
That, NEXT TO HEAVEN, OUR NATIVE LAND!

And I will not retract—ah, no!—
 What, in my pride of home, I said,
That "*I would give my son to go
 Where'er our* HERO RULER *led!*"
The mother's heart may burst, but still
Make it, O God, to know Thy will!

NEW ORLEANS, May 1, 1861. —*N. O. Delta.*

A MOTHER SENDING THREE SONS TO THE ARMY.

BY "L. F."

A mother sends her jewels,
 Three gems from out her store;
What would you ask, O countrymen!
 What could she give you more?

O soldiers, then, who leave your homes,
 For battle-field and strife,
Remember her who gave her three!
 The jewels of her life.

She'll pray for you, for them, for all;
 Her heart is brave and true;
Be honor yours throughout the fight,
 The victor's wreath your due.

She'd go with you to heal your wounds,
 But daughters hold her here;
Their brothers' swords they've girded on,
 Though not without a tear.

Their prayers will waft you on your way,
 The prayers of sisters true;
May God's protecting care surround
 The patriot's cause anew.

NEW ORLEANS, *April 25.* —*N. O. Picayune.*

A BEAUTIFUL POEM.

The rare merit and appositeness of the following masterpiece of Mr. Hope's patriotic muse will strike every mind. The author is one of the most gifted of the poets of America, and has a heart as true and bold as his pen is bright and beautiful.

A POEM WHICH NEEDS NO DEDICATION.

BY JAMES BARRON HOPE.

I.

What! you hold yourselves as freemen?
 Tyrants love just such as ye!
Go! abate your lofty manner!
 Write upon the State's old banner,
 "A furore Normanorum,
 Libera nos, O Domine!"

II.

Sink before the Federal altars,
 Each one, low, on bended knee;
Pray, with lips that sob and falter,
 This prayer from a coward's Psalter:
 "A furore Normanorum,
 Libera nos, O Domine!"

III.

But you hold that quick repentance
 In the Northern mind will be;

This repentance comes no sooner
Than the robber's did at Luna.*
 " A furore Normanorum,
 Libera nos, O Domine ! "

IV.

He repented him ; the Bishop
Gave him absolution free—
Poured upon him sacred chrism
In the pomp of his baptism.
 " A furore Normanorum,
 Libera nos, O Domine ! "

V.

He repented ; then, he sickened—
Was he pining for the sea ?
In extremis he was shriven,
The Viaticum was given :
 " A furore Normanorum,
 Libera nos, O Domine ! "

VI.

Then, the old cathedral's choir
Took the plaintive minor key,
With the Host upraised before him,
Down the marble aisle they bore him.
 " A furore Normanorum,
 Libera nos, O Domine ! "

VII.

And the Bishop, and the Abbot,
And the monks of high degree,
Chanting praise to the Madonna,
Came to do him Christian honor.
 " A furore Normanorum,
 Libera nos, O Domine ! "

VIII.

Now, the Miserere's cadence
Takes the voices of the sea ;—
As the music-billows quiver,
See the dead freebooter shiver !
 " A furore Normanorum,
 Libera nos, O Domine ! "

IX.

Is it that those intonations
Thrill him thus from head to knee ?
So ! his cerements burst asunder !
'Tis a sight of fear and wonder !
 " A furore Normanorum,
 Libera nos, O Domine ! "

X.

Fierce he stands before the Bishop—
Dark as shape of Destinie !
Hark ! a shriek ascends, appalling !
Down the prelate goes, dead—falling ;
 " A furore Normanorum,
 Libera nos, O Domine ! "

XI.

HASTING lives ! He was but feigning !
What ! Repentant ! Never he !

 * The incident with which I have illustrated my opinion
of the policy of those who would have us wait for a " reaction at the North," may be found in *Milman's Latin
Christianity*, vol. iii., p. 133.

Down he smites the priests and friars,
And the city lights with fires.
 " A furore Normanorum,
 Libera nos, O Domine ! "

XII.

Ah ! the children and the maidens,
'Tis in vain they strive to flee !
Where the white-haired priests lie bleeding,
Is no place for tearful pleading.
 " A furore Normanorum,
 Libera nos, O Domine ! "

XIII.

Louder swells the frightful tumult ;
Pallid Death holds reverie ;
Dies the organ's mighty clamor,
By the Norseman's iron hammer.
 " A furore Normanorum,
 Libera nos, O Domine ! "

XIV.

And they thought that he repented !
Had they nailed him to a tree,
He had not deserved their pity,
And—they had not lost their city.
 " A furore Normanorum,
 Libera nos, O Domine ! "

XV.

There's a moral in this story,
Which is plain as truth can be :
If we trust the North's relenting,
We will shriek, too late, repenting :
 " A furore Normanorum,
 Libera nos, O Domine ! "

    —*N. O. Picayune.*

A WAR SONG FOR VIRGINIA.

Sound, Virginia, sound your clarion,
 From your serried ranks of war !
Fall in line with State of Marion,
 And your glittering falchion draw !

Onward, onward, then, to battle !
 For bright freedom points the way ;
Though the grape-shot thickly settle,
 Onward, onward, to the fray !

Though each Northern squadron dashes
 On, as wave up to the rock—
Though each foeman's sword-blade flashes,
 Onward, onward, meet the shock !

Love of freedom, honor, glory,
 Makes each freeman's arm a host ;
This we are taught by minstrel story,
 Tyrants learn but at their cost.

Look, and see " proud Edward's power,"
 Crushed by Bruce at Bannockburn ;
See of Austria's host, the flower
 Bite the dust by Lake Lucerne.

Mark the Persian hordes parading,
 Rushing, flee from Marathon !
And the British lion invading,
 Crouching to your Washington.

So, Virginia, sound your clarion,
  From your serried ranks of war !
Fall in line with State of Marion,
  And your glittering falchion draw !

For the banner which once floated
  Over Freedom's native land—
Flag, to which you are devoted,
  Is borne by a tyrant's band.

Save, oh, save it from pollution,
  Though your noblest sons fall dead !
Save it, though in revolution
  All its stars with blood be red !

Then, with "Southern Cross" emblazon
  Its blue field in colors bold,
So that we may proudly gaze on
  Fifteen clustering stars of gold.
               —*Richmond Enquirer.*

TO THE TORIES OF VIRGINIA.

  " I speak this unto your shame."

In the ages gone by, when Virginia arose
  Her honor and truth to maintain,
Her sons round her banner would rally with pride,
  Determined to save it from stain.

No heart in those days was so false or so cold,
  That it did not exquisitely thrill
With a love and devotion that none would withhold,
  Until death the proud bosom should chill.

Was Virginia in danger ? Fast, fast at her call,
  From the mountains e'en unto the sea,
Came up her brave children their mother to shield,
  And to die that she still might be free.

And a coward was he, who when danger's dark cloud
  Overshadowed Virginia's fair sky,
Turned a deaf, careless ear, when her summons was
    heard,
  Or refused for her honor to die.

Oh ! proud are the mem'ries of days that are past,
  And richly the heart thrills whene'er
We think of the brave, who, their mother to save,
  Have died, as they lived, without fear.

But, *now*, can it be that Virginia's name
  Fails to waken the homage and love
Of e'en one of her sons ? Oh ! cold, cold must be
  The heart that her name will not move.

When she rallies for freedom, for justice, and right,
  Will her sons, with a withering sneer,
Revile her, and taunt her with treason and shame,
  Or say she is moved by foul fear ?

Will they tell her her glories have fled, or grown
    pale ?
  That she bends to a tyrant in shame ?
Will they trample her glorious flag in the dust,
  Or load with reproaches her name ?

Will they fly from her shores, or desert her in need ?
  Will *Virginians* their backs ever turn
On their mother, and fly when the danger is nigh,
  And her claim to their fealty spurn ?

False, false is the heart that refuses to yield
  The love that Virginia doth claim ;
And base is the tongue that could utter the lie,
  That charges his mother with shame.

A blot on her 'scutcheon ! a stain on her name !
  Our heart's blood should wipe it away ;
We should die for her honor, and count it a boon,
  Her mandates to heed and obey.

But never, oh, never, let human tongue say
  She is false to her honor or fame !
She is true to her past—to her future she's true—
  And Virginia has never known shame.

Then shame on the dastard, the recreant fool,
  That *would strike, in the dark,* at her now ;
That would coldly refuse her fair fame to uphold,
  That would basely prove false to his vow.

But no ! it cannot—it can never be true,
  That Virginia claims one single child,
That would ever prove false to his home, or his God,
  Or be with foul treason defiled.

And the man that could succor her enemies *now*,
  Even though on her soil he were born,
Is so base, so inhuman, so false, and so vile,
  That Virginia disowns him with scorn !
          —*Richmond Examiner, May* 18.

LIEUT. GREBLE'S GALLANT CONDUCT AT GREAT BETHEL.—The *Philadelphia Inquirer* has details of the part borne by Lieut. Greble in the Great Bethel affair. It is printed *verbatim* from the rough notes of a friend of Lieut. Greble, who kindly furnished them for the purpose :—

As soon as the confusion arising from the mistake (the cross firing) was over, Gen. Pierce ordered the troops to advance. No scouts were thrown out, nor were troops aware of the vicinity of the enemy's batteries until they came within their fire. Lieut. Greble was ordered to unlimber his gun. He advanced, firing his gun alternately, until he came within two hundred yards of the masked battery of the rebels.

Soon after the firing commenced, he was left alone with his original command of eleven men, in an open road, the volunteers having retreated before the telling fire of the rifled cannon.

He worked his guns until he had silenced all those of the enemy, except one rifled cannon.

The Zouaves made a demonstration, and only desired permission to storm the fort, but no general officer was seen from the commencement of the action, and 1,500 were kept lying on the ground, for an hour and forty minutes, waiting for a command.

Lieut. Greble stood the brunt of the action for two hours ; he was begged by several officers to retreat, but he refused. Lieut. Butler asked him at least to take the same care of himself that the rest did, and dodge. He replied, " I never dodge, and when I hear the notes of the bugle calling a retreat, I shall retreat, and not before." The enemy made a sortie. Lieut. Greble said to Capt. Bartlett, who was standing alongside of him, " Now, Charley, I have something to fire at, just see how I will make them scamper." He immediately loaded with grape, and fired, when the enemy at once retreated behind their intrenchment.

Seeing himself left entirely alone, with five men at his own gun, he turned to Corporal Peoples, and said,

"All he could do would be useless—limber up the gun and take it away." At this moment a shot struck him on the left temple. He immediately fell, and his only exclamation was, " Oh ! my gun ! " The same ball went through the body of another man, and took the leg off a third.

Throughout the firing he had sighted every gun himself, and examined the effect of every shot with his glass. It was remarked by his own men, that every ball was placed in the very spot that he aimed for. The men say that he exhibited the same coolness that he would on parade.

The enemy did not come out again until the Federal troops had been withdrawn a half hour.

Lieut. Greble did not spike his gun, but kept it charged in preparing to withdraw his command. The sergeant spiked it after the lieutenant was killed.

The Mobile *Tribune* proposes " Cousin Sally " as a pet name for the Confederate States. The name is rather effeminate, but then her male fire-eating cousins could very appropriately be called Sally-manders. —*Louisville Journal, June* 17.

REPUDIATION.

'Neath a ragged palmetto, a Southerner sat,
A-twisting the band of his Panama hat,
And trying to lighten his mind of a load,
By humming the words of the following ode :
    " Oh ! for a nigger ! and oh ! for a whip ;
    Oh ! for a cocktail ! and oh ! for a nip ;
    Oh ! for a shot at old Greeley and Beecher !
    Oh ! for a crack at a Yankee school-teacher !
    Oh ! for a captain ! and oh ! for a ship ;
    Oh ! for a cargo of niggers each trip ! "
And so he kept oh-ing for all he had not,
Not contented with owing for all that he'd got.
                            —*N. Y. Tribune, June* 17.

Memphis, Tenn., *June* 6.—John Beman is the name of the watchman on the steamer Morrison, who was hung near Mound City. He was a native of Norway, came to this county in 1811, and lived in Boston, where he has children. He was first examined by a committee, was proven to have said that he hoped Lincoln would come down the river and take every thing ; that he would die rather than live in the Southern States, and much more of the same sort, that it is needless to repeat. The committee proposed to forgive him if he would take an oath to support the Southern States. He indignantly repelled the proposition, and said he would die first. Finding that he was determined and malignant, they threw a rope over the limb of a tree, and strung him up 25 feet, where he was hanging last night.—*Memphis (Tenn.) Bulletin, June* 7.

There are many little incidents illustrating the love displayed by some for the power under which they have been nurtured from the cradle to the present time, and gives some assurance that all will soon be well. One incident so reminded me of the spirit of the women of '76, that I must relate it. It may be that you have heard it before, but it will bear repetition :

It appears that when Captain Armstrong was about to surrender the yard at Pensacola, his daughter, after vain endeavors to persuade him not so to act, demanded of him a dozen men, and *she* would protect the place until aid came ; but no—he was a traitor in his heart, and must so act ; the dear old flag was hauled down from where it had so long waved, and the renegade Renshaw run his sword through it, venting his spleen upon the flag which had so long kept him from starvation. Human nature could not stand it, and the brave woman, seizing the flag, took her scissors and cut from it the Union, telling them that the time was not far distant when she would replace it unsullied ; but for the *stripes*, she left them as their legacy, being their just deserts.—*Phila. Press.*

A HEROINE.

June 10.—A short time since, Mr. Harry Robins, from Illinois, settled with his family in York county, near York River, Va. A few weeks since he was waited upon by a company of secessionists, and accused of entertaining views friendly to the Union. After heaping insults upon him, and threatening him with violence, the rebels quitted the place. For two days, however, parties were seen lurking about the place, and at last Mr. Robins, not feeling safe, managed to make his escape to Fortress Monroe, and claimed protection from Gen. Butler, which was cordially granted.

On the day of the engagement at Bethel, Mr. Robins took his place in the ranks, acted as a guide, and did the duty of a soldier on the field in the thickest of the fight on that occasion, hoping, as he said, " We might be able to get far enough up into the country to enable him to get his family ; " but he was doomed to be disappointed, as the retreat cut off all hopes of accomplishing his object.

On the night of the 11th inst., Mrs. Robins, finding her house was still watched, and that Col. Magruder, at Yorktown, had offered a thousand dollars reward for her husband, dead or alive, and that it was the intention of the rebels to take her and her three little children to Yorktown and incarcerate them in the jail, fled from the house. For two nights she slept under a bridge, and on the second night, about two o'clock in the morning, while her children lay under the bridge asleep, she sallied out and succeeded in finding a small boat, into which she put her three children, and, with the aid of her little boy, only twelve years of age, succeeded in rowing across the York river, a distance of three-fourths of a mile, against a strong current.

On landing, she made her way to the house of a Mr. Phillips, whom she found to be the rankest kind of a secessionist. Knowing her company, she was suddenly taken with an implacable hatred to the Northern Yankees, and finally left her warm secession friends without being suspected.

She then made her way through the woods, a distance of some seven miles to Fortress Monroe, and laying down on the sand on the beach, with her children, she slept until daylight, and then reported herself to Gen. Butler.

In passing through the woods, she had to take one of her little children and carry it on a piece, and lay it down, and then go back for the other—the little boy keeping watch over the little one while his mother went ahead with the other.

Mrs. Robins reports that there are about thirty thousand men between Yorktown and Big Bethel ; that several companies had come down from Richmond to assist the rebels in case of another attack upon Big Bethel.

Her statement about the number of the troops between Yorktown and Big Bethel is also corroborated by the flag of truce which was sent out by Col. Duryea to look after the dead and wounded which were left behind, at the time of the retreat.—*N. Y. Express, June* 19.

FIDDLESTRING NOTES.

BY FIDELIA.

Oh, most puissant General Pillow,
Just hang that gun upon a willow,
Or else prepare yourself instead,
To be a *Pillow without a head.*

Beriah Magoffin,
You traitorous *ruffin,*
  I'm sure the community think that you ought,
With kickin' and cuffin',
Laid flat as a muffin,
To have a good stuffin'
Of powder and shot. —*Buffalo Courier.*

FLAG-RAISING AT FORT CORCORAN.

ARLINGTON HEIGHTS, *May* 30.—The Sixty-ninth New York regiment, having transplanted their flag-staff from Georgetown College to their new camp on Arlington Heights, celebrated the raising of the Stars and Stripes. Near sun-set, Col. Corcoran having assembled all the troops, numbering over thirteen hundred, not on duty, he introduced Col. Hunter, of the Third Cavalry U. S. Army, who has just been assigned the command of the brigade of the aqueduct, consisting of the Fifth, Twenty-eighth, and Sixty-ninth New York regiments, and the detachments in the vicinity. Col. Hunter was received with great enthusiasm, and Col. Corcoran made some patriotic allusions to the Flag, and was loudly cheered. Capt. Thos. F. Meagher, having been called upon, made a brief but high-toned and patriotic address, showing the devotion Irishmen should bear to that flag which brought succor to them in Ireland; and to which, upon landing in this country, they swore undivided allegiance. He was heartily applauded throughout.

Col. Corcoran, having announced that Mr. Savage's new national song would be sung, introduced the author, who was received with loud cheering. After it subsided, he sung the following, the whole regiment present joining in the choruses:—

THE STARRY FLAG.

A NATIONAL SONG, BY JOHN SAVAGE.

AIR—"*Dixie's Land.*"

Oh, the Starry Flag is the flag for me!
'Tis the flag of life! the flag of the free!
  Then hurrah, hurrah!
    For the Flag of the Union!
      Oh, the Starry Flag, &c.
We'll raise that starry banner, boys,
  Hurrah, hurrah!
We'll raise that starry banner, boys,
Where no power in wrath can face it!
  On town and field,
  The people's shield,
No treason can erase it!
  O'er all the land
  That flag must stand,
Where the people's might shall place it.

That flag was won through gloom and woe!
It has blessed the brave and awed the foe!
  Then hurrah, hurrah!
    For the Flag of the Union.
      That flag was won, &c.

We'll raise that starry banner, boys—
  Hurrah, hurrah!
We'll raise that starry banner, boys,
Where the Stripes no hand can sever!
  On fort and mast
  We'll nail it fast,
To balk all base endeavor!
  O'er roof and spire,
  A living fire,
The Stars shall blaze forever.

'Tis the people's will, both great and small,
The rights of the States, the Union of all!
  Then hurrah, hurrah!
    For the Flag of the Union!
      'Tis the people's will, &c.
We'll raise that starry banner, boys—
  Hurrah, hurrah!
We'll raise that starry banner, boys—
Till it is the world's wonder!
  On fort and crag
  We'll plant that flag,
With the people's voice of thunder!
  We'll plant that flag,
  Where no hand can drag
Its immortal folds asunder!

We must keep that flag where it e'er has stood,
In front of the free, the wise, and the good;
  Then hurrah, hurrah!
    For the Flag of the Union!
      We must keep that flag, &c.
We'll raise that starry banner, boys—
  Hurrah, hurrah!
We'll raise that starry banner, boys,
On field, fort, mast, and steeple!
  And fight and fall,
  At our country's call,
By the glorious flag of the people!
  In God, the just,
  We place our trust,
To defend the flag of the people.

The effect of some fourteen hundred voices thundering forth the refrain, was one of the most exciting and inspiriting we have ever witnessed. At the close the utmost enthusiasm prevailed, and three cheers for John Savage were given. Lieut.-Col. Nugent, Lieut. E. K. Butler, and Father T. J. Mooney, the popular chaplain of the Sixty-ninth, by song and sentiment contributed to the enjoyment of the occasion.—*National Intelligencer, June* 1.

If the impending war be the most ruthless ever waged, the consciences of our enemies must bear the guilt of the anguish, and misery, and blood. Their course from the beginning of the great movement has been marked by the meanest arts, the hugest falsehoods, the most indecent abuse, the harshest accusations. They have exhausted their cunning by diplomatic trickery, stultified themselves by absurd reasoning, excited contempt by the long views they have persistently taken of high questions, and envenomed hatred by the cool avowal of purposes as base as they are bloody. The feelings now raging fiercely in the bosom of every Southerner have been blown into a tempest by the untold insults, indignities, and wrongs, inflicted since we severed the ties that bound us to despotism and disgrace. Not content with refusing to concede rights guaranteed by the Constitution, they make the tyranny more odious by deception and perfidy. They force upon us the alternative of resistance, and because we placed our flag where theirs once waved, they rush to arms and threaten us with extermination. At first, when gnashing their teeth over their miserable discomfiture, they affected a beautiful sentiment. The symbol of their grandeur and greatness had been lowered at the command of a foe they had taunted with weakness and folly. Swollen with pride, infuriate with passion, and emboldened by the eager rush of numbers to their capitol, they have ceased prating about the honor of their Government; they no longer make specious appeals to patriotism, but, ignoring these high and potent motives, they address brute passions, and deliberately concoct and propose schemes which would shock and disgust savages. Their brutal soldiery are to possess our fair fields; one class of our population are reckoned upon as allies in the execution of their fiendish purposes; Louisiana is to be conquered by letting in upon her the waters of the Mississippi, and the victors are to prey upon the virtue of our wives and daughters. These are the motives and objects loudly proclaimed by the gathering hordes.

Fierce will be the coming strife. Steel, and lead, and iron will be clothed with all their murderous power. The sword will drink its full of blood. Victory will be slaughter.—*Charleston Courier, May* 16.

A WONDERFUL CONVERSION.—The *New York Observer* of this week, in its report of the daily Fulton street Prayer-meeting, states facts which we presume will be new to a great many readers in this city. The report runs:

One day the meeting was near closing, when a man in the uniform of an officer of the army arose and said: "I cannot let this meeting close without saying a word. I came home from the battle-field at Bull Run injured, and saved from instant death as almost by a miracle. I was in the battle of the 21st of July, and in the thickest of the fight, and such were the circumstances of my escape, that I was led to think on my ways. I have been a wicked man. When there was any wickedness going on, I was sure to be foremost in it. Coming home wounded, I had time to ask myself why I had been spared. I was struck down by a squad of the Black Horse cavalry. I never expected to get away alive."

The witness goes on to relate his religious experience, and implore the prayers of the faithful. The writer says:—

After the meeting, we asked some of the particulars of his peril and deliverance. He said: "I was surrounded by the Black Horse men, and two of them seized me, one on each side laying hold of me, and running at full gallop about half a mile, when both were shot, and fell from their horses dead. A Black Horse man, galloping behind me, gave me a severe blow in the back—intended to kill me—which brought me to the ground. The whole of the troop were on the retreat, and many galloped over me, and I was injured by the hoofs of the horses; but, blessed be God, I was spared."

"Had you pious parents?"

"The most godly people that ever lived, and I firmly believe I was spared in answer to their prayers. I arose from the ground with that conviction, and I believed I was spared, too, that I might have space for repentance, and become a good earnest Christian, and then and there I resolved to become one, and here I am, hoping in God's mercy."

"Where did your parents attend church?" we inquired.

"My father and mother were members of the old Garden street Reformed Dutch church."

"Do you know Jim Irving, of your regiment?"

"What! the old comrade of the worst fighters of the city?—he and Orville Gardner at their head? I guess I know him."

"What sort of a man is he in the camp?"

"His is the most beautiful Christian character I ever saw. I never saw any thing like it."

"Does he drink rum?"

"Not a drop."

"Does he attend prayer-meetings?"

"Always will have one going."

"Where is he now?"

"In prison at Richmond, because he considered it his duty to stand to the last, and he was taken."

"Did you know he was accustomed to attend these meetings?"

"I have often heard him speak of these meetings with the profoundest delight. If Jim Irving is not a changed man, I do not know who is. Not a man in the regiment could be found who does not know him and does not believe him to be a Christian."

James Irving was once a notoriously wicked man in this city, and became, by the grace of God, a most interesting Christian—a meek, humble, modest man as to his spirit, but of towering strength as to the mortal part, and, before going to the army, almost daily in the prayer-meeting.—*N. Y. Tribune.*

"E PLURIBUS UNUM."

We have received the following noble, fervid, and patriotic lyric for publication, from its author, Rev. John Pierpont. It proves that the unwearied fire of genius still glows, undimmed by age, in the soul of an honored American poet, whose first production was published half a century ago. Mr. Pierpont is 76 years old, and his poem has the "spirit of '76." As regards mere age, however, time practices on us a deception in regard to him; for his form seems to grow more erect, his gait more vigorous, his mind more vivid and creative, as he advances in years. The soul of youth breathes and burns in his verse, and animates his frame. Indeed, he promises in body to survive even the literary reputation of many of his younger contemporaries; and the hyperbole of good feeling, "may he live a thousand years," is not so extravagant a wish in respect to him as it is to others.—*Boston Transcript.*

I.

The harp of the minstrel with melody rings,
　When the muses have taught him to touch and to tune it;
But though it may have a full octave of strings,
　To both maker and minstrel the harp is a unit.
　　So the power that creates
　　Our Republic of States,
　Into harmony brings them at different dates;
And the thirteen or thirty, the Union once done,
Are "E Pluribus Unum"—of many made one.

II.

The science that weighs in her balance the spheres,
　And has watched them since first the Chaldean began it,
Now and then, as she counts them and measures their years,
　Brings into our system, and names a new planet.
　　Yet the old and new stars,
　　Venus, Neptune, and Mars,
　As they drive round the sun their invisible cars,
Whether faster or slower their races they run,
Are "E Pluribus Unum"—of many made one.

III.

Of that system of spheres, should but one fly the track,
Or with others conspire for a general dispersion,
By the great central orb they would all be brought back,
And held each in her place by a wholesome coercion.
Should one daughter of light
Be indulged in her flight,
They would all be engulfed by old Chaos and Night,
So must none of our sisters be suffered to run;
For, "E Pluribus Unum"—we all go, if one.

IV.

Let the demon of discord our melody mar,
Or treason's red hand rend our Union asunder;
Break one string from our harp, or extinguish one star,
The whole system's ablaze with its lightning and thunder.
Let the discord be hushed!
Let the traitors be crushed!
Though "Legion" their name, all with victory flushed!
For aye must our *motto* stand, fronting the sun:
"E Pluribus Unum"—*though many, we're* ONE.

THE RISING OF THE PEOPLE.

POEM DELIVERED BEFORE THE PHI BETA KAPPA SO-
CIETY OF HARVARD UNIVERSITY, JULY, 1861.

BY ELBRIDGE JEFFERSON CUTLER.

The drum's wild roar awakes the land; the fife is
calling shrill;
Ten thousand starry banners blaze on town, and bay,
and hill;
Our crowded streets are throbbing with the soldiers'
measured tramp;
Among our bladed corn-fields gleam the white tents
of the camp.
The thunders of the rising war hush labor's drowsy
hum,
And heavy to the ground the first dark drops of battle
come.
The souls of men flame up anew; the narrow heart
expands;
And woman brings her patient faith to nerve her
eager hands.
Thank God! we are not buried yet, though long in
trance we lay;
Thank God! the fathers need not blush to own their
sons to-day.

Oh! sad and slow the weeks went by; each held his
anxious breath,
Like one who waits, in helpless fear, some sorrow
great as death.
Oh! scarcely was there faith in God, nor any trust in
man,
While fast along the Southern sky the blighting
shadow ran.
It veiled the stars, one after one; it hushed the
patriots' song;
And stole from men the sacred sense that parteth
right and wrong.
Then a red flash—the lightning across the darkness
broke,
And with a voice that shook the land, the guns of
Sumter spoke:
Wake! sons of heroes, wake! the age of heroes
dawns again;
Truth takes in hand her ancient sword, and calls her
loyal men.
Lo! brightly o'er the breaking day shines Freedom's
holy star,
Peace cannot cure the sickly time. All hail, the
healer, War!

That call was heard by Plymouth rock; 'twas heard
in Boston bay;
Then up the piny streams of Maine sped on its ring-
ing way;
New Hampshire's rocks, Vermont's green hills, it
kindled into flame;
Rhode Island felt her mighty soul bursting her little
frame:
The Empire City started up, her golden fetters rent,
And, meteor-like, across the North, the fiery message
sent;
Over the breezy prairie lands, by bluff and lake it ran,
Till Kansas bent his arm, and laughed to find himself
a man;
Then on, by cabin and by camp, by stony wastes and
sands,
It ran exultant down the sea where the Golden City
stands.

And wheresoe'er the summons came, there rose an
angry din,
As when upon a rocky coast a stormy tide comes in.
Straightway the fathers gathered voice, straightway
the sons arose,
With flushing cheek, as when the east with day's red
current glows.
Hurrah! the long despair is past; our fading hopes
renew;
The fog is lifting from the land, and lo! the ancient
blue!
We learn the secret of the deeds the sires have handed down,
To fire the youthful soldier's zeal, and tend his green
renown.
Who lives for country, through his arm feels all her
forces flow.
'Tis easy to be brave for truth, as for the rose to
blow.

Oh, Law! fair form of Liberty! God's light is on thy
brow,
Oh, Liberty! thou soul of Law, God's very self art
thou.
One the clear river's sparkling flood that clothes the
bank with green;
And one the line of stubborn rock that holds the
water in—
Friends, whom we cannot think apart, seeming each
other's foe:
Twin flowers upon a single stalk with equal grace
that grow.
Oh, fair ideas! we write your names across our banner's fold;
For you, the sluggard's brain is fire; for you, the
coward bold.
Oh! daughter of the bleeding Past! Oh! hope the
prophets saw!
God give us Law in Liberty, and Liberty in Law!

Full many a heart is aching, with mingled joy and
pain,
For those who go so proudly forth, and may not
come again;
And many a heart is aching for those it leaves behind,
As a thousand tender histories throng in upon the
mind.
The old men bless the young men, and praise their
bearing high;
The women in the doorways stand to wave them
bravely by.

One threw her arms about her boy, and said, "Good
    bye, my son;
God help thee do the valiant deeds thy father would
    have done."
One held up to a bearded man a little child to kiss,
And said, "I shall not be alone, for thy dear love
    and this."
And one, a rosebud in her hand, leant at a soldier's
    side;
"Thy country weds thee first," she said, "be I thy
    second bride."

Oh, mothers! when, around your hearths, ye count
    your cherished ones,
And miss from the enchanted ring the flower of all
    your sons;
Oh, wives! when o'er the cradled child ye bend at
    evening's fall,
And voices which the heart can hear across the dis-
    tance call;
Oh, maids! when, in the sleepless nights, ye ope the
    little case,
And look till ye can look no more upon the proud
    young face,
Not only pray the Lord of Life, who measures mortal
    breath,
To bring the absent back unscathed out of the fire of
    death;
Oh, pray with that divine content which God's best
    favor draws,
That, whosoever lives or dies, he save his holy cause!

So out of shop and farmhouse, from shore and inland
    glen,
Thick as the bees in clover time, are swarming arméd
    men;
Along the dusty roads in haste the eager columns
    come,
With flash of sword and musket's gleam, the bugle
    and the drum.
Ho! comrades! see the starry flag, broad waving at
    our head;
Ho! comrades! mark the tender light on the dear
    emblems spread!
Our fathers' blood has hallowed it; 'tis part of their
    renown;
And palsied be the caitiff hand would pluck its glories
    down!
Hurrah! hurrah! it is our home where'er thy colors
    fly;
We win with thee the victory, or in thy shadow die!

Oh, women! drive the rattling loom, and gather in
    the hay;
For all the youth worth love and truth are marshalled
    for the fray.

Southward the hosts are hurrying, with banners wide
    unfurled,
From where the stately Hudson floats the wealth of
    half the world;
From where, amid his clustered isles, Lake Huron's
    waters gleam;
From where the Mississippi pours an unpolluted
    stream;
From where Kentucky's fields of corn bend in the
    Southern air;
From broad Ohio's luscious vines; from Jersey's
    orchards fair;
From where, between his fertile slopes, Nebraska's
    rivers run;
From Pennsylvania's iron hills; from woody Oregon;
And Massachusetts led the van, as in the days of
    yore,
And gave her reddest blood to cleanse the stones of
    Baltimore.

Oh, mothers! sisters! daughters! spare the tears ye
    fain would shed;
Who seem to die in such a cause, ye cannot call them
    dead;
They live upon the lips of men, in picture, bust, and
    song,
And nature folds them in her heart, and keeps them
    safe from wrong.

Oh! length of days is not a boon the brave man
    prayeth for;
There are a thousand evils worse than death or any
    war—
Oppression, with his iron strength, fed on the souls
    of men,
And License, with the hungry brood that haunt his
    ghastly den.
But like bright stars ye fill the eye; adoring hearts
    ye draw;
Oh! sacred grace of Liberty! oh, majesty of Law!

Hurrah! the drums are beating; the fife is calling
    shrill;
Ten thousand starry banners flame on town, and bay,
    and hill;
The thunders of the rising war drown labor's peace-
    ful hum;
Thank God that we have lived to see the saffron
    morning come—
The morning of the battle call, to every soldier dear!
Oh joy! the cry is "Forward!" Oh, joy! the foe is
    near!
For all the crafty men of peace have failed to purge
    the land;
Hurrah! the ranks of battle close! God takes his
    cause in hand!

INDEX.

EXPLANATION OF ABBREVIATIONS IN THE INDEX.

Int. stands for *Introductory Address*; D. for *Diary of Events*; Doc. for *Documents*; and P. for *Poetry, Rumors, and Incidents.*